D0211885

DELPHI PUBLIC LIBRARY
222 East Main Street
Delphi, Indiana 46923
765-564-2929

CRITICAL SURVEY OF

Long Fiction

Fourth Edition

CRITICAL SURVEY OF

Long Fiction

Fourth Edition

Volume 3

H. L. Davis—John Gardner

Editor

Carl Rollyson

Baruch College, City University of New York

SALEM PRESS

Pasadena, California   Hackensack, New Jersey

Cover photo: Louise Erdrich (AP/Wide World Photos)

Some of the essays in this work, which have been updated, originally appeared in the following Salem Press publications: *Critical Survey of Long Fiction, English Language Series* (1983), *Critical Survey of Long Fiction, Foreign Language Series* (1984), *Critical Survey of Long Fiction, Supplement* (1987), *Critical Survey of Long Fiction, English Language Series, Revised Edition* (1991; preceding volumes edited by Frank N. Magill), *Critical Survey of Long Fiction, Second Revised Edition* (2000; edited by Carl Rollyson).

∞ The paper used in these volumes conforms to the American National Standard for Permanence of Paper for Printed Library Materials, Z39.48-1992 (R1997).

Library of Congress Cataloging-in-Publication Data

Critical survey of long fiction / editor, Carl Rollyson. — 4th ed.
p. cm.
Includes bibliographical references and index.
ISBN 978-1-58765-535-7 (set : alk. paper) — ISBN 978-1-58765-536-4 (vol. 1 : alk. paper) — ISBN 978-1-58765-537-1 (vol. 2 : alk. paper) — ISBN 978-1-58765-538-8 (vol. 3 : alk. paper) — ISBN 978-1-58765-539-5 (vol. 4 : alk. paper) — ISBN 978-1-58765-540-1 (vol. 5 : alk. paper) — ISBN 978-1-58765-541-8 (vol. 6 : alk. paper) — ISBN 978-1-58765-542-5 (vol. 7 : alk. paper) — ISBN 978-1-58765-543-2 (vol. 8 : alk. paper) — ISBN 978-1-58765-544-9 (vol. 9 : alk. paper) — ISBN 978-1-58765-545-6 (vol. 10 : alk. paper)
1. Fiction—History and criticism. 2. Fiction—Bio-bibliography—Dictionaries. 3. Authors—Biography—Dictionaries. I. Rollyson, Carl E. (Carl Edmund)
PN3451.C75 2010
809.3—dc22

2009044410

First Printing

PRINTED IN CANADA

CONTENTS

COMPLETE LIST OF CONTENTS

Volume 1

Volume 2

Volume 3

Volume 4

Volume 5

VOLUME 6

Volume 7

Volume 8

Volume 9

Volume 10

PRONUNCIATION KEY

Foreign and unusual or ambiguous English-language names of profiled authors may be unfamiliar to some users of the *Critical Survey of Long Fiction*. To help readers pronounce such names correctly, phonetic spellings using the character symbols listed below appear in parentheses immediately after the first mention of the author's name in the narrative text. Stressed syllables are indicated in capital letters, and syllables are separated by hyphens.

VOWEL SOUNDS

Symbol	***Spelled (Pronounced)***
a	answer (AN-suhr), laugh (laf), sample (SAM-puhl), that (that)
ah	father (FAH-thur), hospital (HAHS-pih-tuhl)
aw	awful (AW-fuhl), caught (kawt)
ay	blaze (blayz), fade (fayd), waiter (WAYT-ur), weigh (way)
eh	bed (behd), head (hehd), said (sehd)
ee	believe (bee-LEEV), cedar (SEE-dur), leader (LEED-ur), liter (LEE-tur)
ew	boot (bewt), lose (lewz)
i	buy (bi), height (hit), lie (li), surprise (sur-PRIZ)
ih	bitter (BIH-tur), pill (pihl)
o	cotton (KO-tuhn), hot (hot)
oh	below (bee-LOH), coat (koht), note (noht), wholesome (HOHL-suhm)
oo	good (good), look (look)
ow	couch (kowch), how (how)
oy	boy (boy), coin (koyn)
uh	about (uh-BOWT), butter (BUH-tuhr), enough (ee-NUHF), other (UH-thur)

CONSONANT SOUNDS

Symbol	***Spelled (Pronounced)***
ch	beach (beech), chimp (chihmp)
g	beg (behg), disguise (dihs-GIZ), get (geht)
j	digit (DIH-juht), edge (ehj), jet (jeht)
k	cat (kat), kitten (KIH-tuhn), hex (hehks)
s	cellar (SEHL-ur), save (sayv), scent (sehnt)
sh	champagne (sham-PAYN), issue (IH-shew), shop (shop)
ur	birth (burth), disturb (dihs-TURB), earth (urth), letter (LEH-tur)
y	useful (YEWS-fuhl), young (yuhng)
z	business (BIHZ-nehs), zest (zehst)
zh	vision (VIH-zhuhn)

CRITICAL SURVEY OF

Long Fiction

Fourth Edition

H. L. DAVIS

Born: Nonpareil, Oregon; October 18, 1894 (possibly 1896)
Died: San Antonio, Texas; October 31, 1960
Also known as: Harold Lenoir Davis

Principal long fiction

Honey in the Horn, 1935
Harp of a Thousand Strings, 1947
Beulah Land, 1949
Winds of Morning, 1952
The Distant Music, 1957

Other literary forms

H. L. Davis first gained public and critical notice as a poet. His earliest poems were published in *Poetry* magazine and were much admired by such writers as Carl Sandburg and James Stevens. Most of Davis's work in fiction before 1947 was in the short-story form. At first he collaborated with Stevens, but in the late 1920's he began publishing on his own, establishing a reputation as a writer of Westerns. Both his poetry and his short fiction focus on western American themes. Davis's poetry is sensitive to the experiences of the people who lived on the western frontier; among his short stories are a number that retain considerable literary merit. These are notable for the universality of their themes and sensitivity to human character.

Achievements

H. L. Davis won the Pulitzer Prize in 1936 for his first novel, *Honey in the Horn*. His subsequent novels enhanced his reputation, yet he has received little serious scholarly attention. Western genre fiction has long been regarded as inferior: Westerns are often formulaic, poorly written, and insubstantial. Many critics have inappropriately associated Davis's complex novels with the typical products of the genre; at his best, Davis imbues the Western with a universality achieved by few other writers of Westerns.

Biography

Harold Lenoir Davis was born in Nonpareil, Oregon, on October 18, 1894, or possibly 1896. Many of the details of Davis's early years are confused by events that he fabricated in later accounts of his life. For example, he turned a few weeks of herding sheep when a youngster into a tale of a job as a cowpuncher; and he turned a short tenure as a military clerk into an adventure with the cavalry in pursuit of Pancho Villa. One can read psychological import into Davis's romanticizing of his youth—perhaps he did so to compensate for his feelings of inadequacy among the elite writers of his day—but he might simply have been following the frontier tradition of duping outsiders with outlandish anecdotes and contradictory details of his life. Davis's work is full of tall tales; his telling such tales about his life should not be surprising.

His parents were James Alexander Davis and Ruth Bridges Davis. Although James Davis had only one leg (the other having been lost in an accident in a sawmill when he was six years old), he was a vigorous man. He was a schoolteacher who taught in one-room schools and took on other jobs when he could in order to support a family that began with Harold and included three other boys. The Davis family moved from town to town in Oregon while James Davis moved from job to job, finally settling in The Dalles, where, in 1908, James was made principal of the high school.

James Davis had a taste for literature and wrote poetry. Even though H. L. Davis does not seem to have liked his father, James Davis inculcated in his son an interest in literature. Writing was initially a secondary interest for Davis. After working and saving money for college, he went, in 1917, to Stanford University with the hope of training to be an engineer. The school was too expensive, however, and he returned to The Dalles.

In 1918, Davis was drafted into the army and sent to Fort McDowell in California. He served as a clerk from September to December, 1918, at which time he was discharged. During 1918, he submitted poems to *Poetry*; they were published in 1919 and won for Davis a moderate recognition among other poets. He worked at various jobs until he began earning money by collaborating on stories with James Stevens.

In 1926, Davis and Stevens alienated much of the Northwest's small literary establishment by writing *Sta-*

tus Rerum: A Manifesto upon the Present Condition of Northwestern Literature Containing Several Near Libelous Utterances upon Persons in the Public Eye. The pamphlet assaulted the members of the literary community of Washington and Oregon for low standards and nepotism, and earned for Davis the long-lasting enmity of many northwestern writers and scholars. He had happier collaborations with Stevens on short stories. Davis needed money, and Stevens was a well-known writer who commanded a higher rate of pay than Davis could expect. (Paul T. Bryant has suggested that two stories written entirely by Davis were published under Stevens's name.) Encouraged by H. L. Mencken and others, faced with difficulty earning money, and newly married in 1928 to Marion Lay, Davis committed himself to writing professionally and began publishing stories under his own name.

Davis and his wife moved to Washington, then to Arizona, back to Washington, and then to Mexico, where they lived on a grant from the Guggenheim Foundation that enabled Davis to concentrate on a major work. The result was his first novel, *Honey in the Horn*, which appeared in 1935 and won both the Harper Novel Prize and the Pulitzer Prize. In his forties, Davis received recognition as a writer with a promising future, and his next novel was highly anticipated. This second novel, however, was delayed for eleven years by a quarrel with Harper & Brothers, publishers of *Honey in the Horn*, and the breakup of Davis's marriage.

Always a private man, Davis refused an offer from Harper & Brothers of an all-expenses-paid trip to New York City to accept the Pulitzer Prize. This initiated a strain on his relationship with the publishing house that developed into a dispute over royalty payments and the right to publish his next book. The dispute, combined with Marion's suit for divorce in 1942 and Davis's recurring ill health, made the period from 1936 to 1947 unproductive for Davis, save for some short stories published before 1941—although he may have had the manuscript for *Beulah Land* ready in the late 1930's. Davis earned money during this period by writing screenplays.

With the publication of *Harp of a Thousand Strings* by William Morrow in 1947, Davis's career and life took a turn for the better. The publication of *Beulah Land* in 1949 secured his place in American letters. His subsequent novels generally enhanced his reputation and gave him financial security. In 1953, he married Elizabeth Tonkin Martin del Campo, and their relationship was a happy one.

While the 1950's brought Davis hard-earned success and happiness, they also saw the worsening of his health. Doctors amputated his left leg in 1956 because of arteriosclerosis. Almost incessant pain did not prevent him from writing essays, finishing his last novel, *The Distant Music*, and pursuing his interest in literature. In October, 1960, he suffered two heart attacks while visiting San Antonio, Texas; he died on October 31.

Analysis

The novels of H. L. Davis are unified by common themes and a common structure: In each novel except for his last, movement from one place to another provides the various backgrounds for the conflicts and growth of the characters. The themes of flight and pursuit dominate all of Davis's novels, even *The Distant Music*, which structurally is an inverted reflection of its predecessors. In it, Davis focuses on what happens to people who are tied to one place and contrasts them to those who are free.

Honey in the Horn

Honey in the Horn relates the adventures of Clay Calvert, Wade Shively, Uncle Preston Shively, Luce, and Luce's father, a horse trader. Typical of Davis's novels, it is populated by many minor characters in addition to the main characters on whom the action focuses. The book is the creation of a mature author who had been writing for most of his adult life; thus its themes are those that concerned Davis most, and its style is consistent and representative of the author's work. Davis was more interested in characters than in plots, more interested in universal human realities than in local customs. In *Honey in the Horn*, the principal characters act out their drama in a plot that twists and turns almost as if at random; the plot relies heavily on coincidences and is held together primarily by Clay Calvert's travels. The novel faithfully depicts the Oregonian settings and the social customs of the time, but broad Christian symbolism sometimes dominates the novel's imagery. Through symbolism, Davis tries to point out the universal significance of his characters.

Honey in the Horn is set in Oregon in the early part of the twentieth century. The principal events are the murder of a gambler, the development of a relationship between Luce and Clay, Clay's accidental killing of a man, the hanging of Wade Shively, and the discovery that Luce had killed the gambler. These often violent events are set against a background of rural areas and wilderness and mark the growth to maturity of Clay and Luce. They are surrounded by violence and the threat of violence; even the meeting with an old tyrannical owner of a lumber mill about the use of land for camping overnight is fraught with overtones of menace and threats of physical harm. Clay, who initially flees violence, is trapped in it; Luce, too, cannot evade the violence in her nature. As the couple learn to accept each other, they also learn to accept the dark aspects of their own natures; neither wholly good nor wholly evil, they are fully human. Focusing on the relationship of Clay and Luce, the novel emphasizes spiritual trial and growth and presents a sad, slightly world-weary view of humanity that is typical of Davis's novels.

The appearance of symbolism in *Honey in the Horn* is sporadic; it almost totally commands some events and disappears afterward. The most striking example of Christian symbolism is the killing of Wade Shively. Although he is an evil man, he plays the role of Christ in his death: He is captured at night, hanged under false pretenses, and buried in a manner suggesting the burial of Christ. The irony of such symbolism serves Davis's purposes well: Human beings are mixtures of good and evil, satanic at one moment and Christlike the next.

Harp of a Thousand Strings

Davis's use of characters to represent ideas is even more pronounced in the presentation of Melancthon Crawford, Commodore Robinette, Apeyahola (Indian Jory), Jean-Lambert Tallien, and Thérèse de Fontenay in *Harp of a Thousand Strings*. These characters are used to illustrate the theme of the title: Each life is part of a vast instrument, the tones of which reverberate from the past, through the present, and into the future. The broad theme of the interrelationships of human lives dominates the novel to the extent that some of Davis's literary strengths are blunted. The satiric humor that enlivens many of his works is almost nonexistent in *Harp of a Thousand Strings*; the characters sometimes move awkwardly as they fulfill their assigned roles and thus lose some of the natural humanity found in characters in Davis's other novels.

Harp of a Thousand Strings is an ambitious work that portrays the broad sweep of history from the French Revolution to Tripoli in 1805, to the American prairie in the mid-nineteenth century. In flashbacks, the story details how Tallien and Fontenay lived through the French Revolution; how they came to Tripoli and saved Crawford, Robinette, and Apeyahola; and how the three saved men eventually built a town on the American prairie and named it after Fontenay.

The novel begins with Crawford being declared mentally incompetent and then being shipped from the town he helped to found back to his grasping relatives in Pennsylvania. Dismayed by the mistreatment of Crawford, Robinette and Apeyahola discuss their collective fates and recall the events that led them to the prairie. They had met during the attack by American forces on Tripoli—after they had escaped from the Barbary forces, which had held them prisoner. They are met by Tallien, the French consul, and Fontenay. Tallien tells his life story to the three men and notes how it illustrates that the pursuit of love, revenge, and ambition leads to failure: He wins as his wife a woman who does not love him; he finds that avenging personal injustices is silly because of the changes in those he hated; and he finds that power, once gained, controls him rather than his controlling it. In their lives, Apeyahola, Crawford, and Robinette represent the desires for love, revenge, and ambition, and their lives illustrate the futility of their efforts to reach their goals. Apeyahola wants to return to his wife; he ends up murdering her because of her infidelity. Crawford at first suffers failures in his quest to become rich and return to his hometown as an important man; he ultimately returns as a wealthy man in name only because his greedy relatives have made him their ward. Robinette's ambitious military career ends in ignominy: the killing of unarmed Mexican soldiers in Texas.

Beulah Land

Harp of a Thousand Strings shows Davis's interest in the large issues that confront human beings and humanity as a whole. It also shows that those issues are important on a personal level as well as on the dauntingly huge scale of human history. In Davis's later novels, the impact of great issues on personal life is more subtly handled. In *Beulah Land*, the scale of events remains large; the novel sweeps from Tennessee through the forced migration of the Cherokee nation to Oklahoma, through the Civil War, and to Oregon. The novel has a sad, compassionate tone and is pervaded by a gentle sense of humor that enlightens rather than mocks.

The central theme of the novel is the failure of love. The characters of *Beulah Land* seek homes—places where they can live in peace. In the Bible, Beulah Land is the prosperous and peaceful home promised to the children of Israel. In Davis's book, it is both a place and a state of mind. Indians and white people both want lands of their own, and they dispute over who owns what land. The rivalry for land leads to betrayal, hatred, and death from the beginning. Sedayah Gallet saves her people, the citizens of Crow Town, from the Cherokee Trail of Tears by helping the army find hiding Indians. She is motivated by love of land and people; the citizens of Crow Town reject her because of her help to the army, even though the army then spares them from the forced march to the Indian Territory. She eventually flees to Ewen Warne and dies after bearing him a daughter.

Love is pursued throughout the novel as if it were a spiritual Beulah Land. Love of children, love of parents, love of wife, love of people, and love of land are sought with determination, in spite of repeated disasters. Ewen Warne, an independent man who works for the Cherokee, wants to take his daughter Elison with him when he moves. She has been living with the Cargills, who want to keep her. In an argument, Warne kills a Cargill and flees, thus losing his daughter. His other daughter, Ruhama, whose mother was an Indian, and a white boy reared by the Cherokee, Askwani, flee with him. The efforts of Ruhama and Askwani to find peace and fulfilling love serve as focus for much of the novel. Their efforts are sometimes misguided and blind and pull them apart. Their dedication to their search for Beulah Land is at once admirable and pathetic; unlike Clay Calvert and Luce in *Honey in the Horn*, they do not grow into a common understanding. Ruhama seems to have gained some resigned understanding of life and an acceptance of its disappointments, but Askwani is still puzzled, even if a bit wiser. As if to emphasize the divergence of Ruhama and Askwani, Davis has their daughters choose two very different lives: one on a reservation and the other with an Englishman.

Beulah Land shares with *Harp of a Thousand Strings* the generally happy notion that people live beyond themselves in the effects they have on others; humanity shares each person's dreams and sorrows. The characters in *Beulah Land* live on through those they meet and their children, but the notion that love leads to vulnerability, then wounds, and then failure creates a background of universal futility. The novel presents no goals that are worthwhile alternatives to love.

Winds of Morning

In contrast to *Beulah Land*, *Winds of Morning* portrays a cynical young man's discovery of innocence and the good in life. The novel blends folktales, humor, a love story, a murder mystery, and travel into a story about injustice and redemption. The cynical young man is Amos Clarke, a deputy sheriff. The other principal character is Pap Hendricks, an old man who seems younger in spirit than Clarke. The relationship between Clarke and Hendricks is the focus of the book.

Clarke arrests Sylvester Busick for killing an Indian. Busick's trial is rigged so that he is acquitted of manslaughter, and Clarke is made to appear a liar. The sheriff sends Clarke to help Hendricks move some horses to high country. To further complicate Clarke's life, the young man is interested in Calanthe, Busick's daughter, who might have helped set Clarke up for his fall. The journey to the high country is marked by the help Hendricks and Clarke provide for those they meet and by clues to the mysterious murder of Farrand, a rancher. They discover that their companion, Estéban d'Andreas, is the supposed murderer. Later, they determine that d'Andreas was tricked by Farrand's wife, who is also Hendricks's daughter. Busick reappears as her foreman; he is blackmailing her because he knows Mrs. Farrand lied about the murder. Hendricks, who has long—and for good reason—kept his distance from his daughter, speaks with her and reveals the strength of a father's love. His help saves his daughter from Busick and d'Andreas from execution.

One of the novel's important themes is that of reconciliation. Although his daughter had falsely accused him of raping her, Hendricks helps her. Whatever her faults, she remains his daughter and his responsibility. The theme of responsibility is also important. Hendricks finds peace within himself when he acknowledges his responsibility for the death of his wife. Reconciliation between friends and relatives is possible through acknowledgment of love and responsibility; reconciliation with one's own past and spirit is also possible. The ultimate reconciliation comes when Hendricks acknowledges Busick as his son. The peace of spirit he attains comes through his acceptance of the consequences of his acts. Clarke learns from observing Hendricks that he can reconcile with Calanthe.

Winds of Morning is set in Oregon in 1927. The scenes are primarily rural and serve to create a pastoral tone for the background of the novel. While traveling through the semiwilderness, Clarke learns that violence and treachery should indeed be watched for, but that they are not all that is to be found in humanity. Oregon provides wide-open spaces for the opening of his spirit.

The Distant Music

In *The Distant Music*, Davis uses Oregon for opposite purposes. In *Winds of Morning*, the land seems liberating, but in *The Distant Music*, it imprisons and rules the main characters. The plot focuses on successive generations of the Mulock family. The first Ranse Mulock settles his homestead along the Columbia River; his wife, a white woman purchased out of bondage from Indians, has a miscarriage of a pregnancy sired by an Indian. An angry, resentful man, the first Ranse Mulock bears a grudge against the Indian and another against the snooping, self-righteous citizens of the local town, Clark's Landing. He drives himself to build his land into something of value. He dies of exposure after gunning down the Indian responsible for his wife's first pregnancy—he seems at peace with himself for the first time after he has murdered the Indian. The succeeding Mulocks are bound to the land by their struggle to preserve it. Claib, the elder son of the first Ranse Mulock, dies when he leaves the land; without it, his life seems to lack meaning. His younger brother, the second Ranse Mulock, takes over the land, even though he wants to leave it. He spends his life subdividing the land and managing it. Betrayed by his supposed friends and business partners and abandoned by an ungrateful wife, he is left with only his land. He never escapes from it.

The hold of the land extends to the next generation, even though the third Ranse Mulock temporarily escapes to work for the railroad. His old father makes his own ineffectual attempt to escape, is beaten by thieves, and is found by young Ranse and Nina, daughter of the elder Ranse's housekeeper, who is in turn the daughter of one of the people who had betrayed the elder Ranse. Young Ranse returns to the land to help his father and, like his father, is trapped.

Travelers, wanderers, and the broad horizon contrast with the lives of bondage of the Mulocks throughout *The Distant Music*. Davis portrays what happened to the settlers of Oregon, their change from free spirits to parochial ones. The book is sketchy; it lacks the depth and detail that a story covering three generations of people should command. The darkness of *The Distant Music* resembles that of *Beulah Land*, but without the hubris that the pursuit of a great—if empty—goal provides the characters of the earlier book. The movement from one generation to the next is worthy of Davis's other novels; *The Distant Music* is broad in its vision of time and of individual people caught in social change.

Davis was a writer of great ambition. He drew on his experiences to create novels that speak of universal human problems. They are consistent in their portrayal of the universality of human experience, whether in France, Tripoli, the Midwest, or Oregon; in their presentation of individual men and women as part of the large family and history of humanity; and in their sympathetic understanding for people, whatever their weaknesses.

Kirk H. Beetz

Other major works

short fiction: *Team Bells Woke Me, and Other Stories*, 1953.

poetry: *Primapara*, 1919; *Proud Riders*, 1942; *The Selected Poems of H. L. Davis*, 1978.

nonfiction: *Status Rerum: A Manifesto upon the Present Condition of Northwestern Literature Containing Several Near Libelous Utterances upon Persons in the Public Eye*, 1926.

miscellaneous: *Kettle of Fire*, 1959; *Collected Essays and Short Stories*, 1986.

Bibliography

Armstrong, George M. "H. L. Davis's *Beulah Land:* A Revisionist's Novel of Westering." In *The Westering Experience in American Literature: Bicentennial Essays*, edited by Merrill Lewis and L. L. Lee. Bellingham: Western Washington University Press, 1977. Maintains that *Beulah Land* is Davis's only novel to make a direct presentation of settling the West as a foolish effort to achieve impossible goals. Davis used history to challenge the conventions of fiction, as his treatment of the Civil War and Indians in *Beulah Land* illustrates.

Bain, Robert. *H. L. Davis*. Boise, Idaho: Boise State University Press, 1974. Informative biography discusses Davis's life and work and also examines the role of the West in American literature in general.

Bryant, Paul T. *H. L. Davis*. Boston: Twayne, 1978. Introductory study of the author includes a brief biography and analysis of his novels, including *Honey in the Horn*, *Harp of a Thousand Strings*, and *The Distant Music*. Discusses the works' main themes and describes the critical reception of each. Final chapter assesses Davis's achievement through analysis of his style, structural techniques, use of folklore and natural landscape, basic themes, and symbolism. Includes chronology, notes and references, selected and annotated bibliography, and index.

_______. "H. L. Davis." In *A Literary History of the American West*. Fort Worth: Texas Christian University Press, 1987. Brief article presents Davis as a paradox: a fine stylist who chose to work in a genre of clichés and a narrator of Western tales who insisted that there was nothing special about the Western experience. As a result, in both his long and short fiction his writing is uneven. Includes a selected bibliography of primary and secondary sources.

"H. L. Davis." In *Twentieth-Century American Western Writers*, edited by Richard H. Cracroft. First series. Vol. 206 in *Dictionary of Literary Biography*. Detroit, Mich.: Gale Group, 1999. Presents a brief biography and analyses of Davis's books, along with a list of his works and a bibliography.

Kohler, Dayton. "H. L. Davis: Writer in the West." *College English* 14 (December, 1952): 133-140. Sketches events in Davis's early life in Oregon to explain his fictional world. Argues that he carefully examines the sociology of the West as a drifting society on a static frontier. Analyzes *Honey in the Horn*, *Harp of a Thousand Strings*, *Beulah Land*, and *Winds of Morning* and asserts that Davis's style sets him apart from more popular writers in the genre, as it evidences a strong sense of the interrelationships among rhythm, tone, imagery, scene, and character.

OSAMU DAZAI

Born: Kanagi, Aomori, Japan; June 19, 1909
Died: Tokyo, Japan; June 13, 1948
Also known as: Shūji Tsushima

Principal long fiction

Shin Hamuretto, 1941
Seigi to bishō, 1942
Udaijin Sanetomo, 1943
Pandora no hako, 1945
Sekibetsu, 1945
Shayó, 1947 (*The Setting Sun*, 1956)
Ningen shikkaku, 1948 (*No Longer Human*, 1958)

Other literary forms

Like many other modern Japanese prose writers, Osamu Dazai (dah-zi) worked in a variety of modes and forms, many of which do not correspond readily to the terminology of modern Western criticism. Although known in the West and indeed in Japan primarily as a novelist, Dazai wrote only two books that might be called novels even in a loose sense. He wrote a number of memoir-type works that describe certain stretches of his life but that also incorporate additional commentary in a manner that casts doubt on the autobiographical authenticity of the account. Some of these works, *Omoide* (1934; memories) and *Tókyó hakkei* (1941; eight views of Tokyo), for example, are fairly lengthy accounts; others, such as "Mangan" (wr. 1938; the vow), and "Kinshu no kokoro" (wr. 1943; what it's like to abstain), are, on the other hand, brief and essentially anecdotal in nature.

In addition to his own experiences, a main source of material for Dazai resides in works of literature and history. Two of his best collections of tales are based on sources in classical Japanese literature. *Otogi zóshi* (1945)—the title refers to a group of miscellaneous stories from medieval times—involves a retelling of four tales, with extensive interpolations and commentary that mark the works as unmistakably by Dazai; *Shinshaku shokoku banashi* (1945) gave Dazai the opportunity to retell twelve tales by the popular sixteenth century novelist and poet Ihara Saikaku. Dazai also used a number of Western sources as inspiration for his writing. William Shakespeare's *Hamlet* (1602) provided the plot for a dramatic farce, *Shin Hamuretto*, and Friedrich Schiller's poem "Die Burgschaft" was retold as an adventuresome moral fable. Dazai even dissected and rewrote an obscure work by the German playwright Herbert Eulenberg. Most important, Dazai familiarized himself with the New Testament and made constant reference to favorite passages. In one case, he constructed a dramatic monologue in which Judas, after the Crucifixion, reveals a very worldly view of Christ. Titled *Kakekomi uttae* (1940; heed my plea), Dazai's work would probably have appealed to the D. H. Lawrence of *The Man Who Died* (1929).

ACHIEVEMENTS

Both in Japan and abroad, Osamu Dazai is most widely known as the author of two novels, *The Setting Sun* and *No Longer Human*, both of which were written shortly after World War II, during the final three years of the author's life. As a result of these works, Dazai was assuredly the most acclaimed writer in Japan in the years following the war. With the exception of a single short story titled "Biyon no tsuma" (1947; "Villon's Wife," 1956), these two novels have had far wider circulation in English translation than any other of the approximately twenty miscellaneous tales and stories by Dazai that have also been rendered into English. Dazai is best known to readers of English as a novelist, and this, in fact, is generally true of the other European languages into which his works have been translated.

In the decades since his death, Dazai has been thoroughly studied by Japanese critics. An enormous number of books have been published, from ponderous tomes on the author's familiarity with Christianity and Communism to enthralling accounts (mainly by fellow writers) of Dazai's various struggles with drugs, drinking, women, and publishers. For a number of years in the 1960's and early 1970's, a periodical called *Dazai Osamu Studies* was issued, one indication of the huge outpouring of scholarly and personal articles on this particular author.

Over the years, wild acclaim has been replaced by a sober assessment of Dazai's achievement. A number of critics regard Dazai as among the greatest Japanese writers of the twentieth century; others, however, express doubts about the permanence of his accomplishment. Much of this disagreement seems to stem from varying interpretations as to what the author was really doing. Some see him as a moralist, others as a very talented raconteur. Most scholars insist that the autobiographical aspects of Dazai's writings are crucial, while a few try to play down this dimension of Dazai. Of one thing there can be no doubt. Dazai remains widely read in Japan, especially among younger readers. His novels and collections of his stories line the shelves of the bookstores of Tokyo and other cities and towns, along with the works of Yasunari Kawabata, Jun'ichiró Tanizaki, Yukio Mishima, Shúsaku Endó, and other writers who have over the years become better known outside Japan than has Dazai.

BIOGRAPHY

Osamu Dazai was born Shūji Tsushima in 1909 in Kanagi, a small town in the Aomori Prefecture of the Japanese island of Honshu. His family held extensive lands, the taxes on which entitled his father, Gen'emon, to move eventually from an elective seat in the lower house into the upper house of the diet. The tenth of eleven children, Dazai was initially cared for by a nursemaid, then later by a favorite aunt and a staff of servants, because his parents were unable to do so. Dazai's mother, Tane, was exhausted by the successive pregnancies, and his father was either preoccupied with financial matters, when at home, or absent from Kanagi altogether during the legislative sessions.

During his childhood, Dazai enjoyed a comparative freedom, as his elder brothers were already being groomed to undertake the responsibility of maintaining the family fortune and reputation. Once his marked intelligence became evident, the family insisted that Dazai excel in his studies, an obligation that he diligently met throughout his elementary schooling in Kanagi. He began to founder, however, at the secondary level, when he encountered the competition of more select students and the severe scrutiny of teachers relatively indifferent to his prestigious name.

Billeted in the higher school town of Hirosaki, some twenty miles from the family home, Dazai began to cultivate certain fashionable tastes, perhaps as an escape from the relentless scholastic demands confronting him. He dressed flamboyantly and attended the local teahouses, took lessons in ballad chanting, and even courted a young geisha named Koyama Hatsuyo, whom he later insisted upon marrying in spite of his family's shocked disapproval.

During his years in higher school, Dazai did not confine his study to the conservative curriculum, in part because of the influence of the radical ideas that made considerable headway in Japan during the 1920's, a period of economic difficulty throughout the country. The impact of these ideas is apparent in his writings, in which he expresses the profound sense of guilt, shared by his older contemporary, Arishima Takeo, toward the tenant-farmers who worked the family lands partly to support his privileged existence. One of his earliest stories, published in 1930, depicts a youngster who joins a peasant band in rebellion against his own elder brother, a rural landowner of tyrannical arrogance.

Dazai turned twenty-one in 1930 and went off to Tokyo, ostensibly to major in French literature at the university. Living several hundred miles from home, Dazai seldom attended classes, although he continued to receive an allowance on the pretext that he was working steadily toward his degree. Much of his time was spent with radical student groups, to whom he gave some financial assistance and on whose behalf he claimed to have carried out seditious acts. By his own admission, however, Dazai was incapable of becoming a full-fledged revolutionary.

At the same time, he could not seek a genuine reconciliation with his family and therefore continued to deceive them about his studies. Finding this position untenable, Dazai attempted suicide three times and became so addicted to drugs that he was committed to an asylum for a time. The tendency toward tuberculosis—a weakness that he shared with others of his family—was aggravated during this period. By 1937, Dazai was living alone in a shabby boardinghouse in Tokyo. His ties with both his family and the university had been formally severed, and the geisha he had so boldly insisted on marrying had returned to her home in northern Japan.

Slowly, Dazai began to hope for a reconciliation as he recognized that the Tsushima family, despite its political standing and economic status, was marked for tragedy. The two oldest sons had died before his birth, and during his first decade in Tokyo two brothers, two sisters, a nephew, and a cousin also died. Gen'emon had died in 1923, when Dazai was only thirteen years old, and although Tane survived until 1942, she remained in frail health to the end. The family encountered mundane problems as well, notably an accusation that Bunji, the oldest surviving son and present head of the family, had won election to a diet seat through fraud.

Concern over Dazai's notoriety prevented any dramatic move by the family toward reconciliation. Nevertheless, the Tsushimas tried to promote his rehabilitation by quietly sanctioning efforts to bring about a marriage between Dazai and Ishihara Michiko, a schoolteacher from the city of Kófu in central Japan. The wedding took place in January, 1939, after which Dazai settled down to a relatively stable life. A few months later, he and his wife moved to Mitaka Village near Tokyo. The first of three children, a daughter, was born in 1941.

During World War II, Dazai gradually established a reputation as a leading writer of his time, a recognition that brought special satisfaction. His brother, Bunji, appreciated literature, occasionally composing a piece himself. From the late 1930's, Dazai had wished for literary success as a means of compensating in his family's eyes for his academic failure, if not for his earlier radicalism. Apart from this strategy, Dazai tried forthrightly to cultivate the goodwill of his elder brothers, returning to Kanagi several times during the final years of the war. When his house in Mitaka was severely damaged in a bombing raid, Dazai went back home with his wife and children, remaining there until November, 1946.

Having returned to Tokyo for the last time, Dazai began to neglect his family for a life of reckless dissipation. The explanations for this lapse are numerous—a foreboding that he, like certain of his kin, was marked for an early death; an inability to cope with the fame earned by his postwar writings; susceptibility to the machinations of discontented women. One such woman, Yamakazi Tomie, evidently persuaded Dazai to commit suicide by entering the swollen waters of the Tomagawa Canal with her. His body was recovered by the police on June 19, 1948, his thirty-ninth birthday.

Analysis

Osamu Dazai cannot be understood solely with reference to any single work, or even to the two postwar novels that tend to dominate discussions of his writing. Literary studies of Dazai in the United States have tended to treat his entire career instead of focusing so steadily on the postwar novels and stories. Dazai's achievement is seen as a kind of mosaic made up of individual works, the rationale of each work being as much in its contribution to the whole as in its worth as a single creation. Except for Masao Miyoshi's essay "Till Death Do Us Part," critics have not accorded this type of treatment to the novels *The Setting Sun* and *No Longer Human*. Perhaps the novels will come to be seen as important and integral parts of the larger mosaic that is Dazai's oeuvre.

The Setting Sun

The title *The Setting Sun* so vividly suggested the decline of the aristocracy in postwar Japan that the term *Shayózoku*, or "setting sun class," became a catchword for the phenomenon. It is debatable how much real understanding Dazai had of the highly restrictive circles of the prewar aristocracy. Dazai's own family was more on the order of nouveau riche and very provincial as well. These qualifications aside, however, in *The Setting Sun*, Dazai assuredly conveyed his private sense of bleakness.

The novel centers on a family of only three people—a genteel and rather pathetic mother, the outwardly gruff but tenderhearted son Naoji, and the increasingly realistic and tough-minded daughter Kazuko. The mother is depicted in the opening scene of the novel spooning soup into her daughter's mouth. Shortly thereafter, she is described as loitering behind a shrub in the family garden. A moment later, she coyly announces to her daughter that she has been urinating while she was out of view. Passages such as these point to one of several basic problems in the novel. The author, through his narrator, Kazuko, suggests that the mother embodies natural aristocratic qualities that are inimitable. Possibly the idiosyncratic behavior of the mother is to be taken as a sly sort of satire on the "declining aristocracy" of the book's title. Much more likely, however, is that the unconventionality of the mother's conduct represents the genuine aristocracy, possibly recalling Marie Antoinette and her circle at Le petit Trianon in Versailles.

In either event, it is clear that both the son, Naoji, and the daughter, Kazuko, regard their mother as a symbol of certain aristocratic values that are on the wane in the face of an alien process of democratization being imposed upon Japan by the U.S. occupation in the aftermath of the surrender. Having lost their father and most of the family wealth, mother and children must fend for themselves as best they can. In fact, the novel might well be read as a treatise on the various fates lying in wait for the disenfranchised members of the aristocracy.

In poor health even at the beginning of the novel, the mother gradually declines and eventually dies a natural and peaceful death. Given her obvious inability to cope with the practical problems of surviving under the new conditions of postwar Japan—she is depicted as totally dependent upon a character called Uncle Wada—her death seems to symbolize the passing of an era. It also signals the need of her two children to come to terms in some way with the new system of values.

Kazuko and her mother are portrayed as personally close to each other. Indeed, a good portion of the narrative is given over to describing their life together—first, in the old Tokyo house that they were forced to give up and, finally, in the cottage at Izu where they can live simply and frugally. Kazuko cares deeply for her mother and tries to protect her. She fears the possible return of her brother, Naoji, who was listed as missing in action in the

South Pacific early in the book. Reckless and, for a time, addicted to drugs, Naoji would almost certainly disrupt the semi-idyllic life that Kazuko would like to have with her mother.

Despite a sharing of interests, Kazuko and her mother are ultimately seen in sharp contrast to each other. The contrast is strikingly evident in the symbolism of the appearance of snakes at certain crucial points in the narrative. In general, snakes seem to signal impending death. Kazuko, however, imagines a snake within her own breast, a snake that threatens the very life of her mother. In fact, as the novel unfolds, Kazuko gradually moves away from the genteel values represented by her mother. She recalls the days of physical work required of her as a young Japanese citizen during the war and finds great pleasure working in the garden at the cottage in Izu.

To all appearances an ally, Kazuko remains inwardly and involuntarily an enemy of her mother. With Naoji, the opposite seems true. After his sudden and dramatic return home, he flaunts his bad manners and rough language, squanders the little money the family possesses on drinking and on women, and does not try to conceal his dissipation. Always indulgent toward her son, the mother is so overjoyed to have him safely home that she cannot summon up even a whimper of protest. With the mother's death, Naoji goes out of control. He ends up committing suicide, explaining with a note to Kazuko that his recklessness was a desperate attempt to join the masses. In the end, he has come to the realization that he is, after all, an aristocrat.

Again, Dazai is possibly making a sly comment about aristocracy. Yet Kazuko takes her brother quite seriously. Indeed, even before Naoji's death, she has been slowly working out a scheme whereby she proves to be the sole survivor of this old-fashioned family. She has come to know a dissolute novelist named Uehara, a friend of her brother (who himself aspires to be a writer). Eventually, Kazuko sees to it that she is seduced by Uehara—not from any attraction for the rather unattractive novelist but simply that she might bear a child able to cope with the future. At the end of the novel, she senses that she is pregnant. Further, while not necessarily expecting a reply, she writes to Uehara asking that he let his own wife hold the child in her arms while he tells her that Naoji had this child by a woman he loved.

A puzzling novel in many respects, *The Setting Sun* has been examined by both Japanese and foreign critics from many points of view. As is often the case with Dazai, the language of the work is conspicuous. When Naoji arrives home, the sudden shift to rough, substandard Japanese from the pleasant chitchat of mother and daughter is almost shocking to a reader of the Japanese original. The fluidly symbolic manner of part of the narrative has also attracted a great deal of comment, one critic referring to *The Setting Sun* as a kind of symphony with a definite arrangement of movements. Most critics, however, see the work as a reflection of the chaotic times in which it was written and, more particularly, as an expression of the desperate state of Dazai's own life in that final year or two before his own suicide.

No Longer Human

While *The Setting Sun* contains echoes of Dazai's life, *No Longer Human* portrays as its main character what most critics would term a genuine surrogate of the author. The very name Óba Yozo is one that Dazai had used in an early work titled "The Flower of Buffoonery" (1935). In "The Flower of Buffoonery," Dazai evokes the strange condition of the survivor of a suicide attempt. The man has hurled himself into the sea near Kamakura, along with a woman he scarcely knew. The woman perishes, and the surviving man has to face a police investigation even while he recuperates in the hospital. All of these things occurred to Dazai himself, not long after he came to Tokyo to study at the university.

The events of *No Longer Human* do not conform so precisely to the known course of Dazai's life as do those of "The Flower of Buffoonery." The association, however, between protagonist and author is suggested in certain indirect ways. Óba Yozo is abandoned by his family, just as Dazai was disinherited. Under the tutelage of a friend, Yozo learns the use of alcohol and drugs. He encounters difficulty in his relations with women and ends up in an asylum for a time. None of this conforms exactly to Dazai's experience, but each aspect has a counterpart of some kind in the author's life. More pertinent, perhaps, the rhetoric—especially the occasionally exaggerated language—applied to Yozo suggests the descriptive manner of Dazai's explicitly autobiographical portraits.

The main text of the work consists of three notebooks, composed by Óba Yozo presumably after his older brother has put him safely away with an old servant in an unnamed village. These notebooks are handed over quite by accident to a certain writer who, in a brief epilogue, announces his intention of publishing them in a magazine. The notebooks themselves detail Yozo's gradual withdrawal from society and its conventions. Even as a boy, he has found it difficult to accept the habitual and practical nature of everyday life. As he matures, he searches for various means of survival, the unique and most enduring one perhaps being a dependence upon clowning as a way of relating to others; he also marries an innocent and trusting girl named Yoshiko. Presently her very trustworthiness results in a seduction accidentally witnessed by Yozo himself.

As in *The Setting Sun*, it is difficult in *No Longer Human* to ferret out the author's intention. The majority of critics take the portrait of Yozo as another instance of autobiography—the author depicting the depths to which he himself fell in his own life.

James O'Brien

OTHER MAJOR WORKS

SHORT FICTION: *Bannen*, 1936; *Tókyó hakkei*, 1941; *Kajitsu*, 1944; *Otogi zóshi*, 1945; *Shinshaku shokoku banashi*, 1945; *Fuyu no hanabi*, 1947; *Dazai Osamu: Selected Stories and Sketches*, 1983; *Self Portraits*, 1991; *Blue Bamboo: Tales of Fantasy and Romance*, 1993.

PLAYS: *Fuyu no hanabi*, pb. 1946; *Haru no kaeha*, pb. 1946.

NONFICTION: *Tsugaru*, 1944 (English translation, 1985; also known as *Return to Tsugaru: Travels of a Purple Tramp*, 1985).

MISCELLANEOUS: *Dazai Osamu zenshū*, 1955-1956 (12 volumes; collected works).

BIBLIOGRAPHY

Cohn, Joel R. "Dazai Osamu." In *Modern Japanese Writers*, edited by Jay Rubin. New York: Charles Scribner's Sons, 2001. Cohn, who has written a book examining Dazai's work, here provides biographical information and literary analyses of Dazai's writings. Includes an extensive bibliography of works by and about Dazai.

_______. *Studies in the Comic Spirit in Modern Japanese Fiction*. Cambridge, Mass.: Harvard University Press, 1998. Examines thematic, structural, and stylistic elements in the works of Dazai, Masuji Ibuse, and Hisashi Inoue, demonstrating how these writers defy the traditional Japanese idea that literary humor must serve a serious purpose. Includes bibliographical references and an index.

Keene, Donald. *Appreciations of Japanese Culture*. 1971. Reprint. New York: Kodansha International, 1991. Of particular relevance is the section on Osamu Dazai in chapter 4, "Three Modern Novelists," which focuses on the difference between Western and Japanese responses to Dazai's fiction, the strongly autobiographical elements in his works, and the style and major themes of his narrative. Supplemented by illustrations and a short reading list.

Lyons, Phyllis I. *The Saga of Dazai Osamu: A Critical Study with Translations*. Stanford, Calif.: Stanford University Press, 1985. The first part of this study examines Dazai's life, including his mental and emotional health; part 2 analyzes his novels from various critical perspectives. Includes a bibliography and an index.

O'Brien, James. *Dazai Osamu*. Boston: Twayne, 1975. An introduction to the author that combines a biography with a chronologically based examination of Dazai's creative output. Preceded by a chronological summary and followed by a select bibliography.

Rimer, J. Thomas. "Dazai Osamu: The Death of the Past, *The Setting Sun*." In *Modern Japanese Fiction and Its Traditions: An Introduction*. Princeton, N.J.: Princeton University Press, 1978. Rimer views the novel *The Setting Sun* as a reflection of the tensions in Japan before, during, and after the war years. The characters and situations relentlessly probe the realities of a transitional period.

Starrs, Roy. "Nation and Region in the Work of Dazai Osamu." In *Japanese Cultural Nationalism: At Home and in the Asia Pacific*, edited by Starrs. Folkestone, England: Global Oriental, 2004. Reprints lectures delivered at a 2002 conference on Japanese cultural nationalism. Starrs's lecture focuses on Dazai's representation of Japan generally and the country's Tsugaru district specifically.

Ueda, Makoto. *Modern Japanese Writers and the Nature of Literature*. Stanford, Calif.: Stanford University Press, 1976. In a chapter on Dazai, Ueda examines Dazai's literary concepts as revealed in his fiction. Underlying his "expansive, emotional, and spontaneous" prose style, with its seeming artlessness, is a view of literature as a "food for losers." Includes a bibliography focusing on Dazai.

Wolfe, Alan Stephen. *Suicidal Narrative in Modern Japan: The Case of Dazai Osamu*. Princeton, N.J.: Princeton University Press, 1990. Wolfe uses contemporary Western literary and cultural theories and a knowledge of Dazai's work within the context of Japanese history to provide a deconstructive interpretation of the author's writings. This analytical study focuses on the connections between autobiography, suicide, alienation, and modernization in Dazai's writings.

DANIEL DEFOE

Born: London, England; 1660
Died: London, England; April 26, 1731
Also known as: Daniel Foe

Principal long fiction

The Life and Strange Surprizing Adventures of Robinson Crusoe, of York, Mariner, Written by Himself, 1719 (commonly known as *Robinson Crusoe*)
The Farther Adventures of Robinson Crusoe: Being the Second and Last Part of His Life, 1719
The History of the Life and Adventures of Mr. Duncan Campbell, a Gentleman Who, Tho' Deaf and Dumb, Writes Down Any Stranger's Name at First Sight, with Their Future Contingencies of Fortune, 1720
The Life, Adventures and Pyracies of the Famous Captain Singleton, 1720
Memoirs of a Cavalier: Or, A Military Journal of the Wars in Germany, and the Wars in England, from the Year 1632 to the Year 1648, 1720
Serious Reflections During the Life and Surprising Adventures of Robinson Crusoe with His Vision of the Angelick World, 1720
The Fortunes and Misfortunes of the Famous Moll Flanders, Written from Her Own Memorandums, 1722 (commonly known as *Moll Flanders*)
The History and Remarkable Life of the Truly Honourable Col Jacque, Commonly Call'd Col Jack, 1722 (commonly known as *Colonel Jack*)
A Journal of the Plague Year, 1722 (also known as *The History of the Great Plague in London*)
The Fortunate Mistress, 1724 (also known as *Roxana*)
The Memoirs of an English Officer Who Serv'd in the Dutch War in 1672, to the Peace of Utrecht in 1713, by Capt George Carleton, 1728 (also known as *A True and Genuine History of the Last Two Wars* and *The Memoirs of Cap George Carleton*)

Other literary forms

Although Daniel Defoe (dih-FOH) is mainly remembered as the author of *The Life and Strange Surprizing Adventures of Robinson Crusoe, of York, Mariner, Written by Himself*, more commonly known as *Robinson Crusoe*, he did not begin to write fiction until he was fifty-nine years old. He spent the earlier part of his writing career primarily in producing essays and political pamphlets and working for strongly partisan newspapers. He also wrote travel books, poetry (usually on political or topical issues), and biographies of rogues and criminals.

Achievements

Daniel Defoe's principal contribution to English literature is in the novel, and he has been called the first English novelist. The extent of his contribution, however, has been debated. A contemporary of Defoe, Charles Gildon, wrote an attack on *Robinson Crusoe*, criticizing, in part, inconsistencies in the narrative. Such problems are not infrequent in Defoe's long and episodic plots. Nevertheless, readers of almost any of Defoe's works find themselves in real and solid worlds, and Defoe's constant enumeration of *things*—such as, in *Moll Flanders*, the layettes for Moll's illegitimate children, the objects she steals, even her escape routes through London—has earned for the author a reputation as a realist and for his style the label "circumstantial realism." To see Defoe as a photographic realist, however, is also to see his limitations, and some of his critics argue that the formlessness of his novels shows his lack of the very shaping power that belongs to great art. Further, even his circumstantial realism is not of the visual sort: Once Moll has named an object, for example, she rarely goes on to describe it in such detail that the reader may visualize it.

In the late twentieth century, Defoe's novels underwent a reassessment, and critics started to see him as more than a mere assembler of objects. Although these critics diverge widely in their interpretation of his techniques, they do agree that Defoe consciously developed themes and used his narratives to shape these themes, all of which center on the conflict between spiritual and earthly values. Instead of viewing Defoe as a plodding literalist, some critics see a keen irony in his work: Moll's actions and her commentary on those actions, they argue, do not always agree. The reader is thus allowed to cultivate a certain ironic detachment about Moll. While few readers would judge Defoe to be a deeply psychological novelist, this double perspective does contribute to a rudimentary analysis of character. Others see a religious vision in his works, one that underwrites an almost allegorical interpretation of his novels: The ending of *Robinson Crusoe*, the killing of the wolves, is seen as Crusoe slaying his earthly passions. While such a reading may seem forced, one should perhaps remember that John Bunyan was a near contemporary of Defoe—he even preached at Morton's Academy at Stoke Newington while Defoe was a student there—and that readers in his time were accustomed to reading allegorically.

Part of the fascination—and achievement—of Defoe may well lie in the tension between realism and allegory that informs his work. Using natural dialogue and a kind of realistic detail, Defoe can yet go beyond these to create events and characters that are, finally, mythic.

BIOGRAPHY

Daniel Defoe was born Daniel Foe in the parish of St. Giles, London, the son of James Foe, a Dissenter and a tallow chandler. (Only after the age of forty did Defoe change his last name, perhaps to seem more aristocratic.) The date of his birth is conjectural: In 1683, he listed his age on his marriage license as twenty-four, but since his sister, Elizabeth, was born in 1659, it is probable that Defoe was born the next year. Not much is known of his early childhood, but his education was certainly important in molding his interests. Being a Dissenter, Defoe was not allowed to attend Oxford or Cambridge; instead, he went to a dissenting academy presided over by the Reverend Charles Morton. While offering a study of the classics, the academy also stressed modern languages, geography, and mathematics, practical subjects neglected at the universities. This interest in the practical seems to have stayed with Defoe all his life: When his library was sold after his death, the advertisements listed "several hundred Curious, Scarce Tracts on . . . Husbandry, Trade, Voyages, Natural History, Mines, Minerals, etc." Defoe's appreciation of the objects and processes by which one is enabled to live in the world is obvious: After making a table and chair, Crusoe reflects that "by stating and squaring everything by reason and by making the most rational judgment of things, every man may be in time master of every mechanic art."

Although his father intended him for the ministry, Defoe became a merchant after leaving school and probably traveled on the Continent as part of his business. In 1684, he married the daughter of another dissenting merchant, and she brought him a considerable dowry. Defoe's fortunes seemed to be rising, but in 1685, he was briefly involved in the duke of Monmouth's rebellion, a Protestant uprising. Although he escaped the king's soldiers, this event illustrates Defoe's willingness to espouse dangerous political causes: Three former schoolmates who joined the rebellion were caught and hanged. While his affairs seemed to prosper during this time,

Daniel Defoe. (Library of Congress)

there were disquieting lawsuits—eight between 1688 and 1694, one by his mother-in-law, whom he seems to have swindled—that cast doubt on both Defoe's economic stability and his moral character. In fact, by 1692 he was bankrupt, a victim of losses at sea and his own speculations. Defoe's character is always difficult to label; while the lawsuits show his unsavory side, he did make arrangements after his ruin to repay his creditors, which he seems to have done with surprising thoroughness.

Defoe then began building a brick factory on some land that he owned in Tilbury. This enterprise went well and, with William and Mary on the throne, Defoe could praise the government with a clear conscience. He admired William's religious toleration, foreign policy, and encouragement of English trade. He wrote several pamphlets supporting William's policy of containing Louis XIV's political aspirations, a policy not always popular in England. When William's followers from Holland were harassed by the English, Defoe wrote *The True-Born Englishman: A Satyr* (1701), a long poem arguing that the English are themselves a mixed race who cannot afford to deride other nationalities.

With the accession of Queen Anne of England in 1702, the Dissenters—and Defoe—suffered serious political grievances. Fiercely loyal to the Church of England, Anne looked with disfavor on other religious groups, and bills were introduced to limit the freedom of Dissenters. While both houses of Parliament debated the Occasional Conformity Bill in 1702—a bill that would have effectually prevented Dissenters from holding political office—Defoe published "The Shortest Way with the Dissenters," an ironic pamphlet urging the government to annihilate this group entirely. At first it was taken at face value and applauded by the High Church party, but when its irony was perceived, a warrant was issued for Defoe's arrest, and he went into hiding.

Fearful of imprisonment and the pillory, Defoe sent letters to Daniel Finch, second earl of Nottingham, the secretary of state, trying to negotiate a pardon: He would raise a troop of horses for the government at his own expense; he would volunteer to fight—and possibly die—in the Netherlands. Nottingham was inflexible, however, and when Defoe was found, he was imprisoned in Newgate, the scene of Moll's incarceration. Two months later, he was fined two hundred marks, forced to stand in the pillory three times, imprisoned at the queen's discretion, and forced to provide sureties for his good behavior for the next seven years. This experience helps, perhaps, to explain Defoe's later political views, which seemed to his contemporaries based on expediency rather than conviction: In a letter to a friend, he said that, after Newgate, he would never feel himself maligned if called a coward. When Defoe describes Moll's stay in prison, he knows whereof he speaks.

How long Defoe might have remained in Newgate at the queen's discretion cannot, of course, be known; certainly the government showed no sign of releasing him during the summer or in the fall. He appealed to Robert Harley, a man destined to take Nottingham's place when the latter had been dismissed by the queen. After leisurely negotiations—perhaps to render Defoe more grateful when his pardon finally did come—Harley obtained Defoe's release in November, 1703, the queen even going so far as to send money to Mrs. Defoe and another sum to Defoe to settle his debt.

Harley continued to be influential in Defoe's life; indeed, popular opinion seems to have been that Defoe prostituted himself, abandoning all political ideals for Harley. Still, it is hard to imagine how a forty-three-year-old ruined businessman, with a wife and seven children to support, could begin life over if not with the help of a powerful ally. Defoe's letters to Harley also suggest that Harley sometimes kept him short of funds on purpose, perhaps to make him more compliant. In any case, Defoe's career was definitely the writing of political pamphlets—usually in favor of Harley's policies—and he also edited and wrote most of *A Weekly Review*, which ran from 1704 to 1713. Perhaps Defoe's most significant work for Harley was the establishment of a spy system in England to determine what the national sentiment was for the government. This project—which was Defoe's own idea—began in 1704 when Harley sent Defoe on a preliminary reconnaissance trip through the country. This was the first of several such trips, including one to Edinburgh, Scotland, in 1706 to determine local opinion about the proposed union of the English and Scottish parliaments. On all these trips, Defoe had to assume fictitious identities, and he seems to have relished this subterfuge; it is perhaps significant that Defoe's characters usually are forced to assume many varied disguises in the course of their eventual lives. Even Defoe's tracts and pamphlets bear witness to his fascination with assuming various roles: One critic has estimated that Defoe created eighty-seven personae in these works.

After Harley's political decline and Queen Anne's death, Defoe continued to work for the government, characteristically, in a role requiring deception. Pretending to be a Tory out of favor with the government, he obtained a job on *Mist's Weekly Journal*, one of the most influential Tory papers. In this way, he was able to temper the writing so that the paper's attacks on the government became less virulent. Defoe's shadowy activities are difficult to follow, but it seems that he was also performing the same service to the government on other papers: *Dyer's News-Letter, Dormer's News-Letter*, and *Mercurius Politicus*. Defoe's easy transition from Harley's Tory government to the succeeding Whig regime angered many people, who claimed that he had no principles. Defoe's reply, difficult to counter, was always that he was working for moderation, no matter on which side.

Only toward the end of his life did Defoe begin to write prose fiction: *Robinson Crusoe* and its sequels, *The Life, Adventures and Pyracies of the Famous Captain Singleton, The Fortunes and Misfortunes of the Famous Moll Flanders, Written from Her Own Memorandums* (commonly known as *Moll Flanders*), *A Journal of the Plague Year, The History and Remarkable Life of the Truly Honourable Col Jacque, Commonly Call'd Col Jack*, and *The Fortunate Mistress* (also known as *Roxana*). Even after completing this enormous output, he continued to produce biographies of criminals and imaginary biographies of soldiers and sailors.

To all appearances, Defoe seemed to embark on a comfortable old age; Henry Baker, his son-in-law, reported that Defoe had retired from London to a handsome house in Stoke Newington, where he lived a leisurely life, growing a garden, pursuing his studies, and writing. In 1730, however, Defoe vanished from his home and, in a rather cryptic letter to Baker, wrote about his "Load of insupportable Sorrows," a "wicked, perjur'd, and contemptible Enemy," and the "inhuman dealing of my own son," who reduced his "dying Mother to beg . . . Bread at his Door." The enemy seems to have been Mary Brooke, the wife of one of Defoe's former creditors. Although Defoe appears to have paid Brooke—at least Brooke's executor accepted Defoe's story—Brooke died before destroying his record of the debt, and his wife was determined to collect it. Once again, Defoe was being hounded by a creditor. His reference to his unnatural son is a bit more puzzling but may show that he had transferred most of his money and property to his son to keep it out of Mary Brooke's hands; if so, his son seems to have abused the trust placed in him. Defoe died in April, 1731, while hiding in a lodging house in Ropemaker's Alley.

Although Defoe's colorful life almost calls too much attention to itself—some critics have tried to deduce his exact birth date through events in his characters' lives—it is hard not to see a link between the elements of disguise and trickery in so many of his novels and his own eventful life, spent, in large part, in fabricating identities for himself in his government work. Like his character Moll Flanders, Defoe had personal experience with

Newgate, and his biographies of criminals and rogues show a fascination with the inventive powers that allow one to thrive in a treacherous world. In this respect, Defoe and his characters seem to have a great deal in common: They are all survivors in an often hostile environment. This sense of alienation may also have a link with Defoe's religion, a creed that was sometimes tolerated but rarely encouraged by the Crown.

Analysis

Although *A Journal of the Plague Year* is not Daniel Defoe's first work of fiction, it offers an interesting perspective from which to examine all of the author's novels. Purporting to be a journal, one man's view of a period in a city's history, this work shows especially well the nexus between realistic reporting and imaginative invention that is the hallmark of Defoe's novels.

A Journal of the Plague Year

Defoe himself lived through one siege of the plague, and although he was only five years old when the disease swept through London, he presumably would have retained some recollections of this catastrophic event, even if only through conversations he would have heard among family members. In *A Journal of the Plague Year*, he also refers frequently to the mortality list, drawing on actual documents of the time to give his narrative a sense of reality. In spite of the realistic foundations of the work, however, its imaginative—not to say fantastic—elements outweigh its realism. Defoe, in fact, often shows a surprising interest in the occult or grotesque for one who is supposedly forging the realistic novel in English. Dreams and premonitions often assail his characters—Crusoe's dream of the angel, Moll's telepathic contact with her Lancashire husband, Roxana's precognitive vision of the dead jeweler—and the utter incomprehensibility of the plague takes this work far beyond cause-and-effect realism.

Perhaps the main thing to consider in *A Journal of the Plague Year* is the narrator, H. L., who, like many of Defoe's characters, is divided spiritually: He must decide whether to flee London or stay and trust God's divine Providence. Like Crusoe, H. L. in times of stress opens the Bible randomly and applies its words to his immediate situation. A problem with theme—often Defoe's weakness—immediately arises, for while the passage that he finds in the Bible convinces him to stay, by the end of the novel he has decided that flight is the only sensible option. His stay in the city is not developed as a moral flaw, however, although, given the religious concerns of the novel, it seems as though it should be: Some critics even see him as guilty of overstraining God's Providence. This view seems inconsistent with the overall sympathetic character of H. L., and one feels that Defoe is not, perhaps, completely in control of his theme.

Even more significant for theme is the origin of the plague. H. L., a sensible, levelheaded man, insists that the plague's cause is natural; he is just as insistent, however, that God has used natural means to bring about the plague. In fact, he makes frequent biblical references that, if not providing specific emblematic types for the plague, do give it a resonance beyond that of a mere disease. Thus, the narrator's insistence on seeing all the horrors of the plague for himself—even though he admits he would be safer at home—has led some critics to see his curiosity as a desire to understand God's workings directly. Again, one encounters an awkward thematic problem. Is H. L. really curious about God's wisdom, or is his seeming inability to stay home simply a narrative necessity? There would, after all, be no journal without an eyewitness. Like many thematic problems in Defoe's works, this becomes one only in retrospect; H. L.'s emphasis on the particulars he describes can be so interesting—even if gruesome—that it is not until the reader has finished the book that these problems surface.

Two episodes from this work show how effective Defoe can be with detail. The first involves H. L.'s journey to the post office. Walking through silent and deserted streets, he arrives at his destination, where he sees "in the middle of the yard . . . a small leather purse with two keys hanging at it, with money in it, but nobody would meddle with it." There are three men around the courtyard who tell H. L. that they are leaving it there in case the owner returns. As H. L. is about to leave, one of the men finally offers to take it "so that if the right owner came for it he should be sure to have it," and he proceeds to carry out an elaborate process of disinfection. This episode, on the surface merely straightforward description, is fraught with drama and ambiguity.

While it is realistic for the streets to be deserted as people take to the safety of their houses, the silence lends an eerie backdrop to this scene. Furthermore, the men's motivations are hardly straightforward. Are they leaving the purse there out of honesty or are they fearful of contamination? Are they simply playing a waiting game with one another to see who leaves first? Does one man finally take the purse to keep it for the owner or for himself? Finally, why does he have all the disinfecting materials—including red-hot tongs—immediately available? Was he about to take the purse before H. L. arrived? H. L.'s remarks about the money found in the purse—"as I remember . . . about thirteen shillings and some smooth groats and brass farthings"—complete this episode: The particularity of the amount is typical of Defoe's realism, and H. L.'s hesitant "as I remember" also persuades the reader that he or she is witnessing the mental processes of a scrupulously honest narrator. In fact, this whole passage is so effective that one tends to overlook an internal inconsistency: Early in the paragraph H. L. says that the sum of money was not so large "that I had any inclination to meddle with it," yet he only discovers the sum at the end of this episode. Defoe is prone to narrative slips of this kind, but, like this one, they are usually unimportant and inconspicuous.

Another vivid episode concerns H. L. going to check on his brother's house while he is away. Next to the house is a warehouse, and as H. L. approaches it, he finds that it has been broken into and is full of women trying on hats. Thievery is by no means uncommon during the plague, although the women's interest in fashion does seem bizarre. What is remarkable about this description, however, is its ambience: Instead of grabbing the hats and fleeing, the women are behaving as if they are at a milliner's, trying on hats until they find those that are most becoming. This scene shows Defoe ostensibly writing realistically when, in fact, he is creating a picture that borders on the surreal.

A Journal of the Plague Year does not always achieve the degree of success that these two episodes display; much of the book is filled with descriptions of the cries and lamentations the narrator hears as he walks the streets. Even horror, if undifferentiated, can become monotonous, and Defoe does not always know how to be selective about details. One device that he employs to better effect here than in his other works is the keeping of lists. Defoe's characters often keep balance sheets of their profits and expenditures, and while this may indicate, as Ian Watt contends, Defoe's essentially materialistic bias, these lists often seem examples of the crudest form of realism. In *A Journal of the Plague Year*, however, the mortality lists scattered throughout are rather more successful and provide almost a thudding rhythm to what is being described: God's terrible visitation.

ROBINSON CRUSOE

Robinson Crusoe, like *A Journal of the Plague Year* and much of Defoe's fiction, is based on a factual event: Alexander Selkirk, a Scottish sailor, lived for four years on the island of Juan Fernandez until he was rescued in 1709. Defoe supplemented accounts of Selkirk's adventures with information from travel books: Richard Hakluyt's *The Principall Navigations, Voiages, and Discoveries of the English Nation* (1589, 1598-1600), William Dampier's *New Voyage Round the World* (1697), and Robert Knox's *An Historical Relation of Ceylon* (1681). Nevertheless, it is as fiction—not a pastiche of other people's books—that *Robinson Crusoe* engrosses the reader.

Because the story centers on one character, it depends on that character for much of its success, and critics have tended to divide into two groups: those who see Crusoe as the new middle-class economic man with only perfunctory religious feelings and those who see him as a deeply spiritual person whose narrative is essentially that of a conversion experience. The answer, perhaps, is that both views of Crusoe coexist in this novel, that Defoe was not sure in this early work exactly where his story was taking him. This ambiguity is not surprising given that the same problem surfaces in *Moll Flanders*; it was not until *Roxana* that Defoe seems to have worked out his themes fully.

The opening frame to Crusoe's island adventure provides a logical starting point for examining his character. Writing in retrospect, Crusoe blames his shipwreck and subsequent sufferings on his "propension of nature," which made him reject his father's counsel of moderation and prompted him to go to sea. His father's speech seems to echo the idea of a great chain of being: Crusoe's life belongs to the "middle state," and he should not endanger himself by reckless acts. If Crusoe's filial disobedience seems trivial to modern readers, it was not to Defoe: His *The Family Instructor, in Three Parts* (1715) and *A New Family Instructor* (1727) make clear how important the mutual obligations of parents and children are. Crusoe himself, recounting his exile from the perspective of old age, talks about his father in biblical terms: After Crusoe's first shipwreck, his father is "an emblem of our blessed Saviour's parable, [and] had even killed the fatted calf for me." When Crusoe reflects, then, on his sinful and vicious life, the reader has to accept Defoe's given: that Crusoe's early giddy nature is a serious moral flaw.

Even with this assumption, however, the reader may have problems understanding Crusoe's character. Throughout the novel, for example, images of prison and capture recur. This makes sense, for the island is both a prison and, if the reader believes in Crusoe's conversion, a means of attaining spiritual freedom. Crusoe himself is imprisoned early in the novel by some Moors and escapes only after two years (the events of which, like the events that take place over many long stretches of time in Defoe's novels, are only briefly summarized) with a boy named Xury, a captive who soon becomes Crusoe's helpmate and friend. Once Crusoe is free, however, he sells Xury willingly and misses him only when his plantation grows so large that he needs extra labor. Indeed, it is indicative of his relations with other people that when Crusoe meets Friday, Friday abases himself to Crusoe, and Crusoe gives his own name as "Master." Perhaps one should not expect enlightened social attitudes about slavery or race in an eighteenth century author. Even so, there seems pointed irony—presumably unintended by Defoe—in Crusoe gaining his freedom only to imprison others; Crusoe's attitude does not seem sufficient for the themes and imagery that Defoe himself has woven into this work.

Crusoe does not behave appreciably better with Europeans. When he rescues Friday and his father, he also rescues a Spaniard who, with a group of Spaniards and Portuguese, has been living peaceably with Friday's tribe. Crusoe begins to think about trying to return to civilization with the Europeans and sends the Spaniard back to Friday's tribe to consult with the others. Before he returns, however, a ship with a mutinous crew arrives on the island. Crusoe rescues the captain and regains control of most of the mutineers. They leave the worst mutineers on the island and sail off for civilization; Crusoe apparently gives no thought to the Spaniard, who will return to the island only to find a motley collection of renegades. Defoe may, of course, simply have forgotten momentarily about the Spaniard as his narrative progressed to new adventures, but if so, this is an unfortunate lapse because it confuses the reader about character and, therefore, about Crusoe's humanity.

Another problem—this time having to do with theme—occurs at the end of the novel. After being delivered to Spain, Crusoe and another group of travelers set out to cross the Pyrenees, where they are beset by fierce wolves. They manage to escape, and Crusoe returns to England, marries, has three children, travels back to his island, and continues having adventures, which, he says, "I may perhaps give a farther account of hereafter." One might argue that the adventures after he leaves the island are anticlimactic, although some critics try to justify them on thematic grounds, the killing of the wolves thus being the extermination of Crusoe's earthly passions. The question remains whether the narrative can bear the weight of such a symbolic—indeed, allegorical—reading. The fact that the sequels to *Robinson Crusoe* are merely about external journeys—not internal spiritual states—shows, perhaps, that Defoe was not as conscious an allegorist as some critics imagine.

Given these thematic problems, it may seem odd that the novel has enjoyed the popularity it has over the centuries. In part, this may simply be due to the element of suspense involved in Crusoe's plight. On one level, the reader wonders how Crusoe is going to survive, although the minute rendering of the day-to-day activities involved in survival can become tedious. Of more interest are Crusoe's mental states: His fluctuating moods after he finds the footprint, for example, have a psychological reality about them. Further, the very traits that make Crusoe unappealing in certain situations lend the novel interest; Crusoe is a survivor, and, while one sometimes wishes he were more compassionate or humane, his will to endure is a universal one with which the reader can empathize.

Aside from the basic appeal of allowing the reader to experience vicariously Crusoe's struggles to survive, the novel also offers the reader a glimpse of Crusoe's soul. While some of Crusoe's pieties seem perfunctory, Defoe is capable of portraying the character's internal states in sophisticated ways. For example, early in his stay on the island Crusoe discovers twelve ears of barley growing, which convinces him "that God had miraculously caused this grain to grow without any help of seed sown and that it was so directed purely for my sustenance on that wild miserable place." Two paragraphs later, however, "it occurred to my thoughts that I had shook a bag of chicken's meal out in that place, and then the wonder began to cease; and I must confess, my religious thankfulness to God's Providence began to abate too." The mature Crusoe who is narrating this story can see in retrospect that "I ought to have been as thankful for so strange and unforeseen Providence as if it had been miraculous; for it was really the work of Providence as to me" that God allowed the seed to take hold and grow. Here the reader finds Defoe using a sophisticated narrative situation as the older Crusoe recounts—and comments on—the spiritual states of the young Crusoe. Indeed, one problem in the novel is determining when Crusoe's egocentric outlook simply reflects this early unregenerate state of which his mature self would presumably disapprove and when it reflects a healthy individualism in which Defoe acquiesces. Perhaps Crusoe is most appealing when he is aware of his own foibles—for example, when he prides himself on building a gigantic canoe only to find that he cannot possibly transport it to water.

COLONEL JACK

If *Robinson Crusoe* shows an uneasy balance between egocentricity and spiritual humility, materialism and religion, *The Life, Adventures and Pyracies of the Famous Captain Singleton*, more commonly known as *Captain Singleton*, displays what Everett Zimmerman calls a "soggy amalgam of the picaresque and Puritan." This problem reappears in *The History and Remarkable Life of the Truly Honourable Col Jacque, Commonly Call'd Col Jack*, known to readers simply as *Colonel Jack*. Jack's motives are often suspect. When he becomes an overseer in Virginia, for example, he finds that he cannot whip his slaves because the action hurts his arms. Instead, he tells the slaves they will be severely punished by an absentee master and then pretends to have solicited their pardon. Grateful for this mercy, the slaves then work for Jack willingly and cheerfully. While Jack describes this whole episode in words denoting charity and mercy, the reader is uneasily aware that Jack is simply playing on the slaves' ignorance. It is method rather than mercy that triumphs here.

MOLL FLANDERS *and* ROXANA

The confusion in *Captain Singleton* and *Colonel Jack* between expediency and morality can also be found in *Moll Flanders* and, to a lesser extent, in *Roxana*. What makes these latter novels enduring is the power of their central characters. Both Moll and Roxana bear many children, and although they manage to dispose of their offspring conveniently so that they are not hampered in any way, their physical fertility sets them apart from Defoe's more sterile male heroes. This fertility may, of course, be ironic—Dorothy Van Ghent calls Moll an earth mother, but only insofar as she is a "progenitrix of the wasteland"—but it adds a dimension to the characters that both Jack and Singleton lack. One also feels that Defoe allows his female characters greater depth of feeling: Each one takes husbands and lovers for whom she has no regard, but Moll's telepathic communication with her Lancashire husband and Roxana's precognitive vision of her jeweler lover's death imply that both women are involved deeply in these relationships—even though Roxana manages to use the jeweler's death as a way of rising in the world by becoming the Prince's mistress. Defoe's heroines may mourn their losses yet also use them to their advantage.

Another difference between the female and male protagonists in Defoe's novels is that neither Moll nor Roxana descends to murder, whereas Defoe's male picaros often do. Although Moll can occasionally rejoice when a criminal cohort capable of exposing her is hanged, she feels only horror when she contemplates murdering a child from whom she steals a necklace. Similarly, while Roxana may share an emotional complicity in Amy's murder of her importunate daughter, she explicitly tells Amy that she will tolerate no such crime. *Roxana* also seems to have more thematic unity than Defoe's other novels: Instead of advocating an uneasy balance between spiritual and material values, *Roxana* shows a tragic awareness that these are finally irreconcilable opposites. Roxana, although recognizing her weaknesses, cannot stop herself from indulging in them, and her keen awareness of what she calls her "secret Hell within" aligns her more with John Milton's Satan than with Defoe's earlier protagonists.

If Defoe begins to solve the thematic problems of his earlier novels in *Moll Flanders* and *Roxana*, he does so through fairly dissimilar characters. Moll equivocates and justifies her actions much more than does Roxana; when she steals the child's necklace, she reflects that "as I did the poor child no harm, I only thought I had given the parents a just reproof for their negligence in leaving the poor lamb to come home by itself, and it would teach them to take more care another time." She also shows a tendency to solve moral dilemmas by the simple expedient of maintaining two opposing moral stances simultaneously. When she meets a man at Bartholomew Fair who is intoxicated, she has sex with him and then robs him. She later reflects on his "honest, virtuous wife and innocent children" who are probably worrying about him, and she and the woman who disposes of her stolen goods both cry at the pitiable domestic scene Moll has painted. Within a few pages, however, she has found the man again and taken him as her lover, a relationship that lasts for several years.

Moll seems to see no conflicts in her attitudes. Her speech also shows her ability to rationalize moral problems, and she often uses a type of equivocation that allows her to justify her own actions. When a thief is pursued through a crowd of people, he throws his bundle of stolen goods to Moll. She feels herself free to keep them "for these things I did not steal, but they were stolen to my hand."

Contrary to the character of Moll, Roxana recognizes her failings. After her first husband leaves her in poverty, her landlord offers to become her lover. Although he has a wife from whom he is separated, he argues that he will treat Roxana in every way as his legal wife. Throughout their life together, Roxana distinguishes between their degrees of guilt: The landlord, she says, has convinced himself that their relationship is moral; she, however, knows that it is not and is thus the greater sinner.

Indeed, Roxana is portrayed in much greater psychological depth than is Moll; one measure of this is the relationship between Roxana and her maid, Amy. While Defoe's characters often have close friends or confidants—Friday in *Robinson Crusoe*, the midwife in *Moll Flanders*, Dr. Heath in *A Journal of the Plague Year*—it is only in *Roxana* that the friend appears in the novel from the beginning to the end and provides an alter ego for the main character. When Roxana is deciding whether to take the landlord as her lover, for example, Amy volunteers several times to sleep with him if Roxana refuses. Once the landlord and Roxana are living together, Roxana decides to put Amy into bed with the landlord, which she does—literally tearing off Amy's clothes and watching their sexual performance. By the next day, the landlord's lust for Amy has turned to hatred and Amy is suitably penitent. The logical question is why Roxana does this destructive deed, and the answer seems to be that, since she herself feels intense guilt at sleeping with the landlord, she wants to degrade Amy and the landlord as well.

Amy, similarly manipulative, is less passive than Roxana. At the end of the novel, Susan, one of Roxana's daughters, appears, guesses her mother's identity, and begs Roxana to acknowledge her. Amy's suggestion is that she kill Susan, who alone can reveal Roxana's past, having been, unknowingly, a maid in her mother's household when Roxana had many lovers. Roxana recoils from this idea although she admits that Amy "effected all afterwards, without my knowledge, for which I gave her my hearty Curse, tho' I could do little more; for to have fall'n upon Amy, had been to have murther'd myself." Some critics argue that Roxana actually acquiesces in Susan's murder, even though she forbids Amy to do it; her statement that to fall upon Amy would be to destroy herself does lend credence to this view. Amy, perhaps, acts out the desires that Roxana will not admit, even to herself.

In fact, both *Moll Flanders* and *Roxana* seem to hint at an irrational perverseness in their characters that explains, in part, their crimes. At one point after beginning her life as a thief, Moll actually tries to earn her living with her needle and admits that she can do so, but temptation makes her return to crime. She appears to enjoy living outside the law, no matter how much she may talk of her fears of Newgate Prison. Similarly, she once steals a horse simply because it is there; she has no way to dispose of it, but the irrational impulse in her that leads her to crime causes her to commit the theft anyway. Defoe is not given to high comedy, but the picture of Moll leading the horse through the streets, wondering how she is ever going to rid herself of it, is a memorably comic scene.

The frequent irrationality of Moll's behavior seems reiterated in the actions of Roxana; without Moll's self-justifying rationalizations, however, Roxana becomes a tragic figure who knows that her behavior is wrong but cannot stop it. About halfway through the novel, for example, she meets a Dutch merchant who helps her out of some difficulties; she has sex with him, but when he proposes marriage she refuses him on the grounds that marriage is a kind of slavery for women. Actually, she fears that he is trying to take over her fortune. When he answers this unspoken objection, promising not to touch her wealth, she is left in the uncomfortable position of having to admit that her initial reluctance was based solely on financial considerations or else continue her spirited defense of female freedom. She chooses the latter option, arguing until the merchant admits defeat. After she is left alone, Roxana regrets her decision and wishes the merchant back, arguing that no "Woman in her Senses" would ever behave as she did.

In these two novels, Defoe seems to be exploring the nature of evil, and it is seen repeatedly as an irrational drive that can deprive its victims of free choice. In fact, *Roxana* is noteworthy for the ambiguously dark atmosphere that pervades the novel, even apart from Roxana's actions. Although *Moll Flanders* touches on incest, madness, and murder, these seem to be the understandable results of understandable causes: If you do not know your mother, you may marry your brother; if your brother-husband discovers your identity, he may go mad with grief; if you steal from a child, you may contemplate murder to cover up your crime. In *Roxana*, however, many of the characters seem motivelessly malignant, obscurely evil. The midwife whom the Prince hires for Roxana seems so murderous that Roxana has him dismiss her, yet there has been no suggestion in the novel that the Prince intends Roxana harm. On the contrary, he seems delighted with her pregnancy and even spends some time with her during labor. The sexual promiscuity found in *Moll Flanders* turns to sexual perversion in *Roxana*: Roxana's final lover before she goes to live with the Quaker disgusts her "on some Accounts, which, if I cou'd suffer myself to publish them, wou'd fully justifie my Conduct; but that Part of the Story will not bear telling."

Even the Quaker is an ambiguous figure. Although strictly truthful—Roxana states several times that the woman will not tell a lie—she hardly seems above reproach: She shows a surprising adeptness at bringing together Roxana and her former lover; she knows how to disguise the smell of alcohol on one's breath; she says at one point that she is almost tempted to abandon her sober Quaker attire and wear Roxana's Turkish costume, although the costume by this time has come to be an emblem of Roxana's sinful life.

Perhaps Defoe's darkening vision is best seen through a comparison of the conclusions of *Moll Flanders* and *Roxana*. After a life of crime—through which she becomes quite wealthy—Moll is finally caught and sent to Newgate. Sentenced to die, she is instead transported, but not before she meets Jemmy, her Lancashire husband, who has been a highwayman and who also ends up in Newgate. They leave for America together, and since they have enough money to pay the captain of the ship handsomely, they are treated like gentry on their voyage. Once in America, they prosper, only returning to England at the end of the novel, presumably repentant but certainly wealthy from their life of crime.

The uneasy balance of religion and roguery in *Moll Flanders*—Moll's pieties interspersed throughout the work sometimes sound as perfunctory as Crusoe's—shifts in *Roxana*, where Defoe's character finally realizes that one cannot reconcile sin and prosperity in the easygoing synthesis that Moll seems to achieve. The novel ends with Susan's death and Amy's desertion; the final paragraph tells the reader that Roxana and her husband prospered for a while but that a "Blast from Heaven" finally destroyed Roxana's tranquillity and she ended her days miserably. The abruptness of this conclusion makes for an unsatisfactory ending, but at least it does show Defoe solving the thematic problems inherent in all his earlier novels: Roxana recognizes a higher power but is unable to obey it. Instead of having the best of two worlds—prosperity and religion—she is doomed by a just Providence that punishes her unrepentance.

If, like Defoe's heroes and heroines, one is given to keeping balance sheets, one might summarize Defoe's weaknesses and strengths easily. On a basic level, Defoe is often slipshod in his handling of narrative: At one point Moll tells the reader how many lovers she has had in her life, but Moll's list of lovers falls far short of the number she mentions in her own narrative. More serious are the thematic problems that Defoe seems to solve only in his final novel. Finally, his realism is quite crude in some places; descriptions of objects assail the reader without having any sensuous reality to them. To Defoe's credit, he is able to establish a convincing conversational tone for most of his characters, and they often have an energy that far exceeds their function as counters through whom Defoe can manipulate his episodic plots. When reading Defoe, however, one does not tend to think in terms of balance sheets. In his best works, the problems in Defoe's writings are so well masked by the vitality of his fiction as to be unnoticeable. Like all artists, Defoe has the ability to make his readers suspend disbelief.

Carole Moses

Other major works

SHORT FICTION: *A True Relation of the Apparition of One Mrs. Veal*, 1706.

POETRY: *The True-Born Englishman: A Satyr*, 1701.

NONFICTION: *An Essay upon Projects*, 1697; *The Shortest Way with the Dissenters*, 1702; *The History of the Union of Great Britain*, 1709; *An Appeal to Honour and Justice*, 1715; *The Family Instructor, in Three Parts*, 1715; *A New Voyage Round the World by a Course Never Sailed*, 1724; *A Tour Thro' the Whole Island of Great Britain*, 1724-1727 (3 volumes); *A General History of the Robberies and Murders of the Most Notorious Pyrates*, 1724-1728 (2 volumes); *The Complete English Tradesman*, 1725-1727 (2 volumes); *The Four Years Voyages of Capt George Roberts*, 1726; *A New Family Instructor*, 1727; *Augusta Triumphans: Or, The Way to Make London the Most Flourishing City in the Universe*, 1728; *A Plan of the English Commerce*, 1728.

MISCELLANEOUS: *The Novels and Miscellaneous Works of Daniel Defoe*, 1840-1841 (20 volumes; Walter Scott, editor); *Romances and Narratives by Daniel Defoe*, 1895 (16 volumes; George Aitken, editor); *The Shakespeare Head Edition of the Novels and Selected Writings of Daniel Defoe*, 1927-1928 (14 volumes).

Bibliography

Blewett, David. *Defoe's Art of Fiction: "Robinson Crusoe," "Moll Flanders," "Colonel Jack," and "Roxana."* Toronto, Ont.: University of Toronto Press, 1979. In an examination of Defoe's letters and nonfiction, Blewett finds a worldview that sees the individual as isolated in an indifferent or hostile universe. Shows how four of Defoe's novels artfully voice this outlook. An epilogue considers Defoe's contribution to the development of prose fiction.

Bloom, Harold, ed. *Daniel Defoe*. New York: Chelsea House, 1987. Contains thirteen essays representing three decades of criticism. Subjects include point of view, theme, style, and characterization. Bloom's introduction, Leo Braudy's "Daniel Defoe and the Anxieties of Autobiography," and John J. Burke, Jr.'s "Observing the Observer in Historical Fictions by Defoe" are of particular interest. Includes chronology, brief bibliography, and index.

Lund, Roger D., ed. *Critical Essays on Daniel Defoe*. New York: G. K. Hall, 1997. Collection of essays discusses Defoe's domestic conduct manuals, his travel books, his treatment of slavery, his novels, and his treatment of the city. Includes an informative introduction and an index.

Novak, Maximillian E. *Daniel Defoe: Master of Fictions—His Life and Ideas*. New York: Oxford University Press, 2001. Biographical study by a leading Defoe scholar focuses on Defoe's writings. Includes analysis of *Robinson Crusoe*, *Moll Flanders*, and other novels as well as discussion of the author's works in other genres.

_______. *Realism, Myth, and History in Defoe's Fiction*. Lincoln: University of Nebraska Press, 1983. Treats various aspects of Defoe's artistry, such as the psychological realism of *Roxana*, the use of history in *A Journal of the Plague Year* and *Memoirs of a Cavalier*, and mythmaking in *Robinson Crusoe*.

Richetti, John J. *Daniel Defoe*. Boston: Twayne, 1987. Argues that examination of Defoe's fiction should be balanced by a careful study of his nonfiction. This valuable work looks at both, noting both similarities and inconsistencies. Includes chronology, biographical overview, notes, and bibliography with secondary sources briefly annotated.

_______. *Life of Daniel Defoe: A Critical Biography*. Malden, Mass.: Blackwell, 2005. Provides a thorough look at Defoe's writing within the context of his life and opinions, including analysis of his fiction and political and religious journalism. Focuses on Defoe's distinctive literary style.

_______, ed. *The Cambridge Companion to Daniel Defoe*. New York: Cambridge University Press, 2008. Collection of essays designed to introduce students to Defoe includes discussions of Defoe and criminal fiction, money and character in Defoe's fiction, Defoe as a narrative innovator, and gender issues in *Moll Flanders* and *Roxana*.

Rogers, Pat, ed. *Daniel Defoe: The Critical Heritage*. 1972. Reprint. New York: Routledge, 1995. Comprehensive collection of critical commentary on Defoe's work is essential for an understanding of such a complex figure. The editor's introduction provides an excellent overview. Includes appendixes, bibliography, and index.

Spaas, Lieve, and Brian Stimpson, eds. *"Robinson Crusoe": Myths and Metamorphoses*. New York: St. Martin's Press, 1996. Collection of essays explores many aspects of the seminal novel. Includes examinations of Crusoe's women and of the novel within the context of eighteenth century history; several essays focus on how other writers and filmmakers have adapted Defoe's novel for their own works.

Watt, Ian. *The Rise of the Novel: Studies in Defoe, Richardson, and Fielding*. 2d ed. Berkeley: University of California Press, 2001. Discusses *Robinson Crusoe*, *Moll Flanders*, and Defoe's contribution to the realistic novel. Relates Defoe's fiction to the social and economic conditions of his age.

West, Richard. *Daniel Defoe: The Life and Strange, Surprising Adventures*. New York: Carroll & Graf, 1998. Covers all aspects of Defoe's careers as journalist, novelist, satirist, newsman, and pamphleteer as well as tradesman, soldier, and spy. Written with considerable flair by a journalist and historian of wide-ranging experience.

JOHN WILLIAM DE FOREST

Born: Humphreysville (now Seymour), Connecticut; March 31, 1826
Died: New Haven, Connecticut; July 17, 1906

Principal long fiction

Witching Times, 1856-1857 (serial), 1967 (book)
Seacliff: Or, The Mystery of the Westervelts, 1859
Miss Ravenel's Conversion from Secession to Loyalty, 1867
Overland, 1871
Kate Beaumont, 1872
The Wetherel Affair, 1873
Honest John Vane, 1875
Playing the Mischief, 1875
Justine's Lovers, 1878
Irene the Missionary, 1879
The Bloody Chasm, 1881
A Lover's Revolt, 1898

Other literary forms

John William De Forest was interested in history; he began his career as a writer with *History of the Indians of Connecticut from the Earliest Known Period to 1850* (1851). He contributed a number of historical essays to leading magazines such as *The Atlantic Monthly*, *Harper's New Monthly Magazine*, and *Galaxy*. A few years before his death, he published a family history, *The De Forests of Avesnes (and of New Netherland)* (1900). His first long work of fiction, *Witching Times*, and his last, *A Lover's Revolt*, are essentially historical novels. He wrote two travelogues (*Oriental Acquaintance: Or, Letters from Syria*, 1856, and *European Acquaintance: Being Sketches of People in Europe*, 1858) as well as important accounts of his experiences in the American Civil War (*A Volunteer's Adventures: A Union Captain's Record of the Civil War*, 1946) and in the Reconstruction (*A Union Officer in the Reconstruction*, 1948). He also published rather undistinguished poetry (*The*

Downing Legends: Stories in Rhyme, 1901, and *Poems: Medley and Palestina*, 1902), much short fiction of uneven quality that has not been collected in book form, and a variety of uncollected essays, the title of the best known of which, "The Great American Novel," has become a famous phrase.

Achievements

Gordon S. Haight, who rescued John William De Forest from oblivion by republishing *Miss Ravenel's Conversion from Secession to Loyalty* in 1939, declared that De Forest was "the first American writer to deserve the name of realist." Bold as that declaration may sound, it follows William Dean Howells's earlier conviction that De Forest was a major novelist but that the reading public did not appreciate him because he did not conform to the literary fashion of his time. Indeed, De Forest's strong and often unvarnished realistic treatment of battle scenes, political corruption, and sexual morals frequently brought him critical acclaim but hardly ever gained his works any popularity. Modern critics tend to be less enthusiastic about De Forest than was Howells, but most do recognize him as an important precursor of literary realism in the United States. De Forest's personal experience as a Union officer and his evenhanded treatment of both sides of the conflict give a balance, authenticity, and honesty to *Miss Ravenel's Conversion from Secession to Loyalty* that make it perhaps the best novel ever written about the American Civil War.

John William De Forest. (Library of Congress)

Biography

Descended from Huguenot immigrants of earliest colonial times, John William De Forest was born on March 31, 1826, in Humphreysville (now Seymour), Connecticut. His father was president of a local manufacturing company and in other ways, too, was one of the small town's most important citizens; his mother was noted for her strong religious beliefs. De Forest's background was thus paradigmatically characteristic of the Protestant ethic, and throughout his entire life he attempted to prove himself worthy of its religion-derived ideology of hard work. An early illness made it impossible for him to attend college; in order to expand his private schooling into an education approximately equivalent to the one he would normally have received at Yale University, and in order to improve his health at the same time, he traveled for some years in the Near East (especially Lebanon, where his brother was a missionary) and central and southern Europe. However formative these years abroad were, they did not lastingly restore his health or significantly broaden his ideological perspective. Not healthy enough or temperamentally suited for a career in business but very conscious of having to do something, De Forest decided to become a writer.

After his return from Europe, De Forest met Harriet Silliman Shepard, the attractive daughter of Dr. Charles Upham Shepard, a famous scientist who taught part of the year in Charleston, South Carolina, and part in Amherst, Massachusetts. De Forest's courtship of and marriage to Harriet brought him into contact with the antebellum South, and his firsthand experience of slavery and southern life made him a more knowledgeable and rational participant in the Civil War than most Union volunteers. He served as a captain in Louisiana and Virginia and, after his discharge, joined the Veteran Reserve Corps with assignments first in Washington and then with the Freedmen's Bureau in the western district of South Carolina. His experience in the war and in the Reconstruction led to his best writing.

De Forest returned to New Haven in 1869 and for a decade attempted to make a living as a writer. He began to realize that the Gilded Age following the Civil War was characterized not by great collective strides toward perfect nationhood but rather by selfish and frequently corrupt business schemes that merely lined the pockets of individual entrepreneurs. De Forest's ideology increasingly came into conflict with his need for royalties: On one hand, he urged his countrymen in his best though rarely remunerative work—through analysis of regional heritage and through political satire—to fulfill America's manifest destiny as the leader and hope of the world; on the other hand, in order to survive financially, he tried to cater to the reading public's taste with artistically weak novels, novelettes, and short stories, some of which are little better than formula fiction and pulp literature.

The unresponsiveness of the reading public, the death of his wife in 1878, intermittent financial difficulties, and advancing age made a disillusioned and sometimes bitter recluse of De Forest for much of the remainder of his life. He abandoned his notion of being an intellectual and artistic herald to his country and reluctantly contented himself with writing of essentially private import. A forgotten man and author, he died in New Haven, Connecticut, on July 17, 1906.

Analysis

John William De Forest's works accurately reflect the phases of his ideology, beginning with high optimism about progress, reaching mature though still visionary belief in America's destiny as a light to the world, passing on to disillusionment about and satiric criticism of the actual course the United States was taking after the Civil War, and ending in melancholy and private resignation over the country's failure to fulfill the American Dream.

Although the panic of 1837 lastingly damaged the fortunes of the family business, De Forest's youth saw a period of phenomenal growth in every area of the economy and constant technological inventions and improvements. Intoxicated by the magnitude and rapidity of progress in the United States, De Forest believed devoutly in the country's future and its mission as the coming leader of the world. While he was alive to the cultural and architectural attractions of Europe and the Near East, he compensated for any feelings of cultural inferiority by noticing and describing in detail the many and varied signs of decadence and decay in the Old World and holding them up for comparison with American progress. His travelogues about central and southern Europe and the eastern Mediterranean reaffirm the worth and superiority of American democracy, just as his *History of the Indians of Connecticut from the Earliest Known Period to 1850* concludes that it was morally right and historically inevitable for white American civilization to have superseded the anachronistic, barbarous mode of living of the native American Indians.

In the development of De Forest's ideology, the moral element is of particular importance, for he had been exposed to a religious environment in his childhood. Somewhat later, he read John Bunyan's *Grace Abounding to the Chief of Sinners* (1666) and *The Pilgrim's Progress* (1678, 1684) as well as Nathaniel Hawthorne's New England romances (1850-1852). These works tempered his easy belief in progress by their insistence on the moral weakness of all human beings. De Forest began to understand that outward progress was hollow unless it was accompanied by inward progress: It was not only the gross national product that needed to grow but the human soul as well. In his first novels, *Witching Times* and *Seacliff*, De Forest outlines the nature of this inward growth and establishes the cultivation of the virtues of the New Testament—faith, hope, and charity—as the moral equivalent of economic progress and as the most important requirement for America's impending role as world leader.

During his courtship of Harriet Shepard and during the first few years of their marriage, De Forest spent considerable time in Charleston, South Carolina. Firsthand observation of African Americans and a realization of the magnitude of the problem that emancipation would present kept him from becoming an abolitionist; he felt instead that slavery might melt into serfage and finally disappear altogether over a span of six generations. He did not consider southern white society contemptible because of its adherence to slavery; he saw that the system was indefensible, but he also recognized and respected the personal dignity and integrity of high-toned southerners. De Forest never doubted, however, that slavery had to cease: It was morally wrong, it had been the subject of harsh criticism by the Europeans that De Forest had met during his early travels abroad, and it had become so topical an issue that it might become a real crisis at any time.

The outbreak of the Civil War destroyed De Forest's hopes for a gradual disappearance of slavery, and, making a virtue of necessity, he came to see the war as something of a godsend, as an opportunity for America to mend the one great imperfection in the national fabric. The extraordinary sacrifices required by the war could indeed be made to appear sensible only if they served a great end, the unimpeded progress of the United States to human and societal perfection. De Forest's actual experience in the war and the Reconstruction, however, together with his interest in the theories of Charles Darwin and Herbert Spencer on biological and societal evolution, confirmed him in his opinion that racial equality would be achieved only gradually in the United States rather than swiftly and that the fostering of individual worthiness and responsibility was prerequisite to the ultimate realization of a perfect society. The United States, De Forest concluded, had a long way to go after all, and along the way it would need the guidance of the best and the brightest of its citizens.

Accordingly, De Forest developed in his novels, from *Miss Ravenel's Conversion from Secession to Loyalty* to *The Wetherel Affair*, as well as in several essays, the concept of the worthy gentleman of democracy. It is particularly noteworthy that this concept is not purely northern but rather a synthesis of northern morals and southern manners. *Miss Ravenel's Conversion from Secession to Loyalty* describes the breakthrough of a new relationship between North and South, the end of all bitterness, and the renewed hope for a great national future. The essays "Two Girls" and "The 'High-Toned Gentleman'" (1868) suggest ways to draw on the abilities of the American woman and the high character of the defeated southerners in the continuing and indeed renewed effort to realize the American Dream; "The Great American Novel" of the same year defines the function of the American writer as that of a spiritual goal setter, leader, and educator of the vast mediocre masses of democracy and thus expresses the same sentiments Walt Whitman would put forward more poetically in *Democratic Vistas* (1871). In *Overland* and *Kate Beaumont*, De Forest turns west and south, back to the days before the war, in search of a heritage to energize the moral and economic progress of the country after Appomattox. He finds this heritage in exemplary men and women who are just as worthy as their northern postwar counterparts, whom he discusses in *The Wetherel Affair*.

When it appeared, however, that most Americans were interested in more mundane matters than the moral and intellectual progress of civilization, De Forest attacked the rampant political corruption of Ulysses S. Grant's presidential administration and the underlying money-grubbing philosophy of the postwar Gilded Age in two satiric novels, *Honest John Vane* and *Playing the Mischief*. Increasingly, he had to admit to himself that the lofty goal of the American millennium was in reality taking on the shape of the lowly goal of the American "millionairium," that the Civil War had in fact opened the way not to moral glory but to materialistic go-getting, that the great dream was being perverted to what would become the Horatio Alger myth, and that the worthy gentleman of democracy was being pushed aside by the political boss.

The defeat of his mission also meant De Forest's defeat as a writer. His final works were nostalgic (*A Lover's Revolt*, for example, invokes the glorious spirit of the Founding Fathers through a highly idealized portrayal of General Washington during the early stages of the War of Independence), and they increasingly served only the purpose of De Forest's demonstrating to himself and to the few people who still cared to read him that he himself had at least always attempted and generally managed to follow his ideal of the worthy gentleman of democracy.

De Forest's technical development as a writer seems by and large to parallel the phases of his ideology from youth to old age. As the message of his early writings is overconfident and youthfully chauvinistic, so their technique is imitative and their tone sentimental, melodramatic, and brash. His work of the war years and the early 1870's gives a well-balanced assessment of the state of the nation; personal maturity and significant firsthand experience find their stylistic equivalent in reasoned, realistic, pointed expression that generally frees itself from its literary models and becomes authentic. De Forest's late works stylistically resemble his early ones, except that in keeping with the change from relatively unquestioned belief in the American Dream to severe disappointment over its failure, their tone is mostly muted and resigned.

Witching Times

De Forest had begun his career as a writer with the scholarly but ideologically biased *History of the Indians of Connecticut from the Earliest Known Period to 1850*, in which he had ascribed the decline of the American Indians to their own weaknesses and had cited the inevitability of progress to justify the takeover by the white man. The accounts of his foreign travels, *Oriental Acquaintance* and *European Acquaintance*, take a sometimes chauvinistically pro-American stance. His first piece of long fiction, *Witching Times* (serialized but never published in book form during De Forest's lifetime), returns to an epoch of American colonial history but draws no racial or international comparisons. Disturbed by his reading of Nathaniel Hawthorne's *The House of the Seven Gables* (1851), De Forest investigated the Salem witchcraft trials of 1692-1693, probing the various layers of sin and evil present in the leading historical figures of that occurrence. Magistrates such as Stoughton and Hawthorne's ancestor are shown to corrupt justice, but even greater blame is reserved for those Puritan ministers who, purporting to do battle for Christ, forget Christian virtue. Elder Parris is a glutton ruled by jealousy and hate; Elder Noyse is a scheming lecher; and Cotton Mather is almost Antichrist because of his pride, ruthlessness, and excessive ambition. De Forest charges the threesome with a complete perversion of true ministry.

A group of four characters opposes these perverted Puritan leaders: the physically and intellectually strong, fiercely independent Henry More; his daughter Rachel; her husband Mark Stanton; and gentle Elder Higginson. Henry More strongly resists the witchcraft delusion but has too much of a temper, too much pride, and not enough understanding of and rapport with the common people to succeed; on the contrary, he becomes the most prominent victim. Rachel and Mark are more balanced; where More is hopelessly idealistic and unbending and goes to his death, they are practical without sacrificing their integrity, and thus they survive. Higginson, however, is the true minister who lives and pronounces the book's message, namely, that life and therefore progress must be directed by the three cardinal virtues of the New Testament: faith, hope, and charity.

Miss Ravenel's Conversion from Secession to Loyalty

De Forest became active in the Civil War as a Connecticut volunteer in January, 1862, completing his active duty in December, 1864. During that time, he saw much action in Louisiana and in Virginia. He described his war experience in a number of articles, short stories, and poems, but most extensively in letters to his family that he later organized into a book manuscript that was not published until forty years after his death (*A Volunteer's Adventures*). Much of this observation of war entered his novel *Miss Ravenel's Conversion from Secession to Loyalty*, but it would be erroneous to assume, as some critics have done, that De Forest wrote the novel to give the reading public a true picture of what war is really like and that he added the characters and the love plot only to satisfy the most elementary formal requirements of a novel of the time. Quite on the contrary, De Forest insists authorially that the book is concerned with a great change in the life of his heroine and that the military aspects of the war are not the book's main theme.

Edward Colburne is an upright but somewhat shy young man from "New Boston," where he makes the acquaintance of Dr. Ravenel, a scientist and abolitionist, and his daughter Lillie, who have had to leave secessionist New Orleans. Colburne falls in love with Lillie, who has much of the charm and attitude of a young southern belle, but Lillie is attracted to the dashing, virile Colonel Carter, whom she marries after her return to New Orleans. Carter is a gentleman from Virginia by birth, a West Point graduate, and an officer in the Union army. He is a good soldier but unfortunately has little moral fiber: He swears, drinks, has an affair with a French Creole widow, and embezzles government funds. Not entirely a negative character, Carter has enough integrity to regret his fraud and his unfaithfulness, and De Forest gives him an honorable death on the battlefield.

The course of her marriage, the course of the war, the moral authority of her father, and the devotion of

Colburne—which is as steady to her as it is to the Union—ultimately affect Lillie's conversion from secession to loyalty: Just as her early adherence to the South changes to an understanding and acceptance of the Union cause, so her private allegiance shifts from the memory of the unworthy Carter to the living presence of the worthy Colburne. Lillie's marriage to Colburne in the end symbolizes the reunion of the repentant and matured South with the forgiving and faithful North. Lillie's and Carter's little boy, who resembles his maternal grandfather, is no hindrance to Colburne but a joy instead: The end of the war also means the end of the sins of the fathers, and no previous errors are held against those whose new life is before them.

De Forest integrates the ideological, military, and amatory elements of his narrative into a convincing whole; *Miss Ravenel's Conversion from Secession to Loyalty* is the summary of a painful but necessary and highly gratifying process of individual and national maturing, at the end of which stands a hard-won reaffirmation of the great purpose and promise of the United States of America as the true and tested leader in the progress of the human race.

Kate Beaumont

De Forest's firsthand experience of the South before, during, and after the war made him understand more fully its strengths and shortcomings. Evaluating these, he gives in *Kate Beaumont* a balanced picture of those southern elements it had been necessary to destroy and those it was necessary to preserve for the good of the nation.

De Forest's Protestant ethic is offended by the unwillingness of the antebellum planters to work and by their failure to make slavery a truly profitable enterprise. The South's economic system encourages idleness on the part of the ruling class; idleness in turn leads to vice. The Beaumonts are a typical South Carolina planter family; they are basically good but headstrong and misguided people who have few goals in life. Although two of the young Beaumonts have a professional education, they rarely use it, instead whiling away the day with drink and cultivating the family feud with the McAlisters.

Noble Frank McAlister and sweet Kate Beaumont are De Forest's Romeo and Juliet, except that they finally overcome the barbarian senselessness of the *code duello* by their marriage. Through Kate and Frank, but especially through Kate's grandfather Colonel Kershaw, De Forest makes the point that there is much that is admirable about the high-toned southerner; both Frank and Kershaw are likened to the archetypal American gentleman, George Washington himself, and both are depicted as men of high moral and intellectual caliber. The South's real problem, De Forest suggests, is its frivolity, which in turn stems from a wrong attitude toward work; its great contribution to the nation's fabric is the highly civilized character of the best members of its aristocracy, a contribution much needed to keep the level of democracy high. Frank and Kershaw are more progressive than their relatives; Frank in particular is ready to put his scientific education to use for the economy of the South the moment it becomes acceptable for a gentleman to concern himself with something other than cotton.

Kate Beaumont is an important book primarily because of De Forest's careful analysis of the Old South. He not only excoriates the weaknesses of the South but also (and more constructively) identifies its strengths and insists on making them fruitful for the entire nation. Despite the unhappiness of some contemporaneous southern reviewers, it is hard to deny that De Forest was successful in his attempt to give a fair and balanced view of the Old South. The thematic and analytic merit is matched by the technical quality of the book. It provides an impressive range of realistically drawn characters and situations, including an authentic use of dialect; from William Dean Howells's favorite De Forest heroine, Nellie Armitage, and her drunken husband to Peyton Beaumont, readers are given such a comprehensive and forthright picture of the Old South that they cannot help but forgive the sentimentality of the love story.

Honest John Vane

The indispensability of men such as Edward Colburne or Frank McAlister for the advance of American democracy became painfully evident in the political scandals of the Grant administration. The Crédit Mobilier affair in particular made it obvious to De Forest that patient persuading of the American public to assert itself against corrupt leadership had to give way to sound scolding. In *Honest John Vane*, De Forest functions in the manner of an irate Puritan preacher who thunders a jeremiad at his stubborn congregation. Modeling his story on Bunyan's *The Life and Death of Mr. Badman* (1680), De Forest chronicles the rise of his title character from unassuming small-town citizen to fraudulent and hypocritical congressman.

Unfortunately, Vane is not an isolated case, nor does De Forest imply that the fault lies solely or even primarily with politics. The real villain is the gullible, plebeian American public that is too comfortable in its moral mediocrity to desire the leadership of the elite. The modern American woman also comes in for severe criticism: Vane's wife, Olympia, not only does not work but also spends extravagantly and therefore drives her husband, whose moral bulwarks are weak to begin with, into debt and then into venality. Still, De Forest shows that he has not given up hope; he still believes in the basic soundness of the democratic enterprise and of the American people, whom he expects to clean house, reform, and then continue on their way toward the great national goal, the perfection of the American Dream.

Frank Bergmann

Other major works

POETRY: *The Downing Legends: Stories in Rhyme*, 1901; *Poems: Medley and Palestina*, 1902.

NONFICTION: *History of the Indians of Connecticut from the Earliest Known Period to 1850*, 1851; *Oriental Acquaintance: Or, Letters from Syria*, 1856; *European Acquaintance: Being Sketches of People in Europe*, 1858; *The De Forests of Avesnes (and of New Netherland)*, 1900; *A Volunteer's Adventures: A Union Captain's Record of the Civil War*, 1946; *A Union Officer in the Reconstruction*, 1948.

Bibliography

Becker, Stephen. "On John William De Forest's *Miss Ravenel's Conversion from Secession to Loyalty*." In *Classics of Civil War Fiction*, edited by David Madden and Peggy Bach. 1991. Reprint. Tuscaloosa: University of Alabama Press, 2001. Presents analysis of the novel and argues that De Forest "was America's first literary realist" who wrote "one enduring, flawed novel that stands as a milestone . . . not merely realistic but wise."

Bergmann, Frank. *The Worthy Gentleman of Democracy: John William De Forest and the American Dream*. Heidelberg, Germany: C. Winter, 1971. Brief biography provides information on De Forest that serves as useful background to the study of his fiction.

Buckley, William K. *Senses' Tender: Recovering the Novel for the Reader*. New York: Peter Lang, 1989. Examination of literary realism in the novels of several authors includes an analysis of *Miss Ravenel's Conversion from Secession to Loyalty*. Designed for upper-division college students.

Gargano, James W., ed. *Critical Essays on John William De Forest*. Boston: G. K. Hall, 1981. Collection of twentieth century essays on De Forest is aimed primarily at scholars, but included is a rich selection of reviews written in De Forest's own time that may be of interest to students at any level.

Hijiya, James A. *John William De Forest and the Rise of American Gentility*. Hanover, N.H.: University Press of New England, 1988. Comprehensive biography covers the events of De Forest's life and the social context in which he worked. Contains some interesting references to De Forest's novels.

Light, James F. *John William De Forest*. New York: Twayne, 1965. Introductory study of De Forest comments briefly on each of his novels. Provides a chronology and an annotated bibliography.

Schaefer, Michael W. *Just What War Is: The Civil War Writing of De Forest and Bierce*. Knoxville: University of Tennessee Press, 1997. Part 1 discusses the components of realism in the works of De Forest and Ambrose Bierce. Part 2 concentrates on De Forest and explores what it means to depict war in a "realistic" fashion. Discusses De Forest's influences and the extent to which firsthand experience matters in authors' depictions of war. Includes detailed notes and an extensive bibliography.

Wilson, Edmond. *Patriotic Gore*. New York: Oxford University Press, 1966. Classic study of the literature of the American Civil War includes a long chapter on De Forest and "the chastening of American prose style" that constitutes one of the most succinct introductions to De Forest available in print.

WALTER DE LA MARE

Born: Charlton, Kent, England; April 25, 1873
Died: Twickenham, Middlesex, England; June 22, 1956
Also known as: Walter John de la Mare; Walter Ramal

Principal long fiction

Henry Brocken, 1904
The Return, 1910
The Three Mulla-Mulgars, 1910 (reprinted as *The Three Royal Monkeys: Or, The Three Mulla-Mulgars*, 1935)
Memoirs of a Midget, 1921
At First Sight: A Novel, 1928

Other literary forms

Walter de la Mare (deh-luh-MAYR) was a prolific author of poetry, short stories, and nonfiction. Like his novels, de la Mare's poetry and short fiction range from works written explicitly for children (for which he is best remembered) to works intended for adults. Poetry collections such as *Songs of Childhood* (1902) and *A Child's Day: A Book of Rhymes* (1912) reveal his understanding of the pleasures and frustrations of childhood, an understanding that made *The Three Mulla-Mulgars* a favorite with children. De la Mare's poetry for adults embodies his belief that human beings live in two coexistent worlds: the world of everyday experience and the world of the spirit, which is akin to dreaming.

Dreams and the nature of the imagination are frequent themes in both de la Mare's fiction and his poetry. These and other interests are more explicitly revealed in his essays and in his work as an editor. Not much given to analysis, de la Mare was primarily an appreciative critic. Of the anthologies he edited, *Behold, This Dreamer!* (1939) is perhaps the most revealing of the influences that shaped his work.

Achievements

Walter de la Mare published only five novels, one of which, *At First Sight*, is more a long short story than a true novel. His fiction is metaphorical and resembles his poetry in its concerns. Much of what he wanted to communicate in his writing is best suited to short works, and therefore his novels are haphazardly successful. In spite of the difficulties of his novels, his contemporary critics in general had a high regard for him as a novelist. Edward Wagenknecht, an important historian of the novel, ranked *Memoirs of a Midget* as one of the best twentieth century English novels. Indeed, in his essay on de la Mare in *Cyclopedia of World Authors* (1958), Wagenknecht emphasizes *Memoirs of a Midget* at the expense of de la Mare's other writings.

De la Mare's novels, however, were not as widely read in their time as his poetry and short fiction, and today they are seldom read at all. The lack of modern attention to de la Mare's novels is caused less by any absence of merit than by the predictable drop in reputation that many authors undergo in the literary generation after their deaths. Although his novels are unlikely to regain their popularity with a general readership, serious students of twentieth century English literature will almost certainly return to de la Mare's novels as his generation's writings are rehabilitated among scholars.

Biography

Judging from the few published accounts of those who knew him, Walter de la Mare was a quiet and unpretentious man. One can reasonably infer from the absence of autobiographical material from an otherwise prolific writer that he was a private man. He seems to have lived his adventures through his writing, and his primary interests seem to have been of the intellect and spirit.

Walter John de la Mare was born in Charlton, Kent, on April 25, 1873, to James Edward de la Mare and Lucy Sophia Browning de la Mare, a Scot. While attending St. Paul's Cathedral Choir School, Walter de la Mare founded and edited *The Choiristers' Journal*, a school magazine. In 1890, he entered the employ of the Anglo-American Oil Company, for which he served as a bookkeeper until 1908. During these years, he wrote essays, stories, and poetry that appeared in various magazines, including *Black and White* and *The Sketch*. In 1902, his first book—and one of his most lastingly popular—was published, the collection of poetry *Songs of Childhood.* He used the pseudonym "Walter Ramal," which he also used for the publication of the novel *Henry Brocken* in 1904, then dropped. He married Constance Elfrida Igpen in 1899, with whom he had two sons and two daughters. His wife died in 1943.

De la Mare's employment at the Anglo-American Oil Company ended in 1908, when he was granted a Civil List pension of a yearly one hundred pounds by the British government. Thus encouraged, he embarked on a life of letters during which he produced novels, poetry, short stories, essays, one play, and edited volumes of poetry and essays. These many works display something of de la Mare's intellect, if not of his character. They reveal a preoccupation with inspiration and dreams, an irritation with Freudians and psychologists in general (too simplistic in their analyses, he believed), a love of romance, and a love for the child in people. The works indicate a complex mind that preferred appreciation to analysis and observation to explanation.

Analysis

Walter de la Mare's novels are diverse in structure, although unified by his recurring themes. *Henry Brocken* is episodic, with its protagonist moving from one encounter to another. *The Return* has all the trappings of the gothic, with mysterious strangers, supernatural events, and unexplained happenings. *The Three Mulla-Mulgars* is a children's story, with a direct narrative and a clear objective toward which the novel's actions are directed. *Memoirs of a Midget* is Victorian in structure and is filled with incidents and coincidences; it emphasizes character over the other aspects of novel writing. *At First Sight* is really a long short story, what some might call a novella; its plot is simple, the problem its protagonist faces is straightforward, and it has only the barest attempt at a subplot.

Henry Brocken

Early in his literary career, de la Mare concluded that there were two ways of observing the world: inductive and deductive. Induction was a child's way of understanding his environment, through direct experience, whereas deduction was associated with adolescents and adults—the environment was kept at an emotional and intellectual distance. De la Mare believed that reality is best understood in relation to the self and best interpreted through imagination; childlike—as opposed to *childish*—observation is subjective, and childlike imagination can make and remake reality according to the imaginer's desires. Henry Brocken, the eponymous protagonist of de la Mare's first novel, is such a childlike observer. Critics are often confused by his adult behavior; they fail to understand that Brocken is intended to be childlike rather than childish.

Dreams are a part of the human experience that can be made and remade according to the subjective dictates of the self; de la Mare believed that dreams revealed a truer reality than that found in the waking experience. Given de la Mare's beliefs, Brocken's use of dreams to meet with famous literary characters seems almost natural. Brocken is able to converse with characters from the works of such authors as Geoffrey Chaucer, Jonathan Swift, and Charlotte Brontë. The characters are often liv-

Walter de la Mare. (Library of Congress)

ing lives that are barely implied in their original author's works. Jane Eyre, for instance, is with Rochester long after the conclusion of Brontë's *Jane Eyre* (1847). *Henry Brocken* is about imagination and what it can do to reality. Great literary characters can seem more real than many living people. De la Mare represents this aspect of the imaginative response to literature by showing characters maturing and changing in ways not necessarily envisioned by their creators. Criseyde, for example, is not only older but also wiser than in Chaucer's *Troilus and Criseyde* (1382). What is imagined can have a life of its own, just as dreams can be more alive than waking experience.

The Three Mulla-Mulgars

The Three Mulla-Mulgars seems to be an interruption in the development of de la Mare's themes of imagination, dreams, and reality. In it, three monkeys—called "Mulgars"—search for the Valley of Tishnar and the kingdom of their uncle Assasimmon. During their travels, the three—Nod, Thimble, and Thumb—have adventures among the various monkey species of the world and encounter danger in the form of Immanala, the source of darkness and cruelty. Although a children's story, and although humorous and generally lighthearted, *The Three Mulla-Mulgars* contains the spiritual themes typical of de la Mare's best work. Nod, although physically the weakest of the three monkeys, is spiritually gifted; he can contact the supernatural world in his dreams and is able to use the Moonstone, a talisman; Immanala is essentially a spiritual force; it can strike anywhere and can take any form; it can make dreams—which in the ethos of de la Mare are always akin to death—into the "Third Sleep," death. The quest for the Valley of Tishnar is a search for meaning in the Mulla-Mulgars' lives; their use of dreams, a talisman, and their conflict with Immanala make the quest spiritual as well as adventurous.

The Return

The Return represents a major shift in de la Mare's approach to fiction, both long and short. Before *The Return*, he presented his iconoclastic views in the guise of children's stories and allegories—as if his ideas would be more palatable in inoffensive fantasies than in the form of the adult novel. In *The Return*, de la Mare took an important step toward his masterpiece, *Memoirs of a Midget*, by creating a novel featuring adult characters with adult problems.

The Return seems gothic on its surface. Arthur Lawford, weak from a previous illness, tires while walking in a graveyard. He naps beside the grave of Nicholas Sabathier, a man who committed suicide in 1739. Lawford awakens refreshed and vigorous, but to his dismay he discovers that his face and physique have changed. Later, a mysterious stranger, Herbert Herbert, reveals that Lawford resembles a portrait of Sabathier, and Herbert's sister Grisel becomes a powerful attraction for Lawford—she seems to be an incarnation of the lover who may have driven Sabathier to kill himself. The plot, when examined by itself, seems trite and melodramatic, yet de la Mare makes the events frightening, in part because he imbues the novel with genuine metaphysical questions and in part because he believes in his story.

Belief is always a problem in fiction, particularly fantastic fiction. Part of what makes hackwork poor literature is insincerity in the author—that is, the author does not believe that the work is valid, important, or worthy of belief. De la Mare clearly believes that the love story in *The Return* is important, that the novel's themes are valid, and that its events can be believed. His sincerity endows the novel's events with poetic power. The question of Lawford's identity thus becomes disturbing for the reader: De la Mare is saying that no one's identity is certain. Soon after Lawford's physical metamorphosis, his speech takes on a dual sound, as if he and Sabathier are speaking simultaneously. His conversations with Grisel are discussions between the corporeal Lawford and Grisel and between Sabathier and his past love.

In *The Return*, de la Mare's notions about the human spirit being part of two coexistent worlds are made graphic. Lawford becomes a citizen of everyday reality and of the greater reality of the spirit. He can see the world out of time, past and present; he battles both corporeal and supernatural foes; he is at once Sabathier and an ordinary, middle-aged Englishman. Although a part of two realities, he is accepted by neither. His friends and neighbors want him jailed or locked up in a madhouse; Grisel tells him that he cannot have her, although she shares his love, because he is not free of the burdens of his old world. The dilemma of Lawford, trapped as he is between the two worlds, is representative of the human condition: everyone is trapped between two realities because everyone, whether he chooses to recognize it or not, is spiritual as well as physical. So thick with double meanings and disturbing confusions is *The Return* that its almost too convenient resolution—on All Angels Eve, the night on which Sabathier had committed suicide, Lawford is freed of Sabathier's spiritual tug—is a relief. Lawford is free to pretend that what he sees is all that exists, and so is the novel's reader.

Memoirs of a Midget

Greeted from its publication with praise for its characterization and graceful prose, *Memoirs of a Midget* is generally regarded by critics as de la Mare's masterpiece. The novel allows multiple readings; most critics readily recognize de la Mare's unusually successful development of a character's point of view, and they note the subtlety of his social commentary, but they often fail to recognize the novel's informing purpose. The story is simple on its surface. Miss M., also known as Midgetina, is a perfectly formed midget. The novel describes her childhood and emergence as an adult. Her point of view as a small adult is carefully created. The bulk of the novel is devoted to her twentieth year, during which she confronts her selfhood and comes to understand that there is a world of the spirit that is greater than the physical one in which she is a social amusement.

The novel has a Victorian flavor, and many of the characters have a Dickensian vitality. One of the most memorable characters is Mr. Anon, a misshapen hunchback who is only a little taller than Miss M. Mr. Anon transforms Miss M. from a social manipulator into a thoughtful person. He loves her—probably, he says, because she is one of the few people close to his size. His ugliness is repulsive, and Miss M. wants to keep him as a friend, but not as a lover. She joins a circus in order to become independent and quickly becomes a main attraction. In order to save Miss M. from possible recognition when Mrs. Monnerie, Miss M.'s former patroness, attends the circus, Mr. Anon takes her place in a pony-riding act. He is thrown from the pony and is injured; he later dies in Miss M.'s arms. Some critics contend that at Mr. Anon's death Miss M. finally loves him. What is probable is that she believes that his inner self—his spirit—is beautiful and more real than his ugly physical form. Later, Miss M. disappears from a locked room. Her housekeeper, Mrs. Bowater, who commands the only entrance and exit to the room, hears a male voice from within even though no one had entered through the door. Upon investigation, Mrs. Bowater finds a note that reads, "I have been called away."

The character of Miss M. is well suited to de la Mare's purposes. She is small and treated like a child by other characters, and thus her perspective is like that of a child. Reared in seclusion by indulgent parents, she emerges into society with much of her childlike ability to experience the world inductively still intact. She is an adult with an adult's thinking capacity, enabling her to understand as well as know the world. She is an excellent vehicle for de la Mare's ideas about the nature of the human spirit. She observes the best and worst in people, and she sees that the unhappiest people are those who see the world as something to be manipulated, who take without giving. Mr. Anon gives all he has without expectation of receiving what he wants, Miss M.'s love. *Memoirs of a Midget* is more than a story of a social outcast's view of society; it is a depiction of spiritual conflict and revelation.

De la Mare was a seeker, a questioner, and an observer; the endings of his novels are suggestive but provide few answers. A skilled and demanding craftsman, he never failed to entertain his readers, but he employed his storyteller's gift in the service of the lifelong spiritual quest that animated all of his works.

Kirk H. Beetz

Other major works

SHORT FICTION: *Story and Rhyme: A Selection*, 1921; *The Riddle, and Other Stories*, 1923; *Ding Dong Bell*, 1924; *Broomsticks, and Other Tales*, 1925; *Miss Jemima*, 1925; *Readings*, 1925-1926 (2 volumes); *The Connoisseur, and Other Tales*, 1926; *Old Joe*, 1927; *Told Again: Traditional Tales*, 1927; *On the Edge*, 1930; *Seven Short Stories*, 1931; *The Lord Fish*, 1933; *The Nap, and Other Stories*, 1936; *The Wind Blows Over*, 1936; *Animal Stories*, 1939; *The Picnic*, 1941; *The Best Stories of Walter de la Mare*, 1942; *The Old Lion, and Other Stories*, 1942; *The Magic Jacket, and Other Stories*, 1943; *The Scarecrow, and Other Stories*, 1945; *The Dutch Cheese, and Other Stories*, 1946; *Collected*

Stories for Children, 1947; *A Beginning, and Other Stories*, 1955; *Ghost Stories*, 1956; *Short Stories, 1895-1926*, 1996 (Giles de la Mare, editor); *Short Stories, 1927-1956*, 2001 (Giles de la Mare, editor).

PLAY: *Crossings: A Fairy Play*, pr. 1919.

POETRY: *Songs of Childhood*, 1902; *Poems*, 1906; *A Child's Day: A Book of Rhymes*, 1912; *The Listeners, and Other Poems*, 1912; *Peacock Pie: A Book of Rhymes*, 1913; *The Sunken Garden, and Other Poems*, 1917; *Motley, and Other Poems*, 1918; *Flora: A Book of Drawings*, 1919; *Poems 1901 to 1918*, 1920; *Story and Rhyme*, 1921; *The Veil, and Other Poems*, 1921; *Down-Adown-Derry: A Book of Fairy Poems*, 1922; *Thus Her Tale*, 1923; *A Ballad of Christmas*, 1924; *Stuff and Nonsense and So On*, 1927; *Self to Self*, 1928; *The Snowdrop*, 1929; *News*, 1930; *Poems for Children*, 1930; *Lucy*, 1931; *Old Rhymes and New*, 1932; *The Fleeting, and Other Poems*, 1933; *Poems, 1919 to 1934*, 1935; *This Year, Next Year*, 1937; *Memory, and Other Poems*, 1938; *Haunted*, 1939; *Bells and Grass*, 1941; *Collected Poems*, 1941; *Collected Rhymes and Verses*, 1944; *The Burning-Glass, and Other Poems*, 1945; *The Traveller*, 1946; *Rhymes and Verses: Collected Poems for Young People*, 1947; *Inward Companion*, 1950; *Winged Chariot*, 1951; *O Lovely England, and Other Poems*, 1953; *The Complete Poems*, 1969.

NONFICTION: *Rupert Brooke and the Intellectual Imagination*, 1919; *The Printing of Poetry*, 1931; *Lewis Carroll*, 1932; *Poetry in Prose*, 1936; *Pleasures and Speculations*, 1940; *Chardin, J.B.S., 1699-1779*, 1948; *Private View*, 1953.

EDITED TEXTS: *Come Hither*, 1923; *The Shakespeare Songs*, 1929; *Christina Rossetti's Poems*, 1930; *Desert Islands and Robinson Crusoe*, 1930; *Stories from the Bible*, 1930; *Early One Morning in the Spring*, 1935; *Animal Stories*, 1939; *Behold, This Dreamer!*, 1939; *Love*, 1943.

Bibliography

Campbell, James. "A Kind of Magic." *The Guardian*, June 10, 2006. Profile of de la Mare, written on the fiftieth anniversary of his death, focuses primarily on the writer's life but provides some information on his poetry and novels. Notes that although de la Mare's use of language was "at odds with the realism of his contemporaries," he became one of England's "best-loved poets and storytellers."

Hopkins, Kenneth. *Walter de la Mare*. Rev. ed. London: Longmans, Green, 1957. Slim volume touches on de la Mare's life as well as his prose and verse writings, providing a useful introduction to the author. Hopkins, an ardent admirer of de la Mare, briefly examines all of his major works. Supplemented by a select bibliography.

McCrosson, Doris Ross. *Walter de la Mare*. New York: Twayne, 1966. Presents a good critical introduction to de la Mare. Examines at length his total literary output, concentrating particularly on the novels, which McCrosson argues are not only neglected but also contain the clearest statement of his vision of life. Points out that de la Mare's fascinating quest into the mysteries of life never coalesced into a coherent vision. Complemented by a chronology and a select bibliography.

Manwaring, Randle. "Memories of Walter de la Mare." *Contemporary Review* 264 (March, 1994): 148-152. Reminiscence by a longtime acquaintance of de la Mare comments on his style and his influence. Reflects de la Mare's childish delight in simple things that is so often reflected in his fiction.

Megroz, R. L. *Walter de la Mare: A Biographical and Critical Study*. London: Hodder & Stoughton, 1924. Classic work—more an appreciation than a critical examination—is the first book-length study of de la Mare's work. Megroz professes deep admiration for de la Mare, sketches a brief biography, comments on personal impressions, and then devotes the rest of his discussion to de la Mare's poetry.

Wagenknecht, Edward. *Seven Masters of Supernatural Fiction*. Westport, Conn.: Greenwood Press, 1991. Chapter on de la Mare includes a brief biographical sketch and discusses his fiction in the context of the English literary tradition. Addresses both the short and the long fiction, providing a succinct overview of de la Mare's body of work in prose.

Whistler, Theresa. *The Life of Walter de la Mare*. London: Duckworth, 2003. Interesting biography draws on previously unavailable information about the author. Includes discussion of de la Mare's novels; Whistler argues that de la Mare's work is deserving of serious critical reevaluation.

SAMUEL R. DELANY

Born: New York, New York; April 1, 1942
Also known as: Samuel Ray Delany, Jr.

PRINCIPAL LONG FICTION

The Jewels of Aptor, 1962
Captives of the Flame, 1963 (revised as *Out of the Dead City*, 1968)
The Towers of Toron, 1964
The Ballad of Beta-2, 1965
City of a Thousand Suns, 1965
Babel-17, 1966
Empire Star, 1966
The Einstein Intersection, 1967
Nova, 1968
The Fall of the Towers, 1970 (includes revised versions of *Out of the Dead City*, *The Towers of Toron*, and *City of a Thousand Suns*)
The Tides of Lust, 1973 (also known as *Equinox*)
Dhalgren, 1975
Triton, 1976 (also known as *Trouble on Triton*)
Empire, 1978
Tales of Nevèrÿon, 1979
Neveryóna: Or, The Tale of Signs and Cities, 1983
Stars in My Pocket Like Grains of Sand, 1984
Flight from Nevèrÿon, 1985
The Bridge of Lost Desire, 1987 (also known as *Return to Nevèrÿon*)
Hogg, 1993
They Fly at Çiron, 1993
The Mad Man, 1994
Phallos, 2004
Dark Reflections, 2007

OTHER LITERARY FORMS

Samuel R. Delany is known for his work in a number of literary forms other than the novel, including the short story, autobiography, and, most notably, literary criticism and theory. Delany's short stories have been collected in *Driftglass: Ten Tales of Speculative Fiction* (1971), and some have been reprinted along with new stories in *Distant Stars* (1981). *Heavenly Breakfast: An Essay on the Winter of Love* (1979) is a memoir describing Delany's experiences as a member of a commune in New York. *The Motion of Light in Water: Sex and Science-Fiction Writing in the East Village, 1957-1965* (1988) is an autobiography covering Delany's youth and the early part of his writing career.

Delany has also published a number of important essays on science fiction, some of which have been collected in *The Jewel-Hinged Jaw: Notes on the Language of Science Fiction* (1977), *Starboard Wine: More Notes on the Language of Science Fiction* (1984), *The Straits of Messina* (1987), and *Longer Views* (1996). In addition to other, uncollected essays, introductions, and speeches, Delany has written *The American Shore: Meditations on a Tale of Science Fiction by Thomas M. Disch* (1978), a structuralist-semiotic study of Disch's short story "Angouleme," and *Silent Interviews* (1994), a collection of what Delany calls "written interviews." With his then-wife Marilyn Hacker, Delany coedited the journal *Quark: A Quarterly of Speculative Fiction* in 1970-1971. He has also written for comic books, including a large-format "visual novel," *Empire* (1978), and he made two experimental films, *Tiresias* (1970) and *The Orchid* (1971).

ACHIEVEMENTS

Samuel R. Delany is one of a handful of science-fiction writers to have been recognized by the academic community as well as by authors and fans of the genre. Unlike such similarly successful figures as Kurt Vonnegut and Margaret Atwood, however, who refuse to accept the "science fiction" label for their relevant work, Delany has always been a vigorous defender and promoter of genre fiction in general and science fiction in particular. In his criticism as well as in his practice, he has continually stressed the importance of care, thought, and craft in writing. His own work, like that of those writers he most consistently praises (including Joanna Russ, Thomas Disch, and Roger Zelazny), is marked by its attention to language and its concern with issues other than science and technology, particularly with the roles of language and myth in society and the potential of and constraints on human behavior within different social constructs.

Delany's own background informs these social concerns: One of a handful of African American science-fiction writers, he also developed an intense interest in sexuality by virtue of his own homosexuality. His criticism and his fiction writing converged over the years, as Delany sought to incorporate his theoretical interests and insights into his fiction and further develop them in that practical context, using both activities to inform his teaching of creative writing. Although the intense intellectualism of Delany's theoretical investigations alienated many of the fans of his early, more colorful fiction, he gained other readers by way of compensation. He has long been one of the foremost contemporary writers, theoreticians, and critics of science fiction, and he successfully expanded this interest in the latter part of his career to wider enterprises in literary theory and more varied literary endeavors.

Samuel R. Delany. (Courtesy, University Press of Mississippi)

Biography

Samuel Ray Delany, Jr., was born in Harlem in New York City on April 1, 1942, to an upper-middle-class black family. His father was a prominent Harlem funeral director and was active in the National Association for the Advancement of Colored People (NAACP). Delany attended the prestigious Dalton School, noted for its progressive curriculum and eccentric teachers and staff. Tensions with his father and a learning disability that would later be diagnosed as dyslexia marred Delany's childhood and teenage years somewhat, but he found compensation in his interests in theater, science, gymnastics, and—most especially—writing.

After graduating from Dalton in 1956, Delany attended the Bronx High School of Science, where he was encouraged in his writing by some of his teachers and by a fellow student and aspiring poet, Marilyn Hacker. After high school graduation in 1960, Delany received a fellowship to the Bread Loaf Writers' Conference in Vermont, where he met Robert Frost and other professional writers. Delany enrolled in City College of New York but dropped out in 1961. He continued to write, supporting himself as a folksinger in Greenwich Village clubs and cafés. On August 24, 1961, he and Marilyn Hacker were married.

Although their marriage of more than thirteen years was open and loosely structured—the couple often lived apart—Hacker and Delany were highly influential on each other as he developed his fiction and she her poetry. It was at Hacker's instigation that Delany submitted his first published book, *The Jewels of Aptor*, to Ace Books, where she worked. He followed up that novel with a trilogy, *The Fall of the Towers*, and in 1964 he reenrolled at City College of New York, where he edited the campus poetry magazine, *The Promethean*. He soon dropped out again, and in 1965, after completing *The Ballad of Beta-2*, he went with a friend to work on shrimp boats in the Gulf of Mexico.

Delany used the advances earned by *Babel-17* and *Empire Star* to tour Europe during 1965 and 1966, an experience that influenced his next two novels, *The Einstein Intersection* and *Nova*. When he returned to the

United States, Delany became more involved in the science-fiction community, which was beginning to take notice of his work. In 1967, the Science Fiction Writers of America awarded *Babel-17* the Nebula Award for best novel (shared with *Flowers for Algernon* by Daniel Keyes), and in 1968 he won two Nebulas, for *The Einstein Intersection* and the short story "Aye, and Gomorrah . . . ."

During the winter of 1967, while Hacker was living in San Francisco, Delany moved in with a New York rock group called the Heavenly Breakfast, who lived communally. This experiment in living, recorded in *Heavenly Breakfast*, is also reflected in *Dhalgren*. By 1968, when *Nova* was his first publication in hardcover, Delany was beginning to receive critical acclaim from outside science-fiction circles; he spoke at that year's Modern Language Association's annual meeting in New York. During the next few years, while working on *Dhalgren*, he devoted himself to a number of other projects, including reviewing and filmmaking. He received the Hugo Award in 1970 for his short story "Time Considered as a Helix of Semi-precious Stones," and in the same year began coediting *Quark* with Marilyn Hacker; the journal ceased publication after only four issues.

On January 14, 1974, Hacker gave birth to a daughter, Iva Hacker-Delany, in London, where the couple lived for more than a year. Delany returned to the United States later that year to serve as Visiting Butler Chair Professor of English at the State University of New York at Buffalo—a post offered to him by Leslie Fiedler. At this time, Hacker and Delany agreed to a separation and Hacker returned to London. A divorce followed in 1980, with Delany taking primary responsibility for their daughter. After completing *Triton* in 1976, Delany accepted a fellowship at the University of Wisconsin-Milwaukee's Center for Twentieth Century Studies. In 1977, he collected some of his critical essays in *The Jewel-Hinged Jaw* and in 1978 published *The American Shore*, a book-length study of a Disch short story.

Delany spent much of the 1980's living in New York, writing, and looking after Iva. His major project in that decade was the creation of a "sword-and-sorcery" fantasy series comprising *Tales of Nevèrÿon*, *Neveryóna*, *Flight from Nevèrÿon*, and *The Bridge of Lost Desire*. The impact of the acquired immunodeficiency syndrome (AIDS) crisis is seen in the latter two books, especially *Flight from Nevèrÿon*. In 1984, Delany collected more of his criticism in *Starboard Wine* and also received the Pilgrim Award for achievement in science-fiction criticism from the Science Fiction Research Association. He began work on another epic science-fiction project, but the projected diptych stalled when the intimate relationship mirrored in the novel broke up; the first part appeared as *Stars in My Pocket Like Grains of Sand*, but the second, which was to have the title "The Splendor and Misery of Bodies, of Cities" (modeled on the title of a volume from Honoré de Balzac's *La Comédie humaine*, 1829-1848), was never completed. In 1988, Delany published his autobiographical recollections about his earlier years in *The Motion of Light in Water*, and he became a professor of comparative literature at the University of Massachusetts, Amherst.

The most controversial of Delany's subsequent publications were two pornographic novels, *Hogg* and *The Mad Man*, which reflected his continuing interest in "paraliterature"—a fascination further extended in his comic-book-format erotic autobiography, *Bread and Wine*. Delany also published two significant nonfiction works in *Silent Interviews*, a collection of written interviews with subjects ranging from racism to aesthetic theory, and *Longer Views*, a collection of Delany's major essays on art, literature, and culture. He also published *Atlantis*, a collection of three naturalistic novellas, and the fantasy novel *They Fly at Çiron*. Delany won the Bill Whitehead Award for Lifetime Achievement in Gay Literature in 1993 and was the guest of honor at the World Science-Fiction Convention at London, England, in 1995.

In January, 2001, Delany was appointed professor of English and creative writing at Temple University. Two novels he produced in the early years of the twenty-first century, *Phallos* and *Dark Reflections*, reflect his increasing involvement in academic endeavor and the reminders of mortality provided by his own aging process. Delany is the subject of a documentary film appropriately titled *The Polymath: Or, The Life and Opinions of Samuel R. Delany, Gentleman*, which was first shown at the Tribeca Film Festival in April, 2007.

Analysis

Rather than seeking to enhance the value of science fiction, as a writer or critic, by attempting to produce or detect the presence of "literary" elements and properties, Samuel R. Delany proposes that the reader and critic must employ a set of "reading protocols" as a methodology for tapping the richness and complexity of science fiction. The protocols one applies to reading science fiction of necessity must be different from the protocols one applies to "mundane" literature, because the writer—and therefore the reader—must construct whole and distinctive worlds (or universes) as backgrounds for each and every narrative.

To illustrate this point in his critical writing, Delany frequently cites a sentence from a Robert A. Heinlein novel: "The door dilated." Given only these three words, he argues, one can make a wealth of suppositions about a culture that needs doors that dilate rather than swing or slide open and shut and that has the technology to manufacture and operate such doors. Delany's own writing carefully deploys such cues; in *Babel-17*, Mollya explains her desire to aid the heroine, Rydra Wong, by stating, "I was dead. She made me alive"—a sentence meant literally rather than metaphorically, in that Mollya had been "discorporate" before she was revitalized by Rydra, who needed a new crew member. It is by virtue of its potential to "refresh" language in this way, Delany suggests, that science fiction is the form of prose that is closest to poetry.

Delany's novels, therefore, trace the growth and increasing maturity of a literary artist as well as a reasoned mutation of prevalent themes and images. Most of his science-fiction novels feature quests for identity and meaning undertaken or observed by young men—usually artists of some sort; *Babel-17*, with its female hero, modeled on Marilyn Hacker, is a notable exception. These characters are in varying stages of development, but their quests usually culminate in their reaching some kind of "conceptual breakthrough." A major concern in the background to these quests is the author's fascination with the function of language and myth, issues central to *The Einstein Intersection*, *Nova*, and *Dhalgren* and theoretically complicated to an unprecedented extent in the Nevèrÿon cycle.

In his mature works, from *Babel-17* on, Delany's characterizations and plots have taken on new levels of depth and complexity as he has increasingly cultivated the conviction that neither individuals nor societies are stable, unitary entities, and that the relationships and interactions between them are intricate and complicated. This realization is manifested in two images that recur throughout Delany's fiction and criticism. The first is the palimpsest—the inscribed sheet that has been imperfectly erased and reinscribed several times, creating a rich and difficult multilayered text whose meanings may be incomplete and can never be reduced to any one reading. The Nevèrÿon cycle is an extreme instance: a densely layered text that comments on its own narrative, its generic counterparts and origins, and its own composition. The second image is that of the web, which is multidirectional rather than linear and in which the individual points are no more important than the connections between them. To recognize the web is to understand its structure and learn how to use it or at least work within it, possibly even to break or reshape it.

In these complementary images of palimpsest and web, Delany echoes modern thought in many disciplines. Some psychologists assert that the individual ego is illusory, a construct to give the semblance of unity to the multiple and conflicting layers of desire and repression that constitute the subject. Anthropologists and sociologists define society by the interactions within its patterns and structures rather than as a unitary and seamless "culture" or even a collection of such cultures. Linguists stipulate that one cannot determine the meanings of individual utterances by isolating individual parts of speech, that in fact the concepts "noun" and "verb" have no individual meaning except in relation to whole statements and the contexts within which they occur. Finally, post-Einsteinian physics has demonstrated that matter itself is not composed of stable, unitary particles but that atoms and their components might be better visualized as "energy packets" the characteristics and behavior of which depend on the expectations of observers and the contexts in which they are observed. Delany is aware of all these intellectual currents and is in fact a part of this "web" of thought himself; within this pattern of relationships he has set a standard for all writers, whether fantastic or mainstream.

Delany has been referred to in jest as the "ultimate

marginal writer"—a black, gay, poststructuralist writing in a despised genre—but those very margins serve to offer a critique of what is missing in the center and a vision of what could be found there instead. Increasingly, Delany's work has come to stand for openness, diversity, randomness, and the provisional; it opposes closure and stagnation, hierarchies and fixities, providing a continuing challenge to common assumptions about sex, race, and social roles as well as about what fiction is and how it should be read.

BABEL-17

Babel-17 marked the beginning of a dramatic sophistication in Delany's work, following the colorful odysseys in exotica contained in *The Jewels of Aptor*, *The Fall of the Towers*, and *The Ballad of Beta-2*. Its major thematic concern is the power of language in shaping awareness. Its heroine, the poet and space captain Rydra Wong, is fluent in many languages, including those of body movements; she is an ideal candidate for a mission to interpret and discover the source of an enemy alien language, Babel-17. In fulfilling the mission, she discovers a way of thinking that is highly analytical and marvelously efficient and compact but is also dangerous; having no concept of "I" or "you," the language can induce psychotic and sociopathic behavior in those who use it.

EMPIRE STAR

Empire Star features a human habitation of that name established at the gravitational center of the most massive multiple star in the galaxy, the many components of which perform an intricate dance around it. The awesome strain to which space-time is subjected "parts the fibers" of reality, so that the temporal present becomes entangled with both the spatial past and the possible future. Only "multiplex" minds can hope to maintain their spatiotemporal situations and perspectives within it; more primitive "simplex" or "complex" minds are likely to suffer radical disorientation and displacement. It is a hypothetical ultimate of all potentiality: a multiplex forge upon which psychological and physical reality are constantly worked and shaped into something humanly usable.

The short novel's hero, young Comet Jo, is the product of a simplex culture who comes into possession of a Jewel—the story's narrative voice—which is actually a multiplex consciousness that requires him to complete its interrupted delivery to Empire Star. In order to do that, Comet Jo must take a crash course in the differences among simplex, complex, and multiplex thinking and confront some of their many manifestations within the many-layered and multifaceted galactic civilization centered on Empire Star. No other science-fiction story packs such awesome richness and complexity into such a narrow narrative space.

THE EINSTEIN INTERSECTION

The Einstein Intersection is set on a future Earth abandoned by human beings, who have evolved beyond any further need of it but have left their bodies and minds behind for newcomers to occupy. These inheritors embark on an intensive recapitulation of their predecessors' mythologies, aided by an ancient computer system employed by humans for Psychic Harmony Entanglements and Deranged Response Associations (PHAEDRA), which now resides in a radioactive Underworld but is still capable of providing illusory gratifications for any and all desires.

The myths recapitulated by PHAEDRA and transfigured as they are acted out by the characters in the novel are various, ranging from the classical (Orpheus and Jesus) to the ultramodern (Billy the Kid and Jean Harlow), but they are all subject to the same process of calculated adaptation to a species whose existential situation is different from human nature in several ways—most significant is the fact that the species has three sexes rather than two. As usual, the novel's hero, Lobey—its Orpheus—starts off with all kinds of misconceptions regarding himself and his world, and his learning process is a difficult and painful one.

NOVA

In *Nova*—which Delany wanted to describe as a "space opera," although he was advised against it on the grounds that the term, however apt it might have been in terms of the novel's echoes of Richard Wagner's *Parsifal*, had too many negative connotations—space captain Lorq von Ray sets out on a quest for the "grail" that will enable him to seize economic control of the galaxy from his ambitious rivals: the mysterious element Illyrion, formed in the heart of exploding stars, from which it is understandably difficult to recover. The novel's narrative voice is provided by one of his helpers, the relatively innocent artist Katin, who gradually comes to grips with the inordinately complicated web that binds the story together with the galactic culture that is at stake in the plot.

Dhalgren

The amnesiac protagonist of *Dhalgren* wanders into Bellona, a midwestern city that has suffered an unidentified catastrophe that has left a residue of odd side effects. In the course of the novel's 880 pages, he encounters the city's remaining residents; goes through various mental, physical, and sexual adventures; becomes a local legend; and eventually leaves. The rest of the country and the world are unaffected; separated from outside electronic communication and abandoned by the larger society, Bellona has become a quasi-anarchic center of attraction for outcasts and drifters of all descriptions as well as remaining a home to its own disenfranchised, notably the city's black population.

The protagonist, who comes to be known as The Kid, initially goes to work for the Richards family, who are trying (in vain) to maintain a semblance of the old normality; he helps them move upstairs in their apartment complex, away from a "nest" of "Scorpions," the street gangs who wander through the city. In the meantime, he begins to write poetry in a notebook he has found. When his "employment" peters out, he becomes a Scorpion himself, eventually the leader of a nest. His poetry is published, and he becomes famous, at least locally. Near the end of the novel, The Kid believes that he has discovered his name, but when he leaves Bellona, his fate is still obscure.

Dhalgren is a tacit palimpsest, offering new explanations on each reading. Its construction echoes an "optical chain" made of mirrors, prisms, and lenses that The Kid and other characters wear. Events and phrases within the book do not exactly repeat but imprecisely mirror one another. Delany's epigraph reads, "You have confused the true and the real."

Triton

Triton has some significant similarities to *Dhalgren*, but it turns the premises of the earlier novel inside out. Once again, a protagonist is introduced into a society of near-total freedom, but this time the setting is an established and elaborately planned society on Neptune's moon Triton in the year 2112; the protagonist, Bron Helstrom, is a worker in "metalogics" for a company (termed a "hegemony") located there. On Triton people are free to behave and live in almost any social, sexual, or religious pattern; they also may change their residences, their physical sex, and their psychological sexual orientation almost at will. Not everyone can cope with the responsibilities that these freedoms entail, however, and Bron—a recent immigrant from Mars—is one of those who cannot.

In the course of the novel, Triton becomes allied with the other Outer Satellites of the worlds beyond Jupiter in a highly destructive war against Mars and Earth, but the book's main focus is Bron's obsession with an itinerant roaming actress and theatrical producer called The Spike. Her rejection of him drives him into a psychological crisis, precipitating gender reassignment surgery that does not have the desired result. Triton's social system, designed to accommodate anyone and everyone—one of its rules requires a subsidiary location where the rules do not apply—still cannot accommodate someone like Helstrom, who does not share the presuppositions on which this system is founded.

Triton is subtitled *An Ambiguous Heterotopia*—a riposte to the subtitle of Ursula K. Le Guin's *The Dispossessed: An Ambiguous Utopia* (1974). Although Triton's society is quasi-utopian, offering a near-ideal model of future society, the model it provides, like all utopias, is inherently insufficient. In contrast to utopias, which attempt to provide solutions to social problems and consolation to their readers, heterotopias are deliberately disturbing and disruptive. Triton cannot "hold together" metaphorically or literally; it cannot accommodate a Helstrom, just as it might lose its artificial gravity by virtue of a random incoherence of the subatomic particles in its energy field. *Triton* also includes two appendixes, one of them comprising notes on and omitted segments from the novel and the other excerpts from "lectures" by a Martian scholar, titled "Some Informal Remarks Toward the Modular Calculus, Part Two." These additions are integral to the novel, serving to remind the reader of the book's own artificiality and inevitable incompleteness.

Nevèrÿon tetralogy

Although three of the books comprising the Nevèrÿon sequence—*Tales of Nevèrÿon*, *Flight from*

Nevèrÿon, and *The Bridge of Lost Desire*—are collections of "tales" rather than unitary novels, the whole enterprise is a single vast, multifaceted text. In keeping with Delany's insistence on the importance of the provisional, the random, and the contradictory as features to be accepted in life and in literature, however, the parts are not entirely coherent and may be read in different orders. Myth and language, and their relationship to social order—with particular respect to the institution of slavery—provide the central subject matter of the tetralogy, but the texts also play with the concept of utopia. The name Nevèrÿon—"never/there"—is a play on the word "utopia," construed as "no place," as well as a calculated analogue of "New York."

As issued by its publishers, the series begins and ends with the novella "The Tale of Gorgik," whose first version opens the first volume and whose revised version closes the fourth. The first volume has four other stories, "The Tale of Old Venn," "The Tale of Small Sarg," "The Tale of Potters and Dragons," and "The Tale of Dragons and Dreamers"—the first and third of which are also novellas—and an appendix describing the discovery and translation of the series' (imaginary) root text by "K. Leslie Steiner." The second volume, *Neveryóna*, subtitled *The Tale of Signs and Cities*, is a novel. The third includes two long novellas and two appendixes, the first of which is a hybrid of fact and fiction about the advent of AIDS in New York City called "The Tales of Plagues and Carnivals."

Delany's original intention had been to end the series after three volumes, and he had already begun the projected two-volume novel whose first volume appeared as *Stars in My Pocket Like Grains of Sand*, but when he could not finish the second part he began work on a volume that he intended to call *Return to Nevèrÿon*, although the title was changed to *The Bridge of Lost Desire* at the behest of an editor. It consists of two long novellas, "The Game of Time and Pain" and "The Tales of Rumor and Desire," plus the revised "Tale of Gorgik" and a flirtatiously ironic appendix perversely described as a "preface."

The central thread running through the series is the history of Gorgik the Liberator, the slave-turned-statesman who brings about the abolition of slavery in the empire but retains a powerful interest in the apparatus of slavery—embodied and symbolized in a shackle worn as a collar—as an accessory in homosexual intercourse. Gorgik's early biography, described in the first tale, is carried forward in "The Tale of Small Sarg" and "The Tale of Fog and Granite"; he plays a subsidiary role in *Neveryóna* and then looks back on his life in "The Game of Time and Pain." The counterpoint to Gorgik's slightly ambiguous career as a liberator is a complementary series of narratives with female protagonists—or female objects of desire—that explore and develop the author's fascination with feminist aspects of sexual politics.

The series is far more naturalistic than the promiscuously syncretic mock-medieval background that has been standardized by genre fantasy. Indeed, some observers might dismiss it from the genre on the grounds that a key definitive feature—workable magic—is missing. Although the native fauna includes dragons, which are occasionally encountered in the stories, that inclusion seems calculated to emphasize by its singularity that all the other inventions featured in the series are cultural. It *is* a fantasy, however, not merely because it abstracts cultural elements from a more considerable chronological range than could ever have been brought together in one place at one time, but also because it uses their alchemical fusion for both analytic and creative purposes. It is a genre fantasy from which the customary froth of wish fulfillment has been carefully skimmed, precisely in order that the psychology of wish fulfillment can be taken back to its roots.

Stars in My Pocket Like Grains of Sand

Given the kinds of metafictional games played in the Nevèrÿon series, the publication of which *Stars in My Pocket Like Grains of Sand* interrupted, it is not entirely inappropriate that the larger work of which it was intended to form a part remained frustratingly incomplete. Its two major protagonists are Rat Korga and Marq Dyeth, the former an illiterate slave who is filled with knowledge by technological information devices, the latter a descendant of an ancient family and "industrial diplomat." The reader is deliberately tantalized with uncertainty regarding the sex of the two lovers, because the denizens of this future universe classify all humans as "women" and refers to them as "she" regardless of actual sex. Although travel and communication cut across vast distances between planets and galaxies, the social complexities and contradictions within the populations of individual planets can make worlds seem both large and strange. Although Marq communicates with the inhabitants of many other planets with relative ease, it is much harder for him to travel on his own home planet and communicate with other members of his own "family."

The loving relationship between Marq and Rat is complicated by the social and political structures within which they exist. There is an all-embracing power struggle between the Family, which seeks universal dominance to impose a restrictive, authoritarian system of belief and behavior, and the Sygn, an anarchic alliance that seeks power only to abnegate its use in any restrictive sense. Complicating this conflict are the Web, the information link that connects the planets, and the Xlv, a nonhuman species capable of space travel, which might have destroyed Rat's home planet. As the first half of the diptych ends, however, everything still awaits the remotest possibility of resolution.

They Fly at Çiron

They Fly at Çiron was an early novel that Delany had abandoned in 1962. James Sallis had completed a novelette based on the fragment, but Delany returned to it in order to develop it in a different direction. Like the Nevèrÿon series, it is set in a fantasy realm where civilization is just getting started. Çiron is a peaceful, pastoral region whose inhabitants are suspicious of the Winged Ones, flying humans who inhabit the nearby mountains, but when their idyllic way of life is brutally disturbed, the Çironians join with the Winged Ones to resist the invasion. The defenders are able to prevail thanks to a crucial friendship that has developed among a Çironian, Rahm; a Winged One, Vortcir; and a renegade officer of the Empire, Kire. The Çironians' innocence is lost, however; the "virus" of civilization has infected them, and they are already planning to strike back.

Phallos

Like *Empire Star* and many of the components of the Nevèrÿon tetralogy, *Phallos* is short by the standards of modern novels, but it makes up for its lack of length with an awesome complexity. The central narrative has two frames, one briefly recording the external narrator's quest to locate a "lost" pornographic novel published in the late 1960's, the other describing an admittedly false historical context making out the text to be an ancient document known to the likes of Walter Pater and "Baron Corvo." The text itself—described only in synopsis, with excerpts—tells the story of Neoptolemus, a youth from Syracuse whose elaborate sexual odyssey, which begins in the company of a Roman merchant, involves him in the murder of Antinous, the favorite of the Roman emperor Hadrian. The murder is somehow linked to the worship of a "nameless god" whose worship is linked to the prehistory described in the Nevèrÿon series. The process of synopsization removes most of the novel's alleged pornographic content and (in the context of its supposed 1969 publication) presumed raison d'être while preserving the material that is (in the context of Delany's work) its true heart and soul.

Dark Reflections

Dark Reflections is compounded out of three novellas that offer snapshots of the life of Arnold Hawley, an African American poet. The three are presented in reverse chronological order, the snapshots of his middle age and youth being seen from his viewpoint at the age of sixty-seven. Delany was sixty-five when the novel was published, but its first part is set twenty years before publication, so Hawley belongs to a generation preceding the author's, and that is the whole point of the text; it is, in essence, an account of what Delany's life might have been like had he not been fortunate enough to be born in his own time.

Although Delany was not untouched by racial and sexual prejudice, they did not hold him back in his life and career; Hawley, born into a poorer family in a more hostile era, suffers the full stifling effects of both. In the first section he has just won a prize for the poetry he has been publishing from small presses for many years—a welcome belated acknowledgment, but one of insufficient value to allow him to retire early from his job teaching at a community college. The second section describes a brief and horribly disastrous marriage that he was unwisely led to contract in his mid-thirties, after many miserable years living in the closet, too frightened and ashamed of his homosexuality to express it. The third section describes his formative years and details the manner in which his potential as an artist and human being was ruthlessly expunged by evil (but commonplace) circumstance. Read in juxtaposition with Delany's own experiments in autobiography, the novel provides a deft and thorough analysis of the sometimes-unsung benefits of the historical changes that overtook the United States—or, more specifically, New York—in the latter half of the twentieth century.

Donald F. Larsson; John Nizalowski
Updated by Brian Stableford

OTHER MAJOR WORKS

SHORT FICTION: *Driftglass: Ten Tales of Speculative Fiction*, 1971 (revised and expanded as *Aye and Gomorrah*, 2003); *Distant Stars*, 1981; *Atlantis: Three Tales*, 1995.

NONFICTION: *The Jewel-Hinged Jaw: Notes on the Language of Science Fiction*, 1977; *The American Shore: Meditations on a Tale of Science Fiction by Thomas M. Disch*, 1978; *Heavenly Breakfast: An Essay on the Winter of Love*, 1979; *Starboard Wine: More Notes on the Language of Science Fiction*, 1984; *The Straits of Messina*, 1987; *The Motion of Light in Water: Sex and Science-Fiction Writing in the East Village, 1957-1965*, 1988 (memoir); *Silent Interviews*, 1994; *Longer Views*, 1996; *Bread and Wine: An Erotic Tale of New York City, an Autobiographical Account*, 1998; *Shorter Views: Queer Thoughts and the Politics of the Paraliterary*, 1999; *Times Square Red, Times Square Blue*, 1999; *Nineteen Eighty-Four: Selected Letters*, 2000; *About Writing: Seven Essays, Four Letters, and Five Interviews*, 2005.

EDITED TEXT: *Quark: A Quarterly of Speculative Fiction*, 1970-1971 (with Marilyn Hacker).

BIBLIOGRAPHY

Broderick, Damien. "The Multiplicity of Worlds, of Others." In *Reading by Starlight: Postmodern Science Fiction*. New York: Routledge, 1995. Analyzes Delany's work within the context of postmodern theory.

Dery, Mark. "Black to the Future: Interviews with Samuel R. Delany, Greg Tate, and Tricia Rose." *South Atlantic Quarterly* 92 (1993): 735-778. Examines why so few African American authors write science fiction despite the fact that it is a genre in which encounters with the Other are central.

Freedman, Carl. "About Delany Writing: An Anatomical Meditation." *Extrapolation* 47, no. 1 (2006): 16-29. Attempts to apply the prescriptive account offered by Delany's *About Writing* to an understanding of the author's own work, especially *Dhalgren* and *Triton*.

_______. *Critical Theory and Science Fiction*. Hanover, N.H.: Wesleyan University Press, 2000. Scholarly work devotes a chapter to a reading of *Stars in My Pockets Like Grains of Sand*. Freedman is the author of an informative introduction to a new edition of the novel published in 2004.

McEvoy, Seth. *Samuel R. Delany*. New York: Frederick Ungar, 1984. Provides biographical information as well as discussion of Delany's own interpretations of his early works. Draws on personal interviews that McEvoy conducted with Delany.

Reid-Pharr, Robert F. "Disseminating Heterotopia." *African American Review* 28 (Fall, 1994): 347-357. Discusses how Delany confronts traditional ideas of proper identity and community politics, deconstructing lines between black and white communities and between homosexual and heterosexual communities.

Review of Contemporary Fiction 16, no. 3 (Fall, 1996). Special issue on Delany features essays on his novels and on his science-fiction theory and criticism. Includes an interview with Delany in which he discusses his theory of science fiction and his ideas about science fiction as a genre and a way of reading.

Sallis, James, ed. *Ash of Stars: On the Writing of Samuel R. Delany*. Jackson: University Press of Mississippi, 1996. Collection of essays is an excellent source of information on Delany's life and work.

Tucker, Jeffrey Allen. *A Sense of Wonder: Samuel R. Delany, Race, Identity, and Difference*. Middletown, Conn.: Wesleyan University Press, 2004. Presents a sophisticated analysis of Delany's work within the framework of postmodernism, reflecting the author's own interests and compositional methods.

Weedman, Jane. *Samuel R. Delany*. Mercer Island, Wash.: Starmont House, 1982. Provides biographical information on Delany and discusses a wide range of subjects, including influences on his writing, the stylistic and critical concepts in his work, and his development as a writer. Includes a detailed chronology and annotated primary and secondary bibliographies.

GRAZIA DELEDDA

Born: Nuoro, Sardinia, Italy; September 27, 1871
Died: Rome, Italy; August 15, 1936
Also known as: Grazia Cosima Deledda

Principal long fiction

La via del male, 1896
Il tesoro, 1897
La giustizia, 1899
Il vecchio della montagna, 1900
Dopo il divorzio, 1902 (*After the Divorce*, 1905; republished as *Naufraghi in porto*, 1920)
Elias Portolu, 1903 (English translation, 1992)
Cenere, 1904 (*Ashes*, 1908)
Nostalgie, 1905
L'edera, 1906
L'ombra del passato, 1907
Il nostro padrone, 1910
Sino al confine, 1910
Nel deserto, 1911
Colombi e sparvieri, 1912
Canne al vento, 1913 (*Reeds in the Wind*, 1999)
Le colpe altrui, 1914
Marianna Sirca, 1915 (English translation, 2006)
L'incendio nell' oliveto, 1918
La madre, 1920 (*The Woman and the Priest*, 1922; better known as *The Mother*, 1923, 1974)
Il segreto dell'uomo solitario, 1921
Il Dio dei viventi, 1922
La danza della collana, 1924
La fuga in Egitto, 1925
Annalena Bilsini, 1927
Il vecchio e i fanciulli, 1928
Il paese del vento, 1931
L'argine, 1934
La chiesa della solitudine, 1936 (*The Church of Solitude*, 2002)
Cosima, 1937 (English translation, 1988)
Romanzi e novelle, 1941-1969 (5 volumes)
Opere scelte, 1964
Romanzi e novelle, 1971 (one-volume reprint of the 1941-1969 multivolume edition)

Other literary forms

All through her life, Grazia Deledda (day-LEHD-dah) wrote short fiction. After publication in periodicals, most of the short stories were collected in volumes, which number at least twenty-two. The early short pieces were exercises and appeared in local journals or women's magazines; those written from 1899 to 1912 were of higher quality. Those were Deledda's best years for long fiction also, so that the two aspects of her creativity seem to have nourished each other. As the writer's fame grew, she was asked to contribute more and more frequently to popular magazines; like other writers of her generation, she provided the flourishing business of the periodical press with a steady flow of material. Although those short stories were designed to please the public and therefore were often trite, melodramatic, and full of the worst stereotypical characters and situations, they provide useful information on the cultural milieu of the twentieth century in Italy.

Deledda's best collection of short stories is *Chiaroscuro* (1912). She employs a variety of styles and themes in the twenty-two pieces collected under that title: They are inspired by the traditional tale, the ghost story, the fairy tale (Deledda wrote many stories for children, too), the humorous anecdote, and the sentimental story. The most frequently used themes, however, and the most successfully treated, are those inspired by Deledda's half-remembered, half-imagined Sardinia. These short stories are usually fast paced and colorful. The locations and the situations remind the reader of certain scenes from the best Western films: a village square or the stony loneliness of the hills in the white heat of the sun; small groups of people telling one another stories or listening to some handsome stranger's boastings; furious loves, mysterious events, and vendettas. The ingredients are used effectively, and the themes are the same as those that appear in Deledda's major fiction: the power of economic necessity, the greater power of sexual desire, and the uselessness of the wisdom of old people.

Achievements

Critical statements about Grazia Deledda's fiction are contradictory, at times negative, and yet they all acknowledge the power of her imagination and style. What makes a critical evaluation of her work difficult is her apparent isolation from prevailing literary currents.

When Deledda published her first novels and short stories, at the end of the nineteenth century, the emerging current was *Verismo*, or verism, which had largely taken over the tenets of French naturalism. With *Verismo*, human experience is bound to its social context. The author must let characters and events speak directly; the phenomena of everyday life—actions, rites, customs, language—are of greater interest than the probing of psychology. At first, Deledda seemed to have much in common with *Verismo*; the warm welcome that *Veristi* such as Giovanni Verga and Luigi Capuana extended to the young writer was in part the result of Deledda's sensitivity and loyalty to the culture of Sardinia. The critics of the early twentieth century, however, questioned Deledda's *Verismo* and saw it as a limitation and a superficial element in her fiction; they expressed admiration, instead, for the epic aura they found in her novels. While the critics debated Deledda's problematic position in literary history, readers from the urban middle class became her devoted public. For them, she was the very voice of Sardinia, a mysterious and therefore fascinating island, and she was quintessentially a narrator, prolific and attuned to the times.

In the view of some critics, Deledda was a "spontaneous" writer whose immediacy owed almost nothing to literary tradition, a writer not so much ignorant of as uninterested in that tradition, preferring to remain within an archaic, lyric world elaborated by her memory—a world that she called Sardinia. For some, her "illiteracy"—that is, her position outside the literary tradition—her "barbaric" or "primitive" sensibility, were admirable qualities; for others, they were disconcerting liabilities. Critics such as Emilio Cecchi and Eurialo De Michelis have argued that Deledda was in fact deeply responsive to the artistic currents of her time. Pointing to the allusive quality of her writing, the musical and symbolic dimensions of her narratives, they see her as representative of *Decadentismo* or, more generally, of the European Symbolist movement.

Recent analyses have looked more closely at the themes, the imagery, and the language of Deledda's fiction. They confirm the unity of her experience and her marginal relation to the conventional literary tradition, but they also bring out her modernity and her kinship with other solitary figures of early twentieth century Italian literature such as Luigi Pirandello, Italo Svevo, and Federigo Tozzi. Deledda's is a European voice—the voice of an era that was disappointed by the myth of progress and torn between latter-day Romanticism and Symbolism. Her concern with the conflict between the passions of the individual and the needs of an ordered community is the same as that addressed by such different minds as D. H. Lawrence and Sigmund Freud.

Biography

Grazia Deledda was born Grazia Cosima Deledda in Nuoro, Sardinia, on September 27, 1871, the fourth of six children. Her family was moderately well-to-do. Deledda attended three elementary classes, and then repeated the third one, to receive as much schooling as possible—a common practice at that time for a boy from the lower classes or a girl who was unusually bright. Thereafter, Deledda received haphazard tutoring from a professor who happened to be in Nuoro and knew the family. She also read on her own: Eugène Sue, Alexandre Dumas, *père*, Sir Walter Scott, the Bible, Honoré de Balzac, Homer, and Victor Hugo. Soon, constant writing and dreaming of glory became Deledda's occupations.

By the time Deledda was sixteen years old, she had established a network of correspondents in Sardinia and on the Continent, through the little magazines she read. In 1886, she published her first short story, in 1888 and 1889, her first *feuilleton*. From that point on, Deledda published children's stories, essays on regional customs, short stories, and *feuilletons*, becoming a steady contributor to several literary and women's magazines.

No matter what her ambition and her successes may have been, Deledda had soon become aware of the need to comply with the conventions of her provincial town: Her behavior, although girlish at times, was respectful of traditional rules. Nuoro society was irritated when it discovered that a local girl was drawing material for fictional and ethnographic work from its life and customs. In addition, Deledda was a pragmatic person from a tender age; as she observed the world around her, she saw what burdens romantic attachments and unwise unions could place on women. She was fully conscious of her total commitment to her writing career.

Feeling constrained and isolated during all of those years, Deledda yearned to leave Nuoro. That desire was satisfied when she met Palmiro Madesani, a functionary of the Italian government, in 1900. They married and moved to Rome, where Deledda remained during the course of a serene married life that included two children, Sardus and Franz. After 1900, her biography is the record of her literary activity. She continued to publish at a sustained pace, obtaining public favor and critical acclaim. Her success was internationally acknowledged when she was awarded the Nobel Prize in Literature in 1926. She lived a very private life, fulfilled and joyful, which is substantiated by her correspondence with her friends. Deledda died in Rome, Italy, on August 15, 1936.

Grazia Deledda. (© The Nobel Foundation)

Analysis

A prolific writer is often viewed as a force of nature, and Grazia Deledda's writing has been called "instinctual," yet her letters and her autobiographical novel, *Cosima*, written in the last year of her life and published posthumously, testify to her conscious determination to be a writer and to perfect her skills. Deledda's work is the product not only of a facile gift but also of an apprenticeship. There were three periods in her career. The first one, extending to 1900, included at least sixteen volumes of long and short fiction. It was a period of training, when her major themes and images emerged from a mass of second-rate prose. From 1900 to 1915, Deledda wrote all of her best novels, establishing herself as a major novelist on the European scene. During the last twenty years of her life, although she continued to publish at an impressive rate, she failed to reach her earlier effectiveness. Only with *Cosima*, as she looked upon her years in Nuoro, did she again find her voice, speaking of that youthful "Other" whose willfulness and vitality could not be suppressed by family tragedy or dismal circumstances.

Two basic elements of Deledda's fiction must be considered first: the setting and the influence of the female experience. The setting of almost all Deleddian fiction is Sardinia, an island that had always been cut off from the life of the mainland. Until the twentieth century, it remained a land of wild natural beauty and ancient customs, inhabited by shepherds and hostile to the powers that ruled it from afar. Deledda grew up in Sardinia, conscious of the rigid local customs yet separated from "the people" by her social status as the daughter of a landowning family. Her early short stories and novels described the Sardinian environment with clarity but as if from the outside, as an ethnological phenomenon and a picturesque setting.

In *La via del male*, one of her first significant novels, the author indulged in descriptions of the island's beauty; at the same time, she wove a love story based on the devotion of the "primitive soul" of a servant-shepherd, the repressed sexuality of male serf and female landowner, and a code reminiscent of the tradition of courtly love, filtered through folklore. Progressively, however, Sardinia became an integral element of Deledda's fictional world. As she moved to the Continent, she began to appropriate the geographically identifiable Sardinia, to transform it into a land of her imagination. This Sardinia endured as the background against which she drew her characters, the passions, and rituals of her scenario; the island landscape in its changeability became the visible manifestation of states of mind. Seldom did Deledda use urban settings for her novels, and when she did, the city would only be vaguely sketched—as, for example, in *La danza della collana*.

The other major element in Deledda's fiction is the female experience, which in many ways parallels the experience of the Sardinian: It is secretive, marginal, in conflict with itself, and yet it is also a source of strength and a fierce sense of identity. At the age of seventeen, she wrote in a letter that

> Whole months without going out of the house . . . a cheerful house, but looking onto a street where there is never a passer-by. . . . I am not allowed to do anything in the house, except engage in those ethereal occupations that increase boredom.

Inaction and solitude fed Deledda's ambition and helped her to focus her energies. In her novels, the rules of silence and submission exasperate the passions of her characters. Once again, Deledda draws from an experience that is intimately familiar to her. Metaphors and images come frequently from domestic activities, from the universe of female experience, feelings, and values. Her protagonists, male and female, are described in terms of femaleness. Physically, they tend toward androgyny; as they struggle to submit to the prescriptions of an archaic culture, they become aware of their profound "difference." Sensuous and passionate in a world hemmed in by taboos, they retreat into themselves. The contemplation of nature brings them peace; secrecy and silence become sources of strength and guarantee them a measure of personal freedom. The motifs belonging to the two main sources of Deledda's inspiration thus find their confluence.

The world vision of the novelist, however, was a complex one. Deledda knew the impact of different factors impinging upon human experience. In some novels, such as *Ashes* and *Marianna Sirca*, she gave particular attention to the barrier separating classes that lived in daily intimacy; in others, such as *Reeds in the Wind*, she concentrated on the economic imperative. In all of her novels, Deledda spoke of the subversive power of sexuality and of the contradictory demands made by the pagan and the Christian traditions, one ruled by the mystique of blood vengeance, the other by a message of peace.

No matter what the emphasis, each novel is built around a cluster of recurrent themes. Passion is at the center; it may involve desire for power, wealth, or freedom, but it is always manifested as erotic desire. Sexuality is the impulse that cannot be denied, and it is the first spark in the challenge to any taboo. This centrality of the sexual dimension, as the primary subverter of order, places Deledda's fictional universe well within the sensibility of the early part of the twentieth century, when the exploration of the role of human sexuality was central in literature and science.

Desire causes transgression. Here, Deledda's characters reveal their weakness, their tendency toward ambivalence and self-deception. They do not rebel fully and do not consent to their "sin," but they are unable to abide by the ancient rules. Guilt is inevitable for them, and with it an obsessional need for expiation. Deledda has been compared to the great Russian novelists because of her insistence on the themes of sin, guilt, and expiation, yet the similarities are only superficial. For Deledda, the taboos cannot but be challenged, even if the transgressors must suffer for their acts and sometimes for their very wishes; the defeat of desire can only be acknowledged with sadness.

Deledda's protagonists, as most critics have observed, are not the object of psychological study; they are not meant to be. Rather, they reenact a cycle of rebellion and defeat in a context where the forces of clan, class, and religion necessarily overpower the individual. Pietro Benu, the servant-shepherd in *La via del male*, may obtain Maria Noina in marriage after many struggles, but the crimes he has committed transform their union into a punishment, a tool for atonement. In *Ashes*, Olì's ardent sensuality will be expiated through her own and her son's suffering; to this suffering, mother and son will desperately consent. Marianna, the outlaw's lover in *Marianna Sirca*, can be the handsome bandit's wife only at his deathbed; they both pay for falling in love "in a far away, otherworldly place" when they see their faces reflected together in the water of a deep well.

While Deledda's protagonists reenact this bitter cycle, her peripheral characters look on helplessly. Deledda frequently assigns such peripheral roles to old people who have known life's errors, often sinners who have moved into the mountains in order to find peace. Their wisdom, however, cannot influence fate. They are sought after for advice, but their advice is not heeded. They are the archetypal images of a conscience that can only weep over the ruins caused by passion and transgression.

Deledda's style has baffled her critics. To what extent her Sardinian language influenced her writing would be difficult to assess. Her early readings were hardly a school for writing excellence, and that may explain Deledda's long apprenticeship and her lapses into the worst commonplaces in her lesser works. The strength of her prose comes from her attention to gesture and action, her ability to create an atmosphere, her sense for color. There was a dilemma that all Italian writers of her time had to solve: the choice between a dialect that is intimately known but regional, and an imperfectly learned standard language, a bookish language rarely spoken but widely used in writing. Without hesitation, Deledda opted for the Italian that the educated middle class was accustomed to reading. She became the voice of the emerging Italian bourgeoisie, and today her work remains accessible to a wide audience. Her best writing blends the simplicity of the Italian language, which was the medium of the educated class, with the richness of the stylistic devices used by late Romantic authors, and with the flavor of expressions, proverbs, and sayings obviously incorporated from the Sardinian.

The most frequent device used by Deledda is the descriptive passage, a pause in the narration that focuses on a natural scene, a religious festivity, or a character's appearance. In her early works, such passages are frequently an end in themselves, but in her mature works they are functional and fully integrated. In particular, the descriptions of religious pilgrimages are significant, as such communal festivities are emblematic of the connection among religious feeling, natural scenery, and human conscience. Against the background of the mountains in their seasonal splendor, the pilgrims travel on horseback, clad in resplendent costumes, to reach a sanctuary where they customarily perform a ritual. The contrast between the anguish of the protagonists and the beauty of the festive days in their quasi-biblical society is the focal point of Deledda's description.

Elias Portolu

Elias Portolu, one of Deledda's finest novels, opens with a family celebration for Elias upon his return from a penitentiary on the Continent. Two other festive gatherings, one for a pilgrimage to a sanctuary and one for the Mardi Gras, will mark the turning points of the story, dramatizing the conflict between the protagonist and the culture to which he has returned. Elias, who is at the center of the rejoicing of his community, immediately appears alone, an outsider in the tribal unity. The prison experience, his "misfortune," as they call it, has created a distance between him and his culture that allows him to gain a critical perspective; it has also brought out in him an awareness of his own difference, an awareness that contradicts the ethos of the clan. The taboo is an a priori reality in Deledda's universe, but it is Elias's unavoidable obstacle because he is sensitized to its presence, and his changed sensibility leads him to acknowledge his individual desires.

Deledda's characters speak of the taboo in terms of fate; in effect, the mechanism of transgression and punishment is set in motion only under certain circumstances, as if it were lying in wait for a destined victim. Elias self-indulgently probes his discontent; he experiences a sort of existential guilt. His "fate" is made evident also by a "sign" that is given prominence from the very beginning of the novel, his androgynous appearance. By his culture's standards, he is "like a woman in man's clothing": His skin is white as a woman's, his hands are beautiful and white, and he is tall and lean with delicate features. Male society requires coarseness, aggressiveness, and a demeanor rigidly obedient to social conventions. His temperament, gentle and reserved, with sudden bursts of emotion, marks him as "a child," a misfit, as someone who is doomed to violate the laws of custom.

During the cavalcade and the activities of the pilgrimage, Elias falls in love with Maddalena, his brother's fiancé, and the radical weakness of his personality is revealed: He is ambivalent, unable to accept his difference and assert his individual will yet also incapable of denying himself and respecting the taboo. During the Mardi Gras, when masked costumes and dances allow a controlled weakening of the rules governing the community, Elias and Maddalena—who is by now his sister-in-law—begin an incestuous relationship. Torn between decisions he cannot make, Elias retreats into the priesthood, adding the obstacles of new taboos to repress his desire. The burden of expiation will be carried by both lovers, as first Maddalena's husband and then the lovers' child die. By the boy's deathbed, Elias, who is now a very tormented priest, finds some sort of peace, a joy resembling "a vaporous veil." Moments of turmoil alternate with moments of reflection as the protagonist wavers between opposite moods. Although he has discovered the power of desire, the egotism of the self, Elias is paralyzed by his awe for a code of conduct that condemns all impulses that threaten to disrupt the ordered universe of his culture.

The characters around Elias perform a choral function, as the duel between Elias's opposing temptations takes place. There is Maddalena, passionate and sacrificing; the family, unable to understand Elias's "illness"; the mother, the image of the "sainted" female whose embrace promises the peace of renouncement; and a priest and an old hermit, who advise Elias and are not heeded. Deledda also skillfully incorporates dream sequences into the narration, as well as details of the many activities of the shepherd's lives. All around loom the mountainous regions of the island, where nature is order and beauty. There, conflict ceases, overwhelmed by the colors, the fragrances, and the sounds of a primitive Eden. Only wise men, though, Deledda says, can live there, after they have made their peace with the world and with themselves.

Reeds in the Wind

Deledda's personal favorite among her novels was *Reeds in the Wind*, a melancholy tale of three unmarried sisters and their manservant, Efix. Here, Deledda's style is as nuanced as the themes are richly woven. Realistic in the dialogues, her writing becomes lyric in the descriptions of nature, male beauty, and sensual life, suggesting a synesthesia of human experience.

Paradoxically, Efix, who is old and guilty of a double transgression against the taboo of caste and the authority of the father/master, has become the protective figure for the surviving members of the noble family. In a journey of penance, he succeeds in repairing the damage caused within the ancient order by the young people he loves. He will attain his goal of restoring the family's fortunes when he is able to make them obey the law that commands acceptance of suffering and submission: "We are born to suffer like the Christ. We must weep and keep silent."

Another novelist treating the same material might focus on the inevitable conflicts within a static society still faithful to feudal values. Deledda, however, veers away from that set of questions, preferring to explore the stages of a purificatory journey within the majestic environment of her island. The significant theme for her is that of redemption through suffering; the figure of the pure of heart, the simple man, is central to it. This is particularly evident in the episode of Efix's journey in the company of beggars, which is a *mise en abîme* of the role of that character in the novel. In the universe of male values, between the violence of the father and the rebelliousness of the young, Efix embodies the virtues that guarantee endurance. They are the traditional female virtues: patience, resignation, and love of peace. Efix is described in terms of feminine submission: He is "the good servant" who keeps quiet even when he knows, who simulates ignorance, humiliated and yet convinced of the appropriateness of his subservience. His caring love is a kind of motherly nurturing: "He wished that he could lean over the unhappy boy, and tell him: 'I am here, I'll provide!'—but he could only offer him the wine gourd, as a mother offers her breast to her crying baby." The novel closes with a moving account of the death of the servant who has accomplished his task, in a further parallelism with other mother figures in several of Deledda's other works.

The Mother

In *The Mother*, with unusual structural simplicity and the most economical means, Deledda explores again the conflicts of passion and taboo and the problematical issue of expiation. There are only two characters here, the mother and her son, the priest; two locations, the house and the church; and a time span that is both very short and immeasurable, like the time of a fairy tale. A third character, Agnes, is barely sketched, and the choral presence of the villagers, with their primitive celebrations, serves only as a distancing device underlining the loneliness of the protagonists. The almost schematic appearance of the text contradicts its complexity at the stylistic level: The novel partakes of several genres, partly religious drama, partly fantastic tale, and partly symbolic poem.

The passion that leads to transgression here is dual: It is the furious sexual desire that almost overcomes Don Paulo as he begins his pastoral career in a mountain parish, but it is also the ambition of his mother, who "had wanted to return to give orders where she had been a servant" and who thought she had managed to fulfill this ambition by rearing her son for the priesthood. The sexual transgression is avoided in a struggle between Paulo's desire and his fears, but only at the price of the death of the mother, who thus expiates also for her sin of pride. Her death may appear melodramatic, an unconvincing device, but it is consistent with Deledda's development of her story in a symbolic mode. Without perhaps fully realizing it, Deledda deepens her exploration of the connections between sexual taboo and power and the relationship between the traditionally separate male and female universes. Maria Maddalena and Paulo are as one in their symbiotic closeness: mother and son, female and male, one conscience torn between passion and renouncement. On one hand, they harbor a mistrust of the flesh, a fear of all joyous abandon, having internalized their society's condemnation of individual fulfillment; on the other hand is their conviction, persistently voiced, that passion is the only authentic voice of humanity.

Deledda uses visions, dreams, ghostly dialogues, metaphors, and images inspired by fairy tales to create an atmosphere of mystery. The furious wind of the highlands becomes one with the characters' spiritual and physical anguish; the priest's black cloak beats the air like the wings of a bird of prey, and doors open and close as if by magic, hiding forever what is on the other side. This is a journey inside the ambiguity of human experience.

D. H. Lawrence, in his preface to the English translation of the novel, offers, among many questionable statements, the wrongheaded observation that Deledda does not give her book a conclusion because she has divided feelings: She is impatient with her characters and confuses the issues, Lawrence says, resorting to the elimination of the mother because she resents Maddalena's final triumph, resents her as an obstacle to Paulo's sexual satisfaction. Concerned with what he calls primitive and instinctual passionality, Lawrence does not see that Paulo and Maddalena are two faces of the same divided self. As a price for attaining peace, the female figure must die, for she is the one who grieved "in her flesh" for Paulo's renunciation, and it was she, the servant, who had silently questioned the rule of priestly celibacy. The closing of the novel sanctions, and obscurely laments, precisely the end of that tormented ambiguity, the irrepressible joy of that physical communion.

Angela M. Jeannet

Other major works

Short fiction: *Amori moderni*, 1907; *Chiaroscuro*, 1912; *Il fanciullo nascosto*, 1915; *Il ritorno del figlio, La bambina rubata*, 1919; *Il flauto nel bosco*, 1923; *Il sigillo d'amore*, 1926; *La casa del poeta*, 1930; *La vigna sul mare*, 1932; *Sole d'estate*, 1933; *Il cedro del Libano*, 1939; *Chiaroscuro, and Other Stories*, 1994.

Bibliography

Amoia, Alba della Fazia. "Grazia Deledda: The Scandal of a Woman Writer." In *Twentieth-Century Italian Women Writers: The Feminine Experience*. Carbondale: Southern Illinois University Press, 1996. Amoia begins her examination of eleven Italian women writers by analyzing Deledda's work, pointing out feminist themes in her fiction and comparing them to similar themes in the work of the other studied authors in this collection.

Aste, Mario. *Grazia Deledda: Ethnic Novelist*. Potomac, Md.: Scripta Humanistica, 1990. Aste's biography also provides a detailed analysis of the cultural, philosophical, sociolinguistic, and literary dimensions of Deledda's works, and places the writings within the context of Sardinian traditions. Includes a bibliography.

Heyer-Caput, Margherita. *Grazia Deledda's Dance of Modernity*. Buffalo, N.Y.: University of Toronto Press, 2008. Examines Deledda's work within the context of literary modernism and of philosophy, including positivism and the ideas of Friedrich Nietzsche and Arthur Schopenhauer. Heyer-Caput focuses on Deledda's novels, addressing elements of regionalism, decadence, and verism and the influence of other literary movements with which Deledda has been associated.

King, Martha. *Grazia Deledda: A Legendary Life*. Leicester, England: Troubador, 2005. King's biography chronicles Deledda's unlikely evolution from a young girl in nineteenth century Sardinia to a Nobel Prize-winning novelist. A good starting point for any study of Deledda and her life and work. Includes a bibliography.

Kozma, Janice M. *Grazia Deledda's Eternal Adolescents: The Pathology of Arrested Maturation*. Madison, N.J.: Fairleigh Dickinson University Press, 2002. A study of Deledda's depictions of men in her novels and short stories. According to Kozma, Deledda believed that many men fail to mature and become full adults, and she superimposed her understanding of this psychopathology upon her male characters.

Merry, Bruce. "'Dolls or Dragons': The Depiction of Women in Grazia Deledda's Novels." In *Women in Modern Italian Literature: Four Studies Based on the Work of Grazia Deledda, Alba de Céspedes, Natalia Ginzburg, and Dacia Maraini*. Townsville: James Cook University of North Queensland, 1990. Deladda is one of four authors whose work is analyzed in this study of the depiction of women characters in Italian fiction. Includes a bibliography.

Pacifici, Sergio. *The Modern Italian Novel from Capuana to Tozzi*. Carbondale: Southern Illinois University Press, 1973. Pacifici, the author of several surveys of Italian fiction, profiles Deledda and nine other Italian novelists.

MIGUEL DELIBES

Born: Valladolid, Spain; October 17, 1920
Also known as: Miguel Delibes Setién

Principal long fiction

La sombra del ciprés es alargada, 1948
Aún es de día, 1949
El camino, 1950 (*The Path*, 1961)
Mi idolatrado hijo Sisí, 1953
Diario de un cazador, 1955
Diario de un emigrante, 1958
La hoja roja, 1959
Las ratas, 1962 (*Smoke on the Ground*, 1972)
Cinco horas con Mario, 1966 (*Five Hours with Mario*, 1988)
Parábola del náufrago, 1969 (*The Hedge*, 1983)
El príncipe destronado, 1973
Las guerras de nuestros antepasados, 1974 (*The Wars of Our Ancestors*, 1992)
El disputado voto del señor Cayo, 1978
Los santos inocentes, 1981 (novella)
Cartas de amour de un sexagenario voluptuoso, 1983
El tesoro, 1985
377A, Madera de héroe, 1987 (*The Stuff of Heroes*, 1990)
Señora de rojo sobre fondo gris, 1991
Diario de un jubilado, 1995
El hereje, 1998 (*The Heretic*, 2006)

Other literary forms

Though primarily a novelist, Miguel Delibes (deh-LEE-bays) has published several books of travel impressions, including *Por esos mundos* (1961; round about the world), *Europa, parada, y fonda* (1963; Europe, stops, and inns), *USA y yo* (1966; U.S.A. and I), and *La primavera de Praga* (1968; springtime in Prague); short narratives, including the collections *La partida* (1954; the departure), *Siestas con viento sur* (1957; siestas with a southern breeze), and *La mortaja* (1970; the shroud); and books on hunting and fishing, including *Aventuras, venturas, y desventuras de un cazador a rabo* (1977; adventures, good and bad luck of a small game hunter) and *Mis amigas las truchas* (1977; my trout friends). He also has published miscellaneous books of articles, commentary, and essays, as well as newspaper articles and comments and impressions written in diary form. Asked by the Spanish government to write a tourist guide of Old Castile, Delibes produced *Viejas historias de Castilla la Vieja* (1964; old tales of Old Castile), a work that for its narrative-descriptive passages of lyric force is one of the author's most memorable and revealing books (though it was unacceptable as a travel guide); it is sometimes classified as a novella.

Achievements

Miguel Delibes is without doubt one of Spain's most significant novelists to emerge since the end of the Spanish Civil War in 1939. His first novel, *La sombra del ciprés es alargada*, published by the Barcelona publisher Destino in 1948, won the prestigious Eugenio Nadal Prize in 1947. Though probably his worst novel, it was decisive in influencing him to continue his efforts at writing fiction, efforts that he has realized while working simultaneously for many years as a professor in the School of Commerce in Valladolid and on the editorial staff of the newspaper *El norte de Castilla*, serving as its director from 1958 to 1963.

As a novelist, Delibes's work has been marked by a steady growth and progression in style and content, causing the critics to observe that each new Delibean book is better than the last one. In general, Delibes has progressively moved away from a traditional and detailed realism reminiscent of the nineteenth century to a more poetic and symbolic realism, experimentation in structure and techniques, and a more economical, direct, and unaffected style. However, his direction toward simplicity has been broken somewhat in some later works, such as *Five Hours with Mario* and *The Hedge*, in which his more complex and convoluted syntax serves the purpose of making style reflect content, especially, according to Janet Díaz, the "troubled psychological atmosphere and torment" of the protagonist. Delibes's novels have been widely translated into the leading European languages. Numerous doctoral theses on his work have been completed in American and European universities.

A strong and independent voice in contemporary Spanish fiction, Delibes has adhered to no group or movement inside or outside Spain, though he has absorbed from them whatever he saw as beneficial to his own character and temperament as a man and as a writer. Though neither a regionalist nor a novelist of customs (*costumbrista*) in the traditional sense, he has continued to live in Valladolid and portray what he knows best: the rural people and landscape of Old Castile. In particular, his distinctive use of rural Castilian speech has won high praise; notable also is his creation of rural Castilian atmospheres and characters.

Biography

Born Miguel Delibes Setién on October 17, 1920, into a bourgeois family in Valladolid, a provincial capital in Old Castile, Delibes was reared as a strict Catholic. Though his father was liberal in his views, his mother was very conservative; in his childhood and adolescence, her orientation seemed to dominate; in adult life, his father's Catholic liberalism prevailed. By the time the Spanish Civil War began, the future novelist, though not yet seventeen years old, had graduated from high school. A year later, he joined the Nationalist navy and served on a cruiser patrolling the Cantabrian Coast.

After the war, Delibes, having been refused reenlistment in the navy because of nearsightedness, took specially provided accelerated courses in both law and business, obtaining degrees in both areas in 1941. In 1943, he took an intensive three-month course in journalism in Madrid. In 1945, through competitive examinations (*oposiciones*), he won the chair of mercantile law in the School of Commerce in Valladolid, succeeding his father. Later he changed his subject to the history of culture. In 1946, he married Angeles de Castro. In 1947, he wrote his first novel-manuscript, partly in an attempt to rid himself of his obsession with death—an obsession he had had since childhood. Submitted to the Nadal competition, the manuscript won its prestigious prize, and it appeared in 1948 as *La sombra del ciprés es alargada*.

During the next several years, Delibes worked on the editorial staff of *El norte de Castilla*, Spain's second oldest continuously operating newspaper, and held his professorial post in the School of Commerce while continuing to write novels. His second novel, *Aún es de día*, appeared in 1949; according to Díaz, it resembles his first novel in its "rather ponderous, rhetorical style." Critics generally agree that Delibes found his proper style in his third novel, *The Path*, published in 1950, a work that, unlike his first two novels, almost instantly became an unqualified critical success. In 1955, *Diario de un cazador* was awarded the Miguel de Cervantes Prize. While continuing his increasingly successful career as a novelist and writer of short fiction, Delibes fulfilled his journalistic duties with distinction, rising to be assistant director of *El norte de Castilla* from 1952 until 1958 and director from 1958 until 1963 (when political pressures from the Franco regime forced his resignation).

Miguel Delibes. (Getty Images)

A Catholic, though liberal in his views, a faithful husband and father of seven children, a passionate lover of nature and an avid fisherman and hunter, Delibes disclaims all pretensions to intellectualism. Gonzalo Sobejano aptly describes Delibes's whole career as a search for authenticity, a search for his own proper path. Delibes has traveled extensively, including in the United States. He has a broad cosmopolitan view and concern for the problems of contemporary humanity, not only for the people of Spain. In 1975, he was admitted to the Royal Spanish Academy, primarily in recognition of his achievements as a novelist.

Analysis

Critics generally divide Miguel Delibes's novels into two periods or types. Written in the first manner are the author's first two novels, *La sombra del ciprés es alargada* and *Aún es de día*, and his fourth novel, *Mi idolatrado hijo Sisí* (my adored son Sisí), published in 1953. With the publication of *The Path* in 1950, his third novel, Delibes inaugurated his second manner, which implied a definite break with his earlier rhetorical, rather sluggish, analytical, and traditionally realistic style. Since 1950, with the exception of his brief reversion to traditional realism in *Mi idolatrado hijo Sisí*, a novel that advances an anti-Malthusian thesis, Delibes has evolved in the direction of freer artistic expression, of what has been called poetic realism (as against his former "analytic realism").

During his second phase, Delibes has experimented freely with new techniques and structures. Plot has all but disappeared and a third-person narrative point of view has been replaced with the author-narrator merging his voice with that of the protagonist to form a central narrative consciousness with a double perspective: that of the narrator and that of the protagonist. Though the two perspectives coalesce, they can be distinguished by the alert reader. Technical and structural innovations made by Delibes are expressive of his continuing search for his own most authentic mode or path of novelization (although he has sometimes been suspected of following current literary vogues in pursuit of critical acclaim). Novels of his second period are generally characterized by a reduction in time and space and by single-minded, simpleminded protagonists; what the works lose in complexity they gain in unity and concentrated force. The action on the primary plane in *The Path* occurs in one night, in *Five Hours with Mario* also in one night, in *The Wars of Our Ancestors* in seven consecutive evenings, and all occur in a single house or room.

In ideology or thematic content, one finds little if any real changes between the author's early and later periods. An intensified anguish over the dangers to humankind's freedom and dignity, inherent in modern technological paternalistic societies, and the growing lack of communication or human solidarity in today's world, however, especially mark some of his more recent novels, notably *Five Hours with Mario* and *The Hedge*. His main motifs, as pointed out by Díaz, remain as constants in his work: the shadow of death, the importance of nature, the life and landscape of rural Old Castile (with its severe socioeconomic problems and abandonment by the Central Spanish Government), a preference for child protagonists (*The Path*, *Smoke on the Ground*, *El príncipe destronado*) or elementary, abnormal, or "primitive" characters (the Rat Hunter in *Smoke on the Ground*, Pacífico Pèrez in *The Wars of Our Ancestors*), and the individual in his difficult relationships with others and with society at large (*The Wars of Our Ancestors*). His more recent novels include biting satire of the Catholic Church's apparent impotence in effecting a genuine spiritual-moral transformation of the Spanish character. Since childhood, Delibes has occasionally suffered from periods of pessimism, a mood that seems to have intensified in his more recent novels.

Pío Baroja and Camilo José Cela appear to be two of the principal influences upon Delibes as a writer of fiction. His irony and his dry, laconic description of gruesome scenes as well as his use of nicknames and repetition of descriptive phrases or tag lines, often ironic, to identify characters (for example, the priest "who was a great saint"), especially recall Cela.

The Path

Through the memory flashbacks of Daniel, the eleven-year-old protagonist of *The Path*, on the night before his expected departure—for further schooling in the city—from the Castilian village in which he was born and has lived all of his life, the reader enters into the "world" of the protagonist. In that "world," Daniel's personal life is projected outward toward the collective life of the village; the individual and his society in this work fuse into an artistic unity. Past and present are also interwoven through Daniel's memory flashbacks, though the narrator often intervenes to provide his own perspective on the events and situations being recalled. The narrator interjects without destroying the reader's illusion that the central narrative consciousness is that of the child-protagonist; in fact his added perspective subtly contributes to the narrative's sense of reality or verisimilitude.

Essentially plotless, a series of anecdotes given unity primarily by the protagonist himself—he is telling his personal story—the work simultaneously draws a vivid portrayal of village life in Spain while elaborating upon the author's favorite themes: death, childhood, nature, and neighbor (or humankind's relationship in society). Daniel, enamored of his life as the son of a poor cheesemaker in the village, believes that his "path" or "way" in life should be to remain where he is. His father, however, wants his son to develop his possibilities to the fullest, and to achieve that end he believes that it is imperative that Daniel acquire a higher education than that available in the village. At great sacrifice, Daniel's father is sending him to the city. Through the opposing views of father and son, important differences between Spanish rural and city life become visible, leading some critics to regard the work as in praise of country life and scorn of life in the city; it can be more accurately described as simply an effort to present the realities of each. Though without a double time dimension, *Smoke on the Ground*, published almost twelve years later, bears close thematic and structural resemblance to *The Path*. In the later work, however, the reader is made much more painfully aware of the cultural, moral, and economic deprivation of life in a Castilian village.

Five Hours with Mario

Five Hours with Mario will undoubtedly remain one of Delibes's most perfectly constructed and important novels. When it appeared in 1966, critics almost universally commented on its seemingly radical break from the novelist's former, more conventional patterns. In a recent study, however, Luis Gonzalez del Valle demonstrates that in structure, narrative techniques, and themes, it bears a marked resemblance to *The Path*. In Gonzalez del Valle's opinion, it constitutes a partial return to the earlier work.

The book opens with a full-page reproduction of an announcement of funeral arrangements for Mario Collado, a professor and unsuccessful writer, who died unexpectedly at the age of forty-nine in March of 1966. Though not named, the setting is a provincial Spanish capital strikingly similar to Valladolid. Following the obituary notice is an untitled chapter, followed by twenty-seven numbered chapters and closing with an untitled chapter, a kind of epilogue. In the untitled introductory chapter, Carmen, Mario's widow of Spanish bourgeois mentality, in her mind and in conversation with her close female friend Valen, reviews the day, which began with the discovery of Mario's death, funeral arrangements, visits to express condolences, and so on. It is now midnight, and she prepares to spend the morning hours by her husband's corpse. The rest of the novel, except for its last short chapter, consists of her interior monologue or unilateral dialogue in which she addresses Mario's corpse in the familiar second person (*tú*), reviewing in flashbacks their life together.

In her harsh, spiteful, and uncomprehending criticism of Mario—a post-Vatican II Catholic who championed the cause of social justice—she gives full vent to her frustration. In a free association of ideas, reiterating certain obsessions, she sometimes rants and raves. In the process of accusing her dead husband of what she perceives to be his many shortcomings, however, she reveals herself to the reader as an ignorant, self-centered, addle-headed hypocrite and thus condemns herself. At the same time, by implication she condemns (unconsciously, of course) the middle-class Spanish society whose values she so faithfully mirrors and of which she is a product. In the final chapter, the couple's oldest son, Mario, thinking that he has heard his mother talking aloud to the corpse, enters the room. By what he says, the reader gathers some hope that the wounds of a divided Spain—as represented by Mario and Carmen—may eventually be healed.

The novel constitutes a study of an absolutely incompatible marriage, but it is more than that. On an allegorical level, Mario comes obliquely to represent an open and democratic Spain, post-Vatican II Catholicism, love and human solidarity, and the abolition of social and economic inequities, while his widow represents a closed and traditional Spain, a dogmatic pre-Vatican II Church, the preservation of social classes, and an unauthentic, materialistic mode of living. By presenting Mario as a corpse and making Carmen express concepts acceptable to the Spanish political regime of the time, Delibes adroitly avoided official censorship while at the same time improving the novel's artistic quality, a masterpiece in irony. The author wisely avoided painting Mario as a hero; he is seen as an ineffectual and impractical idealist and as a mediocre writer. In presenting him in human proportions, often ambiguous, the novel gains in artistic power. It has been adapted for the stage, and it enjoyed a long and successful run in Spanish theaters.

The Hedge

Reminiscent of Franz Kafka's *Der Verwandlung* (1915; *Metamorphosis*, 1936), Eugène Ionesco's *Le Rhinocéros* (1959; *Rhinoceros*, 1960), and Aldous Huxley's *Brave New World* (1932), *The Hedge* portrays in anguished, nightmarish sequences the slow but certain metamorphosis of Jacinto San José, a symbol of the contemporary human in a technological and increasingly uniform and paternalistic society, into a ram, a sacrificial victim of an all-pervasive collectivity that has extracted from him the last vestiges of his individuality and personhood. Some critics saw in the work a radical new direction, an attempt to join the vanguard in novelistic innovation, especially to emulate the latest in Hispanic novels. In reality, however, *The Hedge*, though a parable rather than a realistic novel, with a setting and atmosphere more European than strictly Spanish, is consonant with the nature of Delibes as a man and as a novelist. It once more demonstrates his profound concern for the dignity and freedom of the individual and his relationship with contemporary society. Its unconventional techniques are in accordance with the author's openness to experimentation and are, as Sobejano has indicated, artistically essential to the work as a whole.

Jacinto, a humble and timid bookkeeper working for the gigantic organization presided over by the rotund Don Abdón, dares one day to ask the meaning of what he is doing, whether he is adding zeros or the letter *O*. His lack of total conformity to the organization thenceforth is suspect and leads to his being sent to a rest home in the country where in helpless isolation he is metamorphosed into a ram, having lost his long, desperate, and tormented battle to preserve his human personality. All is experienced by the reader from *inside* the anguished consciousness of Jacinto, an effect primarily achieved through interior monologues of the protagonist but further reinforced through a series of autodialogues in which Jacinto speaks in second person familiar to his image in the mirror and through the tone and perspective of the narrative sections.

A much noted (and irritating) technique is the use through much of the novel of the verbal designations for punctuation rather than their conventional signs; thus comma, period, semicolon, open parenthesis, close parenthesis, and so on, are all spelled out in the text. The effect on the reader is that of listening to a colorless, impersonal office dictation, which thus heightens the sense of alienation experienced by Jacinto. Much of the book is concerned with the degradation of language (as a parallel to the degradation of man), through which Delibes sought to make form reflect content while at the same time parodying some contemporary novelists who propose the destruction of language as one of their missions.

The Hedge is a mixture of realism and fantasy, appropriate to a parable. It constitutes a powerful metaphor of the plight of contemporary humans in a slowly disintegrating, impersonal society, and in its success in communicating the author's (Jacinto's) deep anguish lies its greatest merit.

The Wars of Our Ancestors

In *The Wars of Our Ancestors*, Delibes employs what Díaz calls a "retrospective-reconstructive technique," a technique by which a whole novelistic world is created indirectly through introspection or conversation during a very short period, a technique employed in *The Path* and in *Five Hours with Mario*. The technique is not at all uncommon, though it has many variations; Ramón José Sender, for example, used it with notable effectiveness in *Mosén Millán* (1953; better known as *Réquiem por un campesino español*; *Requiem for a Spanish Peasant*, 1960). In effect, nothing much happens except introspection and conversation in the present, the primary plane of action, while the major action of the novel is that which is evoked from the past, the secondary plane of action and of time.

The Wars of Our Ancestors opens with an untitled brief introductory section or untitled prologue in which a psychiatrist, the fictitious Dr. Burgueño López, tells of his association with Pacífico Pèrez, a convict in a penal sanatorium, and offers to the reader a faithful transcript of taped conversations he had with Pèrez during seven consecutive evenings, May 21 through May 27, 1961; each conversation makes up a chapter. The book closes with a kind of epilogue (slightly more than a page in length) in which Dr. Burgueño López relates the death of Pacífico Pèrez on September 13, 1969. Before dying, Pèrez gives the psychiatrist permission to publish the transcript of the seven conversations. Through the indirect device of presenting the conversations as taped and transcribed by Dr. Burgueño López, Delibes sought to distance himself as author from the text and to lend to it an illusion of a document placed in the hands of the reader without intermediaries.

The novel is a reconstruction in conversations, guided gently by the psychiatrist, of Pacífico Pèrez's upbringing in a small, poverty-stricken Castilian village and his subsequent life in prison. Pèrez speaks in the language of the Castilian peasant, attesting once again the importance Delibes attaches to this element in his work. The book's title refers to humankind's deep propensity for making war on neighbors. Pacífico was brought up by his great-grandfather, grandfather, and father, each of whom had fought for Spain in a war; they regarded it as inevitable that Pacífico would have "his war" and consequently set about educating him for violence. For great-grandfather Pèrez, it was either "sangra o te sangrarán" ("bleed them or they will bleed you"); Pacífico found this philosophy repugnant and turned inward in deep distress. When the brother of his girlfriend surprises Pacífico half naked with his sister, Pacífico impulsively kills the brother—without fear or hate. Refusing to defend himself in court, he is imprisoned. In prison he finds freedom; he would rather live out of society (or at least on its margin) than pay the terrible price of participation, "bleed them or they will bleed you." The conflict between the individual and society remains unresolved for Delibes, just as it did for Baroja before him. In its despairing tone and atmosphere, *The Wars of Our Ancestors* recalls *The Hedge*. Indeed, with advancing age, the author's pessimism seems to have deepened.

Charles L. King

OTHER MAJOR WORKS

SHORT FICTION: *La partida*, 1954; *Siestas con viento sur*, 1957; *La mortaja*, 1970; *Tres pájaros de cuenta y tres cuentos olvidados*, 2003.

NONFICTION: *Por esos mundos*, 1961; *Europa, parada, y fonda*, 1963; *El libro de la caza menor*, 1964; *Viejas historias de Castilla la Vieja*, 1964; *USA y yo*, 1966; *La primavera de Praga*, 1968; *Vivir al día*, 1968; *S.O.S.*, 1976; *Aventuras, venturas, y desventuras de un cazador a rabo*, 1977; *Mis amigas las truchas*, 1977; *Dos viajes en automóvil: Suecia y Países Bajos*, 1982; *El otro fútbol*, 1982; *La censura de prensa en los años 40, y otros ensayos*, 1985; *Castilla habla*, 1986; *Mi vida al aire libre: Memorias deportivas de un hombre sedentario*, 1989; *Pegar la hebra*, 1990; *El último coto*, 1992; *Conversaciones con Miguel Delibes*, 1993; *He dicho*, 1996; *Correspondencia, 1948-1986*, 2002.

BIBLIOGRAPHY

Agawu-Kakraba, Yaw B. *Demythification in the Fiction of Miguel Delibes*. New York: Peter Lang, 1996. Agawu-Kakraba examines several of Delibes's novels, including *Five Hours with Mario*, *The Stuff of Heroes*, *The Path*, *The Hedge*, and *Smoke on the Ground*, to demonstrate how Delibes's fiction criticized the myths of heroism, stoicism, progress, and other elements of Francisco Franco's totalitarian ideology.

Boucher, Teresa Claire. *Existential Authenticity in Three Novels of Spanish Author Miguel Delibes*. Lewiston, N.Y.: Edwin Mellen Press, 2004. Boucher seeks to determine if Delibes has been correctly characterized as a "novelist of authenticity." She analyzes his work in terms of existential philosophy and examines the "existential inauthority" in his novels *Five Hours with Mario, Señora de rojo sobre fondo gris*, and *Cartas de amor con un sexagenario voluptuoso*.

Díaz, Janet W. *Miguel Delibes*. New York: Twayne, 1971. One of the few English-language books about Delibes aimed at the student or general reader. Provides a biography of Delibes and analyses of his works. Includes chronology and bibliography.

Dinverno, Melissa. "Dictating Fictions: Power, Resistance and the Construction of Identity in *Cinco horas con Mario*." *Bulletin of Spanish Studies* 81, no. 1 (January, 2004): 49-76. A study of *Five Hours with Mario*, describing how Delibes's novel charts the fundamental economic, cultural, social, and political changes that were occurring in Spain when the novel was published in 1966.

Meyers, Glenn G. *Miguel Delibes: An Annotated Critical Bibliography*. Lanham, Md.: Scarecrow Press, 1999. Meyers has compiled an extensive annotated bibliography listing literary criticism of Delibes's work. The book also includes a biography tracing Delibes's origins and development as a writer and an analysis of trends in Delibes's criticism.

Schwartz, Ronald. "Delibes and *Parabola del naufrago* (1969)." In *Spain's New Wave Novelists: 1950-1954*: *Studies in Spanish Realism*. Metuchen, N.J.: Scarecrow Press, 1976. Delibes's novel *The Hedge* is one of the books examined in this study of Spanish realism. The book also includes a chapter defining the characteristics of the "Spanish new wave novel" and another chapter placing these novels in their broader literary and historical context.

Don DeLillo

Born: New York, New York; November 20, 1936

Principal long fiction

Americana, 1971
End Zone, 1972
Great Jones Street, 1973
Ratner's Star, 1976
Players, 1977
Running Dog, 1978
The Names, 1982
White Noise, 1985
Libra, 1988
Mao II, 1991
Underworld, 1997
The Body Artist, 2001
Cosmopolis, 2003
Falling Man, 2007

Other literary forms

Although Don DeLillo (duh-LIHL-oh) has focused his major literary efforts on the novel, he has contributed short stories to periodicals, including *The New Yorker*, *Esquire*, *Sports Illustrated*, *South Atlantic Quarterly*, and *The Atlantic Monthly*, and has written a screenplay and several plays.

Achievements

The publication in 1971 of Don DeLillo's first novel, *Americana*, launched the career of one of America's most innovative and intriguing writers. DeLillo has produced satirical novels that drill into and hammer at the chaos of modern society, the lack of coherence and order in institutions, the breakdown of personal relationships, and particularly the failure of language. His driving, mercurial, upbeat prose at times smacks of an idiosyncratic pedantry yet abounds in lyricism and musicality. Some readers have labeled his prose "mandarin," after the fashion of Donald Barthelme and Thomas Pynchon. Pynchon definitely influenced him, but DeLillo has pushed far beyond the limits of imitation or even derivation, asserting a truly independent voice. The promise of prodigious talent inherent in his first novel flowered in later works.

In 1984, the American Academy and Institute of Arts and Letters presented to DeLillo its Award in Literature. *White Noise* won the 1985 National Book Award, *Libra* won the 1989 Irish Times/Aer Lingus International Fiction Prize, *Mao II* won the 1991 PEN/Faulkner Award, and *Underworld* was nominated for the 1997 National Book Award. Additionally, DeLillo was selected as one of two fiction writers to receive the 1995 Lila Wallace-Reader's Digest Award, which provides three years of financial support. In 1999, DeLillo was the first American awarded the Jerusalem Prize, given to writers who contend with the issue of freedom and individuality in society. He received the William Dean Howells Medal and the Riccardo Bachelli International Award for *Underworld* in 2000. DeLillo's novels, although often criticized as plotless disquisitions that never produce anything but comic-strip characters, nevertheless stimulate and excite readers and critics with their musicality, their rhetorical rigor, and their philosophical depth.

Biography

Don DeLillo was born in New York City in November of 1936. He spent his childhood and adolescence in Pennsylvania and the South Bronx. After studying at Fordham University, he lived for a while in Canada and then returned to New York, which he made his home.

Analysis

What little there is of traditional narrative structure in a Don DeLillo novel appears to serve principally as a vehicle for introspective meanderings, a thin framework for the knotting together of the author's preoccupations about life and the world. Thematically, each novel is a profound reworking of the familiar precepts that make up the core of DeLillo's literary belief system. This basic set of ideas includes the function (misfunction) of language as it relates to being, the absurdity of death and the meaning of apocalypse, the complications and chaotic workings of societies (particularly governments and institutions), the ontological purity of women and children, the notion of sacred spaces, and the interrelatedness of time, history, and myth. DeLillo's great facility with a language perfectly tuned for irony and satire allows him to range the breadth and depth of these themes.

AMERICANA

All these thematic strains are present in *Americana*. The problem of language and meaning finds a penetrating focus in the conversation between the protagonist, David Bell, a dissatisfied minor network executive who seizes upon a documentary assignment to make a cross-country odyssey of self-discovery, and Carol Deming, a distracted yet aggressive young actor who reads a part for David's film: The encounter is set up to be sexual but proves to be nothing more than a bizarre verbal tryst, a duel of wacky hyperbole laced with sarcasm. Beneath the words fired rapidly back and forth between David and Carol are the levels of behavior and intensity normally associated with seduction. In this case, words appear to substitute for the great diversity of emotional responses associated with the sex act. The reader, however, knows that verbal intercourse is no substitute for sexual intercourse and commiserates with David on his lack of fulfillment; words are false images that can be made to disguise the multilayered nature of reality. In the end, however, the word is destroyed by the meaning it tries to mask.

This verbal affair takes place in the middle of the United States, in a town called Fort Curtis, the designated location for the filming of David's documentary. He has been commissioned to film the Navajo Indians but decides that the town will be the backdrop for a film about the central moment of his own childhood, the moment he learned that his mother, for him the bastion of health and security, would soon face disintegration and death. Each stop on his "sacred journey" out West holds a numinous attraction for him: the starting point, the chaotic craziness of the network office with its mad memo writer; the garage of Bobby Brand, a friend who uses his van for the trip; Fort Curtis; and ultimately Rooster, Texas, where David's pilgrimage of self-exploration ends in a boozy orgy in the dust.

In Fort Curtis, David hires local people to read absurd lines and then has traveling companion Sullivan, an enigmatic sculptor, play the part of his mother on the day he learned, in the pantry of his parents' home, the tragic truth that women were not what he expected and wanted them to be: They cannot be held as an anodyne against the fear of death. In David's hands, the camera has the power to create from the union of a special place and a particular moment an image that is again an illusion of reality. When he later tries to make a created image real (that is, make Sullivan a real mother figure by having her tell him a precoital bedtime story), he is again instructed in the misalignment between images and the world. DeLillo, by constantly emphasizing the impossibility of the world's true representation in time and place via the word (history), mythologizes his characters and frees them from the bounds of historicity.

END ZONE

One of DeLillo's mythic characters, Myna Corbett, appears in *End Zone*, the one novel that most of the author's critics agree is a brilliant piece. Myna, a student at Logos College in West Texas, is typical of DeLillo's female characters: She is big, carrying 165 pounds, which she refuses to shed because of her desire not to have the "responsibility" of being beautiful; she fills her mind with trivial matter (she reads science-fiction novels); and

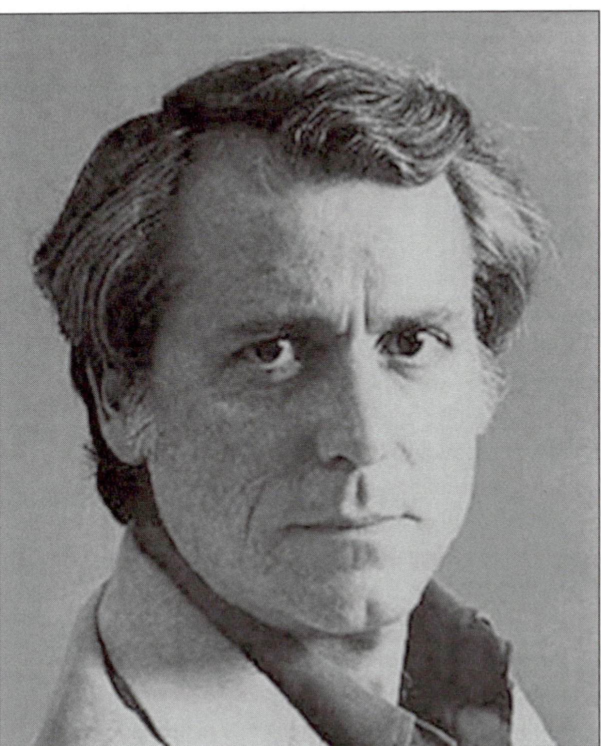

Don DeLillo. (Thomas Victor)

she has large breasts in which Gary Harkness, the protagonist, hopes to find solace from the world.

Gary is a talented but eccentric football player at Logos College who, because of his strange behavior, has been cut from the team rosters of larger institutions such as Penn State and Syracuse. He does not change his ways at Logos, walking off the field during the last game, high on marijuana and very hungry. He has a fascination with war and audits the Reserve Officers' Training Corps classes that have to do with mass killing strategy. When Colonel Staley asks him to become a cadet, Gary refuses, saying that he wants only to fantasize about nuclear war. He enjoys playing nuclear destruction games with the colonel, but he will not prepare himself to become an Air Force officer: He will not drop real bombs.

When not engaged in his graphic war daydreams, Gary is either playing football, an abstraction of war, or having picnics with Myna. If war is organized, palpable death, then Myna must be its opposite, an image of life and a defense against the fear of death. The tension between women (as the word or image of antideath) and harsh reality finds expression in the scene in which Gary undresses Myna in the library stacks. He says to himself that it is important to have her completely nude in the midst of the books containing millions of words. He must see her as the word (the image of harmless, uncomplicated femaleness) made flesh. He wants to see Myna, as the embodiment of the illusion of safety that words give, appear to belie the truth behind the image, the truth that women are not immune from the dread of death and therefore cannot offer the security that he seeks. He does not want to confront the mystery and lure of feminine beauty: He is upset when Myna loses weight. When she returns from vacation slender, it is he who does not want the responsibility of Myna's beauty. Women's love can lead to death, and words can have deadly connotations.

Great Jones Street

DeLillo further explores his themes dealing with language, death, women, and time in *Great Jones Street*, the story of a rock star, Bucky, who grows tired of the business, leaves his band in Houston, and returns to a hovel of an apartment in New York City. There his seclusion is destroyed when Skippy, a hippie girl, leaves with him a box full of a special kind of dope that is untested but is thought to be extremely powerful and is therefore of great interest to a number of people. The rest of the novel focuses on the many people who want to get the drugs. One of the agents sent for the drugs is Opel, who eventually dies in Bucky's bed. She is only an image of a living woman as she lies in the bed; the anti-image, death, is the reality of her being there. When she dies, Bucky can contemplate only her dead self; once people leave one extreme of being, they must become the other.

Bucky tries to make his apartment a refuge from the relentless roll of time and the world. He talks into a dead phone, stifling any possibility that words can reach their destination and complete the communication process. He refuses to wind the clock, hoping to arrest time, that hard reality that lies beneath the illusory image of stasis. Opel, although safe in bed in Bucky's timeless, wordless (telephoneless) world of the apartment, dies nevertheless.

The song that has made Bucky famous, "Pee-Pee-Maw-Maw," provides grist for another favorite DeLillo theme, that children, because of their few years, have no thoughts or fears of dying and therefore are immune from death. Bucky sings in the simple, life-giving syllables of children. The Mountain Tapes, traded for the drugs by a boy named Hanes, bring the same release as do the drugs in the box: They reduce language to nonmeaning. Later, when Bucky is injected against his will with the drug, he loses the power of speech; he is silent. Childish babble and wordlessness are equated with a loss of the fear of death and, consequently, a loss of humanity. Only humans fear death, says Bucky.

Ratner's Star

A child is the central character in *Ratner's Star*, a dense and overly long novel about the shortcomings of modern science. Billy, a fourteen-year-old mathematical genius who has just won the first Nobel Prize in Mathematics, is called to a futuristic think tank to help decipher a signal presumed to be a communication from Ratner's Star. The boy eventually finds the answer: The pulses of the message are really from Earth as it existed long ago. The meaning of the mathematical "words," the exact time of day as Billy looks at the clock on the wall (and coincidentally the exact time as an unscheduled eclipse of the Sun), is that the secret of all knowledge is what one has at a particular place at the present time. All the supposed power of the modern scientific community can be reduced to the utter simplicity of the time of day in a child's room on our own planet in our own time. When a spontaneous heavenly movement takes place, it is announced first to the child's mind.

Through their utter egregiousness, the adult scientists with whom Billy is obliged to interact offer DeLillo myriad openings for the insertion of biting satirical barbs. Endor, for example, the world's greatest mathematician, has given up solving the mystery of the pulses and has gone to live in a mud hole, living off worms and roots that he digs from the ground. Fitzroy-Tapps, the rat-talk scholar, hails from Crutchly-on-Podge, pronounced Croaking-on-Pidgett. Representative of the resident staff are Hoy Hing Toy, the obstetrician who once ate a newborn placenta; Grbk, who has to be officially reprimanded for showing his nipples to young children; and Armand Verbene, S.J., a practitioner of red-ant metaphysics. Of these bizarre characters, one in particular provides DeLillo with an excellent opportunity to hold forth on the meaning of language. Young Billy, a Nobel laureate by virtue of his having conceived the mathematical notion of the zorg (an entity reduced as far as it can be—that is, to nothing), confronts the astronomical mind of Lazarus Ratner. It is necessary to say that Billy confronts the "mind" of Ratner because that is practically all that is left of the man. He is kept from collapsing in on himself by constant silicone injections, and his bodily functions are kept going mechanically inside a protective bubble. Billy sits astride the biotank, talks to Ratner (who will speak to nobody but the child), and translates what the great scientist says for those who stand near.

DeLillo uses this conversation between the old man and the boy to explore provocative notions about language, knowledge, and God. Ratner tells the boy about the Kabbala: The hidden and unknowable name of God is a literal contraction of the superdivinity. The contraction of divine anti- or other-being, *en sof*, makes possible the existence of the world. Being (God) is somewhere on a spectrum between light and darkness, something and nothing, between an integer and a zorg, in Billy's mathematical code. Divinity (pure being) is revealed in the expansion of matter. As the universe expands, human beings, as part of that expansion, come into existence. Existence, then, is like the birth and death of stars, says Ratner: It is manifested with the expansion and perishes with the contraction of its mass. Thus, as elements, or *sephiroth*, of the primal being, humans are like tiny sparks of Ratner's Star. Human names, the words that equate with human existence, are merely artificial and abstract images of a constant expansion and contraction. Real being consists of the flux and levels of being behind the image.

Billy puts this theory into simple, incomplete terminology that, complains Ratner, is not fully expressive of the reality of what is being communicated. Here again is the old problem: Words, as images of reality, cannot possibly convey the entire dimension of the meaning of the world. Those who listen to Billy as he interprets Ratner are able to glean only a small portion of the content of Ratner's words.

The Names

Of DeLillo's novels from the 1980's onward, *The Names* and *White Noise* offer the most moving and powerful treatment of the author's recurring themes. *The Names* features the decay of the typical American marriage. James and Kathryn are married, have a son named Tap, and live happily for a time on an island in the eastern United States. They live peacefully until the bright image of marital bliss splinters, broken into a multileveled subset of hard problems, the first of which is separation. Kathryn, yielding to her fascination for digging in the ground in search of lost messages, commits herself to a life of archaeological digging; she travels to an excavation site on an island in Greece. James, wanting to be near his fractured family, gets a job in Greece as a so-called risk analyst.

Even though this bit of darkness has tarnished the core of the little family, they live on a reasonably even keel until archaeologist Owen Brademas begins an investigation of a cult of hammer killers. These cultists occasionally pound to death a chosen victim who happens to wander into a town with initials that match the initials of the victim's name: For example, they kill Michaelis Kalliambestos as he enters Mikro Kamini. Brademas, whose profession it is to find and translate ancient script written in stone, really is more interested in the kabbalistic power of the alphabet as it is combined and recombined to reveal the hidden names of God. He finds the Names, as the members of the hammer cult refer to themselves, becomes one of them in spirit, witnesses a ritual hammer murder (death comes to the person who finds, even if by accident, correspondence in letters and reality), and then retires to read stones and live unmolested in his final sacred place, a hotel room in Bombay.

Owen Brademas seems to be merely a mythic extension of an innocent, babbling language spoken by Kathryn and her sister as children and used by Kathryn and her son: The language inserts the syllable "ob" among the syllables of real words to create a special code. The initials of wordmonger Owen Brademas's name happen to be O. B. He seeks the meaning of alphabetic combinations even when they lead to death: He is the one who figures out the workings of the Names. In many ways, he is the shadow image of Kathryn's husband, a writer, who lives by the combination of words and who follows Brademas in search of the cult. James finds his place of revelation in a Roman ruin just as Brademas finds his in a hotel room. Brademas is also an alter ego of Kathryn, who seeks hidden wisdom by a kind of mindless digging at the site, yet he takes archaeological inquiry to the ultimate degree and ends in a room with nothing but ordered space, a perfect stasis, a state much like death.

In the same way, James's job is nothing but a cover for an operation conducted by the Central Intelligence Agency (CIA). His image of a harmless and rather pleasant way of life in Greece is destroyed: He experiences a dark underside of intrigue and deception. It seems that the surface of daily life can never remain innocuously in place; there is always a seepage of antilife. His wife and profession appear to be entities resting on shifting sands; only his son, the child, who writes away at a nonfiction novel, can be counted on for authenticity.

White Noise

White Noise is a thematic duplicate of *The Names*. The characters are cartoons. Babette is the physically large wife to whom Jack Gladney, her husband, looks for a peaceful domestic life totally removed from danger. Babette, also called Baba, appears to be very capable of fulfilling her husband's needs: She is the perfect image of easygoing housewifery. She volunteers for community service, she shops constantly in the supermarket, and she lovingly cares for the children. The children are precocious and serious-minded. Heinrich, the oldest boy, seems to know much more than his father, a college professor, about the real world. The girls, especially Denise, are concerned about Babette's health, hiding her drugs and looking for hidden habits that might bring her danger or death. Husband and wife, lost in trivialities, make inconsequential or erroneous statements, whereas the children speak with precision and maturity. The roles of parent and child are reversed; these children, therefore, are not as innocent as are typical DeLillo child figures. Only Wilder, the baby, embodies the ideal of the deathless child hero: At the end of the novel, he rides his tricycle across a four-lane street teeming with speeding vehicles, onto the grass of the opposite shoulder, miraculously escaping death.

Babette crumbles as the symbolic shield against fear; she is exposed as a woman so terrified of death that she trades sex for a special kind of drug that causes one to forget about the fact that one must die. She takes these pills on the sly and is finally found out by her snooping family. Jack has been happy with Babette because she is open and guileless, unlike his previous wives, who were mysterious, complicated secret agents who worked for the CIA. His illusion is destroyed when he finds out about her pills. Her complicity in this kind of intrigue reinforces his recently discovered vulnerability to death (a physical examination has revealed that his exposure to a toxic chemical spill may leave him only a short time to live). Even Baba, the large, comfortable, unbeautiful, unmysterious, faithful wife, who has consoled Jack as he has lain with his face between her large breasts, proves to be full of duplicity and treachery.

This complication leads Jack to reflect on what Murray Siskind, a fellow faculty member, has told him regarding death: Death, says Siskind, can be purged only by killing. Jack has already intuited this precept on his own; his success as a professor of "Hitler studies" (which he established as a full-fledged academic discipline) depends in part on his awareness of the peculiar fascination of the Nazis. Ultimately, Jack shoots Willie Mink, a seedy drug dealer who dispenses death-forgetting pills to women in exchange for sex. He enjoys the bleeding of his wife's seducer for a while but then takes pity on the mindless Mink, a victim of his own pills, and drags him by the foot to a hospital. The nuns who attend the wounded man destroy the last great image of security that Jack has left: Jack learns that those whom he had always thought of as sainted women, women firm in their faith that death's dominion has been crushed by the resurrection of Christ, have no more faith in salvation than he, his wife, or anybody else. The white noise of death silences any voice that would offer human beings a verbal sanctuary from its assault.

Libra

DeLillo followed *White Noise* with *Libra*, a novel about the assassination of President John F. Kennedy; atypically for a DeLillo novel, *Libra* enjoyed a run on the national best-seller lists while winning critical acclaim. *Libra* is, in a sense, two novels in one. It is, first, a fictional re-creation of the assassination and the events leading up to it. In the book's opening pages, and at intervals throughout, the reader shares the consciousness of Lee Harvey Oswald. From Oswald's point of view and the points of view of many others as well, DeLillo constructs his scenario of this still-enigmatic and much-disputed moment in American history. While DeLillo's version departs from the conclusions of the official report of the Warren Commission (he posits a second gunman and a fortuitous confluence of conspirators, including rogue CIA agents and Cuban exiles who want Fidel Castro overthrown), much of the speculation is grounded in the public record.

At the same time, *Libra* is a novel about the making of fiction and, more broadly, about the way in which people make sense of their lives. The novelist's alter ego is Nicholas Branch, a retired senior analyst for the CIA, hired by the agency in the 1980's to write the "secret history" of the assassination. This device allows DeLillo to sketch for the reader the process he went through in order to re-create happenings of the 1960's: sifting through the incredible profusion of evidence (he describes the twenty-six-volume Warren Report as "the Joycean Book of America, . . . the novel in which nothing is left out"), discovering strange patterns of coincidence. Novelists and conspiracy theorists, DeLillo suggests, are in the same business.

Mao II

Continuing DeLillo's preoccupation with the making of fictions, *Mao II* juxtaposes writers, terrorists, and crowds. Narratively similar to *Libra*, the novel interweaves scenes of reclusive novelist Bill Gray; Scott Martineau, his assistant; Brita Nilsson, the photographer assigned to take Gray's photograph as part of the publicity for his new book; and a Swiss United Nations worker and poet, Jean-Claude Julien, who is held hostage in Beirut by a Palestinian group so shadowy that the only knowledge that exists about them is that they have taken him hostage. The first half of the novel gives an intimate view of the writer, the different machinations and rationalizations that sustain his work, and the attempts made by his publishers to get Gray to finish his novel and allow his image to be publicized. DeLillo contrasts the image of the writer, continually rewriting and withholding his latest book, solitary in modern, media-saturated society, with images of crowds: China, the Moonies, mass marriages, terrorist movements.

It is terrorism that undoes Bill Gray in the second half of the novel. When Gray is asked to help in the attempt to get Julien released, he goes to London and then to Beirut, where he dies of untreated injuries sustained in a random automobile accident in London. Along the way, on this journey of unmaking, he has cut off all contact with Martineau, who in his absence goes about the process of organizing all of Gray's papers, taking the reader backward in time via a lifetime's worth of detritus. Accompanying this deconstruction of the archetypal writer is the rise of scenes of terrorism, which take away from the novelist's ability to influence people. Faceless groups displace the writer's power to make societal change possible. Replacing Bill Gray in the narrative's coda is the terrorist leader, Abu Rashid, and the "rising movement" he represents. Ironically, the final scene in the novel is Nilsson's interviewing and photographing of Rashid.

Mao II draws a desolate picture of life at the end of the twentieth century. Where once there had been the importance of solitary individuals struggling to present their understanding of the world, what is left at the end of the novel is faceless violence, mass influence in the form of religiously or ideologically inspired movements, and the hypermediated publicity machine that broadcasts these images to the world.

Underworld

Perhaps because of the bleakness at the end of *Mao II*, DeLillo's next novel seems to be an attempt to understand the world after World War II. A synthesis of many of the concerns in his previous ten novels, *Underworld* may be seen as perhaps DeLillo's magnum opus. Beginning with the simultaneous events of October 3, 1951—Bobby Thompson's home run, "The Shot Heard 'Round the World," and the Soviet Union's conducting of a second nuclear bomb test—the novel jumps back and forth from the early 1950's to the late 1990's. This process repeatedly grounds the language and institutions of the Cold War in a diverse range of contexts, including 1950's schoolchildren huddling under their desks during practice responses to nuclear attack, the week of the Cuban Missile Crisis (October, 1962), the compartmentalized world of the 1970's bomb makers, the 1980's construction of waste storage, and 1990's post-Cold War Russia's elimination of nuclear waste via nuclear explosions. Simultaneously, *Underworld* is also a story of degrees of separation, mingling together the lives of brothers Nick and Matt Shay, the former running a waste-management company, the latter a designer of nuclear weapons; Klara Sax, a found-object artist and the Shays' childhood Brooklyn neighbor; Albert Bronzini, Klara's ex-husband and Matt's chess teacher; and Sister Edgar, a nun in the slums of New York and the brothers' former teacher. Additionally, the novel is the tale of Thompson's home-run baseball and its journey from owner to owner, particularly the crucial first day after the game, when the African American child who caught the ball, Cotter Martin, has it stolen from him and sold by his father, Manx Martin.

What is revealed again and again in the novel is the underworld of modern life: never-mentioned family stories of an absent father; the charity work done by nuns in the forgotten inner cities of the United States; the inner life of the director of the Federal Bureau of Investigation (FBI), J. Edgar Hoover; the transformation of stockpiled and rusting B-52 bombers into acres-long pieces of art; the creation of landfills for America's ever-increasing garbage; and the waste that results from fifty years of nuclear stockpiling. Like DeLillo's previous novels, *Underworld* offers a picture of life at the end of twentieth century that is extremely conflicted, with resolution an impossibility. Through it all, however, the underworld of civilization's forgotten garbage continues to increase, revealing what sustains human lives.

The Body Artist

The Body Artist moves away from DeLillo's epic themes and timelines to examine personal tragedy. Just weeks after beginning a vacation in a rented seaside house, Lauren Hartke discovers that her husband, Rey Robles, has returned to New York, to the apartment of his first wife, to shoot himself in the head. Soon thereafter, Lauren discovers that a strange young man, whom she calls Mr. Tuttle, is living in an empty room on the third floor of the rental house. The intruder, whose age and mental capacity remain ambiguous, is a remarkable ventriloquist, able to mimic both Lauren's and her husband's voices, a skill that makes Lauren's recovery from loss even more difficult.

In its replication of others' voices, Mr. Tuttle's ventriloquism is not unlike Lauren's body art, a choreography of the movements of strangers and friends. That repetition of voices and gestures recalls the preoccupation with simulacra that dominates so much of DeLillo's earlier work. Throughout the novel, the reader sees Lauren practicing her body art, but it is not until the end of the novel that the reader witnesses her performance, an amalgamation of all the experiences of the past few months—her observations of random passersby, her more intimate acquaintance with the stranger living in her house, and her own response to her loss—expressed through gestures rather than words. The novel's spareness speaks to its recognition that language is perhaps not the best way to deal with trauma and grief, particularly not for a "body artist."

Cosmopolis

Published in 2003, *Cosmopolis* is not the post-9/11 novel most readers anticipated from DeLillo. It is, instead, an examination of materialism, a portrayal of urban gridlock punctuated with terrorists, suicide bombers, and protesters, and, as such, might be construed as the precursor to the tragedy of September 11, 2001. DeLillo's recurrent themes are at play here: American excess and waste, increased local and global terrorism, the inadequacy and beauty of language.

Set in New York City in April, 2000, *Cosmopolis* chronicles a day in the life of Eric Packer, a twenty-eight-year-old wizard in the financial sector. Exiting his forty-eight-room apartment on the East Side, Eric slowly makes his way to Manhattan's West Side for a haircut appointment. En route, Eric has three adulterous assignations, is stalked by a former employee, kills his bodyguard, witnesses a rap star's funeral and a

Times Square protest, and loses his wife's money just before realizing that he loves her. His marriage to Elise, effectively arranged to conjoin old and new money, is marked by the absence of intimacy or even simple understanding as these characters connect only when their separate paths serendipitously collide. Ironically, this novel about going somewhere not so fast focuses on a man who is so obsessed with the future that he marks the passage of time by noting the imminent obsolescence of words such as "skyscraper" and "office" and so fully engaged in capitalism, an enterprise defined by his financial therapist as an urge to "destroy the past," that it kills him.

Falling Man

Beginning with Keith Neudecker's escape from the twin towers of the World Trade Center on September 11, 2001, and his eventual arrival at the apartment of his former wife, Lianne, *Falling Man* follows the lives of a handful of characters in the aftermath of the terrorist attacks in New York City. The reunion is less a reconciliation than a temporary respite from reality, as Keith begins an affair with another survivor and devotes himself to poker, a game that simultaneously tethers him to the attacks—a fellow poker player died on 9/11—and separates him from the reality of the present and past. Concerned that she may be losing her mind, in part because of her father's own dementia, Lianne continues working with people with Alzheimer's disease who frantically write their memories and dreams, narratives designed to define them before their identities slip away. The impending loss of self tragically suffered by these patients is writ large in all the novel's characters, as is the attempt to gain some control in the aftermath of catastrophe. Characters' feeble attempts to master their situation include Lianne's counting backward from one hundred by sevens ("her form of lyric verse, subjective and unrhymed, a little songlike but with a rigor, a tradition of fixed order") and Keith's compulsive attention to physical therapy:

> It was not the MRI and not the surgery that brought him closer to well-being. It was this modest home program, the counting of seconds, the counting of repetitions, the times of day he reserved for the exercises, the ice he applied following each of the sessions.

The novel also offers glimpses into the minds of two very different terrorists, Hammad, one of those who perpetrated the attacks on September 11, and Martin Ridour, the European lover of Lianne's mother, Nina.

Repercussions of the attack insinuate themselves into daily life as Lianne finds herself irate at her Muslim neighbor's music and her son becomes preoccupied with a man called Bill Lawton, a name coined from the boy's misunderstanding of "Bin Laden." Lianne's glimpses of the Falling Man of the title, a performance artist dressed in business attire who suspends himself from buildings in simulations of the businessman photographed falling from one of the World Trade Center's towers after the attacks, complete her disorientation.

The novel's temporal experimentation, shifting between present and past, exacerbates the fragmentation and discontinuity characteristic of earlier DeLillo novels, as characters fail to connect with each other. In gruesome irony that only serves to highlight the isolation of people living in close proximity, a doctor treating Keith after the attack describes "organic shrapnel": "small fragments, tiny fragments of the suicide bomber's body . . . get trapped in the body of anyone who's in striking range." The novel concludes at the moments prior to its beginning, as the airliners hit the towers and Keith negotiates his way out of the collapsing structure, offering a circularity that suggests that these characters' exits from disorientation and distance are convoluted and meandering, if they are any exits at all.

Watson Holloway; Joshua Stein
Updated by Laura Barrett

Other major works

Short fiction: "Pafko at the Wall," 1992.

Plays: *The Engineer of Moonlight*, pb. 1979; *The Day Room*, pr. 1986; *The Rapture of the Athlete Assumed into Heaven*, pb. 1990; *Valparaiso: A Play in Two Acts*, pr., pb. 1999; *Love-Lies-Bleeding*, pr., pb. 2005; *The Word for Snow*, pr. 2007.

Bibliography

Bizzini, Silvia Caporale. "Can the Intellectual Still Speak? The Example of Don DeLillo's *Mao II*." *Critical Quarterly* 37, no. 2 (Summer, 1995): 104-117. Discusses the "transformation" of the writer in

Mao II using the theories of Roland Barthes and Michel Foucault. Provides an interesting examination of the writer in postmodern society and a helpful introduction to the uses of both critics' ideas within textual criticism.

Bloom, Harold, ed. *Don DeLillo's "White Noise."* New York: Chelsea House, 2002. Wide-ranging collection of essays presents an overview of critical reactions to DeLillo's novel.

Boxall, Peter. *Don DeLillo: The Possibility of Fiction.* New York: Routledge, 2006. Examines DeLillo's novels through the lens of the "exhaustion" of literature, presenting interesting readings of individual works.

Civello, Paul. *American Literary Naturalism and Its Twentieth-Century Transformations: Frank Norris, Ernest Hemingway, Don DeLillo.* Athens: University of Georgia Press, 1994. Devotes three chapters to DeLillo's work, showing how his texts fit within the lineage of the naturalistic novel and create a "postmodern transformation" of the "scientific assumptions" that undergird literary naturalism.

Cowart, David. *Don DeLillo: The Physics of Language.* Athens: University of Georgia Press, 2002. Astute examination of the theme of language in DeLillo's novels, particularly his desire for a "linguistic sublime" that moves beyond the well-established notion of language as a prison house.

Dewey, Joseph. *Beyond Grief and Nothing: A Reading of Don DeLillo.* Columbia: University of South Carolina Press, 2002. Provides an informative overview of DeLillo's career, with a chronological and developmental exploration of his novels, essays, short stories, and plays.

Dewey, Joseph, Steven G. Kellman, and Irving Malin, eds. *UnderWords: Perspectives on Don DeLillo's "Underworld."* Newark: University of Delaware Press, 2002. Collection of essays focuses on DeLillo's award-winning novel.

DiPietro, Thomas, ed. *Conversations with Don DeLillo.* Jackson: University Press of Mississippi, 2005. Collection of interviews with the author—culled from *Rolling Stone*, *The New Yorker*, and other magazines—spans the years 1982 to 2001. Wealth of information on DeLillo's views on the role of the novelist, the relationship between fact and fiction, and his own work habits.

Kovaldo, Jesse. *Don DeLillo: Balance at the Edge of Belief.* New York: Peter Lang, 2004. Argues against postmodern approaches in the readings of DeLillo's novels.

Mullen, Bill. "No There There: Cultural Criticism as Lost Object in Don DeLillo's *Players* and *Running Dog*." In *Powerless Fictions? Ethics, Cultural Critique, and American Fiction in the Age of Postmodernism*, edited by Ricardo Miguel Alfonso. Atlanta: Rodopi, 1996. Intense, close reading of connections between two of DeLillo's novels, and a thought-provoking discussion of his uses and abuses of official history.

Osteen, Mark. *American Magic and Dread: Don DeLillo's Dialogue with Culture.* Philadelphia: University of Pennsylvania Press, 2000. Dissects DeLillo's engagement with American culture and institutions, both respecting their power and integrity and denouncing the dangerous repercussions of their acts.

ANITA DESAI

Born: Mussoorie, India; June 24, 1937
Also known as: Anita Mazumbar

Principal long fiction

Cry, the Peacock, 1963
Voices in the City, 1965
Bye-Bye, Blackbird, 1971
Where Shall We Go This Summer?, 1975
Fire on the Mountain, 1977
Clear Light of Day, 1980
In Custody, 1984
Baumgartner's Bombay, 1988
Journey to Ithaca, 1995
Fasting, Feasting, 1999
The Zigzag Way, 2004

Other literary forms

In addition to her novels, Anita Desai (duh-SI) has published many short stories. Her first story was published in 1957, when she was twenty years old. Since then, she has contributed stories to various magazines and periodicals, including the London publication *Envoy*; Indian periodicals *Quest*, *The Illustrated Weekly of India*, and *Miscellany*; and the American magazine *Harper's Bazaar*. Some of her stories have been collected in *Games at Twilight, and Other Stories* (1978) and *Diamond Dust: Stories* (2000). Desai has also written three books for children, *The Peacock Garden* (1974), *Cat on a Houseboat* (1976), and *The Village by the Sea: An Indian Family Story* (1982). Two of her works have been adapted to film: *The Village by the Sea* in 1992 and *In Custody* in 1993.

Achievements

Anita Desai is among the more prominent Indian English novelists of the late twentieth and early twenty-first centuries. With her first novel, *Cry, the Peacock* (1963), she added a new psychological dimension to Indian English fiction. Desai was probably the first Indian English novelist to be concerned primarily with the inner lives of her characters—their fleeting moods, wisps of memory, subtle cerebrations. In her novels, Desai succeeds in capturing these evanescent moments of consciousness, preserving them from oblivion and investing them with the permanence of art. The result is that Desai not only creates something of value for herself out of the endless flux of her own psyche but also provides for readers the opportunity to share this rich inner life through her characters.

Desai's stylistic accomplishment is noteworthy as well. Unlike many other Indian English novelists, Desai does not find it necessary to experiment with language. In her novels, no clash between English, her medium of expression, and the Indian subject matter is apparent. Indeed, her use of the language is natural and unselfconscious. Her writing is both supple and precise. Though each sentence is carefully crafted, the overall manner is easy, not precious or labored. Stylistically, Desai is thus in the mainstream of twentieth century English novelists.

Desai is a writer of considerable achievement, perhaps the best contemporary Indian English woman novelist. Critical interest in her work has grown steadily since her first novel was published. She received the Royal Society of Literature Winifred Holtby Prize in 1978 and the Sahitya Akademi of India Award in 1979; she has been a member of the Sahitya Akademi English Board since 1972, a fellow of the Royal Society of Literature since 1978, a fellow of Girton College, Cambridge, and a visiting fellow at Balliol College, Oxford. For *The Village by the Sea* she received the Guardian Award for children's fiction in 1982. Her novels *Clear Light of Day*, *In Custody*, and *Fasting, Feasting* were all shortlisted for the Booker Prize.

Biography

Anita Mazumbar was born in Mussoorie, India, and grew up in Delhi. Her father, D. N. Mazumdar, was a Bengali businessman, and her mother, Toni, was German. Her parents met when her father was a student in Germany; they married and then moved to India in the late 1920's. As a child, Desai spoke German at home and Hindi to her friends and neighbors. She then learned English once she started school. She grew up during the

World War II years of the late 1930's and early 1940's, sensing the anxiety in her mother about the situation in Germany. Fearing the devastation and change wrought by the war, Desai's mother never returned to Germany, a fact that probably inspired some of the facets of the character Hugo Baumgartner in Desai's novel *Baumgartner's Bombay*.

Desai was educated at Queen Mary's School, Delhi, and then at Miranda House at the University of Delhi. At Miranda House she studied English literature, receiving her B.A. in 1957. Her studies helped to fuel her passion for writing, a compulsion that began at the age of seven. After working for a year in Max Muller Bhavan, Calcutta (now known as Kolkata), she married Ashwin Desai, a business executive, in 1958. Since then, she has lived in Kolkata, Mumbai (formerly known as Bombay), Chandigarh, Delhi, and Pune. She and her husband had four children: Rahul, Tani, Arjun, and Kiran.

Desai's writing came to be respected worldwide, and she became a fellow of the Royal Society of Literature in London and of the American Academy of Arts and Letters in New York, as well as a fellow of Girton College, Cambridge. Desai has taught writing at both Smith College and Mount Holyoke College in the United States. In 1993 she became a professor of writing at Massachusetts Institute of Technology.

Anita Desai. (Getty Images)

ANALYSIS

Anita Desai's novels reveal certain recurring patterns in plots, settings, and characterizations. The plots of her novels fuse two opposing propensities—one toward the gothic mystery and the other toward the philosophical novel. The gothic orientation, which Desai probably derived from Emily Brontë's *Wuthering Heights* (1847), is evident in varying degrees in all her novels. *Fire on the Mountain*, the novel that comes closest to being purely a psychological thriller, ends with a half-insane, reptile-like child setting fire to the forest surrounding her house; in *Cry, the Peacock*, Maya, the neurotic heroine, kills her husband, thereby fulfilling the prophecy of an albino sorcerer; in *Voices in the City*, Monisha, an unsettled, manic-depressive housewife, pours kerosene over herself and burns herself to death. On the other hand, most of Desai's novels also contain a deep-rooted, philosophical concern about the meaning of life. From Maya to Matteo, most of Desai's protagonists, dissatisfied with their routine existence, search for a more meaningful life. Such a spiritual orientation is reminiscent of similar concerns in novels such as E. M. Forster's *Howards End* (1910) and Virginia Woolf's *Between the Acts* (1941).

Desai's novels also evolve a typical setting or "world" of their own. Most are set in the city, which comes to represent the undesirable, unimaginative reality; most also have a romantic counterpoint to the city in a hill station or an island that seems to represent the remote, romantic, ideal but is revealed to be an unreal or unsatisfying delusion. At the hearts of the novels are usually big, old houses with several verandas, green shutters, gardens, servants, and pets. The garden is extremely important in Desai's world because her characters show an unusual sensitivity to it. Trees, creepers, tendrils, flowers, fruits, seasons, pets—the concerns of the so-called woman's world—are more vividly perceived in Desai's novels than anywhere else in Indian English fiction. Also part of Desai's world is a brooding, Faulknerian obsession with the past; the present is usually seen by the characters as a decadent remnant, a husk of a glamorous past. Finally, the characters are all members of the upper class who belong to once-affluent, now-decaying families. The city, the hill station, the big house with a garden, a decadent family, an obsession with the past—these make up the typical world of a Desai novel.

Desai's protagonists can be divided into essentially two types: One type possesses a neurotic, hypersensitive, artistic sensibility; the other is cynical, tough, and acerbic. Maya, Monisha, Sarah, Sita, Tara, and Matteo belong to the first category, while Nirode, Amla, Dev, Nanda, Bim, and Sophie belong to the second. In addition to these are two types of supporting characters: the old, ugly, sterile crone, who has been a failure, and the mysterious, insulated character, intriguing but ultimately inscrutable. The best example of the former is Ila Das of *Fire on the Mountain*; of the latter, Dharma of *Voices in the City*. The rest of the characters are the common crowd against whom the protagonist defines him- or herself: They have given up trying to make their lives meaningful and have accepted the full mediocrity of a futile existence. Against such a backdrop, Desai's protagonists struggle to come to terms with their lives. They are usually in a state of conflict, either with themselves or with their environment. The results of this basic conflict are murder, insanity, suicide, compromise, death, or, in the rare instance of Desai's best novel, *Clear Light of Day*, balance, reconciliation, rich acceptance of reality, and a resolution of the conflict.

In the mid-1980's, Desai started to look more closely at the lives of the less privileged. *In Custody* is an ironic story told with humor about literary traditions and academic illusions in a world dominated by men. The central characters are Nur, an Urhi poet, who has fallen on hard times, and Deven, a professor of Hindi. In *Baumgartner's Bombay*, Desai goes back to her parental heritage as she zeroes in on a German Jew who seeks refuge in India. *Journey to Ithaca* is much like *Baumgartner's Bombay* in that it also approaches India through Europeans who are attracted to the mystic India.

Desai's novels since the mid-1990's have continued to explore a concern with imagery built on places, cities that affect her characters who are uprooted or alienated, living away from their homelands and disturbed by their own inner conflicts. In *Fasting, Feasting*, Desai contrasts the American and Indian cultures as well as male and female roles, as Arun leaves India to study in Massachusetts while his sister Uma lives in a small provincial city in India. In *The Zigzag Way*, Desai departs from her familiar territories, setting her story of self-discovery in twentieth century Mexico.

Cry, the Peacock

Cry, the Peacock, Desai's first novel, is divided into three sections: a short introduction and conclusion in objective, third-person narrative, and a long subjective middle section narrated by the neurotic heroine, Maya. In Maya's narrative, Desai employs stream of consciousness to fill in details of Maya's past and to chronicle the progressive deterioration of both Maya's relationship with her husband, Gautama, and her own mental poise and sanity. In the climax, Maya, a slave to the fate she has feared, kills Gautama in accordance with the prophecy of an astrologer. The novel ends with her total mental collapse.

Maya is the sensitive, poetic, intuitive, and unstable type of personality that appears consistently in Desai's fiction. She is extremely sensitive to the beauty around her—the flowers and fruits in the garden, the trees and plants, the sky and the seasons, her pets and other animals—in brief, the whole gamut of nature. Gautama, her husband, is her opposite: He is insensitive to transient beauty; a pure rationalist, he is concerned only with absolutes. The characters' names themselves epitomize their irreconcilability: Maya means "illusion," and Gautama is the name of the Buddha, who was able to rend the veil of maya. Thus, while Maya revels in the world of the senses, Gautama rejects it entirely. According to the astrologer's prophecy, one of them must die. Maya decides to kill Gautama because, in her view, he has rejected all that makes life worth living; hence, to her, he is already "dead." Unable to resolve her conflict with Gautama, Maya pushes him from a terrace, thereby terminating her struggle.

Voices in the City

Desai's second novel, *Voices in the City*, is more ambitious than her first but also noticeably flawed. The narrative centers on the effect of Calcutta on Nirode and his two sisters, Monisha and Amla. The novel is divided into three sections: "Nirode," "Monisha," and "Amla." Nirode is the first of Desai's tough, cynical protagonists, a type that finds fruition in Bim, the heroine of *Clear Light of Day*, fifteen years later. Nirode, realizing that his uncreative job at a respectable newspaper will never allow him to live meaningfully, quits. He refuses support from his rich, widowed mother, who lives in the hills; instead, he sinks from failure to failure, cynically awaiting the bottom. He starts a magazine that fails after a brief run; his subsequent attempts to be a writer fail, too, when his brutally honest play is rejected by a theater group. Nirode envisions himself as fighting Calcutta, the city of Kali, the city that destroys all that is worthwhile in its denizens. Surrounded by quitters, he refuses to compromise, to succumb to an existence he despises.

Monisha, Nirode's elder sister, is the sensitive, neurotic type, like Maya in *Cry, the Peacock*. Married into a traditional Bengali family, she has, to all appearances, accepted the compromise of a routine existence. In fact, however, Monisha leads a secretive inner life that is inviolate despite the ugliness of her surroundings. For example, her inability to bear a child symbolizes her refusal to allow another life into what is, to her, a meaningless and loathsome world. Her section of the novel—a sort of compressed version of Maya's long narrative in *Cry, the Peacock*—takes the form of a diary. Amla, the youngest sibling, is a muted version of Nirode. Beneath the surface, all three characters struggle against Calcutta, fighting to preserve their inner integrity. Of the three, Amla seems the most likely to succeed because she has neither the excessive cynicism of Nirode nor the neurosis of Monisha.

An interesting minor character is Dharma ("righteousness"), the unflappable painter who has left Calcutta but who, upon discovering an ideal model in Amla, returns, following a drastic revolution in his painting. Though Dharma is shown to be the only character who has survived against Calcutta, his inscrutability renders him incomprehensible to Nirode and Amla, as well as to the reader.

The novel has a sensational climax and a somewhat contrived ending. Monisha triumphs by burning herself to death in her bathroom. Her death brings her mother down to Calcutta from the hills. Nirode has a vision of his mother as Kali, the preserver and the destroyer; apparently, his conflict is thus resolved. Nirode, therefore, becomes the initiate, and Amla's more promising efforts at wisdom are sidestepped. In fact, Amla is the only character out of the three whose spiritual growth is utterly convincing; after her encounter with Dharma, she becomes more reconciled to Calcutta. Disregarding the triviality of her job in an advertising agency, she manages to do something that truly satisfies her—making sketches for Professor Bose's translations from the *Panchatantra*. Amla's progress, however, is not allowed fruition; it is neglected in favor of the more artificial vision of Nirode. Part of the problem lies in Desai's definition of the central conflict in the novel; by pitting three individuals against an entire city, the novelist, in effect, disallows the possibility of a single creative, balanced, and happy person in the whole city. Such an opposition is precarious because the reader questions the stance of the protagonists instead of accepting the destructiveness of their environment. Thus, when Nirode's very ordinary mother, who has retreated to the hills, is suddenly revealed to be the goddess Kali, Nirode's vision and the novel's resolution seem to be mere impositions of the novelist.

Bye-Bye, Blackbird

In Desai's third novel, *Bye-Bye, Blackbird*, the action shifts to England. The novel, like the two earlier works, has a tripartite structure: arrival, "Discovery and Recognition," and "Departure." The three main characters are Dev, who has recently arrived in London from India when the novel begins, his friend Adit, with whom he is staying, and Adit's British wife, Sarah. All three characters are in conflict with their environment. Sarah is an unstable wife (in the tradition of Maya and Monisha) who finds herself playing two roles, that of an Indian at home and that of a Britisher outside; all the while, she questions who she really is. Dev and Adit are, in a sense, doubles like Nirode and Amla. Dev is the more cynical and aggressive of the two, while Adit, though essentially the same, is muted at the beginning. The novel follows a pattern like that of Henry James's *The Ambassadors* (1903): Adit, who thought he had felt at home in England, returns to India, while Dev, the militant cynic who has reviled Adit for staying, takes Adit's place after his departure, accepting a job in Adit's firm and moving to Adit's apartment.

Bye-Bye, Blackbird is a satisfying novel partly because Desai builds an inevitability into the narrative; characters are subordinated to pattern and rhythm. Dev's and Adit's decisions, hence, do not have to be fully explained. Their conflicts are not resolved so much as exchanged; the pleasure at the end is as much formal as it is emotional.

Where Shall We Go This Summer?

In Desai's fourth novel, *Where Shall We Go This Summer?*, all of her pervasive themes return: the neurotic heroine, the dissatisfaction with the here and now, the obsessive search for the meaning of existence. Sita, the wife of an industrialist, is disgusted with her indifferent husband, her meaningless life in their Bombay flat, and her selfish, uncaring children. Her memory of an idyllic childhood with her father on a nearby island, Manori, keeps haunting her as a reminder of what life can be. After becoming pregnant with a fifth child, she decides not to continue the charade; she visits the island again to regain the secret magic of life that she had experienced as a child. To her dismay, she realizes that her father, instead of being the great leader she has thought him to be, was really a charlatan. She has glamorized the past, and she now realizes that her memory has deceived her. Completely disillusioned, she waits for her drab husband to take her back to Bombay.

Toward the close of the novel, Sita's conflict appears to have found its solution when she recalls a verse from D. H. Lawrence that has eluded her for a long time. With the recollection, she feels she knows all the answers and can explain everything to her husband. This euphoria, however, is short-lived, ending with her realization that she cannot connect psychologically with her husband. The novel thus ends with a compromise after a false resolution; Sita is back where she began. Commenting that if she had been younger when she wrote the novel she might have ended it with Sita's suicide, Desai has explained that her less melodramatic conclusion is more in keeping with the realities of middle age. Hence, although Sita continues living, her conflict is not resolved; instead, she accepts defeat and compromise.

Fire on the Mountain

In *Fire on the Mountain* Desai reverts to the psychological thriller form exemplified by her first novel. In this work the narrative builds to a superb pitch of suspense and tension, only to end in sensational melodrama: the rape and murder of an old, ugly woman and a forest fire started by a demented child. Embittered by the indifference and infidelity of her husband, worn out from the rearing of several children and grandchildren, and now abandoned by her relatives, Nanda Kaul lives alone in her mountaintop cottage in Kasauli, surrounded by a pine forest. She tries to conceal her bitterness and loneliness behind a facade of cold, cynical aloofness, pretending that she does not need anyone, that she is living in Kasauli out of choice, and that she is in happy retirement after a rich and fulfilling life. When Raka, her great-granddaughter, comes to live with her, Nanda's craving for contact is revived. She tries to win the child by various devices, telling her wild stories, going for walks with her, and bribing her with food. Raka, who is as inscrutable and self-sufficient as a reptile, rebuffs the old woman. Into this situation steps Ila Das, Nanda's childhood friend, a complete failure, a pathetic harridan who has descended into desperate poverty after the ruin of her once-rich, decadent family. It is only when Ila is raped and murdered that Nanda is willing to acknowledge the lie at the core of her life; just then, Raka, the strange, half-crazy child, informs her that she has set the forest on fire.

Fire on the Mountain is superbly narrated but does not aim at being much more than a thriller. Nanda's quest for a meaningful life is subordinated to the demands of the plot. The novel is interesting, however, for at least two reasons. First, the hill station, usually the romantic contrast to the anticreative life of the city, here becomes a horrifying place of ghosts, mad dogs, demented women, impoverished hags, lonely great-grandmothers living in illusions, and demented children; the fantasy has turned into a nightmare. To the Kasauli of *Fire on the Mountain*, even the Calcutta of *Voices in the City* seems preferable. Second, Ila and Raka are two of Desai's most disturbing characters: Both are consistently sketched in animal and reptile imagery, and both are, in a sense, unhinged. They represent the extremes of the fondness for the bizarre that lurks in all of Desai's fiction.

Clear Light of Day

Clear Light of Day is one of Desai's most accomplished novels. In it, the typical elements of her art merge to create a unique artistic triumph. The plot, for example, is a fine blend of the gothic and the philosophical, each strengthening the other. The mysterious well in the back, the drowned cow, Mira Masi's alcoholic disintegration, Tara's fear that her mother was murdered by her father, Baba's idiocy—all these contribute to the final resolution of the novel. One by one, these events are put into their place by the two heroines, Bim and Tara; the mystery, horror, or shame enveloping these events is slowly peeled away, and the past emerges in a new light of clarity and understanding.

The setting of *Clear Light of Day* has the typical Desai elements—the ugly city, the large house with verandas, the garden, the servants' quarters, upper-class characters, and decadent families. These elements, however, are augmented by acute social observation and particularity of place and time. Not only the inner life of the characters but also their milieu is fully developed. Perhaps no other English novel so successfully immortalizes mid-twentieth century Delhi and its locales—Civil Lines, the old Delhi convent school, the Jamuna, Connaught Circus, Hindu College, Darya Ganj, Chandni Chowk, the Ridge, and the Lodi Gardens. *Clear Light of Day* is thus also valuable as a sociohistorical document, a feat rare in Desai's canon.

Desai's main concern, of course, remains with the characters and their conflicts. Bim is the tough, cynical heroine, the one who refuses to compromise. Tara is her softer, more sensitive, counterpart. Raja, the deserter, their brother, is Bim's double. Mira Masi and the sisters next door are the hags. Bakul, Tara's husband, is a shallower, stupider version of Gautama. Bim, Tara, and Raja share the same determination to live meaningfully, without compromise. At the beginning of the novel, when Tara returns to the old house, both sisters are equally distant from resolving their conflicts: While Tara is too weak, Bim is too harsh, too bitter. Both are uncertain about their past, about their relationships to each other and Raja, about the meaningfulness of their lives. Together, they slowly relive their entire past, which leads to a marvelous reconciliation in the last few pages of the novel. Bim, to her astonishment, realizes that Tara—despite her marriage to Bakul and several mundane years as the wife of a diplomat—whom she has always despised, is just like her, and that Tara, too, has managed to preserve her integrity. Tara and Bim reach a new understanding for the first time; through Tara, Bim at last relinquishes her grudge against Raja, reconciling herself to him again.

After Tara's departure, Bim and Baba listen to Mulk and his Guru; Mulk is not after all merely a slothful drunkard as Bim has thought—he *can* sing, he is an artiste. Bim realizes that she does not have to degenerate into another Mira Masi; she fathoms the truth of T. S. Eliot's line from *Four Quartets* (1943): "Time the destroyer is also time the preserver." Bim's conflict ceases, dissolves; she transcends her duality and her contradictions. She can face reality without bitterness or neurosis. Her fancy ceases to cheat her; her imagination no longer makes her despise the reality around her. Instead, she realizes that ordinary life has its moments of fulfillment too. *Clear Light of Day* thus ends in balance, harmony, reconciliation, and resolution, not in murder, suicide, death, insanity, or compromise, as do all of Desai's earlier novels and as does *Baumgartner's Bombay*.

Baumgartner's Bombay

In *Baumgartner's Bombay*, the main character is neither Indian nor English—he is a German Jew. The story follows Hugo Baumgartner from childhood in pre-World War II Germany to his death in Bombay, India. The novel, however, starts with the ending (though the reader cannot realize it until the actual end of the book) and then jumps to the middle of the story. Baumgartner's past is relayed in a series of flashbacks from his time in India.

Baumgartner is forced to leave Germany when the Nazis' rise to power can no longer be ignored. Indeed, by the time Baumgartner leaves, his father has already committed suicide after being sent to a concentration camp, though he was later released. Interestingly, Desai has said about *Baumgartner's Bombay* that she "wasn't writing about the Nazis. I was writing about random evil." Baumgartner himself never expresses much feeling about the injustices done to him; about his six years in a British internment camp for German nationals, Baumgartner protests that "they were not such bad days."

Baumgartner's escape from Germany takes him to Venice, where he is to catch a boat for India. Venice remains in Baumgartner's mind as a kind of paradise, despite the troubles he has there and the fact that he is in the city for less than a week. These fabled and probably half-imagined qualities of Venice contrast sharply with the squalor and degradation of Bombay and of Baumgartner's life there. In fact, he spends most of his time going from restaurant to restaurant trying to find scraps for the multitude of cats with which he shares his dingy little flat. Ironically, Baumgartner does die at the hands of a German, though not a Nazi; rather, a German junkie whom Baumgartner has offered a place to stay kills him for his silver trophies.

Baumgartner's Bombay marks a return for Desai to the twin themes of hopelessness and despair. Baumgartner, his aging friend Lotte, Julius Roth—all are stranded in India; none can return to Germany because the old Germany is gone forever, and they do not fit into the new Germany. Indeed, it is the new Germany that becomes the death of Baumgartner in the shape of the brutal junkie. Desai's picture of foreigners, or *firanghi*, as the Indians label these outcasts, is that they can never fit into Indian society no matter how hard they try. It is Desai's great talent, however, to be able to make these characters compelling despite their obvious fate, which is to be forgotten. They leave no mark or memory when they die, though Desai ensures that they remain with the reader long past the end of the novel.

Journey to Ithaca

Desai's ninth novel, *Journey to Ithaca*, continues certain structures and themes of the earlier novels. It, too, has three parts: prologue, text (divided into chapters), and epilogue. The characters' search for spiritual meaning prompts the action of the story. The title is an allusion to the Greek island home of Homer's Odysseus, who made one of fiction's greatest journeys.

Set in the 1970's, the story is about Sophie and Matteo, two wealthy Italian young people who travel to India on a lark. Matteo, the more emotionally sensitive of the two, is quickly swept up in the spirituality of India, and eventually the couple find themselves in an ashram run by a spiritual leader called Mother. The conflicts created by the personal nature of a journey to enlightenment are manifest as Sophie and Matteo produce two children. Matteo is drawn into the rhythms and beliefs of Mother's ashram, but Sophie, the more practical and cynical of the pair, cannot fathom the attraction, let alone the squalor and deprivation she experiences. Upset, she leaves India and returns to Italy with the children.

In time, Sophie is summoned back to India because Matteo is deathly ill; she leaves the children to go to him. Sick as he is, Matteo is an unrepentant follower of Mother and wishes only to continue his spiritual studies. Shocked and angered, Sophie begins her own journey to understand him. She literally traverses the world to learn who Mother is and how she came to command such devotion. She discovers that Mother was once a young Egyptian girl named Laila and that even as a child Laila sought deeper meaning in life. While attending school in Paris, Laila encountered a troupe of Indian dancers and was taken into the group by the charismatic male lead dancer, Krishna. Through the troupe she learned to employ her dance as a means to spirituality. The story of Laila and her ultimate arrival in India is interwoven with Sophie's search for her, and it introduces the third journey in the novel.

Journey to Ithaca relates the experiences of three people seeking enlightenment. Desai's contribution to this type of literature is that she illustrates the consequences of a spiritual journey, which by its very nature must be personal if not solitary. For the seeker, the arduousness of the search is a reward in itself. Moments of illumination, large or small, are worth striving for. On the journey, however, others are excluded. Matteo's devotion to Mother leaves no room for his family. Sophie at one point recognizes that she has abandoned her children in an obsessive search to discover the truth about Mother. Mother steps on the careers of others and abandons Krishna to seek God in the Himalayas. The journey to Ithaca is a difficult and sorrowful one.

The novel's construction emulates a journey to spiritual enlightenment; it does not follow a simple chronological pattern. The story begins when Sophie has been summoned back to India because Matteo is sick. It then returns to their children, Isabel and Giacomo, in Italy. Then it reverts to Matteo's childhood, his marriage to

Sophie, and their trip to India. Next, the action returns to Italy, then back to India, followed by Sophie's pursuit of Mother, retracing her history from Egypt to Europe to the United States and finally back to India. The path to spirituality is a jagged one, sometimes moving forward, sometimes moving backward or even sideways.

Fasting, Feasting

Desai's tenth novel, *Fasting, Feasting*, deals with themes of suppression and escape. It also deals with oppression and the objectification of women in a sensitive and thoughtful way. The story contrasts the cultures of the United States and India, particularly male and female roles in the two countries. The parents of the two main characters do not consider the possibility that their children have their own lives to live; daughter Uma is a victim of patriarchy, and son Arun is trapped in the education meant to liberate him. The title *Fasting, Feasting* signifies deprivation and abundance, whether of food or of emotional sustenance. Uma is deprived of attention, and Arun is deprived of his freedom of choice. Feasting can be identified in the excesses and opulence in the American lifestyle to which Arun is exposed.

The story depicts the struggles of Arun and his older sister Uma as the siblings attempt to strike a balance between their parents' expectations and their own. Arun studies in Massachusetts while Uma lives in a small provincial Indian city with their parents, to whom she refers collectively as "MamaPapa." Structured in two parts, the story is told first from Uma's point of view, then from Arun's. The first part takes place in India and tells the story of Uma, the eldest daughter of an educated Indian family; the father is a lawyer, but he is provincial and traditional at heart. Uma is not necessarily ugly but she is awkward; her younger sister, Aruna, is the pretty and vivacious one who makes a successful marriage. Uma's celebrated younger brother, Arun, makes it to the United States to study. Meanwhile, Uma stays at home to serve their parents, embarrassed by one failed attempt after another to marry her off; Uma's every chance to find some freedom and space is thwarted by her possessive parents. Even if Uma is not smart, she has a kind heart and a strong willpower, and she grows immensely in spirit throughout the life-changing events in her life, so that by the end of the novel she finds a place for herself in Indian society where she can show her individuality.

The second part of the book focuses on Arun, Uma's younger brother who is attending college in Massachusetts. During the summer, when school is out, he stays with a local family, the Pattons. This section of the book comments on American society through the Patton family, particularly the diminishment of the family structure in the United States and the American obsession with materialism. It also touches on the issue of eating disorders. Arun's childhood was one of oppression—he has been constantly coached and pushed by a domineering father, and initially when he was sent to the United States, his life was still farmed out to family friends through an arrangement made back in India. Arun changes and grows through his experiences in the United States, however. At the American university, Arun finds himself isolated in every way from his peers and from his culture, even others from India. His isolation is more or less his own choice; after his oppressive upbringing, he wants space and freedom. His isolation echoes Uma's as she escapes to the privacy of her room in India—the siblings are in different cultures, but they are equally sad.

Makarand Paranjape; Judith L. Steininger
Updated by Tel Asiado

Other major works

short fiction: *Games at Twilight, and Other Stories*, 1978; *Diamond Dust: Stories*, 2000.

screenplay: *In Custody*, 1993 (adaptation of her novel; with Shahrukh Husain).

children's literature: *The Peacock Garden*, 1974; *Cat on a Houseboat*, 1976; *The Village by the Sea: An Indian Family Story*, 1982.

Bibliography

Afzal-Khan, Fawzia. *Cultural Imperialism and the Indo-English Novel: Genre and Ideology in R. K. Narayan, Anita Desai, Kamala Markandaya, and Salman Rushdie*. University Park: Pennsylvania State University Press, 1993. Scholarly examination of postcolonial Indian fiction places Desai's work in historical context.

Bande, Usha. *The Novels of Anita Desai: A Study in Character and Conflict*. New Delhi: Prestige Books, 1988. Briefly surveys the critical material written on Desai and then provides detailed discussion of each of her novels up to *In Custody*.

Budholia, O. P. *Anita Desai: Vision and Technique in Her Novels*. Delhi: B. R., 2001. Presents a formalistic analysis of Desai's work.

Choudhury, Bidulata. *Women and Society in the Novels of Anita Desai*. New Delhi: Creative Books, 1995. Focuses on Desai's treatment of female characters and their circumstances.

Dash, Sandhyarani. *Form and Vision in the Novels of Anita Desai*. New Delhi: Prestige, 1996. Examines the style of Desai's writing and the themes that recur throughout her works. Includes bibliographical references and an index.

Jena, Seema. *Voice and Vision of Anita Desai*. New Delhi: Ashish, 1989. Concentrates on the place of Desai among female Indian novelists, with discussion of the individual novels' plots and characters.

Khanna, Shashi. *Human Relationships in Anita Desai's Novels*. New Delhi: Sarup & Sons, 1995. Offers a thoughtful examination of Desai's characters and their relationships. Includes bibliographical references.

Prasad, V. V. N. Rajendra. *Five Indian Novelists: B. Rajan, Raja Raa, R. K. Narayan, Arun Jashi, Anita Desai*. Oxford, England: Advent Books, 1997. Presents a study of the self, family, and society in the novels of the five authors.

Rege, Josna. "Codes in Conflict: Post-independence Alienation in Anita Desai's Early Novels." *Journal of Gender Studies* 5, no. 3 (November, 1996): 317-329. Provides a detailed discussion of *Cry, the Peacock*, *Voices in the City*, and *Where Shall We Go This Summer?* in the context of the conflict between the interests of Indian nationalists and women's interests in the postindependence era.

Tandon, Neeru. *Anita Desai and Her Fictional World*. New Delhi: Atlantic, 2008. Examines Desai's contributions to Indian English fiction, assessing the individual novels through *The Zigzag Way*.

PETER DE VRIES

Born: Chicago, Illinois; February 27, 1910
Died: Norwalk, Connecticut; September 28, 1993

PRINCIPAL LONG FICTION

But Who Wakes the Bugler?, 1940
The Handsome Heart, 1943
Angels Can't Do Better, 1944
The Tunnel of Love, 1954
Comfort Me with Apples, 1956
The Mackerel Plaza, 1958
The Tents of Wickedness, 1959
Through the Fields of Clover, 1961
The Blood of the Lamb, 1962
Reuben, Reuben, 1964
Let Me Count the Ways, 1965
The Vale of Laughter, 1967
The Cat's Pajamas and Witch's Milk, 1968
Mrs. Wallop, 1970
Into Your Tent I'll Creep, 1971
Forever Panting, 1973
The Glory of the Hummingbird, 1974
I Hear America Swinging, 1976
Madder Music, 1977
Consenting Adults: Or, The Duchess Will Be Furious, 1980
Sauce for the Goose, 1981
Slouching Towards Kalamazoo, 1983
The Prick of Noon, 1985
Peckham's Marbles, 1986

OTHER LITERARY FORMS

In addition to his work as a novelist, Peter De Vries (duh VREEZ) was a short-story writer of some repute; a number of his stories are collected in *No, but I Saw the Movie* (1952) and *Without a Stitch in Time: A Selection of the Best Humorous Short Pieces* (1972). He also collaborated with Joseph Fields in writing a stage version of one of his novels, *The Tunnel of Love: A Play* (pb. 1957), and wrote the play *Spofford* (pb. 1968). In addition, he published a handful of essays and interviews.

Achievements

In the 1950's, Kingsley Amis called Peter De Vries the "funniest serious writer to be found either side of the Atlantic." De Vries was certainly a clever punster and wit, a master of situation comedy, and a devastating observer of the foibles of suburbia. His droll humor often involves the amorous adventures of the middle-aged suburban male, torn between the sophisticated mores of Connecticut suburbia and his simpler childhood roots, usually in the Dutch Reformed Church or some other equally strict background. De Vries writes knowingly about the same suburban milieu as that of John Updike and John Cheever, but with less overt seriousness and more sheer fun. In fact, he resisted the label of "serious writer" (or, for that matter, "religious writer"), although he dealt extensively with serious topics, including religion, in most of his works. The predominant tone of his writing, with the exception of *The Blood of the Lamb*, is comic and even lighthearted.

De Vries was a prolific novelist, with more than two dozen novels published, along with several collections of short stories reprinted from *The New Yorker*. With so many novels to his credit, there is bound to be some repetitiveness, and De Vries often uses the same basic plot situation—the comic mischances of the lecherous suburban male who is thwarted by his moral scruples, his underlying decency, the vestiges of his past, or simply unlucky circumstances. There is a sameness about so many of his protagonists—particularly in their recollections of their strict religious backgrounds and their ambiguous attempts to "liberate" themselves from middle-class conventionality—that some critics have accused De Vries of being too autobiographical.

What saves his novels from redundancy is the variety of his humor: the puns, witticisms, drollery, repartee, lampoons, parodies, caricatures, and spoofs. De Vries displays the comic instincts of a cartoonist or a comedian, the ability to coin phrases or epigrams so funny that they are almost distracting. His fictional scenes seem to be built around the humorous or witty line, sometimes to the detriment of plot, narrative, or characterization. Given that De Vries repeatedly insisted that his primary purpose as a humorist was to entertain, the loose structure of his work may be judged a necessary evil.

The targets of De Vries' humor are the pretenses and absurdities of modern, affluent suburbia. In an interview, the author once commented, "I'm a regionalist, like Thomas Hardy. And I love those yokels who get off the same bar car at the same time every night and have never swum in anything but a pool in their own backyards. It's really a new provincialism." His "Avalon" and "Decency" are the fictional counterparts of the wealthy, exclusive suburbs, such as Greenwich, Darien, Stamford, and Westport, along Connecticut's "Gold Coast." His characters—or sometimes caricatures—show all the vanities, postures, and affectations of wealth, education, and "good breeding" that might be expected of sophisticated Connecticut suburbanites, yet De Vries is never harsh or satiric, commenting that the purpose of humor, unlike satire, is not to kill one's prey but to bring it back alive to be released. De Vries' humor is thus more charitable than satire; he invites humankind "to laugh at itself."

De Vries is a master of the humorous scene and the comic caricature. Many of his characters are immediately recognizable as "types"—the ultraliberal clergyman, the suave newspaper columnist, the lecherous poet, the hick farmer, the small-town atheist, the unsuccessful artist, and the television game-show host—and they behave in predictable ways. The humor occurs as De Vries builds his scenes toward a hilarious climax—such as the cup of bourbon switched with the teacups at the church ladies' reception in *The Mackerel Plaza* or the social worker's visit to a disorganized family in *The Tunnel of Love*.

Often the comedy takes the form of a continuation of James Thurber's "battle of the sexes," with De Vries' male characters seeking a worldly sophistication and urbanity in which to live out their fantasies, only to be thwarted by the forces of female respectability. Virtually all of De Vries' novels have a male protagonist, and he wrote from a decidedly male perspective on the themes of sex and marriage, explaining once in an interview that bawdy literature is written predominantly by men. His characters *think* they want the freedom and irresponsibility of a carefree bachelor life, with its worldliness and sophistication, but they seem bewildered or disappointed if they get what they seek. The theme of many of his comic novels (and hence the source of their humor) is the shallowness and superficiality of the sophisticated suburban life.

Perhaps the key to De Vries' best work is in the tragicomic tone of his humor—that urge to laugh so as not to cry that marks the grotesque "as a blend of the tragic and comic." Too often in De Vries' novels, however, the comic is present without the tragic, the burlesque and farcical without the serious note that could redeem the work from being merely superficial entertainment. De Vries' inferior works always seem to verge on situation comedy, with their frequently contrived or manufactured scenes, and it is not surprising that he collaborated on a successful Broadway production based on his novel *The Tunnel of Love*. *The Blood of the Lamb* is incomparably De Vries' best novel, with its poignant mixture of humor and pathos; coming at midcareer, it is the touchstone against which the remainder of his novels must be measured. The earlier works in comparison seem to strain after a false sophistication, and the later novels appear increasingly superficial, employing forced gags and contrived situations and depending too heavily on topical humor and burlesque of current trends and fashions.

Peter De Vries. (Library of Congress)

Biography

Peter De Vries was born in Chicago, Illinois, on February 27, 1910. His parents, Joost and Henrietta De Vries, emigrated from Holland and settled in a closely knit Dutch Calvinist community on Chicago's South Side. De Vries' father was an iceman and furniture mover who started with "a one-horse outfit that he gradually built to a sizeable warehouse business." During De Vries' boyhood, the family lived in a three-room apartment behind his father's business office.

The De Vries family were members of the strict Dutch Reformed Church, and their domestic life was probably much like that described in the autobiographical *The Blood of the Lamb*: a large, contentious family with parents and in-laws forever arguing about some obscure point of theology or church doctrine. Apparently, such disagreements were commonplace in the Dutch Reformed Church, for in the novel *The Mackerel Plaza*, when someone boasts to the protagonist's father that *his* denomination has not had a schism in the past one hundred years, the father replies, "Rotten wood you can't split." De Vries' parents were also strict about forbidding any form of worldliness: Card playing and watching motion pictures were forbidden, and Bible reading and theological discussions were encouraged. During his adolescence, De Vries rebelled against these strictures, but he later expressed fond memories of the Dutch-language services and hymns of his childhood.

Young De Vries attended the Chicago Christian High School of the Dutch Reformed Church and then entered Calvin College in Grand Rapids, Michigan, a private liberal arts college founded by the same denomination. There he won a Michigan state extemporaneous speaking contest and graduated with a degree in English in 1931. That summer he also studied briefly at Northwestern University. His family had hoped that he would enter the ministry after graduation, but instead he decided to become a writer and embarked on a series of odd jobs in Chicago to support himself. He edited a community newspaper, tended vending machines, peddled candy apples, served as a radio actor, and spoke before women's clubs.

From 1938 to 1944, he served capably as an editor of *Poetry* magazine. There he met his future wife, Katinka Loeser, who was a poetry contributor and later became a short-story writer of some note. They were married on October 16, 1943. During this time, De Vries had published three early novels, *But Who Wakes the Bugler?*, *The Handsome Heart*, and *Angels Can't Do Better*, which earned him some critical notice but met with only limited financial success. In 1943, De Vries invited James Thurber to speak at a Chicago benefit for *Poetry* magazine and Thurber subsequently persuaded De Vries to go east and write for *The New Yorker*. De Vries joined the staff of *The New Yorker* in 1944 and served as a contributor and cartoon editor until his death. At *The New Yorker*, he worked with editor Harold Ross and such famous humorists as E. B. White and Thurber on a staff that had once included Robert Benchley and S. J. Perelman.

De Vries settled with his wife in suburban Westport, Connecticut. They reared three children—Jan, Peter Jon, and Derek. A fourth child, Emily, died of leukemia before adolescence, a deep personal loss registered in De Vries' most serious novel, *The Blood of the Lamb*, in which a similar event occurs. Unlike the zany characters in many of his novels, De Vries was a man of conventional tastes, happily married and devoted to his family.

During his long career, De Vries published more than two dozen novels, along with his collections of short stories. He won wide critical acclaim for his humorous novels, and he received grants from the American Academy of Arts and Letters and the National Institute of Arts and Letters, of which he was a member. He died on September 28, 1993, in Norwalk, Connecticut.

Analysis

"If I spent my time portraying life as it actually is," Peter De Vries once remarked, "I think I would go insane with boredom inside of two weeks." Eschewing the realistic novel, De Vries has instead concentrated on entertaining his readers with witty and humorous works, filled with hilarious but highly improbable incidents. He was satisfied to write a good comic novel without aiming for any higher artistic qualities. This self-acknowledged limitation has been the source of much of the unevenness in De Vries' work, with the overemphasis on humor weakening the structure of his novels—often to the neglect of narrative continuity, consistent point of view, clear transitions, and strong characterizations. In fact, many of his novels are so seriously flawed as scarcely to be considered novels at all; rather, they are loosely constructed narratives that simply provide a framework for the author's comic genius.

Beyond the purpose of sheer entertainment, De Vries was ambiguous about the intent of his humor, minimizing the social commentary and underlying seriousness of his work so that it is difficult to categorize him as a comic novelist of manners or a satirist. Like his mentor, James Thurber, De Vries chose to limit the scope of his humor and to evoke laughter through grotesque or absurd depictions of modern suburban life, but as his later novels suggest, he risked reducing his work to formulaic entertainment or, worse, self-parody. Stylistically, De Vries is not as original as Thurber, but he is perhaps at his best as a parodist of other writers, or as a writer of brilliant puns and epigrams rather than as the creator of a unified and coherent comic vision. His weakness as a comic novelist comes from his failure to unify his material and to offer an implicit corrective vision to the world he ridicules.

The Tunnel of Love

De Vries' first three novels are of slight artistic value. His first novel of note, and still perhaps his most popular, is *The Tunnel of Love*. Here one enters the affluent world of Connecticut suburbia as seen through the eyes of the first-person narrator, a New York magazine cartoon editor much like De Vries himself. The focus of the novel, however, is on the comic imbroglios of his next-door neighbors, Augie and Isolde Poole, a young, well-to-do, "artistic" couple who try to adopt a child to save their marriage. The novel alternates between Manhattan and Avalon, Connecticut, through a round of weekend cocktail parties and dinners that provide a backdrop for De Vries' wit and cleverness. De Vries peoples the book with a humorous collage of "artsy" types—would-be actresses and directors, abstract painters, mediocre illustrators, poets manqués, affected snobs, precious aesthetes, and other rarefied types. In short, one finds all the empty worldliness of "Vanity Fair," which De Vries is quick to mimic and satirize, yet one also feels the narrator's attraction to these values, which lends the novel a curiously mixed tone of admiration and ridicule. De Vries is a shrewd observer of suburban language and behavior, with a good ear for nuances of conversation, and he creates a wonderful satire of the pretentious cocktail chitchat about creativity and neuroses that the characters employ to boost their sagging egos and disguise from themselves the truth of their mediocrity.

The protagonist, Augie Poole, is a good gag writer though a poor cartoonist who cannot sell his work, so he turns to profligacy to salve his ego. A self-confessed "rotter," he is never quite as wicked as he pretends to be. Superficially a glib and literate ladies' man, he is basically shallow and conceited, though not beyond eventual redemption through the responsibilities of parenthood. The Pooles ironically adopt the illegitimate child of Augie and his artist mistress, but not before a comic series of mishaps during the adoption process. Augie is forced to compromise his "artistic integrity" and sells his gags without the cartoons to prove himself a responsible prospective parent with a steady income. Much of the humor is generated in the domestic life of the narrator, however, in a genial "battle of the sexes" with his wife and family. In conversations with his wife, the narrator of course defends Augie, while she defends Isolde, with predictable results.

In *The Tunnel of Love*, husbands and wives are torn between the routines of respectable suburban life and the allure of a self-indulgent and liberated "artistic" life, with its glamour and sophistication. De Vries contrasts the romantic myth of personal creativity and self-indulgence with the more staid world of middle-class marriage and commuter life. His characters enjoy all the luxuries of suburban affluence, yet they seem to yearn for a vague "something more"—a vicarious excitement missing from their lives and beckoning from the bohemian life or from the narrator's vicarious dreamworld of "Moot Point," a Hollywood fantasy-world of cinema clichés. The comedy is generated by the clash of illusion and reality as Augie and the narrator slowly learn to accept the world as it is; "Moot Point" is eventually replaced by "Drowsy Dell," the summer cabin on a New Hampshire lake that both families enjoy.

The Mackerel Plaza

After De Vries' commercial success with *The Tunnel of Love*, he adapted the novel for stage and screen, and the play ran for a year on Broadway. His fiction writing continued in the same comic vein with his next three novels, *Comfort Me with Apples*, *The Mackerel Plaza*, and *The Tents of Wickedness*. Once more he took aim at the hollow values and assumptions of modern suburbia, particularly the jargon of psychology and adjustment, though not necessarily to replace them with more traditional values, but simply to show their comic inadequacy. The protagonist of *The Mackerel Plaza* is a pompous, ultraliberal minister, the Reverend Andrew Mackerel, as rigid and narrow in his "advanced thinking" as the fundamentalists he opposes. His People's Liberal Church, a nondenominational congregation, is the "first split-level church in America," with a church clinic and psychiatric facilities designed to meet all the needs of modern humanity. Mackerel preaches short, iconoclastic sermons intended to demolish whatever remains of his parishioners' traditional Christian beliefs, though he is the one who ultimately loses his faith in unbelief. A young widower, he is thwarted in his desire to marry an aspiring actress by the forces of New England respectability in his congregation and by an elderly parishioner's desire to erect a memorial to his late wife.

None of the characters is really convincing in this book, and De Vries seems to play off orthodox beliefs against liberal Christianity merely for laughs, without either appearing credible. Mackerel loses his actor, Molly Calico, to a Romanian director and ends up marrying his own sister-in-law, Hester, a caricature of New England primness and domesticity. Like Flannery O'Connor, De Vries uses the humor of the grotesque to show the inadequacy of secular humanism and to point to religious concerns, though not with as much intensity, conviction, or originality as the Georgia writer.

The Tents of Wickedness

In *Comfort Me with Apples* and *The Tents of Wickedness*, De Vries introduces Chick Swallow, a suave newspaper columnist who dispenses inept advice to his readers and generally muddles their lives with his well-intentioned but wrongheaded amateur therapy. Chick and his brother-in-law, Nickie Sherman, are self-styled Oscar Wilde types, adept at café repartee and clever rejoinders but unable to manage their lives or marriages. The pair continually confuse literature and life, and Swallow, who narrates *The Tents of Wickedness*, insists on viewing his personal crises through the eyes of famous writers, which allows De Vries to display clever parodies of the styles of Thurber, J. P. Marquand, William Faulkner, Marcel Proust, Ernest Hemingway, Graham Greene, Henry James, Theodore Dreiser, Franz Kafka, James Joyce, and others.

The plot of *The Tents of Wickedness* consists of a series of thinly contrived situations involving Swallow's blundering attempts to mend his brother-in-law's split personality and to advise Sweetie Appleyard, an innocent young poetess whom he urges to take up the bohemian life, with disastrous results. Nickie vacillates between private detective and a Raffles-like jewel thief, while Sweetie is transformed from a Pre-Raphaelite poetaster to a liberated Greenwich Village type who persuades Swallow to father the child she wants in order to fulfill herself as an "emancipated woman." The action alternates between Greenwich Village and Decency, Connecticut, with De Vries predictably contrasting middle-class and beatnik lifestyles. Without De Vries' clever stylistic parodies and his brilliant verbal wit, this would be unlikely material even for a comic novel. *The Tents of Wickedness* strains credulity with its clumsy social satire and wooden characterizations. Unfortunately, De Vries never allows his characters lives of their own; instead, they serve merely as mouthpieces for his humor. These same flaws are evident in *Through the Fields of Clover*, which takes as its occasion a New England family's fortieth wedding anniversary for De Vries' satire of modern notions of family and marriage.

The Blood of the Lamb

De Vries' next novel, *The Blood of the Lamb*, marked a sharp departure from the slapstick comedy of his earlier novels. In what is undoubtedly his finest book, he blends comedy and pathos in the story of Don Wanderhope, an obviously autobiographical character who breaks away from Chicago and his strict Dutch Calvinist background and goes east to work in a New York advertising agency. The focus of the novel is on the relationship between the protagonist and his daughter Carol, a graceful and precocious child who is stricken with leukemia. Her illness, suffering, and eventual death test Wanderhope's faith, and, through the example of his daughter's courage, lead him back to grace. *The Blood of the Lamb* contains a depth and seriousness otherwise missing in De Vries' work, since it is based on the author's loss of his own daughter Emily to the same disease. Here De Vries finds a theme that permits him to move beyond cleverness for its own sake and create characters of substance and credibility.

"What people believe is a measure of what they suffer," remarks Don Wanderhope, who is himself tried by a series of misfortunes, including the death of his older brother Louie, his father's insanity, his wife's suicide, and finally his daughter's death. Since De Vries' characters are for the most part unable to accept the consolations of traditional belief, and since they are uneasy with modern, relativistic assumptions, their suffering often seems grotesque, and it is from this quality that De Vries extracts much of his humor. This "gallows humor" is what ultimately saves Wanderhope from despair, as when, in a scene of bitter poignancy after he learns of his daughter's death, he pitches her birthday cake at a statue of the suffering Christ. The theme of the novel seems to be that, contrary to received opinion, suffering does not teach one anything; hence, laughter is the best antidote to despair.

There are some very funny episodes in *The Blood of the Lamb*, such as when Wanderhope and his future wife, Greta, are caught in bed together by Greta's parents in a model home that her parents are showing to a client. The emotional center of the book, however, is Carol, especially after her mother's suicide. Carol is the most compelling and believable character in any of De Vries' books. She is, of course, the "Lamb," and her blood is shed gratuitously to a disease for which there is no cure. "The blood of the Lamb" does not redeem anything (except perhaps the protagonist, though that point remains deliberately ambiguous), and hence her suffering and that of the other children in the leukemia hospital remains meaningless. It recalls King Herod's slaughter of the innocents. One's only defense against such realities is to laugh at the tragic absurdity of life; this tragicomic note is best illustrated by the birthday party in the hospital for the young leukemia patients.

Once Carol's illness has been diagnosed, Wanderhope must race against time to cherish every moment with his daughter while sparing her the truth of her condition. As he observes, in such a case "the greatest experience open to man is the recovery of the commonplace." In another moment of bitter emotional truth, a parent remarks to Wanderhope that grief does not unite people, it separates them. De Vries' personal credo may be reflected in the philosophical statement written by Wanderhope for his alma mater, which is read back to him in a tape recording by his daughter Carol: that man has only "Reason, Courage, and Grace" to see him through.

Later novels

Though De Vries never achieved the same artistic success with any of the novels that followed *The Blood of the Lamb*, he managed in several books to temper the humor with serious themes. In *Reuben, Reuben*, his longest novel, De Vries returned to suburban situation comedy and his burlesque of artsy sophistication. Written in three parts, the novel shifts from Frank Spofford, a shrewd chicken farmer, to Gowen McGland, a crude and dissolute Welsh poet, to Alvin Mopworth, a hapless English journalist, all of whose lives become entangled in a humorous chain of events.

In *Let Me Count the Ways*, agnostic piano mover Stan Waltz is pitted against his fundamentalist wife Elsie. *The Vale of Laughter* finds comedian Joe Sandwich trading witticisms with his humorless rival, Wally Hines, a dull professor of humor; and the novellas *The Cat's Pajamas* and *Witch's Milk* deal with characters dissatisfied with their professions or marriages. *Mrs. Wallop*, another situation comedy, finds a middle-aged woman taking on the forces of modernism.

Following the publication of these novels, De Vries proceeded to lampoon modern art and the sexual revolution in a short-story collection, *Without a Stitch in Time*, and a series of unimpressive novels: *Into Your Tent I'll Creep*, *Forever Panting*, *I Hear American Swinging*, *Madder Music*, and *Consenting Adults*.

One of De Vries' few novels that does not deal with sexual comedy is *The Glory of the Hummingbird*, an account of a likable young couple of Dutch Reformed background who, unable to have a child of their own, decide to adopt a teenage juvenile delinquent in the hope of reforming him. The protagonist, Jim Tickler, gravitates from advertising to television, where he eventually comes to host a rigged game show called the "Little Red Poolroom," where in a variation of the "Fortunate Fall," as one critic points out, he wins his foster son's affection after the show is exposed and Jim and his wife Amy are shown to be fallible.

De Vries' novels of the 1980's continued to play out clever variations of the battle of the sexes in a world of changing social mores. In *Sauce for the Goose*, Daisy Dobbin, a young feminist writer from Terre Haute, Indiana, escapes to New York to take a position at the *Metropole* magazine in order to expose the sexual harassment of women and ends by falling in love with the publisher, Dirk Dolfin, a wealthy Dutch businessman. An unconvincing feminist, Daisy betrays her "cause" in a conflict between head and heart, implying that her feminism is an inadequate substitute "religion." In *Slouching Towards Kalamazoo*, Maggie Doubloon, another liberated heroine, attempts to capitalize on her unwed motherhood by marketing T-shirts emblazoned with a scarlet "A+" after she is impregnated by one of her students. Despite its many puns and literary allusions, the novel teeters between comedy and vulgarity.

The Prick of Noon and *Peckham's Marbles* both involve picaresque rascals who attempt to rise in social class or redeem their failed literary careers by using others. In *The Prick of Noon*, Eddie Teeters, a successful pornographic film director from Backbone, Arkansas, attempts to crash into the genteel country-club society of Merrymount, Connecticut, through his affair with socially prominent Cynthia Pickles. Teeters yearns for a world that he cannot enter. Since marriage with Cynthia is out of the question, Teeters eventually settles for an attractive waitress, Toby Snapper, who shares his modest background. In *Peckham's Marbles*, Earl Peckham, a failed novelist, pursues Nelly DelBelly, the wealthy, overweight owner of the Dappled Shade rest home, and Poppy McCloud, the young author of best-selling romances, in a humorous quest for love and money.

Despite the large number of books he wrote, De Vries was essentially a one-book novelist, with *The Blood of the Lamb* rising above the level of his other works, which remain primarily entertainment. Distracted by his own cleverness, De Vries did not employ his humor in the service of any coherent social vision. Unlike Miguel de Cervantes, William Shakespeare, Mark Twain, or any of the other great comic writers, De Vries did not humanize his readers so much as divert them temporarily from the human condition. Because his characters are for the most part weakly drawn, one does not empathize with them; rather, one merely enjoys a laugh at their expense and then turns away without having gained in any measure. This lack of depth, along with the sameness of so much of his work, marks the failure of De Vries to move beyond wit to an underlying seriousness of purpose in his art.

Andrew J. Angyal

Other major works

SHORT FICTION: *No, but I Saw the Movie*, 1952; *Without a Stitch in Time: A Selection of the Best Humorous Short Pieces*, 1972.

PLAYS: *The Tunnel of Love: A Play*, pb. 1957 (adaptation of his novel; with Joseph Fields); *Spofford*, pb. 1968.

Bibliography

Boston, Richard. *An Anatomy of Laughter*. London: Collins, 1974. Study of laughter includes analysis of De Vries' work. Boston considers De Vries among the best humorists of his generation. Includes bibliography.

Bowden, Edwin T. *Peter De Vries*. Boston: Twayne, 1983. Concise critical biography provides an informative overview of De Vries' life and works. An introductory biographical chapter is followed by discussion of each of the major novels. Includes a chronology, notes, and a selected bibliography of primary and secondary works.

Campion, Dan. *Peter De Vries and Surrealism*. Lewisburg, Pa.: Bucknell University Press, 1995. Discusses De Vries' literary life, his encounter with Surrealism in the 1930's, his novel *But Who Wakes the Bugler?*, and his use of humor. Includes detailed notes and bibliography.

Davies, Robertson. *A Voice from the Attic: Essays on the Art of Reading*. Rev. ed. New York: Penguin Books, 1990. Collection of essays about literature and reading includes discussion of De Vries' fiction. Robertson, a noted Canadian novelist and playwright, lauds De Vries' ear for language and defends his relaxed use of first-person narrators.

De Vries, Peter. "An Interview in New York with Peter De Vries." Interview by Richard B. Sale. *Studies in the Novel* 1 (1969): 364-369. De Vries discusses his writing habits and answers questions about the type of humor in his novels and his view of the world.

_______. "An Interview with Peter De Vries." Interview by Douglas M. David. *College English* 28 (April, 1967): 524-530. De Vries answers some interesting questions about his style of humor in this lively interview. He also discusses his use of suburban settings, his character types, and his humorous attitude toward sexuality.

Frank, Jeffrey. "Riches of Embarrassment." *The New Yorker* 80, no. 13 (May 24, 2004). Presents a detailed examination of De Vries' life and novels. Frank concludes that "few writers have understood literary comedy as well as De Vries, and few comic novelists have had his grasp of tragedy."

Jellema, Roderick. *Peter De Vries: A Critical Essay*. Grand Rapids, Mich.: Wm. B. Eerdmans, 1966. Critical study of De Vries' first eight novels points to the religious issues that are often overlooked in discussions of De Vries as a humorist.

Kort, Wesley A. *Shriven Selves: Religious Problems in Recent American Fiction*. Philadelphia: Fortress Press, 1974. Examines fiction by De Vries and other writers in which the main characters are "shriven" or confessed selves. Kort sees De Vries as someone comfortable neither in the community of faith nor outside it.

Yagoda, Ben. "Being Seriously Funny." *The New York Times Magazine*, June 12, 1983. Feature article presents a portrait of De Vries and an overview of his literary career. Offers a good introduction to the writer and his work.

PHILIP K. DICK

Born: Chicago, Illinois; December 16, 1928
Died: Santa Ana, California; March 2, 1982
Also known as: Philip Kindred Dick

PRINCIPAL LONG FICTION

Solar Lottery, 1955 (also known as *World of Chance*, 1956)
The Man Who Japed, 1956
The World Jones Made, 1956
Eye in the Sky, 1957
Time Out of Joint, 1959
Dr. Futurity, 1960
Vulcan's Hammer, 1960
The Man in the High Castle, 1962
The Game-Players of Titan, 1963
Clans of the Alphane Moon, 1964
Martian Time-Slip, 1964
The Penultimate Truth, 1964
The Simulacra, 1964
The Three Stigmata of Palmer Eldritch, 1964
Dr. Bloodmoney: Or, How We Got Along After the Bomb, 1965
The Crack in Space (Cantata 140), 1966
Now Wait for Last Year, 1966
The Unteleported Man, 1966 (also known as *Lies, Inc.*, 1984)
Counter-Clock World, 1967
The Ganymede Takeover, 1967 (with Ray Nelson)
The Zap Gun, 1967
Do Androids Dream of Electric Sheep?, 1968 (reissued as *Blade Runner*, 1982)
Galactic Pot-Healer, 1969
Ubik, 1969
A Maze of Death, 1970
Our Friends from Frolix 8, 1970
The Philip K. Dick Omnibus, 1970
We Can Build You, 1972
Flow My Tears, the Policeman Said, 1974
Confessions of a Crap Artist, 1975
Deus Irae, 1976 (with Roger Zelazny)
A Scanner Darkly, 1977
The Divine Invasion, 1981
Valis, 1981
The Transmigration of Timothy Archer, 1982
The Man Whose Teeth Were All Exactly Alike, 1984
In Milton Lumky Territory, 1985
Puttering About in a Small Land, 1985
Radio Free Albemuth, 1985
Humpty Dumpty in Oakland, 1986
Mary and the Giant, 1987
The Broken Bubble, 1988
Voices from the Street, 2007 (wr. 1953)

OTHER LITERARY FORMS

Before he began writing long fiction, in 1955, Philip K. Dick went through an extraordinarily prolific period as a short-story writer. His first story, "Beyond Lies the Wub," appeared in 1952. In both 1953 and 1954, Dick published twenty-eight short stories per year. His total output in this genre is more than one hundred stories, most of which he wrote early in his career. Many have been reprinted in his collections *A Handful of Darkness* (1955), *The Variable Man, and Other Stories* (1957), *The Preserving Machine, and Other Stories* (1969), *I Hope I Shall Arrive Soon* (1985), and elsewhere. A five-volume collection, *The Collected Stories of Philip K. Dick*, was published in 1987. He also collaborated on novels, including *The Ganymede Takeover* (with Ray Nelson) and *Deus Irae* (with Roger Zelazny).

ACHIEVEMENTS

In all histories of science fiction, Philip K. Dick is hailed as one of the greatest and most distinctive exponents of the genre. Literary awards, however, came his way surprisingly rarely. He received the Hugo Award (which is decided by vote of science-fiction fans attending the annual World Science Fiction Convention) for the best novel of the year 1962, for *The Man in the High Castle*. He received the John W. Campbell Award (decided by a panel of writers and critics, and also administered by the World Science Fiction Convention) for *Flow My Tears, the Policeman Said*, in 1975. More recognition might have been expected, and would surely have been forthcoming, if it were not for two things. One is that Dick was, for a while, an amazingly prolific author (five novels were published, for example, in 1964), yet one who wrote very few evidently weak or minor novels. His high level of productivity and consistency have accordingly made it difficult for single novels to be chosen as superior to others. Probably few critics would agree even on which are the best ten of his nearly forty novels. A further point is that Dick, while a writer of amazing power and fertility, also was prone to convolution and to the pursuit of personal obsessions.

Biography

Philip Kindred Dick was born in Chicago in 1928, but he lived most of his life in California. He studied for one year at the University of California, Berkeley, but he did not earn a degree. He held several jobs for short periods, then began writing science fiction with great speed and immediate success, first short stories and then novels. His output slowed markedly at the beginning of the 1970's, as a result of personal problems, involvement with drugs, strong discontent with American society in the Vietnam era, and a sequence of failed relationships. When he resumed writing, his books were significantly more personal and more propagandist. He died on March 2, 1982, following a stroke.

Philip K. Dick. (Courtesy of the Philip K. Dick Society)

Analysis

Philip K. Dick's novels are, without exception, distinctive in style and theme. Their style may be characterized relatively easily: Dick writes clearly and plainly and is a master of realistic dialogue. He is, however, also a master of the art of "cutting." Frequently, a chapter or a scene will end with a short summary statement, often of doubt, bewilderment, or unease, only to be followed in the next chapter by a longish sentence introducing a new character going about his daily concerns in a manner that seems—but only seems—to have no connection with the foregoing. For all of his plainness, Dick furthermore makes considerable use of words of his own coinage—for example, "flapple," "quibble" (a kind of vehicle), "thungly," "gubbish," and "kipple." The last of these has even achieved a certain currency outside its novel (*Do Androids Dream of Electric Sheep?*) to mean the morass of useless objects, such as gum wrappers or junk mail, that seems to reproduce by itself in any modern dwelling. The overall effect of Dick's style is to give an impression of plainness and superficial normality but to suggest strongly that beneath this surface things are going on that are ominous, disastrous, and inexplicable.

This preoccupation is clearly mirrored in Dick's characteristic themes, many of which are shared with the body of science fiction at large. He often writes of androids, simulacra, and mechanical men. He bases several plots on consciousness-raising drugs. His later works in particular tend toward the dystopian, presenting visions of a future America as a vast gulag or a slave-labor state. The notions of alternate worlds and of post-Holocaust societies are often exploited. Where Dick differs from other users of these themes is in the strange insecurity that he generates while handling them. Androids are common in science fiction, and so are plots in which androids cannot be distinguished from people. Only Dick produces plots in which the test to distinguish human from android is so deeply infected with the bureaucratic mentality that even people are likely to fail and be eliminated. Only Dick has a hero giving himself his own test, having come (for good reason) to doubt his own humanity. Similarly, Dick is capable of writing a story that appears to be set in an alternate world but then begins to suggest that the real world never existed and is merely a drug-induced hallucination—only to switch back again, deny its own hypothesis, and leave the reader quite unsure even of the bases of judgment. Dick is fascinated by forgeries and by coincidences. In scene after scene, he presents a hero doubting even his own identity, and doing so with total rationality on the basis of all the evidence in the world around him.

Most readers soon realize that the common concern that binds Dick's repeated themes and plot elements is the very nature of reality itself, and that Dick doubts common notions of reality more sincerely and more corrosively than almost any writer in any genre. Dick could be described as the poet of paranoia, yet his cool and sensible style enables him to present horrifying alienations in a way with which even the sanest reader can sympathize.

Solar Lottery

Dick's overriding concerns are quite apparent in even his earliest novels. *Solar Lottery*, his first novel, presents a future society that is dedicated entirely to chance, as a result of "extrapolation," first of the then-new phenomenon of the television quiz show, and second (as one might have expected) of the uncertainty principle as a basic rule of the universe. In this world, all authority devolves on the Quizmaster, but the Quizmaster may be deposed at any moment from his position by a "twitch of the bottle," an event determined by the intrinsically unpredictable forces of submolecular physics. The bottle twitches. Reese Verrick the Quizmaster is deposed. His place goes to an unknown fanatic called Cartwright, whose only interest is the search for a (mythical?) tenth planet. Caught up in all these events is a hero who has had the colossal bad luck to swear irrevocable fealty to Verrick just before he fell from power. Already the sense of an unpredictable world where anything can go wrong is very marked.

Eye in the Sky

Even more revealing is *Eye in the Sky*, in which eight characters caught up in a scientific accident find themselves exploring what they slowly realize are the worlds of one another's minds: first that of a total believer in an obscure fundamentalist sect, then that of an inhibited housewife, a borderline paranoid, a fanatical communist, and so on. The worlds themselves are presented with great verve. In the first, for example, a man going for a job asks not about pay but about credits for salvation, and if he presses his question he is told that in his position the God of this world, "Tetragrammaton," will probably grant his prayers to the extent of four hundred (dollars?) a week. The job may be constructing a grace reservoir, or improving the wire to Heaven. There is in fact an "eye in the sky," belonging to the unnameable (Tetragrammaton). Underlying the structure of the whole novel, however, is the notion that each person's individual universe is not only private but unreachable; most people are mad. In view of Dick's later development it is also interesting that the novel is strongly anti-McCarthyite, even though one of the characters (ironically a security chief) is indeed a Communist agent.

Time Out of Joint

The novel that best sums up Dick's earliest phase as a novelist, however, is *Time Out of Joint*. The book appears for quite some time not to be science fiction at all. It reads instead as a pleasantly pastoral, perhaps rather dull, account of life in a small American town of the 1950's. The only odd feature is that the hero, Ragle Gumm, makes his living by continually winning a newspaper contest called Where Will the Little Green Man Be Next? Slowly, however, this idyllic setting begins to drift by quarter-tones to nightmare. Gumm does not recognize a picture of Marilyn Monroe (something unthinkable if he were really of that time and place). An old phone book found in some ruins has his name in it, with eight phone numbers for all hours of the day and night. A boy's crystal radio picks up voices saying in effect "That's *him* down there, Ragle Gumm." It transpires that the small town with its idealized families is a total deception, all created to shield Ragle Gumm and maintain him in his stress-free delusion while he performs his real job—using extrasensory powers to predict the fall of enemy rockets on Earth, under the fiction of the newspaper contest.

The Man in the High Castle

In *Time Out of Joint*, Ragle Gumm is mad at the start. When he thinks he is going mad, he is learning the truth. There is no way to prove that reality is not a perfectly rehearsed plot. This latter is a classic Dick conclusion. In *The Man in the High Castle*—Dick's most famous but not most characteristic work—the reader is plunged into an alternate reality in which the Allies lost World War II, California is occupied by the Japanese, and the inhabitants rather like it. The hero here, Robert Childan, is a seller of "ethnic" American curios, such as Mickey Mouse watches and Civil War handguns, for which the conquerors have an insatiable appetite. His problem is that some of the guns are fakes. The problem of the man who made the fake guns, Frank Frink, is that he is a Jew and could be deported to German-controlled areas. Still, the predictable theme of resistance, triumph, and escape to the real universe where the right side won, hardly materializes. Instead, the reader is presented with a complex argument in favor of Japanese sensitivity, with strong underlying hints that even the "alternate worlds" of this "alternate world" would not be the same as our world. The novel suggests powerfully that history is chance, merely one possibility among a potential infinity of realities.

The Penultimate Truth

By 1964, Dick was at the height of his power as a writer, and almost any of the fifteen novels published between this year and 1969, including *The Simulacra*, *Dr. Bloodmoney*, *Counter-Clock World*, or *Galactic Pot-Healer*, would find admirers. Some especially significant themes emerge, however, from five novels in this group: *The Penultimate Truth*, *Martian Time-Slip*, *The Three Stigmata of Palmer Eldritch*, *Do Androids Dream of Electric Sheep?*, and *Ubik*. The first of these returns to the theme of total, deliberate illusion. In the future imagined in this novel, most of the inhabitants of Earth live underground, in ant-tanks, under the conviction that World War III is still going on and that if they emerge from hiding they will die from the Bag Plague, the Stink of Shrink, Raw-Claw-Paw, or one of a multitude of human-made viruses. In reality, however, the war stopped long ago, and Earth is a park, divided up into the demesnes of the ruling classes. Like Ragle Gumm, one character digs his way out to discover the truth and to try to lead these latter-day Morlocks up to the light. The particular point that Dick wishes to make here, however, is that even outside science fiction, people are genuinely at the mercy of their television screens. They cannot tell whether they are watching truth or a construct. They usually have no way of telling true history from the false varieties that Dick makes up. The end of the novel declares that what is essential—and not only in the novel—is a ferocious skepticism. People are too gullible, too easily deceived.

Martian Time-Slip

There is no such overt political thesis in *Martian Time-Slip*, of the same year, but in this work Dick creates one of his most likable sets of characters in Jack Bohlen, the Martian repairman, and Arnie Kott, senior member of the Waterworkers' Union—naturally a privileged body on arid Mars, though no one had previously been mundane enough to say so. Dick also brings into the novel what seems to be a personal image of the Tomb World, a world in which everything is rotten and decaying, with buildings sliding to ruin and bodies to corruption. This world is perceived only by an autistic child, but that child's perceptions seem stronger than the grandiose claims of governments and land speculators. Still another route into horror is via drugs.

The Three Stigmata of Palmer Eldritch

The Three Stigmata of Palmer Eldritch moves rapidly from a protagonist who has the seemingly harmless job of guessing fashion for dolls and dollhouses to the notion of exploitation—for these Perky Pat Layouts, as they are called, can be experienced only by people who take the drug Can-D to let them into the doll-world—to menace and terror. Can-D is about to be superseded by Chew-Z, a drug allegedly harmless, nonaddictive, and government sponsored. This drug, however, puts its users (as in *Eye in the Sky*) in the world of Palmer Eldritch, a demon figure with steel teeth, artificial hands, and mechanical eyes. Nor can users return from it. Chew-Z takes one into a variant, one might say, of the Tomb World.

Ubik

The hero of *Ubik*, Joe Chip, finds the Tomb World happening around him. Cigarettes he touches fall into dust, cream turns sour, mold grows on his coffee, and even his coins turn out of date. Then he himself starts to age. The only thing that can cure him is a spray of "Ubik," a material that halts the race to corruption and obsolescence. In a memorable scene near the end of the book, Joe Chip reaches a drugstore just before it closes, to demand Ubik, only to find that the store is closing, the stock is out, and spray cans too have aged, becoming cardboard packets. What force is doing all this? Are the characters in fact already dead, now existing only in a bizarre afterlife? For whose benefit is the spectacle being played out? Once again, Dick creates a happy ending, but more strongly than usual, one believes that this ending is demanded by the conventions of the field rather than by the logic of the plot.

Do Androids Dream of Electric Sheep?

For depth of paranoia, the prize should go to *Do Androids Dream of Electric Sheep?* This novel is best known as the source material for the 1982 film *Blade Runner*, both book and film centering on a bounty hunter whose job is to kill androids. What the film could not do is show the depth of devotion that the characters in the book—who live in a world so radioactive that almost all unprotected creatures have died—give to their pets. Deckard the bounty hunter has a counterfeit electric sheep because he is too poor to afford a real one, but like everyone in the book he consistently consults the manual of animal prices. If he kills three more androids, could he buy a goat? If he spares one, will they give him an owl (thought to be extinct)? Would it be an artificial owl? The pitiless slaughter of androids is balanced against the extraordinary cosseting of every nonartificial creature, down to spiders. Yet what is the basis of the division? In a heartrending scene, after Deckard has wiped out his androids, another android comes and kills his goat. Before then, however, Deckard himself has been accused of being an android, been taken to the Hall of Justice, and been quite unable to prove his own identity—because, as soon becomes clear, all the authorities are themselves androids. The notions of undetectable forgery, total illusion, and unanimous conspiracy combine to make the central scenes of this novel as disorienting as any in Dick's work.

Somewhere near this point, Dick's development ended. He wrote most movingly on the subject in the author's note to *A Scanner Darkly*. This novel, he says, is "about some people who were punished entirely too much for what they did." They were real people, the author's friends. They took drugs, like children playing; it was not a disease, it was an error of judgment, called a "life-style." He then lists seven of his friends who have died, three more with permanent brain damage, two with permanent psychosis, one with permanent pancreatic damage—the list goes on. How deeply Dick himself was involved in late 1960's California drug culture, one cannot say. He himself insists this was exaggerated. For whatever cause, however, Dick wrote less, and his mood became angrier, less playful.

Flow My Tears, the Policeman Said

The great surprise of *Flow My Tears, the Policeman Said* is its ending. In this world—a dystopia based on the Richard Nixon era in the United States—students are persecuted, the "nats" and the "pols" run identification checks in the streets, a quota of persons are taken off daily to slave camps, and civil liberties have vanished. Through the world wanders Jason Taverner, in the first chapter a rich and fantastically successful entertainer, who finds himself suddenly (in dream, psychosis, or alternate reality?) in a place where everything is familiar, but no one knows him. His hunter is Police General Felix Buckman, as it were the arch-bogey of the liberal conscience, the policy maker for the police state. Yet at the end, with his sister dead and Taverner arrested, a weeping Buckman finds himself at an all-night garage. He climbs out of his "quibble" and goes over to hug a lonely black person—one of the very few black people in this world to have survived the sterilization programs.

The moral of the story is unexpected, as a reaction to incidents such as the Kent State University shootings. It is that even police officers can love. Even persons who are systematically evil can abandon the system. The ending of this novel comes over as an extraordinarily generous gesture from an embittered man. As with the very strongly antidrug stance of *A Scanner Darkly*, this scene shows that Dick, for all his liberalism, is not prepared to accept the complete antiestablishment package.

Nevertheless, from this point Dick's works grow weirder and more connected. Some of his later novels, such as the posthumously published *Radio Free Albemuth*, were either not submitted or not accepted for publication. This later group also includes the best of Dick's non-science-fiction novels, *Humpty Dumpty in Oakland*, a book most easily described as a sequel to John Steinbeck's *The Grapes of Wrath* (1939), recounting what happened after the so-called Okies got to California in the 1930's: They settled down, lost their way, ran used-car lots, and became "humpty dumpties"—passive spectators of the American Dream. The central idea of the last set of Dick's science-fiction novels, however, is a form of Gnosticism, the ancient Christian heresy that insists that the world contains two forces, of good and evil, in eternal conflict, with only a remote or absent God trying occasionally to get through. Dick writes variations on this theme in *Valis*, *The Divine Invasion*, *The Transmigration of Timothy Archer*, and *Radio Free Albemuth*, mentioned above.

Valis

Valis, at least, makes a direct assault on the reader by including the character Horselover Fat, a transparent translation of Dick. He hears voices, very like the characters from Berkeley in *Radio Free Albemuth*, who believe they are being contacted by a sort of divine transmission satellite. What the voices say are variations on the view that the world is ruled by a Black Iron Empire, by secret fraternities in Rome or the United States; that the president of the United States, Ferris F. Fremont, has "the number of the beast" in his name; that true believers are exiles from another world. Is this mere madness? Horselover Fat remarks himself that the simplest explanation is that the drugs he took in the 1970's have addled his mind in the 1980's. Still, he has to believe his voices. One might say that Dick's corrosive skepticism has finally developed a blind spot or, alternatively, that the novelist has become sadder and wiser. Whatever the decision, Dick's last novels could be characterized not as science fiction but as theological fiction.

Dick's work as a whole shows clear evidence of his deep social concerns, reacting against Senator Joseph McCarthy and President Nixon, first praising and then condemning drugs, testing one notion after another concerning the limits of government. Yet it also remained solidly consistent in its private and personal quest for a definition of reality that will stand any trial. It could be said that Dick's work is obsessive, introspective, even paranoid. It has also to be said that it very rarely loses gentleness, kindness, even a rather wistful humor. Dick certainly contributed a wealth of first-class novels to science fiction, more than most writers in the field, and he convinced many also of the genre's ability to cope with serious reflections on the nature of humanity and of perception.

T. A. Shippey

Other major works

SHORT FICTION: *A Handful of Darkness*, 1955; *The Variable Man, and Other Stories*, 1957; *The Preserving Machine, and Other Stories*, 1969; *The Book of Philip K. Dick*, 1973 (also known as *The Turning Wheel, and Other Stories*, 1977); *The Best of Philip K. Dick*, 1977; *The Golden Man*, 1980; *I Hope I Shall Arrive Soon*, 1985; *Robots, Androids, and Mechanical Oddities: The Science Fiction of Philip K. Dick*, 1985; *The Collected Stories of Philip K. Dick*, 1987 (5 volumes); *Selected Stories of Philip K. Dick*, 2002 (Jonathan Lethem, editor).

NONFICTION: *In Pursuit of Valis: Selections from the Exegesis*, 1991 (Lawrence Sutin, editor); *The Selected Letters of Philip K. Dick*, 1991-1993 (Don Herron, editor); *The Shifting Realities of Philip K. Dick: Selected Literary and Philosophical Writings*, 1995 (Sutin, editor); *What If Our World Is Their Heaven: The Final Conversations of Philip K. Dick*, 2000 (Gwen Lee and Elaine Sauter, editors).

MISCELLANEOUS: *The Dark Haired Girl*, 1988.

Bibliography

Carrère, Emmanuel. *I Am Alive and You Are Dead: A Journey into the Mind of Philip K. Dick*. New York: Henry Holt, 2004. Carrère seeks to recapture Dick's spirit, taking an often painful but well-examined journey into the writer's mind. This biography describes how Dick transformed the conventions of science fiction to create novels reflecting the anxiety of America in the 1950's and 1960's.

Dick, Anne R. *Search for Philip K. Dick, 1928-1982: A Memoir and Biography of the Science Fiction Writer*. Lewiston, N.Y.: Edwin Mellen Press, 1995. Dick's wife recounts her husband's life in candid detail, providing details about the sources of his fiction and the circumstances in which his novels were written.

DiTommaso, Lorenzo. "Redemption in Philip K. Dick's *The Man in the High Castle*." *Science-Fiction Studies* 26, no. 1 (March, 1999): 91-119. Discusses the role of Christian theology in Dick's fiction, particularly gnostic Christian dualism and fundamental Pauline theology. Discusses *The Man in the High Castle* as an important stage in the development of Dick's thought.

Mckee, Gabriel. *Pink Beams of Light from the God in the Gutter: The Science-Fictional Religion of Philip K. Dick*. Lanham, Md.: University Press of America, 2004. Mckee examines Dick's religious experiences and demonstrates how he communicated these experiences in his fiction. Chapter 2 focuses on the novel *A Scanner Darkly*. Includes bibliography and index.

Mackey, Douglas A. *Philip K. Dick*. Boston: Twayne, 1988. A book-length study of Dick. After a sketch of Dick's life, Mackey provides a comprehensive survey of his fiction from the 1950's through the 1980's. Supplemented by a chronology, notes, an extensive bibliography of primary sources, an annotated list of selected secondary sources, and an index.

Palmer, Christopher. *Philip K. Dick: Exhilaration and Terror of the Postmodern*. Liverpool, England: Liverpool University Press, 2003. Palmer provides a postmodern interpretation of Dick's work. He explores Dick's reactions to postmodern ideas about humanism and his use of images related to movement and stasis. Includes analysis of many of his novels, including those published in the 1950's.

Robinson, Kim Stanley. *The Novels of Philip K. Dick*. Ann Arbor, Mich.: UMI Research Press, 1984. A survey of Dick's narrative structures and fictional techniques by a highly respected science-fiction writer.

Science-Fiction Studies 2, no. 1 (March, 1975). This issue of the journal is devoted to the work of Dick and contains essays by writers eminent in the field of science-fiction criticism.

Sutin, Lawrence. *Divine Invasions: A Life of Philip K. Dick*. New York: Harmony Books, 1989. Sutin has written a well-researched biography that includes some discussion of Dick's work.

Umland, Samuel J., ed. *Philip K. Dick: Contemporary Critical Interpretations*. Westport, Conn.: Greenwood Press, 1995. An indispensable collection of essays on Dick's varied body of work. Umland has compiled extremely valuable primary and second bibliographies. Like Umland's introduction, the essays take careful note of the body of critical literature already published on Dick.

Warrick, Patricia S. *Mind in Motion: The Fiction of Philip K. Dick*. Carbondale: Southern Illinois University Press, 1987. Excellent studies of eight of Dick's novels that Warrick believes are representative of his best work, including *The Man in the High Castle* and *Do Androids Dream of Electric Sheep?*

CHARLES DICKENS

Born: Portsmouth, Hampshire, England; February 7, 1812

Died: Gad's Hill, near Rochester, Kent, England; June 9, 1870

Also known as: Charles John Huffam Dickens

Principal long fiction

Pickwick Papers, 1836-1837 (serial), 1837 (book; originally published as *The Posthumous Papers of the Pickwick Club*)

Oliver Twist: Or, The Parish Boy's Progress, 1837-1839 (serial), 1838 (book; originally published as *The Adventures of Oliver Twist*)

Nicholas Nickleby, 1838-1839 (serial), 1839 (book; originally published as *The Life and Adventures of Nicholas Nickleby*)

The Old Curiosity Shop, 1840-1841 (serial), 1841 (book)

Barnaby Rudge: A Tale of the Riots of '80, 1841

Martin Chuzzlewit, 1843-1844 (serial), 1844 (book; originally published as *The Life and Adventures of Martin Chuzzlewit*)
Dombey and Son, 1846-1848 (serial), 1848 (book; originally published as *Dealings with the Firm of Dombey and Son, Wholesale, Retail, and for Exportation*)
David Copperfield, 1849-1850 (serial), 1850 (book; originally published as *The Personal History of David Copperfield*)
Bleak House, 1852-1853 (serial), 1853 (book)
Hard Times, 1854 (originally published as *Hard Times for These Times*)
Little Dorrit, 1855-1857 (serial), 1857 (book)
A Tale of Two Cities, 1859
Great Expectations, 1860-1861 (serial), 1861 (book)
Our Mutual Friend, 1864-1865 (serial), 1865 (book)
The Mystery of Edwin Drood, 1870 (unfinished)

Other literary forms

All of Charles Dickens's novels were published in bound form after serialization, the Oxford edition being the most complete modern collection. A prolific writer, Dickens also published a number of other works. He founded and edited the periodicals *Master Humphrey's Clock* (1840-1841), *Household Words* (1850-1859), and *All the Year Round* (1859-1870), in which many of his essays, collaborative works, and Christmas stories were originally published. Some of the essays have been collected: *Sketches by Boz* (1836), for example, comprises Dickens's periodical contributions from 1833 to 1836, and *The Uncommercial Traveller* (1860) reprints essays from *All the Year Round*. In addition to the Christmas stories, Dickens published five Christmas books, all collected in 1852. He recorded his travel experiences as well: *American Notes* (1842) depicts his first tour of the United States, and *Pictures from Italy* (1846) is a collection of essays first printed in the *Daily News*. Finally, the texts of his public readings have appeared, along with reprints of his dramatic productions. Many of Dickens's works have been anthologized and adapted for stage and screen, and the definitive Pilgrim Edition of his letters, *The Letters of Charles Dickens*, was completed in 1995.

Achievements

Known for his biting satire of social conditions as well as for his comic worldview, Charles Dickens began, with *Pickwick Papers*, to establish an enduring novelistic reputation. In fourteen completed novels and countless essays, sketches, and stories, he emerged as a champion of generosity and warmth of spirit, those human traits most likely to atrophy in an industrialized society. In his own day, he appealed to all levels of society but especially to members of the growing middle class, whose newfound literacy made them educable to eradicate the social evils they themselves had fostered. Dickens was extremely popular in the United States despite his ongoing attack on the lack of an international copyright agreement, an attack directed in part against the Americans who had a financial stake in pirated editions of his works.

Above all, Dickens appealed to his readers' emotions and, through them, to an awakened social sense. To be sure, Dickens's sentimentality offends as many modern readers as it pleased Victorian ones. Indeed, the twenty-first century reader may study his novels primarily for the enjoyment of his craft, but to do so is to ignore Dickens's purpose: to argue on the side of intuition against materialism, as Angus Wilson puts it, or on the side of the individual against the system, as Philip Hosbaum has commented. In his facility for comic language, for example, Dickens created the unforgettable Sairey Gamp, Flora Finching, and Alfred Jingle, whose manic lingo creates worlds with a preposterous logic of their own, but such lingo is sometimes a shield for a warm heart and sometimes an indicator of fragmentation and despair. The reader also finds that Dickens's attacks on certain social institutions, such as the Poor Law in *Oliver Twist* or the Court of Chancery in *Bleak House*, are actually attacks on universal human evils—the greed, hypocrisy, and lust for power that lead to dehumanization and make, for example, a "species of frozen gentleman" out of Mr. Dombey instead of a warm, affectionate human being.

Biography

Born on February 7, 1812, in Portsmouth, on Portsea Island, England, Charles John Huffam Dickens was the son of John Dickens, a Naval Pay Office employee, and Elizabeth Barrow, the daughter of the Naval Conductor of Moneys. John Dickens's largely unsuccessful struggle to gain middle-class respectability was hampered not only by his parents' career in domestic service but also by the disgrace of his father-in-law, who left the country to avoid the consequences of a petty embezzlement. John Dickens's seaport life left a lasting impression on his son, to be recorded partly in Rogue Riderhood's river activities in *Our Mutual Friend* and partly in metaphor, as in *Dombey and Son*, where the running of the river into the ocean represents the passage of life into immortality. John Dickens's improvidence and inevitable bankruptcy is reflected in the impecunious but absurdly hopeful Mr. Micawber and, more abstractly, in Dickens's ambiguous attitude toward wealth, which he viewed as a highly desirable tool but worthless as a gauge of human value, as in *Our Mutual Friend*, in which money is equated with an excremental dust heap. An inordinate number of Dickens's deserving characters acquire wealth fortuitously: Oliver Twist, the parish boy, finds his near relatives; Nicholas Nickleby becomes clerk to the generous Cheerybles; and Esther Summerson comes under the protection of the well-to-do Jarndyce.

Charles Dickens. (Library of Congress)

Childhood associations were incorporated into Dickens's stories as well. His nurse, Mary Weller, by her own dogmatic adherence, inculcated in him a distaste for Chapel Christianity; his childhood taste for theatricals blossomed into a lifelong fascination. (In fact, in 1832, only illness prevented him from auditioning at Covent Garden.) Perhaps no other circumstance, however, had so profound an effect on Dickens as his father's incarceration in the Marshalsea (a London prison) for bankruptcy, well chronicled in *David Copperfield*. John Forster, Dickens's friend and biographer, records the author's bitterness at being put to work at Warren's Blacking Factory. Even worse than the degradation of the job for the young Dickens was the feeling that he had been abandoned. Although his period of employment in the factory could be measured in months, the psychological scars lasted for the rest of Dickens's life, as witnessed by his novelistic preoccupation with orphans and adopted families: Oliver Twist, Amy Dorrit, Pip, Little Nell—all abandoned in some sense and forced into precocity, some, in effect, reversing roles with their parents or guardians to become their protectors.

At the age of fifteen, Dickens was apprenticed as a law clerk in Doctor's Commons, certainly the source of his profound dislike for the pettifoggery exhibited in the Jarndyce case in *Bleak House*. He then became a reporter in Parliament and, at the age of seventeen, fell in love with Maria Beadnell, the daughter of a banking family who discouraged the attentions of the impoverished young man. This experience, as well as his unsuccessful marriage to Catherine Hogarth, daughter of the editor of the *Morning Chronicle*, contributed much to his alternate idealization of women (such as Dora in *David Copperfield*) and mockery of feminine foibles.

At the time of his marriage, Dickens had been writing a serial for Robert Seymour's sporting drawings—a work that became *Pickwick Papers* upon Seymour's suicide. Dickens's success came quickly: He became editor of *Bentley's Miscellany* (1836), and in February, 1837, *Oliver Twist* began to appear, one month after the birth of the first of his ten children. Before *Oliver Twist* had finished its serial run, Dickens had begun *Nicholas Nickleby*, in which he drew on his dramatic interests to create the Crummles provincial acting company. Then, in 1840, Dickens arranged to edit *Master Humphrey's Clock*, which became a vehicle for both *The Old Curiosity Shop* and *Barnaby Rudge* (the story of the 1780 Gordon riots). Some of his immense creative energy came from the early happiness of his marriage, but some also came from an effort to forget the death of his beloved sister-in-law Mary, who died in his arms when she was seventeen.

This period of activity ended in 1842 with a six-month visit to the United States. In letters, in *American Notes*, and in *Martin Chuzzlewit*, Dickens reveals his double vision of America. Welcomed in Boston by such literati as Henry Wadsworth Longfellow, Dickens moved from the cultivated bluestocking milieu into a furious newspaper war that was waged over the lack of an international copyright agreement. Dickens came to believe that while democracy did exist in such model factory towns as Lowell, Massachusetts, America's much-vaunted freedom was an excuse for vulgarity on one hand and hypocrisy on the other. He was appalled at the conditions of slavery in St. Louis and dismayed by the flat stretches of the Great Plains and by the ever-present concern for partisan politics, money, and power. All of these he satirized bitterly in the American section of *Martin Chuzzlewit*.

At home again, Dickens installed his sister-in-law Georgina in her lifelong role of housekeeper to counter what he judged to be Catherine's growing indolence, surely symptomatic of his and his wife's growing disillusionment with each other. Two years later, he began publication of *Dombey and Son*, his first planned novel. His next, the autobiographical *David Copperfield*, contains advice by the novel's heroine, Agnes, that he applied to his own life: "Your growing power and success enlarge your power of doing good." In March, 1850, Dickens founded *Household Words*, a periodical that featured short stories, serialized novels, poetry, and essays. Dickens and his writers published exposés of hospitals, sanitary conditions, political affairs, education, law, and religion, all expressed in a characteristically fanciful style. In these years, Dickens was engaged in amateur theatricals, partly to raise money to endow an impoverished actors' home.

Between 1852 and 1857, he wrote three novels: *Bleak House*, his experiment in first-person narration; *Hard Times*, an attack on utilitarianism; and *Little Dorrit*, a semiautobiographical work. Becoming more and more estranged from his wife, he engaged in a strenuous and highly popular series of readings from his works, again bringing his dramatic talent into play. In June, 1858, he published a much-criticized apologia for his marital separation; then, chafing at the restrictions imposed on *Household Words* by the publishers, Edward Chapman and William Hall, Dickens severed the connection and began *All the Year Round*, a new periodical of the same type.

His liaison with the actor Ellen Ternan continued in this period, during which he wrote *A Tale of Two Cities*, *Great Expectations*, and *Our Mutual Friend*, his last completed novel. He undertook another exhausting series of public readings, his reenactment of Nancy's murder in *Oliver Twist* proving the most demanding. In 1867, he left for a successful tour of the United States. He continued public readings until the end of his life.

Dickens died at Gad's Hill, near Rochester, on June 9, 1870, and is buried in Westminster Abbey. His last unfinished novel, *The Mystery of Edwin Drood*, appeared posthumously.

Analysis

The "Dickens World," as Humphrey House calls it, is one of sharp moral contrast, a world in which the self-seeking—imprisoned in their egotism—rub shoulders with the altruistic, freed from the demands of self by concern for others; a world in which the individual achieves selfhood by creating a "home" whose virtues of honesty and compassion are proof against the dehumanizing "System"; a world in which all things are animate and where, indeed, metaphors for moral perversity take on lives of their own, like the miasma of evil that hangs above the houses in *Dombey and Son*.

Many of Charles Dickens's most memorable characters are those whose language or personality traits are superbly comic: Sairey Gamp, the bibulous nurse in *Martin*

Chuzzlewit, with her constant reference to the fictitious Mrs. 'Arris; Flora Finching, the parodic reincarnation of a stout, garrulous Maria Beadnell in *Little Dorrit*; and Turveydrop, the antediluvian dandy in *Bleak House*. Providing characters with distinguishing traits is, of course, a dramatic device (to see red hair and a handkerchief is to be reminded of Fagin, and knitting, of Mme DeFarge); more important, however, such traits carry a moral resonance. While Dickens's villains grow more complex as his writing matures, most share an overriding egotism that causes them to treat people as things. Perhaps that is why things become animate; in a world in which human traits are undervalued, objects achieve a life and controlling power of their own. The miser Harmon disposes of Bella Wilfer in *Our Mutual Friend* as if she were a property to be willed away; the convict Jaggers creates a "gentleman" out of Pip in *Great Expectations*; both Carker and Dombey see Edith as a valuable objet d'art in *Dombey and Son*.

Dickens's later heroes and heroines are characterized by their movement toward self-actualization. In the early novels, Rose Maylie, Mr. Brownlow, Tom Pinch, Nicholas Nickleby, and even Pickwick represent compassionate but stereotyped models. Later, however, Dombey is thawed by his daughter Florence's love; Eugene Wrayburn, the blasé lawyer, is humanized by Lizzie Hexam; and Bella Wilfer gives up self-seeking for John Rokesmith. Some, however, must go through the reverse process of acquiring self-assertiveness. Florence Dombey is such a one; only by fleeing her father's household and establishing a family of her own can she achieve perspective. Amy Dorrit is another; she must grow up and then willfully become as a child again for the benefit of Arthur Clennam, who needs to be convinced of his worth. Esther Summerson is yet a third; persuaded of her worthlessness because of her illegitimacy, she must learn a sense of self-worth before she can marry Allan Woodstone.

Many of the heroes and heroines are tested by touchstone figures, such as Smike, Jo, Mr. Toots, Maggie, and Sloppy—unfortunates whose lack of mental capability or personal disfavor provides a test for altruism. Many of Dickens's child characters serve a similar purpose, from Oliver Twist and his famous request for more gruel to the itinerant Little Nell.

All of the characters are subject to the effects of the "System," in whatever shape it takes: Dotheboys Hall and the Gradgrind's school, the Circumlocution Office, the middle-class complacency of Podsnappery, the unsanitary conditions of Tom All Alone's, or the financial shenanigans of Montague Tigg's Anglo-Bengalee Disinterested Loan and Life Insurance Company. Far worse are the hypocrisy of Pecksniff, the concupiscence of Gride, the utilitarianism of Gradgrind, and the lovelessness of Estella, but all are personal evocations of the evils of the "System." Even as early as *Oliver Twist*, Dickens seemed to recognize that no one individual could rectify evil. As Stephen Marcus has observed: "*Pickwick Papers* is Dickens's one novel in which wickedness, though it exists, is not a threat. The unfortunate and the deprived . . . have only to catch a glimpse of Pickwick in order to be renewed, for this is the world of the 'good heart,' that thaumaturgic resource of spirit." When Nicholas breaks up Dotheboys Hall by whipping Squeers, all that one can do is succor the runaways; when the law is befogged by obscurities as in the Jarndyce case, all one can do is provide a warm, loving household. This, in fact, seems to be Dickens's solution, for despite his call for reforms, he was, at heart, a conservative, more likely to help Angela Burdett-Coutts set up a home for "fallen women" and to campaign against public executions than to lead riots in the streets. Dickens, then, might say with Voltaire's Candide, "Let us cultivate our garden."

NICHOLAS NICKLEBY

Nicholas Nickleby, an ebullient novel loosely patterned on such picaresque models as Henry Fielding's *Tom Jones* (1749), is ostensibly an attack on the abusive Yorkshire schools that served as repositories for unwanted children. It is, as well, a depiction of Dickens's theatrical concerns, a condemnation of greed, a mystery story, and a conventional romance. To be sure, as Bernard Bergonzi has noted, it has been criticized for its lack of a tightly woven plot as well as for its lack of a "significant moral pattern"; nevertheless it stands as the first of Dickens's full-scale, complex novels.

Dickens went to some trouble to establish the realistic fabric of the novel. Dotheboys Hall is modeled on William Shaw's notorious Bowes Academy, and the generous Cheeryble brothers, who give employment to the titular hero, mirror the merchants William and Daniel Grant. More important than the realistic antecedents, however, is what they represent: The schoolmaster Squeers and the Cheerybles are at opposite moral poles. Indeed, Nicholas's encounter with Dotheboys, his self-defense against Squeers, and his decision to "adopt" the enfeebled and mistreated Smike are preparation to confront his uncle Ralph, whose ungenerous nature is paradigmatic of moral usury. Even Nicholas's accidental joining with the Crummleses and their Infant Phenomenon is a way for him to act out his confrontation with pasteboard sword, for certainly, despite Crummles's benevolence, the closed world of the theater betrays as much selfishness as the world Nicholas eventually joins.

As Angus Wilson has suggested, the foe that Nicholas confronts is more complex than generally recognized. Ralph, driven by the desire for money, is also driven by a desire for power. His belittlement of his clerk, Newman Noggs, is comically reflected in Miss Knag's spitefulness and in Mr. Lillyvick's patronizing attitude toward his relatives; more seriously in Arthur Gride, the miser who charily serves an old wine—"liquid gold"—on his wedding day; and in Walter Bray, who affiances his daughter Madeline to Gride for a retirement stipend. Ralph is powerless, however, against generosity. Cast off by his uncle, Nicholas, like a hero in a French comedy of manners, rescues his sister Kate from the unwelcome advances of Sir Mulberry Hawk, one of Ralph's procurers; he is befriended by Noggs, with whose help he eventually rescues Madeline; and he is given a livelihood by the Cheerybles. In setting up a home for his mother, his sister, and Smike, Nicholas establishes a center of domestic harmony independent of his uncle's world yet connected to that of the Cheerybles, who inculcate similar homely virtues in their business. Indeed, as Nicholas gathers friends around him, Ralph is slowly denuded of his power. Both plot strands meet in the Gride/Bray association, where Ralph faces a double loss, material and psychological: Not only does Gride's loss of valuable deeds spell the beginning of Ralph's financial downfall, but Ralph's scheme to marry Madeline to Bray also is foiled by his nephew, against whom he feels growing resentment.

Nicholas's circle of friends thus comes to dominate Ralph's circle of power. Ralph's bankruptcy is, moreover, symbolic of spiritual bankruptcy, for his ultimate ignominy is discovering that Smike, whom he had persecuted in an attempt to wound Nicholas, is his own son. That the enfeebled boy turned to Nicholas for help is, for Ralph, a final, inescapable bitterness. As Ralph's wheel of fortune reaches its nadir, he hangs himself, cursing the hope of the New Year that brings to Nicholas a marriage and a new family.

Martin Chuzzlewit

Partly the product of Dickens's 1842 trip to America, *Martin Chuzzlewit* takes as its theme the effects of selfishness. Some critics, such as Barbara Hardy, find this theme to be fragmented, insofar as the characters are so isolated that their moral conversions produce no resonance. Critic John Lucas locates the flaws not only in narrative sprawl and faulty timing but also in Dickens's indecision as to "whether he is writing a realistic study or a moral and prescriptive fable." The fabular element is indeed strong. Young Martin is a developing hero whose American experiences and the selflessness of his companion Mark Tapley bring him to recognize his flaws, while his father, Old Martin, serves in his wealth and eccentricity as a touchstone for cupidity. In studying the cumulative effects of selfishness, Dickens portrays a number of family groups and also presents an effective psychological study of a murderer.

Pecksniff, ostensibly an architect and Young Martin's teacher, is the root of hypocrisy in the novel. He imposes on the gullible Tom Pinch; he raises his daughters, Charity and Mercy, to be spiteful and thoughtless; he tries to seduce Martin's fiancé, then accuses Tom of the action; and he attempts to influence Old Martin to disinherit his grandson. Like Molière's Tartuffe, Pecksniff only appears to be virtuous. His assistant, Tom Pinch, is the reader's surrogate; honest, consistent, and generous, Pinch is exiled from Pecksniff's house and goes to London, where he is aided by John Westlock, a former pupil who has come into his inheritance. Tom's household, where he installs his sister Ruth (rescued from being a governess to a highly inconsiderate family), is in direct contrast to Pecksniff's in its innocent, loving companionship. Other family groups appear as contrasts as well, not the least being that of Anthony Chuzzlewit, brother to Old Martin. Anthony's miserly ways have inculcated in his son Jonas so grasping a nature that Jonas attempts to poison his father. Another kind of family group may be seen at Todgers' Commercial Boarding House, where the Pecksniffs stay and where Mercy, eventually married to the brutal Jonas, finds understanding from Mrs. Todgers. The association between young Martin and Mark Tapley may be contrasted with that between Pecksniff and Pinch, for Mark moves from the character of servant to that of friend. While Mark's Pollyannaish attitude—that one must be "jolly" under all circumstances—has annoyed many critics, he is a descendant of the comedy of humors and serves as an important antidote to Martin's selfishness. In setting Martin's conversion (a purgative illness) in the swamps of America, Dickens suggests that hypocrisy, greed, and false pride are not simply manifestations of the British social milieu but flourish even in the "City of Eden," which that worshiper of freedom, Major Hannibal Chollop, praises so highly.

Jonas, on the other hand, undergoes no such conversion, although Mercy fills a role similar to that of Mark. As an investor in a pyramid scheme, the Anglo-Bengalee Company, he is blackmailed into procuring Pecksniff as an investor by Montague Tigg, who is privy to Jonas's poisoning scheme. Fearing exposure, Jonas murders Tigg. Dickens's portrayal of the murderer's frame of mind is exceptional, accompanied as it is by a study of Nadgett, the self-effacing paid informer who shadows Jonas like conscience itself. Even more telling is the disclosure that the deed was unnecessary, for Anthony, who had discovered his son's scheme and foiled it, is said to have died of a broken heart.

The regrouping that occurs at the end when Old Martin confesses his own kind of selfishness, that of suspicion of others, is a reestablishment of an extended family and a casting out of Pecksniff as a kind of scapegoat. Martin and Mary, and Ruth Pinch and John Westlock, are affianced; only Tom Pinch, hopelessly in love with Mary, remains unwed, to be a source of financial support for Pecksniff and Charity, who cadge small amounts from him. In the final analysis, Dickens has performed an "anatomy of selfishness" that is especially powerful because some of his characters have exhibited moral development. To be sure, Old Martin's pretended subservience to Pecksniff and final revelations may be seen as contrivances making possible a deus ex machina ending; yet, for all their artificiality, the conversions seem as true in spirit as do Jonas's terrified and cowardly maunderings.

DOMBEY AND SON

Dombey and Son is considered to be the first novel of Dickens's maturity. Indeed, as John Butt and Kathleen Tillotson have pointed out, it is the first for which he worked out a complete plot outline; therefore, the subplots are controlled, and a fully orchestrated set of symbols emerges. John Lucas has observed that *Dombey and Son* presents the social panorama of the new, industrialized England, allowing "patterns of behavior and language to suggest connections more deeply insistent than blood-ties."

In this story of a middle-class merchant prince who must learn to place heart above head, Dickens produces one of his most moving and powerful studies of childhood, not only in Florence, the neglected daughter, but also in Paul, whom Dombey regards as a small version of himself. Paul is portrayed as an "old-fashioned" boy, one who astonishes his father by asking what money is. Unlike Oliver Twist, who seeks to find a way into society, Paul runs counter to its expectations, resisting his father's attempt to make him into a grown-up before he has been a child. Alive to the world of the imagination, Paul is left untouched by Blimber's educational establishment, described as a hothouse where young minds are forced to produce before their time. Mr. Toots, one of Dickens's divine fools, is intellectually blasted by the process but retains a sweetness of soul that adds poignancy to his comic diction.

When Paul dies in Florence's arms, Dickens illustrates his pervasive water imagery in a masterly way. Paul, rocked gently out to sea in a flood of divine love, has come "to terms with the watery element," as noted by Julian Moynihan; only by close association with the sea is anyone in *Dombey and Son* saved from an atrophying of the affections. Paul's death is but one step in the education of Dombey, whom it initially hardens rather than softens: Dombey blames all of those Paul loved—Polly Toodle, his wet nurse; Walter Gay, one of Dombey's clerks in love with Florence; and Florence herself—for alienating Paul's affections. Another important step comes from Dombey's second marriage, which is to Edith Granger, a young widow put on the marriage market by her Regency mother, the artificial Mrs. Skewton. Bought for her accomplishments and ability to bear sons, Edith sets her will against Dombey's, determined to scorn his material success. She elopes with John Carker, the manager to whom Dombey had entrusted not only his domestic troubles but also his business affairs. Outraged, Dombey strikes Florence when she tries to comfort him. Florence runs away, taking refuge with a friend of Walter's uncle. Edith eventually runs away from Carker, for her motive was not adultery but vengeance. Carker, while trying to escape from the pursuing Dombey, is hit by a train. As Marcus has noted, the railroad is Dickens's "great symbol of social transformation" as well as Carker's nemesis.

That Florence takes refuge with Captain Cuttle, a friend of Walter's uncle, shows the way in which the ocean theme is invoked even in a comic way, for Captain Cuttle is a peg-legged, Bible-quoting sea dog, yet he proves to be a tenderhearted surrogate father to Florence. Her affiancement to Walter, who, at Dombey's instigation, has been sent to the West Indies and shipwrecked, is another blow to Dombey, for it allies him not only with a class he shuns but also with an individual he believes had stolen his son's affections.

The last step in the education of Dombey is the failure of his business, largely through Carker's machinations. Left alone in his empty mansion to be pitied by Miss Tox, an old-maid figure whose ridiculousness, like Captain Cuttle's, is belied by her warmth of heart, Dombey meditates on the remembered figure of his daughter. His contemplation of suicide is interrupted, however, when Florence unexpectedly returns. For Dickens, Florence serves as the model of Christian, womanly behavior, of unselfish self-abnegation that, founded upon love, redeems her father. She returns because, as a mother, she can imagine what desertion by a child would be like.

The story of Dombey was a powerful parable for the middle classes, for whom, Dickens believed, overconcentration on such firms as Dombey and Son led to dehumanization, to a buying and selling not of goods but of people. That Paul's old-fashioned, loving nature could evoke responses in such unlikely quarters as in the pinched and spare Miss Tox or in the schoolmarmish Cornelia Blimber, or that Florence could melt both the disdainful Edith and her hardhearted father, is testimony to Dickens's optimism. In keeping with the theme, all of the characters, no matter how comic, are invariably treated as more than comic elements. Mr. Toots and his fascination with the boxer, the Game Chicken; Miss Tox's futile hope to become Mrs. Dombey; the straitlaced Mrs. Pipchin; and the seaman's caricature, Captain Cuttle himself, are integrated with the plot and ranged on the side of heart.

Little Dorrit

While *David Copperfield* is considered to be Dickens's autobiographical novel par excellence, *Little Dorrit* explores some of the same themes through the metaphor of the imprisonment that had so deep an effect on the Dickenses' family fortunes. Critical opinion ranges from Angus Wilson's comment that the "overcomplicated plot" weakens the imprisonment/release theme, to Lionel Trilling's assessment that the novel is "one of the most profound . . . and most significant works of the nineteenth century." In *Little Dorrit*, imprisonment has many facets. The initial and end scenes are set in the Marshalsea, where William Dorrit, imprisoned like Dickens's father for debt, has set up a social circle whose obsequiousness and class consciousness are simply a reflection of the society outside the prison. The resemblance suggests, in fact, that the large, self-seeking society without is itself a prison, for even when William Dorrit is freed by a legacy (as was John Dickens), he carries the taint of the Marshalsea with him, attempting to conform to social conventions so rigid that they dehumanize him, and hiring the "prunes and prisms" Mrs. General to tutor his daughters. That Dorrit, in ill health, should break down at Mrs. Merdle's state dinner to babble about the prison is indicative that he has never, indeed, left it but has merely called it by different names.

Some prisons are built to contain those like Blandois, an evocation of the evil principle; others are less obvious, like the workhouse, for example, where old Nandy lives, or Bleeding Heart Yard, whose tenants are imposed upon by the patriarchal landlord Casby, or the Circumlocution Office—an accurate representation of the futile motions of a government bound by red tape. People, as well, create their own prisons: Miss Wade, for example, writes "The History of a Self-Tormentor"; Flora Finching is, as Wilson puts it, an "embodiment of romantic love that persists against all reason and propriety"; even Cavalletto is sequestered by his inability to speak English fluently. Amy, or Little Dorrit, is held in bondage not only by her selfless love for her father but also by her neurotic refusal to be anything but a child. Her sister Fanny willfully contracts a marriage with the dandified Edmund Sparkler, a marriage that guarantees her social respectability at the price of a fool for a husband. Fanny's prison becomes even smaller when her father-in-law, Mr. Merdle, commits suicide before his financial chicanery is discovered; without the emollient of money, Fanny spends her days in social battle with her mother-in-law, leaving her children in Little Dorrit's care.

For Arthur Clennam, to return home to his mother's house is to return to imprisonment, where the walls are walls of the spirit, built of her unforgiving nature and her Calvinism that judges by the letter, not by the spirit of the ethical law. Clennam, however, carries his prison with him in the form of diffidence, for it is a lack of self-confidence that prevents him from proposing to Pet Meagles and almost prevents him from believing in the redeeming love of Little Dorrit herself (whom Lionel Trilling sees finally as "the Paraclete in female form"). In the end, he deliberately takes responsibility for his friend Doyce's financial trouble and is imprisoned in William Dorrit's old room. It is fitting that Amy should tend him there, for just as she held the key of affection to lead her father from the prison of self, so she holds the key of love that frees Clennam. In this respect, she radically differs from Clennam's mother, who, knowing that Arthur Clennam is her husband's illegitimate child, takes her vengeance accordingly.

Clearly, in *Little Dorrit*, the individual is both the jailer and the jailed, the cause of suffering and the sufferer; perhaps nowhere else does Dickens so emphasize the intertwined fates of all humans. At this stage in his life, when he was actively involving himself in a number of projects and coming to understand that his marriage was failing, Dickens's view of the human condition had little of the sunny hope exhibited, for example, in *Pickwick Papers*, or little of the simplistic interpretation of motivation found in *Nicholas Nickleby*. Indeed, the last lines of the novel sound a quiet note: Little Dorrit and Clennam go down into the midst of those who fret and chafe as if entering a prison; their only hope is "a modest life of usefulness and happiness." Their ability to quell the "usual uproar" seems severely limited.

OUR MUTUAL FRIEND

According to J. Hillis Miller, "*Our Mutual Friend* presents a fully elaborated definition of what it means to be interlaced with the world." In this last completed novel, Dickens has indeed relinquished the idea that evil or, in fact, the redemption of society resides in any one individual or institution. The Poor Law in *Oliver Twist*, the effects of education in *Nicholas Nickleby*, and the law itself in *Bleak House* represent abuses that are manifestations of a larger illness permeating society. This view, which Dickens begins to develop in *Little Dorrit*, is clear in *Our Mutual Friend*. From the violent, repressed sexuality of the schoolmaster Bradley Headstone to the cool indifference of Eugene Wrayburn, who would despoil Lizzie Hexam to satisfy a whim, all society is affected with a kind of moral (and financial) selfishness that was a matter of parody in *Martin Chuzzlewit*. Even the heroine, Bella Wilfer, becomes, as she calls herself, a "mercenary little wretch," consciously weighing her desire for a wealthy marriage against love for John Rokesmith. The exuberance of subplotting evident in Dickens's early novels is again evident here, although in this case he provides a more disciplined framework, giving the reader not only a central symbol—money (represented as an excremental dust heap) inherited by the Boffins from the miser John Harmon—but also a central character, the enigmatic John Rokesmith, Harmon's son and therefore rightful heir to the fortune.

The central plot that devolves from a single generous act—the Boffins returning to Rokesmith his inheritance—is illustrative of the title, the significance of which Arnold Kettle has explored in terms of the mutuality of relationships, insofar as the activities of Rokesmith/ Harmon interweave all social levels, from Wegg and Venus to the Podsnaps. The novel, moreover, contains elements of the masquerade in *Martin Chuzzlewit* as well as the motif of educating the affections in *Dombey and Son*. Boffin pretends to be a miser and Rokesmith an impoverished clerk to convince Bella that grasping for wealth deadens the heart. Her happy marriage is contrasted with that of her mother, whose perpetual toothache, tender temperament, and mortuary-like deportment minister to her pride but not to the comfort of her family. Indeed, other marriages in the book are hardly preferable: The nouveau-riche Veneerings, who make good friends of strangers in order to entertain them at a sumptuous board, are one example; another is the Lammles, who, sadly deceived in their original estimate of each other's wealth, set out to defraud the world. Likewise, the Podsnaps, an embodiment of the solid, tasteless, and pretentious middle class, are concerned not, for example, with the emotional state of the much-repressed Georgiana but rather with their place on the social scale, and they are therefore willing to entrust her to the Lammles, whose intention it is to procure her in marriage for the moneylender "Fascination Fledgeby."

Our Mutual Friend is about the use and misuse of childhood as well. It offers a panoply of unnatural parents, among them Jesse Hexam, who forces Lizzie to dredge corpses from the Thames, and the bibulous "Mr. Dolls," whose crippled daughter Fanny ("Jenny Wren") is a dolls' dressmaker. There are adoptive parents as well—some, like the Lammles, shamming affection to benefit themselves; others, like Lizzie, mothering her selfish brother Charley; or Riah, giving Lizzie fatherly protection; or Betty Higden, showing kindness to her diminutive boarders. The prime example is, of course, the Boffins, who nurture a series of children, young and old, beginning with John Harmon, for whom their kindness created a home in his father's cold house; then Bella, who they felt had been harmed by the dictates of Harmon's will, being, as she was, ceded in marriage to a stranger; then Johnny, the orphan who dies; and finally, Sloppy, an idiot foundling. Their adoption of Sloppy, an unprepossessing individual, is the key to the series, for Sloppy is another of Dickens's touchstone figures.

The subplot that runs parallel to the education of Bella is that of Lizzie Hexam's wooing by Eugene Wrayburn. While Bella originally refuses Rokesmith because of his supposed poverty, Lizzie evades Wrayburn because of his wealth, fearing that she will become his mistress rather than his wife. Again, while Bella can accept Rokesmith's proposal without knowing his true identity, Lizzie flees Wrayburn to a factory town (perhaps an evocation of Lowell, Massachusetts, where Dickens visited on his American tour). Even Bella's moment of bravery, in which she relinquishes all hope of inheriting the Boffins' money in favor of defending Rokesmith, whose dignity she thinks Boffin is maligning, has a parallel, albeit on a more earthy level: Lizzie rescues Wrayburn from the murderous attack of Headstone, thereby putting to use the skills she had learned when working with her father. Wrayburn's proposal of marriage to her is his recognition that financial and class standing are irrelevant in matters of the heart.

It is, in fact, their marriage that is central to the "trial" scene at the end of the novel, in which the Veneerings convene their friends to pass judgment on Wrayburn's action. Mr. Twemlow, a minor character with romantic notions and little apparent strength of character, nevertheless rises to the occasion, as he had in agreeing to help warn the Podsnaps that their daughter was in danger of a mercenary scheme. He asserts, with finality and against the general disparagement, that if Wrayburn followed his "feeling of gratitude, of respect, of admiration and affection," then he is "the greater gentleman for the action." Twemlow's voice is clearly not the voice of society; rather, it is the voice of the heart, and it is to him that Dickens gives the closing word.

Patricia Marks

OTHER MAJOR WORKS

SHORT FICTION: *Sketches by Boz*, 1836; *A Christmas Carol*, 1843; *The Chimes*, 1844; *The Cricket on the Hearth*, 1845; *The Battle of Life*, 1846; *The Haunted Man*, 1848; *Reprinted Pieces*, 1858; *The Uncommercial Traveller*, 1860; *George Silverman's Explanation*, 1868; *Christmas Stories*, 1871.

PLAYS: *The Strange Gentleman*, pr. 1836; *The Village Coquettes*, pr., pb. 1836; *Mr. Nightingale's Diary*, pr., pb. 1851 (with Mark Lemon); *No Thoroughfare*, pr., pb. 1867 (with Wilkie Collins).

NONFICTION: *American Notes*, 1842; *Pictures from Italy*, 1846.

CHILDREN'S LITERATURE: *A Child's History of England*, 1851-1853 (serial), 1852-1854 (book; published with Jane Austen's *The History of England* as *Two Histories of England*, 2006); *The Life of Our Lord*, 1934.

EDITED TEXTS: *Master Humphrey's Clock*, 1840-1841 (periodical); *Household Words*, 1850-1859 (periodical); *All the Year Round*, 1859-1870 (periodical).

Bibliography

Ackroyd, Peter. *Dickens*. London: Sinclair-Stevenson, 1990. Biography by a major English novelist warrants the characterization of being Dickensian both in its length and in the quality of its portrayal of the nineteenth century writer and his times. In re-creating that past, Ackroyd has produced a brilliant work of historical imagination.

Davis, Paul B. *Charles Dickens A to Z: The Essential Reference to His Life and Work*. New York: Facts On File, 1998. Excellent encyclopedia for the student of Dickens. More than twenty-five hundred entries include articles about all of his novels, each containing a story synopsis, commentary, criticism, and information about adaptions. Also features information about each of Dickens's characters, his life and family, and Victorian England.

Epstein, Norrie. *The Friendly Dickens: Being a Good-Natured Guide to the Art and Adventures of the Man Who Invented Scrooge*. New York: Viking Press, 1998. Provides a succinct, informative, and entertaining overview of Dickens's life and work aimed at the general reader. Includes summaries of each of the novels, illustrations, bibliographical references, index, and filmography.

Hobsbaum, Philip. *A Reader's Guide to Charles Dickens*. Syracuse, N.Y.: Syracuse University Press, 1998. Presents an overview of Dickens's work for the general reader. After a brief discussion of Dickens's political reportage and his pamphlets advocating prison reform, each chapter provides a detailed discussion of one of Dickens's books.

Jacobson, Wendy S., ed. *Dickens and the Children of Empire*. New York: Palgrave, 2000. Collection of fourteen essays focuses on child images and colonial paternalism in the work of Dickens.

Johnson, Edgar. *Charles Dickens: His Tragedy and Triumph*. 2 vols. New York: Simon & Schuster, 1952. This classic work was perhaps the first major scholarly biography of Dickens. Integrated within the biographical material are excellent discussions and analyses of Dickens's writings.

Jordan, John O., ed. *The Cambridge Companion to Charles Dickens*. New York: Cambridge University Press, 2001. Collection of fourteen essays provides information on Dickens's life and times, analysis of his novels, and discussions of his representations of the city, childhood, gender, and the family. Another essays examines Dickens and the form of the novel.

Kaplan, Fred. *Dickens: A Biography*. New York: William Morrow, 1988. An interesting, comprehensive, and well-written biography. Published a generation later than Edgar Johnson's study of Dickens (cited above), this work is more forthright about Dickens's family life and personal qualities, especially his relationship with the actor Ellen Ternan.

Ledger, Sally. *Dickens and the Popular Radical Imagination*. New York: Cambridge University Press, 2007. Examines the relationship between Dickens and the popular British radical culture, including the Chartist political and social reform movement and eighteenth and nineteenth century radical writers. Analyzes Dickens's novels to demonstrate how they reflected the populist ideas of his time.

Newsom, Robert. *Charles Dickens Revisited*. New York: Twayne, 2000. Provides biographical information and examines Dickens's major novels from modern-day critical perspectives. Explains why Dickens remains important to twenty-first century readers and writers.

Reed, John Robert. *Dickens and Thackeray*. Athens: Ohio University Press, 1995. Discusses how beliefs about punishment and forgiveness affected how Dickens and William Makepeace Thackeray told their stories. Discusses Dickens's major fiction in terms of moral and narrative issues.

Smiley, Jane. *Charles Dickens*. New York: Viking Press, 2002. Smiley, a noted novelist herself, focuses on what Dickens reveals about his life in his writings, interpreting many of his novels in the process. Acknowledging that "countless" Dickens biographies have been published, she explains her intention to present a portrait of the author "as he might have seemed to his contemporary audience, to friends and relatives, to intimate acquaintances, to himself, filling in the background only as he became willing to address it in his work."

JAMES DICKEY

Born: Atlanta, Georgia; February 2, 1923
Died: Columbia, South Carolina; January 19, 1997
Also known as: James Lafayette Dickey

Principal long fiction

Deliverance, 1970
Alnilam, 1987
To the White Sea, 1993

Other literary forms

James Dickey's early fame as a writer was based on several volumes of poetry. He also published books of criticism and collections of children's poetry.

Achievements

At the age of thirty-eight, in the middle of a successful career as an advertising executive, James Dickey became a full-time poet. Five years later, in 1966, he won the National Book Award for a collection of poems titled *Buckdancer's Choice* (1965), and he was appointed poetry consultant to the Library of Congress. In 1967, his collection *Poems, 1957-1967* won critical praise. Dickey's first novel, *Deliverance*, was published in 1970 and was a best seller. His second novel, *Alnilam*, appeared in 1987 after a seventeen-year conception.

Biography

Born and reared in Atlanta, Georgia, James Lafayette Dickey attended public schools and experienced a typical twentieth century boyhood and adolescence. He excelled in sports and became a notable football player at Clemson University. During World War II and the Korean War, Dickey flew more than one hundred night combat missions. Returning to the United States after World War II, he enrolled at Vanderbilt University. There the subjects of his compositions for a writing course, based on his war experiences, made Dickey stand out from other students, who were writing about their summer vacations.

At Vanderbilt, Dickey absorbed the literary tradition established by the Fugitive poets, such as John Crowe Ransom, Allen Tate, and Robert Penn Warren, and discovered himself to be a poet. He graduated with honors and went on to finish a master's degree before taking a job teaching English in college. He left teaching for immediate success in advertising, first in New York and later in Atlanta. A grant allowed him to retire from advertising in his mid-thirties and pursue writing full time. He became convinced of the absolute necessity and worth of writing, of writing as a calling demanding total commitment and absorption. His poems were the narration of intense experiences both imaginary and real, whether the dreamlike falling of a flight attendant into a midwestern cornfield or the shark-fishing experience of young boys. As he wrote his poems as extended narratives, it was natural for Dickey also to write novels. Like his poems, his novels deal with human intensities on a visceral level, where the limits of human vulnerability and endurance are explored.

Analysis

James Dickey's first two novels, *Deliverance* and *Alnilam*, were published seventeen years apart, and the chronological separation parallels the levels of difference in their content and style. *Deliverance*, written by Dickey when he was in his forties, is more conventional in form and more accessible to a popular readership. The reader is quickly plunged into the equivalent of an adventure story, as four middle-aged men take a canoe trip in North Georgia and a malevolent pair of mountain men force them into a primal life-or-death encounter. *Alnilam*, a formidably physical book of almost seven hundred pages, defies the reader in many ways, including the intermittent use of experimental double-column pages where the simultaneous narration of the blind character's perception and the seeing narrator is developed. The blind man, Frank Cahill, is physically incapable of the more conventionally heroic feats performed by the narrator of *Deliverance*. This limitation of the main character seems a deliberate aim of Dickey, as he is writing a book about the delusions human beings sustain in their assumed youth and strength. Yet Dickey is also concerned with physical reality, and the task of characterizing the blind Cahill gives Dickey's imagination a broad field of sensations to explore.

Though different in many ways, the novels share a concern with men struggling to survive. *Deliverance* considers the angst of middle-aged suburban males and the efforts they make to escape their civilized imprisonment while dreading the alternative of survival in the wild. *Alnilam* takes the he-man Cahill—a carpenter and lover of boards and nails—and, by making him become blind, places him in a wilderness of greater darkness than the North Georgia forests of *Deliverance*; the normal world becomes as mysterious and untrustworthy as wild nature. Both novels consider the questions quoted from David Hume in an epigraph to *Alnilam*: "Where am I, or what? From what causes do I derive my existence, and to what condition do I return? Whose favour shall I court, and whose anger must I dread? What beings surround me?"

Deliverance

Deliverance conjures the world of modern America in the commercial South of the 1960's. The four male characters have jobs that are typical of this world: bottle distribution, mutual fund sales, advertising, and apartment rental. The main character, Ed Gentry, becomes increasingly aware that running an advertising agency is death in life. He admires the survivalist Lewis, who has honed his body to a muscular perfection through constant exercise and is devoted to a hypothetical future fantasy in which his physical superiority will keep him alive. Dickey is both critical and supportive of Lewis's point of view. He suggests there is in men a need to be tested, to be physically pitted against stress, as a daily fact of life. The modern world has eliminated this part of what it means to be human, and the restlessness of men such as Ed and Lewis to polish their survival skills and instincts indicates a real human need. The modern world has replaced the world where such skills were practiced, however, and men look ridiculous if they believe and behave as sincerely as Lewis. Thus, Lewis must manufacture his own wilderness, must find it before it is buried by developers.

Lewis discovers his dangerous place in North Georgia: a river to explore by canoe. Ed and Lewis are joined by Bobby and Drew, who are less avid but ready for a change of scene. Though the river has treacherous places and does damage to the novice canoers, it is human ugliness that is revealed to be the main danger. Two hillbillies appear to Bobby and Ed on the second day. They are repulsive, lacking teeth and manners, and they sodomize Bobby and prepare to do worse to Ed before Lewis kills one of the mountain men with an arrow through his chest. The four suburbanites are faced with a decision: Do what civilization dictates and face the local authorities, or bury "the evidence" and hope to escape. Lewis argues that survival dictates the latter, and Bobby and Ed agree. After burying the attacker and continuing down the river, Drew is shot and killed by the other hillbilly, the two canoes capsize, and the three survivors are battered by water and stones before landing in a gorge. With Lewis's broken leg and Bobby's general cowardice, Ed is left to scale the gorge walls and kill the sniper with his bow and arrow. The three make it to a town, ultimately escape the local law, and live to savor the next year's

James Dickey. (Washington Star Collection, D.C. Public Library)

damming of the river, which creates a recreational lake that hides all evidence of their experience.

Ed has been tested—a good thing, as implied by the title of the novel, but horrible. Ed has taken the blood and life of another man who had wanted his own. Had he not, he and his friends would have perished. He has also been delivered into an understanding of something disturbing about being human, about what humans carry inside them. This knowledge is good because it is truth, and nothing more. Dickey is aware that men in World War II learned to kill thousands from bombers without seeing their faces or hearing their screams. *Deliverance* presents its main character with an enemy who must be killed face-to-face, as men killed one another before modern warfare. There is a kind of joy for Ed in this combat, but he must return to Atlanta for a lifetime of remembering while he pursues the art of advertising. Dickey intimates that, after such a deliverance experience, the spiritual corrosion of civilization—designing ads for women's underwear—will not so completely dampen Ed Gentry's spirit as it had before.

Alnilam

Deliverance is an unabashedly self-reflective book. At the time that he wrote it, Dickey's passions for archery and the guitar, which Drew plays in the novel, were well documented in magazine articles. Ed Gentry, the narrator, works in the field of advertising, where Dickey spent many successful years. With *Alnilam*, however, Dickey projects a persona whose similarities to himself are more metaphorical than literal. Frank Cahill is an Atlanta carpenter with a high school education who loves to build things, look at blueprints, construct an amusement park labyrinth with his bare hands, and run a swimming pool for the public. Then, in middle age, he becomes blind from diabetes. Suddenly, a man who had loved to be in the visible world, making new things appear with hammer, wood, and nails, is now closed off permanently from being that man. Cahill does not complain and listens to the doctor, who suggests that blindness, rather than killing him, can make Cahill alive in a new way. Another epigraph from David Hume suggests how this might occur: "May I not clearly and distinctly conceive that a body, falling from the clouds, and which, in all other respects, resembles snow, has yet the taste of salt or feeling of fire?"

The reader senses the test Dickey is giving himself as a writer. All characterization demands empathy, but it is more difficult to imagine what one is not than what one is. Also, Dickey is passionate about the world, and a blind narrator forces him to view it through a new dimension. Blindness, while closing off the visible, sharpens touch, smell, hearing, and, most satisfying to Cahill, memory. Cahill's memories, whether of roller-skating all day on Atlanta streets, watching a boy fly a rubber-band-powered airplane in a park, or coming upon a waterfall during a picnic hike, become etched messages that repeatedly appear and a measure for all the unseeableness of his present world. Cahill in his blindness is a metaphor for the private consciousness to which everyone is confined, and the replays of memory allow Dickey to emphasize this point. Cahill, divorced, having never seen his son, and regretting neither the divorce nor the sonlessness, has unashamedly accepted his privacy and distance. Blinded, however, he makes a pilgrimage into the land of other selves.

With Cahill drawn in such a manner that he cannot be easily identified with the author, Dickey places him in a world very familiar to the younger Dickey: a training base for World War II pilots. Cahill's son, Joel, a pilot trainee, has died in a crash during a forest fire in the North Carolina hills. Cahill comes to the base in his new blindness accompanied by his version of a Seeing Eye dog. Zack is not a graduate from a training school for guide dogs but part shepherd and part wolf; Cahill and a friend trained him before Cahill went blind. Zack possesses a blend of viciousness and loyalty that Cahill adores.

Mystery surrounds the death of Joel, and initially Cahill suspects foul play. Joel had been an inspiration to his fellow trainees, and a secret society developed, with Joel as the leader. Cahill's conversations with Joel's friends reveal the society's name, Alnilam (the middle star of the constellation Orion's belt), and intention: the mystical union with other young pilots across the nation leading to a destruction of all war and the means to wage war.

By novel's end, this scheme will be revealed for what it is—high-minded but naïve youthful rebellion against authority. Yet Joel was an extraordinary young man. He innately grasped the subtleties of flying and developed a hypnotic training called "Death's Baby Machine," which struggling young pilots received sitting in an ordinary chair. In his mind, Cahill is able to create a psychological and physical portrait of Joel from questioning those who knew him on the base, and he realizes that giftedness mixed with unwillingness to obey rules constituted Joel's essence. Cahill, who never saw Joel alive or made any effort to that end, can now clutch the few personal remnants of his son in his coat pockets: the pilot's broken goggles, a burned zipper from his boot found near the crash, a piece of wire from the airplane. Cahill steadily contemplates the tangible remains while absorbing the memory fragments from the other pilots. His boy is alive in his head. Cahill, in this blitz of story and memorabilia, is learning to love, but the word does little to indicate the combination of physical impressions and the straining for meaning that come to make up Joel in Cahill's consciousness.

Dickey's creation of a blind character allows him to exploit his bias toward the physical. The world has never been so mediated as felt. Even when the seeing, right-hand column is being read, the experience is emphatically visceral. A bus drives away at the novel's end: "The gears gathered, smashed and crowded, found each other; the bus straightened onto the highway. . . . The highway came to exist in the bodies of the passengers, as the driver brought it into himself, and with it made the engine hoarse and large."

Dickey shows that Cahill, while now blind, has never been so fully *in* the world, and a dead son has never been more alive for him. Joel's Alnilam brothers show a film of their group's arrival at the base. Cahill, privy to their secrets because of their perception of his own arrival as part of Joel's master plan, is present at the showing and asks for a description of Joel when the projector sends out his image. Hearing of a curl of hair across the forehead, Cahill strains out of his chair in an effort to see his son. Later, taking a bath and speaking aloud of the wondrous good things there are in the world, such as a hot bath to soak in and a bottle of gin to swallow, Cahill hears Joel speak. Zack hears him as well and tears up the room. A ghost is as real and sensible as hot water. The world is full of marvels, and human beings are rich creatures both to be and to know.

This message might be a summation of what Dickey wrote fiction about. He would not leave disenchanted suburbanites amid unmitigated ennui. *Deliverance* claims that a man has things to prove to himself. *Alnilam* claims that a man is composed of more than he knows and lives in a world of presences and forces that he tends to ignore or disbelieve. In Cahill, Dickey creates a primal character, a sort of caveman, through whom Dickey as a writer can imagine all sensations anew, from the feeling of snowflakes to the taste of water. Dickey wants to go back to humanity before it was dulled by civilization, and in *Deliverance* and *Alnilam* he imagines characters who experience their basic vitality as living creatures.

Bruce Wiebe

Other major works

POETRY: *Into the Stone, and Other Poems*, 1960; *Drowning with Others*, 1962; *Helmets*, 1964; *Two Poems of the Air*, 1964; *Buckdancer's Choice*, 1965; *Poems, 1957-1967*, 1967; *The Eye-Beaters, Blood, Victory, Madness, Buckhead, and Mercy*, 1970; *The Zodiac*, 1976; *The Strength of Fields*, 1977; *Head-Deep in Strange Sounds: Free-Flight Improvisations from the UnEnglish*, 1979; *The Early Motion*, 1981; *Falling, May Day Sermon, and Other Poems*, 1981; *Puella*, 1982; *The Central Motion: Poems, 1968-1979*, 1983; *The Eagle's Mile*, 1990; *The Whole Motion: Collected Poems, 1945-1992*, 1992.

SCREENPLAY: *Deliverance*, 1972 (adaptation of his novel).

TELEPLAY: *The Call of the Wild*, 1976 (adaptation of Jack London's novel).

NONFICTION: *The Suspect in Poetry*, 1964; *A Private Brinkmanship*, 1965 (address); *Spinning the Crystal Ball*, 1967; *From Babel to Byzantium*, 1968; *Metaphor as Pure Adventure*, 1968; *Self-Interviews*, 1970; *Sorties*, 1971; *The Enemy from Eden*, 1978; *In Pursuit of the Grey Soul*, 1978; *The Starry Place Between the Antlers: Why I Live in South Carolina*, 1981; *The Poet Turns on Himself*, 1982; *The Voiced Connections of James Dickey*, 1989; *Striking In: The Early Notebooks of James Dickey*, 1996 (Gordon Van Ness, editor); *Crux: The Letters of James Dickey*, 1999; *The One Voice of James Dickey: His Letters and Life, 1942-1969*, 2003 (Van Ness, editor); *Classes on Modern Poets and the Art of Poetry*, 2004; *The One Voice of James Dickey: His Letters and Life, 1970-1997*, 2005 (Van Ness, editor).

children's literature: *Tucky the Hunter*, 1978.

miscellaneous: *Night Hurdling: Poems, Essays, Conversations, Commencements, and Afterwords*, 1983; *The James Dickey Reader*, 1999.

Bibliography

Baughman, Ronald, ed. *The Voiced Connections of James Dickey: Interviews and Conversations*. Columbia: University of South Carolina Press, 1989. Collection of important and lively interviews covers Dickey's career from the mid-1960's to the late 1980's. Includes chronology of Dickey's life and career and index.

Calhoun, Richard J., and Robert W. Hill. *James Dickey*. Boston: Twayne, 1983. First book-length study of Dickey's work attempts to analyze virtually everything Dickey wrote during a twenty-two-year period, so that at times the discussion is not very deep. Provides a solid introduction to Dickey's fiction nonetheless.

Clabough, Casey Howard. *Elements: The Novels of James Dickey*. Macon, Ga.: Mercer University Press, 2002. Traces the common elements among *Deliverance*, *Alnilam*, and *To the White Sea*. Also discusses Dickey's unpublished fiction, including a novel manuscript and five screenplay prospectuses.

Dickey, Christopher. *Summer of Deliverance: A Memoir of Father and Son*. New York: Simon & Schuster, 1998. Dickey's son recalls the corrosive effects of fame on his father, describing how his father's drinking and his destructive relationship with his family intensified after the release of the film adaptation of *Deliverance*.

Dickey, James. *The One Voice of James Dickey: His Letters and Life, 1942-1969*. Edited by Gordon Van Ness. Columbia: University of Missouri Press, 2003.

_______. *The One Voice of James Dickey: His Letters and Life, 1970-1997*. Edited by Gordon Van Ness. Columbia: University of Missouri Press, 2005. Letters in these two volumes were culled from Dickey's voluminous correspondence in order to chart the chronological development of his literary career, his attempts to steer that career, his other interests, and the components of his personality. Editor's commentary provides a psychological interpretation of Dickey's personality and places his work within a broader literary and cultural context.

Hart, Henry. *James Dickey: The World as a Lie*. New York: Picador USA, 2000. Narrative biography details the rise and self-destruction of a literary reputation. Argues that lying was a central theme in Dickey's art and life.

Kirschten, Robert, ed. *Critical Essays on James Dickey*. New York: Maxwell Macmillan International, 1994. Collection presents early reviews of Dickey's work as well as a selection of later scholarship. Includes essays by Robert Bly, Paul Carroll, James Wright, and Wendell Berry.

_______. *Struggling for Wings: The Art of James Dickey*. Columbia: University of South Carolina Press, 1997. Compilation of reviews and essays about Dickey's work, as well as interviews with the author, focuses primarily on Dickey's poetry, but the novel *Deliverance* is also addressed.

DENIS DIDEROT

Born: Langres, France; October 5, 1713
Died: Paris, France; July 31, 1784
Also known as: Pantophile

Principal long fiction

Les Bijoux indiscrets, 1748 (*The Indiscreet Toys*, 1749)
Jacques le fataliste et son maître, 1796 (wr. c. 1771; *Jacques the Fatalist and His Master*, 1797)
La Religieuse, 1796 (*The Nun*, 1797)
Le Neveu de Rameau, 1805 (in German; 1821 in French; 1891 complete edition; wr. 1761-1774; *Rameau's Nephew*, 1897)

Other literary forms

Although the official complete edition of the novels of Denis Diderot (DEED-uh-roh) is found in the twenty-volume *Œuvres complètes* (1875-1877), edited by Jean Assézat and Maurice Tourneax, the novels are readily available in the Classiques Garnier, edited by Henri Bénac (1962). An edition of *Œuvres complètes* (1975-1995) has been updated under the editorship of Herbert Dieckmann, Jean Fabre, and Jacques Proust. All the novels are available in English in various popular editions.

Diderot began his literary career with translations, the most important of which are *L'Histoire de Grèce* (1743), a translation of the English *Grecian History* (1739) by Temple Stanyan; *Principes de la philosophie morale: Ou, Essai de M. S.*** sur le mérite et la vertu, avec réflexions* (1745), of the earl of Shaftesbury's *An Inquiry Concerning Virtue and Merit* (1699); and *Dictionnaire universel de médecine* (1746-1748), of Robert James's *A Medical Dictionary* (1743-1745).

Diderot was a prolific essayist. His first important essay, *Pensées philosophiques* (1746; English translation, 1819), was immediately condemned for its rationalistic critique of supernatural revelation. It is available in English in *Diderot's Early Philosophical Works* (1916), translated by Margaret Jourdain. *La Promenade du sceptique* (1830; the skeptic's walk), which was written in 1747, was described by Diderot himself as a "conversation concerning religion, philosophy, and the world." *De la suffisance de la religion naturelle* (on the sufficiency of natural religion), written the same year but not published until 1770, extols natural religion. The famous *Lettre sur les aveugles* (1749; *An Essay on Blindness*, 1750; also as *Letter on the Blind* in Jourdain's book) puts forth Diderot's ideas on the supremacy of matter; this work was the cause of his imprisonment at Vincennes. It was followed in 1751 by the *Lettre sur les sourds et muets* (*Letter on the Deaf and Dumb* in Jourdain's book), which was circulated by tacit permission of the authorities and which contains important ideas on music and poetry. *Pensées sur l'interprétation de la nature* (1754; thoughts on the interpretation of nature) explores some implications of the scientific method.

In 1759, Diderot began his contributions to Friedrich Melchior von Grimm's *Correspondance littéraire*, a periodical that had a very limited circulation among the aristocracy abroad, reporting on the latest happenings in French arts and letters. Diderot's art criticism, contained in the famous *Les Salons* (1845, 1857), first appeared there. These annual reviews of Paris exhibitions were published from 1759 to 1781, the most famous being those of 1761, 1763 (considered the best), 1765, 1767, and 1769. Other essays during this time include the famous *Le Rêve de d'Alembert* (1830; *D'Alembert's Dream*, 1927), written in 1769, which contains scientific and philosophical ideas together with an exploration of dreams. *Entretien d'un père avec ses enfants* (1773; *Conversations Between Father and Children*, 1964) and *Paradoxe sur le comédien* (1830; *The Paradox of Acting*, 1883), written in 1773, are among other important essays. Diderot's last philosophical work was his *Essai sur Sénèque* (1778; essay on Seneca), which was revised as *Essai sur les règnes de Claude et Néron* (1782), a digressive amplification of the former. Both of these essays mix autobiographical material with an exposition of Diderot's ideas on politics and morality. All of these works are included in the *Œuvres complètes*; they are also found in the Classiques Garnier volumes, *Œuvres philosophiques* (1956), *Œuvres esthétiques* (1959), and *Œuvres politiques* (1962). In addition to

Diderot's Early Philosophical Works, English editions include *Diderot, Interpreter of Nature: Selected Writings* (1937), translated by Jean Stewart and Jonathan Kemp, and *Selected Writings* (1966), edited by Lester Crocker.

In 1757, Diderot began to write for the theater. Although he developed a new genre, the so-called *drame bourgeois*, he was not a successful playwright, for his plays lack dramatic qualities. *Le Fils naturel: Ou, Les Épreures de la vertu* (*Dorval: Or, The Test of Virtue*, 1767) was published in 1757 but not staged until 1771. It was followed by an essay, *Entretiens sur "Le Fils naturel"* (1757; conversations on "The Natural Son"). *Le Père de famille* (1758; English translation, 1770; also as *The Family Picture*, 1871) was staged in 1761. This play, too, was followed by an important essay, *Discours sur la poésie dramatique* (1758; English translation of chapters 1-5 in *Dramatic Essays of the Neo-classical Age*, 1950). Diderot's last play, *Est'il bon? Est'il méchant?* (pr. 1781; Is it good? Is it bad?), is considered his best.

In addition to long fiction, Diderot also wrote several short stories. They include "L'Oiseau blanc" (the white bird), written and published in 1748, and several stories written in 1772 that were published at later dates: "Les Deux Amis de Bourbonne" (1773; "Two Friends from Bourbonne," 1964), "Ceci n'est pas un conte" (1798; "This Is Not a Story," 1960), "Madame de la Carlière: Ou, Sur l'inconséquence du jugement public de nos actions particulières" (1798), and *Supplément au voyage de Bougainville* (1796; *Supplement to Bougainville's Voyage*, 1926). Several of these stories are available in English in Ralph Bowen's translation *Rameau's Nephew, and Other Works* (1964).

Diderot's voluminous correspondence is collected in sixteen volumes by George Roth (1955-1970). The most famous of these letters are the 187 extant to his mistress Sophie Volland (1755-1774). Other important letters are those to Paul Landois on determinism (1756); those to the princess of Nassau-Saarbruck (1758), translated as *Concerning the Education of a Prince* (1941); and the farewell letter to Catherine II of Russia (1774). Finally, Diderot wrote many articles in the famous *Encyclopédie: Ou, Dictionnaire raisonné des sciences, des arts, et des métiers* (1751-1772), many of which are unsigned. Some of these are available in English in the Bobbs-Merrill edition, *Encyclopedia* (1965), translated by Nelly S. Hoyt and Thomas Cassirer.

Achievements

Although Denis Diderot is one of the major novelists of the eighteenth century, it is as the editor of the *Encyclopedia* that he is most remembered. Along with Jean le Rond d'Alembert, who was to abandon the project in 1758, he began in 1746 what was intended to be a translation of Ephraim Chambers's major English reference work, *Cyclopedia* (1728). Diderot's version later became a compendium of knowledge in seventeen volumes of text and eleven volumes of plates, published from 1751 to 1772 amid countless difficulties and attacks by clergy and government. Diderot was not only the principal, and eventually sole, editor but also the author of numerous articles, many of which were unsigned in later volumes, and some mutilated by André Le Breton. It is particularly through Diderot's articles that his philosophical ideas come to light, as demonstrated in Arthur M. Wilson's masterful 1972 study and confirmed by numerous other scholars.

Diderot was above all else a philosophe, one of the great eighteenth century Enlightenment figures who prepared the way for modern thought. The philosophes were not philosophers in the classical sense. In fact, they criticized many such thinkers, although Diderot had great respect for Plato, to the extent of using ideas from the Socratic dialogues as the basis for many of his works, at least in the opinion of Donal O'Gorman. The philosophes, Diderot among them, believed strongly in personal freedom, as seen in *The Indiscreet Toys* and *The Nun*; in reason and progress, the whole thesis of the *Encyclopedia*; and in a more representative government. Generally they were Deists, although Diderot himself was associated with the atheist circle of Baron Paul-Henri-Dietrich d'Holbach.

Diderot as a philosophe explored the question of morals, of virtue and vice—which he named *bienfaisance* and *malfaisance*, or good-doing and evildoing. He concluded that morality as such is the result of naturalistic and materialistic causes that determine a person's conduct—hence, that traditional morality has no meaning. *Rameau's Nephew* and *Jacques the Fatalist and His*

Master explore essentially the question of the modifiability of human behavior, determinism, and freedom. Diderot also attributes pleasure to natural causes, becoming one of the forerunners of "sensibility," the Romantic emphasis on feeling and the heart. His novels bear the stamp of Samuel Richardson and Laurence Sterne and anticipate the reign of Romanticism. Diderot's sensitivity to aesthetic beauty is expressed in the art criticism contained in *Les Salons*; it is also reflected in his fiction, notably in the digressions in *The Indiscreet Toys* and the musical discussions in *Rameau's Nephew*.

As a novelist, Diderot was an innovator. *The Nun* anticipates twentieth century psychological fiction, especially in its exploration of the abnormal. *Jacques the Fatalist and His Master* is, by Diderot's own description, an antinovel, a forerunner of the twentieth century New Novel, which is not really a story but rather a collaboration between author and reader. *Rameau's Nephew* is a fascinating study of the paradox of the human personality. The independence of thought that distinguishes all of Diderot's works is particularly evident in his fiction; he produced novels with few models and with rich possibilities for further development.

Denis Diderot. (Library of Congress)

BIOGRAPHY

Denis Diderot was born on October 5, 1713, in Langres, France, one of the seven children of the master cutler Didier Diderot and Angélique Vigneron. The family of the future anticleric was pious and devout, and Diderot's youngest brother, Didier-Pierre, was later to become a canon at Langres, deeply alienated from the great writer. Diderot's younger sister, Angélique, died insane in a convent; her cruel fate inspired Diderot's invective against convents in *The Nun*. Although Diderot began his studies at home, he was an excellent student of the Jesuits from 1723 to 1728, receiving several prizes. He also began his study of Latin and Greek with them, and he remained devoted to the classics throughout his life. He even received the tonsure in 1726, in the hope of a benefice from his uncle's inheritance, and later passed through some periods of religious fervor.

In 1728, Diderot went to Paris, where he was to spend the rest of his long life. Very little is known about his activities during the subsequent fifteen years, other than that he received his master's degree from the University of Paris in 1732 and led a fairly dissolute, though not degenerate, life. In 1743, he fell in love with Anne-Toinette Champion, a modest lace maker, and asked his father's permission to marry her. His father not only refused but also had his son imprisoned in a monastery. Diderot escaped and married Anne-Toinette secretly. It was, however, to be a tumultuous and basically unhappy marriage, from which only Angélique, of the four children born to the Diderots, was to survive. Well educated by her father, she was to become the author of several memoirs that are very valuable to Diderot studies.

Diderot's sensual nature was soon awakened in a liaison with a certain Madame de Puisieux, about whom little is known, except that Diderot wrote his first novel, *The Indiscreet Toys*, to raise money for her. It was around this time, in the late 1740's, that Diderot became associated with d'Alembert, Étienne Bonnot de Condillac, and Jean-Jacques Rousseau. He began working on the *Encyclopedia* with them and Le Breton. Soon,

Diderot and d'Alembert became coeditors, and after 1758 Diderot assumed total responsibility for the work. The production of the *Encyclopedia* was Diderot's greatest achievement and essentially his lifework. By no means a child prodigy, he had produced almost nothing in the literary field until that time, but he immediately threw himself into the new project and other philosophical works.

In 1749, Diderot found himself in prison as a result of his controversial writings, particularly his *Letter on the Blind*. Diderot's brief and not uncomfortable imprisonment was perhaps more noteworthy for Rousseau than for him. It was on his way to visit the incarcerated Diderot that Rousseau experienced his famous "illumination" that led to his *Discours sur les sciences et les arts* (1750; *The Discourse Which Carried the Praemium at the Academy of Dijon*, 1751; better known as *A Discourse on the Arts and Sciences*, 1913), which won for Rousseau the prize of the Academy of Dijon. Diderot's release did not bring an end to his clashes with the law, the harsh censorship of the day, and the criticism of the Jesuits against the *Encyclopedia*. In 1752, the first two volumes were suppressed, and Diderot's papers were confiscated. Because of the support of the honest and liberal censor Chrétien-Guillaume de Lamoignon de Malesherbes and the influence of Madame de Pompadour, Louis XV's favorite, the work continued under a "tacit permission," but its publication was fraught with difficulties. The contributors often quarreled among themselves, the most noteworthy division being that between Rousseau and d'Alembert (and ultimately Diderot), and the attacks from the outside continued.

Nevertheless, Diderot's assiduous work brought him increasing financial independence and a reputation among scholars in France and abroad. It also brought him the love and support of Sophie Volland, whom Diderot met in 1755 and continued to see at least until 1774. Their liaison was characterized by a passionate and intellectual correspondence, of which 187 letters from Diderot are extant, although none of Volland's has survived. In 1757, Diderot began to write plays, creating a new type that became known as the *drame bourgeois*, or bourgeois drama; at the same time, he continued to produce essays and carried on, almost single-handedly, the editorship of the *Encyclopedia*.

The year 1759 was a difficult one for Diderot. His father died, the privilege for printing the *Encyclopedia* was revoked, and the work was condemned by Pope Clement XIII. The difficulties of Diderot's domestic life were intensified by quarrels and jealousy between his wife and Volland. Shortly afterward, Charles Palissot de Montenoy's satiric play *Les Philosophes* (pr. 1760) greatly offended Diderot, although it became one of the sources of inspiration for his masterpiece, *Rameau's Nephew*. Not all was somber, however. Diderot's friends, Grimm, d'Holbach, and his disciple and future editor Jacques-André Naigeon, proved very faithful. Catherine the Great of Russia offered her support to Diderot, purchasing his library for fifteen thousand livres and allowing him to use it for the rest of his life. She invited him to Russia, where he eventually spent the year 1773 to 1774. He was also responsible for selling her several famous art collections and for sending the noted French sculptor Étienne-Maurice Falconet to execute the famous statue of Peter the Great. Toward the end of Diderot's stay in Russia, Catherine's enthusiasm for his ideas waned, as the times were not favorable to the types of reforms that he advocated.

Diderot's last years were filled with literary activity and interest in his newly married daughter Angélique, now Madame de Vandeul. Although his troubles with the authorities continued on a minor scale, he was honored at his native Langres, and he posed for busts by sculptors Jean-Baptiste Pigalle and Jean-Antoine Houdon. In 1783, he became seriously ill, and he died on July 31, 1784, on not unfriendly terms with the Church. He received Christian burial and was interred at the Church of Saint-Roch, where Pierre Corneille is also buried—an unusual setting for a militantly anticlerical philosophe, an avowed materialist, and a sometime atheist.

Analysis

One of Denis Diderot's shorter works of fiction is titled "This Is Not a Story." He might have said of any one of his characteristic works of long fiction, "This is not a novel." At first sight, all of his novels, with the exception of *The Nun*, look like plays. That is because Diderot's favorite method is the dialogue; even many of his philosophical works, such as *D'Alembert's Dream* and *The*

Paradox of Acting, are written in this form. It is in the give-and-take of dialogue that Diderot excels, and his dramatic power, though not of first-rate quality on the stage, comes to life here. The unusually extensive use of dialogue, however, leads to a blurring of genres and a consequent disorder in all of Diderot's works. Critics such as Crocker, O'Gorman, and Francis Pruner have sought to bring order out of this chaos—much to the dismay of others, who see the disorder as the message.

As novels, all of Diderot's fictional works are weak in plot. *The Indiscreet Toys* consists of a series of licentious anecdotes. *Jacques the Fatalist and His Master* is a trip from somewhere to nowhere, with intermittent stops here and there. *Rameau's Nephew* consists of a single conversation in which the two participants discuss everything from seduction to French and Italian music. *The Nun*, which comes closest to the traditional idea of plot, does have a beginning and end but does not use any forward or backward reflection. Although it is based on memory, all is told in a kind of eternal present.

As with plot, the timelines are also weak in Diderot's novels. With the exception of *The Nun*, all of his novels are poorly marked in time and lack traditional novelistic beginnings or ends. They are also vaguely situated in space. *The Indiscreet Toys* takes place in a harem in the Congo, a rather incongruous juxtaposition lacking in credibility. *Jacques the Fatalist and His Master* is situated in France but, despite the efforts of critics to identify the towns and cities that figure in the narrative, there is very little local color to guide the reader. *Rameau's Nephew*, situated in the café du Palais Royal, and *The Nun*, at the convents of Longchamp and Arpajon, are a bit more localized, yet Diderot could have put them anywhere, for his scenery is subservient to the representation of the characters.

Of all the fictional qualities in his works, it is in the portrayal of character that Diderot excels, although his best characters are in fact caricatures. He dislikes the literary portrait and provides little, if any, physical description of his characters; the reader knows nothing of their size, facial expressions, or clothing. Their personalities are revealed by contrast with those of other characters: Jacques is played against his master, Lui against Moi, Sister Suzanne against the three superiors.

Instead of well-rounded, complex characters, Diderot creates striking types. Among the most memorable are Jacques the Fatalist and Rameau's nephew, the latter simply called Lui, or He. Jacques is a picaresque hero in the tradition of Panurge, Cacambo, and the Spanish Lazarillo de Tormes. In contrast to his dull master, who spends his time looking at his watch and sniffing tobacco, Jacques is clever, witty, independent; indeed, not unlike Pierre-Augustin Caron de Beaumarchais's Figaro, he is clearly superior to his master. Lui, vaguely modeled on Jean-François Rameau, is a parasite raised to heroic proportions, a seducer, procurer, and indolent cynic who nevertheless excels in pantomime and offers brilliant reflections on society and its morals.

Having produced such picaresque and cynical heroes, it is not surprising that Diderot expends his flair for satire in other directions. Throughout his novels, Diderot attacks the institutions of eighteenth century France. Like Voltaire, Diderot regarded the clergy and the religious—that is, those who had taken monastic orders—as his greatest enemies. Again and again, he reproached the monasteries for infringing on civil and social freedom and for imposing celibacy on their members. Diderot saw hypocrisy in his society, not only in the court but also in the social conventions that people accepted as a kind of false morality; he censures such conventions with particular force in *Rameau's Nephew*.

In the *esprit gaulois* of Renard the Fox and the fabliaux and the Rabelaisian spirit so close to nature, Diderot delights in the details of sexual passions. He sees the genital act as simply a phenomenon of nature, as a purely physical act like eating and smelling. Although he champions women's rights in *The Indiscreet Toys*, women in his novels are presented as essentially unfaithful and little more than objects of desire for men, although Amisdar looks for fidelity and devotion in a wife. The cynic Lui in *Rameau's Nephew* regrets that his beautiful wife has died, for she might have become the mistress of a wealthy *fermier-général* (tax collector). *Jacques the Fatalist and His Master* is based on the amorous exploits of both Jacques and his master, all of which are totally devoid of any spiritual attraction. By contrast, *The Nun* shows the abnormalities and excesses that result from the frustration of nature.

Diderot's novels are essentially philosophical explorations. In his materialistic system, intuition is ruled out as a cause of human behavior, and free will also becomes questionable, although Diderot was a champion of freedom and human rights. All is the result of predetermined natural causes, a doctrine given symbolic expression by Jacques's "great scroll" and his refrain that "all is written on high." His fatalism is really Diderot's determinism. Diderot, however, observed the role of chance and coincidence in life and was torn by the paradox of freedom and necessity. His two major novels, *Rameau's Nephew* and *Jacques the Fatalist and His Master*, explore this tension in a most creative way, without solving the dilemma.

Diderot is an excellent stylist. As well as a knowledge of music (so aptly related in *Rameau's Nephew*), he had an ear for harmony. His style can be witty, full of plays on words, fast-paced, with the give-and-take of quick argument. It can also be passionate, even mystical—most notably in the moment of physical desire expressed by the superior of Arpajon for Sister Suzanne and in the two pantomimes of Lui in *Rameau's Nephew*, especially the pantomime of the orchestra. In fact, the novels of Diderot reveal a marked talent for mimicry and pantomime, a talent better displayed in his fiction than in his theater.

The Indiscreet Toys

Despite their very readable and attractive prose, Diderot's novels, as vehicles of what was regarded as dangerous philosophical propaganda, were not likely candidates for the ordinary publisher. None of them was published in France when written. *The Indiscreet Toys* was written and published in 1748. Diderot wrote this first work of long fiction to help defray the mounting expenses he incurred in his liaison with Madame de Puisieux. Madame de Vandeul, Diderot's daughter, maintained that her father wrote the book in two weeks, to prove that such a novel could be composed very quickly, provided one had a workable idea. It sold well, with six editions in several months, and was immediately translated into English and German. Reprinted several times in Diderot's lifetime, it continues to be his most popular book.

Although the novel contains social and political allusions to the reign of Louis XV, it is by no means hostile to the king, portrayed as the Sultan Mangogul, or to his favorite, Madame de Pompadour, represented by Mirzoza. It does, however, reveal the licentious behavior of the court in the confessions made by the indiscreet jewels. The king, Mangogul, bored with his court and his harem, consults the genie Cucufa and asks for a means to discover the secrets of the women at his court. Cucufa gives him a magic ring that will make him invisible and will make the women's jewels reveal their wearers' secret passions. Throughout the thirty episodes of the book, licentious secrets entertain both the king and the reader.

While the plot lacks substance and depth, *The Indiscreet Toys* is important because it is one of the earliest works in which Diderot reveals his philosophical preoccupations. He discusses the scientific and metaphysical views of Sir Isaac Newton and René Descartes, satirizes religious practices, ventures into literary criticism (concerning the lack of naturalness on the French stage), and compares the music of Jean-Baptiste Lully and Jean-Philippe Rameau, thus anticipating *Rameau's Nephew*. He also parodies a sermon (his daughter said that he had composed and sold real sermons) and investigates dreams, a phenomenon that he was to explore later, especially in *D'Alembert's Dream*. He already extols the scientific method, and even in the most licentious scenes he shows a naturalistic and methodical bent.

The Nun

Diderot's second novel, *The Nun*, shows a marked advance in technique over *The Indiscreet Toys*, perhaps in part as a result of Diderot's reading of Richardson. Like all of Diderot's novels, *The Nun* had a fascinating origin. Based partly on a true story and partly on a hoax, it lay dormant for twenty years before Diderot even considered publication. The idea for the novel began with a lawsuit in Paris from 1755 to 1758 in which a certain Marguerite Delamarre—whose story has been illuminated through the research of Georges May—applied for dispensation from her religious vows. Her request was refused as contrary to the authority of parents over their children. A friend of Diderot, Marquis de Croismare, had tried to support the nun. Diderot and his friends wrote a series of forged letters to Croismare, supposedly from the nun, who ostensibly had escaped from her convent. Croismare took such an interest in her that his friends were forced to "kill her off" in 1760. Croismare did not discover the hoax until 1768, but in the meantime Diderot had prepared the greater part of the manuscript, which, after revision in 1780, he offered to Grimm's successor, Jakob Heinrich Meister, for the *Correspondance littéraire*. The novel was first published by Naigeon in 1796.

The Nun is a simple, rapidly moving story featuring deep psychological analysis and great artistic restraint. It tells the story of Suzanne Simonin, whose parents force her into a convent because she is illegitimate. She at first refuses to make her vows but is forced into a second convent, where she does make her profession. Her first superior is gentle and maternal, but the second is cruel and vindictive and treats her with extreme brutality. Although Suzanne manages to receive support for a plea to be dispensed from her vows, the request is rejected, and she is sent to another convent, at Arpajon. There the discipline is lax, and the superior makes lesbian advances to Suzanne. This arouses the jealousy of the superior's former favorite, which eventually drives the superior to madness and the unsuspecting Suzanne to flight. The ending is disappointing and illogical, as Suzanne, weakened from her escape, dies.

Although Diderot has frequently been accused of immorality in *The Nun*—a film based on his book was temporarily banned in France in 1966—his intentions were, rather, to show the injustice of the enforced cloister and its dangerous effects on the subjects. His technique is masterful, for he presents a young woman who is not tempted to break her vows by the desire for marriage or a lover but who simply finds she does not have a vocation to the cloister. She is innocent, observant of the discipline in the convent, and even unaware of the significance of the advances made by the superior at Arpajon. Diderot's treatment of the physical desire expressed by the superior is artful and delicate, quite different from his open and licentious descriptions in *The Indiscreet Toys* and in *Jacques the Fatalist and His Master*. The psychological analysis of Sister Suzanne, of her jealous rival, Sister Thérèse, and of the three superiors with whom Suzanne lives is excellent, making *The Nun* a forerunner of the works of Marcel Proust and André Gide.

RAMEAU'S NEPHEW

The story of Diderot's third novel, generally acknowledged as his masterpiece, is even more fascinating than those of the two preceding ones. Evidently begun in 1761, *Rameau's Nephew* was revised by Diderot in 1762, 1766, 1767, and 1775, but—no doubt because of the allusions to his enemies, especially Palissot—was never published during his lifetime, nor did it appear in Naigeon's edition of Diderot's works, *Œuvres* (1798; 15 volumes). In 1805, a German translation by Johann Wolfgang von Goethe was published, and in 1821 the text was retranslated into French, by this time substantially altered. Several other undocumented versions appeared in the nineteenth century, and it was not until 1891 that a genuine text was published by Georges Monval from a manuscript he had located at a *bouquiniste*'s stall in Paris.

Written in the form of a dialogue, *Rameau's Nephew* was staged at the Théâtre Michodière in 1963, starring Pierre Fresnay. Whether it is a novel is debatable; Diderot called it "Satire seconde" (second satire), and its dramatic possibilities are evident. It is, however, a witty, exuberant, rapid exchange of conversation between two characters, Moi and Lui. Lui is vaguely based on Jean-François Rameau, the nephew of the great French musician Jean-Philippe Rameau, whose French severity Diderot disliked, preferring Italian spontaneity. Moi is vaguely reminiscent of Diderot, at least in some biographical details, such as the education of his daughter. Critics have advanced innumerable theories concerning the identities of the characters Moi and Lui. Some say that they are two aspects of Diderot's personality, others that Lui is the id and Moi the ego, still others that they are literally Rameau's nephew and Diderot. Perhaps the most original interpretation is that of O'Gorman, who sees the work both as a Horatian satire and as a Socratic dialogue with the figures of Apollo and Marsyas, and who also identifies Rameau's nephew with Rousseau.

Rameau's Nephew, which discusses music, anti-Rousseauesque education, the hypocrisy of society, the art of seduction, and numerous other themes, opens as a casual conversation at the café du Palais Royal during a chess game. It is also a searching inquiry into the basis of morality and a study of the paradox involved in determining the right way to live. For Diderot, morality is nonexistent, because all is based on natural phenomena and matter is the root of human behavior. Yet the existence of a cynical parasite such as Rameau's nephew, who contends that his way of life is the best, poses a problem to Diderot's materialistic system, for society cannot survive with a number of Rameau's nephews. The debate is never neatly resolved; Diderot's dialectical method in the novel has been much praised by Marxist critics, who differ from many readers in finding a clear message within the twists and turns of the dialogue.

Jacques the Fatalist and His Master

Diderot continued his metaphysical speculations on the paradox of morality in his last novel, *Jacques the Fatalist and His Master*, which rivals *Rameau's Nephew* as his masterpiece. Like the two preceding novels, it was not published during his lifetime, although it was written probably around 1771 and revised during or after his stay in Russia of 1773 to 1774, as evidenced by the travel theme. Diderot gave the manuscript to the *Correspondence littéraire* before 1780, but the work was not published until 1796, by Buisson. It was inspired by a passage from Laurence Sterne's *The Life and Opinions of Tristram Shandy, Gent.* (1759-1767), which Diderot had read in English.

Constructed along the lines of Miguel de Cervantes' *Don Quixote de la Mancha* (1605, 1615), *Jacques the Fatalist and His Master* is, however, quite different in tone from the great Spanish masterpiece. It is the most disorderly of all of Diderot's "chaotic" works, with interruptions of interruptions, interference by the author (who holds dialogues with his reader), and unfinished stories left to the reader's imagination. Jacques, a sort of Figaro, accompanies his rather empty-headed master, not unlike Count Almaviva, on a trip. In order to entertain his master, Jacques relates the story of his amorous exploits, and various interruptions preclude a real end to his tale. At the end, the master also tells his story; it is not unlike Jacques's, but it lacks his sparkling wit.

Their stops at inns along the way precipitate other tales, the two most important of which are the stories of Madame de la Pommeraye and Père Hudson. Madame de la Pommeraye is resentful of her lover's unfaithfulness and decides to avenge herself. She hires a prostitute and her mother to pose as a respectable young woman accompanied by her devout widowed mother. This done, Madame de la Pommeraye arranges to have her former lover, Monsieur des Arcis, fall in love with the prostitute. The day after the marriage, Madame de la Pommeraye tells him the truth, but the revenge is thwarted because he really loves his new wife and forgives her completely. Père Hudson is a sensual and domineering superior who reforms a monastery but exempts himself from its discipline. He arranges for the two priests sent to investigate his conduct to be trapped with a young woman he has seduced, thus escaping censure himself.

Despite the adventures and interruptions, the real theme of the book is the paradox of freedom and necessity. Jacques the Fatalist is really a determinist who, like Diderot, believes that "all is written on high," that one cannot change one's destiny. The very form of the novel, however, proves that chance does indeed exist. All of this seems to rule out freedom, which, like good and evil, becomes a mere illusion.

Crocker's observations on why *Jacques the Fatalist and His Master* is a great work but not a great novel may serve to classify all of Diderot's novels. A great novel must embody human life in all of its emotional and intellectual range, in all of its intensity. It must contain a view of human life in terms of concrete problems and human suffering. By contrast, *Rameau's Nephew* and *Jacques the Fatalist and His Master* are preoccupied with abstract philosophical problems. Although these two works may be Diderot's most profound fictions, it is perhaps *The Nun* that comes closest to the ideal of the novel. Diderot himself wept over *The Nun*; its characters and their suffering were real to him, as they are to his readers.

Irma M. Kashuba

Other major works

Short fiction: "L'Oiseau blanc," 1748; "Les Deux Amis de Bourbonne," 1773 ("The Two Friends from Bourbonne," 1964); *Supplément au voyage de Bougainville*, 1796 (*Supplement to Bougainville's Voyage*, 1926); "Ceci n'est pas un conte," 1798 ("This Is Not a Story," 1960); "Madame de la Carlière: Ou, Sur l'inconséquence du jugement public de nos actions particulières," 1798; *Rameau's Nephew, and Other Works*, 1964.

Plays: *Le Fils naturel: Ou, Les Épreuves de la vertu*, pr., pb. 1757 (*Dorval: Or, The Test of Virtue*, 1767); *Le Père de famille*, pb. 1758 (*The Father of the Family*, 1770; also known as *The Family Picture*, 1871); *Est'il bon? Est'il méchant?*, pr. 1781.

NONFICTION: *Pensées philosophiques*, 1746 (English translation, 1819; also known as *Philosophical Thoughts*, 1916); *Lettre sur les aveugles*, 1749 (*An Essay on Blindness*, 1750; also known as *Letter on the Blind*, 1916); *Notes et commentaires*, 1749; *Lettre sur les sourds et muets*, 1751 (*Letter on the Deaf and Dumb*, 1916); *Pensées sur l'interprétation de la nature*, 1754; *Entretiens sur "Le Fils naturel,"* 1757; *Discours sur la poésie dramatique*, 1758 (English translation of chapters 1-5 in *Dramatic Essays of the Neo-classical Age*, 1950); *Les Salons*, 1759-1781 (serial; 9 volumes), 1845, 1857 (book); *Éloge de Richardson*, 1762 (*An Eulogy of Richardson*, 1893); *De la suffisance de la religion naturelle*, 1770 (wr. 1747); *Entretien d'un père avec ses enfants*, 1773 (*Conversations Between Father and Children*, 1964); *Essai sur Sénèque*, 1778 (revised and expanded as *Essai sur les règnes de Claude et de Néron*, 1782); *Essais sur la peinture*, 1796 (wr. c. 1765); *Pensées détachées sur la peinture*, 1798; *Plan d'une université pour le gouvernement de Russie*, 1813-1814 (wr. c. 1775-1776); *Paradoxe sur le comédien*, 1830 (wr. 1773; *The Paradox of Acting*, 1883); *La Promenade du sceptique*, 1830 (wr. 1747); *Le Rêve de d'Alembert*, 1830 (wr. 1769; *D'Alembert's Dream*, 1927); *Diderot's Early Philosophical Works*, 1916 (includes *Letter on the Blind*, *Letter on the Deaf and Dumb*, *Philosophical Thoughts*); *Concerning the Education of a Prince*, 1941 (wr. 1758); *Correspondance*, 1955-1970 (16 volumes); *Œuvres philosophiques*, 1956; *Œuvres esthétiques*, 1959; *Œuvres politiques*, 1962.

TRANSLATIONS: *L'Histoire de Grèce*, 1743 (of Temple Stanyan's history); *Principes de la philosophie morale: Ou, Essai de M. S.*** sur le mérite et la vertu, avec réflexions*, 1745 (of the earl of Shaftesbury's essay); *Dictionnaire universel de médecine*, 1746-1748 (of Robert James's dictionary).

EDITED TEXTS: *Encyclopédie: Ou, Dictionnaire raisonné des sciences, des arts, et des métiers*, 1751-1772 (17 volumes of text, 11 volumes of plates; partial translation *Selected Essays from the Encyclopedy*, 1772; complete translation *Encyclopedia*, 1965).

MISCELLANEOUS: *Œuvres*, 1798 (15 volumes); *Œuvres complètes*, 1875-1877 (20 volumes); *Diderot, Interpreter of Nature: Selected Writings*, 1937 (includes short fiction); *Selected Writings*, 1966.

BIBLIOGRAPHY

Creech, James. *Diderot: Thresholds of Representation*. Columbus: Ohio State University Press, 1986. Presents a very clear explanation of Diderot's aesthetics that enables readers to appreciate the originality of Diderot's art criticism. Also shows how Diderot utilized these theories in representing social reality in his fiction.

Cronk, Nicholas. "Reading Expectations: The Narration of Hume in *Jacques le fataliste*." *Modern Language Review* 91 (April, 1996): 330-341. Argues that David Hume's ideas of causation and determinism influenced Diderot's philosophical voice and narrative structure. Asserts that Diderot exemplifies the compatibility of the apparently contradictory positions of "reader-freedom" and "reader-direction."

Curran, Andrew. *Sublime Disorder: Physical Monstrosity in Diderot's Universe*. Oxford, England: Voltaire Foundation, 2001. Examines Diderot's fascination with anatomical monstrosity and analyzes how he represents the physically grotesque in his novels and other works. Includes bibliography and index.

Fellows, Otis. *Diderot*. Rev. ed. Boston: Twayne, 1989. Offers an excellent short introduction to the works of Diderot. Describes very well Diderot's evolution as a writer despite the fact that censorship prevented him from publishing his major works during his lifetime. Includes a good annotated bibliography.

Furbank, Philip Nicholas. *Diderot: A Critical Biography*. New York: Alfred A. Knopf, 1992. Excellent biography of the philosopher-writer includes analysis of Diderot's works, including the novels *The Nun*, *Jacques the Fatalist and His Master*, and *Rameau's Nephew*.

Goodden, Angelica. *Diderot and the Body*. Oxford, England: Legenda, 2001. Examines Diderot's fiction and other works to describe his ideas about the relationship of the body to the mind, anatomy, ethical extensions of the body, sensuality, sexuality, and other concerns.

Loy, Robert J. *Diderot's Determined Fatalist*. New York: King's Crown Press, 1950. Focuses on *Jacques the Fatalist and His Master* but argues persuasively that Diderot's experimentation with various narrative techniques in this novel enables readers to understand his originality as a writer of other works of long fiction.

Rex, Walter E. *Diderot's Counterpoints: The Dynamics of Contrariety in His Major Works*. Oxford, England: Voltaire Foundation, 1998. Examines Diderot's works in relation to his era, including analysis of the novels *Rameau's Nephew* and *Jacques the Fatalist and His Master*. Includes bibliographical references and index.

Umdank, Jack, and Herbert Joseph, eds. *Diderot: Digression and Dispersion, a Bicentennial Tribute*. Lexington, Ky.: French Forum, 1984. Presents nineteen essays that cover Diderot's many activities and interests. In their diversity, the contributions mirror the editors' view that Diderot did not seek unity but rather regarded diversity as the rule of nature.

Werner, Stephen. *Socratic Satire: An Essay on Diderot and "Le Neveu de Rameau."* Birmingham, Ala.: Summa, 1987. Begins with an introduction that explores Diderot's view of satire, and subsequent chapters analyze different forms of satire as they apply to Diderot and to his conception of irony. Includes notes and substantial bibliography.

Wilson, Arthur M. *Diderot*. New York: Oxford University Press, 1972. Essential and well-researched biography includes insightful analyses of Diderot's major works. Defines Diderot's importance in the development of the French Enlightenment and the critical reception of his works since the eighteenth century. Includes notes and bibliography.

JOAN DIDION

Born: Sacramento, California; December 5, 1934
Also known as: Joan Reese

Principal long fiction

Run River, 1963
Play It as It Lays, 1970
A Book of Common Prayer, 1977
Democracy, 1984
The Last Thing He Wanted, 1996

Other literary forms

Joan Didion (DIHD-ee-uhn) is respected as a novelist, but she is even more highly acclaimed as an essayist. Her career as a writer was launched by a piece of nonfiction; in 1956, during Didion's senior year at the University of California at Berkeley, her article on the San Francisco architect William Wilson Wurster won *Vogue*'s Prix de Paris contest for young writers, and she was awarded a job with that magazine. Although she resigned her position at *Vogue* in 1963 to devote more time to her fiction, she continued as a film critic for the magazine and began publishing regularly in the *Saturday Evening Post*. She also wrote articles for periodicals such as *The American Scholar*, *The New York Times Magazine*, *National Review*, *Esquire*, *New West*, and *The New York Review of Books*. Didion also collaborated with her husband, John Gregory Dunne, on several screenplays.

Didion achieved national recognition with her first collection of essays, *Slouching Towards Bethlehem* (1968); her second collection, *The White Album* (1979), was a best seller. Her books *Salvador* (1983) and *Miami* (1987) are overtly political and aroused considerable controversy. *After Henry* (1992), her third essay collection, largely concerns California subjects. This return to her original source of topics was well received by many critics. *Political Fictions* (2001) deals with, among other things, the effect of big money on American politics and the lack of interest in voting among most Americans as well as with censorship and "compassionate conservatism." Dedicated to her husband, John Gregory Dunne, and to the editor of *The New York Review of Books* (Robert Silvers), who, in 1988, asked her to cover the American national elections that year, the book argues that big money has helped make political party differences irrelevant to the governing of the nation.

Where I Was From (2003) is a collection of essays about California, tracing the state's history as well as Didion's family's history as generations of her ancestors settled in and flourished in California until the end of the twentieth century, when dislocations in the aircraft industry radically changed large segments of the population. In *Fixed Ideas: America Since 9-11* (2003), Didion argues that there is a gap between the American government and the American people, and that since the terrorist attacks on New York and Washington, D.C., of September 11, 2001, the United States has become an imperial nation unilaterally trying to enforce its will on the rest of the world.

In the autobiographical book *The Year of Magical Thinking* (2005), Didion addresses the death of her husband and discusses her life in the year after his death. Didion adapted the book into a one-woman show that opened on Broadway in 2007 starring Vanessa Redgrave. The book was accepted for publication shortly before Didion's thirty-nine-year-old daughter, Quintana Roo, died after a long illness. Although the book includes extensive discussion of the daughter's illness, Didion refused to revise it to include her daughter's death. The play, however, actually treats about one and one-half years of Didion's life and does include the death of her daughter.

Achievements

Joan Didion's achievements are somewhat paradoxical. Despite her claims that she speaks only for herself, she became a spokeswoman for the anxiety-ridden generation of the late 1960's and early 1970's; as surely as F. Scott Fitzgerald became the chronicler of the Jazz Age, she became the chronicler of a generation living, in her terms, "close to the edge." Didion developed a reputation for cool, detached observation and for a syncopated but elegant style. Poet James Dickey called her "the finest woman prose stylist writing in English today," and even some who dismiss her as intellectually shallow respect her craftsmanship.

Didion's accomplishments were formally recognized in 1996 when she was awarded the Edward MacDowell Medal for outstanding contributions to the arts. Previous recipients have included Robert Frost, Lillian Hellman, and Mary McCarthy. In 1999 she was given a Columbia Journalism Award by Columbia University's Graduate School of Journalism. In 2005, *The Year of Magical Thinking* won the National Book Award for nonfiction, and Didion received the 2006 Hubert Howe Bancroft Award, given for "significant achievements in support of historical research and scholarship." In 2007, she won the Evelyn F. Burkey Award from the Writer's Guild of America, East, an honor given in recognition of writers whose "contributions have brought honor and dignity to writers everywhere." In the same year she won the National Book Foundation Medal for Distinguished Contribution to American Letters in recognition of her achievements as a novelist and essayist.

Biography

Joan Didion was born to Frank Reese and Eduene Jerrett Didion on December 5, 1934, in Sacramento, California. Both the date and the place are significant. Though Didion had just turned seven when the Japanese attacked Pearl Harbor, she is not, strictly speaking, a child of the post-World War II generation. This fact might explain some of her detachment from the 1960's and some of the nostalgia she evidently feels even when she is pointing out the shortcomings of the more traditional and more orderly values of prewar America.

Didion's place of birth is even more important. Didion is a child of the West—not the West of Los Angeles, but of the more pastoral Sacramento Valley. The land on which Didion lived had been in her family for five generations, and as a child, she was expected to absorb the myth that America was a new Eden. In *Slouching Towards Bethlehem*, Didion reports that her Episcopal Sunday school teacher used to ask the children, "In what ways does the Holy Land resemble the Sacramento Valley?" Didion explores—and largely explodes—the myth of the Sacramento Valley as Eden in her first novel, *Run River*. Eden, however, is not lost—or rejected—without some sense of regret, and Didion's novel reflects nostalgia for the lost paradise and the passing of innocence.

Didion's intellectual break from a more traditional world may have begun in high school, when she discovered literature, and it must have been accelerated by her studies at the University of California at Berkeley, where she majored in literature; read the works of Ernest Hemingway, Joseph Conrad, Henry James, and Albert Camus; moved out of her sorority house; and did not, as she points out with some regret, make Phi Beta Kappa. She did, however, win first prize in *Vogue*'s Prix de Paris contest. Given as an award the choice of a trip to Paris or a job on the magazine, Didion chose the more practical option and moved to New York.

At *Vogue*, Didion learned to write for the general public, and she began writing for several other magazines as well. She also seriously began writing fiction, and *Run River* was published in 1963. Her time in New York, then, was important for her development as a writer, and, judging from her essay "Good-bye to All That," she enjoyed her first few years there. Unfortunately, as the essay continues, she began to believe that "it is distinctly possible to stay too long at the fair." Disenchantment turned to depression. In January, 1964, in lieu of seeing a psychiatrist, Didion married John Gregory Dunne, also a writer, and the couple moved to Los Angeles. They adopted a daughter, Quintana Roo, in 1966.

In Los Angeles, Didion's writing continued to go well—she published *Slouching Towards Bethlehem* in 1968, and she and Dunne wrote the screenplay for *The Panic in Needle Park* (1971)—but for some time she continued to suffer from the depression and sense of disorientation she describes in *The White Album*. Her marital problems were publicized in her own essays and in Dunne's. In the 1970's, however, both her marriage and her emotional state improved, and her literary success continued to grow: *Play It as It Lays*, *The White Album*, and *A Book of Common Prayer* were all best sellers. Financial success also came, not so much from the books as from Didion and Dunne's collaborations on screenplays, many of which were never filmed. In addition to *The Panic in Needle Park* and the film adaptation of Dunne's novel *True Confessions*, the couple worked on the script for the 1976 version of *A Star Is Born*. According to Dunne, that motion picture "made us a fortune." Didion and Dunne also cowrote scripts for cable television films. Their work on the theatrical release *Up Close and Personal* (1996) was highly publicized and became the subject of Dunne's book *Monster: Living off the Big Screen* (1997), a less-than-fond look at the world of filmmaking.

Joan Didion. (Quintana Roo Dunne)

Didion's journalism has also remained an important part of her career. She reported on the 1988 and 1992 U.S. presidential campaigns, a detail of her life that resurfaces in her novel *The Last Thing He Wanted*; the novel's protagonist, Elena McMahon, begins the story as a reporter for *The Washington Post* who is covering the 1984 presidential election. Praise for Didion's journalism was particularly effusive after she published "Trouble in Lakewood" in *The New Yorker* in July, 1993; the story described the Los Angeles suburb's many social problems after the drastic contraction of the defense industry in Southern California.

Didion and Dunne continued to live in the Los Angeles area until 1988, when they returned to Manhattan to be closer to their business interests and friends. Nevertheless, Didion continued to write about California while managing to avoid being labeled a regional writer. Despite the atmosphere of angst and dread that pervades much of Didion's writing, Dunne wrote in the June, 1990, issue of *Esquire* magazine that his and his wife's epitaph could well read, "They had a good time."

On December 30, 2003, John Gregory Dunne died. Didion claimed to have finished writing *The Year of Magical Thinking* exactly one year and one day after his death. On August 26, 2005, at age 39, Quintana Roo died.

Analysis

Almost all of Joan Didion's works are concerned with similar themes, and there is an interesting complementary relationship between her essays and her novels. Her essays generally seem intended to force the reader to strip away illusions about contemporary life and accept realities, even if they are bleak. The novels are generally explorations of characters crippled by illusions. To some extent, in each novel, the heroine is disabused of her illusions. The fragile hope that each novel holds out, however, is offered not in terms of this disillusionment but in terms of new illusions and almost meaningless gestures. Each novel ends with the heroine learning to care for others—for a husband, for a lover, for children, for friends—and yet this caring is generally based on illusion and seems doomed to failure. Didion's final implication, then, seems to be that people need to strip away all illusions, except those that help them to care for others. Such illusions—even though they are doomed to lead to failure—are sacred. These sacred illusions might be fictional, as stories are fictional, but, as Didion has said, "We tell ourselves stories in order to live . . . or at least we do for a while."

Run River

Although Didion's first novel, *Run River*, is not autobiographical, it does explore the myth she absorbed in her childhood, the myth of America as the new Eden, the new Promised Land. This myth was brought to the New World by the earliest settlers of Virginia and Massachusetts, but it took special form with the westward expansion. Lily Knight, the heroine of *Run River*, expresses her faith directly: "She believed that it was America's mission to make manifest to the world the wishes of an Episcopal God, [and] that her father would one day be Governor of California." The novel can be quickly summarized. It begins—and finally ends—on the night that Everett McClellan, Lily's husband, kills Ryder Channing, Lily's lover, and then himself. The novel backtracks to trace the lives of the main characters and returns full circle to the murder and suicide. Along the way, it suggests that Lily, Everett, and Everett's sister Martha have been shattered because of a misplaced faith in traditional, romantic notions about their lives and about their home, the Sacramento Valley.

Lily, after she admits to herself that she probably will not be offered the lead role in the film version of *Gone with the Wind*, accepts a traditional, passive woman's role. After passively "accepting" Everett twenty-seven times, she agrees to marry him: "It seemed as inescapable as the ripening of the pears, as fated as the exile from Eden." Unfortunately, she finds the role of river matron less than satisfactory, and she continues to accept men—first Joe Templeton and later Ryder Channing—for little more reason than that they desire her. Through it all, Lily fails to come to terms with who she is and what she really wants.

The traditional dream of ranch and family no longer works for Everett, either. Ironically, he seems happy only when he runs away from the ranch, his wife, and his sister to join the army during World War II. When his father dies, however, he feels bound by duty to return to the ranch, to try to make it work, and to take care of his wife and sister. It does not work; his wife is unfaithful, his sister is destroyed by the "lack of honor" in the world, and his son obviously intends to abandon the homestead.

Martha, Everett's sister, is perhaps the most utterly destroyed character in the novel. She cannot act out her incestuous feelings for her brother, and the man she does accept as a lover, Ryder Channing, is no gentleman. After he is married to another woman and their affair is over, he almost brutally "seduces" her again. Martha is forced to admit that she is not a "lady"—their affair had not been a great romantic passion, but what advice columnist Ann Landers might describe as "chemistry." Stripped of her illusions, she cannot live. Her brother cannot protect her—a fact that will make him, a romantic gallant, feel even more guilty—and she kills herself.

All of the romantic illusions of the traditional world come crashing down when Everett kills Ryder Channing and then himself. It could be argued that the traditional world has not failed these characters; rather, they have failed it. After all, a good river matron should not have an affair while her husband is serving his country, Everett should have been stronger, and Martha should have had more self-respect than to take up with a man such as Ryder. Such an argument, however, would simply ignore too much of the characters' background. Lily's father, Walter Knight, was not so shining as Lily had thought. He does not become governor of California. He is a near alcoholic, and he carries on an adulterous relationship with Rita Blanchard, another "good spinster" who proves no better and no worse than Martha. Walter is no more a rancher than Everett; his Mexican foreman Gomez is the one who keeps the place going. Finally, he can no more protect his Rita than Everett can protect Martha; both he and Rita drown when he accidentally drives into the Sacramento River.

The novel, then, shows the myth of the Sacramento Valley as a second Eden to be a second-generation failure. The book might seem to imply that it is World War II that renders this idyllic world "gone with the wind," but it is doubtful that Didion believes that things were really better in the old days. Her vision of the settling of the West seems centered on the Donner-Reed party; her great-great-great-grandmother had been part of that party originally, but she left it before the group was stranded by winter snows and the members were forced to eat their own dead to survive. In her essay "On Morality," Didion equates morality with not leaving the dead to the coyotes, and she writes of the Donner-Reed party: "We were taught instead that they had somewhere abdicated their responsibilities, somehow breached their primal loyalties or they would not have found themselves helpless in the mountain winter . . . would not have failed." At the end of *Run River*, all three major characters have failed to live up to their primal loyalties of wife to husband, husband to wife, brother to sister, sister to sister-in-law. They have been "immoral," not because of their sexual misconduct, but because they have failed to take care of one another.

There is, perhaps, some hope for Lily at the end. She has survived, not by virtue but by luck, and she may have learned. Looking at Everett's body, she finally—perhaps for the first time—tries to talk to him. She recalls the good times and realizes the importance of their love: "She hoped that . . . he would rise thinking of her, *we were each other, we were each other, not that it mattered much in the long run but what else mattered as much*." "Not that it mattered much" is vintage Didion, but the "what else mattered as much" seems heartfelt. The hope that lovers will rise thinking of each other "through all eternity" has the ring of romantic illusion, but at this point, such a hope constitutes the only possible relationship left for Lily and Everett. At the end of the novel, she is left thinking about what she will say to her children. To sustain them, she will probably be compelled to sustain an illusion about the man she has come to love too late: "She did not know what she could tell anyone except that he had been a good man. She was not certain that he had been but it was what she would have wished for him, if they gave her one wish."

The ease with which *Run River* can be explained as an explosion of traditional American myths probably suggests why the novel is generally considered Didion's most modest achievement. So many people have exploded traditional American myths since 1963 that it does not seem necessary to reread *Run River* to see it done again. In *Play It as It Lays*, however, Didion does something few writers have done as well as she; she turns the tables and explodes the myths and illusions of the contemporary sensibility.

Play It as It Lays

Perhaps no setting could be more appropriate for an illusion-hunter than Los Angeles. In *Play It as It Lays*, Didion places her heroine Maria (pronounced "Mar-eye-ah," like the west wind in the musical *Paint Your Wagon*) squarely in the fast lane of life in Southern California. The novel opens with Maria in a psychiatric ward. She has been placed there, presumably, for her failure to attempt to stop a friend from committing suicide in her presence. As the novel unfolds (like *Run River*) backward into the past, however, the reader comes to realize that if Maria has become unhinged, it is probably a result of the cumulative effect of her abortion, her divorce, and the miscellaneous acts of casual sex, drugs, and other perversities one might expect in a novel about Hollywood.

Didion does not condemn the fast lane from a traditional moral perspective; that would have been too easy, and probably not very convincing or interesting. Besides, Didion's target is not simply the sexual mores of contemporary culture. Rather, she explores the popular "philosophy" or worldview that so many have accepted since the collapse of the traditional morality—a "philosophy" that might be called sloppy existentialism, extreme relativism, or simply nihilism. Maria states the key tenet of this philosophy on the second page of the novel: "NOTHING APPLIES."

Maria herself was not reared with the traditional American values. Instead of the Puritan work ethic ("God helps those who help themselves"), she was taught the gambler's code: "My father advised me that life itself was a crap game." That view was infused with a faith in good luck: "I was raised to believe that what came in on the next roll would always be better than what went on the last." For a long time, Maria was content to wait for the rolls, to go with the flow, and to "play it as it lays." Unfortunately, Maria's luck runs out. The bad roll is an unwanted pregnancy. She thinks, but is not sure, that Carter, her husband, is not the father. He demands that she have an abortion and threatens to take away Kate, their brain-damaged daughter, if she refuses. Maria acquiesces, and her mental deterioration begins.

If Maria could completely accept the mores of her set, she would have no problem; for them, neither abortion nor divorce is anything to lose one's composure over. Maria, however, does cling to one traditional dream: She wants a family. She fantasizes about living a simple life with Kate and some man—in almost identical fantasies, the man is either Ivan or Les, two of her steadier lovers. Abortion—the termination of another possible child—is almost more than Maria can contemplate, yet she undergoes the procedure.

Maria's reaction to the abortion is not philosophical, moral, or religious; it is emotional, physical, and psychological. She cries; she hemorrhages; she reaches a point where she cannot easily use plumbing because she imagines pipes clogged with chopped-up pieces of flesh.

Didion does not attempt to make an abstract moral issue out of abortion. Maria's reaction is almost primitive, in the sense of being immediate and unreflecting. In a real sense, however, to return to Didion's essay "On Morality," abortion is a denial of the most basic social responsibility, that of mother to child (it is hard here not to recall Didion's own traumatic miscarriage and her devotion to her adopted daughter). In *Play It as It Lays*, even more emphatically than in *Run River*, characters fail to fulfill their primal social responsibilities. Carter, Les (even Les's wife), Maria's friends Helene and BZ, and a number of others all say that they are "seriously worried" about Maria as she slips more and more into self-destructive behavior; they say that they care, but none of them can reach her, none of them can take care of her. Some of their protestations are hard to take seriously; Carter humiliates Maria on a number of occasions, and Helene and BZ use her—while she is drunk and only half-conscious—for obscure and unpleasant sexual purposes.

Most of these characters profess not to be concerned with the sexual conduct of their spouses. When Helene, BZ's wife, drifts into an affair with Carter, BZ asks Maria if she cares. For a time, Maria tries to insist that she does care, but as the novel draws to a conclusion, BZ forces her more and more to a nihilistic position: "'Tell me what matters,' BZ said. 'Nothing,' Maria said." The "nothing" here is Ernest Hemingway's "nada," and at the end of the novel, BZ, like Hemingway, kills himself. BZ, however, does not use a gun. He goes out with a bottle of vodka and a grain and a half of Seconal. When Helene and Carter force their way into the room, BZ is dead and Maria is asleep next to him, holding his hand.

On the last page of the novel, Maria, from the psychiatric ward, affirms BZ's nihilism, if not his suicide: "I know what 'nothing' means, and keep on playing. Why, BZ would say. Why not, I say." That, however, is not all there is to it. Maria has already made it clear that she is playing for Kate. She wants to take Kate away from the hospital; she wants them to have a home by the sea where they can live a simple life. Given Kate's condition—to say nothing of Maria's—this future does not sound very likely. Despite her acceptance of nihilism, Maria holds on to one last romantic notion. Perhaps she realizes how illusory her hope is, but, like Lily's hope that Everett will rise thinking of her, the illusion and the hope are necessary. They keep her in the game and away from the Seconal.

A Book of Common Prayer

Run River and *Play It as It Lays* demonstrate the failures both of traditional American myths and of more current nihilistic lifestyles. Lily Knight McClellan and Maria Wyeth both survive, but both are sustained by hopes that seem largely based on illusion. In Didion's third novel, *A Book of Common Prayer*, the reader is told on the first page that the protagonist, Charlotte Douglas, does not survive. The narrator, however, comments that "she died, hopeful." Whether Charlotte's hope is also illusory is a central question of the novel.

It is the question that the narrator, Grace Strasser-

Mendana, née Tabor, is trying to answer throughout the novel. Grace, originally from the United States, "married into one of the three or four solvent families in Boca Grande," the small Central American republic in which Charlotte Douglas is finally killed (or murdered; as Grace says, neither word seems to work). The death of Grace's husband has left her "in putative control of fifty-nine-point-eight percent of the arable land and about the same percentage of the decision-making process in La Republica." From this position of power, Grace observes the political scheming of her family. She also watches Charlotte walk barefoot into the scene and become caught up in it. Grace leaves the country before Charlotte dies, and the novel is her attempt to understand Charlotte. As she says, "Call it my witness to Charlotte Douglas."

At the very beginning of her witness, Grace comments that Charlotte "dreamed her life," and much of what Grace says makes Charlotte seem a woman even more given to illusion than is Lily Knight McClellan or Maria Wyeth. Grace insists that Charlotte was the "usual child of comfortable family in the temperate zone." She had been supplied with all the material benefits and easy optimism of an affluent American. As a child, she was given a carved Austrian angel that listened to her bedside prayers: "In these prayers the child Charlotte routinely asked that 'it' turn out all right, 'it' being unspecified and all-inclusive, and she had been an adult for some years before the possibility occurred to her that 'it' might not."

Like Maria, Charlotte loses some of the optimism; her luck runs out. The more traditional lifestyle fails her. Her first husband, Warren Bogart (perhaps the name is meant to be halfway between Warren Beatty and Humphrey Bogart), had been "raised to believe not in 'hard work' or 'self reliance' but in the infinite power of the personal appeal." He is also sadistic, sexually perverse, and alcoholic. Charlotte is not perfect, either; one Easter, while their child Marin is still a baby, she gets drunk and sleeps with a man she does not even like (she later conveniently forgets the episode). Warren hits her, and she finally walks away from the marriage.

Her second marriage is not unlike Maria's life in the fast lane, except that the game is no longer motion pictures but radical politics. Her husband is not a director but a radical-chic lawyer who flies from one center of revolution to another. Leonard does seem to care for Charlotte genuinely, but there are complications. Marin, Charlotte's child by Warren, turns revolutionary; she and her friends hijack a jetliner, burn it in the desert, and join the underground.

Charlotte's main illusion, like Maria's, is centered on her daughter. She later tells Grace that she and Marin were "inseparable" (a term she also uses to describe her relationship with Warren), and she spins out fantastic accounts of their visit to the Tivoli Gardens. As might be expected, the revolutionary Marin claims to have little use for her bourgeois mother.

After a disastrous reunion with Warren and after the birth and almost immediate death of her child by Leonard, Charlotte drifts to Boca Grande, where she meets Grace. At first, Charlotte gives Grace every reason to think that she is dreaming her life; for quite a while, she goes to the airport every day on the offhand chance that Marin will pass through Central America; she drifts aimlessly into sexual relations with Victor, Grace's brother-in-law, and then with Gerardo, Grace's son; she seems not to notice the growing signs of revolution; she refuses the attempts of Gerardo, Leonard, and Grace to persuade her to leave; finally, the revolution begins, and she is arrested and killed. Her body is dumped on the lawn of the American embassy.

All this does seem to add up to a life of dreams and illusions, yet throughout the novel, Charlotte proves herself to be capable of very practical behavior. She kills a chicken with her bare hands, she skins an iguana for stew, she performs an emergency tracheotomy with a penknife, and she inoculates people against an epidemic of cholera for thirty-four hours without a break. Although Charlotte often seems not to notice what is going on around her, she corrects people who claim to know what is happening; she reminds a reporter that Marin's comrade killed himself in Arizona, not Mexico, and she later corrects Gerardo on a technical point: "'Carmen wasn't using an M-3.' Charlotte said. She leaned forward slightly and her face was entirely grave. 'Antonio was. Carmen was using an M-16.'"

If Charlotte is not as out of touch as she seems, why then does she stay in Boca Grande and risk her life? In her last conversation with Leonard, she says very simply, "I walked away from places all my life and I'm not going to walk away from here." In another context, one could imagine John Wayne speaking those lines. In this context, however, there is no sense of the heroic. For a moment, Leonard seems to misunderstand this, and he warns her, "You don't get any real points for staying here, Charlotte." Charlotte understands perfectly: "'I can't seem to tell what you do get the real points for,' Charlotte said. 'So I guess I'll stick around for a while.'" Didion does not glorify Charlotte's decision to stay; it is not a self-defining existential act. She simply returns to her work at a birth control clinic (an ironic job for a woman whose passport lists her occupation as *"madre"*). Her work is not particularly meaningful, since Charlotte routinely advises women to use the diaphragm while the clinic stocks only intrauterine devices (IUDs). In any event, no clients come on Charlotte's last day of work, the last day of her life. In deciding to stay, Charlotte maintains something of her integrity, what Didion would call "character," but Didion allows the reader no illusions about the act; it is the integrity of a card player playing out a losing hand.

Charlotte's integrity can be appreciated only in comparison to the values of the other characters, particularly Grace. Even though Grace has been trying to understand Charlotte throughout the novel, she is as much a victim of delusion as Charlotte is. For some time, Grace has realized the difficulty in understanding things, in trying to get the story straight. She had abandoned her first discipline before the beginning of the novel: "I am an anthropologist who lost faith in her own method, who stopped believing that observable activity defined anthros." She turned to biochemistry, but that, too, failed: "Give me the molecular structure of the protein which defined Charlotte Douglas." When Leonard reveals to her that her husband Edgar had been involved with the guerrillas himself, Grace is finally forced to realize that her life, as much as Charlotte's, has been one of delusion.

Grace's statement "We all remember what we need to remember" is one of the lessons of the novel; all people prefer to believe their own versions of the stories in which they are trapped; all people accept delusions. Grace finally realizes that "I am more like Charlotte Douglas than I thought I was." Perhaps Charlotte's death was something of a meaningless gesture, but beside her coffin, Grace can only make a small meaningless gesture of love; she places a T-shirt painted like an American flag on the casket. By way of comment, she borrows a phrase from Charlotte and Leonard: "There were no real points in that either."

Neither Grace nor Charlotte—perhaps none of Didion's characters in any of her novels—scores any real points in the end. They try to take care of one another, but they fail. Grace and Leonard try to take care of Charlotte, but they fail. Charlotte would like to take care of Marin, but she cannot. Warren wants Charlotte to take care of him, but it does not work. As cynical as Warren is, he may have the final judgment in the novel: "It doesn't matter whether you take care of somebody or somebody takes care of you. . . . It's all the same in the end. It's all the same." Warren dies alone; Charlotte dies alone. Grace will die—as she says—very soon, and she will be alone. It is all the same in the end. At least Charlotte does to some degree shape her own life toward the end. The night she was arrested, she was, Grace imagines, "walking very deliberately."

Democracy

The protagonist of Didion's fourth novel, *Democracy*, is Inez Christian Victor, the daughter of a prominent Honolulu family and the wife of a liberal U.S. senator from California who narrowly lost the Democratic nomination for president in 1972. The love of her life, however, is a shadowy soldier of fortune named Jack Lovett. She follows him to Southeast Asia on the eve of the fall of Vietnam (to retrieve her daughter—a heroin addict who has drifted to Saigon because she hears that employment opportunities are good there) and sees him drown in a hotel pool in Jakarta. She brings the body back to Hawaii to be buried under a jacaranda tree at Schofield Barracks and returns to Kuala Lumpur to work with refugees.

In *Democracy*, one finds evidence of two of Didion's most prominent characteristics as a writer—her acute sense of place and her fascination with the American West. While these twin aspects of her muse have always been evident in her writings about California, she has occasionally cast her glance farther westward to Hawaii. In *Slouching Towards Bethlehem*, she states, "I sat as a child on California beaches and imagined that I saw Hawaii, a certain shimmer in the sunset, a barely perceptible irregularity glimpsed intermittently through squinted eyes." In a column written more than a decade later for *New West* magazine, she revealed that she kept a clock set at Honolulu time in her bedroom in Los Angeles.

When Didion, however, tried to write a novel about feudal Hawaii (originally titled "Pacific Distances"), she produced a book that is only marginally about that subject. In *Democracy*, Hawaii is less important as a society in transition than as a way station between the mainland and America's ultimate western frontier, Southeast Asia. (In *Slouching Towards Bethlehem*, she speaks of sailors who got drunk in Honolulu because "they were no longer in Des Moines and not yet in Da Nang.") As Walt Whitman proclaimed more than a century earlier in his poem "Passage to India" (1871), the roundness of the earth leads not to some apocalyptic West but back east whence we came. America's Manifest Destiny, however, has not even produced a mystical passage to India, but rather helicopters lifting off the roof of the American embassy in Saigon during the final days of the only war the United States has ever lost.

In this imagistic, elliptical novel, much is left to conjecture. More than in any of her previous works, Didion helps fuel this conjecture through an almost compulsive literary allusiveness. Certainly the most significant allusion is to Henry Adams, who in 1880 published a novel titled *Democracy*. Although in her review of Didion's novel Mary McCarthy made nothing of the novels having the same name, Thomas R. Edwards saw both Didion and Adams as displaced aristocrats who with "irony and subtlety confront a chaotic new reality that shatters the orderings of simpler, older ways," and other critics have seen Adams's view of history as informing Didion's in several of her works, especially *Democracy*.

From a purely technical standpoint, the most controversial and problematic aspect of *Democracy* is its point of view. Departing from the more conventional narrative techniques of her earlier novels, Didion inserts herself into *Democracy* and claims to have been acquainted personally with her characters. Although this device may appear to make Didion's tale a postmodernist novel about novel writing, it also places her in the decidedly premodernist company of George Eliot and William Makepeace Thackeray, both of whom inserted themselves into their fiction.

By revealing her problems in writing this book and by treating her characters as if they are as real as the figures in her journalism, Didion may be trying to collapse the distinction between fiction and nonfiction narrative. If the New Journalism brings the techniques of fiction to the writing of fact, this novel brings the illusion of fact to the writing of fiction. Such a device is for *Democracy* what the title *A Book of Common Prayer* is for Didion's earlier novel—a reason for telling the story.

The Last Thing He Wanted

In *The Last Thing He Wanted*, Didion's technique of writing fiction as though it were fact becomes much more assured. She creates a journalist narrator who claims not only to be the novel's author but also to have written about one of the story's characters for *The New York Times Magazine*, the type of high-profile periodical in which readers would expect to find an article by the real Joan Didion. In contrast to *Democracy*, however, Didion does not identify herself as the narrator. "For the record," she writes, "this is me talking. You know me, or you think you do. The not quite omniscient author." Readers may be tempted to think that the "me" refers to Didion herself, but the novel's characters are clearly fictional, and the narrator belongs to the same created world as the characters. Instead, the "me" seems to refer more to the idea of the narrator as "not quite omniscient author." Unlike true omniscient authors, who know everything that goes on in their stories, this narrator-author has a limited view. She must piece together the story of Elena McMahon, the novel's heroine, from transcripts of tape recordings, news articles, diplomatic reports, and interviews with not-always-truthful sources.

Out of these fragments the narrator-author constructs a story that explains Elena's mysterious death. After Elena walks away from her job covering the 1984 presidential campaign for *The Washington Post*, her seriously ill father, who is an arranger of ambiguous "deals," asks her to fly to the Caribbean to deliver something for him. The plane does not land exactly where Elena expects it to, and the something turns out to be illegal arms for the Contras, a counterrevolutionary group that opposed the Sandinista government of Nicaragua in the 1980's. Once Elena reads in a U.S. paper that her father has suddenly died, she (along with the reader) realizes that her life is in extraordinary danger. Ultimately, she is framed for an assassination attempt on Treat Morrison, a U.S. operative with whom Elena has a fleeting romance. The attempt ends with Elena shot dead and Morrison gravely wounded. The novel itself ends two brief chapters later, as the narrator-author tries to reshape the story so that it ends with Elena and Morrison still together, a form the story's narrator-author finds more pleasing than the "actual" one.

Perhaps Didion's greatest achievement in this novel is the complexity that she wrings out of its lean, deceptively easy-to-read prose. Although several critics in the 1990's noted that her fiction was becoming ever more spare and her nonfiction was growing in length and density, *The Last Thing He Wanted* merges both characteristics. The novel's language makes it seem simple on its surface, but keeping track of the story requires the reader to maneuver through murky, difficult-to-follow conspiracies involving rival government factions, just as did the actual 1980's news coverage of alleged (and illegal) U.S. government support of the Contras. Although not all critics agreed that the novel broke new ground for Didion, it received mostly positive reviews—tribute to Didion's position as one of the most highly regarded writers of her generation.

James Reynolds Kinzey; Kelly Fuller
Updated by Richard Tuerk

OTHER MAJOR WORKS

SHORT FICTION: *Telling Stories*, 1978.

SCREENPLAYS: *The Panic in Needle Park*, 1971 (with John Gregory Dunne); *Play It as It Lays*, 1972 (with Dunne); *A Star Is Born*, 1976 (with Dunne and Frank Pierson); *True Confessions*, 1981 (with Dunne); *Up Close and Personal*, 1996 (with Dunne).

TELEPLAYS: *Hills Like White Elephants*, 1990 (with John Gregory Dunne); *Broken Trust*, 1995 (with Dunne).

NONFICTION: *Slouching Towards Bethlehem*, 1968; *The White Album*, 1979; *Salvador*, 1983; *Joan Didion: Essays and Conversations*, 1984 (Ellen G. Friedman, editor); *Miami*, 1987; *After Henry*, 1992 (also known as *Sentimental Journeys*, 1993); *Political Fictions*, 2001; *Fixed Ideas: America Since 9-11*, 2003; *Where I Was From*, 2003; *Vintage Didion*, 2004; *The Year of Magical Thinking*, 2005; *We Tell Ourselves Stories in Order to Live: Collected Nonfiction*, 2006.

BIBLIOGRAPHY

Felton, Sharon, ed. *The Critical Response to Joan Didion*. Westport, Conn.: Greenwood Press, 1994. Collection of reviews and scholarly essays discusses Didion's novels through *Democracy* as well as several of her major works of nonfiction. Includes chronology, bibliography, and indexes.

Hall, Linda. "The Writer Who Came in from the Cold." *New York* 29 (September, 1996): 28-33, 57. Published shortly after the release of *The Last Thing He Wanted*, this profile is particularly informative concerning Didion's early career and the influence of her former mentor Noel Parmentel, a political essayist and journalist.

Hanley, Lynne. *Writing War: Fiction, Gender, and Memory*. Amherst: University of Massachusetts Press, 1991. Two chapters of this elegantly written study discuss Didion's depictions of war in *A Book of Common Prayer*, *El Salvador*, and *Democracy*.

Henderson, Katherine Usher. *Joan Didion*. New York: Ungar, 1981. Brief introductory study, appropriate for a general audience, provides information on Didion's life and work up through *The White Album*.

Parrish, Tim. "After Henry Adams: Rewriting History in Joan Didion's *Democracy*." *Critique* 47 (Winter, 2006): 167-184. Discusses the influence of Henry Adams's view of American history on Didion, especially as it relates to the novel *Democracy*.

Spencer, Nicholas. "Territoriality and the Lost Dimension: Joan Didion and Don DeLillo." In *After Utopia: The Rise of Critical Space in Twentieth-Century American Fiction*. Lincoln: University of Nebraska Press, 2006. Addresses the relationship between power and landscape in Didion's novels.

Stout, Janis P. *Strategies of Reticence: Silence and Meaning in the Works of Jane Austen, Willa Cather, Katherine Anne Porter, and Joan Didion*. Charlottesville: University Press of Virginia, 1990. Chapter 5 treats at length Didion's use of silence in her first four novels.

Winchell, Mark Royden. *Joan Didion*. Rev. ed. Boston: Twayne, 1989. Updated version of the first book-length study of Didion's work follows its subject's career up through *Miami*. Written for a scholarly audience but accessible to the general reader.

ANNIE DILLARD

Born: Pittsburgh, Pennsylvania; April 30, 1945
Also known as: Annie Doak

Principal long fiction

The Living, 1992
The Maytrees, 2007

Other literary forms

Annie Dillard has received critical acclaim for her ability to write in many forms. Highly regarded as a writer of nonfiction, memoirs, essays, and philosophy, she has made many contributions to such periodicals as *The Atlantic Monthly*, *American Scholar*, *Harper's*, *Esquire*, *The Yale Review*, and *The New York Times Magazine*. Her first publication, *Tickets for a Prayer Wheel* (1974), is a book of poems about her search for God. Her 1974 nonfiction book *Pilgrim at Tinker Creek*, which earned a 1975 Pulitzer Prize for general nonfiction, remains the author's most popular book. Also in nonfiction, *Holy the Firm* (1977), *Living by Fiction* (1982), and *Encounters with Chinese Writers* (1984) received high literary praise, while her memoir *An American Childhood* (1987) received similar acclaim.

Achievements

Annie Dillard has earned most of her many prestigious nonfiction awards for *Pilgrim at Tinker Creek*. In addition to a Pulitzer Prize, she was honored with the Washington State Governor's Award for Literature (1977), and she received grants from the National Endowment for the Arts in 1982. She was honored with the Appalachian Gold Medallion from the University of Charleston and the St. Botolph's Club Foundation Award, both in 1989. In 1993, she received the History Maker Award from the Historical Society of Western Pennsylvania and the Connecticut Governor's Arts Award, the Campion Medal from *America* magazine, and the Milton Prize the following year. In 1997, she was inducted into the Connecticut Women's Hall of Fame. She also received an Academy Award in Literature from the American Academy of Arts and Letters in 1998 and became a fellow of that academy in 1999. Dillard also has honorary degrees from Boston College (1986), Connecticut College (1993), and the University of Hartford (1993).

Biography

Annie Dillard, born Annie Doak in 1945, is the oldest of three daughters and was raised in a wealthy Pittsburgh, Pennsylvania, family. Her mother, Pam Lambert Doak, and father, Frank Doak, raised her in the Presbyterian faith, encouraged her to pursue a wide range of interests, and pushed her especially to explore the natural world. Her unique childhood is described at length in her 1987 memoir *An American Childhood.* During high school the future author rebelled against her parents' wealth and had a turbulent time as a student. At this point, she developed an interest in poetry and took particular interest in the work of Ralph Waldo Emerson and Henry David Thoreau.

After studying English, theology, and creative writing, Dillard received a B.A. in 1967 and an M.A. in 1968 from Hollins College near Roanoke, Virginia. Her master's thesis, which focused on Thoreau's *Walden* (1845), directly influenced her work on the hugely popular *Pilgrim at Tinker Creek.* After graduation, Dillard began writing in earnest and published several poems. In 1971, after an exceptionally bad bout of pneumonia that almost took her life, she moved to live near Tinker Creek in Virginia's Roanoke Valley, the setting for *Pilgrim at Tinker Creek*. She spent a year living alone, closely observing both the beauty and the violence of the changing seasons. Classified in some realms as a theology book, *Pilgrim at Tinker Creek* incorporates aspects of Buddhism, Sufism, and Christianity, among other philosophies and religions.

Dillard then moved to a cabin on an island in Puget Sound in Washington State, the setting for her 1992 Western novel *The Living*. An opportunity to teach at Wesleyan University brought her to Connecticut, and she began serving as professor emeritus at Wesleyan in 1999. In 1964, Dillard had married her writing professor, Richard Dillard. After divorcing Richard, she married writer Gary Clevidence in 1980. This marriage also ended in divorce. In 1988, she married award-winning historical biographer Robert D. Richardson, Jr.

Dillard gained fame as a voracious reader—typically reading more than one hundred books a year on an enormous variety of subjects. After years of searching among various religions, she settled on Roman Catholicism. Whether by writing essays or fiction, Dillard captures the essence of what it is to be human.

ANALYSIS

Annie Dillard's writing is difficult to classify. Indeed, readers often gain a far greater knowledge of subjects such as history, theology, natural science, and ethnography from reading her works, fiction as well as nonfiction. The influence of Dillard's masterpiece *Pilgrim at Tinker Creek* pervades her fiction, and the inseparability of nature and humanity is a central premise in Dillard's oeuvre. One of the central characters in *The Living*, Clare Fishburn, simply could not exist without Washington's Bellingham Bay. The landscape, the place itself, defines him. Similarly, Lou Maytree, one of the primary characters in *The Maytrees*, would lose depth and definition entirely without Maryland's Chesapeake Bay.

THE LIVING

James Joyce's 1907 short-story masterpiece "The Dead" comes to mind when reading Dillard's *The Living*, which was first written as a short story. In Joyce's story, no one actually dies, but the characters are Dublin's "walking dead." In *The Living*, many of the unforgettable characters face horrific deaths from disease, drowning, and natural disaster, but they lived full lives. They had lived with the vital life force inherent in the early American settlers who forged west into Whatcom's gigantic forest on Bellingham Bay in Washington State.

Spanning the second half of the nineteenth century, Dillard's elegant novel is made up of five sections. It begins with the story of as-strong-as-steel pioneers Ada and Rooney Fishburn, who travel over mountain passes and deserts to the Pacific Northwest. On the way, they lose a child, and soon after their arrival, Ada loses Rooney, who dies while digging a well. They are followed by the next wave of settlers, Minta and Eustace Honer, who decide to shun their stifling wealthy lives of leisure in Baltimore and buy farming land in Washington State. Similarly, Eustace will die young, caught in a logjam. Minta's house burns down with her babies inside and she, in turn, adopts three Native American children and turns her land into a profitable hops ranch. The new family lives among the gentle Lummi and Nansook Indians, who befriend them, nurture them, and eventually marry them.

The next generation of families consists of Clare Fishburn, who enjoys life to the fullest, and June Randell, Minta's wealthy sister from the East who comes west to visit and decides to stay. They provide for their families in periods of great economic growth, but also when the banks fail and they lose everything except their cows.

The Living is also a celebration of the natural world, which includes human nature. To illustrate, Dillard shows that, in the realm of nature, humans are vulnerable, given that their skeletons are inside their bodies; insects, by contrast, are less vulnerable because they have

Annie Dillard. (Courtesy, Harper & Row)

an outside armor to protect them. Humans live a short time on Earth; they die easily and, not unlike insects and other animals, can die violently and unexpectedly. Near the end of the novel, the gentle yet bearlike Clare Fishburn, who joyously plays a fiddle and lives each moment absolutely to the fullest, calls out a great "no" against Beal Obenchain, the dark stalking figure who represents impending death. Clare nevertheless jumps off a train trestle. As he falls through the air he sees a farmer plowing, and he comes to realize that humans, too, are plowed into Earth by nature to make way for new generations of humans. Clare also realizes that his life on Earth was a blessing.

The novel abounds with wondrous anecdotes of human behavior that make up living: the man who plants sunflowers in Alaska, only to have their "heads" twist off when the Sun fails to set; the family who washes their clothes by dangling them from a boat they row; the ominous man, Obenchain, who lives in the stump of a giant cedar tree; and the Lummi mother, who dashes a cup of cold water into her baby's face to quiet the child.

In *The Living*, Dillard goes far beyond giving her readers a good story. Indeed, each character encounters and resolves a metaphysical dilemma in the search for his or her own meaning of life, and this, in turn, prompts readers to examine their own lives.

The Maytrees

Although much slimmer than the pioneer epic *The Living*, *The Maytrees* is a comparable family saga about three generations of the Maytree family. After the poet Toby Maytree returns from World War II, he falls passionately in love with tall and silent Lou Bigelow, also an intellectual. They marry and live happily together in a beach house in Provincetown on Cape Cod. Their happiness is complete with the birth of their son Pete. Lou adores her husband and Toby adores his wife. Toby then falls in love with a vagabond beach woman named Deary, a friend of Lou, and leaves his family to live with her on an island in Maine the morning after Pete, the son he will not see for twenty years, is hospitalized with a broken leg.

After fourteen years of marriage, the aging Toby realizes that he was not in love with Lou in the first place and that he was only flattered by how much she loved him. In Deary, he thinks, he has found his true life mate. With her, he works as a carpenter on the island and finds peace.

Unlike her mother before her, who also had to cope with a philandering husband, Lou tries but fails to hold herself together. Eventually, however, after her son leaves home to become a fisherman, she appreciates her solitude, in which life holds "no schedule but whim" and where she does not have to please anyone but herself.

Twenty years later, Toby and Deary have changed from "roughing it" on the Maine island to becoming socially and professionally successful. Deary, who was poor before meeting Toby, is now an architect in Camden, and the couple is wealthy. In time, Toby reconciles with his fisherman son Pete, who marries and has a son of his own, whom he adores. Deary's health begins to fail, and she is diagnosed with congestive heart failure. While attempting to carry her, Toby breaks both of his arms in a fall and becomes helpless. In time, they realize they have no one to help them. Friends and relatives scatter. Toby shows up one particularly dark night on the beach to face the woman he left years ago to beg her help in caring for Deary. Lou takes her friend Deary and her wandering husband into her home and nurses them until Deary dies of heart failure.

Within a brilliant literary network of nature in the form of seascape, Dillard forces her readers to embrace the metaphysical construct that time heals all wounds. All the characters experience betrayal and intense psychic suffering, inflicted by the ones they love, yet they remain, despite years apart, lovingly attached through time.

M. Casey Diana

Other major works

POETRY: *Tickets for a Prayer Wheel*, 1974; *Mornings Like This: Found Poems*, 1995.

NONFICTION: *Pilgrim at Tinker Creek*, 1974 (nature); *Holy the Firm*, 1977 (theology); *Living by Fiction*, 1982 (criticism); *Teaching a Stone to Talk: Expeditions and Encounters*, 1982 (essays); *Encounters with Chinese Writers*, 1984 (essays); *An American Childhood*, 1987 (autobiography); *The Writing Life*, 1989; *For the Time Being*, 1999.

EDITED TEXTS: *The Best American Essays 1988*, 1988; *Modern American Memoirs*, 1995 (with Cort Conley).

Bibliography

Johnson, Sandra Humble. *The Space Between: Literary Epiphany in the Work of Annie Dillard.* Kent, Ohio: Kent State University Press, 1992. Scholarly work that focuses on the epiphanies inherent in Annie Dillard's works. Also examines the particular influence of Romantic poet William Wordsmith on Dillard.

McClintock, James. *Nature's Kindred Spirits: Aldo Leopold, Joseph Wood Krutch, Edward Abbey, Annie Dillard, and Gary Snyder.* Madison: University of Wisconsin Press, 1994. Illustrates how a variety of writers, including Dillard, interacted with nature and came away changed, deeply influencing their writing.

Parrish, Nancy C. *Lee Smith, Annie Dillard, and the Hollins Group: A Genesis of Writers.* Baton Rouge: Louisiana State University Press, 1999. A volume of the Southern Literary Studies series, this work examines the Hollins Group—women, including Dillard, who graduated from Hollins College in 1967 and achieved literary fame.

Smith, Linda. *Annie Dillard.* Boston: Twayne, 2002. Part of the Twayne American Authors series, this work includes scholarly essays and biographical material on Dillard.

ALFRED DÖBLIN

Born: Stettin, Germany (now Szczecin, Poland); August 10, 1878
Died: Emmendingen, West Germany (now in Germany); June 26, 1957
Also known as: Bruno Alfred Döblin

Principal long fiction

Die Ermordung einer Butterblume, 1913 (novella)
Die drei Sprünge des Wang-lun, 1915 (*The Three Leaps of Wang Lun*, 1991)
Die Lobensteiner reisen nach Böhmen, 1917 (novella)
Wadzeks Kampf mit der Dampfturbine, 1918
Der schwarze Vorhang, 1919
Wallenstein, 1920
Berge, Meere, und Giganten, 1924 (revised as *Giganten: Ein Abenteuerbuch*, 1932)
Berlin Alexanderplatz: Die Geschichte vom Franz Biberkopf, 1929 (*Alexanderplatz, Berlin*, 1931; better known as *Berlin Alexanderplatz*)
Babylonische Wandrung: Oder, Hochmut kommt vor dem Fall, 1934
Pardon wird nicht gegeben, 1935 (*Men Without Mercy*, 1937)
Amazonas, 1937-1948, 1963 (also known as *Das Land ohne Tod: Südamerika-Roman in drei Teilen*; includes *Die Fahrt ins Land ohne Tod*, 1937; *Der blaue Tiger*, 1938; and *Der neue Urwald*, 1948)
Der Oberst und der Dichter: Oder, Das menschliche Herz, 1946 (novella)
Verratenes Volk, 1948 (*A People Betrayed*, 1983)
Heimkehr der Fronttruppen, 1949 (*The Troops Return*, 1983)
Karl und Rosa, 1950 (*Karl and Rosa*, 1983)
Hamlet: Oder, Die lange Nacht nimmt ein Ende, 1956 (*Tales of a Long Night*, 1984)
November 1918: Eine deutsche Revolution, 1978 (collective title for *Verratenes Volk*, *Heimkehr der Fronttruppen*, and *Karl und Rosa*; *November 1918: A German Revolution*, 1983)
"Jagende Rosse," "Der schwarze Vorhang," und andere frühe Erzählwerke, 1981

Other literary forms

Under a liberal definition of the form, one would probably consider two additional works by Alfred Döblin (DOH-bleen) as novels: *Manas: Epische Dichtung* (1927; Manas: a verse epic) and *Die Pilgerin Aetheria* (1978; Aetheria the pilgrim). The consciously archaic verse form of the first and the relative brevity of the second exclude them from the category of novels in the view of at least some scholars.

Döblin also wrote short stories throughout his literary career, though the majority of them were written before 1933 and were typically first published in well-known literary journals of their time: *Der Sturm*, *Der neue Merkur*, *Die neue Rundschau*, and *Die literarische Welt*. Eighteen of these earlier stories were reprinted, together with six new ones, in collections in 1913 and 1917. Between 1906 and 1931, Döblin experimented four times with drama. All four plays saw production (in Berlin, Darmstadt, Leipzig, and Munich), but their respective legal, political, and critical consequences outshone their dramatic quality.

The best known of Döblin's novels, *Berlin Alexanderplatz*, was adapted as a radio play, with script by Döblin and the radio director Max Bings, in 1930. In the following year, it became a film success in an adaptation written by Döblin in collaboration with Hans Wilhelm. (The overwhelming international acclaim given German cinema director Rainer Werner Fassbinder's fifteen-hour-plus screen adaptation, *Berlin Alexanderplatz*, 1980, attests the continuing impact of Döblin's epic vision.) Döblin's second venture in screenwriting came during his exile in California, where in 1940 and 1941 he contributed to the scripts for Metro-Goldwyn-Mayer's *Mrs. Miniver* and *Random Harvest*, a possible source of ideas for his own novel *Tales of a Long Night*. A number of autobiographical writings shed some light on Döblin's aesthetic development and literary career; his major essays on philosophy, religion, literature, and the other arts help to reveal the intellectual underpinnings of his often experimental creative works.

The Berlin house of S. Fischer Verlag published all of Döblin's novels through 1932. Following the Nazi takeover and the banning of his writings, Döblin was able to place his work with the exile publishing firm Querido-Verlag, in Amsterdam. The books written in the United States and following his return to Germany in 1945 appeared under the imprints of various German companies; only since the posthumous publication of his collected works was begun, by Walter-Verlag in 1960, has Döblin's literary and theoretical production become generally accessible.

Achievements

Two years before his death, Alfred Döblin complained, "Whenever my name was mentioned, they always added the name *Alexanderplatz, Berlin*. But my path was still far from ended." The overshadowing success of that work does in part account for Döblin's failure to establish a secure reputation for his entire literary output, and there are Döblin specialists who maintain that this novel represents the height and the end of his significant development. The other major obstacle to Döblin's full recognition, during his lifetime and since, is his resistance to philosophical, theoretical, and literary classification. Thus, the daily *Frankfurter Rundschau* could characterize him as "a shrewd but uncommonly unstable writer who was incapable at any time of rationally disciplining his emotions and impulses." It is perhaps an extreme portrayal, but nevertheless symptomatic.

Most serious critics attribute the difficulty in placing Döblin among twentieth century German novelists to his constant questioning of his own position, which for him meant no less than the examination and testing of the foundations of human existence. He had expressed that compulsion in the 1919 statement: "We only live once, it seems. Then existence must be the burning question for us." Even near the end of his life, a convert to Roman Catholicism, Döblin would not retreat into a sham doctrinaire certainty of his own position but remained ever the questioner and ironic self-examiner.

Döblin's public reception in postwar Germany was far from gratifying. A number of circumstances and personal traits may have contributed to Döblin's postwar disappointments: the changed literary tastes of his former public—or what remained of it; the general discrediting of the German émigré writers; displeasure with Döblin's "provocative" return in the uniform of a French colonel; his sometimes gratuitous attacks on other writers, particularly Thomas Mann; a public coolness toward his conversion to Christianity; and almost certainly his tendency to isolate himself from other opinions and sides of issues. He has not, however, been without influence on other novelists; one acknowledged pupil, Günter Grass, portrayed Döblin in 1967 as unacceptable to radicals and conservatives alike, unsuited to either adult or juvenile audiences. As Grass summed it up, "The value of Döblin's stock did not and still does not appear in the market quotations."

Largely on the strength of his achievements in the novel form before his exile, Döblin is a generally acknowledged force among German writers of the first third of the twentieth century. His pioneering creation of the montage as a structural principle for the novel, his development of a philosophy of the individual in the natural world, his portrayal of the modern existential tension between the individual will and the anonymous forces against which it must assert itself, and his efforts toward the democratization of art are achievements for which few would deny him credit. Failures, however, accompanied his successes: Döblin did not succeed, either in his personal life or in those of his fictional heroes, in finding the bridge from the self to the community, from personal transformation to politically relevant action. Whenever it happened that Döblin found no clear echo—hence, whenever his social relevance was in doubt—he was conscious of his isolation. In a sense, this amounted to an "exile before the fact," being cut off artistically both before and after his physical exile, as well as during the years of emigration.

It is no longer quite accurate to state, as Grass did in 1967, that Döblin's worth remains unevaluated. The German edition of his collected works is now much more nearly complete than when Grass acknowledged his debt to his predecessor, and the major scholarly studies of his life and work almost all date from 1970 and later. Disagreement remains over the continuity and the literary stature of the later novels, especially of *November 1918* and *Tales of a Long Night*.

Alfred Döblin. (Getty Images)

BIOGRAPHY

Bruno Alfred Döblin was born on August 10, 1878, in the Baltic port city of Stettin, the former Pomeranian capital (now Szczecin, Poland). His father, Max Döblin, operated a clothing shop until its failure forced him into the tailor's trade. Max Döblin was intelligent and sensitive but also passive and unambitious, a Western European Jew separated from his people's traditions and sense of identity. Döblin's mother, Sophie, was two years older than her husband and very different from him—sober, practical, and materialistic. She had come to the marriage from better economic circumstances, and she was its dominant partner. Many of the disparities and conflicts in Döblin's life can be found partially rooted in his parents' dissimilarities. In 1888, when Döblin was ten years old, his father abandoned the family for a young woman employed in his shop and left Stettin. His mother moved with the children to Berlin that same year, hoping to find among relatives there some assistance in supporting her children and meeting the heavy debts left behind by her husband. The emotional effect on Döblin was predictably traumatic. Attempts to mend the marriage came to nothing, but it was not until 1908 that his parents' divorce was finally granted.

Döblin asserted later in life that the move to Berlin in 1888 had been his "real birth," for he regarded the capital from then onward as his true home, and himself as a Berliner. He completed his secondary schooling there in 1900, began studying medicine and philosophy at the university, and began writing his first stories. He transferred to Freiburg University, where he specialized in psychiatry and neurology, and after earning his degree there in 1905, he served a year of internship in a mental hospital near Regensburg. The following year, he returned to Berlin and remained on hospital staffs until he could establish a private practice in neurology and internal medicine in 1911. All the while, the newly settled doctor in working-class East Berlin was combining a medical and a writing career, as he would continue to do until 1933. In 1910, he became the cofounder, with writer and art critic Herwarth Walden, of the expressionist journal *Der Sturm*, a publication that attracted the contributions of many antibourgeois writers of apolitical and anarchist persuasion.

In Berlin, Döblin also met Erna Reiss, a medical student ten years younger than he, whom he married in 1912, but not before having an affair with a younger woman who was neither Jewish nor of a well-to-do family. Döblin's mother strictly opposed a marriage with her, and he yielded, though with a heavy sense of guilt—not least of all for having fathered her illegitimate child. He found in Reiss a wife in many ways like his strong-willed mother. From 1912 to 1926, four sons were born to Erna and Alfred Döblin. He spent most of the war years, from 1914 to 1918, as a military doctor stationed on the western front in Lorraine and Alsace.

Returning then to Berlin as "the only city" where he could live and work, Döblin joined the Independent Social Democratic Party and, after its split in 1921, the Social Democratic Party. These were the years of his greatest political activity, during which he wrote satiric pieces critical of conditions in the infant Weimar Republic under the pen name Linke Poot (dialect for "left paw"). A trip to Poland in 1924 brought devout Catholicism to his attention for the first time, but, more important, it afforded him an insight into the spiritual identity of the unassimilated Eastern Jew as a still intact, self-assertive member of the natural order, at a time when Döblin was occupied with developing his philosophy of self and cosmos.

In mid-decade, Döblin was a member of several writers' organizations, some with clearly leftist political tendencies. In 1928, he was elected to membership in the rather more conservative literary section of the Prussian Academy of Arts. When, in 1933, the section's chair, Heinrich Mann, was forced to resign his office on account of his pro-Communist political statements, Döblin sealed his own fate as an enemy of the National Socialist wing by openly criticizing the Academy's action. On February 28, urged by friends, he made a trip to Switzerland; in November he traveled to Paris. As a Jew and a leftist intellectual whose books had been publicly burned in Germany, he realized the impossibility of returning soon to Berlin. Exile also meant the end of his medical career, since he could not practice as an alien in host countries.

During the years in France, Döblin enjoyed particularly the support of Robert Minder, a Germanist at the University of Nancy who became a lifelong friend and an advocate of the novelist's works and literary reputation. Döblin was naturalized a French citizen in 1936, and in 1939 he worked under Jean Giraudoux in the French information ministry. Still not at ease in the language, and prompted by the fear of the imminent German invasion of France, he fled in 1940 with his wife and youngest son, by way of Spain and Portugal, to New York.

In Hollywood, where friends suggested he go, Döblin's existence was made difficult by economic dependence on refugee aid societies and uninspiring work in the film industry, by his artistic isolation and inability to publish anything more than some fragments of *November 1918* in the United States, and, again, by the language barrier. There, in 1941, he made his controversial decision to become a Roman Catholic. Among his German fellow intellectuals, this step only aggravated his isolation.

At war's end in 1945, Döblin returned at once, first to Paris, then to Baden-Baden in the French Occupation Zone. There, he was attached to the military public information bureau and for five years published a journal called *Das goldene Tor*, which he envisioned as an instrument for restoring a healthy literary life to Germany. In 1949, he helped to reestablish the Mainz Academy of Sciences and Literature. Neither these efforts nor his artistic and personal life, however, bore good fruit. Politically and professionally, Döblin seemed condemned to frustration. He moved to Mainz in 1949, to Paris in 1953, then back to southwest Germany, where his failing health obliged him to make a succession of stays in hospitals and sanatoriums. On June 26, 1957, he died in the clinic at Emmendingen near Freiburg.

Analysis

In view of the iconoclastic literary principles that Alfred Döblin championed and the considerable modifications to which he subjected his style and method over the span of his creative life, it may be surprising to note that his abiding concern was with the simple telling of stories. That, at least, is what he asserted in the retrospective epilogue sketched in 1948. It is known that he considered himself—or aspired to be—an epic writer in the original sense of that word, a teller of tales. This is not to suggest that he aimed at the telling of simple, linear plots, for he avowed a preference for depicting complex totalities in his novels. The stress should rather be on the epic's immediacy, that quality for which Döblin, in 1917, paid respect to Homer, Dante, Miguel de Cervantes, and Fyodor Dostoevski, and that he had demanded perhaps most succinctly, in 1913, with the statement, "The whole must not appear as if spoken, but as if present." This view of the novel's purpose and execution was directly opposed to the idea of the polyhistorical, intellectual novel—rooted in the nineteenth century bourgeois cultural tradition, larded with ostentatious knowledge, and diluted with narrative digression and commentary—as practiced by Hermann Broch, Thomas Mann, Robert Musil, and others.

Nor did Döblin have any patience with the psychological novel, another of the early twentieth century's favorites. He did not accept the isolated individual, created in a vacuum by authors of studio exercises, as a means of depicting the world. Instead, Döblin desired the dismantling of the individual, who otherwise constituted, like the intrusive narrator, an obstacle to the epic's direct presentation of the infinitely varied world. Confrontation with that world, with the whole of nature, was for Döblin the modern human condition and the object of art: the reader standing before the "stone facade" of the novel. Later in his career, he rejected as inhuman this radical call for depersonalization in the novel and modified it. One clear beneficiary of the modification was the once-banished narrator, whose presence is increasingly evident in the progression of his works from *The Three Leaps of Wang Lun* to *Berlin Alexanderplatz*.

Much of the thematic import of Döblin's literary output until about 1930 can be traced through his development of a philosophy of the human individual's place and function in the natural world. Having abandoned the Nietzschean concept of individual development and the cult of the "great personality" in the first years of the century, Döblin expressed, notably in "Der schwarze Vorhang" (the black curtain), the despair of the confined, powerless self confronting the superior force of a meaningless environment. He accordingly searched for some encompassing meaning to which humans could willingly submit themselves—whether as submission to "fate" (in *The Three Leaps of Wang Lun*) or to the cosmic wholeness of all living matter (in *Berge, Meere, und Giganten*; mountains, seas, and giants).

Döblin finally synthesized his view of individual passivity and individual self-assertion in the essay *Das Ich über der Natur* (1927; the ego above nature), which postulated a "naturalism" of balance between self and creation, the ego as part and counterpart of nature, simultaneously creature and creator. The result for Döblin was a new image of the individual and a new view of art, clearest perhaps in *Berlin Alexanderplatz*, both as Franz Biberkopf swims in the stream of life and as the story's creator responds to the primordial rhythms of the narrative stream he has set flowing.

Döblin saw the naturalism of *Das Ich über der Natur* distorted and perverted by Nazism in Germany after 1933, however, and his novels, beginning with *Babylonische Wandrung* (Babylonian migration), betray the confusion that resulted for him. "I was examining in my mind how it had all come to pass," he recalled in 1948. Finally he turned to religion and the search for a personal God as a means to rebuilding his philosophical position, but he could not recover the former union of his philosophy and his art. *Tales of a Long Night* and the works that came after it do not resonate with their author's idea as *Berlin Alexanderplatz* does.

Since the deep rupture in Döblin's philosophical reflections makes it difficult to analyze the post-1933 novels with reference to his "naturalistic" postulates, one might better ask what his exile and the related external circumstances meant for his literary activity. He had only begun the writing of *Babylonische Wandrung* in Berlin; most of the work on it was done in Zurich and Paris. As his first literary reaction to the catastrophic situation in Germany, the novel makes its serious point with its theme of guilt and penance, but the liberties Döblin took in its composition expose characters, the author, reality, and the epic form itself to ridicule. *Men Without Mercy* is, by contrast, spare in its composition, partially autobiographical, and formally a throwback to the realistic narrative tradition. When Döblin spoke of this as one of the novels through which he "examined how it had all come to pass," he undoubtedly had in mind its theme of the German bourgeoisie's betrayal of the ideals of freedom whose guardian that class had once been. In *Das Land ohne Tod* (land without death), he removed the novel's setting to another age and another continent. Still, it relates the unhappy condition of the "modern" (post-Renaissance) European, the conqueror whose spiritual poverty and faith in technological progress bar him from mystical union with nature as it is known by the South American Indians.

Döblin had set out initially to fashion epic works of immediate directness—what he had defined as his "stone style" or "facade" of the novel—that would represent a world in complex totality and depict the relationship of the individual to cosmic nature and its forces. At the culmination of this effort, with *Berlin Alexanderplatz*, he found that individual in equilibrium, part and counterpart of the natural world, and there had been a reemergence of the personal narrator and the individual hero. With the dislocation of Döblin's theoretical base in the events of 1933, however, his novels ceased to be controlled experiments in the epic form and tended instead to mark his coming to terms with past and present—his country's and his own.

The Three Leaps of Wang Lun

To write an epic of the complex and diverse totality of the world, Döblin chose as his subject in *The Three Leaps of Wang Lun* life in eighteenth century China and made it a reflection of the world in his own age and place. Like many of his German contemporaries early in the second decade of the twentieth century, he was fascinated by Chinese culture and philosophy. His persistent habit of researching the subject matter and background of his novels began with the preparation of this book, and the result is impressive. Historical episodes, parables and anecdotes, social and political systems, culture, climate, and geography—all attest the exhaustive scholarly groundwork and contribute to the presence of "world" in *The Three Leaps of Wang Lun*. Daoist philosophy in particular was fashionable in early twentieth century Germany, and Döblin incorporated various literal extracts from Daoist writings in this novel—the fable of the man who tries to escape his own shadow and to leave no footprints, for example.

The novel's characters, while distinguished by names and fixed roles, are defined exclusively by their visible behavior and evident moods; their psychic interiors are not explored. There is, moreover, the prominent part that Döblin gives to human masses, but not ones brought to the level of some "collective hero," as they might have appeared in other contemporary works, the expressionist dramas particularly. Rather it is in their anonymity, into which certain of the individual characters themselves return, that the masses of people are important here. They serve more to remind us of individual insignificance than to assert identities of their own. Similarly, Döblin avoids what he considered the inappropriateness of unusual or exotic, "artful" imagery. The unfamiliar Asian world might easily have furnished exotic motifs for the Western writer, but Döblin had expressly rejected facile "artifice" and built instead with abundant but objective, careful detail.

In the fable of the man who fears his shadow and hates his footprints, he runs to the point of exhaustion in the attempt to escape them and dies from the effort: "He did not know that he had only to sit in the shade somewhere to be rid of his shadow, that he had only to remain still in order to leave no footprints." This little story exemplifies the thematic point of the whole novel. The problem, and the dilemma of modern Europeans as well, is the choice between action and inaction, rebellion and submission in the world.

Wang-lun is the son of a fisherman and leader of a passive sect, the Truly Weak Ones, the Wu-wei, who at the story's beginning await their annihilation by the imperial troops. The novel traces how this destruction of the Wu-wei came about, but the important chain of events is that involving Wang-lun, their leader. His career takes him first from his village to refuge in the mountains, where he formulates his doctrine of nonresistance. He returns to the fisherman's life and marriage but also to rebellion against the emperor. Yet another reversal takes him back to the side of the submissive doctrine.

These are the three "leaps" that he illustrates by jumping three times over a stream. Paradoxically, however, passivity cannot be tolerated, because it denies the forces of fate; these dominant forces are to be placated, as Wang-lun ultimately realizes, only by resistance to them. He knows at the end that "to submit is the pure way," but he cannot live the truth he knows. Döblin, too, regarded it as an immediate dilemma.

Berge, Meere, und Giganten

Even from a writer who aspired to depict the endlessly changing totality of nature and its enormous forces, *Berge, Meere, und Giganten* is an ambitious work. Its story begins in the twentieth century and goes forward into another half millennium of a visionary future. Its physical setting includes Europe and extends from Asia to Greenland. Its human masses are vast. In a procedure rare for Döblin, he furnished a simultaneous account of the writing of this novel, and he tells in it how the earth itself, as it were, implanted the germ of the epic idea in his mind. Stones idly picked up along the Baltic shore gave the first unclear impulse to his musings and gradually drew him to the study of various branches of biology and geology. Only later, Döblin claims, did he recognize and begin to compose a novel as the consequence of this intellectual captivation. It is instructive to observe that he began the writing, well before the whole plan was clear to him, not with the novel's beginning chapters, but with a "gigantic expedition." "It was to become a tellurian adventure, a wrestling with the earth," he says. The masses of humanity "take up the arrogant, imperious struggle with the earth itself."

The result, which occupies books 6 and 7 (of the novel's nine), is a tremendous westward expedition to colonize Greenland by melting its ice sheet with energy generated in the volcanoes of Iceland. Preceding this major segment of the epic is the story of centuries-long human technological development to the point of its final breakdown. The assault on the Greenland ice releases monstrous forces of Cretaceous life—a retaliation by the earth—and the following books depict humanity's efforts to resist. Those who acknowledge nature's superior force and willingly surrender themselves to fusion with the elements attain reunion with the cosmic whole in their deaths. The physical survivors, a remnant of settlers, are humbled and led into a future devoid of technology, but thereby into harmony with nature and reverence for it.

The sense of the individual's inclusion in such an anonymous, collective relationship to elemental forces suggests a certain affinity with the expressionists, whom Döblin otherwise viewed with reserve by this time, while, with its overtones of irrational mysticism, the work maintains a safe distance from the intellectual novel already mentioned as a style Döblin found distasteful. As for the individuals themselves, he asserts that, in keeping with his epic intentions, they still are not personal characters, but only "voices of the mass." Even though this novel still owes a certain debt to the Futurist concept of dynamics and speed and periodically exhibits that concept in its language, it also has its more ponderous, inflated sections that dull its linguistic contours. This stylistic inconsistency may reflect (in its racing intensity) the Promethean activism of Döblin's human actors but also (in its heavy solemnity) the doomed hubris of their assault on the earth.

A distorted image of the novel's structure will result if one considers only the progression of these events, however, for this constitutes only the epic "report." Four years later, in 1928, Döblin would deliver a lecture titled "Der Bau des epischen Werks" (the structure of the epic), perhaps his single most important theoretical piece. In it, he called for discarding the "forced mask of reporting" and for expanding the means for epic portrayal and depiction; this kind of narrative modification was already taking shape in *Berge, Meere, und Giganten*. Döblin admits to having sought relief during the writing by creating "oases" for himself, by means of a freer, more expansive treatment of numerous episodes. As a result, the "reportorial" structure supports an overgrowth of more freely imaginative episodic sections, especially those in which Döblin explains technological inventions and procedures of the future. The method he had called his stone facade was yielding gradually to rediscovery of the personal narrator, whom he later (in the 1928 lecture) acknowledged as necessary to the epic form.

Berlin Alexanderplatz

Two years before the appearance of *Berlin Alexanderplatz*, in 1929, Döblin's *Manas* had become a moderate publishing failure. *Berlin Alexanderplatz*, which treats essentially the same idea—the overcoming of the old and birth of the new person—was easily his greatest success. From the mythological realm of India in the verse epic, Döblin brought his idea to the contemporary metropolis. East Berlin was his terrain, and he could make it ring more true than any other place. This novel is therefore filled with what *Manas* had most lacked: the familiar—the language, appearance, and life of an everyday, working-class city.

Authentic representation of the familiar may account for the book's popularity, but it does not explain its greatness. Its stature as a landmark among German novels of the twentieth century is the result of Döblin's integration of the diverse forms and fragments of the world of Berlin into cogent totality. It represents his mastery of narrative montage and thus his ultimate realization of the attempt to represent a world at once whole and multifarious. Moreover, he brought the human individual into the most refined expression of his relationship with this world and, by referring every fragment of the environment to this central figure, gave the novel its final cogency.

The very looseness of structure in *Berlin Alexanderplatz* permits its unified wholeness. The shifting narrative perspectives, the free-association technique, the interior monologue and free indirect discourse, the prefiguration and retrospection, cross-references, illustrative parallels, and recurring rhythms large and small, all function both as fragmenting and as reconnecting devices. Franz Biberkopf is central even when not physically present, since he can be recalled, explicitly or by subtle association, at any time. At times, one cannot be certain who is speaking—the narrator, Biberkopf, or some interpolated, seemingly unrelated source. It becomes clear, however, that all of these voices, the author's included, are speaking to Biberkopf, that most of the novel is a multiple voice speaking to him.

At the beginning of the book, Biberkopf emerges into Berlin from the gate of Tegel Prison, where he has served his term for a violent crime. He is determined to "go straight" and "keep his nose clean." The narrator says, "The punishment begins." Biberkopf's subsequent fortunes show what is meant by this curious remark. All that he has to learn still lies ahead of him. He is mistaken to believe that serving a prison sentence has made a new man of him; in fact, he has learned nothing. With good intentions and unwarranted self-confidence he believes he can do it alone. He is struck down three times by fate, each time more brutally than the last, but the assaults are ones that he himself has defiantly provoked in his moments of greatest satisfaction with his own progress. In fact, as the author has hinted in his preface, the unexpected force that strikes Biberkopf down only "looks like a fate." Not until the final blow is struck and Biberkopf finds himself implicated in a murder trial and committed to a mental hospital does he recognize the fate as Death, which has spoken to and in him throughout the novel. When finally Death speaks plainly to him, it says that it is life, since only death can lead the submissive individual back into the eternal anonymity that the self-confident Biberkopf has sought to deny. True to its rhythmic-repetitive pattern, the world of the Alexanderplatz in Berlin goes on—and so does Biberkopf, but broken outwardly and inwardly, no longer self-reliant, now a willing part of the anonymous world in which he understands his place.

Whether and how much Döblin may have borrowed from the techniques of James Joyce's *Ulysses* (1922) or John Dos Passos's *Manhattan Transfer* (1925) is subject to dispute. Both of these novels had appeared in German translations in 1927, but Döblin denied that either had any significant influence on *Berlin Alexanderplatz*. As the models for his montage technique, he cited instead the expressionists and Dadaists and the techniques of filmmaking. The more important point here is that the montage furnished Döblin with the means for overcoming, insofar as that is possible, the sequential nature of narrative art and lending it an illusion of simultaneity that relates the seemingly unrelated in a single image of countless parts. *Berlin Alexanderplatz* is thus an intimation of the infinitesimal and the infinite combined, an extraordinary example of "narrated world."

November 1918

During his exile in France, and with little time lost following the completion of his South American novel, Döblin began work on *November 1918*, now republished as the four-volume edition it might have been much earlier but for the complications of exile and its aftermath. This expansive work is a pairing of two concurrent narratives: the story of the World War I veteran Friedrich Becker and his return to defeated Germany; and the fictionalized historical account of the events most Germans would associate with its title—the failed Communist revolution of November and December, 1918, immediately following the collapse of the German Empire. As one form of Döblin's coming to terms with his own and Germany's fate, the work mixes individual and political-historical probing and psychological and epic processes.

The psychological component is the great innovation of *November 1918* for Döblin's literary development. The collective anonymity of human masses, familiar already from his early novels, finds expression in the depiction of the 1918 revolutionary turmoil; the probings into individual consciousness are undertaken most fully, but not exclusively, with the character of Becker, a man physically and psychologically disabled by the war. His sense of sharing in Germany's guilt and his powerlessness to effect change in the German mind by precept or by force torment him to the point where he becomes a fanatical seeker of God. Döblin's extension of interest from the collective to the individual psychological level is surely a reflection of his personal questioning and searching, marked clearly by his conversion to Christianity in 1941. It would be unfair, however, to say that he accepted the validity of the psychological novel he had eschewed earlier in his career, since his analysis of Becker's condition is not a "studio exercise" in the abstract, but an expression of urgent personal doubts.

Doubts and reservations affect the tone of the novel. Both Becker and the Spartacist revolutionary leaders have their doubts about the rightness of their cause, and both the revolutionary and the religious quests in *November 1918* come to unhappy ends. The Berlin revolts are frustrated until they can be crushed by the reactionary forces, and Becker falls the victim of a familiar error: the fatal hubris of believing he can stand alone. Döblin's ambivalent attitude toward the leftist cause, although he was generally in sympathy with it, is evident in farcical, satiric, and ironic passages. The style tends toward objective sobriety and understatement, placing Döblin in the company of other post-World War II German realists with their sense of minimal intact resources for artistic expression.

The narrative control, once so sure in *Berlin Alexanderplatz*, gives evidence of weakening in *November 1918*. Sharply drawn individual scenes contrast with an absence of clear overall structure. In fact, the attitude—or pretense—of narrative helplessness may be the more honest gesture for one writing in the early 1940's. Friedrich Becker surely reflects Döblin's thoughts on Germany when, near the end of the novel, he talks about Richard Wagner's *Tristan und Isolde*: "The opera is a terrifying document of the times. Love-death, alcohol-death, opium-death, war-death; what death will people flee to next?"

Tales of a Long Night

Tales of a Long Night, written in 1945 and 1946 and bridging Döblin's exile and repatriation, is again the story of a war veteran who returns home with severe physical and emotional wounds. This "Hamlet" is an Englishman, however, not a German, and the war from which he returns is World War II. Thus, Döblin chose characters and a setting in which he could analyze the human conflicts and relationships much more intensely than he had done in *November 1918*. The probings of *Tales of a Long Night* are Döblin's most direct confrontation with his own childhood experience of the tensions in his parents' marriage and the emotional complex brought on by the nature of their separation.

Like Friedrich Becker of *November 1918*, the principal figure in *Tales of a Long Night*, Edward Allison, returns home in confusion, questioning the sense of the war. Like his Shakespearean namesake, he finds there a tangle of lies and deceit that he must cut apart in the search for his own identity. For his parents, whose marriage is a bond of love and hate, the result is disastrous. For Allison himself, once "the long night of lies is past," the revelation is poor comfort, since it has shown him that dark instincts indeed seem to dominate human fate. Döblin originally had Allison enter a monastery at the novel's close. The publisher preferred—and received—a more optimistic ending in which "a new life began" for Edward Allison. Perhaps characteristically, Döblin left the literary world without a clear statement of his own wishes regarding the revised ending. His last major work thus remains as ambiguous in its philosophical conclusions as many of its predecessors; for a writer who saw the epic as a never-ending form, the lack of a final answer seems fully in character.

Michael Ritterson

Other major works

SHORT FICTION: *Märchen vom Materialismus: Erzählung*, 1959; *Gesammelte Erzählungen*, 1971; *Erzählungen aus fünf Jahrzehnten*, 1977; *Die Pilgerin Aetheria*, 1978.

PLAYS: *Lydia und Mäxchen: Tiefe Verbeugung in einem Akt*, pb. 1906; *Lusitania*, pb. 1919; *Die Nonnen von Kemnade*, pb. 1923; *Die Ehe*, pb. 1930.

POETRY: *Manas: Epische Dichtung*, 1927.

NONFICTION: *Der deutsche Maskenball von Linke Poot: Wissen und Verändern!*, 1921 (essays); *Das Ich über der Natur*, 1927 (philosophy); *Alfred Döblin im Buch, zu Haus, auf der Strasse*, 1928 (with Oskar Loerke); *Wissen und Verändern! Offene Briefe an einen jungen Menschen*, 1931 (essays); *Die deutsche Literatur im Ausland seit 1933*, 1938 (criticism); *Jüdische Erneuerung*, 1933 (religion; *Jews Renew Yourselves!*, 1935); *Unser Dasein*, 1933 (philosophy); *Der unsterbliche Mensch: Ein Religionsgespräch, Der Kampf mit dem Engel, Ein Gang durch die Bibel*, 1946 (religion); *Die literarische Situation*, 1947 (criticism); *Unsere Sorge der Mensch*, 1948 (religion); *Schicksalsreise: Bericht und Bekenntnis*, 1949 (autobiography; *Germany Is No More*, 1946); *Die Dichtung, ihre Natur und ihre Rolle*, 1950 (criticism); *Aufsätze zur Literatur*, 1963 (criticism); *Reise in Polen*, 1968 (*Journey to Poland*, 1991); *Briefe*, 1970; *Schriften zur Politik und Gesellschaft*, 1972 (essays); *Autobiographische Schriften und letzte Aufzeichnungen*, 1977; *Gespräche mit Kalypso: Über die Musik*, 1980.

Bibliography

Barta, Peter I. "Walking in the Shadow of Death: *Berlin Alexanderplatz*." In *Bely, Joyce, and Döblin: Peripatetics in the City Novel*. Gainesville: University Press of Florida, 1996. An analysis of three novels about cities—Döblin's *Berlin Alexanderplatz*, James Joyce's *Ulysses*, and Andrei Bely's *Petersburg*. Barta argues that these novels juxtapose descriptions of the city with descriptions of the characters' rambling thoughts in order to show how the city creates a sense of psychic displacement and tension in its residents. Includes notes and a bibliography.

Dollenmayer, David B. *The Berlin Novels of Alfred Döblin: "Wadzek's Battle with the Steam Turbine," "Berlin Alexanderplatz," "Men Without Mercy," and "November 1918."* Berkeley: University of California Press, 1988. In addition to separate chapters on the novels, Dollenmayer includes an introduction surveying Döblin's career and a first chapter titled "The City Theme in Döblin's Early Works." Includes notes and a bibliography.

Dollinger, Roland, Wulf Koepke, and Heidi Thomann Tewarson, eds. *A Companion to the Works of Alfred Döblin*. Rochester, N.Y.: Camden House, 2004. A collection of scholarly essays analyzing the full range of Döblin's works, including *Berlin Alexanderplatz*, *Tales of a Long Night*, *November 1918*, and other novels.

Graber, Heinz, ed. Introduction to *Reise in Polen*, by Alfred Döblin. New York: Paragon House, 1991. In his introduction to Döblin's account of his trip to Poland, Graber contrasts Döblin's attitudes toward Germany and Poland and compares the author's work to that of other Central European novelists.

Koepke, Wulf. *The Critical Reception of Alfred Döblin's Major Novels*. Rochester, N.Y.: Camden House, 2003. This critical study examines the reviews of Döblin's novels that were written before and after 1933—the year he went into exile. Koepke also analyzes the scholarly articles that were written about the novels, placing them in historical context. Includes a chapter discussing Döblin's impact on other writers as well as a bibliography and an index.

Kort, Wolfgang. *Alfred Döblin*. New York: Twayne, 1974. A reliable introductory work with chapters on Döblin's life as a German intellectual; his literary beginnings; his theory of the epic and his philosophy of nature; his handling of imagination and reality, history and science fiction, and mythology and modern existence; and his attitude toward writing and toward Europe. Includes a chronology, notes, and an annotated bibliography.

Midgley, David. "Radical Realism and Historical Fantasy: Alfred Döblin." In *German Novelists of the Weimar Republic: Intersections of Literature and Politics*, edited by Karl Leydecker. Rochester, N.Y.: Camden House, 2006. Döblin is one of twelve writers whose work is analyzed in this study of Weimar literature. The essays focus on the authors' response to the political, social, and economic instability of that era.

O'Neill, Patrick. *Alfred Döblin's "Babylonische Wandrung": A Study*. Bern, Switzerland: Herbert Lang, 1974. Part 1 of this study is an introduction to Döblin and his literary career. Part 2 concentrates on the development of the novel *Babylonische Wandrung*. Part 3 explores matters of form, structure, style, sources, materials, and humor. Notes and bibliography.

E. L. DOCTOROW

Born: New York, New York; January 6, 1931
Also known as: Edgar Lawrence Doctorow

Principal long fiction

Welcome to Hard Times, 1960
Big as Life, 1966
The Book of Daniel, 1971
Ragtime, 1975
Loon Lake, 1980
World's Fair, 1985
Billy Bathgate, 1989
The Waterworks, 1994
City of God, 2000
The March, 2005

Other literary forms

E. L. Doctorow (DOK-tur-oh) has seldom ventured outside the novel genre. He has, however, written a play, *Drinks Before Dinner* (pr. 1978) and has published two collections of short stories, *Lives of the Poets* (1984) and *Sweet Land Stories* (2004), as well as collections of essays, including *Jack London, Hemingway, and the Constitution: Selected Essays, 1977-1992* (1993), *Reporting the Universe* (2003), and *Creationists: Selected Essays, 1993-2006* (2006). Doctorow has also published a prose poem in a collection of photographs by David Finn, *Lamentation 9/11* (2002).

Achievements

Ragtime, a popular and critical success, catapulted E. L. Doctorow into prominence as one of the finest and most exciting novelists of his generation. With *Welcome to Hard Times* and *The Book of Daniel*, he had already established a solid reputation, but the rave reviews he received for *Ragtime* and the subsequent film and Broadway musical adaptations of the novel secured his place in the contemporary culture. *Ragtime* won the National Book Critics Circle Award in 1976, *World's Fair* won the American Book Award in 1986, and *Billy Bathgate*—nearly as successful as *Ragtime*—won the 1990 National Book Critics Circle Award and the PEN/Faulkner Award for Fiction the same year. Among the awards Doctorow has received for lifetime achievement are the 1996 Medal of Honor for Literature from the National Arts Club and the 1998 National Humanities Medal. *The March*, Doctorow's highly praised Civil War novel, was a finalist for the Pulitzer Prize and the National Book Award and won both the PEN/Faulkner Award and the National Book Critics Circle Award in 2005.

Biography

Edgar Lawrence Doctorow was born in the Bronx in 1931, and his fiction returns again and again to urban themes, particularly to the life of New York City at the beginning of the twentieth century and in the 1920's and 1930's. He graduated from Kenyon College with a major in philosophy, and after serving in the U.S. Army he worked for publishers in New York City, editing important writers such as Norman Mailer. His philosophical training is evident in his novels, in which he tries to infuse serious ideas into popular genres such as the Western (*Welcome to Hard Times*), science fiction (*Big as Life*), and detective fiction (*The Waterworks*).

Identifying with the downtrodden, with immigrants, criminals, and political protesters, Doctorow fashions fiction with a leftist orientation, and on occasion he has joined in public protests against government censorship and other forms of tyranny. With residences in New York City and New Rochelle, New York, he divides his time between the city and the suburbs. He has taught at several colleges and universities, including Sarah Lawrence College and Princeton. In 1982, he began teaching at New York University, where he became Loretta and Lewis Glucksman Professor of English and American Letters. He provides a partial account of his life in "Childhood of a Writer," which is included in *Reporting the Universe*.

E. L. Doctorow. (Barbara Walz)

Analysis

E. L. Doctorow's work is concerned with those stories, myths, public figures, and literary and historical forms that have shaped public and political consciousness, even when his subject is not overtly political. In his first novel, *Welcome to Hard Times*, he uses the genre of the Western to comment on the American sense of crime and justice. The Western has often been a vehicle for the celebration of American individualism and morality, but in this fablelike novel Doctorow questions American faith in fairness and democracy. At the same time, he follows the conventions of the genre by maintaining the customary strong opposition between good and evil, between the "bad guys" and the "good guys," and by fashioning a simple but compelling plot line.

Welcome to Hard Times

The struggle in *Welcome to Hard Times* is between the Man from Bodie, who in a fit of rage destroys a town in one day, and Blue, the tragic old man who almost single-handedly tries to rebuild the town. The plot and characters echo classic Western films such as *High Noon* (1952), with their solitary heroes who oppose villains who tyrannize communities. Doctorow's vision, however, is much bleaker than that of the traditional Western and cannot be encompassed by the usual shoot-out or confrontation between the sheriff and the outlaw. In fact, Doctorow's novel implies that the West was chaotic and demoniac, and order was not usually restored in the fashion seen in Hollywood Westerns. The reality of American history has been much grimmer than its literature or its popular entertainment has ever acknowledged. Indeed, Doctorow's fiction shows again and again an America whose myths do not square with its history.

It is a paradoxical aspect of Doctorow's success that his parodies of popular genres are themselves usually best sellers. Perhaps the reason is that alongside his ironic use of popular genres runs a deep affection for the literary forms he burlesques. The title of *Welcome to Hard Times*, for example, is a kind of genial invitation to have some fun with the pieties and clichés of the Western. Doctorow is deadly serious about the "hard times" and grave flaws in American culture, but he usually finds a way to present his criticisms in a comic vein.

The Book of Daniel

Doctorow's fiction is often set in the past, during identifiable historical periods such as the 1870's, the 1920's, the Great Depression era of the 1930's, or the 1950's. Characteristic of Doctorow's deft handling of important political themes and historical periods is *The Book of Daniel*, a major political novel about the Cold War period of the 1950's. Centering on a couple (who bear a striking resemblance to spies Ethel and Julius Rosenberg) who were executed for espionage (supposedly for stealing the "secret" of the atomic bomb for the Soviet Union), the story is narrated by one of their children, Daniel. He sets out to investigate what happened to his parents while trying to come to terms with his own 1960's brand of radicalism. Concerned less with whether the couple were actually guilty of spying than with uncovering his own identity, Daniel tracks down and interviews those who had been closest to his parents. Through this personal story, Doctorow conducts an analysis of the failure of American radicalism and of one generation to speak to another. By and large, 1960's radicals did not know much about the history of the Left, and the traditional Left had done little to pass on its past, so that young men like Daniel felt isolated, bereft, and angry about their lack of connection to a heritage of social protest.

Daniel mourns the loss of his family. Unable to cope with his parents' sacrifice of themselves to a political movement, he allows his own marriage to deteriorate as he is racked by memories of what it was like for his parents to be harassed constantly for their political beliefs. Daniel is embittered by the human costs of political activism, but those costs are also what make him fiercely determined to gain some truth out of what happened to his parents and to confront those relatives who seem to have collaborated in his parents' execution.

From the point of view of 1960's radicalism, Daniel has a certain contempt for his parents and their attorney, who tried scrupulously to accommodate themselves to the American judicial system rather than challenging that system outright by calling the trial political and acting in court—as some protesters did in the 1960's—as defiant political prisoners. In the novel, politics serves as the metaphor for the divisions in family life. In other words, there is a merging between the private and public realms, between individuals and political movements, just as the narrative swings between Daniel's first-person (intimate) and third-person (impersonal) points of view. In his great trilogy *U.S.A.* (1937), John Dos Passos separates elements of history and fiction with discrete sections called "Camera Eye" and "Newsreel." It is Doctorow's achievement to have fused the personal and the public, the fictional and the historical, into one narrative voice, suggesting the indivisibility of history and the individual's perceptions of it. There is no "history" out there, he implies; there is only the "history" within the minds of the people who live it and re-create it.

Near the end of *The Book of Daniel* is a brilliant set-piece description of Disneyland, which comes to stand for the forces in American life that threaten any complex sense of history. On the grounds of the theme park, which resembles a film set, are arranged figures and artifacts of American history, the symbols and tokens of the national heritage, wrenched from their social and historical context and abstracted into a series of entertainments for customers who do not have to analyze what is presented to them. This spectacle of history substitutes for the real thing, demeaning the past and replacing it with a comfortable, pacific, and convenient product that need only be enjoyed and consumed.

Ragtime

In *Ragtime*, Doctorow goes even further in suggesting that much of American history has been turned into a myth. In this novel, historical figures have the same status as fictional creations. The novelist's Sigmund Freud—who appears in *Ragtime* going through the Tunnel of Love with Carl Jung, one of his disciples (and later a rival)—and the historical Freud are equally products of the imagination, of the language that is used to invent both history and fiction. So convincing is Doctorow in inserting famous people such as J. P. Morgan, Henry Ford, and Emma Goldman into his narrative that many readers are led to wonder which incidents in the novel are "true." Doctorow has implied in interviews that in a sense it is all "true," since the imagination has such power to reconfigure history. *Ragtime* is surely one of the most subversive novels ever written by an American, for it suggests that history can be viewed as a consummate fiction.

Like *The Book of Daniel*, *Ragtime* is anchored in the story of a family—this time of a boy who grows up in New Rochelle, New York, at the beginning of the twentieth century, during a time of polar exploration, the development of great inventions such as motion pictures, and political upheavals led by radicals such as Emma Goldman. From his naïve viewpoint, the small boy observes the explosive changes and the stresses of a society that does not know how to handle its own dissenting elements. One of these is Coalhouse Walker, a proud black man who is insulted by a group of white firemen and who resorts to violence and hostage taking, demanding that society recognize his rights after his wife, Sarah, is killed while trying to petition a politician on Coalhouse's behalf. While the boy sees his society falling apart, it is also reconstructing itself. He sees his mother take into their home Sarah and the child she had with Coalhouse, and the boy later sees his uncle join the Coalhouse gang.

A third family important to the novel is an immigrant family of Eastern European Jews: Tateh, Mameh, and their little girl. After a financial crisis causes Mameh to resort to prostitution, Tateh expels her from the family, becomes increasingly desperate in his attempts to get money, and finally, after leaving his past behind, manages in Horatio Alger fashion to make a fortune as a film director. The final interweaving of the novel's families occurs when the mother of the New Rochelle family marries Tateh and they move to California with their two children and the black child they have adopted, the son of Coalhouse and Sarah.

If the actions of Coalhouse Walker seem more appropriate to the 1960's than to early twentieth century America, it is Doctorow's way of exaggerating those elements of the future that inhere in the past. The rage that Walker feels is both a personal and a historical rage; the insult is to him and to his race. If a black man in the age of J. P. Morgan would not in fact take over the financier's library full of art treasures, the truth is (Doctorow implies) that the conditions for such terrorism were brewing for a long time in the United States. Such an act could almost have happened then. That the seemingly stable world before World War I was on the verge of cataclysm is suggested at the end of the novel's first chapter, when the boy exclaims, "Warn the duke"—referring to the assassination of the Archduke Ferdinand, the event that precipitated World War I.

Ragtime is similar to *Welcome to Hard Times* in that it has a fairy-tale quality. The prose is quite simple, descriptive, and declarative: Doctorow could almost begin with the phrase "Once upon a time." It is clear, however, that his point is to link the past and the present, to show that the craving for mass entertainment at the beginning of the twentieth century naturally had its outlet in the invention of motion pictures, just as the urge of Robert Edwin Peary and other explorers to roam the world had its counterpart in the mass production of the automobile. Repeatedly, Doctorow links the innovations in domestic life with great public adventures and events, fusing public and private affairs in an almost magical, uncanny manner.

The very title of the novel, *Ragtime*, refers not merely to the syncopated, accented music of the time but also to the quality of the period, with its fragmented, volatile changes that transformed the character of the United States. This was the beat, the rhythm of the period, Doctorow implies. Time was being given a different tempo by the inventions, innovations, and struggles of immigrants, African Americans, and the underclass, even as Americans of an earlier generation took refuge in patriotism and public displays that excluded these groups.

Loon Lake

The class distinctions that play an important role in *Ragtime* become the focal element of *Loon Lake*, which, like *The Book of Daniel*, contains a double narrative perspective. *Loon Lake* shifts between the experiences of a poet on a rich man's isolated estate and a poor man's picaresque adventures across 1930's America. Somehow the power of the materialist, the millionaire capitalist, is meant to be balanced by the imagination of the poet, but the novel fails to measure up to *Ragtime*'s astonishing feat of fusing the different realms of fiction and history.

The poetic interludes in *Loon Lake* are reminiscent of the stream-of-consciousness "Camera Eye" sections of Dos Passos's *U.S.A.* trilogy. *Loon Lake* also has a haunting, ineffable quality, evoking a metaphorical but almost tangible sense of history that is akin to the novel's image of the lake: a dazzling surface of ever-shifting and widening perspectives and hinted-at depths. History as mirror—refracting, distorting, highlighting, and obscuring human actions—is a palpable presence. A great social novelist, Doctorow manages to describe every level and grouping of society in the soup kitchens, monasteries, mansions, and assembly lines in the United States between the two world wars.

World's Fair

In comparison to Doctorow's earlier novels, *World's Fair* seems remarkably straightforward. It resembles a work of conventional nonfiction, and, like a memoir, it is largely bound by a chronological structure. While a few sections resemble oral-history accounts from other characters' perspectives, much of the action is seen through the consciousness of a young boy, Edgar, living in the Bronx during the 1939-1940 New York World's Fair. Given the main character's name and background, it is difficult not to conclude that Doctorow has himself and his family in mind. He had already used his New Rochelle house as a model for the house in *Ragtime* and the mind of a young boy as the intuitive medium through which many of the domestic, private events of that novel are filtered. Doctorow's interest in the way the fictional and factual impinge on each other naturally led to this exercise in quasi-autobiography, in which the materials from his own background underpin the plot. The World's Fair becomes a metaphor for the boy's growing up and for the maturation of the United States.

Unlike many American novelists, Doctorow does not merely criticize American materialism, seeing in the emphasis on things a soul-deadening culture that is antithetical to the artist's imagination. On the contrary, he enjoys playing with the nation's materiality, decrying, to be sure, the way in which the culture turns its important figures and events into toys and commercials for capitalism, but also capturing—and honoring—the American delight in inventiveness and machinery. In *World's Fair*, he triumphantly combines the personal and familial aspects of life with the way a society celebrates itself. In doing so, he recovers the synthesis of history and literature that make *Ragtime* such a resounding success.

Billy Bathgate

In most of Doctorow's work there is a tension between a naïve, childlike point of view, often fresh with perception, and an older, ironic, detached perspective. Sometimes this split is expressed in terms of first- and third-person narration, as in *The Book of Daniel*. In *Ragtime*, the narrator seems to be simultaneously the little boy and his older self, both observing for the first time and remembering the past. Like *World's Fair*, *Billy Bathgate* seems more conventional than Doctorow's earlier novels, for it is told from the standpoint of its main character, a mature man reviewing his past. The novel unfolds with such immediacy, however, that it appears to be taking place as the narrator tells it.

The first long sentence of *Billy Bathgate* launches right into a scene in which Dutch Schultz is disposing of a disloyal associate, Bo Weinberg. The setting is described by fifteen-year-old Billy Bathgate, the novel's narrator, who is impressed with the smooth running of the Dutchman's criminal enterprise. A car drives up to a dark dock, and without using any light or making a sound, Dutch's crew gets on the boat with Bo and his girl, Drew Preston. Dutch's control over the situation is inspiring for the young boy, who has been given the honor of running errands and performing other chores for the famous gang.

Doctorow exquisitely handles the feeling of an adult remembering his adolescent self and the sheer excitement of being privy to the most secret counsels of criminals. Billy describes, in fascinating detail, the process by which Bo's feet are encased in concrete. Facing the torture of drowning, Bo taunts Dutch, hoping to provoke his famous temper so that Dutch will shoot him so he can die quickly rather than make him suffer the agony of a slow death. Dutch keeps calm, however, while Bo retails instances of Dutch's violent and ungiving nature. Dutch takes his revenge by appropriating Bo's mistress, Drew.

Billy fears but is also fascinated by Dutch's violence, for Dutch cuts a great figure in the world, with minions to serve him and women to fawn over him. Billy's Irish mother has occasional periods of dementia (pushing around a baby carriage full of garbage), and his Jewish father long ago abandoned his family. Dutch provides a glamorous alternative to this grim life, and the gang a surrogate family for the neglected boy. The Dutchman sees him juggling on the street and takes a shine to him, eventually calling Billy his "pro-to-jay." Billy is, in Dutch's words, "a capable boy."

Dutch has a way of utterly changing the face of

things, and for a long time working for him has a fairy-tale quality. No sooner is Bo Weinberg overboard with his cement overshoes than Dutch is making love to Drew Preston—a socialite who is fascinated, for a while, by his presence and energy. She even accompanies him to Onondaga in upstate New York, where Dutch takes over a town, plying the locals with gifts and setting up a cozy atmosphere in preparation for what he rightly expects will be a favorable jury verdict in the case brought against him for tax evasion.

Dutch has the power to create his own world, staying for days at a time in his hotel room with Drew. There is something engaging and down-to-earth in his crude, raw energy, which is perhaps why Drew finds herself attracted to a man so unlike her husband and his rich cronies. Drew's involvement with Dutch is reminiscent of Evelyn Nesbit's fascination with Tateh, the Jewish immigrant, and his daughter in *Ragtime*, for they represent a life of the streets, a flavor of what is going on in the lower orders, which is at once alien and appealing to those living a highly stylized and often-repressed life in the upper classes.

Dutch's great strength is also his great weakness. By making all of his business revolve around himself, he fails to see how crime is becoming organized and corporate. His way of doing business is almost feudal—depending on violence and on the loyalty of subordinates—and he has no grasp of how to put together an organization that can compete with the government or his rival, Lucky Luciano. Dutch wants to personalize everything, so that it all evolves out of his own ego. That ego is unstable, however; on an impulse, Dutch kills an uncooperative colleague in an Onondaga hotel, one of many instances in which he goes berserk against his opponents.

Members of Dutch's gang—particularly his accountant, Abbadabba Berman—sense that the old ways of doing things are nearly finished. Bo's defection is only the beginning of events that put Dutch on the defensive and that culminate in his gangland murder. Abbadabba tries to convince Dutch to recognize that he is part of a larger crime network, but Dutch can think only in terms of his own ambitions and calls off plans to join with Lucky Luciano and other gangsters. In compensation, perhaps, for Dutch's inability to adapt to new times, Abbadabba turns to Billy, making him an apprentice and lavishing attention on the boy.

Through Abbadabba and Drew, Billy gains perspective on Dutch. Drew, Billy finds, has her own sort of power and sense of ease. When she tires of Dutch, she simply leaves him, conveying to Billy the impression that Dutch's charisma has its limits. Billy never dares to think of actually leaving the gang, but he keeps his own counsel and is prepared to take care of himself when Dutch is murdered. At the death scene, in which Dutch, Abbadabba, Lulu, and Irving have been shot, Billy learns from Abbadabba the combination of the safe where Dutch has stashed much of his loot. Evasive about his subsequent career, Billy intimates at the end of the novel that he has indeed gained the Dutchman's fortune, but he does not explain what he will do with it.

Billy's reticence is a perfect foil to the Dutchman's very public career: Even Dutch's last delirious words are taken down by a stenographer and published in the newspapers. Dutch never learns to be circumspect and even plans to assassinate Thomas E. Dewey, the district attorney who made it his mission to put Dutch in prison. By the end of his career, Dutch has not only alienated his gangland associates but has also made it impossible for corrupt Tammany politicians to accept his bribes. He is a relic of an earlier age of unbridled individualism. Billy, on the other hand, hides Dutch's fortune, goes back to school, graduates from an Ivy League college, and becomes an army officer in World War II and then a business entrepreneur—an inconceivable career in Dutch Schultz's world.

Billy Bathgate is a combination of Huck Finn, Tom Sawyer, and Horatio Alger. He is a hero who is prudent, yet an adventurer who risks making love to Drew Preston, even though he knows that it means certain death if the Dutchman finds out. He keeps a cool head even when the Dutchman is punishing him for not having provided a piece of vital information sooner. Billy is a romantic, melting at the sight of Drew and hardly believing that they have been sexual partners. He is also a rationalist, realizing that his best chance of survival is to play the role of the loyal Bronx kid.

As Billy prospers and gets to know the different worlds to which he has been introduced, he finds it impossible to return as he was to his old neighborhood. He dresses differently, carries himself differently, and has a consciousness of a world that extends far beyond Bathgate Avenue, from which he has derived his assumed name. Billy becomes, in other words, a self-invented figure, transcending his origins not only in the actions he narrates but also in his very language, a blend of popular and sophisticated vocabulary that precisely captures the boy and the man who has become the narrator of this novel.

The Waterworks

The possibility that even a child like Billy Bathgate may be destroyed by adults is suggested by *The Waterworks*, in which the industrialism and politics of 1870's New York threaten all children. In some ways Doctorow's bleakest novel, *The Waterworks* has elements of a detective tale by Edgar Allan Poe. Unlike Doctorow's novels in which a young man's viewpoint is central, *The Waterworks* is narrated by a mature journalist, McIlvaine, who sees the victimization not only of the masses of homeless, abandoned children wandering New York but also of youth at the top of the social scale. McIlvaine's young freelance writer Martin Pemberton, son of the corrupt businessman Augustus Pemberton, finds himself first disinherited by his father and eventually made a subject for experiments by the novel's mad scientist, Dr. Wrede Sartorius.

When Martin abandons his fiancé, Emily Tisdale, disappearing after announcing that he has seen his supposedly dead father still alive and riding through the streets in an omnibus, McIlvaine joins with an honest policeman (a rare creature in this time of the Tweed Ring) to solve the mystery. They discover that old men are faking their deaths, abandoning their wives and children, and turning their wealth over to Sartorius, who will keep them alive as long as possible by injecting them with bodily fluids taken from children. The casket in which August Pemberton's wife and sons thought they had buried him is discovered to hold a child's body. While the conspiracies against children are apparently defeated by the novel's end and two marriages appear to give the work a happy ending, McIlvaine concludes his tale with little faith that children (or adult women, for that matter) can do anything to defend themselves against predatory men.

McIlvaine comments on the difficulty of pinning down the source of evil in his story. Sartorius can be given alibis, much of the evil activity is learned about through rumor, evil characters are glimpsed rather than caught in spotlights. It is as if the city itself is evil, or as if evil is in the water. Even more troubling are McIlvaine's similarities to his supposed villains, for he too takes advantage of young people in order to produce his book. *The Waterworks* shares with several other Doctorow novels a thematic concern for the role of the writer in society, and like Blue in *Welcome to Hard Times*, McIlvaine may create evils in the course of trying too hard to cover up horror. Insofar as *The Waterworks* is read as a prologue to Doctorow's other New York novels, it casts a pall over them. This novel allows the reader less ability to accept what looks like a loophole for optimism in another book, because it instructs the reader on the ways civilization ignores or forgets its errors, the ways civilization chooses to remember what supports its illusions.

Doctorow's novels contain acute perceptions of the way the public makes its selections about what it will remember about the past, aided by the film industry and Disneylands of the culture. Gangsters, film stars, cowboys—all have a certain glamour in Doctorow's fiction because they have that glamour in the popular genres he mimics. As models for a rational, democratic society, these stock types fail, and Doctorow is fully aware of that reality. He cannot abandon them, however, for these amusements reflect the core of the American psyche, the overwhelming urge to mythologize history, to make it amenable to human desires and hopes.

City of God

Set in New York City, *City of God* is nothing less than a meditation on the nature of the universe, of God, the role of religion, and, of course, New York itself, a world city that expresses the powerful countervailing forces that Saint Augustine explored in his book of the same title. Is religion, for example, a force for good or an irrelevance in the modern world beset by horrifying phenomena such as the Holocaust and acts of mystifying blasphemy? An eight-foot brass cross is stolen from St. Timothy's Episcopal Church in the East Village and placed on the roof of a small synagogue situated in an uptown brownstone. Is this an anti-Semitic act or even—as a rabbi proposes—possibly an attack by an ultra-Orthodox Jewish group upset with those attempting to update Judaism?

The novel begins with an account of the creation of the world derived from the study of contemporary physics. The traditional religious accounts of creation cannot square with a God of physics that would, in the narrator's words, represent a deity that seems out of reach—not merely all-powerful but inscrutable. Can efforts pursued by the Manhattan-based congregation of the Synagogue for Evolutionary Judaism (EJ) integrate science in a religious worldview? The congregation includes a Nobel laureate in physics who seeks a meaning in the universe that his science cannot yield.

The Reverend Thomas Pemberton, known as Pem, has essentially lost his congregation and is attracted to the notion of an evolutionary Judaism, which attempts to take into account the changing historical conceptions of God and God's role in the world. Complicating Pem's response is his attraction to Sarah Blumethal, the daughter of Holocaust survivors and a rabbi who has, along with her husband, Joshua Gruen, established the EJ movement. What is motivating Pem? Like Augustine, Doctorow probes the intersection between human desire and religious belief.

Complicating this novel is yet another strand of story involving Everett, a writer, who reports his dialogues with Pem in a workbook. Everett is attempting to make a novel out of Pem's quest to make Christianity relevant to the modern world. Pem speaks in paradoxes, saying, for example, that he has never felt more like a Christian than while studying for his conversion to Judaism and marriage to Sarah (her husband Joshua having died in his quest to expose a Holocaust perpetrator).

Critics have split in their assessment of this novel—some have deemed it too diffuse and overwrought, whereas others have called it an ambitious and bravura blending of theology, science, and fiction. Like Doctorow's other works, *City of God* is an effort to stretch the reach of contemporary fiction. The question on which many of the novel's detractors and supporters focus is whether Doctorow's hybrid of philosophy and story justifies the fragmentary, decentered structure of the work.

The March

The title of *The March* refers to General William Tecumseh Sherman's devastating invasion of the South during the last year of the American Civil War. His army of sixty thousand men burned and tore their way through Georgia, intent on bringing the war to a swift end. Doctorow does not moralize about the cruelty of this episode; rather, he treats it as human phenomenon with ramifications beyond Sherman's or anyone else's control.

Sherman is a very well-drawn character. Focused on his mission, he bridles when Secretary of War Edwin M. Stanton arrives to chafe the general about his troops' treatment of the South's freed slaves. Sherman points out that he cannot possibly care for the thousands who are now abandoning slavery and flocking to the Union lines. He cannot advance if he allows questions of emancipation or even human rights to interfere with his strategy. In an especially vivid scene, Sherman poses for a photograph; the moment recalls Doctorow's musing in *Ragtime* on motion pictures and way the modern media change the ways in which events are recorded and indeed are shaped by the mechanisms brought to bear on them.

Instead of making any direct critique of Sherman's march, Doctorow presents a set of fascinating characters who embody the contradictions and challenges of war. Wrede Sartorius (who appears also in *The Waterworks*), for example, is a brilliant if cold surgeon, pioneering new methods of saving lives and reducing the mutilations of the wounded but also contemptuous of most medical practices and indifferent to the larger war aims or even to taking a human interest in his patients. On the other end of the spectrum is Pearl, a "white Negro," the daughter of a plantation owner and one of his slaves; Pearl disguises herself as a drummer boy in the Union army as she tentatively explores the opportunities freedom offers her. The planter class and rank-and-file Confederate soldiers also make convincing appearances—none more so than Arly, a rascal who garbs his nefarious and self-serving deeds in colorful religious language. Readers of *Ragtime* will revel in the story of Coalhouse Walker, the father of the rebellious black man in the denouement of Doctorow's earlier novel.

Doctorow's ear for dialogue is extraordinary, providing an immediacy to the re-creation of the past that seems spontaneous, not studied. Abraham Lincoln and Ulysses S. Grant figure in brief but arresting scenes, the former seeming like a modest man in Wrede Sartorius's presence and yet one who in retrospect grows in stature as Sartorius appreciates the enormity of Lincoln's task.

Although some critics have asserted that *The March* is too congested with characters and subplots, the panoramic approach of the novel does justice to the history-making events it depicts. The strategic goals and the human costs of war are finely balanced in this deftly wrought narrative. *The March* is not as daring as *Ragtime*, which treats historical and fictional characters more insouciantly—for instance, in contriving meetings between Emma Goldman and Evelyn Nesbit—but its sober realism and precise diction make *The March* superior to the conventional historical novel.

Carl Rollyson
Updated by Marshall Bruce Gentry

Other major works

SHORT FICTION: *Lives of the Poets*, 1984; *Sweet Land Stories*, 2004.

PLAY: *Drinks Before Dinner*, pr. 1978.

SCREENPLAYS: *Three Screenplays*, 2003.

NONFICTION: *Jack London, Hemingway, and the Constitution: Selected Essays, 1977-1992*, 1993; *Poets and Presidents*, 1993; *Conversations with E. L. Doctorow*, 1999; *Reporting the Universe*, 2003; *Creationists: Selected Essays, 1993-2006*, 2006.

EDITED TEXT: *The Best American Short Stories 2000*, 2000.

Bibliography

Bloom, Harold, ed. *E. L. Doctorow*. New York: Chelsea House, 2001. Collection of essays offers an overview of Doctorow's career and works from a variety of perspectives. Intended as a starting point for students first reading the author.

_______. *E. L. Doctorow's "Ragtime."* New York: Chelsea House, 2002. Collection of essays illuminates the historical context of Doctorow's work and also offers literary analysis.

Fowler, Douglas. *Understanding E. L. Doctorow*. Columbia: University of South Carolina Press, 1992. Introduces the reader to Doctorow and his works on a basic level, surveying arguments of other critics and noting Doctorow's links to other writers. Emphasizes the extent to which family life is Doctorow's most enduring thematic concern.

Harris, Stephen. *The Fiction of Gore Vidal and E. L. Doctorow: Writing the Historical Self*. New York: Peter Lang, 2002. Provides a valuable introduction to the way Doctorow situates himself in the tradition of the historical novel and, more specifically, in American literary work that focuses on how history shapes and is shaped by the individual.

Harter, Carol, and James R. Thompson. *E. L. Doctorow*. Boston: Twayne, 1990. Emphasizes Doctorow as an artist rather than as a politician or experimental historian. More than other scholars, Harter and Thompson discuss significant differences among Doctorow's works and see Doctorow himself moving toward autobiography over the course of his career.

Morris, Christopher D., ed. *Conversations with E. L. Doctorow*. Jackson: University Press of Mississippi, 1999. Reprints more than twenty interviews with Doctorow in which he discusses a wide range of topics, including his goals in his fiction, his themes, and his approach to his work.

Siegel, Ben, ed. *Critical Essays on E. L. Doctorow*. New York: G. K. Hall, 2000. Collection features essays on Doctorow's fiction by important writers such as Edmund White, Garry Wills, and Hilton Kramer.

Tokarczyk, Michelle M. *E. L. Doctorow's Skeptical Commitment*. New York: Peter Lang, 2000. Presents a political literary analysis of Doctorow's works. Covers all the novels through *The Waterworks*.

Williams, John. *Fiction as False Document: The Reception of E. L. Doctorow in the Postmodern Age*. Columbia, S.C.: Camden House, 1996. Reviews and analyzes important criticism on Doctorow, including major reviews, especially in relation to how criticism has promoted Doctorow's reputation, used postmodernism to understand Doctorow, and used Doctorow's texts to promote postmodern critical theories.

HEIMITO VON DODERER

Born: Weidlingau, near Vienna, Austro-Hungarian Empire (now in Austria); September 5, 1896
Died: Vienna, Austria; December 23, 1966
Also known as: Franz Carl Heimito Ritter von Doderer

Principal long fiction

Die Bresche, 1924
Das Geheimnis des Reichs, 1930
Ein Mord den Jeder begeht, 1938 (*Every Man a Murderer*, 1964)
Ein Umweg, 1940
Die erleuchteten Fenster, 1950
Die Strudlhofstiege: Oder, Melzer und die Tiefe der Jahre, 1951
Das letzte Abenteuer, 1953 (novella)
Die Dämonen: Nach der Chronik des Sektionsrates Geyrenhoff, 1956 (*The Demons*, 1961)
Die Merowinger, 1962
Roman No. 7, Erster Teil: Die Wasserfälle von Slunj, 1963 (*The Waterfalls of Slunj*, 1966)
Roman No. 7, Zweiter Teil: Der Grenzwald, 1967 (fragment)

Other literary forms

In addition to novels, Heimito von Doderer (DOHD-ehr-ur) published several volumes of short stories, poems, aphorisms, and essays, as well as his diary for the period from 1940 to 1950.

Achievements

The mention of Heimito von Doderer's name among people familiar with German literature invariably evokes the image of Austria, particularly of the last few decades of the Austro-Hungarian Empire, which ceased to exist in 1918, and of the first Austrian Republic, which came to an end when Adolf Hitler annexed it to Germany in 1938. Doderer's major novels contain not only detailed and loving depictions of the Austrian landscapes and of the cityscape of Vienna but also fascinating social panoramas of these singularly troubled periods in the country's history. Perhaps most important, these social panoramas are made up of characters whose personalities reflect the author's deeply felt concerns about the essence of modern humanity.

Biography

Heimito von Doderer was born Franz Carl Heimito Ritter von Doderer on September 5, 1896, in Weidlingau, near Vienna. His father was Wilhelm Ritter von Doderer, a government architect and the builder of the Karawankenbahn and other Alpine railways. Doderer spent his youth in Vienna, where he attended secondary school. During World War I, he served as an officer of the Dragoons in the imperial Austrian army. In 1916, he was captured on the Russian front and spent the next four years in various prisoner-of-war camps in Siberia.

In 1920, Doderer escaped from Siberia by walking across the Kirghiz Steppe. He returned to Vienna and studied history and psychology at the university there. In 1921, he wrote his first novel, *Die Bresche* (pb. 1924), and in 1925, he received his doctorate in history. Beginning in 1927, he wrote for several newspapers, an activity that he gave up in 1931 to devote himself exclusively to his own literary production. In 1930, Doderer married Gusti Hasterlik; they were divorced in 1934. In 1933, he joined the outlawed Austrian National Socialist Party. When he moved to Munich in 1936, however, he came into direct contact with the political reality of Nazi Germany, particularly since he could find lodgings only in Dachau, a Munich suburb that was the site of a concentration camp. When he returned to Vienna shortly before the Anschluss, Doderer left the National Socialist Party and warned his Jewish friends of the impending danger. During World War II, he served as a captain in the German air force and in that capacity spent varying periods of time in France, Russia, Germany, Austria, Czechoslovakia, and Norway, where he was captured by the British in 1945.

During the period from 1946 to 1948—the worst postwar hunger years—Doderer completed the manuscript of his most humane and lighthearted novel, *Die Strudlhofstiege*. When this work and *Die erleuchteten*

Fenster were published, Doderer was firmly established as a major literary figure. In 1952, he married Maria Emma Thoma. From 1950 to 1956, Doderer worked on his magnum opus, *The Demons*. It was published on his sixtieth birthday. Shortly afterward, in 1957, *The Times Literary Supplement* called him "the most formidable German-speaking novelist now living." In 1958, he received the Austrian State Prize for Literature, the first of several awards from various parts of the German-speaking world.

During the last years of his life, Doderer worked on a series of four novels that were to stand in the same thematic arrangement to one another as the four movements of a symphony. In their totality, these four parts were to constitute a panorama of the modern age, as seen from an Austrian vantage point. Unfortunately, Doderer was able to write only one complete novel of this series, *The Waterfalls of Slunj*, and a fragment of a second one, *Der Grenzwald*. He died of cancer in Vienna on December 23, 1966.

Analysis

One of the most striking impressions one receives from a reading of Heimito von Doderer's novels is that most of his characters are somehow incomplete. At the outset of the novels, the physical, intellectual, and emotional circumstances of his personages are usually presented in great detail, and they often appear to be quite commonplace and normal to the reader, yet, by various means, Doderer always manages to convey the notion that they are deficient in some way. Their deficiency often consists of the preponderance of one character trait at the expense of others or of the domination of one part of human nature (such as intellect) over another one (such as emotion). Such one-sidedness results in disharmony between the character concerned and the world around him or her and, in Doderer's terms, constitutes a deficiency in that character's humanity.

Heimito von Doderer. (Getty Images)

In the course of the novels, some of his characters achieve a complete integration of the various aspects of their personalities and hence what he considers their true humanity. The successful integration of the characters' personalities establishes harmony between them and the world, or to use Doderer's terms, their universality. In Doderer's view, *Homo universalis* must be able to come to grips with the rational and irrational forces within and outside him- or herself, with beauty and ugliness, with richness and poverty—in short, he or she must accept life in all of its manifestations and must reconcile all of its extremes. The general theme of Doderer's novels is humankind's achievement of its own humanity.

According to Doderer, the universal man must be free in the Schillerian sense; he (or she) should do by inclination that which it is his duty to do. He must, of his own accord, accept life as it is, and he must participate in it to the best of his ability. Having understood Doderer's standard, one can proceed to the deviations from it that constitute the points of departure for his plots. Anyone who has a fixed notion as to what his life or his environment ought to be or why it does not correspond to his notion, and who consequently attempts to change his life or his environment, is caught in a situation that Doderer calls "the second reality." He is caught within the confines of ideology, idiosyncrasy, milieu, or whatever the case may be; he sees everything through glasses of a certain tint, his actions are conditioned in a certain manner, and he moves in a reality different from the generally accepted normalcy as postulated by Doderer. One such character is Frau Schubert, a middle-aged servant who wants to get married, even though there is not a chance in a million that she will find a husband. Nevertheless, she makes preparations, quits her job, rents a flat, buys furniture, and finally commits suicide out of desperation about her deceived hopes.

The plots of Doderer's novels are invariably concerned with the liberation of the protagonist from his or her second reality. The treatment of the subject may at times be comical (as in the character Schlaggenberg's *chronique scandaleuse* in *The Demons*), but the basic problem is Doderer's most serious concern and directly related to some of the larger issues of the twentieth century. In his epilogue to the novella *Das letzte Abenteuer*, he differentiates between a pragmatic way of life ("thinking commensurate with life") and an ideological way of life ("living commensurate with thought"), and he considers the latter doomed to end in doctrinairism, in reformism, and finally in the totalitarian state. Elaborating on this point, Doderer says in the same epilogue that during World War II, he discovered

> how much more important it is to see what is, than to ascertain what ought to be, for the latter leads to the refusal of apperception, i.e. to that devastating form of modern stupidity which, by means of so-called convictions . . . makes impossible any communication about the simplest things.

Every Man a Murderer

The theme of humankind's achievement of humanity is presented throughout Doderer's novels with increasing emphasis. Some of his early works could conceivably be read as "stories" (to use E. M. Forster's term), without an awareness of the theme. This is particularly true of the second half of *Every Man a Murderer*, which has all the suspense of a whodunit.

Conrad Castiletz, the protagonist of this novel, becomes obsessed with the idea of discovering the murderer of his wife's sister, whose death occurred eight years earlier. Conrad neglects his wife and starts on a wild-goose chase, searching for the jewelry that the woman in question had carried with her and for the one suspect in the case, whom the police had been compelled to release for want of evidence. In the end, Conrad finds out that he himself, together with a group of students in a train, unintentionally killed the woman. After this discovery, Conrad makes another one—namely, of his wife's infidelity. The next morning he dies in an explosion. Conrad's obsession with his wife's sister constitutes his second reality, which he is unable to leave in spite of several warnings by friends and associates, who admonish him to lead and enjoy his life in the normal "first reality." When he is finally forced to accept the irrefutable evidence of his own unwitting complicity in his sister-in-law's death, he cannot live with this knowledge.

Conrad is the only character in *Every Man a Murderer* that is caught in the second reality. This is typical of Doderer's early novels, where there are usually only a few characters directly concerned with his central theme. As Doderer develops, the number of characters in his novels increases, as does the complexity of their plots, but his central theme—humankind's attainment of true humanity—remains paramount.

Die Strudlhofstiege *and* The Demons

In *Die Strudlhofstiege*, Doderer presents this theme by means of a vast and complex array of characters. It is true that the protagonist (Lieutenant Melzer) is the only character who is involved in all the essential events of the novel, but the events do not take place solely because of him or for the sake of his development. The process of Melzer's complete humanization serves as a basis for comparison and contrast to various other characters whose humanization is achieved only partially or not at all.

Die Strudlhofstiege is in many ways a precursor of *The Demons*: Many of the characters of the earlier novel reappear in the later one. The German title of Doderer's novel, *Die Dämonen*, was adopted from the identical German title of the work by Fyodor Dostoevski, which is known in English as *The Possessed* or *Devils*.

There are several thematic and structural similarities between Dostoevski's and Doderer's works. The main difference on the thematic level lies in the nature of the characters who are caught in the second reality, of those who are possessed. In Dostoevski's work, the primary concern is with a group of fanatical ideologists whose ill-defined political pursuits bring harm to the lives of others. In Doderer's novel, all the major characters are possessed or, to use his terminology, have entered a second reality. Only those characters whose illusions and activities are on a political plane, however, bring permanent misfortune and doom upon themselves and others.

In *The Demons*, the theme of humankind's attainment of true humanity is presented by means of a multitude of interrelated actions involving a total of 142 characters. While most of the principal characters are members of the upper middle class and professionals, the scope of the novel also includes members of the highest ranks of the aristocracy as well as criminals and prostitutes. The main events of the novel take place between the fall of 1926 and July 15, 1927, the day of the general strike and the burning of the Palace of Justice in Vienna. Most of the many strands of the action, both private and political, are parts of the tissue of a conventional, almost classical, plot centered on the unveiling of the origin of a natural daughter and the bringing to light of a previously suppressed last will.

A synopsis of the plot of so long a novel (1,345 pages) must necessarily be incomplete and selective. For the sake of the present discussion, the fates, actions, and developments of seven key characters have been chosen for a detailed examination: Georg von Geyrenhoff; René von Stangeler and his fiancé, Grete Siebenschein; Kajetan von Schlaggenberg and his supposed sister, Charlotte; and Leonhard Kakabsa and his beloved, Mary K.

Geyrenhoff, a bachelor and a high-ranking civil servant, has recently regained a considerable sum of money that had been deposited in England and was thus inaccessible during World War I and for some time thereafter. Because of his financial independence and because of his dissatisfaction with his work, he retires prematurely from the civil service and devotes himself to the writing of a chronicle about the activities of a group of friends who are usually referred to as Our Crowd. At first, he stands aloof from the lives of his friends and simply observes and records them, but soon he becomes intellectually and emotionally involved in their affairs; it is he who is responsible for bringing to light the suppressed last will, and in the end he marries Friederike Ruthmayr, the rich widow of Charlotte's father.

Stangeler, a recently graduated historian, at first is seen as struggling for intellectual, personal, and financial independence. He does not want a regular appointment (such as a professorship), and he does not want to be tied to the woman he loves, Siebenschein. Siebenschein, on the other hand, has to contend with her solidly middle-class family, as well as with her own often ruffled pride and self-respect. Their relationship and their lives change for the better when Stangeler is offered a job as a consultant by Jan Herzka, a businessman who inherits a castle in Carinthia. This job leads to a permanent position as librarian and book buyer for Herzka; it also helps to establish Stangeler's scholarly reputation because of his excellent critical edition of an original medieval manuscript that he discovers in the castle. Now that he feels financially and professionally independent and secure, Stangeler has much more self-assurance in his dealings with Siebenschein and her family, and at the end of the book he refers to her as his fiancé.

Kajetan and Camy von Schlaggenberg's marriage has been a failure because of a fundamental emotional incompatibility. At the beginning of the novel, their definite separation has just taken place, and Kajetan suffers great emotional pain that impairs his creativity as a novelist. In addition, he has pecuniary problems and is forced to waste much time on journalistic hackwork. After he receives some financially important commissions from a large newspaper concern, he is in a position to pursue his theory of sexuality—that of the Fat Females. According to this theory, only experienced, rather abundantly endowed middle-aged women who have no ambitions regarding marriage and family life are suitable mates for men of the postwar generation. He unfolds a great flurry of activity and wastes much money on this project until he eventually realizes how foolish and ridiculous it is.

Meanwhile, his supposed sister, Charlotte, is in dire financial straits as she practices her violin, preparing for a career as a soloist. During her first important audition, the insurmountable tremor of her hands (of which she had been aware all along) becomes evident once more, and the conductor for whom she auditions persuades her to abandon her goal. Upon returning to her home, she finds a letter informing her of a legacy of 250,000 schillings, which, however, is only a fraction of the fortune that she will eventually inherit. Even though she learns shortly afterward that she is not Kajetan's sister, she gives him a considerable sum of money. Kajetan is thus able to take a trip to London, where he has one last brief encounter with his wife. After this painful experience, he begins to devote himself to his real literary work. Charlotte marries Géza von Orkay, a Hungarian diplomat who is Geyrenhoff's cousin.

Kakabsa, a simple worker, one day follows an impulse to buy a Latin grammar. He begins to study Latin and in the course of his studies develops a very keen understanding of grammar, which leads him in turn to master standard German diction. At first, he applies this diction only in his thoughts, nourished by the Greek classics, which he reads in German translations. He cultivates an acquaintance with several young persons, some of whom attend the *Gymnasium* (college-preparatory secondary school). One of them introduces him to her mother, Mary K. This strikingly beautiful widow has managed to overcome the effects of an accident in which one of her legs was cut off above the knee. She does not hobble about with her artificial leg but has learned to control it completely, and thus she continues not only to appear but also be graceful and poised. Her physical victory and Leonhard's intellectual victory at once point to an affinity in spirit. They are attracted to each other, fall in love, and accept this love, with all of its implications.

In *The Demons*, the theme of humanization is presented by means of one main motif that pervades the entire novel and involves all the major characters. This motif is humankind's passage from its self-constructed second reality into the factual, everyday reality. Motifs from Doderer's earlier novels, such as confinement and freedom, or imperceptiveness and perceptiveness, are all present in *The Demons*, but they are integrated or submerged in the main motif. While the various characters are in their second reality, they are represented as being confined, as being unable to lead their own lives, and as being imperceptive in the sense that they have no understanding of their own afflictions or of their unsatisfactory relationships with others. At the end of their development—that is, once they have attained humanity in Doderer's sense—they understand and accept their own personalities and their positions in the world. Once they have attained this understanding and acceptance, they become sovereign masters of their own lives.

The main characters of the novel could well be categorized with respect to the amount of imagination they possess and the measure in which they are involved in a second reality: The spectrum would range from Camy von Schlaggenberg, who is represented as completely matter-of-fact and self-contained, to Alois Gach, an instinctively integrated personality, to Leonhard Kakabsa, whose initial mania for independence and noninvolvement is already somewhat akin to a second reality, to René, Geyrenhoff, Charlotte, Kajetan, and Jan Herzka, not to speak of the political agitators or of Achaz von Neudegg, the medieval witch hunter and sex pervert. One cannot but agree with H. M. Waidson when he says that "the really interesting people in the novel are those whom the second reality has invaded, but who are capable, even if only with great effort, of focusing the double vision into one, subduing the imagination within its limits."

The question arises how the author conveys the idea that a given character has reached the turning point, that he or she has managed to "focus the double vision into one." There are several instances in the novel where choral characters make general philosophical statements on behalf of the author. These abstract statements, however, are outweighed by the all-pervading patterns of imagery that Doderer uses in applying his theory to particular characters and situations. The existence of a given character within a second reality, his realization of being in this state, and his eventual attainment of true humanity—that is, his acceptance of factual reality—these phases of his development are indicated by means of telltale images, thoughts, and occurrences. In this manner, a certain rhythm is established that is very helpful for purposes of orientation within the many different strands of action in this long and complex novel.

At the end of the novel, all the major characters, with the sole exception of the political fanatics, have entered or reentered factual reality. They have learned to accept life as it is; they have attained true humanity. This affirmation of life is expressed in an almost ritualistic manner through the many marriages that conclude the novel.

THE WATERFALLS OF SLUNJ

No consideration of Doderer's novels would be complete without at least mentioning *The Waterfalls of Slunj*, his last complete novel, a work that is masterfully constructed according to the sonata form. It includes all of his usual motifs and images, but they are subordinated to the overall musical structure. It is certainly a masterpiece and makes one regret that the author was unable to complete the remaining three parts of his projected tetralogy.

Franz P. Haberl

OTHER MAJOR WORKS

SHORT FICTION: *Die Posaunen von Jericho*, 1958; *Die Peinigung der Lederbeutelchen*, 1959; *Meine neunzehn Lebensläufe und neun andere Geschichten*, 1966; *Unter schwarzen Sternene*, 1966; *Frühe Prosa*, 1968; *Die Erzählungen*, 1972; *A Person Made of Porcelain, and Other Stories*, 2005; *Divertimenti and Variations*, 2008.

POETRY: *Gassen und Landschaft*, 1923; *Ein Weg im Dunkeln*, 1957.

NONFICTION: *Der Fall Gütersloh*, 1930; *Julius Winkler*, 1937; *Grundlagen und Funktion des Romans*, 1959; *Tangenten: Tagebuch eines Schriftstellers, 1940-1950*, 1964 (diaries); *Repertorium*, 1969; *Die Wiederkehr der Drachen*, 1970; *Commentarii: Tagebücher, 1951 bis 1956*, 1976; *Commentarii: Tagebücher, 1957-1966*, 1986; *Heimito von Doderer-Albert Paris Gütersloh: Briefwechsel, 1928-1962*, 1986; *Tagebücher, 1920-1939*, 1996; *Von Figur zu Figur*, 1996.

BIBLIOGRAPHY

Bachem, Michael. *Heimito von Doderer*. Boston: Twayne, 1981. This volume in the Twayne World Authors series contains a biography as well as close analysis of Doderer's works. Includes a bibliography of primary and secondary sources.

Embry, Charles R. "'A Secret Between Man and God': Second Reality in Heimito von Doderer's *The Demons*." In *The Philosopher and the Storyteller: Eric Voegelin and Twentieth-Century Literature*. Columbia: University of Missouri Press, 2008. In the first part of this book, Embry analyzes the work of Eric Voegelin, a twentieth century political philosopher who also theorized about literature. In the second part, Embry employs Voegelin's concepts to analyze three literary works, including Doderer's novel *The Demons*.

Hesson, Elizabeth. *Twentieth Century Odyssey: A Study of Heimito von Doderer's "Die Dämonen."* Columbia, S.C.: Camden House, 1983. A thorough analytical study of Doderer's most important novel, *The Demons*. Includes a bibliography and an index.

Jones, David L. "Heimito von Doderer and Man's 'Existential Fear.'" *Papers on Language and Literature* 20, no. 2 (Spring, 1984). Jones discusses Doderer's life and his novels, providing background information, psychological and philosophical analysis, and an examination of the issues emphasized in the works.

Luft, David S. *Eros and Inwardness in Vienna: Weininger, Musil, Doderer*. Chicago: University of Chicago Press, 2003. An examination of Doderer, Robert Musil, and Otto Weininger—three twentieth century Viennese authors whose work presented radically new concepts of sexuality. Luft describes how Doderer portrayed his personal sexual obsessions to understand the power of National Socialism and other forms of totalitarianism.

Pfeiffer, Engelbert. *The Writer's Place: Heimito von Doderer and the Alsergrund District of Vienna*. Translated by Vincent Kling. Riverside, Calif.: Ariadne Press, 2001. The Alsergrund district was the location of two of Doderer's novels. Pfeiffer, the Doderer curator at the Alsergrund District Museum of Vienna, describes the role that Alsergrund played in Doderer's life and works. Kling's afterword places Doderer within a broader literary context.

HARRIET DOERR

Born: Pasadena, California; April 8, 1910
Died: Pasadena, California; November 24, 2002
Also known as: Harriet Huntington

Principal long fiction

Stones for Ibarra, 1984
Consider This, Señora, 1993

Other literary forms

Although known primarily for her novels, Harriet Doerr (dowr) also published short stories and essays. Most of her shorter works are collected in a volume of short stories, *Under an Aztec Sun* (1990), and in *The Tiger in the Grass: Stories and Other Inventions* (1995). Many pieces appeared first in anthologies, such as *The Best American Short Stories* (1989, 1991), or in magazines, such as *Poets and Writers Magazine* and *The New Yorker*.

Achievements

Harriet Doerr was the recipient of numerous awards, including the Wallace Stegner Fellowship in Creative Writing to Stanford University, 1980-1981; the *Transatlantic Review*'s Henfield Foundation Prize (London) for her short stories, 1982; a National Endowment for the Arts grant in 1983 for the manuscript of *Stones for Ibarra*; and the American Book Award for first fiction in 1984 for *Stones for Ibarra*. In 1985 she received five fiction awards for *Stones for Ibarra*: awards from the Bay Area Book Reviewers Association, the PEN Center U.S.A. West, and the American Academy and Institute of Arts and Letters as well as the Gold Medal for fiction from the Commonwealth Club of California and the Harold D. Vursell Memorial Award for quality of prose style from the American Academy and Institute of Arts and Letters. Her seemingly simple prose is carefully crafted and polished to eliminate any unnecessary language, yet each phrase sparkles with meaning and poetic brilliance. *Stones for Ibarra* and *Consider This, Señora* both take place in Mexico, and Doerr manages to describe and bridge the gap between the native Mexicans and transplanted Americans, presenting a more accurate and more just portrayal of Mexicans than is typical of American fiction. *Stones for Ibarra* was adapted for a two-hour television film for the Columbia Broadcasting System's Hallmark Hall of Fame in 1988.

Biography

Harriet Doerr was born Harriet Huntington in Pasadena, California, one of six children of a well-to-do family. She grew up in a household with gardeners and cooks. Her father died when she was eleven; her mother never worked outside the home. In 1926, when Harriet was sixteen, she first met her future husband, Albert Doerr. After graduating from high school in 1927, she went east to Smith College in Northampton, Massachusetts. She attended Smith for a year, and then, continuing her history major, she transferred to Stanford University, where Albert was studying. They married in 1930, and Doerr left Stanford without graduating. For the next many years, she spent much of her time raising their two children—a son, Michael, and a daughter, Martha.

In 1935, Doerr and her husband, now an engineer, went to Mexico together for the first of what would be many visits to oversee his family's mining interests. Albert had been born in Mexico, and when his father died in 1950 he and Harriet moved to Mexico City for a year to take charge of extensive family land holdings, including the copper mine that would later figure in *Stones for Ibarra*. After subsequently living in California for ten years, they returned to live in a small town in Mexico. Over the course of several trips and sojourns, Doerr spent a total of fifteen years in Mexico. Other than the Mexican years and a brief stay in Philadelphia, Doerr lived in California.

In 1962 Albert Doerr was diagnosed with leukemia. He died in 1972. Three years later, rising to the challenge given by her son and daughter, Harriet Doerr returned to college at the age of sixty-five. She began at Scripps College in Claremont, where she took Spanish, music, and creative writing, then moved to Stanford to complete the degree she had begun more than forty years earlier. She graduated in 1977. At Stanford she submitted some stories she had written at Scripps to the writer John

L'Heureux in order to get into his writing class. Though she had planned to stay only a few months to finish her degree, she stayed in the creative-writing program at his invitation. Although decades older than the other student writers, she managed to fit in with the other members of the workshops. The weekly deadlines, combined with the workshop members' critiques, kept Doerr writing regularly.

L'Heureux encouraged his students to submit their work for publication, and several of Doerr's stories were published. In 1982, she received the *Transatlantic Review*'s Henfield Foundation Prize. On that basis, she signed on with a literary agent, but the agent had little success representing her. Publishers liked her work but did not know how to classify it: Were the pieces she wrote stories or reminiscences? Then the Viking Press's London scout sent some of Doerr's stories to Corlies Smith at Viking's New York office. Smith had no knowledge of Doerr's age and assumed she was British. Smith asked for more, and then suggested that the stories be turned into a novel. With the help of L'Heureux, Doerr decided on an order for the stories, making them chronological, and wrote some new and linking texts. *Stones for Ibarra* was published in 1984, when Doerr was seventy-three years old. The novel was an immediate critical and popular success. Doerr spent nearly a decade writing her second novel, *Consider This, Señora*, partly because of her age and partly because she feared that reviewers would be more critical of her work after the tremendous success of her first book.

At the behest of her son, who was dying of brain and lung cancer, Doerr wrote *The Tiger in the Grass*, which contains some autobiographical pieces. In the late 1990's, despite her normal reticence and her near blindness because of glaucoma, Doerr undertook work on her autobiography at her home in Pasadena, California. The work was not completed by the time Doerr died in November, 2002, of complications from a broken hip.

Analysis

Harriet Doerr's novels share a common episodic structure and a Mexican setting, and they have similar characters and related themes. Both novels are written in a thoroughly crafted prose in which each sentence is pared down and polished until only the essential innermost gem remains, resulting in what one critic has called a "crystalline prose." The reader is able to discover in Doerr's spare phrases the meaning and emotion the characters themselves hesitate to reveal. Critics have commented on the sense of oral storytelling of *Stones for Ibarra* in particular and Doerr's use of vignettes to advance the story.

Both of her novels reveal as much about the "lost" North American expatriates as they do about the Mexican natives, and, by shifting perspectives, they allow the reader to see each group or individual through the eyes of the other. Compared with the Mexico in novels by such authors as Graham Greene, Malcolm Lowry, and D. H. Lawrence, Doerr's Mexico is a friendlier, more humane place, where the Mexicans are as perplexed about the North Americans as the North Americans are about the Mexicans. It is a no less tragic Mexico, but tragedy is quotidian, a normal part of life for natives and expatriates. Despite their differences, despite the clash of cultures in the conflict zone of cultural interaction, their shared sense of tragedy and search for saving grace unites Mexican and North American.

Stones for Ibarra

Stones for Ibarra began as a series of short stories that share a general location in a central Mexican town so small that it does not appear on the map of Mexico. Doerr claimed that only about 10 percent of *Stones for Ibarra* is autobiographical, but the framework of the novel recalls the Doerr family's forays to Mexico.

Like the Doerrs, the fictional Sara and Richard Everton go to Mexico from San Francisco to reclaim the family estate and reopen a copper mine abandoned since the Mexican Revolution of 1910. Not long after their arrival at the unexpectedly dilapidated house (it falls far short of both the faded family photographs and the Evertons' dreams), Richard is diagnosed with leukemia; the estimate is that he has six years to live. Doerr's prose is so restrained that Richard's illness and impeding death are treated no more dramatically than any number of other elements in the novel. The vignettes that constitute the work's eighteen chapters chronicle a series of events that focus on one character of Ibarra after another; they are connected by the passage of time between the arrival of Richard and Sara Everton and Sara's departure six years later.

"The Red Taxi," for example, tells the story of Chuy Santos, whose two friends, El Gallo and El Golondrino, or the Rooster and the Swallow, work at the Everton mine. Together the three men decide to buy an aged Volkswagen and become partners in a taxi service. Unfortunately, the two friends, working in unsafe conditions after hours in order to make enough money to meet the purchase deadline for the car, die in a mine accident. Chuy mourns the loss of his friends; nonetheless, when the Evertons give him the money to buy two coffins in which to bury them, he buys the cheapest ones he can and uses the difference to buy the car that was the original cause of the accident. One story after another describes death and loss, but these are not macabre tales that horrify or elicit pity. Doerr portrays people and events with such tranquillity that the reader bears witness to what the Evertons see as a "national peculiarity": "a disregard for danger, a companionship with death."

Indeed, it is this companionship with death that Sara Everton must learn as she comes to terms with her husband's impending death and her initial denial moves toward acceptance. The novel closes with an incident that explains its title. According to ancient Mexican custom, the site of a fatal accident is marked by a cross to remind others of the tragedy. As people pass and remember, each leaves a stone. The road across from the gates of the widow Everton's house is marked by a pile of stones. "An accident has happened here. Remember the place. Bring stones," thinks Sara on the eve of her departure. She has accepted her husband's death and accepted, as well, the Mexican interpretation of it.

Consider This, Señora

Doerr spent almost ten years writing her second novel. The enormous popularity of her first made her strive for a proper encore. Furthermore, as Doerr herself once said, she was perfectly happy to work on a single sentence for an hour or more, to find the right word or phrase needed. Like *Stones for Ibarra*, *Consider This, Señora* began as three short stories published in journals and only later acquired life as a novel.

Consider This, Señora consists of ten chapters of interlocking stories of the lives of a small group of expatriate North Americans who have relocated to the small Mexican village of Amapolas (Poppies). Though five expatriates live in the small community, the novel focuses in particular on three women. Susan Ames is an artist who divorced her mountain-climbing husband after finding him in bed with another woman. Frances Bowles is a twice-divorced travel writer desperately trying to hang on to her handsome Mexican lover. Her mother, Ursula Bowles, is an elderly widow born in Mexico who has come back to the land of her childhood to die. One male expatriate is Bud Loomis, an annoying and crass exploiter who has fled the United States to escape paying taxes and perhaps imprisonment; he has bought land in partnership with Sue Ames. The other is Herr Otto, a former pianist with the telltale numbers of a concentration camp tattoo on his wrist; he repeatedly plays a single note on the piano.

The land and people of Mexico, which Doerr describes with exquisite clarity and precision, bring about a healing process in each of these lost exiles. Sue Ames suffers from her husband's betrayal, but she blossoms as a painter and artist. Her ex-husband comes for her, even though she has not answered any of the many letters he has written. He finds her a changed and better woman—a new, mysterious, self-satisfied woman—and they reunite. Frances Bowles finishes her travel book, *Your Mexico*, which all knowledgeable readers agree is inaccurate in its generous descriptions of hotels, meals, and local color. She sadly gives up her lost lover, only to find a truly compatible mate in an archaeologist she meets in the Yucatán Peninsula. After months of playing only one note, the A above middle C, Herr Otto starts to play again. Bud Loomis impregnates his young housekeeper; to the surprise of everyone, he marries her and acclimates completely to Mexico. The widow Bowles finds the quiet death she was seeking, carefully organizing all her effects in her last days.

All the expatriates except Sue Ames eventually sell their houses in Amapolas. Sue installs a caretaker, Patricio, who eventually marries and raises a family there. Though she never returns to Amapolas, Sue claims, when interviewed after a showing of her paintings, that the paintings divide her "between Mexico and here." The simplicity of Doerr's prose does not hide the central theme of this novel, the search for and receiving of a saving grace.

Linda Ledford-Miller

OTHER MAJOR WORKS

SHORT FICTION: "Edie: A Life," 1989; *Under an Aztec Sun*, 1990; *The Tiger in the Grass: Stories and Other Inventions*, 1995.

BIBLIOGRAPHY

Alarcón, Daniel Cooper. *The Aztec Palimpsest: Mexico in the Modern Imagination*. Tucson: University of Arizona Press, 1997. Analyzes works by Mexican and non-Mexican writers to demonstrate how Mexico and the concept of "Mexicanness" have been defined and depicted. Includes *Stones for Ibarra* in an examination of classic Anglo-American writings about Mexico.

Doerr, Harriet. "Enough About Age." Interview by Pamela Warrick. *Los Angeles Times*, August 27, 1993. An interview with Doerr on the publication of *Consider This, Señora*. Doerr talks about her decision to get her college degree after her husband's death in 1972 and her experience in the creative-writing program at Stanford University. She also discusses the importance of memory, saying that no experience one has had is ever lost.

_______. "Harriet Doerr: When All of Life Is Important, the Search for the Right Word Is Endless." Interview by Steve Profitt. *Los Angeles Times*, December 31, 1999. In this interview, Doerr talks about the lessons she learned from her life in Mexico, her matter-of-fact style, the importance of memory in her work, and her attitude toward mortality. She notes that she sees no harm in the fact that the older one gets, the more memory and imagination become the same.

_______. "A Sleeve of Rain." In *New Essays in New Territory*. Vol. 2 in *The Writer on Her Work*, edited by Janet Sternburg. New York: Norton, 1991. Through the lens of the homes in which she spent her life, Doerr reminisces and shares autobiographical details.

Henderson, Katherine Usher. "Harriet Doerr." In *Inter/View: Talks with America's Writing Women*, edited by Mickey Pearlman and Katherine Usher Henderson. Lexington: University Press of Kentucky, 1990. Offers tributes to creative-writing professors who encouraged Doerr to publish and discusses her creative process and her favorite writers—Katherine Anne Porter, Eudora Welty, Gabriel García Márquez, and Juan Rulfo.

King, Rosemary A. "*Stones for Ibarra*, by Harriet Doerr." In *Border Confluences: Borderland Narratives from the Mexican War to the Present*. Tucson: University of Arizona Press, 2004. Analysis of *Stones for Ibarra* is included in a volume that examines fiction written by authors living on the border between the United States and Mexico. Argues that "the effect of the border on the region as an agent of cultural differences influences the ways writers construct narrative space and the ways their characters negotiate those spaces."

Oliver, Myrna. "Harriet Doerr, 1910-2002: Novelist Published First of Three Gem-like Books at Age 74." *Los Angeles Times*, November 26, 2002. One of the more detailed obituaries published upon Doerr's death. Includes information about her life, her novels, and the critical reception of her books.

Reynolds, Susan Salter. "Haunted by Memory." *Los Angeles Times Magazine*, February 8, 1998. Extensive article provides a biographical sketch supplemented by Doerr's memories of her childhood drawn from an interview with the author. Includes Doerr's discussion of her nurse Edie Pink, the subject of her best-known story, "Edie: A Life" (1989), and other autobiographical sources of her work.

See, Lisa. "Harriet Doerr." In *Writing for Your Life, Number Two*, edited by Sybil Steinberg. New York: Publishers Weekly, 1995. Focuses on Doerr's experiences in Mexico and their relationship to *Stones for Ibarra* and *Consider This, Señora*. Also discusses the effects of her age on Doerr's writing.

Silko, Leslie Marmon. "Pablo, Domingo, Richard, and Sara." Review of *Stones for Ibarra*, by Harriet Doerr. *The New York Times Book Review*, January 8, 1984. Argues that the village of Ibarra takes over as the central interest in the novel, and the American couple serve only as a point of departure for the reader. Calls the work a poet's novel and a tribute to the native culture and the basic human impulse to tell a story.

J. P. DONLEAVY

Born: Brooklyn, New York; April 23, 1926
Also known as: James Patrick Donleavy

Principal long fiction

The Ginger Man, 1955, 1965
A Singular Man, 1963
The Saddest Summer of Samuel S, 1966
The Beastly Beatitudes of Balthazar B, 1968
The Onion Eaters, 1971
A Fairy Tale of New York, 1973
The Destinies of Darcy Dancer, Gentleman, 1977
Schultz, 1979
Leila: Further in the Destinies of Darcy Dancer, Gentleman, 1983
De Alfonce Tennis, the Superlative Game of Eccentric Champions: Its History, Accoutrements, Rules, Conduct, and Regimen, 1984
Are You Listening, Rabbi Löw?, 1987
That Darcy, That Dancer, That Gentleman, 1990
The Lady Who Liked Clean Rest Rooms: The Chronicle of One of the Strangest Stories Ever to Be Rumoured About Around New York, 1995
Wrong Information Is Being Given out at Princeton, 1998

Other literary forms

All of the principal works produced by J. P. Donleavy (DUHN-lee-vee) are novels, but some of the protagonists and central situations of these novels are explored in other literary forms. *A Fairy Tale of New York* is derived from the play *Fairy Tales of New York* (pb. 1961) and the short story "A Fairy Tale of New York" (1961), later collected in Donleavy's volume of short stories *Meet My Maker the Mad Molecule* (1964). Donleavy adapted several of his published novels for the stage: *The Ginger Man* (pr. 1959), *A Singular Man* (pb. 1965), *The Saddest Summer of Samuel S* (pb. 1972), and *The Beastly Beatitudes of Balthazar B* (pr. 1981). He also wrote a book of satiric nonfiction, *The Unexpurgated Code: A Complete Manual of Survival and Manners* (1975). Among Donleavy's limited production of occasional pieces are two important autobiographical essays: "What They Did in Dublin," an introduction to his play *The Ginger Man*, and "An Expatriate Looks at America," which appeared in *The Atlantic Monthly* in 1976. He explored his Irish heritage in *J. P. Donleavy's Ireland: In All Her Sins and Some of Her Graces* (1986), *A Singular Country* (1990), and *The History of the Ginger Man* (1994).

Achievements

The prevailing literary image of J. P. Donleavy is that of the one-book author: He gained celebrity status of a notorious sort with his first novel, *The Ginger Man*, but his subsequent novels failed to generate equal interest. Reactions to *The Ginger Man*, a book that did not appear in an unexpurgated American edition until ten years after its first publication, ranged from outraged condemnations of it as obscene in language and immoral in content to later appreciations of it as a comic masterpiece. The later novels have been received with moderate praise for their style and humor and with slight dismay for their lack of structure or apparent intent. Donleavy himself remained confidently aloof from all critical condemnation, exaltation, and condescension. He continued to pursue his private interests in fiction, to discourage academic interest in his work, and to express, when pressed, bemusement at literary frays of any sort. His work is difficult to place in standard literary traditions: His residency in Ireland and fondness for Irish settings seem to place his work outside American literature, but his birth and use of American protagonists seem to place it outside Anglo-Irish literature as well.

Biography

James Patrick Donleavy was born of Irish parents in Brooklyn, New York, on April 23, 1926. After being educated at private schools, he served in the U.S. Navy during World War II. He saw no action in the service, but he did encounter the work of James Joyce through an English instructor at the Naval Preparatory School in Maryland. This combination of family background and reading interests led to his enrollment in Dublin's Trinity College from 1946 to 1949, on funds provided by the American G.I. Bill. There he was registered to read natural sciences, but he has readily admitted that most of his energies were devoted to pub crawls with fellow American students such as Gainor Crist, the model for Sebastian Dangerfield in *The Ginger Man*, and A. K. O'Donoghue, the model for O'Keefe in the same novel.

Donleavy married Valerie Heron after leaving Trinity and briefly considered pursuing a career as a painter. He returned to the United States, where he finished *The Ginger Man* in 1951, but the novel was rejected by one publisher after another on the basis of its supposed obscenity. On his return to Dublin in 1954, he became friends with playwright and man-about-town Brendan Behan. Through Behan's efforts, *The Ginger Man*, having been refused by some thirty-five American and British publishers, was accepted for publication in 1955 by the Olympia Press of Paris, a house whose main list of pornography enabled it to gamble on unusual literary properties such as Behan's works and Samuel Beckett's novel *Watt* (1953). Donleavy's book was greeted rudely by the British press and by the British courts, where it was prosecuted for censorship violations, but the ensuing publicity, combined with the enthusiasm of early critics and readers, led to the publication of expurgated English (1956) and American (1958) editions that brought Donleavy financial stability and an enviable literary reputation for a first novelist. These editions also marked the beginning of a series of lawsuits filed against Donleavy by Olympia Press over the rights to republish the novel. The litigation ended with appropriate irony when Donleavy acquired the ownership of Olympia Press after decades of legal maneuvering, a story told in his *The History of the Ginger Man*. After that time, he made his home in Ireland, on Lough Owel in Westmeath, in rather baronial circumstances that resembled the affluence of his later characters rather than the student poverty of *The Ginger Man*.

After his marriage to Valerie Heron ended in divorce in 1969, Donleavy married Mary Wilson Price. Each of his marriages produced one son and one daughter. He became an Irish citizen in 1967 and settled in a twenty-five-room mansion on a 180-acre estate near Mullingar, about sixty miles from Dublin. Fittingly, descriptions of his house appear in James Joyce's early *Stephen Hero* (1944), providing yet another link to the writer with whom Donleavy is most frequently compared. Donleavy is also known as a serious artist whose numerous paintings have appeared at many exhibitions.

Analysis

In an interview published in the *Journal of Irish Literature* in 1979, J. P. Donleavy said: "I suppose one has been influenced by people like Joyce. But also possibly—and this is not too apparent in my work—by Henry Miller who was then literally a private god." Appreciation of Donleavy's work is indeed improved by cognizance of these two acknowledged predecessors, and it is entirely appropriate that the former is Irish and the latter American and that all three expatriates have been subject to censorship litigation.

The influence of James Joyce is most apparent in Donleavy's style, and it should be noted that the Ireland of Donleavy's work scarcely overlaps with that of

J. P. Donleavy. (Library of Congress)

Joyce's work. Joyce made self-conscious and even self-indulgent style a necessity for the serious modern novelist, and Donleavy creates his own evocation of Dublin and other Irish environs in an intricate prose style characterized by minimal punctuation, strings of sentence fragments, frequent shifts of tense, and lapses from standard third-person narration into first-person stream of consciousness. The single most obvious indication of Donleavy's stylistic ambitions is his habit of ending his chapters with brief poems.

The influence of Miller is most apparent in the fact that Donleavy's novels, for all their supposedly "graphic" language and sexual encounters, create a world that is a patent fantasy. As in Miller's case, the primary aspect of the fantasy is a distinctly male fabrication based on unending sexual potency and invariably satisfying liaisons with uniformly passionate and voluptuous women. To this, Donleavy adds fantasies about immense wealth, requited infantile eroticism, Dionysian thirst, and spectacular barroom brawls. Because of this comic freedom from actual contingencies, his work satirizes absurd caricatures of recognizable social evils.

The central concern of all of Donleavy's novels is the fortune of a single male protagonist isolated from family and country and pursuing a lifestyle that is improvised and erratic. The great exemplar of this essential situation is *The Ginger Man*, a novel that weighs the joys of decadent drunkenness and ecstatic sex against spiritual fears of loneliness and death. After that first novel, which left the future of its protagonist ambiguous, Donleavy went through a period of bleak despair over the viability of a free lifestyle and emerged from it into a period of wholehearted endorsement of its pleasures. In the process, his view of the world changed from a belief in its essential malevolence to an assertion of its essential benevolence. He thus confronted the problem of the value of independence from social conformity from two wholly different perspectives.

The Ginger Man

The Ginger Man, Donleavy's famous first novel, opens with a pair of subordinate clauses; the first celebrates the spring sun, and the second laments Dublin's workaday horse carts and wretched child beggars. It is between these two emotional poles that the Ginger Man, Sebastian Dangerfield, vacillates throughout the novel. He will be exalted by visions of freedom and possibility, but he will also be crushed by fears and depressions. In *The Ginger Man*, freedom is revolt against the forces of social conformity and rigidity, a casting over of the bulwark virtues of thrift, reverence, and self-discipline. The fear, however, is of the ultimate victory of those same forces and values. The novel refuses to resolve these oppositions neatly. Dangerfield, subject to reckless extremes throughout, finally remains both the Ginger Man, an alias suggestive of spirit and mettle, and Sebastian, the namesake of a betrayed and martyred saint.

One of the novel's achievements is its candid admission of the most deplorable aspects of a quest for freedom such as Dangerfield's. It is appropriate and commonplace in contemporary fiction that an alienated protagonist should court his wife for her dowry and run into debt with landlords, shopkeepers, and other pillars of middle-class society. Donleavy, however, proceeds beyond this comfortable degree of roguery to a proposal of a more complete anarchy that is the novel's most compelling and disturbing quality. Dangerfield also beats his wife, abuses his child, senselessly vandalizes the property of strangers, and is otherwise selfishly destructive because of a self-proclaimed natural aristocracy, a phrase crucial to Donleavy's later novels. In this respect, he sins far more than he is sinned against, and one measure of the novel's complexity is the fact that its most sympathetic character is a matronly Miss Frost, who is devoted to Sebastian but is abandoned by him when her finances have been consumed. *The Ginger Man* is superior to many contemporary novels contemptuous of society because of this admission of the sheer egotism and selfishness underlying such contempt.

Dangerfield's redeeming features, which make him an antihero rather than a villain, are his invigorating bohemian bravura and his true appreciation of life's quiet beauties. The novel is appropriately set in Dublin, mirroring a fine appetite for great talk and plentiful drink. On one level, the novel is about the meeting of the vital New World with the stagnant Old World, for Dangerfield and his Irish American cronies flamboyantly outtalk and outdrink the Irish, who are portrayed as a mean and frugal people who can only be bettered by insult. Dangerfield's appreciation of subtler sensual delights, however, is as essential to his character as those more raucous tastes. His love of the smell of freshly ground coffee wafting from Bewley's in Grafton Street is as important to this novel as its more notorious adventures with whiskey and women. In these aesthetic moments, including the appreciation of the rising sun in the opening of the novel, Sebastian provisionally justifies his sense of aristocracy and demonstrates a kind of moral purity not shared by the novel's other characters.

In conjunction with the picaresque comedy and titillation of Dangerfield's more preposterous adventures, there remains the essentially naïve and ultimately unfulfilled desire for a simpler, solitary bliss. *The Ginger Man* is Donleavy's salient novel because it manages this balance between frivolity and remorse, between freedom and surrender, an opposition resolved in different ways in all of his subsequent novels.

A Singular Man

His second novel, *A Singular Man*, was also held up by worries about censorship, and it was published only after Donleavy threatened to sue his own publisher. Donleavy left the bohemian lifestyle that gave Sebastian Dangerfield vitality for the opulent but gloomy existence of George Smith, whose freedoms have been lost to the encroachments of great wealth. The premise of the novel has obvious autobiographical relevance to the success of *The Ginger Man*; George Smith is accused by his estranged wife of sneaking into society, and he is in fact bewildered by his inexplicable attainment of sudden wealth and fame. The novel frustrates autobiographical interpretation, however, because it represents the emergence in Donleavy's work of the caricatured environment common in his later novels. The nature of Smith's industrial empire is mysterious, but he travels through surroundings with names such as Dynamo House, Electricity Street, and Cinder Village, and makes his home in Merry Mansions.

Smith's only obvious claim to singularity is his solitary appreciation of the hollowness of material wealth, and the novel records his increasing disillusionment and despair. The only satisfying one of his several love affairs is with the sassy Sally Thompson, doomed by the sorrowful machinations of the plot to death in an automobile accident. Smith's only respite from the responsibilities of his financial empire is the construction of a fabulous mausoleum under the pseudonym "Doctor Fear." *A Singular Man* is controlled completely by the obsession with death that was always counterpointed in *The Ginger Man* with a potential for sudden joy, and its style reflects this severe introversion in its reliance on more extended passages of stream-of-consciousness narration than is common in Donleavy's novels.

The Saddest Summer of Samuel S

While *A Singular Man* explored the despair of wealth, *The Saddest Summer of Samuel S* broadened the gloom of Donleavy's post-*Ginger Man* novels by exploring the despair of a vagrant lifestyle. An expatriate American living in Vienna, Samuel S is an overage Ginger Man whose misery is caused by the stubborn isolation from society that was at least a mixed virtue in Donleavy's first novel. In this novel, the only humor is provided by Samuel's bleak confessions to his shocked psychoanalyst Herr S, who functions as a socially acclimated if complacent foil to the alienated but determined Samuel S. The comedy is, however, completely overwhelmed by Samuel's inability to accept the apparent happiness of a relationship with an invigorating American student named Abigail. It is as if Donleavy set out to correct simplistic praise for *The Ginger Man* as an unambiguous paean to rootlessness by stressing in *The Saddest Summer of Samuel S* the costs of bohemian disregard for domestic and social comforts. The novel presents no acceptable alternative to Samuel's self-destructive insistence on alienation for its own sake, none of the moments of happy appreciation of life that redeemed Sebastian Dangerfield.

The Beastly Beatitudes of Balthazar B

Balthazar B is Donleavy's most withdrawn and morbid protagonist, and the novel named for him represents the author's most consistent use of religious resignation as a metaphor for a passive secular disengagement from a malevolent world. The presence of his prep school and college classmate Beefy adds a raucous dimension reminiscent of *The Ginger Man*, however, and *The Beastly Beatitudes of Balthazar B* resuscitates the power of outrageous farce in Donleavy's work. Balthazar, another Donleavy protagonist who is fatherless and without a surname, progresses only from childhood fantasies about African pythons to more adult but equally futile ones about sex in aristocratic surroundings. Throughout the novel, he provides naïve perspective that enables

Donleavy to satirize social pretensions and rampant materialism. The beatitudes that govern most of the novel are Beefy's, which bless the beastly virtues of complete decadence and joyful carnality but prove inadequate in the face of repressive social conformity. The ultimate beatitudes of the novel, however, are Balthazar's, which emerge late in the work and resemble those delivered in the Sermon on the Mount. Having accompanied Beefy on his salacious adventures and seen his companion undone, Balthazar—who, like Donleavy's other early protagonists, identifies with martyrs—is left only with a saintly hope for later rewards such as those in the beatitudes recorded in Matthew's gospel.

The Onion Eaters

Like Balthazar B, Clementine of *The Onion Eaters* is a protagonist plagued by lonely remorse and surrounded by a dynamism in others that he is unable to emulate. He is a young American heir to a medieval British estate, a situation whose effect is that of placing an introspective and morose modern sensibility in the raucous world of the eighteenth century novel. As in most of Donleavy's novels, the central theme is the vicissitudes of a natural aristocracy, here represented by the fortunes of Clementine of the Three Glands in a chaotic world of eccentric hangers-on and orgiastic British nobility. The emotional tension of the novel is based on a deep desire for the freedom of complete decadence in conflict with a more romantic yearning for quieter satisfactions. That conflict enables Donleavy, as in parts of *The Ginger Man*, to create a titillating fantasy while concurrently insisting on a sort of innocence, for Clementine survives his picaresque adventures with his essential purity intact. The significant contemporary revision of an older morality, however, lies in the fact that in Donleavy's fiction such virtue goes unrewarded.

A Fairy Tale of New York

In Donleavy's later work, fantasy is allowed to prevail over remorse, and this new direction emerges first in *A Fairy Tale of New York*, in which a protagonist named Christian is tempted by the evils of the modern metropolis much as the traveler Christian is tempted in John Bunyan's *The Pilgrim's Progress* (1678, 1684). This novel has a special interest within Donleavy's work for its description of a return from Ireland to New York City, which is characterized in the novel by gross consumerism. In *A Fairy Tale of New York*, Christian is more a protector of real virtues than a seeker of them, and the novel ends with a comment on life's minor and earthy beauties rather than the plea for mercy that is common in Donleavy's earlier works. A brief vignette of the same title published a decade earlier provided the opening of *A Fairy Tale of New York*, and the intervening years saw a change in Donleavy's literary interests that enabled him to pursue a fulfilling fantasy beyond the limits of vignette. The result, however it may finally be judged, is a sacrifice of the emotional tension of his finest earlier work in favor of the pleasure of unconstrained fabrication, a surrender of psychological depth for a freer play of literary imagination.

The Destinies of Darcy Dancer, Gentleman

Returning to the spirit of the eighteenth century novel that animated *The Onion Eaters*, *The Destinies of Darcy Dancer, Gentleman* evokes a world of baronial splendor, earthy servants, seductive governesses, and naïve tutors without apparent concern for the forces of modern technology and consequential social ills common to the contemporary novel. It is a stylish and literate entertainment without moral pretensions, a vein of fiction entirely appropriate to the alliance with freedom of imagination arduously explored in the course of Donleavy's work.

There are allusions to a darker world beyond the novel's immediate environs, such as housekeeper Miss von B.'s wartime experiences in Europe, but these serve only to stress the value of the free lifestyle pursued by Darcy Dancer without guilt and without controls beyond a decent sense of chivalry. One indication of the shift from morbidity to frivolity apparent in Donleavy's work is the fact that the setting here is Andromeda Park, named for a goddess whose miseries were relieved rather than for a saint who was martyred. Yet *Leila*, sequel to *The Destinies of Darcy Dancer, Gentleman*, retains the tone of upper-class superficiality while reintroducing a darker view: In this novel, Dancer becomes enamored of a woman but is left helpless when his love is married to another.

Schultz

Schultz is similar to *The Ginger Man* but expresses no remorse or recrimination. Its operative assumption and central motif is a concept of the world as a pointless Jewish joke, and this permits the London theatrical impresario Sigmund Schultz to exploit materialism without moral doubts and Donleavy to create a world in which even the sinfully rich prove ultimately benevolent. Class consciousness and privilege are a matter for comedy rather than bitterness in this novel, and the foul-mouthed American social climber Schultz is accepted with amusement rather than repelled with horror by English royalty.

The perspective of the novel is so completely comic that venereal diseases are presented as mere inconveniences, the political world is represented by the monarch of an African nation named Buggybooiamcheesetoo, and the romantic liaisons are unabashed and masturbatory fantasies. The most important distinction between *The Ginger Man* and *Schultz* is that in Donleavy's first novel the world was seen as malevolent and in the latter it is seen as benign. In accordance with this movement, the author has shifted from a celebration of gallant but doomed improvised lifestyles to a forthright assertion of their superiority to accepted and inherited modes of behavior.

The style and structure of Donleavy's work continued to evolve: *De Alfonce Tennis, the Superlative Game of Eccentric Champions*, for example, is such a mishmash of story, satire, and whimsy that one would be hard-pressed to categorize it. Despite the negative critical response to *Schultz*, Donleavy's public proved loyal, justifying an even less distinguished sequel, *Are You Listening, Rabbi Löw?* Donleavy's fiction of this period deliberately deprives itself of the emotional conflicts central to his earlier, saintlier protagonists. It represents as well an insolent abrogation of the traditional concerns of "serious" fiction. By contrast, *The Ginger Man* was superior to the bulk of postwar novels about bohemian expatriates in Europe because of its sense of the limitations of that lifestyle as well as its potential. His nonfiction of the same period includes two books about his adoptive country, the largely autobiographical *J. P. Donleavy's Ireland* and *A Singular Country*.

THAT DARCY, THAT DANCER, THAT GENTLEMAN

That Darcy, That Dancer, That Gentleman completes the trilogy of Darcy novels, which collectively provide the high point of Donleavy's later work as a novelist. Although ostensibly set in twentieth century Ireland, the focus is on traditional, even anachronistic Irish rural life and values, which impelled Donleavy to make important stylistic modifications to fit the leisurely milieu, particularly in slowing the pace of events and descriptions to mirror the setting. This well-integrated juxtaposition of plot and characters drawn from the tradition of the eighteenth century novel with Donleavy's distinctively modernist style accounts for much of the freshness of the three works.

Darcy's battle to keep Andromeda Park afloat as his resources run out depends on his finding a wealthy wife, but the only woman he can imagine truly loving, Leila, is lost beyond hope of recovery as a marchioness in Paris. Among the unsuitable matches he considers are his neighbor Felicity Veronica Durrow-Mountmellon and two American heiresses from Bronxville, Florida, and Virginia. Rashers Ronald plays a large role in the book as Darcy's virtually permanent houseguest and best, though most unreliable, friend. The novel's climax is a chaotic grand ball at Darcy's estate, at which virtually every character to have been featured in the trilogy makes an appearance. At the end of the book, Ronald is engaged to Durrow-Mountmellon and Darcy is finally reunited with Leila, providing unusually traditional closure for a Donleavy novel, perhaps by way of winding up the trilogy.

WRONG INFORMATION IS BEING GIVEN OUT AT PRINCETON

Donleavy's next full-length novel, *Wrong Information Is Being Given out at Princeton*, presents the first-person narrative of Alfonso Stephen O'Kelly'O, in some ways a typical Donleavy hero. He is a social outsider with no money and expensive tastes, a problem he thinks he has solved in marrying the daughter of a wealthy family. Stephen differs from most of his predecessors, however, in that he is a dedicated musician, composer of a minuet that has been offered a prestigious opening performance by the book's end. While most of Donleavy's protagonists have artistic sensibilities, Stephen is one of the few who manages to be genuinely productive. His devotion to his work provides him with a moral and ethical center that often outweighs his hedonistic impulses, making him to some extent a principled rebel rather than just another of Donleavy's failed would-be conformists.

John P. Harrington
Updated by William Nelles

Other major works

SHORT FICTION: *Meet My Maker the Mad Molecule*, 1964.

PLAYS: *The Ginger Man*, pr. 1959 (adaptation of his novel; also known as *What They Did in Dublin, with The Ginger Man: A Play*); *Fairy Tales of New York*, pb. 1961 (adaptation of his novel *A Fairy Tale of New York*); *A Singular Man*, pb. 1965; *The Plays of J. P. Donleavy: With a Preface by the Author*, 1972; *The Saddest Summer of Samuel S*, pb. 1972 (adaptation of his novel); *The Beastly Beatitudes of Balthazar B*, pr. 1981 (adaptation of his novel).

NONFICTION: *The Unexpurgated Code: A Complete Manual of Survival and Manners*, 1975; *J. P. Donleavy's Ireland: In All Her Sins and Some of Her Graces*, 1986; *A Singular Country*, 1990; *The History of the Ginger Man*, 1994; *An Author and His Image: The Collected Shorter Pieces*, 1997.

Bibliography

Contrucci, Lance. "Revisiting *The Ginger Man*." *Poets and Writers* 31, no. 5 (September/October, 2003). Profile of Donleavy includes background information on his life, a description of his writing process, and an account of the success of *The Ginger Man*.

Donleavy, J. P. "The Art of Fiction: J. P. Donleavy." Interview by Molly McKaughan. *The Paris Review* 16 (Fall, 1975): 122-166. Lengthy interview includes Donleavy's discussion of the complex publishing history of *The Ginger Man*, the painful process of writing, the differences between his characters and himself, his preference for reading newspapers and magazines rather than novels, his life on his Irish farm, and his attitudes toward critics, New York, and death.

_______. "I Have an Aversion to Literature and Writing." In *Endangered Species: Writers Talk About Their Craft, Their Visions, Their Lives*. Cambridge, Mass.: Da Capo Press, 2001. An interview in which Donleavy addresses a range of topics, including his life as a writer, his writing style, and the influence of other writers on his work.

_______. "Only for the Moment Am I Saying Nothing: An Interview with J. P. Donleavy." Interview by Thomas E. Kennedy. *Literary Review* 40, no. 4 (Summer, 1997): 655-671. In this wide-ranging interview, conducted at Donleavy's mansion in Ireland, the author discusses issues from all periods of his literary career and personal life. Particular attention is afforded to the details of his methods of writing and the status of his manuscripts. Includes a bibliography of Donleavy's works.

Keohan, Joe. "A Man Amuck." *Boston Globe*, February 19, 2006. Revisits *The Ginger Man* on the occasion of its fiftieth anniversary and provides background about Donleavy's life. Summarizes the novel's plot, and defines the book's theme as "resistance for its own sake. Resistance as a moral virtue."

Lawrence, Seymour. "Adventures with J. P. Donleavy: Or, How I Lost My Job and Made My Way to Greater Glory." *The Paris Review* 33, no. 116 (Fall, 1990): 187-201. Donleavy's first American editor reveals the inside story behind the complicated negotiations, fueled by fears of obscenity prosecution, that plagued the first two novels, *The Ginger Man* and *A Singular Man*. Lawrence eventually had to publish under his own imprint the first unexpurgated American edition of *The Ginger Man*, followed by eleven subsequent Donleavy books.

LeClair, Thomas. "A Case of Death: The Fiction of J. P. Donleavy." *Contemporary Literature* 12 (Summer, 1971): 329-344. Shows how Donleavy's protagonists are both classical rogues in the tradition of Henry Fielding's Tom Jones and modern victims resembling Franz Kafka's Joseph K. One of the best analyses available of Donleavy's obsession with death, which LeClair identifies as the controlling element in his fiction.

Masinton, Charles G. *J. P. Donleavy: The Style of His Sadness and Humor*. Bowling Green, Ohio: Bowling Green State University Popular Press, 1975. Pamphlet-length study of Donleavy's fiction through *A Fairy Tale of New York* places him in the American black humor tradition. Notes that although Donleavy's characters are increasingly morose and withdrawn, the fiction is most notable for its humor and irony. Includes a brief bibliography.

Morse, Donald E. "American Readings of J. P. Donleavy's *The Ginger Man*." *Eire-Ireland: A Journal of Irish Studies* 26 (Fall, 1991): 128-138. Explores the treatment of the novel in American criticism and discusses reactions in the United States to the use of slang, myth, and Irish values depicted in the novel.

Norstedt, Johann A. "Irishmen and Irish-Americans in the Fiction of J. P. Donleavy." In *Irish-American Fiction: Essays in Criticism*, edited by Daniel J. Casey and Robert E. Rhodes. New York: AMS Press, 1979. Examines Donleavy's attitudes toward his native and adopted countries in *The Ginger Man*, *The Beastly Beatitudes of Balthazar B*, and other works, and concludes that the author has grown more hostile toward the United States while gradually accepting a romanticized view of Ireland. Presents an excellent discussion of Donleavy's use of Ireland. Includes a bibliography.

JOSÉ DONOSO

Born: Santiago, Chile; October 5, 1924
Died: Santiago, Chile; December 7, 1996
Also known as: José Donoso Yañez

Principal long fiction

Coronación, 1957 (*Coronation*, 1965)
Este domingo, 1965 (*This Sunday*, 1967)
El lugar sin límites, 1966 (*Hell Has No Limits*, 1972)
El obsceno pájaro de la noche, 1970 (*The Obscene Bird of Night*, 1973)
Tres novelitas burguesas, 1973 (novellas; *Sacred Families*, 1977)
Casa de campo, 1978 (*A House in the Country*, 1984)
La misteriosa desaparición de la Marquesita de Loria, 1980
El jardín de al lado, 1981
La desesperanza, 1986 (*Curfew*, 1988)
Taratuta; Naturaleza muerta con cachimba, 1990 (novellas; *"Taratuta" and "Still Life with Pipe,"* 1993)
Donde van a morir los elefantes, 1995
El Mocho, 1997

Other literary forms

José Donoso (doh-NOH-soh) was a superb storyteller, and his first literary efforts were in the area of the short story (curiously, his first stories were written in English and published in the Princeton University literary review *MSS*). His collections of stories include *Veraneo, y otros cuentos* (1955; summer vacation, and other stories); *Dos cuentos* (1956; two stories); *El Charlestón* (1960; abridged as *Cuentos*, 1971; *Charleston, and Other Stories*, 1977); and *Los mejores cuentos de José Donoso* (1965; the best stories of José Donoso). Little if any significant thematic or technical distinction can be drawn between Donoso's novels and shorter fiction, other than those imposed by the limits of the genres themselves. Regardless of length, all are superb blends of sociological observation and psychological analysis, in which realism never quite manages to eliminate fantasy, where madness, the supernatural, and the unknown hover just beyond the bounds of consciousness and reason.

Donoso also wrote essays of literary criticism and attracted attention with *Historia personal del "boom"* (1972; *The Boom in Spanish American Literature: A Personal History*, 1977). His *Poemas de un novelista* (1981) is a collection of thirty poems with a twelve-page authorial introduction explaining the personal circumstances that occasioned the verse.

Achievements

Each of José Donoso's novels had its special success, and the writer's prestige grew with each stage of his career. Despite a slow beginning (he came to the novel at age thirty-three), Donoso published no novel that could be classed a failure by critics or the public, and several of his works have received awards, the most acclaimed being *The Obscene Bird of Night* (a favorite of reviewers and literary critics) and *A House in the Country*, which received the Spanish Critics' Prize, a coveted award despite its lack of endowment, since it reflects the esteem of the country's professional critics as a whole. Donoso was the recipient of two grants from the Guggenheim Foundation for the furthering of works in progress and served as writer-in-residence at various American universities, with stints at the University of Iowa Writers' Workshop (1965-1967) and teaching positions at Princeton University and Dartmouth College. In demand as a distinguished lecturer, he also held a number of editorial posts. His powers of sociopsychological penetration and his marvelous irony and skillful use of allegory, together with his masterful handling of existential themes and the abnormal or psychotic narrative perspective, place Donoso in the forefront of international fiction.

Biography

José Donoso is one of Chile's most widely known writers of prose fiction and one of the most outstanding and prestigious figures of his generation of narrators in Latin America. He was born José Donoso Yañez into an upper-middle-class family of Spanish and Italian descent in Santiago on October 5, 1924. His father (for whom Donoso was named) was a physician; his mother, Alicia Yáñez, came from a prominent Chilean family. It was she who, with the couple's servant, Teresa Vergara, reared Donoso and his two brothers. Until her death in 1976, Donoso's mother continued to live in the spacious home where the future novelist was born, and the atmosphere of decrepitude and decay in the labyrinthine mansion (property of Dr. Donoso's three elderly great-aunts) haunts his fiction.

When Donoso was seven years old, his father hired an English governess, the foundation of his excellent knowledge of the language, which he continued to study at the Grange, an English school in Santiago, from 1932 to 1942. During this period, Donoso's maternal grandmother returned from Europe to make her home with the family, an event that (together with her deteriorating mental and physical condition) left a mark on the future writer's development. A teenage rebel who disliked school and his father's imposition of the British sports ethic (personified in a boxing instructor), Donoso began feigning stomachaches, which led to a real appendectomy and subsequently an equally real ulcer.

Never serious about religion, Donoso proclaimed himself an atheist at the age of twelve. Equally cavalier about classes, he cared only for reading, and in 1943, he dropped out of school. After two years, during which he had not managed to hold a job for more than a few months, he set out for Magallanes at the southern tip of Chile, where he worked as a sheepherder on the pampas for about a year, subsequently hitchhiking through Patagonia to Buenos Aires, where he lived as a dockhand until he contracted measles, which obliged him to return home. He finished high school in 1947, enrolling in the University of Chile with a major in English and completing his bachelor of arts degree at Princeton in 1951. His study with Allen Tate and his discovery of Henry James, as well as his introduction to the great paintings of the world, would all influence his future writings.

Returning to Chile, Donoso worked as a teacher, journalist, and literary critic but found himself estranged from his homeland and dissatisfied with his work. His ulcer returned, and he began psychoanalysis. He collaborated in launching the newsmagazine *Ercilla*, which he edited, and in 1954, his first short story written in Spanish ("China") was included in an anthology of Chilean short fiction. The following year, his first book, the collection *Veraneo, y otros cuentos*, was published and had a favorable critical reception, winning the Santiago Municipal Short Story Prize. This success and that of his first novel notwithstanding, Donoso found Chilean society oppressive and moved on to Buenos Aires, where he met his future wife and stayed for two years. He published his second collection of short stories upon his return to Santiago, and he became a leading literary critic, which led to teaching in the Writers' Workshop at the University of Iowa; he abandoned this position in order to move to Spain and finish a novel begun years before, which would become *The Obscene Bird of Night*.

Donoso and his wife, Mará del Pilar Serrano, whom he had married in 1961, adopted an infant daughter in Madrid and settled in Mallorca in 1967. Donoso's first Guggenheim award (1966) was followed by a lectureship at Colorado State University (1969). While in Colorado, his hemorrhaging ulcer required surgery; because of his inability to tolerate painkilling drugs, he subsequently went through a period marked by hallucinations, schizophrenia, and paranoia that resulted in suicide attempts. He returned to Mallorca, moved his family to Barcelona, and began to rewrite his novel, incorporating his nightmarish illness. Subsequently, still recuperating, he bought a seventeenth century home in Calaceite, remodeled it, and in 1971 moved to this village of some two thousand inhabitants in the center of Spain. Both his critical history, *The Boom in Spanish American Literature*, and his novellas in *Sacred Families* were published in Spain.

Donoso's second Guggenheim Fellowship, in 1973, enabled him to work on *A House in the Country*. His first trip to Chile in some nine years had to be canceled because of the military coup there (an event that colors both *A House in the Country* and *El jardín de al lado*). His next move, to the Mediterranean fishing and resort village of Sitges (1976), has obvious resonances in *El jardín de al lado*, which, like all of the author's fiction, has a strong autobiographical substratum. Donoso returned to Chile in 1980, winning the Chilean Premio National de Literatura in 1990. He died in Santiago in 1996.

José Donoso. (© Layle Silbert)

Analysis

José Donoso's first two novels are similar in a number of ways, which makes it convenient to consider them together, despite significant and perhaps fundamental differences in the level of style and technique. Both involve upper-class, traditional Chilean families, a decaying mansion, and the problem of the generation gap; both treat psychological abnormalities in a rigidly stratified society where a rich, decadent minority is contrasted with an impoverished lower class; and in both, members of the aristocracy become emotionally involved with members of the lower class. In *This Sunday*, however, there is a more adroit utilization of innovative techniques and more subtle thematic development, a contrapuntal effect and stream-of-consciousness narration rather than the omniscient narrator of *Coronation*, who summarizes events and describes places and people in photographic fashion, sharpening the narrative perspective and involving the reader's collaborative effort, using secondary characters as third-person reflectors.

Time in *Coronation* is treated in a linear, chronological manner, but in *This Sunday* it is subjected to a more fluid handling, reflecting the philosophical and literary theories of Henri Bergson and Marcel Proust while intensifying the latent Freudian and existential concepts of the first effort, with the result that the aesthetic and intellectual density of *This Sunday* is considerably greater.

Coronation

Misiá Elisa Grey de Abalos in *Coronation* is a wealthy, demented nonagenarian who lives with her fiftyish bachelor grandson, Andrés, an asexual aesthete whose life is a prime example of abulia and existential inauthenticity, a man addicted to French history and collecting canes (possibly symbolic of his not standing on his own in life). Andrés's world, like that of his grandmother, is hermetic, monotonous, isolated from the "real" workaday world; virtually his only human contact is his lifelong friend, Dr. Carlos Gros. The two aging servants, Rosario and Lourdes, have devoted their lives to the service of the Abalos family but become unable to cope with and care for the bedridden Misiá Elisa; Estela, a sensual country wench, is brought in to care for her, introducing a new element into the previously closed system. Estela is something of a catalyst, awakening Andrés's dormant sexuality and introducing the neighboring shantytown's societal dregs into the mansion (and the novel) via her affair with Mario (whose older half brother, René, is a link with the criminal element).

Coronation is traditional in its technique and employs an almost naturalistic cause-and-effect sequence, portraying most of the characters as products of their environment, although Donoso's interest in psychological analysis transcends the usual naturalistic characterization. Social determinism underlies the formation both of Andrés, who studied law in his youth because it was the thing for young men of his class to do, and of Misiá Elisa, who is pathologically repressed, molded by the religious education and bourgeois puritanism of her family. A similar social determinism is responsible for Mario's fear of entrapment (partly cultural, partly based on his brother's unhappy marriage); Estela's pregnancy thus inspires in Mario panic and instinctive flight.

Following Freudian psychology, Donoso stresses the importance of early-childhood experiences, the power of the unconscious, and the central role of sexuality in other areas of human life, with much of the characters' conduct being irrational, neurotic, or motivated by repressed erotic urges. In her senile dementia, Misiá Elisa becomes overpoweringly obsessed with sexuality, which she suppressed during most of her life, and gives way to obscene outbursts. Obsessions are a recurring motif in *Coronation* and in Donoso's fiction as a whole, and often are associated with recurring symbols, false rituals, repetitive or symbolic dreams, existential themes, and rigid daily routines that acquire an unconscious, magical, or supernatural character for the participants. Any break in the routine, therefore, is a transcendent disruption of order—hence the ultimately catastrophic ramifications of bringing Estela, the new servant, into the rigid and ritualistic existence of the mansion.

Misiá Elisa's conversations with Estela include warnings of the dangers of seduction and reveal that she considers all men "pigs" while considering herself a saint (having never let her husband see her naked). Life for the old lady is a gutter, a sewer, a cesspool from which religion is the only escape; thus she is also obsessed with sin, although for her, sexuality and sin are essentially identical. His grandmother's stern warnings and prohibitions and the inculcation of childhood fears and exaggerated taboos fill the boy Andrés with dread and apprehension, leading ultimately to his falsifying his first confession and, disappointed that instant fire and brimstone is not the result, to a loss of faith and rejection of religion, without any accompanying loss of inhibitions.

Plagued by a recurring nightmare in which a long bridge over an abyss suddenly ends, precipitating him into the void, Andrés experiences extreme existential anguish as he comes to realize the inability of philosophy or science to replace the security promised by faith and to assuage the fear of death, of the infinite, and of nothingness. Existentially, he is also radically alone, his solitude and loneliness so extreme that his abulia and inability to act are the visible result of the isolation and meaninglessness of his life. More than two decades spent in idle alienation, avoiding any engagement with life, end abruptly for Andrés when the terror inspired by his grandmother's approaching death is combined with the disturbing attraction of Estela's presence, bringing the realization that he has never really lived (in contrast with his friend, Carlos Gros, who represents an acceptance of life and love, believes both in science and religion, and exemplifies an existential exercise of free will). Where Misiá Elisa sees life as a sewer, Andrés sees it as chaos, terror, absurdity, a mad trick played upon humankind by an unjust or insane god. Both grandmother and grandson thus exemplify alienation so extreme that it borders upon the psychotic, their fragile equilibrium maintained by a series of obsessive routines and rituals—as in the case of Andrés limiting his cane collection to ten.

Donoso employs an indirect, third-person narration or monologue (comparable to the procedure of James) to plumb the psychological depths of his characters and thereby provide a multiplicity of perspectives, augment dramatic intensity, and allow the reader to identify more directly with a given character's viewpoint. The novel raises serious psychological, social, and philosophical issues, often through Andrés's very avoidance of them (an ironic technique that requires the reader to face the conclusions that Andrés has refused to contemplate), but Donoso also employs humor and numerous aesthetic ingredients. Incongruity is essential to many moments of humor, with the best examples involving Misiá Elisa, who, in her madness, swings like a pendulum from prudishness to obscenities to exaggerated religiosity. Similarly, the ironic contrast between Andrés's adolescent ignorance (in flashbacks to his childhood and youth) and the mature knowledge of narrator and reader provides much black comedy; for example, the young Andrés imagined that there was some connection between hell and the school restroom because the latter was a filthy place, and it was there that he first overheard a conversation about sex.

One of the recurring symbols or images of Donoso's fiction is the decaying mansion, often a Victorian monstrosity replete with gables and turrets, balconies whose only function is decorative, passages leading nowhere, closed or walled-up rooms, and other elements representative of a decadent or outmoded lifestyle. The mansion in *Coronation*, similarly constructed, also exemplifies Donoso's fascination with Art Nouveau—with its opulence of detail, decorative floral borders, and curving lines—while the depictions of the grandmother, her "coronation" and death (amid rococo bows, streamers, and billowing folds of cloth), function to complement and emphasize the theme of conspicuous consumption. The decadent mansion is a transparent allegory of a decadent upper class, while on an individual, psychological level, it also frequently symbolizes existential or emotional emptiness, isolation or alienation, and lack of contact with reality.

Another important symbol in *Coronation* is Andrés's collection of canes, rigidly limited to ten to exteriorize or make visible the rigid, self-imposed limits on his sterile, monotonous, routine existence. When the existential crisis provoked by confrontation with two of life's most powerful forces—love and death, both of which he has previously avoided—obliges Andrés to take radical measures, the one step he is able to visualize is raising the limit on his cane collection. He visits the home of an antique dealer whose wife—with her pink shawl and naked palms, evoking a powerful subconscious association with Estela—profoundly disturbs him; thus brought to an awareness of his desire for Estela, he resolves to win her, a decision that, if carried out, would constitute his first step toward existential engagement and authenticity. As he returns home, however, an accidental glimpse of the girl with her lover beneath a streetlight mortifies him and brings realization of his own absurdity and that of his situation; unable to return to his once-comfortable abulia and solitude, he gradually retreats into madness (a denouement that, in naturalistic terms, might be implicit in his heredity), succumbing to the pernicious influence of his grandmother, whose pervasive madness has gradually undermined his own rationality.

Similarly, Mario's fear of becoming a criminal, arising from his brother's criminal nature, the family's increasingly desperate financial straits, and the injustices of society, presages his fall into crime: He is induced to participate in the theft of the Abalos family silver, thereby setting the stage for the grotesque denouement that combines the frustrated robbery attempt, Andrés's madness, and Misiá Elisa's death.

This Sunday

The themes of alienation and existential anguish reappear in *This Sunday*, but Donoso's interest in abnormal psychology and the exploration of the unconscious of each of his protagonists are much more visible than in the earlier novel. Don Alvaro Vives and his wife, Chepa, a wealthy, middle-aged couple, live in another of Donoso's mansions, where they are visited by their five grandchildren (one of whom narrates portions of the novel). Other characters include Violeta, a retired former servant of the Vives household and onetime mistress of Alvaro; Maya, a lower-class psychopath who has been convicted of murder; Marujita, a peddler; Mirella, Violeta's illegitimate daughter; and her husband, Fausto.

In brief, the plot revolves around the activities of Chepa, a volunteer welfare worker, and her infatuation with Maya and use of the family's influence to obtain his parole. Settled by Chepa in Violeta's house, Maya is both attracted to his benefactor and fearful of her, and his pathology determines a path of escape through violence once again—this time through the murder of Violeta, which allows him to return to the comfortable alienation of prison, where no existential decisions are required. Rather than a straightforward narrative, *This Sunday* employs an ironic alternation between the naïve or limited vision of characters—first-person narrators who are participants in the action—and the occasional interventions of an omniscient narrator, thereby stressing the characters' ingenuousness, self-deception, or unawareness.

Much of the narrative is retrospective, via the use of Proustian flashbacks (for example, Alvaro's recollections of the beginning of his affair with Violeta are stimulated by the smell of meat pastries, experienced years previously when he had gone to her house). Free association and indirect third-person, stream-of-consciousness narrative are combined in reconstructing Alvaro's life as a weak young man whose social position enabled him to exploit Violeta without assuming responsibilities, avoiding the threats represented by both university girls and prostitutes while preventing the servant girl from living an authentic existence of her own. A victim of the social conventions by which "decent" girls of his own class were sacred, meant only for marriage, Alvaro is unable to truly love Chepa and other upper-class girls, although on the basis of established mores, he assumes that he will love her; actually, he manages to consummate the marriage only by closing his eyes and imagining that he is making love to Violeta.

In their fifties, Alvaro and Chepa have ceased sleeping together, and both live behind masks, maintaining a facade that serves as a substitute for authentic relationships as well as an escape from unpleasant reality. Alvaro's inability to love having become more pronounced with time, he appears narcissistic, withdrawn, and slightly ridiculous—aspects emphasized by his grandchildren's nicknaming him the Doll, his interminable games of chess and solitaire, his deafness, his lack of concern for things other than his health, and his rituals. Chepa, a victim of a loveless marriage that has increased her basic insecurity, provides a self-portrait in a number of interior monologues, most of them precipitated by contact with Maya. As a lonely, aging woman whose children have left home, she seeks to give some meaning to her existence by works of charity—by helping the poor and through her work at the prison—in an attempt to compensate for the knowledge that for Alvaro she is an object devoid of significance.

A good deal of sadomasochism inheres in Chepa's relationships with "her" poor; she imagines herself as "a littered bitch" with a compulsive need to feed the hungry mouths fastened to her. Her philanthropy is a substitute for the normal human relationships that are lacking in her life as well as a mask for less admirable motivations of her own, the desire to dominate or control, and to indulge her more (or less) than maternal interest in Maya. She helps him to set up a leather-goods shop, but her vigilance arouses his resentment and desire to escape; despite his derangement, Maya intuits in Chepa the devouring female, the Jungian evil mother.

Seeking Maya at Violeta's house, Chepa learns both that he has become Violeta's lover and that Violeta had an affair with Alvaro before his marriage to Chepa, provoking the latter's decision to throw off convention and look for Maya in the shantytown. Unfamiliar with the sprawling slums, she becomes lost in the twilight maze of alleys, but she fortuitously encounters Maya's mistress, Marujita, whose revelations of Maya's mixed emotions concerning Chepa inflame her and bring on a surrealistic, nightmarish experience as she is set upon by slum children who rob her of her furs and purse and leave her exhausted, on a trash heap. The inferno of the slums into which Chepa descends is a symbolic, expressionistic representation of her own subconscious with its hidden, conflicting sexual desires. Maya's murder of Violeta has been seen by critics as an instance of transferring his repressed aggression for Chepa to one socially weaker; the murder frees him from his obligations to her as benefactor, and to society.

The differences between Alvaro and Chepa are not so marked as the grandchildren imagine; their inability to communicate with Alvaro leads them to see him as cold, absurd, and slightly grotesque, while the grandmother is perceived in an unrealistically positive fashion as generous and loving (perhaps a result of her own altruistic self-image), a participant in the children's games of fantasy. Actually, both Alvaro and Chepa suffer from inauthenticity, solitude, and unfulfilled emotions, but Chepa is close to achieving authenticity when she recognizes and accepts her desire for Maya and determines to seek him, while Alvaro has lived so long in egotistic aloofness, exploiting without giving, that no self-redemption appears possible.

The novel's title refers to the family's habitual Sunday gatherings for dinner at the grandparents' residence, highlighting an incident of one specific Sunday, when Chepa searches for Maya, returning from the slums so traumatized that her subsequent life is almost that of a catatonic. Maya's murder of Violeta, who is vicariously Chepa, symbolically signals Chepa's death, and although she lives for many years, she spends them in isolation, essentially as dead to her grandchildren as if she were deceased. The rituals in the lives of adults are paralleled by the children's games, and additional parallels and contrasts throughout the novel lend symmetry: Alvaro's relationship with Violeta is socially similar to that of Chepa with Maya (a superior-inferior involvement); Alvaro and Violeta are passive, inert, making no effort to change their lives, while Chepa and Maya are active, attempting to improve their situations or to change them. *This Sunday* explores more complicated relationships, with more tragic repercussions, than those plumbed in *Coronation*, and it does so in a more objective fashion, given the lessening of authorial intervention. Both novels, however, re-create the surrealistic and nightmarish effects of subconscious, irrational, or instinctive forces, achieving especially memorable portraits in the matriarchs (Misiá Elisa and Chepa), who undoubtedly hark back to the mental deterioration of Donoso's own maternal grandmother.

Hell Has No Limits

Hell Has No Limits, which was published one year after *This Sunday*, provides a departure from the novelist's previous urban settings, being set in a somber, sordid brothel in a backwater rural winegrowing area. Although the existential issues of authenticity and alienation, solitude, and a lack of communication found in the earlier novels are again present to some degree, there is an increased emphasis on absurdity and the grotesque, and Donoso begins to employ mythic elements and ambiguity, symbolically alluding to biblical myths of the Creation and the Fall in depicting the results of a failed economic experiment by a local politician, Don Alejo, who is a sort of local god, even said to resemble the Lord.

The village, Estación El Olivo, created by Don Alejo, a wealthy landowner and area boss, was touted as an earthly paradise at its inception, but some twenty years later, during the novel's present, it has become a caricature of itself, where physical and moral stagnation make it something of a hell on earth. Don Alejo had originally owned the brothel, but as the result of a bet between himself and the madam, Big Japonesa, he signed the property over to her (the wager involved Japonesa's managing to seduce Manuela, a gay cross-dresser who imagines that he is a flamenco dancer). Japonesa won, thanks to her astuteness in manipulating Manuela's erotic fantasy and a promise to make him her partner in the brothel, but during the incident she became pregnant and subsequently gave birth to an unattractive girl, Japonesita, who operated the brothel business following her mother's death. Japonesita, at the age of twenty still a virgin despite her managing a house of prostitution, is a rival of her gay father in a subliminal competition for the affections of Pancho Vega, a truck driver, bully, and closeted gay man whose return precipitates the novel's climax.

Although Don Alejo, as "creator" of Estación El Olivo, is a benign god figure, he is ambiguous by reason of being politically and morally corrupt (he also plots the destruction of the town, since he has decided to convert the whole area to vineyards). His wager, the precipitating factor that brings Manuela's family into being, is a parodic perversion of the concept of Christian marriage, and his association with the powers of evil is symbolized by four vicious black dogs that accompany him (similar dogs appear in *The Obscene Bird of Night*). The ambiguity of Manuela is primarily sexual, for he desires ardently to be a woman; some similar ambiguity appears in Pancho, who is muscular and seemingly virile but in reality is cowardly and in the closet. The ambiguity of Japonesita, virgin madam of the bordello, is underlined by her lack of sexual maturity, her exaggerated thrift, and illusions that hinge on her buying a phonograph—a pathetically unrealistic hope, given the reality of her economic situation.

The catalyst in *Hell Has No Limits* is Pancho, who decides after a meeting with Don Alejo that he will enjoy one last spree at the brothel. He makes sexual advances toward Japonesita, but having aroused her (all the while thinking of his truck—both a Freudian sexual symbol and an instrument of suicidal escape), he sadistically rejects her for Manuela, whose dance provokes him, not so much to sexual desire as to murderous fantasies of disemboweling and leaving her lifeless.

The novel's brutal climax resolves Manuela's existential identity crisis (brought on by age and the depressing material situation). Leaving the brothel with Pancho and his brother-in-law, Octavio, after the flamenco performance, Manuela makes the mistake of kissing Pancho, who fears exposure of his homosexuality; this unleashes a nightmarish flight-and-pursuit sequence in which Manuela is beaten and attempts to seek refuge in the home of Don Alejo. Caught and beaten again, Manuela is sodomized by Pancho and Octavio and left nearly dead by the river. Whether this episode is fatal is also ambiguous; the novel ends on a note of pessimism as Japonesita extinguishes the brothel light and retires to the howling of Don Alejo's dogs and the sobs of a prostitute's child, traditional motifs of doom that combine with the blackness of night to underscore the impression of impending death and oblivion. Because of his psychological complexity, existential revolt, and commitment to ideals of art and beauty, Manuela is one of Donoso's most memorable characters.

The Obscene Bird of Night

The Obscene Bird of Night, considered by critics an antinovel because of Donoso's abandonment of traditional plot, character, and thematic development in favor of a more spontaneous depiction of reality and a virtuosic display of stylistic artistry, is the author's most complex work. Filled with grotesque fantasies, characters with multiple and fluctuating identities or protean, disintegrating personalities, the novel does away with conventions of logic and of mimetic literature, discarding any portrayal of objective reality to present the dilemma of humanity before the existential void.

Humberto Peñaloza, narrator and protagonist, begins as an incipient or would-be writer whose poverty obliges him to accept the job of secretary to Don Jerónimo Azcoitía, a wealthy aristocrat and influential politician. Jerónimo's wife, Inés, inspires Humberto's erotic fantasies, although her witchlike old servant, Peta Ponce, intrudes upon many of them, preventing the consummation—even in his mind—of Humberto's desire. When Jerónimo and Inés fail to have a son to carry on the family's distinguished name, Peta Ponce supposedly arranges for Humberto to have intercourse with Inés, who conceives and gives birth to Boy, a repugnant little monster, deformed to such an extreme that Jerónimo has him reared on an isolated, distant estate that is placed under the direction of Humberto. Whether Humberto fathers Boy is highly questionable; it may be only another fantasy, as are many other incidents in the novel (the ultimate reality of Boy is also questionable).

The distant estate, La Rinconada, peopled by monsters—gathered by Jerónimo so that Boy will not believe himself abnormal—is a grotesque, absurd mirror image of the Azcoitía estate and a possible expressionist allegory of Chilean society. Years later, after surgery for an ulcer, Humberto becomes obsessed with the notion that his physician, Dr. Azula, has removed eighty percent of his organs; Humberto abandons La Rinconada to take refuge in La Casa—a former convent that has become a domicile for retired female servants—where he retreats into silence and is called Mudito (mute).

Inés, now aging and frustrated in her aspirations to maternity, fails in a mission to the Vatican in which she seeks symbolic perpetuity, via the quest for beatification of a homonymic forebear, and also takes refuge in La Casa, where she spends her time despoiling the grotesque old inmates of their few miserable belongings in a dog-racing game that she always wins. Or does she? The visionary and phantasmagoric world of the protagonist-narrator is so fluctuating, so surrealistic and ambiguous, that the reader assumes the narrative consciousness to be schizophrenic or psychotic and mistrusts his representation of events. Humberto's schizophrenic symptoms include withdrawal from reality, hallucinations, living in a world of fantasy, systems of false selves, masks or personas, fear or terror of engulfment by others or the world, a feeling of imprisonment, and the imagining of himself as an infant. Donoso's uncanny capturing of the schizophrenic's perceptions undoubtedly owes something to his own experience of mental illness, with transient schizophrenia and paranoia induced by his inability to tolerate the painkillers given him after his operation. It is possible—and even plausible—that most of the novel's characters are phantoms generated by Humberto's deteriorating mind, and that the two worlds of the Azcoitía estate and the isolation of La Rinconada respectively represent the rational world of visible reality and the dangers of the invisible world of the unconscious.

A HOUSE IN THE COUNTRY

Although the labyrinthine, dilapidated casa has been seen as an archetypal Jungian symbol of terror, it may also be related to Donoso's use of the decaying mansion throughout his fiction as a symbol of Chilean society with its archaic social structures and decadence. Yet another such house, a seemingly limitless labyrinth with miles of underground passages, secret rooms, false or hollow walls, and hidden doors, appears in *A House in the Country*, seen by some as an allegory of Chilean politics and referring concretely to the military coup of 1973, following in the wake of other novels about Latin American dictators, such as Alejo Carpentier's *El recurso del método* (1974; *Reasons of State*, 1976), Augusto Roa Bastos's *Yo el Supremo* (1974), and Gabriel García Márquez's *El otoño del patriarca* (1975; *The Autumn of the Patriarch*, 1975). If this is true, Donoso's novel does not present the biography of a dictator so much as the ideological configurations of a historical event, alluding to the opponents, victims and villains, the personal concentration of power and attendant aspiration to perpetuity, physical and intellectual repression, official rhetoric, and external intervention, with the house or mansion and its surrounding outbuildings constituting a metaphor for the totalitarian state, especially for the political prison, concentration camp, or detention center.

Beyond allusions to specific concepts or historically recognizable persons, *A House in the Country* is significant for its portrayal of a general problem in Latin America, a vast complex transcending geographical and political boundaries and involving the unholy alliance between oligarchies and foreign interests, militarism and dictatorships, the exploitation of the lower class and the lack of freedom of speech and of the press. It is an abstract political allegory of the abuse of power based on bureaucratic structures, the novel of a family dynasty whose fortune is based on mining in a remote rural area of lush vegetation and unreal, stylized geography, with significant subthemes such as adolescent rebellion, the conflict between idealism and materialism, the generation gap, psychosexual repression, conformism and hypocrisy, inauthentic values and lifestyles, and radical solitude and the inability to communicate.

Set in an imaginary country whose flora and fauna appear to be drawn from all of South America, *A House in the Country* employs a vague chronology, as befits its mythic and ahistorical nature. As something of a dystopia with strong existentialist undercurrents, it portrays a Kafkaesque world where utopia has gone awry via the symbolic narration of a "revolution": Children who take advantage of their elders' absence on an extended and unexplained trip take over the estate and set up their own regime, instituting some reforms among the natives but eventually quarreling among themselves and finally being discovered and chastised after a parental display of force involving the use of troops. *A House in the Country* is thus no more a realistic portrayal of recognizable reality than is *The Obscene Bird of Night*, although powerful realities of another order are captured and conveyed with forceful impact.

Donoso's later novels also display vanguardist tendencies, employing variants of the metanovel and self-conscious fiction, the purpose of which is to erase the boundaries between the real and fictitious worlds, with the author being simultaneously creator and novelistic character, the novel both that which the reader peruses and another work whose genesis is subject or problem of the text at hand. The problem of the relationships among author, text, and reader is a leitmotif in *The Obscene Bird of Night*, *A House in the Country*, and *El jardín de al lado*, where it assumes preponderant proportions. In an encounter between the novelist and one of the Ventura dynasty in *A House in the Country*, the character criticizes many details of the narrative, a situation elaborated in *El jardín de al lado*; in both works, Donoso presents his literary theories or comments upon them, burlesques the expectations of the reader of conventional novels, parodies literary convention, and repeatedly destroys the mimetic illusion in favor of an investigation into the problems of the novel as genre, thereby further separating his last five novels from those of the 1950's and 1960's. Without ceasing to write of Chile, he became more cosmopolitan in his choice of settings and characters; without abandoning social concerns, he incorporated broader themes and more universal literary preoccupations.

Janet Pérez

OTHER MAJOR WORKS

SHORT FICTION: *Veraneo, y otros cuentos*, 1955; *Dos cuentos*, 1956; *El Charlestón*, 1960 (abridged as *Cuentos*,

1971; *Charleston, and Other Stories*, 1977); *Los mejores cuentos de José Donoso*, 1965; *Cuentos*, 1971; *Seis cuentos para ganar*, 1985.

PLAYS: *Sueños de mala muerte*, pb. 1985; *Este domingo: Versión teatral de la novela homónima*, pb. 1990.

POETRY: *Poemas de un novelista*, 1981.

NONFICTION: *Historia personal del "boom,"* 1972 (*The Boom in Spanish American Literature: A Personal History*, 1977).

Bibliography

Callan, Richard J. *Jung, Alchemy, and José Donoso's Novel "El obsceno pájaro de la noche."* Lewiston, N.Y.: Edwin Mellen Press, 2000. Examines *The Obscene Bird of Night* from the perspective of Carl Jung's analytical psychology. Callan explains how Donoso created his own literary version of Jungian psychology to focus on themes of imprisonment and disguise.

Carbajal, Brent J. *The Veracity of Disguise in Selected Works of José Donoso: Illusory Deception*. Lewiston, N.Y.: Edwin Mellen Press, 2000. Carbajal discusses the use of masks, both literal and metaphorical, in four of Donoso's novels. One chapter focuses on the role of the double in his lesser-known novel *Donde van a morir los elefantes*.

Finnegan, Pamela May. *The Tension of Paradox: José Donoso's "The Obscene Bird of Night" as Spiritual Exercises*. Athens: Ohio University Press, 1992. Finnegan examines the novel as an expression of humanity's estrangement from the world. A difficult but rewarding study for advanced students. Includes a bibliography.

Friedman, Mary Lusky. *The Self in the Narratives of José Donoso: Chile, 1924-1996*. Lewiston, N.Y.: Edwin Mellen Press, 2004. A detailed examination of a major theme in Donoso's writing: the perils of establishing a self. Friedman focuses on his later works, including the novels *The Garden Next Door*, *Curfew*, and *Donde van a morir los elefantes*, to describe how Donoso's works expressed his conception of selfhood.

González Mandri, Flora. *José Donoso's House of Fiction: A Dramatic Construction of Time and Place*. Detroit, Mich.: Wayne State University Press, 1995. A study of Donoso's incorporation of masks and houses in his fiction, the latter implicating allusions to Henry James. González Mandri focuses on his novels and the novella *Taratuta* (1990). Includes detailed notes, an extensive bibliography, and an index.

King, Sarah E. *The Magical and the Monstrous: Two Faces of the Child-Figure in the Fiction of Julio Cortázar and José Donoso*. New York: Garland, 1992. Informative, although the short citations in Spanish are not translated into English. Nevertheless, this comparative study of two figures of the Spanish American boom in literature is valuable.

McMurray, George R. *Authorizing Fictions: José Donoso's "Casa de Campo."* London: Tamesis Books, 1992. Chapters on Donoso's handling of voice and time, his narrative strategies (re-presenting characters), and his use of interior duplication and distortion. Includes a bibliography.

_______. *José Donoso*. Boston: Twayne, 1979. An excellent introductory study, with chapters on Donoso's biography, his short stories, *The Obscene Bird of Night*, and *Sacred Families*. Includes a chronology, detailed notes, and an annotated bibliography.

Magnarelli, Sharon. *Understanding José Donoso*. Columbia: University of South Carolina Press, 1993. Thoroughgoing study of Donoso's works. The first chapter, "How to Read José Donoso," offers an introduction to his work. Separate chapters analyze his novels *Coronation*, *This Sunday*, *Hell Has No Limits*, *The Obscene Bird of Night*, *A House in the Country*, and *Curfew*.

ARIEL DORFMAN

Born: Buenos Aires, Argentina; May 6, 1942
Also known as: Vladimiro Dorfman

PRINCIPAL LONG FICTION

Moros en la costa, 1973 (*Hard Rain*, 1990)
Viudas, 1981 (*Widows*, 1983)
La última canción de Manuel Sendero, 1982 (*The Last Song of Manuel Sendero*, 1987)
Máscaras, 1988 (*Mascara*, 1988)
Konfidenz, 1994 (English translation, 1995)
The Nanny and the Iceberg, 1999
Terapia, 1999 (in Portuguese; in Spanish, 2001; *Blake's Therapy*, 2001)

OTHER LITERARY FORMS

In addition to his novels, Ariel Dorfman has written short stories, poems, essays, and plays. Probably his best-known work is the play *Death and the Maiden* (pr. 1990), which he also adapted as a screenplay and an opera. He has written seven plays and one musical. He also has published collections of short stories and poems, and his essays deal with subjects including political oppression, American foreign intervention, and exile. His memoir, *Heading South, Looking North: A Bilingual Journey*, was published in 1998.

ACHIEVEMENTS

Ariel Dorfman received honorary doctorates from Illinois Wesleyan University (1989), Wooster College (1991), Bradford College (1993), and American University (2001). His novels and plays have garnered many awards. Chile-Films, Santiago, named his unproduced screenplay *Balmaceda* the best screenplay in 1972. The novel *Hard Rain* was accorded the Premio Ampliado Sudamericana-La Opinión in 1973. His play *Death and the Maiden* has outdone all other writings in terms of awards: In London, it won the *Time Out* Award and the Sir Laurence Olivier Award, both for best play of the season (1991-1992). In Korea, the play won the Dong Award for best play (1992-1993), and in Canada, it won several Dora Mavor Moore Awards, including for outstanding play or musical (1994). It also won Japan's Yoshiko Yuasa Prize for best foreign play (1999).

Dorfman also received two Kennedy Center Theater Awards: the Kennedy Center/American Express New Plays Award for *Widows* and the Roger L. Stevens Award for Extraordinary Playwriting for *Reader*. In 1995, the Writers Guild of Great Britain recognized *Prisoners in Time* as the best television drama; it was written with his son Rodrigo. Dorfman also won the ALOA Prize in Denmark for his memoir *Heading South, Looking North* in 2002. He served as the Walter Hines Page Distinguished Professor of Literature and Latin American Studies at Duke University.

BIOGRAPHY

Ariel Dorfman might be described as a multinational, or as someone in search of a country. His parents emigrated to Argentina to avoid the persecution of Jewish people in Ukraine (in the case of his father, Adolfo), and in the region of Romania/Russia/Moldavia (in the case of his mother, Fanny). Dorfman was born in Buenos Aires, Argentina, on May 6, 1942. From this time forward, through most of his life, Dorfman has been "moving" from one country to another. Indeed, his name reflects this shifting cultural identification: At birth, he was named Vladimiro by his father as a tribute to Vladimir Ilich Lenin. Dorfman later shed that name in favor of Edward, wanting to be associated with the United States. When he became disillusioned with the United States, he chose to associate himself with South America by using his middle name, Ariel, given him by his mother. She took the name from a work by Uruguayan writer José Enrique Rodó, who contrasted North and South America through two characters from William Shakespeare's *The Tempest:* the earth-bound, materialistic creature Caliban, and the airy, spiritual Ariel.

In 1945, when Dorfman was just three years old, his family fled the oppressive regime in Argentina and emigrated once more, to the United States. His father, who had become a prominent economist and the author of an important book on the industrial economy of Argentina, became a diplomat with the United Nations in New

York. The McCarthy years and the Red Scare drove the family out of the United States in 1951, and they spent the next few years in Europe. In 1954, they settled in Chile.

In 1964, back in the United States, Dorfman spent a year and a half at the University of California, Berkeley, on a study grant. On his return to Chile, he became deeply involved in President Salvador Allende's campaign to establish an open, democratic, socialist government. Eventually, in 1970, Dorfman joined Allende's government. The overthrow of that government by Augusto Pinochet Ugarte in 1973 forced Dorfman to escape to Argentina. Juan Perón's oppressive regime in Argentina, however, prompted Dorfman to flee once again, first to France (where he taught at the Sorbonne), then to Holland (where he taught at the University of Amsterdam), and then to the United States, where he taught at Duke University. In 1990, democracy returned to Chile with the government of Patricio Aylwin Azócar, and Dorfman finally could return. With his wife, Angélica, he has two sons, Rodrigo and Joaquin, both of whom have collaborated with their father in writing. Dorfman became a U.S. citizen in 2004.

Ariel Dorfman. (WireImage)

Analysis

Ariel Dorfman takes his subject matter from his experience with the cultural and political crosscurrents that cause much of the suffering of ordinary people, who often cannot speak for themselves and are disenfranchised, powerless, and segregated. They also may be "absented," that is, forcibly "disappeared" by the ruling classes (including repressive governments), or even killed. Dorfman's novels, short stories, poems, and plays often depict individuals caught in mysterious, ominous, and threatening circumstances that are manipulated by amorphous political powers, powers embodied in distant yet ubiquitous governing bodies. There is a certain kinship with the novels of Franz Kafka.

Dorfman's memoir *Heading South, Looking North* takes its title from Dorfman's own constant movement between the United States and South America, between English and Spanish, and between life and the threat of death. The narrative of his works often traces a character or a group trying to survive or at least circumvent some form of oppression. No doubt, much of his inspiration derives from his life in Chile under Pinochet, Argentina under Perón, and the United States under the thumb of Senator Joseph McCarthy or in the middle of concealed machinations of the Central Intelligence Agency. His own perpetual exile over so many years certainly contributed to a feeling of displacement and rootlessness.

In terms of style, all these experiences led him to adopt a multilayered structure to his novels, juxtaposing reflections, parallel action, surveillance, mystery, uncertainty, and distrust. What happens on one level has reverberations on another level. Almost always, some malevolent force operates at the most basic level. This appears, for example, in the voice at the other end of the telephone line in the novel *Konfidenz*, in the deceptions and betrayals in *Mascara*, the frightening distrust in the play *Death and the Maiden*, and even in the threats of the wolves in the children's story "The Rabbits' Rebellion," published in book form in 2001.

WIDOWS

Written in 1982, when Chile was still under the oppressive regime of Pinochet, *Widows* portrays the frightening mystery of "disappearing persons." In several countries, including Chile, Argentina, and El Salvador, certain people were taken from their homes—often in the dead of night—by state police, and were never heard from again. Dorfman initially planned to publish this novel as if written by "Eric Lohmann," a resistance fighter in Nazi-occupied Denmark. That fictional author disguised his true subject by placing the action of *Widows* in a fictional town in Greece under Nazi domination. The original plan was to publish the novel in Danish, with later translations into English and Spanish. When the publisher balked, Dorfman authorized its publication in the United States under his own name, but he retained the original "voice" of Lohmann. Sirgud Lohmann, the putative son of Eric Lohmann, contributed a foreword to his "father's" book, explaining that it had been completed just before the Gestapo took his father away. Only much later, according to Sirgud Lohmann's account, was the "Widows" manuscript discovered among other papers and periodicals in a trunk at Sirgud's aunt's home.

With this as a framework, the novel portrays a fictitious Greek town under a fascist regime whose orders are carried out by a nameless captain newly appointed to this command. His predecessor, Captain Gheorghakis, had been very efficient and managed to disappear thirty-seven men, leaving behind thirty-seven widows. Not long before the new Captain arrives, a mangled corpse washes up on the riverbank. One of the widows, Sofia Angelos, claims the corpse is that of her father and demands that Gheorghakis give her the body so that she can carry out her duty and give him a proper Christian burial. The Captain refuses, having already buried the corpse in an unmarked grave. Sofia had lost four men in her family, all of them disappeared: her father, Karoulos Mylonas; her husband, Michael Angelos; and her two sons, Dimitriou and Serguei. Now she brings her demand to the new Captain. He inherits this delicate problem, compounded by the arrival on the riverbank of yet another mangled corpse. Sofia claims this one also, insisting it is the body of her husband, Michael. Both corpses are mutilated beyond recognition, but that only makes Sofia and the other women of the town more demanding.

The new Captain is caught in a dilemma. On one hand he must exert control over the area, even if it calls for violence, and on the other hand he must maintain an appearance of civility, according to the dictates of the Supreme Government. He only has two assistants: the Orderly, a local youth knowledgeable about the town that hates him, and Lieutenant Constantopoulos, the rigid, unflinching son of a general to whom he would certainly report any weakness he saw in the Captain. He tries to enlist the support of the parish priest, Gabriel, and, failing that, seeks the intervention of the Kastorias, the rich landed family living on the mountainside above the town. Eventually, all thirty-seven widows become involved, each of them claiming a corpse as her own. In frustration, the Captain attempts to bring Sofia under his control by threatening to disappear her grandson, Alexis, but she will not break.

As a public relations stunt, the Captain invites a prominent journalist to town and stages a "reappearance" of the disappeared Alexis. The journalist does not take the bait. New pressure on the Captain comes with the arrival of a German general. With the prodding of the Lieutenant, the Captain's forces march on the widows at the riverbank, only to encounter yet another washed-up corpse.

Widows contains not just a narrative of gamesmanship. The novel takes in a panoramic portrait of a particular society: its military, government, courts of justice, and class divisions. The peasant world becomes a pocket of poverty and desperation under the tight control of the military, which is acting on orders of a fascist regime itself controlled by the corporate world (represented by the Kastoria family). The whole of the affair relies on the reader's awareness of the Holocaust and of the many disappeared people of countries such as Chile and Argentina. As a gentle reminder, Sirgud intrudes into the narrative to inform the reader that section 10 of chapter 6 is missing from the novel, leaving a gap in the story that creates its own mystery.

Blake's Therapy

Blake's Therapy is the story of Graham Blake, the chief executive officer of an industrial firm called Clean Earth, which manufactures herbal goods. He inherited the Philadelphia factory from his father and built a second, more modern and productive one in Houston with the guidance and ingenuity of Jessica Owens, a bioengineer and now his former wife.

Blake has become sick mentally. He cannot sleep. He lives with his young mistress, Natasha, but he has lost interest in touching her. The reader is introduced to all of this by way of surveillance cameras and recordings shared by Dr. Tolgate with his staff at the therapeutic clinic, the Corporate Life Therapy Institute. Blake is about to enter the clinic for a one-month stay to undergo an arduous therapy designed by Dr. Tolgate to ease his mind and enable him to sleep and live normally.

The therapy is bizarre and deeply unsettling. Blake is put in a room, where he witnesses the life of an entire family via cameras located throughout their apartment. The daughter, Roxanna, will become the focus of Blake's attention and therapy. He is given the power to do anything to the family that suits him. At first he refuses to participate, but gradually he begins to enjoy having such complete power over other people. Exercising that control leads him to do more and more disruptive and cruel things, beginning with having the police break into the apartment and arrest Johnny, Roxanna's boyfriend, on a drug charge. Things get worse for every member of the family, until at last Blake sees Roxanna take a fistful of pills to kill herself. With the help of a staff member, he runs through the streets to the apartment and arrives in time to save Roxanna's life—only then to find out that everything had been staged in the first place and that all involved are actors.

This farce is his therapy, and it leads him to another family, this time real but bearing an uncanny resemblance to the fake family. The real family includes a young woman named Rose. Blake becomes a voyeur with a full array of surveillance equipment of his own. He assumes a false identity to intervene in the family's affairs and to help make their fortune. He becomes so obsessed that he loses his mental bearings. He loses his job. Worse still, he turns the family against him. At the novel's end, it is hinted that this "real" family, too, may have been a fiction played out by actors hired by Dr. Tolgate.

Stanley Vincent Longman

Other major works

SHORT FICTION: *Cría ojos*, 1979 (*My House Is on Fire*, 1990); *Acércate más y más: Cuentos casi completos*, 2002.

PLAYS: *Widows*, pr. 1988 (adaptation of his novel); *Death and the Maiden*, pr. 1990; *Reader*, pb. 1995; *Resistance Trilogy*, 1998 (includes *Widows*, *Death and the Maiden*, and *Reader*); *The Other Side*, pr. 2005.

POETRY: *Pastel de choclo*, 1986 (*Last Waltz in Santiago, and Other Poems of Exile and Disappearance*, 1988); *In Case of Fire in a Foreign Land: New and Collected Poems from Two Languages*, 2002.

TELEPLAY: *Prisoners in Time*, 1995 (with Rodrigo Dorfman).

NONFICTION: *Para leer al Pato Donald*, 1971 (with Armand Mattelart; *How to Read Donald Duck: Imperialist Ideology in the Disney Comic*, 1975); *The Empire's Old Clothes: What the Lone Ranger, Babar, and Other Innocent Heroes Do to Our Minds*, 1983; *Some Write to the Future: Essays on Contemporary Latin American Fiction*, 1991; *Heading South, Looking North: A Bilingual Journey*, 1998 (memoir); *Más allá del miedo: El largo adiós a Pinochet*, 2002 (*Exorcising Terror: The Incredible Unending Trial of Augusto Pinochet*, 2005); *Other Septembers, Many Americas: Selected Provocations, 1980-2004*, 2004; *Desert Memories: Journeys Through the Chilean North*, 2003.

CHILDREN'S LITERATURE: *Burning City*, 2003 (with Joaquín Dorfman).

Bibliography

Hassett, John J. "Dictatorship, Memory, and the Prospects for Democracy: The Fiction of Ariel Dorfman." *Third World Quarterly* 13, no. 2 (1992): 393-398. Explores Dorfman's message of necessary democracy in countries ruled as dictatorships.

McClennen, Sophia A. *The Dialectics of Exile: Nation, Time, Language, and Space in Hispanic Literatures*. West Lafayette, Ind.: Purdue University Press. 2002.

A comparative analysis of the works of Dorfman as well as other "exile writers": Juan Goytisolo of Spain and Cristina Peri Rossi of Uruguay. McClennen explores these authors' representations of "exile identity" and how exile formed their sense of a broader cultural identity.

_______. "An Interview with Ariel Dorfman," *World Literature Today* 78, nos. 3/4 (September-December, 2004): 64-67. McClennen interviews Dorfman, offering a fuller study of his writings and how they engage the concepts of exile, culture, and cultural identity.

JOHN DOS PASSOS

Born: Chicago, Illinois; January 14, 1896
Died: Baltimore, Maryland; September 28, 1970
Also known as: John Roderigo Dos Passos

Principal long fiction

One Man's Initiation—1917, 1920
Three Soldiers, 1921
Streets of Night, 1923
Manhattan Transfer, 1925
The 42nd Parallel, 1930
1919, 1932
The Big Money, 1936
U.S.A., 1937 (includes *The 42nd Parallel*, *1919*, and *The Big Money*)
Adventures of a Young Man, 1939
Number One, 1943
The Grand Design, 1949
Chosen Country, 1951
District of Columbia, 1952 (includes *Adventures of a Young Man*, *Number One*, and *The Grand Design*)
Most Likely to Succeed, 1954
The Great Days, 1958
Midcentury, 1961
World in a Glass, 1966
Century's Ebb: The Thirteenth Chronicle, 1975

Other literary forms

John Dos Passos (duhs PAS-uhs) published only one collection of poetry, *A Pushcart at the Curb* (1922), which re-creates a journey through crowded streets and countryside of Spain and the Near East. He also published a collection of plays, *Three Plays* (1934), written and produced during the author's experimentation with the expressionistic techniques of the New Playwright's Theatre group.

In addition to Dos Passos's many long fictions, which he called contemporary chronicles, he also published many volumes of historical narratives, essays, and reportage. Among his books of travel and reportage, which spanned his entire career, were *Rosinante to the Road Again* (1922), *Orient Express* (1927), *In All Countries* (1934), *Journeys Between Wars* (1938), *State of the Nation* (1944), *Tour of Duty* (1946), *The Prospect Before Us* (1950), *Brazil on the Move* (1963), *The Portugal Story* (1969), and *Easter Island: Island of Enigmas* (1971).

Most of Dos Passos's historical narratives were written in his later years and reflect the shift in his political stance; they include *The Ground We Stand On: Some Examples from the History of a Political Creed* (1941), *The Head and Heart of Thomas Jefferson* (1954), *The Men Who Made the Nation* (1957), *Mr. Wilson's War* (1962), *Thomas Jefferson: The Making of a President* (1964), and *The Shackles of Power: Three Jeffersonian Decades* (1966).

Achievements

John Dos Passos's importance cannot be highlighted with one literary accomplishment or summarized with a list of singular achievements. Rather, Dos Passos offered a constant but integrated response to the nation and to the new. Throughout his writing career of fifty years, he was committed to exploring individual freedom and utilized every literary means to that end. Combining his interest in history with his experience as a journalist and artist, Dos Passos produced a remarkable number of novels, poems, plays, essays, and various nonfictional pieces. They are important for their intrinsic merit as well as for their great documentary value. In addition to his extensive list of publications, Dos Passos was a loyal and impassioned correspondent; his letters to significant literary figures and friends also serve as chronicles of the age.

Finally, and unknown to many of his readers, Dos Passos was a talented painter. His sketchbooks, watercolors, and drawings—which date from his youth to his last days—are evidence of Dos Passos's fascination with the visual innovations and artistic movements of his lifetime. His painting had a significant influence on his methods as a writer.

Although Dos Passos experienced a decline in popularity when the critics believed he had abruptly shifted his political views to the right, there is now a revived interest in his best works, which are acknowledged as among the most inventive pieces of the twentieth century.

Biography

From the start of his life, John Roderigo Dos Passos was the victim of circumstances that would set him on an isolated course. In 1896, he was born illegitimately in a Chicago hospital. His father, John R. Dos Passos, Sr., was a famous defense lawyer, a stock market expert, and a writer of brokerage texts. His mother, Lucy Addison Sprigg, was of a fine southern stock. Apparently, his birth was never recorded: This would have meant a scandal for Dos Passos, Sr., whose Catholic wife, Mary Dyckman Hays Dos Passos, was disabled.

For the most part, Dos Passos's childhood was spent with his mother in Brussels, London, or the United States, where reunions with his father were possible. From time to time, he was able to visit his father along the New Jersey shore or in New York, but only in a formal gathering where the affections of the boy for his "guardian" were repressed. Dos Passos's own account of his father's rare presence and peculiar hold are captured poignantly in *The Best Times* (1966).

Dos Passos's father, however, managed to shape the boy's intellect and attitudes, not through fatherly attentions but with books and clear opinions about politics and through his son's elitist schooling. Dos Passos attended Peterborough Lodge, outside London, and the Choate School after returning to the United States. In 1910, Mary Dos Passos died; the boy's mother and father were married, and Dos Passos was given his actual surname. This new life and early schooling culminated in a grand tour of Europe and the Near and Middle East, complete with a mentor—Virgil Jones, a Dominican candidate. At this point, Dos Passos's great interest in art, architecture, and history was kindled. Ironically, he returned home to find that his mother, like Mary, had become disabled.

The following autumn, Dos Passos entered Harvard, and the great avenues were opened for the nurturing of his writing, his political and social tendencies, and his artistic abilities. He ardently read both the classics and the moderns, as well as *Insurgent Mexico* (1914) by John Reed, an activist and a Harvard contemporary. Outside Harvard's walls, Dos Passos and his friends absorbed such artistic events as the Boston Opera, Sergei Diaghilev's ballet, the sensational Armory Show of modernist paintings, and the approach of World War I.

Dos Passos's final year in school was somewhat sad, for his mother died, deepening his sense of isolation. It was also a springboard for his literary career, since it afforded the opportunity to collect and edit material and negotiate funds from his father for *Eight Harvard Poets*. He wrote for various Harvard publications, especially *The Harvard Monthly*, for which he was secretary and editor.

In 1916, Dos Passos studied architecture in Spain—an experience that would color his perspective on the civil war there and alienate him from his friend, Ernest Hemingway. It was at this time, too, that Dos Passos's father died of pneumonia; his subsequent feeling of abandonment can be traced through correspondence with friends in *The Fourteenth Chronicle* (1973).

During "Mr. Wilson's War," as he dubbed it, Dos Passos, like many writer friends, joined the selective Norton-Harjes Ambulance Unit, serving France and Italy. Following the war, he was considered to be a member of the so-called lost generation, but always remained somewhat apart. Dos Passos immersed himself in and

John Dos Passos. (National Portrait Gallery, Smithsonian Institution)

contributed to the artistic excitement in Paris. Designing and painting sets for the ballet and writing consistently for the first time, Dos Passos also observed the peace conference and the postwar unrest.

Travels took Dos Passos to the Basque country, to New York, and to the Near East on the trans-Siberian railroad. There, the danger of the desert, the stench of the cities, and the exotic activity greatly affected Dos Passos's creative notions. Back in New York by 1924, he rode on the wave of socialism, jazz, and the fragmentation of the postwar period—precisely the right mixture for his highly stylized work, *Manhattan Transfer*. Simultaneously, he directed the New Playwright's Theatre group, which produced his dazzling, expressionistic productions on labor issues: *The Moon Is a Gong* (1925), *Airways, Inc*. (1928), and *Fortune Heights* (1933).

In 1928, Dos Passos met and married Katy Smith, a writer and friend of the Hemingways. Her temperament, wit, and goodness seemed to be the perfect match for Dos Passos's solitary nature and restless spirit. The couple enjoyed years of extensive travel and literary success before Katy was killed in a tragic automobile accident, in which her husband was driving. As for his political development during these years, Dos Passos supported the labor cause and the more universal cause for justice and individual freedom. When the Spanish Civil War broke out, however, and the making of a film rallied writers to Spain, Dos Passos's reaction to the execution of his friend, the poet José Robles, caused a serious rift with Hemingway.

The 1940's and 1950's marked a transition away from the political left: For Dos Passos, it was a natural shift to maintain his defense of freedom; for others, it remained a puzzling and outrageous movement to the right. During this period, Dos Passos was a war correspondent in the Pacific theater during World War II; after the war, he married a widow, Elizabeth Holdridge, with whom he had a daughter, Lucy. He spent his remaining years traveling widely—particularly to South American countries such as Chile, Argentina, and Brazil, and also around the United States. Discomfort due to a serious heart condition plagued him.

On September 28, 1970, Dos Passos died of a heart attack in an apartment near Baltimore. He is buried near Spence's Point, his family's home in the northern neck of Virginia.

Analysis

Readers of John Dos Passos's unusual novels have attempted to define the writer as a chronicler, a historian, or a critic of twentieth century America. To these titles, Dos Passos added another dimension by calling himself "an architect of history." Indeed, his works move in skillfully drawn directions—horizontally across continents, vertically through socioeconomic strata, temporally to the deepest places of memory. Considering further Dos Passos's training in architecture and painting, it is not solely by conventional literary means that students can come to grips with his novels; the reader must also be a good viewer. In fact, in the best of his long fiction—*Three Soldiers*, *Manhattan Transfer*, and the *U.S.A.* trilogy—the image and the word are often synonymous.

Three Soldiers

Three Soldiers emerged from Dos Passos's post-World War I travels through Italy, Portugal, and Spain. Published in 1921, it was not the writer's first novel, but it refined an artistic process he had begun during his ambulance service, a process that yielded his first novel, *One Man's Initiation*, in 1920. Both this novel and *Three Soldiers* were drawn from sketchbooks of notes, highly descriptive entries, and diagrams and sketches of landscapes, characters, and confrontations. While they are both antiwar books, *Three Soldiers* is clearly a better experiment in realism. Recalling Stephen Crane's *The Red Badge of Courage* (1895), the novel presents war through the eyes of the common soldier in France. Widening the range, Dos Passos poignantly captures the disillusionment and dehumanization of war for all soldiers.

True to his architectural design, Dos Passos allows for three geographical and individual perspectives—that of Don Fuselli, a Californian; Chrisfield, a restless Indiana farmer boy; and Andrews, a Virginian and a composer. Through a thick buildup of violent encounters, he vividly portrays the Army's destruction of the individual. Each responds to the regimentation and absurd conformity in different ways. Dan accepts the fantasy that conforming will result in promotion and the ultimate possession of his girl. Chrisfield plans to avenge himself on the hated sergeant. Andrews, the artist, struggles to find his creative place. In a series of violent confrontations, each soldier fails miserably to achieve his personal goals. Dan is promoted to corporal, but only after total exploitation by his superiors; Mabe, his girlfriend, has married another man. Chrisfield vows to murder the sergeant. Having practiced on a solitary German in an abandoned house, he throws his last two grenades at the wounded sergeant in the woods. Dos Passos focuses on the artist, Andrews, who has managed to study legitimately in Paris and meet a sympathizer, Geneviève. Finally, he decides to go absent without leave (AWOL) and is discovered and beaten by military police officers. As Andrews is dramatically removed from his hiding place, a gust of wind scatters his unfinished composition "John Brown," an homage to the liberator of slaves.

Although simplistic when compared to the later works, *Three Soldiers* is an exercise in an important visual process. First, he planned his novel from collected verbal and visual sketches. Second, his strong sense of painterly composition allowed for three diverse perspectives in Chrisfield, Fuselli, and Andrews. The reader will discover this geographical interest later in the *U.S.A.* trilogy, as well. Finally, he positioned images of violent confrontations against serene French landscapes. The violent action is shockingly portrayed while the images of the countryside are almost nostalgically impressionistic. The effect is similar to the anxiety created in cubist paintings, where familiar objects and spaces are reshaped and limited. In the juxtaposition of images, the reader will sense Dos Passos's extreme personal disdain for war and his appreciation of a lost world.

Manhattan Transfer

The writing that followed *Three Soldiers* was not so much a further refinement as it was a sudden explosion of artistic innovation, yet the germination of *Manhattan Transfer* was like that which produced Dos Passos's first two novels: a rich collage of images, impressions, notes, and sketches. Just as *Three Soldiers* is critical of war, so *Manhattan Transfer* focuses on the dehumanizing effects of the city, particularly on immigrants and other outsiders.

To convey his theme, Dos Passos transformed the conventional components of character, setting, and plot in much the same way that cubist painters distorted familiar objects and transformed the viewer's perception of them. New York, for example, is not really a setting or a backdrop, to use a visual term, but a major and monstrous character. Similarly, while there are approximately twelve identifiable characters out of the masses, they are important only as facets of the portrait of the real antagonist, the city. Finally, while there is a complicated network of overlapping and chaotic activities among and between the characters, there is no single plot. Instead, the novel is like a roller coaster or rapid transit ride; the reader experiences flashes of sense, sound, color, and conflict. It is, then, a collective novel—a compilation of the notes and pictures created while Dos Passos himself was in motion as a traveler.

The novel is divided into three sections, demarcated not by logical, literary closures but by highly visual introductory commentaries. Each section also contains several divisions, the headings of which allude to the metals and myths of great cities: "Ferryslip," "Tracks," "Rollercoaster," "Steamroller," "Revolving Doors," "Skyscrapers," and "The Burthen of Nineveh." What occurs within each division is not an unfolding of ideas or action but an envelopment of the reader into a frenzy of lives colliding in the city's mainstream.

To create this collage, Dos Passos welds fragments of dialogue, action, newspaper clippings, signs, city sights, and time. In "Ferryslip," a child is born to an uncertain father, Ed Thatcher, and a hysterical mother, Susie. The child suddenly becomes Ellie, Ellen, or Elaine, depending upon the fortunes and fame of the gentlemen she lures. In "Tracks," the reader meets Jimmy Herf, an immigrant newspaper reporter who is the only figure eventually to escape the city's grasp. There is George Baldwin, a manipulative attorney who turns politician; Congo and Emile, two Frenchmen who represent the extremes of survival in a new land—one marries and conforms while the other returns to sea. Joe O'Keefe, a labor organizer, is juxtaposed with a successful Broadway producer, Harry Goldweiser. Almost all the characters collide with one another, or else their adventures are butted against one another's in the same section of the novel. Herf provides the final view as he waits for a ferry to take him from Manhattan. Broken by every component of life in New York, he decides to hitchhike out of the city on a furniture truck, glistening and yellow. He provides the reader with an uncertain perspective; when asked how far he is going, Herf replies aimlessly that he wants to go far away.

Recalling the collective portrayal of the Army in *Three Soldiers*, *Manhattan Transfer* captures the entirety and enormity of the city. The realism of *Three Soldiers*, however, was brilliantly and vividly transformed into a masterful expressionistic style. Instead of a conventional linear narrative about the dehumanization of the modern city, Dos Passos chose to re-create the eclectic experience of Manhattan. He verbally reproduced the rhythms, forms, plasticity, and chaotic activity of the city without the traditional literary processes of describing, developing, or narrating. The novel initially shocks the reader, forces a complicated sensual experience, and convinces the reader of the city's power by its sheer visual frenzy. The innovative techniques of *Manhattan Transfer* won for Dos Passos the praise of eminent contemporaries: Sinclair Lewis compared the novel to the modernist masterpieces of Gertrude Stein, Marcel Proust, and James Joyce. Certainly, Dos Passos had concocted a work in which the mass of the image and the word were of equal weight.

U.S.A. trilogy

If *Manhattan Transfer* represented a heightened style and structure in comparison to *Three Soldiers*, then the *U.S.A.* trilogy was the apex of Dos Passos's expressionistic novels; generally acknowledged as his masterpiece, it is on this work that his reputation rests. The trilogy is a panoramic fictional history of the United States in the first three decades of the twentieth century.

The title of the first novel in the trilogy, *The 42nd Parallel*, suggests the sweep of the work, across the United States from Plymouth, Massachusetts, through the industrial centers of Detroit and Chicago, over to the gold coast of Northern California. Along the way, history is not remembered or narrated, but reproduced by a series of modernist devices.

Dos Passos composed his trilogy with fragments of American life—newsreels, headlines, songs, letters, placards, colloquialisms, and biographical pieces of fictional and nonfictional figures. These fragments click away like an early film or newsreel itself, which captures the reader's attention for the narrative that follows. Dos Passos embellished this superstructure, more elaborate in scope than the divisions of *Manhattan Transfer*, with illustrations and with the ingenious and provocative device of the Camera Eye. Interspersed and intruding into the narrative, the Camera Eye is composed of images in such a way as to reproduce memory, probably the writer's memory. The voice seems both deterministic and vulnerable to all that happens around it. Its focus set, the epic catalog of characters, real and imagined, is called to action.

The 42nd Parallel

The characters in the trilogy are representative figures intended to form a composite of the American soul. In *The 42nd Parallel*, there is Mac McCreary, a printer who eventually joins the revolutionary movement in Mexico, following disillusionment with marriage. J. Ward Moorehouse, a charismatic and powerful figure, is then introduced; the reader follows him throughout the trilogy as he is transformed from a public relations man and government servant in France to a wealthy advertising executive. Among the female characters is Eleanor Stoddard, an artsy interior decorator at Marshall Field's in Chicago; she eventually makes the acquaintance of Moorehouse. There is also Charley Anderson, an opportunist whose mechanical inventiveness leads him to become an airplane manufacturer. The reader observes his steady decline. These are but a few of the many contrasting characters sketched throughout the trilogy.

The historical portraits are of eloquent and eccentric figures of the period: Eugene V. Debs, the labor organizer jailed by U.S. president Woodrow Wilson; William Jennings Bryan, the silver-tongued midwestern orator and frequent presidential candidate; the socialist mathematician Charles Proteus Steinmetz who, as the property of General Electric, developed the law of hysteresis that produced electrical transformers for the world. The novel is a portrait collection of real and imagined people. Some are creative, cunning, impassioned; most are naïve. To link them, Dos Passos develops a kind of self-portrait through the Camera Eye series. The reader traces the Eye's consciousness from young and constant traveler in Europe and feisty adolescent to observer of labor rallies. The very last Camera Eye in *The 42nd Parallel* parallels the final sequence of Charley Anderson's crossing to war-torn France. The Eye pans out on the *Espagne*, dangerously crossing the Atlantic, its passengers caught in ironic responses to the great fear of destruction. The Eye moves quickly to death in the trenches, to the prosperity of vine growers, to a town in France unpleasantly interrupted by agents searching bags in well-known hotels. Through one Eye, then, and through the other biographies, the reader views rather than reviews the transition of Americans from naïveté to anticipation of some inevitable doom.

1919

If *The 42nd Parallel* finishes in fearful anticipation, then *1919* fills the void with the thunder of World War I and the frightened inner voices of the characters. Far more tragic and total a portrayal of war than *Three Soldiers*, *1919* unmasks the entire absurdity, debauchery, and waste of "Mr. Wilson's War" at home and abroad. This second volume in the trilogy opens with a grimly ironic headline concerning the "great" Battle of Verdun. The horror implicit in this headline is counterpointed by domestic suffering, by scenes of a United States in which the wealthy few prosper at the expense of the masses.

Against this panorama of war and an industrializing nation, Dos Passos paints his imaginary portraits. There is Dick Savage, a literary Harvard graduate who resembles the author in several ways. He serves in the ambulance corps, caring for the mutilated and deranged. His horror is juxtaposed with a farcical censuring and punishment by the Army for his mild criticism of war in a letter to a friend. (In a similar incident, Dos Passos himself had been expelled from the Red Cross.) Dick eventually finds his way into J. Ward Moorehouse's association after the war. There is also Ben Compton, the son of a Jewish immigrant, who travels north, south, east, and west as a political agitator at home. He is jailed, persecuted, and finally broken by the forces of law and order. Eleanor Stoddard begins her climb to the top through a series of affairs ultimately leading to Moorehouse in Paris. Together, they exploit all around them to buy into the power of "Big Business" back home.

The historical figures expand Dos Passos's portrayal of this contradictory world at war. There is Jack Reed, the Harvard man who spoke and wrote revolution. Theodore Roosevelt is portrayed by a series of vivid anecdotes. He was, for Dos Passos, the last major figure of everything American, what Teddy characterized as "bully." The great J. P. Morgan is last. His family's empire built upon warmongering, Morgan's portrait prepares the reader for the monsters to come in *The Big Money*.

Just as in *The 42nd Parallel*, the Camera Eye moves the reader's view from the dying and dead in ambulance vans, to harlots, to soldiers running for cover in city streets, and finally to civilians collecting scrap iron at the war's end. Moreover, Dos Passos adds to the collage scraps of headlines of suicides and murders at home, uprising of the workers, and bits of melancholy American and French war songs. These grim scraps are collected for the future recycling of postwar industrial and political figures in *The Big Money*. The reader experiences the change in American consciousness from innocent anticipation to horror.

The end of *1919* is quite poignant both in technique and in meaning. Dos Passos blends the essence of the "newsreels," the Camera Eye, and the biographies to create a moving elegiac portrait of the Unknown Soldier.

From the almost flippant choosing among pieces of bodies in France, to the imagined home and youth of the anonymous man, to the placing of Wilson's bouquet of poppies at the Tomb, Dos Passos movingly portrays the common dehumanizing experience of all soldiers and the unique and sacred individuality of every human being.

The Big Money

Following the brilliant design of the first two volumes of the trilogy, *The Big Money* picks up the pace of *1919* and brings the author's rather cynical perspective into perfect focus. Against the scenes of war's end and the anticipation of the Great Depression, Dos Passos draws his ultimate conclusion—that the simple individual, as an American ideal, was not strong enough to confront the new powers of the modern world. It is not so much the individual against the world that is of importance here, however, as it is the composite view of America as one character after all, a collection of all the victims and aggressors of the early twentieth century. America is both protagonist and antagonist in *The Big Money*; both Dos Passos's subject and his means of painting it are unsettling.

Exploiting the technical innovations of the previous volumes, Dos Passos paints a pessimistic picture of Americans coming to terms with the twentieth century. Charley Anderson, corrupted by money, booze, and sexual affairs, drives south and dies in a car crash in Florida. Eveline Johnson, reaching her lowest point of boredom with Moorehouse and company, takes her life with sleeping pills. Margo Dowling, the ultimate plastic Hollywood starlet, is created and controlled by her powerful producer-husband, Sam Mongolies. In contrast, Mary French remains honest, constant, and determined in her work for the Communist Party, particularly in her protest against the executions of Nicola Sacco and Bartolomeo Vanzetti. Among the real biographies, there is Isadora Duncan, who danced for the sake of art, accidentally drowned her children, and died in a joyride when her neck scarf caught in the wheel of an automobile. There is Frank Lloyd Wright, whose functional designs for the rich were not beauty enough to disguise his ugly family squabbles, bankruptcy, and scandalous affairs. Even the Wright brothers, whose flying machine becomes a new war machine, present no triumph for the common person—at least, not at first—but they are admiringly portrayed.

The Camera Eye seems surer, more direct than before, more focused as it captures the Depression era. The man behind the camera was older, more experienced. The Eye in *The Big Money* is not reminiscent, as in *The 42nd Parallel*, or horrified, as in *1919*, but strong and clear about the plight of the social worker, the immigrant, and the laborer; about the triumph of the rich, the powerful, and the political. In fact, one of the last Camera Eyes of the trilogy forces the reader to view finally two nations in one, two languages, two experiences—that of the poor and that of the wealthy. Somehow, nevertheless, through Dos Passos's concentration on the common American, the nation seems on the brink of renewal.

The use of the now-familiar experimental tools of newsreels and cultural fragments is also sharper in *The Big Money*, especially in Dos Passos's juxtapositions of realities and absurdities, a technique begun in *1919*. One newsreel, for example, proclaims in archaic speech and images that the steel corporation is a marvelous colossus, while bomb scares, suicides, and Georgia's new controversial dance, Shake That Thing, are stated matter of factly. Another announces America's air supremacy and a boom year ahead while it simultaneously lists a massacre of six hundred in Canton, the production of gas for warfare, and the use of machine guns and steamrollers on strikers. The musical fragments come from the blues and from poetic choruses written for the unemployed. What seems hidden in the portrayal of America as shaken, explosive, and cruelly challenged is a wishful portrait of America as diversified, creative, and positively evolving.

Although Dos Passos continued to explore the themes of his great trilogy in seven subsequent novels, none of them was as provocative, as innovative in visual techniques, or as critically acclaimed as his masterpiece *U.S.A.*

Mary Ellen Stumpf

Other major works

PLAYS: *The Garbage Man*, pr., pb. 1926 (pr. as *The Moon Is a Gong*, 1925); *Three Plays*, 1934.

POETRY: *A Pushcart at the Curb*, 1922.

NONFICTION: *Rosinante to the Road Again*, 1922; *Orient Express*, 1927; *In All Countries*, 1934; *Journeys Between Wars*, 1938; *The Ground We Stand On: Some Examples from the History of a Political Creed*, 1941; *State of the Nation*, 1944; *Tour of Duty*, 1946; *The General*, 1949; *The Prospect Before Us*, 1950; *The Head and Heart of Thomas Jefferson*, 1954; *The Theme Is Freedom*, 1956; *The Men Who Made the Nation*, 1957; *Prospects of a Golden Age*, 1959; *Mr. Wilson's War*, 1962; *Brazil on the Move*, 1963; *Lincoln and the Gettysburg Address*, 1964; *Occasions and Protests*, 1964; *Thomas Jefferson: The Making of a President*, 1964; *The Best Times: An Informal Memoir*, 1966; *The Shackles of Power: Three Jeffersonian Decades*, 1966; *The Portugal Story*, 1969; *Easter Island: Island of Enigmas*, 1971; *The Fourteenth Chronicle*, 1973; *John Dos Passos: The Major Nonfictional Prose*, 1988 (Donald Pizer, editor).

Bibliography

Becker, George J. *John Dos Passos*. New York: Frederick Ungar, 1974. A critical biography that describes Dos Passos's major works, his artistic observations, and his treatment of American social institutions. Includes a bibliography and an index.

Carr, Virginia Spencer. *Dos Passos: A Life*. Garden City, N.Y.: Doubleday, 1984. In this detailed biography, Carr examines the contradictions in Dos Passos's life and provides critical insight into the personal and political influences on his fiction.

Casey, Janet Galligani. *Dos Passos and the Ideology of the Feminine*. New York: Cambridge University Press, 1998. Discusses Dos Passos's female characters, placing them within the context of the gender representations and ideas about gender that were prevalent in the 1920's and 1930's. Includes bibliographical references and an index.

Colley, Iain. *Dos Passos and the Fiction of Despair*. Totowa, N.J.: Rowman & Littlefield, 1978. One of the most frequently cited texts in Dos Passos scholarship. Colley analyzes *Manhattan Transfer* and other works, citing how Dos Passos was influenced by the "true experimentalists," including Theodore Dreiser, James Joyce, and Gertrude Stein.

Harding, Desmond. "*Ulysses* and *Manhattan Transfer*: A Poetics of Transatlantic Literary Modernism." In *Writing the City: Urban Visions and Literary Modernism*. New York: Routledge, 2003. Although the book focuses on James Joyce's depiction of Dublin, Ireland, this chapter discusses Dos Passos, comparing how he and Joyce envisioned city life in their novels *Manhattan Transfer* and *Ulysses*, respectively.

Ludington, Townsend. *John Dos Passos: A Twentieth Century Odyssey*. Rev. ed. New York: Carroll & Graf, 1998. Standard biography first published in 1980; revised edition contains a new introduction by the author. Comprehensively chronicles Dos Passos's artistic endeavors and political leanings.

McGlamery, Tom. *Protest and the Body in Melville, Dos Passos, and Hurston*. New York: Routledge, 2004. In his introduction, McGlamery states that this book is "about three authors and the way their bodies manifest in their texts." Chapter 2, "Producing Remembrance: John Dos Passos's Body in the Text," provides biographical information and an analysis of *U.S.A*.

Maine, Barry, ed. *Dos Passos: The Critical Heritage*. New York: Routledge, 1988. Devoted to the contemporary critical reception of Dos Passos's individual novels. Divided into twelve sections, each covering a major work. These chapters contain between two (*Number One*, *The Grand Design*) and twelve (*The Big Money*) different reviews, taken from publications ranging from *American Mercury* to the *Daily Worker*.

Nanney, Lisa. *John Dos Passos Revisited*. New York: Twayne, 1998. An excellent introductory study of Dos Passos and his works. Nanney draws on previously untapped sources to describe how Dos Passos's own paintings, his interest in the visual arts, and his friendship with artists affected his development as a modernist.

Strychacz, Thomas. "Reading John Dos Passos Reading Mass Culture in *U.S.A.*" In *Modernism, Mass Culture, and Professionalism*. New York: Cambridge University Press, 1993. A study of Dos Passos and three other modernist writers in the period from 1880 to 1940. Strychacz argues that contrary to most scholarship, these writers were influenced by, and not opposed to, mass culture, although they sought to create works that were more esoteric than the popular fiction of their times.

FYODOR DOSTOEVSKI

Born: Moscow, Russia; November 11, 1821
Died: St. Petersburg, Russia; February 9, 1881
Also known as: Fyodor Mihaylovich Dostoevski; Feodor Dostoyevsky; Feodor Dostoevsky

Principal long fiction

Bednye lyudi, 1846 (*Poor Folk*, 1887)
Dvoynik, 1846 (*The Double*, 1917)
Netochka Nezvanova, 1849 (English translation, 1920)
Unizhennye i oskorblyonnye, 1861 (*Injury and Insult*, 1886; also known as *The Insulted and Injured*)
Zapiski iz myortvogo doma, 1861-1862 (*Buried Alive: Or, Ten Years of Penal Servitude in Siberia*, 1881; better known as *The House of the Dead*)
Zapiski iz podpolya, 1864 (*Letters from the Underworld*, 1913; better known as *Notes from the Underground*)
Igrok, 1866 (*The Gambler*, 1887)
Prestupleniye i nakazaniye, 1866 (*Crime and Punishment*, 1886)
Idiot, 1868 (*The Idiot*, 1887)
Vechny muzh, 1870 (*The Permanent Husband*, 1888; also known as *The Eternal Husband*)
Besy, 1871-1872 (*The Possessed*, 1913; also known as *The Devils*)
Podrostok, 1875 (*A Raw Youth*, 1916)
Bratya Karamazovy, 1879-1880 (*The Brothers Karamazov*, 1912)
The Novels, 1912 (12 volumes)

Other literary forms

The collected works of Fyodor Dostoevski (dahs-tuh-YEHF-skee) are available in many Russian editions, starting from 1883. The most carefully prepared of these, comprising some thirty volumes, is the Leningrad Nauka edition, which began publishing in 1972. A wide variety of selected works are also available in English. While the novels dominate Dostoevski's later creative period, he began his career with sketches, short stories, and novellas, and he continued to write shorter pieces throughout his working life. These works do not exhibit the same unity of theme as the major novels, though many of them in one way or another involve Dostoevski's favorite topic, human duality.

Dostoevski's nonfictional writing is diverse. In his monthly *Dnevnik pisatelya* (1876-1877, 1880-1881; *The Diary of a Writer*, 1949), he included commentary on sociopolitical issues of the time, literary analyses, travelogues, and fictional sketches. He also contributed many essays to his own journals and other publications. The nonfictional writings often clash with the views expressed in the novels and consequently enjoy wide circulation among specialists for comparative purposes. Equally popular is his correspondence, comprising several volumes in his collected works. The notebooks for the major novels, as well as other background comments, are also included in the collection. They became available in English in editions published by the University of Chicago Press during the 1960's and 1970's.

Achievements

Both Leo Tolstoy and Fyodor Dostoevski, the giants of the Russian novel during the era preceding the 1917 October Revolution, are firmly part of the Western literary tradition today, but whereas Tolstoy's outlook is solidly rooted in the nineteenth century, Dostoevski's ideas belong to modern times. His novels go far beyond the parameters of aesthetic literature; they are studied not only by literary historians and critics but also by psychologists, philosophers, and theologians the world over. Each discipline discerns a different drift in Dostoevski's work, and few agree on what the author's basic tenets are, but all claim him as their hero. His contemporaries, too, were at a loss to categorize him, primarily because his style and subject matter had little in common with accepted literary norms. Russia's most prominent writing, as espoused by Ivan Turgenev and Tolstoy, was smooth and lyric. While Turgenev analyzed topical social problems in a restrained, faintly didactic manner, and Tolstoy presented panoramic visions of certain Russian social classes and their moral problems, Dostoevski brought an entirely new style and content to Russian writing. He disregarded his colleagues' logically progressing, chronological narrative mode and constructed his stories as mosaics or puzzles, often misleading the audience, experimenting with peculiar narrative voices, allowing his pathological figures to advance the plot in disconcertingly disorienting ways, and in general forcing the reader to reevaluate and backtrack constantly. Dostoevski was also revolutionary in his choice of subjects, introducing characters whose perception of outside reality essentially mirrored their own skewed personalities.

Dostoevski thus rendered obsolete both his contemporaries' classical realism and the prevailing superficial treatment of the human psyche. In his choice of settings, he disdained the poetic landscapes preferred by others and concentrated on the teeming of the city or the starkly barren aspects of the countryside. Because of this preference for the seamy side of life, he is often linked to Nikolai Gogol, but Dostoevski's descriptions of deviant behavior have a decidedly more modern flavor than do Gogol's. During his enforced proximity to criminals, Dostoevski applied his powers of observation to their perverted worldview and, in the process, developed a new approach to literary portraiture; Sigmund Freud praised him for anticipating modern psychological approaches, and twentieth century psychologists on the whole have accepted Dostoevski's observations as valid.

Dostoevski tended to be conservative and didactic in his nonfictional writings, though his often cantankerous and controversial assertions contributed to the lively journalistic interplays of the time; to this day, there is disagreement over whether he affected a conservative public stance in order to be trusted with censorially sensitive material in his fiction or whether conflicting elements were actually integral to his personality. In either case, Dostoevski is responsible for leading Russian literature away from its often tranquilly harmonious narratives, with their clearly discernible authorial points of view, to a polyphonic plane.

During Joseph Stalin's reign as leader of the newly formed Soviet Union, severe censorial strictures limited the average Soviet reader's access to Dostoevski, yet interest in him remained undiminished, and he returned to his prominent place after Stalin's death. Outside his homeland, Dostoevski's influence has been immeasurable. Albert Camus—to cite only one among countless examples of twentieth century writers awed by the power of Dostoevski's metaphysical dialectics—transformed *The Possessed* into a gripping play, *Les Possédés* (pr., pb. 1959; *The Possessed*, 1960), because he saw in Dostoevski's tortured protagonists the forerunners of today's existentialist heroes. Dostoevski's work thus has remained topical and continues to appeal to widely divergent views.

Biography

There was little in the childhood of Fyodor Mihaylovich Dostoevski to presage his achievements as a writer of world-famous novels. Born into a middle-class family of few cultural pretensions, he received a mediocre education. His father, a physician at a Moscow hospital for the poor, ruled the family with a strict hand and enforced observance of Russian Orthodox ritual at home. When Dostoevski entered the St. Petersburg Military Engineering School in 1838, he found himself unprepared for academic life; nevertheless, he enjoyed his first exposure to literature and soon immersed himself in it. The elder Dostoevski's murder at the hands of his serfs (he had in the meantime become a modest landowner) and the first signs of his own epilepsy upset Dostoevski's academic routine, delaying his graduation until 1843.

Dostoevski worked only briefly as a military engineer before deciding to pursue a literary career. When the efforts of acquaintances resulted in the publication of his first fictional work, *Poor Folk*, his excitement knew no bounds, and he envisioned a promising writing career. His initial success led easily to publication of several additional pieces, among them the uncompleted *Netochka Nezvanova* and the psychologically impressive *The Double*. While these works are not considered primary by Dostoevski scholars, they hint at what was to become the author's fascination with humankind's ambiguous inner world.

The perfecting of this artistic vision was interrupted by Dostoevski's encounter with the realities of czarist autocracy under Nicholas I. Dostoevski was active in the Petrashevsky Circle, one of many dissident groups engaged in underground dissemination of sociopolitical pamphlets. Dostoevski's arrest and death sentence in

1849, commuted at the last moment to prison and exile, initiated a terrible period for the young author. On Christmas Eve of that year, he left St. Petersburg in chains to spend four years in the company of violent criminals in Omsk, Siberia. The inhuman conditions of his imprisonment severely taxed his mental stability, especially because he was forbidden to write or even read anything, except religious matter. He later recorded these experiences graphically in *The House of the Dead* (initially translated as *Buried Alive: Or, Ten Years of Penal Servitude in Siberia*), immediately catching public attention for his psychological insight into pathological and criminal behavior. He spent an additional five years (1854-1859) as a political exile in a Siberian army contingent.

In 1857, after recovering somewhat from the ravages of incarceration, which had exacerbated his epilepsy, Dostoevski married a widow, Maria Isayeva, and hesitantly resumed his writing career. Upon his return to St. Petersburg in 1859, he was drawn into a hectic pace of literary activity. Turgenev and Tolstoy occupied first place among writers, leaving the unfortunate ex-convict to rebuild his career almost from scratch. To facilitate the serial printing of his work, he ventured into publishing. Together with his brother Mikhail, he started the journal *Vremya* in 1861, using it as a vehicle to publish his not very successful novel *The Insulted and Injured*, which he had written primarily to alleviate financial pressures. When he visited Western Europe for the first time in 1862, his observations also appeared in *Vremya* as "Zimnie zametki o letnikh vpechatleniyakh" (1863; "Winter Notes on Summer Impressions," 1955). Before he could reap substantial material benefit from his enterprise, government censors closed the magazine in 1863 because a politically sensitive article on Russo-Polish affairs had appeared in its pages.

At this inopportune moment, Dostoevski indulged himself somewhat recklessly by revisiting Europe on borrowed funds in order to pursue a passionate love interest, Apollinaria Suslova, and to try his luck at German gaming tables. Unsuccessful in both pursuits, he returned to Russia in 1864 to risk another publishing venture, the periodical *Epokha*, which folded in less than a year, though he managed to print in it the initial installments of his first successful longer fiction, *Notes from the Underground*, before its demise. His personal life, too, did not proceed smoothly. The deaths of his wife, with whom he had shared seven unhappy years, and of his brother and business partner Mikhail in 1864 brought enormous additional debts and obligations, which led him to make hasty promises of future works. To extricate himself from one such contract, he interrupted work on *Crime and Punishment* and hastily put together a fictional version of his gambling experiences and his torrid love affair with Suslova. To speed the work, he dictated the text to a twenty-year-old stenographer, Anna Snitkina. With her expert help, *The Gambler* was delivered on time. Dostoevski and Snitkina married in 1867, and she is generally credited with providing the stability and emotional security that permitted the author to produce his last four novels at a more measured pace.

Fyodor Dostoevski. (Library of Congress)

Despite the success of *Crime and Punishment*, Dostoevski still ranked below Turgenev and Tolstoy in popular esteem by the end of the 1860's, partly because their wealth allowed them leisure to compose carefully edited works that appealed to the public and their gentry status opened influential doors, and partly because Dostoevski's writings were uneven, alternating between strange psychological portraits and journalistic polemics, all produced in a frantic haste that seemed to transmit itself to the text. Dostoevski spent the first four years after his marriage to Snitkina in Europe, largely to escape creditors but also to feed his gambling mania, which kept the family destitute. He completed *The Idiot* abroad and accepted a publisher's large advance in 1871 to facilitate return to his homeland. His remaining ten years were spent in more rational pursuits.

Between 1873 and 1874, he edited the conservative weekly *Grazhdanin* and initiated a popular column, *Diary of a Writer*, which in 1876 he turned into a successful monthly. The appearance of the politically provocative *The Possessed* and of *A Raw Youth* kept him in the public eye, and he was finally accorded some of the social acknowledgments previously reserved for his rivals Turgenev and Tolstoy. The duality of his writings, at once religiously conservative and brilliantly innovative, made him acceptable to government, Church, and intellectuals alike. This philosophical dichotomy remained characteristic of Dostoevski to the end. In 1880, he delivered an enthusiastically received speech during the dedication of the Alexander Pushkin monument in Moscow, in which he reiterated patriotic sentiments of a rather traditional tenor. At the same time, his last novel, *The Brothers Karamazov*, expressed doubts about a single, traditional view of life. When he died two months after completing the novel, an impressive public funeral attested his stature as a major Russian writer.

Analysis

Fyodor Dostoevski's creative development is roughly divided into two stages. The shorter pieces, preceding his imprisonment, reflect native and foreign literary influences, although certain topics and stylistic innovations that became Dostoevski's trademarks were already apparent. The young author was fascinated by Gogol's humiliated St. Petersburg clerks and their squalid surroundings, teeming with marginal, grotesque individuals. These elements are so abundant in all of Dostoevski's fiction that he labeled himself a disciple of Gogol. Traces of E. T. A. Hoffmann's fantastic tales are evident in the young Dostoevski's preference for gothic and Romantic melodrama. What distinguishes Dostoevski from those influences is his carnivalistically exaggerated tone in describing or echoing the torments of members of the lower classes. He not only imbues them with frantic emotional passions and personality quirks in order to make them strangers to their own mediocre setting but also endows them with precisely the right balance between eccentricity and ordinariness to jar the reader into irritated alertness. While other writers strove to elicit public sympathy for the poor, Dostoevski subtly infused an element of ridiculousness into his portrayals, thereby reducing the social efficacy of the genre while enhancing the complexity of literary expression.

In Dostoevski's later, post-Siberian novels, this delicate equilibrium between empathy and contempt for the downtrodden is honed to perfection. The author supplements his gallery of mistreated eccentrics with powerful, enigmatic, ethically neutral supermen—highly intelligent loners whose philosophies allow simultaneously for self-sacrifice and murder. Other favorite types are passionate females, aborting good impulses with vicious inclinations, and angelic prostitutes, curiously blending religious fanaticism with coarseness.

This multiplicity is the dominant characteristic of Dostoevski's style. It is for the most part impossible to discern in his works an authorial point of view. By using a polyphonic approach, Dostoevski has characters arguing diametrically opposed concepts so convincingly and in such an intellectually appealing fashion that readers are prevented from forming simplistic judgments. Most readers are held spellbound by the detective quality of Dostoevski's writing. On the surface, the novels appear to be thrillers, exhibiting the typical tricks of that genre, with generous doses of suspense, criminal activity, confession, and entrapment by police or detectives. While viewing the works from this angle alone will not yield a satisfactory reading, it eases the way into the psychologically complex subtext. Not the least of Dostoevski's appeal lies in his original development of characters, prominent among them frantically driven types who bare their psyches in melodramatic confessions and diaries while at the same time confusing the reader's expectations by performing entirely contradictory deeds. Superimposed on these psychological conflicts are other metaphysical quandaries, such as passionate discussions about good and evil, church and state, Russia and Western Europe, free will and determinism. These struggles often crowd the plot to the point of symbolic overload, thereby destroying any semblance of harmony.

That Dostoevski is avidly read by the general public and specialists alike attests his genius in fusing banalities with profound intellectual insights. Nevertheless, a certain unevenness in language and structure remains. The constant pressure under which Dostoevski worked resulted in incongruities and dead spots that are incompatible with expert literary craftsmanship, while the installment approach forced him to end segments with suspense artificially built up to ensure the reader's continuing interest. Some of these rough spots were edited out in later single-volume editions, but the sense of rugged style persists, and reading Dostoevski is therefore not a relaxing experience. No reader, however, can easily forget the mental puzzles and nightmarish visions generated by Dostoevski's work.

NOTES FROM THE UNDERGROUND

Notes from the Underground, Dostoevski's first successful longer work, already contained many elements found in the subsequent novels. The nameless underground man is a keenly conscious misogynist who masks excessive pride with pathological submissiveness. In his youth, his need for self-esteem led him into disastrous social encounters from which he usually emerged the loser. For example, his delusion of being ignored by a social superior, who is not even aware of him, has caused him to spend years planning a ridiculous, and in the end miscarried, revenge. Dostoevski liked to use noncausal patterning in his compositional arrangements to enhance a sense of discontinuity. Thus, *Notes from the Underground* begins with the forty-year-old protagonist already withdrawn from society, spewing hatred, bitter philosophy, and ridicule at the imaginary reader of his journals. Only in the second part of the novel, which contains the underground man's actual confrontations, does it become clear that he has no choice but to hide himself away, because his twisted personality is incapable of even a casual positive human interaction. His very pronouncement is a contradiction, uttered in a continuous stream without developing a single argument, so that the overall effect is one of unordered dialectical listing.

On one level, *Notes from the Underground* was written to counter Nikolay Chernyshevsky's *Chto delat'?* (1863; *What Is to Be Done?*, c. 1863), which stresses the benefits of scientific thinking and considers self-interest beneficial to all society. Through the underground man's irrational behavior and reasoning, Dostoevski ridicules Chernyshevsky's assumptions. He makes his hero a living refutation of scientific approaches. If human logic can be corrupted by the mind's own illogic, no strictly logical conclusions are possible. By indulging in actions injurious to himself, the underground man proves that human beings do not act solely out of self-interest, that they are, in part at least, intrinsically madcap. Thus, any attempt to structure society along scientific lines, as suggested by Chernyshevsky, is doomed to failure. The duality of the hero is such, however, that rational assertions, too, receive ample exposure, as the underground man refutes his own illogic and spins mental webs around the imaginary listener. *Notes from the Underground* is difficult to read, especially for those unfamiliar with Chernyshevsky's novel. The unprogressively flowing illogicalities, coupled with an elusive authorial voice, render the narrative undynamic and tax even the intellectually committed reader. Dostoevski himself realized an insufficiency in the work but blamed it partly on censorial editing of an obscure religious reference, according to which the hero saw a glimmer of hope for himself in Christianity. The deleted comments, however, do not carry such a weighty connotation, and Dostoevski made no effort to restore the cut text later, when he might have done so. In its emphasis on the dual qualities of human endeavor, *Notes from the Underground* is firmly linked to the subsequent novels, in which this theme is handled with more sophistication.

CRIME AND PUNISHMENT

The wide appeal of *Crime and Punishment* results partly from its detective-story elements of murder, criminal investigation, evasion, confession, and courtroom drama. Dostoevski immediately broadens the perspective of the genre, however. Readers not only know from the outset who the murderer is but also are at once made part of his thinking process, so that his reasoning, motivations, and inclinations are laid bare from the start. The enigmatic element enters when readers come to realize, along with the murderer, and as slowly and painfully as the murderer, that he cannot assign a purpose to the crime, that human motivation remains, in the end, an unsolved mystery.

The very name of the hero, Raskolnikov, is derived from the Russian word for "split," and his entire existence is characterized by a swiftly alternating, unsettling duality. Raskolnikov is introduced as an intense former student who is about to put a carefully constructed theory into action. The opening chapters chronicle the confused state of his mental processes. He plans to rid the world of an evil by killing a pawnbroker who is gradually ruining her customers, Raskolnikov among them, and plans to use her hoarded wealth for philanthropical purposes in justification of the crime. Almost immediately, other motives call the first into question. Raskolnikov's mother threatens to sacrifice her daughter to ensure his financial well-being. An encounter with a derelict drunkard, Marmeladov, strengthens Raskolnikov in his resolve to kill, for Marmeladov keeps himself in drink and out of work by drawing on the pitiful earnings of his young daughter, Sonia, whom he has sent into prostitution. Raskolnikov notes in horror that he may force his sister into a similar situation through the legal prostitution of a sacrificial marriage. The crime itself renders all of Raskolnikov's musings invalid. He brutally murders a second, innocent victim, takes very little money, does not spend what he does steal, and will have nothing to do with his family.

From this point on, the novel focuses on Raskolnikov's struggle within himself. His prominently present but long repressed humanity asserts itself against his will to demolish arguments against confession provided by the proud part of his personality. Dostoevski uses the device of multiple alter egos in projecting Raskolnikov's dichotomy onto other characters. At one extreme pole stands the personification of Raskolnikov's evil impulses, the suspected killer and seducer Svidrigaïlov. Time and again, Raskolnikov confronts the latter in attempts to develop a psychological affinity with him. Raskolnikov's subconscious moral restraints, however, prevent such a union. Svidrigaïlov, and by extension Raskolnikov, cannot bring himself to perform planned abominations or live peacefully with already committed ones. Svidrigaïlov exits through suicide at about the same time that Raskolnikov is more urgently drawn to his other alter ego, the self-sacrificing, gentle prostitute Sonia.

Whereas Svidrigaïlov is a sensually vibrant figure, Sonia is basically colorless and unbelievable, but as a symbol of Raskolnikov's Christian essence, she turns out to be the stronger influence on him. She is not able to effect a moral transformation, yet she subtly moves into the foreground the necessity of confession and expiation. Raskolnikov never truly repents. He has, however, been forced to take a journey into his psyche, has found there an unwillingness to accommodate murder, and, almost angrily, has been forced to acknowledge that each life has its own sacramental value and that transgression of this tenet brings about psychological self-destruction. The final pages hint at Raskolnikov's potential for spiritual renewal, a conclusion that many critics find artistically unconvincing.

Intertwined with this primary drama are related Dostoevskian themes. Raskolnikov, in one of his guises, imagines himself a Napoleonic superman, acting on a worldwide stage on which individual killings disappear in the murk of historical necessity. On another plane, Dostoevski weaves Raskolnikov's mother, his landlady, and the slain pawnbroker into a triangle that merges the figures in Raskolnikov's confused deliberations, so that murderous impulses toward one are sublimated and redirected toward another. Similarly, the figures of Sonia, Raskolnikov's sister Dounia, and the pawnbroker's sister Lizaveta, also killed by Raskolnikov, are symbolically linked. Raskolnikov directs Dounia away from his lecherous alter ego Svidrigaïlov toward his proper, good-hearted embodiment and friend, Razumihin, while he himself, in expiation for killing Lizaveta, becomes a brotherly friend to Sonia. An important and cleverly presented role is reserved for the detective Porfiry, whose cunning leads Raskolnikov to confess a moral as well as a legal transgression. *Crime and Punishment* remains Dostoevski's most popular novel.

The Idiot

The author's narrative mode does not differ drastically in the remaining novels. Though each work is built on a different drama, all are developed along Dostoevski's favorite lines of human duality, alter ego, and authorial ambiguity. These qualities find expression in a most controversial way in *The Idiot*, the incongruous, almost sacrilegious portrayal of a Christlike figure. While the devout and selfless Sonia of *Crime and Punishment* occupies a position secondary to that of the central hero and thus lacks extensive development, Dostoevski makes the similarly self-sacrificing Prince Myshkin into the pivotal character of *The Idiot*. Through him, the author unfolds the notion that compassion and goodness, no matter how commendable on a theological plane, are insufficient to counter the less desirable aspects of reality.

The manner of Myshkin's presentation immediately challenges the reader's expectation of a "perfectly beautiful human being," as Dostoevski called his hero in preparatory notes. Myshkin—the name derives from the root of the Russian word for "mouse"—enters the novel as an insecure, epileptic, naïve young man, characterized by boundless goodwill, an immense capacity for humiliation, and a willingness to take the blame for the loathsome actions of others. He is a rather vapid personality, totally out of tune with existing human realities. Socially inept because of a long absence from Russia, ill at ease and inexperienced in confrontation with women, Myshkin is unable to establish satisfactory relationships. His kindness and empathy with suffering cause him to intervene repeatedly in other affairs, only to run afoul of the intense passions motivating his friends, and his interventions eventually lead to tragedy all around. Far from serving as counselor and redeemer, Myshkin is the cause of several calamities. Unversed in the intricacies of human interaction, created insufficiently incarnate by Dostoevski, the hapless protagonist leaves a path of misery and destruction before sinking totally into idiocy.

As he blunders his way through many unhappy encounters, several other themes emerge. The virginal hero actually has a sexually vicious and otherwise offensive double in Rogozhin, with whom he retains a close bond to the end, when both seemingly merge into one over the body of their mutual love, Nastasya Filipovna, freshly murdered by Rogozhin. Dostoevski assured outraged moralist critics that he had intended to create a perfect saint in Myshkin and implied that he had perhaps failed to create believable separate identities for Myshkin and Rogozhin, but Dostoevski's public assertions often contradicted the thrust of his novels, and it is more likely that here, too, he employed his favorite device of embodying the multifaceted human psyche in diametrically opposed figures.

In most of Dostoevski's novels, male characters are placed at center stage, leaving women to embody a given alter ego, highlight certain aspects of the protagonist, or echo other major concerns. *The Idiot* differs in presenting Nastasya Filipovna as Myshkin's primary antagonist. She is given scope and complexity in bringing to the surface Myshkin's temperamental inadequacy; in revenging herself for having been made concubine to the man appointed to be her guardian; in being torn by pride, guilt, and frustration; in vacillating between Myshkin and Rogozhin; and finally in orchestrating her own destruction. The other major female, Aglaya, receives less psychological expansion, but even here Dostoevski gives an interesting portrayal of a goodly woman unable to accept the humiliations associated with being Myshkin's companion. Dostoevski favored females of devious intensity, as typified by Nastasya Filipovna. In *Crime and Punishment* and *The Brothers Karamazov*, this type is marked by the identical name of "Katerina Ivanovna." Analysts interested in linking biography to plot perceive in these women an echo of Dostoevski's equally cruel and passionate friend, Apollinaria Suslova, as well as traits of his first wife, Maria Isayeva.

The preparatory notes to the novel reveal that Dostoevski changed perspective several times in shaping his guiding theme. In early drafts, Myshkin is a genuine double, possessed of many violent traits later transferred to Rogozhin. As Myshkin is stripped of negative features in later versions, he acquires the characteristics of a "holy fool," a popular type in pre-nineteenth century Russian literature, the mental defective as sweet, innocent, and specially favored by God. In the end, however there emerges the idea that an overflow of goodwill cannot vouchsafe positive results and can easily have the opposite effect. A certain meandering in the second part of the novel still reflects the author's hesitation in deciding on a direction. Earlier scholarship, unwilling to accept the fact that Dostoevski had depicted a failed saint in such a controversial manner, saw in *The Idiot* an unsuccessful attempt to portray a wholly Christian figure, but careful study of the text and background material reveals an intentional and original portrayal of a Christian dilemma. In succeeding works, too, Dostoevski's integrity as novelist took precedence over personal theological convictions.

The Possessed

In *The Possessed*, Dostoevski centered his attention on a very different type, the emerging Russian nihilist-atheist generation of the latter half of the nineteenth century. While the political aspect of the work occupies the general background, metaphysical and moral issues soon find their way into the narrative, as do satiric portraits of prominent Russians, among them a caricature of Turgenev, depicted in the ridiculous figure of Karmazinov. On the political level, Dostoevski demonstrates that revolutionary nihilism inevitably turns into a greater despotism than the order it intends to replace. One unscrupulous gang member, Shigalev, advocates a dictatorship of select revolutionaries and absolute submission on the part of the governed. For this reason, *The Possessed* faced long censorial repression in the Soviet Union, and former Soviet critics still find it awkward to present credible analyses of the novel.

The novelistic conspiracy is headed by a bloodthirsty degenerate, Pyotr Verkhovensky. Like Raskolnikov's murder in *Crime and Punishment*, Verkhovensky's killing is based on an actual event, the extermination of a student by the political terrorist Sergey Nechayev in 1869. Dostoevski's correspondence reveals that he was disturbed by the perverse publicity attending Nechayev's notoriety and intended to incorporate the incident into *The Possessed* for the purpose of deglamorizing such nihilistic misdeeds. In this he succeeded without question. Verkhovensky is shown to manipulate followers whose brutality and narrow-mindedness easily fashion them into blindly obedient puppets.

The focus of the novel, however, is on an enigmatic atheist, Stavrogin, who is only passively interested in external events. Stavrogin has no plans, preferences, illusions, beliefs, or passions, and his actions are accordingly illogical. For example, he engages in duels although he does not believe in them; marries a mental defective on a wager; bites his host, the governor of the province, on the ear; and calmly accepts a slap in the face from a subordinate. His very indifference to everyone and everything has made him into a charismatic figure whom Verkhovensky and his revolutionaries revere as a deity.

Stavrogin is depicted in such a shadowy manner that no coherent portrait emerges. The notebooks for *The Possessed* record the author's difficulties in creating the character: In early versions, Stavrogin is more fleshed out and clarified, but in the end Dostoevski chose to present him as a riddle, to demonstrate that an incorporeal image, by its very nature, exacts the deepest loyalties. Stavrogin's disinterest in the world eventually leads to inner dissatisfaction and suicide. An interesting part of his portrayal, his confession to a priest that he is responsible for the death of a child whom he raped, was excised by the censors and never restored by Dostoevski. Omission of this episode strips Stavrogin of the feeling of regret implied in the confession and intensifies the impression of absolute ethical neutrality assigned to his personality. Stavrogin is the opposite of Prince Myshkin in every respect—uninvolved rather than concerned, bored rather than active, cruel and unpredictable rather than steadfastly compassionate—yet their endeavors lead to the same tragic end. Neither manages to cope with reality and both abandon the world, Myshkin through madness, Stavrogin through suicide.

Another major character carrying a symbolic burden is Kirillov, whose inner conflicts about the existence or nonexistence of God also drive him to self-extinction. Kirillov is Western-educated, influenced by the scientific discoveries of the age; an avowed atheist, he transfers godlike attributes to himself. As Dostoevski traces Kirillov's inner reasoning, he reveals Kirillov to be a philosophical extremist. Because he no longer believes in an afterlife but is inexplicably afraid of death, he conquers that fear by annihilating himself. His opposite, Shatov, a believer in the Orthodox Church and in the special status of the Russian people, ends as a victim of the conspirators; once more, the author's plot line follows two diametrically opposed figures to the same fatal end.

Both *The Idiot* and *The Possessed* lack a hopeful view of the future. The society and mores in which the major figures operate reflect moral confusion and material corruption, a Babylonian atmosphere that Dostoevski subtly ascribes to erosion of faith. As always, it is difficult to say exactly where the author stands. Clearly, he refutes the terrorism exercised by Verkhovensky and his gang. Their political intrigue assumes the metaphysical quality of biblical devils "possessed" by love of ruin and chaos. The grisly demise of the other major characters suggests that Dostoevski also considered their approaches inadequate. The philosophical arguments, however, are presented with such conviction and honesty that no point of view is totally annihilated.

For most of the 1870's, Dostoevski was able to work at a leisurely pace, free from the material wants and deadline pressure of the preceding decades. It is all the more surprising, then, that *A Raw Youth*, composed in those tranquil years, is his least successful major novel. The reasons are painfully clear. The author overloaded the plot with poorly integrated, unrelated themes. What is worse, he let the rhetorical expression of his pet ideas overwhelm the artistic structure. The basic story deals with the illegitimate "raw youth" Arkady Dolgoruky, who is engaged in winning some recognition or affection from his biological father, Versilov. The narrative soon shifts to Versilov, a typical Dostoevskian dual type, motivated simultaneously by cruel passions and Christian meekness. Versilov carries additional symbolic burdens relating to Russia's alleged spiritual superiority over Western Europe. While Dostoevski fails to tie the many strands into a believable or even interesting panorama, he does attempt a symbolic scheme. Arkady's mother, Sofia, embodies "Mother Russia." She is on one side linked by marriage to a traditional peasant, Makar Ivanitch. At the same time, Sofia has been seduced by and continues to be involved with Versilov, the representative of the Western-educated nobility. The hapless Arkady, the disoriented offspring of this unconsecrated union, is driven to drastic schemes in an effort to find his place in life.

THE BROTHERS KARAMAZOV

Together with *Crime and Punishment, The Brothers Karamazov* continues to be Dostoevski's most widely read and discussed work. The author introduces no new concepts or literary devices in the novel, but this time he is successful in casting his themes into a brilliantly conceived construct. The conflict between a cruelly uncaring father and his vengeance-bound sons receives the artistic treatment missing in *A Raw Youth*. The metaphysical arguments, especially the dialectic between atheism and Christianity, are dealt with at length. Finally, the behavioral complexities of bipolar personalities are depicted in a most sophisticated manner.

The plot of the novel revolves around parricide. Four brothers, one illegitimate, have been criminally neglected by their wanton father, Fyodor Pavlovich, and subconsciously strive to avenge this transgression. The abominations of old Karamazov, some brutally indulged in the children's presence and partly involving their respective mothers, settle in the brothers' subconscious and motivate all of their later actions and behaviors. For most of the novel, none of the adult brothers is ever completely aware of the now-sublimated parricidal impulses, but all silently play their parts in seeing the old man murdered. The three legitimate brothers cope by nurturing father substitutes with whom they enter into complicated relationships. The oldest, Dmitri, fights his surrogates, almost murdering one, while the youngest, Alyosha, a novice, faces deep mental anguish in cultivating a father figure in his spiritual superior, Father Zossima. Ivan, the middle brother, has transferred his hatred of his father to a metaphysical plane, where he spars with a cruel God about the injustice of permitting mistreatment of children. In his prose poem "The Legend of the Grand Inquisitor," Ivan creates a benevolent father figure who shields his human flock from such suffering. Only Smerdyakov, the illegitimate offspring, keeps his attention focused on the primary target and actually kills old Karamazov, though his inner understanding of the factors motivating him is equally fuzzy. In desperation at not being fraternally acknowledged by his brothers, even after murdering for them, Smerdyakov implicates them in the crime and removes himself through suicide. The other three undergo painful self-examination from which they emerge as better human beings but not victorious. Dmitri, officially convicted of the crime, faces long imprisonment; Ivan's mind has given way as hallucinations plague him; and Alyosha seeks ways to combine his faith in a merciful God with the catastrophes of his actual experience.

Dostoevski has the major characters respond in different ways to their situation, developing each in terms of a specific psychological or metaphysical problem. Through Ivan, the author demonstrates the inadequacy of intellect where subconscious motivation is concerned. Ivan is educated, rational, atheistic, given to abstraction, loath to enter into close personal relationships, and proud of his intellectual superiority. Yet his wish to see his father dead is so powerful that it leads him into a silent conspiracy with Smerdyakov, whom he despises on a rational plane. The author attaches a higher moral value to Dmitri's type of personality. Dmitri represents an emotionally explosive spirit, quick to engage in melodramatic outbursts and passionate displays of surface sentiment. He instinctively grasps the moral superiority of the earthy, morally lax Grushenka to the socially superior, moralizing Katerina Ivanovna. His reckless nature leads him into many transgressions and misjudgments, but at a crucial point, when he has sought after opportunity to murder his parent, a deeply embedded reverence for life stays his hand. Alyosha acts as Dostoevski's representative of the Christian faith, and, like all other Dostoevskian Christian heroes, he is subjected to severe spiritual torments. His faith is tested as the externals and rituals of religion to which he clings prove elusive, if not false, and he is made to reach for a more profound Christian commitment within himself in order to survive the violence engendered by the Karamazov heritage. He is given the privilege, rare among Dostoevskian heroes, of affecting his environment in a wholesome fashion, especially at the end of the novel.

Each of the three brothers is rendered more complex in the course of his spiritual odyssey. The atheistic Ivan defends the cause of the Orthodox Church in his formal writings and in the end loses all pride and reason as he humbles himself in a futile attempt to save the innocent Dmitri from imprisonment. Dmitri acquires a measure of philosophical introspection as he learns to accept punishment for a murder he ardently desired but did not commit. Alyosha, too, despite largely positive patterning, is shown to let hidden desire neutralize religious conviction. Charged by Father Zossima with acting as Dmitri's keeper, the otherwise conscientious and compassionate Alyosha simply "forgets" the obligation and thereby fails to prevent his father's murder and his brother's entrapment. Dostoevski envisioned a larger role for Alyosha in a sequel to *The Brothers Karamazov* that never materialized. For this reason, Alyosha exits the work somewhat incomplete, incongruously engaged to a cunning, cruel cripple, Liza, who serves as his own unholy alter ego in the parricidal scheme.

The work abounds in secondary plots and figures, all interconnected and echoing the primary drama in intricate ways. Prominent among these plots is the legend of the Grand Inquisitor and the refutation of the legend by Father Zossima. Through the Grand Inquisitor, Dostoevski argues that Christian ideals are set too high for ordinary mortals, who prefer security and comfort to difficult individual choices. The Grand Inquisitor, in a dramatic encounter with Christ, thoroughly defends a benign kingdom on earth as most suitable for the masses. This argument is countered by Zossima's restatement of basic Christian theology, which does not answer the Grand Inquisitor's charges but simply offers traditional belief and practice of Christian tenets as an alternative perspective. The very type of behavior that proved ruinous to Prince Myshkin is in Zossima's actions converted into a richly beneficial model. By presenting the discourse in this fashion, Dostoevski cleverly juxtaposed humanistic and Christian arguments without resolving them. He thus once more implied that all so-called issues contain their own contradictions, that life and truth are indeed multiple.

By devoting his novels to the exploration of the mind, Dostoevski extended the intellectual horizons of his day. Although publicly a conservative of Russian Orthodox conviction, Dostoevski produced works that continuously challenge the notion that atheism inevitably engenders wanton amorality. It is this recognition of human complexity, coupled with a fascinating narrative style, that gives Dostoevski his modern flavor.

Margot K. Frank

Other major works

SHORT FICTION: *Sochineniya*, 1860 (2 volumes); *Polnoye sobraniye sochineniy*, 1865-1870 (4 volumes); *Povesti i rasskazy*, 1882; *The Gambler, and Other Stories*, 1914; *A Christmas Tree and a Wedding, and an Honest Thief*, 1917; *White Nights, and Other Stories*, 1918; *An Honest Thief, and Other Stories*, 1919; *The Short Novels of Dostoevsky*, 1945.

NONFICTION: "Zimniye zametki o letnikh vpechatleniyakh," 1863 ("Winter Notes on Summer Impressions," 1955); *Dnevnik pisatelya*, 1876-1877, 1880-1881 (2 volumes; *The Diary of a Writer*, 1949); *Pisma*, 1928-1959 (4 volumes); *Iz arkhiva F. M. Dostoyevskogo: "Idiot,"* 1931 (*The Notebooks for "The Idiot,"* 1967); *Iz arkhiva F. M. Dostoyevskogo: "Prestupleniye i nakazaniye,"* 1931 (*The Notebooks for "Crime and Punishment,"* 1967); *F. M. Dostoyevsky: Materialy i issledovaniya*, 1935 (*The Notebooks for "The Brothers Karamazov,"* 1971); *Zapisnyye tetradi F. M. Dostoyevskogo*, 1935 (*The Notebooks for "The Possessed,"* 1968); *Dostoevsky's Occasional Writings*, 1963; *F. M. Dostoyevsky v rabote nad romanom "Podrostok,"* 1965 (*The Notebooks for "A Raw Youth,"* 1969); *Neizdannyy Dostoyevsky: Zapisnyye knizhki i tetradi 1860-1881*, 1971 (3 volumes; *The Unpublished Dostoevsky: Diaries and Notebooks, 1860-1881*, 1973-1976); *F. M. Dostoyevsky ob iskusstve*, 1973; *Selected Letters of Fyodor Dostoyevsky*, 1987.

TRANSLATION: *Yevgeniya Grande*, 1844 (of Honoré de Balzac's novel *Eugénie Grandet*).

MISCELLANEOUS: *Polnoe sobranie sochinenii v tridtsati tomakh*, 1972-1990 (30 volumes).

BIBLIOGRAPHY

Adelman, Gary. *Retelling Dostoyesvky: Literary Responses and Other Observations*. Lewisburg, Pa.: Bucknell University Press, 2001. Provides information on Dostoevski's life and works by examining how nine twentieth century authors re-created *Crime and Punishment* and other Dostoevski novels. Describes how Dostoevski deeply influenced Joseph Conrad, Richard Wright, Vladimir Nabokov, Bernard Malamud, David Storey, Leonid Leonov, J. M. Coetzee, Frank Herbert, and Albert Camus.

Bloom, Harold, ed. *Fyodor Dostoevsky*. New York: Chelsea House, 2005. Collection of essays includes a biography, analyses of Dostoevski's works, and discussions about the characters in *The Brothers Karamazov* and Dostoevski's detractors and defenders. Also reprints "The Idea in Dostoevsky," an essay by Russian philosopher and literary critic Mikhail Bakhtin.

Catteau, Jacques. *Dostoevsky and the Process of Literary Creation*. Translated by Audrey Littlewood. New York: Cambridge University Press, 1989. Excellent resource offers detailed textual analysis and factual information on Dostoevski. Provides a thematic overview of the pressures and inspirations that motivated the author. Includes extensive notes, bibliography, and index.

Frank, Joseph. *Dostoevsky: The Seeds of Revolt, 1821-1849*. Princeton, N.J.: Princeton University Press, 1976.

_______. *Dostoevsky: The Years of Ordeal, 1850-1859*. Princeton, N.J.: Princeton University Press, 1983.

_______. *Dostoevsky: The Stir of Liberation, 1860-1865*. Princeton, N.J.: Princeton University Press, 1986.

_______. *Dostoevsky: The Miraculous Years, 1865-1871*. Princeton, N.J.: Princeton University Press, 1995.

_______. *Dostoevsky: The Mantle of the Prophet*. Princeton, N.J.: Princeton University Press, 2002. Monumental five-volume biography is one of the best sources on Dostoevski's life and art available in English. Frank subordinates details about the writer's private life in favor of tracing his connection to the social and cultural history of his time.

Kjetsaa, Geir. *Fyodor Dostoevsky: A Writer's Life*. Translated by Siri Hustvedt and David McDuff. New York: Viking Press, 1987. Thorough and compelling work on Dostoevski's life seeks to shed light on the creation of his fiction, citing letters and notes as artistic points of departure for the author.

Leatherbarrow, W. J., ed. *The Cambridge Companion to Dostoevskii*. New York: Cambridge University Press, 2006. Collection of essays examines the author's life and works, discussing his relationship to Russian folk heritage, money, the intelligentsia, psychology, religion, the family, and science, among other topics. Includes chronology and bibliography.

McReynolds, Susan. *Redemption and the Merchant God: Dostoevsky's Economy of Salvation and Antisemitism*. Evanston, Ill.: Northwestern University Press, 2008. Argues that readers cannot fully understand Dostoevski's writings without understanding his obsession with the Jews. Analyzes not only the elements of anti-Semitism in his works but also examines his views of the Crucifixion, Resurrection, morality, and other aspects of Christian doctrine.

Miller, Robin Feuer. *Dostoevsky's Unfinished Journey*. New Haven, Conn.: Yale University Press, 2007. Examines Dostoevski's works from numerous perspectives, analyzing the themes of conversion and healing in his fiction, questioning his literary influence, and exploring what happens to *Crime and Punishment* when it is taught in the classroom.

Scanlan, James P. *Dostoevsky the Thinker: A Philosophical Study*. Ithaca, N.Y.: Cornell University Press, 2002. Analyzes Dostoevski's novels, essays, letters, and notebooks to provide a comprehensive account of his philosophy, examining the weakness as well as the strength of Dostoevski's ideas. Concludes that Dostoevski's thought was shaped by anthropocentrism—a struggle to define the very essence of humanity.

Straus, Nina Pelikan. *Dostoevsky and the Woman Question: Rereadings at the End of a Century*. New York: St. Martin's Press, 1994. Argues that Dostoevski's compulsion to depict men's cruelties to women is an important part of his vision and his metaphysics. Maintains that Dostoevski attacks masculine notions of autonomy and that his works evolve toward "the death of the patriarchy."

ELLEN DOUGLAS

Born: Natchez, Mississippi; July 12, 1921
Also known as: Josephine Ayres Haxton

Principal long fiction

A Family's Affairs, 1962
Where the Dreams Cross, 1968
Apostles of Light, 1973
The Rock Cried Out, 1979
A Lifetime Burning, 1982
Can't Quit You, Baby, 1988

Other literary forms

Ellen Douglas's second book was a collection of short stories called *Black Cloud, White Cloud* (1963; rev. 1989), which was well-received critically, making the *New York Times* year's best fiction list. She continued to write and publish short stories in various periodicals across her career. Douglas also wrote the nonfiction study *A Long Night* (1986), about the integration of the University of Mississippi. In 1987, she published a collection of fairy tales, myths, and legends, *The Magic Carpet, and Other Tales*, to accompany illustrations by the celebrated Mississippi artist Walter Anderson. *Truth: Four Stories I Am Finally Old Enough to Tell* (1998), which Douglas herself calls fiction, is autobiographical and tells stories from several generations of her family's history, culminating in the tale of their involvement in the execution of several slaves in 1861 because of a purported rebellion. Finally, *Witnessing* (2004) collects forty years of essays, those published elsewhere and some written for this book.

Achievements

Ellen Douglas's first novel, *A Family's Affairs*, won the Houghton Mifflin Esquire Fellowship Award for the best new novel. *A Family's Affairs* and her second book, *Black Cloud, White Cloud*, were both named among the ten best works of fiction of the year by *The New York Times*. Douglas received two National Endowment for the Humanities Fellowships. Her 1982 novel *A Lifetime Burning* won the Mississippi Institute of Arts and Letters Award.

Douglas is an elected member of the Fellowship of Southern Writers (FSW). The success of her 1988 novel *Can't Quit You, Baby* earned for her FSW's first Hillsdale Prize for fiction. In 1999, the University Press of Mississippi held a symposium on Douglas's life and work. She won a literature prize in 2000 from the American Academy of Arts and Letters, and in 2008 received the Mississippi Institute of Arts and Letters' (MIAL) lifetime artistic achievement award. She has twice been awarded prizes by MIAL for her fiction (1979 and 1983).

BIOGRAPHY

Ellen Douglas was born Josephine Ayres in Natchez, Mississippi, on July 12, 1921, the second child of Laura Davis and Richardson Ayres. Because her father was a civil engineer, the family moved much, living in both Arkansas and Louisiana. Douglas's mother, not a writer herself, nevertheless inspired in her children a love of books. Douglas's paternal grandmother wrote children's books and also—along with the stories, conversations, and unusual behavior of her extended family—contributed to Douglas's love of words. Douglas's family has deep roots in the state's history.

From 1938 to 1939, Douglas attended Randolph-Macon Woman's College, but she finished her degree in 1942 at the University of Mississippi in Oxford. She married Kenneth Haxton, a composer, on January 12, 1945, and they soon settled in Greenville, Mississippi, in the region known as the Mississippi Delta. Greenville is a place rich in history and culture. The couple had three sons, Richard, Ayres, and Brooks, before they were divorced in 1980.

Douglas became friends with historian and writer Shelby Foote, writer Walker Percy, and Hodding Carter III, the newspaper editor renowned for his liberal voice during the civil rights struggles in Mississippi. In such an environment, Douglas began to write seriously, though she had written stories beginning in sixth grade.

The birth of *A Family's Affairs* was a bet she made with her husband and another friend about who could finish a novel in the least amount of time. When Houghton Mifflin wanted to publish it, she was reluctant because of the potential effect of its autobiographical content on her family. With the permission of her two aunts, she published the novel, using the pseudonym Ellen Douglas. *A Family's Affairs* met with much critical praise and was reissued by Louisiana State University in 1990 as part of its Voices of the South series.

Beginning in 1976, Douglas taught creative writing at Northeastern State University of Louisiana (now Louisiana State University, Monroe), and she served as a writer-in-residence at the University of Mississippi (1979-1983) and visiting professor at the University of Virginia (1984). She was named Welty Professor of Southern Studies at Millsaps College in Jackson, Mississippi, in 1988.

ANALYSIS

Because of the autobiographical nature of Ellen Douglas's novels, it is noteworthy that her family's heritage is deeply rooted in the history of Mississippi. She comes from what could be called the landed aristocracy. Some of her ancestors held land and slaves, and in subsequent generations entered professions that gave them significant community and social standing. During the economic depression in the South that began around the time of the American Civil War, they were, however, impoverished, and still of the genteel class. The genteel class, and their conflicts and concerns, predominate in Douglas's novels. Through their eyes and voices she describes the South's legacy of racial conflict as well as the changes wrought within the region's families and communities by economic forces, and, some say, encroaching New South values.

Douglas's novels also have complex and strong women characters for whom changing gender roles bring struggle. These women marry, raise children, live as responsible members of extended families and in small-town communities, and try to age with dignity. Clearly, the theme of family resonates in her work, but like so many important southern writers of her generation, Douglas is always exploring the burden of the past, especially as it is learned—and remembered—through story, as well as the individual's responsibility to that past. Her fiction raises the question, Given the circumstances of personal and public history, what was, indeed what is, the right thing to do?

Though Douglas continued to write about the complexity of life in small-town Mississippi, and though her "voice" remained consistent, she also experimented with point of view. For example, *A Family's Affairs* employs an omniscient narrator, but the perspective of Anna—daughter, granddaughter, and sister—predominates. While *Apostles of Light*, a later novel, also uses an omniscient narrator, Douglas creates here the increasingly confused interior world of the elderly Martha as she endures the stresses of aging. *A Lifetime Burning* is the fictional diary of a sixty-two-year-old college professor whose husband has an affair. She then has to deal with her life with him after the affair. The diary is sometimes addressed to her children and even includes a diary within her own, that of her husband's grandmother.

Then, in *Can't Quit You, Baby*, Douglas invents a third-person female narrator who sometimes intrudes into the narrative with her own comments. Here, too, this omniscient narrator takes the reader into the confused and grief-deadened mind of Cornelia, the novel's protagonist.

Douglas also is known for the realism of her descriptions of small-town life in the Deep South—its gardens, small businesses, conversations—the rhythms of both everyday life and special, sacred occasions. Her detailed descriptions of the natural world, however, make nature the most compelling aspect of these small towns and their surrounds. Many of her characters are deeply in tune with the land—its trees, shrubs, and flowers; insects, birds, and small creatures, both domestic and wild; the way scents and sounds change according to the time of day and the season. The loss of this connection with nature is a sign of spiritual atrophy in Douglas's fictional worlds.

Finally, though her novels could never be described as polemical, Douglas does not shy from the social issues that plagued the modern South. Race relations are a major topic of her fiction, as might be expected of a southern writer, but she also takes on the struggles of the aging, drug abuse, the complexities of human sexuality—including homosexuality—the environment, and the consequences of unchecked materialism, especially as it plays against the genteel, dignified poverty and making-do of earlier generations.

A Family's Affairs

A Family's Affairs tells the story of the matriarch and widow Kate Anderson and her family as they struggle and endure in Homochitto, Mississippi. The family lives in genteel poverty at the start of the story, but the realities of World War I and the economic depression that follows affect the family even further. As a single mother, Kate raises four daughters—Charlotte, Sara D., Katherine (Sis), and Anna—and a son, Will. The novel, told pri-

Ellen Douglas. (AP/Wide World Photos)

marily through daughter Anna's point of view, spans much of Kate's adult life, beginning with the marriage of her oldest daughter, Charlotte, to Ralph McPherson and ending with Kate's decline and death. Anna, at this point, is married with children of her own, but no longer living in Homochitto.

A Family's Affairs is a story of courtships and marriages, as Kate has to settle four daughters who, too, must consider the futures of their own children. The novel begins with a wedding and ends with a funeral, as if to suggest the overriding significance of such rituals. These rituals address beginnings and endings; communion, community, and solitariness; and the enduring nature of the ties of family—by blood and by marriage.

Bracketed within the novel are individual stories of Charlotte's successful marriage; Sarah D.'s loving but difficult union; Sis's disastrous marriage to a man beneath her in class and an outsider to the South as well, and their divorce; and Will's alcoholism. All the while, Anna is watching and learning, finally marrying outside the community and clan. Her new husband's father is a northerner and his mother is a southern Jew. The novel ends with the minister's prayer and blessing: "But let none of us be outside at last. Let not one man be outside another's pale. Let the inside be opened instead."

Apostles of Light

Douglas's third novel, *Apostles of Light*, explores the plight of the aging, though ultimately it is the story of a family and the way they take care of each other—or fail to. Martha Clarke and her longtime friend and lover, Dr. Lucas Alexander, are at the center of the story. Martha's family tries to deal with her aging, though without consulting her much.

The family home, Martha's home, is turned into a retirement facility, overseen by a third or fourth cousin, Howie Snyder. The novel becomes increasingly frightening as Martha and Lucas, the most aware of those ensconced in this new "home," lose their autonomy while Howie introduces more and more corruption into the running of what is for him clearly a business venture. The two protagonists are driven to desperate measures as they try to wrest their freedom from Howie and a family who initially mean well but fail in their responsibility to their own and to the community as a whole through carelessness.

As in all of Douglas's work, the small-town scene is rendered in great detail, especially the old family home full of heirlooms and memories. In the transition to a retirement home, the place is sanitized and fitted with plastic and cheap prints. Balancing these changes are the unchanging land, levee, and river surrounding the house. Through Martha's consciousness of this precious place, Douglas names and describes the home's sounds and fragrances, its stunning green beauty. Here, too, however, the ravages of change soon take affect: Howie removes trees and has plans to raze parts of the property to accommodate his cheapened taste.

Douglas masterfully writes Martha's increasing stress and mental confusion as her "home" is transmogrified into "the home." The old woman has waking dreams, and she mistakes visions of the past for the present. She becomes hyper-aware of the cats on her property. In her mind, the cats become ever more predatory, symbolic of her own entrapment and helplessness. Finally, the cats become part of her hallucinations and become metaphors for what has happened to her and her once-beloved home.

A Lifetime Burning

In *A Lifetime Burning*, Douglas experiments with a first-person narrator, Corinne, the sixty-two-year-old protagonist. Corinne relates the story of her life, mostly of her relationship with her husband, George, through a journal addressed to the couple's three grown children—Corinne, William, and James.

Over a six-month period, Corinne pieces memories together, though never in chronological order, as she attempts to understand and explain her relationship with George and their betrayal of each other. She seeks to penetrate the mystery of her husband, a man whom she feels has always held himself apart. Her journal, addressed in the end to "American History~~, children, American History~~ George," is her attempt both to understand and to close that distance.

Corrine begins by telling a story about George's affair with a woman she calls The Toad. As it turns out, Corinne invented this relationship, which she admits when she begins to tell the real story of his affair with a younger man, whom she calls Musk-rat. As the novel—the journal—progresses, the reader discovers that Corinne, as a young married woman, had an affair with a colleague, a woman who taught photography at the college. She, too, is married and with a child. The affair ends when the woman's husband, who is mentally ill, relapses, and the family moves from town.

Can't Quit You, Baby

In *Can't Quit You, Baby*, Cornelia is the source of her family's consternation for her remoteness, symbolized in the hearing aid she turns on and off at whim. Many of Douglas's important themes come together in this novel: family, marriage and sexuality, the individual's responsibility to his or her family, storytelling, change, and, as always, the southern landscape. For the first time, however, the protagonist visits a city, New York, and undergoes life-changing experiences there. The issue of race becomes embodied in the relationship between the affluent and white Cornelia and her African American maid, Tweet, or Julia, as Cornelia sometimes calls her.

Cornelia is happily married, content with her two grown children, her and her husband's book business, and her beautiful home. Tweet is introduced to the reader as she tells a long story to Cornelia while the two work side by side in the kitchen. Perhaps Cornelia listens; clearly, she tunes out some of Tweet's story. However, the reader is privy to the entire tale. In yet another experiment in point of view and narrative technique, Douglas creates an omniscient narrator, one who tells the reader something about herself and who comments on the story of the two women.

Before the sudden death of her husband, Cornelia begins to awaken to the realities of the lives all around her. John's death, however, finds her more remote and withdrawn than ever, dangerously so, and only her trip to New York and Tweet's serious illness brings her back and able to face the world as it is. Tweet, too, is central to the novel, and her story both parallels that of Cornelia and diverges in ways that suggest the unbreachable barrier of race. Once the women confess that they "hate" each other, they begin to build a real connection.

Douglas underscores the illusions and distances that keep people apart. References to Rapunzel and Cornelia's tower bedroom suggest her dreamy perspective on life as well as her remoteness. Her hearing aid and Tweet's loss of her ability to speak because of an aneurism are powerful symbols of the silence between them. Only after Tweet begins to sing and Cornelia takes up these songs—gospel and blues—can they make their healing confessions.

Susie Paul

Other major works

short fiction: *Black Cloud, White Cloud*, 1963 (revised 1989).

nonfiction: *Walker Percy's "The Last Gentleman,"* 1969; *A Long Night*, 1986 (essay); *Truth: Four Stories I Am Finally Old Enough to Tell*, 1998; *Conversations with Ellen Douglas*, 2000 (Panthea Reid, editor); *Witnessing*, 2004.

children's/young adult literature: *The Magic Carpet, and Other Tales*, 1987.

Bibliography

Lancaster, Sonya. "Too Many Cooks: Contested Authority in the Kitchen." *Southern Literary Journal* 38, no. 2 (Spring, 2006): 113-130. Lancaster examines the place of "cross-racial relationships": white women's kitchens, one of the only places in which women of different races could intermingle during segregation in the United States.

Manning, Carol S. "Ellen Douglass: Moralist and Realist." In *Women Writers of the Contemporary South*, edited by Peggy Whitman Prenshaw. Jackson: University Press of Mississippi, 1984. A discussion of Douglas's work through *A Lifetime Burning*, with an emphasis on the themes of responsibility and morals.

Tate, Linda. *A Southern Weave of Women: Fiction of the Contemporary South*. Athens: University of Georgia Press, 1994. In the chapter "Race and Region: Black and White Sisters of the Now South," Tate includes an extensive discussion of the relationship between Cornelia and Tweet in Douglas's novel *Can't Quit You, Baby*.

ARTHUR CONAN DOYLE

Born: Edinburgh, Scotland; May 22, 1859
Died: Crowborough, East Sussex, England; July 7, 1930
Also known as: Arthur Ignatius Conan Doyle

Principal long fiction

A Study in Scarlet, 1887 (serial), 1888 (book)
The Mystery of Cloomber, 1888
Micah Clarke, 1889
The Firm of Girdlestone, 1889
The Sign of Four, 1890 (also known as *The Sign of the Four*)
Beyond the City, 1891
The Doings of Raffles Haw, 1891
The White Company, 1891
The Great Shadow, 1892
The Refugees, 1893
The Parasite, 1894
The Stark Munro Letters, 1895
The Surgeon of Gaster Fell, 1895
Rodney Stone, 1896
The Tragedy of the Koroska, 1897 (also known as *A Desert Drama*)
Uncle Bernac, 1897
A Duet, with an Occasional Chorus, 1899 (revised 1910)
The Hound of the Baskervilles, 1901-1902 (serial), 1902 (book)
Sir Nigel, 1905-1906 (serial), 1906 (book)
The Lost World, 1912
The Poison Belt, 1913
The Valley of Fear, 1914-1915 (serial), 1915 (book)
The Land of Mist, 1926

Other literary forms

In his lifetime, Arthur Conan Doyle (doyuhl) was far better known for his short stories than for his novels. Until he became interested in science fiction (a medium he found better suited to shorter fiction) after 1900, Doyle concentrated his creative energies on his novels, those works by which he felt posterity would judge him, and took a purely monetary interest in the short-story format. Ironically, contemporary readers and critics continue to value the Sherlock Holmes short stories and largely ignore Doyle's historical novels.

One of the most prolific in an era of prolific authors, Doyle also dabbled in the theater. The most commercially successful of his dramas was the stage version of *Sherlock Holmes*, first produced in 1899, starring William Gillette. Doyle frequently financed his own plays, such as the violent and realistic *The Fires of Fate* (pr. 1909, from his novel *The Tragedy of the Koroska*), a dramatization of a river-pirate raid on a party of English tourists in Egypt, an adventure based—like so many of Doyle's works—on his own experiences.

Doyle's nonfiction was largely polemical. He chronicled and defended the course of the British involvement in the Boer War in his *The Great Boer War*, published in 1900, and *The War in South Africa: Its Cause and Conduct* (1902). His efforts at defending government policy, as well as his own medical service during the war, were largely responsible for his knighthood. Doyle also wrote extensively about other causes: the reform of the divorce laws, the denial of the vote for women, the abolition of ostrich-feather hats. He reserved his greatest energy, however, for his popularizing and propagandizing of spiritualism, a doctrine with which he had toyed from his youth and to which he became devoted after the death of his eldest son in World War I. Indeed, the last fifteen years of his life were spent in furthering the spiritualist cause through writings and lectures.

Achievements

"Come, Watson. The game's afoot." Few words by any author evoke a clearer picture in the public's mind. Individuals who have never read a Sherlock Holmes story can immediately conjure up a vision of two distinctive figures leaving the fog-shrouded entrance to 221-B Baker Street: Sherlock Holmes, tall and skeletal, pale from his sedentary existence and haggard from his addiction to cocaine, wearing his famous deerstalker cap; Dr. Watson, short and stolid, though limping from an old bullet wound, one hand nervously hovering over the pocket that holds his trusted revolver. Indeed, few, if any, imaginary addresses have received the bulk of mail that continues to be sent to Holmes's Baker Street apartment; few fictional characters have been the subject of even a single "biography," let alone the great number of books that purport to document the life of Sherlock Holmes; and certainly few authors have cursed the success of one of their creations as much as Arthur Conan Doyle did that of Sherlock Holmes.

When the struggling young Portsmouth physician first wrote down the name of "Sherringford Hope," soon changed to "Sherlock Holmes" in honor of the American writer Oliver Wendell Holmes, he did not dream of fame or literary immortality but merely of some means of augmenting his income, for he had a wife as well as a younger brother and an impoverished mother to support. In fact, as soon as *A Study in Scarlet* had been sent off to a prospective publisher in early 1887, Doyle was hard at work on *Micah Clarke*, the novel he felt would represent "a door . . . opened for me into the Temple of the Muses." Two years later, Doyle wrote the second Holmes novel, *The Sign of Four*, as a *jeu d'esprit* after a convivial dinner with Oscar Wilde, an unlikely admirer of *Micah Clarke*, and James Stoddart, the editor of *Lippincott's Monthly Magazine*, who challenged both Doyle and Wilde to supply him with suitable mystery manuscripts. Doyle's real interest at the time was in the completion of his "masterpiece," the historical novel *The White Company*, and its acceptance for serialization in the *Cornhill Magazine* beginning in January, 1891, seemed to him a far better harbinger of literary fame.

The unexpected success of Sherlock Holmes stories as they appeared in *The Strand Magazine* in the early 1890's quickly established Doyle's reputation as, in the opinion of Greenough Smith, literary editor of the magazine, the greatest short-story writer since Edgar Allan Poe, but Doyle continued to churn out a seemingly endless series of historical and semiautobiographical novels, most of which are read today only by scholars. The commercial success of these novels (*The Firm of Girdlestone*, *Beyond the City*, *The Great Shadow*, *The Refugees*, *The Parasite*, *The Stark Munro Letters*, *Rodney Stone*, *Uncle Bernac*, and *Sir Nigel*, among others), his numerous collections of short stories, his occasional ventures into drama, and his essays and pamphlets on social and political issues (such as reform of the divorce laws and the conduct of the Boer War) all depended in large part on Doyle's popularity as the creator of Sherlock Holmes. Throughout his life, however, he never saw the stories and novels featuring Holmes and Watson as much more than potboilers. Even the famous "resurrection" of Holmes in 1903 was an attempt to capitalize financially on the success of the London opening of the play *Sherlock Holmes*, starring William Gillette. Doyle saw his real life's work, up until he became a propagandist for spiritualism at the end of his life, as writing fiction that would amuse and distract "the sick and the dull and the weary" through the evocation of the heroic past.

Biography

The idealization of the past served other purposes for Arthur Ignatius Conan Doyle, who had been born into genteel poverty in Edinburgh on May 22, 1859, and named for King Arthur: It gave him a model to live by and to instill in his sons, and it diverted him from the disappointments of life that frequently threatened to overwhelm him. From his earliest childhood, his mother, Mary Doyle, the daughter of the keeper of a lodging house who believed herself a descendant of the Plantagenets, indoctrinated her eldest son in tales of his aristocratic ancestry and the virtues of medieval chivalry. Doyle's father, Charles, although employed throughout his son's childhood as a municipal architect in Edinburgh, was the youngest son of a highly gifted and artistic family. Charles Doyle's father, John Doyle, was the talented caricaturist "H. B."; his maternal uncle Michael Edward Conan was an artist as well as the art and drama critic and Paris correspondent for *Art Journal*; his brother Richard was a graphic artist for *Punch* and later an illustrator for John Ruskin, Charles Dickens, and William Makepeace Thackeray; another brother, Henry, was a painter before becoming director of the National Gallery of Ireland; a third brother, James, was a famous mid-Victorian portrait painter. Charles Doyle himself, who had suffered since early childhood from epilepsy and emotional disturbances, supplemented his salary with sketches of famous criminal trials and illustrations of fairy tales and historical romances. By the time his older son reached adulthood, Charles Doyle had descended through alcoholism into incurable insanity, retreating from a world he found uncongenial to his artistic temperament.

Mary Doyle necessarily became the central figure in her children's lives and continued to be so after they grew up. When Doyle first considered killing off Sherlock Holmes in November, 1891, his mother convinced him not to do so, thus reprieving the famous detective for a year. She also supplied her son with ideas for the Holmes stories. Throughout his childhood, Doyle's mother managed the practical necessities of life for an improvident husband and eight children on £180 per year and also instilled a vision of the ideal gentleman in her eldest son. In contrast to his father's instability and impracticality, Doyle grew into the epitome of the Victorian male: respectable, decent, cautious, thrifty, stolid. Only his writing—with its predilection for the codes of chivalry and honor and its preoccupation with a romantic past and his later obsession with spiritualism—betrayed the influences of Doyle's belief in his descent from kings and his father's retreat into a world of fantasy.

Arthur Conan Doyle. (Library of Congress)

Doyle's family was Catholic, and he was educated first at a Catholic preparatory school and then at Stonyhurst, the foremost Jesuit educational institution in England. He hated both, finding Stonyhurst rigid, backward, superstitious, narrow, and, above all, dull. Unpopular with the masters because of his frequent protests against physical punishment, Doyle survived his school days because of his ability at games, his preeminence among his schoolmates, and his aptitude at diverting himself through reading and writing about a more glorious and exciting past. In his five years at Stonyhurst he had no formal holidays, but he managed one visit to his uncle Richard Doyle in London, where the highlight of his stay was a visit to the Chamber of Horrors at Mme Tussaud's on Baker Street. During this period, he began to read the short stories of Poe, which later influenced him through their fascination with the macabre as well as through the characterization of Poe's intellectual detective, C. Auguste Dupin, who was one of the models for Sherlock Holmes. When Doyle entered Stonyhurst, the Jesuits had offered free tuition if he would train for the priesthood; fortunately, his mother refused the offer for him in spite of the advantages such an arrangement would have held. Ironically, the reactionary atmosphere at Stonyhurst contributed to Doyle's loss of faith, a faith he would not regain until his adoption of spiritualism forty years later.

Leaving school, Doyle found himself with three choices: the priesthood, law, or medicine. His loss of faith ruled out the first alternative and his lack of influential connections the second, so he entered Edinburgh University to study medicine in 1877. Although he was once again not a particularly brilliant student, he was deeply influenced by two of his professors, Dr. Joseph Bell, who became a prototype for Sherlock Holmes, and Dr. Andrew Maclagan, an instructor of forensic medicine, who served as a model for Professor Challenger in Doyle's later science-fiction novels. The School of Medicine at Edinburgh formed both the setting and the subject of his early and happily forgotten novel *The Firm of Girdlestone*.

Doyle's university days were punctuated with two spells as a ship's surgeon. The first voyage was aboard the *Hope*, an Arctic fishing boat. The seven-month trip was one of the highlights of Doyle's life. Seemingly indifferent to the bloody spectacle of the slaughter of whales and seals, he remembered only the sense of adventure and camaraderie among the crew. After graduation, he took a similar job aboard the passenger ship *Mayumba* on a voyage to the Gold Coast. This trip was in stark contrast to the first. Passengers and crew were struck down with tropical fevers that the young doctor was unable to treat. This experience so depressed Doyle that he gave up his plans for a career as a ship's surgeon and took up a position as an assistant to a doctor who turned out to be incompetent. When Mary Doyle objected to this association, her son left his employer and went to Portsmouth, where he opened his first practice.

Since the first years of his practice were not prosperous, Doyle returned to writing to occupy his time and to supplement his earnings. He also began to toy with an interest in the supernatural that is reflected in his later fiction and in his obsession with spiritualism. He attended his first séance in 1879 and worked on a number of bizarre stories. His poverty was such (he earned only about fifty pounds a year from his writing, and not much more from his practice) that his nine-year-old brother Innes, who was living with him at the time, had to usher patients into his surgery. His mother sent sheets and other household necessities from Edinburgh.

One of Doyle's greatest strokes of good fortune was the death of a patient. When a young boy collapsed of meningitis, then an incurable illness, outside his office, Doyle took the patient in and nursed him until his death. The boy's mother was so grateful for the doctor's solicitude, if not his medical skill, that she introduced Doyle to her daughter, Louise Hawkins, known as Touie. The young couple were married on August 6, 1885, and Touie Doyle became the perfect Victorian wife. Not only was she gentle, undemanding, and industrious but she also possessed a small yearly income that nicely supplemented her husband's earnings. The Doyles eventually had two children, Mary Louise and Alleyne Kingsley, before Touie developed consumption, the disease that doomed her to an early death and Doyle to years of celibacy.

Doyle's *Beyond the City* and *A Duet, with an Occasional Chorus* chronicle their married life. *Beyond the City* is set in Upper Norwood, the London suburb to which they moved in 1891, and details the days of their early married life: quiet afternoons spent bicycling together, equally quiet evenings with Touie sewing and her husband reading or writing. *A Duet*, written after Touie's fatal illness had been diagnosed, is silly and sentimental but ends with the deaths of the main characters in a train crash. Although Doyle remained devoted to assuring his wife's happiness until her death in 1906, he had fallen in love again in the mid-1890's. How much the fictionalized death of Touie in *A Duet* may have represented wish fulfillment remains conjecture.

The 1890's were years of contradiction for Doyle. His rise to literary prominence was paralleled by great personal distress. Although he had enjoyed moderate success as an author beginning with the publication of *A Study in Scarlet* in 1887, he still doubted that he could support his family by his pen. Early in 1891, he and Touie went to Austria, where he attempted to study ophthalmology; unsuccessful in this, he returned to England and moved his wife and daughter to London, where he set up a practice that drew even fewer patients than the one in Portsmouth. He had arrived back in England at a fortuitous moment for his career as a writer, however, as *The Strand Magazine* had decided to bolster its circulation by abandoning the traditional serial novel for a series of short stories featuring a continuing character. Hearing of this, Doyle decided to revive his Sherlock Holmes character. In less than two weeks, he wrote two more Holmes stories, "A Scandal in Bohemia" and "The Red-Headed League," which were immediately accepted by Greenough Smith, literary editor of *The Strand Magazine*. The two stories, which were published with illustrations by Sidney Paget, were instant and enormous successes. Doyle found himself an overnight celebrity.

This, however, was not the type of literary fame for which Doyle had hoped. Although he continued to turn out Holmes stories for *The Strand Magazine*, he worked more diligently on two new novels, *The Refugees*, another historical tale, and *Beyond the City*. By November, 1891, just five months after Holmes first appeared in *The Strand*, his creator had decided to end the detective's life. Only the influence of Mary Doyle and the temptation of the one thousand pounds the magazine was offering for a new series to run throughout 1892 made Doyle reconsider.

The second Holmes series confirmed Smith's opinion that Doyle was among the masters of the short-story form. Doyle himself found the format tedious; he always thought up the solution to the mystery first and then concocted the story in such a fashion as to obscure the true outcome from the reader as long as possible. His real affinity was for the historical novel, which he felt comfortable in writing and which he felt represented the true and highest purposes of art. In 1892, *The Great Shadow*, another example of his fondness for this genre, was published. It was extremely popular only because its author was the creator of Sherlock Holmes.

The continued ill health of Doyle's wife (her tuberculosis was finally diagnosed in 1893) required frequent journeys to the Continent. Churning out a story a month to meet his commitment to *The Strand Magazine*, concerned about Touie's health, constantly on the move, unhappy with the format in which he was forced to write, Doyle became more and more dissatisfied with his literary detective. If he did not exactly grow to hate Sherlock Holmes, he found the process of inventing new adventures for him more and more distasteful. He informed the magazine that Holmes's final case, recorded in "The Final Problem," would appear in their December, 1893, issue. No entreaties or offers of higher payments would change his mind. After the account of Holmes's death was published, more than twenty thousand subscribers to *The Strand* canceled their subscriptions.

With Sherlock Holmes seemingly permanently out of his life, Doyle devoted himself to a renewed interest in the psychic research of his youth and to public affairs. Since his wife's illness precluded sexual intercourse, Doyle's writings of this period reverted to his earlier preoccupation with a connection between sex and death. Doyle's 1894 novel *The Parasite* deals with the relationship between Professor Gilroy, a Holmesian figure who has retreated to the world of the intellect, and Helen Penclosa, a beautiful clairvoyant. At first a skeptic, Gilroy becomes increasingly obsessed with the beautiful young woman until, unable to withstand the passion that has made him lock himself in his own room, he rushes to her flat and makes love to her. Overcome immediately by guilt, he flees from her room, only to discover later that she has mesmerized him and forced him to rob a bank. As his obsession grows, Gilroy is dismissed from his post at the university and becomes increasingly erratic in his behavior. The more unstable Gilroy becomes, the weaker Penclosa grows, her power obviously transferring itself into his mind. In a moment of madness, Gilroy attempts to murder his fiancé, then decides to free himself by killing Penclosa. When he arrives at her flat, he finds her already dead and himself returned to sanity.

The public Doyle, however, continued to be the respectable man of affairs. Another historical novel, *Rodney Stone*, the story of a Regency dandy who becomes a "man" in the end, appeared in 1896. *Round the Red Lamp: Being Fact and Fancies of Medical Life*, a collection of ghost stories Doyle wrote for his children, was published in 1894. He continued his travels in search of renewed health for Touie, journeying back and forth to Switzerland and spending the winter of 1896-1897 in Egypt.

In private, Doyle was increasingly troubled by the complications of his love for Jean Leckie, to whom he was originally attracted because of her descent from the Scottish hero Rob Roy. Although he confessed his love for Jean to his mother and other family members, he resisted all their advice that he divorce Touie. Vowing never to consummate his relationship with Jean until Touie's death, he instructed his family never even to hint of the affair to his wife. His "code of honor" as a gentleman mandated that he cherish and protect Touie at the cost of his own happiness. Jean, with whom he had never quarreled, agreed. They continued to see each other, but Touie was kept ignorant of her husband's love for another woman. Doyle and Jean even waited the requisite year of mourning after Touie's death before they were finally married in 1907.

Although he had returned to an English setting for *Rodney Stone*, Doyle was fascinated by the events of the French Revolution and the Napoleonic Wars. In 1896 and 1897, after a spell in Egypt as a war correspondent during the Sudanese War, he published *The Exploits of Brigadier Gerard*, the first of a series of stories about the picaresque hero to appear in novel form. He also wrote *Uncle Bernac*, another Napoleonic novel, and *The Tragedy of the Koroska*, a melodrama about his adventures with paddleboat bandits in Egypt.

In the late 1890's and the first years of the new century, Doyle increasingly turned to the horror story. One particular story, "Playing with Fire," published in 1900, combined his interest in psychic phenomena with his love for animals and suggested that animals, too, survive the grave. "The King of Foxes" (1903) dealt with Jean Leckie's favorite sport, foxhunting, in a bizarre and macabre form. Also in this period, to make money and to forestall another dramatist from seizing on the idea, Doyle adapted the character of Sherlock Holmes for the American stage, emphasizing that the play that would make actor William Gillette famous was not a new adventure but related events that had occurred before Holmes's "death."

The outbreak of the Boer War in October, 1899, gave Doyle the outlet he needed for his interest in public affairs. He first attempted to enlist in the army and then accepted the position of senior surgeon with John Longman's private field hospital. He saw his service at Bloemfontein in 1900 as that of a medieval knight seeking to help those less fortunate than he. His heroic efforts with inadequate equipment, his propaganda pamphlet *The War in South Africa: Its Cause and Conduct*, and later his history of the war, *The Great Boer War*, combined to win him knighthood in 1902.

While in South Africa, Doyle had read of the story of the Cabell family, which was haunted by a ghostly hound. He saw in this the germ of a new Holmes novel, and *The Hound of the Baskervilles* was duly published in 1901-1902. He was still not committed to bringing Holmes back to life and insisted once again that *The Hound of the Baskervilles* was an earlier adventure only now coming to light. Although he continued to write horror stories, he was unable to resist the financial lure of more Holmes tales, and, consequently, in October, 1903, the first adventure of the "resurrected" Sherlock Holmes appeared.

During the last two decades of Doyle's life, his fame and finances were assured by the popularity of Sherlock Holmes. His private life, after his marriage to Jean Leckie and the birth of their three children, was that of an Edwardian paterfamilias. With the exception of *Sir Nigel*, he finally abandoned the historical novel in favor of science fiction. Politically reactionary, Doyle nevertheless was respected for his warnings about the outbreak of World War I. His greatest preoccupation, however, was with the cause of spiritualism; his final "conversion" to absolute belief in the phenomenon that had fascinated him for years resulted from the deaths of his brother Innes and eldest son Kingsley during World War I. To the end of his life, he was convinced that he was in frequent touch with the spirits of his loved ones and thus devoted all the proceeds from his novels and lectures to the "cause."

In the early 1920's, he once again announced Holmes's departure, this time to honorable retirement as a beekeeper on the Sussex Downs. Doyle brought him back only once, in a 1924 story written expressly for Queen Mary's Dolls' House, an elaborate dollhouse created for Queen Mary in the 1920's. His literary reputation suffered because of his involvement in spiritualism, and his excellent science-fiction novels, many of which rival those of Jules Verne, were ridiculed by the critics more for their author's peculiarities than for their own lack of merit. Doyle died on July 7, 1930; his wife Jean claimed to receive a spirit message from him less than twenty-four hours later. His epitaph, however, looked back to earlier decades, to the little boy named after King Arthur who had resolved to live his life according to knightly ideals: "STEEL TRUE/BLADE STRAIGHT."

Analysis

Arthur Conan Doyle's epitaph can also serve as an introduction to the themes of his novels, both those that feature actual medieval settings and those that center on Sherlock Holmes. Doyle's central character is always the knight on a quest, living and battling according to chivalric ideals. Micah Clarke, Alleyne Edricson, and Sir Nigel Loring all engage in real battles; Sherlock Holmes combats villains on behalf of distressed young women and naïve and frightened young men; Professor Challenger takes on the unknown—a prehistoric world, the realm of the spirit, the threatened extinction of life on Earth.

Micah Clarke

Doyle's first historical novel, *Micah Clarke*, is set in seventeenth century England against the background of Monmouth's Rebellion. As he always did in his historical fiction, in which he intended to portray the actual conditions of life at the time the novels were set, he paid meticulous attention to actual detail. In the Sherlock Holmes stories, Doyle seems not to have cared whether Dr. Watson's old war wound was in his shoulder or his knee, whether the good doctor's Christian name was John or James, whether there were one or two Mrs. Watsons, but his period novels show none of this casualness. For *Micah Clarke*, the author had carefully explored the area around Portsmouth, where most of the action takes place. He also did careful research into the dress, customs, and speech of the era. Indeed, it was its "mode of speech" that caused both Blackwoods and Bentley, Ltd. to reject the novel; this same period diction makes the novel extremely slow going for the modern reader.

Like most of Doyle's characters, those in *Micah Clarke* are modeled on real individuals. Micah Clarke, the gallant young man fighting zealously for a lost cause, is largely based on young Doyle himself, protesting hopelessly at Stonyhurst against outmoded courses of study, unfair punishments, and censorship of his letters home. Ruth Timewell, the cloyingly sweet young heroine, depicts the quiet, meek Touie Doyle, who at the time the novel was written represented her husband's ideal of womanhood. In spite of the critical acclaim *Micah Clarke* received when it was originally published, few people would consider it the stirring tale of adventure that its author did, although parts of it, especially the description of the climactic Battle of Sedgmoor and the portrait of the evil Judge Jeffreys, retain some interest for the modern reader.

The White Company

The White Company, Doyle's second venture into the historical genre, and its companion piece, *Sir Nigel*, have worn slightly better. Like its predecessor, *The White Company* is distinguished by its scrupulous re-creation of the entire spectrum of life in fourteenth century England. Once again, Doyle's preoccupation with noble causes is reflected in the interests of his characters, members of a small but dedicated mercenary company who set off for the Continent to fight for England during the Hundred Years' War.

The hero of *The White Company*, after whom Doyle later named his eldest son, is Alleyne Edricson, a landless young squire who leaves the monastery where he has been reared with his two companions, the lapsed monk Hortle John and the former serf Samkin Aylward, to join the White Company under the command of Sir Nigel Loring. Alleyne, his friends, his leader, and later his prince represent a microcosm of English society in the Middle Ages, depicting an idealized vision of the English character and contrasting with that of the country's main enemies: the French, the Spanish, and the Germans. Departing from his usual historical accuracy, Doyle presents the Germans as the worst foes of the English, reflecting his own late Victorian perspective. Alleyne and his friend are mercenaries who live by their wits, but their fighting, looting, and pillaging are always conducted according to the rules of the chivalric game. At the end of the novel, Alleyne wins his knighthood, his inheritance, and his lady fair in the person of Sir Nigel's daughter Maude. The virtues Sir Nigel embodies and Alleyne learns are those that Doyle taught his own sons: sympathetic treatment of social inferiors, courtesy and respect for women, and honesty in financial dealings.

The novel is particularly interesting for its two main themes: the rise of the English middle class and of English patriotism. *The White Company* depicts a world where individuals are judged not by their birth but by their accomplishments, in much the same manner as Doyle rose from poverty to affluence through his own efforts. The book, however, also reflects its author's belief that the English character was the best in the world; Doyle clearly insists that the language, history, customs, and beliefs of England are far superior to those of any other nation.

Sherlock Holmes novels

At first glance, the four Sherlock Holmes novels (*A Study in Scarlet*, *The Sign of Four*, *The Hound of the Baskervilles*, and *The Valley of Fear*) might seem to have little in common with Doyle's historical fiction. A closer look, however, shows that whatever the surface differences, the author's underlying concerns and prejudices are the same. Indeed, Sherlock Holmes can be seen as a knight-errant who ventures forth from Baker Street on a series of quests. In the earlier novels and stories, he battles dragons of crime on behalf of individuals. Mary Morstan in *The Sign of Four* is the epitome of a damsel in distress. In Holmes's later adventures, both the suppliants and the dragons are different. There is an increasing tendency for those seeking Holmes's assistance to be representatives of the government itself or, as in "The Illustrious Client," a person no less exalted than King Edward VII himself, and for the villains to be international criminals or even foreign governments.

Holmes's relationship with Dr. Watson reflects that of a knight and his squire. The detective and his intellect operate according to the rules of detection that Holmes himself establishes at the beginning of *The Sign of Four*, rules analogous to the chivalric code, and squire Watson accompanies Holmes as much to learn how to conduct himself according to these rules as to assist in the solution of the crime. Dull, plodding, faithful Watson may never win his spurs, but at least he wins the hand of Mary Morstan.

The Holmes novels also exhibit Doyle's characteristic xenophobia. With the possible exception of Moriarty, who, after all, is an international rather than an English criminal, the villains with whom Holmes contends frequently are foreigners, or else the crimes he investigates have their origins in foreign or distant events. *A Study in Scarlet* is a story of the revenge exacted for a crime committed in the mountains of Utah twenty years earlier. The novel's "victims" are in fact villains who have mistreated an old man and a young girl, those most deserving of protection, and so deserve their own deaths, while its "villain" is a just avenger who is saved from the gallows by a "higher judge" and dies with a smile on his face as if looking back on a deed well done. The crime in *The Sign of Four* similarly has its origins years before in India, and its victims also turn out to have brought their doom on themselves. Rodger Baskerville, the father of Stapleton the naturalist, who perpetrated the hoax in *The Hound of the Baskervilles*, had fled to South America before his son was born. As in the fictional press report at the end of *A Study in Scarlet*, Doyle appears eager to distance the true Englishman from responsibility for crime.

The Lost World

Although Doyle himself favored his historical fiction while the public preferred the Sherlock Holmes adventures, the author's finest works have largely been ignored. *The Lost World, The Poison Belt*, and *The Land of Mist* are novels that belong to a series of science-fiction works featuring the eccentric Professor George Edward Challenger. By the time *The Lost World* was published in 1912, Doyle was already becoming a figure of fun among the intelligentsia because of his ardent defense of psychic phenomena and his reactionary political views. The critics' disdain for this series unfortunately affected its popularity, and in subsequent years scholars and others have had a consequent tendency to overlook them as examples of Doyle's literary skill at its finest.

The Lost World resulted from Doyle's interest in prehistoric footprints near his home in the New Forest. After he made casts of the prints, he consulted with zoologist Edwin Ray Lankester and came away with the idea for the novel. *The Lost World* is narrated by Edward Dunn Malone, a journalist who comes to act as a Watson-like chronicler of the exploits of Professor Challenger, an eccentric scientist with a great physical resemblance to Arthur Conan Doyle. After knocking Malone down the stairs at their first meeting, Challenger recruits him for a proposed expedition to South America in search of a prehistoric monster believed to exist on a plateau in the Amazon River basin.

Doyle's penchant for realistic description deserts him in *The Lost World*. His details are fifty years out of date; he instead presents a fantastically imaginative vision of the unexplored jungle wilderness. The beauty of the jungle vanishes as the explorers reach the historic plateau. With almost surrealistic horror, Doyle depicts the filthy, fetid nesting ground of the pterodactyls and the dank and dirty caves of the ape-men who inhabit the plateau. A marvelous comic ending has Challenger revealing the results of the expedition to a skeptical London audience of pedants by releasing a captured pterodactyl over their heads.

The characterization in *The Lost World* is among Doyle's finest achievements. The members of the expedition are well balanced: the eccentric and pugnacious Challenger, the naïve and incredulous Malone, the cynical and touchy Summerlee, and the great white hunter Lord John Roxton. The one woman in the novel, Malone's fiancé, Gladys, bears no resemblance to the Ruth Timewells and Lady Maudes of Doyle's earlier work. She is spunky and independent, refusing to marry Malone until he has done something worth admiring, and in his absence marrying someone else because she decides money is a more practical basis for marriage than fame.

Later works

The series retains its high quality in *The Poison Belt*, but the subsequent related works are less consequential. In *The Land of Mist*, Challenger becomes a spiritualist convert when the spirits of two men whom he believes he has killed return to tell him of his innocence. "When the World Screamed," one of the stories in *The Maracot Deep, and Other Stories* (1929), reverts to the morbid sexuality of *The Parasite*. When Challenger attempts to drill a hole to the center of the earth, the world turns out to be a living female organism. When Challenger's shaft penetrates the cortex of her brain, she screams, setting off earthquakes and tidal waves.

Few of Doyle's writings from the last decade of his life are read by other than specialists, dealing as they do with the propagation of spiritualism. The canon of his fiction can thus be said to have ended with science-fiction novels. These novels too all deal with Doyle's characteristic themes and concerns. Challenger and Maracot uncover hidden truths about the nature of the past, the present, the future, and life after death much in the same way Sherlock Holmes discovered the truth about human nature in the course of his investigation of crime. The historical fiction had sought to explore the truth about a specialized human nature, that of the archetypal Englishman, in the same manner. Even the obsession with spiritualism that cost him his credibility among intellectual circles was but another example of Doyle's lifelong search for the truth about human existence.

In whatever guise he portrayed that search, Doyle never deviated from the devotion to the ideals that were instilled in him in childhood and that are recorded on his gravestone. Similarly, all his literary protagonists embody these same ideals: a devotion to truth and a belief in the rightness of their cause. Few other authors have managed to create such a coherent body of work as did Arthur Conan Doyle, and fewer have matched the content of their work so closely to the conduct of their lives.

Mary Anne Hutchinson

Other major works

SHORT FICTION: *Mysteries and Adventures*, 1889 (also known as *The Gully of Bluemansdyke, and Other Stories*); *The Captain of Polestar, and Other Tales*, 1890; *The Adventures of Sherlock Holmes*, 1892; *My Friend the Murderer, and Other Mysteries and Adventures*, 1893; *The Great Keinplatz Experiment, and Other Stories*, 1894; *The Memoirs of Sherlock Holmes*, 1894; *Round the Red Lamp: Being Fact and Fancies of Medical Life*, 1894; *The Exploits of Brigadier Gerard*, 1896; *The Man from Archangel, and Other Stories*, 1898; *The Green Flag, and Other Stories of War and Sport*, 1900; *The Adventures of Gerard*, 1903; *The Return of Sherlock Holmes*, 1905; *Round the Fire Stories*, 1908; *The Last Galley: Impressions and Tales*, 1911; *One Crowded Hour*, 1911; *His Last Bow*, 1917; *Danger!, and Other Stories*, 1918; *Tales of Terror and Mystery*, 1922 (also known as *The Black Doctor, and Other Tales of Terror and Mystery*); *Tales of the Ring and Camp*, 1922 (also known as *The Croxley Master, and Other Tales of the Ring and Camp*); *Tales of Twilight and the Unseen*, 1922 (also known as *The Great Keinplatz Experiment, and Other Tales of Twilight and the Unseen*); *Three of Them*, 1923; *Last of the Legions, and Other Tales of Long Ago*, 1925; *The Dealings of Captain Sharkey, and Other Tales of Pirates*, 1925; *The Case-Book of Sherlock Holmes*, 1927; *The Maracot Deep, and Other Stories*, 1929; *The Final Adventures of Sherlock Holmes*, 1981 (revised and expanded 2001); *Uncollected Stories: The Unknown Conan Doyle*, 1982.

PLAYS: *Foreign Policy*, pr. 1893; *Jane Annie: Or, The Good Conduct Prize*, pr., pb. 1893 (with J. M. Barrie); *Waterloo*, pr. 1894 (also known as *A Story of Waterloo*); *Halves*, pr. 1899; *Sherlock Holmes*, pr. 1899 (with William Gillette); *A Duet*, pb. 1903; *Brigadier Gerard*, pr. 1906; *The Fires of Fate*, pr. 1909; *The House of Temperley*, pr. 1909; *The Pot of Caviare*, pr. 1910; *The Speckled Band*, pr. 1910; *The Crown Diamond*, pr. 1921; *Exile: A Drama of Christmas Eve*, pb. 1925; *It's Time Something Happened*, pb. 1925.

POETRY: *Songs of Action*, 1898; *Songs of the Road*, 1911; *The Guards Came Through, and Other Poems*, 1919; *The Poems: Collected Edition*, 1922.

NONFICTION: *The Great Boer War*, 1900; *The War in South Africa: Its Cause and Conduct*, 1902; *The Case of Mr. George Edalji*, 1907; *Through the Magic Door*, 1907; *The Crime of the Congo*, 1909; *The Case of Oscar Slater*, 1912; *Great Britain and the Next War*, 1914; *In Quest of Truth, Being a Correspondence Between Sir Arthur Conan Doyle and Captain H. Stansbury*, 1914; *To Arms!*, 1914; *The German War: Some Sidelights and Reflections*, 1915; *Western Wanderings*, 1915; *The Origin and Outbreak of the War*, 1916; *A Petition to the Prime Minister on Behalf of Roger Casement*, 1916(?); *A Visit to Three Fronts*, 1916; *The British Campaign in*

France and Flanders, 1916-1919 (6 volumes); *The New Revelation*, 1918; *The Vital Message*, 1919; *A Debate on Spiritualism*, 1920 (with Joseph McCabe); *Our Reply to the Cleric*, 1920; *Spiritualism and Rationalism*, 1920; *The Evidence for Fairies*, 1921; *Fairies Photographed*, 1921; *The Wanderings of a Spiritualist*, 1921; *The Case for Spirit Photography*, 1922 (with others); *The Coming of the Fairies*, 1922; *Our American Adventure*, 1923; *Memories and Adventures*, 1924; *Our Second American Adventure*, 1924; *The Early Christian Church and Modern Spiritualism*, 1925; *Psychic Experiences*, 1925; *The History of Spiritualism*, 1926 (2 volumes); *Pheneas Speaks: Direct Spirit Communications*, 1927; *What Does Spiritualism Actually Teach and Stand For?*, 1928; *A Word of Warning*, 1928; *An Open Letter to Those of My Generation*, 1929; *Our African Winter*, 1929; *The Roman Catholic Church: A Rejoinder*, 1929; *The Edge of the Unknown*, 1930; *Arthur Conan Doyle on Sherlock Holmes*, 1981; *Essays on Photography*, 1982; *Letters to the Press*, 1984; *Arthur Conan Doyle: A Life in Letters*, 2007 (Jon Lellenberg, Daniel Stashower, and Charles Foley, editors).

TRANSLATION: *The Mystery of Joan of Arc*, 1924 (of Léon Denis's biography).

EDITED TEXTS: *Dreamland and Ghostland*, 1886; *D. D. Home: His Life and Mission*, 1921 (by Mrs. Douglas Home); *The Spiritualist's Reader*, 1924.

MISCELLANEOUS: *The Sir Arthur Conan Doyle Reader*, 2002.

Bibliography

Barsham, Diana. *Arthur Conan Doyle and the Meaning of Masculinity*. Burlington, Vt.: Ashgate, 2000. Examines Doyle's depiction of masculinity, delving into all of his works, including his war correspondence and travel writings. Demonstrates how Doyle sought to alter the idea of manliness at a time of shifting gender identity.

Booth, Martin. *The Doctor, the Detective, and Arthur Conan Doyle: A Biography of Arthur Conan Doyle*. London: Hodder & Stoughton, 1997. Well-written, astute biography provides details about the full range of Doyle's activities and writings. Demonstrates how Doyle's accomplishments extended far beyond his creation of Sherlock Holmes.

Carr, John Dickson. *The Life of Sir Arthur Conan Doyle*. London: John Murray, 1949. One of the first biographies of Doyle not written by a relative, this straightforward account gives a good overview of Doyle's life. Quotes copiously from Doyle's letters, but offers little discussion of the stories. Includes a list of sources and an index.

Edwards, Owen Dudley. *The Quest for Sherlock Holmes: A Biographical Study of Arthur Conan Doyle*. New York: Barnes & Noble Books, 1983. Concentrates on the first twenty-three years of Doyle's life. Explains how various aspects of Doyle's early life influenced his writing, such as his love of history and Celtic lore, the impoverished and Catholic Edinburgh of his youth, and his alcoholic father.

Jaffee, Jacqueline A. *Arthur Conan Doyle*. Boston: Twayne, 1987. Solid study combines biography and a critical discussion of Doyle's novels and stories. Supplemented by an index, a bibliography of Doyle's work, and an annotated bibliography.

Jann, Rosemary. *The Adventures of Sherlock Holmes: Detecting Social Order*. New York: Twayne, 1995. Slim volume is divided into two parts, the first of which places the great detective in a literary and historical context, followed by Jann's own reading of Arthur Conan Doyle's Sherlockian approach to detective fiction. Includes a brief chronology of Doyle's life and work as well as a selected bibliography.

Lycett, Andrew. *The Man Who Created Sherlock Holmes: The Life and Times of Sir Arthur Conan Doyle*. New York: Free Press, 2007. Comprehensive and detailed biography is based in part on materials in Doyle's personal archive that were not available to researchers until 1997. Describes the events of the author's life and the variety of his writings, explaining how the author who created one of the world's most rational detectives was a believer in spiritualism and the supernatural.

Orel, Harold, ed. *Critical Essays on Sir Arthur Conan Doyle*. New York: G. K. Hall, 1992. Collection of essays presents both evaluations by Doyle's contemporaries and later scholarship, some of it commissioned specifically for inclusion in this volume. Divides the discussion into three sections: "Sherlock Holmes," "Other Writings," and "Spiritualism." Orel opens the collection with a lengthy and comprehensive essay, which is followed by essays by such literary lights as Dorothy L. Sayers, George Bernard Shaw, Max Beerbohm, and Heywood Broun.

Simmons, Diane. *The Narcissism of Empire: Loss, Rage, and Revenge in Thomas De Quincey, Robert Louis Stevenson, Arthur Conan Doyle, Rudyard Kipling, and Isak Dinesen*. Brighton, England: Sussex Academic Press, 2007. Analyzes the works of five authors who helped popularize the goals of imperialism, arguing that they all bore scars of traumatic childhoods and sought to bolster their fragile egos through dreams of imperial domination.

Stashower, Daniel. *Teller of Tales: The Life of Arthur Conan Doyle*. New York: Henry Holt, 1999. Excellent, thorough biography focuses less on the Holmes novels than have other biographers and more on Doyle's historical novels, personal crusades, and spiritualism. This work received the 1999 Edgar Award for Best Biographical Work.

RODDY DOYLE

Born: Dublin, Ireland; May 8, 1958

Principal long fiction

The Commitments, 1987
The Snapper, 1990
The Van, 1991
The Barrytown Trilogy, 1992 (includes the previous 3 novels)
Paddy Clarke, Ha-Ha-Ha, 1993
The Woman Who Walked into Doors, 1996
A Star Called Henry, 1999
Oh, Play That Thing, 2004
Paula Spencer, 2006

Other literary forms

In addition to his novels, for which he is best known, Roddy Doyle wrote several highly successful plays, including *Brownbread* (pr. 1987), *War* (pr., pb. 1989), and *The Woman Who Walked into Doors* (pr. 2003), which is based on his 1996 novel. *Family* (1994), a four-part television play, was highly controversial for its treatment of domestic abuse. While the subject of the abusive husband and father was by no means new in Irish literature, the play's widespread distribution through television provoked public debate over the representation of the working-class Irish family.

Doyle also wrote many short stories, including the collection *The Deportees, and Other Stories* (2008), and he wrote several books for children and teenage readers, including *Not Just for Christmas* (1999), *The Giggler Treatment* (2000), *Rover Saves Christmas* (2001), *The Meanwhile Adventures* (2004), and *Wilderness* (2007). He also contributed to the collaborative novels *Finbar's Hotel* (1999, with others) and *Yeats Is Dead!* (2001, with others). In 2002, he published an oral history-memoir about his parents, *Rory and Ita*.

Achievements

Roddy Doyle's earlier novels are recognized for their unique and original representation of contemporary working-class family life in suburban Dublin. The novels that comprise the Barrytown trilogy (*The Commitments*, *The Snapper*, and *The Van*; all three published later as *The Barrytown Trilogy*) are celebrated for their honest, realistic portrayal of family dynamics and socioeconomic conditions as an antidote to the often romanticized depictions of life in earlier Irish novels. Perhaps as a result of this unique focus, the Barrytown trilogy has enjoyed a rare combination of critical acclaim and popular commercial success. *The Van*, the most serious of the three novels, was nominated for the Booker Prize, which is awarded annually to the best novel in English from the Commonwealth or the Republic of Ireland. All three novels of the Barrytown trilogy have been made into major motion pictures.

Doyle's next novel, *Paddy Clarke, Ha-Ha-Ha*, went

on to win the Booker Prize in 1993. With its innovative narrative technique and disturbingly honest portrayal of childhood at the brink of adolescence, *Paddy Clarke, Ha-Ha-Ha* is widely acknowledged to be Doyle's masterpiece. In 1998, Doyle was awarded an honorary doctorate from Dublin City University.

Roddy Doyle. (AP/Wide World Photos)

Biography

Roddy Doyle was born May 8, 1958, in Dublin, one of four children born to Rory and Ita Doyle. His father was a printer and his mother worked as a secretary. As a child, Doyle attended schools in the suburbs to the north of the city. He later earned a degree in English and geography from University College, Dublin, and became a teacher. He worked as a schoolteacher from 1979 until 1993, when, after considerable critical and commercial success, he resigned to work full time as a writer.

Doyle seems to have drawn upon the neighbors and neighborhoods of his childhood for his earlier novels, set as they are in Barrytown, a fictional working-class suburb north of Dublin. His interest in portraying the resilience and ingenuity of average people makes this a fertile source of inspiration. Doyle's work with schoolchildren must have been a direct influence on his highly insightful novel *Paddy Clarke, Ha-Ha-Ha*, which portrays the dissolution of a marriage from the point of view of a young boy.

Doyle dabbled in writing for periodicals before seriously attempting to write fiction. His first attempt at a novel was not published, and his second, *The Commitments*, was originally published by a company that Doyle and a friend began just for that purpose. Printed and distributed on borrowed money, *The Commitments* eventually attracted the notice of a major publishing house, which republished the novel for a broad and appreciative audience. Although Doyle is one of Ireland's best-known writers, he has shunned the public limelight and remained a very private person.

Analysis

One of Roddy Doyle's greatest attributes as a writer is his ear for voice and dialogue, and his first five novels in particular display this gift to excellent effect. With minimal third-person narration, Doyle uses realistic dialogue—such as profanities and regional dialect—to achieve vivid characterization. It is not surprising that several of his novels have been adapted effectively for film, since his dialogue-heavy expository technique is essentially dramatic, or cinematic.

Some commentators, however, claim that Doyle's emphasis on dialogue detracts from the novels' plots. Character takes precedence in these novels over author, narrator, and plot. Considered chronologically, Doyle's novels demonstrate an increasingly complex interaction between dialogue and narration. Because his characters do most of their speaking for themselves, there is little evidence of an authoritative, controlling consciousness in his novels. This technique empowers Doyle's characters even as it deprives readers of a comforting narrative guide; whether Doyle is using first-person or third-person narration, there is no concrete, objective perspective with which to compare and measure the perspective of the protagonist.

Doyle's dialogue has attracted much commentary because his characters belong to an economic and social class underrepresented in literature. Prior to Doyle's Barrytown novels, the contemporary, urban, working class of Dublin was an uncommon subject in the Irish novel.

While several of Doyle's novels are notable for their treatment of contemporary Dublin, the past plays a vital role throughout his works. In *The Commitments*, the young protagonist forms a band that plays soul music from the 1960's, hearkening back to an earlier, perhaps more innocent time. *Paddy Clarke, Ha-Ha-Ha* is set in 1968, and young Paddy and his father reflect both on nationalism in Irish history as well as on more contemporary events. The historical novels that comprise the Last Roundup series foreground Doyle's preoccupation with early twentieth century Ireland and with American culture.

The Barrytown trilogy

Doyle's interest in the frank exploration of family dynamics is evident in the three novels that make up the Barrytown trilogy. (The three novels were later published in a single volume under the same title.) While the notion of family values is by no means idealized in these novels, Doyle focuses on the large, resilient Rabbitte family, a family of survivors.

These novels display narrative immediacy because of their emphasis on dialogue and a near absence of intrusive narration. This immediacy is intensified by the pervasive contemporary slang and profanity in the dialogue. In *The Commitments*, young Jimmy Rabbitte, Jr., attempts to bring soul music back to Dublin by bringing together an array of talented musicians (most of them young) and then rehearsing them. He then has to market them as a rhythm-and-blues (R & B) band called the Commitments, to a skeptical public. The trumpet player, an older man who claims friendship with the African American R & B musician Wilson Pickett, is the band's most direct connection to the tradition they are trying to revive. Jimmy understands that the appeal of this genre is not nostalgia, but rather its association with sex and an affinity he perceives between African American culture and the urban, Irish working class. Jimmy's enthusiasm and entrepreneurial skills are impressive but are ultimately not equal to the self-destructive forces that pull the band apart on the eve of its success.

While the Rabbitte family remains in the background through most of *The Commitments*, the family is the focus of *The Snapper*. The book's title refers to Dublin slang for an infant, and the novel centers on the unwanted pregnancy of the eldest daughter, Sharon, and the family's struggle to accept her decision to give birth and to raise the child without revealing the identity of the father, who turns out to be a friend of her own father. Jimmy Rabbitte, Sr., vacillates between disgust, embarrassment at the community's almost tribal reaction to his family's predicament, and, ultimately, acceptance of his daughter's decision. His skirmishes with Sharon form the major conflict of the novel.

The Van tells the story of the business partnership between Jimmy Rabbitte, Sr., and his friend Bimbo after they both lose their jobs. Jimmy has been struggling with unemployment; he takes the opportunity to spend time with his granddaughter but misses the male social interaction provided through work and evenings at the pub. Bimbo buys an old fish-and-chips van, and Jimmy joins him on his new job. At first, all goes well, but business and legal problems strain the friendship and, eventually, Bimbo drives the van into the sea. It is not clear whether the friendship can survive, but it appears Jimmy will with the support of his wife and family.

Paddy Clarke, Ha-Ha-Ha

While *Paddy Clarke, Ha-Ha-Ha* has earned many critical comparisons to James Joyce's autobiographical novel *A Portrait of the Artist as a Young Man* (1916), it is important to note that Doyle's novel does not seem to draw directly upon his own childhood experiences but rather upon his interactions with his own students and their parents. This novel shares a setting with the Barrytown trilogy as well as a reliance on dialect for character and exposition, and some critics have failed to detect a plot—a criticism levied at Doyle's earlier novels as well. However, there is a story in *Paddy Clarke, Ha-Ha-Ha*, though the narrator, and therefore the reader, becomes aware of it only late in the novel: A marriage dissolves because of economic and other pressures, and children struggle to deal with the consequences during a time (the novel is set in 1968) when broken marriages carried considerable social stigma.

The novel is narrated by ten-year-old Paddy, and the events he describes are those that would likely preoccupy a boy of his age in that time and place. At the beginning of the novel, he is part of the "in" crowd, though not a leader. His hobbies are soccer, picking at scabs, and tormenting his younger brother, Francis, whom he calls Sinbad. His relationship with Sinbad is ambivalent; his younger brother's soccer skills exceed his own, and Paddy is confused by the mixed feelings of pride and hatred this causes him. He tortures Sinbad but defends him from others. Their fellow students are known by their actions: Some are pathetic and to be made fun of, some are strong and to be feared and appeased. The adults in Paddy's life, the ones outside his family, are ancillary for the most part.

Some of the novel's most significant moments are to be found in Paddy's conversations with his father about patriotism and Irish independence, the Cold War, and the Middle East. At the novel's conclusion, Paddy's social status among his peers changes due to his father's departure.

The Woman Who Walked into Doors

Doyle's consideration of family dynamics takes a darker turn in *The Woman Who Walked into Doors*. Paula Spencer is abused at the hands of her husband, Charlo. The protagonist demonstrates a complicated mix of denial and inner strength. She recognizes that her situation, raising four children and living in constant fear, is at once very complicated and very simple. Her drinking, at first an apparent solution, eventually becomes a problem in its own right. The novel is ultimately a story of endurance and survival; the protagonist's story of recovery continues in Doyle's novel *Paula Spencer*.

A Star Called Henry *and* Oh, Play That Thing

A Star Called Henry and *Oh, Play That Thing* mark a substantial departure for Doyle; the two novels are works of historical fiction, a challenging mixture of historical fact and invention. The first novel describes the early life of Henry Smart and his experiences and exploits during and after the Easter Uprising of 1916. He encounters many of the famous historical figures who played public roles in the uprising and himself takes active part in the ensuing war for independence, even as he grows increasingly disillusioned over the lack of prospects either side offers for the poor and disenfranchised.

Oh, Play That Thing follows Henry Smart to America, in flight from his former Irish Republican Army associates. He works his way into the world of crime in New York through the gateway of advertising, eventually getting involved with bootlegging and pornography. He then flees to Chicago and befriends Louis Armstrong, whom he assists as a manager and bodyguard.

James S. Brown

Other major works

short fiction: *The Deportees, and Other Stories*, 2008.

plays: *Brownbread*, pr. 1987; *War*, pr., pb. 1989; *The Woman Who Walked into Doors*, pr. 2003 (adaptation of his novel).

screenplays: *The Commitments*, 1991 (adaptation of his novel; with Dick Clement and Ian La Frenais); *The Snapper*, 1993 (adaptation of his novel); *The Van*, 1996 (adaptation of his novel).

teleplay: *Family*, 1994.

children's/young adult literature: *Not Just for Christmas*, 1999; *The Giggler Treatment*, 2000; *Rover Saves Christmas*, 2001; *The Meanwhile Adventures*, 2004; *Wilderness*, 2007.

Bibliography

Booker, M. Keith. "Late Capitalism Comes to Dublin: 'American' Popular Culture in the Novels of Roddy Doyle." *Ariel* 28, no. 3 (1997): 27-46. This article examines the portrayal of American popular culture in the novels of Doyle. Examines as well the development of the books around the theme of multinational popular culture.

McCarthy, Dermot. *Roddy Doyle: Raining on the Parade*. Dublin: Liffey Press, 2002. This guide to Doyle's fiction (through *The Woman Who Walked into Doors*) focuses on Doyle's "counter-mythological" depiction of contemporary urban Ireland and his characters' disengagement with or rejection of traditional Irish nationalism and colonialism.

McGlynn, Mary. "'But I Keep on Thinking and I'll Never Come to a Tidy Ending': Roddy Doyle's Useful Nostalgia." *LIT: Literature Interpretation Theory* 10, no. 1 (July, 1999): 87-105. This article begins by examining Doyle's use of nationalistic color symbolism in *Paddy Clarke, Ha-Ha-Ha* and describes a shift from the insular nationalism of the first part of the twentieth century to an outward-looking construction of nation, focusing on the role of nostalgia.

McGuire, Matt. "Dialect(ic) Nationalism? The Fiction of James Kelman and Roddy Doyle." *Scottish Studies Review* 7, no. 1 (Spring, 2006): 80-94. This article contrasts the use of dialect in the works of Scottish novelist James Kelman and Irish novelist Doyle. Examines their novels in relationship to the respective Scottish and Irish historical contexts of their settings as well as the times in which they were written.

Marsh, Kelly A. "Roddy Doyle's 'Bad Language' and the Limits of Community." *Critique* 45, no. 2. (Winter, 2004): 147-159. This article analyzes self-censorship in Doyle's novels, examining changes in the use of "bad" language from the Barrytown trilogy to the later novels *Paddy Clarke, Ha-Ha-Ha* and *The Woman Who Walked into Doors*. Discusses the significance of censorship and free speech in preserving community.

Mildorf, Jarmila. "Words that Strike and Words that Comfort: Discursive Dynamics of Verbal Abuse in Roddy Doyle's *The Woman Who Walked into Doors*." *Journal of Gender Studies* 14, no. 2 (July, 2005): 107-122. This article uses sociolinguistic and literary analysis to examine characters' use of language in *The Woman Who Walked into Doors*. Studies slang and sexist language and explores how verbal abuse ultimately empowers the novel's protagonist and provides her with a means of retaliation.

Reynolds, Margaret, and Jonathan Noakes. *Roddy Doyle: The Essential Guide*. New York: Vintage, 2004. This book is an interactive reading guide to Doyle's novels, devoting a chapter to each covered novel and including questions for discussion and analysis. Also provides a short interview with Doyle.

MARGARET DRABBLE

Born: Sheffield, South Yorkshire, England; June 5, 1939
Also known as: Lady Holroyd

Principal long fiction

A Summer Bird-Cage, 1963
The Garrick Year, 1964
The Millstone, 1965 (also known as *Thank You All Very Much*)
Jerusalem the Golden, 1967
The Waterfall, 1969
The Needle's Eye, 1972
The Realms of Gold, 1975
The Ice Age, 1977
The Middle Ground, 1980
The Radiant Way, 1987
A Natural Curiosity, 1989
The Gates of Ivory, 1991
The Witch of Exmoor, 1997
The Peppered Moth, 2000
The Seven Sisters, 2002
The Red Queen, 2004
The Sea Lady: A Late Romance, 2006

Other literary forms

Margaret Drabble has combined literary scholarship with her career as a novelist. Among other works, she has published a short critical study of William Wordsworth, *Wordsworth: Literature in Perspective* (1966), and has edited a collection of critical essays about Thomas Hardy, *The Genius of Thomas Hardy* (1975). Over the years, she has edited or written introductions for most of Jane Austen's works for various publishers, including *Lady Susan*, *The Watsons*, and *Sanditon*. She has also edited editions of Thomas Hardy's *The Woodlanders* and Emily Brontë's *Wuthering Heights* and *Poems*. In 1989, she published her Gareth Lloyd Evans Shakespeare Lecture at Stratford-Upon-Avon as *Strat-*

ford Revisited: A Legacy of the Sixties. She has also written two major biographies: *Arnold Bennett* (1974) and *Angus Wilson* (1995). Her literary travelogue *A Writer's Britain: Landscape in Literature* was published in 1979, and she is well known for editing the fifth edition of *The Oxford Companion to English Literature* (1985, revised 2000).

In addition, Drabble has had a long-standing connection with drama. Her works include *Bird of Paradise* (pr. 1969), a stage play; *A Touch of Love* (1969), a screenplay based on her novel *The Millstone*; and *Laura* (1964), a play for television. Drabble has also written a fair number of short stories that are as yet uncollected and only partially available to American audiences. In 1978, she published the children's book *For Queen and Country: Britain in the Victorian Age*.

Achievements

Margaret Drabble's novels charm and delight, but perhaps more significant is that they reward their readers with a distinctively modern woman's narrative voice and an unusual blend of Victorian and modern structures and concerns. Although there seems to be critical consensus that Drabble has, as Bernard Bergonzi has said, "devised a genuinely new character and predicaments," the exact nature of this new voice and situation has not been precisely defined. Bergonzi sees the new character as an original blend of career woman and mother, yet Drabble's career woman begins to appear only in her seventh novel, *The Realms of Gold*. Her earlier, equally freshly portrayed heroines are often not mothers—for example, Sarah in *A Summer Bird-Cage* or Clara in *Jerusalem the Golden*. Most of the mothers who precede Frances Wingate in *The Realms of Gold* can in no way be considered career women. Rose Vassiliou in *The Needle's Eye* does not work; Rosamund Stacey in *Thank You All Very Much* works only sporadically to support her baby, and her job can hardly be considered a career.

Other critics have claimed that the new voice involves an unprecedented acquaintance with the maternal attitude toward children. This is the voice Erica Jong predicted would emerge once motherhood was no longer thought incompatible with literary artistry. In fact, only three Drabble novels can be said to contain this voice—*Thank You All Very Much*, *The Ice Age*, and *The Middle Ground*—yet all the novels seem to present something original in their female point of view.

Female characters have illuminated literature for more than a thousand years, but until relatively recently they have appeared as secondary figures. The female has been present, but her point of view and voice have been lacking. Drabble seems to be able to evoke not only the female point of view but also the cadence of the female voice. Her ear for speech rhythms is exceptional, and each central female character has a distinct speech pattern and cadence. This is, of course, more intensely true in the first-person narratives of Drabble's earlier novels, but it is also true of her later novels in which the heroine's interior life is rendered by an omniscient narrator who mimes her speech in order to discuss her feelings and thoughts. Perhaps Drabble's artistry in portraying the sound of the female voice is among her most significant accomplishments, more simple and more complex than the evocation of a maternal career woman or of the mother-child bond.

Drabble has also begun to experiment with the return of the outspoken omniscient narrator. Drabble's rediscovery of an old literary technique seems timely rather than regressive. She does not embed the characters in the amber of the narrator's point of view, preventing them from dramatizing themselves. Drabble's omniscient narrator gives the reader a sense of place, a sense of location and history, without forcing the characters to bear the burden of carrying all that perception in their minds. It frees the characters to notice only what they perceive within the confines of their personalities, for there is a narrative voice to create the density of the social and physical scene.

The narrator's involvement in place and history has important thematic implications for Drabble's fiction. Drabble departs from the prevalent modern emphasis on the centrality of the individual sensibility, reaching back instead to the tradition of two authors she admires, Arnold Bennett and George Eliot. She explores modern fragmentation as a function, to some extent, of human choice. She explores the consequences of choosing to submit to centrifugal forces as opposed to struggling against them in an effort to be true to one's roots. This original blend of a deep concern for society's conventions and origins and an unusually sensitive evocation of the individual female sensibility gives Drabble's works their particular flavor.

Drabble's novels have won many prizes, including the John Llewelyn Rhys Memorial Award (1966), the James Tait Black Memorial Prize (1968), the Book of the Year Award from the *Yorkshire Post* (1972), and the E. M. Forster Award of the American Academy of Arts and Letters (1973). Drabble has received honorary D.Litt. degrees from many universities, including Sheffield, Manchester, Keele, Bradford, Hull, East Anglia, and York. She was made an honorary fellow of the Sheffield City Polytechnic in 1989. In 1980, she was made a Commander of the Order of the British Empire; in 2008, she was promoted to Dame Commander.

Margaret Drabble. (© Jerry Bauer)

BIOGRAPHY

Margaret Drabble was born into a family that reflects at once the breakup of old patterns and the power of conventions, which may account for her receptiveness to both aspects of modern England. Her parents, John Frederick Drabble and Kathleen Marie (Bloor) Drabble, were the first of their families to attend university. The results of her parents' upward mobility were both creative and destructive. Her father became a barrister and then a judge; her mother suffered the dislocations that attend such rapid social changes. She became an atheist and thus estranged herself from her religious fundamentalist parents. Drabble has stated that her mother was released from the harshness of her religious training when, as a young woman, she read George Bernard Shaw. As she turned the pages she had a revelation that there is no God. "One could say," says Drabble, "that that was a revelation from God not to worry about him because it was going to drive her mad if she did." Drabble's mother struggled against clinical depression until her death.

Margaret Drabble is the second of three daughters. Her sisters are Dr. Helen Langdon, a scholar, and Susan Duffy, a novelist, whose pen name is A. S. Byatt. She also has a brother, Richard J. B. Drabble. She attended a Quaker boarding school in York, The Mount School, and then read English at Newnham College, Cambridge, where she finished among the top of her class. In 1960, in the week that she finished at Cambridge, she married Clive Swift.

Swift was an aspiring actor who worked with the Royal Shakespeare Company. In the early years of their marriage, Drabble spent much of her time having three children, writing novels, and acting in bit parts and understudying for the Royal Shakespeare Company. While she was writing *The Garrick Year*, she understudied Imogen in *Cymbeline*, played a fairy in *A Midsummer Night's Dream*, and had a bit part in *The Taming of the Shrew*. Drabble separated from her husband in 1972; their divorce became final in 1975.

Drabble is a member of the National Book League and served as its chair from 1980 to 1982. During the 1980's she devoted much of her energy to revising *The Oxford Companion to English Literature* for its fifth edition. In 1982, she married the biographer Michael Holroyd. They settled in the Notting Hill district of London and at Porlock Weir, Somerset.

Analysis

Margaret Drabble's novels begin as female arias in the bel canto style, predominantly elaborate embellishments on a simple series of events relative only to the first-person narrator, events that reflect a brief but formative time in the narrator's life. The early novels deal with the lives of rather ordinary middle-class girls and, but for their sensitivity and subtlety of insight, come dangerously close to being considered women's magazine fiction. The later novels are more complex, exploring the delicate webs of social interconnections and covering longer periods of time in which the convergences of many lives on one another effect subtle and not-so-subtle changes. Both the early and later novels express Drabble's concern with finding the legitimate sources of growth and development. Her later novels explore global concerns in addition to the domestic. Throughout the entire canon of Drabble's novels one finds the use of irony and the display of comedic wit, sometimes in the form of black comedy.

A Summer Bird-Cage

Drabble's distinctive narrative voice is clear in her first novel. Sarah Bennett, a recent college graduate, is the protagonist of *A Summer Bird-Cage* but figures mainly as a witness to her sister Louise's marriage. From her older sister's mistakes, Sarah learns about her own attitude toward the future. The novel begins as Sarah returns from Paris to attend Louise's marriage to Stephen Halifax, a boring, trendy, wealthy, satirical novelist. Louise is a stunning and exciting raven-haired beauty, and Sarah cannot understand why she is marrying the bloodless Stephen. Sarah and her friends attempt to puzzle this out through the progress of the novel, especially as it becomes increasingly obvious that Louise has been having an affair with a very attractive actor, John Connell. In the end, Sarah learns directly from Louise what was obvious all the while: Louise married Stephen for his money. Rather than seeming anticlimactic, this knowledge solidifies Sarah's growing understanding of what fidelity and betrayal are about. Despite its socially sanctioned position, the marriage Louise has contracted is in fact adulterous because it is a betrayal of her heart and affections. The technical adultery is an act of faith.

Louise divorces Stephen to take her chances with John, and Sarah ends the novel with a forged bond of affection with Louise. Sarah is thus prepared for the return of her boyfriend, Francis, from America. Having observed Louise, Sarah realizes that fidelity to her vow to marry Francis is not as important as waiting to see if in fact their relationship has its roots in truth. Sarah will only marry if the action follows from an authentic feeling.

Jerusalem the Golden

In her fourth novel, *Jerusalem the Golden*, Drabble experimented for the first time with omniscient narration, maintaining an ironic distance from her protagonist. Clara Maugham, a provincial girl from Northam, a small town in the North of England, is that young woman all too familiar in fiction, the woman whose capacities for development are greater than the opportunities presented by her narrow circumstances. In general, such a character is often created by a writer who has escaped the clutches of small minds and tight social structures; an identity of author and character is usually suspected. The character becomes a vehicle through which the author gets back at the tormentors of his or her youth; the character finds dazzling fulfillment in the city.

Clara Maugham, then, comes out of this tradition, but she does not lead the reader into the usual pitfalls. Drabble considers the problems of leaving one's roots for fuller possibilities. As impoverished as one's heritage may be, it provides one with a foothold in reality. Hence the title of the novel is a mocking one—it alludes to the utopian dream that emerges from a hymn to which Clara is attracted as a schoolgirl:

> Jerusalem the Golden
> With Milk and Honey blest
> Beneath thy contemplation
> Sink heart and voice oppressed.
> I know not, oh, I know not
> What social joys are there
> What radiance of glory
> What light beyond compare.

For Clara, the mysteries of ecstasy counterpoint the threadbare, wretched, familiar world. For her there is nothing in between, and she leaves Northam only to find a sham Jerusalem in London.

Clara begins life believing that she is doomed to be as her mother is, a woman without hope who remarks that when she is dead the garbage collector can cart her off. Mrs. Maugham is a jealous, inconsistent woman who verbally snipes at her neighbors behind her lace curtains because of their concern for their proprieties, and then she outdoes them in cheap ostentation. Rejecting such a life, Clara finds hope in literary images. Metaphors provide avenues of escape, as in the hymn; so too does a children's story that makes a deep impression on her, *The Two Weeds*. The story presents the choices of two weeds. One decides on longevity at the cost of a miserly conservation of its resources, growing "low and small and brown"; the other longs for intensity, the spectacular but short life, and puts its efforts into fabulous display. Each weed achieves its goal. The small, plain one survives, as it had hoped. The magnificent, attractive weed is plucked and dies happily at the bosom of a lovely girl. What impresses Clara about this story is the offer of any possibility other than the low road of mere survival. Little by little, Clara chooses the mysteries of ecstasy.

Clara has to make her way to these mysteries by rejecting a more moderate course, thus losing real opportunities to grow and succeed. Her intellect is widely despised by the good people of Northam, although it is valued by some of her teachers, who fight to attach her to their subjects. She is also revered by a boy named Walter Ash, who values culture and comes from a family tradition that stresses intellectual stimulation. Clara is cynical about her teachers' admiration; she does not value their esteem. She allows Walter to go out with her, but she has little regard for him. She ultimately rejects him, thinking, "I shall get further if I'm pulled, I can't waste time going first."

This cryptic remark makes sense only in the light of her choices in London, to which she goes on scholarship to attend Queens College. By chance, she meets Clelia Denham at a poetry reading. This meeting drives her to an instinctual attachment to the girl and subsequently to her family, especially Clelia's brother Gabriel, with whom she has an affair. Although her attachments to the Denhams "pull her," and she does not need to "go first," it is questionable whether they take her anywhere. Indeed, the Denhams provide her the accoutrements of ecstasy. The life she leads with them, however, having torn herself away from her unsatisfactory family, is not one that she builds herself. It is one that envelops her in a "radiance of glory."

The Denhams are rich, and their money is old. Their family house is exquisitely done in tile, with fireplaces, pictures, and mirrors—old, good things. Outside the house is a terraced garden that to Clara is the original Eden. The Denhams themselves are good-looking people who dress well and speak cleverly. Mrs. Denham is a writer known professionally as Candida Grey. Mr. Denham is a lawyer. Magnus, the oldest boy, is a rich capitalist. Gabriel is in television, and Clelia works in a chic art gallery.

To the detached eye, the Denham children seem smothered by this "good life." The oldest child, no longer living in the Denham house, has gone crazy. Clelia is startlingly infantile. She speaks in all situations as if to a close relative, never using tact or discretion. Although twenty-seven years old, she lives at home, seemingly unable to establish herself on her own as wife, mother, or career woman. The job she holds in the gallery is purely decorative, one she obtained through family connections, and on which she could never support herself. Her extremely chic room contains her childhood toys as part of the decor. Clara interprets their presence as part of Clelia's enviable sense of continuity with a happy childhood. Unfortunately for both Clelia and Clara, they are signs of a childhood that has never ended.

Gabriel is married and lives with his wife and children in one of those fashionable sections of London that are emerging from slum conditions. He has a good job with Independent Television and makes a good salary. He and his wife, Phillipa, make stunning personal impressions. When Clara visits the couple, however, she is appalled to find that their home is in a state of chaos. The house is potentially as beautiful as others in the neighborhood that have been renovated, but nothing has been done to it. The floors are pitted and worn, the walls are badly in need of paint, the ancient wallpaper hangs in tatters, and the rooms are poorly lit. The kitchen is a war zone in which the litter of cracking plaster vies with expensive cooking equipment. Phillipa is unable to provide food for her family or any kind of supportive attention to the children. Gabriel is unable to organize a life of his own, so dependent is he on the glorious life of his parents' house. Gabriel becomes obsessively attracted to

Clara and dreams of a ménage à trois between them and Clelia.

Magnus is an industrial mogul, a bachelor who becomes parasitically and emotionally attached to Gabriel's women. At first in love with Phillipa, when he senses the affair between Gabriel and Clara he begins an erotic flirtation with Clara. Clara gives herself over emotionally to all the Denhams, and sexually to the brothers Magnus and Gabriel. She feels little for them, or anyone, but the lust for inclusion in a beautiful life. She acts out increasingly more elaborate scenes with them, climaxed by a visit to Paris with Gabriel. During this journey, a flirtation between Clara and Magnus sends Gabriel back to the hotel where he and Clara are staying. Clara outdoes him by leaving him sleeping to miss his plane while she returns to London alone. Once there, she discovers that her mother is dying of cancer.

Clara visits her mother, but there is no feeling between them. Returning to London, her connections to her childhood severed, she finds that the affair with the Denhams is just beginning. Despite the seemingly decisive break in Paris, Clara is now well into Denham games. Her future is to be composed of "Clelia, and Gabriel and she herself in shifting and ideal conjunctions." There is no mention of the development of her intellect or talents.

Clara, at last, contemplates her victory: her triumph over her mother's death, her triumph over her early life, her survival of all of it. "Even the mercy and kindness of destiny she would survive; they would not get her that way, they would not get her at all." These final words are fully ironic: Clara has not triumphed over anything. She is a victim of her own fear of life. Her evasion of a nebulous "them" is a type of paranoid delusion that amounts to a horror of life. Clara has been true to her need to expand but false to what she is. The outcome is not a joyous one. She has achieved a perverse isolation in a bogus, sterile Jerusalem.

The Waterfall

The same themes are explored in Drabble's next novel, *The Waterfall*. Though rendered in the first person by the central character, Jane Grey, *The Waterfall* is a highly ironic, fearfully complex exploration of the question that informs *A Summer Bird-Cage* and *Jerusalem the Golden*: To what must one be true? A vast variety of claims are made on one's fidelity, and these claims frequently pull in different directions. Shall one be true to one's family? One's religion? One's friends? One's heart? One's sexuality? One's intellect? Even from the simple personal perspective, Drabble arrives at an impasse from which the protagonist herself cannot reckon her obligations or even the main issue deserving of her attention.

Jane Grey begins her story giving birth, overwhelmed, that is, by her biology, shaped and determined by her gender, her flesh, her sexuality. This is confirmed by her statement to her husband, Malcolm, who has left her before the birth of their second child, "If I were drowning, I couldn't reach out a hand to save myself, so unwilling am I to set myself up against my fate."

Jane Grey is a woman who does not give allegiance to anything that requires conscious choice. She cannot sustain a marriage, a career, or any affiliation that calls for directed will. She is faithful only to what takes her, overwhelms her, leaving her no choice—her sexuality. Thus she can be a mother, but not a wife. She can be a lover, but not a companion. The result is that she becomes the adulterous, almost incestuous lover of James, her cousin Lucy's husband. This comes about in a way that can be seen as nothing less than a betrayal of a number of social norms.

Because Jane has been deserted by Malcolm, Lucy and James alternate visits to assist her. Lucy, who has been like a sister to Jane, initiates these visits without Jane's request. Jane's breaking of her marriage vows and her betrayal of Lucy are not as uncomplicated as Louise's affair with John in *A Summer Bird-Cage*. Louise has violated nothing more than the law; Jane has violated the bonds of her heart, since Lucy has been so close to her, and the bonds of family and morality, as well as the bonds of law and ethics. Nevertheless, there is a fidelity in Jane's choice. She and James, whose name is deliberately the male reflection of hers, are, in being overwhelmed by each other, satisfying the deepest narcissistic sexuality in each other. It is, of course, true that in so doing they create social limbo for their mates and their children, and for themselves.

Their adultery is discovered when they are in an automobile accident. James's car hits a brick, although he is driving carefully, as they begin a weekend outing together with Jane's children. The car turns over; only James is hurt, and he recovers almost fully. Jane and James continue with their ordinary life. Neither Malcolm nor Lucy exacts any payment from them. The lovers meet when they can. The novel ends with their only full weekend together after the accident. Jane and James climb the Goredale Scar, one of England's scenic wonders. They are there because someone described it so enthusiastically to Jane that it became her goal to see it herself. The Scar is the quintessential female sexual symbol, a cavernous cleft in the mountains, flushed by a waterfall and covered by a pubic growth of foliage. Drabble then sends the lovers back to their hotel room to drink Scotch inadvertently dusted by talcum powder, which leaves a bad taste in their mouths. They have been faithful in their own minds to a force validated by nature.

THE NEEDLE'S EYE

The Needle's Eye, regarded by many readers as Drabble's finest novel, takes its title from Jesus' proverbial words to a rich young man: "It is easier for a camel to go through the eye of a needle, than for a rich man to enter into the kingdom of God" (Matthew 19:24). At the center of the novel are Simon Camish, a barrister from a poor background who would seem to have regretfully gained the world at the expense of his soul, and Rose Bryanston Vassiliou, a rich young woman who compulsively divests herself of the benefits of her inheritance but is not fully enjoying her flight into the lower classes.

Rose, a pale, timid girl, had created a tabloid sensation by marrying out of her class. Her choice was the disreputable, seedy, sexy Christopher Vassiliou, son of Greek immigrants whose pragmatic financial dealings are not solidly within the boundaries of the law. Rose sought to escape from the evils of wealth through Christopher, one of the downtrodden. Much to her consternation, however, Christopher is not a "happy peasant." He detests poverty, legitimately, and associates it not with virtue but with humiliation and deprivation, both of which he has endured.

Christopher's dream is to make something of himself. This dream is strengthened by the birth of their three children, for whom Christopher wants "only the best." He sees in Rose's war on wealth nothing but perverse self-destructiveness. His fury vents itself in physical abuse. Frail, pale Rose is equally adamant in the protection of her children's future. To her mind, "the best" means freedom from possessions. Again Rose and Christopher become figures of tabloid fantasy, this time in a dramatic divorce case.

Rose is working out her divorce settlement when she meets Simon. Simon is introduced to the reader on the same night that he is introduced to Rose; the reader first sees him in a store, buying liquor. Simon feels estranged from the lower-class types who frequent and staff the store. Soon thereafter, this isolation is established as a sharp discontinuity in Simon's life, for he has risen from these ranks. He has been pushed upward by a mother embarrassed by the meanness of her lower-class life and determined that her son will have what she never had. Ironically, the essential gap in his mother's life is also left unfilled in Simon's; that is, the need for warmth and affection. Simon tried to marry into an inheritance of warmth and wealth by his alliance with what he thought was a good-natured girl of the comfortable upper-middle class, Julie Phillips. Their marriage, however, only revealed her fear and insecurity, her essential coldness. What Simon had mistaken for warmth was merely superficial brightness, a by-product of the Phillipses' affluence.

Rose and Simon have attempted to gain what each personally lacked through marriage, as if one could graft onto oneself a human capacity with a wedding ring. Such marriages are doomed to failure. Also doomed has been Rose's attempt to meet human needs with "filthy lucre." She has given a huge portion of her inheritance to a schoolhouse in a lonely, little-known part of Africa. Within months, the school was demolished in the chaos of a civil war, along with approximately one hundred children. Rose does not attempt to deny the futility of what she has done.

Simon and Rose strike up a professional acquaintance, casually, it seems, because Christopher has begun some devious maneuvers to get his children away from Rose. As he becomes increasingly involved in helping Rose, Simon realizes that he is in love with her. Rose reveals but a few of her feelings on this issue, but she does indicate the joy she takes in his company. While Rose and Simon are chasing around after Christopher, who appears to be in the process of abducting the children and taking them out of England, Simon finally tells Rose that, were they at liberty, he would marry her. He blurts out this sentiment as they are walking in a woodland setting. The moment of his revelation finds them in sudden confrontation with a dead stoat hanging grotesquely in front of them, a dried-up little corpse. According to the narrator, this is "a warning" to Simon and Rose.

The satisfaction that Rose and Simon might find together is based on their shared concern for their obligations and duties. To turn to each other, a temptation for both of them, would be a betrayal of the very basis of their attraction to each other, as it would necessitate shirking their responsibilities. It is the grace in them that understands commitments beyond the self. Understanding this, Simon and Rose remain friends; Christopher and Rose are reunited. Rose has achieved a modus vivendi with Christopher, who goes to work for her father. There is no fully articulated happiness, but a kind of integrity exists at the heart of Rose's and Simon's arrangement.

In the novel's final tableau, Rose is looking at a vandalized plaster lion outside a second-rate British edifice called the Alexandra Palace. The lion's head is broken, revealing a hollow inside. It has been spray-painted red with the name of a local gang, but Rose decides that she likes it. Although it began life as an anonymous, mass-produced piece of kitsch, the lion has been worn into something unique: "It had weathered into identity. And this she hoped for every human soul." Rose's final wish accepts the uniqueness of life, the beauty of its mere being. She rejects the vision of a life that is continually being held up to an intellectual ideal, by which standards the lion, like her life, is an awful mess.

Drabble has said in an interview that, had she written *The Needle's Eye* after her husband left her, she might have altered Rose's destiny; perhaps she meant that Rose might have been sent off with Simon after all. Perhaps these words reveal something of the personal Drabble, but they are a betrayal of the novel. The delicacy of Simon and Rose's poise in front of the dead stoat and the final image of the lion resist second thoughts.

The Realms of Gold

Drabble has called *The Realms of Gold* her only comedy. It is the most elaborately plotted of her novels, and Drabble has observed that comedies are permitted such carefully structured plots. Perhaps Drabble defends her plot to excuse herself for pivoting the outcome of her story on the delay in the mail of a postcard, consciously parodying the tragic turn of William Shakespeare's *Romeo and Juliet* (pr. c. 1595-1596), when Romeo's letter from Friar Laurence is delayed. Unlike the passion of Romeo and Juliet, however, the passion of the lovers in *The Realms of Gold*, Frances Wingate and Karel Schmidt, is not "too swift, too unadvised." Frances and Karel are survivors, and it is for this reason that true love between them is possible.

The novel begins in a hotel room. Frances is on a lecture tour, giving talks about her discovery of an ancient city, Tizouk. One evening, in a fit of loneliness, she writes a postcard to Karel, whom she capriciously rejected six months previously. She now regrets her action. Impulsively, she writes on the card, "I miss you. I love you." She is bothered when she receives no response, ignorant of the fact that the card has not been delivered, having been mislaid by the European mail system. Frances is distraught, but she carries on as mother to her four children, as a professional, and as a member of her family.

Karel, too, carries on, thinking hopelessly about Frances, his lost love, puzzled by her rejection of him, suffering at the hands of his deranged wife and his students at the polytechnic, where he is a lecturer in history. Both wife and students continually take advantage of Karel's patience and good nature, and he, not quite understanding why, allows them to victimize him.

Karel and Frances's professional interests, history and archaeology, bring to the novel the long view of continuity. This view is partially what sustains Karel and Frances, whose families cannot or will not support them. Karel has been cut off from his family by the horrors of history. He is Jewish, the only member of his immediate family to survive World War II. Frances, on the other hand, has a large family, but it is wracked with odd and self-destructive behavior: alcoholism, suicide, depression. Frances's family is composed of two estranged branches, isolated from each other by an ancient quarrel—that no one can remember—between two brothers. During the course of the novel, the branches are reconciled. The healing begins when Frances discovers her cousin David, of whom she was previously unaware. She meets him professionally at a conference of the

United Nations Educational, Scientific, and Cultural Organization (UNESCO) in Adra.

The conference has taken Frances away from England at a particularly crucial time in the life of her family. In Tockley, in the English Midlands, an old lady discovered dead of starvation turns out to be Frances's estranged great-aunt. As Frances's family is a prominent one, there is a scandal about this shocking neglect of a family member. Frances is called home from the conference and discovers another lost cousin, Janet Bird, the last person to see their great-aunt alive. Meanwhile, Frances's cousin David is surprised at the conference by the arrival of Karel, who, finally receiving the delayed postcard, flies heedlessly to join Frances at the conference and must be escorted by David back to Tockley. The results of these and more complications are the marriage of Karel and Frances and the reunification of Frances's family.

Frances and Karel synthesize stability and freedom; their marriage triumphantly asserts the victory of human freedom through history, continuity, and culture. The horrors of history—present in the Nazi persecution of the Jews, Frances's blighted family history, and the evidence of child sacrifice that Frances has found in her ancient city Tizouk—do not lead to a rejection of continuity but to the passion to grow through it and outlive the evil it contains.

The major image of *The Realms of Gold* incarnates the comic attitude necessary if one is to lay hands on that hard-won treasure known as life. Shortly before Frances had rejected Karel, causing the long separation that was to end in Tockley, Frances and Karel were enjoying a vacation together. Endeavoring to spend a pleasant day in the country, they had driven their car into the mud, resulting in the bespattering of their persons in a most unromantic way. In the midst of their predicament, they heard a strange, almost ominous sound. An investigation turned up hundreds of frogs simply honking away in a drainage pipe in a ditch. Frances and Karel were flooded with affection and amusement at this gratuitously joyous spectacle. The image of it never leaves them and becomes a sustaining force during their ordeal of separation. Perhaps this is Drabble's best image of a realistic optimism in a very flawed world: joy spontaneously uttered from a muddy ditch.

The Ice Age

In *The Ice Age*, Drabble considers the problem of survival within a dying tradition. England is enduring an ice age: Its social structure is collapsing. In a brilliantly dark vision, Drabble surveys the challenge this poses to personal resources.

As the novel begins, a reckless real estate speculator, Len Wincobank, is serving time in Scratby Open Prison for fraud. Len's technically innocent accomplice, Maureen Kirby, is wondering how to fit the pieces of her life back together again. A teenage girl, Jane Murray, daughter of an extremely beautiful former actor, Alison Murray, is on trial in the remote Communist country of Wallachia. Anthony Keating, a charming author of musical comedies turned real estate speculator, is recovering from a heart attack and the collapse of his financial empire.

All the characters are suffering through imprisonment in England. It is a time in which Max and Kitty Friedman are the victims of an Irish Republican Army (IRA) terrorist attack as they are having an anniversary dinner. England is plagued by degenerate youth, a situation frightening in what it portends for the future. Jane Murray is an angry, shallow child, seemingly incapable of love or of true civility. Anthony Keating finds two young squatters on the empty floor of his former home. The girl is a heroin addict, pregnant and in labor. The boy is drunk and stoned, unable to summon assistance for the girl. Anthony's chance visit to his old house means that the girl will get to the hospital, but she will die and her baby will be born suffering from prenatal heroin addiction.

Through the gloom of England's dark night, Drabble feels her way toward dawn, steadfastly refusing to deny the value of principle because history is suffering temporarily from chaos. She paints a damning picture of a contemporary of Anthony, Mike Morgan, a comedian who pointlessly and viciously ridicules his audience because he mistakes a bad patch for the end of coherence. She also, however, defends the human being as a flexible, creative source of energy not to be trapped within rigidities of principle.

Alison Murray emerges as the polar opposite to Mike Morgan. She too is a doomed soul, because as England flails about, she has chosen the sterility of a noble perfection over the struggles of possibility. Alison's choice has been to devote herself to her brain-damaged daughter, Molly, rather than to her normal daughter, Jane. Molly can never develop and grow, despite Alison's martyrdom, and Jane is wild and sullen as a result of her displacement. Drabble shows that Alison's choice is at least as bad as Mike's, leading directly to her own misery and indirectly to Jane's self-imposed troubles in Wallachia. Alison's choice also leads indirectly to Anthony Keating's downfall.

Anthony, Alison's lover, goes to Wallachia to escort Jane home when the authorities suddenly decide to return her to England. A civil war erupts, randomly freeing Jane and trapping Anthony. He is mistaken for a British spy and remanded to a Siberian-style forced-labor camp.

Between the extremes of Mike Morgan and Alison Murray lies the possibility of working one's way back to continuity by keeping the spirit free. The major examples of such survival in the novel are Maureen Kirby and Anthony Keating. Maureen is a lower-class girl, sexy rather than beautiful, who falls somewhat short of conventional morality. Hardly a person who eschews extremes, Maureen has been the partner of Len Wincobank in his whirlwind financial spree. She has also temporarily retreated into her own selfish, protected world when Len is imprisoned, but she is resilient. In a striking narrative device, Drabble looks into the future at the end of the novel, coolly summarizing the fates of her characters. Maureen is projected as a woman of the 1980's who ultimately marries well and becomes a role model to young women. Her coarse-grained vitality and common sense lack the charm of Alison's elegant self-immolation, but they radiate the warmth of survival.

Anthony Keating, in his frozen Wallachian prison, the ice age of England made palpable, turns also toward life in the only way that is available to him. He becomes enthralled with watching birds, symbols of his spirit, which, despite everything, remains untrammeled.

At the close of the novel, the state of the nation is given a good prognosis. It will recover, asserts the narrator. Anthony has come to terms. Len will surely go on to further development and a financial comeback. Maureen's trajectory is in ascent, but, asserts the narrator, Alison Murray will never recover. The doom of Alison Murray strongly suggests that her kind of retreat from possibility is the worst prison of all, subject to no reprieve or amelioration. Here Drabble seems to have found the limits of what critics have called her conservatism. Cutting off from one's roots to rise in the world brings peril, and denying one's context in order to acquire more brings suffering; these may reveal the flaws in the liberal dream. The ultimate horror, however, would seem to be turning away from growth, regardless of the reason.

The Radiant Way

In her novels of the 1980's—*The Middle Ground*, *The Radiant Way*, and *A Natural Curiosity*—Drabble continued to work in the manner of *The Realms of Gold* and *The Ice Age*. Her intrusive narrators continued to reflect on the nature of fiction and to make arch asides to the reader. All three of these novels center on well-educated characters of the upper middle class whose domestic concerns are intertwined with larger social issues.

The Radiant Way, *A Natural Curiosity*, and a long novel published in 1991, *The Gates of Ivory*, form a trilogy that follows a number of characters through the 1980's and beyond. *The Gates of Ivory* is not only a long book but also a demanding one. It moves from England to Thailand and back and seems to take as its subject not only the state of England but also the state of the world. In the book's opening sentence, Drabble understandably wonders whether it is a novel at all.

There is no doubt that the first two books in the trilogy are novels. As *The Ice Age* had shown Britain's suffering during a Labour government, so these novels show national life under Prime Minister Margaret Thatcher. At the center of the novels are three women friends: Liz Headleand, a psychotherapist; Alix Bowen, an idealistic social worker; and Esther Breuer, a mysterious art historian who focuses on minor figures of the Italian Renaissance. The title *The Radiant Way* refers both to a book that Liz's husband, Charles, read as a boy and to a television documentary he made in the 1960's. It also provides the novel's double-edged central symbol: the radiant personal sun of achievement that many of its youthful characters once envisioned and a radiant national future of justice and harmony. The novel's other pervasive symbol is a web—a vast and complicated web of interconnections in which the characters live.

The novel begins at Liz's New Year's Eve party in the last minutes of 1979. The 1980's get off to a bad start when Charles announces that he is leaving her. Things get worse nationally as relations between social classes deteriorate and as the gap between the North and South of England widens. Alix, the most political of the three friends, finds that her efforts to help the underprivileged not only bear no fruit but also lead to horrible violence. She loses faith in her husband's old-fashioned lower-class values and is content to sift through the papers of an old poet. Liz finds herself enmeshed in a personal web with her sister, Shirley Harper, unhappily married back in their home in the North of England, and with their mother, Rita. The Dickensian secret that Rita Ablewhite keeps is one of even more interrelationships.

A Natural Curiosity

By means of a loosely constructed narrative that shifts from plot thread to plot thread, *A Natural Curiosity* enables readers to follow the stories of the three women up to the point where *The Gates of Ivory* begins. In *A Natural Curiosity*, Liz and her former husband try to discover what has happened to a friend of theirs who is being held hostage. Liz also worries about the fate of another friend, a novelist named Stephen Cox. (The story of Stephen Cox forms the backbone of the plot of *The Gates of Ivory*.) Alix, now living in the North, visits the murderer who was introduced in the previous novel and brings him books. In order to try to understand him, she tracks down and confronts his unpleasant father and even more unpleasant mother. Shirley Harper is more prominent in this book; she finds herself free for the first time in her adult life and flees to Paris and a wild affair. Liz and Shirley find that the Ablewhite family mysteries deepen and go in new directions; these lead in turn to new revelations and new energy. Drabble's narrative voice is more intrusive in this novel than in her previous works.

The Gates of Ivory

The final novel of the trilogy that includes *The Radiant Way* and *A Natural Curiosity*, *The Gates of Ivory* follows Liz Headleand's investigation into the disappearance of Stephen Cox, who had traveled to Southeast Asia ostensibly to research Pol Pot in order to write a play. After a discursive section on "Good Time" and "Bad Time," the novel begins with the opening of a mysterious package delivered to Liz. The first items Liz finds are two finger bones. Also included are newspaper clippings, notebooks, postcards, a poem by Arthur Rimbaud, and photographs. One photograph is of a Khmer woman, Mme Savet Akrun, with the caption, "Where is my son?" In addition, Liz finds pages of an apparent novel in progress, which begins, "And he came to a land where the water flows uphill." Discovering the handwriting of Stephen Cox, Liz is propelled into the full mystery of Stephen's disappearance, the atrocities of a faraway land, and questions concerning the moral integrity of humanity itself.

In this novel, Drabble uses a nonchronological narrative from multiple points of view. A frequent ironic tone complicates the narration. Though largely told in third person through the perspectives of individual characters, primarily Liz Headleand, Alix Bowen, and Esther Breuer, in addition to a panorama of minor characters, *The Gates of Ivory* introduces a new character, Hattie Osborne, who speaks in first person. Hattie, whom Drabble describes as "dottie," is living in Stephen's apartment while he is away and serves as his unofficial literary executor. Interestingly, no one can remember how long ago Stephen left; was it one year, two years, or was it three? Though Liz is in charge, other characters take part as well; however, the entire investigation is frequently interrupted by the concerns of daily life in England. Within the narration, Drabble moves from England to Southeast Asia and back again, from present time to the past. One technique holding it all together is repetition—for example, the repeated image of Stephen's white suit, the caption "Where is my son," and phrases about water flowing uphill, as well as references to the sound of "spade on skull."

Finally Liz is on her way to Bangkok, following the same trail as Stephen Cox, staying in the same hotel, meeting the same characters. She travels to Site Ten, a refugee camp, where she meets Mme Savet Akrun, and back to Bangkok, learning nothing of Stephen's whereabouts. In a restaurant, she runs into old friends who tell her of Stephen's apparent death. They are thinking about making a documentary film of the Booker Prize-winning novelist's excursion to locate Pol Pot and his resulting death. Liz returns to England, where she organizes a memorial service for Stephen. Following the service, the novel closes anticlimactically, at a party at Liz's house, where she and Alix and Esther propose a vacation, bringing the trilogy full circle to where it began.

The Red Queen

The Red Queen, subtitled *A Transcultural Tragicomedy*, continues Drabble's exploration of the East. The novel is divided equally into two parts, the first titled "Ancient Times" and the second "Modern Times." In addition, a short section titled "Postmodern Times" concludes the novel. Part 1 is told in first person through the voice of the eighteenth century Korean crown princess Hong, who is apparently still in search of the meaning of her own story. Interestingly, she speaks with knowledge of late twentieth century intellectual theory and scholarship; death has not hindered her education, but neither has her continued education served to enlighten her. Part 2 is told in third person through the eyes of Barbara Halliwell, a twenty-first century scholar on sabbatical at Oxford, who reads Hong's memoirs on a flight to deliver a paper at an academic conference in South Korea. The immediate connection between Hong and Halliwell, and even between both and Drabble herself (as indicated by the novel's afterword), is a fondness for the color red. Each harbors a fondness for red clothing. In the novel, beginning with this one connection, Drabble attempts to collapse the dichotomies of East and West, past and present. Despite postmodern theory's demanding cultural relativism, Drabble attempts to locate a universal human personality.

The crown princess tells her story in the form of a chronological narrative. Hers is the story of a woman groomed from the age of nine to become a future queen of Korea. Korean life in the eighteenth century, based on Confucianism, was wrought with societal stresses; royal life was even more so. Hong begins her tale with a discussion of the pressure of examinations as experienced by her father. Quickly she is moved to the palace, where her daily behavior, even from childhood, is held to close scrutiny. She virtually grows up with her future husband and king, Prince Sado. Sado is constricted by his own pressures. He acquires a clothing fetish, which further creates economical stress. As pressure in the royal household mounts, his psychological problems escalate. He becomes a sadistic murderer, until he is, at last, forced to commit a ritual suicide by suffocation in a rice chest. All the while, Hong is cognizant of her own tenuous position in the royal household.

Barbara Halliwell's story is also told chronologically. On the plane, she is immediately captured by Hong's story. Arriving at her hotel in Korea, Barbara meets Dr. Oo, who is attending another local conference, through a mix-up in luggage. Dr. Oo serves as Barbara's escort as she visits locations significant in the memoir of the crown princess. At the conference, Barbara meets the scholar Professor Jan van Jost, with whom she has a brief affair. Van Jost delivers a paper filled with images of entombment; Barbara finds the work largely incomprehensible. Later, van Jost dies in her bed.

The novel ends happily with a meeting between Jan van Jost's wife, who has adopted an infant from China, and Barbara. Barbara returns to London, where she teaches and writes. Polly Usher, a character from earlier Drabble novels, makes an appearance. Margaret Drabble herself makes a cameo appearance at the novel's end, "looking older than she did on her book jackets."

Martha Nochimson; George Soule
Updated by Nettie Farris

Other major works

play: *Bird of Paradise*, pr. 1969.

screenplays: *Isadora*, 1969 (with Melvyn Bragg and Clive Exton); *A Touch of Love*, 1969 (also known as *Thank You All Very Much*; adaptation of her novel *The Millstone*).

teleplay: *Laura*, 1964.

nonfiction: *Wordsworth: Literature in Perspective*, 1966; *Arnold Bennett: A Biography*, 1974; *A Writer's Britain: Landscape in Literature*, 1979; *The Tradition of Women's Fiction: Lectures in Japan*, 1982; *Safe as Houses*, 1990; *Margaret Drabble in Tokyo*, 1991 (Fumi Takano, editor); *Angus Wilson: A Biography*, 1995.

children's literature: *For Queen and Country: Britain in the Victorian Age*, 1978.

edited texts: *Lady Susan; The Watsons; Sanditon*, 1974 (by Jane Austen); *The Genius of Thomas Hardy*, 1975; *The Oxford Companion to English Literature: New Edition*, 1985 (revised 6th edition, 2000).

Bibliography

Brownley, Martine Watson. "Mothers and Capitalists in International Politics: Margaret Drabble's *The Gates of Ivory*." In *Deferrals of Domain: Contemporary Women Novelists and the State*. New York: St. Martin's Press, 2000. Presents a sociopolitical analysis of *The Gates of Ivory* through the lens of feminist theory.

Leeming, Glenda. *Margaret Drabble*. Tavistock, England: Northcote House, 2006. Focuses on Drabble's use of narrative technique, often citing the author herself from published interviews. Includes a bibliography of interviews as well as critical works on Drabble.

Myer, Valerie Grosvenor. *Margaret Drabble: A Reader's Guide*. New York: St. Martin's Press, 1991. Informative volume identifies allusions in Drabble's works, places the works within historical and literary contexts, and summarizes critical opinions on them.

Rose, Ellen Cronan, ed. *Critical Essays on Margaret Drabble*. Boston: G. K. Hall, 1985. Collection includes important critical writings on Drabble's early works as well as an informative introduction that presents an overview of Drabble's career.

Rubenstein, Roberta. "Fragmented Bodies/Selves/Narratives: Margaret Drabble's Postmodern Turn." *Contemporary Literature* 35 (Spring, 1994): 136-155. Analyzes Drabble's novels of the 1980's and 1990's and shows how they are fragmented in postmodern ways.

Sadler, Lynn Veach. *Margaret Drabble*. Boston: Twayne, 1986. Offers a balanced and readable appraisal of Drabble's work. A brief biographical sketch is followed by a chronological survey of Drabble's novels through *The Middle Ground* and a coda titled "Drabble's Reputation." Includes an extensive bibliography.

Skoller, Eleanor Honig. "Margaret Drabble." In *The In-Between of Writing: Experience and Experiment in Drabble, Duras, and Arendt*. Ann Arbor: University of Michigan Press, 1993. Argues that many critics misread Drabble and asserts that, contrary to the popular opinion that she uses a traditional nineteenth century narrative approach to fiction, Drabble displays many postmodern techniques.

Soule, George. *Four British Women Novelists: Anita Brookner, Margaret Drabble, Iris Murdoch, Barbara Pym*. Lanham, Md.: Scarecrow Press, 1998. Annotated critical bibliography provides analysis and evaluation of most of the critical books and articles on Drabble's fiction through 1996.

Sullivan, Mary Rose. "Margaret Drabble: Chronicler, Moralist, Artist." In *British Women Writing Fiction*, edited by Abby H. P. Werlock. Tuscaloosa: University of Alabama Press, 2000. Provides a short chronological analysis of Drabble's novels through *The Gates of Ivory*. Includes both a bibliography of critical works on Drabble and an extensive bibliography of works by Drabble, including her scholarly publications and short stories.

Uniyal, Ranu. *The Fiction of Margaret Drabble and Anita Desai: Women and Landscape*. New Delhi: Creative Books, 2004. Analyzes Drabble's use of geography and images of landscape in her fiction. Also includes an interview between the author and Drabble.

THEODORE DREISER

Born: Terre Haute, Indiana; August 27, 1871
Died: Hollywood, California; December 28, 1945
Also known as: Theodore Herman Albert Dreiser

Principal long fiction

Sister Carrie, 1900
Jennie Gerhardt, 1911
The Financier, 1912, 1927
The Titan, 1914
The "Genius," 1915
An American Tragedy, 1925
The Bulwark, 1946
The Stoic, 1947

Other literary forms

The scope of literary accomplishment found in the work of Theodore Dreiser (DRI-sur) includes attempts in every major literary form, including autobiography and philosophy. Dreiser's poetry is generally of poor quality; his plays have been produced on occasion, but drama was not his métier. His sketches, such as those included in *The Color of a Great City* (1923), are vivid and accurate, but they seem to be only workmanlike vignettes that Dreiser developed for the practice or for later inclusion in one of his many novels. His short stories are, like the sketches, preparation for the novels, but the compression of scene, character, and idea necessary for the short story lends these pieces a life of their own, distinct from the monolithic qualities of the novels. Dreiser's philosophical works, such as *Hey, Rub-a-Dub-Dub!* (1920), and his autobiographical forays are the product of an obsession with explaining himself; the philosophy is often obscure and arcane, and the autobiography is not always reliable. Dreiser's letters have been collected and offer further insight into the man, as do the massive manuscript collections that are the products of his tortuous composition and editing processes.

Achievements

The enigma that is Theodore Dreiser divides the critical world into two clearly identifiable camps: those who despise Dreiser and those who honor him just short of adulation—there is no middle ground. With the publication of *Sister Carrie* in 1900, Dreiser committed his literary force to opening the new ground of American naturalism. His heroes and heroines, his settings, his clear dissection of the mechanistic brutality of American society, and his frank discussion, celebration, and humanization of sex—all were new and shocking to a reading public reared on genteel romances and adventure narratives. *Jennie Gerhardt*, the Cowperwood trilogy (at least the first two volumes), and *An American Tragedy* expand and clarify the themes introduced in *Sister Carrie*. Dreiser's genius was recognized and applauded by H. L. Mencken, who encouraged him, praised his works publicly, and was always a valued editorial confidant, but the general reaction to Dreiser has always been negative. He has been called a "crag of basalt," "solemn and ponderous," and "the world's worst great writer," but his influence is evident in the works of Sherwood Anderson, Sinclair Lewis, Ernest Hemingway, and James T. Farrell, among others. Lewis refused the 1925 Pulitzer Prize, which probably should have gone to Dreiser for *An American Tragedy*, and in 1930 took the Nobel Prize Committee to task for choosing him as the first American Nobelist in literature instead of Dreiser.

Dreiser's political and social activism during the long hiatus between *An American Tragedy* and *The Bulwark*, and his never-ending battle against censors and censorship, kept him in the public eye, and the failure of *The Bulwark* and *The Stoic* consigned him to years of neglect after his death. His works' technical and stylistic faults have often obscured their real value, but the effects of Dreiser's works are still rippling through American fiction. He was the first to point out the fragile vulnerability of the facade that was understood to be the American Dream and to depict the awful but beautiful reality that supports the facade.

Biography

Theodore Herman Albert Dreiser was born in Terre Haute, Indiana, on August 27, 1871, into a family of German Americans. His father, John Paul Dreiser, was a weaver by trade, and from the time of his entry into the

United States (in 1846), he had worked westward in an attempt to establish himself. He induced Sarah Schanab (later shortened to Shnepp), the daughter of an Ohio Moravian, to elope with him, and they settled near Fort Wayne. John Paul became the manager in a woolen mill and soon amassed enough funds to build his own mill in Sullivan, Indiana. In 1870, the year before Theodore's birth, the mill burned, John Paul was seriously injured, Sarah was cheated out of the family property by unscrupulous "yankee trickery," and the family was forced to move to Terre Haute, where Theodore was born the eleventh of twelve children, ten of whom survived to adulthood.

After the family misfortunes, John Paul never recovered physically and sank into a pattern of paternal despotism and narrow religious fervor, against which Theodore and the rest of the children could only express contempt and revolt and from which their only haven was the open, loving character of their mother. In 1879, with the family teetering on the edge between poverty and penury, Sarah took Theodore and the youngest children to Vincennes, Indiana, and the girls stayed with John Paul in Terre Haute in an attempt to economize. There then followed a series of moves that took the two parts of the family from Vincennes back to Sullivan, to Evansville to live with Theodore's brother Paul (who had succeeded in the vaudeville circuit), to Chicago, and finally to Warsaw, Indiana. This nomadic life only deepened the destitution of the family and heightened the children's craving for the material part of life they never had. In 1887, after the move to Warsaw, sixteen-year-old Theodore announced that he was going back to Chicago; his mother, characteristically, gave him six dollars of her savings and her blessing, and Theodore went on his way back to the most wonderful city he had ever seen.

As a sixteen-year-old alone in Chicago, Dreiser, like Carrie Meeber, could find only menial labor, first as a dishwasher, later working for a hardware company. In 1889, however, a former teacher who believed in his latent abilities encouraged him to enroll at Indiana University and subsidized his enrollment. After a year of frustrated attempts to break into the fraternity social life of Bloomington, Dreiser left Indiana University and returned to Chicago.

After another series of menial jobs, including driving a laundry delivery wagon, Dreiser managed to land a job with the *Chicago Globe* as a reporter. After a few months, he was invited to take a position on the *St. Louis Globe-Democrat and Republic* staff, and he moved to St. Louis. In St. Louis, he covered the usual types of news events and met Sara (Sallie) White, to whom he found himself unaccountably attracted. In 1895, after brief periods on newspaper staffs in St. Louis, Toledo, Cleveland, and Pittsburgh, Dreiser took up residence in New York City. Even after his newspaper success in St. Louis and Chicago, however, Dreiser could only find freelance work in New York City until his brother Paul, by then a successful songwriter and publisher, persuaded his publishers to make Dreiser the editor of their newly established music periodical, *Ev'ry Month*, for which he wrote monthly editorial columns. This forum for Dreiser's talents was the beginning of a long editorial career that led him to editorships at *Smith's Magazine* and *Broadway Magazine* as well as editorial positions with

Theodore Dreiser. (Library of Congress)

Street & Smith and with Butterick. During this period he published *Sister Carrie*, separated from his wife, Sallie White, whom he had married in 1898, suffered the death of his brother Paul, began work on *Jennie Gerhardt*, and quit his position at Butterick to avoid scandal and to devote his time to fiction.

After the publication of *Jennie Gerhardt*, Dreiser's career is the story of one laboriously prepared work after another. Even at the end, he was working on *The Stoic*, the last of the Cowperwood trilogy, almost as if it were unfinished business. He died in Hollywood on December 28, 1945.

Analysis

Literary historians have shown, by identifying sources and characters, that Theodore Dreiser, even in his fiction, was a capable investigative reporter. His reliance on research for setting, character, and plot lines is evident in *The Financier* and *The Titan* and, most important, in *An American Tragedy*, but Dreiser was not bound by his investigative method. He went often to his own memories for material. Only when Dreiser combines autobiographical material with his research and reportage does his fiction come alive.

Dreiser's youth and early manhood prepared him for the themes he developed. His unstable home life; the dichotomy established between a loving, permissive mother and a narrow, bigoted, dogmatic, penurious father; abject poverty; his own desires for affluence, acceptance, sexual satisfaction, and recognition—all were parts of his fictional commonplace book. His sisters' sexual promiscuity was reflected in Carrie and Jennie, and his own frustrations and desires found voice in, among others, Clyde Griffiths. The character of Frank Cowperwood was shaped in Dreiser's lengthy research into the life of Charles Tyson Yerkes, but Cowperwood was also the incarnation of everything that Dreiser wanted to be—handsome, powerful, accepted, wealthy, and capable. Dreiser projected his own dreams onto characters such as Griffiths and Cowperwood only to show that human dreams are never ultimately fulfilled. No matter for what man (or woman) contested, "his feet are in the trap of circumstances; his eyes are on an illusion." Dreiser did not condemn the effort; he chronicled the fragile nature of the pursued and the pursuer.

Sister Carrie

The genesis of *Sister Carrie*, Dreiser's first novel, was as fantastic as the work's appearance in Victorian America. In Dreiser's own account, he started the novel at the insistence of his friend Arthur Henry, and then only to appease him. In order to end Henry's wheedlings and annoyances, Dreiser sat down and wrote the title of the novel at the top of a page. With no idea of a program for the novel or who the basic characters were to be, Dreiser began the book that did more to change modern American fiction than any since.

The amatory adventures of Dreiser's sisters in Indiana and his own experiences in Chicago and in New York were the perfect materials for the story of a poor country girl who comes to the city to seek whatever she can find. The one thing she is certain of is that she does not wish to remain poor. With this kind of material, it is surprising that Dreiser escaped writing a maudlin tale of a fallen girl rescued at the end or an Algeresque tale of her rise from rags. *Sister Carrie* is neither of these. Carrie does rise, but she does so by the means of a male stepladder. She is not a simple gold digger; she is much more complex than that. Her goals are clothes, money, and fame, and the means by which she achieves them are relatively unimportant. More important, however, is that Carrie is a seeker and a lover. She cannot be satisfied. She must always have a new world to conquer, new goals to achieve. In New York, when she has finally acquired all that she has sought, Ames shows her that there is a world beyond the material—a world of literature and philosophy; it is an aesthetic world of which Carrie has not dreamed and that she recognizes as a new peak to conquer and a new level to achieve. There is a hint that this new level is more satisfying than any she has reached, just as Ames seems more interesting and satisfying than either of her previous lovers, Drouet and Hurstwood, but the novel ends with Carrie still contemplating her attack on this new world.

Carrie subordinates everything to her consuming ambition. She comes to understand the usefulness of sex, but she also understands the emotional commitment necessary to love, and she refuses to make that commitment. In the pursuit of the fullest expression and fulfillment of life she can achieve, human attachments are only transitory at best, and Drouet and Hurstwood are only means to an end for Carrie.

Drouet, a traveling salesman whom Carrie meets on the train to Chicago, becomes her first lover after she has had time to discover the frustration of joblessness and sweatshop employment and the despair of the poverty in which the relatives with whom she is staying live. Drouet ingratiates himself with Carrie by buying her dinner and then by slipping two ten-dollar bills into her hand. Not long thereafter, Drouet outfits a flat for her, and they set up housekeeping together. Drouet is, for Carrie, an escape. She does not love him, but his means are a source of amazement, and she recognizes that the relative opulence of his chambers and of the apartment he procures for her are the signs of that for which she is striving. She recognizes very early that Drouet is static, a dead end, but he is only an intermediary in her movement from poverty to affluence.

Hurstwood is the bartender and manager of a prominent Chicago tavern. As he watches Carrie perform in a cheap theatrical, he is smitten by her youth and her vitality. A middle-aged, married man possessed of a virago of a wife, he is naturally attracted to Carrie. Carrie in turn recognizes the quality of Hurstwood's clothes, his style, and his bearing as distinct improvements on Drouet and makes it clear she will accept his advances. Hurstwood's wife uncovers the subsequent affair, a messy divorce threatens Hurstwood's stability and prestige in his job, fortuity brings him to embezzle ten thousand dollars from the bar safe, and he flees with Carrie first to Montreal and then to New York. Once the couple arrive in New York, the chronicle becomes the tale of Hurstwood's steady degeneration and Carrie's alternatively steady rise to stardom on the stage.

Hurstwood does not carry his status with him from Chicago to New York. In New York, he is merely another man who either cannot hold or cannot find a job. His funds are seriously depleted in the failure of an attempt to open his own saloon, and the more he fails, the further he withdraws from life and from Carrie, until he becomes completely dependent on her. When Carrie leaves him because she cannot support both of them and buy the clothes necessary to her profession, he drifts deeper and deeper into New York's netherworld until he commits suicide by turning on the gas in a Bowery flophouse. Typically, Carrie never knows or cares that Hurstwood is dead. If Drouet is a dead end, Hurstwood is a weak man trapped by circumstance and by his unwillingness or inability to cope with situations he recognizes as potentially disastrous. His liaison with Carrie is based on mutual attraction, but he is also enamored of his daily routine and of the prestige that accompanies it. Only when his wife threatens him with exposure is he forced to make the final commitment to Carrie and, eventually, to the gas jet.

Carrie's desertion of Hurstwood can be interpreted as cold and cruel, but she stays with him until it is clear that there is nothing anyone can do to save him. To try to save him would only mire her in his downward spiral. The counterpoint of Carrie's rise and Hurstwood's fall is the final irony of the novel. Carrie and Hurstwood reach their final disappointments in almost the same basic terms. Hurstwood dies tired of the struggle, and Carrie realizes that she has finally arrived and there is nothing more to conquer or achieve. Only the promise of an aesthetic world beyond material affluence offers hope for Carrie, and that hope seems illusory. The ubiquitous rocking chair is the perfect symbol for *Sister Carrie*. It is an instrument that forever moves but never goes anywhere and never truly achieves anything. Carrie's every success is ultimately unsatisfying, and every new horizon offers only a hollow promise.

Sister Carrie was stillborn in the first edition. Published but suppressed by the publisher, it did not reach the public until seven years later, when it was given to a new publisher. The novel contains the seeds of most of Dreiser's recurrent themes.

Jennie Gerhardt

The protagonist of *Jennie Gerhardt*, Dreiser's second novel, is Carrie's natural sister or, perhaps, her alter ego. Jennie is also the product of Dreiser's early family life, of his sisters' fatal attraction to men and the natural result. When Dreiser turned to *Jennie Gerhardt* while still embroiled in the publication problems of *Sister Carrie*, he drew upon the events in the life of his sister Mame, who was seduced, abandoned, and ended up living successfully with another man in New York City. From this basic material, Dreiser created a girl much like Carrie in origin, who has the same desires for material ease but none of the instincts Carrie possesses or has the same instincts channeled into a different mode of expression.

Jennie Gerhardt is divided into two parts. In the first, as the daughter of a poor washerwoman, Jennie is noticed by Senator Brander Matthews, another older man attracted by youth and vitality; he is kind, tips her heavily for delivering his laundry, and eventually seduces her. Matthews is, however, more than a stereotype. He has a real need for Jennie and a fatherly attachment to her. Jennie, who is more than a "fallen angel," as some have seen her, responds in kind. Surrounded by conventional morality and religious prohibitions, represented by Old Gerhardt and others, Jennie, unlike Carrie, has a desperate need to give in order to fulfill herself. Despite the veneer of indebtedness Jennie brings to her seduction by Matthews (he arranges the release of her brother from jail, among other things), there is a surprisingly wholesome atmosphere to the affair. Matthews is solicitous and protective, and Jennie is loving and tender. When Jennie becomes pregnant, Matthews plans to marry her, put her parents in a more comfortable situation, and, in short, do the right thing. Matthews dies, however, and Jennie gives birth to his illegitimate child; she is condemned by her parents and society, and her previous joy and prospects dissolve before her eyes.

Dreiser's portrayal of Jennie does not allow the reader to feel sorry for her. Vesta, Jennie's child, is not the product of sin but the offspring of an all-suffering, all-giving earth mother. Dreiser's depiction of Jennie as a child of nature verifies this impression. Despite society and its narrow views, Jennie is not destroyed or even dismayed. She is delighted with her child and thus snatches her joy and fulfillment from a seeming disaster. As long as she can give, be it to child or lover, she is unassailable.

The second seduction occurs when the Gerhardts, except for Old Gerhardt, move to Cleveland at the behest of brother Bass and supposedly at his expense. Bass is expansive and generous for a while, but he begins to demand more and more until Jennie must take a position as a chambermaid at the Bracebridge house, where she meets Lester Kane. Once again, as with Brander Matthews, the seduction wears the facade of obligation—this time because Lester Kane helps the family when Old Gerhardt suffers debilitating burns that deprive him of his glassblowing trade, his sole means of support. Lester has pursued Jennie, and his help fosters the ensuing affair. Like the first seduction, however, the second is not the simple matter it seems.

Lester Kane is Dreiser's portrayal of the enlightened man—the man who has serious doubts about religion, morality, societal restrictions, and mores. He serves the basic needs of Jennie's character; he also understands his own needs for the devotion, care, and understanding that Jennie is able and willing to give. With his willingness to make a more or less permanent commitment to Jennie, he seems to be a match, but Lester also understands the restrictions of class that forbid him to marry Jennie and feels the strong pull of family duty, which requires that he play a vital part in shaping the family's considerable enterprises. Lester, then, is caught with Jennie, as Dreiser puts it, between the "upper and nether millstones of society."

When Jennie and Lester set up their clandestine apartment in Chicago, they are enormously happy until they are discovered by Lester's family; the newspapers make front-page news of the discovery, and Jennie reveals to Lester that she has hidden the existence of her daughter, Vesta, from him. Amazingly, Lester weathers all these shocks and even brings Vesta and Old Gerhardt to share the apartment with them, but Lester's "indiscretions" have allowed his less heroically inclined brother to take control of the family business, and when his father dies, his will decrees that Lester must make a choice. If he marries Jennie, he gets a pittance; if he leaves her, he gets a normal portion. At this point, Letty, an old flame of Lester—of the "right" class—surfaces, and Jennie, fully recognizing the mutual sacrifices she and Lester will have to make whether he leaves or stays, encourages him to leave her.

Lester eventually marries Letty and claims his inheritance. Jennie sacrifices Lester and in rapid succession sees Old Gerhardt and Vesta die. Deprived of her family, she manufactures one by taking in orphans. The device is not satisfying, and the worldly refinement she has assimilated in her life with Lester is not enough to succor her, yet she survives to be called to Lester's death bed. Lester tells her that he has never forgotten her and that he loves her still, and Jennie reciprocates. The scene brings together a man and a woman who have given away or had taken away everything they loved through no particular fault of their own.

Lester is a weak man, like Hurstwood, but unlike Hurstwood he does not give up; he is beaten until he can no longer resist. Unlike Carrie, Jennie is brought to the point of emptiness not by achievements but by losses. Her nature has betrayed her, and when one sees her hidden in the church at Lester's funeral, unrecognized by his family, one senses the totality of her loss. One also senses, however, that she has emerged a spiritual victor. She seems to have grown more expansive and more generous with each loss. Her stature grows until she looms over the novel as the archetypal survivor. She has been bruised, battered, and pushed down, but she has not been destroyed. She cannot be destroyed so long as she can give.

THE FINANCIER

In *The Financier*, the first of the three novels known collectively as the Cowperwood trilogy or the Trilogy of Desire (the others are *The Titan* and *The Stoic*), perhaps more than in any other of his works, Dreiser relied on research for character, setting, plot, and theme. The characters are not drawn from memories of his family or his beloved Chicago, at least not exclusively or primarily; the themes are most clearly the result of Dreiser's enormous reading.

"*Genus Financierus Americanus*," or the great financial wizards of the United States in the early twentieth century, fascinated Dreiser, and in their world of amorality, power, money, and materialism, he saw the mechanism that led America. Frank Cowperwood is a fictional representation of Charles T. Yerkes, a relatively obscure name but one of the movers in American finance in that period. Dreiser encountered Yerkes in Chicago and New York and watched his machinations from a reporter's and an editor's vantage point. Yerkes was no worse or better than the Rockefellers or Goulds, but by the time Dreiser started the trilogy, Yerkes was dead and his career could be studied in its totality. In addition, Yerkes' career was extensively documented in newspaper accounts, a fact that facilitated Dreiser's research, and that career had the advantage of a wife and a mistress and the final breaking up of Yerkes' empire by his creditors—all of which fit nicely into Dreiser's plan. The failure by one of the "titans of industry" to leave an indelible mark on humanity or on his immediate surroundings is the key to Dreiser's "equation inevitable," a concept first clearly worked out in *The Financier*.

Dreiser's readings of Arthur Schopenhauer, Friedrich Nietzsche, Karl Marx, Herbert Spencer, Jacques Loeb, and others confirmed his idea that the strong are meant to fulfill their course, to alter the pattern of life, and to "be a Colossus and bestride the world." At the same time, other strong individuals or groups (the "masses" were a real but troublesome entity for Dreiser) appear with equal strength but opposite intentions specifically intended by nature to maintain an equilibrium—a sort of cosmic system of checks and balances. For Dreiser, "no thing is fixed, all tendencies are permitted, apparently. Only a balance is maintained." All people, significant and insignificant, are tools of nature and all are, in some way, a part of the equation. From Cowperwood's youth, the equation is seen in action. His victory in a boyhood fight confirms his trust in strength and resolution (or the first lick), and the now-famous lobster/squid narrative clarifies his understanding of the operation of nature. If the squid is prey for the lobster and the lobster prey for man, then man must also be prey, but only to man. These early insights are borne out in Cowperwood's Philadelphia life.

Cowperwood's early successes and his dealings with Colonel Butler are built on his philosophy of prey, but they are also founded on his realization that form and substance are separate. In order to succeed, one must maintain the semblance of propriety while carrying on normal business, which is ruthless and unfeeling. When he is jailed, he does not consider it a defeat, only a setback. Cowperwood is basically a pragmatist who does what is necessary to please himself. Aside from this pragmatic nature, however, Cowperwood has another side that seems anomalous in his quest for power.

The other side of Cowperwood is epitomized by his simultaneous lust for and pride in his women and his art collection. Often styled by his quest for the beautiful, Cowperwood's desire for women and art, no matter which woman or which masterpiece, is still a facet of his acquisitive nature, but it is a facet that reflects the hidden recesses of his spirit. Inside the ruthless, conniving, buccaneering entrepreneur is a man seeking to outdo even nature by acquiring or controlling the best of nature's handiwork, but there is also a closely guarded, solidly confined sensibility. This artistic sensibility is confined because it is the antithesis of strength and power and because Cowperwood understands that if he yields to it, he will no longer be in control of his life, his fortune, and his world.

Morality has no relevance in Cowperwood's understanding of the equation. He and his desires are all that exist. His desires are completely carnal in relationships with women. Even with Aileen, who understands him best, there is only lust, never love, because love is a part of that hidden Cowperwood, which he knows he must suppress. The implication is that if he ever loved, Cowperwood would no longer be the financier; he would become simply human.

Aside from the development of the equation and its workings in Cowperwood's world, *The Financier* is a faintly realized novel when set against *Sister Carrie* or *An American Tragedy*. Cowperwood's motto, "I satisfy myself," is the prevailing motto, and his failure to satisfy himself, his wife, his competitors, or anyone or anything else provides the answer to the motto's arrogance.

An American Tragedy

An American Tragedy is Dreiser's acknowledged masterpiece; of all his novels, it most successfully blends autobiography with the fruits of the author's painstaking research. In the work, Dreiser was interested in exposing the flaws in the seamless fabric of the American Dream. He had seen the destructive nature of the untempered drive for success and he understood that such a drive was an unavoidable result of the social temperament of the times. He also understood that the victims of that destructive urge were those who strove, not fully understanding why they struggled or why they failed. His criticism is thus aimed both at those who struggle for an unattainable dream and at the society that urges them on and laughs when they fall. His research led Dreiser to the case of Chester Gillette and the narrative skeleton for *An American Tragedy*.

The events leading to Gillette's murder of Grace Brown in 1906 and the circumstances of his early life were amply documented in the sensational, yellow-press coverage of the Gillette trial, and they provide a circumstantial sketch of the events of Clyde Griffiths's life and times. Gillette and Griffiths also bear the marks of a common background with Dreiser. The poverty-stricken youth, the desire for success and material things, the sexual frustrations, and the attraction to beautiful, well-placed women are all parts of Dreiser's youth and young manhood. If one adds Dreiser's later unhappy marriage, his philandering, and his tense relationship with Helen Richardson, one has all the pieces that produced Dreiser's empathy for and attraction to Chester Gillette and, ultimately, Clyde Griffiths. Thus, in addition to the dramatic possibilities of the Gillette case, Dreiser felt a kinship with his protagonist that allowed him to portray him as a pitiable, arresting, trapped creature.

Clyde Griffiths, in Dreiser's vision, is trapped by forces over which he has little or no control. The "chemisms" of Clyde's life trap him: He no more has control over his desires for success, sex, and material goods than he has over the voice that urges him during the accident/murder that kills Roberta. In short, Clyde has no control over the irresistible American Dream. Writing of the Gillette case, Dreiser observes that Chester Gillette, if he had not committed murder, "was really doing the kind of thing which Americans should and would have said was the wise and moral thing to do" by trying to better his social standing through a good marriage. Gillette did, however, commit murder; Clyde Griffiths, on the other hand, intends to commit murder but loses his nerve in the boat with Roberta. When she falls into the water after he accidentally hits her with a camera, she drowns only because of Clyde's inaction. Faced with the decision to save her or not, Clyde cannot or will not make the decision, and his inaction damns him. The evidence against him is circumstantial at best, and objective examination allows doubt as to his guilt. That doubt intensifies Clyde's entrapment. It is a trap of his own making, but the reader is never sure if he deserves his fate.

In the trial scenes and the events surrounding the trial, Dreiser shows all the external forces that work against Clyde to seal that fate. Political pressures on the defense attorneys and the prosecutors, the prejudice of the rural jury impaneled to try Clyde, the haste with which his wealthy cousins disavow him in order to save their social standing, and Clyde's own ineptitude as a liar form a second box around him, enclosing the first box of his own desires and failures.

Clyde's inevitable conviction and death sentence place him in the final box—his prison cell. This final enclosure is the ultimate circumstance over which Clyde has no control. There is no exit after the governor is convinced of Clyde's guilt by Clyde's mother and his clergyman. When Clyde is finally executed, his inexorable fall is complete.

Clyde's doom is sealed in his tawdry youth, first as a member of an itinerant evangelist's family, later in his work at the Green-Davidson, and ultimately in his fatal liaison with his wealthy Lycurgus cousins. He is not clever enough to help himself, is not wealthy enough to pay anyone to help him (especially during Roberta's pregnancy), and his "chemisms" drive him on in spite of his limitations. When he has his goal of wealth and success in sight, the only obstacle in his path, the pregnant Roberta, must be discarded at any cost without a thought of the consequences. His dreams are the driving force, and those dreams are the product of forces over which he has not a shred of control. When he attempts to force his dreams to fruition, he further commits himself into the hands of those forces, and they lead him to his death.

Clyde lacks Carrie's inherent sense for survival and success, Jennie's selflessness and resilience, and Cowperwood's intelligence and wealth, but for all that, he is a reflection of all of them and of the society in which they function. Clyde commits the crime and is punished, but Dreiser indicts all of society in Clyde's execution. Clyde's death sounds the knell for the romance of success and heralds the vacuum that takes its place. Clyde is not strong and falls; Cowperwood is strong and falls anyway. Carrie finds there is no fulfillment in success and feels the emptiness of her discovery; Jennie is beaten down again and again until she finds that she is living in a void that cannot be filled even with her abundant love. Clyde is thus not only the natural product of all these characters and of Dreiser's development but also the symbol of Dreiser's worldview: a relentless vision that permanently altered American literature.

Clarence O. Johnson

Other major works

SHORT FICTION: *Free, and Other Stories*, 1918; *Chains: Lesser Novels and Stories*, 1927; *Fine Furniture*, 1930; *The Best Stories of Theodore Dreiser*, 1947 (Howard Fast, editor); *Best Short Stories*, 1956 (James T. Farrell, editor).

PLAYS: *Plays of the Natural and Supernatural*, pb. 1916; *The Girl in the Coffin*, pr. 1917; *The Hand of the Potter: A Tragedy in Four Acts*, pb. 1919; *The Collected Plays of Theodore Dreiser*, 2000.

POETRY: *Moods: Cadenced and Declaimed*, 1926, 1928; *The Aspirant*, 1929; *Epitaph: A Poem*, 1929.

NONFICTION: *A Traveler at Forty*, 1913; *A Hoosier Holiday*, 1916; *Twelve Men*, 1919; *Hey, Rub-a-Dub-Dub!*, 1920; *A Book About Myself*, 1922 (revised as *Newspaper Days*, 1931); *The Color of a Great City*, 1923; *Dreiser Looks at Russia*, 1928; *My City*, 1929; *Dawn*, 1931 (autobiography); *Tragic America*, 1931; *America Is Worth Saving*, 1941; *Letters of Theodore Dreiser*, 1959; *Letters to Louise*, 1959; *Notes on Life*, 1974 (Marguerite Tjader and John J. McAleer, editors); *American Diaries, 1902-1926*, 1982; *An Amateur Laborer*, 1983; *Selected Magazine Articles of Theodore Dreiser*, 1985; *Dreiser's Russian Diary*, 1996 (Thomas P. Riggio and James L. W. West, editors); *Theodore Dreiser's "Ev'ry Month,"* 1996 (magazine articles; Nancy Warner Barrineau, editor); *Art, Music, and Literature, 1897-1902*, 2001 (Yoshinobu Hakutani, editor); *Theodore Dreiser's Uncollected Magazine Articles, 1897-1902*, 2003 (Hakutani, editor).

Bibliography

Cassuto, Leonard, and Clare Virginia Eby, eds. *The Cambridge Companion to Theodore Dreiser*. New York: Cambridge University Press, 2004. Collection of twelve essays discusses the novelist's examination of American conflicts between materialistic longings and traditional values. Includes essays on Dreiser's style, Dreiser and women, and Dreiser and the ideology of upward mobility.

Gerber, Philip. *Theodore Dreiser Revisited*. New York: Twayne, 1992. Includes chapters on all of Dreiser's major works, three chapters on the development of Dreiser studies, a chronology, notes and references, and an annotated bibliography.

Gogol, Miriam, ed. *Theodore Dreiser: Beyond Naturalism*. New York: New York University Press, 1995. Collection of essays presents interpretation of Dreiser's work from the perspectives of new historicism, poststructuralism, psychoanalysis, feminism, and other points of view. Gogol's introduction advances the argument that Dreiser was much more than a naturalist and deserves to be treated as a major author.

Juras, Uwe. *Pleasing to the "I": The Culture of Personality and Its Representations in Theodore Dreiser and F. Scott Fitzgerald.* New York: Peter Lang, 2006. Examines how the two authors depicted the newly emerging concept of personality, defined as the outward presentation of self, in their work. Includes discussion of Dreiser's novels *Sister Carrie*, *Jennie Gerhardt*, *The Financier*, *The Titan*, *The "Genius,"* and *An American Tragedy*.

Kazin, Alfred, and Charles Shapiro, eds. *The Stature of Theodore Dreiser: A Critical Survey of the Man and His Work.* Bloomington: Indiana University Press, 1965. Well-selected anthology of articles, essays, and personal reminiscences by noted authors and critics on Dreiser the man and the writer. A perceptive introduction by Kazin sets the tone. Includes a lengthy bibliography.

Lingeman, Richard. *At the Gates of the City, 1871-1907.* Vol. 1 in *Theodore Dreiser.* New York: Putnam, 1986.

_______. *An American Journey, 1908-1945.* Vol. 2 in *Theodore Dreiser.* New York: Putnam, 1990. Comprehensive two-volume biography places Dreiser's personal life within the context of American history during the Gilded Age and the Progressive Era. Recounts how Dreiser became one of the most influential American writers of his time.

Loving, Jerome. *The Last Titan: A Life of Theodore Dreiser.* Berkeley: University of California Press, 2005. Written by a distinguished biographer, this engrossing survey of the author's life and work is a welcome addition to Dreiser scholarship. Focuses on Dreiser's work, including his journalism, discussing the writers who influenced him and his place within American literature.

Pizer, Donald. *The Novels of Theodore Dreiser: A Critical Study.* Minneapolis: University of Minnesota Press, 1976. Solid study provides a good introduction to Dreiser's eight published novels. Examines each work as a separate unit and points out its respective merits and flaws.

Shapiro, Charles. *Theodore Dreiser: Our Bitter Patriot.* Carbondale: Illinois University Press, 1962. Shapiro expands his original dissertation study into a critical and illuminating examination of the underlying themes found in Dreiser's works. Argues that *An American Tragedy* is Dreiser's most important work because of its thematic richness.

Swansberg, W. A. *Dreiser.* New York: Charles Scribner's Sons, 1965. Classic biography has stood the test of time and ranks with the best. Swansberg is not a literary critic and is less interested than other scholars in Dreiser the artist, concentrating instead on Dreiser the man.

ALEXANDRE DUMAS, *PÈRE*

Born: Villers-Cotterêts, France; July 24, 1802
Died: Puys, France; December 5, 1870
Also known as: Dumas Davy de la Pailleterie

Principal long fiction

Acté, 1838 (English translation, 1904)
Le Capitaine Paul, 1838 (*Captain Paul*, 1848)
La Salle d'armes, 1838 (includes *Pauline* [English translation, 1844], *Pascal Bruno* [English translation, 1837], and *Murat* [English translation, 1896])
La Comtesse de Salisbury, 1839
Le Capitaine Pamphile, 1840 (*Captain Pamphile*, 1850)
Othon l'archer, 1840 (*Otho the Archer*, 1860)
Aventures de Lyderic, 1842 (*Lyderic, Count of Flanders*, 1903)
Ascanio, 1843 (with Paul Meurice; English translation, 1849)
Le Chevalier d'Harmental, 1843 (with Auguste Maquet; *The Chevalier d'Harmental*, 1856)
Georges, 1843 (*George*, 1846)
Amaury, 1844 (English translation, 1854)
Une Fille du régent, 1844 (with Maquet; *The Regent's Daughter*, 1845)
Les Frères corses, 1844 (*The Corsican Brothers*, 1880)
Gabriel Lambert, 1844 (*The Galley Slave*, 1849; also known as *Gabriel Lambert*, 1904)
Sylvandire, 1844 (*The Disputed Inheritance*, 1847; also known as *Sylvandire*, 1897)
Les Trois Mousquetaires, 1844 (*The Three Musketeers*, 1846)
Le Comte de Monte-Cristo, 1844-1845 (*The Count of Monte-Cristo*, 1846)
La Reine Margot, 1845 (with Maquet; *Marguerite de Navarre*, 1845; better known as *Marguerite de Valois*, 1846)
Vingt Ans après, 1845 (with Maquet; *Twenty Years After*, 1846)
La Guerre des femmes, 1845-1846 (*Nanon*, 1847; also known as *The War of Women*, 1895)
Le Bâtard de Mauléon, 1846 (*The Bastard of Mauléon*, 1848)
Le Chevalier de Maison-Rouge, 1846 (with Maquet; *Marie Antoinette: Or, The Chevalier of the Red House*, 1846; also known as *The Chevalier de Maison-Rouge*, 1893)
La Dame de Monsoreau, 1846 (*Chicot the Jester*, 1857)
Les Deux Diane, 1846 (with Meurice; *The Two Dianas*, 1857)
Mémoires d'un médecin, 1846-1848 (with Maquet; also known as *Joseph Balsamo*; *Memoirs of a Physician*, 1846)
Les Quarante-cinq, 1848 (with Maquet; *The Forty-five Guardsmen*, 1847)
Le Vicomte de Bragelonne, 1848-1850 (with Maquet; *The Vicomte de Bragelonne*, 1857; also published as 3 volumes, *The Vicomte de Bragelonne*, 1893; *Louise de la Vallière*, 1893; and *The Man in the Iron Mask*, 1893)
La Véloce, 1848-1851
Le Collier de la reine, 1849-1850 (with Maquet; *The Queen's Necklace*, 1855)
La Tulipe noire, 1850 (with Maquet and Paul Lacroix; *The Black Tulip*, 1851)
Ange Pitou, 1851 (*Six Years Later*, 1851; also known as *Ange Pitou*, 1859)
Conscience l'innocent, 1852 (*Conscience*, 1905)
Olympe de Clèves, 1852 (English translation, 1894)
Isaac Laquedem, 1852-1853
La Comtesse de Charny, 1853-1855 (*The Countess de Charny*, 1858)
Catherine Blum, 1854 (*The Foresters*, 1854; also known as *Catherine Blum*, 1861)
Ingénue, 1854 (English translation, 1855)
Le Page du duc de Savoie, 1854 (*Emmanuel Philibert*, 1854; also known as *The Page of the Duke of Savoy*, 1861)
El Saltéador, 1854 (*The Brigand*, 1897)

Les Mohicans de Paris, 1854-1855
Salvator, 1855-1859 (with *Les Mohicans de Paris*, abridged as *The Mohicans of Paris*, 1875)
Charles le Téméraire, 1857 (*Charles the Bold*, 1860)
Les Compagnons de Jéhu, 1857 (*Roland de Montrevel*, 1860; also known as *The Companions of Jéhu*, 1895)
Les Meneurs de loups, 1857 (*The Wolf Leader*, 1904)
Ainsi-soit-il!, 1858 (also known as *Madame de Chamblay*, 1862; *Madame de Chamblay*, 1869)
Le Capitaine Richard, 1858 (*The Twin Captains*, 1861)
L'Horoscope, 1858 (*The Horoscope*, 1897)
Le Chasseur de sauvagine, 1859 (*The Wild Duck Shooter*, 1906)
Histoire d'un cabanon et d'un châlet, 1859 (*The Convict's Son*, 1905)
Les Louves de Machecoul, 1859 (*The Last Vendée*, 1894; also known as *The She Wolves of Machecoul*, 1895)
Le Médecin de Java, 1859 (also known as *L'Île de feu*, 1870; *Doctor Basilius*, 1860)
La Maison de Glace, 1860 (*The Russian Gipsy*, 1860)
Le Père la Ruine, 1860 (*Père la Ruine*, 1905)
La San-Felice, 1864-1865 (*The Lovely Lady Hamilton*, 1903)
Le Comte de Moret, 1866 (*The Count of Moret*, 1868)
La Terreur prussienne, 1867 (*The Prussian Terror*, 1915)
Les Blancs et les bleus, 1867-1868 (*The Whites and the Blues*, 1895)
Le Chevalier de Sainte-Hermine, 1869 (serial), 2005 (book; *The Last Cavalier: Being the Adventures of Count Sainte Hermine in the Age of Napoleon*, 2007)
The Romances of Alexandre Dumas, 1893-1897 (60 volumes)
The Novels of Alexandre Dumas, 1903-1911 (56 volumes)

Other literary forms

Other novels are attributed to Alexandre Dumas, *père* (dyew-MAH pehr), that some scholarship, such as that by Douglas Munro, Gilbert Sigaux, and Charles Samaran, credits more to his collaborators. Of the many editions of Dumas's works, the standard edition, *Œuvres complètes* (1846-1877), in 301 volumes by Calmann-Lévy, is not always authoritative. The best editions of the novels are those in *Œuvres d'Alexandre Dumas* (1962-1967; 38 volumes), published by Éditions Rencontre, with excellent introductions to the novels by Sigaux. Munro lists at least fifteen English editions of Dumas prior to 1910, and countless others have appeared since. *The Romances of Alexandre Dumas*, published by Little, Brown and Company, has been updated several times. Virtually all of Dumas's novels are available in English and many other languages.

Dumas also wrote many plays, several in collaboration with other authors and a number based on his novels. A total of sixty-six are generally ascribed to him, among them *Henri III et sa cour* (pr., pb. 1829; *Catherine of Cleves*, 1831, also known as *Henry III and His Court*, 1904), *Christine: Ou, Stockholm, Fontainebleau, et Rome* (pr., pb. 1830), *Kean: Ou, Désordre et génie* (pr., pb. 1836, with Théaulon de Lambert and Frédéric de Courcy; *Edmund Kean: Or, The Genius and the Libertine*, 1847), *Mademoiselle de Belle-Isle* (pr., pb. 1839; English translation, 1855), *Un Mariage sous Louis XV* (pr., pb. 1841; *A Marriage of Convenience*, 1899), *Les Demoiselles de Saint-Cyr* (pr., pb. 1843; *The Ladies of Saint-Cyr*, 1870), and *L'Invitation à la valse* (pr., pb. 1857; adapted in English as *Childhood Dreams*, 1881). The plays are available in the *Œuvres complètes*, occupying twenty-five volumes in the Calmann-Lévy edition. The best contemporary edition is *Théâtre complet*, edited by Fernande Bassan.

Dumas's other writings include histories, chronicles, memoirs, travel notes, articles, and essays. Among the more interesting of these are "Comment je devins auteur dramatique" ("How I Became a Playwright"), "En Suisse" (in Switzerland), *Quinze Jours au Sinai* (1838; *Impressions of Travel in Egypt and Arabia Petraea*, 1839), *Excursions sur les bords du Rhin* (1841, with Gérard de Nerval; excursions on the banks of the Rhine), *Le Midi de la France* (1841; *Pictures of Travel in the*

South of France, 1852), *Le Spéronare* (1842; travels in Italy), *Le Corricolo* (1843; travels in Italy and Sicily), *Mes Mémoires* (1852, 1853, 1854-1855; *My Memoirs*, 1907-1909), *Causeries* (1860), *Les Garibaldiens* (1861; *The Garibaldians in Sicily*, 1861), *Histoires de mes bêtes* (1868; *My Pets*, 1909), and *Souvenirs dramatiques* (1868; souvenirs of the theater).

Achievements

The Larousse *Grand Dictionnaire du XIX siècle* of 1870 described Alexandre Dumas, *père*, as "a novelist and the most prolific and popular playwright in France." Today his novels are regarded as his most durable achievement; they are known to every French person and to millions of other people through countless translations. Indeed, for innumerable readers, French history takes the form of Dumas's novels, and seventeenth century France is simply the France of the Three Musketeers. Dumas was an indefatigable writer, and his production is impressive by its volume alone: more than one hundred novels, including children's stories and tales. Although Dumas worked with many collaborators—the most famous being Auguste Maquet, Paul Meurice, Hippolyte Augier, Gérard de Nerval, and Auguste Vacquerie—a Dumas novel is readily distinguishable by its structure and style, sparkle, wit, rapid action, and dramatic dialogue.

Dumas's narratives teem with action and suspense; like the works of Eugène Sue, Frédéric Soulié, Honoré de Balzac, and Fyodor Dostoevski, most of Dumas's novels were first published in serial form, appearing in *La Presse*, *Journal des débats*, *Le Siècle*, and *Le Constitutionnel*, and later in his own journals, such as *Le Mousquetaire* and *Le Monte-Cristo*. He thus attracted a continuation. Sometimes he himself was uncertain what direction the plot of a given novel would take, and certain inconsistencies and discrepancies occasionally resulted from the serial format, but these are generally insignificant and surprisingly few in number. Often melodramatic, Dumas's novels nevertheless combine realism with the fantastic. Historical personages in his fiction maintain their roles in history yet sparkle with life: the haughty Anne of Austria, the inflexible Cardinal Richelieu, the independent Louis XIV. Like a careful puppeteer, Dumas never allows the intricate plot to escape him, nor does he resolve it until the end.

A gifted dramatist, Dumas was above all a master of dialogue. The critic Isabelle Jan has analyzed Dumas's dialogue as the very life's breath of his characters, noting that Dumas succeeded in making even the dumb speak—the mute Noirtier in *The Count of Monte-Cristo*. Dumas's characters communicate by gestures and body language as well as by speech; indeed, in Dumas's fictions even stovepipes and scaffold boards are eloquent. The action in a Dumas novel is carried forward through dialogue; a Dumas plot is not described, it is enacted.

Though Dumas did not possess Balzac's profound analytic intelligence, he shared Balzac's powers of observation. Lacking Victor Hugo's awareness of the abyss and his visionary gift, Dumas nevertheless had Hugo's sparkle and wit. Indeed, both Balzac and Hugo admired Dumas greatly, as did Nerval, one of his collaborators,

Alexandre Dumas, père. (Library of Congress)

with whom he shared a taste for the occult and the supernatural. Unlike Stendhal, whose unhappy Julien Sorel was created "for the happy few," yet, like him, a true Romantic in spirit, Dumas wrote for all, proving that the novel could be both popular and memorable.

Biography

On July 24, 1802, Alexandre Dumas was born in Villers-Cotterêts, a suburb of Paris with souvenirs of eighteenth century royalty that was to figure in many of his novels. From his father, Thomas-Alexandre Dumas Davy de la Pailleterie, a general in Napoleon I's service who dared to defy the emperor and hence lost possibilities of future honors, he received an adventurous spirit and a mulatto ancestry. His father died in 1806, and young Alexandre was brought up by his mother with little formal education and a love for the country and its woods. In 1818, Adolphe de Leuven and Amédée de la Ponce began to initiate him into German and Italian studies, and later into the works of William Shakespeare and a love for the theater.

In 1823, Dumas left Villers-Cotterêts and, with little more than a few coins and a letter of introduction (the minimum that d'Artagnan also carried), found a job as a copyist for the future Louis-Philippe through the intermediary of his father's former colleague General Foy. Dumas's passion for women developed alongside his love for the theater, and in 1824 he had a child, Alexandre Dumas, *fils*, by Catherine Labay. Dumas's first successful play, *Henri III and His Court*, was staged at the Comédie-Française in 1828. Thereafter his plays succeeded one another as rapidly as his liaisons, many with actresses, notably Mélanie Waldor; Mélanie Serre (Belle Krelsamer), the mother of Marie-Alexandrine Dumas; and Ida Ferrier, later his wife. He rapidly became acquainted with the most notable authors and artists, including Balzac, Hugo, Alfred de Vigny, and Eugène Delacroix. In 1831, Dumas officially recognized Alexandre as his son, separating son from mother and beginning a turbulent existence with his son that was to last his entire life.

After Dumas had received the Croix de la Légion d'Honneur and was reconciled with Hugo in 1836 (earlier, Dumas had thought that Hugo, whom he regarded as a close friend, had taken portions of *Christine* to use for his own work *Marie Tudor*, 1833), the two of them operated the famous Théâtre de la Renaissance. At this time, historical novels in the manner of Sir Walter Scott became popular in France, and Dumas tried his hand at them. With many collaborators, the most important being Auguste Maquet, Dumas produced a tremendous output of fiction, particularly between 1844 and 1855—so great that Eugène de Mirecourt, in his 1845 "Fabrique de romans: Maison Alexandre Dumas et Cie.," accused Dumas of running a "novel factory." As the result of a lawsuit, Mirecourt was convicted of slander, and Dumas continued to write prodigiously, acquiring an immense fortune and spending his money with equal prodigality. In 1847, he received six hundred guests at the housewarming of his Château de Monte-Cristo, a lavish estate that he was to occupy for little more than a year.

The Revolution of 1848 curtailed Dumas's career as it did Hugo's. The Théâtre Historique, which Dumas had founded principally as a showcase for his own works, closed, and Dumas, like Hugo, went to Belgium in 1851, though Dumas's reasons were less political than financial, for he was pursued by his creditors. After reaching an arrangement with them in 1853, he returned to Paris, where he undertook publication of successive journals, such as *Le Mousquetaire* (1853-1857) and *Le Monte-Cristo* (1857-1860). He traveled extensively, always writing travel impressions of each place he visited. In 1860, his liaison with Émilie Cordier led him to Italy and brought him another daughter, Micaëlla; he later visited Germany, Austria, and Russia. Among his many interests was cooking, and in 1869 he undertook a *Grand Dictionnaire de cuisine*, which was completed by Anatole France and published in 1873. In 1870, at the declaration of war, Dumas returned to Paris from the South. After a stroke, he returned to his son's home at Puys, where he died on December 5, 1870. In 1872, his remains were transferred to Villers-Cotterêts, and his fame continued to spread far and wide.

Analysis

Alexandre Dumas, *père*, arrived at the novel indirectly, through the theater and an apprenticeship with history and chronicles. By the time he turned to the novel in the style of Sir Walter Scott, then intensely popular in France, he had already dealt with historical subjects in his plays and had explored the Hundred Years' War, the French Revolution, and the Napoleonic era in his chronicles. Indeed, one can follow French history from the Middle Ages, though rather incompletely, up to the nineteenth century through Dumas's novels. His most successful cycles are set in the sixteenth century (especially the reign of the Valois), the seventeenth (especially the periods of Richelieu and Cardinal Mazarin), and the French Revolution, and the novels set in these periods are his best-known works—with the exception of *The Count of Monte-Cristo*, which is not really a historical novel but is rather a social novel or a *roman de moeurs*. His best historical fiction was written in the years from 1843 to 1855. Dumas's novels after 1855 are chiefly concerned with the French Revolution, the Directory, and the nineteenth century, and are less well known than his earlier works.

Among Dumas's medieval novels are *Otho the Archer*, which evokes a German medieval legend; *Lyderic, Count of Flanders*, set in seventh century Flanders; and *The Bastard of Mauléon*, which covers the period from 1358 to 1369, the earlier part of the Hundred Years' War. Dumas treats the period from 1500 to 1570 in greater detail, in scattered novels from 1843 to 1858. *The Brigand* treats the period from 1497 to 1519 and focuses on the youth of Charles V. *The Two Dianas* and *Ascanio*, written with the collaboration of Meurice, treat the reign of François I and the presence of sculptor Benvenuto Cellini at the French court. The two Dianas are Diane de Castro and Diane de Poitiers. *The Page of the Duke of Savoy*, set in the years 1555 to 1559, with an epilogue that takes place in 1580, is a companion to *The Two Dianas*. The final novel of the series, *The Horoscope*, treats the beginning of the reign of François II.

The Valois cycle, which covers the period from August, 1572, to June, 1586, comprises three of the most successful and popular of Dumas's historical romances. *Marguerite de Navarre* treats the period from 1572 to 1575, beginning with the wedding of Marguerite de Valois and Henri de Navarre and focusing on their various romantic intrigues; the novel concludes with the famous Saint Bartholemew's Day Massacre. The second book in the cycle, *Chicot the Jester*, is the most popular and introduces one of Dumas's finest creations: Chicot, a rival of d'Artagnan and similar to him in many ways. The novel covers the period from 1578 to 1579 under Henri III and focuses on the death of Bussy d'Amboise. The last book in the cycle, *The Forty-five Guardsmen*, covers the years from 1582 to 1584; it tells of the Ligue, the duc de Guise, and the vengeance of the duc d'Anjou for Bussy's murder.

Unquestionably Dumas's best-written and most popular cycle, however, is that of d'Artagnan, which covers the period from 1625 to 1673. It includes *The Three Musketeers*, the immortal story of Athos, Porthos, and Aramis, who, together with d'Artagnan, interact in the stories of Richelieu, Louis XIII, Anne of Austria, and the Duke of Buckingham from 1625 to 1628. *Twenty Years After*, as the title indicates, takes place in 1648 and finds the same characters involved with Anne of Austria and Mazarin, the Fronde, and the Civil War in England. *The Vicomte de Bragelonne*, a lengthy account largely set in the period from 1660 to 1673, focuses less on the musketeers than on Louis XIV, Fouquet, and the Man in the Iron Mask. The intervening years (1628 to 1648) are covered in three less important novels, the best being *The War of Women*, which deals with the new Fronde of 1648 to 1650.

The century from 1670 to 1770 is the subject of four novels, of which the best known are the companion works *The Chevalier d'Harmental* and *The Regent's Daughter*, both of which deal with the Cellamare conspiracy of 1718. The Marie Antoinette cycle, often referred to collectively by the title of the first volume, *Memoirs of a Physician*, takes place between 1770 and 1791 and is also a very popular series. The first book in the cycle, written in collaboration with Maquet, covers the period between 1770 and 1774, including the death of Louis XV and the marriage of Marie Antoinette to Louis XVI. *The Queen's Necklace* focuses on the scandal of the Queen's diamond necklace and her love affair with Charny from 1784 to 1786. *Taking the Bastille* covers only four months in 1789, the period of the taking of the Bastille. Finally, *The Countess de Charny* begins in 1789, covers the King's flight to Varennes in 1791 and the destinies of Andrée and Charny, and concludes with the King's execution in 1793. Although the series lacks a strong central character, with the possible exception of Joseph Balsamo, it is important for its emphasis on women.

Five other novels cover the intervening period until 1800, of which *The Whites and the Blues*, showing the influence of the novelist Charles Nodier, is the best known. Six novels treat the Napoleonic period, the Restoration, and the reign of Louis-Philippe. Of these, *The Mohicans of Paris*, dealing with the revolution under the Restoration in the 1820's, and *Salvator*, its companion, together form Dumas's longest novel; although not his most popular, it is a highly representative work.

In Dumas's many social novels, there are frequent historical excursions; among his finest and most popular works in this genre is *The Count of Monte-Cristo*, which begins with Napoleon's exile at Elba, the Hundred Days, and the second Restoration. In the manner of Balzac, this great novel depicts the greed and selfishness of the Parisian aristocracy and the consuming passion of ambition. Dumas treated racial prejudice in *George*, set in Mauritius, and depicted his own native town in three novels known as the Villers-Cotterêts cycle: *Conscience*, *Catherine Blum*, and *The Wolf Leader*.

In virtually all of his novels, Dumas excels in plot and dialogue. His most successful works blend history or social observation with fantasy, and his plots nearly always involve mystery and intrigue. Usually they concern romantic involvements, yet there are relatively few scenes of romance.

Although Dumas's novels are rich with memorable characters, he does not focus on psychological development. A given character remains essentially the same from the beginning to the end of a work. Despite the disguises and the mysteries that often surround a character's name—even the three musketeers have strange aliases—there is never an aspect of personality that remains to be discovered. Dumas's characters are not inspired by moral idealism; they are usually motivated by ambition, revenge, or simply a love for adventure. Dumas does not instruct, but he also does not distort the great movements of history or of social interaction. He aims principally to entertain, to help his readers forget the world in which they live and to move with his characters into a fantastic world that is sometimes truer to life than reality.

The famous d'Artagnan trilogy, which is made up of *The Three Musketeers*, *Twenty Years After*, and *The Vicomte de Bragelonne*, has three differing basic texts: the first, the original published in *Le Siècle*; the second in pirated Belgian texts; the third published by Baudry; many other versions exist as well. The series covers the period from 1625 to 1673, focusing on the events during the period of Richelieu, Mazarin, and Louis XIV. The main characters, and even some secondary ones, have their sources in history, although their interaction with the major historical figures is often imaginary. Dumas's primary source is the *Mémoires de M. d'Artagnan* (1700), a fabricated account of d'Artagnan's life by Gatien de Courtilz de Sandras. The trilogy provides an excellent introduction to Dumas's use of historical sources, his storytelling technique, his dramatic power, and his creation of character.

The Three Musketeers

The Three Musketeers begins in April, 1625, at Meung-sur-Loire, where the Quixote-like d'Artagnan, a young Gascon of eighteen years, is making his way to Paris with a letter of introduction to Monsieur de Tréville, the captain of the King's musketeers. It is here that he meets the Count of Rochefort, Richelieu's right-hand man, and "Milady," a beautiful and mysterious woman whose path will cross his throughout the novel and whose shadow will haunt him for the next twenty years. In Paris, d'Artagnan becomes fast friends with Athos, Porthos, and Aramis, the three musketeers who share his adventures throughout the novel. D'Artagnan falls in love with Constance Bonacieux, his landlord's wife, also a lady-in-waiting to the Queen, Anne of Austria. He thus becomes involved in recovering the Queen's diamond studs, a present from the King that she has unwisely given to her lover, the handsome Duke of Buckingham, Richelieu's rival in both political and amorous intrigue. D'Artagnan falls in love with the bewitching Milady and discovers her criminal past, for which knowledge she begins an inexorable pursuit of him.

Meanwhile, the siege of La Rochelle permits the four friends to display their bravery and to develop a plot against Milady, who in a very complex intrigue becomes an agent in Buckingham's assassination. Milady's revenge leads her to poison Constance, and for this final crime she is tried and condemned by the four musketeers and her brother-in-law, Lord de Winter. Since the siege of La Rochelle ends to Richelieu's advantage through the invaluable assistance of the musketeers, d'Artagnan becomes a friend of Richelieu and a lieutenant of the musketeers. Porthos marries his mistress, the widowed Madame Coquenard; Aramis becomes a priest; and Athos, or the Comte de la Fère, after a few more years of military service, retires to his estate in Roussillon.

TWENTY YEARS AFTER

Twenty Years After, as the title indicates, begins in 1648, twenty years after the conclusion of *The Three Musketeers*; Mazarin is at the helm of the government, and Paris is on the verge of the Fronde, a rebellion of the nobles against the regent. The lives of the four musketeers have been singularly without adventure during the preceding twenty years; d'Artagnan, still a lieutenant in the musketeers, lives with "the fair Madeleine" in Paris; Athos, Comte de la Fère, spends his time bringing up his son, Raoul de Bragelonne; Porthos, now Comte du Vallon and master of three estates, is dissatisfied with his lot and aspires to become a baron; Aramis, formerly a musketeer who aspired to be an abbé, is now the Abbé d'Herblay and longs to be a musketeer again.

The four men, now a bit distrustful of one another, are unable to join forces since Athos and Aramis are *frondeurs* and d'Artagnan and Porthos are cardinalists. They meet on opposite sides in their first encounter with the Duke of Beaufort, who escapes from d'Artagnan. Subsequently in England, during Cromwell's overthrow of Charles I, they find themselves opponents but join in an unsuccessful attempt to save the King. Their efforts in this and other intrigues are thwarted by Mordaunt, Milady's son, who seeks to avenge his mother and finally meets with a violent death at sea. Their united support of Charles I wins the four imprisonment from Mazarin, whom they in turn abduct and coerce into signing certain concessions to the *frondeurs*. At the end, d'Artagnan becomes captain of the musketeers and Porthos, a baron.

THE VICOMTE DE BRAGELONNE

The third novel in the series, *The Vicomte de Bragelonne*, which is twice as long as the two previous novels together, covers the period from 1660 to 1673, from Louis XIV's visit to Blois in 1659 and his marriage to Marie-Thérèse of Spain to the death of d'Artagnan. It has four centers of interest: the Restoration of Charles II of England; the love affair of Louis XIV and Louise de la Vallière; the trial of Fouquet; and the famous tale of the Man in the Iron Mask. The musketeers are no longer in the foreground; in fact, they do not even appear in several episodes, and the novel as a whole is more disconnected than its predecessors in the trilogy. The main character, Raoul de Bragelonne (Athos's son), is unconvincing, though Louis XIV in particular emerges as a well-developed figure. Indeed, the historical characters dominate the novel, giving it the quality of a "sweeping pageant," as Richard Stowe describes it.

The d'Artagnan novels, especially *The Three Musketeers*, are Dumas at his best. They include his most successful character portrayals, both the primary historical figures—Richelieu, Mazarin, Anne of Austria, and Louis XIV—and the musketeers, who also have a basis in history. D'Artagnan especially is an immortal creation, partaking at once of Don Quixote, the clown, and Ariel; he is a creature of the air and the night whose age hardly seems to matter and whose sprightly, carefree manner is balanced by his inflexible loyalty to his three musketeer friends and to his masters. The three books in the trilogy, more successfully than any others, combine history and fiction and are perhaps the most popular novels produced in the nineteenth century.

THE COUNT OF MONTE-CRISTO

Rivaling the d'Artagnan saga in popularity is *The Count of Monte-Cristo*. Incredible as the adventures of Monte-Cristo may seem, they are based on reality. In 1842, Dumas visited Elba with Prince Jérôme, son of Napoleon's youngest brother, and sailed around the island of Monte-Cristo. Dumas said that he would someday immortalize it. At about the same time, he was approached by Béthune and Plon to write a work titled "Impressions de voyage dans Paris" (travel impressions in Paris). Béthune and Plon did not want an archeological or scientific work, but rather a novel like Eugène Sue's *Les Mystères de Paris* (1842-1843; *The Mysteries of Paris*, 1843). Dumas found the germ of a plot in "Le diamant et la vengeance," a chapter in *Mémoires tirés des archives de la Police de Paris* (1837-1838) by Jacques Peuchet, referred to by Dumas in his *Causeries* as "État civil du 'Comte de Monte Cristo.'" The main character of *The Count of Monte-Cristo* is based on an unjustly imprisoned shoemaker named François Picaud.

The Count of Monte-Cristo first appeared serially, in

Le Journal des débats, with the spelling *Christo*, a spelling also used in the Belgian pirated editions. Unlike Dumas's historical novels, *The Count of Monte-Cristo* is set in contemporary France and, except for short passages relating to Napoleon and Louis XVIII, is almost totally a *roman de moeurs*.

The lengthy novel is divided into three unequal parts—based on the cities in which the action takes place: Marseilles, Rome, and Paris—the last being by far the longest. Part 1 opens in 1815, in Marseilles, where Dumas introduces the attractive first mate of the ship *Pharaon*, Edmond Dantès, soon to be promoted to captain. He is celebrating his impending marriage to his beautiful Catalan sweetheart, Mercédès, when he is suddenly arrested. Earlier, the dying captain of the *Pharaon* had given him a letter to deliver to a Bonapartist group in Paris, and because of this he has been accused of treason by two jealous companions: Danglars, the ship's accountant, and Fernand, Dantès's rival for the hand of Mercédès. Caderousse, a neighbor, learns of the plot against Dantès but remains silent. Villefort, the *procureur du roi*, is sympathetic to Dantès until he discovers that the letter is intended for his father, whose Bonapartist and Girondist political views he despises, seeing them as a threat to his own future. He therefore allows Dantès to be condemned to solitary confinement at the nearby Château d'If. Dantès, resentful and despairing, remains in prison for fourteen years, during which time he makes the acquaintance of the Abbé Faria (a character based on a real person), who instructs Dantès in history, mathematics, and languages and wills him the fabulous treasure that the Abbé has hidden on the island of Monte-Cristo. At the Abbé's death, Dantès changes places with his corpse in the funeral sack, is thrown into the sea, and swims to safety.

Once free, Dantès claims the treasure and learns the whereabouts of his betrayers: Danglars has become a successful banker, while Fernand, after acquiring wealth by betraying Pasha Ali in the Greek revolution, has gained the title of Count de Morcerf and has married Mercédès. Shortly afterward, Dantès, now the Count of Monte-Cristo, assumes the persona of Sinbad the Sailor and entertains the Baron Franz d'Épinay at Monte-Cristo. An atmosphere reminiscent of *The Arabian Nights' Entertainments* (fifteenth century) dazzles Franz, who hardly knows if what he sees is real or imaginary. Later, Franz, in the company of his friend Albert de Morcerf, the son of Mercédès and Fernand, again meets Monte-Cristo in Rome, where Monte-Cristo saves Morcerf from the kidnapper Luigi Vampa. Albert invites Monte-Cristo to visit him in Paris, thus introducing part 3.

Part 3 is, properly speaking, the story of Dantès's vengeance and takes place twenty-three years after he was first imprisoned. Disguised sometimes as Monte-Cristo, sometimes as the Abbé Busoni, sometimes as Lord Wilmore, Dantès dazzles all of Paris with his endless wealth, powerful connections, and enigmatic manner. Meanwhile, he slowly but surely sets the stage for his revenge. Directly attacking no one, he nevertheless brings his four enemies to total ruin by intricate and complex machinations. The greedy Caderousse, who gave silent assent to Dantès's imprisonment, is killed by an anonymous assassin while attempting to rob Monte-Cristo's rich hotel on the Champs-Élysées. Before his death, he learns Monte-Cristo's real identity. Danglars is the next victim; by means of false information, Monte-Cristo succeeds in ruining him financially and exposing his wife's greed and infidelity. Fernand is brought down in turn when Monte-Cristo, with the aid of his adopted daughter, Haydée (the natural daughter of Pasha Ali), brings to light several acts of cowardice of which Fernand was guilty during his army service. Fernand's son Albert challenges Monte-Cristo to a duel, but through the intercession of Mercédès, who recognizes her fiancé of many years before, Albert's life is spared.

The last victim is Villefort, whose daughter Valentine is in love with Maximilien Morrel, the son of a shipping master who had aided Dantès and his father long ago. Monte-Cristo encourages Madame de Villefort's greedy efforts to acquire the wealth of Valentine (who is her stepdaughter), and the Villefort family is all but destroyed by the poison Madame de Villefort administers as part of her plan; Valentine herself is an apparent victim. Saved by Monte-Cristo, she is at last reunited with her lover on the island of Monte-Cristo, which Edmond Dantès reveals to the lovers as the site of the treasure he bequeaths to them. He sails off in the distance, his revenge complete. The revenge has also brought about a second transformation in Dantès, for he is now a man who, "like Satan, thought himself for an instant equal to God, but now acknowledges, with Christian humility, that God alone possesses supreme power and infinite wisdom."

Irma M. Kashuba

OTHER MAJOR WORKS

PLAYS: *La Chasse et l'amour*, pr., pb. 1825 (with Adolphe de Leuven and P.-J. Rousseau); *La Noce et l'enterrement*, pr., pb. 1826; *Henri III et sa cour*, pr., pb. 1829 (*Catherine of Cleves*, 1831; also known as *Henry III and His Court*, 1904); *Christine: Ou, Stockholm, Fontainebleau, et Rome*, pr., pb. 1830; *Antony*, pr., pb. 1831 (English translation, 1904); *Charles VII chez ses grands vassaux*, pr., pb. 1831; *Napoléon Bonaparte: Ou, Trente Ans dans l'histoire de France*, pr., pb. 1831; *Richard Darlington*, pr. 1831; *La Tour de Nesle*, pr., pb. 1832 (redrafted from a manuscript by Frédéric Gaillardet; English translation, 1906); *Le Fils de l'émigré: Ou, Le Peuple*, pr. 1832 (selections pb. 1902); *Le Mari de la veuve*, pr., pb. 1832; *Teresa*, pr., pb. 1832 (based on a draft by Auguste Anicet-Bourgeois); *Angèle*, pr. 1833; *Catherine Howard*, pr., pb. 1834 (English translation, 1859); *La Vénitienne*, pr., pb. 1834; *Cromwell et Charles 1*, pr., pb. 1835 (with E.-C.-H. Cordellier-Delanoue); *Don Juan de Marana: Ou, La Chute d'un ange*, pr., pb. 1836; *Kean: Ou, Désordre et génie*, pr., pb. 1836 (with Théaulon de Lambert and Frédéric de Courcy; *Edmund Kean: Or, The Genius and the Libertine*, 1847); *Caligula*, pr. 1837; *Piquillo*, pr., pb. 1837 (libretto; with Gérard de Nerval); *Le Bourgeois de Gand: Ou, Le Secrétaire du duc d'Albe*, pr., pb. 1838 (with Hippolyte Romand); *Paul Jones*, pr., pb. 1838; *L'Alchimiste*, pr., pb. 1839 (with Nerval); *Bathilde*, pr., pb. 1839 (with Auguste Maquet); *Léo Burckart*, pr., pb. 1839 (with Nerval); *Mademoiselle de Belle-Isle*, pr., pb. 1839 (English translation, 1855); *Jarvis l'honnête homme: Ou, Le Marchand de Londres*, pr., pb. 1840 (originally credited to Charles Lafont); *Jeannic le Breton: Ou, Le Gérant responsable*, pr. 1841 (with Eugène Bourgeois); *Un Mariage sous Louis XV*, pr., pb. 1841 (*A Marriage of Convenience*, 1899); *Halifax*, pr. 1842 (with Adolphe D'Ennery?); *Lorenzino*, pr., pb. 1842; *Le Séducteur et le mari*, pr., pb. 1842 (with Lafont); *Les Demoiselles de Saint-Cyr*, pr., pb. 1843 (*The Ladies of Saint-Cyr*, 1870); *L'École des princes*, pr. 1843 (with Louis Lefèvre); *Louise Bernard*, pr., pb. 1843 (with Leuven and Léon Lhérie); *Le Mariage au tambour*, pr., pb. 1843 (with Leuven and Lhérie); *Un Conte des fées*, pr., pb. 1845 (with Leuven and Lhérie); *Le Garde forestier*, pr., pb. 1845 (with Leuven and Lhérie); *Les Mousquetaires*, pr., pb. 1845 (with Maquet; adaptation of Dumas's novel *Vingt Ans aprés*); *Sylvandire*, pr., pb. 1845 (with Leuven and Louis-Émile Vanderburch); *Échec et mat*, pr., pb. 1846 (with Octave Feuillet and Paul Bocage); *Une Fille du régent*, pr., pb. 1846; *Le Chevalier de Maison-Rouge*, pr., pb. 1847 (with Maquet; *The Chevalier de Maison-Rouge*, 1859); *Hamlet, prince de Danemark*, pr. 1847 (with Paul Meurice; adaptation of William Shakespeare's play); *Intrigue et amour*, pr., pb. 1847 (adaptation of Friedrich Schiller's play *Kabale und Liebe*); *La Reine Margot*, pr., pb. 1847 (with Maquet; adaptation of Dumas's novel); *Catilina*, pr., pb. 1848 (with Maquet); *Monte-Cristo*, parts 1 and 2, pr., pb. 1848 (with Maquet; *Monte-Cristo*, part 1, 1850); *Le Cachemire vert*, pr., pb. 1849 (with Eugène Nus); *Le Chevalier d'Harmental*, pr., pb. 1849 (with Maquet; based on Dumas's novel); *Le Comte Hermann*, pr., pb. 1849; *Le Connétable de Bourbon: Ou, L'Italie au seizième siècle*, pr., pb. 1849 (with Eugène Grangé and Xavier de Montépin); *La Guerre des femmes*, pr., pb. 1849 (with Maquet; based on Dumas's novel); *La Jeunesse des mousquetaires*, pr., pb. 1849 (with Maquet; based on Dumas's novel *Les Trois Mousquetaires*; *The Musketeers*, 1850); *Le Testament de César*, pr., pb. 1849 (with Jules Lacroix); *La Chasse au chastre*, pr., pb. 1850 (with Maquet?; based on Dumas's story); *Les Chevaliers du Lansquenet*, pr., pb. 1850 (with Grangé and Montépin); *Pauline*, pr., pb. 1850 (with Grangé and Montépin; based on Dumas's novel *Pauline*); *Urbain Grandier*, pr., pb. 1850 (with Maquet); *Le Vingt-quatre février*, pr., pb. 1850 (adapted from Zacharias Werner's play *Der 24 Februar*); *Le Comte de Morcerf*, pr., pb. 1851 (with Maquet; part 3 of *Monte-Cristo*); *Villefort*, pr., pb. 1851 (with Maquet; part 4 of *Monte-Cristo*); *Romulus*, pr., pb. 1854; *L'Orestie*, pr., pb. 1856; *L'Invitation à la valse*, pr., pb. 1857 (adapted in English as *Childhood Dreams*, 1881); *L'Envers d'une conspiration*, pr., pb. 1860; *Le Roman d'Elvire*, pr., pb. 1860 (with Leuven); *La Veillée allemande*, pr. 1863 (with Bernard Lopez); *Madame de Chamblay*, pr. 1868; *Les Blancs et les bleus*, pr., pb. 1869 (adaptation of part of Dumas's novel); *Théâtre complet*, 1873-1876 (25 volumes); *The Great Lover, and Other Plays*, 1979.

NONFICTION: *Gaule et France*, 1833 (*The Progress of Democracy*, 1841); *Impressions de voyage*, 1833, 1838, 1841, 1843 (*Travels in Switzerland*, 1958); *La Vendée et Madame*, 1833 (*The Duchess of Berri in La Vendée*, 1833); *Guelfes et Gibelins*, 1836; *Isabel de Bavière*, 1836 (*Isabel of Bavaria*, 1846); *Napoléon*, 1836 (English translation, 1874); *Quinze Jours au Sinai*, 1838 (*Impressions of Travel in Egypt and Arabia Petraea*, 1839); *Crimes célèbres*, 1838-1840 (*Celebrated Crimes*, 1896); *Excursions sur les bords du Rhin*, 1841 (with Gérard de Nerval); *Le Midi de la France*, 1841 (*Pictures of Travel in the South of France*, 1852); *Chroniques du roi Pépin*, 1842 (*Pepin*, 1906); *Jehanne la Pucelle, 1429-1431*, 1842 (*Joan the Heroic Maiden*, 1847); *Le Spéronare*, 1842; *Le Corricolo*, 1843; *Mes Mémoires*, 1852, 1853, 1854-1855 (*My Memoirs*, 1907-1909); *Souvenirs de 1830 à 1842*, 1854-1855; *Causeries*, 1860; *Les Garibaldiens*, 1861 (*The Garibaldians in Sicily*, 1861); *Histoires de mes bêtes*, 1868 (*My Pets*, 1909); *Souvenirs dramatiques*, 1868; *Grand Dictionnaire de cuisine*, 1873 (with Anatole France); *On Board the Emma*, 1929; *The Road to Monte-Cristo*, 1956.

TRANSLATION: *Mémoires de Garibaldi*, 1860 (of Giuseppe Garibaldi's *Memorie autobiografiche*).

CHILDREN'S LITERATURE: *La Bouillie de la Comtesse Berthe*, 1845 (*Good Lady Bertha's Honey Broth*, 1846); *Histoire d'un casse-noisette*, 1845 (*Story of a Nutcracker*, 1846); *Le Roi de Bohème*, 1853 (also known as *La Jeunesse de Pierrot*, 1854; *When Pierrot Was Young*, 1924); *Le Sifflet enchanté*, 1859 (*The Enchanted Whistle*, 1894).

MISCELLANEOUS: *Œuvres complètes*, 1846-1877 (301 volumes); *Œuvres d'Alexandre Dumas*, 1962-1967 (38 volumes).

Bibliography

Beaujour, Elizabeth Klotsky. "Dumas's Decembrists: *Le Maitre d'Armes* and the *Memoirs* of Pauline Annenkova." *Russian Review* 59, no. 1 (2000): 38-51. Describes Dumas's meeting with the Russian subjects of a historical novel he had written eighteen years previously and considers the relationship between history and fiction in the author's works.

Bell, A. Craig. *Alexandre Dumas: A Biography and Study*. London: Cassel, 1950. Helpful and thorough guide pays significant attention to both the life and the work of Dumas. Introduction deals succinctly with the phenomenon of Dumas's popularity and the need for a careful treatment of his entire body of work.

Bell, David F. *Real Time: Accelerating Narrative from Balzac to Zola*. Urbana: University of Illinois Press, 2004. Cites examples from novels and short stories to explore how the accelerated movement of people and information in the nineteenth century was a crucial element in the work of Dumas and three other French authors.

Fabre, Michel. "International Beacons of African-American Memory: Alexandre Dumas père, Henry O. Tanner, and Josephine Baker as Examples of Recognition." In *History and Memory in African-American Culture*, edited by Genevieve Fabre and Robert O'Meally. New York: Oxford University Press, 1994. An examination of Dumas's African heritage is included in a collection of essays that focuses on how African Americans' historical identity has been represented in literature and other media.

Galan, F. W. "Bakhtiniada II, *The Corsican Brothers* in the Prague School: Or, The Reciprocity of Reception." *Poetics Today* 8, nos. 3/4 (1987): 565-577. Approaches Dumas's *The Corsican Brothers* using the critical apparatus of Russian literary critic Mikhail Bakhtin.

Lucas-Dubreton, J. *The Fourth Musketeer: The Life of Alexandre Dumas*. New York: Coward-McCann, 1938. Provides a lively introduction to Dumas's life and career for the general reader.

Maurois, André. *Alexandre Dumas: A Great Life in Brief*. Translated by Jack Palmer White. New York: Alfred A. Knopf, 1964. Offers a good introduction to the life of Dumas, providing the basic facts in readable but limited fashion, including information on the novels. Maurois is one of the recognized authorities on Dumas.

_______. *The Titans: A Three-Generation Biography of the Dumas*. Translated by Gerard Hopkins. 1957. Reprint. Westport, Conn.: Greenwood Press, 1971. A classic in Dumas studies by a seasoned biographer, recounting the life of Dumas, his father, and his son. Includes notes, bibliography, and illustrations.

Nesci, Catherine. "Talking Heads: Violence and Desire in Dumas *père*'s (Post-)Terrorist Society." *SubStance* 27, no. 2 (1998): 73-92. Presents a poststructuralist reading of two of Dumas's novels about the French Revolution, *The Thousand and One Ghosts* and *The Woman with a Velvet Necklace*.

Stowe, Richard S. *Alexandre Dumas père*. Boston: Twayne, 1976. One of the best short introductions to Dumas available in English, with a chapter of biography followed by chapters on Dumas's dramas, novels, and other fiction. Includes notes, chronology, and annotated bibliography.

DAPHNE DU MAURIER

Born: London, England; May 13, 1907
Died: Par, Cornwall, England; April 19, 1989
Also known as: Lady Daphne Browning

Principal long fiction

The Loving Spirit, 1931
I'll Never Be Young Again, 1932
The Progress of Julius, 1933
Jamaica Inn, 1936
Rebecca, 1938
Frenchman's Creek, 1941
Hungry Hill, 1943
The King's General, 1946
The Parasites, 1949
My Cousin Rachel, 1951
Mary Anne, 1954
The Scapegoat, 1957
Castle Dor, 1962 (with Arthur Quiller-Couch)
The Glass-Blowers, 1963
The Flight of the Falcon, 1965
The House on the Strand, 1969
Rule Britannia, 1972

Other literary forms

In addition to her many novels, Daphne du Maurier (dew MOHR-ee-ay) wrote and edited biographies, collections of letters, travel books, plays, and short stories. Her biographical works include *Gerald: A Portrait* (1934), the life story of her actor father; *The du Mauriers* (1937), the inside story of her famous family of actors, dramatists, and novelists; and *The Young George du Maurier: A Selection of His Letters, 1860-1867* (1951), a collection of her caricaturist-novelist grandfather's letters. She earned a place among playwrights with *The Years Between* (pr. 1944) and *September Tide* (pr. 1948). Her travel book *Vanishing Cornwall* (1967) describes the rugged coastal area of southwestern England, where she set so many of her novels and stories. Often weaving elements of the supernatural into her tales of mystery and romance, du Maurier produced several notable volumes of short stories, including *Echoes from the Macabre* in 1976 and *Classics of the Macabre* in 1987.

Achievements

The theatrical quality of Daphne du Maurier's novels is evidenced by the frequency and reported ease with which her works have been adapted for the big screen. Alfred Hitchcock directed film versions of *Jamaica Inn* (1939) and her best-selling gothic novel *Rebecca* (1940). The latter won an Academy Award for Best Picture. Paramount Pictures released *Frenchman's Creek* in 1944, and Universal Pictures released a film adaptation of *Hungry Hill* in 1947, for which du Maurier herself wrote the first draft of the screenplay. *My Cousin Rachel* became a Twentieth Century Fox production in 1952, and Metro-Goldwyn-Mayer released *The Scapegoat* in 1959. Hitchcock turned her story "The Birds" into a highly successful motion picture of the same title in 1963, and her story "Don't Look Now" became a hit film in 1973.

Rebecca won an award from the American Booksellers' Association in 1939. In 1969, du Maurier was named a Dame Commander of the Order of the British Empire.

Biography

Daphne du Maurier was born to a theatrical family. Her father, Gerald, was an actor and manager; her mother, Muriel Beaumont, was an actor. Du Maurier was educated in both England and France. Plagued from childhood by feelings of self-doubt and inadequacy, she turned to writing to achieve the solitude she desperately craved. She preferred fantasy to reality and shunned social engagements. She began writing stories and poems in her teens. By the time she was in her twenties, she was selling regularly to magazines such as *The Bystander* and the *Sunday Review*.

She wrote her first novel, *The Loving Spirit*, when she was only twenty-two years old. This romantic family saga earned both critical acclaim and best-seller status. It so impressed a major in the Grenadier Guards that he arranged a meeting with its author. The two soon developed an attachment, and in 1932 du Maurier married Major Frederick Arthur Montague Browning, whom she called Tommy. He later earned the rank of lieutenant general, became Chancellor of the Exchequer in the household of Princess Elizabeth, and became treasurer to the Duke of Edinburgh. The couple had three children: daughters Flavia and Tessa and son Christian. Browning died in 1965.

In 1943, du Maurier fulfilled a childhood dream and moved into Menabilly, a seventy-room manor house in Cornwall that inspired Manderley, the eerie setting for *Rebecca*. She adored the reputedly haunted house, asserting that it whispered its secrets to her in the solitude of midnight. Never one for social life, she preferred solitary walks in the woods to bustling cities and glittering social gatherings. Her family life was seldom serene, with du Maurier's troubled and erratic spirit manifesting itself in frequently problematic ways; in addition, Browning was plagued with psychological problems and poor physical health, both associated with his chronic abuse of alcohol.

A rocky marriage was only one of the writer's torments. Biographer Margaret Forster asserts that du Maurier's stories and novels reflected severe emotional turbulence. Du Maurier had, according to Forster, a stifling relationship with her father, a complicated extramarital affair, and a lesbian relationship with actor Gertrude Lawrence. The details of daily life troubled her, and she frequently retreated from family and friends to find solace in make-believe. Twice she faced plagiarism charges and endured the agonies of court hearings as a result of claims that she had stolen the second-wife theme used in *Rebecca*. Although she was acquitted in both instances, the publicity wearied and shamed her, and she grew increasingly reclusive in later life. Du Maurier died in Cornwall, England on April 19, 1989.

Analysis

Daphne du Maurier came naturally by her dramatic bent. Having eschewed a career in acting, she turned instead to writing, creating the settings of her novels as a vivid stage on which her melodramas could unfold. Most often, she wrote about what she knew: the craggy, tempestuous coasts and climate of Cornwall. With the playwright's flare, she elicited as much suspense from her setting as from her characters and plots. Du Maurier yearned to write light romance, but it was not in her nature. "I may determine to write a gay, light romance. But I go for a walk on a moor and see a twisted tree and a pile of granite stones beside a deep, dark pool, and *Jamaica Inn* is born," she told *Current Biography* in 1940. Du Maurier's readers can only be glad for the writer's solitary walks, for *Jamaica Inn* and the writer's many other haunting novels and stories rank among the finest spine-tingling page turners ever written. Her books contain passion, jealousy, evil, and murder, with surprise heaped upon surprise.

While du Maurier's works may not probe the depths of human experience, they create worlds and peoples that haunt long after the books are finished. Du Maurier believed in her own brand of predestination, a reincarnation of the human spirit. Evil is inevitable, in her view, but not insurmountable. People are, however, condemned by their very nature to a vision that exceeds their grasp. Du Maurier's interest in character took a backseat to her fascination with personality types symbolic of abstract qualities of good and evil. She told Barbara Nichols in an interview for *Ladies' Home Journal*,

> I am not so much interested in people as in types—types who represent great forces of good or evil. I don't care very much whether John Smith likes Mary Robinson, goes to bed with Jane Brown and then refuses to pay the hotel bill. But I *am* [emphasis in original] passionately interested in human cruelty, human lust, and human avarice—and, of course, their counterparts in the scale of virtue.

Although critics have complained about her melodrama, plot contrivances, shallow characterization, romanticism, sentimentality, vague motivations, and moralizing, such commentary probably misses the point. Du Maurier's unfailing appeal to her readers is fundamental: She tells a good story, and she tells it well. Unsurpassed as a teller of gothic tales tinged with horror or the supernatural, she is worth studying if only for her pacing, which moves from plot twist to plot twist with consummate ease. A romance writer in the best sense of the label, she creates engaging heroines blessed with immense inner strength. Her heroes helped to establish the model for modern romances: dark of complexion, dark of spirit, silent, enigmatic, harboring some unspeakable secret. Her settings evoke the foreboding ambience of Cornwall's precipitous cliffs and misty moors, the perfect backdrop for the dramatic events that so astonish and delight du Maurier's readers.

Daphne du Maurier. (Popperfoto/Archive Photos)

Rebecca

Among the most memorable opening lines in English literature is the first sentence of du Maurier's best-known work, *Rebecca*: "Last night I dreamt I went to Manderley again." In a landscape of words, du Maurier takes her readers to Manderley to hear the rustle of leaves, smell the flowers in the garden, luxuriate in the opulence of the estate's drawing room. As ominous waves pound the Cornish coast, the dark tale unfolds. Maxim de Winter, the brooding, detached master of Manderley, marries in haste while abroad and brings his new bride home to Cornwall. The new Mrs. de Winter (whose given name is never revealed) recounts her tale entirely in flashback, compelling the reader to stay with her as the reason for her departure from Manderley is slowly brought to light.

What begins as a Cinderella story—this young girl of modest means swept off her feet by a wealthy, powerful gentleman—soon turns sinister. The narrator is haunted by the lingering influence of Maxim's first wife, Rebecca, who died in a sailing accident. Rebecca's presence is perpetually felt; even the name of Rebecca's boat, *Je reviens* (French for "I return"), suggests its owner will not depart, either in body or in spirit. Manderley itself seems keeper of Rebecca's mystique, with its forbidden halls, haunted rooms, and secret passages accidentally discovered. Beautiful, witty, flirtatious, and strong, Rebecca looms large—her power all the greater, even as a memory, for its contrast to the reticent nature of de Winter's diffident second bride. The narrator imagines she can hear Rebecca calling to the dogs and Rebecca's evening dress rustling on the stairs. The housekeeper, Mrs. Danvers, exhibits fierce loyalty to the first Mrs. de Winter and sullen contempt for the second. Cruelly, she plots to displace the narrator from Manderley and drive a wedge between its master and mistress.

The ensuing labyrinth of deceptions, betrayals, and revelations spellbinds readers and proves that the new Mrs. de Winter is not without resources. Determined to uncover the truth and break free of Rebecca's legacy, she counters the housekeeper's wicked lies and her husband's silent brooding with a resolute search for the truth. In a surprise ending, she rises whole and victorious, her nightmare ended and justice served. Manderley was great and corrupt, just as was Max's dead wife. Readers find it satisfying to learn that love can be deep and enduring enough to overcome an adversary as powerful as Rebecca.

Jamaica Inn

Critics praised *Jamaica Inn* as a tale nineteenth century adventure writer Robert Louis Stevenson would have been proud to write, and du Maurier admitted it was similar to—and inspired by—his *Treasure Island* (1883). The rain-swept Cornish coast in raw November portends danger, but orphan Mary Yellan is determined to keep the promise she made to her dying mother—to make her home with her victimized Aunt Patience and brutish Uncle Joss. Working at the dilapidated Jamaica Inn, where thieves and smugglers come to divide their spoils and pirates plot their next raids, Mary discovers a secret about her father's death. Alone and afraid, Mary feels a sexual (although not romantic) attraction to Jem Merlyn, Joss's younger brother and a domineering ruffian not above violence. In the background lurks the mysterious vicar of Altarnum, who hides a few secrets of his own. With its twisted motives, midnight crimes, smugglers, and secrets, this is du Maurier at her best. Although depicting a rather pessimistic view of the plight of women as helpless and subservient, the fast-paced adventure gains fresh popularity with each new generation of readers who discover it.

The House on the Strand

In du Maurier's penultimate novel, *The House on the Strand* (the last among five du Maurier books featuring a male protagonist), the narrator, Dick, travels back to fourteenth century England, his journeys made possible by an experimental drug concocted by his scientist friend and mentor, Magnus. A stereotypical "nice guy," Dick marries an American who is already mother to two sons. Dick is no fan of women (including his wife), judging the feminine point of view trivial and restrictive, but he changes his mind when he becomes entranced with Isolda, a woman of the fourteenth century who is saddled with a faithless husband. Dick develops as a pathetic character who longs for perceived glories of the past but can find no fulfillment in any epoch, past or present.

Combining historical fact with psychological analysis, the book paints the same haunting atmosphere so apparent in du Maurier's earlier works, this time using the Kilmarth house in Cornwall and its rich history as both setting and theme. Dick's unwillingness to be pulled away from his time travels reflects du Maurier's own total immersion in her fantasy worlds. When writing, she lost herself in the lives of her characters, finding real life little more than a distraction and an annoyance.

Faith Hickman Brynie

Other major works

SHORT FICTION: *Come Wind, Come Weather*, 1940; *Happy Christmas*, 1940; *The Apple Tree: A Short Novel and Some Stories*, 1952 (also known as *The Birds, and Other Stories* and as *Kiss Me Again, Stranger: A Collection of Eight Stories*); *Early Stories*, 1955; *The Breaking Point*, 1959 (also known as *The Blue Lenses, and Other Stories*); *The Treasury of du Maurier Short Stories*, 1960; *Not After Midnight, and Other Stories*, 1971 (also known as *Don't Look Now*); *Echoes from the Macabre*, 1976; *The Rendezvous, and Other Stories*, 1980; *Classics of the Macabre*, 1987.

PLAYS: *Rebecca: A Play in Three Acts*, pr. 1940 (adaptation of her novel); *The Years Between*, pr. 1944; *September Tide*, pr. 1948.

NONFICTION: *Gerald: A Portrait*, 1934; *The du Mauriers*, 1937; *The Infernal World of Branwell Brontë*, 1960; *Vanishing Cornwall*, 1967; *Golden Lads: Sir Francis Bacon, Anthony Bacon, and Their Friends*, 1975; *The Winding Stair: Francis Bacon, His Rise and Fall*, 1976; *Growing Pains: The Shaping of a Writer*, 1977 (also known as *Myself When Young: The Shaping of a Writer*); *The Rebecca Notebook, and Other Memories*, 1980; *Letters from Menabilly: Portrait of a Friendship*, 1994 (Oriel Malet, editor).

EDITED TEXTS: *The Young George du Maurier: A Selection of His Letters, 1860-1867*, 1951; *Best Stories of Phyllis Bottome*, 1963.

Bibliography

Auerbach, Nina. *Daphne du Maurier, Haunted Heiress*. Philadelphia: University of Pennsylvania Press, 1999. Auerbach discusses her literary passion for du Maurier and demonstrates how du Maurier's work has been inaccurately categorized as romance fiction. Includes a chapter on du Maurier's family that examines how du Maurier's fiction was a reaction to her male heritage.

Cook, Judith. *Daphne: A Portrait of Daphne du Maurier*. London: Bantam Books, 1991. Thorough biography offers perceptive insights into du Maurier's life and work.

Du Maurier, Daphne. *Letters from Menabilly: Portrait of a Friendship*. Edited by Oriel Malet. New York: M. Evans, 1994. Presents a selection of du Maurier's correspondence with writer Oriel Malet, which took place for about thirty years beginning in the 1950's. Some of du Maurier's letters describe her family, her marriage to General Sir Frederick Browning, and her past life.

Forster, Margaret. *Daphne du Maurier: The Secret Life of the Renowned Storyteller*. New York: Doubleday, 1993. A candid, meticulous, and riveting biography, prepared with cooperation of the du Maurier family after du Maurier's death. Focuses on the motivations behind the author's works.

Horner, Avril, and Sue Zlosnik. *Daphne du Maurier: Writing, Identity, and the Gothic Imagination*. New York: St. Martin's Press, 1998. Evaluates du Maurier's fiction from historical, cultural, geographic, and female gothic literary perspectives. In addition to a discussion of *Rebecca*, presents analyses of her lesser-known novels, including *I'll Never Be Young Again* and *The Flight of the Falcon*.

Kelly, Richard Michael. *Daphne du Maurier*. Boston: Twayne, 1987. Provides a solid introduction to the author's works. Includes bibliography and index.

Leng, Flavia. *Daphne du Maurier: A Daughter's Memoir*. Edinburgh: Mainstream, 1994. In recounting her childhood, Leng provides a powerful portrait of her mother, Daphne du Maurier. Describes du Maurier's love for Cornwall and her estrangement from family and friends.

Taylor, Helen, ed. *The Daphne du Maurier Companion*. London: Virago, 2007. Collection of essays presents a reassessment of du Maurier's work, with essays examining her novels, short stories, and biographies. Includes analyses of the film adaptations of her works, such as director Alfred Hitchcock's films *Rebecca* and *The Birds*.

JOHN GREGORY DUNNE

Born: Hartford, Connecticut; May 25, 1932
Died: New York, New York; December 30, 2003

Principal long fiction

True Confessions, 1977
Dutch Shea, Jr., 1982
The Red White and Blue, 1987
Playland, 1994
Nothing Lost, 2004

Other literary forms

In addition to his novels, John Gregory Dunne produced a distinguished body of nonfiction, including a memoir, *Harp* (1989), and other personal and autobiographical essays. One of his primary subjects was Hollywood, the focus of both *The Studio* (1969) and *Monster: Living off the Big Screen* (1997). His first book, *Delano: The Story of the California Grape Strike* (1967, revised 1971), reflects his early career in journalism. He combined his talents as autobiographer and reporter in *Vegas: A Memoir of a Dark Season* (1974), which recounts a time of crisis in his marriage and in his writing career, set in the milieu of a stunning cast of characters who thrive in the mecca of legal gambling. Dunne's travel writing is featured in *Crooning* (1990), a collection of essays that also contains a number of his reflections on

Hollywood, the American West, and politics. *Quintana and Friends* (1978), another collection of essays, is autobiographical (Quintana is the name of his adopted daughter) and focuses on his personal account of moving from his roots in the eastern United States to a career as a Hollywood screenwriter. Uniting much of Dunne's fiction and nonfiction are his concerns with his Irish background and sensibility as well as the world of urban crime and scandal and the role of institutions such as the family, the Roman Catholic Church, politics, and the entertainment industry. *Regards: The Selected Nonfiction of John Gregory Dunne* (2006) includes several essays published in the last fifteen years of his life and previously uncollected in book form, as well as his 1996 *Paris Review* interview.

Achievements

John Gregory Dunne's fiction falls within the tradition of the crime novel as developed by Dashiell Hammett and Raymond Chandler. Like Hammett's, Dunne's novels feature a gritty realism, although his detectives tend to be less hard-boiled and romanticized than those of his predecessors. Dunne shares much of Chandler's fascination with Los Angeles. In other words, Dunne's obsession with crime and detection reveals a profound concern with the corruption of urban society. Also like Hammett and Chandler, Dunne is an elegant stylist. Although his sense of plot construction is not as acute as that of the greatest detective novelists, his probing of characters and milieu is reminiscent of writers such as F. Scott Fitzgerald and Nathanael West. Like Fitzgerald and West, Dunne sets some of his fiction in Hollywood, where Americans seem particularly free to invent themselves.

Dunne's fiction recalls Fitzgerald's *The Last Tycoon* (1941) and *The Great Gatsby* (1925), for it takes up the theme of the easterner who moves West to find his fortune and a new identity. Dunne, however, adds a keen concern with ethnicity and religion that earlier crime and mystery writers confront only fleetingly and with embarrassing stereotypes. Dunne's Irish men and women, for example, are not only sophisticated and working class, white and blue collar, powerful politicians and churchmen, but also immigrants and criminals. Dunne's unique contribution to the crime novel was to give it a sociological context and a depth of background without sacrificing the drama and intense curiosity about events and people that are requisite in mystery fiction. Dunne's final novel, published in 2004 shortly after his death, exploits his deft understanding of politics and the legal system and shows no diminution of his narrative powers or of his ability to create memorable characters.

Biography

John Gregory Dunne, born on May 25, 1932, in Hartford, Connecticut, was the fifth of six children born to Richard Edward and Dorothy Burns Dunne. In many ways, Dunne's family enjoyed the typical immigrant success story. His maternal grandfather arrived in the United States from Ireland shortly after the American Civil War, an uneducated boy who could not read. He became a grocer and then a banker in Frog Hollow, Hartford's Irish ghetto. Dunne grew up with stories about his Irish ancestors' assimilation in America and with a sense of being a "harp," a derogatory term for the Irish, who were considered inferior by the city's Anglo-Saxon establishment.

An indifferent student, Dunne nevertheless managed to complete four years at Princeton University and earn an undergraduate degree. Not knowing what to do after graduation, he enlisted in the U.S. Army, a decision he credits in *Harp*, his autobiography, with helping to ground him with a sense not only of society's complexity but also of its very rich resources in humanity. Had he remained in the elitist milieu of Princeton, Dunne suggests, his career as a writer would have been seriously limited, if not entirely vitiated, by the lack of worldly experience he deemed necessary for a writer.

Dunne's development as a novelist proceeded slowly. He began writing short pieces for newspapers before landing a job on the staff of *Time* magazine. There he labored for six years in New York City, meeting writer Joan Didion, whom he married on January 30, 1964. Although she was already an accomplished journalist and novelist, Didion found herself undergoing a creative crisis, and the couple decided to move to California, where Didion had grown up and where Dunne hoped to find the material to begin writing both fiction and nonfiction. Husband and wife also began collaborating on screenplays as a way of supporting themselves while they worked on longer fiction and nonfiction projects. After two decades of residence in California, Dunne and Didion moved back to New York City, continuing to collaborate on screenplays as well as working separately on their fiction and nonfiction. Dunne continued to write essays for *The New York Review of Books*. He suffered from a heart condition that worsened during the last decade of his life, and he died of a heart attack at his Manhattan home on December 30, 2003.

John Gregory Dunne. (Time & Life Pictures/Getty Images)

Analysis

All of John Gregory Dunne's novels are about power and personal integrity. The power is exercised by Roman Catholic prelates, the police, criminals, studio bosses and producers, quasi-legitimate businessmen, and politicians. The person of integrity is often the estranged member of a family, such as Jack Broderick in *The Red White and Blue* and *Playland* or Tom Spellacy in Dunne's brilliant debut novel, *True Confessions*. The head of the family—Jack's father, Hugh Broderick, or Tom Spellacy's brother, Des (Desmond), for example—stands for the patriarchal and corrupt aspects of society. Tom Spellacy may have spurned his brother Des's ambitious careerism in the Church, but he has also been a bagman for a local crime king. Jack Broderick has not followed his father into the world of high-stakes politics and business, yet he writes screenplays for craven Hollywood producers. In other words, even Dunne's moral characters are compromised. They come by their moral code precisely because they are flawed figures. Dunne's early exposure to Roman Catholicism is most telling in his awareness of how virtue and vice coincide.

True Confessions

True Confessions begins and ends in the 1970's, when Tom Spellacy has retired from the police department and his brother Des, an ambitious Catholic clergyman, is spending the last of his thirty years of exile in a small, neglected parish. Somehow Tom's actions have led to his brother's downfall, and the heart of the novel, "Then" (set in the 1940's), tells the story that leads to "Now," the first and last chapters.

The first "Now" section centers on Des's call to his brother Tom. Why, Tom wonders, has Des summoned him to his parish in the desert? The brothers have been intensely preoccupied with each other and yet estranged. Although one has chosen a career in the police department and the other the Church, they are both worldly men. Tom cannot seem to live down his corrupt period on the vice squad, when he was "on the take," a bagman for Jack Amsterdam, a supposedly legitimate contractor and a pillar of the Church, but in fact a thug with numerous illicit enterprises. Amsterdam is the link between the careers of the two brothers, since Des has relied on Amsterdam to construct many of his parish's impressive church buildings, even though Des knows that Amsterdam has padded his payroll and physically intimidated other contractors so that they have not put in bids for the construction projects. Des has also functioned as a kind of enforcer for Cardinal Danaher, who is trying to centralize power by depriving parish priests of their autonomy.

When the two brothers meet in the opening section of the novel, Des tells Tom that he is dying. It is this announcement that precipitates the action of the novel, as Tom remembers the events that have led to his brother's dramatic announcement.

"Then" begins as a traditional murder mystery. A woman is found with her body hacked in two. There is no blood, which suggests the body has been moved from another location. The cut is clean, indicating that a very sharp instrument was used.

Tom Spellacy is goaded into action by his boss, Fred Fuqua, who is yearning to become chief of police. Fuqua is a systems man. He claims to be able to find patterns in crime, though he has little sense of street life or of how crimes are committed. What also goads Tom, however, is his intuition that larger forces—namely, Jack Amsterdam—are somehow connected to the mutilated body. Tom's search for the murderer and his gunning for Amsterdam also set in motion the forces that expose Des's complicity in evil and lead to his banishment from the center of power.

DUTCH SHEA, JR.

Dutch Shea, Jr. is one of Dunne's darkest novels. It includes an epigraph by the poet Gerard Manley Hopkins, "I awake and feel the fell of dark, not day." Its second epigraph provides a hint of understanding, if not redemption: "for we possess nothing certainly except the past"—a line from novelist Evelyn Waugh. Significantly, both Hopkins and Waugh were Catholics who found in their religion a way of analyzing and coping with the world's corruption and blindness. This novel of occluded vision is reminiscent of Saint Paul's admonition that "we see as through a glass darkly."

Dutch Shea's father was sent to prison for embezzlement, and attorney Dutch is well on the way to committing a similar crime, having held back money owed to one of his clients, now in a nursing home. Dutch's demons also drive him, however, to defend criminal suspects that other attorneys spurn. His wife has left him, and he is carrying on a covert relationship with a female judge. He mourns his adopted daughter, who was blown up in an Irish Republican Army (IRA) bombing in London, but he has also seduced his surrogate father's Irish immigrant servant. He suspects that his surrogate father was somehow involved in the crime that put his father in prison, and much of the novel deals with Dutch's conflicted feelings: He is at once burning to know exactly how and why his father turned to crime and terribly afraid of knowing the worst. What Dutch never sees, however, is that the story he is investigating—his attempt to find the Irish immigrant girl he seduced—will lead him to a confrontation not only with the mystery of why his father sinned and committed suicide in prison but also with his own failings as husband and lover.

Like *True Confessions*, *Dutch Shea, Jr.* thrives on lively dialogue and shrewd character assessments. It lacks the drive of Dunne's first novel, however, perhaps because it does not have a tightly constructed plot and its themes seem not only derivative of *True Confessions* but also devoid of fresh treatment.

THE RED WHITE AND BLUE

Whereas *True Confessions* centers on Los Angeles and is tightly woven around the tensions between Tom and Des, and *Dutch Shea, Jr.* explores the career of a disaffected and down-and-out lawyer trying to regain a coherent life for himself and a tolerable vision of the world, *The Red White and Blue* functions on a broader canvas, as an ambitious novel that represents Dunne's bid to encompass the epic sweep of contemporary American history. The Broderick family of the novel vaguely resembles the Kennedy family of American politics. Again there is a struggle between two brothers, Bro (another ambitious churchman) and Jack (the less determined screenwriter). Both brothers, however, disappoint their father, Hugh, a kind of Joseph Kennedy figure, the confidant of presidents and other power brokers, an amoral man who finds Bro's talents wasted on the Church and Jack's lack of drive pathetic and almost beneath his notice.

As the novel's narrator, Jack resembles Tom Spellacy, for, as is true of Tom, it is Jack's nearness to power coupled with his distaste for it that makes him both keen observer and critic. Each of the male Brodericks focuses, in turn, on Leah Kaye, a radical attorney whose moral and political principles are opposed to the Brodericks'.

Leah becomes sexually involved with all three of the Broderick men, and her personal and political entanglements are further examples of the difficulty of separating the worlds of virtue and vice in Dunne's fiction.

Like *Dutch Shea, Jr.*, *The Red White and Blue* seems a falling off from *True Confessions*. All three novels are immensely polished performances, yet only the first seems original in its intensity and language, while the second seems repetitive and the third too diffuse. The machinations of the Brodericks are less intricate and tawdry than those of their real-life models, the Kennedys.

PLAYLAND

Dunne's fourth novel represents a recovery of the author's full novelistic powers. It not only has the intensity of *True Confessions* but also manages to incorporate the broader canvas that seems too thin in *The Red White and Blue*. Jack Broderick is the narrator, and Dunne puts his own experience as a Hollywood screenwriter into full play, as Jack sets off on a quest to find the reclusive Blue Tyler, a child star of the 1930's rumored to be living in a trailer park in Hamtramck, Michigan.

As Jack is researching Tyler's life and interviewing her, he is negotiating with Hollywood producer Marty Magnin to turn the project into a film. Bits of screenplay are interwoven throughout the narrative, as Broderick writes and rewrites Tyler's life, realizing that he is often speculating, turning guesses into narrative even as he tries to resist the Hollywood touches on which his producer insists.

Playland's gangster character, Jacob King, is reminiscent of Fitzgerald's Jay Gatsby, and Jack's quest to understand the King-Tyler love affair by interviewing various witnesses also calls to mind the 1941 film *Citizen Kane*. The humor, sex, and violence are as crude as in the cheapest crime novels, but Jack's desire to get the story right, even as he realizes there cannot be a single authentic version, elevates *Playland* to the ranks of the most distinguished works about Hollywood, including Fitzgerald's *The Last Tycoon* and Norman Mailer's play *The Deer Park* (pb. 1967). *Playland* also includes stunning settings in Las Vegas and Detroit, giving the novel the all-encompassing geographic and historical reach that Dunne had been working toward since the brilliant success of *True Confessions*.

NOTHING LOST

Dunne's last novel is set in the small town of Regent, South Midland—apparently a fictional version of South Dakota. At any rate, this heartland setting is the locus for a brutal murder: A well-liked African American man is bludgeoned to death and then stripped of his flesh. Although this would seem an obvious case of a racially motivated crime, in fact the story of Edgar Parlance's gruesome death is far more elusive and ambiguous than either the court system or the press can fathom. The novel's narrator, Max Cline, a prosecutor turned defense attorney, gradually pieces together part of what happened to Parlance, assembling testimony from a cast of characters with varying degrees of reliability. In the end, vital aspects of the Parlance case remain unresolved in favor of a nuanced and sharply observant portrayal of a people and a place reminiscent of William Faulkner's best work, such as *Absalom, Absalom!* (1936), or of the greatest nonfiction as exemplified in Rebecca West's classic essay "Mr. Setty and Mr. Hume" in *A Train of Powder* (1955).

Cline is a superb choice for a narrator because he has worked for the establishment and yet is an outsider. Jewish and gay, he had only a short-lived career in the attorney general's office, and his switch to defense work makes him a pariah among law-enforcement types and in his community, since he is regarded as protecting the very kinds of criminals he used to incarcerate. Cline sports his outsider credentials wryly, so that while he may irritate the establishment, nothing in his behavior actually can be charged with causing offense. He thus insinuates himself into the action, so to speak, avoiding confrontations but picking up bits of evidence overlooked by the police. In the Parlance case, he has a cocounsel, Teresa Kean, whose own story and affair with J. J. McClure, the prosecutor and ostensibly her adversary, complicates Cline's work but also leads him closer to the reality of what happened to Parlance.

Cline works with the sensibility of a novelist. Indeed, it has been noted that Cline's voice resembles the one Dunne employed in his nonfiction. Perhaps because Cline has been the object of hate and ridicule, he is slow to sit in judgment of McClure's and Kean's unethical behavior and Kean's efforts to hide her affair from Cline. Kean, like Duane Lajoie, the man she is defending, is the product of a fraught background and of forces she ultimately finds it impossible to control.

Not much more can be said of the plot of *Nothing Lost* without giving away the secrets Cline so assiduously explores. Suffice it to say that a number of critics have asserted that *Nothing Lost* is Dunne's finest novel. It has been compared to the best work of John D. MacDonald and John O'Hara because of Dunne's sure handling of both the novel's mystery elements and its social observations.

Carl Rollyson

Other major works

SCREENPLAYS: *The Panic in Needle Park*, 1971 (with Joan Didion); *Play It as It Lays*, 1972 (with Didion); *A Star Is Born*, 1976 (with Didion); *True Confessions*, 1981 (with Didion); *The War*, 1994 (with Didion); *Up Close and Personal*, 1996 (with Didion).

TELEPLAYS: *Hills Like White Elephants*, 1990; *L.A. Is It*, 1991.

NONFICTION: *Delano: The Story of the California Grape Strike*, 1967 (revised 1971); *The Studio*, 1969; *Vegas: A Memoir of a Dark Season*, 1974; *Quintana and Friends*, 1978; *Harp*, 1989; *Crooning: A Collection*, 1990; *Monster: Living off the Big Screen*, 1997; *Regards: The Selected Nonfiction of John Gregory Dunne*, 2006.

Bibliography

Dunne, John Gregory. *Harp*. New York: Simon & Schuster, 1989. Dunne's memoir is one of the best sources available for both biographical information on the author and insight into the sources and themes of his fiction.

Edwards, Thomas R. "The Awful Truth." *The New York Review of Books*, June 24, 2004. Long, thoughtful review of *Nothing Lost* takes into account the entire trajectory of Dunne's career. Provides especially perceptive discussion of the connections between Dunne's fiction and his nonfiction.

Fanning, Charles. *The Irish Voice in America: 250 Years of Irish-American Fiction*. 2d ed. Lexington: University Press of Kentucky, 2000. Comprehensive scholarly work includes discussion of Dunne as an Irish American writer.

Keane, James. T. "Savagery in South Midland." *America*, February 21, 2005. Review of *Nothing Lost* commends Dunne for creating a notable cast of characters and for his satiric portrayal of the American media as well as of the conniving practices of both local, state, and national politicians.

Thomson, David. "*Playland*." *The New Republic*, August 22, 1994. Highly critical review of the novel includes an astute assessment of Dunne's style and his handling of Hollywood themes.

Winchell, Mark Roydon. *Joan Didion*. Rev. ed. Boston: Twayne, 1989. Includes brief discussion of Dunne's work and the Dunne-Didion marriage. Chapter 1 provides a good overview of Dunne's and Didion's reactions to the American East and West Coasts in their writing.

_______. *John Gregory Dunne*. Boise, Idaho: Boise State University Press, 1986. Brief work provides a solid introduction to Dunne's biography and to the backgrounds of his fiction. Discusses only the first two novels and Dunne's early nonfiction. Includes a useful bibliography.

MARGUERITE DURAS

Marguerite Donnadieu

Born: Gia Dinh, Indochina (now Vietnam); April 4, 1914

Died: Paris, France; March 3, 1996

Also known as: Marguerite Donnadieu

Principal long fiction

Les Impudents, 1943
La Vie tranquille, 1944
Un Barrage contre le Pacifique, 1950 (*The Sea Wall*, 1952; also known as *A Sea of Troubles*, 1953)
Le Marin de Gibraltar, 1952 (*The Sailor from Gibraltar*, 1966)
Les Petits Chevaux de Tarquinia, 1953 (*The Little Horses of Tarquinia*, 1960)
Le Square, 1955 (*The Square*, 1959)
Moderato Cantabile, 1958 (English translation, 1960)
Dix heures et demie du soir en été, 1960 (*Ten-Thirty on a Summer Night*, 1962)
L'Après-midi de Monsieur Andesmas, 1962 (*The Afternoon of Monsieur Andesmas*, 1964)
Le Ravissement de Lol V. Stein, 1964 (*The Ravishing of Lol Stein*, 1966)
Le Vice-consul, 1966 (*The Vice-Consul*, 1968)
L'Amante anglaise, 1967 (English translation, 1968)
Détruire, dit-elle, 1969 (*Destroy, She Said*, 1970)
Abahn Sabana David, 1970
L'Amour, 1971
India Song: Texte-théâtre-film, 1973 (English translation, 1976)
La Maladie de la morte, 1982 (*The Malady of Death*, 1986)
L'Amant, 1984 (*The Lover*, 1985)
Emily L., 1987 (English translation, 1989)
Les Yeux bleus, cheveux noirs, 1987 (*Blue Eyes, Black Hair*, 1987)
La Pluie d'été, 1990 (*Summer Rain*, 1992)
L'Amant de la Chine du Nord, 1991 (*The North China Lover*, 1992)
Yann Andrea Steiner, 1992 (*Yann Andrea Steiner: A Memoir*, 1993)

Other literary forms

In addition to her novels (most of which were published by Gallimard, with the exception of *Moderato Cantabile* and *Destroy, She Said*, which were published by Minuit, the press favored by the New Novelists), Marguerite Duras (dew-RAH) published a collection of short stories, *Des journées entières dans les arbres* (1954; *Days in the Trees*, 1967), and two short texts, *L'Homme assis dans le couloir* (1980; *The Man Sitting in the Corridor*, 1991) and *L'Homme atlantique* (1982; *The Atlantic Man*, 1993). Duras was also known as a prolific playwright, and her plays were regularly performed on the French stage. In 1969, Duras turned to filmmaking as her principal activity, perhaps encouraged by the success of her scenario for director Alain Resnais's *Hiroshima mon amour* (1959; *Hiroshima mon amour: Text by Marguerite Duras for the Film by Alain Resnais*, 1961). In 1961, she collaborated with Gérard Jarlot on the script for *Une Aussi Longue Absence* (English translation, 1966), directed by Henri Colpi, and in 1969, she wrote and directed her first film, *Détruire, dit-elle*, avowedly inspired by the May, 1968, leftist revolution. Her other films include *Nathalie Granger* (1972), *La Femme du Gange* (1973), *Baxter, Véra Baxter* (1976), *Son nom de Venise dans Calcutta désert* (1976), *Des journées entières dans les arbres* (1976), *Le Camion* (1977), *Aurélia Steiner* (1979), *Agatha: Ou, Les Lectures illisibles* (1982), and *L'Homme atlantique* (1982). Duras evolved a new "hybrid" genre with works such as *India Song*, subtitled *Texte-théâtre-film*, and *Le Navire "Night"* (1979). *India Song*, the 1973 film, was awarded a special prize at the Cannes Film Festival in 1975.

Achievements

In 1984, Marguerite Duras's novel *The Lover* won the Prix Paris Ritz Hemingway and the coveted Prix Goncourt. Despite her affinities with the New Novelists, who gained prominence in the 1950's and 1960's

(Nathalie Sarraute, Michel Butor, Alain Robbe-Grillet, Claude Simon, and Robert Pinget), Duras steadfastly refrained from aligning herself with any one school of literature. She had a deep concern for human values, and some of her fiction of the early 1970's is definitely marked by the events of May, 1968, which proclaimed an end to excessive governmental control in France and sought a more egalitarian society. For the most part, however, Duras's novels address political issues indirectly. Her talents as a writer lie in character portrayal, particularly in her studies of female protagonists caught in the imaginative re-creation of a passionate love. In her later works, Duras eschews straightforward analysis of characters' emotions for an allusive style that evokes fantasies and imaginations through a lyric, often fragmented, prose. As a result of numerous interviews in periodicals and on television and through her prodigious output in fiction, drama, and film, Duras became a highly visible, often controversial, figure on the French literary scene. Her work has gained recognition abroad as well, and most of her novels have been translated into English.

Biography

Marguerite Duras was born Marguerite Donnadieu on April 4, 1914, in Gia Dinh, Indochina (now Vietnam), where her parents came to teach from northern France. Her father died when she was young, and her mother undertook the rearing of two sons and a daughter by farming a government land grant. Duras's attachment to her older brother and her ambivalent feelings toward her feisty and domineering mother are sketched in many of the novels but most particularly in *The Sea Wall*. The exotic landscape of Indochina, where Duras attended the *lycée* and took her *baccalauréat* in Vietnamese and French, colors her fiction. She excels at evoking a steamy, although often suffocating, atmosphere in settings that are rich in sensual vegetation.

In 1931, Duras went to Paris to continue her education, earning a *licence* in law and political science in 1935. A secretary for the Colonial Ministry from 1935 to 1941, she married Robert Antelme, an active member of the Communist Party and author of *L'Espèce humaine* (1947). Her own membership in the party and her participation in the Resistance movement during World War II bespoke a strong sense of political commitment, which she later rejected. It was during the war that she began to work at Gallimard and to write fiction. Although her first manuscript, "La Famille Taneran," was never published, she was encouraged by Raymond Queneau to continue writing. Divorced from Antelme, Duras met Dionys Mascolo, a fellow Communist and author of a book about the Communist Party; they had a son, Jean. In 1950, Duras was one of a number of intellectuals excommunicated from the French Communist Party. As a result of this experience and, later, the revolution of May, 1968, she advocated a rejection of all ideology and a negation of bourgeois values and social conventions.

During the 1960's, Duras was a journalist and conducted interviews on French television. In 1963, she achieved notoriety for her exposé of the Ben Barka affair during the Algerian revolt. She has also written articles for *Vogue* magazine and published short texts for feminist publications such as *Sorcières*. Duras lightheartedly satirized her own milieu, the intellectual Saint-Germain-des-Prés area of Paris, in a short story, "Madame Dodin." Her country home in Neauphle-le-Château, outside Paris, served as the setting for some of her films. Duras died on March 3, 1996, after a long battle with alcoholism.

Analysis

All of Marguerite Duras's novels revolve around the central theme of love, a necessary and impossible passion that is most often addressed in a climate of violence and left unsatisfied. Several studies of Duras's fiction divide the novels into three groups or periods. The first includes the traditional, autobiographical novels, often referred to as an American-inspired type of fiction, emulating the Hemingwayesque novel of adventure. These early works set forth most of the themes that are elaborated in subsequent novels. *Les Impudents*, *La Vie tranquille*, and *The Sea Wall* are concerned with young heroines in search of a lover or husband to fill the emptiness of their existence. Passive, lethargic women, they seek incarnation in the other, and their inner void is indistinguishable from the ennui and stagnation of their environment. They must wrench themselves from the domination of a brother or a mother, and, at the novel's conclusion, their success is ambiguous.

The second phase of Duras's novelistic career begins with *The Sailor from Gibraltar*; in this novel and its kin, the protagonists are preoccupied with unhappy love affairs from the past, which they attempt to reenact in the present. Similarly, in the screenplay *Hiroshima mon amour*, the French actress confuses her adolescent affair during World War II with an illicit affair in the present in a city that is a constant reminder of a tragic past. In *Ten-Thirty on a Summer Night*, a married couple turns to infidelity in order to mediate their past desires for each other. The wife's encounter with a criminal in a city besieged by violent storms is Duras's indirect affirmation of the destructive aspect of their love. Anne, in *Moderato Cantabile*, reenacts with Chauvin a crime of passion that they have both witnessed at the beginning of the novel. Eros and Thanatos are clearly linked in these novels, where the re-creation of love provokes desires and fantasies associated with crime, disorder, death, and destruction. In this second group of novels, Duras's style begins to conform to her subject matter. The verbosity of description and the careful delineation of narrative events that marked the earlier works are discarded for a more poetic, allusive style in which characters' motives and incidents of plot are evoked in a gesture or setting and emphasized through repetition. The atmosphere of violence associated with destructive passion begins to affect textual structure and style.

The Ravishing of Lol Stein begins a third group of novels. Duras said of this text that, whereas *Moderato Cantabile* is a finished product, the story of Lol was continually in the process of being written. For the most part, Duras's subsequent fiction embodies fragments both of *The Ravishing of Lol Stein* and of her earlier works. Text thus mirrors content (characters' memory or re-creation of past events), and it becomes clear that protagonists' desires are equated with memory and writing, equally fictitious. The incipient stylistic and structural violence of the second group of novels is accentuated in this third group. Sentences and paragraphs are reduced to lyric fragments of the story, decor is stylized, characters' identities are blurred, chronological time yields to phenomenological duration, and narrative control is abandoned in favor of poetic evocation. What has come to be known as the India cycle, comprising *The Ravishing of Lol Stein*, *The Vice-Consul*, *L'Amour*, and *India Song*, is but a series of decanted versions of the same story, one that springs from Duras's childhood and adolescent experiences in French Indochina. In a sense, the story of love and desire is progressively internalized and made to reverberate in its repetitions.

THE SEA WALL

Because of its critical success, *The Sea Wall* marks a turning point in Duras's career as a novelist. Published in 1950, the novel was translated into English in 1952 and was adapted for the screen by René Clément in 1967. Often compared with the fiction of Ernest Hemingway, *The Sea Wall* is a fictionalized account of Duras's experiences in colonial Indochina—the sentimental education of its eighteen-year-old protagonist Suzanne and, to a lesser degree, of her older brother Joseph. It is also the story of the siblings' mother, known as Ma. Like Duras's own mother, Ma is a widowed French teacher who had settled with her husband in the colonial city of Ram, near

Marguerite Duras. (New Press)

the Gulf of Siam. Forced to support the children after the death of her husband, she works nights as a piano player at the Éden Cinéma (whence comes the title of Duras's 1977 play) in order to buy a land grant from the French government. Her dreams of establishing a fortune by farming are shattered when she realizes that she, like the other settlers in the area, has been sold an uncultivable tract of land by the corrupt colonial government. The farmland is inundated by the Pacific during the summer rainy season. Ma's story is one of a Herculean, almost ludicrous attempt to hold back the forces of nature by constructing a dam at the ocean's edge. Her revolt against the Pacific and her angry protests against government corruption are evidence of her undaunted and overweaning spirit. Suzanne and Joseph must liberate themselves from their mother's control if they are to pass from adolescence to adulthood.

Most of the novel centers upon Suzanne's relationship with the men who actively court her. The wealthy Monsieur Jo represents release from the hardships of life on the plains and from Joseph and Ma. Suzanne feels nothing for him, but she prostitutes herself in order to satisfy her family's materialistic longings. Passivity characterizes most of Duras's protagonists: Their desires remain lodged in the imagination. Suzanne's concept of love derives from long afternoons watching romantic films at the Éden Cinéma. A modern-day Emma Bovary, Suzanne's interpretation of the stormy, passionate affairs that she sees on the screen is that love is destructive and tinged with violence, a conclusion emblematic of her own repressed desire. Like so many Durasian heroines, Suzanne fantasizes love, and, although she succeeds in working out some of her fantasies in other relationships, particularly with Jean Agosti, her emotional involvement is still characterized by passivity, and she retreats into a bitter stoicism. In the subplot concerning her brother, Joseph turns to women and drink to escape from the quotidian boredom in this desolate outpost. At the novel's end, however, the only true release for the siblings comes with their mother's death.

The exotic Vietnamese landscape is a lush background for this novel of thwarted dreams and repressed sexuality. Duras's descriptions of the tropical forest and the forceful powers of the sea are rich in a feminine sensuality. The spiritual and physical misery of life on the plains, together with the sexual awakening of Suzanne and Joseph, bathe the novel in an atmosphere of morbidity and longing. The theme of desire is firmly implanted in the Durasian corpus, to be picked up and elaborated in succeeding novels. The memories of a harsh yet sensuous childhood spent in Vietnam haunt the author and are reflected in practically everything that she has written. Her talent for dialogue—which sparks her plays and films—is evident in this novel, in which characters seem to talk past one another and in which the revelation of feeling resides in what is left unsaid rather than in what is explicitly stated.

Moderato Cantabile

Like *The Sea Wall*, *Moderato Cantabile* is the study of a female protagonist caught in a web of fantasy and repressed desire. Duras's most critically acclaimed novel, *Moderato Cantabile* is a masterpiece of stylistic control and emotional transport. Duras prefers to call this text a poem rather than a novel and refers to it as a "metaphysical adventure organically experienced in a blinding moment of near-imbecility." Clearly, the rational forces of order (the *moderato* principle) in this work are in constant conflict with the disorder of a passionate madness (the *cantabile*) in a poetic evocation of an inner experience. Duras eschews the direct, linear narrative of the first group of novels for a more lyric prose.

The central character, whose inner adventure governs the telling of the tale, is Anne, the wife of a prominent factory owner in an unidentified port town. She encounters Chauvin, an unemployed former worker in her husband's factory, at the scene of a crime of passion: the murder of an unfaithful wife by her madly jealous husband. Duras has indicated that the entire novel—and thus fantasy—was generated from this initial scene, in particular from the morbidly erotic image of the husband licking the blood from his dead wife's face, a strange expression of desire in his eyes. Against this backdrop, Anne Desbaresdes and Chauvin meet almost daily in the café to work out in their imaginations the motivation for the crime. The theme of writing and remembering the past as pure fantasy or desire is accentuated as the novel develops and as the reader realizes that Anne and Chauvin are writing their own story of desire, intertwining inventions of possible motivations for the crime with fragments of their own lives. Self-conscious narration, along with a blurring of events and character psychology, aligns this work with the New Novel.

The story unfolds in a contrapuntal fashion best illustrated by the title; it refers to the weekly piano lesson to which Anne accompanies her free-spirited little boy, who refuses to heed his teacher's injunction to play a sonatina *moderato cantabile*. The sonatina is closely associated with the murder, because the crime (the gunshots and cries of the townspeople) interrupts the piano lesson in the opening scene of the novel. The basic conflict between order and disorder is amplified by the very impossibility of the task imposed upon the child. Oppositions in character and plot (between the disorderly child and the disciplined teacher, the bourgeois wife and the mother-adultress, musical culture and crime) are carried out in a quasi-mathematical fashion. Anne and Chauvin meet five times in the course of nine days in a re-creation of the emotional event that is itself a structure of opposites: The control of ritual alternates with the intoxication of liberated desires. These conflicts are buttressed by contrasting motifs in scenic descriptions. The tale is exploded into fragments of decor that are adumbrated in musical modulations. For example, in chapter 1, the pounding surf is indistinguishable from the woman's cry, the murmuring of the onlookers, and the child's attempt to attain the desired *moderato cantabile* at the piano. Throughout the text, scenic motifs, together with Anne and Chauvin's snatches of conversation, are introduced separately, intertwined, and intensified in an orchestration that leads to the climax of *moderato cantabile* at several different textual levels: the child's glorious rendition of the sonatina as marked, the orgasmic moment of the crime of passion, and finally the verbal consummation of Anne and Chauvin's imagined affair. When Chauvin symbolically kills Anne at the end ("I wish that you were dead"), she accepts it with relief ("So be it"), having worked out, in the realm of fantasy, her desires. The insistence on imagination and the almost fatalistic passivity with which Anne undergoes the ritual of self-negation with Chauvin link her to other Durasian protagonists, victims of a desire that they constantly seek to exorcise but that they are doomed to work out in their imaginations. *Moderato Cantabile*'s power lies in its musical resonance, prompting one critic to refer to this novel as "*Madame Bovary* rewritten by Béla Bartók."

The Ravishing of Lol Stein

The story of repressed desire that structures the plot of both *The Sea Wall* and *Moderato Cantabile* also informs Duras's 1964 novel, *The Ravishing of Lol Stein*. Like the preceding works, this text excels in character portrayal and evocation of decor; its protagonist, a sensitive but passive young woman who thrives on reliving a thwarted passion, is but another version of Suzanne and Anne. In narrative form, however, *The Ravishing of Lol Stein* goes further than either of the two earlier works in its subversion of traditional novelistic techniques. Conflicting elements of order and disorder, reason and madness, Eros and Thanatos, narrative control and narrative abdication serve to anchor the text in a series of contradictions. The very title, for example, suggests a dual interpretation of the heroine's predicament; the English title is an unfortunate mistranslation of the French. *Ravissement* is more accurately rendered as "ravishment," which can mean both ecstasy and ravage. This ambiguity recalls the juxtaposition of two contrary worlds implied by the title *Moderato Cantabile*. The contrapuntal technique continues to dominate Duras's style.

The Ravishing of Lol Stein marks a reorientation in Duras's writing; successive works, including those works of the India cycle, espouse a more open, less controlled form in a radical portrayal of the negation of self implicit in Duras's treatment of desire. These texts, in particular *The Vice-Consul*, *L'Amour*, *India Song*, and the film *Son nom de Venise dans Calcutta désert*, seem to flow musically from *The Ravishing of Lol Stein*, elaborating in fuguelike fashion its basic themes.

Set in a seaside village referred to as S. Thala, the decor is a stylized reflection of the lush, tropical landscape of Duras's youth in Vietnam. The site is emotionally charged in the novel and haunts the heroine of the story, Lola Valerie Stein, as a reminder of an unrequited love experienced when she was nineteen years old. At that time, she was engaged to be married to Michael Richardson, but, at a ball held at nearby T. Beach, she watched helplessly as her fiancé was seduced by an older, beautifully mysterious woman, Anne-Marie Stretter. In voyeuristic fashion, Lol observes their dance of desire from behind a row of plants. The scene of rejection that opens the novel has the same impact on Lol as the passionate crime that generates the action of *Moderato Cantabile*. It crystallizes Lol's identity in a "lack"; the center of her personality (which, the narrator informs the reader, has always been distant and difficult to grasp) is paradoxically "grounded" in negation and unfulfilled desire. Although she later marries, has children, and leads a "respectable" life, an undercurrent of violent desire threatens to burst forth at any moment. As in the case of Anne Desbaresdes, Lol's passion is triggered by an amorous encounter that is a reliving of the primal scene of triangular desire and exclusion.

The alliance of form and content already present in the second group of novels is perfected in the third group. The triangular mediation of desire that serves as catalyst for the plot is underscored by the novel's tripartite division. Part 1 relates Lol's initial rejection and her temporary madness. Part 2 deals with her marriage and espousal of bourgeois values, reflected in an excessive orderliness of manner. In both parts, the style is clean and direct, and the narrative is in the straightforward mode of the third person. In part 3, the breakdown of Lol's compulsive behavior, induced by an affair, is reflected in the narrative style, which becomes rambling and confused. When Lol is seduced by Jacques Hold, the lover of her best friend, Tatiana, she is thrust once again into a triangular situation; part 3 repeats part 1. The revelation, by a sudden intrusion of first-person narration, that the narrator is Jacques Hold and that the reader's perspective on preceding events has been manipulated by an interested character-narrator casts a different light on the story and accounts for the narrative confusion. Jacques's constant reminders in part 3 that he can only "believe" what happened and that he is "inventing" Lol's story erode the reader's confidence and underline the theme of memory as a fictive replay or rewriting of the past. Visually, the text betrays this erosion. Question marks, suppositions, hypothetical formulations, unfinished sentences, and blank spaces on the page convey an abdication of control and the very uncertainty of the text that is being read. Desire as lack is translated both formally and thematically.

Stylistic and narrational violence are complemented by subversive elements in time and place that enhance the portrayal of desire. Part 3, a replay or remembering of part 1 (which is itself a replay of preceding texts), continues the theme-and-variations pattern that characterizes the novel. The continual return to an elusive and illusional past succeeds in collapsing distinctions between past and present—a confusion supported by associations in the setting. Lol's seduction by Jacques Hold in part 3 takes place in a room reminiscent of the ballroom in part 1, to which Jacques and Lol make a pilgrimage. The site is consecrated as a sacred place of desire, like the café to which Anne and Chauvin return to reenact the passionate crime. Ambiguities resulting from confusion of past and present, ballroom and hotel room, occur also in character portrayal. The three female protagonists, Tatiana, Anne-Marie Stretter, and Lol, are variously described by the same characteristics of desire and death. They, like the entire Durasian corpus, take on the attributes of allegory in a progressively stylized and thus universalized story of absolute passion.

India Song

The publication of *India Song* in 1973 culminated the India cycle (which includes play and film); indeed, *India Song* is a transparent text through which are filtered the essential themes, characters, and events of Duras's novelistic world. It might be regarded as the allegorical blueprint of all Duras's preceding novels, containing them yet transcending them in an increasingly fragmented rendition of what Duras maintains in the preface to *India Song* to be the essence of her story, "a story of love immobilized in the culminating moment of passion."

The Malady of Death

In *The Malady of Death* the narrator, an unnamed woman, is paid to be at a man's disposal for several nights. The woman is seen as a commodity that can be purchased. Although the woman is not a prostitute, she allows herself to be bought by the man. The male, also unnamed, has total control of the female (in fact, she is to be paid only if she remains submissive to his oppression). The seduction in the novel is sparsely told by the female speaker. As the nights go by, the narrator speaks for the male who, though he exerts his power of silencing the female, has no voice of his own. At first he wants her silent; he does not want to know her. He eventually wants to know more about the woman and releases her from her silence by asking her why, if she is not a prostitute, she has accepted his offer: She answers that as soon as she saw him, she knew he was afflicted with a malady of death. During the first days of the relationship, she did not know how to name that malady, and then she found her voice. She calls him a dead man because he has never loved or desired a woman.

Once awakened, she will no longer play the part of the silent, submissive prostitute. He attempts to engage her on a more maternal level, begging her to listen to the story of his childhood. Again she refuses to be what he wants her to be. By not exerting her power, by not recognizing her power until she recognizes his malady, she gains power over him. No longer willing to play his game, she ends it by leaving.

The Lover

Duras's final group of novels is characterized by her sparse prose and stories shifting both in time and narration. This kaleidoscopic shifting is most evident in *The Lover*. The story of the protagonist's relationship with her Chinese lover is told in the midst of a swirl of images, shifting points of view, and brutal violence. The story is narrated by a female speaker, and it leaps startlingly back and forth in time; the periods of the speaker's life are marked as happenings before the seduction, at the time of the affair, and after the seduction. The three time periods structure the narrative, with the seduction at the center. Past and future come together in Duras's novel, and it is not clear who has been, or who is being, seduced—the Chinese man or the narrator.

At the beginning of the story the narrator is a fifteen-year-old boarding school student in Saigon. The meeting with her Chinese lover is yet another fictionalized telling of the Durasian mythology. His relationship to the young girl is at once paternal, erotic, and, after the introduction to her family, violent. The lover is afraid to make their affair known, not only because he is Chinese and she is white, but because he is twelve years older than her.

The narrative shifts between the first person and the third person, especially in violent scenes. When her mother suspects that she is having an affair with the Chinese man, the narrator talks of herself in the first person while the scene unfolds. However, when her mother begins beating her, she shifts into the third person, distancing herself from the violence of her mother's blows. Duras's manipulation of the narrative continually challenges the reader.

Carol J. Murphy
Updated by Patricia Kennedy Bankhead

Other major works

short fiction: *Des journées entières dans les arbres*, 1954 (*Days in the Trees*, 1967); *L'Homme assis dans le couloir*, 1980 (*The Man Sitting in the Corridor*, 1991); *L'Homme atlantique*, 1982 (*The Atlantic Man*, 1993); *La Pute de la côte Normande*, 1986 (*The Slut of the Normandy Coast*, 1993); *Two by Duras*, 1993 (includes *The Slut of the Normandy Coast* and *The Atlantic Man*).

plays: *Le Square*, pr. 1957 (*The Square*, 1967); *Les Viaducs de la Seine-et-Oise*, pr., pb. 1960 (*The Viaducts of Seine-et-Oise*, 1967); *Les Papiers d'Aspern*, pr. 1961 (with Robert Antelme; adaptation of Michael Redgrave's adaptation of Henry James's novella *The Aspern Papers*); *La Bête dans la jungle*, pr. 1962 (with James Lord; adaptation of Henry James's story "The Beast in the Jungle"); *Miracle en Alabama*, pr. 1962 (with Gérard Jarlot; adaptation of William Gibson's play *The Miracle Worker*); *Des journées entières dans les arbres*, pr. 1965 (*Days in the Trees*, 1967); *Les Eaux et forêts*, pr., pb. 1965 (*The Rivers and Forests*, 1965); *La Musica*, pr., pb. 1965 (*The Music*, 1967); *Théâtre*, 1965-1999 (4 volumes; volume 1 includes *Les Eaux et forêts*, *Le Square*, and *La Musica*; volume 2 includes *Suzanna Andler* [English translation, 1973], *Des journées entières dans les arbres*, *Yes, peut-être*, *Le Shaga*, and *Un Homme est venu me voir*; volume 3 includes *La Bête dans la jungle*, *Les Papiers d'Aspern*, and *La Danse de mort*; volume 4 includes *Véra Baxter*, *L'Éden cinema*, *L'Amante anglaise*, *Home*, and *La Mouette*); *Three Plays*, 1967 (includes *The Square*, *Days in the Trees*, and *The Viaducts of Seine-et-Oise*); *L'Amante anglaise*, pr., pb. 1968 (*A Place Without Doors*, 1970); *Un Homme est venu me voir*, pr., pb. 1968; *La Danse de mort*, pr. 1970 (adaptation of August Strindberg's play *Dösdansen, andra delen*); *Home*, pb. 1973 (adaptation of David Storey's play); *India Song: Texte-théâtre-film*, pb. 1973 (English translation, 1976); *L'Éden Cinéma*, pr., pb. 1977 (*The Eden Cinema*, 1986); *Agatha*, pb. 1981 (English translation, 1992); *Savannah Bay*, pr., pb. 1982 (English translation, 1992); *La Mouette*, pb. 1985 (adaptation of Anton Chekhov's play *The Seagull*); *La Musica, deuxième*, pr., pb. 1985; *Four Plays*, 1992 (includes *La Musica*, *Eden Cinema*, *Savannah Bay*, and *India Song*).

screenplays: *Hiroshima mon amour*, 1959 (*Hiroshima mon amour: Text by Marguerite Duras for the Film by Alain Resnais*, 1961); *Une Aussi Longue Absence*, 1961 (with Gérard Jarlot; English translation, 1966); *La Musica*, 1966 (with Paul Seban); *Détruire, dit-elle*, 1969; *Nathalie Granger*, 1972; *La Femme du Gange*, 1973; *India Song: Texte-théâtre-film*, 1973; *Baxter, Véra Baxter*, 1976; *Des journées entières dans les arbres*, 1976; *Son nom de Venise dans Calcutta désert*, 1976; *Le Camion*, 1977; *Le Navire "Night,"* 1978; *Aurélia Steiner*, 1979; *Cesarée*, 1979; *Les Mains négatives*, 1979; *Agatha: Ou, Les Lectures illisibles*, 1982; *L'Homme atlantique*, 1982.

nonfiction: *Les Parleuses*, 1974 (*Woman to Woman*, 1987); *Les Lieux de Marguerite Duras*, 1977; *Outside: Papiers d'un jour*, 1981 (*Outside: Selected Writings*, 1986); *La Douleur*, 1985 (*The War: A Memoir*, 1986); *La Vie matérielle*, 1987 (*Practicalities: Marguerite Duras Speaks to Jérôme Beaujour*, 1990); *Les Yeux verts*, 1987 (*Green Eyes*, 1990); *Ecrire*, 1993 (*Writing*, 1998); *Outside II: Le Monde extérieur*, 1993; *C'est tout*, 1995 (*No More*, 1998); *Wartime Writings, 1943-1949*, 2008.

Bibliography

Adler, Laure. *Marguerite Duras: A Life*. Translated by Anne-Marie Glasheen. Chicago: University of Chicago Press, 2000. Portrait of the novelist offers a comprehensive account of Duras's life. Especially interesting is this work's examination of Duras's previously little-known activities during World War II.

Crowley, Martin. *Duras, Writing, and the Ethical: Making the Broken Whole*. New York: Oxford University Press, 2000. Closely examines all of Duras's written works, focusing on the ethical questions that arise out of experiences of both passion and excess. Includes bibliography and index.

Glassman, Deborah N. *Marguerite Duras: Fascinating Vision and Narrative Cure*. Madison, N.J.: Fairleigh Dickinson University Press, 1991. Begins with an overview of Duras's life and career, and then focuses on her novels in succeeding chapters. Among the works discussed are *The Ravishing of Lol Stein*, *The Vice-Consul*, and *India Song*. Includes detailed notes and extensive bibliography.

Schuster, Marilyn R. *Marguerite Duras Revisited*. New York: Twayne, 1993. Updates and thoroughly revises the original Twayne volume of 1971. Takes into account Duras's later fiction and the growing body of criticism on her work. Includes chapters on Duras's life, her coming-of-age stories, her work in films, and her major novels. Supplemented by a chronology and an annotated bibliography.

Vircondelet, Alain. *Duras: A Biography*. Translated by Thomas Buckley. Normal, Ill.: Dalkey Archive Press, 1994. English translation of the first biography of Duras, which appeared in France in 1991. Vircondelet's preface describes his approach to Duras's life and work and the problems he confronted in writing a biography of this complex figure. Includes an extensive bibliography.

Willging, Jennifer. *Telling Anxiety: Anxious Narration in the Work of Marguerite Duras, Annie Ernaux, Nathalie Sarraute, and Anne Hébert*. Toronto, Ont.: University of Toronto Press, 2007. Analyzes the representation of anxiety in the works of the four women writers, explaining how their depictions reflect postwar skepticism about the ability of language to express the death and destruction of World War II.

Williams, James S. *The Erotics of Passage: Pleasure, Politics, and Form in the Later Work of Marguerite Duras*. New York: St. Martin's Press, 1997. Scholarly study of Duras's later fiction, films, and work in other media is aimed at advanced students. Analyzes Duras's work from a variety of perspectives, including psychoanalytic, comparative, and linguistic.

Willis, Sharon. *Marguerite Duras: Writing on the Body*. Urbana: University of Illinois Press, 1987. Addresses Duras's entire career—her fiction and her film work—with separate chapters on *Hiroshima mon amour*, *The Ravishing of Lol Stein*, *The Vice-Consul*, and *L'Amour*, emphasizing the erotic figure of both the author and her fiction. Includes detailed notes and bibliography.

Winston, Jane Bradley. *Postcolonial Duras: Cultural Memory in Postwar France*. New York: Palgrave, 2002. Examines Duras's role as an intellectual force in a colonizing power, particularly valuable in the light of her early life in French Indochina and her continued use of the region as a setting.

LAWRENCE DURRELL

Born: Julundur, India; February 27, 1912
Died: Sommières, France; November 7, 1990
Also known as: Lawrence George Durrell; Gaffer Peeslake; Charles Norden

Principal long fiction

Pied Piper of Lovers, 1935
Panic Spring, 1937 (as Charles Norden)
The Black Book, 1938
Cefalû, 1947 (also known as *The Dark Labyrinth*, 1958)
Justine, 1957
Balthazar, 1958
Mountolive, 1958
Clea, 1960
The Alexandria Quartet, 1962 (includes previous 4 novels)
Tunc, 1968
Nunquam, 1970
Monsieur: Or, The Prince of Darkness, 1974
Livia: Or, Buried Alive, 1978
Constance: Or, Solitary Practices, 1981
Sebastian: Or, Ruling Passions, 1983
Quinx: Or, The Ripper's Tale, 1985
The Avignon Quintet, 1992 (includes previous 5 novels)

Other literary forms

Lawrence Durrell (DUR-uhl) was a prolific writer in many genres. As a successful poet, he published many books, including *Ten Poems* (1932), *Bromo Bombastes* (1933), *Transition: Poems* (1934), *A Private Country* (1943), *Cities, Plains, and People* (1946), *On Seeming to Presume* (1948), *Deus Loci* (1950), *The Tree of Idleness, and Other Poems* (1955), *Private Drafts* (1955), *The Ikons, and Other Poems* (1966), *The Red Limbo Lingo: A Poetry Notebook for 1968-1970* (1971), *Vega, and Other Poems* (1973), and *Collected Poems, 1931-1974* (1980). He wrote three plays in verse, *Sappho* (pr. 1950), *An Irish Faustus* (pb.1963), and *Acte* (pr. 1964). He also published travel books such as *Prospero's Cell* (1945), *Reflections on a Marine Venus* (1953), *Bitter Lemons* (1957), *Sicilian Carousel* (1977), and *The Greek Islands* (1978). His essays and letters have been published in several volumes, including *A Key to Modern British Poetry* (1952), *Art and Outrage* (1959), *Lawrence Durrell and Henry Miller: A Private Correspondence* (1963), edited by George Wickes, and *Spirit of Place: Letters and Essays on Travel* (1969), edited by Alan G. Thomas. His publisher apparently persuaded him to identify one of his books, *White Eagles over Serbia* (1957), as being "for juveniles." He translated Greek poetry by C. P. Cavafy, George Seferis, and others, as well as *The Curious History of Pope Joan* (1954; revised as *Pope Joan*, 1960) by Emmanuel Royidis. He published widely in periodicals as various as *Mademoiselle*, *Quarterly Review of Literature*, *New Statesman*, *T'ien Hsia Monthly of Shanghai*, and *Réalités*, and he edited anthologies of poetry and collections of letters. He also spent some time working on the screenplay for the 1963 film *Cleopatra*. His last book published during his lifetime was a nonfiction work titled *Caesar's Vast Ghost: A Portrait of Provence* (1990). Since his death, additional volumes of his writings have appeared; these include *Lawrence Durrell: Conversations* (1998), edited by Earl G. Ingersoll, and *The Lawrence Durrell Travel Reader* (2004), edited by Clint Willis.

Achievements

Although Lawrence Durrell was highly respected as a poet and travel writer, it is generally agreed that his greatest accomplishments were *The Alexandria Quartet* and *The Avignon Quintet*. There is little doubt that Durrell's place in twentieth century literature rests on these extraordinary works. Throughout his career, Durrell had a sensuous, ornate, and lyrical style that sometimes degenerated into overwriting—a tendency to which he freely admitted. In his best books, however, the style reflected his Mediterranean surroundings of Greece, Egypt, or Provence, France. Influenced by Henry Miller but by no means an imitator of him, Durrell appealed to so-called literary tastes beginning with *The Black Book*. The popularity of *The Alexandria Quartet*, however, seems to be the result of the blend of an exceptional style with an exotic setting and characters, wit, and exciting plot elements such as murder, conspiracy, and unrequited love. *The Avignon Quintet* has these same elements and is no less a literary triumph for its lack of public acclaim.

Biography

Lawrence George Durrell was born in Julundur, India, on February 27, 1912, to Lawrence Samuel Durrell, an English engineer who built the Tata Iron and Steel Works, and Louise Florence "Dixie" Durrell, of Irish heritage. Both his parents' families had been in India for some time. When the boy was very young, the Durrells moved to Kurseong, near the Himalayas, so that the elder Durrell could accept a three-year contract on a mountain railway to Darjeeling. The sight of the mountains made a strong impression on the boy, so much so that he once described his childhood in a letter to Henry Miller as "a brief dream of Tibet." While in Darjeeling, he began his education at the College of St. Joseph and received the first encouragement for his writing from a Belgian priest, Father Joseph De Guylder.

At twelve, Durrell was sent to England with his brother Leslie "to get the hall-mark," as his father said, of a public school education. He attended St. Olave's and St. Saviour's Grammar School, where he developed his lifelong interest in Elizabethan writers, and later entered St. Edmund's School in Canterbury. Despite several attempts, he was never admitted to Cambridge University and would later write of his life in England, "That mean shabby little island . . . wrung my guts out of me and tried to destroy anything singular and unique in me."

The death of his father left Durrell with a small income, which he used to move to Bloomsbury in order to become a writer. During his Bloomsbury years, Durrell held a number of odd jobs, including jazz pianist and composer, race-car driver, and real estate agent. During this period he also met his first wife, Nancy Myers, a student at the Slade School, with whom he ran a photo studio for a time. At nineteen, he met John Gawsworth in a café after fleeing from an upstairs window during a police raid on the Blue Peter nightclub, where Durrell was playing piano. Awed by Gawsworth's personal knowledge of many famous authors, Durrell became his friend, and though they often disagreed on literary matters—Gawsworth was a very conservative poet who admired the literature of the 1890's and had little respect for W. H. Auden and Stephen Spender—Gawsworth helped Durrell to get his first poems published. *Ten Poems* was published in 1932 under the pseudonym "Gaffer Peeslake" by Caduceus Press, founded by Durrell, his wife, and George Wilkinson.

Durrell began his first novel, *Pied Piper of Lovers*, while he and Nancy lived for a year in a Sussex cottage with George and Pam Wilkinson. After the Wilkinsons emigrated to Corfu, Greece, Durrell lived with his mother, sister, and two brothers in Bournemouth, where they received glowing letters from the Wilkinsons. Excited by the idea of the warm climate, Durrell left his novel under consideration at Cassell's and departed for Corfu. When the rest of his family followed a few weeks later, they bore the news that the book had been accepted, confirming Durrell in his notion to take up writing as a profession, though very few copies of the book would sell. The residence in Corfu had two important results for him. First, it began his long association with Greece, its poetry, and language; and second, it led to his discovery of *Tropic of Cancer* (1934) by Henry Miller.

The latter was probably the most significant development in the young Durrell's career. He wrote a letter of praise to Miller, who responded warmly, saying that the letter was the most intelligent he had yet received from a Briton about his book. By 1936, Durrell was clearly under the influence of Miller, apologizing for his second novel and engrossed in writing *The Black Book*. The next year, Durrell announced that he was the "first writer to be fertilized by H. M." and sent *The Black Book* to Miller, who paused in the writing of *Tropic of Capricorn* (1939) to type out (with Anaïs Nin) three copies to be sent to Herbert Read, T. S. Eliot, and Jack Kahane. Kahane published it in Paris, and Eliot endorsed it as "the first piece of work by a new English writer to give me any hope for the future of prose fiction." Durrell visited Paris, and Miller later visited Corfu, solidifying a friendship that would last until the latter's death, despite Durrell's forthright, often scathing, reviews of Miller's later works.

World War II interrupted Durrell's idyllic life in Corfu. He moved to Athens in 1940, where he worked for the British embassy, and then was posted to the Institute of English Studies in Kalamata. While in Athens, he met George Katsimbalis and George Seferis, both of whose works he would later translate. In 1941, he was forced to escape the Nazi invasion with Nancy and their daughter Penelope Berengaria in an old caïque bound for Crete. From Crete, they went on to Egypt, where Durrell served as a foreign press service officer for the British Information Service. Nancy and Penelope spent the war in Palestine, and the marriage deteriorated, resulting in a divorce in 1947. Durrell soon married Eve Cohen, a dark-eyed Alexandrian woman who may have partly inspired the character of Justine.

Happy to escape from Egypt, Durrell lived for a time on Rhodes, then in Argentina and Yugoslavia, disliking both places. In the early 1950's, he left Yugoslavia for Cyprus, where he bought a home, taught school, and, during the developing civil war, became public relations officer for the British government. His second marriage deteriorated early in his stay on Cyprus, but by 1956, he had completed *Justine*, the first novel of *The Alexandria Quartet*. Late that year, he moved on to Dorset with Claude-Marie Vincenden (who would later become his third wife), where he worked on *Bitter Lemons*, a book drawing on his experiences in Cyprus.

Financially exhausted but unable to live away from the Mediterranean area for very long, Durrell and Claude began to look for a home in the Midi. Virtually overnight, Durrell became a world-renowned author when *Justine*, *Bitter Lemons*, *White Eagles over Serbia*, and *Esprit de Corps: Sketches from Diplomatic Life* were published in 1957. His works were translated into numerous foreign languages and he was able to devote his entire time to writing. With his favored mode of work being intense days of some fourteen hours of writing, he allegedly produced *Justine* in four months, *Balthazar* in six weeks, *Mountolive* in twelve weeks, and *Clea* in eight.

For thirty years or so, Durrell lived a settled life in Provence, with occasional travel. On March 27, 1961, he and Claude were married, and in 1966, they moved into a larger house in Sommières to accommodate their guests, Claude's children by a previous marriage, Penelope, and their daughter Sappho-Jane. After a period of declining health, Claude died on New Year's Day, 1967. In 1973, Durrell married Ghislaine de Boysson, but by 1986 his fourth marriage was finished. The five novels of *The Avignon Quintet* appeared between 1974 and 1985 to mixed reviews, but there is no question that this thirteen-hundred-page sequence is a tour de force of the first order.

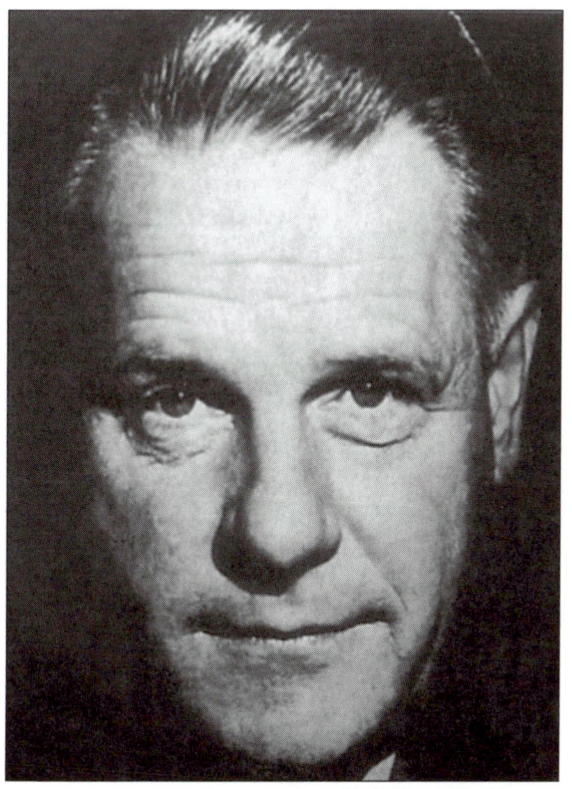

Lawrence Durrell. (© Rosemarie Clausen)

Lawrence Durrell died on November 7, 1990, at the age of seventy-eight in his home in Provence. His literary reputation, which rests chiefly on *The Alexandria Quartet*, is higher on the Continent and in the United States than in Great Britain.

Analysis

Lawrence Durrell's first novel, *Pied Piper of Lovers*, is a story of life among the bohemians at Bloomsbury. It was sufficiently dismal to provoke a publisher to advise him to offer *Panic Spring* under the pseudonym of Charles Norden, so that the latter, a slightly better book, would not be associated with its predecessor. *Panic Spring* has been described as being influenced by, even imitative of, the works of Aldous Huxley; even as it was published, Durrell was writing an apology to Henry Miller for his "new and facile novel." In essence, Durrell's early career was characterized by a search for a paradigm or form for his talent, a search that ended with his discovery of *Tropic of Cancer*.

The Black Book

The impact of Miller's novel on the young Durrell was enormous. A comparison of his earlier works with his third novel, *The Black Book*, reveals a dramatic transformation. His creative impulses have been freed. As he described it in 1959, *The Black Book* is "a two-fisted attack on literature by a young man in the thirties," taking its aggressive intent from Miller's all-out assault on the literary establishment. The narrator, Lawrence Lucifer, recounts his experiences in a seedy London hotel from the perspective of his life on Corfu. In the hotel he finds the diary of Herbert Gregory, which relates experiences that overlap with his own. There are numerous other characters and much obscurity as to the details of time and event. There is a great deal of erotic content, both homosexual and heterosexual, as the characters betray and cuckold one another. The novel's themes are revealed not through a carefully constructed plot but through a series of scenes, reminiscences, and vignettes.

Durrell later wrote the following in the 1959 introduction to the second edition of *The Black Book*:

> With all its imperfections lying heavy on my head, I can't help being attached to it because in the writing of it I first heard the sound of my own voice, lame and halting, perhaps, but nevertheless my very own.

In this work, the reader finds the first cry of Durrell's literary voice, his exotic characters, his sensual and sensuous prose, and his experiments with narrative time. When it was published, T. S. Eliot (among others) was perspicacious enough to recognize the voice of a major new talent. Had Durrell ended his career with *The Black Book*, it would most likely be forgotten. Burdened with an excessively baroque style, it is of interest chiefly because of its place in his career.

The Dark Labyrinth

Cefalû, Durrell's next novel (reissued as *The Dark Labyrinth* after *Justine* had assured Durrell a place in twentieth century literature), can be viewed in much the same way as *The Black Book*. In it, Durrell seems to be discovering himself, experimenting, finding the form and style that would achieve maturity in *The Alexandria Quartet*. One also sees a tugging away from Miller's influence—only a few years later, Durrell would write a scathing indictment of Miller's *Sexus* (1949)—and a reversion to the influence of Aldous Huxley that had been so apparent in *Panic Spring*. *The Dark Labyrinth* has extensive allegorical elements, reminiscent of Huxley: The characters are trapped in a labyrinth in Crete, and each finds in the maze that for which he or she has been looking. The book was written quickly—which was not unusual for Durrell—and seems rather derivative in structure, though the writing itself often attains his characteristic brilliance.

The Alexandria Quartet

The four novels that compose *The Alexandria Quartet* are collectively one of the greatest achievements in the modern novel. Like many modern works, *The Alexandria Quartet* often seems to be about the creation of fiction. Darley, the narrator of *Justine* and *Balthazar*, is a novelist, as are two other characters. Diversity in point of view is regularly exploited through the use of diaries, letters, and recounted experiences. Truth becomes subjective and layered. The characters' knowledge is limited to what they perceive, and numerous questions are left unanswered.

The Alexandria Quartet is also an examination of love in the modern world as the characters pass through convoluted interrelationships. Sex and love, like art, become ways of glimpsing underlying truths, of developing one's knowledge of reality. Durrell stated that *The Alexandria Quartet* consists of four parts because he was attempting to produce a novelistic version of Albert Einstein's universe. Relativity (or subjectivity) thus appears as a justification for the exploitation of point of view, for the questionable reliability of narrators, and for an exploration of time and memory. Durrell was careful, however, despite the modern and postmodern objectives of *The Alexandria Quartet*, to hang all the theory on a generous structure of narrative. The works involve a number of stories of betrayal, murder, love, devotion, and tragedy intertwined, and although they are elusive, they make the tetralogy accessible in a way that many "experimental" works are not, without compromising the artistic integrity of the work.

Finally, Durrell's extraordinary prose, his poetic, lyrical, and erotic use of language, elevates *The Alexandria Quartet* above most modern fiction, although this talent was manifest as early as *The Black Book*, provoking Miller to write of Durrell, "You are *the* master of the English language." Some critics have regarded Durrell's prose as excessive, overdone, a flamboyant collection of purple clichés and Victorian decadence. In each of his major works, however, and especially in *The Alexandria Quartet*, it is difficult to imagine a prose style without his deliberate rhythms and cadences that would be suitable to his themes and extraordinary settings.

The chief characters of *The Alexandria Quartet* may be loosely based on people Durrell had known. Darley has a number of characteristics in common with the author: They are both novelists, three women (up to the writing of the novel) have played major parts in both their lives, and they have held similar jobs. Other resemblances between characters and certain "real people" might be noted, but these would only contribute to the thematic question of how reality is transformed by experience, recollection, and novelization. The whole question adds another layer to the multiple levels among which the tetralogy moves.

Justine is one of the most haunting characters in the tetralogy. Born in Alexandria, she is a dark, beautiful Jewess with an intense sexuality and an obscure background. She runs the gamut of sexual pleasure and is seen from a variety of viewpoints, including the romanticized memories of Darley's love, the cynical stance of the novelist Pursewarden, and the roman à clef of her first husband, Arnauti. Though not really in love with Nessim Hosnani, a Copt, she marries the devoted Egyptian on the condition that he help her find her kidnapped child. Nessim becomes involved in gunrunning into Palestine because of his hatred of the English. Narouz—Nessim's harelipped, violent, and earthy brother—becomes a force in the second and third volumes of the tetralogy. Balthazar, a physician, gives his name to the second volume, which he also partly narrates, though he is present throughout the books. A mystic homosexual, he seems to know most of the other characters' secrets, and his illuminations of Darley's perceptions provide new insights into the situations. Mountolive is a diplomat who has an affair with Leila Hosnani, Nessim's mother, who later contracts smallpox, loses her beauty, and engages in a lengthy correspondence with Mountolive, who falls in love with Pursewarden's blind sister, Liza.

Alexandria, with its convoluted intrigues, gradually wears away the English confidence of the diplomat as Nessim and others betray him as he investigates the circumstances of Pursewarden's suicide. Clea is a superstitious artist, beloved of Narouz, lover of Justine, Dr. Amaril, and, eventually, Darley. With blond hair and blue eyes, Clea's northern European beauty contrasts with Justine's Mediterranean beauty.

Even this short summary of the characters reveals the complexity of the story line of *The Alexandria Quartet*, and there are even more characters who play important roles: Scobie, the transvestite who becomes a saint; Cohen, who plots to liberate Palestine; Dr. Amaril, who loves the noseless Semira; Mnemjian, the dwarf barber; Pombal, involved in espionage; Capodistria of the great sexual prowess; and Toto de Brunel, who is murdered with a hatpin, probably by mistake. A complete list of characters would number more than one hundred.

Alexandria itself has often been discussed as playing a character-like role in the tetralogy. Like James Joyce's Dublin, Marcel Proust's Paris, and William Faulkner's Yoknapatawpha County, the landscape exhibits a crucial influence on the characters, determining their behavior. Sometimes characters seem to be mere expressions of some element of the landscape, appearing and disappearing into the textures of Alexandrian life, just as the "reality" of Scobie is absorbed into the legend of "El Scob." Alexandria is mysterious, full of deception and treachery. There are always murderous undercurrents, such as when Justine suspects Nessim's plans to kill Darley at the duck shoot and when Toto is murdered at the masked ball, probably in Justine's place. Even Narouz's frustration at being unable to satisfy his love for Clea seems to explode out of his harpoon gun after his death, the accident nearly causing her to drown when her hand is staked to a sunken ship.

A brief discussion of *The Alexandria Quartet* can hardly do justice to the complexity of the work. With no ostensible intention of making a moral statement, Durrell's foremost intention was the creation of a work of art that reflected the relativistic sensibility of the modern world, yet he carefully maintained an absorbing plot to serve as a skeleton on which to flesh out his musings on love, sex, art, writing, memory, and time. Although Durrell celebrates life in a way many contemporary artists do not, *The Alexandria Quartet* also reveals ambiguities and darknesses. The tetralogy cannot be reduced to story, theme, or message. Its lush writing becomes a sensory experience of a world with overlapping, often conflicting layers of reality.

Tunc *and* Nunquam

Tunc and *Nunquam*, the pair of novels that followed *The Alexandria Quartet*, have much in common with the tetralogy, despite the great difference in subject matter. Felix Charlock invents a computer, named Abel, which can recall or predict virtually anything. Charlock soon finds himself under contract to a huge conglomerate headed by Julian Merlin, a mysterious character who seems to control, through business connections, most of the people in the world. To join Merlin is to be assured of comfort but also to give up individual freedom. *Tunc* and *Nunquam* contain Durrell's usually rich selection of characters, including the neurotic Benedicta, Julian's sister; Iolanthe, a prostitute-become-film-star; and Caradoc, a wordplaying architect.

In style, *Tunc* and *Nunquam* are similar to *The Alexandria Quartet*, despite the science-fiction mise-en-scène. When Merlin creates a robotic duplicate of Iolanthe, which can hallucinate eating and other bodily functions even though it does not do these things, Charlock comes to identify with the robot's quest for freedom, seeing in it his own struggle to remain an individual despite his absorption into Merlin's world. This thematic concern with individual freedom in the contemporary world does not play a large part in *The Alexandria Quartet*, but *Tunc* and *Nunquam* exhibit the tetralogy's themes of time, space, art, love, and sex, as well as a masterful use of language.

The Avignon Quintet

With the five novels that constitute *The Avignon Quintet* (*Monsieur*, *Livia*, *Constance*, *Sebastian*, and *Quinx*), Durrell recapitulates the themes of a lifetime with self-conscious exuberance, like a magician putting on his show for the last time. Shifts of viewpoint are kaleidoscopic in effect: bright, dazzling, patterned, but ambiguous as to meaning. He presents two novelists, Aubrey Blanford and Robin Sutcliffe, who explore the theme of novel writing to a fare-thee-well. Durrell creates two different fates for each of these characters, as if his world suddenly split in two and his personae lived out opposing potentialities. Duality is rife in *The Avignon Quintet*, as one can see from the double titles of all the novels.

One underlying idea, however, permeates everything: entropy, the tendency for orderly systems to dissolve in anarchy and death. Taking the period from 1938 to 1945, with the whole of World War II occurring in *Constance*, Durrell shows entropy at work in Europe under the impact of Nazism, entropy in the failure of Western rationalism to stem the "deathdrift" of society or individuals, and entropy in the breakdown of personality in the forms of insanity and suicide. Against entropy, Durrell poses the forces of love and art. Even these, however, succumb to chaos and death.

As an author, Durrell is like the "Lord of Misrule," the comic king of festival, in *The Avignon Quintet*. His world is one in which social disorder reigns amid drinking and feasting. In fact, *The Avignon Quintet* describes celebrations and banquets frequently, often at the ends of the novels, and often with something sinister at their cores. Durrell's comic tone and exuberance just barely conceal a deeply pessimistic outlook, like gallows humor.

The Provence town of Avignon is the geographic and spiritual center of the quintet. With its dual legacy, very much present in these novels, of having been the center of Catholicism and of the heretical Knights Templar in the Middle Ages, Avignon represents the opposing pulls of reason and mysticism, West and East, and life and death on the characters. Egypt stands for the East, for Gnostic mysticism (linked with the Templar heresy), and for death throughout *The Avignon Quintet*. Geneva is the site of safety and reason during World War II, an outpost of civilized Western values in an era turned savage and suicidal. Each locale—Avignon, Egypt, and Geneva—has its own distinct flavor and ambiguity, and each is fully realized artistically. Durrell's unique descriptive prose and his use of vignette and narrative event are matchless in creating the feel of place.

Most of the main characters are on quests of some kind: some for love (Blanford, a novelist; Constance, a psychoanalyst; Chatto, a consul), some for sexual adventure (Livia, Prince Hassad), some for wealth (Lord Galen, Smirgel), some for revenge (Quatrefages, Mnemidis), and some for a sacrificial death at the hands of a Gnostic cult (Piers de Nogaret, Sebastian Affad). Several of these private quests are subsumed under one last, collective quest: the search for the lost Templar treasure, hidden centuries ago in a labyrinth of caves near the Roman aqueduct at Avignon, caves mined with explosives by Austrian sappers in the closing days of World War II. On a Friday the thirteenth, Blanford and Constance enter the caves, following a group of intoxicated revelers from a banquet at which Death has just appeared. The inconclusive end of this quest for treasure hints strongly that some poor fool set off the dynamite, sending *The Avignon Quintet* into the silence of extinction.

In the end, three aspects of life matter to Durrell: love as the means to truth, art as the mirror of truth, and a joyful acceptance of both life and art as the final consummation of truth. By facing down entropy, his own and his world's, Durrell achieved a rare and disturbing kind of wisdom.

J. Madison Davis

Other major works

SHORT FICTION: *Esprit de Corps: Sketches from Diplomatic Life*, 1957; *Stiff Upper Lip: Life Among the Diplomats*, 1958; *Sauve Qui Peut*, 1966; *The Best of Antrobus*, 1974; *Antrobus Complete*, 1985.

PLAYS: *Sappho*, pr. 1950; *An Irish Faustus*, pb. 1963; *Acte*, pr. 1964.

POETRY: *Quaint Fragment: Poems Written Between the Ages of Sixteen and Nineteen*, 1931; *Ten Poems*, 1932; *Bromo Bombastes*, 1933; *Transition: Poems*, 1934; *Proems: An Anthology of Poems*, 1938 (with others); *A Private Country*, 1943; *Cities, Plains, and People*, 1946; *On Seeming to Presume*, 1948; *Deus Loci*, 1950; *Private Drafts*, 1955; *The Tree of Idleness, and Other Poems*, 1955; *Selected Poems*, 1956; *Collected Poems*, 1960; *Penguin Modern Poets One*, 1962 (with Elizabeth Jennings and R. S. Thomas); *Beccafico = Le Becfigue*, 1963 (includes French translation by F. J. Temple); *Selected Poems, 1935-1963*, 1964; *The Ikons, and Other Poems*, 1966; *The Red Limbo Lingo: A Poetry Notebook for 1968-1970*, 1971; *On the Suchness of the Old Boy*, 1972; *Vega, and Other Poems*, 1973; *Collected Poems, 1931-1974*, 1980; *Too Far to Hear the Singing: Poems*, 2005 (Francoise Hestman Durrell, editor).

NONFICTION: *Prospero's Cell*, 1945; *A Landmark Gone*, 1949; *A Key to Modern British Poetry*, 1952; *Reflections on a Marine Venus*, 1953; *Bitter Lemons*, 1957; *Art and Outrage*, 1959; *Lawrence Durrell and Henry Miller: A Private Correspondence*, 1963 (George Wickes, editor); *Spirit of Place: Letters and Essays on Travel*, 1969 (Alan G. Thomas, editor); *The Big Supposer: Dialogues with Marc Alyn/Lawrence Durrell*, 1973; *Sicilian Carousel*, 1977; *The Greek Islands*, 1978; *Literary Lifelines: The Richard Aldington-Lawrence Durrell Correspondence*, 1981; *The Durrell-Miller Letters, 1935-1980*, 1988; *Caesar's Vast Ghost: A Portrait of Provence*, 1990; *Lawrence Durrell: Conversations*, 1998 (Earl G. Ingersoll, editor); *The Lawrence Durrell Travel Reader*, 2004 (Clint Willis, editor).

TRANSLATIONS: *Six Poems from the Greek of Sekilianos and Seferis*, 1946; *The King of Asine, and Other Poems*, 1948 (of George Seferis' poetry); *The Curious History of Pope Joan*, 1954 (of Emmanuel Royidis' biography; revised as *Pope Joan*, 1960).

CHILDREN'S LITERATURE: *White Eagles over Serbia*, 1957.

Bibliography

Bengal, Michael H., ed. *On Miracle Ground: Essays on the Fiction of Lawrence Durrell*. Lewisburg, Pa.: Bucknell University Press, 1990. Limited to Durrell's major fiction, these essays reflect the variety of critical responses the novels elicited, including analyses from the perspectives of metafiction, deconstruction, and reader-response theory. In his essay "Overture," Durrell provides his own understanding of the forces that shaped him. Contains a useful bibliography of secondary sources.

Bowker, Gordon. *Through the Dark Labyrinth: A Biography of Lawrence Durrell*. New York: St. Martin's Press, 1997. Reveals Durrell to be a complex man beset at times by incredibly painful circumstances that he was somehow able to transmute into his fiction. Includes bibliography and index.

Fraser, George S. *Lawrence Durrell*. London: Longman, 1970. Perceptive pamphlet-length study addresses Durrell's major literary output up to 1970, tracing the themes and plot of *The Alexandria Quartet* with admirable clarity. Includes a select bibliography.

Friedman, Alan Warren. *Lawrence Durrell and "The Alexandria Quartet": Art for Love's Sake*. Norman: University of Oklahoma Press, 1970. Pioneering study of Durrell's writing concentrates on *The Alexandria Quartet* as the culmination, at the time, of his writing. Places Durrell as a leading experimental novelist in the traditions of the impressionists and the stream-of-consciousness novelists.

Herbrechter, Stefan. *Lawrence Durrell: Postmodernism and the Ethics of Alterity*. Atlanta: Rodopi, 1999. Presents an investigation of the notions of alterity that underlie the work of Durrell and postmodernist theory. The introduction sketches the ethics of alterity as conceived by French philosopher Emmanuel Lévinas and reevaluates Durrell's fiction within the context of these postmodern ideas.

Kaczvinsky, Donald P. *Lawrence Durrell's Major Novels: Or, The Kingdom of the Imagination*. London: Associated University Presses, 1997. Provides excellent discussion of Durrell's seminal works, including his early novel *The Black Book* and *The Alexandria Quartet*. Describes how these novels feature artist-heroes who come into contact with debilitating cultures and places.

Kersnowski, Frank, ed. *Into the Labyrinth: Essays Concerning the Art of Lawrence Durrell*. Rochester, N.Y.: University of Rochester Press, 1991. Collection of critical essays and biographical reminiscences analyzes all forms of Durrell's writing and painting. Includes material not readily available elsewhere, such as in the reproduction of Durrell's art and in a chronology of his life.

MacNiven, Ian. *Lawrence Durrell: A Biography*. London: Faber & Faber, 1998. With Durrell's cooperation, MacNiven had extraordinary access to both his subject and his papers, including notebooks and letters. Interviews with Durrell's friends and lovers are integrated into a probing look at the sources of Durrell's writing. Includes illustrations, chronology, family tree, and notes.

Morrisson, Ray. *A Smile in His Mind's Eye: A Study of the Early Works of Lawrence Durrell*. Toronto, Ont.: University of Toronto Press, 2005. Focuses on the work Durrell produced before World War II, stressing how the author's interest in Daoism enabled him to move from a male-centered Western worldview to a more female-oriented Eastern consciousness.

Weigel, John A. *Lawrence Durrell*. Rev. ed. Boston: Twayne, 1989. Provides a clear overview of Durrell's life and writing as well as discussion of individual works. Includes discussion of Durrell's poetry, drama, and criticism, but focuses on the novels. Useful for students approaching Durrell for the first time.

E

JOSÉ MARIA DE EÇA DE QUEIRÓS

Born: Póvoa de Varzim, Portugal; November 25, 1845
Died: Paris, France; August 16, 1900
Also known as: José Maria de Eça de Queiróz

Principal long fiction

O crime do Padre Amaro, 1876, 1880 (*The Sin of Father Amaro*, 1962)
O Primo Basílio, 1878 (*Dragon's Teeth*, 1889; better known as *Cousin Bazilio*, 1953)
O mandarim, 1880 (*The Mandarin*, 1965)
A relíquia, 1887 (*The Relic*, 1925)
Os Maias: Episódios da vida romântica, 1888 (*The Maias*, 1965; also known as *The Maias: Episodes from Romantic Life*, 2007)
A ilustre casa de Ramires, 1900 (*The Illustrious House of Ramires*, 1968)
A cidade e as serras, 1901 (*The City and the Mountains*, 1955)
A Capital, 1925 (*To the Capital*, 1995)
Alves e Cia, 1925 (*Alves and Co.*, 1988; also known as *The Yellow Sofa*, 1993)
O Conde de Abranhos, 1925
A tragédia da rua das Flores, 1979, 1980 (*The Tragedy of the Street of Flowers*, 2000)

Other literary forms

The first fictional work of José Maria de Eça de Queirós (AY-sah-theh-kay-ee-ROHSH) was a parody of the romantic "mystery" novel, *O misteério da estrada de Sintra* (1885; the mystery of Sintra Road), which was written in collaboration with his friend, Ramalho Ortigão (1836-1915). It is not considered a significant work, although it does present themes that Eça de Queirós later developed in a serious manner. Complete satisfaction with his texts was an elusive goal; as a result, Eça de Queirós withheld publication of many works. The posthumously published works, edited by his son, his daughter, and others, are pertinent to the study of the thematic and technical development of Eça de Queirós's fiction. Several novels were to form a Balzacian "Scenes of Portuguese Life" in conjunction with *The Maias*, *O Conde de Abranhos*, and *Alves and Co.*

In 1979 and 1980, two different editions were published of a long-suppressed novel, *The Tragedy of the Street of Flowers*; the difficulty in deciphering Eça de Queirós's handwriting led to great variations in interpretations of words and constructions in the two competing editions. A collection of Eça de Queirós's short stories was published under the title *Contos* (1902; stories); some of these stories were the seeds for later novels. Eça de Queirós's journalistic collaborations, his letters and impressions about life abroad, and his personal correspondence have also appeared. A translation into Portuguese of H. Rider Haggard's *King Solomon's Mines* (1885), *As minas de Salomão* (1891), is attributed to Eça de Queirós and included among his works; it is now believed, however, that the translation was prepared by his sister-in-law and only revised by Eça de Queirós.

From the 1920's through the early 1970's, Eça de Queirós's works were published by the Livraria Lello and Irmão of Oporto. Livraria Lello's fifteen-volume *Obras de Eça de Queiróz* (1960-1972) is the most comprehensive of the various editions of the author's complete works. As a result of a lawsuit brought by Eça de Queirós's heirs against Lello and Irmão and a change in the Portuguese copyright law, many of Eça de Queirós's works are no longer protected under Portuguese copyright provisions. At present, the principal Portuguese publisher of Eça de Queirós's work is Editora Livros do Brasil of Lisbon.

Achievements

José Maria de Eça de Queirós's adversary stance toward the ultraromantic trend of Portuguese culture was well established prior to the publication of his first novel. Indeed, this stance conditioned the Portuguese critical evaluation and attitude toward his works throughout his lifetime. Eça de Queirós's early novels were scorned by the national literary establishment as nothing more than poor imitations of the French naturalists. Violent polemics, charges of plagiarism, and legitimate criticisms of his art resulted. The most significant evaluation of these early works was by the Brazilian writer Joaquim Maria Machado de Assis. Rather than discourage Eça de Queirós's literary output, these criticisms helped him to become a more sensitive artist.

Eça de Queirós's wide reading in foreign literatures and philosophy as well as his sojourns abroad provided a reference point for the analysis of Portuguese society and an awareness of the literary art that no other previous Portuguese writer had enjoyed. His fiction not only touched on the situation of Portuguese existence in the late nineteenth century but also confronted the more serious question of a Portuguese identity within a European context.

Through his novels, Eça de Queirós revitalized and brought new depth to all aspects of Portuguese fiction. His creation of a personalized linguistic style is of particular distinction. The most revealing testaments to Eça de Queirós's significance for Portuguese fiction are the enduring shadow his works have cast over twentieth century writers and the continuous critical attention that he attracts. Although widely read and influential in Brazil, Spain, and Spanish America, his major novels have been translated into English, French, and other languages only within recent years. Eça de Queirós has won the critical attention of important European and American literary critics, but he has yet to achieve the international recognition that his works so justly merit.

Biography

José Maria de Eça de Queirós was born out of wedlock on November 25, 1845, in Póvoa de Varzim, a village in northern Portugal. Although his parents, members of the rural upper bourgeoisie, married in 1849, Eça de Queirós spent his childhood with a nursemaid and later with his paternal grandmother. His illegitimacy was a subtle preoccupation that often surfaced in his personal activities as well as in his fiction. It was not until 1885, the year of his own marriage, that Eça de Queirós was officially recognized by his parents.

In 1861, Eça de Queirós began to study law at the University of Coimbra. He also became an active member of the school's literary and theatrical clique. Through his friendship with the poet-philosopher Antero de Quental (1842-1891), Eça de Queirós's sociopolitical formation was initiated with readings of Auguste Comte, Pierre Proudhon, Ernest Renan, and a wide acquaintance with French literature. After law school, Eça de Queirós combined his professional life with his journalistic and literary activities; he wrote for Portuguese newspapers on literary and social questions throughout his life. After a short stint as editor of the political opposition's newspaper in Évora in 1867, Eça de Queirós returned to Lisbon to begin a diplomatic career. A trip to Egypt in 1869 to attend the opening of the Suez Canal included visits to the Holy Land's sacred shrines.

In Lisbon in 1871, the Cenacle, Eça de Queirós's literary circle, launched a series of conferences that proposed revolutionary alternatives to the "backwardness" of Portuguese culture in relationship to the rest of Europe. Inspired in his readings of the social philosophers and the events of the Paris Commune, Eça de Queirós's conference propounded a realist social ethic for Portuguese literature.

Eça de Queirós's administrative and diplomatic career was harmoniously combined with his literary pursuits. His brief appointment as town administrator in rural Leiria in 1871 provided material for *The Sin of Father Amaro* and *Cousin Bazilio*. His posting to Havana, Cuba, from 1872 to 1874 brought him into contact with the dire conditions of the Portuguese-Chinese emigrant workers, which he officially protested in *A emigração como força civilizadora* (1979; emigration as a civilizing force). Eça de Queirós visited the United States but was not impressed by its large cities or its reliance on machines. As Portuguese consul in Newcastle upon Tyne, England, he finished two versions of *The Sin of Father Amaro* and *Cousin Bazilio*, as well as *The Mandarin*. Eça de Queirós spent his vacations in Portugal, where he maintained strong links with Portuguese traditions and problems and often engaged in polemics over national problems with ultrachauvinists.

In 1885, Eça de Queirós visited Émile Zola in Paris, and later that year, he married Emília de Resende. In 1887, *The Relic* was published and denied an important literary prize. In 1888, the year that his masterpiece *The Maias* was published, Eça de Queirós was named Portuguese consul in Paris. His Parisian years were spent as an almost complete social and literary recluse. The Dreyfus affair caused him great disappointment with the personal, moral, and social levels of his once idealized French society. His prime attention turned toward the future of the Portuguese identity, as evident in *The Illustrious House of Ramires* and *The City and the Mountains*. Eça de Queirós died in Paris on August 16, 1900.

Analysis

In the course of his novels, José Maria de Eça de Queirós vividly dissected a society lost in past centuries, oblivious to any contemporary political, social, or cultural ideology. Initially, he censured Portugal's backwardness in *romans à thèse* that presented a rather confused, even naïve, comprehension and literary application of the social theories of Proudhon, the religious doctrines of Renan, and the literary aims of Gustave Flaubert. As he discovered his own literary persona, these influences gradually became secondary.

Several thematic and technical interests are recurrent in Eça de Queirós's literary voyage from naturalism and realism to his unique personal style, independent of any literary school. His own parentless childhood is often invoked through numerous characters in odd family situations—orphans, wards, widowers, loners without family—and through the theme of incest. Further, Eça de Queirós's "presence" in the attributes of his novels' characters appears to be an attempt to examine and resolve the extremes of his own personality: the spirit of a romantic dandy with the mind of a practical realist. Finally, his concern with the Portuguese identity led him to examine repeatedly its traditional components: rural existence, the Roman Catholic tradition, and the national preoccupation with and glorification of past centuries' achievements.

The Sin of Father Amaro *and* Cousin Bazilio

The Sin of Father Amaro and *Cousin Bazilio* are closely related in Eça de Queirós's early development. Both have a basis in actual events that occurred prior to his arrival as administrator of the city of Leiria. The publication history of *The Sin of Father Amaro* is indicative of the almost maniacal search for an appropriate, personalized style, which Eça de Queirós pursued and which limited his publications. The original version was serialized in the Lisbon *Revista ocidental* in 1875, when the author was in England, and he entrusted the editing to his friends Ramalho Ortigão and Antero de Quental, but he was rather dissatisfied with their efforts. After the serialization, Eça de Queirós wrote a "definitive" version with substantially developed characters and preponderant social themes.

José Maria de Eça de Queirós. (Biblioteca Nacional de Portugal)

Father Amaro is an orphan who, through the graces of "benefactors," is ordained and obtains a desirable parish in Leiria. He becomes enamored of his landlady's daughter, the innocent Amélia, who gives herself to Amaro in a spiritual trance of religious possession. Her pregnancy results in guilt, the murder of the child, and her own death. Unrepentant, Amaro travels on to another parish. The rural existence in general and the role of the corrupt priests of the Church in particular are the targets of Eça de Queirós's censure. Graphic scenes of sexual encounters and blasphemous presentations of religious activities led to hostile commentaries that branded the novel anticlerical and pornographic. A "completely new, revised, and rewritten edition" appeared in 1880, owing to the influence of Machado de Assis, who wrote a sharp criticism of the "definitive" edition and Eça de Queirós's second novel, *Cousin Bazilio.*

Set in upper-middle-class Lisbon society, *Cousin Bazilio* was written within a few short months of 1877 and reveals the impact of Flaubert's *Madame Bovary* (1857; English translation, 1886) on Eça de Queirós. Luiza is a slightly educated woman living in a world of romantic fantasy. When her husband, Jorge, goes off on business, she becomes involved in an affair with her Cousin Bazilio, who is on a visit from Paris. Luiza's maid, Juliana (one of Eça de Queirós's finest creations), discovers several discarded love letters from Luiza to Bazilio and decides to blackmail her mistress and thus avenge her unfortunate proletarian life. Juliana dies of a fear-provoked stroke, and Luiza succumbs to "brain fever." As in Eça de Queirós's first novel, there are lurid sexual encounters and a general attack on the aimless existence of Portuguese women.

The essential criticism of both of these novels was provided in a review by Machado de Assis, which appeared in 1878 in a Rio de Janeiro newspaper. Although Machado de Assis found merits in Eça de Queirós's writings, he rejected Eça de Queirós's reliance on the descriptive extremes of the naturalist school, which, he believed, went against Eça de Queirós's abilities and artistic aims. He cited Eça de Queirós's plagiarism of parts of Zola's *La Faute de l'Abbé Mouret* (1875; *The Abbé's Temptation*, 1879; also known as *Albine: Or, The Abbé's Temptation*, 1880; better known as *The Sin of Father Mouret*, 1904, 1969) in *The Sin of Father Amaro*, and the device of the stolen letters as an awkward plot element that proved detrimental to the character development in *Cousin Bazilio*. Eça de Queirós made a weak attempt at defending himself in the preface to the 1880 edition of *The Sin of Father Amaro*. A more vituperative self-defense, written at the time, appeared in a posthumously published article, "Idealism and Realism."

These two novels present a remarkable overview of Portuguese society. Eça de Queirós admirably captured the essential traits of various classes. Indeed, he was at his best as a caricaturist; he produced an inimitable Portuguese type in *Cousin Bazilio*: the much-respected expounder of trite clichés, the Counselor Acácio. The petty intrigues of liberals, monarchists, and republicans that kept Portuguese political society afloat are a continuous source of satire in Eça de Queirós's novels.

The Mandarin *and* The Relic

In the important letter/preface to *The Mandarin* (included with the romance since its fifth edition), Eça de Queirós described his "pointless" dedication to realism and his need as an artist to create fantasy. *The Mandarin* and *The Relic* are two related realizations of this creative need. This flight from the reality of realism was to bring about a major revision of Eça de Queirós's literary aims and artistic techniques.

Fantasy for Eça de Queirós was, nevertheless, rooted in reality—his own reality. Thus, Teodoro, the protagonist of *The Mandarin*, has much in common with Eça de Queirós himself—a harassed bureaucrat living alone in a mediocre Lisbon pensione. The financially attractive Faustian offer to kill a Chinese mandarin leads Teodoro to brief wealth, but then to repentance and a begrudging return to his bourgeois existence. With no direct social criticism and only minimal interest in psychological character development, Eça de Queirós was preoccupied with stylistic simplicity and directness. A notable narrative structure that Eça de Queirós employed in many subsequent novels appears in *The Mandarin*: the antithetic comparison. In *The Mandarin*, two very different worlds are juxtaposed: late nineteenth century Portugal and exotic China.

The Relic involves two principal antitheses: spatial (Portugal and Jerusalem) and chronological (hypocritical nineteenth century Portuguese Roman Catholicism and the mystical origins of Christianity). As a reward for his piousness, Teodorico is sent by his sanctimonious aunt on a pilgrimage to the Holy Land, where, aside from engaging in a series of love affairs, he becomes involved in a vivid dream voyage to the beginnings of Christianity. The basis for this dream includes not only Eça de Queirós's remembrances of his trip to Egypt but also the contemporary positivistic attitudes toward religion. Eça de Queirós achieved a comic satire of religious life; it also attests the author's ever-growing interest in hagiography.

Eça de Queirós indicated in the letter/preface to *The Mandarin* that he would begin to pay attention to "fine sentences rather than fine notions." Indeed, linguistic creation and technical originality became his prime concerns. This reorientation is evident in his masterpiece *The Maias*, which was written, reworked, and rewritten over several years.

The Maias

Aristocratic society is the background for *The Maias*. Three generations of a family representing traditional Portugal and the new and future Portugal are lost in their daily existences. Afonso de Maia had been a respected diplomat with a broad knowledge of European life. His grandson, Carlos, a doctor, has all the necessary opportunities but is unable to achieve any goal. He falls passionately in love with Maria Eduarda, who turns out to be his half sister; thus, the family "curse" leads to its ruin. Many brilliant caricatures of Portuguese social life are drawn—the Englishman, the Jewish banker, the homosexual, the ultraromantic poet. Eça de Queirós himself is present in the moralizing voice of João da Ega.

The lurid sex scenes and the plot detail of Eça de Queirós's early naturalistic novels are no longer present in *The Maias*. Eça de Queirós attained an admirable psychological depth in characterization and an innovative, almost poetic use of the Portuguese adjective. He employed indirect free discourse here and throughout his remaining novels as a means of diminishing authorial presence.

Neither of Eça de Queirós's final two novels, *The Illustrious House of Ramires* and *The City and the Mountains*, was completely revised by him prior to his death in 1990, but both reveal the author's continuing concern with the questions of artistic technique and his love for Portugal, conditioned by his realization of its limited future.

The Illustrious House of Ramires *and* The City and the Mountains

In *The Illustrious House of Ramires*, Gonçalo Ramires, the last scion of an ancient Portuguese noble family, is preparing his family history for "political" reasons. The intertwining of the Portuguese past and present results in a series of antitheses of satiric and allegorical proportions. Gonçalo cannot live up to the standards of his ancestors, just as Portugal can no longer be what it was in the past. Eça de Queirós skillfully manipulates both "historical plots" and thus compares time, space, and characters. Ultimately, he reveals eternal Portuguese qualities: innocence, good-heartedness, nostalgia for the past, all mixed with shades of laziness.

To this list of Portuguese characteristics can be added the "rural inclination," as is evident in *The City and the Mountains*. The antithesis here is between the ultramodern city of Paris and the backwardness of the Portuguese countryside. The city dweller Jacinto resides at 202 Champs Elysées and believes that "Absolute Knowledge × Absolute Power = Absolute Happiness." This formula holds true until all of his gadgets and machines begin to fail. His ennui causes a dreaded return to his native rural Portugal. There, Jacinto discovers the simple pleasures of life and resolves his existence.

For Eça de Queirós, no doubt, this novel was a resolution of his own reality, or indeed the Portuguese reality: an adventurer in his diplomatic and literary careers, but at heart a "poor man from Póvoa de Varzim."

Irwin Stern

Other major works

SHORT FICTION: *A correspondência de Fradique Mendes*, 1900; *Contos*, 1902 (includes *O Defunto* [*Our Lady of the Pillar*, 1906]; *José Mathais* [English translation, 1947]; *Perfection*, 1923; and *The Sweet Miracle*, 1904); *Cartas inéditas de Fradique Mendes e mais páginas esquecidas*, 1928; *The Mandarin, and Other Stories*, 1965.

NONFICTION: *Prosas Bárbaras*, 1903; *Cartas de Inglaterra*, 1905 (*Letters from England*, 1970); *Ecos de Paris*, 1905; *Notas contemporâneas*, 1909; *Cartas familiares e bilhetes de Paris*, 1912; *Ultimas páginas*, 1912; *A catástrofe*, 1925; *Correspondência*, 1925; *Cronicas de Londres*, 1944; *Folhas soltas*, 1966; *Prosas esquecidas*, 1966; *A emigração como força civilizadora*, 1979.

MISCELLANEOUS: *Obras completas*, 1948; *Obras de Eça de Queiroz*, 1960-1972 (15 volumes).

Bibliography

Bloom, Harold. *Genius: A Mosaic of One Hundred Exemplary Creative Minds*. New York: Warner Books, 2002. Eça de Queirós is one of the "geniuses" whose life and work is discussed in this collection of vignettes about significant literary figures.

Coleman, Alexander. *Eça de Queirós and European Realism*. New York: New York University Press, 1980. A biography placing Eça de Queirós in the context of his literary contemporaries, focusing on his promotion of realism as a literary genre. Includes an index and a bibliography.

Demetz, Peter. "Eça de Queiróz as a Literary Critic." *Comparative Literature* 19 (Fall, 1967): 289-307. One of the few studies in English of Eça de Queirós's nonfiction, namely his literary criticism.

Mónica, Maria Filomena. *Eça de Queiroz*. Translated by Alison Aiken. Woodbridge, England: Tamesis, 2005. The first biography of Eça de Queirós available in English, this book places the author within the context of nineteenth century Portuguese history. Includes thirty black-and-white photographs.

Pritchett, V. S. *The Myth Makers: Essays on European, Russian, and South American Novelists*. London: Chatto & Windus, 1979. Eça de Queirós is discussed in this collection of essays by Pritchett, himself a noted English author.

Scott, Paddy. *Women in the Novels of Benito Pérez Galdós and Eça de Queiroz*. Lewiston, N.Y.: Edwin Mellen Press, 2008. Scott analyzes the representation of women in the work of the two novelists, examining the themes of women and education, religion, and work from a feminist perspective.

Stevens, James R. "Eça and Flaubert." *Luso Brazilian Review* 3, no. 1 (1966). Discusses and compares the two masters of nineteenth century realism.

UMBERTO ECO

Born: Alessandria, Italy; January 5, 1932

Principal long fiction

Il nome della rosa, 1980 (*The Name of the Rose*, 1983)
Il pendolo di Foucault, 1988 (*Foucault's Pendulum*, 1989)
L'isola del giorno prima, 1994 (*The Island of the Day Before*, 1995)
Baudolino, 2000 (English translation, 2002)
La misteriosa fiamma della regina Loana, 2004 (*The Mysterious Flame of Queen Loana: An Illustrated Novel*, 2005)

Other literary forms

Umberto Eco (EHK-oh) is known primarily for his scholarly work in semiotics and his extensive writing on language and culture. He has published numerous essays, book chapters, and encyclopedia articles in works including *Enciclopedia filosofica* and the *Encyclopedic Dictionary of Semiotics*. He has been a columnist for *Il Giorno*, *La Stanma*, and other newspapers and magazines. His essays and reviews have also been published in *L'Espresso*, *Corriere della sera*, *Times Literary Supplement*, and *Nouvelle revue française*. Essay collections include *Cinque scritti morali* (1997; *Five Moral Pieces*, 2001), *Il secondo diario minimo* (1992; *How to Travel with a Salmon, and Other Essays*, 1994), and *Travels in Hyper Reality: Essays* (1986). Well-known scholarly pieces include *Semiotica e filosofia del linguaggio* (1984; *Semiotics and the Philosophy of Language*, 1984), *The Limits of Interpretation* (1990), and *La ricerca della lingua perfetta nella cultura europea* (1993; *The Search for the Perfect Language*, 1995). Eco has two works of juvenile fiction to his credit—*I tre cosmonauti* (1988; *The Three Astronauts*, 1995) and *La bomba e il generale* (1989; *The Bomb and the General*, 1989).

Achievements

Umberto Eco has received twenty-four honorary doctorates from universities in Europe, North America, and South America. He has served on the editorial boards of several scholarly publications, including *Semiotica*, *Poetics Today*, *Structuralist Review*, *Text*, and *Alfabeta*. He also founded and edited the journal *VS: Versus—Quaderni di studi semiotici*.

For his novel *The Name of the Rose*, Eco won several prizes and nominations, including the Italian Premio Strega and Premio Anghiari (1981); the Prix Medicis for best foreign novel (1982); a *Los Angeles Times* fiction prize nomination (1983); and an award for best fiction book from the Association of Logos Bookstores. In 1986, Jean-Jacques Annaud directed a film adaptation of *The Name of the Rose*, starring Sean Connery as William of Baskerville. Eco also received the Columbus Award of the Rotary Club of Florence (1983); the Commander of the Order of Arts and Letters (France, 1985); the Marshall McLuhan Award-UNESCO Canada; and an award from the Canadian communications company Teleglobe.

Eco was a professor of semiotics at the University of Bologna in Italy, where he also directed programs for communication sciences and publishing. He also was a visiting professor or guest lecturer at many of the Western world's most prestigious universities, including Cambridge, Oxford, Harvard, and Columbia. Beginning in 1992, he was a member of the UNESCO International Forum and of the Académie Universelle des Cultures in Paris. His novels have been translated into many languages and have enjoyed remarkable international success.

Biography

Umberto Eco was born on January 5, 1932 in Alessandria, a small city east of Turin and south of Milan in the northwestern Italian province of Piedmont. He had a home in the Piedmont region his entire life. His father, Giulio Eco, was an accountant in a firm that manufactured bathtubs. His mother was Giovanna Bisio Eco. The

Umberto Eco. (Guido Harari/Contrasto/Redux/ Courtesy, Harcourt Books)

young Eco entered the University of Turin and graduated in 1954 with a degree in philosophy. His thesis, *Il problema estetico in San Tommaso* (1956), was translated into English as *The Aesthetics of Thomas Aquinas* (1988). In 1961, he received a *libera docenza* (a degree roughly equivalent to the doctorate) in aesthetics.

On September 24, 1962, Eco married Renate Ramge, a German-born teacher. The couple had two children, Stefano (born 1963) and Carlotta (born 1964). Eco's first job after graduate school was as cultural editor at the Milan studio of Radiotelevisione Italia (RAI), the Italian radio and television network. With RAI he learned about the workings of popular culture and acquired an intellectual interest in novels, motion pictures, comic books, and in other mass media. After five years at RAI, he began work as a nonfiction senior editor at Casa Editrice Bompiani, a Milan publishing house. During the 1950's and 1960's, he taught at the universities of Turin, Milan, and Florence on subjects ranging from aesthetics and architecture to visual communication. During this time as well, Eco developed the concept of the "open work" or "open text." For Eco, an open text is a text that allows and invites a variety of readings; a "closed work" or "closed text," in contrast, has a narrow range for interpretation.

Eco maintained a lifelong interest in popular culture and has written on the James Bond novels, detective fiction, and Superman comic books, analyzing their narrative structures and ideological content. Eco also began to organize his ideas about semiotics—the study of the signs and symbols through which cultures communicate. His first book solely on that subject was *La struttura assent* (1968; the absent structure), which was revised and then published as *A Theory of Semiotics* (1975). This work marks his shift from an interest in medieval aesthetics to a more general interest in cultural values, literature, and literary criticism. In 1971, he joined the faculty of the University of Bologna, Europe's oldest university, as its first professor of semiotics, a position he held for more than three decades.

Long respected as a language and culture scholar, Eco's life took an interesting turn in the 1980's when he became a celebrated novelist with the publication of *The Name of the Rose*. The success of the novel surprised Eco, and his novels have since sold millions of copies.

Even though he has earned recognition for his novels, Eco's scholarly work has not abated. He has garnered high academic and public distinctions, teaching and lecturing all over the world while continuing to write. He formed a close association with Indiana University Press, which published a number of his works in English. Eco wrote into his seventies, including writing a weekly column for *L'Espresso*.

Analysis

Umberto Eco's five novels are known throughout the Western literary world. The first two, *The Name of the Rose* and *Foucault's Pendulum*, were best sellers. The first four novels might be called historical mysteries. They show Eco's wide ranging knowledge of the culture and history of the ancient and medieval worlds, as well as his fascination with the scientific history of the sixteenth and seventeenth centuries. The novels show an interest in maps, signs, logic, and the way in which texts interact. Indeed, all of his novels reveal his academic and intellectual interests to one degree or another. The narrator of his novel *The Mysterious Flame of Queen Loana*, Giambattista Bodoni, tells the story of his own attempt to regain the memory of his existence. He remembers everything he has ever read but, curiously, because of a stroke, he has lost the facts of his own life. He sets out to recover his memories by sifting through his childhood reading.

The Name of the Rose

The Name of the Rose was one of the most successful novels of the 1980's. Its labyrinthine plot embraces many of Eco's intellectual interests, namely semiotics, medieval religion and aesthetics, and detective stories. The narrative has a triple frame. In a preface and note, readers learn that the narrator was given a translation, by Abbé Valet, of a manuscript written in Latin by Adso of Melk. Adso, a young Benedictine novice of the monastery of Melk at the time of the story, has written of his adventure with Brother William of Baskerville. William is a learned Franciscan undertaking an important mission; Adso becomes his scribe and disciple.

The main thrust of the plot concerns the murder of several monks at a northern Italian abbey in 1327. Like Sherlock Holmes, of whom Brother William certainly reminds readers, William traces clues to find the party responsible for the murders. Involved in the plot is a book containing the second part of Aristotle's *Poetics*, the part devoted to comedy. Adso chronicles William's movements and methods as he solves the mystery with his logic, knowledge of language, and ability to find and interpret the meaning of clues.

Foucault's Pendulum

Foucault's Pendulum takes place in the years 1970 to 1984. Three men—Belpo, Diotallevi, and Causaubon—working at a Milan publishing house amuse themselves by putting information about occultism and conspiracy groups from manuscripts they have reviewed for publication into a computer program called The Plan. The program produces a map suggesting that the geographical point at which the powers of the earth can be controlled is at Foucault's Pendulum in Paris. This elaborate joke is taken seriously, however, by Satanists and other occultists, who pursue the three editors—to the death in one case—to find the "secret" to world power.

The novel offers readers a staggering amount of information about subjects such as the Knights Templar, the Cabala, the Masons, the Jesuits, the Nazis, and the Rosicrucians. Some critics faulted the novel for giving too much arcane information. Others felt Eco was not fully successful in conveying the many layers of meaning he intended. One critic suggested the novel was really about the act of interpretation itself. Herbert Mitgang said in *The New York Times* that the book

> is a quest novel that is deeper and richer than *The Name of the Rose*. It's a brilliant piece of research and writing—experimental and funny, literary and philosophical—that bravely ignores the conventional expectations of the reader.

The elusive, encyclopedic style was denounced by some as not appropriate for the novel form. In objection to Eco's habit of using lengthy lists of items, Leon Wieseltier declared in *The New Republic* that the book "was not written, it was compiled." Anthony Burgess, in *The New York Times*, called it "an encyclopedic detective story" and commented

> For while it is not a novel in the strict sense of the work, it is a truly formidable gathering of information delivered playfully by a master manipulating his own invention—in effect, a long erudite joke.

Both *Foucault's Pendulum* and *The Name of the Rose* involve maps, signs, and secrets, but they focus on the complex ways in which people come to understand the world. Both novels also expose the dangers of fanaticism.

The Island of the Day Before

Eco sets his third novel, *The Island of the Day Before*, in the first half of the seventeenth century, an age of daring voyages and scientific discovery. He has devised a curious frame to tell the story of Roberto della Griva, a young man who has sailed on the vessel *Amaryllis*. After a tempest, Roberto becomes shipwrecked on the *Daphne*. The *Daphne* lies anchored within sight of a tropical island, but Roberto cannot reach it because all the lifeboats are gone and Roberto cannot swim. The narrator of the story claims to have acquired various pieces of writing that Roberto created while stranded on the *Daphne*, and that he has pieced the writings into a narrative. Among other things, Roberto had written letters and a romance to a beloved.

Roberto has sufficient provisions to survive for some time on the ship. After many musings about his past, his family, science, and the natural world, he sets himself adrift. In a colophon, the narrator tells readers that no one knows for certain what happened to Roberto. The narrator also tells readers how Roberto's papers were found, possibly with information about finding the secret to plotting a ship's longitudinal position at sea; it was this secret that Cardinal Mazarin had sent Roberto to find in the first place.

Some reviewers found the novel dense and somewhat dull despite its playful presentation of knowledge and narrative. Robert Kelly, however, writing for *The New York Times Book Review*, declared the novel "a grand and entertaining book" that "belongs in the great tradition of the *conte philosophique* (philosophical story), like [Jonathan] Swift's *Gulliver's Travels* . . . and Voltaire's *Candide*."

Toni J. Morris

Other major works

NONFICTION: *Il problema estetico in San Tommaso*, 1956 (also known as *Il problema estetico in Tommaso d'Aquino*; *The Aesthetics of Thomas Aquinas*, 1988); *Sviluppo dell'estetico medievale*, 1959 (*Art and Beauty in the Middle Ages*, 1986); *Opera aperta*, 1962 (*The Open Work*, 1989); *Apocalittici e integrati*, 1964 (revised 1977; *Apocalypse Postponed*, 1994); *Le poetiche di Joyce: Dalla "Summa" al "Finnegans Wake,"* 1966 (*The Aesthetic of Chaosmos: The Middle Ages of James Joyce*, 1982); *La struttura assente*, 1968; *Opera aperta, la definizione dell'arte*, 1968; *Le forme del contenuto*, 1971; *A Theory of Semiotics*, 1976; *The Role of the Reader: Explorations in the Semiotics of Texts*, 1979; *Postille a "Il nome della rosa,"* 1983 (*Postscript to "The Name of the Rose,"* 1984); *Sette anni di desiderio: Chronache 1977-1983*, 1983; *Semiotica e filosofia del linguaggio*, 1984 (*Semiotics and the Philosophy of Language*, 1984); *Faith in Fakes*, 1986; *Travels in Hyper Reality: Essays*, 1986; *Diario minimo*, 1988 (*Misreadings*, 1993); *The Limits of Interpretation*, 1990; *Il secondo diario minimo*, 1992 (*How to Travel with a Salmon, and Other Essays*, 1994); *Interpretation and*

Overinterpretation, 1992 (with Richard Rorty, Jonathan Culler, and Christine Brooke-Rose); *La ricerca della lingua perfetta nella cultura europea*, 1993 (*The Search for the Perfect Language*, 1995); *Six Walks in the Fictional Woods*, 1994; *In cosa crede chi non crede?*, 1996 (with Carlo Maria Martini; *Belief or Nonbelief? A Confrontation*, 2000); *Cinque scritti morali*, 1997 (*Five Moral Pieces*, 2001); *Serendipities: Language and Lunacy*, 1998; *La bustina di Minerva*, 1999; *Conversations About the End of Time*, 1999; *Kant e l'ornitorinco*, 1999 (*Kant and the Platypus: Essays on Language and Cognition*, 1999); *Experiences in Translation*, 2001; *Sulla letteratura*, 2002 (*On Literature*, 2004); *Dire quasi la stessa cosa: Esperienze di traduzione*, 2003; *Mouse or Rat? Translation as Negotiation*, 2003; *A passo di gambero: Guerre calde e populismo mediatico*, 2006 (*Turning Back the Clock: Hot Wars and Media Populism*, 2007).

CHILDREN'S LITERATURE: *I tre cosmonauti*, 1988 (*The Three Astronauts*, 1995); *La bomba e il generale*, 1989 (*The Bomb and the General*, 1989).

EDITED TEXTS: *Storia figurata delle invenzioni: Dalla selce scheggiata al volo spaziali*, 1961 (with G. Zorzoli; *The Picture History of Inventions from Plough to Polaris*, 1963); *Il caso Bond*, 1965 (with Oreste del Buono; *The Bond Affair*, 1966); *I fumetti di Mao*, 1971 (with J. Chesneaux and G. Nebiolo; *The People's Comic Book: Red Women's Detachment, Hot on the Trail, and Other Chinese Comics*, 1973); *A Semiotic Landscape*, 1979 (with Seymour Chatman and Jean-Marie Klinkenberg); *The Sign of the Three: Dupin, Holmes, Peirce*, 1984 (with Thomas A. Sebeok); *Meaning and Mental Representations*, 1988 (with Marco Santambrogio and Patrizia Violi); *Povero Pinocchio*, 1995; *Storia della bellezza*, 2004 (*History of Beauty*, 2004; also known as *On Beauty*, 2004); *On Ugliness*, 2007.

Bibliography

Bondanella, Peter. "Umberto Eco." In *Postmodernism: The Key Figures*, edited by Hans Bertens and Joseph Natoli. Malden, Mass.: Blackwell, 2002. A brief introduction to Eco as a key figure in postmodernism.

_______. *Umberto Eco and the Open Text: Semiotics, Fiction, Popular Culture*. New York: Cambridge University Press, 1997. The first comprehensive English-language study of Eco's work. The author considers Eco's well-known texts and traces his intellectual development from medieval aesthetics to popular culture, postmodernism, and semiotic theory. One chapter each is devoted to Eco's first three novels.

Francese, Joseph. *Socially Symbolic Acts: The Historicizing Fictions of Umberto Eco, Cincenzo Consolo, and Antonio Tabucchi*. Madison, N.J.: Fairleigh Dickinson University Press, 2006. Close readings of the fiction of Eco and two other prominent Italian novelists. Provides an analysis of Eco's first three novels.

Rice, Thomas J. "Mapping Complexity in the Fiction of Umberto Eco." *Critique* 44, no. 4 (Summer, 2003): 349-368. A substantial article that addresses a new style of novel—the novel of complexity. Rice explores Eco's first three novels by defining them as a mapping problem, as all three novels are centrally concerned with mapmaking.

Ross, Charlotte, and Rochelle Sibley, eds. *Illuminating Eco: On the Boundaries of Interpretation*. Burlington, Vt.: Ashgate, 2004. A collection of ten essays approaching Eco's work from several disciplinary perspectives. Includes analysis of Eco's fiction and his theories of interpretation and translation.

Streufert, Paul D. "The Liar, the Forger, the Actor: The Idea of 'Author' in *The Name of the Rose* and *The Island of the Day Before*." *RLA: Romance Languages Annual* 11 (1999): 380-384. Streufert analyzes the two novels looking through the lens of Eco's essay "The Semiotics of Theatrical Performance." Specifically, he explores the narrative framing texts employed by Eco.

MARIA EDGEWORTH

Born: Black Bourton, Oxfordshire, England; January 1, 1768
Died: Edgeworthstown, Ireland; May 22, 1849

PRINCIPAL LONG FICTION

Castle Rackrent: An Hibernian Tale, 1800
Belinda, 1801
Leonora, 1806
Ennui, 1809
The Absentee, 1812
Vivian, 1812
Patronage, 1814
Harrington, 1817
Ormond, 1817
Helen, 1834

OTHER LITERARY FORMS

Like a number of late eighteenth century and early nineteenth century authors, Maria Edgeworth did not intend to become a novelist; rather, she began writing extended prose fiction as an outgrowth of other kinds of literary production. Her first works were children's tales, usually short and always with a clear and forcefully advanced didactic thesis—a few titles suggest the nature of the themes: "Lazy Laurence," "Waste Not, Want Not," "Forgive and Forget." Many of these stories were assembled under the titles *The Parent's Assistant: Or, Stories for Children* (1796, 1800) and *Moral Tales for Young People* (1801), the first of which encompassed six volumes, while the second filled five volumes.

These tales were written largely at the behest of Edgeworth's father, Richard Lovell Edgeworth, who was a deeply committed moralist and is still considered a notable figure in the history of education in England and Ireland. Both father and daughter collaborated on many of the stories, as they did on most of what Maria Edgeworth wrote. As a sort of commentary on the works of short fiction and certainly as an adjunct to them, the essays on education collected in *Essays on Practical Education* (1798) were designed to advance the liberal but moralistic theories on child rearing that the elder Edgeworth had imbibed in part from Jean-Jacques Rousseau and had transmitted to his daughter. Richard Edgeworth's credentials for such a piece of writing were perhaps enhanced by the fact that he fathered no fewer than twenty-two children with four wives.

Apart from further essays (again, chiefly written either in collaboration with her father or under his watchful eye) on education, morals, Ireland, and culture, Edgeworth's primary emphasis was on fiction, usually of novel length (her "novels" range in length from the quite short *Castle Rackrent*, merely one hundred pages, to *Belinda*, which extends to almost five hundred pages). The only other form she attempted—one in which, like many nineteenth century authors, she had no publishing success—was the drama. Her plays were composed essentially for the pleasure of the family, as were the first drafts of the majority of her fiction works, and the volume containing the best of the plays, *Comic Dramas in Three Acts* (1817), is now almost universally unread.

ACHIEVEMENTS

During her long lifetime, Maria Edgeworth helped to make possible the Victorian novel. Reared with a rich background in the high achievements of Henry Fielding, Samuel Richardson, and Tobias Smollett, she began to write at a time when female novelists were just beginning to be accepted; a few of them, such as Fanny Burney and Elizabeth Inchbald, managed to attain some popularity. The novel of manners was the prevailing genre produced by these "lady writers." It had affinities with the lachrymose novel of sensibility (the classic example of which, *The Man of Feeling*, was penned in 1771 by a man, Henry Mackenzie), and the tight focus and excessively delicate feelings exhibited in this form limited its appeal and artistic possibilities. It lay to Jane Austen to instill clever and penetrating satire, along with a much greater sense of realism in regard to human behavior, and to Maria Edgeworth to extend its bounds of character depiction, to include persons of the lower classes, and to broaden its range: Men are seen at the hunt, in private conference, and in all manner of vigorous activity unknown in Austen's fiction.

Edgeworth is, of course, bound to be compared with

Austen, to the former's derogation; there can be no doubt that the latter is the greater novelist, from an artistic standpoint. This judgment should not blind the reader to Edgeworth's accomplishment, however. As P. N. Newby has observed, although "Jane Austen was so much the better novelist," yet "Maria Edgeworth may be the more important." Her significance rests chiefly on two achievements: She widened the scope of the "female" novel (the emphasis on female sensibility in her work is considerably less than in Austen's novels, though it can be detected), and, as Newby has noted, in her careful and detailed treatment of Ireland and its people she "gave dignity to the regional subject and made the regional novel possible." Today, readers tend to take for granted the insightful historical works of, for example, Sir Walter Scott; they often do not realize that, had it not been for Edgeworth, Scott might not have attempted the monumental effort that he began in *Waverley: Or, 'Tis Sixty Years Since* (1814), in the preface of which he gives Edgeworth full credit for inspiring him to essay the regional fiction in which his work became a landmark. It has also been claimed that such disparate figures as Stendhal and Ivan Turgenev were influenced by Edgeworth's sympathetic treatment of peasants. Some critics and literary historians have gone so far as to claim for her the title of the first intelligent sociological novelist in English literature. More than any author up to her time, Edgeworth revealed human beings as related to, and partially formed by, their environments.

Biography

January 1, 1767, is usually accepted as the birth date of Maria Edgeworth, but, in *Maria Edgeworth: A Literary Biography* (1972), Marilyn Butler asserts that Maria herself "seems to have considered 1768 correct, and the Black Bourton records on the whole support her." This is one of the few uncertainties in a life dedicated to family, friends, and literature. Edgeworth was born in England, the child of Richard Lovell Edgeworth (an Anglo-Irish gentleman with extensive estates in county Longford, about sixty miles from Dublin) and his first wife, Anna Maria Elers Edgeworth, who died when Maria was five years old. By all accounts, Maria got along well with her three siblings, two sisters and a brother (another child died before she was born), and with her father's next three wives and her seventeen half brothers and half sisters, most of whom she helped to rear. The general harmony in the Edgeworth household may be seen as all the more remarkable when one considers that Richard Edgeworth's last wife, Frances Anne Beaufort Edgeworth (with whose family Maria became quite friendly), was a year or two younger than Maria.

Much of this impressive concord can be credited to Richard Lovell Edgeworth, a man of enormous confidence and personal force. He took the not untypical eighteenth century view that, as the father in the household, he was the lord and master in a literal sense. Fortunately, he was a benevolent master. Although he believed firmly that he knew what was best for all his wives and children, what he believed to be best was their relatively free development, confined only by his sense of what was morally right and socially proper. Maria evidently accepted her father's guidance to the point of seeking and welcoming his advice.

Richard Edgeworth had such confidence both in the good sense of his children and in his own principles of education, which were patterned on those of his eccentric friend Thomas Day (author of the once-famous novel of education *The History of Sandford and Merton*, 1783-1789), that he informed his family of the reasons for nearly all of his decisions, and certainly for the important ones. The most important of these was his resolve to settle on his family estate in Ireland (he had been living in England for a number of years, having left Ireland about 1765; and Maria had visited Ireland only briefly, in 1773). One reason for the election to live in Ireland—Edgeworth could have afforded to stay in England, since he received rents from his Irish property—was that Richard Edgeworth was convinced by his reading and by the course of national affairs (one feature of which was the harsh economic treatment of Ireland because of the great expense incurred by England in its war with the American colonies) that Ireland could be one of the best and most productive areas in the British Empire.

To achieve the goal of proper estate management, a subject that was to engage the interest of Maria Edgeworth for the rest of her life, her father had to revolutionize the way in which his lands and tenants were cared for. The salient aspect of the change was a greater concern for genuine productivity and less for high rents. He was

Maria Edgeworth. (Library of Congress)

quite successful, partly because of the help of his adoring and sensible daughter. The estate and the family survived riots, famines, and the very real threat of a French invasion of Ireland during the Napoleonic campaigns. From the time the Edgeworth family relocated to Edgeworthstown, in 1782, until her death, Maria Edgeworth lived in the family homestead—the constancy of her residence there being broken by only a few trips to England, France, and Scotland and brief visits to other countries on the Continent. During these sojourns, she managed to become acquainted, largely through her father's influence, with some of the leading thinkers and artists of the day, notably Sir Walter Scott, with whom she formed a warm personal friendship and for whom she had a great admiration, which was reciprocated. Edgeworth was one of the first readers to recognize that the anonymously published *Waverley* was the work of "the Wizard of the North."

While visiting France in 1802, Edgeworth met the Chevalier Abraham Niclas Clewberg-Edelcrantz, a Swedish diplomat to whom she was introduced in Paris. For this somewhat shy, very small, not particularly attractive woman, the encounter was extraordinary. Edelcrantz was not handsome, and he was forty-six years old. On the positive side, he was very intelligent and quite well educated, a fact that appealed to Edgeworth. Although evidently astounded and pleased by Edelcrantz's proposal of marriage, she was wise enough to realize that his devotion to Sweden, which he could not think of leaving as his home, and hers to Ireland posed an absolute barrier to any happiness in such a union. Richard Edgeworth was apparently in favor of the marriage, but he did nothing to persuade Maria to accept the Swede, and he received her decision with equanimity.

Apart from helping her father to manage the estate—managing it herself almost single-handedly after his death in 1817—and looking after the family, Edgeworth devoted herself almost exclusively to writing. Some of her novels began as very short tales written (usually on a slate, so that erasures and improvements could be made readily) for the entertainment of the younger members of the family circle. Richard Edgeworth, however, persuaded her to take her writing seriously. This she did for some fifty years, until shortly before her death in 1849, by which time she had become respected and, to a degree seldom achieved by a female author, famous.

Analysis

The novels of Maria Edgeworth are, to the modern reader, an odd combination of strengths and weaknesses. This phenomenon is not really very strange, given the times in which she lived and the progress of fiction writing in the early nineteenth century. The work of all the novelists of that period may be considered strongly flawed and yet often unexpectedly effective (Sir Walter Scott is the obvious example, but the same might even be said of much of the work of Charles Dickens). What is perhaps more surprising is that Edgeworth herself was aware of the defects of her work. She knew, for example, that her writings were didactic to an often annoying degree. Her father, who had a great deal to do with her conviction that fiction should aim to elevate the morals of its readers, even comments on the fact in one of his prefaces to her novels and claims that a severe attempt had been made to subdue the moralistic features. By modern standards, the attempts never fully succeeded in any of Edgeworth's novels.

One reason for the "failure" is simply the prevalence of the late eighteenth century belief that behavior can be modified by edifying reading and that character can be formed and, possibly more important, reformed by acts of the will. Those of Edgeworth's tales titled with the name of the central character, such as *Ormond*, *Belinda*, and *Vivian*, are thus the stories of how these young people come to terms with society and their responsibilities—in short, how they grow up to be worthy citizens. The concept itself is not ludicrous; literature is replete with studies of the ways in which young people come of age successfully. What is distressing in Edgeworth's "moral tales" (and those of many other writers of the era) are the improbable turns of plot such as those by which poor but honest people are suddenly discovered to be heirs to great properties, those believed to be orphans are revealed as the offspring of noble houses, and so forth. This sort of device has a long history in both fiction and drama, but it is especially dismaying in a work that is otherwise, and by clear intention, realistic. The distracting and hardly credible process by which Grace Nugent, in *The Absentee*, is proved legitimate so that Lord Colambre can in good conscience marry her (the moral logic behind his reluctance to wed her, blameless as she is for the situation of her birth, may repel modern readers who are not familiar with the depth of the eighteenth century conviction concerning the influence of a flawed family background) is needlessly detailed. Such a device also intrudes on a story that is otherwise filled with convincing details about estate management (and mismanagement) in Ireland and fairly realistic studies of the lives of the common people.

Richard Edgeworth was blamed, perhaps unjustly, for the excess of didacticism in his daughter's novels (it is surely no accident that the only work lacking such material, *Castle Rackrent*, was her most popular title and is today her only novel still read); some of the tiresome passages of "uplifting" commentary do sound as if they came from his eloquent but ponderous pen, as in Belinda's comment in a letter, "Female wit sometimes depends on the beauty of its possessor for its reputation; and the reign of beauty is proverbially short, and fashion often capriciously deserts her favourites, even before nature withers their charms." To his credit, however, Richard Edgeworth is now known to have done a great deal to provide his daughter with ideas for stories and plot sequences.

Perhaps the most important artistic flaw to which the younger Edgeworth pleaded guilty was a lack of invention, and critics over the decades have noticed that she depends to excess on details and facts, many of which she collected from her own family's records and memoirs. The rest she gathered by direct (and penetrating) observation, as in the realistic farm scenes in the Irish tales and the believable pictures of society gatherings in London and Paris. One of the most obvious indications of Edgeworth's failure to devise plots artfully is her reliance on the retrospective strategy of having a character reveal his or her background by telling it to another. Certainly, the review of her own life that Lady Delacour provides for Belinda is not without interest and is necessary to the story, yet it seems cumbersome, appearing as it does in two chapters that occupy more than thirty pages near the opening of the novel.

The two types of novels that Edgeworth wrote—the Irish tales and, as the title of one collection indicates, the *Tales of Fashionable Life* (1809-1812)—manifest the poles of her thematic interest. She believed, as did her father, that Ireland could benefit and even prosper from a more responsible aristocracy, landowners who lived on their property and saw that it was fairly and efficiently managed. In her three best Irish tales, *Castle Rackrent*, *The Absentee*, and *Ormond*, Edgeworth underlines the virtues of fair play with tenants, caution in dealing with hired estate managers (the wicked Nicholas Garraghty in *The Absentee* should be warning enough for any proprietor), and close attention to details of land and equipment. The years that Edgeworth spent aiding her father at Edgeworthstown bore impressive fruit in her grasp of the problems and difficulties faced by owners of large estates.

Because the sectarian, political, and economic problems that faced Ireland have tended to persist into the present, while the aspects of fashionable life have not, the "society" novels in Irish literature are almost unknown by the reading public today. In any case, Edgeworth was much more intellectually involved in the politics and social problems of her homeland than she was in the vagaries and evils of society life in big cities. Much as she believed that a great deal can be learned about the proper way to live one's life by observing society closely, she was personally never so involved in that topic as she was in such concerns as the injustices created by absentee landlords and the abuse of tenants by land agents hired by the absentees and given enormous power. Thus, while Belinda, Vivian, and Helen do hold some interest for the reader, their problems and challenges are dated. The modern reader has difficulty taking seriously the follies of Vivian, who manages to misjudge nearly everybody in the novel, leading to his not unexpected demise, which is sad but far from tragic. The peculiarities of King Corny in *Ormond*, however, as when it is revealed that he is elevating the roof of his large house so that he can construct attics under it, help to provide the reader with a more substantial grasp of the great power, the tendency toward eccentricity, and the frequent good-heartedness of Irish estate owners.

Edgeworth usually dealt with events and conditions in the fairly recent past; as such, she can be considered a historical novelist. Her emphasis on what can be viewed as an international theme, however (the relationship between English and Irish characters and attitudes), is thought by many to be the most significant aspect of her novels. Critics have even suggested that her treatment of the topic prefigures the more detailed analyses by Henry James.

Edgeworth appeared on the literary scene at the best possible moment for her career and the future of the English novel. Her own records designate the amounts that she was paid by her publishers for each major work, and the list of payments is, by the standards of the time, impressive. For example, the minor novel *Patronage* earned Edgeworth twenty-one hundred pounds, at that time an enormous sum. The influence that she had on the course of the historical and regional novel is proof of her little-known but vital contribution toward the development of the English novel.

CASTLE RACKRENT

In his introduction to the Oxford English Novels edition of *Castle Rackrent* (1964), George Watson claims for this unusual book the distinction of being "the first regional novel in English, and perhaps in all Europe." Certainly, the work is a tour de force, all the more impressive because it was, by most accounts, achieved virtually by accident. Richard Edgeworth had on the estate a steward named John Langan. His opinions and mode of expression so struck Maria Edgeworth that she began to record his comments and became an able mimic of his dialect and turns of speech. Her letters to her father's sister, Mrs. Margaret Edgeworth Ruxton, one of her favorite correspondents, inspired this sympathetic lady to encourage her niece to develop the material into a story. Thus was born Maria Edgeworth's only substantial piece of fiction written during Richard Edgeworth's lifetime in whose composition he evidently did not play a part.

Edgeworth claimed that only the narrator was based on a real-life person, Langan; some scholars have suggested that one or two other characters might have been fashioned after people known to her. An example is the entertaining character Sir Conolly "Condy" Rackrent, who may have been broadly patterned on Edgeworth's maternal grandfather. However great or small its basis in real life, the novel has the air of reality about it. The actions and the motivations ring true to life. *Castle Rackrent* is often praised for its lack of an obtrusive moral emphasis, but it would be a mistake to read the novel as having no message. The decline and fall of the Rackrent family is the story of irresponsibility and extravagance, an unfortunately common phenomenon in the history of Irish landowners.

The narrator, Thady Quirk, commonly called honest Thady, tells the dismal but occasionally humorous tale of the several masters under whom he has served: Sir Patrick O'Shaughlin, who drinks himself to death early in the story; Sir Murtaugh Rackrent, who dies in a paroxysm of anger over a legalistic contretemps; Sir Kit Rackrent, who dies in a duel over the controversy stemming from his indecision regarding the choice of a new wife, when his first spouse seems on the point of death; and Sir Conolly Rackrent, whose narrative is longer than the tale of the first three owners of Castle Rackrent. Another innovative aspect of the novel, aside from the use of such an authentic narrator, is the consistent employment of dialect. The text is not difficult to read, but many of the expressions are not easily comprehensible to a reader unfamiliar with the Irish speech and mores of that era. Wisely, Edgeworth—with her father's help—appended a glossary that explains, occasionally in needless detail, many of Thady's locutions and references. That Thady opens his memoir on a Monday morning might have little special significance unless the reader is informed by the glossary that "no great undertaking can be auspiciously commenced in Ireland on any morning but *Monday morning*."

Perhaps the chief appeal of the work to the modern reader lies in the personality of Thady and in the folkways he embodies. On the first page, he tells of his "great coat," which poverty compels him to wear winter and summer but which is "very handy, as I never put my arms into the sleeves, (they are as good as new,) though come Holantide next, I've had it these seven years." The extraordinary loyalty of Thady to a family that seems not to deserve such fidelity is both exasperating and admirable. Thady is not, however, overcome with emotion when unfortunate circumstances arise. Though he cannot recall the drinking habits of Sir Patrick without the brief aside, "God bless him!," he speaks of a shocking event at the funeral with relative calm: "Happy the man who could get but a sight of the hearse!—But who'd have thought it? Just as all was going on right, through his own town they were passing, when the body was seized for debt." Thady is moved enough to call the creditors "villains," but he swiftly moves on with his tale: "So, to be sure, the law must take its course—and little gain had the creditors for their pains." The old man spends more time on the legal implications of the seizure than on the event itself. This passage displays Edgeworth's understanding of the contentious element in the Irish personality and the formidable grasp of the law that even poorly educated people often had. Indeed, lawsuits and legal technicalities abound in Edgeworth's fiction.

Thady's almost eccentric equanimity and generous nature are further revealed when, after Sir Kit has gambled away virtually all the assets of the Rackrent estate, including the goodwill of his wealthy wife, the old retainer remarks, "the Castle Rackrent estate was all mortgaged, and bonds out against him, for he was never cured of his gaming tricks—but that was the only fault he had, God bless him!" Further, Thady seems untroubled by the confinement of Sir Kit's wife for seven years in her apartments (an incident based on the actual imprisonment of a Lady Cathcart, in 1745, who was kept locked up by her husband for a much longer period), apparently lost in admiration of the fierce temper of his master, which not only caused the drastic action but also discouraged anyone from asking him about it.

The first part of *Castle Rackrent* is titled "An Hibernian Tale." It is indeed very "Hibernian," but no more so than the story of Sir Conolly Rackrent, whom Thady refers to as "ever my great favorite, and indeed the most universally beloved man I had ever seen or heard of." Condy's chief attractions are a good nature and a propensity to spend excessively. Both of these qualities contribute to the further impoverishment of the estate, a condition that he does little to alleviate. Even his marriage to the daughter of a wealthy landowner on a nearby estate (who promptly disinherits his offspring as soon as he learns of the wedding, thus frustrating even this half-hearted attempt to repair the Rackrent fortunes) is a matter of chance: Condy, who actually loves Thady's pretty but fortuneless grandniece, Judy M'Quirk, flips a coin to determine whether he will propose to Judy or the moneyed Isabella.

Despite the disinheritance, Sir Condy is fond of Isabella; when financial disaster looms, he attempts to provide her with a generous allotment in his will. The closing of the novel exposes another theme that may be derived from the plot. The villain who buys up Sir Condy's debts and brings on his personal ruin is Thady's own son, the self-serving Jason. Edgeworth possibly had in mind to make some point about the difference between the single-minded loyalty and honesty of the older generation and the selfish heartlessness of the younger. Even the attractive Judy, when Thady suggests that she might become the next mistress of Castle Rackrent (Isabella has had an accident from which Thady believes she will die), tells him there is no point in marrying a poor man; she has evidently set her sights on Jason, much to Thady's dismay.

Typically, the novel ends with a lawsuit. Lady Condy, after her husband's death from drinking, sues for the title to the estate. Thady does not know how the suit will end, and he seems not to care: "For my part, I'm tired wishing for any thing in this world, after all I've seen in it." With this touching close to what is considered Edgeworth's best novel, the reader may well believe that the author has provided the opportunity for a greater understanding of those elements of Irish culture and history that impelled her to devote a lifetime of study to them.

THE ABSENTEE

During Edgeworth's lifetime, *The Absentee* was probably her most influential work. The central problem addressed in the novel is that of the absentee landlords, who left the management of their often vast Irish estates in the hands of inept and frequently unscrupulous agents. These agents robbed the landlords as well as the tenants, but the indifferent landowners took little interest in the lands so long as the rents were paid on time. As Edgeworth makes eminently clear by the contrast between the sensible and benevolent Mr. Burke, one of Lord Clonbrony's agents, and the other, Nicholas Garraghty, who is scheming and dishonest, not all agents were bad; the trouble was that the owners had no accurate way of knowing, since they were almost never on the scene.

The hero of this novel, Lord Colambre, is the son of Lord and Lady Clonbrony; it is around this unbelievably virtuous and somewhat stuffy young man that the several subplots and themes are centered. Each subplot is designed to underline an obvious theme, and Colambre is a vital, if artificial, unifying element in a novel whose general absence of unity is disquieting. The main plot line has to do with the Clonbronys, who live in London because Lady Clonbrony believes that high society is indispensable to her happiness (typically, the other members of the "smart set" find her pretensions ridiculous; Edgeworth explores a number of opportunities to satirize the false values of such people). Lord Clonbrony would not mind returning to the family estate, and he realizes that remaining away may be ruinous, since he is already in considerable debt. Lord Colambre visits his father's lands in disguise, where he identifies the problem and recognizes the virtues and evils of the two agents. After vigorous efforts to repay his father's debts, he saves the situation and persuades his mother to return to Ireland.

A related theme concerns the actions that Colambre will not take in order to pay the debts—chiefly, he will not marry for money, a time-honored method of acquiring funds in a short time. Edgeworth offers several illustrations of the folly of such a practice, though perhaps to the modern reader her emphasis on the legitimacy of the birth of Grace Nugent, Colambre's cousin, as a criterion for his proposing to her may seem artificial and even essentially immoral. Interestingly, when Miss Nugent (who has been unaware of the "disgrace") learns of the reason for Colambre's erstwhile restraint, she fully agrees that it would have been improper for him to offer marriage when her birth seemed under a cloud. Through an unlikely and tiresome concatenation of circumstances and accidents, the problem is solved: It is proved that Grace's birth was legitimate, and the marriage is approved, even by Lady Clonbrony, who for most of the story has been trying to persuade her son to wed the wealthy Miss Broadhurst.

The Absentee is filled with flat characters created in the heroic mold, most of whom befriend Colambre and impress him with a variety of sensible insights: the positive aspects of life in Ireland; the joys and satisfactions of the quiet country life (the O'Neill family, tenants on the Clonbrony estate, underline this point; they, too, are so honest and good-hearted as to be difficult to accept); the emptiness and falseness of "society"; and the great importance of taking responsibility and performing one's duty well. *The Absentee* emphasizes two aspects of Edgeworth's philosophy of life. She fully accepted the eighteenth century conviction that the class structure of society was inevitable and proper, and she wholeheartedly believed in the primacy of duty (a word iterated by her father as the chief element of a worthy life) as everyone's first responsibility. Thus, in *The Absentee* there is an interesting mingling of liberal attitudes toward the rights of the peasants and conservative views regarding the propriety of aristocratic privilege.

At the close of a long and complicated reticulation of plot lines, Edgeworth had the clever notion of ending the story simply and even humorously (there is an unfortunate paucity of humor in this novel) by completing the tale through the device of a letter written by an Irish coach-driver to his brother, who currently lives in England, telling him of the happy return of the Clonbronys to the estate and the upcoming marriage of Colambre and Grace, and urging him to come back to Ireland, since "it's growing the fashion not to be an Absentee." *The Absentee* lacks the humor and directness of *Castle Rackrent*, but it makes its thematic points forcefully, and in Sir Terence O'Fay, Edgeworth has created a revealing, rounded portrait of an interesting Irish type: a good-natured wastrel who is no one's enemy but his own. His function in the plot is minimal, but he displays some of the most engaging features of the Irish personality.

Ormond

Unlike *The Absentee*, whose title indicates that the subject is a general phenomenon, *Ormond*, as its title suggests, is about the development of a single individual. The novel is based on the view that young people can change their character by learning from their experiences and exerting their will. Although Harry Ormond is not exactly Rousseau's "noble savage," he is clearly intended to be the image of an untutored, raw personality, full of fine possibilities that must be cultivated to be realized. During the long, complex advance of the story, this is just what happens.

The lad has been reared by an old friend of his father, who died in India, a minor aristocrat named Sir Ulick O'Shane, who believes that educating the boy would be a waste of time, since he is destined to be a poor dependent for life. The contrast between Harry Ormond and Ulick's own son, Marcus, a formally educated but weak and ineffective youth, is one of several that give the novel a sense of polarity. Ulick is contrasted with his cousin, Cornelius O'Shane, the King Corny who takes over the care of Harry when he is forced to leave Ulick's estate after a shooting incident; Dora O'Shane, the daughter of Corny, with whom for a while Harry believes himself to be in love, is seen as quite different from the modest and highly moral Florence Annaly, whom he does love and finally marries; White Connal, Dora's first suitor, is, even by his name, contrasted with his brother, Black Connal, who ultimately is the man who marries Dora.

Harry Ormond is placed in the care of a succession of older men, and from each he learns things that help him grow into a responsible and sensitive man. Ulick teaches him some of the complexities of business and helps him to understand the difficulty of judging character in another; King Corny instructs him in the need for bold action and in the excellences to be found in the primitive personality; Dr. Cambray, a clergyman, starts Harry on his formal education; and, while staying with the Annaly family, Harry perceives the delights of a well-ordered life in a well-regulated family, something he has never before experienced.

The essence of the book, apart from Ormond's development into a mature person, is his ultimate winning of the girl he truly loves. His material dependence is easily (and, again, incredibly) solved by the discovery that his father has left him a fortune. His only real problem, then, is to pass a series of moral tests created by Edgeworth to prove that he is a worthy, responsible man. The novel is marked by a number of traditional devices, such as the timeworn "While Sir Ulick is drinking his cup of cold coffee, we may look back a little into his family history," which is done for some six and a half pages. Frequent references to Ormond as "our hero" remind the reader that this is his story and that Harry is to be thought of as heroic, no matter what mistakes he makes (and he does blunder now and then, usually on the side of excessive credulity). The author does not hesitate to intrude into the story, to proclaim ignorance ("What he said, or what Florence answered, we do not know"), or to move the plot along with phrases such as "We now go on to," or "We now proceed to." *Ormond* is thus in many ways a traditional novel of the period, but it achieves a level of social criticism—of French society (a number of scenes are set in Paris) as well as of English and Irish ways—seldom found before William Makepeace Thackeray in the history of the English novel. This tale, unlike *The Absentee*, is also enlivened by humor.

Edgeworth's novels are unfortunately little read today, except by students of the English novel. Aside from plainly revealing the significant lines of tradition and transition from the eighteenth century to the nineteenth century novel, Edgeworth's work is enjoyable in itself. Nowhere else can one find such a lively and fairly balanced picture of the life and values found in the Ireland and England of the late Georgian period.

Fred B. McEwen

Other major works

short fiction: *The Modern Griselda*, 1805; *Tales of Fashionable Life*, 1809-1812; *Tales and Miscellaneous Pieces*, 1825; *Garry Owen: Or, The Snow-Woman, and Poor Bob, the Chimney-Sweeper*, 1832; *Orlandino*, 1848; *Classic Tales*, 1883.

plays: *Comic Dramas in Three Acts*, 1817.

nonfiction: *An Essay on the Noble Science of Self-Justification*, 1795; *Letters for Literary Ladies*, 1795; *Practical Education*, 1798 (with Richard Lovell Edgeworth; also known as *Essays on Practical Education*); *A Rational Primer*, 1799 (with Richard Lovell Edgeworth); *Essay on Irish Bulls*, 1802 (with Richard Lovell Edgeworth); *Essays on Professional Education*, 1809 (with Richard Lovell Edgeworth); *Readings on Poetry*, 1816 (with Richard Lovell Edgeworth); *Memoirs of Richard Lovell Edgeworth Esq.*, 1820 (vol. 2); *Thoughts on Bores*, 1826; *A Memoir of Maria Edgeworth*, 1867 (Francis Edgeworth, editor); *Archibald Constable and His Literary Correspondents*, 1873; *The Life and Letters of Maria Edgeworth*, 1894 (Augustus J. Hare, editor); *Chosen Letters*, 1931 (F. V. Barry, editor); *Romilly-Edgeworth Letters, 1813-1818*, 1936 (Samuel H. Romilly, editor); *Letters from England, 1813-1844*, 1971 (Christina Colvin, editor).

TRANSLATION: *Adelaide and Theodore*, 1783 (of comtesse de Stephanie Felicite Ducrest de Saint Aubin Genlis's system of education).

CHILDREN'S LITERATURE: *The Parent's Assistant: Or, Stories for Children*, 1796 (3 volumes), 1800 (6 volumes); *Frank, I-IV*, 1801 (with Richard Lovell Edgeworth; this and the two previous titles known as *Early Lessons*); *Harry and Lucy, I and II*, 1801 (with Richard Lovell Edgeworth); *The Mental Thermometer*, 1801; *Moral Tales for Young People*, 1801; *Rosamond, I-III*, 1801 (with Richard Lovell Edgeworth); *Popular Tales*, 1804; *Continuation of Early Lessons*, 1814; *Rosamond: A Sequel to Early Lessons*, 1821; *Frank: A Sequel to Frank in Early Lessons*, 1822; *Harry and Lucy Concluded*, 1825; *Little Plays for Children*, 1827; *The Purple Jar, and Other Stories*, 1931.

MISCELLANEOUS: *Tales and Novels*, 1832-1833 (18 volumes).

BIBLIOGRAPHY

Butler, Marilyn. *Maria Edgeworth: A Literary Biography*. Oxford, England: Clarendon Press, 1972. Standard biography on Edgeworth is strongest when dealing with the complex and voluminously documented Edgeworth family history. Provides a comprehensive sense of the author's immediate family background. The overall social and cultural context of Edgeworth's work receives less detailed treatment, and literary criticism as such is kept to a minimum.

Gilmartin, Sophie. "Oral and Written Genealogies in Edgeworth's *The Absentee*." In *Ancestry and Narrative in Nineteenth-Century British Literature: Blood Relations from Edgeworth to Hardy*. New York: Cambridge University Press, 1998. Chapter on *The Absentee* is included in a volume that explores the importance of the concept of ancestry in Victorian England by examining novels from that era. Includes bibliographical references and an index.

Harden, Elizabeth. *Maria Edgeworth*. Boston: Twayne, 1984. Survey of Edgeworth's life and works is organized around the theme of education. This approach reveals in broad outline the range of Edgeworth's sympathies and activities. Supplemented by an excellent bibliography.

Hollingworth, Brian. *Maria Edgeworth's Irish Writing*. New York: St. Martin's Press, 1997. Focuses on Edgeworth's Irish works, especially the novels *Castle Rackrent* and *Ormond*, to explore the author's attitudes toward language and regionalism. Includes detailed notes and bibliography.

Kaufman, Heidi, and Chris Fauske, eds. *An Uncomfortable Authority: Maria Edgeworth and Her Contexts*. Newark: University of Delaware Press, 2004. Collection of scholarly essays examines Edgeworth's works through attention to various cultural and ideological contexts. Presents analysis of the novels *Ormond*, *Castle Rockrent*, *Ennui*, and *Belinda*. Includes bibliography and index.

McCormack, W. J. *Ascendancy and Tradition in Anglo-Irish Literary History from 1789 to 1939*. Oxford, England: Clarendon Press, 1985. Intellectually far-reaching essay in the sociology of Irish literature firmly establishes the ideological lineage of Edgeworth's work, with special reference to the writings of Edmund Burke. Also assesses the role of Edgeworth's work in articulating the outlook of the author's social class.

Manly, Susan. "Maria Edgeworth and 'the Genius of the People.'" In *Language, Custom, and Nation in the 1790's: Locke, Tooke, Wordsworth, Edgeworth*. Burlington, Vt.: Ashgate, 2007. Analyzes Edgeworth's novels, demonstrating how these books, which were written during a period of Irish rebellion, reflect the contemporary political situation by their use of a vernacular language.

Nash, Julie. *Servants and Paternalism in the Works of Maria Edgeworth and Elizabeth Gaskell*. Burling-

work on *The Leader*. Victorian laws made divorce virtually impossible and prohibitively expensive; the fact that Lewes had accepted Hunt's child as his own precluded his citing adultery as possible grounds.

Under the circumstances, Eliot and Lewes had the choice of living together in a common-law marriage or not living together at all. They chose the former, and on July 20, 1854, traveled to Germany as husband and wife. Eliot wrote to her friends to explain her new status and to ask that henceforth they address her as Marian Lewes.

Although the couple had no children, their relationship was in many respects a model Victorian marriage. They lived happily together until Lewes's death in 1878; with their writing, they supported not only themselves but also Lewes's four sons and Agnes and her children by Hunt. Lewes's sons appeared to regard Eliot with great affection. In other respects, however, the irregularity of their relationship cut Eliot off from much of the social life of the time, since only the most courageous Victorian women dared risk their own respectability by calling on her. Eliot's family, especially her brother Isaac, also cut her off, condemning her relationship with Lewes as adulterous.

Encouraged by Lewes, Eliot published her first work of fiction, "The Sad Fortunes of the Reverend Amos Barton," in *Blackwood's Magazine* in January, 1857. Because Eliot wished to protect her standing as an editor and reviewer and because she feared that her unconventional marriage to Lewes would prejudice the reception of her fiction, she published under the pseudonym George Eliot. Encouraged by the favorable reception of these stories and protected by Lewes from adverse criticism, Eliot published her first full-length novel, *Adam Bede*, in 1859.

For the next two decades the chief events in Eliot's life were the publications of her novels—*The Mill on the Floss*, *Silas Marner*, *Romola*, *Felix Holt, the Radical*, *Middlemarch*, and *Daniel Deronda*. Of these novels, only *Romola*, a meticulously researched historical novel set in fifteenth century Florence, was less than successful; the others won Eliot both an enthusiastic popular audience and critical recognition as the major English novelist of her time.

George Eliot. (Library of Congress)

As the success of Eliot's novels and the continuing acceptance of Lewes's articles and books also brought considerable prosperity, the Leweses' life together was punctuated by trips to various parts of England and the Continent and by a series of moves to houses in more attractive parts of London. In November, 1878, only a few months after they moved to a long-sought-after house in the country, Lewes died.

Devastated by the loss of the emotional support that Lewes provided, on May 6, 1880, Eliot married John Cross, who, although twenty years younger than she, had long been a close friend and frequent visitor to the Lewes household. In the eyes of her sternly conventional brother Isaac, this marriage conferred respectability; he wrote to his sister for the first time since 1854 to offer his "sincere congratulations." Their marriage, though happy, was brief: Eliot died in December, 1880.

Analysis

Discussions of George Eliot's fiction often begin by quoting chapter 17 of *Adam Bede*, in which she makes one of the most persuasive statements of the creed of the realistic novelist to be found in nineteenth century literature. Indicating that she is seeking that "rare, precious quality of truthfulness that I delight in [in] many Dutch paintings," she goes on to state the need for "men ready to give the loving pains of a life to the faithful representing of commonplace things—men who see beauty in these commonplace things, and delight in showing how kindly the light of heaven falls on them." Through the truthful and sympathetic rendering of a fictional world no better than the actual one "in which we get up in the morning to do our daily work," novelists should win the reader's sympathy for "the real breathing men and women, who can be chilled by your indifference or injured by your prejudice, who can be cheered and helped onward by your fellow-feeling, your forbearance, your outspoken, brave justice." These statements suggest that Eliot conceived of fiction as a moral force, not because it is didactic in any narrow sense but because it inculcates in the reader an attitude of sympathy for his or her fellow people, which in turn leads to everyday acts of justice and compassion that lighten the burden of the human lot.

Fiction, then, performs one of the functions that is commonly associated with the church as a Christian community by reminding readers of Christ's second commandment, that they love their neighbors as themselves. Indeed, although Eliot's belief in Christian theology waned when she was in her twenties, her devotion to the major elements of Christian morality as she understood them remained steadfast throughout her life and provided the moral framework for her fiction. Her practice as a novelist eventually goes beyond her statement in *Adam Bede* in both complexity and subtlety, but this statement remains as the foundation of her creed as a novelist.

As her career developed, Eliot's characters became complex moral paradigms that could serve her readers as both examples and warnings. The highest moral achievement of her characters is renunciation of their own claims to happiness in order to minister to the needs of others, sometimes less deserving, whose lives impinge on theirs. The act of renunciation involves acknowledgment of the claims of community and often provides a sense of continuity with the character's past or traditions. Conversely, the characters whom Eliot condemns most severely are those who evade their responsibilities by a process of self-delusion or self-indulgence, avoiding hard choices and hoping that chance will deliver them from the consequences of selfish actions. Characters are often moved toward renunciation by others who act as "messengers"—almost secularized angels—to guide them; their acts of renunciation and sense of community are often associated with the sacraments of baptism or communion. The process of egotistical self-indulgence, on the other hand, is often associated with a sexual relationship that is clearly inappropriate, although not necessarily illicit. Later in her career, Eliot treated the difficulty of finding an arena for purposeful life in the England of her time, but she never abandoned her intense commitment to individual moral responsibility.

Adam Bede

Eliot's first full-length novel, *Adam Bede*, is built on two pairs of contrasting characters, one male and one female. Adam, a carpenter of consummate skill, is a model of rectitude and self-discipline whose only flaw is his intolerance of any weakness in others. Contrasting with Adam is Arthur Donnithorne, a well-intentioned young landowner whose moral weakness causes the principal catastrophe of the novel. There is a similar contrast between the two major female characters: Dinah Morris, a self-effacing Methodist preacher whose primary concern is doing what she can for others, and Hetty Sorrel, a young farm girl whose kittenish appeal conceals a hard core of egotism. The fact that both Adam and Arthur love Hetty intensifies the contrast between them. Adam, captivated by her charms, admires her as a paragon of femininity without ever perceiving her indifference to him. Arthur, without really intending to, takes advantage of Hetty's self-deluding dreams of being a wealthy landowner's wife to indulge in an affair with her. Frightened when she discovers that she is pregnant, Hetty runs away from home in a vain attempt to find Arthur, who has gone to rejoin his regiment. After her baby is born, she abandons it in a forest, where it dies of exposure. When she is arraigned for child murder, she appears hard and indifferent until Dinah moves her to repentance. Although Arthur succeeds in obtaining a pardon that saves Hetty from hanging, the young woman disappears from the story and, like the overwhelming majority of fallen women in Victorian fiction, dies. The somewhat improbable marriage of Adam and Dinah provides the happy ending that the contemporary audience expected.

The melodramatic aspects of *Adam Bede* tend to obscure, especially in summary, Eliot's primary concerns in the novel. Most conspicuously, the relationship between Arthur and Hetty is not simply a trite story of a sexual encounter between a wealthy young man and a simple farm girl; the sexual aspect of their relationship is less important than their self-delusion, self-indulgence, and egotism. Both characters embody moral issues that Eliot returned to again and again in her career: Arthur is attractive, likable, and well-intentioned, but he lacks both strength of purpose and self-knowledge. Intending to break off his relationship with Hetty, he finds himself contriving meetings with her; dreaming of being a model landowner, he comes near to destroying the happiness of his best tenants. Hetty's flaw is even more damaging: Although she appears to be a creature of simple charm with the "beauty of young frisking things, round-limbed, gambolling, circumventing you by a false air of innocence," her egotism makes her indifferent to almost everything except her own beauty and her self-deluding dreams.

Similarly, Dinah's success in leading Hetty to repentance is a prototype of much more complex processes that occur in later novels, when characters who have greater potential for moral growth than Hetty are enabled to develop that potential. Dinah's willingness to take on responsibility for sympathetically ministering to the needs of people around her—a moral virtue Eliot lauds above all others—has to be learned by Adam, whose own stalwart rectitude causes him to scorn weakness in others. His success in learning sympathy is symbolized by his acceptance of a meal of bread and wine in an "upper room" the morning of Hetty's trial—one of several instances in Eliot's fiction where objects associated with a Christian sacrament are used to suggest the establishment of a sense of community.

Although it is a major achievement for a first novel, *Adam Bede* pales in comparison to Eliot's later fiction. Eliot's depiction of the self-deception and egotism of Arthur and Hetty looks ahead to the fuller development of this theme in later novels, but neither the characters nor their situation provides the opportunity for the depth of psychological insight Eliot shows later. Similarly, Arthur's last-minute rescue of Hetty from the very foot of the gallows is reminiscent of the clichés of nineteenth century melodrama and seems almost pointless in the light of Hetty's immediate disappearance from the story and her early death. The marriage of Adam and Dinah caters too obviously to the Victorian taste for this kind of conventional "happy ending" and seems inconsistent with the earlier description of Dinah. Adam himself is too idealized a character to be convincing.

Many minor characters, however, demonstrate Eliot's impressive gift for characterization. Mr. Irwine is the first of several Eliot clergymen who are virtuous but hardly spiritual; Mrs. Poyser's pungent sayings indicate Eliot's humor; and Adam's mother Lisbeth combines maternal love with grating querulousness and self-pity.

The Mill on the Floss

More than any of Eliot's other novels, *The Mill on the Floss*, her second novel, focuses on a single character—Maggie Tulliver. Considered one of Eliot's most complex creations, Maggie embodies both the tendency toward self-indulgence that Eliot condemns elsewhere and the earnest desire for moral achievement by renunciation of one's own happiness that is the hallmark of the characters of whom Eliot appears to approve most highly.

These conflicting tendencies in Maggie, although evident in the long childhood section of the novel, assume their full significance when Maggie begins a series of secret meetings with Philip Wakem, the crippled son of a lawyer whom Maggie's father regards as a mortal enemy. In some respects, these meetings are innocent enough: Philip and Maggie are both lonely, as Philip is set apart by his physical handicap and Maggie is isolated by her family's financial distresses, and their conversations provide them with companionship they find nowhere else. More significant, however, is that Maggie's meetings with Philip are wrong because they require her to deceive her family and because they would, if discovered, add to her father's already overflowing cup of grief and bitterness. Although the standard of conduct that Maggie is being asked to meet seems almost pointlessly rigid, Eliot makes it clear that Maggie errs by not meeting it. When Maggie's narrowly righteous brother Tom discovers the meetings and harshly puts a stop to them, even Maggie feels that the "sense of a deliverance from concealment was welcome at any cost."

Maggie's failure to meet the standards of conduct required of her has much more serious consequences when she allows herself to go away with Stephen Guest, a young man who is virtually engaged to her cousin Lucy. Although Maggie rejects Stephen's offer of marriage, their apparent elopement causes a scandal that prostrates Lucy and bitterly divides Maggie's family. Tom is especially adamant in condemning her.

Maggie is a character who is sometimes almost painful to read about, for she has too little self-discipline to avoid slipping into actions that she knows to be wrong and too sensitive a conscience not to feel acutely the consequences of her errors. The ideal of conduct that she longs for and ultimately achieves when she decides to reject Stephen's second proposal of marriage is expressed by passages marked in an old volume of Saint Thomas à Kempis that is in a package of books given to Maggie in the depths of the Tullivers' poverty. Reading the words "Forsake thyself, resign thyself, and thou shall enjoy much inward peace," Maggie seems to see "a sudden vision" and feels this "direct communication of the human soul's belief and experience . . . as an unquestioned message."

Maggie is spared further conflict by the melodramatic conclusion of the novel. A flood gives her the opportunity to demonstrate her love for Tom by rescuing him from the mill. Maggie and Tom are briefly reconciled; then a floating mass of machinery bears down on their boat, drowning them both. Their epitaph—"In death they were not divided"—suggests a harmony that Maggie hungered for but seldom achieved in life.

The collision that results in the drowning of Maggie and Tom is, in fact, a kind of deus ex machina employed to achieve a resolution for Maggie that would be hard to envision otherwise. More intelligent and gifted than any of the other women in the novel, Maggie would hardly have found the fulfillment in marriage that appears to be the only resource for the women of the village, especially since marriage to Philip would have brought her into irreconcilable conflict with Tom and marriage to Stephen could have been achieved only at the cost of Lucy's happiness. Finally, since Maggie's sensitive compassion has conflicted with Tom's narrow dogmatism throughout the novel, it seems unlikely that their reconciliation could have been permanent. Even the renunciation she learns about in Thomas à Kempis seems to offer more a model of resignation than a pattern for a fruitful and fulfilling life. In the melodramatic ending, therefore, the issues raised by the novel finally remain unresolved.

As in *Adam Bede*, Eliot's brilliant creation of minor characters is one of the finest achievements of *The Mill on the Floss*. Especially noteworthy are the Dodson sisters, Maggie's aunts, who embody the common qualities of a proud and clannish family and yet have traits that clearly distinguish them according to their ages, degrees of prosperity, and individual temperaments.

SILAS MARNER

Eliot's third and most perfectly constructed novel, *Silas Marner*, embodies her complex moral vision with the precision of a diagram. Like *Adam Bede*, the novel is built on morally contrasting characters, but Silas Marner and Godfrey Cass reveal with much greater clarity than any of the characters in the earlier novel Eliot's concern with the moral patterns of renunciation and self-indulgence.

In a sort of prologue to the main action of the novel, Silas, a linen weaver who is a member of a pious religious sect in a large industrial city, is accused of stealing church funds by a close friend who actually stole the money. When a trial by lots sponsored by the sect declares Silas guilty, he loses faith in God and humanity and flees to a distant country village, where he isolates himself from the community and finds solace in constant weaving, like a "spinning insect."

Through years of weaving, Silas accumulates a hoard of gold coins that become the only object of his affections. When his gold is stolen by Godfrey Cass's irresponsible brother Dunstan, Silas is utterly devastated, until Godfrey's daughter by a secret marriage toddles into his house after her mother dies of exposure and an overdose of laudanum. The presence of this child, whom Silas takes in and rears as his own, restores the contact with his fellow men and women that Silas had lost; Eliot compares the girl to the "white-winged angels" that "in old days . . . took men by the hand and led them away from the city of destruction."

Almost every act that Silas performs in relation to the loss of his gold and the rearing of the child takes on near-symbolic significance. His spontaneous turning to the men assembled at the village tavern when his gold is stolen and to the New Year's assemblage at the Cass house when he finds the child suggest an instinctive searching for community. His heeding of the parish clerk's admonition not to accuse the innocent after his gold is stolen and his choice of his younger sister's "Bible name" of Hepzibah (shortened to Eppie) for the child suggest the reestablishment of ties to his past. In particular, his acceptance of lard cakes with "I.H.S." (a Christogram derived from the first three letters of the Greek name for Jesus) pricked on them from his kindly neighbor Dolly Winthrop provides a secularized communion that suggests that ties between human beings and God may be replaced in importance by ties between individuals, as Eppie has replaced the white-winged angels of older days. It may also be significant that Silas spends Christmas in lonely isolation, while Eppie comes to his house on New Year's Eve.

Similarly, Godfrey embodies the consequences of a self-indulgent avoidance of one's responsibilities. Prevented by his secret marriage to the dissolute mother of Eppie from marrying Nancy Lammeter, he weakly trusts to chance, "the god of all men who follow their own devices instead of obeying a law they believe in," to relieve him somehow of the consequences of his actions. Godfrey has none of the malice of his younger brother Dunstan; nevertheless, his anxiety is so great that his "one terror" when Silas comes to his house with Eppie is that his wife might *not* be dead. He sees that the child is his but fails to acknowledge her, salving his conscience by giving Silas a half-guinea when he finds that Silas has determined to keep her.

The chance that has relieved Godfrey of the consequences of his secret marriage eventually brings retribution. His marriage to Nancy is childless, and when Dunstan's body is discovered with Silas's long-lost gold, Godfrey finally tells Nancy that Eppie is his child. Their plan of relieving their childlessness by adopting Eppie comes to nothing when Eppie tells them that she can only think of Silas as her father. With poetic justice that even Godfrey recognizes, the man who admits that he "wanted to pass for childless once" will now "pass for childless against my wish."

Middlemarch

Middlemarch is unquestionably Eliot's finest achievement as a novelist. Whereas *Silas Marner* presents the moral patterns of renunciation and self-indulgence with unparalleled clarity, *Middlemarch* explores them with profound subtlety and psychological insight. The vast scope of *Middlemarch*—the novel is more than twice the length of *Adam Bede* or *The Mill on the Floss*—gives Eliot room for a panoramic view of provincial life, and her focus on the upper middle class and gentry gives her an opportunity to deal with characters whose experience is wider and whose motives are more sophisticated and complex than those of many of the characters in the early novels. In this "study of provincial life," as the novel's subtitle describes it, Eliot explores the familiar moral territory of renunciation and self-indulgence by developing four more or less distinct plot lines. The most important of these concern Dorothea Brooke and Tertius Lydgate, but Fred Vincy and Nicholas Bulstrode also claim a substantial amount of Eliot's attention.

This vast novel is unified not only by Eliot's moral concerns and by various cross-connections among the plot lines but also by a pervasive theme of reform. The implied contrast between the climate for "far-resonant" action that existed when a "coherent social faith" allowed Saint Theresa to find "her epos in the reform of a religious order" and the time of the novel, which ends "just after the Lords had thrown out the Reform Bill [of 1832]," suggests the difficulty of achieving meaningful action in the fragmented world of contemporary England. More than any previous novel, *Middlemarch* explores the moral achievements and failures of individuals against the background of an entire society, a society that does not provide many opportunities for people to put their best talents to use.

These issues are perhaps most fully embodied in Dorothea Brooke, a young heiress with "a nature altogether ardent, theoretic and intellectually consequent" who is "struggling in the bands of a narrow teaching, hemmed in by a social life which seemed nothing but a labyrinth of petty courses, a walled-in maze of small paths that led no whither." Seeking a way to give her life consequence and purpose, she marries Edward Casaubon, a desiccated pseudoscholar, whom she naïvely thinks of as a John Locke or a John Milton, a "winged messenger" who can guide her along the "grandest path." She soon discovers that Casaubon is not a great man; rather, he is pathetic egotist who is morbidly sensitive to real or imagined criticism of his work, pettishly jealous of Dorothea's friendship with his nephew Will Ladislaw, and incapable of offering her any real affection. She also learns that his projected work, grandly titled "Key to All Mythologies," is nothing but a monumental collection of trivia already rendered obsolete by superior German scholarship. Nevertheless, Dorothea prepares to promise her husband, who is suffering from a "fatty degeneration of the heart," that she will continue his work after his death, a sacrifice from which she is saved by his timely demise.

Like Dorothea, Tertius Lydgate finds his ambitions for significant achievement frustrated by social pressures, but unlike Dorothea he adds to his difficulties by a tendency toward heedless self-indulgence. His well-intentioned plans for medical reform are jeopardized by his lack of sensitivity to the feelings of both patients and other practitioners and by his regrettable involvement with Nicholas Bulstrode, an unpopular but powerful leader in community affairs. More important, he shackles himself by marriage to Rosamond Vincy, the beautiful and self-centered daughter of the mayor of Middlemarch. This marriage, which Lydgate slips into more or less intentionally, blights his hopes of success. He gets heavily into debt as both he and Rosamond carelessly incur expenses on the unconsidered assumption that they ought to live well. Rosamond, utterly unwilling to make any sacrifices, simply blames him for their problems.

These two plot lines come together when Dorothea, deeply moved by Lydgate's marital and financial problems and eager to clear him from blame in a scandal involving Bulstrode, offers to call on Rosamond. She finds Rosamond in what appears to be a compromising tête-à-tête with Will, whom she had come to love since Casaubon's death. Deeply distressed by what she assumes about Will's conduct, she nevertheless forces herself to "clutch [her] own pain" and think only of the "three lives whose contact with hers laid an obligation on her." Feeling "the largeness of the world and the manifold wakings of men to labour and endurance," she compels herself to make a second visit. She has some success in reconciling Rosamond to Lydgate and finds that Will's conduct was indeed blameless.

Although Dorothea's renunciation of herself has the unexpected result of opening the way for her marriage to Will, she never achieves her potential as a latter-day Saint Theresa, "for the medium in which [her] ardent deeds took shape is forever gone." Her "full nature" spends itself "in channels which had no great name on earth" but that nonetheless bring benefits to her fellow men and women. Lydgate, who allowed himself to slip into marriage with the paralyzingly egotistical Rosamond, achieves financial success as a society doctor but "always regarded himself as a failure; he had not done what he once meant to do."

The other two plot lines, although less important than those centering on Dorothea and Lydgate, afford Eliot opportunity to round out her study of provincial life. Fred Vincy, who is Rosamond's brother, overcomes his tendency to fritter away his money in casual pleasures when he realizes the distresses that his failure to pay a debt will cause the Garth family, who represented security for him, and recognizes that Mary Garth will not marry him unless he undertakes a worthwhile career. The plot line centering on Nicholas Bulstrode, although the least extensive of the four, contains some of Eliot's most perceptive explorations of self-delusion. Bulstrode, who had gathered a fortune dealing in stolen goods before coming to Middlemarch, aspires to leadership in the community as a banker and as an Evangelical Christian. Although he assiduously conceals his former life, he is no simple hypocrite; rather, he is an ambitious man who aims at "being an eminent Christian," capable of deluding himself even in his prayers. His lifetime habit of confusing his own desires with God's will comes to a climax when he allows his housekeeper to administer brandy to an alcoholic former associate who has been blackmailing him—a treatment that, although common at the time, has been forbidden by Lydgate. Only after the man dies does Bulstrode discover that the former associate has already revealed Bulstrode's long-guarded secrets in his drunken ramblings.

Although the principal themes of *Middlemarch* are developed primarily in the four major plot lines, the novel's extraordinary richness of minor characters is surely one of its outstanding features. Mr. Brooke, Dorothea's uncle, is one of Eliot's supreme comic creations, a man "of acquiescent temper, miscellaneous opinions, and uncertain vote." Caleb Garth, "one of those rare men who are rigid with themselves and indulgent to others," is a model of sturdy rectitude. The description of Mrs. Bulstrode's loyal support of her guilty husband and her acceptance of "a new life in which she embraced humiliation" is one of Eliot's finest passages. The list could be continued almost at will, amply justifying the claim of the novel's subtitle to be a "study of provincial life."

The subtitle is also appropriate in that it calls attention to Eliot's recognition, more fully expressed in this novel than in any of her earlier ones, of the ways in which the circumstances of society limit her characters' options. Dorothea achieves the ideal of self-renunciation that characters in the earlier novels strive for, but the conditions of her life prevent her from achieving her potential; Lydgate fails not only because of his ill-advised marriage but also because the community views his eagerness to advance medical practice with suspicion and prejudice. Conditions of society, as well as moral flaws, frustrate the ambitions of even the worthiest characters.

Daniel Deronda

Daniel Deronda, Eliot's final novel, emphasizes the search for purpose more than the ideal of renunciation. Eliot continues her examination of egotism and self-indulgence, but these themes are muted with pathos in the portrayal of Gwendolen Harleth. In subject matter, Eliot also takes another step or two up the social ladder, dealing in this novel with the wealthy upper middle class and aristocracy.

The protagonist, Daniel Deronda, is such a paragon at the beginning of the novel that he has little need of the lessons in renunciation that Eliot's other protagonists must learn. Handsome, well-educated, and generously supported by Sir Hugo Mallinger, Deronda is concerned only with finding something purposeful to do with his life. His only burden is the assumption that he is Sir Hugo's illegitimate son. His discovery of a cause to which he can dedicate himself proceeds by easy stages. His rescue of Mirah, a Jewish singer who is preparing to drown herself, prompts his interest in Judaism. He succeeds in reuniting Mirah with her terminally ill brother, Mordecai, a visionary Jewish mystic. When Mordecai sees Deronda from a bridge, which he describes as "a meeting place for spiritual messengers," he assumes that Deronda has been sent to bring him "my new life—my new self—who will live when this breath is all breathed out." Finally, Deronda discovers that he is actually the son of a distinguished Jewish singer who had asked Sir Hugo to bring him up as an Englishman. The discovery that he is Jewish enables him to marry Mirah, take up the torch from the dying Mordecai, and dedicate himself to the "restoration of a political existence to my people, giving them a national center, such as the English have." (In assigning this cause to Deronda, Eliot anticipated the Zionist movement by some twenty years and, indeed, gave powerful stimulus to the movement for the development of a Jewish national state.)

In Gwendolen Harleth, Eliot examines again the anatomy of egotism. Concerned only with her own comforts, Gwendolen rules imperiously over the household of her twice-widowed mother, Mrs. Davilow. Gwendolen's manifest dislike of men and her habit of sleeping in her mother's bedroom suggest sexual frigidity. Nevertheless, she is on the verge of marrying Henleigh Grandcourt, Sir Hugo's nephew and heir, when she discovers that Grandcourt has had four children by a mistress who deserted her own husband and whom Grandcourt still supports. An invitation to visit Germany with some family friends allows Gwendolen to evade a decision, but when her family loses its fortune, she decides on marriage rather than having her mother live in painfully reduced circumstances while she is forced to take the ignominious position of governess.

Gwendolen's motives in marriage are intriguingly mixed. To be sure, she is essentially egotistical and assumes that she will be able to control her husband. The family's dismal prospects after their catastrophic financial losses inevitably influence her. She is especially concerned for her mother, the one person for whom she feels genuine affection. Nevertheless, she also suffers an agony of guilt in her sense that her marriage has deprived Grandcourt's illegitimate children of any claim to his wealth.

Once they are married, the ruling hand is entirely Grandcourt's. Gwendolen bears his elegantly polite sadism with proud reserve, but is inwardly tormented by dread that her fear and hatred of her husband may drive her to some desperate act. When he drowns, perhaps because she fails to throw him a rope, she is overwhelmed with guilt. Desolated by the marriage of Deronda, whom she has turned to as a moral guide and mentor, she takes solace in Deronda's admonition that she "may live to be one of the best of women," although, as she adds in a final letter to Deronda, "I do not yet see how that can be."

Although Gwendolen's willingness to accept suffering scourges her egotism and brings her to a prospect of redemption that Rosamond Vincy glimpses only briefly, *Daniel Deronda* is in most ways Eliot's bleakest novel. An air of futility hangs like a pall over most of the characters; without a tradition of commitment to some place or purpose, they lack a future also. Mrs. Davilow moves from one rented house to another, and the estates passed down to Sir Hugo from the time of William the Conqueror will finally be inherited by Grandcourt's illegitimate son. Jewish characters such as Mirah's father and Deronda's mother wander over Europe, rejecting even an obligation to their own children. Only the dedication to art of Herr Kelsmer, a German musician, and the acceptance of Mordecai's dream of a national Jewish homeland by Deronda provide a sense of purpose or direction, and these vocations are ones from which most of the characters are inevitably excluded. Except in unusual cases, it appears that even the desire to renounce oneself may not be efficacious. The very circumstances of modern life work against moral achievement.

Erwin Hester

OTHER MAJOR WORKS

SHORT FICTION: *Scenes of Clerical Life*, 1858.

POETRY: *The Spanish Gypsy*, 1868; *The Legend of Jubal, and Other Poems*, 1874.

NONFICTION: *The Impressions of Theophrastus Such*, 1879; *Essays of George Eliot*, 1963 (Thomas Pinney, editor); *The Journals of George Eliot*, 1998 (Margaret Harris and Judith Johnston, editors).

TRANSLATIONS: *The Life of Jesus Critically Examined*, 1846 (with Mrs. Charles Hennell; of David Friedrich Strauss's philosophical history); *The Essence of Christianity*, 1854 (of Ludwig Feuerbach's philosophical history).

BIBLIOGRAPHY

Ashton, Rosemary. *George Eliot: A Life*. New York: Penguin Books, 1997. Introduction to Eliot's life and work by an admirer of her fiction. Interlaces discussions of Eliot's life with analysis of her fiction and the context of her work within Victorian society and social thought. Argues that Eliot's novels most often focus on characters out of step with their culture.

Dodd, Valerie A. *George Eliot: An Intellectual Life*. New York: St. Martin's Press, 1990. Part 1 gives the intellectual background of Victorian England, discussing writers such as John Stuart Mill and Thomas Carlyle; part 2 discusses Eliot's work in relation to that intellectual background. Includes a useful bibliography.

Ermarth, Elizabeth Deeds. *George Eliot*. Boston: Twayne, 1985. Excellent short reference work on Eliot provides a biographical sketch and outlines Eliot's career, including analyses of *Middlemarch*, *Silas Marner*, *Romola*, and other novels. The select bibliography is helpful, as is the chronology.

Hardy, Barbara. *George Eliot: A Critic's Biography*. London: Continuum, 2006. Presents an examination of Eliot's life combined with an analysis of her works; intended for readers with some prior knowledge of her writings. Includes an outline of Eliot's works in the context of the events in her life.

Harvey, W. J. *The Art of George Eliot*. New York: Oxford University Press, 1962. Addresses the structure of Eliot's work—the omniscient narrator, the treatment of time, and characterization. A helpful source for a close study of Eliot's work. Supplemented by a short bibliography.

Hughes, Kathryn. *George Eliot: The Last Victorian*. London: Fourth Estate, 1998. Good standard biography suitable for the general reader. Includes bibliographical references and index.

Hutchinson, Stuart, ed. *George Eliot: Critical Assessments*. 4 vols. East Sussex: Helm Information, 1996.

Volume 1 consists of biography, nineteenth century reviews, and responses; volume 2 contains perspectives from 1900-1970 on Eliot's work; volume 3 provides critical essays on individual works; volume 4 includes perspectives from the 1970's to the mid-1990's.

Karl, Fred. *George Eliot: Voice of a Century*. New York: W. W. Norton, 1995. Biography draws on previously unavailable archival material and on feminist criticism, depicting Eliot as an author whose work symbolized "the ambiguities, the anguish, and divisiveness of the Victorian era."

Levine, George, ed. *The Cambridge Companion to George Eliot*. New York: Cambridge University Press, 2001. Collection of essays analyzes Eliot's works, including her early and late novels, from various perspectives. Addresses Eliot's realism and her approaches to philosophy, science, politics, religion, and gender.

Menon, Patricia. *Austen, Eliot, Charlotte Brontë, and the Mentor-Lover*. New York: Palgrave Macmillan, 2003. Examines and compares how Jane Austen, Eliot, and Brontë handled matters of gender, sexuality, family, behavior, and freedom in their work.

Rignall, John, ed. *Oxford Reader's Companion to George Eliot*. New York: Oxford University Press, 2000. Encyclopedic volume contains entries that cover everything about the novelist, including her pets and homes as well as the themes in her fiction and the various contexts in which to place her works.

Taylor, Ina. *A Woman of Contradictions: The Life of George Eliot*. New York: William Morrow, 1989. Interesting and provocative book focuses on Eliot's personal life. Taylor claims to work from sources different from those on which all previous biographies drew—all of which, she says, come from one beginning: Eliot's husband, John Cross. Includes photographs of Eliot, her family, and friends.

STANLEY ELKIN

Born: Brooklyn, New York; May 11, 1930
Died: St. Louis, Missouri; May 31, 1995
Also known as: Stanley Lawrence Elkin

Principal long fiction

Boswell: A Modern Comedy, 1964
A Bad Man, 1967
The Dick Gibson Show, 1971
The Franchiser, 1976
George Mills, 1982
Stanley Elkin's the Magic Kingdom, 1985 (also known as *The Magic Kingdom*)
The Rabbi of Lud, 1987
The MacGuffin, 1991
Mrs. Ted Bliss, 1995

Other literary forms

Stanley Elkin published two collections of his short fiction, *Criers and Kibitzers, Kibitzers and Criers* (1965) and *Early Elkin* (1985); three collections of novellas, *Searches and Seizures* (1973), *The Living End* (1979), and *Van Gogh's Room at Arles* (1993); one collection titled *Stanley Elkin's Greatest Hits* (1980); and another of essays, *Pieces of Soap* (1992). He also wrote a film script, *The Six-Year-Old Man* (1968), and edited several collections of short fiction. *Why I Live Where I Live*, a memoir, was published in 1983.

Achievements

Since their emergence in the mid-1960's, Stanley Elkin's novels and short fiction have been praised by critics as some of the best satiric writing in American literature. The novels tend to be darkly comedic performances of unusually articulate, marginal characters struggling to define themselves in a confusing and harsh modern world. Elkin's writing career was generously acknowledged in the form of numerous grants and awards. In 1962 Elkin won the Longview Foundation

Award, and in 1964 he received the Paris Review John Train Humor Prize. In 1966 he was awarded a Guggenheim Fellowship, in 1968 a Rockefeller Fellowship, in 1971 a National Endowment for the Arts grant, in 1974 an American Academy grant, in 1980 a Rosenthal Foundation Award, in 1981 a *Sewanee Review* award, and in 1983 a National Book Critics Circle Award. Three of his books were nominated for the National Book Award, and *Van Gogh's Room at Arles* was a PEN/Faulkner Award finalist.

Stanley Elkin. (Miriam Berkley)

Biography

Stanley Lawrence Elkin was born on May 11, 1930, in Brooklyn, New York. His father, a traveling salesman and noted storyteller, later moved to the Chicago area, where Elkin spent his early childhood. At the age of twenty-two, while enrolled at the University of Illinois at Urbana, Elkin married Joan Marion Jacobson, an aspiring young artist. Two years later, in 1955, he enlisted in the U.S. Army, where he served two years in the field of radio communications. After his tour of duty, Elkin and his wife spent some time in Europe, especially Rome and London, where he began writing what would later be his first novel, *Boswell*. Returning to the United States, Elkin resumed his studies at the University of Illinois at Urbana, continuing his graduate work in English and working for the student magazine, *Accent*, which published his first short story, "Among the Witnesses," in 1959.

Before receiving a Ph.D. from the University of Illinois at Urbana in 1961, Elkin took a position teaching English at Washington University in St. Louis. He was visiting lecturer at institutions such as Smith College, the University of California at Santa Barbara, the University of Wisconsin at Milwaukee, Yale University, and Boston University. Beginning in 1983, he held the title of Kling Professor of Modern Letters at Washington University. Elkin died of a heart attack in St. Louis in 1995, after long suffering from multiple sclerosis, first diagnosed in 1961. He was survived by his wife and three children (a daughter and two sons).

Analysis

Often erroneously categorized as a "black humorist," Stanley Elkin wrote novels and short stories that bristle with a kind of modern satiric language and a blending of the ordinary and the bizarre that characterize much of the black humor that emerged in the 1960's. Unlike contemporaries such as Joseph Heller, J. P. Donleavy, and Kurt Vonnegut, however, Elkin did not produce works that are particularly pessimistic or given to excessive lamentations over the inadequacies of contemporary culture. The world Elkin depicts in his fiction is indeed bleak, desolate, and unforgiving, but Elkin's characters always seem to manage somehow, always seem to exhibit a certain kind of moral fortitude that enables them to persevere.

It is Elkin's treatment of his characters that is perhaps the most striking element in his fiction, causing his work to stand apart from that of the black humorists. Unlike many of his contemporaries, Elkin does not disrespect the characters he satirizes, even when those characters have despicable traits or engage in criminal—even cruel—behavior. In addition, his characters have the ability to make moral choices, a characteristic lacking in most protagonists in works of black humor. Despite Elkin's elaborate, artful characterizations, however, his fiction—because of his overpowering style, his artful use of language and metaphor (far beyond the characters to which he typically ascribes the gift of language), and his lack of emphasis on plot—has been somewhat of an enigma to literary scholars, who have struggled to understand the significance of his works and their place in the context of contemporary American literature.

Boswell

Elkin's first novel, *Boswell*, centers on the protagonist James Boswell, conceived as a loose parody of the eighteenth century biographer who pursued the most eminent man in the London of his day, Samuel Johnson, eventually befriending him and writing his biography. Elkin's Boswell is also a pursuer of celebrities, but in twentieth century America, the task is more complicated—and the reasons for undertaking the task more pathological. Boswell is obsessed with death: the certainty of death and the prospect of having lived a meaningless life. In this regard, *Boswell* seems almost existential in nature. Unlike the earlier existential novelists, however, and unlike Elkin's contemporaries, who often see life in the modern world as vacuous and absurd, Elkin pushes past this categorization, causing his protagonist to make a life-affirming gesture, to take from the confusion and chaos of modern life some organizing principle, or affirmative stance, that can overcome his oppressive feelings of meaninglessness. In Boswell's case, as he stands outside, unable to cross the police barrier in front of the hotel where celebrities are gathering at his own request, he finally comes to understand the inherent injustice of a world that gives special status, even immortal status, to certain individuals while others are left in meaningless obscurity. The novel ends with Boswell's uncharacteristically democratic gesture: He begins to shout opposition to these celebrities, choosing to remain an outsider just on the eve of his acceptance into their circle.

Boswell was received rather cautiously by critics and reviewers. The work's lack of plot—not much really "happens" in the novel—and Elkin's intense, almost overwhelming rhetorical style, with his seemingly inconsistent juxtaposition of formal speech and street slang (often coming from the same character, in the same paragraph), caused several critics to denounce the work as too artificial, too self-conscious, and too uncontrolled. Peter J. Bailey, in defense of Elkin, has argued that the early characterizations of Elkin were unfair for a number of reasons. For one thing, Elkin's literary antecedents were misunderstood. He was not trying to write realistic plot-based fiction and failing; instead, he was writing antirealistic, comedic novels of excess, very much like his contemporaries Thomas Pynchon, Robert Coover, and Donald Barthelme. The confusion, according to Bailey, comes about because other such novelists use language that is extravagant, rhetorically excessive, and comical. With Elkin, the language is the language one hears every day, the language of shopkeepers and grocers. This realistic speech in the midst of bizarre situations makes Elkin's work more insidious—and, Bailey argues, more effective.

A Bad Man

With his second novel, *A Bad Man*, Elkin continues what he began in *Boswell*. Like most of Elkin's novels, it focuses on a single protagonist who tells his own story, a protagonist who seeks to heal his disparate, chaotic life through a single profession, or obsession, as the case may be. Leo Feldman, a department store magnate, seeking a way to test his resolve, strength, and fortitude, has himself put into prison for doing his customers illegal favors. In prison, Feldman confronts the system, personified by the warden, and ultimately confronts death itself in many guises, just as Boswell had done before him. The consummate salesman, Feldman is keenly aware of the art of selling himself, promoting the self, and he seeks to do this as he fights the warden and the system.

The Dick Gibson Show

In his third novel, *The Dick Gibson Show*, Elkin turns to the world of radio broadcasting, a perfect medium for the depiction of the loner, the orphan (a characteristic of many Elkin protagonists), the marginal modern hero who lives isolated from others yet seeks a kind of renewal, a connection with an understanding, sympathetic "audience." The novel spans Gibson's career (which coincides with the introduction of radio as a mass medium). The format at which he excels is the talk show and, later, the telephone call-in shows that became popular in the 1960's. The callers telephone to articulate their despair, their feelings of inadequacy, and their inability to order their lives—feelings Gibson shares. Rather than succumb to these feelings, however, Gibson uses his position as adviser to help himself overcome them. In the callers themselves he finds a substitute for the family he has spent his life seeking in vain.

The Franchiser

The Franchiser, Elkin's fourth (and, some argue, his best) novel, was published in 1976. The protagonist, Ben Flesh, is yet another loner—a man living on the road in a late-model Cadillac, opening franchises across the country—but a loner who feels at home anywhere in the United States. The opening sentence of the novel catalogs the various places to which he travels: Wherever he is, "he feels he is home." Putting absolute faith in the newly emerged system of franchising, Flesh seeks to celebrate and homogenize the United States itself. For him the franchising system is the perfect democratic scheme, the means by which all Americans can participate. The novel ultimately shows the scheme to be misleading, but despite Flesh's setbacks—his businesses begin to fail, he is diagnosed with multiple sclerosis—the novel does not end in despair. Flesh recovers and begins again, revealing an indomitable spirit, a certain moral fortitude that is characteristic of Elkin's heroes.

George Mills

Elkin is perceived, even by those who look disparagingly at his fiction, as a master of the depiction of American popular culture, the world of hamburger joints, radio spots, and storefronts, the language of the jingle, shoptalk, and the hype of the sales floor. American consumer culture is Elkin's peculiar specialty, and his poetic treatment of it raises it almost to the level of myth. In Elkin's fifth novel, *George Mills*, he attempts to reveal the extent of these mythic proportions.

The story of George Mills, a blue-collar worker in St. Louis, is depicted in the context of his ancestry: He comes from a long line of "working stiffs," beginning with a stable boy during the Fifth Crusade. It is as though George's bloodline had been cursed: Each generation passes on a peculiar capacity to serve, each generation is destined to be followers, never leaders, and each generation is doomed to retain forever the hope that somehow God will come through in the end, that at the last minute something will happen to change their fate. The world of *George Mills* is a world where God is a trickster and a bully. Life is absurd, because what happens to people is merely God's trick, "God's fast one." Somehow Mills manages to retain his dignity, however, managing a kind of embrace of all those who are also the butt of God's jokes.

Stanley Elkin's the Magic Kingdom

In *Stanley Elkin's the Magic Kingdom*, Elkin carries the idea of life being God's practical joke to an even more poignant level. The novel probes the obsession of Eddy Bale, a Londoner who has recently lost his son to a terminal illness, to take a group of terminally ill children from their home in England to Disney World and the Magic Kingdom in Florida. The effort he expends to raise the money, make the travel arrangements, and orchestrate the medical needs of the children is enormous—his own personal battle against the inevitable. He hires a nurse, Mary Cottle, who is thirtyish, a self-imposed exile from romantic relationships because she is a disease carrier (every child born to her would be destined to be diseased and blind). Again the reader sees Elkin's dark vision of the world, a vision that critics justly compare to that of the nihilists, the black humorists, but Elkin's dark vision somehow refuses to remain dark. After losing a child during their week in Florida, and after making the arrangements for the body to be returned, Bale and Cottle end the novel in a frenzied sexual encounter that is, in an odd, perhaps perverted way, a gesture of renewal, a feeble attempt to repopulate the world, to replace the diseased children, even if they must be replaced with more diseased children.

The Rabbi of Lud

The Rabbi of Lud explores Elkin's Jewish heritage: It concerns a rather cynical rabbi of Lud, New Jersey, by the name of Jerry Goldkorn. In the opening chapters, Elkin presents a series of descriptions that suggest his vision of the modern landscape: desolate, dirty, and reeking of death. The town's major feature, indeed its major business, consists of cemeteries and mortuaries. Lud, as

Elkin describes it, is a closed system, a place he calls "thanatopsical," after the Greek word for death. It is the quintessential wasteland, T. S. Eliot's image that overwhelmed twentieth century fiction and poetry—the empty, spiritually defunct landscape of modern humanity. Rabbi Goldkorn is in a spiritual crisis, or rather a series of spiritual crises, involving his family and his career. He eventually moves to Alaska to be the rabbi of the Alaskan pipeline, a typically Elkian metaphor for the ultimately useless career.

Despite this rather forbidding depiction of modern life, however, and despite the trials that beset the rabbi, Goldkorn is basically happy in his long-standing marriage to his wife, Shelley, and he enjoys his work—even finds it noble to a degree, despite the inevitability of its failure. The end of the novel characteristically reveals Elkin's refusal to paint a completely dismal picture of modern life. Obligated to deliver a eulogy for his friend Joan Cohen, Rabbi Goldkorn—after discussing the hopelessness of life and the inevitability of death—delivers a rather strange, visionary series of blessings that catalog the things in life there are to celebrate, small things such as eating fruit and smelling wood.

The MacGuffin

At fifty-eight, Robert "Bobbo" Druff finds himself "on the downhill side of destiny" in *The MacGuffin*. A streets commissioner in an unnamed midsize American city reminiscent of Elkin's own St. Louis, Druff sees his own health declining just as federal highway funds are drying up (a situation that is this novel's version of the energy crisis in *The Franchiser*). He cannot get any respect, from others or even from himself. His seething resentment fuels his paranoid fantasies and his raging, often misdirected rants in which the pathos of Arthur Miller's delusional Willy Loman is transformed into pure spiel. He and his maker play a variation on the familiar Descartean theme: not a philosophical *Cogito, ergo sum*, but a self-assertive "I rage, therefore I am."

The novel's title alludes to the filmmaker Alfred Hitchcock's love of arbitrary narrative contrivances to keep his plots moving, and as such it underscores the absurdity of Druff's "pointless odyssey." In a life, and a novel, filled with non sequiturs, Druff compensates for life's indignities by imagining plots in which he figures prominently, especially plots to dethrone, or decommission him. In this way, he salvages some measure of dignity from his otherwise clownish life. Although *The MacGuffin* is wildly funny, it is Druff's fears and frustrations, along with a sense of personal injustice, that drive both the novel's streets commissioner and Elkin's high-energy prose.

Other works

The same combination of fear, frustration, rage, and revenge figures prominently in the three novellas that make up *Van Gogh's Room at Arles*. In *Her Sense of Timing*, the wife of a suffering but insufferable wheelchair-bound professor of geography leaves him at a particularly inopportune moment. In the title novella, a small-time college teacher wins a foundation grant only to find that entry into the select company of academic powerhouses makes him feel even more unworthy and resentful. The third novella features an English working-class girl snubbed by the royal family. She reveals all to a British tabloid in *Town Crier Exclusive, Confessions of a Princess Manqué: "How Royals Found Me 'Unsuitable' to Marry Their Larry."*

The combination is also present in *Mrs. Ted Bliss*, albeit in a different key. Far less pyrotechnic than most of Elkin's earlier novels, *Mrs. Ted Bliss* depicts one of Elkin's most likable (as well as most passive) protagonists. She is a former butcher's wife, now a widow (widowhood being her occupation), who has traveled from Russia to Chicago only to find herself, in her eighties, virtually imprisoned in a Miami condominium tower. As if caught in a parody of a fairy tale, she is cut off from and fearful of the outside world.

Her losses, particularly that of her husband, leave her in much the same condition the unraveling myelin of Elkin's own multiple sclerosis left him: exposed, irascible, tragicomically human. Stubbornly, helplessly trapped in her evacuated building as a hurricane approaches, she becomes Elkin's King Lear on the stormy heath. Where Lear rages, however, she merely waits, in the company of the building's security guard: a small comfort, but a comfort nonetheless. They do what they can to see each other through the storm. "Everything else falls away," Elkin writes, brilliantly and elegiacally, at novel's as well as career's end: "Family, friends, love fall away. Even madness stilled at last. Until all that's left is obligation."

Again and again, Elkin shows his readers the resilience of the human spirit, the ability humans have to cope with the chaos of modern life, the meaninglessness of human values, and the entropy from which cultural systems suffer. The major characters in Elkin's novels, novellas, and collections of short fiction share the black humorist's understanding of the condition of modern culture yet ultimately offer a constructive, if not ideal, response. All of his characters share a certain morality, a willingness to admit life's meaninglessness, but also a necessity of struggling against it with whatever strength they can muster. This almost dignified response in the face of life's absurdity is Elkin's particular legacy and is the measure by which his works are best understood.

Edward W. Huffstetler
Updated by Robert A. Morace

Other major works

short fiction: *Criers and Kibitzers, Kibitzers and Criers*, 1965; *The Making of Ashenden*, 1972; *Searches and Seizures*, 1973; *The Living End*, 1979; *Stanley Elkin's Greatest Hits*, 1980; *Early Elkin*, 1985; *Van Gogh's Room at Arles: Three Novellas*, 1993.

screenplay: *The Six-Year-Old Man*, 1968.

nonfiction: *Why I Live Where I Live*, 1983; *Pieces of Soap: Essays*, 1992.

Bibliography

Bailey, Peter J. *Reading Stanley Elkin*. Urbana: University of Illinois Press, 1985. Study of Elkin's fiction examines the works' major themes in order to counteract misreadings of Elkin as another in a series of black humorists, especially given Elkin's association with black humorists of the 1960's. Each of the seven chapters discusses a separate theme or thematic element in Elkin's work. Includes a comprehensive index.

Bargen, Doris G. *The Fiction of Stanley Elkin*. Frankfurt, Germany: Verlag Peter D. Lang, 1980. The first book-length work of criticism on Elkin includes an interview with the author and an extensive biography. Examines Elkin's association with the literary movements of metafiction, black humor, American Jewish writers, and popular-culture novels, and argues that his work is similar in some ways to all of these but dissimilar enough to resist categorization. Supplemented with a comprehensive bibliography and an index.

Cohen, Sarah Blacher, ed. *Comic Relief: Humor in Contemporary American Literature*. Urbana: University of Illinois Press, 1978. Collection of essays discusses the role of humor in the works of American writers who emerged in the 1960's and 1970's, with Elkin figuring prominently in the discussion. Aligns Elkin with black humorists, identifying their common traits, such as their need to laugh at the absurdity of modern culture.

Dougherty, David C. "A Conversation with Stanley Elkin." In *The Muse upon My Shoulder: Discussions of the Creative Process*, edited by Sylvia Skaggs McTague. Madison, N.J.: Fairleigh Dickinson University Press, 2004. Elkin is one of thirteen authors who discuss the process of writing, their inspiration to write, and their relationship to their readers in this collection of interviews.

_______. *Stanley Elkin*. Boston: Twayne, 1990. Discusses all of Elkin's fiction through *The Rabbi of Lud*, including stories and novellas, emphasizing Elkin's almost poetic use of language and sense of vocation. Chronology, brief biography, bibliography of secondary works, and discussion of the uses and limitations of classifying Elkin as a Jewish American writer, a satirist, a black humorist, and a metafictionist make this an especially useful work.

Olderman, Raymond M. *Beyond "The Waste Land": The American Novel in the Nineteen Sixties*. New Haven, Conn.: Yale University Press, 1972. The first treatment of Elkin's fiction in the context of other emerging authors of the 1960's. Discusses Elkin and others of his generation, repudiating the image of modern society as the wasteland depicted in T. S. Eliot's landmark 1922 poem. Olderman identifies a new kind of idealism emerging in modern fiction.

Pughe, Thomas. *Comic Sense: Reading Robert Coover, Stanley Elkin, Philip Roth*. Boston: Birkhäuser Verlag, 1994. Analyzes the major works of Elkin and the other authors from a postmodernist perspective, focusing on their use of humor and their sense of the comic.

Review of Contemporary Fiction 15, no. 2 (Summer,

1995). Special issue on Elkin features contributions by Jerome Klinkowitz, Jerome Charyn, William H. Gass, and others. Includes an interview with Elkin in which he discusses the mystery in his fiction, the nature of plot, the essence of story, and his prose style.

Tristman, Richard. "Tragic Soliloquy, Stand-up Spiel." *New England Review* 27, no. 4 (Fall, 2006): 36-40. Presents an analysis of the comic themes in Elkin's writing, including a discussion of the characters, whom Tristman describes as being "drawn from the ordinary and even tawdry precincts of life."

Vinson, James, ed. *Contemporary Novelists*. 2d ed. New York: St. Martin's Press, 1976. Comprehensive and broad study includes Elkin in an overview of writers from the 1960's and 1970's. The section that covers Elkin most comprehensively is written by David Demarest, Jr., who discusses Elkin's place among his contemporaries.

RALPH ELLISON

Born: Oklahoma City, Oklahoma; March 1, 1914
Died: New York, New York; April 16, 1994
Also known as: Ralph Waldo Ellison

Principal long fiction

Invisible Man, 1952
Juneteenth, 1999 (John F. Callahan, editor; revised and expanded as *Three Days Before the Shooting*, 2010, Callahan and Adam Bradley, editors)

Other literary forms

Ralph Ellison's reputation rests primarily on *Invisible Man*, but *Shadow and Act* (1964), a collection of nonfiction prose, established Ellison as a major force in the critical theory of pluralism and in African American aesthetics. Arranged in three thematically unified sections, the essays, most of which appeared originally in journals such as *Antioch Review*, *Partisan Review*, and *The New Republic*, emphasize the importance of folk and popular (especially musical) contributions to the mainstream of American culture. Several of the essays from *Shadow and Act* are recognized as classics, notably "Richard Wright's Blues," "Change the Joke and Slip the Yoke," and "The World and the Jug." In addition, Ellison published several excellent short stories, including "Flying Home" and "Did You Ever Dream Lucky?" Collections of his essays include *Going to the Territory* (1986), *The Collected Essays of Ralph Ellison* (1995), and *Living with Music: Ralph Ellison's Jazz Writings* (2001).

Achievements

Ralph Ellison occupies a central position in the development of African American literature and of contemporary American fiction. Equally comfortable with the influences of Fyodor Dostoevski, Mark Twain, Louis Armstrong, Igor Stravinsky, James Joyce, and Richard Wright, Ellison was the first African American writer to attain recognition as a full-fledged artist rather than as an intriguing exotic. Whereas Caucasian critics had previously, and unjustly, condescended to African American writers such as Langston Hughes, Zora Neale Hurston, and Wright, most granted Ellison the respect given Euro-American contemporaries such as Norman Mailer and Saul Bellow. A 1965 *Book World* poll identifying *Invisible Man* as the most distinguished postwar American novel simply verified a consensus already reflected in the recurrence of the metaphor of invisibility in countless works by both Caucasians and African Americans during the 1950's and 1960's.

Within the African American tradition itself, Ellison occupies a similarly prominent position, although his mainstream acceptance generates occasional reservations among some African American critics, particularly those committed to cultural nationalism. A *Black World* poll, reflecting these reservations, identified Wright rather than Ellison as the most important black writer. The discrepancy stems in part from the critical image in the late 1960's of Ellison and James Baldwin as leading figures in an anti-Wright "universalist" movement in African American culture, a movement that some critics viewed as a sellout to Euro-American aesthetics. In the late twentieth century, however, both Euro-American and African American critics recognized Ellison's synthesis of the oral traditions of black culture and the literary traditions of both his black and his white predecessors. The consensus of that time viewed Ellison as clearly more sympathetic than Wright to the African American tradition. As a result, Ellison seems to have joined Wright as a major influence on younger black fiction writers such as James Alan McPherson, Leon Forrest, Toni Morrison, and David Bradley.

Ellison's most profound achievement, his synthesis of modernist aesthetics, American romanticism, and African American folk culture, embodies the aspirations of democratic pluralists such as Walt Whitman, Twain, and Hughes. His vernacular modernism earned Ellison an international reputation while exerting a major influence on the contemporary mainstream. With a reputation resting almost entirely on his first novel, Ellison's career is among the most intriguing in American literary history.

Biography

Despite Ralph Ellison's steadfast denial of the autobiographical elements of *Invisible Man* and his insistence on the autonomy of the individual imagination, both the specific details and the general sensibility of his work clearly derive from his experience of growing up in a southern family in Oklahoma City, attending college in Alabama, and residing in New York City during most of his adult life. Ellison's parents—whose decision to name their son Ralph Waldo Ellison, for American philosopher and essayist Ralph Waldo Emerson, reflected their commitment to literacy and education—moved from South Carolina to the comparatively progressive Oklahoma capital several years before their son's birth. Reflecting on his childhood, which was characterized by economic hardship following his father's death in 1917, Ellison emphasized the unusual psychological freedom provided by a social structure that allowed him to interact relatively freely with both whites and blacks. Encouraged by his mother, Ida, who was active in socialist politics, Ellison developed a frontier sense of a world of limitless possibility rather than the more typically southern vision of an environment filled with dangerous oppressive forces.

During his teenage years, Ellison developed a serious interest in music, both as a trumpet player and as a composer-conductor. Oklahoma City offered access both to formal classical training and to jazz, which was a major element of the city's nightlife. The combination of Euro-American and African American influences appears to have played a major role in shaping Ellison's pluralistic sensibility. After he graduated from high school in 1933, Ellison accepted a scholarship to the Tuskegee Institute, where he remained for three years, studying music and literature, until financial problems forced him to drop out. Although he originally planned to finish his studies, his subsequent relocation to New York City marked a permanent departure from the South.

Arriving in the North in 1936, Ellison established contacts with African American literary figures, including Hughes and Wright, who encouraged him to develop his knowledge of both the African American literary world and Euro-American modernism, especially that of T. S. Eliot and James Joyce. Never as deeply involved with leftist politics as Wright, Ellison nevertheless began developing his literary ideas in reviews and stories published in radical magazines such as *New Masses*. In 1938, Ellison, who had previously supported himself largely as a manual laborer, worked for the Federal Writers' Project, which assigned him to collect urban folklore, providing him direct contact with northern folk culture to complement his previous knowledge of southern folkways. Ellison's short fiction began appearing in print in the late 1930's and early 1940's. After a short term as managing editor of *Negro Quarterly* in 1942, he briefly left New York, serving in the merchant marine from 1943 to 1945. Awarded a Rosenwald Fellowship to write a novel, Ellison returned to New York and married Fanny McConnell in 1946.

Invisible Man, which took Ellison nearly seven years to write, was published in 1952, bringing him nearly instantaneous recognition as a major young writer. The novel won the National Book Award in 1953, and its reputation has continued to grow. Starting in 1952, Ellison taught at Bard College, Rutgers University, New York University, and other institutions. From 1955 to 1957, he was the American Academy Fellow in Rome. In addition, he delivered public lectures, wrote essays, and worked on a second novel.

Less inclined to direct political involvement than contemporaries such as Amiri Baraka and James Baldwin, Ellison participated in the Civil Rights movement in a relatively quiet manner. He nevertheless attracted political controversy during the rise of the African American nationalist movements in the mid-1960's. Refusing to endorse any form of cultural or political separatism, Ellison was attacked as an aesthetic European and a political reactionary, especially after he accepted appointments to the American Institute of Arts and Letters (1964) and to the National Council on the Arts and Humanities, acts that were interpreted as support for the Lyndon B. Johnson's presidential administration's Vietnam policy. During the mid-1970's, however, these attacks abated as nationalist critics such as Larry Neal rose to Ellison's defense and a new generation of African American writers turned to him for aesthetic inspiration.

Ralph Ellison. (National Archives)

From 1970 to 1980, Ellison was Albert Schweitzer Professor of Humanities at New York University. He then retired from full-time teaching and continued to work on his second novel, *Juneteenth*, which was delayed both by his own perfectionism and by a house fire that destroyed much of the manuscript. The novel was incomplete at the time of his death on April 16, 1994, in New York.

Analysis

Ellison's artistic vision is not impaired by blind spots related to racially divided cultures. While he acknowledges the expression of racial divisions in the works of such authors as Richard Wright and Langston Hughes, he is also critical of stereotyped images of blacks in fiction by white authors. Ellison's mature attitude toward American pluralism made him aware that racism is a common phenomenon that both whites and blacks need to transcend in order to coexist.

A masterwork of American pluralism, Ralph Ellison's *Invisible Man* insists on the integrity of individual vocabulary and racial heritage while encouraging a democratic acceptance of diverse experiences. Ellison asserts this vision through the voice of an unnamed first-person narrator who is at once heir to the rich African American oral culture and a self-conscious artist who, like T. S. Eliot and James Joyce, exploits the full potential of his written medium. Intimating the potential cooperation between folk and artistic consciousness, Ellison confronts the pressures that discourage both individual integrity and cultural pluralism.

Invisible Man

Invisible Man is a story about the gradual awakening of an African American man concerning his role in a multicultural democracy. The novel's narrator-protagonist introduces Ellison's central metaphor for the situation of the individual in Western culture in the first paragraph: "I am invisible, understand, simply because people refuse to see me." As the novel develops, Ellison extends this metaphor: Just as people can be rendered invisible by the willful failure of others to acknowledge their presence, so by taking refuge in the seductive but ultimately specious security of socially acceptable roles they can fail to see *themselves*, fail to define their own identities. Ellison envisions the escape from this dilemma as a multifaceted quest demanding heightened social, psychological, and cultural awareness.

The style of *Invisible Man* reflects both the complexity of the problem and Ellison's pluralistic ideal. Drawing on sources such as the blindness motif from William Shakespeare's *King Lear* (pr. c. 1605-1606), the underground man motif from Fyodor Dostoevski, and the complex stereotyping of Wright's *Native Son* (1940), Ellison carefully balances the realistic and the symbolic dimensions of *Invisible Man*. In many ways a classic *Künstlerroman*, the main body of the novel traces the protagonist from his childhood in the deep South through a brief stay at college and then to the North, where he confronts the American economic, political, and racial systems.

This movement parallels what Robert B. Stepto in *From Behind the Veil* (1979) calls the "narrative of ascent," a constituting pattern of African American culture. With roots in the fugitive slave narratives of the nineteenth century, the narrative of ascent follows its protagonist from physical or psychological bondage in the South through a sequence of symbolic confrontations with social structures to a limited freedom, usually in the North. This freedom demands from the protagonist a "literacy" that enables him or her to create and understand both written and social experiences in the terms of the dominant Euro-American culture. Merging the narrative of ascent with the *Künstlerroman*, which also culminates with the hero's mastery of literacy (seen in creative terms), *Invisible Man* focuses on writing as an act of both personal and cultural significance.

Similarly, Ellison employs what Stepto calls the "narrative of immersion" to stress the realistic sources and implications of his hero's imaginative development. The narrative of immersion returns the "literate" hero or heroine to an understanding of the culture he or she symbolically left behind during the ascent. Incorporating this pattern in *Invisible Man*, Ellison emphasizes the protagonist's links with the African American community and the rich folk traditions that provide him with much of his sensibility and establish his potential as a conscious artist.

The overall structure of *Invisible Man*, however, involves cyclical as well as directional patterns. Framing the main body with a prologue and epilogue set in an underground burrow, Ellison emphasizes the novel's symbolic dimension. Safely removed from direct participation in his social environment, the invisible man reassesses the literacy gained through his ascent, ponders his immersion in the cultural art forms of spirituals, blues, and jazz, and finally attempts to forge a pluralistic vision transforming these constitutive elements. The prologue and epilogue also evoke the heroic patterns and archetypal cycles described by Joseph Campbell in *The Hero with a Thousand Faces* (1949). After undergoing tests of his spiritual and physical qualities, the hero of Campbell's "monomyth"—usually a person of mysterious birth who receives aid from a cryptic helper—gains a reward, usually of a symbolic nature involving the union of opposites. Overcoming forces that would seize the reward, the hero returns to transform the life of the community through application of the knowledge connected with the symbolic reward.

To some degree, the narratives of ascent and immersion recast this heroic cycle in specifically African American terms: The protagonist first leaves, then returns to his or her community bearing a knowledge of Euro-American society potentially capable of motivating a group ascent. While it emphasizes the cyclic nature of the protagonist's quest, the frame of *Invisible Man* simultaneously subverts the heroic pattern by removing the protagonist from his community. He promises a return, but the implications of the return for the life of the community remain ambiguous.

This ambiguity superficially connects Ellison's novel with the classic American romance that Richard Chase characterizes in *The American Novel and Its Tradition* (1975) as incapable of reconciling symbolic perceptions with social realities. The connection, however, reflects Ellison's awareness of the problem more than his acceptance of the irresolution. Although the invisible man's underground burrow recalls the isolation of the heroes of the American romance, he promises a rebirth that is at once mythic, psychological, and social:

> The hibernation is over. I must shake off my old skin and come up for breath. . . . And I suppose it's damn well time. Even hibernations can be overdone, come to think of it. Perhaps that's my greatest social crime, I've overstayed my hibernation, since there's a possibility that even an invisible man has a socially responsible role to play.

Despite the qualifications typical of Ellison's style, the invisible man clearly intends to return to the social world rather than light out for the territories of symbolic freedom.

The invisible man's ultimate conception of the form of this return develops out of two interrelated progressions, one social and the other psychological. The social pattern, essentially that of the narrative of ascent, closely reflects the historical experience of the African American community as it shifts from rural southern to urban northern settings. Starting in the deep South, the invisible man first experiences invisibility as a result of casual but vicious racial oppression. His unwilling participation in the "battle royal" underscores the psychological and physical humiliation visited upon southern blacks. Ostensibly present to deliver a speech to a white community group, the invisible man is instead forced to engage in a massive free-for-all with other blacks, to scramble for money on an electrified rug, and to confront a naked white dancer who, like the boys, has been rendered invisible by the white men's blindness.

Escaping his hometown to attend a black college, the invisible man again experiences humiliation when he violates the unstated rules of the southern system—this time imposed by blacks rather than whites—by showing the college's liberal northern benefactor, Mr. Norton, the poverty of the black community. As a result, the black college president, Dr. Bledsoe, expels the invisible man. Having experienced invisibility in relation to both blacks and whites and still essentially illiterate in social terms, the invisible man travels north, following the countless southern blacks involved in the "Great Migration."

Arriving in New York, the invisible man first feels a sense of exhilaration resulting from the absence of overt southern pressures. Ellison reveals the emptiness of this freedom, however, stressing the indirect and insidious nature of social power in the North. The invisible man's experience at Liberty Paints, clearly intended as a parable of African American involvement in the American economic system, emphasizes the underlying similarity of northern and southern social structures. On arrival at Liberty Paints, the invisible man is assigned to mix a white paint used for government monuments. Labeled "optic white," the grayish paint turns white only when the invisible man adds a drop of black liquid. The scene suggests the relationship between government and industry, which relies on black labor. More important, however, it points to the underlying source of racial blindness/invisibility: the white need for a black "other" to support a sense of identity. White becomes white only when compared to black.

The symbolic indirection of the scene encourages the reader, like the invisible man, to realize that social oppression in the North operates less directly than that in the South; government buildings replace rednecks at the battle royal. Unable to mix the paint properly, a desirable "failure" intimating his future as a subversive artist, the invisible man discovers that the underlying structure of the economic system differs little from that of slavery. The invisible man's second job at Liberty Paints is to assist Lucius Brockway, an old man who supervises the operations of the basement machinery on which the factory depends. Essentially a slave to the modern owner/master Mr. Sparland, Brockway, like the good darkies of the plantation tradition, takes pride in his master and will fight to maintain his own servitude. Brockway's hatred of the invisible man, whom he perceives as a threat to his position, leads to a physical struggle that culminates in an explosion caused by neglect of the machinery. Ellison's multifaceted allegory suggests a vicious circle in which blacks uphold an economic system that supports the political system that keeps blacks fighting to protect their neoslavery. The forms alter, but the battle royal continues. The image of the final explosion from the basement warns against passive acceptance of the social structure that sows the seeds of its own destruction.

Although the implications of this allegory in some ways parallel the Marxist analysis of capitalist culture, Ellison creates a much more complex political vision when the invisible man moves to Harlem following his release from the hospital after the explosion. The political alternatives available in Harlem range from the Marxism of the "Brotherhood" (loosely based on the American Communist Party of the late 1930's) to the black nationalism of Ras the Exhorter (loosely based on Marcus Garvey's pan-Africanist movement of the 1920's). The Brotherhood promises complete equality for blacks and at first encourages the invisible man to develop the oratorical talent ridiculed at the battle royal. As his effectiveness increases, however, the invisible man finds the Brotherhood demanding that his speeches conform to its "scientific analysis" of the black community's needs. When he fails to fall in line, the leadership of the Brotherhood orders the invisible man to leave Harlem and turn his attention to the "woman question."

Without the invisible man's ability to place radical politics in the emotional context of African American culture, the Brotherhood's Harlem branch flounders. Recalled to Harlem, the invisible man witnesses the death of Tod Clifton, a talented coworker driven to despair by his perception that the Brotherhood amounts to little more than a new version of the power structure underlying both Liberty Paints and the battle royal. Clearly a double for the invisible man, Clifton leaves the organization and dies in a suicidal confrontation with a white policeman. Just before Clifton's death, the invisible man sees him selling Sambo dolls, a symbolic comment on the fact that blacks involved in leftist politics in some sense remain stereotyped slaves dancing at the demand of unseen masters.

Separating himself from the Brotherhood after delivering an extremely unscientific funeral sermon, the invisible man finds few political options. Ras's black nationalism exploits the emotions the Brotherhood denies. Ultimately, however, Ras demands that his followers submit to an analogous oversimplification of their human reality. Where the Brotherhood elevates the scientific and rational, Ras focuses entirely on the emotional commitment to blackness. Neither alternative recognizes the complexity of either the political situation or the individual psyche; both reinforce the invisible man's feelings of invisibility by refusing to see basic aspects of his character.

As he does in the Liberty Paints scene, Ellison emphasizes the destructive, perhaps apocalyptic, potential of this encompassing blindness. A riot breaks out in Harlem, and the invisible man watches as DuPree, an apolitical Harlem resident recalling a number of African American folk heroes, determines to burn down his own tenement, preferring to start again from scratch rather than even attempt to work for social change within the existing framework. Unable to accept the realistic implications of such an action apart from its symbolic justification, the invisible man, pursued by Ras, who seems intent on destroying the very blackness he praises, tumbles into the underground burrow. Separated from the social structures, which have changed their facade but not their nature, the invisible man begins the arduous process of reconstructing his vision of America while symbolically subverting the social system by stealing electricity to light the 1,369 lightbulbs on the walls of the burrow and to power the record players blasting out the pluralistic jazz of Louis Armstrong.

As his frequent allusions to Armstrong indicate, Ellison by no means excludes the positive aspects from his portrayal of the African American social experience. The invisible man reacts strongly to the spirituals he hears at college, the blues story of Trueblood, the singing of Mary Rambro after she takes him in off the streets of Harlem. Similarly, he recognizes the strength wrested from resistance and suffering, a strength asserted by the broken link of chain saved by Brother Tarp. These figures, however, have relatively little power to alter the encompassing social system. They assume their full significance in relation to the second major progression in *Invisible Man*, that focusing on the narrator's psychological development.

As he gradually gains an understanding of the social forces that oppress him, the invisible man simultaneously discovers the complexity of his own personality. Throughout the central narrative, he accepts various definitions of himself, mostly from external sources. Ultimately, however, all definitions that demand he repress or deny aspects of himself simply reinforce his sense of invisibility. Only by abandoning limiting definitions altogether, Ellison implies, can the invisible man attain the psychological integrity necessary for any effective social action.

Ellison emphasizes the insufficiency of limiting definitions in the prologue when the invisible man has a dream-vision while listening to an Armstrong record. After descending through four symbolically rich levels of the dream, the invisible man hears a sermon on the "Blackness of Blackness," which recasts the "Whiteness of the Whale" chapter from Herman Melville's *Moby Dick* (1851). The sermon begins with a cascade of apparent contradictions, forcing the invisible man to question his comfortable assumptions concerning the nature of freedom, hatred, and love. No simple resolution emerges from the sermon, other than an insistence on the essentially ambiguous nature of experience. The dream-vision culminates in the protagonist's confrontation with the mulatto sons of an old black woman torn between love and hatred for their father. Although their own heritage merges the "opposites" of white and black, the sons act in accord with social definitions and repudiate their white father, an act that unconsciously but unavoidably repudiates a large part of themselves. The hostile sons, the confused old woman, and the preacher who delivers the sermon embody aspects of the narrator's own complexity. When one of the sons tells the invisible man to stop asking his mother disturbing questions, his words sound a leitmotif for the novel: "Next time you got questions like that ask yourself."

Before he can ask, or even locate, himself, however, the invisible man must directly experience the problems generated by a fragmented sense of self and a reliance on others. Frequently, he accepts external definitions, internalizing the fragmentation dominating his social context. For example, he accepts a letter of introduction from Bledsoe on the assumption that it testifies to his ability. Instead, it creates an image of him as a slightly dangerous rebel. By delivering the letter to potential employers, the invisible man participates directly in his own oppression. Similarly, he accepts a new name from the Brotherhood, again revealing his willingness to simplify himself in an attempt to gain social acceptance from the educational, economic, and political systems. As long as he accepts external definitions, the invisible man lacks the essential element of literacy: an understanding of the relationship between context and self.

His reluctance to reject the external definitions and attain literacy reflects both a tendency to see social experience as more "real" than psychological experience and a fear that the abandonment of definitions will lead to total chaos. The invisible man's meeting with Trueblood, a sharecropper and blues singer who has fathered a child by his own daughter, highlights this fear. Watching Mr. Norton's fascination with Trueblood, the invisible man perceives that even the dominant members of the Euro-American society feel stifled by the restrictions of "respectability." Ellison refuses to abandon all social codes, portraying Trueblood in part as a hustler whose behavior reinforces white stereotypes concerning black immorality. If Trueblood's acceptance of his situation (and of his human complexity) seems in part heroic, it is a heroism grounded in victimization.

Nevertheless, the invisible man eventually experiments with repudiation of all strict definitions when, after his disillusionment with the Brotherhood, he adopts the identity of Rinehart, a protean street figure who combines the roles of pimp and preacher, shifting identities with context. After a brief period of exhilaration, the invisible man discovers that "Rinehart's" very fluidity guarantees that he will remain locked within social definitions. Far from increasing his freedom at any moment, his multiplicity forces him to act in whatever role his "audience" casts him. Ellison stresses the serious consequences of this lack of center when the invisible man nearly becomes involved in a knife fight with Brother Maceo, a friend who sees only the Rinehartian exterior. The persona of "Rinehart," then, helps increase the invisible man's sense of possibility but lacks the internal coherence necessary for psychological, and perhaps even physical, survival.

Ellison rejects both acceptance of external definitions and abandonment of all definitions as viable means of attaining literacy. Ultimately, he endorses the full recognition and measured acceptance of the experience, historical and personal, that shapes the individual. In addition, he recommends the careful use of masks as a survival strategy in the social world. The crucial problem with this approach, derived in large part from African American folk culture, involves the difficulty of maintaining the distinction between external mask and internal identity. As Bledsoe demonstrates, a protective mask threatens to implicate the wearer in the very system he or she attempts to manipulate.

Before confronting these intricacies, however, the invisible man must accept his African American heritage, the primary imperative of the narrative of immersion. Initially, he attempts to repudiate or to distance himself from the aspects of that heritage associated with stereotyped roles. He shatters and attempts to throw away the "darky bank" he finds in his room at Mary Rambro's. His failure to lose the pieces of the bank reflects Ellison's conviction that stereotypes, major aspects of the African American social experience, cannot simply be ignored or forgotten. As an element shaping individual consciousness, they must be incorporated into, without being allowed to dominate, the integrated individual identity. Symbolically, in a scene in which the invisible man meets a yam vendor shortly after his arrival in Harlem, Ellison warns that one's racial heritage alone cannot provide a full sense of identity. After first recoiling from yams as a stereotypical southern food, the invisible man eats one, sparking a momentary epiphany of racial pride. When he indulges the feelings and buys another yam, however, he finds it frost-bitten at the center.

The invisible man's heritage, placed in proper perspective, provides the crucial hints concerning social literacy and psychological identity that allow him to come provisionally to terms with his environment. Speaking on his deathbed, the invisible man's grandfather offers cryptic advice that lies near the essence of Ellison's overall vision: "Live with your head in the lion's mouth. I want you to overcome 'em with yeses, undermine 'em with grins, agree 'em to death and destruction, let 'em swoller you till they vomit or bust wide open." Similarly, an ostensibly insane veteran echoes the grandfather's advice, adding an explicit endorsement of the Machiavellian potential of masking:

> Play the game, but don't believe in it—that much you owe yourself. Even if it lands you in a straitjacket or a padded cell. Play the game, but play it your own way—part of the time at least. Play the game, but raise the ante, my boy. Learn how it operates, learn how *you* operate. . . . that game has been analyzed, put down in books. But down here they've forgotten to take care of the books and that's your opportunity. You're hidden right out in the open—that is, you would be if you only realized it. They wouldn't see you because they don't expect you to know anything.

The vet understands the "game" of Euro-American culture, while the grandfather directly expresses the internally focused wisdom of the African American community.

The invisible man's quest leads him to a synthesis of these forms of literacy in his ultimate pluralistic vision. Although he at first fails to comprehend the subversive potential of his position, the invisible man gradually learns the rules of the game and accepts the necessity of the indirect action recommended by his grandfather. Following his escape into the underground burrow, he contemplates his grandfather's advice from a position of increased experience and self-knowledge. Contemplating his own individual situation in relation to the surrounding society, he concludes that his grandfather "*must* have meant the principle, that we were to affirm the principle on which the country was built but not the men." Extending this affirmation to the psychological level, the invisible man embraces the internal complexity he has previously repressed or denied: "So it is that now I denounce and defend, or feel prepared to defend. I condemn and affirm, say no and say yes, say yes and say no. I denounce because though implicated and partially responsible, I have been hurt to the point of abysmal pain, hurt to the point of invisibility. And I defend because in spite of all I find that I love. In order to get some of it down I *have* to love."

"Getting some of it down," then, emerges as the crucial link between Ellison's social and psychological visions. In order to play a socially responsible role—and to transform the words "social responsibility" from the segregationist catchphrase used by the man at the battle royal into a term responding to Louis Armstrong's artistic call for change—the invisible man forges from his complex experience a pluralistic art that subverts the social lion by taking its principles seriously. The artist becomes a revolutionary wearing a mask. Ellison's revolution seeks to realize a pluralist ideal, a true democracy recognizing the complex experience and human potential of every individual. Far from presenting his protagonist as a member of an intrinsically superior cultural elite, Ellison underscores his shared humanity in the concluding line: "Who knows but that, on the lower frequencies, I speak for you?" Manipulating the aesthetic and social rules of the Euro-American "game," Ellison sticks his head in the lion's mouth, asserting a blackness of blackness fully as ambiguous, as individual, and as rich as the whiteness of Herman Melville's whale.

JUNETEENTH

Forty-seven years after the release of *Invisible Man*, Ellison's second novel was published. Ellison began working on *Juneteenth* in 1954, but his constant revisions delayed its publication.

Juneteenth is about a black minister, Hickman, who takes in and raises a little boy as black, even though the child looks white. The boy soon runs away to New England and later becomes a race-baiting senator. After he is shot on the Senate floor, he sends for Hickman. Their past is revealed through their ensuing conversation. The title of the novel, appropriately, refers to a day of liberation for African Americans. June 19, 1865, which came to be known as Juneteenth, was the day on which Union forces announced the emancipation of slaves in Texas. The title applies to the novel's themes of evasion and discovery of identity, themes that Ellison explores so masterfully in *Invisible Man*.

Although the novel was unfinished at the time of Ellison's death, only minor edits and revisions were necessary to publish the book, first in 1999 with some chapters previously published in various magazines and in a more complete edition, retitled *Three Days Before the Shooting*, in 2010.

Craig Werner
Updated by Mabel Khawaja

Other major works

SHORT FICTION: *Flying Home, and Other Stories*, 1996.

NONFICTION: *Shadow and Act*, 1964; *The Writer's Experience*, 1964 (with Karl Shapiro); *Going to the Territory*, 1986; *The Collected Essays of Ralph Ellison*, 1995 (John F. Callahan, editor); *Conversations with Ralph Ellison*, 1995 (Maryemma Graham and Amritjit Singh, editors); *Trading Twelves: The Selected Letters of Ralph Ellison and Albert Murray*, 2000; *Living with Music: Ralph Ellison's Jazz Writings*, 2001 (Robert O'Meally, editor).

Bibliography

Applebome, Peter. "From Ellison, a Posthumous Novel, with Additions Still to Come." *The New York Times*, February 11, 1999. Provides information on the origins of *Juneteenth*, both historical and personal to Ellison.

Benston, Kimberly, ed. *Speaking for You: The Vision of Ralph Ellison*. Washington, D.C.: Howard University Press, 1987. Useful resource reprints critical responses to Ellison's fiction and essays. Also includes an extensive bibliography of his writings.

Busby, Mark. *Ralph Ellison*. Boston: Twayne, 1991. Provides a concise, excellent introduction to Ellison's life and work.

Hill, Michael D., and Lena M. Hill. *Ralph Ellison's "Invisible Man": A Reference Guide*. Westport, Conn.: Greenwood Press, 2008. Analytical study addresses the content of the novel, the context in which it was written, its critical reception, and the work's artistic merit.

Jackson, Lawrence. *Ralph Ellison: Emergence of Genius*. New York: John Wiley & Sons, 2002. First book-length study of Ellison's life is a good source of information on the novelist's early life and career. Jackson, however, ends his study in 1953, shortly after the publication of *Invisible Man*.

O'Meally, Robert G., ed. *New Essays on "Invisible Man."* New York: Cambridge University Press, 1988. Collection of essays includes the responses of many critics and scholars to questions raised by earlier commentators on Ellison's novel.

Posnock, Ross, ed. *The Cambridge Companion to Ralph Ellison*. New York: Cambridge University Press, 2005. Collection of essays offers analysis of Ellison's life and interests. Includes a biographical chronology.

Rampersad, Arnold. *Ralph Ellison: A Biography*. New York: Alfred A. Knopf, 2007. Definitive biography draws extensively on Ellison's correspondence.

Rice, William H. *Ralph Ellison and the Politics of the Novel*. Lanham, Md.: Lexington Books, 2003. Addresses an unanswered question implied in *Invisible Man* regarding the politics of redefining the American novel and whether it is possible to ignore an author's ethnicity.

Schor, Edith. *Visible Ellison: A Study of Ralph Ellison's Fiction*. Westport, Conn.: Greenwood Press, 1993. Excellent study of all of Ellison's fiction that was generally available at the time, including his short fiction, which had not yet been collected in book form. A good starting place for any study of Ellison's work.

BUCHI EMECHETA

Born: Yaba, Lagos, Nigeria; July 21, 1944
Also known as: Florence Onye Buchi Emecheta

Principal long fiction

In the Ditch, 1972
Second-Class Citizen, 1974
The Bride Price, 1976
The Slave Girl, 1977
The Joys of Motherhood, 1979
Destination Biafra, 1982
Double Yoke, 1982
Adah's Story, 1983 (includes *Second-Class Citizen* and *In the Ditch*)
The Rape of Shavi, 1983
A Kind of Marriage, 1986 (adaptation of her teleplay)
Gwendolen, 1989 (also known as *The Family*, 1990)
Kehinde, 1994
The New Tribe, 2000

Other literary forms

Books written by Buchi Emecheta (eh-mee-CHEH-tah) include a number of works for a juvenile audience, such as *The Moonlight Bride* (1980) and *The Wrestling Match* (1980). Two others, *Titch the Cat* (1979) and *Nowhere to Play* (1980), are based on stories by her daughters. Emecheta has also published an autobiography—*Head Above Water* (1986)—screenplays, and articles in prominent British journals and newspapers, including *New Statesman*, *The Times Literary Supplement*, and *The Guardian*.

Achievements

Described by M. Keith Booker as "probably Africa's best known and most widely read woman novelist," Buchi Emecheta has gained a reputation and readership that extend far beyond her native land and her adopted country of Great Britain. Her novels have been translated into many European languages, including Danish, Finnish, Greek, Hungarian, and Swedish, and also into Korean, Tamil, and Sinhalese. She was invited by the World Population Foundation to contribute an article to its *Brief aan de 6 miljardste wereldburger* (1999; letters to the sixth billionth world citizen). Emecheta's article, along with those of such major literary figures as Ariel Dorfman, Salman Rushdie, and Pramoedya Ananta Toer, was translated into Dutch and then published in Hebrew (*Mikhtavim le-ezrah ha-shishah-mili'ard*, 1999). She won the 1978 *New Statesman*/Jock Campbell Award for *The Slave Girl*, was named the Best Black Writer in Britain in 1980, and was named one of the best young British writers in 1983. In 2005, she was appointed an honorary officer of the Order of the British Empire.

Biography

Readers of Buchi Emecheta's heavily autobiographical fiction will see its inspiration in the events of her life. Florence Onye Buchi Emecheta was born July 21, 1944, in modest circumstances to Igbo parents in Yaba, near Lagos, when Nigeria was still a British colony. Her father, described in the dedication to her novel *In the Ditch* as a "Railwayman and 14th Army Soldier in Burma," died when she was nine years old. Despite economic disadvantages and racial and gender biases, Emecheta rose above her life circumstances. She won a scholarship to the Methodist Girls' High School, staying there for half a dozen years until her marriage, at the age of sixteen, to Sylvester Onwordi. Following Igbo practice, she was engaged to Onwordi at the age of eleven. In 1962, she moved to London, where Onwordi had relocated one year earlier to study accounting.

Despite an abusive marriage and the births of five children in six years, Emecheta focused on the two activities that would save her from poverty and degradation: She learned how to write, and she developed a career that would lead her to academia. From 1965, still in London, Emecheta began to work outside the home, first in the library of the British Museum and later for the Inner London Education Authority as a youth worker and sociologist. She left her husband in 1966, kept custody of her children, and entered the University of London, where she earned a bachelor's degree in sociology in 1972. She earned a doctorate from the same institution in 1991.

Emecheta's academic qualifications, coupled with increasing fame as a writer, led to several academic posts. For most of the decade after 1972, she was a visiting professor at various American universities, including Pennsylvania State; the University of California, Los Angeles; the University of Illinois at Urbana-Champaign; and Yale. She also taught at the University of Calabar in Nigeria (1980-1981) and at London University (beginning in 1982); in addition, she became a fellow at London University in 1986.

Aware from childhood that she had literary talent and ambitions, Emecheta began keeping a diary while living impoverished and being abused by her husband. She soon published short pieces about the lives of black Britons. Parts of her first novel, *In the Ditch*, an account of a single black mother living a life of precarious survival and comradeship in a squalid North London apartment, first appeared in serial form in the left-wing weekly *New Statesman*. Her work has earned her recognition as perhaps the foremost African woman writer, and one of a dozen or so of the most significant postcolonial African novelists.

In 1979, Emecheta became a member of the British Home Secretary's Advisory Council on Race. She was a member of the Arts Council of Great Britain from 1982 to 1983.

Analysis

Buchi Emecheta's novels deal principally with the life experiences of Nigerian women, who are subordinated in an indigenous society deeply influenced by the Western values introduced by British colonists. Other Nigerian women, those who have relocated to England, for example, often suffer the emotional effects of being suddenly immersed into an alien country. Their lives are further complicated by the power that Nigerian men, following traditional beliefs, still have over them. Emecheta, who struggled in Nigeria to get an education and who suffered abuse in England by her Nigerian husband, reproduces these and other experiences in fictionalized form. Whether at home or in the imperial metropolis, Nigerian women in Emecheta's novels experience both sexism and racism in a world of African—and Western—traditions.

Second-Class Citizen

A prequel to *In the Ditch*, *Second-Class Citizen* explains how Adah became a single parent in a North London slum. At the age of eight she first noticed a "Presence" accompanying her, a wish to acquire education despite her inferior status as a girl. Resisting pressure to leave school at the age of eleven and eventually to marry and become a submissive wife, she wins a scholarship with full board to the Methodist Girls' School, where she does well. At the end of her stay at the school she marries Francis, but she does so simply to acquire a stable and socially acceptable home. Adah and Francis, who is studying to become an accountant, then move to London.

A defeatist Francis tells Adah that the color of her skin makes her a second-class citizen, her educational achievements notwithstanding. Adah, however, sets out to prove Francis wrong: She gets and keeps a "white man's" job in a library, where she is accepted by her white coworkers; she refuses to foster out her children, as do many African women in London, and instead finds a nursery for them; and she laments the jealousy directed at her as an ambitious Igbo by other blacks, including West Indians, considering this jealousy as harmful as white prejudice. Adah undergoes other trials. It is difficult for her family to find accommodations, as explicit racist exclusion is still legal ("Sorry, no coloreds"). Francis, unable to cope with British life, not only stops studying but is repeatedly unfaithful while demanding submission and sex from Adah. In response, Adah experiments unsuccessfully with birth control in an attempt to avoid the financial catastrophe of yet another pregnancy.

Later in the novel, Adah is introduced to black writers, including James Baldwin, by a fellow worker, and her own ambition to write begins to form. After Francis burns the manuscript of her novel, Adah takes the couple's four children and leaves him; she soon realizes that she again is pregnant.

Second-Class Citizen is unpretentiously written and compelling. It is an autobiographical story of an intelligent and resilient woman who is determined not to let sexism and racism limit her life or her talents. Although the book has been criticized for its portrayal of Nigerian society and Nigerian men, it is free of apparent bitterness and explicit special pleading. *Second-Class Citizen* captures a phase in the relationship between Britain and one of its African colonies, explaining why some Nigerians left for Britain in the late 1940's and what happened to those who failed there. The novel is also insightful in discussing the experiences of immigrants who arrived in Britain in the 1960's shortly after Nigeria's independence. Still, *Second-Class Citizen*, the work of a young writer, is lumpily episodic in structure, and its ending is disconcertingly abrupt.

The Bride Price

The name of Aku-nna, the central character of *The Bride Price*, translates as "father's wealth." Knowing the importance her loving father places on her bride price, the sum paid to the family of a bride by the family of a suitor, Aku-nna determines to marry a rich man with a substantial bride price. However, after the death of her father, Aku-nna, her brother, and their mother move from pluralistic Lagos to traditional Ibuza, where Aku-nna's mother marries Okonkwo, her own brother-in-law, according to custom.

Okonkwo's social ambitions require money. He permits Aku-nna to continue her education because it will increase her bride price, which will now go to him, but he has no interest in her personal wishes. Meanwhile, Aku-nna and Chike, her schoolmaster, fall in love, but Chike, the descendant of slaves, is subordinated and limited by traditional views as well. When Aku-nna can no longer hide that she is menstruating, and thus marriageable, Okonkwo, in a display of male power, tells her that she must let her friendship with Chike die. Aku-nna is kidnapped for marriage by Okoboshi, a classmate, in a tradition that is tolerated by Igbo society, but she is rejected by him when she falsely claims that she is not a virgin. She is able to escape with Chike, marries him, but dies giving birth to a daughter.

Emecheta's own fears of powerlessness and loss of autonomy in a male-dominated society are here projected onto an exclusively Nigerian setting and are more extensively fictionalized than in her first two novels. There is, furthermore, the introduction of a new theme, the destructive effects of the caste system within African society: Chike, too, is marginalized. Indeed, the repressive forces that threaten Aku-nna's happiness are indigenous rather than imported.

Despised by Okoboshi and his relatives when they think she has lost her virginity, Aku-nna reflects that she will be killed by Okonkwo if she runs away from him, and that she will die of shame and rejection if she stays. The point of these psychological pressures is to bring about the very death that is traditionally predicted for those who break custom and taboo. When Aku-nna dies during labor because of her youth, physical frailty, and malnutrition, the omniscient authorial voice informs the reader that Aku-nna's story is told to every girl in Ibuza: Women who do not accept the man chosen by their people and whose bride price is not paid will die while giving birth to their first child. Ironically, even the rebel against traditional customs and constraints reinforces these traditions by the manner of her death.

The Joys of Motherhood

Nnu Ego, the central character of *The Joys of Motherhood*, whose life and sufferings will dramatize the story's main points, is the illegitimate daughter, by a fiercely proud mistress, of the local chief in rural Ibuza. Nnu Ego's inability to bear children with her first husband causes her father to arrange a second marriage, to Nnaife Owulum, who works in Lagos for an English family. Nnu Ego submits to marrying a man she has never met; indeed, when she does meet him, she finds in him neither esteem nor attractiveness. When Nnaife's older brother dies, his wife, Adaku, becomes the younger brother's junior wife. Nnaife is conscripted into the British army for action in World War II, and his two wives are left to their own resources. Adaku becomes a prostitute and does well financially; Nnu Ego remains respectable and does not. When Nnaife returns, he acquires a third wife, sixteen-year-old Okpo. Nnu Ego's sons, as boys, are favored in society, and decide to continue their education in the United States and in Canada. Nnu Ego's own life continues to be subordinated to men and their privileged status. Nnaife, after serving a brief prison sentence for attacking a man of a different tribe who wanted to marry one of his daughters, returns to Ibuza, with the young Okpo. Nnu Ego, disowned, dies in Ibuza obscurely, and a shrine is built for her so any infertile granddaughters can pray to her.

A mesh of interconnected themes is developed in *The Joys of Motherhood*. At one stage, Nnu Ego thinks that if she were in Ibuza she would have her own hut and be given respect; in colonized Lagos, she has the worst of both worlds—polygamy and exploitation. She has been given to a man who is subservient before his English masters, as if he were a woman, but who still tries to exact complete obedience in the home, as if he were part of an organic social system of give and take that justified such demands. Her boys, to whom she has sacrificed everything, end up living in the New World, the epitome of modernity, and do not correspond with their mother. Nnu Ego has obeyed all the old rules but is still taken advantage of, and abandoned in old age.

M. D. Allen

Other major works

TELEPLAYS: *A Kind of Marriage*, 1976; *Family Bargain*, 1987.

RADIO PLAY: *The Ju Ju Landlord*, 1976.

NONFICTION: *Head Above Water*, 1986 (autobiography).

CHILDREN'S LITERATURE: *Titch the Cat*, 1979; *The Moonlight Bride*, 1980; *Nowhere to Play*, 1980; *The Wrestling Match*, 1980; *Naira Power*, 1982.

Bibliography

Booker, M. Keith. "Buchi Emecheta: *The Joys of Motherhood*." In *The African Novel in English: An Introduction*. Portsmouth, N.H.: Heinemann, 1998. A good account and overview of critical responses to Emecheta's novel.

Cox, C. Brian, ed. *African Writers*. 2 vols. New York: Charles Scribner's Sons, 1997. This compilation on African writers includes a biographical and critical overview of Emecheta and her writings. Also includes a brief bibliography.

Derrickson, Teresa. "Class, Culture, and the Colonial Context: The Status of Women in Buchi Emecheta's *The Joys of Motherhood*." *International Fiction Review* 29, nos. 1/2 (2002): 40-51. An examination of women in Igbo society and their place in colonial Nigeria. Discusses how women's status is reflected in *The Joys of Motherhood*.

Fishburn, Katherine. *Reading Buchi Emecheta: Cross-Cultural Conversations*. Westport, Conn.: Greenwood Press, 1995. A more demanding postmodernist approach. For advanced readers with some knowledge of literary and cultural theories.

Ogunyemi, Chikwenye Okonjo. "Buchi Emecheta: The Shaping of a Self." *Komparatistische Hefte* 8 (1983): 65-77. A general, and sometimes hostile, account of Emecheta's writings and themes through *The Joys of Motherhood*.

Umeh, Marie, ed. *Emerging Perspectives on Buchi Emecheta*. Trenton, N.J.: Africa World Press, 1995. A diverse collection of essays that show ever-changing interpretations of Emecheta's works.

Uwakweh, Pauline Ada. "Carving a Niche: Visions of Gendered Childhood in Buchi Emecheta's *The Bride Price* and Tsitsi Dangarembga's *Nervous Conditions*." *African Literature Today* 21 (1998): 9-21. A comparative essay arguing, in part, that gender identity, as evidenced in Emecheta's novel *The Bride Price*, is created by socialization.

SHŪSAKU ENDŌ

Born: Tokyo, Japan; March 27, 1923
Died: Tokyo, Japan; September 29, 1996
Also known as: Paul Endō

Principal long fiction

Shiroi hito, 1954
Kiiroi hito, 1955
Umi to dokuyaku, 1957 (*The Sea and Poison*, 1972)
Kazan, 1959 (*Volcano*, 1978)
Obakasan, 1959 (*Wonderful Fool*, 1974)
Watashi ga suteta onna, 1963 (*The Girl I Left Behind*, 1994)
Ryugaku, 1965 (*Foreign Studies*, 1989)
Chinmoku, 1966 (*Silence*, 1969)
Taihen da, 1969
Kuchibue o fuku toki, 1974 (*When I Whistle*, 1979)
Samurai, 1980 (*The Samurai*, 1982)
Sukyandaru, 1986 (*Scandal*, 1988)
Hangyaku, 1989 (2 volumes)
Kessen no tiki, 1991
Otoko no issho, 1991
Yojo no gotoku, 1991
Aio chiisana budo, 1993
Fukai kawa, 1993 (*Deep River*, 1994)
Shukuteki, 1995

Other literary forms

In Japan, Shūsaku Endō (ehn-doh) is known as a versatile, prolific author of novels, short stories, plays, and essays on history and theology. Only three works in these other genres, however, have been translated into English. *Ogon no kuni* (pr. 1966; *The Golden Country*, 1970), a three-act play, dramatizes basically the same historical events as those portrayed in the novel *Silence* and was first performed in Japan shortly after the publication of the book. Endō's best-known work in the West, aside from his novel *Silence*, is probably his *Iesu no shōgai* (1973; *A Life of Jesus*, 1978), an interpretive biography that attempts to reintroduce the person of Christ to skeptical Asian readers; it was joined in 1977 by the companion work *Kirisuto no tanjō* (the genesis of Christ), which won the Yomiuri Literary Prize. *Juichi no irogarasu* (1979; *Stained-Glass Elegies*, 1984) collects eleven elegantly crafted Endō short stories drawn and translated from two of his earlier Japanese anthologies. In 1992, a collection of some of Endō's short works was published in English as *To Friends from Other Lands: A Shūsaku Endō Miscellany*.

Achievements

Shūsaku Endō's fiction won for him numerous awards in Japan, including the prestigious Akutagawa Prize, the Mainchici Cultural Prize, the Shincho Prize, and the Noma Prize. In 1981, Endō was elected to the Japan Arts Academy. He is widely regarded as one of Japan's most important novelists and during his lifetime was hailed by Western writers such as Graham Greene, John Updike, and Irving Howe as perhaps the most significant religious novelist writing in any language. That Endō achieved this recognition writing as a believing Christian in a non-Christian culture generally resistant to Western religious philosophy is all the more remarkable.

Of all postwar Japanese novelists, Endō's work is the most accessible to the West. This is partly because he explicitly made it his mission to explore and explain the chasm between the two cultures, especially the spiritual abyss that separates them, a theme he pursued from the time his first published essay, "The Gods and God," appeared in 1947. Endō's oeuvre is thus unique in the history of modern Japanese literature, illuminating the struggle of Christianity to survive and thrive in the Orient while providing Western readers with new perspectives for examining their own religious heritage and commitment. Translations of his work have appeared in more than ten languages.

Biography

Shūsaku Endō was born on March 27, 1923, in Tokyo, Japan, but he spent his early years in Dalian, Manchuria. After divorcing his father, Endō's mother took her two sons back to Tokyo and, with her sister, converted to Catholicism. This religious conversion was the single most important event in Endō's life, since he and his brother soon followed her in accepting the Catholic faith. Though he little understood at the time what a momentous decision he was making, and though he wrestled in his later youth with doubts about his own commitment to Christianity, the adult Endō eventually embraced fully this Western faith.

After he graduated from the Japanese equivalent of high school, Endō enrolled at Keio University at the age of sixteen, studying Catholic philosophy. Unable to serve in the armed forces during World War II because of his poor health, he continued his education there in French literature, taking his B.A. in 1949. Eventually, Endō became one of the first Japanese to study in Europe after the war, attending the University of Lyons in France from 1950 to 1953, studying French Catholic writers Jacques Maritain, Georges Bernanos, and François Mauriac. His submersion in European culture intensified his appreciation for the impact of Christianity on the West and forced him to recognize the spiritual vacuum in Japan, which made belief in a transcendent deity difficult, if not impossible.

Chronic heart and lung problems prevented Endō from extending his stay in Europe, and he returned home to begin an ambitious career as a novelist and critic. Between 1953 and 1959, he wrote fiction that chronicled the religious indifference of the East and the widening disaffection between Eastern and Western cultures. From 1960 to 1963, Endō underwent a series of major surgical procedures, including the removal of one lung. During his long convalescence in the hospital, Endō renewed his literary craft, developing new themes that explored the possibility of developing a stronger, more indigenous version of Christianity in his native land.

Directly after this period, Endō's reputation and popularity began to grow both within Japan and internationally as he pursued the most important fiction of his career. At home in Japan, Endō was known not only as a writer of serious fiction and nonfiction but also as a television personality, humorist, and uniquely gifted public figure whose opinions and viewpoints were sought and respected by both the cultural elite and the Japanese population at large. After years of poor health, Endō died in Tokyo on September 29, 1996.

Analysis

Shūsaku Endō has been called a "Japanese Graham Greene" by several enthusiastic Western critics. For a writer to be so compared with a successful, highly visible novelist such as Greene is frequently a heavy burden. Whatever the actual merits of a writer so described, a reader too often reminded of a resemblance to another writer will be tempted to dismiss the writer's work as either inferior to that of the presumed counterpart or merely derivative. In introducing a Japanese writer to a Western audience, however, such comparisons can be useful, even indispensable—and, in this case, entirely apropos. Endō was one of the few Catholic novelists in the East, and his compelling though sinful and often stumbling characters captivate and endear themselves to the reader in the same way that Greene's faltering saints do.

A more pertinent comparison, however, could be drawn between Endō and the American Catholic novelist Walker Percy. Percy's seriocomic exploration of the disintegration of authentic Christianity in the jaded West and his attempts to redeem it novelistically from its secular trappings resemble Endō's own agenda in addressing both his Eastern and his Western readers. Like Percy himself, Endō saw his task as taking Jesus out of the realm of commonplaces in his native culture, disarming his Japanese readers and getting past their syncretizing defenses. The key themes in his work are nearly always intertwined with an evocation of Japan as a "mudswamp," that is, a land pervaded by moral apathy and a desperate need to find an ethical center rooted in eternal values—something that, in Endō's view, only Christianity can ultimately provide.

Endō's Christianity emanates from a childhood conversion to Catholicism, a Catholicism tempered by an education in France, where he was exposed to such French Catholic writers as François Mauriac, Paul Claudel, and Georges Bernanos. Endō recognized that as a Japanese Christian he was a walking oxymoron, an anomaly in his native culture. His own faith, he candidly admits in *Silence*, was a struggle against tradition and cultural identity:

> For a long time I was attracted to a meaningless nihilism and when I finally came to realize the fearfulness of such a void I was struck once again with the gran-

> deur of the Catholic Faith. This problem of the reconciliation of my Catholicism with my Japanese blood . . . has taught me one thing: that is, that the Japanese must absorb Christianity without the support of a Christian tradition or history or legacy or sensibility.

When Endō looked at his nation through the eyes of a believing Christian, he saw a "swamp" that "sucks up all sorts of ideologies, transforming them into itself and distorting them in the process." As a Christian novelist whose readers have no "objective correlatives" for the concepts he wished his fiction to incarnate, Endō saw his personal task as a novelist much differently from his contemporaries in Japan. Rather than mirroring the moral and social malaise about him, Endō sought to foster and exemplify such religious concepts as sin, redemption, and resurrection.

Like most works in translation, Endō's novels have been brought into English not in the order in which they appeared in his native country but in the order of the prestige and interest they have engendered in the West. It is possible, then, to get a somewhat distorted view of Endō's concerns and craft if one considers his work only in terms of what is available in English translation. In fact, Endō's long fiction shows clear signs of development and maturation over time, and can be best and most conveniently discussed and analyzed within two main periods.

FIRST PERIOD

The first period covers 1953-1959, the years immediately following his return to Japan from France and during which Endō wrote the short work *Aden made* (1954; till Aden) and five novels. Each dramatizes, in Endō's words, the Japanese "numbness to sin and guilt" by juxtaposing it to the conventional Christianized conscience of postwar Europe. Endō's earliest novels, untranslated into English, bear the marks of a genuinely talented writer who is still seeking the most appropriate voice and characterization to express his thematic vision. The early short piece *Aden made* and the novels *Shiroi hito* (white men), and *Kiiroi hito* (yellow men) deal graphically with the spiritual contrasts between East and West in the postwar period but with thin characterization and heavy sentimentality.

THE SEA AND POISON *and* VOLCANO

Endō's first two important novels, *The Sea and Poison* and *Volcano*, emerged as flawed but stirring problem works that scathingly indict the Japanese conscience for its insensitivity to the basic humanitarian impulse Endō saw in Western Christian nations. Set six months before the atomic bombings of Hiroshima and Nagasaki, *The Sea and Poison* stands out as particularly stirring and harrowing thematically in its exploration of the inhumane operations performed by the Japanese on captured American pilots during World War II and their impact on two young medical interns. *Volcano* is the first Endō novel that features fully drawn, credible characters, examining the complex relationship between a defrocked French priest and a Japanese volcanologist as they grapple with the natural and the supernatural at the foot of a newly active volcano.

WONDERFUL FOOL

At the end of this period, Endō published what may be his most characteristic and ultimately most enduring novel for Western readers, *Wonderful Fool*. Because *Wonderful Fool* is a transitional work that demonstrates Endō's versatility as a novelist with a penchant for combining humor and pathos in his pursuit of a serious theme, and that bridges the gap between Endō's two periods, it warrants special attention. In this novel, Endō's comic narrative style merges with a mature grasp of characterization to balance his central themes. *Wonderful Fool* features as protagonist the bumbling Gaston "Gas" Bonaparte, a "fool for Christ's sake" whose selflessness and genuine love for his fellow humans reflect the Christlike attributes that Endō wants his reader to recognize. Gaston is a "fool" in a Shakespearean sense, one who may unexpectedly speak as well as live the truth in a most poignant way.

Set twelve years after the end of World War II, *Wonderful Fool* tells the story of Gaston Bonaparte, a bona fide descendant of Napoleon himself, who arrives in Japan on a third-rate steamer, surprising his sometime pen pal, Takamori, a clerk, and Takamori's sister, Tomoe. After their first meeting, neither Takamori nor Tomoe could have suspected that Gas, as they come to call him, is a failed French seminary student who has launched out on his own to spread the news of faith and love to the long-neglected Orient. Upon first acquaintance, Gas seems to be a bumbling, clumsy oaf, well-intentioned but utterly ineffectual. In an early encounter, the gangly, uncoordinated Frenchman scandalizes his Japanese hosts by brandishing a loincloth in the place of table napkin. Later, he mistakes the advances of a prostitute for the simple congeniality of Japanese people.

Gas is clearly a stranger in a strange land, a wayfarer whose language and whose thought processes set him apart from everyone. Eventually Gas leaves behind the warmth and comfort of Takamori's home to set out on his own pilgrimage, accompanied only by the mongrel dog that has taken up with him. As Gas moves through the squalor of Tokyo's underworld, he steadily gropes toward his own destiny, toward his own Gethsemane and later his own Golgotha.

The key relationship in the novel, however, occurs between Gas and the gangster Endō. Kidnapped by Endō, Gas repeatedly manifests the innocence and love that is uncommon in the streets of Tokyo, endearing himself to the hardened and morally drained underworld figure. Compelled by Endō to assist him in getting revenge against another criminal, Gas thwarts him twice and eventually dies in saving both men from killing each other. Gas's climactic and heroic acts on behalf of two criminals beyond redemption earn for him the reverence from Takamori and Tomoe that his tenderness and tolerance so clearly warrant. In a final scene, Gas, apparently drowned in his mission of mercy, is remembered as a "lone egret, flapping snow-white wings," a traditional Japanese figure of peace and transfiguration.

Wonderful Fool is thus a parable about faith, the inevitable fate of a trusting soul who determinedly opens his life and his heart to all he encounters. His naïveté leads him to offend every significant social norm of Japanese society and even most patterns of everyday common sense. The final scenes of the novel powerfully capture Endō's vision of contemporary Japan: a mudswamp in which a wise fool battles with all of his strength to redeem two hoodlums who want neither redemption nor life, but whom he redeems all the same.

Second period

The second period in Endō's development as a novelist comprises his work after 1963 and includes his most celebrated works, exemplified in *Silence*, *When I Whistle*, and *The Samurai*. *Silence* and *The Samurai* are historical novels that focus attention intently on Japan's often ferocious rejection of Christianity in the seventeenth century and mirror its modern-day ambivalence toward Christianity; these works are best examined together.

Because few of Endō's lighter, more comic novels and his numerous historical and theological essays—works no less interesting and provoking than his other works—have been translated for Western readers, it is possible for such readers to form a view of Endō as a rather somber, overly moralistic writer. Certainly, if one knew only Endō's interpretive biography, *A Life of Jesus*, and his historical novels, *Silence* and *The Samurai*, one would gain a distorted picture of both his range of concerns and his innovation as a writer. Nevertheless, *Silence* and *The Samurai* are rightly regarded as two of Endō's major works, and clearly they have drawn the most critical attention and applause in the West. They detail the dismal record of Christianity in Japan, bitterly chronicling both the shallow ambitions of the missionaries who dared to invade the Japanese shores in the seventeenth century and the moral malaise of the Japanese themselves, who first welcomed the visitors and then condemned them to brutal martyrdom.

Silence

Silence is a dark epistolary novel of apostasy and betrayal, a narrative as told from the perspective of a Portuguese missionary priest. It is a tale of faith and faithlessness among both Western and Eastern men, men whose integrity as believers and as human beings is under constant attack. At the beginning of the seventeenth century, the Edo emperors came to the conclusion that Christianity did not "fit" Japan, banishing Christian missionaries and persecuting their flocks of converts. In *Silence*, Endō turns that conclusion on its head, establishing that Christianity and Christ fit nowhere yet everywhere, inasmuch as they dramatize and respond to humankind's homelessness in the world, the loneliness of human beings, and their forlorn hope of finding compensation for the pain of life in eternity, if at all.

The Samurai

In *The Samurai*, written nearly fifteen years after *Silence*, Endō again picks up the themes of martyrdom and betrayal. As a novel, it reminds many readers of Grahame Greene's *The Power and the Glory* (1940) and its heroic whiskey priest. *The Samurai* focuses on the enduring faith of a humble, despised servant, Rokuemon Hasekura, a warrior in the service of a powerful feudal lord in seventeenth century Japan, and his cohorts, who escort Father Velasco, an overly ambitious Franciscan missionary, from Japan to Mexico to Rome in his attempt to secure Japanese trading privileges with the West. Velasco's aim is to use his diplomacy to become bishop of Japan. Hasekura is a reluctant envoy who first despises the emaciated man on the cross who serves as the symbol of this baffling faith Velasco represents and later embraces him as the only light in a civilization growing darker day by day. *The Samurai* takes the reader on the ill-fated diplomatic journey of Velasco and Hasekura, during which both men, stripped of their illusions about self and motive, embrace a common faith. The two return to Japan as fools for Christ's sake, true believers without pretense or pride, facing inevitable martyrdom.

When I Whistle

Between these two historical novels, Endō wrote *When I Whistle*, a study of contemporary Japan and the relationship between two generations that focuses on a father and son. Here Endō reveals another aspect of his talent, the ability to write with realism and subtlety, avoiding sentimentality while evoking the antiseptic, forbidding images of hospitals and technology gone mad. Effectively using flashbacks from prewar and postwar Japan, Endō ironically juxtaposes the "new" Japan with the old and finds modern Japan, presumably more open to the West, in its own way even less congenial to Christian values and to simple human kindness. Ozu, the protagonist, is a humble clerk; his ignorance and general nostalgia for the older Japan are in vivid contrast to the preoccupations of his more successful and sophisticated son, Eiichi.

Eiichi is an opportunistic doctor willing to do anything to rise within his profession. His Japan is that of the grim Japanese novelist Yukio Mishima: minimalistic, technological, spiritually barren. Ozu longs for the Japan just after the attack on Pearl Harbor, in which "at last the time for a confrontation between the spiritual civilization of Japan and the material civilization of a foreign country has come!" Father and son are united at the hospital bed of Ozu's old flame from grammar school days, Aiko, who is dying of cancer. For Eiichi and the other young doctors, Aiko is not a person deserving of care, attention, and love but a convenient depository for experimental cancer treatments. Ozu parts from his old love and his son in muffled despair, confronting a predatory Japan conquering no longer with bayonets or aircraft but with sheer economic and technological prowess, devoid of a spiritual center.

Christian vision

Endō's early works, such as *Volcano* and *The Sea and Poison*, cleared his vision and provided the foundation for transitional works such as *Wonderful Fool* and, later, more mature works such as *Silence* and *When I Whistle*. The backdrop for each of these novels and, indeed, all of Endō's works is the congenital failure of Japanese culture to nurture a transcendent faith and to recognize the eternal relevance of such a faith for its people. In the novels, Endō attempts to craft an authentically Eastern vision of Christian faith obstinate enough to endure even in soils that have never been fertile for its growth.

The Christian vision of Shūsaku Endō thus has at its center a dramatically Eastern Jesus, the humble but single-minded "fool" who abandons all to reach those who are not so much hostile as they are indifferent, not so much faithless as they are cynical. This "foolish" Jesus—distinguished from the often bombastic and authoritarian Jesus imported from the West—drives his readers beyond the shallow, impotent Christianity lurking behind much modern faith. To reach them, Endō is challenged to defamiliarize Christ in his conventionally distant and supernaturally holy character, portraying him instead as a profoundly self-sacrificing, tender, and moral human being—an elder brother, not an omnipotent Lord.

Saint Cyril of Jerusalem, Endō's ancient brother in the Catholic faith, once wrote, "The dragon sits by the side of the road, watching those who pass. Beware lest he devour you. We go to the Father of Souls, but it is necessary to pass by the dragon." In commenting on this passage, the American Catholic writer Flannery O'Connor once remarked, "No matter what form the dragon may take, it is of this mysterious passage past him, or into his jaws, that stories of any depth will be concerned to tell, and this being the case, it requires considerable courage at any time, in any country, not to turn away from the storyteller." Shūsaku Endō refuses to turn away from the dragon or the storyteller, and he asks of his audience—East or West—the same courage.

Bruce L. Edwards, Jr.

Other major works

SHORT FICTION: *Aden made*, 1954; *Endō Shūsaku shū*, 1960; *Aika*, 1965; *Endō Shūsaku yūmoa shōsetsu shū*, 1969-1973 (2 volumes); *Gekkō no domina*, 1972; *Endō Shūsaku misuteri Shōsetu shū*, 1975; *Juichi no irogarasu*, 1979 (*Stained-Glass Elegies*, 1984); *The Final Martyrs*, 1993; *Five by Endo: Stories*, 2000.

PLAYS: *Ogon no kuni*, pr. 1966 (*The Golden Country*, 1970).

NONFICTION: *Furansu no Daigakusei*, 1953; *Gūtara seikatsu nyūmon*, 1967; *Iesu no shōgai*, 1973 (*A Life of Jesus*, 1978); *Shikai no hotori*, 1973; *Seisho no naka no joseitachi*, 1975; *Tetsu no kubikase*, 1976; *Watakushi no lesu*, 1976; *Kirisuto no tanjō*, 1977; *Ningan no naka no X*, 1978; *Jū to jūjika*, 1979; *Watakushi no ai shita shōsetsu*, 1985; *Haru wa basha ni notte*, 1989 (essays); *Honto no watakushi o motomete*, 1990; *Iesu ni atta onnatachi*, 1990; *Ihojin no tachiba kara*, 1990 (essays); *Kirishitan jidai: Junkyo to kikyo*, 1992; *Kokoro no sunadokei*, 1992 (essays).

MISCELLANEOUS: *To Friends from Other Lands: A Shūsaku Endō Miscellany*, 1992.

Bibliography

Beverly, Elizabeth. "A Silence That Is Not Hollow." *Commonweal* 116 (September 22, 1989): 491-494. Asserts that Endō's writing is inspired by two elemental aspects of his identity: the Japanese culture and Catholicism. Argues that Endō's embrace of both often made his life difficult and perilous, but that the labor of fiction made it bearable.

Bussie, Jacqueline Aileen. *The Laughter of the Oppressed: Ethical and Theological Resistance in Wiesel, Morrison, and Endo*. New York: T & T Clark International, 2007. Analyzes the depictions of the persecuted Japanese Christians in Endō's work, arguing that their ability to find humor in their fate is a means of resisting their oppression.

Gessel, Van C. "The Voice of the Doppelgänger." *Japan Quarterly*, no. 38 (1991): 198-213. Examines four postwar Japanese novelists, including Endō, and notes how the postwar fiction differs from the prewar tradition of the "I story," in which author and persona are one. Discusses Endō's *Scandal* as a model of the new treatment, in which the doppelgänger actually mocks the protagonist who represents the novelist, thus introducing aesthetic distance and irony.

Mase-Hasegawa, Emi. *Christ in Japanese Culture: Theological Themes in Shusaku Endo's Literary Works*. Leiden, Netherlands: Brill, 2008. Analyzes *Silence*, *The Samurai*, *Deep River*, and other works from a theological perspective, demonstrating how Christian doctrine has been adapted by the Japanese. Charts the development of Endō's thoughts on this adaptation (or "inculturation") during his career.

Mathy, Francis. "Endō Shūsaku: White Man, Yellow Man." *Comparative Literature* 19, no. 1 (1967): 58-74. Mathy, a Jesuit, explores Endō's fiction and essays and produces a clear and comprehensive treatment of the cultural conflict between Japan and Western Europe, especially as this conflict relates to religion and notions of beauty and morality. Shows how Endō experienced strong opposition between his Japanese heritage and the Christian view of life that he was taught by his mother and by Christian missionaries.

_______. "Shūsaku Endō: Japanese Catholic Novelist." *America* 167 (August 1-8, 1992): 66-71. Presents a biographical account of Endō's life, from his childhood and his education through the development of his most important works. Also surveys Endō's work and analyzes the themes presented in his early essays.

Netland, John T. "From Resistance to Kenosis: Reconciling Cultural Difference in the Fiction of Shūsaku Endō." *Christianity and Literature* 48 (Winter, 1999): 177-194. Discusses Endō's translation of the polemics of cultural difference into art; claims that his works replace a simple binary postcolonial tension with a three-dimensional configuration of Christian, Eastern, and European perspectives.

Quinn, P. L. "Tragic Dilemmas, Suffering Love, and Christian Life." *Journal of Religious Ethics* 17 (1989): 151-183. Provides a comprehensive description and analysis of Endō's *Silence*, in which the life of the Portuguese priest Sebastian Rodrigues, who became an apostate by trampling on an image of Christ to save his parishioners from torture and death by the governmental authorities, is reflected upon in the hope of enriching ethical thought.

Reinsma, Luke M. "Shūsaku Endō's River of Life." *Christianity and Literature* 48 (Winter, 1999): 195-211. Contribution to a special issue devoted to Endō discusses the natural world, particularly the river, as a metaphorical backdrop for his work. Argues that Endō shifted from landscapes and waters ravaged by a Father God in his early work to lush vegetation in his later fiction.

Williams, Mark. *Endō Shūsaku: A Literature of Reconciliation.* New York: Routledge, 1999. Interesting examination of Endō's fictive technique includes analysis of all of the major novels. Williams takes exception to the common characterization of Endō as the "Japanese Graham Greene" and locates the cultural and political contexts that differentiate Endō's work. Includes bibliography.

LOUISE ERDRICH

Born: Little Falls, Minnesota; June 7, 1954
Also known as: Karen Louise Erdrich

Principal long fiction

Love Medicine, 1984 (revised and expanded 1993)
The Beet Queen, 1986
Tracks, 1988
The Crown of Columbus, 1991 (with Michael Dorris)
The Bingo Palace, 1994
Tales of Burning Love, 1996
The Antelope Wife, 1998
The Last Report on the Miracles at Little No Horse, 2001
The Master Butchers Singing Club, 2003
Four Souls, 2004
The Painted Drum, 2005
The Plague of Doves, 2008
Shadow Tag, 2010

Other literary forms

In addition to long fiction, Louise Erdrich (UR-drihk) has published poetry, books for children, nonfiction, and short fiction. Many chapters in her novels were originally published as short stories in various periodicals. Her early books of poetry *Jacklight* (1984) and *Baptism of Desire* (1989) present vivid North Dakota vignettes as well as personal reflections on Erdrich's relationships with her husband and children. Several of the poems in these volumes, together with nineteen new ones, are included in *Original Fire: Selected and New Poems* (2003). Erdrich's memoir of her daughter's birth, *The Blue Jay's Dance: A Birth Year*, was published in 1995, and her travel memoir *Books and Islands in Ojibwe Country* appeared in 2003.

Achievements

A poet and poetic novelist, Louise Erdrich learned to draw on her Ojibwa (also known as Chippewa) and German-immigrant heritage to create a wide-ranging chronicle of Native American and white experience in twentieth century North Dakota and Minnesota. She received fellowships from the MacDowell Colony in 1980 and from Dartmouth College and Yaddo Colony in 1981. Since she began to publish her fiction and poetry in the early 1980's, her works have garnered high critical praise, and her novels have been best sellers as well.

Erdrich was awarded a National Endowment for the Arts Fellowship in 1982, the Pushcart Prize in 1983, and a Guggenheim Fellowship in 1985-1986. Her first novel, *Love Medicine*, won the National Book Critics Circle Award in 1984, and three stories that became chapters in that book were also honored: "The World's Greatest Fishermen" won the 1982 Nelson Algren Fiction Award, "Scales" appeared in *The Best American Short Stories 1983*, and "Saint Marie" was chosen for *Prize Stories 1985: The O. Henry Awards* (1985). Two of the stories included in the novel *Tracks* also appeared in honorary anthologies: "Fleur" in *Prize Stories 1987: The O. Henry Awards* and "Snares" in *The Best American Short Stories 1988*. Erdrich's 2001 novel *The Last Re-*

port on the Miracles at Little No Horse was a finalist for the National Book Award for fiction, and her children's book *The Game of Silence* (2005) received the Scott O'Dell Award for Historical Fiction.

Erdrich's works often focus on the struggles of Native Americans for personal, familial, and cultural survival. Her treatment of white characters and of characters of mixed Native American and white blood, however, reveals an empathetic understanding of the ways in which people of all races long for closer connection with one another and the land.

Biography

Karen Louise Erdrich, whose grandfather was tribal chair of the Turtle Mountain Band of the Ojibwa Nation, grew up in Wahpeton, a small town in southeastern North Dakota. Both of her parents—Ralph Erdrich, the son of a German immigrant, and Rita Gourneau Erdrich, who is three-quarters Ojibwa—taught at the Wahpeton Indian Boarding School. Erdrich's mixed religious and cultural background provided a rich foundation for her later poetry and fiction.

Erdrich earned two degrees in creative writing, a B.A. from Dartmouth College in 1976 and an M.A. from Johns Hopkins University in 1979. In 1981, she married Michael Dorris, a professor of anthropology and head of the Native American Studies Program at Dartmouth. Erdrich and Dorris devoted much of their married life to ambitious family, literary, and humanitarian goals. Dorris, who was three-eighths Modoc Indian, had previously adopted three Lakota Sioux children; together Erdrich and Dorris had three daughters. Professionally, they collaborated on virtually all the works that either one published—whether fiction, poetry, or nonfiction. Erdrich has thus acknowledged Dorris's important contribution to her earlier fiction; similarly, she collaborated with him on his first novel, *A Yellow Raft in Blue Water* (1987), and on his study of fetal alcohol syndrome (FAS), *The Broken Cord* (1989). Erdrich and Dorris donated money and campaigned for legislation to combat FAS, which afflicts the lives of many Native American children born to alcoholic mothers.

Unfortunately, their private lives became difficult. All of their adopted children were permanently affected by the alcoholism of their mothers and led troubled lives

Louise Erdrich. (Michael Dorris)

as adults. One son attempted to extort money from Dorris and Erdrich, and their daughter became estranged from them. Their oldest adopted child, Abel (renamed Adam in *The Broken Cord*), was struck by a car and killed in 1991, an event that deeply affected the marriage.

Erdrich and Dorris eventually moved from New Hampshire to Minneapolis and later separated after fifteen years of marriage. During subsequent divorce proceedings, Dorris, who had been profoundly depressed since the second year of their marriage, attempted suicide twice. He succeeded on April 11, 1997.

In 2000, Erdrich established Birchbark Books, a small independent bookstore in Minneapolis; she gave birth to another daughter the following year. She continues to incorporate her study of the Ojibwa language and culture into her writing.

Analysis

In a 1985 essay "Where I Ought to Be: A Writer's Sense of Place," Louise Erdrich states that the essence of her writing emerges from her attachment to her North Dakota locale. The ways in which Erdrich has brought this region to literary life have been favorably compared by critics to the methods and style of William Faulkner, who created the mythical Yoknapatawpha County out of his rich sense of rural Mississippi. Like Faulkner, Erdrich has created a gallery of diverse characters spanning several generations, using multiple points of view and shifting time frames. Erdrich's fiction further resembles Faulkner's in that the experiences of her characters encompass a broad spectrum, ranging "from the mundane to the miraculous," as one critic has put it.

Erdrich's stories generally begin with realistic bases of ordinary people, settings, and actions. As the tales develop, however, these people become involved in events and perceptions that strike the reader as quite extraordinary—as exaggerated or heightened in ways that may seem deluded or mystical, grotesque or magical, comic or tragic, or some strange mixture of these. Thus, one critic has described Erdrich as "a sorceress with language" whose lyrical style intensifies some of the most memorable scenes in contemporary American fiction.

Love Medicine

Erdrich's first novel, *Love Medicine*, spans the years 1934-1984 in presenting members of five Ojibwa and mixed-blood families, all struggling in different ways to attain a sense of belonging through love, religion, home, and family. The novel includes fourteen interwoven stories; though the title refers specifically to traditional Ojibwa magic in one story, in a broader sense "love medicine" refers to the different kinds of spiritual power that enable Erdrich's Native American and mixed-blood characters to transcend—however momentarily—the grim circumstances of their lives. Trapped on their shrinking reservation by racism and poverty, plagued by alcoholism, disintegrating families, and violence, some of Erdrich's characters nevertheless discover a form of "love medicine" that helps to sustain them.

The opening story, "The World's Greatest Fishermen," begins with an episode of "love medicine" corrupted and thwarted. Though June Kashpaw was once a woman of striking beauty and feisty spirit, by 1981 she has sunk to the level of picking up men in an oil boomtown. Unfortunately, June fails in her last attempts to attain two goals that other characters will also seek throughout the novel: love and home. Although she appears only briefly in this and one other story, June Kashpaw is a central character in the novel, for she embodies the potential power of spirit and love in ways that impress and haunt the other characters.

The second part of "The World's Greatest Fishermen" introduces many of the other major characters of *Love Medicine*, as June's relatives gather several months after her death. On one hand, several characters seem sympathetic because of their closeness to June and their kind treatment of one another. Albertine Johnson, who narrates the story and remembers her Aunt June lovingly, has gone through a wild phase of her own and is now a nursing student. Eli Kashpaw, Albertine's granduncle, who was largely responsible for rearing June, is a tough and sharp-minded old man who has maintained a time-honored Ojibwa way of life as a hunter and fisherman. Lipsha Morrissey, who, though he seems not to know it, is June's illegitimate son, is a sensitive, self-educated young man who acts warmly toward Albertine. In contrast to these characters are others who are flawed or unsympathetic when seen through the eyes of Albertine, who would like to feel that her family is pulling together after June's death. These less sympathetic characters include Zelda and Aurelia (Albertine's gossipy mother and aunt), Nector Kashpaw (Albertine's senile grandfather), and Gordon Kashpaw (the husband whom June left, a hapless drunk). Worst of all is June's legitimate son King, a volatile bully. King's horrifying acts of violence—abusing his wife Lynette, battering his new car, and smashing the pies prepared for the family dinner—leave Albertine in dismay with a family in shambles.

Love Medicine then shifts back in time from 1981, and its thirteen remaining stories proceed in chronological order from 1934 to 1984. "Saint Marie" concerns a mixed-blood girl, Marie Lazarre, who in 1934 enters Sacred Heart Convent and embarks on a violent love-hate relationship with Sister Leopolda. In "Wild Geese," also set in 1934, Nector Kashpaw is infatuated with Lulu Nanapush, but his affections swerve unexpectedly when he encounters Marie Lazarre on the road outside her convent. By 1948, the time of "The Beads," Marie has married Nector, had three children (Aurelia, Zelda, and Gordie), and agreed to rear her niece June. Nector, however, is drinking and philandering, and June, after almost committing suicide in a children's hanging game, leaves to be brought up by Eli in the woods. "Lulu's Boys," set in 1957, reveals that the amorous Lulu Lamartine (née Nanapush) had married Henry Lamartine but bore eight sons by different fathers. Meanwhile, in "The Plunge of the Brave," also set in 1957, Nector recalls the development of his five-year affair with Lulu and tries to leave his wife Marie for her, but the result is that he accidentally burns Lulu's house to the ground.

The offspring of these Kashpaws and Lamartines also have their problems in later *Love Medicine* stories. In "A Bridge," set in 1973, Albertine runs away from home and becomes the lover of Henry Lamartine, Jr., one of Lulu's sons, a troubled Vietnam War veteran. "The Red Convertible," set in 1974, also involves Henry, Jr., as Lyman Lamartine tries unsuccessfully to bring his brother out of the dark personality changes that his time in Vietnam has wrought in him. On a lighter note, "Scales," set in 1980, is a hilarious account of the romance between Dot Adare, an obese clerk at a truck weighing station, and Gerry Nanapush, one of Lulu's sons who is a most unusual convict: enormously fat, amazingly expert at escaping from jail, but totally inept at avoiding capture. "Crown of Thorns," which overlaps with the time of "The World's Greatest Fishermen" in 1981, traces the harrowing and bizarre decline of Gordie Kashpaw into alcoholism after June's death.

Though in these earlier *Love Medicine* stories the positive powers of love and spirit are more often frustrated than fulfilled, in the last three stories several characters achieve breakthroughs that bring members of the different families together in moving and hopeful ways. In "Love Medicine," set in 1982, Lipsha Morrissey reaches out lovingly to his grandmother Marie and to the ghosts of Nector and June. In "The Good Tears," set in 1983, Lulu undergoes a serious eye operation and is cared for by Marie, who forgives her for being Nector's longtime extramarital lover. Finally, in "Crossing the Water," set in 1984, Lipsha helps his father, Gerry Nanapush, escape to Canada and comes to appreciate the rich heritage of love, spirit, and wiliness that he has inherited from his diverse patchwork of Ojibwa relatives—especially from his grandmother Lulu, his great-aunt Marie, and his parents, June and Gerry.

The Beet Queen

In *The Beet Queen*, her second novel, Erdrich shifts her main focus from the American Indian to the European-immigrant side of her background, and she creates in impressive detail the mythical town of Argus (modeled on Wahpeton, where she was reared, but located closer to the Ojibwa reservation) in the years 1932-1972. The opening scene of *The Beet Queen*, "The Branch," dramatizes two contrasting approaches to life that many characters will enact throughout the novel. On a cold spring day in 1932, two orphans, Mary and Karl Adare, arrive by freight train in Argus. As they seek the way to the butcher shop owned by their Aunt Fritzie and Uncle Pete Kozka, Mary "trudge[s] solidly forward" while Karl stops to embrace a tree that already has its spring blossoms. When they are attacked by a dog, Mary runs ahead, continuing her search for the butcher shop, while Karl runs back to hop the train once again. As the archetypal plodder of the novel, Mary continues to "trudge solidly forward" throughout; she is careful, determined, and self-reliant in pursuit of her goals. On the other hand, Karl is the principal dreamer—impressionable, prone to escapist impulses, and dependent on others to catch him when he falls.

The Adare family history shows how Karl is following a pattern set by his mother, Adelaide, while Mary grows in reaction against this pattern. Like Karl, Adelaide is physically beautiful but self-indulgent and impulsive. Driven to desperation by her hard luck in the early years of the Great Depression, Adelaide startles a fairground crowd by abandoning her three children (Mary, Karl, and an unnamed newborn son) to fly away with the Great Omar, an airplane stunt pilot.

In Argus, Mary tangles with yet another beautiful, self-centered dreamer: her cousin Sita Kozka, who resents the attention that her parents, Pete and Fritzie, and her best friend, the mixed-blood Celestine James, pay to Mary. Mary prevails, however, and carves a solid niche for herself among Pete, Fritzie, and Celestine, who, like Mary, believe in a strong work ethic and lack Sita's pretentious airs.

A number of episodes gratify the reader with triumphs for Mary and comeuppances for the less sympathetic characters Karl, Adelaide, and Sita. Mary becomes famous for a miracle at her school (she falls and cracks the ice in the image of Jesus), gains Celestine as a close friend, and in time becomes manager of the Kozka butcher shop. By contrast, Karl becomes a drifter who finds only sordid momentary pleasure in his numerous affairs. Meanwhile, Adelaide marries Omar and settles in Florida, but she becomes moody and subject to violent rages. Similarly, Sita fails in her vainglorious attempts to become a model and to establish a fashionable French restaurant; she escapes her first marriage through divorce and becomes insane and suicidal during her second.

Even as Erdrich charts the strange and sometimes grotesque downfalls of her flighty characters, however, she develops her more sympathetic ones in ways that suggest that the opposite approach to life does not guarantee happiness either. Mary is unsuccessful in her attempt to attract Russell Kashpaw (the half brother of Celestine), and she develops into an exotically dressed eccentric who is obsessed with predicting the future and controlling others. Like Mary, Celestine James and Wallace Pfef are hardworking and successful in business, but their loneliness drives each of them to an ill-advised affair with Karl, and he causes each of them considerable grief. In addition, the union of Celestine and Karl results in the birth of Dot Adare (who grows up to be the ill-tempered lover of Gerry Nanapush in the *Love Medicine* story "Scales"); since Celestine, Mary, and Wallace all spoil the child, Dot turns out, in Wallace's words, to have "all of her family's worst qualities." As a teenager, Dot herself comes to grief when she is mortified to learn that the well-meaning Wallace has rigged the election for queen of the Argus Beet Festival so that she, an unpopular and ludicrously unlikely candidate, will win.

In addition to the defeats and disappointments that all the characters bear, Erdrich dramatizes the joy that they derive from life. The compensations of family and friendship—ephemeral and vulnerable as these may be—prove to be significant for all the characters at various times in the story, particularly at the end. The irrepressible vitality of these people, troublesome as they often are to one another, keeps the reader involved and entertained throughout the novel.

Tracks

Erdrich's third novel, *Tracks*, is concentrated, intense, and mystical. It is shorter than the previous novels, covering a time span of only twelve years and alternating between only two first-person narrators. This compression serves the story well, for the human stakes are high. At first, and periodically throughout the novel, the Ojibwa characters fear for their very survival, as smallpox, tuberculosis, severe winters, starvation, and feuds with mixed-blood families bring them close to extinction. Later in the novel, government taxes and political chicanery threaten the Ojibwas' ownership of family and tribal land. In response, Erdrich's Ojibwa characters use all the powers at their command—including the traditional mystical powers of the old ways—to try to survive and maintain their control over the land.

Nanapush, one of the novel's two narrators, is an old Ojibwa whom Erdrich names for the trickster rabbit in tribal mythology who repeatedly delivers the people from threatening monsters. In *Tracks*, Erdrich's Nanapush often does credit to his mythological model, Nanabozho, by wielding the trickster rabbit's powers of deliverance, wiliness, and humor. He saves Fleur Pillager, a seventeen-year-old girl who is the last but one of the Pillager clan, from starvation. Later he delivers young Eli Kashpaw from the sufferings of love by advising him how to win Fleur's heart. Also, Nanapush is instrumental in saving the extended family that forms around Fleur, Eli, and himself. This family grows to five when Fleur gives birth to a daughter, Lulu, and Eli's mother, Margaret Kashpaw, becomes Nanapush's bedmate. As these five come close to starvation, Nanapush sends Eli out to hunt an elk; in one of the most extraordinary passages of the novel, Nanapush summons a power vision of Eli hunting that the old man imagines is guiding Eli to the kill. Nanapush also demonstrates the humor associated with his mythological model in his wry tone as a narrator, his sharp wit in conversation, and the tricks that he plays on his family's mixed-blood antagonists, the Morrisseys and the Lazarres.

Foremost among these antagonists is the novel's other narrator, Pauline Puyat. A "skinny big-nosed girl with staring eyes," Pauline circulates in Argus from the Kozkas' butcher shop to the Sacred Heart Convent, and on the reservation from the Nanapush-Pillager-Kashpaw group to the Morrissey and Lazarre clans. At first attracted to Fleur by the beauty and sexual power that she herself lacks, Pauline later takes an envious revenge by concocting a love potion that seems to drive Fleur's husband, Eli, and Sophie Morrissey to become lovers. Ironically, though one side of her believes in a Catholic denial of her body, Pauline later gives birth out of wedlock to a girl named Marie, and at the end of her narrative Pauline enters the convent to become Sister Leopolda—the cruel nun who later torments her own daughter, Marie Lazarre, in *Love Medicine*.

Though Erdrich clearly feels passionately about the sufferings visited on her Ojibwa characters in *Tracks*, she treats this politically charged material with her usual disciplined restraint. Her dispassionate, deadpan use of first-person narrators (never broken by authorial commentary) matches the understated, stoic attitude that Nanapush adopts toward the numerous waves of hardship and betrayal that the Ojibwas must endure.

If in some ways *Tracks* seems to conclude with a feeling of fragmentation and defeat, in other ways it strikes positive notes of solidarity and survival, especially when considered in relation to *Love Medicine* and *The Beet Queen*. Fleur disappears, leaving her husband and daughter, but Nanapush uses his wiliness to become tribal chairman and then to retrieve Lulu from a distant boarding school. At the end, the reader is reminded that Nanapush has addressed his entire narrative to Lulu: The old man hopes that his story will convince Lulu to embrace the memory of Fleur, "the one you will not call mother." Further, the reader familiar with *Love Medicine* will realize how this young girl, who becomes Lulu Lamartine, carries on the supernaturally powerful sexuality of her mother Fleur and the wily talent for survival of Nanapush, the old man who gave her his name and reared her.

The Bingo Palace

The Bingo Palace takes place roughly ten years after the end of *Love Medicine* and follows several characters introduced in Erdrich's first three novels. Primary among these is June Kashpaw's luckless son Lipsha Morrissey, back on the reservation after a series of failed jobs. His uncle, shrewd businessman Lyman Lamartine, offers Lipsha a job at his bingo parlor as a part-time bartender and night watchman. After his dead mother June appears with bingo tickets that are destined to change his luck significantly, gentle Lipsha not only wins a prize van but also pockets more of Lyman's money by continuing to win. A further complication in their relationship is Shawnee Ray Toose (Miss Little Shell), champion jingle-dress dancer, with whom Lipsha is promptly smitten, even though she has had a son by Lyman.

This loosely structured novel recounts Lipsha's sweet but faltering courtship of Shawnee, who rebuffs both of her suitors; Lyman's schemes to erect a splendid bingo palace on the last bit of Pillager land; and a joint vision quest that is serious for Lyman but comic for Lipsha, whose vision animal turns out to be a skunk that really sprays him. Lipsha has another abortive reunion with his father, escaped convict Gerry Nanapush, and is left stranded in a stolen car in a blizzard until his great-grandmother Fleur Pillager steps in. Erdrich employs techniques of Magical Realism as the dead speak and the lake monster Misshepeshu continues to strike terror into the hearts of all except the dauntless Fleur.

The Antelope Wife

Erdrich's seventh novel, *The Antelope Wife*, shifts to a new set of characters and a new locale, Minnesota. A young cavalry private, Scranton Roy, is sent to quell an American Indian uprising but mistakenly attacks a neutral Ojibwa village. Realizing his error, he manages to rescue a baby whom he then nurses with his own miraculous milk and raises to adulthood. In this way the white Roy family begins a relationship that spans five generations with two Ojibwa families.

The infant's grieving mother marries a man named Showano and bears twin girls. Her twin granddaughters Zosie and Mary Showano figure prominently as the wife and the lover of Scranton Roy's grandson and as the two mothers of Rozina Roy Whiteheart Beads, herself the mother of twin daughters. Rozina wants to leave her husband Richard for a Minneapolis baker, Frank Showano. Although this novel was completed just before Michael Dorris's death, it is uncomfortably prescient in its account of the unhappy marriage between Rozina and her suicidal husband.

This is a novel of repeated family patterns (lost mothers, lost daughters), emphasized by the linking imagery of the archetypal beaders that introduce each section. In this subtle and seamless blending of Ojibwa myth with contemporary life, Magical Realism becomes even more pronounced. Frank Showano's brother Klaus is nearly destroyed by his infatuation with a seductive, shape-shifting antelope woman. The windigo, a cannibal hunger spirit, is a very real presence and threat, and some chapters are narrated by a talking dog named Almost Soup. *The Antelope Wife* affirms the vitality of Ojibwa culture on and off the reservation.

THE LAST REPORT ON THE MIRACLES AT LITTLE NO HORSE

Erdrich's darkly comic eighth novel, *The Last Report on the Miracles at Little No Horse*, revisits several of the characters from earlier books, particularly Father Damien Modeste, the mild old priest at Little No Horse reservation in North Dakota. Erratically spanning the years from 1910 to 1996, this book offers an account of his unusual history, including the revelation that he is not only a woman, Agnes DeWitt, but a former nun and farm wife to whom a piano, even a simple Chopin nocturne, presents an occasion of sin. Swept in by the flooding Red River, he arrives on the reservation to assume the identity of a recently drowned priest and begin a life of service. As Father Damien, he enjoys a deepening friendship with the Ojibwa elders Kashpaw and Nanapush as well as with their extended families. He also endures the unwelcome visit of a foul black dog that thrusts its paw into his soup, bargains for his soul, and presents him with an irresistible temptation.

A second story line involves an initial inquiry into purported miracles that were worked by the late Sister Leopolda (formerly Pauline Puyat), as the first step toward her possible canonization. Enigmatic Leopolda, skeletal and bone-white, appears only briefly as a figure from the past, although her memory looms large in the present. Prior to entering the novitiate, Pauline had tirelessly attended the sick and dying during the devastating influenza epidemic of 1918. On the reservation, people still recall stories of her stigmata, the imprints of Christ's wounds on her body, and a mysterious paralysis that caused her to fold like a jackknife. As the nun's only surviving contemporary, Father Damien supposedly knows the real truth about her and has been writing desperate, unanswered letters to the Vatican ever since his arrival.

At last the Vatican sends Father Jude Miller to investigate. Eager to discover a new saint, Father Jude embarks on a series of interviews with various residents who offer guarded recollections of Sister Leopolda. Father Damien, on the other hand, has developed serious misgivings about the nun's sanctity and harbors no illusions about his own. His hard-earned wisdom leads him to a question that Erdrich has implied before: He fears that all his good intentions have been futile, that the government schools and forced conversion of the Ojibwas to Christianity have been horrible mistakes, offering the people little more than a destructive, alcohol-soaked alternative to their own culture.

Erdrich's books are seldom predictable, but life at Little No Horse offers more surprises than most with its splendid procession of mystery, mysticism, gravity, and humor. The hilarious account of Nanapush's death at the mercy of a runaway moose (and his subsequent resurrection) is one of the highlights of the novel.

THE PLAGUE OF DOVES

Erdrich returns to the familiar plains of North Dakota for *The Plague of Doves*, but, as in *The Antelope Wife*, with completely new characters whose lives are intertwined. This time her setting is near Argus, in the fictional town of Pluto, whose sparse population consists of Germans, Norwegians, and Ojibwas from the neighboring reservation. The present is filled with dizzying relationships, interspersed with tales from the past that reveal the origins and history of the community.

The novel opens in 1911, immediately after the horrific slaughter of a whole family, save for an infant, then shifts back fifteen years to the time when a sudden plague occurred. Invading doves blackened the skies like locusts and settled over the land, devouring everything. In desperation, people attempted to drive them away, while the local Catholic priest organized a procession of the mixed-blood population to pray for deliverance. During this event a young altar boy, Seraph Milk, took advantage of the confusion to run off with his future wife, to become the progenitor of the Milk-Harp family around which the story centers.

In this novel, Erdrich employs three main narrators as well as several minor ones. The first is Evelina (Evey) Harp, the granddaughter of Seraph Milk, who is now called Mooshum (Grandfather). Evey reveals her childhood crushes on a mischievous classmate, Corwin Peace, and on her sixth-grade teacher, whom the children call Sister Godzilla. Later, Evey becomes a psychiatric aide in the state mental hospital, eventually signing herself in as a patient after a bad experience with some

LSD that Corwin has given her. (In an Erdrich novel, at least one character is always slightly mad.) Other narrators include a judge whose grandfather, as a member of an ill-fated surveying party, had a hand in the founding of Pluto, and a naïve teenager who marries Corwin's charismatic uncle, an evangelist who founds a dangerous cult.

Mooshum is another of Erdrich's delightfully roguish old men, as is his crippled brother Shamengwa, who plays a magical violin in spite of his damaged arm. The two elders relish teasing Mooshum's daughter by sneaking forbidden whiskey past her, which they manage whenever an unpopular priest, Father Cassidy, comes calling in another attempt to save their souls. Because Shamengwa long ago left the Catholic Church to return to traditional beliefs, any hope of his conversion is doomed, but Mooshum enjoys sparring with the frustrated priest.

One of the tales that Mooshum relates to Evey is a shameful secret widely known in the community yet seldom repeated—the story of an Ojibwa youth who was a distant relative. Dying from tuberculosis, the boy's pious mother nailed wooden crosses to her son's boot soles to protect him from the disease, so that his footprints revealed crosses, a holy track, which then became his nickname. Holy Track, whom Erdrich modeled on a historical figure of the same name, was one of four innocent Ojibwas hanged by an angry mob of Pluto's white citizens, believing that the men were responsible for murdering the baby's family.

Like most of Erdrich's work, this is a story of connections, mixing regional and human history with fiction and elements of the supernatural. Descendants of the lynch mob and of their victims now live side by side in Pluto. Erdrich exposes the underlying wounds between Ojibwas and whites that still remain, but silence helps to preserve the amenities of everyday living, and even reconciliation, in a town where some secrets are not spoken yet are shared by all.

If Louise Erdrich had been born two hundred years earlier, she might have become a traditional Ojibwa storyteller, whose tales would have reminded her listeners of their unchanging relationship to the land and to the mythic and legendary characters who inhabited it. Several generations removed from such a stable and undamaged culture, Erdrich nevertheless has been able to create a richly neotribal view of people and place. Her novels testify to the profound interrelatedness of her characters—Native American and white, contemporaries and ancestors—both with one another and with their midwestern homeland.

Terry L. Andrews
Updated by Joanne McCarthy

Other major works

SHORT FICTION: "The Red Convertible," 1981; "Scales," 1982; "American Horse," 1983; "Destiny," 1985; "Saint Marie," 1985; "Fleur," 1987; "Snares," 1987; "Matchimanito," 1988; *The Red Convertible: Selected and New Stories, 1978-2008*, 2009.

POETRY: *Jacklight*, 1984; *Baptism of Desire*, 1989; *Original Fire: Selected and New Poems*, 2003.

NONFICTION: *The Blue Jay's Dance: A Birth Year*, 1995; *Books and Islands in Ojibwe Country*, 2003.

CHILDREN'S LITERATURE: *Grandmother's Pigeon*, 1996 (illustrated by Jim LaMarche); *The Birchbark House*, 1999; *The Range Eternal*, 2002; *The Game of Silence*, 2005.

EDITED TEXT: *The Best American Short Stories 1993*, 1993.

Bibliography

Beidler, Peter G., and Gay Barton. *A Reader's Guide to the Novels of Louise Erdrich*. Columbia: University of Missouri Press, 1999. Informative handbook for students of Erdrich's fiction covers geography, chronology, and character relationships in her novels through *The Antelope Wife*.

Brehm, Victoria. "The Metamorphoses of an Ojibwa *Manido*." *American Literature* 68 (December, 1996): 677-706. Traces the evolution of the legendary Ojibwa water monster Micipijiu (Misshepeshu), with a fascinating section on the symbolism and significance of the monster in Erdrich's *Love Medicine*, *Tracks*, and *The Bingo Palace*.

Chavkin, Allan, ed. *The Chippewa Landscape of Louise Erdrich*. Tuscaloosa: University of Alabama Press, 1998. Collection of original essays focuses on Erdrich's writings that are rooted in the Ojibwa experience. Premier scholars of Native American literature investigate narrative structure, signs of ethnicity, the notions of luck and chance in Erdrich's narrative cosmology, and her use of comedy in exploring American Indians' tragic past.

Chavkin, Allan, and Nancy Feyl Chavkin, eds. *Conversations with Louise Erdrich and Michael Dorris*. Jackson: University Press of Mississippi, 1994. Collection contains several articles and twenty-five interviews with the couple, including an interview conducted by Abenaki author and storyteller Joseph Bruchac.

Ferguson, Suzanne. "The Short Stories of Louise Erdrich's Novels." *Studies in Short Fiction* 33 (1996): 541-555. Provides an excellent discussion of four short stories—"Saint Marie," "Scales," "Fleur," and "Snares"—and how Erdrich modified them when they became chapters in her novels. Argues that the short stories should be read differently when they stand on their own compared with when they are presented as chapters in novels.

Smith, Jeanne Rosier. *Writing Tricksters: Mythic Gambols in American Ethnic Literature*. Berkeley: University of California Press, 1997. Presents a thorough examination of ethnic trickster figures as they appear in the works of Erdrich, Maxine Hong Kingston, and Toni Morrison. Chapter 3 explores the trickster characteristics of Old Nanapush, Gerry Nanapush, Lipsha Morrissey, Fleur Pillager, and others found in Erdrich's novels.

Stookey, Lorena Laura. *Louise Erdrich: A Critical Companion*. Westport, Conn.: Greenwood Press, 1999. Study of Erdrich's works presents biographical information, an examination of Erdrich's place in literary tradition, and analysis of each novel through *The Antelope Wife*. Includes bibliographical references and index.

Treuer, David. *Native American Fiction: A User's Manual*. St. Paul, Minn.: Graywolf Press, 2006. An Ojibwa author offers an intriguing perspective on the work of several contemporaries, including Erdrich. The chapter "Smartberries" praises Erdrich's modern literary techniques in *Love Medicine*, but in other chapters Treuer questions what in fact constitutes "authentic" Native American writing.

Wong, Hertha D. Sweet. *Louise Erdrich's "Love Medicine": A Casebook*. New York: Oxford University Press, 2000. Presents documents relating to the historical importance of *Love Medicine*, representative critical essays, and excerpts from several interviews with Erdrich and Michael Dorris.

PERCIVAL EVERETT

Born: Fort Gordon, Georgia; December 22, 1956
Also known as: Percival Leonard Everett

PRINCIPAL LONG FICTION

Suder, 1983
Walk Me to the Distance, 1985
Cutting Lisa, 1986
For Her Dark Skin, 1990
Zulus, 1990
God's Country, 1994
Watershed, 1996
Frenzy, 1997
Glyph, 1999
Erasure, 2001
Grand Canyon, Inc., 2001 (novella)
A History of the African-American People (Proposed) by Strom Thurmond, 2004 (with James Kincaid)
American Desert, 2004
Wounded, 2005
The Water Cure, 2007
I Am Not Sidney Poitier, 2009

OTHER LITERARY FORMS

In addition to long fiction, Percival Everett has published short stories, poetry, and works he has characterized as "multimedia," such as *Re: f (gesture)* (2006). In 1992, he published a children's book, *The One That Got Away*. His most notable collections of short stories are *Big Picture* (1996) and *Damned If I Do* (2004). Everett also served as the fiction editor for the journal *Callaloo* (1994), and his work was featured in a special issue of that journal in 2005. His collection of poetry *Abstraktion und Einfühlung* was published in 2008.

Everett, a prolific and eclectic writer, challenges the conventions of genre in works such as *A History of the African-American People (Proposed) by Strom Thurmond*, a collaborative work that plays with the conventions of the epistolary novel and the slave narrative. His novel *Walk Me to the Distance* was adapted as a film for television under the title *Follow Your Heart* (1990). In his work, Everett draws on a background in ordinary language philosophy from his academic studies as well as his passions for horse training, woodworking, and fly fishing. He has said that he would rather paint than write, and he has exhibited his abstract paintings.

Achievements

Percival Everett's novel *Zulus* won the New American Writing Award, and *Erasure*, his biting parody of race in the world of publishing, received the Hurston/Wright Legacy Award. Everett has also been the recipient of a PEN USA Literary Award and of a Literature Award from the American Academy of Arts and Letters. He has held fellowships from the Lila Wallace-Reader's Digest Foundation and from the University of New Mexico.

Biography

Percival Leonard Everett was born in 1956 in Fort Gordon, Georgia, and was raised in Columbia, South Carolina, where he graduated from A. C. Flora High School. His father was a sergeant in the U.S. Army when Everett was born on the military base just outside Augusta, but he went on to become a dentist. Everett received a B.A. in philosophy with a minor in biochemistry in 1977 from the University of Miami, Florida, and continued the study of philosophy at the University of Oregon from 1978 to 1980. He left the study of philosophy for creative writing, moving to Brown University, where he earned an M.A. in fiction in 1982.

For brief periods, Everett worked as a jazz musician, as a hand on a sheep ranch, and as a high school teacher. He served as an associate professor on the faculty of the University of Kentucky from January, 1985, to January, 1988, and then joined the faculty of the University of Notre Dame as a full professor. He left Notre Dame in 1991 for the University of California, Riverside, and finally moved to the University of Southern California in 1998, where he was named a distinguished professor of English in March, 2007. He has also taught at Bennington College and the University of Wyoming.

Analysis

Percival Everett has developed a reputation for frustrating expectations with each new work he brings to the public. The experimental chances he takes in his writing make his novels difficult to classify and therefore difficult to publish through mainstream presses. Although he has made the shift to major publishers, he has been consistently published by the small, nonprofit Graywolf Press and maintains a relationship with his editor there, Fiona Macrae.

Everett's first novel, *Suder*, met with success in part because it was readily identifiable as "African American" literature. The main character plays third base for the Seattle Mariners baseball team and embarks on a series of unlikely encounters during a dry spell in his career; Suder works in the tradition of the picaresque, and he is not unlike Charles Johnson's protagonist in *Middle Passage* (1990). Everett readily acknowledges his debt to Laurence Sterne, and in particular to that author's *The Life and Opinions of Tristram Shandy, Gent.* (1759-1767), an eighteenth century classic considered by many critics as the first postmodern novel.

Critiques of Everett's work often question his reconstruction of the dialogue around race. Novels such as *Cutting Lisa* and *Frenzy* contain no racial markers, and others, such as *Glyph*, *Wounded*, and *Erasure*, implicitly or explicitly challenge assumptions about race. The writing of *Erasure*, in fact, was partly motivated by Everett's wish to respond more fully to what he regards as the narrow categorization of his fiction.

Everett also thematizes violence in his novels, sometimes in the form of dark humor and sometimes in more troubling ways. In *Erasure*, the narrator's sister is the victim of random violence in the poor Washington, D.C., neighborhood she serves as a doctor. In *Frenzy*, the bloody rites of the worshipers of Bacchus are vividly detailed, and *For Her Dark Sin* incorporates the murders associated with the stories of Medea, including the murders of her children. This theme surfaces in *Watershed* and *Wounded* in the more traditional setting of the murder mystery, but even so Everett brings out the moral dilemma raised by the need for self-defense and revenge.

With each successive novel, Everett has changed paradigms; *Walk Me to the Distance* and *Cutting Lisa* in some ways fit the genre of the problem novel, featuring troubled characters struggling with their own violent natures. *Zulus* operates within the expectations of science fiction but bends those expectations. Everett revises the story of Medea in *For Her Dark Skin* and takes up the stories surrounding the god Dionysus in *Frenzy*. With *Watershed* and *Wounded*, Everett continues the revisionist reading of the American West that he began in *God's Country*.

Despite Everett's reputation as an iconoclast, each of the novels contains a recognizable narrative thread around human relationships; even *Frenzy*, which features a god as its central character, narrates through a character who is struggling to become human and to connect with the all-too-human worshipers and enemies of his master, Dionysus.

God's Country

In *God's Country*, a parody of the traditional Western, Everett pairs black scout Bubba with broadly drawn white rancher Curt Marder to set off on an eventful exploration of the myth of the West. Everett characterizes this novel as following in the tradition of Thomas Berger's *Little Big Man* (1964) and E. L. Doctorow's *Welcome to Hard Times* (1960) in terms of its manipulation of the conventions of the Western. The novel opens with the narrator, Marder, looking at the ruins of his ranch, which has been destroyed by "fake Indians." This evocation of John Wayne's role in the 1956 film *The Searchers* is quickly undercut by the encounters between Marder and his peers, which show his lack of heroic qualities and the contempt in which they hold him. The scout, Bubba, emerges as the hero, and the surprise ending of the novel suggests that he is larger than life: Marder shoots him repeatedly but is unable to kill him. Bubba may well represent the inescapable presence of racism in white society while at the same time embodying the resilience of African Americans within that racist world.

Glyph

With *Glyph*, Everett takes up the parody of the academy, joining that tradition as represented in *Lucky Jim* (1954) by Kingsley Amis and more recently revised in David Lodge's *Small World* (1984) and Ishmael Reed's *Japanese by Spring* (1993). The protagonist, baby Ralph, embodies the novel's critique of poststructuralist theory because Ralph is, himself, a sign, a glyph. He comes into the world fully formed in terms of written language and is able to read anything. This prodigy chooses writing as his only form of communication. Ralph, like the figures in many of Everett's novels, rushes through a series of

Percival Everett. (F. Everett)

unexpected and hilarious adventures. He is kidnapped and caged by a psychology researcher who wants to study him, then taken by federal agents, and is finally rescued by a childless couple who want him to become their own son. Here, as in all the novels, violence plays a role, however humorous it may seem. The reader may laugh while Ralph manages to elude exploitation by scientists and government officials, but the fact that he is imprisoned as a baby still evokes a darker response.

Douglas, Ralph's father, is a university professor angling for tenure who considers himself a sophisticated poststructuralist theorist, only to have his pretensions undercut by his infant son. His self-image is further eroded by a wickedly funny encounter with Roland Barthes, one of the major figures of poststructuralist thought. The marriage between Ralph's parents falls apart in tandem with the disintegration of Douglas's career. As Douglas becomes more uncertain of his intellectual ground, Ralph's mother begins to explore her gift for visual art. She makes herself independent of her husband and can then offer Ralph a home. Reunited with his mother in a chaotic final clash of all the forces that pursue him, Ralph makes the decision to step away from his identity in writing and become an ordinary human baby. This choice is mediated by Everett's interruption of Ralph's story with quotations, poetry, and imaginary dialogues between famous figures. These apparent digressions provide a running interpretive commentary on the main narrative. *Glyph* closes with the single observation "*The line is all*," returning to Everett's commitment to that narrative thread of human experience through time.

Erasure

In *Erasure*, his most widely known novel, Everett takes on the giants of the African American literary canon, Ralph Ellison and Richard Wright. The main character, Thelonius Ellison, nicknamed "Monk," embodies a revision of Ellison's *Invisible Man* (1952), in addition to paying homage to the jazz musician for whom he is named. Monk is a writer whose novels have been neglected because they fail to reflect the "African American experience" accepted in popular culture. On an impulse, Monk pens *My Pafology*, a thinly disguised parody of Wright's *Native Son* (1940), and this novel makes him a huge success. The full text of *My Pafology* appears within *Erasure*, and Monk's alter ego, Stagg R. Leigh (the pseudonym under which he publishes *My Pafology*), begins to take over his life, erasing the boundary between fiction and reality.

Everett parallels the story of his protagonist's trials in the publishing industry with the story of Monk's trials with his family. His sister, a doctor serving a poor community in Washington, D.C., is murdered, leaving Monk to care for his mother, who has Alzheimer's disease. Through the course of Monk's interactions with his sister before she dies, with his brother, whose homosexuality has alienated him from the family, and with the lifelong family servant, Lorraine, a complex and nuanced portrayal of one particular African American experience balances the stereotypes of *My Pafology*. To complicate the questions of race and class further, Monk discovers that his father has an illegitimate daughter, the result of an ongoing affair with a white woman. He seeks her out and finds her living a very impoverished life in comparison with his own. Ironically, Monk's creation, Stagg Leigh, seems to have the last word in the novel: Monk looks into a mirror and sees the face of his creation rather than his own familiar face. Throughout *Erasure* Everett picks up themes from Ellison's writing, and this figure, Stagg Leigh, reprises Rinehart from *Invisible Man*, the troubling alter ego of Ellison's nameless narrator.

The Water Cure

Another example of Everett's ongoing experimentation in the genre of the novel, *The Water Cure* recounts the harrowing story of the aftermath of the kidnapping and murder of a young girl told through the perspective of her father. Like his other novels, the story contains multiple layers, one of which can be read as an allegory of the American condition in the age of the war on terrorism.

The narrator, Ishmael Kidder, earns his living writing romance novels under the pseudonym Estelle Gilliam, but he has submerged his work and identity into finding and punishing his daughter's killer. The man has been freed on a technicality, allowing Kidder to find and kidnap him. He subjects the man to torture, interrupting the narration of revenge with philosophical discourses featuring Socrates, René Descartes, and Pope Gregory as he interrogates both the kidnapper and the nature of evil. The novel also contains passages of Joycean language experimentation in which the narrator transforms ordinary speech through a process of multilingual puns and interchanging of syllables. The blending of words reaches the edges of intelligibility, as does the blending of identities between criminal and victim. The pages of the novel also contain progressive line drawings that gradually build up to readable images, once more raising the theme of the written word versus the drawn image seen in *Glyph*. This question, of course, as the narrator of *The Water Cure* makes explicit, originates in Plato's discussion of the arts in the *Republic*.

Amee Carmines

Other major works

SHORT FICTION: *The Weather and Women Treat Me Fair*, 1987; *Big Picture*, 1996; *Damned If I Do*, 2004.

POETRY: *Re: f (gesture)*, 2006; *Abstraktion und Einfühlung*, 2008.

CHILDREN'S LITERATURE: *The One That Got Away*, 1992.

Bibliography

Everett, Percival. "The Satiric Inferno." Interview by Peter Monaghan. *Chronicle of Higher Education* 51, no. 23 (2005): A18-A20. Everett answers questions about his influences, his style, and his intended audience. Provides overview and analysis of Everett's major publications.

"Percival Everett: A Special Section." *Callaloo* 28, no. 2 (Spring, 2005): 291-342. Volume of the noted African American literary journal devotes a substantial section to Everett. Includes an interview, personal tributes, images of Everett's paintings, and substantial critical essays on *God's Country*, *Glyph*, *Erasure*, and *Watershed*. Fiona Macrae, Everett's editor at Graywolf Press, contributes a brief discussion of *Frenzy*, and a dialogue is presented between Everett and James Kincaid, a professor of English at the University of California and Everett's collaborator on *A History of the African American People*.

Ramsey, W. M. "Knowing Their Place: Three Writers and the Postmodern South." *Southern Literary Journal* 37, no. 2 (Spring, 2005): 119-139. First formulates the concept of the "postmodern South" and then places African American authors Yusef Komunyakaa, Percival Everett, and James McBride within that context. Offers substantive analyses of Everett's novels *Glyph* and *Erasure*.

Sanchez-Arce, Ana Maria. "'Authenticism': Or, The Authority of Authenticity." *Mosaic* 40, no. 3 (September, 2007): 139-155. Frames an analysis of *Erasure* with the concept of "authenticity" as defined by Lionel Trilling, Edward Said, Gayatri Chakravorti Spivak, and Jean-François Lyotard.

F

J. G. FARRELL

Born: Liverpool, England; January 23, 1935
Died: Bantry Bay, Ireland; August 12, 1979
Also known as: James Gordon Farrell

Principal long fiction

A Man from Elsewhere, 1963
The Lung, 1965
A Girl in the Head, 1967
Troubles, 1970
The Siege of Krishnapur, 1973
The Singapore Grip, 1978
The Hill Station: An Unfinished Novel, 1981

Other literary forms

J. G. Farrell is known primarily for his novels. His perceptive and entertaining account of his 1971 visit to India, posthumously titled "Indian Diary," is appended to *The Hill Station*, an unfinished novel that was published after Farrell's death.

Achievements

In the main, J. G. Farrell's early efforts—*A Man From Elsewhere*, *The Lung*, and *A Girl in the Head*—fail to display the power, intricacy, and inventiveness that characterize his fourth book, *Troubles*, and the rest of his completed fiction. Set in rural Ireland in the years 1919 to 1921—a period of bloody civil war—*Troubles* earned for Farrell the Geoffrey Faber Memorial Prize and signaled his interest in producing carefully documented and closely detailed historical fiction. Farrell's fifth novel, *The Siege of Krishnapur*, takes place in India in 1857, when protest of the British presence in that country suddenly grew violent and widespread. *The Siege of Krishnapur* was awarded Britain's prestigious Booker Prize and convinced many critics that Farrell, not yet forty, was fast on his way to a spectacular career. Set during the 1930's in what was then British Malaya, Farrell's sixth book, *The Singapore Grip*, was generally less enthusiastically received than *The Siege of Krishnapur*. Tragically, Farrell's life was cut short when, in 1979, he drowned in waters off Ireland's southern coast. Still, on the basis of his later work, Farrell must be considered a highly original talent and can be ranked among the finest historical novelists of his generation.

Biography

Though born in Liverpool, England, James Gordon Farrell had strong family ties to Ireland, which he visited regularly as a child and as an adolescent. After completing his public school training at Rossall, in Lancashire, Farrell worked briefly as a firefighter along a North Atlantic Treaty Organization (NATO) defense line in the Canadian Arctic. In 1956, during his first term at Oxford University, Farrell contracted polio, which left his chest and shoulder muscles permanently weakened. After taking his degree in 1960, Farrell taught in France and traveled to both Africa and the United States but spent the bulk of the following decade living in London, where he formed friendships with many fellow writers and developed the highly disciplined work habits that enabled him to produce a series of increasingly lengthy and complex novels.

In the early 1970's, in the wake of the considerable critical and financial success of *The Siege of Krishnapur*, Farrell traveled throughout Asia, where he conducted extensive research for *The Singapore Grip*. In April, 1979, he moved into an old farmhouse on the Sheep's Head Peninsula of Bantry Bay in Ireland's county Cork. There, while fishing close to his house, Farrell fell from a rock and—according to witnesses—was quickly swept out to sea.

Analysis

J. G. Farrell was essentially a realist whose most accomplished works draw on extensive historical research and are both carefully crafted and meticulously detailed. In each of his historical novels, Farrell focuses on various outposts of British colonialism that are under attack and, by implication, in decline. Often these works bluntly ridicule the cultural codes and biases that made the British Empire possible; indeed, they tend to ridicule narrow-mindedness of any kind and suggest, implicitly, that no religion or ideology can convincingly account for the existence of humankind. Much of Farrell's fiction focuses on the seeming randomness of human life, on the least attractive attributes—particularly the brutality and the greed—that are part of human nature. The tone of his works, moreover, is frequently sardonic and aloof, but it is by no means misanthropic. Instead, as Farrell's friend and fellow novelist Margaret Drabble has observed, "Farrell combined a sense of the pointless absurdity of man with a real and increasing compassion for characters caught up in decay and confusion."

Farrell's first book, *A Man from Elsewhere*, is set in France and focuses largely on a journalist named Sayer, who seeks to expose a former Communist alleged to have dealt too intimately with the Nazis during World War II. In his second novel, *The Lung*, Farrell's principal figure is Martin Sands, a young man confined to an iron lung and in love with Marigold, his stepdaughter and nurse. *A Girl in the Head*, Farrell's third novel, depicts the romantic difficulties of Boris Slattery, a Polish count living in the English resort town of Maidenhair. These novels are certainly not without merit: They contain some fine tragicomic moments, and they feature characters—such as Slattery—that, in some scenes, come convincingly alive. Farrell's early novels, however, are ponderously paced; they tend to reveal the self-consciousness of a beginning writer who is trying hard to be original and clever but failing to conceal his debt to other authors. In *A Girl in the Head*, for example, it is not difficult to detect the presence of Iris Murdoch, whose celebrated first novel, *Under the Net* (1954), similarly and more successfully combines a disaffected young hero and a supporting cast of eccentrics with serious philosophical themes and, throughout, a charmingly whimsical tone.

Troubles

The far better *Troubles* is set in the Irish coastal town of Kilnalough and covers the years between 1919 and 1921—a period in which militant Irish nationalists were beginning to employ violence more frequently as a means of freeing their country from British control. The book's central figure, Major Brendan Archer, is a veteran of World War I who comes to Kilnalough's huge Majestic Hotel, where his fiancé, Angela Spenser, resides with her father, Edward, a jingoistic, increasingly unbalanced man who owns the hotel and must work hard to keep it running. The Majestic is—like the British Empire itself—an aging, sprawling structure in a slow but certain state of decay. The Majestic is dusty, gloomy, and filled with odd, elderly guests; in its lobby, one hears the constant ticking of an ancient pendulum clock.

Unlike the protagonists in Farrell's earlier novels, the Major is neither intellectually nor artistically inclined. He is, in fact, a rather bland figure who enjoys reading serialized adventure stories and who has without reflection absorbed most of the prejudices of his nation and his class. Though not a religious man, he regards with particular prejudice and suspicion the tenets and practices of Roman Catholicism. He also takes for granted the notion that Irish Catholics are still simply too irrational and unruly to be trusted with the task of governing themselves. The Irish Republican movement, he unthinkingly assumes, "was merely an excuse for trouble-makers moved more by self-interest than patriotism." Still, Archer is so well rounded that he cannot be dismissed as a mere bigot and an utterly unsympathetic character. The Major, Farrell makes clear, has been keenly disappointed both in life and in love; as a veteran of trench warfare, he has been on close terms with hunger, fear, and death. Early in *Troubles*, the Major—fresh from war—is shown attending a tea party and causing some discomfort among his fellow guests because of the intensity with which he studies their heads, arms, and legs: "He was thinking: 'How firm and solid they look, but how easily they come away from the body!' And the tea in his cup tasted like bile."

Troubles does contain many comical characterizations and scenes, including a failed sexual interlude that features a pair of fumbling young men and a set of naïvely flirtatious twins and that balances, with a stunning deftness, the pathetic and the ribald. Most of *Troubles*, however, focuses bluntly on the brevity of life, on the sobering reality of change and decay. The Majestic, for example, literally crumbles bit by bit throughout the novel: It becomes overrun with weeds and rats and—at the novel's close—burns to the ground after being shelled by Irish rebels. Images of skulls and skeletons abound; the silent, mysterious Angela quietly suffers from leukemia and suddenly dies. Meanwhile, not far from the hotel—and, Farrell keeps noting, throughout much of the rest of the world—men continue to slaughter men with brutal gusto. Indeed, by alluding frequently to newspaper accounts of the world's never-ending wars and riots, Farrell not only lends an element of authenticity to his work but also underlines the point that, unfortunately, bloody "troubles" fester wherever human beings gather; because humans are territorial and animalistic, they will invariably fail in their attempts to construct a serene and civilized world.

The Siege of Krishnapur

The theme of human brutality is even stronger in *The Siege of Krishnapur*. This work shows the effect of the Sepoy Rebellion of 1857 on some of the English who were then helping rule India in the name of the British-owned East India Company. The novel's principal character, Mr. Hopkins—"the Collector," or chief administrator, at the British outpost at Krishnapur—is a sober, optimistic man who early in the work proclaims his belief that the perfection of humankind will surely be achieved through "Faith, Science, Respectability, Geology, Mechanical Invention, Ventilation, and the Rotation of Crops." Another principal character is George Fleury, a young, melancholic, rather overly sensitive Englishman who is fond of Romantic poetry and no longer certain of the tenets of orthodox Christianity. Fleury—a recognizable Victorian "type," like all the principal characters in *The Siege of Krishnapur*—must then suffer the fulsome proselytism of the Reverend Mr. Hampton, a boorish Anglican clergyman identified throughout the novel as "the Padre."

The early chapters of *The Siege of Krishnapur* portray well-settled British characters in a world of poetry readings and cricket matches, of elegant meals served by obsequious native servants who, in some cases, must bear with a smile the insulting nicknames their masters have bestowed on them. As the remainder of the novel reveals, however, that cozy, very Victorian world is utterly shattered when mutinous Indian soldiers—or "sepoys"—begin an attack on the British compound at Krishnapur that drags on for months and that results not only in countless Indian and English casualties but also in—for the English—severe shortages of ammunition and food. Eventually, the survivors find themselves filthy, disease-ridden, rag-clad, and so famished that they willingly devour their horses and prey upon bugs. In the end, they are saved by British reinforcements, but by then, as one of their rescuers observes, they look less like gentlemen and gentlewomen than do the pathetic untouchables whom they once automatically scorned.

The Siege of Krishnapur is full of extremely well-paced, graphically described battle scenes. Like *Troubles*, and like Alfred, Lord Tennyson's *In Memoriam* (1850)—perhaps the greatest and most representative poetical work of the Victorian era—*The Siege of Krishnapur* also frequently addresses the most basic of philosophical questions: Does God exist? What is the true nature of humankind? Is there a divine plan that can account for the ruthlessness of nature and the universality of human pain? In several amusingly constructed scenes, Farrell portrays the Padre arguing at length in favor of the existence of a Supreme Intelligence and offering as proof dozens of such ingeniously practical phenomena as the eel's eyes, the boar's tusks, and the bee's proboscis. Like *Troubles*, however, *The Siege of Krishnapur* focuses principally on a world of nature that is, in Tennyson's famous phrase, "red in tooth and claw"; it conveys strongly the impression that the god or gods who designed the world now seem quite uninterested in its day-to-day operation. It suggests that the margin between civilization and barbarism is frighteningly narrow and that, moreover, the codes and biases by which men and women order their lives are not only arbitrary but also often bizarre. Indeed, at the conclusion of *The Siege of Krishnapur*, the Collector, older and more cynical and back in England, asserts bluntly that "culture is a sham. It's a cosmetic painted on life by rich people to conceal its ugliness."

The Singapore Grip

The Singapore Grip, Farrell's final completed novel, is a particularly lengthy work that, some critics have suggested, occasionally bogs down under the weight of too many characters and documentary details. Set entirely in Singapore, it focuses principally on the years just prior to December, 1941, when all of British Malaya was rapidly overrun by the Japanese. Its principal characters are related to a large British rubber company run by Walter Blackett, who takes for granted the invincibility of British power in the Pacific and so—like other Britons portrayed in the book—fails to comprehend the seriousness of the Japanese threat. Blackett, who is described as having hairy "bristles" that run up and down his back, is probably too much the stereotypical big-business tycoon: He is aggressive, envious, calculating. Far more appealing is Brendan Archer, who is retired from the military but who, as in *Troubles*, retains the title "the Major." Some of the most poignant scenes in *The Singapore Grip* show Archer "fixed in his habits, apparently suspended in his celibacy like a chicken in aspic," and living out his remaining days in modest quarters in Singapore, surrounded by old, bleary-eyed dogs he no longer likes, but—out of a continuing sense of obligation—continues to board.

The Singapore Grip makes clear that Farrell likes the Major not only for his pluck and respect for duty but also for the many quirks he has accumulated over the years. Indeed, as in *Troubles* and *The Siege of Krishnapur*, Farrell in *The Singapore Grip* reveals a continuing fondness for harmless eccentrics—and underdogs—of all sorts. By focusing extensively on Blackett and his operations, however, Farrell also makes obvious his continuing disdain for cultural chauvinism and the blundering pursuit of profit at any cost. By filling *The Singapore Grip* with vivid, unsettling scenes of war, Farrell also once again indicates his belief that the study of human history is essentially the study of brutality and folly, that only by self-deception can one insist on the universality of human goodness and the inevitability of a saner, more harmonious world.

Brian Murray

BIBLIOGRAPHY

Bergonzi, Bernard. "Fictions of History." In *The Contemporary English Novel*, edited by Malcolm Bradbury and David Palmer. London: Edward Arnold, 1979. Informative piece of criticism discusses Farrell in the context of English historical fiction and emphasizes his concern with the lives of individuals.

Binns, Ronald. *J. G. Farrell*. London: Methuen, 1986. First full-length study of Farrell traces the development of the idiosyncratic Anglo-Irish novelist's career.

_______. "The Novelist as Historian." *Critical Quarterly* 21 (Summer, 1979): 70-72. Offers clearly written, insightful discussion of *The Singapore Grip*, the last of Farrell's novels about the decline of the British Empire, as well as his other two novels on the subject.

Blamires, Harry, ed. *A Guide to Twentieth Century Literature in English*. New York: Methuen, 1983. Entry on Farrell describes his early novels as dabbling in "the bizarre and the grotesque." Praises *The Siege of Krishnapur* and *The Singapore Grip*, however, for their "meticulously researched" emphasis on the rhythms of everyday life in a time of political upheaval.

Crane, Ralph J., ed. *J. G. Farrell: The Critical Grip*. Dublin: Four Courts Press, 1999. Collection of essays discusses various aspects of Farrell's work. Works analyzed include *The Singapore Grip* and *The Siege of Krishnapur*. Supplemented with a bibliography of primary and secondary sources.

Crane, Ralph J., and Jennifer Livett. *Troubled Pleasures: The Fiction of J. G. Farrell*. Dublin: Four Courts Press, 1997. Presents a critical reassessment of Farrell's fiction and asserts that Farrell was a major twentieth century novelist whose works were early examples of "postmodern historiographic metafiction." Analyzes his works from numerous perspectives, including those of Marxism and postcolonialism.

Greacen, Lavinia. *J. G. Farrell: The Making of the Writer*. London: Bloomsbury, 1999. First biography of the novelist is greatly enhanced by Greacen's access to Farrell's family and his private papers. Provides a comprehensive account of Farrell's life.

Morey, Peter. *Fictions of India: Narrative and Power*. Edinburgh: Edinburgh University Press, 2000. Analyzes works of fiction about India, including Farrell's novel *The Siege of Krishnapur*, to examine their narrative techniques and their treatments of colonialism and other issues of political power.

Prusse, Michael C. *"Tomorrow Is Another Day": The Fictions of James Gordon Farrell.* Tübingen, Germany: A. Francke, 1997. Analyzes each of Farrell's novels, focusing on the opposition of idealism and cynicism in the works. A biographical chapter traces the origins of Farrell's attitudes on this opposition and his use of the siege as a persistent metaphor. Also examines the influence of Albert Camus on Farrell's work.

Wilson, A. N. "An Unfinished Life." *Spectator*, April 15, 1981, 20-21. Admiring piece acknowledges Farrell as an "outstanding novelist of his generation" but points out flaws in Farrell's three British Empire novels.

JAMES T. FARRELL

Born: Chicago, Illinois; February 27, 1904
Died: New York, New York; August 22, 1979
Also known as: James Thomas Farrell

Principal long fiction

Young Lonigan: A Boyhood in Chicago Streets, 1932
Gas-House McGinty, 1933
The Young Manhood of Studs Lonigan, 1934
Judgment Day, 1935
Studs Lonigan: A Trilogy, 1935 (collective title for *Young Lonigan, The Young Manhood of Studs Lonigan*, and *Judgment Day*)
A World I Never Made, 1936
No Star Is Lost, 1938
Tommy Gallagher's Crusade, 1939
Father and Son, 1940
Ellen Rogers, 1941
My Days of Anger, 1943
Bernard Clare, 1946
The Road Between, 1949
This Man and This Woman, 1951
Yet Other Waters, 1952
The Face of Time, 1953
Boarding House Blues, 1961
The Silence of History, 1963
What Time Collects, 1964
Lonely for the Future, 1966
When Time Was Born, 1966
New Year's Eve/1929, 1967
A Brand New Life, 1968
Judith, 1969
Invisible Swords, 1971
The Dunne Family, 1976
The Death of Nora Ryan, 1978
Dreaming Baseball, 2007

Other literary forms

James T. Farrell began his career, as so many other novelists have done, by writing short stories, and his more than two hundred tales are an integral part of the vast world he portrays. Most of his stories have been gathered in collections such as *Calico Shoes, and Other Stories* (1934) and *$1,000 a Week, and Other Stories* (1942), but several stories and manuscript works remain unpublished. His poetry, collected by Farrell himself in a 1965 edition, seems to be the product of early and late speculations—the early poetry probably coming from the period of the Studs Lonigan trilogy and the later poetry seemingly produced during the early 1960's, when he was beginning his "second career" with *A Universe of Time*, an unfinished multicycle series of novels, stories, and poems. All the poetry is uneven in quality and, despite some remarkable effects, is not memorable. Farrell also published volumes of literary criticism, cultural criticism, and essays on a wide range of subjects. *The Mowbray Family* (pb. 1946), a play written with Hortense Alden Farrell, is a dramatic treatment of the same material that he treats brilliantly in his fiction. The drama, however, lacks the vitality of his novels and seems lifeless alongside a work such as *My Days of Anger*. Farrell's letters remain to be collected.

ACHIEVEMENTS

James T. Farrell's career encompassed many diverse literary movements and trends. He was active to the end of a long life, publishing his last novel in the year before his death. On the evidence of his three major complete works, the Studs Lonigan trilogy, the Danny O'Neill series (or the O'Neill-O'Flaherty series, as Farrell preferred to call it), and the Bernard Carr trilogy, Farrell presented urban America and the people who sprang from it with a brutal candor rarely equaled in American literature.

Farrell's youth, spent in Irish Catholic, lower- and middle-class Chicago, gave him the milieu from which a whole society could be examined and explained. His career began with his conscious decision to quit a steady job and become a writer and survived despite reactions to his work that included indifference, shock, bad reviews, prejudice, and ignorance. Farrell's social activism led him into and out of Marxist circles, sustained him through attacks by the Marxist critics who accused him of abandoning the cause, and gave him the focus necessary to show Americans an entire society that survived and prospered in spite of its environment.

Farrell never achieved great popularity; his style was deemed too flat and brusque, his language profane, and his methods inartistic. His fiction was considered basically plotless or merely photographic, and he was condemned, especially by the Marxists, for failing to be didactic. In the years since his death, however, the scope of his urban vision has been recognized; Farrell's fictional world has the breadth of conception associated with greatness and has been compared favorably to that of William Faulkner. Much like Theodore Dreiser, whom he admired, Farrell went his own way when it was extremely unpopular to do so, and his impact on modern fiction remains to be assessed.

BIOGRAPHY

James Thomas Farrell was born on February 27, 1904, in Chicago, where he lived until 1931, except for a short sojourn in New York City during the 1920's. The son of a family of Irish teamsters and domestics, he was the product of a curious dual lifestyle in his youth. One of fifteen children, Farrell was taken, when he was three years old, to live with his maternal grandparents as the result of his own family's impoverished condition. His grandparents, John and Julia Daly, were of the same poor, hardworking stock as his father and mother, but they were somewhat more financially stable and lived a different, more affluent life. The difference in these two families was important in Farrell's development.

Living with the Dalys, Farrell found himself in a neighborhood of modern brick buildings that were a sharp contrast to the poor, wooden-shack neighborhood where his parents lived with the rest of their children. The personal confusion and divisions of loyalties caused by this unusual arrangement were only a part of Farrell's childhood problems. Living in one household and coming from another made Farrell the center of many family tensions and involved him in most of the family's disagreements.

Farrell entered Corpus Christi Parochial Grammar School in 1911, and through the course of his education was a loner and a dreamer. He became an excellent athlete, taking seven letters in sports at St. Cyril High

James T. Farrell. (Library of Congress)

School. He attended St. Cyril after giving up early plans to attend a seminary to become a priest. He excelled in his studies and was active on the St. Cyril *Oriflamme*, the school's monthly magazine, in addition to being an active member of the high school fraternity, Alpha Eta Beta. He was desperately in need of acceptance, but his classmates sensed that he was different, and his social incapacity was another influence on his later life.

After high school, Farrell went to work full time for the Amalgamated Express Company, where he had worked summers while in school. After nearly two years with the express company, Farrell felt trapped by the routine and, in 1924, enrolled in night classes at De Paul University as a prelaw student. He first encountered political and economic theory there and first read Theodore Dreiser. The financial and mental strain eventually became too much for Farrell, and he left De Paul and the express company in 1925. He then took a job as a gas station attendant for the Sinclair Oil and Refining Company and saved part of his wages for tuition at the University of Chicago.

In eight quarters at the university, completed between 1925 and 1929, Farrell became a voracious reader, enjoyed an intellectual awakening that has been compared to Herman Melville's similar awakening in the 1840's, and discovered that he wanted to become a writer. In 1927, he dropped out of school and hitchhiked to New York City, determined to succeed as a writer. He returned to Chicago in 1928, reentered the university, and began to write, placing critical articles and book reviews in campus publications and in Chicago and New York newspapers. By 1929, he had sold his first story, "Slob," to a little magazine, and his career was launched.

Farrell and Dorothy Patricia Butler were secretly married in 1931. (Farrell was to divorce Dorothy later, marry the actor Hortense Alden, whom he also divorced, and remarry Dorothy in 1955.) Farrell and Dorothy sailed for France immediately after their wedding. In France, Farrell discovered that he had little in common with the American expatriates in Paris and that he had important admirers and supporters such as Samuel Putnam, James Henle, and Ezra Pound. The publication of *Young Lonigan* and *Gas-House McGinty* by the Vanguard Press during this period established Farrell as a writer and confirmed his faith in his vision. He began to publish a great number of short stories, and by the time the Farrells returned to New York in 1932, his conceptions for the entire Studs Lonigan trilogy and the first Danny O'Neill novel, *A World I Never Made*, were outlined. He was prepared to become an integral part of American literary history. His contribution to American letters included stormy confrontations with Marxist critics and novelists and a staunch defense of the integrity of art and the artist as opposed to the socialist demands that fiction, and all art, serve the party.

The 1930's were the end of the personal experiences that Farrell used as the material for his major fiction; the Studs Lonigan trilogy, the Danny O'Neill series, and the Bernard Carr trilogy are all drawn from the same well. In describing that world, Farrell was determined to "shake the sack of reality" until it was empty. In 1957, he completed his original life plan for twenty-five volumes that were to be "panels of one work" and had begun a second lifework, called *A Universe of Time*, of which he published seven volumes (*The Silence of History*, *What Time Collects*, *When Time Was Born*, *Lonely for the Future*, *A Brand New Life*, *Judith*, and *Invisible Swords*). Farrell died in New York on August 22, 1979, before this lifework was complete.

Analysis

An understanding of James T. Farrell and his work on the basis of one novel, or even as many as three individual novels, is impossible. Farrell's vision was panoramic, however limited his subject matter may have been, and cannot be understood except in terms of large, homogeneous blocks of fiction. He did not write exclusively of Chicago or of Irish Catholics, but it was on this home "turf" that he most effectively showed the effects of indifference and disintegration on an independent, stubborn, often ignorant, urban subculture. He was at once appalled by and attracted to the spectacle of an entire people being strangled by the city and by their own incapacity to understand their position, and he was most successful when he embodied the society in the life and times of an archetypal individual.

Farrell's three major, complete works total eleven novels; each of the eleven creates another panel in the same essential experience. While the Studs Lonigan trilogy, the five novels of the O'Neill-O'Flaherty series, and the Bernard Carr trilogy have different protagonists, they all share a common impulse and reflect Farrell's almost fanatical obsession with time, society, and the individual's response to both. Studs Lonigan, Danny O'Neill, and Bernard Carr are extensions or facets of Farrell's primal character, pitted against a hostile urban environment.

Studs Lonigan: A Trilogy

The Studs Lonigan trilogy, arguably Farrell's best and certainly his best-known work, is the story of the development and deterioration not only of the title character but also of the Depression-era Irish Catholic Chicago society from which he springs. In the fifteen-year span of *Young Lonigan*, *The Young Manhood of Studs Lonigan*, and *Judgment Day*, Farrell shows the total physical, moral, and spiritual degeneration of Studs Lonigan.

Studs is doomed from the moment he appears just prior to his graduation from grammar school. His announcement that he is "kissin' the old dump goodbye tonight" is ominously portentous. He drops out of high school, goes to work for his father, a painting contractor, and becomes a member and leading light of the gang that hangs out in Charlie Bathcellar's poolroom. The association with the gang is Studs's life—everything else is "plain crap." Through a swirl of "alky," "gang-shags," "craps," and "can-houses," Studs fights to prove himself to be the "real stuff" and ultimately finds himself a frail, thirty-year-old shell of the vigorous youth he once was. The physical ruin of Studs Lonigan, however, is only the result of larger deficiencies.

Studs is a sensitive, moral being who consciously rejects his innate morality as a weakness. He blindly accepts his Catholic upbringing without believing it. There is never a present for Studs Lonigan—there is only a future and a past. In *Young Lonigan*, the future is the vision of Studs standing triumphantly astride the fireplug at 58th and Prairie, proclaiming his ascendancy to the brotherhood of the gang. The past is his rejection of juvenile harassment he suffered as the result of his one moment of ecstasy with Lucy Scanlan in Washington Park. He proclaims himself the "real stuff" and flees from human emotions and the potentialities of those experiences with Lucy.

Studs consistently refuses to allow his emotional sensitivity to mature. The spiritual stagnation that results confines him to dreams of future aggrandizement or of past glories. The future dies, and Studs is left with memories of his degeneracy. His affair with Catherine Banahan awakens new sensibilities in Studs, but he is unable to nurture them, and they die stillborn. His heart attack at the beach, his dehumanizing odyssey through the business offices of Chicago looking for work, his shockingly prurient behavior at the burlesque show, and his final delirium are simply the payment of accounts receivable.

As Studs dies, his world is dying with him. His father's bank has collapsed, the mortgage on his building is due, his fiancé is pregnant, and the gang has generally dispersed. These are not the causes of Studs's failures, however; they are reflections of that failure. Studs is the product and the producer. He is not a blind victim of his environment. He makes conscious choices—all bad. He is bankrupt of all the impulses that could save him. He batters and abuses his body, strangles his emotions, and clings to the stultifying spirituality of a provincial Catholicism. As Lucy Scanlan dances through his final delirium and his family abuses his pregnant fiancé, Studs Lonigan's dying body becomes the prevailing metaphor for the empty world that Studs created and abused, and in which he suffered.

O'Neill-O'Flaherty series

Danny O'Neill, protagonist of the O'Neill-O'Flaherty series, is the product of the same environment as Studs Lonigan, but O'Neill recognizes that he controls his destiny in spite of overbearing environmental pressures and, by the end of the series, seems on the verge of success. If he succeeds, he does so because he refuses to fall into the trap that Studs builds for himself, and he thus escapes into the larger world that Studs never knows. In the five novels of the series, *A World I Never Made*, *No Star Is Lost*, *Father and Son*, *My Days of Anger*, and *The Face of Time*, Danny not only escapes the strictures of environment but also sloughs off the psychological and spiritual bondage of family and religion and creates his own freedom.

Farrell's most clearly autobiographical work, the O'Neill-O'Flaherty series portrays Danny's growth from 1909 to 1927—from a five-year-old child to a man breaking from college and Chicago. Unlike the Studs Lonigan trilogy, the O'Neill series portrays a larger world and more diverse elements of that world. While the Lonigan trilogy is dependent on the portrayal of its central character for action and meaning, Danny's story introduces more people and more settings and thus illustrates one of the major differences between Studs and Danny. Whereas Studs demands his personal image as a loner but actually depends heavily on his gang as a prop, Danny begins as an atypical child—the result of his life in a bifurcated family much like Farrell's own—and learns the hypocrisy of the accepted values around him, which prompts him to formulate and depend on his own personal values.

The process by which Danny reaches this understanding is the contorted progress of a hybrid adolescence. Born to Jim and Lizz O'Neill, a poor, working-class Irish couple, he is taken to live with his grandparents, of the lace-curtain Irish variety, because his parents cannot support their already large family. He is accepted wholeheartedly by his grandmother, and he accepts her as a surrogate mother, but he has problems rationalizing his relatively opulent life while his natural siblings are dying of typhoid and neglect. He also refuses, violently, to return to his natural parents, to the poverty in which they live, and to the oppressive Roman Catholicism that his mother practices.

The tensions forged between the two families are the stuff of which Danny is made, but he is also affected by the lonely, drunken promiscuity of his Aunt Peg, the decorous commercialism of his Uncle Al, and the maternal tyranny of his grandmother, Mary O'Flaherty. Danny grows up alone in a world that he has difficulty understanding and that seems to engulf but reject him summarily. He is not a clear member of either of the families that are the heart of the story, he is rejected by Studs Lonigan's gang because of his youth and because he is considered a neighborhood "goof," and he cannot find the love he desperately seeks. Only late in the series does he understand Jim, his father, and come to accept him for what he is—a hardworking, decent, poor Irish laborer who loves his children desperately enough to thrust them into a better world than he can make for them.

By the time Danny understands his father, Jim is dying, Danny has discovered the importance of books, he has had a hint of love through a college affair, and he has realized that education may be his key to a broader world. In the course of his intellectual discoveries at the University of Chicago, he has rejected religion and become something of a socialist. He has also discovered that New York City is the hub of the world, and, after quitting his job and dropping out of college in order to pursue his dream, seems on the verge of simultaneously discovering himself and success by migrating to New York.

The O'Neill series, then, comes full circle—from Chicago back to Chicago both actually and metaphorically; the distinction is unimportant. For all his effort to escape what he views as mindless and oppressive, Danny finally seems to understand that his basic character is still that of the poor, hardworking Irishman that, with all its flaws, is at least pitiable rather than repugnant. As Danny prepares to escape from Chicago, he has developed a fuller appreciation and self-preserving understanding of his heritage and an ability to progress beyond his previous angry rejections. He does not give up his new certainties, particularly in relation to the Church and religion (he has become an avowed atheist), but he displays a tolerance and acceptance of himself and his culture that are the foreground of promised success.

BERNARD CARR TRILOGY

Bernard Carr seems to take up the story where Danny leaves it. The trilogy—comprising *Bernard Clare* (Farrell changed the name to Carr in the second novel after a man named Bernard Clare brought libel proceedings against him), *The Road Between*, and *Yet Other Waters*—is Farrell's attempt to represent the lives of a generation of artists in New York during the Great Depression and in the circles of politically radical activism.

The trilogy, for the first time in Farrell's fiction, is largely set in New York. Bernard's life in New York, however, is highlighted with periodic flashbacks of Chicago; thus Farrell's integrity of vision is preserved, and Bernard's lower-class origins are discovered. Bernard is the last member of Farrell's Irish Catholic trinity—he is the embodiment of the whole man whom Studs could not become and Danny might well have become had his story been continued.

Bernard's New York is a world of struggling artists and Communists. In the early New York years, Bernard becomes involved with Communists and then rejects them as being little more than a gang—brutes who demand mindless adherence to the party propaganda, no matter what that adherence does to artistic integrity and vitality. He also recognizes that the dogma of Communism is akin to that of Roman Catholicism—that both are crutches for weak men.

Bernard's marriage introduces him to family life and the wonder of birth and rearing a child, and it is the spur in his attempt to recover and understand his family and his heritage. During all of these events, Bernard is achieving a limited success from his writing, and by the end of the trilogy he has brought all the pieces together and has found himself, his vocation, and an enlightened ability to see life for what it is and make the most of it.

The Bernard Carr trilogy does not carry the impact of the Lonigan saga, but the diffusion necessary to present Bernard's story precludes the grim concentration necessary to portray Studs and his life. The world expands for Danny and Bernard, and that expansion naturally admits the people, ideas, ideals, and philosophies that are the components of an expanded sensibility.

The dovetailing of the experiences and environments of his three major characters is what ultimately makes Farrell's work live. Their stories make up a tapestry that mirrors the world from which they sprang and rivals it for true pathos and vitality.

Clarence O. Johnson

Other major works

SHORT FICTION: *Calico Shoes, and Other Stories*, 1934; *Guillotine Party, and Other Stories*, 1935; *Can All This Grandeur Perish?, and Other Stories*, 1937; *Fellow Countrymen: Collected Stories*, 1937; *The Short Stories of James T. Farrell*, 1937; *$1,000 a Week, and Other Stories*, 1942; *Fifteen Selected Stories*, 1943; *To Whom It May Concern, and Other Stories*, 1944; *Twelve Great Stories*, 1945; *More Fellow Countrymen*, 1946; *More Stories*, 1946; *When Boyhood Dreams Come True*, 1946; *The Life Adventurous, and Other Stories*, 1947; *A Hell of a Good Time*, 1948; *An American Dream Girl*, 1950; *French Girls Are Vicious, and Other Stories*, 1955; *An Omnibus of Short Stories*, 1956; *A Dangerous Woman, and Other Stories*, 1957; *Saturday Night, and Other Stories*, 1958; *Side Street, and Other Stories*, 1961; *Sound of a City*, 1962; *Childhood Is Not Forever*, 1969; *Judith, and Other Stories*, 1973; *Olive and Mary Anne*, 1977.

PLAYS: *The Mowbray Family*, pb. 1946 (with Hortense Alden Farrell).

POETRY: *The Collected Poems of James T. Farrell*, 1965.

NONFICTION: *A Note on Literary Criticism*, 1936; *The League of Frightened Philistines, and Other Papers*, 1945; *The Fate of Writing in America*, 1946; *Literature and Morality*, 1947; *The Name Is Fogarty: Private Papers on Public Matters*, 1950; *Reflections at Fifty, and Other Essays*, 1954; *My Baseball Diary*, 1957; *It Has Come To Pass*, 1958; *On Irish Themes*, 1982.

Bibliography

Branch, Edgar M. *James T. Farrell*. New York: Twayne, 1971. After tracing Farrell's "plebeian origin," Branch discusses the author's major works, including the Studs Lonigan trilogy, the O'Neill-O'Flaherty series, and the Bernard Carr trilogy. Includes chronology, notes, selected bibliography, and index.

_______. *Studs Lonigan's Neighborhood and the Making of James T. Farrell*. Newton, Mass.: Arts End Books, 1996. Presents a look at the Chicago neighborhood of Farrell's youth and the inspiration for the Studs Lonigan series. Includes illustrations, maps, bibliographical references, and index.

Fanning, Charles. "Death and Revery in James T. Farrell's O'Neill-O'Flaherty Novels." In *The Incarnate Imagination: Essays in Theology, the Arts, and Social Sciences in Honor of Andrew Greeley*, edited by Ingrid H. Shafer. Bowling Green, Ohio: Bowling Green State University Popular Press, 1988. Analyzes Farrell's novels and other fiction to identify common themes, such as the artist as an isolated being, the role of memory and dreaming in achieving the necessary isolation, and the relationship of the isolation to the experience of death.

_______. "James T. Farrell and Irish-American Fiction." In *The Irish Voice in America: 250 Years of Irish-American Fiction*. 2d ed. Lexington: University Press of Kentucky, 2000. Examines Farrell's place among Irish American novelists; includes discussion of the Studs Lonigan trilogy and other works.

Farrell, Kathleen. *Literary Integrity and Political Action: The Public Argument of James T. Farrell*. Boulder, Colo.: Westview Press, 2000. James T. Farrell's former daughter-in-law charts his life in the 1930's, when he, like many of his contemporaries, was involved in left-wing political causes and sought to create a socialist literature.

Fried, Lewis F. *Makers of the City*. Amherst: University of Massachusetts Press, 1990. Argues that Farrell portrays the city as a liberalizing and democratizing force. Fried does an excellent job of weaving together discussion of Farrell's life, career, and fiction. He also provides a helpful bibliographical essay on other studies of Farrell.

Landers, Robert K. *An Honest Writer: The Life and Times of James T. Farrell*. San Francisco, Calif.: Encounter Books, 2004. A fresh look at the creator of Studs Lonigan, this biography argues for renewed appreciation for the American naturalist, who has fallen out of popular and critical favor.

Pizer, Donald. "James T. Farrell and the 1930's." In *Literature at the Barricades: The American Writer in the 1930's*, edited by Ralph F. Bogardus and Fred Hobson. Tuscaloosa: University of Alabama Press, 1982. Argues convincingly that Farrell's literary roots are in the 1920's, that he owes as much to the Chicago school of philosophical pragmatism as to naturalism, and that James Joyce and Sherwood Anderson also influenced Farrell's fiction. To demonstrate his theses, Pizer analyzes the Studs Lonigan trilogy.

Smith, Gene. "The Lonigan Curse." *American Heritage* 46 (April, 1995): 150-151. Claims that while the character of Studs Lonigan became Farrell's most popular creation, it was also his biggest personal albatross; notes that after killing Studs off, Farrell had trouble getting his work published and came to look back at his earlier work with loathing.

Wald, Alan M. *James T. Farrell: The Revolutionary Socialist Years*. New York: New York University Press, 1978. Chapter titled "The Literary Record" demonstrates the intent of Leon Trotsky's influence on Farrell's fiction. Wald identifies the real persons represented by Farrell's fictional characters and focuses on Farrell's treatment of the plight of the socialist writer. Contains an excellent bibliography with many political entries.

WILLIAM FAULKNER

Born: New Albany, Mississippi; September 25, 1897
Died: Byhalia, Mississippi; July 6, 1962
Also known as: William Cuthbert Falkner

Principal long fiction

Soldiers' Pay, 1926
Mosquitoes, 1927
Sartoris, 1929
The Sound and the Fury, 1929
As I Lay Dying, 1930
Sanctuary, 1931
Light in August, 1932
Pylon, 1935
Absalom, Absalom!, 1936
The Unvanquished, 1938
The Wild Palms, 1939
The Hamlet, 1940
Go Down, Moses, 1942
Intruder in the Dust, 1948
Requiem for a Nun, 1951
A Fable, 1954
The Town, 1957
The Mansion, 1959
The Reivers: A Reminiscence, 1962
The Wishing Tree, 1964 (fairy tale)
Flags in the Dust, 1973 (original version of *Sartoris*)
Mayday, 1976 (fable)

Other literary forms

William Faulkner (FAWK-nur) published two volumes of poetry and several volumes of short stories. Most of his best stories appear in *Knight's Gambit* (1949), *Collected Short Stories of William Faulkner*

(1950), and the posthumously published *Uncollected Stories of William Faulkner* (1979). His early journalistic and prose pieces have been collected and published, as have his interviews and a number of his letters. Also published are several interesting minor works, including a fairy tale, *The Wishing Tree*, and a romantic fable, *Mayday*. New Faulkner material is steadily seeing print, much of it in the annual Faulkner issue of *Mississippi Quarterly*. Scholars are continually making public more information on Faulkner's screenwriting in Hollywood, where he collaborated on such major successes as *To Have and Have Not* (1945) and *The Big Sleep* (1946). Several of his works have been adapted for television and film; notably successful were the 1949 film adaptation of *Intruder in the Dust* and the 1969 adaptation of *The Reivers*.

Achievements

When William Faulkner received the Nobel Prize in Literature in 1949, he completed an emergence from comparative obscurity that had begun three years before. In 1946, when nearly all of Faulkner's books were out of print, Malcolm Cowley published *The Portable Faulkner*. Cowley's introduction and arrangement made clear "the scope and force and interdependence" of Faulkner's oeuvre up to 1945.

Even in 1945, Faulkner was reasonably well known to the readers of popular magazines, his stories having appeared with F. Scott Fitzgerald's and Ernest Hemingway's in publications such as the *Saturday Evening Post*, *Scribner's Magazine*, *Harper's Magazine*, and *The American Mercury*. Despite his success in selling short stories and as a Hollywood screenwriter, Faulkner's novels, except for the notorious *Sanctuary*, had little commercial success until after Cowley's volume and the Nobel Prize. The notoriety of *Sanctuary*, which was widely reviewed as salacious, brought Faulkner to the attention of the film industry; it was his screenwriting that sustained him financially during the years of comparative neglect when he produced the series of powerful novels that constitute one of the major achievements of world fiction. The motion-picture adaptation of his first novel to appear after Cowley's volume, *Intruder in the Dust*, was filmed in Faulkner's hometown, Oxford, Mississippi, and released in 1949.

After the Nobel Prize, honors came steadily. Faulkner was made a member of the French Legion of Honor, received two National Book Awards, for *A Fable* and *Collected Short Stories of William Faulkner*, and received two Pulitzer Prizes, for *A Fable* and *The Reivers*. He traveled around the world for the U.S. Department of State in 1954. During 1957, he was writer-in-residence at the University of Virginia. Recognition and financial security, while gratifying, neither diminished nor increased his output. He continued writing until his death.

Faulkner has achieved the status of a world author. His works have been painstakingly translated into many languages. Perhaps more critical books and articles have been written about him in the late twentieth and early twenty-first centuries than about any other writer with the exception of William Shakespeare. Critics and scholars from all over the world have contributed to the commentary. Faulkner's achievement has been compared favorably with the achievements of Henry James, Honoré de Balzac, and Charles Dickens; many critics regard him as the preeminent novelist of the twentieth century.

Biography

William Faulkner was born William Cuthbert Falkner in New Albany, Mississippi, on September 25, 1897. His ancestors had emigrated from Scotland in the eighteenth century. Faulkner's great-grandfather, William Clark Falkner, was a colonel in the Civil War, wrote the popular romance *The White Rose of Memphis* (1881), and provided a model for the patriarch of the Sartoris clan in *The Unvanquished*. Faulkner's family was very important to him. The eldest son of Maud and Murry Falkner, William Cuthbert later became the head of the family. He took this responsibility seriously, struggling most of his life to care for those whom, whether by blood or moral commitment, he considered members of his family. In 1924, he changed the spelling of his family name to Faulkner.

Faulkner discovered his storytelling gifts as a child, but his writing career did not really begin until after his brief training for the Royal Air Force in Canada, shortly before the World War I Armistice in 1918. He attended the University of Mississippi for one year, worked at odd jobs, and published a volume of poetry, *The Marble Faun* (1924). He took writing more seriously, with encouragement from Sherwood Anderson, while living in New Orleans in 1925. The influence of Anderson, especially his "The Book of the Grotesque" from *Winesburg, Ohio* (1919), seems to pervade Faulkner's work. During his apprenticeship he spent several months traveling in Europe. Out of his experiences in New Orleans and Europe came a number of journalistic sketches, most dealing with New Orleans, and a group of short stories set in Europe.

The early novels are interesting, but Faulkner began to show his powers as a prose stylist and as a creator of psychologically deep and interesting characters in *Sartoris*, which he had originally written as *Flags in the Dust*. Beginning with *The Sound and the Fury* through *Go Down, Moses*, Faulkner wrote the major novels and stories of his Yoknapatawpha series. Of the ten novels he published in these thirteen years, five are generally considered to be masterpieces: *The Sound and the Fury*, *As I Lay Dying*, *Light in August*, *Absalom, Absalom!*, and *Go Down, Moses*. At least two others, *Sanctuary* and *The Hamlet*, are widely studied and admired. The entire series of novels set in the mythical Yoknapatawpha County, Faulkner's "little postage stamp of native soil," is sometimes considered as a great work in its own right, especially when all of the Snopes Trilogy (*The Hamlet*, *The Town*, *The Mansion*) is included with the above-named masterpieces. Stories from his two collections of the 1929-1942 period regularly appear in anthologies; "Old Man" and "The Bear," which are parts of *The Wild Palms* and *Go Down, Moses*, are perhaps his best-known novellas.

Faulkner's personal life was difficult and has provoked much critical interest in tracing relationships between his life and his work. The family-arranged and unhappy marriage to Estelle Oldham in 1929 ended in divorce. Both Faulkner and his wife were subject to alcoholism. He carried on a virtually continuous struggle against debt, resentful and unhappy over the necessity of working in Hollywood in order to keep his family solvent. Though Faulkner was a fiercely loyal husband and father, he was also capable of philandering.

Faulkner preferred to work at home in Mississippi. Still, he traveled a great deal, first for education, later to deal with publishers and to work in Hollywood, and finally as a goodwill ambassador for the United States. He met and formed acquaintances with several important contemporaries, notably Nathanael West, Anderson, and Howard Hawkes.

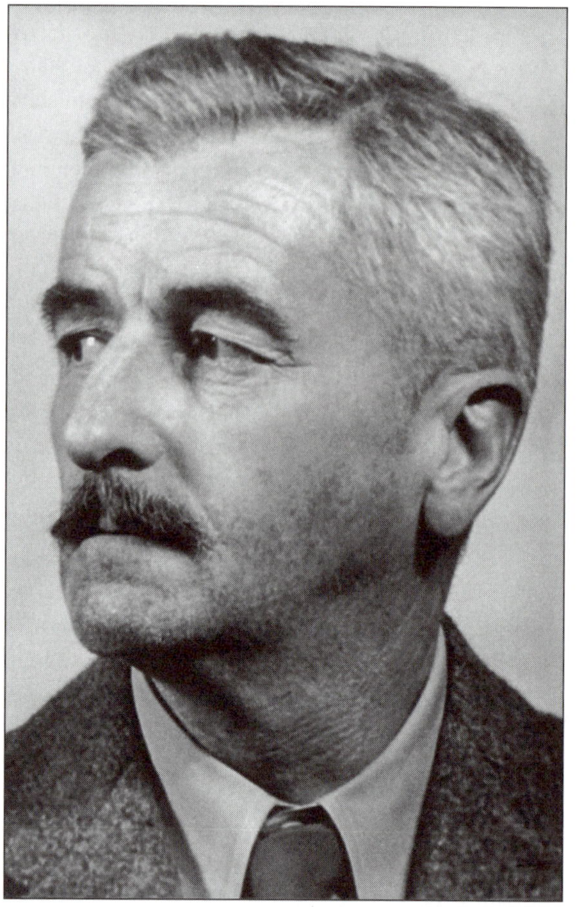

William Faulkner. (© The Nobel Foundation)

Faulkner died of a heart attack on July 6, 1962, after entering the hospital to deal with one of his periodic drinking bouts.

Analysis

When William Faulkner accepted the Nobel Prize in December, 1950, he made a speech that has become a justly famous statement of his perception of the modern world and of his particular place in it. In the address, Faulkner speaks of the modern tragedy of the spirit, the threat of instant physical annihilation, which seems to overshadow "the problems of the human heart in conflict with itself." He argues that all fiction should be universal and spiritually significant, "a pillar" to help humankind "endure and prevail." Literature can be such a pillar if it deals with "the old verities and truths of the heart, the universal truths lacking which any story is ephemeral and doomed—love and honor and pity and pride and compassion and sacrifice."

All of Faulkner's greatest works were written before the first explosion of the atomic bomb, yet in all of them there is an awareness of the threat of annihilation of which the bomb may be only a symptom: a kind of spiritual annihilation. Lewis P. Simpson argues that Faulkner, like the greatest of his contemporaries, dramatizes in most of his novels some version of the central problem of modern man in the West, how to respond to the recognition that man has no certain knowledge of a stable transcendent power that assures the meaning of human history. Panthea Broughton makes this view of Faulkner more concrete: In Faulkner's world, characters struggle to find or make meaning, exposing themselves in various ways to the danger of spiritual self-destruction, of losing their own souls in the effort to find a way of living in a universe that does not provide meaning.

The immense quantity of critical commentary on Faulkner provides several satisfying ways of viewing and ordering the central concerns of his novels. While the way into Faulkner suggested by Simpson and Broughton is only one of many, it seems particularly helpful to the reader who wishes to begin thinking about Faulkner's whole literary career. Broughton demonstrates that the Faulknerian universe is characterized essentially by motion. Human beings need meaning; they need to impose patterns on the motion of life. Out of this need spring human capacities for mature moral freedom as well as for tragic destructiveness. Closely related to this pattern that Broughton sees in Faulkner's stories are his tireless experimentation with form and his characteristic style.

In his essay in *William Faulkner: Three Decades of Criticism* (1960), Conrad Aiken notes the similarities between Faulkner's characteristic style and that of Henry James. The comparison is apt in some ways, for both in their greatest novels seem especially concerned with capturing in the sentence the complexity of experience and of reflection on experience. As Walter Slatoff, in the same volume, and others have shown, Faulkner seems especially drawn to paradox and oxymorons, kinds of verbal juxtaposition particularly suited to conveying the tension between the motion of life and the human need for pattern. Once one notices these aspects of Faulkner's style in a complex novel such as *Absalom, Absalom!*, in which Faulkner's characteristic style finds its ideal subject, much that initially seems obscure becomes clearer.

Faulkner seems to have found most instructive the "loose" forms characteristic of the Victorian panoramic novel as it was developed, for example, by his favorite author, Charles Dickens. Faulkner's novels generally contain juxtapositions of attitudes, narrative lines, voices, modes of representation, and emotional tones. His more radical and probably less successful experiments in this vein include the alternation of chapters from two quite separate stories in *The Wild Palms* and the alternation of fictionalized historical narrative with dramatic acts in *Requiem for a Nun*, a kind of sequel to *Sanctuary*. *Light in August* is his most successful work in this direction. Somewhat less radical and more successful experiments involved the incorporation of previously published stories into "collections" and sustained narratives in such a way as to produce the unity of a novel. Parts of *The Unvanquished*, the Snopes Trilogy, and *A Fable* have led dual lives as stories and as parts of novels. *Go Down, Moses* is probably the most successful experiment in this direction. Faulkner was particularly interested in the juxtaposition of voices. His career as a novelist blossomed when he juxtaposed the voices and, therefore, the points of view of several characters in *The Sound and the Fury* and *As I Lay Dying*. In *Absalom, Absalom!*, the juxtaposition of voices also becomes the placing together of narrative lines, comparable episodes, points of view, modes of narration, attitudes, and emotional tones. This one novel brings together everything of which Faulkner was capable, demonstrating a technical virtuosity that in some ways is the fruit of the entire tradition of the novel. *Absalom, Absalom!* also realizes to some extent a special potential of Faulkner's interest in juxtaposition, the conception of his Yoknapatawpha novels as a saga that displays a unity of its own.

The technique of juxtaposition, like Faulkner's characteristic style, reflects his concern with the problems of living meaningfully within the apparently meaningless flow of time. Because life will not stand still or even move consistently according to patterns of meaning, it becomes necessary to use multiple points of view to avoid the complete falsification of his subject. Juxtaposition, the multileveled and open-ended sentence, and the oxymoronic style heighten the reader's awareness of the fluidity of the "reality" that the text attempts to portray. Faulkner's most tragic characters are those who feel driven to impose so rigid a pattern on their lives and on the lives of others as to invite destruction from the overwhelming forces of motion and change. These characters experience the heart in conflict with itself as the simultaneous need for living motion and meaningful pattern.

The Sound and the Fury

The Sound and the Fury is divided into four parts to which an appendix was later added. Faulkner repeated in interviews that the novel began as a short story that grew into the first section. He then found that the point of view he had chosen did not tell the whole story even though it closely approximated the flow of events before a nonjudgmental consciousness. Gradually, Faulkner found himself retelling the story four and, finally, five times. The effect of reading these juxtapositions may be described as similar to that of putting together a puzzle, the whole of which cannot be seen until the last piece is in place. Like several of Faulkner's novels, notably *Absalom, Absalom!*, *The Sound and the Fury* is not fully comprehendible upon a single reading. The first reading provides a general idea of the whole, and subsequent readings allow one to fill in the details and to see ever more deeply into this moving narrative.

The novel concerns the tragic dissolution of the Compson family. The decline dates decisively from the marriage of Candace (Caddy), the only daughter of Jason Compson III and Caroline Bascomb. Caddy's marriage is not the sole cause of the family's decline; rather, it becomes symbolic of a complex of internal and external forces that come to bear on this Mississippi family early in the twentieth century. Caddy becomes pregnant by Dalton Ames, a romantic, heroic, and apparently devoted outsider. Her mother then seeks out Sydney Herbert Head as a respectable husband for her. After the marriage, Herbert finds he has been gulled and divorces Caddy. These events deprive all the Compson men of their center of meaning. Quentin, the oldest son who loves Caddy not as a sister but as a woman, commits suicide. Jason III drinks himself to death, having lost the children on whom his meaning depended. Jason IV seeks petty and impotent revenge on Caddy's daughter, also named Quentin, because he believes the failure of Caddy's marriage has deprived him of a chance to get ahead. Benjy, the severely retarded youngest brother, suffers the absence of the only real mother he ever had. Control of the family passes to Jason IV, and the family ceases finally to be a place where love is sustained, becoming instead, despite the efforts of the heroic and loving black servant, Dilsey, a battleground of petty scheming, hatred, and revenge.

This general picture emerges from the internal monologues of Benjy, Quentin (male), and Jason IV, from a third-person narrative centering on Dilsey and Jason IV, and from the final appendix. Each of the four main sections is set on a particular day: Benjy's section on his thirty-third birthday, Easter Saturday, 1928; Jason's on Good Friday; and Dilsey's (the fourth section) on Easter Sunday of the same year. Quentin's section is on the day of his suicide, June 2, 1910. As the portrait of the family's decline emerges from these juxtaposed sections, their tragic significance becomes apparent.

Benjamin Compson's internal monologue consists of images, most of which are memories. At the center of his memory and of his stunted life is Caddy, whose "hair was like fire" and who "smelled like trees." Every experience Benjy has that evokes these images or resembles any experience he has had with Caddy automatically triggers his memory. As a result, Benjy lives in a blending together of past and present in which memory and present experience are virtually indistinguishable. The spring of his suffering is that for him the experience of losing Caddy is continuous; the memory of her presence is perfect and the experience of her absence is constant.

This section proceeds by a series of juxtapositions that place Benjy's present, deprived condition starkly beside the richness of his memory. Though the pattern is difficult to see at first, repeated readings show that Faulkner works in this section primarily by pairing certain events: the funeral of Damuddy (Caroline's mother and Benjy's grandmother) and Caddy's wedding with all the attendant suggestions of meaning; Caddy with her boyfriends on the porch swing and Quentin (female) with her boyfriends; Benjy at the gate waiting for Caddy to come home from school one Christmas and Benjy waiting at the gate on the day Jason IV leaves it open. This last event, part of Jason's spitefulness against Caddy, leads to Benjy's castration after he grabs a school girl to ask about Caddy, though he cannot speak. Among the many pairings, the most pathetic appears at the end of the section. Benjy remembers his family long ago:

> Her hair was like fire, and little points of fire were in her eyes, and I went and Father lifted me into the chair too, and Caddy held me. She smelled like trees.
>
> *She smelled like trees. In the corner it was dark, but I could see the window. I squatted there, holding the slipper. I couldn't see it, but my hands saw it.*

The contrast between the firelight of the library, with its mirror and the loving people and the now barren and dark library with only one of Caddy's wedding slippers reveals much of the mood, the meaning, and the effectiveness of technique in Benjy's section.

Quentin's section also proceeds largely by the juxtaposition of memory and present experience. Quentin's memories are triggered by present events and he is sometimes unable to distinguish between memory and external reality. He commits suicide at the end of his first year at Harvard. As he carries out his plans to drown himself, he is caught up in various events that repeat aspects of his loss of Caddy, the last being a picnic with some college classmates during which he remembers his abortive attempt to be the brother who avenges a wronged sister. This memory is simultaneous with and is repeated in a fight with Gerald Bland, the kind of womanizer Quentin wishes Dalton Ames was.

Perhaps the major irony of Quentin's suicide is that the state of being that he desires is in many ways like the state in which his youngest brother suffers. Quentin wishes to be free of time, to end all motion. He gives as a motive his fear that grief over the loss of Caddy will attenuate, for when grief is gone, his sister will have become meaningless and his life utterly empty—yet his grief, of which every event reminds him, is unbearable. He wishes to keep Caddy as she was and to deny the repetitions that force him to remember her loss. Though he sees such a transcendent state in many images in his world, he can only *imagine* himself in that state, for it is impossible in life. Suicide seems his only alternative. In death, he can at least shirk everything, he can at least escape the *again*, which to him is a sadder word than *was*.

Quentin's relationship with Caddy is highly problematic. One fairly simple way of understanding how his sister becomes so important to him that he must commit suicide when she marries is to observe Quentin's and Caddy's relationship with their parents: Jason III does not love Caroline. She believes that he has come to resent the fact that her family is socially inferior. In reality, she is a selfish and stupid woman who is completely inadequate as a mother and wife. Her husband is unable to deal with her. His growing unhappiness and cynicism magnify her weakness. The result is that these children have no real parents, and the responsibility falls on the gifted Caddy. Despite her extraordinary capacity, Caddy is a girl. When she grows into a woman, she must inevitably betray the brothers who depend on her love. Even when she is with them, she cannot love them as an adult would; she cannot teach them to give. Her gifts lead her to another who is also capable of passion, Dalton Ames. This affair exaggerates the meaning of the betrayal by heightening the inadequacy of the family, including Quentin, to meet Caddy's needs. Caddy's sense of her parents' failure is captured in her memory of a picture in a book that made her think of her parents as keeping her from the light. Quentin needs Caddy not only as a mother, a source of pure affection, but also as a center of meaning. She embodies all the forms and traditions to which Quentin clings to escape the despair his father teaches him. Losing her, he loses his life.

Jason's section of the novel is much easier to read, for his interior life is more or less in the present. He neither desires nor even conceives of any transcendent reality; he desires power above all things, even money, though he is well aware that money is, in his world, the superior means to power. He delights in the power to be cruel, to make others fear him, yet he is remarkably impotent. His impotence stems from his inability to imagine in others any motives different from his own. In these respects, his character, as well as the mode in which it is presented, recalls the jealous monk in Robert Browning's "Soliloquy of the Spanish Cloister." Jason's interior monologue is the only one of the three that has all the marks of being spoken. It is as if Jason were two people, one constantly explaining and justifying himself to the other.

Jason tells primarily about his troubles bringing up Caddy's daughter, Quentin. The girl has been left in the care of the family while the divorced Caddy makes her way in the world. Quentin becomes the central instrument of Jason's revenge against Caddy for the failure of her marriage and the disappointment of his hope. Jason is so fixed on his need to exercise cruel power that he is unable to restrain himself sufficiently to keep the situation stable. He drives Quentin out of the family, losing the monthly checks from Caddy that he has been appropriating, the hoard he has collected in part from this theft, and the one person on whom he can effectively take his revenge.

"I've seed de first en de last," says Dilsey. She refers to the beginning and the end of the doom of the Compson family, to Caddy's wedding and Quentin's elopement. Each of these events suggests more meanings than can be detailed here, but the importance of Dilsey's section is that she sees a pattern of human meaning in the events that threaten an end to meaning for so many. Her part in these events has been a heroic struggle to bind the family together with her love and care, a doomed but not a meaningless struggle, for she can still see pattern, order, meaning in all of it. The events of Easter morning, in which Dilsey figures, suggest that at least one source of that power to mean and to love is her community at the African American church service, a community that, in the contemplation of the Christian symbols of transcendence, attains an experience of communion that partakes of the eternal even though it is temporary. Dilsey's church is a model of the family, and her experience there is not unlike Benjy's experience in Caddy's arms on Father's lap before the library fire. The Compson family has somehow lost this experience. As the appendix suggests, all of the Compsons, except perhaps for Benjy, are damned, for they have all, in various ways, come to see themselves as "dolls stuffed with sawdust."

The Sound and the Fury is in part an exploration of the loss of the Christian worldview. Temple and Popeye in *Sanctuary* respond in ways similar to Jason's. Addie in *As I Lay Dying* and Horace Benbow in *Sanctuary* play parts similar to Quentin's. Benbow attempts to prove the truth of the traditional view he has inherited from his family and class, the view that "God is a gentleman" and that Providence takes an active hand in human affairs. He is disastrously and blindly wrong and apparently suffers the loss of his faith. Addie Bundren's attempt to impose order on her world seems even more disastrous because Faulkner centers attention on the suffering she causes her family.

As I Lay Dying

In *As I Lay Dying*, Addie Bundren wants and fails to find a kind of transcendent communion with some other being. When she realizes the inevitable impermanence of such communion, she plans revenge against the people who have failed her, especially her husband, Anse. She makes him promise that he will bury her with her relations in Jefferson. This simple promise is a subtle revenge because it binds Anse with words for which he has too much respect and it becomes a terrible vengeance when Anse comes to fulfill that promise. Addie believes that a word is "a shape to fill a lack." By this she means that the communion she feels when she is pregnant with her firstborn is an essential experience for which words are unnecessary and inadequate. Not only are words inadequate to this experience, but they are also symbols of separation from this experience. At one point Addie reflects, "I would think how words go straight up in a thin line, quick and harmless, and how terribly doing goes along the earth." By making Anse "promise his word," Addie forces her husband to attempt a union of saying and doing, an attempt which sends Addie's entire family on a grotesque and tortured journey along the earth.

Addie imposes a verbal pattern on her family in revenge because pregnancy and passion are temporary. Each pregnancy ends in separation. Her one love affair is with the Reverend Whitfield, whom she describes as "the dark land talking the voiceless speech." When this affair ends in the birth of Jewel, her third son, her despair is complete. The promise she extracts from Anse elicits a catastrophic juggernaut, for she dies at the beginning of a storm that floods the area, making the wagon journey to Jefferson next to impossible.

The novel is presented in a series of monologues similar in depth and intensity to Quentin's in *The Sound and the Fury*. As the narrative emerges from these monologues so do the internal relationships of the family. The reader becomes intensely aware of the feelings and the needs of each family member. Anse is driven not only by his promise but also by the desire to regain the dignity he believes he loses by having no teeth. A sedentary man, he has needed this prod to set him in motion. He eventually returns, not only with teeth and dignity, but with several other new possessions as well, including a new wife. Cash, the oldest son, is the family's repository of technical skill. Almost without questioning, he solves the material problems of the journey. In crossing the flooded river, he breaks his leg, yet he finishes the journey in incredible pain. Darl, the son Addie has rejected, is the most sensitive of her children. He is seemingly capable of a kind of communion that might have fulfilled her, for he seems able to read minds and to know of events he does not see. He opposes the journey at every significant point, understanding that it is Addie's revenge and that it threatens to tear apart the family. Anse finally commits Darl to a mental hospital in order to escape financial responsibility for a barn that Darl ignites in an attempt to burn Addie and end the journey.

Jewel, product of the Whitfield affair, though he is barely articulate, comes to seem the living embodiment of Addie's wordless will to revenge. He saves the coffin from the flood when the wagon overturns in the river and from the fire in the barn. He sacrifices his much prized pony in trade to replace the mules lost in the river crossing. Dewey Dell, the only daughter, is desperate to reach Jefferson where she believes she can get an abortion. She shares Darl's sensitivity and hates it because it makes her feel naked and vulnerable. She violently assists in the capture of Darl for she is glad to be rid of the kind of communion Addie so deeply desired. Vardaman, the youngest son, suffers loss. Drawn along on the journey by promises of bananas and a view of a toy train, he registers all the family's pain: the loss of a mother, the dislocations of the journey, the humiliation as Addie begins to smell, the shiftless poverty of Anse, the sufferings of the brothers, the vulnerability of Dewey Dell and, finally, the loss of Darl. Because the unity of the family is his identity, he suffers a kind of dismemberment.

This brief glimpse hardly conveys the richness and power of this novel. Still it should make clear that part of the novel's meaning derives from Addie's attempt to impose a rigid pattern on a significant part of her family's life and the extreme suffering her success brings about.

Sanctuary

Popeye and Temple in *Sanctuary* are lost children, victims of their moment in history, in that they are without souls. Their culture has failed to give them reasons for doing one thing rather than another. They do not have the natural acquisitiveness of Jason IV and the Snopeses, nor do they have a motive such as revenge to give direction to their lives. Popeye wears the mask of a gangster, though the mask slips occasionally. It is the role itself that gives Popeye substance and makes him appear somewhat like a normal human being. He also has a vague desire that he expresses in his abduction of Temple Drake. He desires to join the human community, to live a meaningful life. Just as he imitates gangsters in order to take possession of some identity, he also imitates the acts of men who reveal themselves to be under the power of a strong motive. He tries to desire and to possess Temple Drake because other men desire her. He fails even to desire her and apparently, as a result of this failure, he gives up his life. He has money, says the narrator, but there is nothing to buy with it.

Temple is perhaps the most fully developed example in early Faulkner of a character who simply flows, who seeks no meanings at all, but merely acts out her impulses. When she is abducted by Popeye, she is freed of the social restraints that have never been made important to her. Nothing in her experience has taught her to internalize social restraints as communal values. She is virtually without values, virtually unable to make moral choices; freed of external restraint, she seeks pointless and ultimately unsatisfying gratification of whatever impulses come to the fore. She becomes capable of killing in order to achieve sexual satisfaction. In her final act in the novel, she pointlessly condemns an innocent man to death as she begins to adopt Popeye's failed strategy, assuming a role to pass the time.

In Temple one sees that the utter surrender to motion is no solution to the search for meaning in Faulkner's world. Neither surrender nor rigid resistance to the flow of events will suffice. Faulkner's heroes, like Dilsey, are generally those who are able to find a balance between what Broughton calls the abstract and the actual, a balance that seems to answer the cry of the heart and to make loving possible. Faulkner's novels suggest that the modern tragedy of a lack of soul, of spiritual annihilation, results from some decisive break in the process by which one generation teaches the next how to love.

Light in August

The central juxtaposition in *Light in August* is between Lena Grove and Joe Christmas. Lena Grove, scandalously pregnant and deserted by Lucas Burch, alias Joe Brown, walks the dirt roads of Alabama, Mississippi, and finally Tennessee in tranquil search of a husband. She is a center of peace and faith and fertility, though all around her may be waste and catastrophe. She is like the peaceful center of Herman Melville's Grand Armada on the outer circles of which the stricken whales murder one another. Byron Bunch, who loves her at first sight even though she is nine months pregnant, tells his friend, the Reverend Gail Hightower, that Lena seems to have two persons inside her, one who *knows* that Lucas Burch is a scoundrel who will never marry her, and another who *believes* that God will see to it that her family will be together when the child is born. God somehow keeps these two persons within Lena from meeting and comparing notes.

When the child is born, there is a family indeed, for Lena seems to attract all the help she needs. Byron is camped outside her door. Gail is there to deliver the child. Joe Christmas's grandparents are present, reliving a past moment which promises them some small redemption. Even Lucas Burch makes a brief appearance before leaving the field open to Byron. Lena's tranquil faith, her trust in the world and its people, and her submission to her natural being make her into a kind of Faulknerian heroine. She is capable of finding meaning for herself in the flow of life, and this meaning attracts and vitalizes others. The images used to describe her are filled with the paradoxes of stillness in motion. This attitude gives her power, not a power that she often consciously uses, but still a real power to draw recluses such as Byron and Gail out of spiritual death and into the flow of living.

While Lena moves peacefully through the book, seeking a husband and bearing a child, Joe Christmas careens through the last days of his life, the culmination of more than thirty years of bigoted education. Joe's life story is the center of a novel that is composed largely of condensed biographies. Of the major characters, only Byron and Lena have relatively obscure pasts. Gail, Joanna Burden, and Joe are presented as the end products of three generations in their respective families. Even Percy Grimm, a relatively minor character, receives a fairly full biography. Each of these lives contrasts starkly with the life of Lena and, eventually, with Lena and Byron's relationship. Gail, Joanna, Joe, and Percy are, in the words of Gail, "lost children among the cold and terrible stars." They are the children of a generation that saw its world crumble and that adopted fanatic versions of Calvinism mixed with an inherited racism in order to resist the flow of history with its threat of meaninglessness. They are products of the failure of love. While Lena, miraculously immunized against lovelessness, is capable of accepting the world and its lawful motion as her home, most of the other major characters resist and reject the world, living in alienation.

Joe's life reveals the sources and meanings of resistance and alienation. The story of his life comes in several blocks. After learning that Joe has murdered Joanna, the reader is plunged deeply into the suffering consciousness of the murderer during the twenty-four hours preceding the crime. Joe is seen as a driven man: He seems to be under the control of the voices that speak inside him, and he is unaware of the loving, caressing voices in his natural environment. This glimpse into his consciousness reveals ambivalent attitudes toward his racial background, a hatred of the feminine, a sense that Joanna has somehow betrayed him by praying over him, and a sense of being an abandoned child who wants to be able to say with conviction, "God loves me, too." The middle section of the novel separates into strands the inner voices that drive Joe to murder, which, in his culture, is tantamount to suicide.

In an orphanage at age five, Joe accidentally provokes the dietician into speeding his placement with a family. His adoptive father, the Calvinist fanatic Simon McEachern, teaches Joe the skills of resistance to nature. He learns to cultivate a rocklike will and an indomitable body. He learns to relate to people impersonally. He grows up not only without love but also in resistance to love: To be a man is not to love. McEachern derives his hatred of the world from his Calvinist theology, while Joe learns to resist the world in defense of his selfhood. Joe is not a Calvinist; he resists the content of McEachern's teachings by mastering its forms. Inside

Joe, the voice perhaps first awakened by a girl who mothered him in the orphanage continues to speak. Joe continues to desire to love, to belong, and ultimately to be free of the voices that drive him.

Of the forms Joe's rebellion against his culture takes, those involving sex and race seem most significant. Joe's desire to love and be loved is revealed and betrayed in his adolescent affair with Bobbie Allen, a local prostitute, a relationship that paradoxically combines intimacy with impersonality. In his adult life, his rebellion often takes the form of asserting his presumed black blood. In doing so, he provokes a ritual reaction that becomes the dominant pattern in his life, the pattern that is worked out in full when he kills Joanna and suffers the consequences.

His affair with Joanna, his life and death in Jefferson, Mississippi, replay the patterns of his life in their full significance, bringing him again to the moment of rebellious protest in which he faces an authority figure in the fullness of his identity and strikes out in murderous self-defense. Joe and Joanna are virtually doubles. They proceed through tortured and perverse phases of sexual relations until they reach a kind of purged state of near normality, a point at which both seem seriously able to contemplate marriage, children, a normal human life. When Joanna enters menopause, however, she is simply unable to accept the natural flow of time. Her "sins" with Joe lose their meaning if they do not lead to marriage, motherhood, and "normal" feminine fulfillment. She reverts to her inherited Calvinism and racism, changing from Joe's double to McEachern's double. Betrayed herself, she betrays Joe, trying to form into a piece of her sick world. Joe responds to this change as he responded to McEachern's attempt to cast him into Hell.

During Joe's flight from the pursuing Jefferson authorities, he comes closer than ever before to the peace, freedom, and love he has desired. In his disorientation and physical suffering, for the first time in his life, he feels unity with the natural world. He partakes of "the peace and unhaste and quiet" that are characteristic of Lena's experience because for the first time he is really free of the compulsive voices of his culture, free to feel at home in his world.

Contrasted to this experience is the story of Joe's first five years as told to Gail by Joe's fanatical grandfather, Doc Hines, and by his grandmother. Doc Hines sees himself as the agent of a Calvinist deity avenging the lust after worldly pleasure symbolized by femininity and the inferior race ("God's abomination upon the earth"). Against these disembodied "voices of the land," Joe emerges as somewhat ambiguously victorious in his death. Joe's death is inevitable. Even though he seems to have found freedom from the internal compulsions that have driven him to self-destruction, he cannot escape the consequences of his actions in the world. He can only accept. The way in which Joe accepts the consequences of his acts suggests for him a kind of heroic status.

Joe's death is inevitable because he has set in motion a deeply embedded social ritual, a fateful machine that cannot stop until it has completed its movement. The community's heritage of Calvinism and racism has produced that ritual machine. In a desperate need to assert control over the flow of history, the culture has embraced the Calvinist denial of all things in this world that might turn one's attention from God.

Among other elements that contribute to the view of Joe as a hero is his effect on Gail. Gail has been on the edges of all the events of these days in Jefferson. He has had several opportunities to mitigate suffering, but he has, on the whole, failed to act. He is afraid to leave his sanctuary in order to help those he could really help. Joe appears at Gail's door, moments before dying, like an avenging god to strike Gail down in a kind of judgment, even as Gail confesses part of his sin. Finally, Joe dies in Gail's house, another sacrifice to the very kinds of rituals and legalisms that Gail has used to buy what he calls peace, the right to sit unmolested in his house dreaming of his grandfather's absurdly heroic death. Gail learns from this experience. He goes on to make, to himself at least, a full confession of his sins. He faces the fact that what he has wanted, a sterile stasis in a dead past moment, was selfish, that this desire has led him to bring about his wife's death, to welcome being ostracized by the town, ultimately to serve his small need at the cost of abandoning those he promised to serve when he became a minister.

The juxtaposition of lives tragically ruined by a heritage of racism and fanatical Calvinism with Lena's life creates an unforgettable and moving work. One of the easily overlooked effects of the whole is the impression it gives of a community whose heart is basically good, which responds, albeit sometimes grudgingly, with sympathy to those in need and with kindness to those in trouble. Lena brings out this side of the community. On the lunatic fringe of the community are those who express the deep compulsions that thrive in the insecurity of modern life. Joe is brought up to evoke this underside of the community that it would like to forget. They are not to forget. The images of horror pass from one generation to the next. The uncertainties of life, especially in a world that seems to have lost the easy comfort of religious consensus, continue to produce personalities such as those of Doc Hines and Percy Grimm, who cannot deal with or bear an indifferent universe. Their rigid imposition of abstraction on the flow of life forces them ever backward to the legalism of their secret rituals. Society is tragically in the grip of the past despite its great desire to be finally free of these compulsions.

Absalom, Absalom!

Absalom, Absalom! juxtaposes differing accounts of the same events. In *The Sound and the Fury*, Faulkner thought of himself as trying to tell the whole story and finding that he had to multiply points of view in order to do so. In *Absalom, Absalom!*, as Gary Stonum argues, "the labor of representation is . . . made a part of the text." The story is only partly known; it is a collection of facts, not all of which are certain, which seem to those who know them profoundly and stubbornly meaningful. The various characters who try their formulae for bringing those facts together into a meaningful whole are the historians of the novel. Faulkner has written a novel about writing novels, about giving meaning to the flow of events. *Absalom, Absalom!* dramatizes so effectively the processes and obstacles to creating a satisfying structure for events and offers such an ideal wedding of structure, content, technique, and style, that many critics regard it as Faulkner's greatest achievement. With *The Sound and the Fury* this novel shares characters from the Compson family and a degree of difficulty that may require multiple readings.

The central concern of the narrative is the life of Thomas Sutpen and his family. Sutpen has appeared out of nowhere to build a vast plantation near Jefferson, Mississippi, in the early nineteenth century. Apparently without much wealth, he nevertheless puts together the greatest establishment in the area, marries Ellen Coldfield, a highly respectable though not a wealthy woman, and fathers two children by her. When Sutpen's son, Henry, goes to college, he meets and befriends Charles Bon. Charles and Sutpen's daughter, Judith, fall in love and plan to marry. For no apparent reason, Sutpen forbids the marriage and Henry leaves his home with Charles. During the Civil War, Ellen dies. Near the end of the war, Henry and Charles appear one day at the plantation, Sutpen's Hundred, and Henry kills Charles. After the war, Sutpen becomes engaged to Rosa Coldfield, Ellen's much younger sister, but that engagement is suddenly broken off. A few years later, Sutpen fathers a daughter with Milly Jones, the teenage daughter of his handyman, Wash Jones. When Sutpen refuses to marry Milly, Jones kills him. Then Sutpen's daughter, Judith, and his slave daughter, Clytie, live together and, somewhat mysteriously, care for the descendants of Charles Bon by his "marriage" to an octoroon.

Though not all the known facts, these constitute the outline of the story as it is generally known in Jefferson. The major mysteries stand out in this outline. Why did Sutpen forbid the marriage? Why did Henry side with Charles and then kill him? Why did Rosa agree to marry Sutpen and then refuse? Why did Sutpen get a squatter's daughter pregnant and abandon her, bringing about his own death? Why did Judith take responsibility for Bon's family? These are the questions to which Rosa Coldfield, Jason Compson III and his father General Compson, and Quentin Compson and his Harvard roommate Shreve McCannon address themselves. A rough chapter outline will give an idea of the novel's structure while suggesting how the various accounts interrelate.

The setting in chapters 1 through 5 is day one of time present, early September, 1909, before Quentin Compson leaves for Harvard. (1) Afternoon, Rosa tells Quentin about Sutpen in summary, painting him as a destructive demon of heroic proportions. (2) Evening, Jason III repeats his father's description of how Sutpen built his empire of one hundred square miles and married Ellen. (3) Evening, Jason III gives the public version, with some inside information, of Rosa's relationship with Sutpen, centering on her involvement with the Judith-Charles relationship and her eventual refusal to marry Sutpen. (4) Evening, Jason attempts to explain why Sutpen forbade the marriage and why Henry killed Charles. He argues that Bon intended to keep his octoroon mistress/wife when he married Judith. Jason offers this explanation as plausible but does not really feel it is adequate. (5) Later that same evening, Rosa tries to explain why she refused to marry Sutpen, giving her own version of how she came to be on the scene and describing the death of Bon and its effect on the family. She ends this part by revealing her belief that the Sutpen mansion contains some secret that she intends to discover that evening.

Chapters 6 through 9 are set in day two of time present, January of 1910; Quentin and Shreve spend an evening in their Harvard dormitory working out their version of the Sutpen story. (6) Quentin has a letter saying that Rosa is dead. The story is recapitulated with more details coming to light and completing the story of the Sutpen line in outline. (7) Quentin and Shreve concentrate on Sutpen's youth, retelling his story up to his death in the light of information Quentin received directly from his grandfather. (8) The boys work out the story of Charles Bon's and Henry Sutpen's relationship, constructing a new answer to the question of why Henry killed Charles. Not only was Charles Henry's half brother, but he also had black blood. (9) Quentin recalls his trip with Rosa to Sutpen's house on the September night and his brief meeting with the returned Henry. They finish Jason III's letter and contemplate the whole story.

The novel's climax comes in chapter 8 when Shreve and Quentin construct their explanation. They "discover" through intense imaginative identification with Henry and Charles a meaning latent in the facts they have gathered. Their discovery implies that Sutpen prevented the marriage and alienated Henry by revealing that Charles and Henry were half brothers. The substance of their discovery is that the first wife whom Sutpen put aside, the mother of Charles, was a mulatto. Sutpen reserves this information as his trump card in case Henry comes to accept an incestuous marriage. Only this revelation could have brought Henry to kill Charles rather than allow him to marry Judith. The means by which the boys arrive at this conclusion reveal much about the meanings of the novel. Not least among these meanings is the revelation of a sickness at the "prime foundation" of the South, the sickness of a planter society that prevents one from loving one's own children.

There is no way for the boys to *prove* this solution. Their discovery is above all an imaginative act, yet it has the ring of truth. No one who is alive, except Henry, knows what passed between Sutpen and Henry in the conversations that broke off the marriage and led to the murder, and Henry tells no one before his own death. The truth is utterly hidden in the past. The materials that make up this truth are fragmentary, scattered in distance, time, and memory. Only through the most laborious process do Quentin and Shreve gather the facts together from the narratives of their elders and a few documents. Informants such as Rosa and Jason III are Sherwood Anderson grotesques; they have chosen simple truths to which they make all their experiences conform. Rosa's portrait of Sutpen grows almost entirely out of Sutpen's proposal that they produce a child before they marry. Jason III's portrait of Charles Bon is an idealized self-portrait. Even eyewitnesses such as General Compson and Rosa have faulty memories and biased points of view. In the world of this novel, the truth is difficult to know because the facts on which it is based are hard to assemble.

When the facts are assembled, they are even harder to explain. Jason realizes that he has "just the words, the symbols, the shapes themselves." Quentin and Shreve are able to explain, not because they find the facts, but because they use their imaginations so effectively as to find themselves in the tent with Sutpen and Henry in 1865 and in the camp when Charles tells Henry that even though they are brothers, Charles is the "nigger" who is going to marry his sister. Quentin and Shreve have felt Thomas Sutpen's motives, his reasons for opposing the marriage. They have felt Charles's reasons for insisting on the marriage and Henry's victimization as an instrument of his father. They have entered into the heart's blood, the central symbolic image of the novel, the symbol of the old verities that touch the heart and to which the heart holds as truth. Sutpen's honor is embodied in the design that will crumble if he accepts Charles as his son or allows the marriage. The love of sons for fathers and of brothers for sisters becomes a tragic trap within that design. If love, honor, courage, compassion, and pride are found at the center of these inexplicable events, then the boys have discovered "what must be true." As Cass Edmonds says to young Ike McCaslin in *Go Down, Moses*, "what the heart holds to becomes truth, as far as we know truth."

In order for Quentin and Shreve to complete this act of imagination, they must come to understand Sutpen more fully than anyone does. The key to understanding Sutpen comes in chapter 6, when Quentin repeats what he has learned from General Compson, to whom Sutpen has confided much of his life story. Sutpen is the child of an independent mountain family who have fallen on hard times and have become tenant farmers. His ambition springs into being on the day he discovers that in the eyes of the plantation owner's black doorman he is insignificant "white trash." On that day, he determines to right this injustice by becoming a planter himself. He dreams that when he is a planter, he will not turn away the boy messenger from his door. He becomes a planter in Haiti, then abandons everything to go to Mississippi. Having built a second plantation there and begun his dynasty again, he sacrifices his son to cancel the son by the first marriage. As General Compson sees it, Sutpen's great weakness is his innocence. Sutpen is never able to understand how history betrays him. By becoming a planter, Sutpen inevitably adopts the material forms that determine the morality of the planter, and he lacks the imagination to circumvent those forms. In fact, Sutpen is so literal, rigid, and puritanical in his adoption of the design that he becomes a grotesque of a planter. The messenger boy who comes to his door is his own mulatto son, yet Sutpen can only turn away without even so much as an "I know you are my son though I cannot say so publicly."

Sutpen's innocence and the rigidity of his design account for many of the mysteries of his life. As General Compson says, Sutpen seems to think of morality, even of life as a whole, as like a cake; if one includes the ingredients and follows the recipe, only cake can result. Supten's design is so abstract that he is utterly blind to the feelings of others. He fails to anticipate Rosa's probable reaction to the second proposal. He never thinks of how Wash will react to his treatment of Milly. He never expects that Charles Bon will be the boy at his door. When Sutpen tells his story to General Compson, he is seeking the missing ingredient that has twice prevented him from completing his design and his revenge. Sutpen's boyhood experience has cut him off from the truth of the heart. He has, instead, rigidly grasped a single truth and has made it into a falsehood in his Olympian effort to make the world conform to the shape of that truth.

Because of Sutpen's failure, many children stand before doors that they cannot pass. Only an act of sympathetic imagination can get one past the symbolic doors of this novel, but most of the children are so victimized that they are incapable of imaginative sympathy. Even Quentin would not be able to pass his door, the subjects of incest and a sister's honor, without help from Shreve. Without Quentin's passion and knowledge, Shreve would never have seen the door. Their brotherhood is a key "ingredient" in their imaginative power.

Many significant elements of this complex novel must remain untouched in any brief analysis. One other aspect of the novel, however, is of particular interest: In *Absalom, Absalom!*, Faulkner suggests the possibility of seeing the Yoknapatawpha novels as a saga, a unified group of works from which another level of significance emerges. He chooses to end *Absalom, Absalom!* with a map of Yoknapatawpha County. This map locates the events of all the preceding Yoknapatawpha novels and some that were not yet written, though the relevant Snopes stories had appeared in magazines. Reintroducing the Compson family also suggests that Faulkner was thinking of a unity among his novels in addition to the unity of the individual works. It seems especially significant that Shreve McCannon, an outsider, neither a Compson nor a southerner nor an American, makes the final imaginative leap that inspirits Sutpen's story with the heart's truth. In this way, that truth flows out of its narrow regional circumstances to a world that shares in the same heart's blood. With *Absalom, Absalom!*, Faulkner may have seen more clearly than before how his novels could be pillars to help men "endure and prevail" by reminding them of those "old verities," the central motives that bind humankind and the Yoknapatawpha novels together.

Go Down, Moses

In *Go Down, Moses*, Faulkner juxtaposes two sides of the McCaslin family. This contrast comes to center on Lucas Beauchamp, a black descendant, and Isaac

McCaslin, a white descendant of L. Q. C. McCaslin, the founder of the McCaslin plantation. Although the novel divides roughly in two and has the appearance of a collection of stories, it is unified as an explanation of the opening phrases that summarize Isaac's life. Ike is distinguished by his refusals to inherit the family plantation or to own any other land because he believes the earth belongs to no man, by his love for the woods, and by the fact that though he has married and is uncle to half a county, he has no children.

"Was," "The Fire and the Hearth," and "Pantaloon in Black" deal primarily with the black McCaslins. Taken together, these stories dramatize the suffering of basically good people, black and white, as they struggle to make and preserve their marriages and to honor their blood ties despite the barrier of racism.

"Was" tells how Tomey's Turl and Tennie arrange their marriage. Turl and Tennie are slaves on neighboring plantations in the days when such farms were half a day's travel apart. In this comic interlude, remembered from before Isaac's birth, Hubert Beauchamp, owner of the neighboring farm, tries without success to marry his sister, Sophonsiba, to Isaac's father, Buck McCaslin. It becomes clear that the plot to land Buck is a cooperative effort among the slave couple and the Beauchamps. The plot ends with a poker game in which Buck's twin, Uncle Buddy, nearly outmaneuvers Hubert. That Turl is the dealer convinces Hubert to settle for the advantages he has gained rather than chance losing everything to Buddy. Buck escapes for the time being, though he eventually marries Sophonsiba, and Tennie and Turl achieve their marriage. These two marriages generate the two main characters of the novel, Lucas and Isaac. From this point of view the tale is funny and almost heartwarming, but it has a tragic undertone, for Turl, it turns out, is half brother to the twins. Even though Buck and Buddy are reluctant and enlightened slaveholders, they try to prevent their brother's marriage and must be tricked into permitting it.

This barrier of race that separates brothers and threatens marriages is the center of "The Fire and the Hearth." This long story dramatizes two pairs of conflicts. In the present, Lucas Beauchamp discovers a gold piece buried on Roth Edmonds's plantation. The Edmondses have become inheritors of the McCaslin land because of Isaac's repudiation. In his mad search for "the rest of the gold," Lucas becomes a barrier to the marriage of his daughter with George Wilkins, a rival moonshiner. To get rid of Wilkins, Lucas uses the very racist rituals that have caused him suffering; he appeals to Roth's paternalistic dominance of his black tenants. This conflict reminds Lucas of his previous conflict with Roth's father, Zack. In this conflict, Zack and Lucas, who were reared as brothers, nearly kill each other because as a black, Lucas simply cannot believe Zack's statement that though he had the opportunity, he has not cuckolded Lucas.

The second present conflict arises when Lucas's wife, Mollie, decides she will divorce her husband because he has become obsessed with finding gold. When she announces this plan to Roth, Roth remembers his own relationship with Lucas and Mollie, especially that Mollie is the only mother he ever had. His childhood memories prominently include the shame he felt when racism came between him and his "family." Now, when he most needs to, he cannot talk with them heart to heart.

In "Was" and "The Fire and the Hearth," the wall of racism divides lovers, brothers, parents, and children. All suffer because what their hearts yearn for is forbidden by their racial experience. Familial love is blocked by racism. "Pantaloon in Black" completes this picture of tragic suffering with a powerful image of what whites, especially, lose by inherited racist attitudes. Rider and Mannie, tenants on Edmonds land, love passionately. When Mannie dies, Rider cannot contain his grief. He moves magnificently toward a complex love-death. Juxtaposed to this image is the marriage of a local deputy that contains no passion or compassion. They live separate lives, the wife's emotional needs satisfied by card parties and motion pictures. Their brief discussion of Rider's grief and death reveals that because they are unable to see their black brothers as human, they are cut off from imagining their feelings, cut off from sympathy and, finally, cut off from their own humanity.

"The Old People," "The Bear," and "Delta Autumn" tell the story of Isaac: of his education for life in the woods, his consecration to that life, the resulting decision to repudiate his inheritance and the consequence of that decision, including his wife's refusal to bear his children.

Isaac's education begins with Sam Fathers. Sam contains the blood of all three races that share in the founding of America. In him the wilderness ideal of brotherhood is made visible. On the other hand, Sam contains the sins of the American Indians who sold land not theirs to sell and then went on to buy and sell men, including Sam, who was sold as a slave by his own father. Sam is the last of the old people and, therefore, figures in both the origins and the victimizations of the races. When Isaac perceives these meanings in Sam's life, his spontaneous response is, "Let him go!" But this Mosaic wish is futile, Ike is told. There is no simple cage that can be unlocked to free Sam. From that moment, Ike tries to discover some effective way to set some of God's lowly people free.

By means of the stories of the old people, Sam teaches Ike that, in the wilderness, all people are guests on the earth. In the wilderness, the hunt becomes a ritual by which man, in taking the gifts of the land for his sustenance, participates in the immortal life processes of the cosmos. Here even the barriers between life and death lack significance. Opposed to this view is the civilization represented by the divided fields outside the wall of the big woods. In this outer world, land ownership divides the haves and the have-nots. Conceiving of the land as dead matter to be bought and sold leads to conceiving of people as beasts to be bought and sold. Ike comes to see this decline in humanity in his own family history as contained in the ledgers of the plantation commissary.

In part 4 of "The Bear," having seen the death of Old Ben, the bear that stands for the life of the old wilderness, Ike explains to his older cousin, Cass Edmonds, why he will not accept his inheritance, the McCaslin plantation. Though quite complex, his argument is mainly that if owning land leads directly to the exploitation of God's lowly people, then refusing to own the land may help end such exploitation. He takes on the responsibility of attempting to realize in civilization the values of the wilderness to which he has consecrated himself. Among the reasons for his choice is the pattern he sees in his family history.

His grandfather, L. Q. C. McCaslin, seems almost incomprehensible to Ike because he bought a beautiful slave, fathered a daughter with her, and then fathered a son, Tomey's Turl, with that daughter. To Ike, these acts represent the worst of the violations that arise from arrogant proprietorship. In his grandfather's will, in the subsequent actions of Buck and Buddy in freeing slaves, in the Civil War and in his own education, Ike sees a pattern that leads him to think his family may have a responsibility to help bring an end to these wrongs. By repudiating his inheritance, he hopes humbly to participate in making love possible between the races.

Critics disagree about whether readers are to see Ike as heroic in the tradition of saintliness or as a fool who hides his light under a bushel by refusing to risk the exercise of power in behalf of his beliefs. While Ike does not fall into Sutpen's trap, largely because he conceives of his mission as acting for others rather than for himself, he may choose too passive a means to his end. It may be that Faulkner intended a suspension between these alternatives that would heighten the tragic dimensions of moral choice in the complex welter of human events. It is difficult to fault Ike's motives or his perception of the situation, but when assessing the effectiveness of his actions, one finds roughly equal evidence for and against his choice.

In "Delta Autumn," Ike is a respected teacher. He speaks with a wisdom and authority that command attention, if not full understanding, from his companions and that speak directly to Roth Edmonds's shame at his inability to marry the mulatto woman he loves and to claim his son by her. While Ike has nothing of which to be ashamed, his refusal of the land has helped to corrupt the weaker Roth. Ike has known that he would probably never see the amelioration for which he has worked and, more than any of his companions, Ike understands that something sacred, which he can call God, comes into being when people love one another. Nevertheless, he must suffer seeing the sins of his grandfather mirrored by Roth, for Roth's mistress is a descendant of Tomey's Turl. Ike must tell that woman to accept the repudiation of her love, and he must accept her accusation that he knows nothing about love. Whether Ike is a saint or a fool seems endlessly arguable. That he is to some extent aware of this dilemma may be part of the tragic significance of his life. He cannot learn whether his example will contribute to ending the shame of denied love that results from racism and that perpetuates it. He can only believe.

"Go Down, Moses," the last story, reemphasizes the desire for spiritual unity between the races and the apparently insuperable barriers that remain. Mollie Beauchamp's grandson, Samuel Worsham Beauchamp, is executed for murdering a Chicago policeman. Sam is the opposite of Sam Fathers. He is the youngest son, sold into the slavery of making money too fast, which devalues human life. Mollie's grieving chant that Roth Edmonds sold her Benjamin into Egypt echoes the imagined grief of the biblical Jacob whom his sons claim will die if they return from Egypt without their youngest brother. Roth has taken responsibility for this young relation and then has repudiated him. Mollie's accusation is fundamentally correct. The sympathetic but paternalistic white community of Jefferson cannot see this connection and so, despite its good heart, it cannot cross the barrier between races and truly enter into Mollie's grief. Gavin Stevens, the community's representative, feels driven from the scene of grief before the fire on the hearth by the intense passion of Mollie's grieving. Ike's sacrifice has changed nothing yet, but whether it was a bad choice remains hard to decide.

Faulkner wrote many fine novels in addition to those discussed here. The Snopes Trilogy and *The Reivers*, for example, are often included among his masterpieces, in part because they reveal especially well Faulkner's great but sometimes overlooked comic gifts. Faulkner's reputation has grown steadily since his Nobel Prize. Some critics are ready to argue that he is the greatest American novelist. They base their claim on the power of his novels to fascinate readers, to provoke serious and profound discussion about the modern human condition while engaging significant emotions, and to give the pleasures of all great storytelling, the pleasures of seeing, knowing, believing in, and caring for characters like oneself at crucial moments in their lives. The quantity and quality of his work, as well as the worthy unity of purpose that emerges from analysis of his career, tend to confirm the highest estimate of Faulkner's accomplishment.

Terry Heller

Other major works

SHORT FICTION: *These Thirteen*, 1931; *Doctor Martino, and Other Stories*, 1934; *The Portable Faulkner*, 1946, 1967; *Knight's Gambit*, 1949; *Collected Short Stories of William Faulkner*, 1950; *Big Woods*, 1955; *Three Famous Short Novels*, 1958; *Uncollected Stories of William Faulkner*, 1979.

POETRY: *The Marble Faun*, 1924; *A Green Bough*, 1933.

SCREENPLAYS: *Today We Live*, 1933; *To Have and Have Not*, 1945; *The Big Sleep*, 1946; *Faulkner's MGM Screenplays*, 1982.

NONFICTION: *New Orleans Sketches*, 1958; *Faulkner in the University*, 1959; *Faulkner at West Point*, 1964; *Essays, Speeches, and Public Letters*, 1965; *The Faulkner-Cowley File: Letters and Memories, 1944-1962*, 1966 (Malcolm Cowley, editor); *Lion in the Garden*, 1968; *Selected Letters*, 1977.

MISCELLANEOUS: *The Faulkner Reader*, 1954; *William Faulkner: Early Prose and Poetry*, 1962.

Bibliography

Bleikasten, Andre. *The Ink of Melancholy: Faulkner's Novels from "The Sound and the Fury" to "Light in August."* Bloomington: Indiana University Press, 1990. Focuses on four of Faulkner's novels—*The Sound and the Fury*, *Sanctuary*, *As I Lay Dying*, and *Light in August*—in offering a wide-ranging study of the writer and the limits of authorship.

Blotner, Joseph. *Faulkner: A Biography*. 2 vols. New York: Random House, 1964. Comprehensive, readable biography remains an important source for details about Faulkner's life. Includes many photographs and a useful index.

Brooks, Cleanth. *William Faulkner: The Yoknapatawpha Country*. 1963. Reprint. Baton Rouge: Louisiana State University Press, 2002. Brooks has written several excellent books on Faulkner, but this venerable classic of Faulkner criticism is one of the best introductions, treating Faulkner's characteristic themes and historical and social background and offering detailed readings of the major novels and stories. Carefully prepared notes, appendixes, and character index are immensely helpful to beginning readers trying to make sense of mysterious events and complex family relations in Faulkner's works.

Broughton, Panthea. *William Faulkner: The Abstract and the Actual*. Baton Rouge: Louisiana State University Press, 1974. One of the best of several fine critical studies available that attempt to see Faulkner whole and understand his worldview, especially for readers just beginning to know Faulkner. Broughton sees the tension between the ideal and the actual as central to understanding the internal and external conflicts about which Faulkner most often writes.

Gray, Richard. *The Life of William Faulkner: A Critical Biography*. Cambridge, Mass.: Blackwell, 1994. A noted Faulkner scholar, Gray closely integrates the life and work. Part 1 suggests a method of approaching Faulkner's life; part 2 concentrates on his apprentice years; part 3 explains his discovery of Yoknapatawpha and the transformation of the region into his fiction; part 4 deals with his treatment of past and present; part 5 addresses his exploration of place; and part 6 analyzes his final novels. Includes family trees, chronology, notes, and bibliography.

Marius, Richard. *Reading Faulkner: Introduction to the First Thirteen Novels*. Compiled and edited by Nancy Grisham Anderson. Knoxville: University of Tennessee Press, 2006. Collection of the lectures that Marius, a novelist, biographer, and devoted Faulkner scholar, presented during an undergraduate course. Provides an approachable introduction to Faulkner.

Minter, David. *William Faulkner: His Life and Work*. Baltimore: Johns Hopkins University Press, 1980. Shorter and less detailed than Blotner's biography (cited above), but valuable for its exploration of the connections between Faulkner's life and his works.

Porter, Carolyn. *William Faulkner*. New York: Oxford University Press, 2007. Concise and informative biographical work spans Faulkner's entire life but focuses primarily on his most prolific period, from 1929 to 1940. Offers insightful analysis of his major works.

Singal, Daniel J. *William Faulkner: The Making of a Modernist*. Chapel Hill: University of North Carolina Press, 1997. Study of the thought and art of Faulkner charts the development of his ideas from their source in his reading to their embodiment in his writing. Depicts two Faulkners: the country gentleman and the intellectual man of letters.

Towner, Theresa M. *The Cambridge Introduction to William Faulkner*. New York: Cambridge University Press, 2008. Accessible resource, aimed at students and general readers, provides detailed analyses of Faulkner's nineteen novels, discussion of his other works, and information about the critical reception for his fiction.

Wagner-Martin, Linda, ed. *New Essays on "Go Down, Moses."* New York: Cambridge University Press, 1996. Collection of essays features a range of approaches to the novel, including from the perspectives of race, environment, gender, and ideology. An editor's introduction summarizes contemporary reception and critical analysis of the novel.

_______. *William Faulkner: Six Decades of Criticism*. East Lansing: Michigan State University Press, 2002. Collection of critical essays presents interpretations of Faulkner's work from perspectives such as language theory, feminism, deconstruction, and psychoanalysis. Includes analyses of many of his novels.

JESSIE REDMON FAUSET

Born: Snow Hill, New Jersey; April 27, 1882
Died: Philadelphia, Pennsylvania; April 30, 1961

PRINCIPAL LONG FICTION

There Is Confusion, 1924
Plum Bun: A Novel Without a Moral, 1928
The Chinaberry Tree: A Novel of American Life, 1931
Comedy, American Style, 1933

OTHER LITERARY FORMS

In addition to her four novels, Jessie Redmon Fauset wrote short stories, poems, nonfictional pieces, and works for children. She also translated the works of some Haitian writers.

ACHIEVEMENTS

Jessie Redmon Fauset was one of the most prolific novelists of the Harlem Renaissance of the 1920's, when her works were highly praised for introducing the reading public to a class of African Americans unknown to whites. Perhaps more important than her own works was her publishing and nurturing of other Harlem Renaissance writers as literary editor of *The Crisis*, the journal of the National Association for the Advancement of Colored People (NAACP), from 1919 to 1926. In that capacity, she published works by Langston Hughes, Claude McKay, Nella Larsen, Jean Toomer, and Countée Cullen. In 1920, Fauset also became the managing editor of the short-lived *The Brownies' Book*, writer W. E. B. Du Bois's magazine for children. Her first novel, *There Is Confusion*, was nominated for the Harmon Award in Literature in 1928.

BIOGRAPHY

Jessie Redmon Fauset, the youngest of seven children born to Redmon Fauset, an African Methodist Episcopal minister, and Annie Seamon Fauset, was born in South Hill, New Jersey, on April 27, 1882. She attended the public schools in Philadelphia and graduated as an honor student from the Philadelphia School for Girls. When she sought admission to Bryn Mawr College, rather than admit her, the college supported her application to Cornell University. Fauset graduated Phi Beta Kappa from Cornell in 1904. Whether she was the first black woman to attend Cornell or to be elected to Phi Beta Kappa, both of which are often speculated, Fauset "was one of the best educated Americans of her generation."

Denied employment in Philadelphia's integrated schools, Fauset began teaching high school in New York in 1905. After a year there and a year in Baltimore, she moved to the M Street High School (later named Dunbar High School) in Washington, D.C., where she taught for fourteen years. In 1921, a few months after receiving her master's degree from the University of Pennsylvania, Fauset joined the staff of *The Crisis* as literary editor. In 1924 she published her first novel. Fauset left *The Crisis* and returned to teaching in 1926. In 1929, she married a businessman, Herbert Harris, and between 1929 and 1933, she completed three other novels. When her husband died in 1958, Fauset returned to Philadelphia, where she died in 1961.

ANALYSIS

Although she had been writing for *The Crisis* since her undergraduate days, it was not literary aspiration that spurred Jessie Redmon Fauset to write novels, but rather the 1922 publication of T. S. Stribling's novel about a middle-class mulatto, *Birthright*. Realizing that there was "an audience waiting to hear the truth about" African Americans, Fauset felt that those who were better qualified than whites to present the truth should do so. In presenting such truth, Fauset wrote about characters she knew best: educated African Americans from respectable family backgrounds who in their values and goals were, as she stated, "not so vastly different from other Americans." Fauset used traditional literary forms in her writing, such as the sentimental novel, Greek tragedy, and fairy tales, and she was criticized for offering nothing innovative during a time when African American writers were experimenting with cultural forms and themes. In addition, because Fauset's novels focused on women and women's issues, they were dismissed in the

Jessie Redmon Fauset. (Courtesy, Moorland-Spingarn Research Center, Howard University)

1930's by both white and black male critics. With the burgeoning interest in African American women's literature in the 1970's, female critics began to discover the complexity of Fauset's novels and to note her treatment of gender, class, and race issues. As a result, Fauset's works have become the focus of increased critical attention.

THERE IS CONFUSION

Fauset's first novel, *There Is Confusion*—a tale of two families—is structured by three separate but connected plot lines, the first of which focuses on the Marshalls, a well-to-do family. Joanna, the youngest of the four children, encouraged by her father's thwarted dreams of greatness, wants to become a dancer. The second plot line focuses on Peter Bye, the fourth-generation descendant of a family whose lives are intertwined with the lives of their wealthy white former owners. While Peter's grandfather, Isaiah, refuses to accept his relative's offer to serve as their coachman and goes on to found a school for black youths in Philadelphia, Peter's dreams of becoming a surgeon are thwarted because he longs to be recognized by the white Byes and is not. Meriwether, Peter's father, deciding instead that "the world owes [him] a living," does nothing. Influenced by his father's attitude, Peter becomes entangled in the legacy of racial hatred and aspires to nothing. It is only when he becomes attracted to Joanna and is influenced by her goals of greatness that he decides, in order to win her love, to become a doctor.

The third plot line, the story of Maggie Ellersley, the daughter of a washerwoman, involves a conventional marriage. Aspiring to the middle class, Maggie begins working for Joanna's father, where she meets and takes an interest in his son, Philip. The interest appears to be mutual; however, Joanna intervenes and tells Maggie that she should marry someone in her own class. A hurt Maggie does so, then becomes a successful businesswoman when the marriage fails. After a second failed marriage, Maggie goes to France to volunteer during World War I and encounters the dying Philip. They marry, and she takes care of him until his death.

Within each plot line, Fauset heavy-handedly reveals the obstacles to the achievement of each character's dreams: Joanna's dream of becoming a professional dancer is thwarted by race; Peter's dream (or lack thereof) is influenced by family legacy; Maggie's dream is hindered by class. Fauset also reveals how each character achieves despite the obstacles. Unable to dance in a white theater troupe, Joanna starts her own dance class but is asked to dance the role of the colored American in "The Dance of the Nations" when the white woman chosen for the part lacks the technique. Joanna attains instant success and is eventually asked to perform three roles.

Peter, because of his love for Joanna, becomes a surgeon; however, she has no interest in assuming the conventional roles of wife and mother. Therefore, caught in the web of circumstances characteristic of sentimental novels, and through a series of contrived coincidences, Peter ends up in Europe during the war and meets one of his white relatives. Young Meriwether dies in Peter's arms, but not before extracting the promise that Peter will visit the senior Meriwether. By moving beyond hate, Peter not only receives long-awaited recognition from the white Byes but also wins Joanna as his wife.

As evidenced by the many hardships that Maggie undergoes, Fauset suggests that Maggie's aspiration—to transcend one's class through marriage—is the most problematic. Maggie achieves her desired middle-class status not through her marriages but rather through her business acumen. Moreover, by developing a political and racial consciousness and selflessness and traveling to Europe to aid black soldiers, she is reunited with her first love. *There Is Confusion* ends, as do all sentimental novels, on a happy note. While many ideas are introduced in the novel, the theme that dominates is, as critic Carolyn Sylvander puts it, that "surviving the hardships engendered by discrimination places the black person and the race in a position of superiority."

Plum Bun

Most critics consider Fauset's second novel, *Plum Bun*, to be her best. As in *There Is Confusion*, a middle-class African American family is at the novel's center, but unlike the earlier work, *Plum Bun* centers on one protagonist, Angela. In addition, the novel is structured in five parts, using a nursery rhyme as its epigraph and unifying element:

> To market, to market
> To buy a plum bun;
> Home again, home again,
> Market is done.

In the first section, titled "Home," readers are introduced to the Murray family: Junius and Mattie and their two daughters, Angela and Virginia. This section also provides the background information important to the rest of the novel. Angela and Virginia are exposed early on to their mother's fairy-tale view of marriage. Just as important, they are exposed to her views on color. Although Junius and Virginia are both brown-skinned, Mattie and Angela are light enough to pass—which they often do "for fun." Junius is not opposed to this as long as no principle is being compromised. The result, however, is that Angela grows up seeing her mother on occasion publicly ignore her darker-skinned husband and daughter. When the parents die within two weeks of each other, Angela decides to move to New York in order to further her personal and professional goals.

In the second section, "Market," Angela becomes the art student Angele Mory and is indoctrinated in the worldly ways of courtship. In the third section, titled "Plum Bun," Angele meets Roger Fielding, an affluent white man, whom she dates and eventually hopes to marry. Roger does not propose marriage but rather cohabitation. Angele does not agree, and he eventually ends the relationship, but not before Angele has publicly denied Virginia, who has also moved to New York. In "Home Again," the novel's fourth section, Angele, in search of companionship, admits her love for Anthony Cross, a fellow art student who is also passing. Having resolved never to marry a white woman, Anthony rejects Angele and becomes engaged to Virginia, unaware that Angele and Virginia are sisters.

In the final section, "Market Is Done," Angele decides to focus on her art. She wins a scholarship to study in Paris but forfeits it by revealing that she, too, is black when fellow student Rachel Powell is denied money for her passage because of her race. Angele decides to support her own study in Paris. Before she leaves the United States, she returns "home" to Philadelphia and is reunited with a former admirer, Matthew Henson. Knowing that Virginia is really in love with Matthew, and learning that Matthew loves Virginia, Angele does not interfere. Instead she moves to Paris, seemingly destined to be alone; however, Anthony appears that Christmas Eve, sent with Matthew and Virginia's love. Like *There Is Confusion*, *Plum Bun* has a happy ending.

By including fairy-tale motifs within the marriage plot, Fauset explores the choices and compromises that women make regarding marriage. The novel "without a moral" indeed has one: Adhering to the traditional conceptions of marriage is problematic when race, class, and gender are factors.

The Chinaberry Tree

Fauset's theme of the effects of race, gender, and class as focused within two-parent, multiple-sibling families is abandoned in her third novel. *The Chinaberry Tree* relates the story of two cousins, Laurentine Strange and Melissa Paul, who are both products of illicit relationships.

Laurentine is the product of an illicit romantic relationship between a master, Colonel Halloway, and his former slave, Sarah. Accepting the community's opinion that she has "bad blood," Laurentine isolates herself from the community, and rejection from a suitor reinforces her feelings of inadequacy and propels her to further isolation. Melissa, the product of an adulterous relationship between Judy Strange and the married Sylvester Forten, is sent to Red Brook to live with her relatives. She meets and falls in love with Malory Forten, who, unknown to her, is her half brother. The novel explores both women's responses to being innocent victims of fate.

The Chinaberry Tree is not merely Fauset's attempt to reveal that "Negroes are not so vastly different" or that their lives are elements of a play falling together, as stated in the novel's foreword. It is a subtle illustration of women making choices and accepting the consequences: Both Sal and Judy Strange choose forbidden loves. In spite of their "bad blood," as the daughters are seemingly tainted by their mothers' choices, Laurentine and Melissa are able to find true love at the novel's end. What appears to be another example of Fauset's blind acceptance of the values of nineteenth century sentimental fiction is a subtle commentary on women refusing to adhere to the constrictions placed on their lives.

Comedy, American Style

Fauset structured her final novel around the elements of drama, with its chapters titled "The Plot," "The Characters," "Teresa's Act," "Oliver's Act," "Phebe's Act," and "Curtain." In this, Fauset's darkest work, she returns to the format of the two-parent family. The novel chronicles the life of Olivia Blanchard Cary, a light-skinned African American who, shaped by two incidents in her childhood, chooses a life of passing. She marries a black doctor, not for love but rather for status, and they have three children. Nonetheless, Olivia's obsession with color consciousness destroys the family. When her oldest child, Teresa, falls in love with the dark-skinned Henry Bates, Olivia intervenes and forces Teresa to marry a Frenchman.

The youngest child, Oliver, suffers the most because of his bronze skin color. Rejected by his mother from birth and often made to play the role of servant or denied in public, he commits suicide. Only Christopher survives intact through his marriage to Phebe Grant. When the novel ends, Olivia has finally achieved her objective: Living alone in France—her husband has divorced her, and her children have abandoned her—she passes as white.

In this, her only novel that does not have a happy ending, Fauset's use of satire is quite evident. One critic, pointing to Fauset's subversion of the Cinderella motif, has noted that neither mother nor daughter is happily married, and both are poor. Another critic has commented on the ironic use of the Snow White motif: Olivia pronounces the bitter truth in her pregnancy with Oliver that he would be "the handsomest and most attractive of us all," and by doing so she unwittingly proclaims that black is beautiful.

Paula C. Barnes

Bibliography

Calloway, Licia Morrow. "Revising the Victorian Maternal Ideal in Jessie Fauset's *There Is Confusion*." In *Black Family (Dys)function in Novels by Jessie Fauset, Nella Larsen, and Fannie Hurst*. New York: Peter Lang, 2003. Examines *There Is Confusion* with a focus on Fauset's treatment of maternity and her handling of the class pressures on upwardly aspiring black characters.

Harker, Jaime. *America the Middlebrow: Women's Novels, Progressivism, and Middlebrow Authorship Between the Wars*. Amherst: University of Massachusetts Press, 2007. Traces the careers of Fauset and several other women authors who published during the 1920's and 1930's and who viewed fiction as a means of reforming society.

Jones, Sharon L. "Deconstructing the Black Bourgeoisie: Subversions and Diversions in the Fiction of Jessie Fauset." In *Rereading the Harlem Renaissance: Race, Class, and Gender in the Fiction of Jessie Fauset, Zora Neale Hurston, and Dorothy West*. Westport, Conn.: Greenwood Press, 2002. Chapter devoted to Fauset's novels is part of a larger analysis of the works of three African American women writers that demonstrates how their fiction challenges conventional ideas about race, class, and gender oppression.

McDowell, Deborah. "Jessie Fauset." In *Modern American Women Writers*, edited by Lea Baechler and A. Walton Litz. New York: Charles Scribner's Sons, 1991. Presents a general discussion of Fauset's role in the Harlem Renaissance as editor and writer, and analyzes Fauset's four novels to illustrate their "thematic and ironic complexity."

McLendon, Jacquelyn Y. *The Politics of Color in the Fiction of Jessie Fauset and Nella Larsen*. Charlottesville: University of Virginia Press, 1995. Addresses the theme of the "tragic mulatto" in the novels of the two writers. The discussion of Fauset's work focuses on the novels *Plum Bun* and *Comedy, American Style*.

Ransom, Portia Boulware. *Black Love and the Harlem Renaissance (the Novels of Nella Larsen, Jessie Redmon Fauset, and Zora Neale Hurston): An Essay in African American Literary Criticism*. Lewiston, N.Y.: Edwin Mellen Press, 2005. Examines how the three writers use their semiautobiographical fiction to focus on the tensions between black men and women who are trying to define themselves.

Sato, Hiroko. "Under the Harlem Shadow: A Study of Jessie Fauset and Nella Larsen." In *The Harlem Renaissance Remembered*, edited by Arna Bontemps. New York: Dodd, Mead, 1972. While asserting that Fauset "is not a first-rate writer," Sato argues that race is the central concern of the middle-class characters in her novels.

Sylvander, Carolyn. *Jessie Redmon Fauset: Black American Writer*. Troy, N.Y.: Whitston, 1981. Definitive critical biography argues that reading Fauset's novels as compared to her life is too simplistic. Provides analysis of Fauset's work in addition to recounting the details of her life.

Wall, Cheryl. *Women of the Harlem Renaissance*. Bloomington: Indiana University Press, 1995. Presents an excellent discussion of all of Fauset's works. Wall asserts that Fauset achieved distinction as a journalist and essayist instead of as a novelist.

EDNA FERBER

Born: Kalamazoo, Michigan; August 15, 1885
Died: New York, New York; April 16, 1968
Also known as: Edna Jessica Ferber

Principal long fiction

Dawn O'Hara: The Girl Who Laughed, 1911
Fanny Herself, 1917
The Girls, 1921
So Big, 1924
Show Boat, 1926
Cimarron, 1930
American Beauty, 1931
Come and Get It, 1935
Saratoga Trunk, 1941
Great Son, 1945
Giant, 1952
Ice Palace, 1958

Other literary forms

In addition to twelve novels, Edna Ferber wrote eight plays, two novellas, eighty-three short stories, and two autobiographies. Although her novels have perhaps been the most enduring part of her work, her short stories and plays were equally or more important during her lifetime. Almost all her works, except the dramas, first appeared serially in magazines. In addition, she wrote numerous short articles and commentaries. Twenty-two Emma McChesney stories made Ferber a best-selling writer. These were first published in *The American Magazine* or *Cosmopolitan* between 1911 and 1915 and later were collected in *Roast Beef Medium* (1913), *Personality Plus* (1914), and *Emma McChesney and Co.* (1915). Emma McChesney also was the heroine of *Our Mrs. McChesney* (pr., pb. 1915), Ferber's first play, which she wrote with George V. Hobart.

The McChesney character was a significant innovation—the first successful businesswoman depicted in popular American literature. Finally, however, Ferber declined *Cosmopolitan*'s proffered contract for as many McChesney stories as she wished to write at a price she could name. Ferber saw herself, instead, as a novelist and dramatist. The plays she wrote with George S.

Kaufman, especially *Dinner at Eight* (pr., pb. 1932), *The Royal Family* (pr. 1927), and *Stage Door* (pr., pb. 1936), enjoyed long Broadway runs and secured her fame as a dramatist. Her autobiographies, *A Peculiar Treasure* (1939, 1960) and *A Kind of Magic* (1963), explain her motivations and detail her writing techniques. The books also are intensely personal and revealing. The second, written after her health began to deteriorate, is rambling and repetitive but essentially completes the story of her active life.

Achievements

Edna Ferber maintained herself as a best-selling author and a popular celebrity from the appearance of the Emma McChesney stories in 1911 to the publication of *Ice Palace* in 1958. During this period, she was cited several times as America's best woman novelist, and literary notables such as William Allen Wright, Rudyard Kipling, and James M. Barrie praised her work. Her reputation, however, abruptly declined in the late 1960's. A resurgence in interest in Ferber's work began in the 1980's, fueled mostly by the publicity surrounding her participation in several social crusades. Her advocacy of social and political causes in her fiction significantly influenced public opinion and policy. Ernest Gruening, territorial senator-elect of Alaska, for example, cited Ferber's *Ice Palace* as important in winning Alaska's statehood.

Ferber's explication of regional history and culture in her novels also played a prominent part in raising pride in American culture after World War I. Her short story "April Twenty-fifth as Usual" (first published in *Ladies' Home Journal* in July, 1918) received the O. Henry Award in 1919, and in 1925, her novel *So Big* won the Pulitzer Prize for fiction. Jerome Kern and Oscar Hammerstein II's classic musical play *Show Boat* (pr. 1927), based on Ferber's novel, was the first American musical with a serious plot derived from a literary source. The story also was used in a successful radio serial program and four films; it made so much money that Ferber referred to it as her "oil well." She associated with many prominent theatrical, literary, and political figures, including members of the Algonquin Round Table, a circle of literary friends who met for lunch regularly at New York's Algonquin Hotel. At least twenty-seven films have been based on her works.

Edna Ferber. (Library of Congress)

Biography

Edna Jessica Ferber was the second daughter of a Hungarian Jewish immigrant storekeeper, Jacob Charles Ferber, and Julia Neuman Ferber, daughter of a prosperous, cultured German Jewish family. She was named Edna because the family, hoping for a male child, had already selected the name Edward. When she was born in Kalamazoo, Michigan, her father owned and operated a general store. Soon the business faltered, and the family moved in with Julia's parents in Chicago. The family moved subsequently to Ottumwa, Iowa, then back to Chicago, then to Appleton, Wisconsin, but Jacob Ferber still failed to prosper as a storekeeper. Though intelligent, kindly, and cultured, he never acquired business skills; in addition, he soon lost his sight. Julia assumed management of the business and became the head of the family. With great personal effort and the active assistance of Edna, she stabilized the business, paid off debts, and maintained the family's independence.

Edna Ferber later described Ottumwa as narrow-minded and sordid. There she experienced anti-Semitism and witnessed a lynching. During her high school years in Appleton, in contrast, she enjoyed pleasant, tolerant, midwestern small-town life. Unable to afford college tuition in 1902, she began her professional writing career as a reporter for the *Appleton Daily Crescent*. Eighteen months later, the editor who had hired her—on the strength of her reportorial writing in her high school paper—left the newspaper, and Ferber was fired. The most credible reason given for her dismissal was her imaginative "embroidering" of news reports. She then became a reporter on the *Milwaukee Journal*. Exhausted by overwork and anemia, she returned home in 1905 and began writing fiction. High school and about five years of newspaper writing constituted Ferber's entire preparation for her literary career.

After Jacob Ferber's death in 1909, Julia sold the store and took her two daughters to Chicago. There, while her mother and sister earned their living, Edna continued writing. In 1912, after selling some of her work, she moved to New York City, but she remained closely attached to her mother. Thereafter, she and her mother resided in hotels or apartments in New York, Chicago, and elsewhere but considered themselves New Yorkers. Though they did not always actually live together, their lives were closely intertwined. In 1938, Edna, who never married, built a house for herself in suburban Connecticut, pointedly leaving her mother in a New York apartment. After Julia died, Edna sold her house and returned to New York to live, taking an apartment. During the last ten years of her life, a painful nervous disorder impaired her writing. She died of stomach cancer in New York City on April 16, 1968.

Analysis

Edna Ferber was a feminist, a conservationist, a crusader for minorities and immigrants, and a staunch believer in the work ethic and American culture. Strong women characters rising above the limitations of birth and gender dominate her novels; most men in her works are weak, and many desert their women and children. Ferber's fiction describes and condemns mistreatment of African Americans, Jews, Latinos, and Native Americans. Her novels decry unrestrained capitalism and wasteful exploitation of natural resources while celebrating regional culture and history in an effective and pleasing style that clearly reflects her journalistic background. Her characterization, however, is less effective, and her plots tend toward melodrama and coincidence.

All of Ferber's novels were commercial successes, and many remained in print for decades after their first publication. Her first novels, *Dawn O'Hara* and *Fanny Herself*, are strongly autobiographical. They remain interesting because they show Ferber's literary growth. The background material in *Great Son*, a later work, is sketchy, the characters are stereotypical, and the plot is contrived. At the time of that novel's writing, during World War II, Ferber was preoccupied with writing propaganda to help in the war effort. Her final novel, *Ice Palace*, is a political tract of little literary merit; Ferber was ill at the time of its writing.

The Girls

Ferber expected *The Girls* to be a best seller and considered it her best novel. The story recounts six decades of Chicago middle-class history and intergenerational conflict. Charlotte Thrift, forbidden to marry an unsuitable boy, loses him to death in the American Civil War. She never marries. Her unmarried niece, Lottie, under her mother's domination, keeps house for her mother and aunt. Lottie finally rebels, joins the Red Cross during World War I, has a brief affair, and returns with her illegitimate daughter, whom she passes off as a French orphan. Charly (Charlotte), Lottie's niece, falls in love with a poet, who is killed in World War I, and moves in with her aunt and great-aunt. All three of these women are strong personalities, whereas their men are either incompetent boors or scoundrels.

So Big

Ferber's first best seller, *So Big*, effectively contrasts humble life in the Halstead Street Market with that of pretentious Chicago society. A genteelly reared orphan, Selina Peake, goes to teach school in a community of Dutch market gardeners, where she must adjust to a brutal existence. Her only intellectual companion is thirteen-year-old Roelf, the artistically talented son of the family with whom she lives. After a year, she marries kindly Pervus DeJong, an unimaginative, unenterprising widower. They have a son, Dirk, nicknamed So Big. After Pervus's death, Selina makes their farm a thriving success. She sacrifices all for So Big, who, after a few years as a struggling architect, shifts to a banking career and high society. In contrast, Selina's first protégé, Roelf, becomes a famous sculptor. At the end, So Big finally realizes that his life is empty. Although the novel was critically acclaimed, the characterization barely develops beyond stereotypes, and many of the anecdotes presented in the work are clichés.

Show Boat

Show Boat describes life aboard late nineteenth and early twentieth century Mississippi River showboats and addresses the cultural significance of these centers of entertainment. Magnolia Hawkes, daughter of Captain Andy and Parthenia Hawkes of the showboat *Cotton Blossom*, marries Gaylord Ravenal, a charming professional gambler. After Captain Andy's death, Magnolia, Gaylord, and their daughter, Kim, move to Chicago, where they squander Magnolia's inheritance. Magnolia, deserted by her wastrel husband, becomes a successful singer and raises Kim to become a successful serious actor. Parthenia inherits and successfully operates the showboat. Parthenia, Magnolia, and Kim are all protofeminist career women. Captain Andy, though competent and wise, defers to Parthenia in almost everything.

In *Show Boat*, Ferber depicts African Americans as patient, upright, and hardworking people. A tragic incident of miscegenation and the injustice of the laws in the American South balance the romanticized account of showboat life, which is charming.

Cimarron

Cimarron is set in Oklahoma in the period between the 1889 land rush and the 1920's oil boom. Sabra Cravat begins life as a genteel, impoverished southern girl but ends up an assured newspaperwoman and member of the U.S. Congress. Her husband, Yancey Cravat, a flamboyant lawyer-newspaperman of dubious background, starts grandiose projects, performs heroic acts, and upholds high ideals, but he accomplishes little. Desertion of his family clears the way for Sabra's rise. These characters exemplify the tension between those who "won" Oklahoma and those who "civilized" it. In addition, in this work interaction between Native Americans and European Americans is perceptively treated.

American Beauty

Ferber rhapsodically describes the Connecticut landscape in *American Beauty*, in which she also chronicles the abuse of land and resources. She presents Polish immigrant culture sympathetically, whereas she depicts the indigenous New Englanders as played-out aristocrats. Judy Oakes and her niece, Tamar Pring, are strong, stubborn women devoted to their aristocratic background and ancestral home. Their hired man, Ondy Olszak, a kindhearted, hardworking, unimaginative Polish immigrant, maintains the farm at just above subsistence level. Tamar seduces and marries Ondy, and their son Orrange combines Ondy's peasant vigor and Tamar's cultural sensibilities. Although Orrange inherits the farm, Ondy's family forces him to sell. Millionaire True Baldwin, who, as an impoverished farm lad, had aspired to marry Judy Oakes, buys it. Fortunately, Baldwin's architect daughter, Candy Baldwin, who is sexually attracted to Orrange, hires him to manage the farm.

Come and Get It

Ferber draws heavily on her own background in *Come and Get It*, a story of resource exploitation, unrestrained capitalism, and social contrast. After lumberjack Barney Glasgow fights his way up to a managerial position at the mill, he marries his boss's spinsterish daughter. The mill's timbering and papermaking thrive under his direction, until he is fatally attracted to Lotta Lindaback, granddaughter of his longtime lumberjack pal Swan Bostrom. Barney's daughter, frustrated by unacknowledged desire for her father, marries a dull young businessman. Bernard, Barney's son, pursues Lotta when Barney restrains his own passion for her. Barney then fights with Bernard and expels him from the house. Immediately afterward, Barney and his family are killed in an explosion. Bernard marries Lotta and builds an industrial empire in steel and paper. Lotta, meanwhile, enters international high society. The Great Depression forces Lotta's return to Wisconsin, where her twins come under the influence of Tom Melendy, an idealistic young man from a mill-hand family. Rejecting their parents' materialism, the twins return to the simple Bostrom ways.

Saratoga Trunk

In *Saratoga Trunk*, Ferber decries the evils of unrestrained capitalism and the decadent snobbery of New Orleans high society. She also promotes women's causes and the conservation of natural resources. Illegitimate Clio Dulain and Texas cowboy-gambler Clint Maroon join forces to extort money from Clio's aristocratic father. They then move to Saratoga, New York, where Clio sets out to snare a rich husband. Although she entraps railroad millionaire Van Steed, she drops him for Clint when Clint is injured fighting for Van Steed's railroad, the Saratoga Trunk. Thereafter, Clio and Clint become railroad millionaires but idealistically give their wealth to charity. Clio subtly manipulates Clint in all important matters.

Giant

Giant, Ferber's flamboyant version of Texas history and culture, exemplifies the Texas mythology; upon publication, the novel earned violent protests from Texans. Ferber's typical strong female central character, Leslie Lynnton, daughter of a world-famous doctor living in genteel shabbiness, is swept off her feet by a visiting Texas rancher. Transported to his gigantic ranch, she finds her husband ruled by his spinster sister, Luz. Luz dies violently, and, with great skill and wisdom, Leslie guides her man through repeated crises as the great cattle and cotton "empires" are hemmed in by vulgar oil billionaires. In this novel, Ferber shows the original Texans, Mexican Americans, as deeply wronged, patient, dignified, and noble. Unfortunately, the book's ending leaves ongoing problems unsolved.

Ralph L. Langenheim, Jr.

Other major works

SHORT FICTION: *Buttered Side Down*, 1912; *Roast Beef Medium*, 1913; *Personality Plus*, 1914; *Emma McChesney and Co.*, 1915; *Cheerful—By Request*, 1918; *Half Portions*, 1919; *Mother Knows Best*, 1927; *They Brought Their Women*, 1933; *Nobody's in Town*, 1938 (includes *Nobody's in Town* and *Trees Die at the Top*); *One Basket*, 1947.

PLAYS: *Our Mrs. McChesney*, pr., pb. 1915 (with George V. Hobart); *$1200 a Year*, pr., pb. 1920 (with Newman A. Levy); *Minick*, pr., pb. 1924 (with George S. Kaufman); *The Royal Family*, pr. 1927 (with Kaufman); *Dinner at Eight*, pr., pb. 1932 (with Kaufman); *Stage Door*, pr., pb. 1936 (with Kaufman); *The Land Is Bright*, pr., pb. 1941 (with Kaufman); *Bravo!*, pr. 1948 (with Kaufman).

NONFICTION: *A Peculiar Treasure*, 1939 (revised 1960); *A Kind of Magic*, 1963.

Bibliography

Antler, Joyce. *The Journey Home: Jewish Women and the American Century*. New York: Free Press, 1997. Ferber is one of the fifty women profiled in this overview of the lives of American Jewish women in the 1890's and the twentieth century.

Batker, Carol. "Literary Reformers: Crossing Class and Ethnic Boundaries in Jewish Women's Fiction of the 1920's." *MELUS* 25, no.1 (Spring, 2000): 81-104. Analyzes the work of Ferber, Fannie Hurst, and Anzia Yezierska, focusing on how Ferber depicted African American characters and class mobility.

Bloom, Harold, ed. *Jewish Women Fiction Writers*. New York: Chelsea House, 1998. Provides biographical information, a wide selection of critical excerpts, and complete bibliographies of Ferber and nine other female Jewish American writers. Designed for high school and undergraduate students.

Botshon, Lisa, and Meredith Goldsmith, eds. *Middlebrow Moderns: Popular American Women Writers of the 1920's*. Boston: Northeastern University Press, 2003. Collection of essays examines the work of writers who were both critically acclaimed and commercially successful in the 1920's. Two chapters are devoted to Ferber: One discusses the "middlebrow regional fiction" of Ferber and Rose Wilder Lane; the other analyzes Ferber's novel *Cimarron*.

Gilbert, Julie Goldsmith. *Ferber: Edna Ferber and Her Circle—A Biography*. New York: Applause, 1999. Well-researched biography calls Ferber a romantic realist. Notes that she was not opposed to working with the system, yet she created her own unique niche within it. Includes an index.

Meade, Marion. *Bobbed Hair and Bathtub Gin: Writers Running Wild in the Twenties*. New York: Nan A. Talese/Doubleday, 2004. Offers a nonscholarly, entertaining look at Ferber, Dorothy Parker, Edna St. Vincent Millay, and Zelda Fitzgerald, chronicling the lives of these writers in the "Roaring Twenties."

Shaughnessy, Mary Rose. *Women and Success in American Society in the Works of Edna Ferber*. New York: Gordon Press, 1977. Examination of Ferber's life and work provides an assessment of the author's place in the women's movement.

Watts, Eileen. "Edna Ferber, Jewish American Writer: Who Knew?" In *Modern Jewish Women Writers in America*, edited by Evelyn Avery. New York: Palgrave Macmillan, 2007. Essay interpreting Ferber's work from the perspective of her Jewish heritage is included in a collection devoted to the discussion of American women writers whose lives and work have been influenced by Judaism.

GABRIEL FIELDING

Alan Gabriel Barnsley

Born: Hexham, Northumberland, England; March 25, 1916

Died: Bellevue, Washington; November 27, 1986

Also known as: Alan Gabriel Barnsley

Principal long fiction

Brotherly Love, 1954
In the Time of Greenbloom, 1956
Eight Days, 1958
Through Streets Broad and Narrow, 1960
The Birthday King, 1962
Gentlemen in Their Season, 1966
Pretty Doll Houses, 1979
The Women of Guinea Lane, 1986

Other literary forms

Gabriel Fielding's literary reputation rests primarily on his prose, but his early work was in poetry, published in two collections, *The Frog Prince, and Other Poems* (1952) and *XXVIII Poems* (1955), neither of which matches his prose in quality or critical acclaim. Fielding also published two books of short stories—*Collected Short Stories* (1971) and *New Queens for Old: A Novella and Nine Stories* (1972)—that are substantial enough in literary quality and theme to form a significant part of Fielding's canon.

Achievements

By 1963, Gabriel Fielding had established the reputation that was maintained, but never enhanced, by his later work. Some critics view Fielding as a Catholic writer, comparable with Graham Greene, Evelyn Waugh, and Muriel Spark, concerned with social and moral issues from a specifically Catholic point of view; this aspect of his work was duly recognized when he was awarded the St. Thomas More Association Gold Medal in 1963 and the National Catholic Book Award in 1964. Other critics, however, see him as a writer belonging to the school of European existentialist writers, sharing their philosophical worldview; this second estimate was expressed in 1963 when Fielding was presented with the W. H. Smith Literary Award.

Biography

Alan Gabriel Barnsley was born in Hexham, Northumberland, England, on March 25, 1916, the fifth of six children of an Anglican vicar. After going to school at St. Edward's, Oxford, he took a B.A. at Trinity College, Dublin, and from there went to St. George's Hospital, London, from which he graduated with a medical degree in 1941. He immediately started his war service in the Royal Army Medical Corps, continuing his service until demobilization in 1946. After the war, he was in general medical practice in Maidstone, Kent, until 1966, part of his duties being those of medical officer for Maidstone Prison, the experience of which contributed significantly to several of his novels. Fielding did not start writing seriously until his middle thirties, and in 1966, when he considered his literary career to be established, he left the medical profession to become author-in-residence and later professor of English at Washington State University, Pullman, a position that he held until retirement. Fielding died in Bellevue, Washington, on November 27, 1986.

Analysis

In the context of British novelists of the twentieth century, Gabriel Fielding presents some characteristics that distinguish his work sharply from that of mainstream novelists and at the same time place him firmly in a tradition that, in fact, goes back to the realistic social novel of Daniel Defoe. Fielding's distinctiveness lies in a steadiness and explicitness of worldview and ethical philosophy that raise his novels well above mere stories or entertainments; his identification with British literary tradition reveals itself in the spell he casts as a storyteller whose characters, plots, and settings have the dramatic quality of those found in the works of Thomas Hardy and Charles Dickens, striking the reader's mind like reality itself and haunting the memory forever. The result of what is, for a British novelist, an unusual combination of philosophical outlook and intensity of fictional realization is an integrated creativity that expresses the writer's unified sensibility of spirit and mind and that evokes within the reader an intense and often uncomfortable urge to reassess his or her own preoccupations and prejudices, yet whose effect is ultimately cathartic.

Fielding's major novels—*In the Time of Greenbloom*, *The Birthday King*, and *Gentlemen in Their Season*—pursue and explore a theme that is found more frequently in the European novel than in the British: that of individual responsibility in an irrational world. Each of the three novels has a different "world" as its setting—a middle-class English county, Nazi Germany, and postwar liberal London—but the dilemmas of decision and action that face the protagonist in each novel are of the same kind. The novels' settings reflect the stages of Fielding's own life: country vicarage and Oxford, wartime military service, and postwar intellectual life in London. In many ways one feels that the novels represent a working-out in fiction of the writer's own perplexities, which were not resolved until his emigration to the United States—to the more primal setting of eastern Washington State and the Moscow Mountains, where it is clear that Fielding found a peace and joy of life, and a professional satisfaction, that had eluded him in England.

The Blaydon novels

The autobiographical element of Fielding's work is seen most clearly in the four novels concerning the Blaydon family. The family name itself is a well-known Northumbrian place-name, while the chronicles of John Blaydon—spanning childhood in *Brotherly Love*, adolescence in *In the Time of Greenbloom*, adulthood and medical studies in *Through Streets Broad and Narrow*, and wartime medical service in *The Women of Guinea Lane*—reflect the early progress of Fielding's own life. Of the three Blaydon novels, *In the Time of Greenbloom* is the most striking, with its presentation of a guilt-ridden and domineering adult society bent on finding sin in the young. In the novel, twelve-year-old John Blaydon is wrongly blamed for the death of his friend Victoria Blount, who has been murdered by a hiker in a cave. He is made the scapegoat for an adult crime, and he is ready to acquiesce in the guilt forced on him by the adult world when he is saved by the ministrations of Horab Greenbloom, an eccentric Jewish Oxford undergraduate who applies to John's sense of guilt a bracing dose of Wittgensteinian positivism and Sartrean existentialism. Greenbloom's therapeutic interest is that of one scapegoat for another, and his remedy is to make John see that the empty, abstract categories of the adult moral scheme lead ultimately to personal irresponsibility and inevitable pangs of guilt that must be transferred to the innocent and vulnerable for punishment.

Fielding had initially explored the theme of blame, and the accompanying figure of the scapegoat, in *Brotherly Love*, in which John observes and chronicles the moral demolition of his older brother, David, by their domineering mother. She forces David to become a priest, thereby perverting his natural creative talents into sordid sexual encounters and alcoholism. In this earlier novel, the adult world is only too successful in transferring its empty notions of duty, faith, sin, and shame to the adolescent, but there is no suggestion of an alternative, redemptive way. *In the Time of Greenbloom* offers hope for redemption in the magus figure of Greenbloom through his resolute opposition to spurious objective abstraction and his insistence that John must make his own moral decisions and not accept those offered by his elders. (In this and in several other respects, Fielding anticipates the concerns and solutions offered in Robertson Davies's *Deptford Trilogy*.)

The Birthday King

The theme of guilt, blame, and the scapegoat principle is one that preoccupies Fielding in all of his major novels, but nowhere does it achieve more compelling realization than in *The Birthday King*, which elevates and generalizes John's suffering in a northern English county to the agony of a whole race in wartime Nazi Germany. The novel chronicles the rise and fall of Nazi Germany through the lives of two Jewish brothers, Alfried and Ruprecht Waitzmann, who are directors of a large industrial group and thus somewhat protected from liquidation by the Nazis. The contrasting responses of the two brothers to the dictatorship of Adolf Hitler represent the twin facts of Jewishness and of humans as a whole in reaction to mindless oppression. Alfried, as a rather self-indulgently pious man, innocent yet provocative, opts for the untidiness of life, represented by the dirty, smelly goat in the Kommandant's garden. His rejection of the hygienic bureaucracy and simple slogans of the Nazis causes him to be imprisoned and tortured in an attempted "cure" of his wayward individuality, and he thus becomes the scapegoat, despised by his friends more than by the Nazis (for whom he actually lightens the burden of guilt). Ruprecht, on the other hand, represents the alternative path: survival at any cost. He is an opportunist and a schemer, preserving the family business by betraying Alfried and running his factories on forced labor for the Nazi regime.

The novel explores the consequences of the brothers' different choices—sacrifice and survival—each of which has been made with existential authenticity, both in their different ways morally "right." Alfried's response, with its mystical innocence and awkward honesty, is that of the child who rejects the adult world of organized belief and consequent absurd moral simplifications. Ruprecht's response is just as true to his own shrewd, aggressive, and lucky nature in a world in which he sees Germany as one gigantic concentration camp in which the only possible choice is for survival. The kind of choice each brother makes is less important than the fact that each actually makes a conscious choice freely, rather than choosing to join the bored sleepwalkers: the camp Kommandant, his puritanical wife, and the aristocratic remnants of old Germany, such as von Hoffbach and von Boehling, who applaud the new Wagnerian romanticism of the Third Reich while sneering at the inferior social status of the Nazi party upstarts. For Fielding, the only corrective to the mind-numbing boredom represented by Nazi Germany is the exercise of free will in subjective decision.

GENTLEMEN IN THEIR SEASON

Boredom provides the focus of *Gentlemen in Their Season* as well, but Fielding narrows his scope to marriage in the postwar, liberated world. In many ways, this novel is more complex than the earlier and, arguably, better novels in that issues are less clear-cut and the possibility of authentic decision is consequently much reduced. Moreover, the setting and characters, in their familiarity and ordinariness, are uncomfortably close to the reader, who is unable to distance himself from the action as he is in *In the Time of Greenbloom* and *The Birthday King*. The plot of *Gentlemen in Their Season* concerns two middle-aged, middle-class liberal intellectuals, Randall Coles and Bernard Presage, whose marriages, to an assertive humanist and a rather religious Catholic, respectively, have stagnated to the point of artificiality, which takes the form of clever parties, esoteric intellectualism, mutual criticism, and automatic churchgoing. Each man drifts into a pointless affair, with tragic consequences for a third party, Hotchkiss, whose simple Christian faith in monogamy has already led to his imprisonment for the manslaughter of his wife's lover, who escapes from prison to confront her current lover, Coles, and to force him to practice the morality that he preaches as director of religious programming for the British Broadcasting Corporation (BBC). In impulsive reaction, and horrified at having to make a simple act of faith in front of Hotchkiss, Coles betrays him to the police, who kill him in their attempted arrest.

This novel, probably the blackest, most ironic, and most comic of all of Fielding's novels, reduces the sleepwalking quality of a whole nation in *The Birthday King* to the level of ordinary, casual, and unthinking behavior of men whose abstract conceptions of what modern marriage should be make them indecisive, vacillating, and morally irresponsible while they continue to justify their behavior on intellectualized principles remote from the concerns of real life. Hotchkiss, by breaking out of prison and confronting Coles, makes the only authentic decision in the whole course of events, and by consciously being an agent, rather than a victim to whom things lamely happen, he forces action on the part of others and thus, in his self-sacrifice, atones for the sins of his intellectual and social superiors.

The central concern in all of Fielding's major novels is the moral necessity for human action in the fullest sense of deliberate, self-aware decisiveness in a society that is largely content to go along with the crowd, to rationalize behavior in terms of social, political, religious, and intellectual abstractions. The actions that result from such decisiveness may, in fact, lead to the protagonist's becoming the scapegoat for society's somnambulistic and self-justifying atrocities but ultimately awaken the sleepwalkers for a while, dazzling people into self-awareness by their enormity. Although this theme is existential, it is a Catholic existentialism, reconciling the principles most fundamental to Christian faith with the natural, human, subjective conscience and promoting will as a necessary accompaniment to belief. Adult institutions of class, politics, and church may, and for most do, substitute slogans for principles and apologetics for action, but the blame lies not in the institutions themselves but in society's slavish and easy acquiescence in the precepts that demand least exercise of will.

The starkness of Fielding's theme associates his work most closely with European preoccupations, constantly reminding the reader of figures such as Jean-Paul Sartre, Albert Camus, Hermann Hesse, and Günter Grass. The only British writer who shares these preoccupations is Graham Greene, whose continentalism makes most British critics, who are more comfortable with what might be called the "cardigan and post office" kind of novel, suspicious of the underlying philosophical concerns of his fiction. The poor critical response in Great Britain to Fielding's work arises, one imagines, from a similar fear of philosophical depth.

Despite the philosophical significance of Fielding's novels, they are works of literature, not of philosophy. What elevates Fielding beyond the level of mere "messenger," didacticist, or programmatic writer is the other face of his work: the elevation of narrative over precept, of imagery and language over naked theme. His novels are by no means mere illustrative allegories of ready-made themes; rather, they are explorations in narrative that lead, perhaps to the surprise of the writer, to inevitable philosophical conclusions. It is the power and richness of plot, character, and language and the concreteness of setting that put Fielding in the grand tradition of the English novel with Dickens, the Brontës, and Hardy, making his novels compelling and memorable in themselves, not merely as vehicles of Catholic-existentialist thought. The elemental images of purifying water and oppressive earth, the institutional images of the prison, the school, the hospital, and the bureaucratic machinery, together with the evocative associations of proper names (Badger, Toad, Greenbloom, Hubertus, and Presage), interweave with one another and with settings rich in symbolism (the cave where Victoria is murdered, the Anglo-Catholic church with its dead image of Christ, the deserted swimming pool where Ruprecht and Carin make love, the camp of forced workers, Alfried's punishment cell, and Hotchkiss's prison cell), creating a text of such richness as to transcend its constituent parts and to enter the reader's consciousness like reality itself. The texture of Fielding's language is that of the best dramatic poetry: Images, allusions, and references, in the vigorous expression of quite ordinary speech, cluster and weave to engender a depth and breadth of experience that triggers unconscious associations supporting the reader's conscious interpretation of plot and character to produce a wholly new, vital, and often disturbing sensibility.

Frederick Bowers

Other major works

SHORT FICTION: *Collected Short Stories*, 1971; *New Queens for Old: A Novella and Nine Stories*, 1972.

POETRY: *The Frog Prince, and Other Poems*, 1952; *XXVIII Poems*, 1955.

Bibliography

Bloom, Harold, ed. *Twentieth Century British Literature*. Vol. 2. New York: Chelsea House, 1986. Entry on Fielding in this encyclopedic collection lists his works up to his novel *Pretty Doll Houses*. Also reprints an interview with Fielding from 1967, titled "The Longing for Spring," that provides much useful information on the author and his work.

Borrello, Alfred. *Gabriel Fielding*. New York: Twayne, 1974. Provides a good introduction to Fielding's life and works. Includes bibliographical references and an index.

Bowers, Frederick. "Gabriel Fielding." In *Contempo-*

rary Novelists, edited by James Vinson. London: St. James Press, 1976. Appraises Fielding in the light of his growing reputation as a major novelist. Presents commentary on three of his novels: *In the Time of Greenbloom, The Birthday King*, and *Gentlemen in Their Season*.

_______. "Gabriel Fielding's *The Birthday King." The Queen's Quarterly* 74 (Spring, 1967): 148-158. Bowers explores the themes of guilt, innocence, and personal responsibility in this novel, comparing the work to that of existentialists Albert Camus and Jean-Paul Sartre.

_______. "The Unity of Fielding's *Greenbloom*." Review of *In the Time of Greenbloom*, by Gabriel Fielding. *Renascence* 18 (Spring, 1966): 147-155. Favorable review asserts that the novel is of "major importance and worth in theme and execution." Comments on the existentialist nature of the novel, comparing it to the philosophy of Søren Kierkegaard, and on the scapegoat theme in this work.

HENRY FIELDING

Born: Sharpham Park, Somersetshire, England; April 22, 1707
Died: Lisbon, Portugal; October 8, 1754

Principal long fiction

An Apology for the Life of Mrs. Shamela Andrews, 1741 (commonly known as *Shamela*)
The History of the Adventures of Joseph Andrews, and of His Friend Mr. Abraham Adams, 1742 (commonly known as *Joseph Andrews*)
The History of the Life of the Late Mr. Jonathan Wild the Great, 1743 (revised 1754; commonly known as *Jonathan Wild*)
The History of Tom Jones, a Foundling, 1749 (commonly known as *Tom Jones*)
Amelia, 1751

Other literary forms

Henry Fielding's literary output, aside from his novels, can be categorized into three groups: plays, pamphlets and miscellaneous items, and journals. In addition, the publication of his three-volume *Miscellanies* (1743) by subscription brought together a number of previously published items as well as new works, including the first version of *Jonathan Wild*, and an unfinished prose work, "A Journey from This World to the Next."

Fielding's dramatic works, many presented with great success at either London's Little Theatre in the Haymarket or the Drury Lane Theatre, include ballad opera, farce, full-length comedy, and adaptations of classical and French drama. Most are overtly political in theme. Because of their contemporary subject matter, few have survived as viable stage presentations, although *The Covent Garden Tragedy* (pr., pb. 1732) was presented by the Old Vic in London in 1968. Fielding also wrote a number of prologues, epilogues, and monologues that were performed in conjunction with other dramatic pieces.

The pamphlets and miscellaneous items that are currently attributed to Fielding, excluding those for which he merely wrote introductions or epilogues, are "The Masquerade" (1728), a poem; *The Military History of Charles XII King of Sweden* (1740), a translation; "Of True Greatness" (1741), a poem; "The Opposition: A Vision" (1741), a poem; "The Vernoniad" (1741), a poem; "The Female Husband" (1746); "Ovid's Art of Love Paraphrased" (1747); "A True State of the Case of Bosavern Penlez" (1749); "An Enquiry into the Causes of the Late Increase in Robbers" (1751); "Examples of the Interposition of Providence in the Detection and Punishment of Murder" (1752); "A Proposal for Making an Effectual Provision for the Poor" (1753); "A Clear State of the Case of Elizabeth Canning" (1753); and *The Journal of a Voyage to Lisbon*, which was published posthumously (1755).

Fielding edited and made major contributions to four

journals: *The Champion* (November 15, 1739-June, 1741; the journal continued publication without Fielding until 1742); *The True Patriot* (November 5, 1745-June 17, 1746); *Jacobite's Journal* (December 5, 1747-November 5, 1748); and *The Covent-Garden Journal* (January 4-November 25, 1752).

Achievements

Fielding's lasting achievements in prose fiction—in contrast to his passing fame as an essayist, dramatist, and judge—result from his development of critical theory and from his aesthetic success in the novels themselves. In the preface to *Joseph Andrews*, Fielding establishes a serious critical basis for the novel as a genre and describes in detail the elements of comic realism; in *Joseph Andrews* and *Tom Jones*, he provides full realizations of this theory. These novels define the ground rules of form that would be followed, to varying degrees, by Jane Austen, William Makepeace Thackeray, George Eliot, Thomas Hardy, James Joyce, and D. H. Lawrence, and they also speak to countless readers across many generations. Both novels, in fact, have been translated into successful films (*Tom Jones* was released in 1963; *Joseph Andrews*, in 1977).

The historical importance of the preface to *Joseph Andrews* results from both the seriousness with which it treats the formal qualities of the novel (at the time a fledgling and barely respectable genre) and the precision with which it defines the characteristics of the genre, the "comic epic-poem in prose." Fielding places *Joseph Andrews* in particular and the comic novel in general squarely in the tradition of classical literature and coherently argues its differences from the romance and the burlesque. He also provides analogies between the comic novel and the visual arts. Fielding thus leads the reader to share his conception that the comic novel is an aesthetically valid form with its roots in classical tradition and a form peculiarly suited to the attitudes and values of its own age.

With his background in theater and journalism, Fielding could move easily through a wide range of forms and rhetorical techniques in his fiction, from direct parody of Samuel Richardson in *An Apology for the Life of Mrs. Shamela Andrews* to ironic inversion of the great man's biography in *Jonathan Wild* to adaptation of classical structure (Vergil's *Aeneid*, c. 29-19 B.C.E.; English translation, 1553) in *Amelia*. The two major constants in these works are the attempt to define a good, moral life, built on benevolence and honor, and a concern for finding the best way to present that definition to the reader. Thus the moral and the technique can never be separated in Fielding's works.

Joseph Andrews and *Tom Jones* bring together these two impulses in Fielding's most organically structured, brilliantly characterized, and masterfully narrated works. These novels vividly capture the diversity of experience in the physical world and the underlying benevolence of the natural order, embodying them in a rich array of the ridiculous in human behavior. Fielding combines a positive assertion of the strength of goodness and benevolence (demonstrated by the structure and plot of the novels) with the sharp thrusts of the satirist's attack on the hypocrisy and vanity of individual characters. These elements are held together by the voice of the narrator—witty, urbane, charming—who serves as moral guide through the novels and the world. Thus beyond the comic merits of each of the individual novels lies a collective sense of universal moral good. The voice of the narrator conveys to the reader the truth of that goodness.

Although the novels were popular in his own day, Fielding's contemporaries thought of him more as playwright-turned-judge than as novelist. This may have been the result of the low esteem in which the novel as a form was held as well as of Fielding's brilliant successes in these other fields. These varied successes have in common a zest for the exploration of the breadth and variety of life—a joy in living—that finds its most articulate and permanent expression in the major novels.

Today Fielding is universally acknowledged as a major figure in the development of the novel, although there is still some debate about whether he or Richardson is the "father" of the British novel. Ian Watt, for example, has asserted that Richardson's development of "formal realism" is more significant than Fielding's comic realism. Other critics, notably Martin Battestin, have demonstrated that Fielding's broader, more humane moral vision, embodied in classical structure and expressed through a self-conscious narrator, is the germ from which the richness and variety of the British novel grows. This disagreement ultimately comes down to personal taste, and there will always be Richardson and Fielding partisans to keep the controversy alive. There is no argument, however, that of their type—the novel of comic realism—no fiction has yet surpassed *Joseph Andrews* or *Tom Jones*.

Biography

Henry Fielding was born April 22, 1707, in Sharpham Park, Somersetshire, to Edmund and Sarah Fielding. His father, an adventurer, gambler, and swaggerer, was a sharp contrast to the quiet, conservative, traditional gentry of his mother's family, the Goulds. In 1710, the family moved to Dorset, where Fielding and his younger brother and three sisters (including the future novelist Sarah Fielding) would spend most of their childhood on a small estate and farm given to Mrs. Fielding by her father, Sir Henry Gould.

The death of Fielding's mother in April, 1718, ended this idyllic life. Litigation over the estate created a series of family battles that raged for several decades. In 1719, Fielding was sent to Eton College, partly because the Goulds wanted him influenced as little as possible by his father, who had resumed his "wild" life in London, and partly because Fielding disliked his father's new Catholic wife. Remaining at Eton until 1724 or 1725, Fielding made many friends, including George Lyttleton and William Pitt. At Eton he began his study of classical literature, which became a profound influence on his literary career.

Few details are known of Fielding's life during the several years after Eton. He spent a good deal of time with the Goulds in Salisbury, but he also led a hectic, boisterous life in London, spending much time at the theater, where the popular masquerades and burlesques influenced him greatly. His visits to the theater stimulated him to try his own hand at comedy, and in February, 1728, *Love in Several Masques*, based on his own romantic adventures of the previous year, was performed at Drury Lane. In March, 1728, Fielding enrolled in the Faculty of Letters at the University of Leyden (Netherlands), where he pursued his interest in the classics. In August, 1729, at the age of twenty-two, he returned to London without completing his degree.

It is clear from his literary output in the 1730's that Fielding was intensely involved in theatrical life. From 1730 through 1737 he authored at least nineteen different dramatic works (as well as presenting revivals and new productions of revised works), most with political themes, at both the Little Theatre in the Haymarket and the Drury Lane. In addition to writing ballad opera, full-length comedies, translations, and parodies, Fielding was also producing, revising the plays of other writers, and managing theater business. He also formed a new, important friendship with the artist William Hogarth.

His theatrical career came to an abrupt halt (although a few more plays appeared in the 1740's) with the passage of the Licensing Act of 1737 which resulted in the closing of many theaters. Fielding's political satire offended Prime Minister Sir Robert Walpole and had been part of the motivation for the government's desire to control and censor the theaters.

In addition to this theatrical activity with its political commentary, Fielding found time in the years 1733-1734 to court and marry Charlotte Cradock of Salisbury. Charlotte's mother died in 1735, leaving the entire estate to the Fieldings and alleviating many of the financial problems caused by the legal disputes over the estate in Dorset. The couple moved from London to East Stour the same year, although Fielding regularly visited London, because he was manager, artistic director, and controller in chief of the Little Theatre. The first of their three children, Charlotte, was born April 17, 1736.

Fielding's relentless energy (and desire to add to his income) compelled him to begin a new career in late 1737, whereupon he began to study law at the Middle Temple. He became a barrister on June 20, 1740, and spent the next several years in the Western Circuit. During this service he became friends with Ralph Allen of Bath. He remained active in the practice of justice, as attorney and magistrate, until he left England in 1754.

Fielding continued to involve himself in political controversy, even while studying law. He edited, under pseudonyms, *The Champion*, an opposition newspaper issued three times a week, directed against Prime Minister Walpole (a favorite subject of Fielding's satire). Later he would edit *The True Patriot* in support of the government during the threat of the Jacobite Rising, *Jacobite's Journal*, and *The Covent-Garden Journal*.

From theater to law to journalism—Fielding had already charged through three careers when the first in-

Henry Fielding. (Library of Congress)

stallment of Richardson's *Pamela: Or, Virtue Rewarded* appeared on November 6, 1740. Deeply disturbed by the artificiality of the novel's epistolary technique, and appalled by its perversion of moral values, Fielding quickly responded with *An Apology for the Life of Mrs. Shamela Andrews*, often referred to as *Shamela*, an "antidote" to *Pamela*. Although published anonymously, Fielding's authorship was apparent and created ill feelings between the two authors that would last most of their lives.

The success of *Shamela* encouraged Fielding to try his hand at a more sustained satire, which eventually grew into *Joseph Andrews*. In 1743 he published, by subscription, the *Miscellanies*, a collection of previously published works, and two new ones: an unfinished story, "A Journey from This World to the Next," and the first version of *Jonathan Wild*.

Although the mid-1740's brought Fielding fame, success, and money, his personal life was beset with pain. He suffered continually from gout, and his wife died in November, 1744. In the following year he became involved in the propaganda battles over the Jacobite Rising. On November 27, 1747, he married his wife's former maid, Mary Daniel, and some sense of peace and order was restored to his private life. They would have five children.

While forming new personal ties and continuing strong involvement in political issues, Fielding was preparing his masterwork, *Tom Jones*. He also took oath as justice of the peace for Westminster and Middlesex, London, in 1748, and he opened an employment agency and estate brokerage with his brother in 1749. His last novel, *Amelia*, was not well received, disappointing those readers who were expecting another *Tom Jones*.

The early 1750's saw Fielding's health continue to decline, although he remained active in his judgeship, producing a number of pamphlets on various legal questions. In June of 1754, his friends convinced him to sail to Lisbon, Portugal, where the climate might improve his health. He died there on October 8, 1754, and is buried in the British Cemetery outside Lisbon. *The Journal of a Voyage to Lisbon*, his last work, was published one year after his death.

Analysis

Analysis and criticism of Henry Fielding's fiction have traditionally centered on the moral values in the novels, the aesthetic structure in which they are placed, and the relationship between the two. In this view, Fielding as moralist takes precedence over Fielding as artist, since the aesthetic structure is determined by the moral. Each of the novels is judged by the extent to which it finds the appropriate form for its moral vision. The relative failure of *Amelia*, for example, may be Fielding's lack of faith in his own moral vision. The happy ending, promulgated by the deus ex machina of the good magistrate, is hardly consistent with the dire effects of urban moral decay that have been at work upon the Booths throughout the novel. Fielding's own moral development and changes in outlook also need to be considered in this view. The reader must examine the sources of Fielding's moral vision in the latitudinarian sermons of the day, as well as the changes in his attitudes as he examined eighteenth century urban life in greater detail, and as he moved in literature from *Joseph Andrews* to *Amelia*, and in life from the theater to the bench of justice.

As is clear from the preface to *Joseph Andrews*, however, Fielding was equally interested in the aesthetics of his fiction. Indeed, each of the novels, even from the first parody, *Shamela*, conveys not only a moral message but a literary experiment to find the strongest method for expressing that message to the largest reading public. This concern is evident in the basic plot structure, characterization, language, and role of the narrator. Each novel attempts to reach the widest audience possible with its moral thesis. Although each differs in the way in which Fielding attempts this, they all have in common the sense that the *how* of the story is as important as the *what*. The novels are experiments in the methods of moral education—for the reader as well as for the characters.

This concern for the best artistic way to teach a moral lesson was hardly new with Fielding. His classical education and interests, as well as the immediate human response gained from theater audiences during his playwriting days, surely led him to see that fiction must delight as well as instruct. Fielding's novels are both exemplars of this goal (in their emphasis on incidents of plot and broad range of characterization) and serious discussions of the method by which to achieve it (primarily through structure and through narrative commentary).

The direct stimulation for Fielding's career as novelist was the publication of Samuel Richardson's *Pamela*, a novel that disturbed Fielding both by its artistic ineptitude and by its moral vacuousness. Fielding was as concerned with the public reaction to *Pamela* as he was with its author's methods. That the reading public could be so easily misled by *Pamela*'s morals disturbed Fielding deeply, and the success of that novel led him to ponder what better ways were available for reaching the public with his own moral thesis. His response to *Pamela* was both moral (he revealed the true state of Pamela/Shamela's values) and aesthetic (he exposed the artificiality of "writing to the moment").

Sermons and homilies, while effective in church (and certainly sources of Fielding's moral philosophy), were not the stuff of prose fiction; neither was the epistolary presentation of "virtue rewarded" of *Pamela* (or the "objectively" amoral tone of Daniel Defoe's *The Fortunes and Misfortunes of the Famous Moll Flanders, Written from Her Own Memorandums*, 1722). Fielding sought a literary method for combining moral vision and literary pleasure that would be appropriate to the rapidly urbanizing and secular society of the mid-eighteenth century. To find that method he ranged through direct parody, irony, satire, author-narrator intrusion, and moral exemplum. Even those works, such as *Jonathan Wild* and *Amelia*, which are not entirely successful, live because of the vitality of Fielding's experimental methods. In *Joseph Andrews* and *Tom Jones*, he found the way to reach his audience most effectively.

Fielding's informing moral values, embodied in the central characters of the novels (Joseph Andrews, Parson Adams, Tom Jones, Squire Allworthy, Mr. Harrison) can be summarized, as Martin Battestin has ably done, as Charity, Prudence, and Providence. Fielding held an optimistic faith in the perfectability of humanity and the potential for the betterment of society, based on the essential goodness of human nature. These three values must work together. In the novels, the hero's worth is determined by the way in which he interacts with other people (charity), within the limits of social institutions designed to provide order (prudence). His reward is a life full of God's provision (Providence). God's Providence has created a world of abundance and plenitude; man's prudence and charity can guarantee its survival and growth. Both Joseph Andrews and Tom Jones learn the proper combination of prudence and charity. They learn to use their innate inclination toward goodness within a social system that ensures order. To succeed, however, they must overcome obstacles provided by the characters who, through vanity and hypocrisy, distort God's Providence. Thus Fielding's moral vision, while optimistic, is hardly blind to the realities of the world. *Jonathan Wild*, with its basic rhetorical distinction between "good" and "great," and *Amelia*, with its narrative structured around the ill effects of doing good, most strongly reflect Fielding's doubts about the practicality of his beliefs.

These ideas can be easily schematized, but the scheme belies the human complexity through which they are expressed in the novels. Tom Jones is no paragon of virtue, but he must learn, at great physical pain and spiritual risk, how to combine charity and prudence. Even Squire Allworthy is, as Sheldon Sacks has observed, a "fallible" paragon. These ideas do not come from a single source, but are derived from a combination of sources, rooted in Fielding's classical education; the political, religious, and literary movements of his own time; and his own experience as dramatist, journalist, and magistrate.

Fielding's familiarity with the classics, begun at Eton and continued at the University of Leyden, is revealed in many ways: through language (the use of epic simile and epic conventions in *Joseph Andrews*), through plot (the symmetry of design in *Tom Jones*), through theme (the importance of moderation in all the novels), and through structure (the relationship of *Amelia* to Vergil's *Aeneid*). The preface to *Joseph Andrews* makes explicit how much Fielding saw in common between his own work and classical literature. His belief in the benevolent order of the world, especially illustrated by country living, such as at Squire Allworthy's estate (Paradise Hall), is deeply rooted in the pastoral tradition of classical literature. These classical elements are combined with the beliefs of the latitudinarian homilists of the seventeenth and eighteenth centuries, who stressed the perfectibility of humankind in the world through good deeds (charity) and good heart (benevolence).

While Fielding's thematic concerns may be rooted in classical and Christian thought, his literary technique has sources that are more complex, deriving from his education, his own experience in the theater, and the influence of Richardson's *Pamela*. It is difficult to separate each of these sources, for the novels work them into unified and original statements. Indeed, *Joseph Andrews*, the novel most closely related to classical sources, is also deeply imbued with the sense of latitudinarian thought in its criticism of the clergy, and satire of Richardson in its plot and moral vision.

The London in which Fielding spent most of his life was a world of literary and political ferment, an age of factionalism in the arts, with the Tory wits (Jonathan Swift, Alexander Pope, John Gay, John Arbuthnot) allied against Colley Cibber, the poet laureate and self-proclaimed literary spokesman for the British Isles. Swift's *Gulliver's Travels* (1726) and Gay's *The Beggar's Opera* (1728) had recently appeared; both were influential in forming Fielding's literary methods—the first with its emphasis on sharp political satire, the second with the creation of a new literary form, the ballad opera. The ballad opera set new lyrics, expressing contemporary political and social satire, to well-known music. Fielding was to find his greatest theatrical success in this genre and was to carry it over to his fiction, especially *Jonathan Wild*, with its emphasis on London low life and its excesses of language.

It was a time, also, of great political controversy, with the ongoing conflicts between the Tories and Jacobites about the questions of religion and succession. Prime Minister Walpole's politics of expediency were a ripe subject for satire. Fielding's career as journalist began as a direct response to political issues, and significant portions of *Joseph Andrews* and *Tom Jones*, as well as *Jonathan Wild*, deal with political issues.

These various sources, influences, and beliefs are molded into coherent works of art through Fielding's narrative technique. It is through the role of the narrator that he most clearly and successfully experiments in the methods of teaching a moral lesson. Starting with the voice of direct literary parody in *Shamela* and moving through the varied structures and voices of the other novels, Fielding's art leads in many directions, but it always leads to his ultimate concern for finding the best way to teach the clearest moral lesson. In *Tom Jones* he finds the most appropriate method to demonstrate that the world is a beautiful place if people practice charity and prudence.

Shamela

The key to understanding how *Shamela* expresses Fielding's concern with both the moral thesis and the aesthetic form of fiction is contained in the introductory letters between Parsons Tickletext and Oliver. Oliver is dismayed at Tickletext's exuberant praise of *Pamela* and at the novel's public reception and popularity. The clergy, in particular, have been citing it as a work worthy to be read with the Scriptures. He contends that the text of *Shamela*, which he encloses, reveals the "true" story of Pamela's adventures and puts them in their proper moral perspective. By reading Oliver's version, Tickletext will correct his own misconceptions; by reading *Shamela* (under the guidance of the prefatory letters), the public will laugh at *Pamela* and perceive the perversity of its moral thesis.

Shamela began, of course, simply as a parody of Richardson's novel, and, in abbreviated form, carries through the narrative of the attempted seduction of the young serving girl by the squire, and her attempts to assert her virtue through chastity or marriage. Fielding makes direct hits at Richardson's weakest points: His two main targets are the epistolary technique of "writing to the moment" and the moral thesis of "virtue rewarded" by pounds and pence (and marriage).

Fielding parodies the epistolary technique by carrying it to its most illogical extreme: Richardson's technical failure is not the choice of epistolary form, but his insistence on its adherence to external reality. Shamela writes her letters at the very same moment she is being attacked in bed by Squire Booby. While feigning sleep she writes: "You see I write in the present tense." The inconsistency of Pamela's shift from letters to journal form when she is abducted is shown through Fielding's retention of the letter form throughout the story, no matter what the obstacles for sending and receiving them. He also compounds the criticism of Richardson by including a number of correspondents in addition to Shamela (her mother, Henrietta Maria Honora Andrews, Mrs. Jewkes, Parson Williams) and including various complications, such as letters within letters within letters.

Fielding retains the essential characters and key scenes from *Pamela*, such as Mr. B's hiding in the closet before the attempted seduction, Pamela's attempted suicide at the pond, and Parson Williams's interference. For each character and scene Fielding adopts Richardson's penchant for minute descriptive detail and intense character response to the event; he also parodies the method and seriousness of the original by revealing the motives of the characters.

The revealing of motives is also Fielding's primary way of attacking the prurience of Richardson's presentation as well as the moral thesis behind it. He debunks the punctilio (decorum) of the central character. Shamela's false modesty ("I thought once of making a little fortune by my person. I now intend to make a great one by my virtue") mocks Pamela's pride in her chastity; the main difference between them is Shamela's recognition and acceptance of the mercenary motives behind her behavior and Pamela's blindness to her own motivation. Richardson never examines the reliability of Pamela's motivations, although he describes her thoughts in detail. Fielding allows Shamela to glory in both her ability to dupe the eager Squire Booby and her mercenary motives for doing so. The reader may, as Parson Oliver wants Tickletext to do, easily condemn Shamela for a villain but never for a hypocrite.

Fielding also attacks Richardson's refusal to describe the sexual attributes of his characters or to admit the intensity of their sexual desires, particularly in the case of Pamela herself. Pamela always hints and suggests—and, Fielding claims, wallows in her suggestiveness. Fielding not only describes the sexual aspects directly, but exaggerates and reduces them to a comic level, hardly to be taken sensually or seriously. *Shamela* quickly, fully, and ruthlessly annihilates the moral thesis of "virtue rewarded" through this direct exaggeration. Fielding does not, however, in his role as parodist, suggest an alternative to *Pamela*'s moral thesis; he is content, for the time, with exposing its flaws.

This first foray into fiction served for Fielding as a testing ground for some of the rhetorical techniques he used in later works, especially the emphasis on satiric inversion. These inversions appear in his reversal of sexual roles in *Joseph Andrews*, the reversal of rhetoric in the "good" and "great" in *Jonathan Wild*, and the reversal of goodness of motive and evil of effect in *Amelia*. Fielding's concern to find a rhetorical method for presenting a moral thesis was confined in *Shamela* to the limited aims and goals of parody. He had such success with the method (after all, he had his apprenticeship in the satiric comedy of the theater), that he began his next novel on the same model.

Joseph Andrews

Like *Shamela*, *Joseph Andrews* began as a parody of *Pamela*. In his second novel, Fielding reverses the gender of the central character and traces Joseph's attempts to retain his chastity and virtue while being pursued by Lady Booby. This method of inversion creates new possibilities, not only for satirizing Richardson's work but for commenting on the sexual morality of the time in a more positive way than in *Shamela*. The most cursory reading reveals how quickly Fielding grew tired of parody and how *Joseph Andrews* moved beyond its inspiration and its forerunner. Even the choice of direct narration rather than epistolary form indicates Fielding's unwillingness to tie himself to his model.

Most readers agree that the entrance of Parson Adams, Joseph's guide, companion, and partner in misery, turns the novel from simple parody into complex fiction. Adams takes center stage as both comic butt, preserving Joseph's role as hero, and moral guide, preserving Joseph's role as innocent.

Adams's contribution is also part of Fielding's conscious search for the best way to convey his moral thesis. The narrative refers continually to sermons, given in the pulpit or being carried by Adams to be published in London. These sermons are generally ineffectual or contradicted by the behavior of the clergy who pronounce them. Just as experience and the moral example of Adams's life are better teachers for Joseph than sermons—what could be a more effective lesson than the way he is treated by the coach passengers after he is robbed, beaten, and stripped?—so literary example has more power for Fielding and the reader. Adams's constant companion, his copy of Aeschylus, is further testament to Fielding's growing faith in his exemplary power of literature as moral guide. In *Joseph Andrews*, narrative art takes precedence over both parody and sermon.

Fielding's concern for method as well as meaning is given its most formal discussion in the preface. The historical importance of this document results from both the seriousness with which it treats the formal qualities of the novel and the precision with which it defines the characteristics of the genre, the "comic epic-poem in prose." The seriousness is established through the careful logic and organization of the argument and through the parallels drawn between the new genre and classical literature (the lost comic epic supposedly written by Homer) and modern painting (Michelangelo da Caravaggio and William Hogarth).

Fielding differentiates the "comic epic-poem in prose" from contemporary romances such as *Pamela*. The new form is more extended and comprehensive in action, contains a much larger variety of incidents, and treats a greater variety of characters. Unlike the serious romance, the new form is less solemn in subject matter, treats characters of lower rank, and presents the ludicrous rather than the sublime. The comic, opposed to the burlesque, arises solely from the observation of nature, and has its source in the discovery of the "ridiculous" in human nature. The ridiculous always springs from the affectations of vanity and hypocrisy.

Within the novel itself, the narrator will continue the discussion of literary issues in the introductory chapters to each of the first three of four books: "of writing lives in general," "of divisions in authors," and "in praise of biography." These discussions, although sometimes more facetious than serious, do carry through the direction of the opening sentence of the novel: "Examples work more forcibly on the mind than precepts." Additionally, this narrative commentary allows Fielding to assume the role of reader's companion and guide that he develops more fully in *Tom Jones*.

While the preface takes its cue from classical tradition, it is misleading to assume that *Joseph Andrews* is merely an updating of classical technique and ideas. Even more than *Shamela*, this novel brings together Fielding's dissatisfaction with Richardson's moral thesis and his support of latitudinarian attitudes toward benevolence and charity. Here, too, Fielding begins his definition of the "good" man in modern Christian terms. Joseph redefines the place of chastity and honor in male sexuality; Parson Adams exemplifies the benevolence all people should display; Mrs. Tow-wowse, Trulliber, and Peter Pounce, among others, illustrate the vanity and hypocrisy of the world.

The structure of the novel is episodic, combining the earthly journey and escapades of the hero with suggestions of the Christian pilgrimage in John Bunyan's *The Pilgrim's Progress* (1678, 1684). Fielding was still experimenting with form and felt at liberty to digress from his structure with interpolated tales or to depend on coincidence to bring the novel to its conclusion. The immediate moral effect sometimes seems more important than the consistency of rhetorical structure. These are, however, minor lapses in Fielding's progression toward unifying moral thesis and aesthetic structure.

JONATHAN WILD

In *Jonathan Wild*, Fielding seems to have abandoned temporarily the progression from the moral statement of parody and sermon to the aesthetic statement of literary example. *Jonathan Wild* was first published in the year immediately following *Joseph Andrews* (revised in

1754), and there is evidence to indicate that the work was actually written before *Joseph Andrews*. This is a reasonable assumption, since *Jonathan Wild* is more didactic in its method and more negative in its moral vision. It looks back toward *Shamela* rather than ahead to *Tom Jones*.

Jonathan Wild is less a novel, even as Fielding discusses the form in the preface to *Joseph Andrews*, than a polemic. Critic Northrop Frye's term "anatomy" may be the most appropriate label for the work. Like other anatomies—Sir Thomas More's *De Optimo Reipublicae Statu, deque Nova Insula Utopia* (*Utopia*, 1551), Swift's *Gulliver's Travels*, and Samuel Johnson's *Rasselas, Prince of Abyssinia* (1759)—it emphasizes ideas over narrative. It is more moral fable than novel, and more fiction than historical biography, altering history to fit the moral vision.

More important, it was Fielding's experiment in moving the moral lesson of the tale away from the narrative (with its emphasis on incident and character) and into the rhetoric of the narrator (with its emphasis on language). Fielding attempted to use language as the primary carrier of his moral thesis. Although this experiment failed—manipulation of language, alone, would not do—it gave him the confidence to develop the role of the narrative voice in its proper perspective in *Tom Jones*.

Fielding freely adapted the facts of Wild's life, which were well known to the general public. He chose those incidents from Wild's criminal career and punishment that would serve his moral purpose, and he added his own fictional characters, the victims of Wild's "greatness," especially the Heartfrees. Within the structure of the inverted biography of the "great" man, Fielding satirizes the basic concepts of middle-class society. He differentiates between "greatness" and "goodness," terms often used synonymously in the eighteenth century. The success of the novel depends on the reader's acceptance and understanding of this rhetorical inversion.

"Goodness," characterized by the Heartfrees, reiterates the ideals of behavior emphasized in *Joseph Andrews:* benevolence, honor, honesty, and charity, felt through the heart. "Greatness," personified in Wild, results in cunning and courage, characteristics of the will. The action of the novel revolves around the ironic reversal of these terms. Although Wild's actions speak for themselves, the ironic voice of the narrator constantly directs the reader's response.

Parts of *Jonathan Wild* are brilliantly satiric, but the work as a whole does not speak to modern readers. Fielding abandoned the anatomy form after this experiment, recognizing that the voice of the narrator alone cannot carry the moral thesis of a novel in a convincing way. In *Jonathan Wild*, he carried to an extreme the role of the narrator as moral guide that he experimented with in *Joseph Andrews*. In *Tom Jones*, he found the precise balance: the moral voice of the narrator controlling the reader's reaction through language and the literary examples of plot and character.

Tom Jones

In *Tom Jones*, Fielding moved beyond the limited aims of each of his previous works into a more comprehensive moral and aesthetic vision. No longer bound by the need to attack Richardson or by the attempt to define a specific fictional form, such as the moral fable or the "comic epic-poem in prose," Fielding dramatized the positive values of the good man in a carefully structured narrative held together by the guiding voice of the narrator. This narrator unifies, in a consistent pattern, Fielding's concern for both the truthfulness of his moral vision and the best way to reach the widest audience.

The structure of *Tom Jones*, like that of *Joseph Andrews*, is based on the secularization of the spiritual pilgrimage. Tom must journey from his equivocal position as foundling on the country estate of Squire Allworthy (Paradise Hall) to moral independence in the hellish city of London. He must learn to understand and control his life. When he learns this lesson, he will return to the country to enjoy the plenitude of paradise regained that Providence allows him. He must temper his natural, impetuous charity with the prudence that comes from recognition of his own role in the larger social structure. In precise terms, he must learn to control his animal appetites in order to win the love of Sophia Western and the approval of Allworthy. This lesson is rewarded not only by his gaining these two goals, but by his gaining the knowledge of his parentage and his rightful place in society. He is no longer a "foundling."

Unlike the episodic journey of *Joseph Andrews*, *Tom Jones* adapts the classical symmetry of the epic in a more conscious and precise way. The novel is divided into eighteen books. Some of the books, such as 1 and 4, cover long periods of time and are presented in summary form, with the narrator clearly present; others cover only a few days or hours, with the narrator conspicuously absent and the presentation primarily scenic. The length of each book is determined by the importance of the subject, not the length of time covered.

The books are arranged in a symmetrical pattern. The first half of the novel takes Tom from his mysterious birth to his adventures in the Inn at Upton; the second half takes him from Upton to London and the discovery of his parentage. Books 1 through 6 are set in Somerset at Squire Allworthy's estate and culminate with Tom's affair with Molly. Books 7 through 12 are set on the road to Upton, at the Inn, and on the road from Upton to London; the two central books detail the adventures at the Inn and Tom's affair with Mrs. Waters. Books 13 through 18 take Tom to London and begin with his affair with Lady Bellaston.

Within this pattern, Fielding demonstrates his moral thesis, the education of a "good man," in a number of ways: through the narrative (Tom's behavior continually lowers his moral worth in society); through characters (the contrasting pairs of Tom and Blifil, Allworthy and Western, Square and Thwackum, Molly and Lady Bellaston); and through the voice of the narrator.

Fielding extends the role of the narrator in *Tom Jones*, as teller of the tale, as moral guide, and as literary commentator and critic. Each of these voices was heard in *Joseph Andrews*, but here they come together in a unique narrative persona. Adopting the role of the stagecoach traveler, the narrator speaks directly to his fellow passengers, the readers. He is free to digress and comment whenever he feels appropriate, and there is, therefore, no need for the long interpolated tales such as appeared in *Joseph Andrews*.

To remind his readers that the purpose of fiction is aesthetic as well as moral, the narrator often comments on literary topics: "Of the Serious in Writing, and for What Purpose it is introduced"; "A wonderful long chapter concerning the Marvelous"; "Containing Instructions very necessary to be perused by modern Critics." Taken together, these passages provide a guide to Fielding's literary theory as complete as the preface to *Joseph Andrews*.

Although in *Tom Jones* Fielding still schematically associates characters with particular moral values, the range of characters is wider than in his previous novels. Even a minor character, such as Black George, has a life beyond his moral purpose as representative of hypocrisy and self-servingness.

Most important, *Tom Jones* demonstrates Fielding's skill in combining his moral vision with aesthetic form in a way that is most pleasurable to the reader. The reader learns how to live the good Christian life because Tom learns that lesson. Far more effective than parody, sermon, or moral exemplum, the combination of narrative voice and literary example of plot and character is Fielding's greatest legacy to the novel.

Lawrence F. Laban

Other major works

PLAYS: *Love in Several Masques*, pr., pb. 1728; *The Author's Farce, and the Pleasures of the Town*, pr., pb. 1730; *Rape upon Rape: Or, Justice Caught in His Own Trap*, pr., pb. 1730 (also known as *The Coffee-House Politician*); *The Temple Beau*, pr., pb. 1730; *Tom Thumb: A Tragedy*, pr., pb. 1730 (revised as *The Tragedy of Tragedies: Or, The Life and Death of Tom Thumb the Great*, pr., pb. 1731); *The Letter-Writers: Or, A New Way to Keep a Wife at Home*, pr., pb. 1731; *The Welsh Opera: Or, The Grey Mare the Better Horse*, pr., pb. 1731 (revised as *The Grub-Street Opera*, pb. 1731); *The Covent Garden Tragedy*, pr., pb. 1732; *The Lottery*, pr., pb. 1732; *The Mock Doctor: Or, The Dumb Lady Cur'd*, pr., pb. 1732 (adaptation of Molière's *Le Medecin malgré lui*); *The Modern Husband*, pr., pb. 1732 (five acts); *The Old Debauchees*, pr., pb. 1732; *The Miser*, pr., pb. 1733 (adaptation of Molière's *L'Avare*); *Don Quixote in England*, pr., pb. 1734; *The Intriguing Chambermaid*, pr., pb. 1734 (adaptation of Jean-François Regnard's *Le Retour imprévu*); *An Old Man Taught Wisdom: Or, The Virgin Unmask'd*, pr., pb. 1735; *The Universal Gallant: Or, The Different Husbands*, pr., pb. 1735 (five acts); *Pasquin: Or, A Dramatic Satire on the Times*, pr., pb. 1736; *Tumble-Down Dick: Or, Phaeton in the Suds*, pr., pb. 1736; *Eurydice Hiss'd: Or, A Word to the Wise*, pr., pb. 1737; *Eurydice: Or, The Devil's Henpeck'd*, pr. 1737 (one act); *The Historical Register for the Year 1736*, pr., pb. 1737 (three acts); *Miss Lucy in Town*, pr., pb. 1742 (one act); *The Wedding-Day*, pr., pb. 1743 (five acts; also known as *The Virgin Unmask'd*); *The Fathers: Or, The Good-Natured Man*, pr., pb. 1778 (revised for posthumous production by David Garrick).

NONFICTION: *The Journal of a Voyage to Lisbon*, 1755.

TRANSLATION: *The Military History of Charles XII King of Sweden*, 1740.

MISCELLANEOUS: *Miscellanies*, 1743 (3 volumes).

Bibliography

Battestin, Martin C. *A Henry Fielding Companion*. Westport, Conn.: Greenwood Press, 2000. Comprehensive reference work covers the life and writings of Fielding in a thorough fashion. Includes sections on where Fielding lived, his family, and significant historical figures and literary influences, in addition to material on Fielding's works, themes, and characters. Includes bibliography and index.

Battestin, Martin C., with Ruthe R. Battestin. *Henry Fielding: A Life*. New York: Routledge, 1989. The *Sunday Times* of London voted this work one of the four best biographies of the year. Based on fourteen years' research, this detailed biography provides a definitive story of Fielding. Includes a useful bibliography of Fielding's writings.

Bertelsen, Lance. *Henry Fielding at Work: Magistrate, Businessman, Writer*. New York: Palgrave, 2000. Presents analysis of Fielding in his roles as writer, magistrate, and businessman, discussing how his various work experiences affected the form and content of his writing. Includes bibliography and index.

Dircks, Richard J. *Henry Fielding*. Boston: Twayne, 1983. Provides a useful introduction to Fielding, integrating his central ideas and vision of life as they are experienced in his works as a novelist, dramatist, journalist, and pamphleteer. Focuses on Fielding's major works. Includes an excellent bibliography and a chronology.

Mace, Nancy A. *Henry Fielding's Novels and the Classical Tradition*. Newark: University of Delaware Press, 1996. Examines the classical influence on Fielding's novels and other writings, discussing his knowledge of classical literature and his use of classical allusions and quotations.

Pagliaro, Harold E. *Henry Fielding: A Literary Life*. New York: St. Martin's Press, 1998. Excellent work presents an interesting account of Fielding's life and writings, with one chapter devoted to his novels and other prose fiction. Includes bibliographical references and index.

Paulson, Ronald. *The Life of Henry Fielding: A Critical Biography*. Malden, Mass.: Blackwell, 2000. Examines how Fielding's literary works—novels, plays, and essays—all contained autobiographical elements. Each chapter begins with an annotated chronology of the events of Fielding's life in the period covered within the chapter. Includes bibliography and index.

Rawson, Claude, ed. *The Cambridge Companion to Henry Fielding*. New York: Cambridge University Press, 2007. Collection of essays, commissioned for this volume, includes an examination of Fielding's life and discussion of his major novels, his style, his theatrical career, and his journalism work.

Rivero, Albert J., ed. *Critical Essays on Henry Fielding*. New York: G. K. Hall, 1998. Interesting collection of essays about Fielding that were published originally in the 1980's and 1990's, including discussions of the novels *Joseph Andrews*, *Tom Jones*, *Amelia*, and *Jonathan Wild*. Includes bibliographical references and index.

Watt, Ian. *The Rise of the Novel: Studies in Defoe, Richardson, and Fielding*. 2d American ed. Berkeley: University of California Press, 2001. Focuses on three novelists—Fielding, Daniel Defoe, and Samuel Richardson—in tracing the social conditions, public attitudes, and literary practices in eighteenth century England that contributed to the emergence of the novel as an important literary genre. Includes a chapter titled "Fielding and the Epic Theory of the Novel" as well as a chapter analyzing *Tom Jones*.

F. SCOTT FITZGERALD

Born: St. Paul, Minnesota; September 24, 1896
Died: Hollywood, California; December 21, 1940
Also known as: Francis Scott Key Fitzgerald

Principal long fiction

This Side of Paradise, 1920
The Beautiful and Damned, 1922
The Great Gatsby, 1925
Tender Is the Night, 1934
The Last Tycoon, 1941

Other literary forms

Charles Scribner's Sons published nine books by F. Scott Fitzgerald during Fitzgerald's lifetime. In addition to the first four novels, there were four volumes of short stories, *Flappers and Philosophers* (1920), *Tales of the Jazz Age* (1922), *All the Sad Young Men* (1926), and *Taps at Reveille* (1935); and one play, *The Vegetable: Or, From President to Postman* (pb. 1923). The story collections published by Scribner's contained fewer than one-third of the 165 stories that appeared in major periodicals during his lifetime; now, virtually all of Fitzgerald's stories are available in hardcover collections. Fitzgerald also wrote essays and autobiographical pieces, many of which appeared in the late 1930's in *Esquire* and are now collected in, among other places, *The Crack-Up* (1945). Fitzgerald's Hollywood writing consisted mainly of collaborative efforts on scripts for films such as *Gone with the Wind* (1939) and others, although during his life and since his death there have been various screen adaptations of his novels and stories. Fitzgerald's notebooks, scrapbooks, and letters also have been published.

Achievements

Curiously, F. Scott Fitzgerald has appealed to two diverse audiences since the beginning of his career: the popular magazine audience and the elite of the literary establishment. His work appeared regularly in the 1920's and 1930's in such mass-circulation magazines as the *Saturday Evening Post*, *Hearst's*, *International*, *Collier's*, and *Redbook*. The readers of these magazines came to ask for Fitzgerald's flapper stories by name, expecting to find in them rich, young, and glamorous heroes and heroines involved in exciting adventures. Popular magazines in the 1920's billed Fitzgerald stories on the cover, often using them inside as lead stories. Long after Fitzgerald lost the knack of writing the kind of popular stories that made him famous as the creator of the flapper in fiction and as the poet laureate of the Jazz Age, magazine headnotes to his stories identified him as such.

Those who recognized the more serious side of Fitzgerald's talent, as it was evidenced particularly in his best stories and novels, included Edmund Wilson, George Jean Nathan, H. L. Mencken, Gertrude Stein, Edith Wharton, and T. S. Eliot, who offered criticism as well as praise. Fitzgerald was generous with advice to other writers, most notably to Ring Lardner, Ernest Hemingway, and Thomas Wolfe, but also to struggling unknowns, who wrote to him asking for advice, and receiving it.

Many of Fitzgerald's critical opinions went into the public domain when he published essays in *Esquire* in the late 1930's, his dark night of the soul. Regarded by some in Fitzgerald's time as self-pitying, these essays are now often anthologized and widely quoted for the ideas and theories about literature and life that they contain. At the time of his death, Fitzgerald seemed nearly forgotten by his popular readers and greatly neglected by literary critics. After his death and the posthumous publication of his incomplete *The Last Tycoon*, a Fitzgerald revival began. With this revival, Fitzgerald's reputation as a novelist (principally on the strength of *The Great Gatsby* and *Tender Is the Night*), short-story writer, and essayist has been solidly established.

Biography

Francis Scott Key Fitzgerald was born in St. Paul, Minnesota, on September 24, 1896. His mother's side of the family (the McQuillans) was what Fitzgerald referred to as "straight 1850 potato famine Irish," but by the time of his maternal grandfather's death at the age of forty-four, the McQuillan fortune, earned in the grocery business, was in excess of $300,000. Fitzgerald's father was a poor but well-bred descendant of the old Maryland Scott and Key families. Always an ineffectual businessman, Edward Fitzgerald had met Mary McQuillan when he arrived in St. Paul to open a wicker furniture business, which shortly went out of business. In search of a job by which he could support the family, Edward Fitzgerald moved his family from St. Paul to Buffalo, New York, in 1898, then to Syracuse and back to Buffalo. When Fitzgerald was eleven years old, he moved with his family back to St. Paul and the security of the McQuillan wealth.

With McQuillan money, Fitzgerald was sent (for two painfully lonely years) to the private Newman School in Hackensack, New Jersey. Discovering there a flair for writing musical comedy, Fitzgerald decided that he would attend Princeton University, whose Triangle Club produced a musical comedy each year. At Princeton, Fitzgerald compensated for his feelings of social inferiority by excelling in the thing he did best, writing for the Triangle Club and the *Nassau Literary Magazine*. During a Christmas vacation spent in St. Paul, Fitzgerald met Ginevra King, a wealthy Chicago debutante whose initial acceptance of Fitzgerald was a supreme social triumph; her later rejection of him became one of the most devastating blows of his life. He kept her letters, which he had typed and bound and which ran to more than two hundred pages, until his death.

F. Scott Fitzgerald. (Library of Congress)

In 1917, Fitzgerald left Princeton without a degree, accepted a commission in the U.S. Army, and wrote the first draft of what was to become his first novel, *This Side of Paradise*. During the summer of 1918, Fitzgerald met Zelda Sayre while he was stationed near Montgomery, Alabama, and having recently received word of Ginevra's engagement, he fell in love with Zelda. Zelda, however, although willing to become engaged to Fitzgerald, did not finally agree to marry him until he could demonstrate his ability to support her. Fitzgerald returned to New York, worked for an advertising firm, and revised his novel, including in it details from his courtship with Zelda. Charles Scribner's Sons agreed in September, 1919, to publish the novel, and Fitzgerald and Zelda were married in April of the following year.

The first two years of their marriage were marked by wild parties, the self-destructive mood of which formed the basis for some of the scenes in Fitzgerald's second novel, *The Beautiful and Damned*. After a trip to Europe, the Fitzgeralds returned first to St. Paul and then to Great Neck, New York, where they lived among the Astors and Vanderbilts while Fitzgerald accumulated material that would figure in *The Great Gatsby*.

In the decade that followed the publication of that novel, the Fitzgeralds lived, among other places, on the French Riviera, which would provide the background for *Tender Is the Night*. Zelda headed toward a mental collapse, a fictionalized version of which appears in the novel; Fitzgerald sank into alcoholism. In 1930, Zelda was institutionalized for treatment of her mental condition. The rest of Fitzgerald's life was spent writing stories and screenplays that would pay for her treatment, both in and out of institutions. In 1937, Fitzgerald went to Hollywood, met Sheila Graham, worked under contract for MGM Studios, and accumulated material for his last novel, while Zelda remained in the East. Fitzgerald died of a heart attack on December 21, 1940, while working on his unfinished novel, *The Last Tycoon*.

ANALYSIS

"The test of a first-rate intelligence," F. Scott Fitzgerald remarked in the late 1930's, "is the ability to hold two opposed ideas in the mind at the same time, and still retain the ability to function." At his best—in *The Great Gatsby*, in parts of *Tender Is the Night*, in the unfinished *The Last Tycoon*, and in parts of his first two novels, *This Side of Paradise* and *The Beautiful and Damned*—Fitzgerald demonstrates the kind of intelligence he describes, an intelligence characterized by the aesthetic principle of "double vision." An understanding of this phrase (coined and first applied to Fitzgerald's art by Malcolm Cowley) is central to any discussion of Fitzgerald's novels.

"Double vision" denotes two ways of seeing. It implies the tension involved when Fitzgerald sets things in opposition such that the reader can, on one hand, sensually experience the event about which Fitzgerald is writing, becoming emotionally immersed in it, and yet at the same time retain the objectivity to stand back and intellectually criticize it. The foundation of double vision is polarity, the setting of extremes against each other; the result in a novel is dramatic tension. By following the changes in Fitzgerald's narrative technique from *This Side of Paradise* to *The Beautiful and Damned* to *The Great Gatsby* and finally into *Tender Is the Night*, one can trace the growth of his double vision, which is, in effect, to study his development as a literary artist.

The major themes of Fitzgerald's novels derive from the resolution of tension when one idea (usually embodied in a character) triumphs over another. Amory Blaine, the protagonist of Fitzgerald's first novel, *This Side of Paradise*, is a questing hero armed with youth, intelligence, and good looks. Anthony Patch in *The Beautiful and Damned* has a multimillionaire grandfather, a beautiful wife, and youth. Jay Gatsby in *The Great Gatsby* possesses power, newly made money, and good looks. Finally, Dick Diver in *Tender Is the Night* has a medical degree, an overabundance of charm, and a wealthy wife. The common denominators here are the subjects with which Fitzgerald deals in all of his novels: youth, physical beauty, wealth, and potential or "romantic readiness"—all of which are ideals to Fitzgerald. Set against these subjects are their polar opposites: age, ugliness, poverty, squandered potential. Such conflict and resulting tension is, of course, the stuff of which all fiction is made.

With Fitzgerald's characters, however, partly because of the themes with which he deals and partly because of his skillful handling of point of view, the choices are rarely as obvious or as clear-cut to the main characters at the time as they may be to a detached observer, or as they may seem in retrospect to have been. Daisy, for example, so enchants Gatsby and the reader who identifies with him that only in retrospect (if at all) or through the detached observer, Nick, does it become clear that she and the other careless, moneyed people in the novel are villains of the highest order. It is Fitzgerald's main gift that he can draw the reader into a web of emotional attachment to a character, as he does to Daisy through Gatsby, while simultaneously allowing him to inspect the complexity of the web, as he does through Nick. That is what Fitzgerald's double vision at its best is finally about.

For the origins of Fitzgerald's double vision, it is helpful to look at several ingredients of his early life, particularly at those facets of it that presented him with the polarities and ambiguities that would later furnish the subjects and themes of his art. "In a house below the average on a block above the average" is the way that Fitzgerald described his boyhood home. A block above the average, indeed. At the end of the "block" on Summit Avenue in St. Paul lived James J. Hill, the multimillionaire empire builder referred to by Gatsby's father in the last chapter of *The Great Gatsby*. The Fitzgerald family, however, nearly in sight of such wealth, lived moderately on the interest from his mother's inheritance, taking pains not to disturb the capital; Fitzgerald's father, in spite of his idealistic gentility and an ancestral line that linked him to the Maryland Scott and Key families, was unable to hold a good job. One of Fitzgerald's most devastating memories was of his father's loss of a job with Procter and Gamble, which left the older Fitzgerald, then beyond middle age, broken and defeated. When Fitzgerald was sent East to boarding school and then to Princeton, it was with his mother's money, less than a generation earned, and with considerably less of it than stood behind most of his classmates.

Early, then, Fitzgerald, a child with sensitivity, intelligence, and good looks—qualities possessed by most of his heroes and heroines—was impressed with the importance of money, at least with the lifestyle of the moneyed class. Yet Fitzgerald's participation in that lifestyle, like that of many of his fictional creations, was limited by something beyond his control: the fixed income of his family. In addition, he watched his father, an idealist unable to compete in a materialistic world, defeated.

With this kind of early life, Fitzgerald was prepared—or, more accurately, left totally unprepared—for the series of events in his life that formed the basis of much of his later fiction. Two of these stand out: his romantic attachment to Ginevra King, a wealthy Chicago debutante who, in his words, "ended up by throwing me over with the most supreme boredom and indifference"; and his relationship with Zelda Sayre, who broke their engagement (because Fitzgerald was neither rich enough nor famous enough for her) before finally marrying him after his first novel was accepted for publication. Fitzgerald emphasizes the importance of the Ginevra King episode in particular and of biographical material in general in his essay "One Hundred False Starts." He wrote,

> We have two or three great and moving experiences in our lives. . . . Then we learn our trade, well or less well, and we tell our two or three stories—each time in a new disguise—maybe ten times, maybe a hundred, as long as people will listen.

The subjects and themes from those experiences formed what Fitzgerald called "my material."

Through Ginevra, Fitzgerald saw the opportunity to be accepted into the wealth that the King family represented. Her father, however, did not conceal his "poor boys shouldn't think of marrying rich girls" attitude, recorded in Fitzgerald's notebooks, and when Fitzgerald was "thrown over" in favor of an acceptable suitor with money and social position, he saw the rejection not only as a personal one but also as evidence that the emergence of an upper caste in American society had rendered the American Dream an empty promise. Curiously though, Fitzgerald's infatuation with wealth and the wealthy, symbolized by the Kings, stayed with him for the rest of his life. As he wrote to his daughter in the late 1930's on the eve of seeing Ginevra for the first time since she had rejected him nearly twenty years earlier, "She was the first girl I ever loved and I have faithfully avoided seeing her up to this moment to keep that illusion perfect." It was this experience, then, coupled with the near loss of Zelda and their subsequent, complex relationship, that would provide his "material." Fitzgerald also describes an attitude that grows out of these experiences of enchantment and loss, and that he identifies variously as his "solid gold bar" or his "stamp": He wrote, "Taking things hard—from Ginevra to Joe Mank. That's the stamp that goes into my books so that people can read it blind like Braille."

Fitzgerald's achievements rest on three obsessions that characterized him as an artist and as a man. The first of these obsessions was "his material." It included the subjects of youth, wealth, and beauty and was an outgrowth of his social background. The second was his "solid gold bar" or his "stamp," which he defined as "taking things hard," an attitude that grew out of his background and was partly rooted in his feelings of social inferiority. The third was his "double vision," an artistic perspective that remained his goal until the end. This double vision matured as he gained objectivity toward his material. With these cornerstones, Fitzgerald constructed a set of novels that document the development of one of the most complex and fascinating literary personalities of modern times, that chronicle a time of unparalleled frivolity and subsequent national despondency in the United States, and that speak with authenticity about an international wasteland almost beyond reclaiming. "The evidence is in," wrote Stephen Vincent Benét regarding the body of Fitzgerald's work in a review of the incomplete *The Last Tycoon*. "This is not a legend, this is a reputation—and seen in perspective, it may well be one of the most secure reputations of our time."

This Side of Paradise

Writing in 1938 about the subject matter of his first novel, Fitzgerald alludes to its origins in his experience: "In 'This Side of Paradise' I wrote about a love affair that was still bleeding as fresh as the skin wound on a haemophile." The love affair that he refers to is his relationship with Ginevra, and it is but one of many episodes from Fitzgerald's life—his courtship with Zelda is another—that are loosely tied together in *This Side of Paradise* to form a bildungsroman. Unlike the novel of "selected incident," the bildungsroman is a novel of "saturation"—that is, a novel in which the hero takes on experiences until he reaches a saturation point; by virtue of his coming to this point, he reaches a higher level of self-awareness. In *This Side of Paradise*, Amory Blaine, the hero and thinly veiled Fitzgerald persona, reaches this point when, at the end of the novel, he rejects all of the values that have been instilled in him, embraces socialism, and yells to the world, "I know myself . . . but that is all."

The route that Amory follows to arrive at this pinnacle of self-knowledge is more a meandering process of trial and error than it is a systematic journey with a clearly defined purpose. His mother, whom Amory quaintly calls by her first name, Beatrice, and whom he relates to as a peer, instills in Amory an egotism (almost unbearable to his own peers as well as to the reader) and a respect for wealth and social position. These qualities make Amory an object of ridicule when he goes away to an eastern boarding school. His years at St. Regis are spent in isolation, and there he finally makes the emotional break with his mother that frees the "fundamental Amory" to become, in Fitzgerald's words, a "personage."

The landmarks of this becoming process are, for the most part, encounters with individuals who teach Amory about himself: "The Romantic Egotist," as he is referred to in book 1 of the novel, is too solipsistic to go beyond himself even at the end of the novel. After learning from these individuals, Amory either leaves or is left by them. From Clara, a cousin whose beauty and intelligence he admires, he learns that he follows his imagination too freely; he learns from his affair with Rosalind, who almost marries him but refuses because Amory lacks the money to support her, that money determines the direction of love. Through Monsignor Darcy, he learns that the Church of Rome is too confining for him, and from half a dozen of his classmates at Princeton, he discovers the restlessness and rebelliousness that lead him to reject all that he had been brought up to believe, reaching out toward socialism as one of the few gods he has not tried.

The reader will perhaps wonder how Amory, whose path has zigzagged through many experiences, none of which has brought him closely in contact with socialism, has arrived at a point of almost evangelical, anticapitalist zeal. It is worth noting, however, that, in addition to its interest to literary historians as an example of the bildungsroman, *This Side of Paradise* also has value to social historians as an enlightening account of Jazz Age manners and morals. One contemporary observer labeled the novel "a gesture of indefinite revolt," a comment intended as a criticism of the novel's lack of focus. The social historian, however, would see the phrase as a key to the novel's value, which view would cast Amory in the role of spokesperson for the vague rebelliousness of the lost generation, a generation, in Amory's words, "grown up to find all gods dead, all wars fought, all faiths in man shaken." As Malcolm Cowley has noted,

> More than any other writer of these times, Fitzgerald had the sense of living in history. He tried hard to catch the color of every passing year, its distinctive slang, its dance steps, its songs . . . its favorite quarterbacks, and the sort of clothes and emotions its people wore.

John O'Hara, for one, recalls the impact of *This Side of Paradise* on his generation:

> A little matter of twenty-five years ago I, along with half a million other men and women between fifteen and thirty, fell in love with a book. . . . I took the book to bed with me, and I still do, which is more than I can say of any girl I knew in 1920.

By Fitzgerald's own account, the novel made him something of an "oracle" to his college readers, and largely on the strength of *This Side of Paradise*, Fitzgerald became the unofficial poet laureate of the Jazz Age.

For those interested in Fitzgerald's development as a novelist, however, the value of *This Side of Paradise* goes beyond its worth as a novel of growth or its importance as a social document. In it are contained early versions in rough form of most of the novels that Fitzgerald later wrote. By the time of its completion, Fitzgerald's major subjects were cast and marked with his stamp: "taking things hard." Amory "takes hard" the breakup with the young, wealthy, and beautiful Isabel, modeled on Ginevra. Amory "takes hard" his rejection by Rosalind by going on an extended drunk, similar to Fitzgerald's response when Zelda refused to marry him until he demonstrated that he could support her. Event after event in the novel shows Fitzgerald, through Amory, "taking hard" the absence of wealth, the loss of youth, and the ephemerality of beauty. Even in the characterization of Amory, who is born moneyed and aristocratic, Fitzgerald seems to be creating his ideal conception of himself, much the way Gatsby later springs from his own platonic conception of himself.

With his subject matter, his themes, and his distinctive stamp already formed, Fitzgerald needed only to find a point of view by which he could distance himself, more than he had through Amory, from his material. He had yet, as T. S. Eliot would have phrased it, to find an "objective correlative," which is to say that he had not yet acquired the double vision so evident in *The Great Gatsby*.

THE BEAUTIFUL AND DAMNED

Although *The Beautiful and Damned*, Fitzgerald's second novel, is usually considered his weakest, largely because of its improbable and melodramatic ending, there is evidence in it of Fitzgerald's growth as a writer. Unlike *This Side of Paradise*, which is a subjective rendering through a thinly disguised persona and which includes nearly everything from Fitzgerald's life and work through 1920 (one critic called it "the collected works of F. Scott Fitzgerald"), *The Beautiful and Damned* moved toward the novel of selected incident. Written in the third person, it shows Fitzgerald dealing in a more objective fashion with biographical material that was close to him, in this instance the early married life of the Fitzgeralds. Whereas *This Side of Paradise* was largely a retrospective, nostalgic recounting of Fitzgerald's recently lost youth, *The Beautiful and Damned* projects imaginatively into the future of a life based on the belief that nothing is worth doing.

In spite of the differences between the two novels, however, particularly in narrative perspective, it is clear that the characters and subjects in *The Beautiful and Damned* are logical extensions, more objectively rendered, of those introduced in *This Side of Paradise*, making the former a sequel, in a sense, to the latter. With slight modifications, Anthony Patch, the hero of *The Beautiful and Damned*, is Amory Blaine grown older and more cynical. Add to Amory a heritage that links him to Anthony Comstock, a mother and father who died in his youth, a multimillionaire grandfather, and half a dozen years, and the result is a reasonable facsimile of Anthony. To Amory's Rosalind (a composite of Ginevra and Zelda), add a few years, a "coast-to-coast reputation for irresponsibility and beauty," and a bit more cleverness, and the result is strikingly similar to Gloria Gilbert, the heroine of *The Beautiful and Damned*, who will, unlike Rosalind, marry the hero.

When Fitzgerald created Rosalind, of course, Zelda had for the time being rejected him. Her reappearance in *The Beautiful and Damned* as the hero's wife reflects Fitzgerald's change in fortune, since he and Zelda had been married for two years when *The Beautiful and Damned* was published. Their life together provided the basis for many of the experiences in the novel, and there is good reason to believe that the mutual self-destructiveness evident on nearly every page of the novel reflects Fitzgerald's fears of what he and Zelda might do to each other and to themselves. In *This Side of Paradise*, Amory knows himself, "but that is all." Anthony carries this knowledge two years into the future and cynically applies it to life: He will prove that life is meaningless and that "there's nothing I can do that's worth doing." His task is to demonstrate that it is possible for an American to be gracefully idle. Gloria's goal is to avoid responsibility forever, which was essentially Rosalind's goal in *This Side of Paradise*. The kind of life that Gloria and Anthony desire is dependent on the possession of wealth, of which Anthony has promise through the estate of his grandfather, a virtual guarantee until the social-reformer grandfather happens into one of the Patches' parties and disinherits Anthony.

The novel could logically end there, but it does not. Instead, its long conclusion leads the reader through a maze of melodramatic circumstances and improbabilities. Gloria and Anthony contest the will and, with dwindling funds, sink into despair and self-destructiveness. Gloria auditions for a part in a motion picture and is told that she is too old; Anthony remains drunk, tries unsuccessfully to borrow money from friends, and finally gets into a senseless fight with the film producer who has given Gloria the news that she is too old for the part she wants. On the day of the trial that will determine whether the will is to be broken, Anthony loses his mind and is capable only of babbling incoherently when Gloria brings him the news that they are rich.

The major flaw in the novel is this long, melodramatic ending and the thematic conclusions it presents. On one hand, Fitzgerald posits the theory that life is meaningless, yet Anthony's life is given meaning by his quest for money, not to mention that the philosophy itself can be practiced only when there is enough money to support it. Certainly Gloria, who is sane and happy at the novel's end, does not seem much impressed by life's meaninglessness, and the reader is left with the feeling that Anthony, when the advantages that his inheritance can offer him are evident, will recover from his "on-cue" flight into insanity. The effect of the ending is to leave the reader with the impression that Fitzgerald had not thought the theme carefully through; or, as Edmund Wilson hints with the following words, that Fitzgerald himself had not taken the ideas in either of his first two novels seriously:

> In college he had supposed that the thing to do was to write biographical novels with a burst of energy toward the close; since his advent into the literary world, he has discovered that another genre has recently come into favor: the kind which makes much of tragedy and what Mencken has called "the meaninglessness of life."

The greater truth suggested by Wilson here is that through 1922 Fitzgerald was writing, in part, what he thought he should write. With the completion of *The Beautiful and Damned*, his apprenticeship was over, and with an artistic leap he moved into his own as an original prose stylist, writing in *The Great Gatsby* what Eliot called "the first step that American fiction has taken since Henry James."

THE GREAT GATSBY

For Amory Blaine in *This Side of Paradise*, there are four golden moments, as many perhaps as there are new and exciting women to meet; for Anthony Patch in *The Beautiful and Damned*, the moment is his meeting with Gloria Gilbert. For Jay Gatsby, the golden moment is the time when "his unutterable vision" meets Daisy's "perishable breath." For Fitzgerald, the artistic golden moment was the creation of *The Great Gatsby*. Critics have marveled that the author of *This Side of Paradise* and *The Beautiful and Damned* could in less than two years after the publication of the latter produce a novel of the stature of *The Great Gatsby*. Clearly, the writer of *This Side of Paradise* did not blossom overnight into the author of *The Great Gatsby*. The process by which Fitzgerald came to create *The Great Gatsby* is a logical one.

From the beginning of his career as a novelist, Fitzgerald stayed with the subjects and themes that he knew well and that were close to him: wealth, youth, and beauty. What did change between the creation of *This Side of Paradise* and *The Great Gatsby* was Fitzgerald's perspective on his material and his ability to objectify his attitudes toward it. In 1925, Fitzgerald was more than five years removed from his affair with Ginevra King, which gave him the distance to be Nick Carraway, the novel's "objective" narrator. Yet he was also near enough in memory that he could recall, even relive, the seductiveness of her world; that is, he was still able to be the romantic hero, Jay Gatsby. In effect, he had reached the pivotal point in his life that allowed him to see clearly through the eyes of both Gatsby and Nick; for the time of the creation of *The Great Gatsby*, he possessed double vision.

The success of the novel depends on Fitzgerald's ability to transfer to the reader the same kind of vision that he himself had: the ability to believe in the possibilities of several opposite ideas at various levels of abstraction. On the most concrete level, the reader must believe that Gatsby will and will not win Daisy, the novel's heroine and symbol of the American ideal. On a more general level, the reader must believe that anyone in America, through hard work and perseverance, can and cannot gain access to the best that America has to offer. Until Daisy's final rejection of Gatsby in the penultimate chapter of the novel, the reader can, indeed, believe in both alternatives because both have been seen, from the perspective of Gatsby (who believes) and from the point of view of Nick (who wants to believe but intellectually cannot).

The central scene in *The Great Gatsby* nicely illustrates how Fitzgerald is able to present his material in such a way as to create dramatic tension through the use of double vision. This scene, which occupies the first part of chapter 5, is built around the reunion of Gatsby and Daisy after a five-year separation. The years, for Gatsby, have been devoted to the obsessive pursuit of wealth, which he wants only because he believes it will win Daisy for him. Daisy, who has married Tom Buchanan, seems to have given little thought to Gatsby since her marriage. The moment of their reunion, then, means everything to Gatsby and very little to Daisy, except as a diversion from the luxurious idling of her daily existence. In this meeting scene, as Gatsby stands nervously talking to Daisy and Nick, Fitzgerald calls the reader's attention to a defunct clock on Nick's mantlepiece. When Gatsby leans against the mantle, the clock teeters on the edge, deciding finally not to fall. The three stare at the floor as if the clock has, in fact, shattered to pieces in front of them. Gatsby apologizes and Nick replies, "It's an old clock."

On the level of plot, this scene is the dramatic high point of the novel; the first four chapters have been devoted to preparing the reader for it. The image of Daisy's desirability as she is seen through Nick's eyes in chapter 1 has been followed with an image at the chapter's end of Gatsby standing, arms outstretched, toward the green light across the bay at the end of Daisy's dock; the image of the emptiness of the Buchanans' world in chapter 1 has been followed with the image in chapter 2 of the valley of ashes, a huge dumping ground in which lives the mistress of Daisy's husband, Tom; the open public gathering of Gatsby's lavish parties in chapter 3 has been set against the mysterious privacy of Gatsby's life. All of these scenes have come to the reader through the central intelligence, Nick, who has learned from Jordan Baker a truth that, at this point, only Gatsby, Jordan, and Nick know: Gatsby wants to turn time backward and renew his relationship with Daisy as if the five years since he has seen her have not gone by. Nick, Daisy's cousin and Gatsby's neighbor, is the natural link that will reconnect Daisy and Gatsby. To the tension inherent in the reunion itself, then, is added the ambivalence of Nick, who despises Gatsby's gaudiness but admires his romantic readiness and who is captivated by Daisy's charm but also, by the time of the meeting in chapter 5, contemptuous of her moral emptiness.

On coming into the meeting scene, the reader is interested, first on the level of plot, to see whether Gatsby and Daisy can renew their love of five years before. In addition, he is interested in the reaction of Nick, on whose moral and intellectual judgment he has come to depend. At a deeper level, he is ready for the confrontation of abstract ideas that will occur in the clock scene. The clock itself, a focal point of the room in which Gatsby and Daisy meet, represents the past time that Gatsby wants to repeat in order to recapture Daisy's love for him. That this clock, which has stopped at some past moment, can be suspended on a mantelpiece in front of them affirms the possibility of bringing the past into the present. Yet, the fact that they all envision the clock shattered on the floor suggests that all three are aware of the fragility of this past moment brought into the present. The fact that the clock does not work hints at the underlying flaw in Gatsby's dream of a relationship with Daisy.

The scene is a foreshadowing of what the rest of the novel will present dramatically: the brief and intense renewal of a courtship that takes place behind the closed doors of Gatsby's mansion, a courtship that will end abruptly behind the closed doors of a Plaza Hotel room after a confrontation between Gatsby and Tom convinces Daisy finally to reject Gatsby. The death of Myrtle, Tom's mistress; Gatsby's murder by Myrtle's husband; Daisy and Tom's "vacation" until the confusion dies down; Gatsby's funeral, whose arrangements are handled by Nick—all follow with an unquestionable inevitability in the last two chapters of the novel. Nick alone is left to tell the story of the dreamer whose dreams were corrupted by the "foul dust" that floated in their wake and of the reckless rich who "smashed up things and people and then retreated back into their vast carelessness, or whatever it was that kept them together, and let other people clean up the mess they had made."

At this endpoint, the reader will recall the ominous foreshadowing of the broken clock: Gatsby cannot, as Nick has told him, repeat the past. He cannot have Daisy, because as Nick knows, "poor guys shouldn't think of marrying rich girls." Gatsby cannot have what he imagined to be the best America had to offer, which Nick realizes is *not* Daisy. The fault, however, does not lie in Gatsby's capacity to dream, only in "the foul dust" that floated in the wake of his dreams—a belief in the money-god, for example—which makes him mistake a counterfeit (Daisy) for the true romantic vision. "No—Gatsby turned out all right at the end," Nick says in a kind of preface to the novel, a statement that keeps Fitzgerald's double vision intact in spite of Gatsby's loss of Daisy and his life. At the highest level of abstraction, the novel suggests that an idealist unwilling to compromise can and cannot survive in a materialistic world, an ambivalent point of view that Fitzgerald held until his death. No longer did he need to write what he thought he should write; he was writing from the vantage point of one who saw that he had endowed the world of Ginevra with a sanctity it did not deserve. Part of him, like Gatsby, died with the realization. The other part, like Nick, lived on to make sense of what he had lost and to find a better dream.

TENDER IS THE NIGHT

For the nine years that followed the publication of *The Great Gatsby* (sometimes referred to as "the barren years"), Fitzgerald published no novels. During the first five of these years, the Fitzgeralds made four trips to Europe, where they met Ernest Hemingway in 1925 and where they lived for a time on the French Riviera, near Gerald and Sara Murphy, prototypes for Dick and Nicole Diver in Fitzgerald's last complete novel, *Tender Is the Night*. In 1930, Zelda had her first mental breakdown and was hospitalized in Switzerland. Two years later she had a second breakdown. For Fitzgerald, the years from 1930 to 1933 were years during which he was compelled to write short stories for popular magazines, primarily the *Saturday Evening Post*, to enable Zelda to be treated in expensive mental institutions. All of these years were devoted to developing a perspective on his experiences: his feelings about Zelda's affair with a French aviator, Edouard Jozan; his own retaliatory relationship with a young film star, Lois Moran; his attraction to the lifestyle of the Murphys; Zelda's mental illness; his own alcoholism and emotional bankruptcy. He carried the perspective he gained through seventeen complete drafts, fully documented by Matthew J. Bruccoli in *The Composition of "Tender Is the Night"* (1963), to its completion in his novel.

Partly because it attempts to bring together so many subjects, partly because it deals with so complex a theme as the decline of Western civilization, and partly because of its experimentation with multiple points of view, *Tender Is the Night* is usually regarded as Fitzgerald's most ambitious novel. The story line of the novel is straightforward and has the recognizable Fitzgerald stamp. Its hero, Dick Diver, is a gifted young American in Europe who studies psychiatry with Sigmund Freud, writes a textbook for psychiatrists, marries a wealthy American mental patient, and over a period of years makes her well, while sinking himself into an emotional and physical decline that leads him away from Europe to wander aimlessly in an obscure part of upper New York state. The plot rendered chronologically can be represented as two *v*'s placed point-to-point to form an *X*. The lower *v* is Dick's story, which follows him from a relatively low social and economic position to a high one as a doctor and scientist and back again to the low point of emotional bankruptcy. The story of his wife Nicole can be represented by the upper *v*, since Nicole starts life in America's upper class, falls into mental illness (caused by an incestuous relationship with her father), and then rises again to a height of stability and self-sufficiency.

Fitzgerald, however, does not choose to tell the story in chronological sequence, electing instead to focus first on Dick at the high point of his career, following him through his training in a flashback and ending the novel with his collapse into anonymity. Nicole's story, secondary to Dick's, is woven into that of Dick's decline, with the implication that she has helped to speed it along. Nor does Fitzgerald select for the novel a single focus of narration, as he does in *The Great Gatsby*. Instead, book 1 of the novel shows Dick in June and July of 1925 at the high point of his life, just before the beginning of his decline, from the viewpoint of Rosemary Hoyt, an innocent eighteen-year-old film star whose innocence Dick will finally betray at his low point by making love to her. Book 2 contains four chronological shifts covering more than a decade, beginning in 1917, and is presented variously from Dick's and then Nicole's perspective. Book 3 brings the story forward one and a half years from the close of book 2 to Dick's departure from the Riviera and Nicole's marriage to Tommy Barban, and it is from the point of view of the survivor, Nicole.

The complicated shifts in viewpoint and chronological sequence are grounded in the complexity of Fitzgerald's purposes. First, he is attempting to document both the external and internal forces that bring about the decline of a gifted individual. In Dick's case, the inward flaw is rooted in an excess of charm and in a self-destructive need to be used, which the reader can best see from Dick's own perspective. From without, Nicole's money weakens his resistance and serves as a catalyst for the breaking down of his willpower, a process more clearly observable in the sections from Nicole's point of view.

The value of seeing Dick at a high point early in book 1 through Rosemary's eyes is that it emphasizes how attractive and desirable he could be; by contrast, the fact of his emotional bankruptcy at the end of the novel gains power.

Fitzgerald, however, is also attempting to equate Dick's decline with the decline of Western society, a subject that had come to him primarily through his reading of Oswald Spengler's *Der Untergang des Abendlandes* (1918-1922; *The Decline of the West*, 1926-1928). As Fitzgerald wrote to Maxwell Perkins, "I read him the same summer I was writing *The Great Gatsby* and I don't think I ever quite recovered from him." The moral "invalids" of the international set, who gather on "the little prayer rug of a beach" in *Tender Is the Night*, are, like the characters in Eliot's wasteland, hopelessly cut off from the regenerative powers of nature. There is evidence that even Nicole, whose strength seems assured at the novel's end, may soon be in danger of being overcome by Barban, whose name hints at the barbarian takeover of Western culture predicted by Spengler.

At first glance, *Tender Is the Night* may appear far removed in theme and narrative technique from *The Great Gatsby*, even farther from the two apprenticeship novels *This Side of Paradise* and *The Beautiful and Damned*. Yet, it does not represent a radical departure from what would seem a predictable pattern of Fitzgerald's growth as a novelist. In *Tender Is the Night*, as in all of his earlier work, Fitzgerald remains close to biographical material, particularly in his drawing on actual people for fictional characters and parts of composite characters. Dick and Nicole Diver are patterned, in part, on Gerald and Sara Murphy, whose "living well" Fitzgerald admired and to whom he dedicated the novel. The Divers are, of course, also the Fitzgeralds, plagued in the 1930's by mental illness and emotional bankruptcy. Similarly, Rosemary, whose innocent and admiring viewpoint sets up the first book of the novel, is patterned on the young actor Lois Moran, and Tommy Barban is a fictional representation of Zelda's aviator, Jozan.

Also, in drawing on subjects and themes that had characterized even his earliest work, especially wealth and its corrosive influence, Fitzgerald was extending his past concerns from as far back as *This Side of Paradise* into the present, most notably in Baby Warren in *Tender Is the Night*, who callously "buys" Nicole a doctor. Finally, the multiple viewpoint of the novel is a logical extension of the narrator-observer in *The Great Gatsby*, an attempt to carry objectivity even further than he does in that novel. Only perhaps in his reaching into historical prophecy does Fitzgerald go beyond his earlier concerns. Yet even *The Great Gatsby*, which Nick calls "a story of the West," appears on one level to address the moral decay of society on an international level. What *Tender Is the Night* finally reflects, then, is a novelist who has gained philosophical insight and technical skill and has added them onto the existing foundation of his craftsmanship.

Bryant Mangum

OTHER MAJOR WORKS

SHORT FICTION: *Flappers and Philosophers*, 1920; *Tales of the Jazz Age*, 1922; *All the Sad Young Men*, 1926; *Taps at Reveille*, 1935; *The Stories of F. Scott Fitzgerald*, 1951; *Babylon Revisited, and Other Stories*, 1960; *The Pat Hobby Stories*, 1962; *The Apprentice Fiction of F. Scott Fitzgerald, 1907-1917*, 1965; *The Basil and Josephine Stories*, 1973; *Bits of Paradise*, 1974; *The Price Was High: The Last Uncollected Stories of F. Scott Fitzgerald*, 1979; *Before Gatsby: The First Twenty-Six Stories*, 2001 (Matthew J. Bruccoli, editor).

PLAY: *The Vegetable: Or, From President to Postman*, pb. 1923.

NONFICTION: *The Crack-Up*, 1945; *The Letters of F. Scott Fitzgerald*, 1963; *Letters to His Daughter*, 1965; *Thoughtbook of Francis Scott Fitzgerald*, 1965; *Dear Scott/Dear Max: The Fitzgerald-Perkins Correspondence*, 1971; *As Ever, Scott Fitzgerald*, 1972; *F. Scott Fitzgerald's Ledger*, 1972; *The Notebooks of F. Scott Fitzgerald*, 1978; *A Life in Letters*, 1994 (Bruccoli, editor); *F. Scott Fitzgerald on Authorship*, 1996; *Dear Scott, Dearest Zelda: The Love Letters of F. Scott and Zelda Fitzgerald*, 2002 (Jackson R. Bryer and Cathy W. Barks, editors); *Conversations with F. Scott Fitzgerald*, 2005 (Bruccoli and Judith S. Baughman, editors).

MISCELLANEOUS: *Afternoon of an Author: A Selection of Uncollected Stories and Essays*, 1958; *F. Scott Fitzgerald: The Princeton Years, Selected Writings, 1914-1920*, 1996 (Chip Deffaa, editor).

Bibliography

Berman, Ronald. *Fitzgerald, Hemingway, and the Twenties*. Tuscaloosa: University of Alabama Press, 2001. An explication of the cultural context of the era and how the works of these two American writers are imbued with the attitudes and icons of their day.

_______. *"The Great Gatsby" and Fitzgerald's World of Ideas*. Tuscaloosa: University of Alabama Press, 1997. Explores Fitzgerald's political and social views within the context of his era and how he incorporated them into his seminal novel. Describes how Fitzgerald was influenced by William James, Josiah Royce, George Santayana, John Dewey, and other philosophers and how the novel raises philosophical and moral questions.

Bloom, Harold, ed. *F. Scott Fitzgerald*. New York: Chelsea House, 2006. An updated edition of the essay collection originally published in 1985. Analyzes Fitzgerald's *The Great Gatsby*, *Tender Is the Night*, *The Last Tycoon*, *This Side of Paradise*, and other works.

Bruccoli, Matthew J. *Some Sort of Epic Grandeur*. New York: Harcourt Brace Jovanovich, 1981. In this outstanding biography, a major Fitzgerald scholar argues that Fitzgerald's divided spirit, not his lifestyle, distracted him from writing. Bruccoli believes that Fitzgerald both loved and hated the privileged class that was the subject of his fiction.

Curnutt, Kirk. *The Cambridge Introduction to F. Scott Fitzgerald*. New York: Cambridge University Press, 2007. A concise overview of Fitzgerald's life and work, including discussions of the composition process; major themes, characters, plots, and motifs; critical reception and contemporary reviews; the Fitzgerald revival; and modern Fitzgerald studies.

Eble, Kenneth. *F. Scott Fitzgerald*. Rev. ed. Boston: Twayne, 1977. A clearly written critical biography, this book traces Fitzgerald's development from youth through a "Final Assessment," which surveys scholarship on Fitzgerald's texts. Includes an index and a bibliography.

Gale, Robert L. *An F. Scott Fitzgerald Encyclopedia*. Westport, Conn.: Greenwood Press, 1998. A wealth of information, including brief biographies of all of Fitzgerald's significant family members, friends, and acquaintances; plot summaries of all of his fictional works; brief descriptions of every named person in all of his works; bibliographies; and chronologies.

Gross, Dalton, and MaryJean Gross. *Understanding "The Great Gatsby": A Student Casebook to Issues, Sources, and Historical Documents*. Westport, Conn.: Greenwood Press, 1998. An excellent study guide for high school and undergraduate students. Discusses why *The Great Gatsby* is a great novel, describes how Fitzgerald's life intertwined with this novel, and provides background information about gender relations, scandals, and money in the 1920's. Includes bibliographical references and an index.

Lee, A. Robert, ed. *Scott Fitzgerald: The Promises of Life*. New York: St. Martin's Press, 1989. An excellent collection of essays by Fitzgerald scholars, this book includes an introduction that surveys scholarship on the texts. Topics addressed include Fitzgerald's treatment of women, his notion of the decline of the West, his "ethics and ethnicity," and his use of "distortions" of the imagination.

Meyers, Jeffrey. *Scott Fitzgerald: A Biography*. New York: HarperCollins, 1994. In this biography, which makes use of newly discovered materials about Fitzgerald's life, Meyers discusses how such writers as Edgar Allan Poe, Ernest Hemingway, and Joseph Conrad influenced Fitzgerald's fiction.

Miller, James E., Jr. *F. Scott Fitzgerald: His Art and His Technique*. New York: New York University Press, 1964. An expanded version of *The Fictional Technique of Scott Fitzgerald*, originally published in 1957, this book emphasizes Fitzgerald's technique, focusing on the impact of the "saturation vs. selection" debate between H. G. Wells and Henry James; it also adds critical commentary and interpretations of the later works.

Prigozy, Ruth, ed. *The Cambridge Companion to F. Scott Fitzgerald*. New York: Cambridge University Press, 2002. Collection of essays examining Fitzgerald's critical reputation and his portrayal of women in his fiction; the novels *The Great Gatsby*, *Tender Is the Night*, and other works; and other aspects of his life.

RICHARD FLANAGAN

Born: Rosebery, Tasmania, Australia; 1961

Principal long fiction

Death of a River Guide, 1994
The Sound of One Hand Clapping, 1997
Gould's Book of Fish: A Novel in Twelve Fish, 2001
The Unknown Terrorist, 2006
Wanting, 2008

Other literary forms

In his journalistic work, Richard Flanagan has focused on Tasmanian issues, from Aboriginal reparations to the logging of Tasmania's forests, and he has been published in *The Guardian*, *The Telegraph*, *The Age*, *The Monthly*, and many other periodicals. In addition, he has written screenplays: *The Sound of One Hand Clapping* (1998), an adaptation of his novel that he also directed, and *Australia* (2008; with Baz Luhrmann, Stuart Beattie, and Ronald Harwood). Before he turned to fiction, Flanagan wrote history books, including *A Terrible Beauty: History of the Gordon River Country* (1985) and *"Parish-Fed Bastards": A History of the Politics of the Unemployed in Britain, 1884-1939* (1991).

Achievements

Richard Flanagan's novels have been published in more than two dozen countries. His first novel, *Death of a River Guide*, was deemed an "auspicious" beginning by *The Times Literary Supplement* and made him a household name in Tasmania. His second novel, *The Sound of One Hand Clapping*, sold more than 150,000 copies in Australia alone. With *Gould's Book of Fish* he gained an international reputation as a writer of genius. Each of his first three novels was short-listed for the Miles Franklin Award.

Death of a River Guide also won the Sheaffer Pen Prize for First Fiction (1995)—a Victorian Premier's Literary Award (VPLA)—and the South Australia Premier's Award for Fiction (National) in 1996. *The Sound of One Hand Clapping* won a 1998 VPLA award for best novel and an award from the Australian Booksellers Association, also in 1998. The film version of *The Sound of One Hand Clapping* (1998), which Flanagan wrote and directed, was nominated for best film at the Berlin Film Festival. *Gould's Book of Fish* won the 2002 Commonwealth Writers' Prize, and another VPLA—the Vance Palmer Prize for Fiction—in 2002. *The Unknown Terrorist* was chosen as *The Washington Post*'s 2007 Book of the Year. In addition, Dreamworks studios optioned *The Unknown Terrorist* for a major film. In 2008, Flanagan received the John Curtain Prize for Journalism for his article "Out of Control: The Tragedy of Tasmania's Forests" (2007, *The Monthly*).

Biography

Richard Flanagan was born in the mining township of Rosebery, Tasmania, in 1961, the fifth of six children in a large Irish Catholic family (he also had more than fifty cousins). He attended local school in Rosebery, which is on the west coast of Tasmania. He left high school when he was sixteen years old to work as a bush laborer, but after a couple of years decided to go to college. He attended the University of Tasmania and won a Rhodes Scholarship to Oxford in England, where he earned a master of letters degree. He soon began work as a roof painter, one of many construction jobs that supported his writing. He also worked as a river guide and became a skilled canoeist. Flanagan and his wife, Majda Smolej, have three daughters, Rosie, Eliza, and Jean. Flanagan's brother is Australian journalist Martin Flanagan.

Flanagan, also a historian and editor, is very much rooted in his homeland. His connection with Tasmania's rivers and his familiarity with the Tasmanian landscape appear in all but one of his novels (*The Unknown Terrorist* is set in Sydney), and he has an appreciation for Tasmania's diverse cultural heritage. Tasmania is a large island on the southeast tip of Australia, with rugged terrain, an intense and variable climate, and a history that includes settlement by convicts and the near-extinction of the Aborigines. For Flanagan, the stories that arise from these elements are as much a part of the world as a tree or a human being. They have power and presence; they can change lives.

Flanagan's first novel, *Death of a River Guide*, initially received little promotion by his publisher and was largely ignored by reviewers; word of mouth sold out the first printing. Flanagan's aim for the novel was to write about the people he knew and the richness of Tasmanian history as it was lived. He got it right: Tasmanians devoured *Death of a River Guide* and made Flanagan a national phenomenon. With each succeeding novel, he broadened his audience and won even more acclaim.

Analysis

Richard Flanagan's first three novels are concerned largely with questions of identity and kinship. In *Death of a River Guide*, he plumbs his childhood in a large Irish Catholic family, one with an oral tradition whose stories, he says, are full of fascinating digressions. In *The Sound of One Hand Clapping* he explores the sorrows and triumphs in his wife's Slovenian ancestry. In *Gould's Book of Fish*, Flanagan uncovers Tasmania's painful history, and in the process finds marvelous treasures.

Flanagan's later novels are at a further remove, though they remain concerned with life's big questions. *The Unknown Terrorist*, Flanagan's response to Australian antiterror laws, is a cry of outrage. In *Wanting*, he unearths material from the past to tell the story of desire, that most basic of human emotions and a driving force that cannot be long suppressed without harm.

Flanagan's overarching theme is that love matters above all else. In the interviews that accompanied the launch of each of his books, he made clear that he believed humans find meaning in life through relationships with other people. His books approach this fundamental issue; love and authenticity can be blocked in innumerable ways, most of them well intentioned. It is inevitable that humans will miss the mark a great deal of the time, but what matters more than individual success or failure is to keep striving toward human connection.

Flanagan makes full use of fiction's ability to "go" wherever it must, though he often finds inspiration in historical facts and artifacts, particularly those of Tasmanian provenance. What drew Flanagan to the writing of history was perhaps a desire to find some sense of his own place in the world as a Tasmanian, as a cultural, if not genetic, descendant of Aborigines, convicts, and immigrants. History, however, is bound by a few facts surrounded by large gaps of information. What cannot be found in the material world must be left out of the story.

In fiction, Flanagan found a way to express what he had learned: that the vitality, intelligence, and creativity of Tasmania's people will see them through, as it always has, and that to look unflinchingly at Tasmania's dark colonial past is to recognize human fallibility and realize that it is possible to learn and move on. Hope, that small green shoot, finds a way to push through the ashes of destruction and despair toward light.

Richard Flanagan. (Peter Whyte)

Flanagan is not stingy with detail, and his dialogue is always true to the character. He bestows great care on every aspect of his work. (Before writing *Gould's Book of Fish*, he made sure to find a book designer, and then worked with him throughout the book's composition.)

In his love of his family, his homeland, and his history, Flanagan is a Tasmanian Walt Whitman, at one with the soul of the place, a love that is as visceral as it is intellectual. He is a writer for whom all the senses matter, for whom all layers of experience are valuable.

Death of a River Guide

Flanagan's first novel was far more successful than the Tasmanian literary community expected it to be. Flanagan had already written a number of historical works, so his ability to write was not in question. It may have been more a matter of a lack of faith in the subject matter—a drowning Tasmanian full of regrets. *Death of a River Guide*, an accessible and even uplifting book, was an ambitious experiment that few would even attempt, but Flanagan succeeded with apparent ease.

Aljaz Cosini, the river guide, is wedged headfirst in rocks in the Franklin River, one hand breaking the surface of the water like a sad flag. As his lungs burn and his body aches, his mind travels, impossibly expanding time, visiting ancestors, past selves, loves, and the events on the river that led to his current predicament. Aljaz is a helpless witness to all that has gone into making who he is, with no choice of where or when he enters or leaves a scene.

Aljaz narrates his story in third person as an observer of his visions and in first person as the one who is drowning. Throughout the story, he is mostly puzzled by his own actions and choices, but he is experiencing more insight into them now, seeing them from the outside, as an observer. Now he can ask questions he did not have the wit or courage to ask while living.

Aljaz was born with a caul, a traditional sign of having second sight. His mother intended to save the caul but soon sold it to a sailor so she could buy little Aljaz some fruit when he fell ill. The midwife, Maria Magdelena Svevo, is a tough, cigar-smoking refugee from Slovenia who came to Australia with Sonja Cosini, Aljaz's mother, and she hangs around. Aljaz's former love is Couta Ho, mother of Jemma, their child, who died in her crib when she was three months old.

Aljaz is a failure, mostly because of his own choices, which seemed right at the time—except for his choice to do one last stint as a river guide. He is out of shape, old for a guide (thirty-six), and ten years removed from his last river run. He knows the trip is not a good idea, but when his former boss offers him the job, he cannot say no.

Drowning, Aljaz sees episodes in the lives of his parents, his grandparents, and even his great grandparents. He discovers that his forebears include a convict and an Aborigine. As his consciousness wanders where it will and Aljaz is drawn in to his own story, he begins to feel far more attached to his life, now that he is about to leave it, than he did while he lived it. In *Death of a River Guide* Flanagan draws from his own experiences to send a message: Life is hard, love hurts. Do not turn away. Look.

The Sound of One Hand Clapping

The Sound of One Hand Clapping was meant to be a screenplay, but Flanagan did not know how to go about writing one, so he wrote it first in prose and then "translated" it. Not surprisingly, the occasional cinematic moment glimmers through the text. Nevertheless, Flanagan has made good use of the novelist's ability to get inside the characters and let the reader see into their hearts. As a result, this novel is intense and emotional, writ large to project off the screen, and then embroidered to fill in the gaps of detail that a film cannot show.

Bojan and Maria Buloh made their way from Slovenia to Tasmania. Bojan was set to work on a hydro dam in Butler's Gorge, leaving behind, the couple hoped, the terrible events of the war years. One snowy night, Maria walked out on Bojan and their small daughter Sonja, never to return.

Sonja, now in her late thirties, decides to visit her father, driven by a need she refuses to define but cannot ignore. She has made it as far from Butler's Gorge as she can, to the big Australian city of Sydney, with its pleasant anonymity. She avoids closeness—life is easier that way. She prefers tiny apartments that are as impersonal as hotel rooms. She drives in from Hobart and visits the hydro dam. The worker's camp is long gone.

Bojan still works in the area as a laborer, drinking too much and avoiding closeness, but he also paints flowers on everything, even his hard hat. He lays out sumptuous meals for himself, food like that from the old country, and buys Tasmanian schnapps from a fellow down the road. Sonja's visit is accepted ungraciously, and she wonders why she came.

Before going back to Sydney, Sonja stops in Hobart to visit Helvi, an old friend of Bojan and Maria, who insists she check out of the hotel for her last night in Tasmania and stay with Helvi and her husband, Jiri. The next morning, Helvi finds out that Sonja is pregnant and has made plans for an abortion in Sydney. Helvi tells her that sometimes having a child breaks a woman down, but sometimes it is healing. At first, Sonja dismisses the idea, but just before she boards the plane, something makes her turn back.

The rest of the novel is a journey backward and forward through time. Sonja stays with Helvi and Jiri, finds a job in a pub, and as her belly grows she remembers events long buried. Flanagan tells the story—in the third person—that remains close to the characters. In lines that often resemble poetry, Flanagan reveals the characters' inner dialogue, and much of it is distress, but some of it is joy. He takes great pains to show the reader where the stories happen, to give details of color, sound, and smell that sweep the reader up into the storms of emotion that Bojan and Sonja struggle through.

Throughout the novel, atmospheric conditions mirror the emotional weather of the novel's characters. Flanagan describes Tasmania's weather as not only extremely changeable, but liable to go from one extreme to another in the course of a day or even an hour. It snows, it rains in sheets and in torrents, ash floats down from raging fires, the sky is dark with smoke, dark with clouds, wind tears at trees, floods roar through gorges, the sky sags with fog. Most often it is rain that provides the backdrop for action, as though the sky is bound to express what the characters cannot. The color red also figures as a motif, and lace, wood, and edelweiss are prominent throughout as well.

As their story unfolds, Bojan and Sonja's complicated relationship begins to make sense. At times, the reader may wonder how the two could ever reconcile. Somehow, though, they do. The journey is exhausting, but well worth the ride—and the scenery is beautiful.

Gould's Book of Fish

Where Flanagan's photograph would normally be on the flap of the hardcover edition of *Gould's Book of Fish*, an old painting takes its place. The painting shows a grinning sailor, the very William Buelow Gould, who is the supposed author of *Gould's Book of Fish*. It is part of the myth of the book that Flanagan does his best to convince the reader, through tangled strands of obfuscation, that there may be some truth to all these sparkling, lavishly illustrated tales.

Gould's Book of Fish pretends to be an aged document uncovered by Sid Hammet, a dealer of fake antiques who provides tourists with the "authenticity" they crave, battering, for example, a cache of old chairs into a condition resembling genuine age. Rummaging under a stack of ladies magazines in an old meat safe, he finds a book glowing with phosphorus and fish scales, written with multicolored ink, and illustrated with watercolors of Australian fish. It is "a novel in twelve fish;" each section, named after a fish, is an episode of Billy's adventures, which overlaps with and sometimes contradicts the others.

The author of this mysterious book could be an ancestor of Hammet. (Most Tasmanians have a convict somewhere in the branches of their family tree.) Hammet becomes obsessed with the book, reading and rereading the words crowding in on the exquisitely painted fish. The words are written from front to back and then—because the writer apparently was unable or unwilling to reach an end—continue back to front, with new lines squeezed between earlier lines. Hammet shows the book to a history professor, who declares it a fake. Hammet then carries it with him to the pub, where he drinks and reads. One day, to his horror, the book disappears, and he determines to re-create it from memory.

Part of the novel's mystery is determining which version of events, if any, one chooses to believe. Gould, as remembered by Hammet and invented by Flanagan, is an unreliable narrator. Gould's voice is an exhilarating invention. His sentences are long. Clogging here to "unjam" there, they unwind in garlands of flowery language, the polyglot of a newly settled land, and the vernacular of a convict. Some critics assail *Gould's Book of Fish* as confusing and frustrating, and others have hailed Flanagan as a postmodern genius.

The fish of *Gould's Book of Fish* are delicate watercolors by the real William Buelow Gould, petty thief and convict, who painted the fish, along with landscapes, portraits, and botanical illustrations, while a prisoner on Sarah Island. (The original paintings of fish are in the Allport Museum and Library of Fine Arts in Tasmania.) In the hardcover version of the novel, the sections are printed in different colored ink, and each is preceded by the watercolor of its namesake. In the paperback version, the text is in black ink and the paintings of fish are collected at the back of the book.

It may be that painting was the only freedom the real Buelow could manage to hold on to. It is certainly the case for the fictional Buelow (both tried to escape Sarah Island in 1831, but drowned in the attempt).

The novel is a combination of tantalizing historical remnants with Flanagan's imaginary fleshing out of what might have truly happened. It is a testament to the power of words and of art to allow readers to escape the confines of whatever prison they may find themselves in, whether self-created or inescapably real.

The Unknown Terrorist

Life changed after the terrorist attacks of September 11, 2001, in the United States, and for more than Americans alone. In 2005, antiterror laws were passed in Australia following terrorist bombings in Bali, Indonesia, that same year; the laws were passed in part because the nightclub targeted was frequented by Australian nationals visiting Bali. *The Unknown Terrorist* questions whether those laws have victimized people already socially marginalized.

Flanagan renders the realms of the lowly with sympathy and even grandeur. The Doll, the main character in the novel, is a pole dancer at the Chairman's Lounge. The Doll is a bit of an orphan, a person adrift, trying to find an identity in expensive clothes, in her dream of someday having a beautiful apartment in a flashy neighborhood. She is paid in cash by the owner of the club, and keeps it hidden in a cubbyhole in the ceiling over her bed.

After she is caught on a surveillance camera in an embrace with a "suspected terrorist" who has gone missing, the Doll's life grows increasingly terrifying. At first, she is disturbed, but not terribly frightened, to hear of the disappearance of the man whose bed she shared the night before. As the days go by, and the media flash her face repeatedly on television and on the cover of tabloids, and identify her by name on radio, the Doll is increasingly desperate to escape. She does not believe the authorities will listen to her after all of the panicked hysteria. With each day, escape becomes less possible.

One of the Lounge's patrons is a newscaster who is getting old and is about to lose his prime-time slot. The Doll once snubbed him when he requested further services. Now he is sure he can make a comeback telling about the pole dancer who is reportedly also a terrorist. He does not find it difficult to rationalize his exploitation of the Doll's predicament—it is a service to the country.

The language of *The Unknown Terrorist*, in contrast to Flanagan's earlier work, is as plain and unadorned as a police report. He tells the story in the same staccato flashes as the evening news, with the same repetitive hyperbole. It is a thriller with social commentary.

Wanting

The story in *Wanting* ricochets between Tasmania in 1839 and London in 1854, two very different worlds linked together, in an odd way, by the writer Charles Dickens. Flanagan was first drawn to the story by the artist-convict Thomas Bock's painting of a young Aborigine girl in a red dress. When he saw that the oval frame was positioned to hide her bare feet, he was touched.

The girl's name was Mathinna, and what is known of her story is mostly tragic, but if the painting is any witness, she was a girl of great beauty. (Her father appears to have been equally vital in a portrait by Gould.) Flanagan's use of Mathinna's bare feet as a motif displays his ability to find symbols that live in both the world of intellectual meaning and the world of sensory experience.

Flanagan makes use of many historical facts, and leaves them more or less unaltered: Dickens did write a play (with Wilkie Collins) called *The Frozen Deep* (pr. 1857), and performed in it to great acclaim; Sir John and Lady Jane Franklin did move to Van Diemen's Land (original colonial name for Tasmania); the Franklins did adopt Mathinna and take her with them to live in Hobart; Sir John did lead a polar expedition, whose members never returned; Lady Jane did ask Dickens to write a story refuting the claim (by a later explorer) that Sir John's party resorted to cannibalism before their final end; and Dickens did fall in love with the actor Ellen Ternan.

With other historical facts he takes great liberties. His aim for *Wanting* was not historical fiction. *Wanting* is about desire, the driving force of the human animal, the essential spark that leads people to their fates, which no religion or rational thought can smother. Desire in its life-giving aspects links the stories of Mathinna and Dickens. Mathinna has no choice in how her life unfolds, and her natural impulse to connect with others is irreparably damaged. Dickens tries to control his own impulses, but it becomes clear to him that the only choice is to starve his soul of sustenance.

Again, Flanagan uses atmospheric details to great effect, though in *Wanting* it is the filth of London's air and streets that figures most prominently, along with the eternal Tasmanian rain. His language—in particular the dialogue—is appropriate to the time, and yet sounds perfectly natural.

Donna Munro

Other major works

SCREENPLAYS: *The Sound of One Hand Clapping*, 1998 (adaptation of his novel); *Australia* (2008; with Baz Luhrmann, Stuart Beattie, and Ronald Harwood).

NONFICTION: *A Terrible Beauty: History of the Gordon River Country*, 1985; "Joyce's Politics and Mine," 1988; *Codename Iago: The Story of John Friedrich*, 1991 (with John Friedrich); *"Parish-Fed Bastards": A History of the Politics of the Unemployed in Britain, 1884-1939*, 1991; "Stripped Naked by Film," 1993; "The Stars and the Mountains: A Politics to Reclaim the Commons," 1995; "Out of Control: The Tragedy of Tasmania's Forests" (2007).

EDITED TEXT: *The Rest of the World Is Watching: Tasmania and the Greens*, 1990 (with Cassandra Pybus).

Bibliography

Flanagan, Richard. "Many Hands Clapping: An Interview with Richard Flanagan." Interview by Murray Waldron. *The Weekend Australian*, 1997. Flanagan discusses his novel *The Sound of One Hand Clapping* as well as his background, his social activism, and the themes of his fiction.

Kellaway, Kate. "Hook, Line, and Thinker." *The Observer*, June 9, 2002. An interview with Richard Flanagan on the launch of *Gould's Book of Fish*.

Polack, Fiona. "Taking the Waters: Abjection and Homecoming in *The Shipping News* and *Death of a River Guide*." *Journal of Commonwealth Literature* 41, no. 1 (2006): 93-109. A scholarly examination, using psychoanalytic and Freudian theories on the uncanny and on abjection, into how Annie Proulx, in her novel *The Shipping News*, and Flanagan, in *Death of a River Guide*, "bring their misfit protagonists back to the islands of their forefathers to undergo a traumatic but effective 'process' of homecoming."

GUSTAVE FLAUBERT

Born: Rouen, France; December 12, 1821
Died: Croisset, France; May 8, 1880

Principal long fiction

Madame Bovary, 1857 (English translation, 1886)
Salammbô, 1862 (English translation, 1886)
L'Éducation sentimentale, 1869 (*A Sentimental Education*, 1898)
La Tentation de Saint Antoine, 1874 (*The Temptation of Saint Anthony*, 1895)
Bouvard et Pécuchet, 1881 (*Bouvard and Pécuchet*, 1896)
La Première Éducation sentimentale, 1963 (wr. 1843-1845; *The First Sentimental Education*, 1972)

Other literary forms

"The novelist's novelist," as Henry James called him, Gustave Flaubert (floh-BEHR) became an undisputed, if controversial, master of prose fiction in a great age of French prose. Celebrated as the founder of the modern novel, especially in its psychological dimensions, Flaubert published no poetry (if one excepts segments of *The Temptation of Saint Anthony*) but did write a great many dramatic scenarios and fragments. Among his early plays is the unpublished "Loys XI" (written in 1838), the last play of his youth; like his later plays, this one clearly demonstrates that, although he was devoted to the drama and infused his novels with dramatic elements and effects, he was not a talented dramatist. Flaubert's *Le Château des cœurs* (pr. 1874; *The Castle of Hearts*, 1904), written in 1863 in collaboration with his lifelong friend Louis Bouilhet, is a *féerie*, a play that highlights and relies on the marvelous to carry it. The one play of his maturity of which he is sole author, a farcical comedy in four acts called *Le Candidat* (pr., pb. 1874; *The Candidate*, 1904), lasted for four performances at the Vaudeville in Paris. Although it was fueled by Flaubert's contempt for the Third Republic and the grasping materialism of its bourgeois industrialists—and thus potentially explosive—the play is full of stereotypes. Edmond de Goncourt characterized it as a particularly painful failure, funereal and glacial.

Flaubert's *Correspondance, 1830-1880* (1887-1893)—especially his frequently unamorous love letters to his mistress, Louise Colet, his epistles to George Sand, Maxime Du Camp, and Ivan Turgenev, and his notes to a host of friends and literary figures of the era—makes for extraordinarily fascinating reading. André Gide, one of many twentieth century writers who have expressed their debt to Flaubert's letters, wrote that for five years the *Correspondance* was his bedside book. The letters provide a particularly useful picture of the inner Flaubert, his life, his theories about art, and his vocation as a writer. They help form a theoretical canon that explicates Flaubert's intentions and works in the way the essays of Jean-Paul Sartre, Albert Camus, or Michel Butor serve to gloss those authors' novels. An accomplished and prolific correspondent, Flaubert appears in his letters in ways he does not overtly appear in his fiction.

Flaubert's travel book *Par les champs et par les grèves* (1885; *Over Strand and Field*, 1904), written with Maxime Du Camp, is an account of their walking tour of Touraine and Brittany from May to July, 1847. The *Dictionnaire des idées reçues* (1910, 1913; *Dictionary of Accepted Ideas*, 1954), most likely an object of the copying efforts of Bouvard and Pécuchet in the projected second volume of his last and unfinished novel, occupied Flaubert from at least 1850 as a possible anthology of idiocy (*un sottisier*), compendium of foolish conventional opinion, and monument to error.

Apart from his novels, Flaubert's greatest contributions to literature and those on which a major portion of his fame rests are contained in the volume *Trois Contes* (1877; *Three Tales*, 1903). These three stories, "Un Cœur simple" ("A Simple Heart"), "La Légende de Saint Julien l'Hospitalier" ("The Legend of St. Julian, Hospitaler"), and "Hérodias," reflect many of Flaubert's historical interests, artistic preoccupations, and themes and are major products of his fully mature artistry.

ACHIEVEMENTS

"If all high things have their martyrs," wrote Gustave Flaubert's English contemporary Walter Pater in his *Appreciations: With an Essay on Style* (1889), "Gustave Flaubert might perhaps rank as the martyr of literary style." Flaubert's great and unquestionable achievement as founder and master of the modern novel lies precisely in his perfection of a literary style that seeks to capture the essential unity of idea and form, a style that seeks, before all, *le mot juste*, a style that, in Pater's (and later T. S. Eliot's) phrase, involves a natural economy "between a relative, somewhere in the world of thought, and its correlative, somewhere in the world of language." This style uses elements of composition functionally and emphasizes the more formal dimensions of the novel; in Flaubert's hands, the novel achieves a beauty of form and a power that relate it to the other arts. Flaubert's influence extends to Guy de Maupassant, Pater, James, Gide, Oscar Wilde, Butor, and Sartre. Sartre's study of Flaubert, *L'Idiot de la famille: Gustave Flaubert, 1821-1857* (1971-1972; partial translation *The Family Idiot: Gustave Flaubert, 1821-1857*, 1981, 1987), stands as a forceful witness to his lengthy engagement with Flaubert's life, meaning, and place in the intellectual life of subsequent generations. No one writing in French can fail to reckon with Flaubert; no one writing in English should fail to do so.

One public distinction accorded Flaubert in his lifetime was one his father had received in 1839 for his work in medicine. On the strength of his writing, especially for *Madame Bovary*, and in part because it attracted the notice of Princess Mathilde and opened the court to him, Flaubert was named Chevalier de la Légion d'Honneur in 1866. In his *Dictionary of Accepted Ideas*, he writes of this title: "Make fun of it, but covet it. When you obtain it, always say it was unsolicited."

The most complete collection of Flaubert's works is the twenty-two volume Conard edition, issued in Paris from 1910 to 1933. His manuscripts are in many locations but principally in the Bibliothèque Nationale (Paris), the Bibliothèque Historique de la Ville de Paris, the Collection Louvenjoul (Chantilly), and the Bibliothèque Municipale (Rouen).

Biography

Born on December 12, 1821, at the Hôtel-Dieu in Rouen, Gustave Flaubert was the fifth of six children and the fourth son of Achille Cléophas Flaubert, director of Rouen's hospital and founder of its medical school, and Caroline (Fleuriot) Flaubert, the daughter of a physician. Only three of the Flaubert children survived infancy: Achille, the eldest (who later became a physician and replaced his father as master of Rouen's hospital), Gustave, and a sister, Caroline, who was Gustave's junior by two and a half years and who died in childbirth at the age of twenty-one. Flaubert's early and prolonged associations with examining rooms, surgeries, dissecting rooms, and the medical scientists who used them left clear marks on his thought and fiction. His formal education began at the age of nine at Rouen's Collège Royal; there he came under the strong influence of Pierre-Adolphe Chéruel, a disciple of the historian Jules Michelet. An avid student of history, young Flaubert won several prizes for historical essays in the course of pursuing the *baccalauréat*, which was awarded to him in 1840.

In some sense, Flaubert's own sentimental education began at the age of fourteen, when he met Madame Maurice Schlésinger (Elisa Foucault), the wife of a music editor, during a family summer vacation at Trouville. Elisa, who was then twenty-six, became for him an ideal of the beloved but inaccessible woman, the object of unrequited (and unexpressed) love. With great acuity, Enid Starkie asserts that in this first meeting with Elisa, "Flaubert experienced the illumination which permanently fixed the pattern of his emotional life." The beautiful and elusive Madame Arnoux of *A Sentimental Education* is modeled on Madame Schlésinger.

Gustave Flaubert. (Library of Congress)

Upon his graduation from Rouen's *lycée*, Flaubert traveled to the south of France and to Corsica before taking up intermittent study of the law in Paris, study that ended in 1844 with his first major attack of epilepsy. This attack did not merely render him an invalid for several months; it profoundly altered the course of his life. During this illness, Dr. Flaubert bought a house outside Rouen at Croisset and moved his family there; in this house, facing the Seine, "the Hermit of Croisset" was to write some of the greatest fiction in the French language. The year 1846 marked Flaubert's decision to remain permanently at Croisset: In January, his father died; in March, his sister, Caroline, died giving birth to a daughter; and he and the only household he would ever have, his mother and his infant niece, took up domestic life together at Croisset.

Somewhat later in 1846, another event took place that would alter Flaubert's life: On July 28, he met Louise Colet, who became his mistress from 1846 to 1848 and again from 1851 to 1854. This passionate, often stormy, and finally disastrous relationship occasioned some of Flaubert's most important letters. It is arguable that after the first rupture between them (1848), he again pursued her in 1851 to study at first hand the Romantic obsessions he would dissect in *Madame Bovary*—that is, at best, a partial explanation of his intense attraction to her. His self-enforced rustication, away from Paris, away from Louise, led to an irrevocable break in 1854.

Flaubert was not, however, simply the Hermit, as several writers have portrayed him. Croisset remained his primary residence and his place to engage in serious writing over the years, but he also moved about a great deal. In 1847, he and Du Camp made their celebrated walking tour of Brittany; early in 1848, Flaubert was an eyewitness to the revolutionary fighting at the Palais-Royal in Paris; from November, 1849, through July, 1851, he journeyed, mainly with Du Camp, throughout the Middle East, Greece, and Italy. With the publication of *Madame Bovary*, Flaubert entered and fully enjoyed Parisian life, dividing his time between Paris and Croisset from 1856 to his death in 1880.

Early in 1857, *Madame Bovary* caused one of the few great public events of Flaubert's life: He was prosecuted on charges of obscenity and blasphemy. The result was the Napoleonic equivalent of a Scotch verdict, with the ruling that the charges were "not proven." After the notoriety of the trial, the remainder of Flaubert's life was spent in comparative quiet, interspersed with some romantic liaisons, some hard financial times through the improvidence of his niece's husband, and, most of all, the work of producing more remarkable fiction. Flaubert was still at work on *Bouvard and Pécuchet* when he died at Croisset of a cerebral hemorrhage on May 8, 1880.

Analysis

Long the subject of a large and still increasing volume of literary criticism and debate, the novels of Gustave Flaubert are susceptible to a variety of approaches. Classified as a realist, his works deprecated by some of his contemporaries as supreme examples of the excesses to which novelistic realism was prone, Flaubert refused to consider himself an advocate of something he so hated—reality. The psychological realism of *Madame Bovary*, for example, as noted by Charles Baudelaire in an early review, clearly strikes a new note in the development of the novel and is one of Flaubert's major contributions to the genre. This realism is, nevertheless, tempered by some elements of Romanticism, even though Flaubert regarded Romanticism not as an intellectual or artistic doctrine to be prized but as a disease. One objective of the Romantic generation of the 1830's, *épater le bourgeois* (to shock the middle class), surely seems to be at work in Flaubert's fiction; just as surely, the manner of accomplishing this artistic task has little in common with the many Romantic efforts of the age. In one of the earliest studies of Flaubert, Guy de Maupassant hailed Flaubert as an advocate of impersonality in art, and Flaubert's method of composition as well as numerous letters seem to bear out this notion. Conversely, while he could write, for example, that there was nothing of himself, his sentiments, or his life in *Madame Bovary*, he could still exclaim, "Madame Bovary, c'est moi!" (I am Madame Bovary!).

Flaubert's intentions, then, and the circumstances of his life have figured significantly in the interpretation and evaluation of his fiction. One useful way of thinking about his work as a writer and the writing he produced is to consider his life and work spent in the service of art, a demanding art that provided a refuge from the world of ordinary provincial and urban affairs, an art that helped him reorder experience into the image of objective reality without sacrificing all the Romantic traits he had developed in his youth. One primary Romantic element in the novels is the sense of disillusionment attendant on the recognition that Romantic ideals themselves are untenable. This sense is usually dominant in the endings of Flaubert's novels, endings that are supremely important in adjusting the reader's perspective. Such Romantic aspects of his novels are usually overlooked—understandably so, because the restrained language, seemingly objective tone, and intense scrutiny of personality overshadow other elements. It has been said that Flaubert, a Romantic by nature, became a realist and a classicist by discipline.

Madame Bovary

Having turned his hand to writing at an early age, Flaubert was thirty-five years old when he published his masterpiece, *Madame Bovary*, a novel that has been variously interpreted and characterized. For every just claim that Flaubert undertook this novel to purge himself of the Romantic disease, there are equally cogent claims that the work is a Romantic novel, though different in kind from its predecessors. Emma Bovary is surely the victim of her own Romanticism and, like the legions of Romantic heroes and heroines, is one who longs for absolutes and seeks after something that either does not exist or exists but imperfectly. Her aspirations are completely out of proportion to her capacities and her situation in life. Thus, while *Madame Bovary* may be seen as a literary tour de force that makes superb use of organization and of great virtuosity in the handling of structure and text, it remains essentially a novel that both eschews the received objective of entertainment and sets forth an argumentative analysis of society as that society encourages Emma's folly, blames her for it, and triumphs over it.

The work is divided into three unequal parts that correspond to the three stages of the lives of Emma and her husband, Charles. Before turning to the story itself, however, it is essential to look closely at the novel's title: Flaubert called the novel not "Emma Bovary" but *Madame Bovary*. The emphases on her married name, on the marriage itself, on her role as wife (and as mother) are paramount. They are the very things that she will betray and that, in her betrayal, will precipitate her ruin. Moreover, Emma can have no place in the work separate from Charles; one particularly important clue to the nature of the work is the narrative device that opens the novel and then disappears as the objective narrator replaces the first voice that the reader hears. This voice belongs to one of Charles's young classmates at the *lycée*, a classmate who begins casually enough ("We were in class") and who then talks about Charles, his provenance, and his inauspicious beginnings, including having to write the conjugation of *ridiculus sum* twenty times. The idea that Charles is, in fact, ridiculous remains central to the novel, a novel that does not end with Emma's death but with his. Shortly before his death, Charles makes what the narrator considers his one great statement in life; speaking to Rodolphe Boulanger, Emma's first seducer, Charles says, "It is the fault of fate." This statement sums up Charles's inability to understand and to act, the foolishness of his perception of life, and the conventionality of its expression in clichés. The work also ends with the factual statement that the monumental stupidity of another character, Homais, the town chemist, has at last gained proper recognition: Homais has received the Croix de la Légion d'Honneur.

The first of the novel's three segments introduces Charles in a sort of choric prologue to this tragedy of dreams. In what Enid Starkie calls a duet between Charles and Emma, Flaubert presents each of the characters in a series of tableaux that leads the reader through the romance of courtship and the marriage of Charles and Emma, and also to Emma's disillusionment with the unexciting marriage. This section ends, symbolically, with the Bovarys' move from Tostes to Yonville, with the news that Emma is pregnant, and with her burning her now desiccated, tattered wedding bouquet. Each of these occasions, like the rest of the events in the novel, is presented in a detached, declarative, unsentimental manner.

Part 2 consists of another series of tableaux featuring a platonic but potentially passionate relationship between Emma and Léon Dupuis and her carefully plotted seduction by Rodolphe. Indeed, by the time Rodolphe appears, Emma has so languished at Yonville and has so nourished fleshly lusts and acquisitive passions that she is ready for an affair. Having yielded to Rodolphe, she continues to respond to him in an aggressively positive way, especially once Charles's stupidity, matched only by the ignorance of Homais, has led to the crippling of the boy Hippolyte and the consequent diminution of Charles in her eyes and of her, by association, in the eyes of the bourgeoisie of Yonville. Just when she thinks she will finally be free of the tedium of Yonville and the boredom of her marriage to Charles by fleeing with Rodolphe, Rodolphe not only fails to take her away but also flees himself, to avoid what he rightly perceives as her possessive nature: Having captured her, his first thought is how to become free of her.

In the novel's final section, Emma has irretrievably abandoned herself to her Romantic notions of how her life ought to be lived, the high passion of her affair with Léon, the possession of fine things, and the indulgence of her whims; she assumes an inexhaustible supply of funds to support her new style. Predictably, her affair with Léon and her neglect of Charles and their daughter, Berthe, bring her to moral bankruptcy, while her constant borrowing and signing of promissory notes bring her and Charles to financial bankruptcy. In the end, she cannot pay, cannot tap Rodolphe or Léon or anyone with sufficient funds who will not exact her favors in return for the money. Having lived beyond her means in many senses, she chooses an excruciatingly painful death by arsenical poisoning. Charles, the physician, is helpless for a second time when death claims his wife, yet so involved is he with her existence that his interest for readers barely survives hers: His own end is a necessary consequence of hers.

Salammbô

Flaubert's second novel, *Salammbô*, is unsettling, entirely different from his first; it is arguably the cruelest novel of the nineteenth century. In a letter to the celebrated critic Charles-Augustin Sainte-Beuve, Flaubert said he wanted "to fix a mirage by applying to antiquity the methods of the modern novel." The mirage he fixes is ancient Carthage, in a novel that has been called both Romantic and anti-Romantic and that, like many of his works, contains both elements. *Salammbô* is a work of picturesque barbarity and gratuitous violence; it is an unrelieved, pathological compendium of atrocities that the Marquis de Sade would have enjoyed thoroughly. Neither a historical novel, a novel of "historical reconstruction" (as Jules Michelet, Augustin Thierry, and other nineteenth century writers defined the genre), nor a psychological novel like his first one, *Salammbô* is a great Parnassian epic that should be judged more as a poem than as a novel. In its last chapters, the nightmarish mirage becomes a surrealistic vision, what Maurice Nadeau calls "a hallucination described in cold blood."

Flaubert achieves these nightmarish effects through his full and objective descriptions of brutality and through his emphasis on the unreality of the landscape, an emphasis achieved through the use of lapidary objects and architecture. These techniques are prime contributions to what Victor Brombert calls an "epic of immobility." The motif of predation, in which birds and animals of prey become recurrent metaphors and evolve into symbols, coalesces with the lapidary metaphors to help create an absolute sense of dehumanization. This sense is never far from the novel's surface and is constantly reinforced by other recurrent elements: the all-pervasive themes of mutilation and self-mutilation, obsessions with disease, the ravages of hunger and thirst, and cannibalism and vampirism. All of these elements and more combine to produce an overwhelming sense of disgust with things as they are.

The story progresses from the colorful opening revels, in which the priestess Salammbô appears on the tower high above the exotic garden in which the mercenaries hold their feast, through Mathô's theft and Salammbô's recovery of the sacred veil of Tanit, to the horrific destruction of Mathô, to the somewhat unexpected but internally logical statement that the story has been told to explain how the priestess came to die for having touched Tanit's veil. Throughout this bizarre tale of the revolt of a mercenary army that the Carthaginians employed in the wars with Rome, there is no character who approaches full humanity. The exaltations of place over person, of the animalistic and supernatural dimensions over ordinary human existence, of solid objects over all, lead the reader less toward any sympathy with the characters than to either impassiveness or revulsion. Salammbô herself is one more beautiful object among many beautiful objects, and, through her death, she achieves oneness with the gorgeous artifacts that surround her. An overblown exotic fantasy of gargantuan proportions, the work may also be read as a parable of waste, futility, decadence, and inhumanity that has direct application not only to the highly stylized Carthaginian world but also to the bourgeois France of Flaubert's own time.

A Sentimental Education

In *A Sentimental Education*, an ironic self-portrait of the artist as a young man, Flaubert's life and times are both at the core and on the surface. Frédéric Moreau, like his creator, is part of a generation of young intellectuals in revolt against the bourgeois mediocrity that surrounds them; in sympathy with the bohemian life, they are in love with love and passionately in love with passion. Also like his creator, Frédéric conceives an inordinate passion for an older, married woman, a love that cannot be requited. When Flaubert wrote this second version of *A Sentimental Education*, he had already changed from a youthful, aspiring law student more interested in being an aspiring writer to an accomplished and widely recognized novelist. His first attempt to write the story of his generation, the earlier version of *A Sentimental Education* (written 1843-1845 and published in 1963 as *The First Sentimental Education*), underwent considerable revision; the celebration of Romanticism and the enthusiasms and sufferings of youth in the first version are replaced by irony and detached and sardonic realism in the second. What remains constant is the notion that life has cheated the characters by replacing their illusions with reality. The great exception is Madame Arnoux: Surely there are lapses when the reader is allowed to see or at least divine her limitations, but in general she is depicted as the apotheosis of both internal and external beauty. Frédéric shares some of the nobility that attaches to Madame Arnoux's character simply because his love for her remains the fixed star of his existence. Otherwise, he is little better than the rest of the odd characters who populate the novel and whose counterparts lived in Flaubert's France.

One of the novel's primary themes is selling—and, in some sense, selling out. From Monsieur Arnoux to Monsieur Dambreuse to Husonnet to Deslauriers, the notion of selling one's wares and oneself is a constant, and the theme of prostitution, literal and figurative, permeates the work. Both the demimonde of Rosanette and the fashionable world of Madame Dambreuse share the same principle, or lack of it, of barter and bargaining. Closely related to this theme is that of betrayal, which exists on every level and in every character (again, with the exception of Madame Arnoux). Both themes work together to form the basis of Frédéric's education.

That education is a series of initiations—into bohemia, high society, finance, and politics—in which Frédéric discovers cheapened ideals, infidelity, and lost innocence; in short, he finds that reality is antithetical to his Romantic vision of the world. In more than one sense, Frédéric's education is truly sentimental. At the novel's close, for example, Frédéric and Deslauriers meet and agree that the best time they ever had was a frustrated adolescent visit to a provincial bordello; in this agreement, the replacement of the present with a nostalgic desire to recapture the past, Flaubert demonstrates the extent to which the sentimental Frédéric has not been fully educated, as evidenced by the tenacity with which he grasps at the few Romantic notions left him.

The Temptation of Saint Anthony

The transition from *A Sentimental Education* to *The Temptation of Saint Anthony* is an abrupt one, even though the latter was in progress almost as long as the former, possibly longer if one reads "Smarh" (written 1839) and other juvenilia as a prelude to it. Both antedate *Madame Bovary* in Flaubert's consciousness and are filled with the elemental novelistic matter he continually reshaped and refined; both very diverse works seem to have held his attention simultaneously over a long period of time. His tale of Saint Anthony as "Smarh" went through three successive versions (1846-1849, 1856, 1870) before he finally published it as *The Temptation of Saint Anthony* in 1874. When he read the first version to Du Camp and Louis Bouilhet, they advised him to burn it, because the Romanticism it exemplified was out of fashion. When Flaubert published part of the work in 1856, Baudelaire accorded it enthusiastic praise. It was still, in 1856, a provisional work; Flaubert struggled on with it, intent on finding the optimum form into which he could pour the myriad ideas, emotions, and suggestions that the legend of Saint Anthony evoked for him.

Like its predecessors, the final version is a "pandemonic prose poem," in Victor Brombert's phrase, that blends dramatic fragments, monologues, proems, and epic conventions. Ostensibly the story of a hermit tempted by the world, the flesh, and the Devil, it is a work of Romantic decadence that explores and exploits such topics as human sexuality, integrity and bad faith, and the credos and desires of Romanticism as those topics relate to the subject of Saint Athanasius's hagiography and to Everyman. It has a particular relevance to Flaubert's own psyche, what Baudelaire called the secret chamber of Flaubert's mind, as tensions between orgy and asceticism, worldly and mystical perspectives, and reality and illusion are played out in the text. A poetic novel of some eroticism, it is firmly imbued with a hatred of the flesh as well as with an unwillingness to part with it. A work that asks fundamental questions about the nature of life, moral choice, and ethical action, it is finally on the side of death. At the bottom of this work, as in much of Flaubert's writing, there exists a disturbing and thoroughly Romantic longing for oblivion; this longing informs and colors Anthony's reactions to most situations and to himself.

The novel is replete with allusions to theological controversies, historic persons and events, and mythological, mystical, and religious lore that strike modern readers, as they struck Flaubert's contemporaries, as bewildering. Enid Starkie is not alone in judging the novel as largely unreadable without fairly large amounts of specialized knowledge. For example, its seven parts or chapters suggest to Michel Butor a pattern based on an analysis of the seven deadly sins, but that scheme does not fit exactly; it is possible that the mystical associations of the number seven are all that Flaubert intended. In any case, the general reader has only limited access to the novel.

Bouvard and Pécuchet

In his last and unfinished novel, *Bouvard and Pécuchet*, Flaubert continued his analysis of the human condition and the human psyche by rendering a nearly perfect double portrait of human stupidity particularized in his two bourgeois antiheroes. The first meeting of two copy clerks on a deserted boulevard on a hot Parisian afternoon in 1838 marks the beginning of an extraordinary friendship. Bouvard soon receives a small but sufficient legacy, and, after a gap of three years, Pécuchet retires from his work; they are now poised for a lifelong venture in retirement in the country place they had sought for the intervening three years. The rest of their story takes place in Chavignoles, Normandy, where they set up as country gentlemen—without, however, having any clear idea of what that may involve. Their rural adventures uniformly end in disaster and are predicated mainly on ignorance and the perfect confidence that if one reads the great books of direction, one will succeed. Disregarding the experience of those around them, the citified bunglers draw down ruin on their garden, farm, produce, and livestock. Their bungling does not end there.

Each new failure drives them further into abstruse research: Instead of becoming apprentices or hiring well-qualified, honest masters, they plunge themselves into a regressive quest after first principles. Their failed attempt at canning, for example, leads them to chemistry, then medicine, archaeology, and the study of evolutionary theory; they come, encyclopedically, a very long way from learning the right way to can vegetables. This pattern of regression away from ordinary life and the daily attention it requires is one they follow throughout the novel. The unbalanced quest for first principles leads them to study history and literature in general; in this quest after the past, they overlook the fact that their present is quickly disintegrating.

Some critics find in the novel's last chapters an increasingly sympathetic presentation of the pair. As their disillusionment—with sex, politics, religion, education, and the law—becomes complete, they seem to emerge as objects of pity as well as of irony. Given the importance Flaubert attached to the endings of his works, it is particularly unfortunate that his last novel remains unfinished. In the face of their abysmal failure, the two old men take up copying, the task they had worked at in Paris; what they copy, the matter of a proposed second volume for the novel, is not fully known, although some hints exist. The copying of words, words of others, and the interjection of their own comments serve as a fitting occupation for Flaubert's characters. Throughout his own career as a writer/copier, Flaubert had consistently stressed the necessity of the right words, the classical, disciplined finish that frequently captured his own regret, and presumably would capture the regrets of Bouvard and Pécuchet, that, after all, things did not work out well. To the last, even in his bitter exposition of Rousseauism, the Enlightenment, and encyclopedism, he was never free of the regret for lost illusions.

John J. Conlon

Other major works

short fiction: *Trois Contes*, 1877 (*Three Tales*, 1903); *Novembre*, 1885 (wr. c. 1840; *November*, 1932).

plays: *Le Candidat*, pr., pb. 1874 (*The Candidate*, 1904); *Le Château des cœurs*, pr. 1874 (wr. 1863; with Louis Bouilhet; *The Castle of Hearts*, 1904).

nonfiction: *Par les champs et par les grèves*, 1885 (with Maxime Du Camp; *Over Strand and Field*, 1904); *Correspondance, 1830-1880*, 1887-1893; *Dictionnaire des idées reçues*, 1910, 1913 (*Dictionary of Accepted Ideas*, 1954); *Notes de voyage*, 1910; *The Letters of Gustave Flaubert*, 1980-1982 (2 volumes; Francis Steegmuller, editor); *Correspondance*, 1981 (Alphonse Jacobs, editor; *Flaubert-Sand: The Correspondence of Gustave Flaubert and George Sand*, 1993); *Gustave Flaubert-Alfred Le Poittevin, Gustave-Flaubert-Maxine Du Camp: Correspondances*, 2000 (Yvan Leclerc, editor).

miscellaneous: *The Complete Works*, 1904 (10 volumes); *Œuvres complètes*, 1910-1933 (22 volumes).

Bibliography

Addison, Claire. *Where Flaubert Lies: Chronology, Mythology, and History*. New York: Cambridge University Press, 1996. Detailed study of Flaubert's life and art focuses on the relationships among his personal life, the historical context within which he lived, and his fiction. Includes bibliography and index.

Bart, Benjamin F. *Flaubert*. Syracuse, N.Y.: Syracuse University Press, 1967. Chronologically arranged, detailed biography places Flaubert's works in the context of the events of his life and provides analyses of his novels. Includes index.

Brombert, Victor. *The Novels of Flaubert: A Study of Themes and Techniques*. Princeton, N.J.: Princeton University Press, 1966. A thorough examination of Flaubert's novels and other works by a noted authority on French literature. Includes bibliography and index.

Brown, Frederick. *Flaubert: A Biography*. New York: Little, Brown, 2006. Critically acclaimed biography is thorough, detailed, and engagingly written. This ambitious work sets Flaubert's life within the cultural history of France in the middle of the nineteenth century.

Lottman, Herbert. *Flaubert: A Biography*. Boston: Little, Brown, 1989. Provides a comprehensive account of Flaubert's personal life, refuting some of the myths about the writer. Includes many previously unknown details about the author's activities.

Porter, Laurence M., ed. *A Gustave Flaubert Encyclopedia*. Westport, Conn.: Greenwood Press, 2001. Alphabetically arranged collection of articles provides a wide range of material, including information on Flaubert's literary works and their sources, on the places and characters in his fiction, on nineteenth century history, and on the writers who influenced and were influenced by Flaubert. Each article concludes with a bibliography.

Ramazani, Vaheed. *The Free Indirect Mode: Flaubert and the Poetics of Irony*. Charlottesville: University Press of Virginia, 1988. Very helpful and detailed study focuses on Flaubert's use of verbal irony, point of view, voice, and language—especially metaphor. Includes notes and bibliography.

Tarver, John Charles. *Gustave Flaubert as Seen in His Works and Correspondence*. 1895. Reprint. Port Washington, N.Y.: Kennikat Press, 1970. Relatively complete early biography interweaves details about Flaubert's life with information about his work, devoting several chapters to analysis of his novels. Includes an index.

Troyat, Henri. *Flaubert*. Translated by Joan Pinkham. New York: Viking Press, 1992. Thorough, engrossing biography reconstructs Flaubert's life based on the novelist's remarkable and prodigious correspondence with family members and friends.

Unwin, Timothy, ed. *The Cambridge Companion to Flaubert*. New York: Cambridge University Press, 2004. Collection of essays includes analyses of Flaubert's works and discussions of his life, his place in literary history, his writing process, and various aspects of his fiction. In the final essay, "Flaubert, Our Contemporary," noted novelist Mario Vargas Llosa assesses Flaubert's continuing relevance.

Wall, Geoffrey. *Flaubert: A Life*. New York: Farrar, Straus and Giroux, 2002. Critically acclaimed, engagingly written narrative biography compares favorably with the excellent Flaubert biographies by Lottman and Troyat (cited above). Offers many previously unpublished details.

Williams, Tony, and Mary Orr, eds. *New Approaches in Flaubert Studies*. Lewiston, N.Y.: Edwin Mellen Press, 1999. Contributors to this collection of essays provide fresh interpretations of Flaubert's works. Topics addressed include Flaubert's depictions of gender roles, his use of flower figures and other imagery, and his classical influences.

KEN FOLLETT

Born: Cardiff, Wales; June 5, 1949
Also known as: Kenneth Martin Follett; Symon Myles; Zachary Stone; Bernard L. Ross; Martin Martinsen

Principal long fiction

The Big Black, 1974 (as Symon Myles)
The Big Needle, 1974 (as Myles; also known as *The Big Apple*, 1975)
The Big Hit, 1975 (as Myles)
The Shakeout, 1975
Amok: King of Legend, 1976 (as Bernard L. Ross)
The Bear Raid, 1976
The Modigliani Scandal, 1976 (as Zachary Stone)
Paper Money, 1977 (as Stone)
Capricorn One, 1978 (as Ross)
The Eye of the Needle, 1978 (also known as *Storm Island*)
Triple, 1979
The Key to Rebecca, 1980
The Man from St. Petersburg, 1982
Lie Down with Lions, 1985
The Pillars of the Earth, 1989
Night over Water, 1991
A Dangerous Fortune, 1993
Pillars of the Almighty, 1994
A Place Called Freedom, 1995
The Third Twin, 1996
The Hammer of Eden, 1998
Code to Zero, 2000
Jackdaws, 2001
Hornet Flight, 2002
Whiteout, 2004
World Without End, 2007

Other literary forms

In addition to his many novels, Ken Follett (FAHL-iht) has written nonfiction, including *On Wings of Eagles* (1983), about American businessman Ross Perot's 1979 rescue of two corporate executives imprisoned in Tehran, Iran; screenplays such as *Fringe Banking* (1978) and *A Football Star* (1979); and children's stories such as *The Secret of Kellerman's Studio* (1976) and *The Power Twins and the Worm Puzzle: A Science Fantasy for Young People* (1976).

Achievements

Among the youngest millionaire authors, Ken Follett has created best sellers characterized by clear-cut prose with multiple subplots and characters. Set amid chaotic sociopolitical milieus, these works suggest the conflicts of an age or of a historical period through the plight of individuals, and depend on ordinary women rising to life's challenges with strength, fortitude, and vision. Follett was not yet thirty years old when he wrote his novel *The Eye of the Needle*, an international success that sold more than ten million copies, was translated into twenty-five languages, won the Edgar Award of the Mystery Writers of America (1979), and was made into a 1981 United Artists film of the same title starring Kate Nelligan and Donald Sutherland. Other film adaptations include two television miniseries (*The Key to Rebecca* in 1985 and *On Wings of Eagles* in 1986) as well as a 1997 television adaptation of *The Third Twin* (to which CBS purchased the rights for $1.4 million).

By 1989, Follett had more than ninety million readers worldwide. In 2003, as part of the British Broadcasting Corporation series *The Big Read*, the British public voted *The Pillars of the Earth* one of that nation's one hundred best-loved novels. Follett received an honorary doctorate from Exeter University in 2008.

Biography

Kenneth Martin Follett was born in Cardiff, Wales, on June 5, 1949, the son of Lavinia C. Evans and Martin D. Follett. His father worked as an inland revenue clerk and then as a lecturer training tax inspectors. Follett's conservative Christian parents barred television in the home and disapproved of films. There were few books in the Follett home, but the young Follett read avidly the works available in the public library. His family moved to London in 1959. At the age of eighteen, Follett married Mary Emma Ruth Elson, who was pregnant, so their son (Emanuele) would not be born out of wedlock. Elson then worked as a bookkeeper, while Follett studied philosophy at the University of London, becoming involved in left-wing politics, participating in anti-Vietnam War and antiapartheid rallies, and graduating in 1970. He worked as a reporter and rock music columnist for the *South Wales Echo* (Cardiff) until 1973, when his daughter Marie-Claire was born, then switched for one year to covering Scotland Yard and crime in general for the *Evening News* (London) before turning his hand to fiction because of financial necessity.

Follett's first novel, *The Big Needle*, a murder mystery in which the father of a comatose drug user brings down heroin dealers, paid for Follett's car repairs and rent. He went to work for a small London publisher, Everest Books, to find out how to write moneymaking books. After being promoted to deputy managing director in 1976 and writing nine more books (at five thousand dollars per book), some under the pseudonyms Symon Myles, Zachary Stone, and Bernard L. Ross, he finally learned how to turn mediocre novels into popular novels. U.S. literary agent Al Zuckerman, whose correspondence included detailed statements of what Follett was doing wrong and what changes he could make to succeed in the U.S. book market, helped the young writer on the path to becoming a popular novelist. The best work of this period is *The Modigliani Scandal*, a classic caper story about a forged masterpiece and risqué European lifestyles.

Follett finally made his breakthrough with *The Eye of the Needle*, which brought him the fame and fortune needed to retire from journalism and to live comfortably in Surrey. Taxes in the 83 percent bracket, however, drove him to Grasse, France, for a few years. Upon his return, he became involved in Labour Party activities and met Barbara Broer, a Labour official and later a parliamentarian who involved him more deeply in politics. He divorced Elson in September, 1985, and married Broer in November of the same year. He played bass guitar for the bands Damn Right I've Got the Blues and ClogIron and has served as president of the Dyslexia Institute.

Analysis

Though he has varied his writing pattern over the years, Ken Follett often concentrates on a time of international crisis (revolution, war, bank failures, plague, terrorist attacks), then creates a fictive exploration of what could have happened. He mixes invented characters with historical figures and invented action with historical records before returning to some type of epilogue that teases the reader with reference to an actual news story or historical text (like the defeat of the Germans in North Africa during World War II or a newspaper notification of a significant death). His family crises often parallel national or international crises, and middle or working-class outsiders rise to the occasion and dramatically outperform the aristocrats. An impoverished miner or circus performer might gain influence and transform

Ken Follett. (Tim Graham/Getty Images)

society by behaving with compassion or defending a just cause.

Follett has been proud of his craft and versatility; he has tried new ideas and striven to improve his work. After a series of successful spy thrillers depicting resourceful agents, Follett turned to historical novels, then in the 1990's returned to modern stories centered on high-tech equipment. In the first decade of the twenty-first century, he wrote about World War II, the fourteenth century, biological terrorism, and Cold War espionage. He includes strong heroines who thrive in tough times, and his ongoing goal as a writer has been to produce works in the middle ground between the serious and the popular.

The Eye of the Needle

The Eye of the Needle is a tightly constructed spy story about Germany's long-term top spy in England, Heinrich von Müller-Güden, codenamed Die Nadel (the Needle). Under the alias Henry Faber, this master spy, a dispassionate loner scornful of German authorities and the National Socialist Party, has discovered dummy aircraft and plywood tanks that mean the Allies will invade at Normandy, not Pas-de-Calais, France. He must board a U-boat and take his photographic evidence to Adolf Hitler.

Faber flees aboard a stolen craft that wrecks on Storm Island off the coast of Aberdeen, Scotland, pursued by medievalist professor Percival Godliman and former Scotland Yard inspector Frederick Bloggs. Bloggs blames Faber's spy reports for his wife's death in a German bombing raid. On the island Faber encounters Lucy and Dave Rose, a dysfunctional couple whose wedding was closely followed by a traffic accident in which David lost both his legs. Lucy and Faber, both emotionally deprived, find kinship and release in each other's arms. Dave, an embittered sheep farmer who has been sexually estranged from his wife since the accident, discovers Faber's photographic negatives and fights him to the death along a cliff top. Lucy remains composed, has sex with Faber, then flees with her son to radio for help. When caught, she axes Faber's hand, knocks out the radio, then shoots Faber when she overtakes him on the beach. In doing so, this lonely, isolated woman determines the fate of millions of people. By humanizing Faber (he falsifies information to save St. Paul's Cathedral from German bombs), Follett establishes a pattern that has become his trademark: balanced portraits of characters on opposite sides of a conflict; understandable villains and flawed heroes.

Triple

Set one year after the Six Day War of June, 1967, *Triple* builds on a striking real-life news story—a 1968 heist of two hundred tons of uranium (enough for thirty nuclear bombs)—to explore a hypothetical explanation of how and why Israel acquired nuclear materials for its weapons program. A newspaper clipping at novel's end suggests readers have the backstory of a world news event. The novel postulates that Israeli intelligence officers, shocked by Egypt's nuclear capability, hijacked the shipload of uranium.

Mossad agent Nat Dickstein, a master of disguise committed to a Jewish homeland, nonetheless loves an attractive Arab woman, Suza Ashford. As Dickstein, aided by a wartime buddy who is now a Mafia don, puts a clever plan in play, a Palestinian triple agent for the Egyptians and Soviets—and a fedayeen, or freedom fighter—Yasif Hassan, and a Russian, David Rostov, seek to thwart the plan. In the process, Dickstein rescues Ashford from Rostov after a hair-raising high-seas chase and sinks the interfering Russian vessel. Follett provides Israeli and Palestinian perspectives, with the Mossad agent suffering strong doubts about his assignment and the Palestinian disturbed at endangering old friends (he went to Oxford with Dickstein and Rostov).

The Key to Rebecca

Set in wartime Cairo and the north African desert lands that German field marshal Erwin Rommel's World War II forces controlled, *The Key to Rebecca* is one of Follett's best works. It is based on the exploits of the real German spy, John Eppler, at the time of Rommel's 1942 move on Alexandria. This well-written, satisfying spy story pits a capable, good-hearted British military intelligence officer against a cruel, psychologically complex spy codenamed Sphinx, who feeds Rommel detailed troop movements. The plot turns on the deciphering of the German spy's secret code, features a young Anwar Sadat, satirizes British *pukka sahibs*, and brings to life the interplay between Cairenes—those from Cairo—and British.

The Man from St. Petersburg

Set in London just before World War I and amid Russian expatriates, *The Man from St. Petersburg* unravels a

Russian anarchist's scheme to keep Russia from signing a treaty supporting England against Germany by assassinating the czarist negotiator. The earl of Walden, who hosts the Russian prince and handles Anglo-Russian treaty negotiations, faces major obstacles, with which a young Winston Churchill assists. The story's focus on eighteen-year-old Lady Charlotte Walden, who rejects her aristocratic roots and plunges into middle-class horrors, brings to the forefront the suffragist movement. In this tale, which is less credible than other Follett stories, the central character is both hero and villain.

Lie Down with Lions

Lie Down with Lions depicts the clash of values at work in Afghanistan during the Russian occupation of that country in the 1980's. The idealistic heroine, whose doctor husband spies on Afghan freedom fighters for the Soviets while supposedly engaged in humanitarian relief efforts, has an affair with Central Intelligence Agency operative Ellis Thaler, a 1960's radical poet who hates his new job. Erotic scenes counter images of intolerant Muslim chauvinism, as when the pregnant heroine, upon seeing a young Afghan lose his hand to a mine, wraps the wound with her blouse and then is beaten by Afghanis angry at her exposed upper torso. When she goes into premature labor as a result, an untrained midwife colors the heroine's forehead blue to combat evil spirits before delivering her daughter. The novel even includes a bibliography of Follett's sources.

The Pillars of the Earth

The Pillars of the Earth, a massive historical romance, broke new territory for Follett, who considers this his finest work. Very precise details about the forty-year building of a medieval cathedral are the centerpiece of a wide-ranging study of the human sacrifices necessitated by such a monumental effort. Set in the twelfth century, the story depicts the murder of Thomas Beckett, the whipping of Henry II, and the struggle for the Crown as the prior, his master builder, and their community toil on, carving out a living for themselves amid the looting and pillaging of the time.

Night over Water

A wartime thriller, *Night over Water* takes place aboard the last transatlantic voyage of a luxurious Pan American clipper plane bound from Southampton to the United States on the eve of war. Its passenger list provides intriguing subplots even as the plane heads for disaster, a planned crash landing off the coast of Maine facilitated by a blackmailed flight engineer whose wife has been kidnapped. Opposites clashing on board (a Nazi sympathizer and a Jewish scientist, an American gangster and his federal escort, a Russian princess and a jewel thief) make for a tense thirty hours.

A Dangerous Fortune

A Dangerous Fortune traces several generations of the Pilasters, a late nineteenth century banking family, whose rise to social position and wealth ends with the failure of their bank. Responsible for the failure are the unscrupulous Augusta Pilaster, family matriarch, who contrives to raise her personal fortune and prestige and ruin her enemies; her dissolute son, Edward, whose sexual obsessions result in a deadly sexually transmitted disease, but not before he has entangled the bank in a disastrous South American scheme; and the unscrupulous son of a brutal, power-hungry South American businessman, Micky Miranda, who uses multiple murders and seduction of mother and son to bend the Pilasters to his will.

Hugh Pilaster's instinct for business and strong work ethic make him the only truly reliable member of his extended family, but the failure of his father's bank makes him the poor relation. A number of lives are interlocked by the unexplained death of an English schoolboy, the first in a series of murders disguised as accidents. The novel deals head-on with nineteenth century British anti-Semitism, homosexuality, and the potential horrors of arranged marriages while providing a Pygmalion tale of a Polish-Jewish circus performer-cum-bareback-rider who becomes a woman of prominence and influence among the London aristocracy.

A Place Called Freedom

In *A Place Called Freedom* a young Scotsman flees the permanent servitude in the mines that will result if he continues to work past the age of twenty-one (a regional tradition for youngsters born to mining families, one unsupported by law). He flees to London, encounters more difficulties when he tries to break a monopoly, and is transported as an indentured slave to the American colonies, where he works on a tobacco plantation. He arrives around the time of the American Revolution and gets caught up in the fervor of the struggle for human rights in Virginia.

The Third Twin

The Third Twin delves into the darker possibilities of biotechnology and genetic research. A university professor, studying twins to test whether or not criminality is genetic, finds the nature-nurture debate played out in the case of law student Steven Logan, accused of sadistic rapes on a peaceful Maryland college campus. His murderous twin is already in jail, but the possibility of a third identical brother raises questions, including: Has Logan been cloned and, if so, by whom?

The Hammer of Eden

In *The Hammer of Eden*, a radical California cult leader named Priest, upon learning that a power plant, dam, and lake will be constructed above his secret commune and its vineyards, retaliates by stealing a seismic vibrator from an oil company and producing earthquakes that threaten San Francisco. Throughout the story, Follett tries to make understandable Priest's actions.

Code to Zero

Code to Zero takes place in 1958, at the height of the Cold War and on the eve of the first launch of a U.S. satellite, Explorer I. The head scientist wakes up with artificially induced amnesia and must recover his life and memories step-by-step to thwart the Russians, who have him under surveillance to prevent the launch. Not knowing whom to trust or where to turn, he experiences flashbacks that gradually permit him to piece together his past and understand his present.

Jackdaws

Jackdaws, a wartime thriller in the tradition of the E. M. Nathanson novel *The Dirty Dozen* (1965), pits a female team of six (including a crack shot, an explosives expert, and a cross-dressing telephone operator) against the Gestapo and Nazi intelligence officers. A British agent and a French Resistance leader attack a telephone exchange but fail to cut off German military communications for the region. With D day just days away, the British agent is airdropped into France with her unlikely team (French-speaking Englishwomen with specialized skills), this time to get the job done. They pose as a local cleaning detail and dismantle the telephone exchange.

Hornet Flight

Hornet Flight is an exciting World War II story of Danish amateurs and resistance fighters trying to figure out exactly where the Germans have hidden their new technology: radar stations that identify British bombing formations to facilitate their annihilation. Eighteen-year-old physics student Harald Olufsen, inspired by his brother's wartime efforts as a Danish military pilot, stumbles upon what the British have been seeking, takes photographs, and eventually restores the Hornet's Moth of the title (a wood-and-linen biplane) to carry the evidence and his Jewish girlfriend to England, despite the efforts of local collaborators, such as a Danish police detective who uses cooperation with the Germans to take on long-time family enemies, the Olufsens. Follett demonstrates the insidious ease with which the conquered yielded to German ways, persecuting Jews and enforcing rigid regulations that intimidated the local population.

Whiteout

In *Whiteout*, biological terrorism strikes over a wintry Christmas holiday in northern Scotland, as the security head of a boutique pharmaceuticals company discovers two doses of an experimental drug—a potential cure for a deadly virus—stolen from her top-secret laboratory along with a sample of the virus. The associates of the gambling-addicted son of the company's founder have committed the robbery. The son, who is deeply in debt to a mobster, plans to sell the drugs and leave the country. Amid complicated family intrigue, all end up at the Oxenford family estate, trapped by a blizzard, fighting over the stolen materials at midnight on Christmas Eve. This is not a cozy mystery.

World Without End

World Without End begins two centuries after the completion of the cathedral built in *The Pillars of the Earth*, with the cathedral and priory again at the crossroads of new ideas in conflict with old and the novel set against the backdrop of the Black Plague. According to Follett, the twelfth century monastery, once a positive force for good in medieval society, encouraging education and technological advance, became a wealthy, conservative opponent of change in the fourteenth century. Four children from different social classes witness a murder that affects each differently; between 1327 and 1361, these four become a peasant's wife, a knight, a builder, and a nun, respectively, whose stories the novel traces as it explores continuity and change. Varied topics include the evolution of cloth weaving, the French-

English Wars, the corruption of the clergy, and the cruelty and greed of nobles.

Gina Macdonald

Other major works

SCREENPLAYS: *Fringe Banking*, 1978; *A Football Star*, 1979 (with John Sealey); *Lie Down with Lions*, 1988 (adaptation of his novel).

NONFICTION: *The Heist of the Century*, 1978 (with René Louis Maurice; as *The Gentlemen of 16 July*, 1980; revised as *Under the Streets of Nice: The Bank Heist of the Century*, 1986); *On Wings of Eagles*, 1983.

CHILDREN'S/YOUNG ADULT LITERATURE: *The Power Twins and the Worm Puzzle: A Science Fantasy for Young People*, 1976 (as Martin Martinsen); *The Secret of Kellerman's Studio*, 1976; *The Mystery Hideout*, 1991.

Bibliography

Dean, John W. "Occupational Hazards." *The New York Times Book Review*, January 14, 2001. Dean, a former White House counsel, examines credibility in the works of Follett and fellow novelist Richard North Patterson.

Ramet, Carlos, and Marshall William Fishwick. *Ken Follett: The Transformation of a Writer*. Bowling Green, Ohio: Bowling Green State University Popular Press, 1999. Ramet focuses on the artistic precursors and cultural implications of Follett's literary canon.

Turner, Richard Charles. *Ken Follett: A Critical Companion*. Westport, Conn.: Greenwood Press, 1996. A thorough study of Follett's life, literary influences, and major works, including various critical approaches to his works.

Van Teeffelen, Toine Van. "(Ex)communicating Palestine: From Best-Selling Terrorist Fiction to Real-Life Personal Accounts." *Studies in the Novel* 36, no. 3 (2004): 438-458. Van Teeffelen compares various writers' stories and representations of Palestine and Palestinians, including those of Follett in *Triple*.

THEODOR FONTANE

Born: Neuruppin, Prussia (now in Germany); December 30, 1819
Died: Berlin, Germany; September 20, 1898
Also known as: Henri Theodor Fontane

Principal long fiction

Vor dem Sturm, 1878 (*Before the Storm: A Novel of the Winter of 1812-13*, 1985)
L'Adultera, 1882 (*The Woman Taken in Adultery*, 1979)
Schach von Wuthenow, 1883 (*A Man of Honor: Schach von Wuthenow*, 1975)
Cécile, 1887 (English translation, 1982)
Irrungen, Wirrungen, 1888 (*Trials and Tribulations*, 1917; also known as *A Suitable Match*, 1968)
Stine, 1890 (English translation, 1969)
Unwiederbringlich, 1892 (*Beyond Recall*, 1964)
Frau Jenny Treibel, 1893 (*Jenny Treibel*, 1976)
Effi Briest, 1895 (English translation, 1914, 1962)
Die Poggenpuhls, 1896 (*The Poggenpuhl Family*, 1979)
Der Stechlin, 1898 (*The Stechlin*, 1996)

Other literary forms

In addition to novels, Theodor Fontane (fahn-TAH-neh) wrote numerous poems, novellas, theater reviews, travel journals, autobiographical writings, four volumes of letters, and essays on literature, history, and art. This extremely prolific writer was a journalist for many years before he was able to devote himself mainly to belles lettres.

Achievements

When considering Theodor Fontane's writing, one thinks not only of nineteenth century Prussia, of its landscapes and cityscapes, of its people—particularly the declining gentry, the prosperous upper middle class, the faithful servants—but also of the emerging working class. Beginning with his *Wanderungen durch die Mark Brandenburg* (1865-1882; journeys through Mark Brandenburg) and culminating in his major novels, Fontane painted a fascinating social panorama of his age.

Biography

Henri Theodor Fontane was born on December 30, 1819, in Neuruppin, Prussia (now in Germany). Both of his parents were of French descent, part of the French Huguenot colony that had existed in Prussia since the Edict of Potsdam of 1685. Fontane's father was a pharmacist. During the first year of his marriage, he acquired a well-established pharmacy in Neuruppin. He was not, however, a good businessman, and he lost considerable amounts of money at the gambling table. In 1827, the elder Fontane sold his pharmacy in Neuruppin and purchased another in Swinemünde.

The Fontane family then moved to Swinemünde, a port town that was much livelier than Neuruppin. For Fontane, Swinemünde was always imbued with a certain poetic quality, and he transmuted it into the setting of a few of his works. He attended the *Gymnasium* (academic high school) in Neuruppin for a few years, but eventually he switched to a vocational school in Berlin and, in 1836, was apprenticed to a pharmacy there. During those years, his father's fortunes went from bad to worse, and his parents eventually separated.

Fontane's father's financial failures meant that, from a very young age, Fontane had to rely almost exclusively on his own resources in order to make a living. While still an apprentice in the pharmacy in Berlin, he wrote poems and novellas, a few of which were published. In April, 1844, he began his one-year military service. During the summer of the same year, he was given leave in order to accompany a friend on a trip to England. He was fascinated by that country and particularly by the city of London. He resolved to find a way to live in England for several years.

In 1847, Fontane received his license as a first-class pharmacist, but he never practiced his profession in any consistent manner. He became active in a few literary societies in Berlin and received several assignments as a journalist. In 1850, he married Emilie Rouanet-Kummer, to whom he had been engaged for five years. In 1851, their first son was born, and the struggle for day-to-day survival intensified.

In 1852, Fontane was sent to London for several months, as a correspondent for the *Preussische Zeitung*. After his return, he published *Ein Sommer in London* (1854; a summer in London), a collection of essays that are full of his admiration for British history and society and for the country's wealth. Fontane did not, however, hesitate to criticize the prevailing materialism and social injustice. His summer in London in 1852 and his knowledge of the English language and of British institutions were important factors when the Prussian government chose a press agent to be sent to London to present its views on world affairs to the British press.

In 1855, Fontane was posted to London for more than three years and, for the first time in his life, had a comfortable income. These years in England were very important to his development: They were a fruitful period of learning, of absorbing a foreign culture, and of contrasting it to his own. Toward the end of his assignment in England, Fontane went on a journey to Scotland, treading in the footsteps of Ossian and Sir Walter Scott. Shortly after his return to Berlin, he published a very personal account of his journey to Scotland: *Jenseits des Tweed* (1860; *Across the Tweed*, 1965), which received favorable critical reviews. More important, Fontane's work on *Across the Tweed* led to a number of insights, comparisons, and transmutations that were to find their way into *Wanderungen durch die Mark Brandenburg*, in which his monumental depiction of the landscape, the towns, the people, and the history of Mark Brandenburg was to set the stage for his novels and novellas.

In 1860, Fontane joined the editorial staff of the conservative *Kreuzzeitung*, not out of political conviction but to have a regular income. Ten years later, he was finally able to break "the chain on which my daily bread dangles." In 1870, he was appointed theater critic of the prestigious (and liberal) *Vossische Zeitung*, with which he remained associated until 1890.

Except for a brief internment by the French during the Franco-Prussian War (Fontane had served as a war correspondent), the last third of his life was relatively free of anxiety. Most of his time was devoted to writing, and he was increasingly recognized as a major literary voice. In 1894, when most of his major works (but not his two greatest novels) had been published, he was awarded an honorary doctorate by the University of Berlin. He was held in esteem by the adherents of naturalism, though their emerging literary form was quite unlike his own. Fontane died on September 20, 1898, apparently from a stroke. One of the papers found on his desk was a list of those people who were to receive copies of his just-published masterpiece, *The Stechlin*.

Theodor Fontane. (Library of Congress)

ANALYSIS

Theodor Fontane's novels may be divided into three categories, according to their subject matter: first, novels dealing with the conflicts arising from class distinctions, frequently involving a young nobleman and a girl from the lower classes; second, novels about marriage, in all cases involving adultery; and third, vast epic panoramas of Prussian society with diffuse plots, skillfully depicted settings, and carefully nuanced utterances by large numbers of characters. This third category includes Fontane's earliest novel, *Before the Storm*, and *The Stechlin*.

A SUITABLE MATCH

Turning to a detailed consideration of the first category, one should look first at *A Suitable Match* and *Stine*. The plot of *A Suitable Match* centers on a love affair between Botho von Rienäcker, an officer of the Prussian nobility, and Lene, a seamstress. Botho is eventually induced by family considerations to marry a rich young woman of his own class. Lene also gets married to an honest man, a Pietist recently returned from America. Fontane uses this simple plot to create realistic yet subtle portraits, not only of the two protagonists but also of the two social strata that they represent.

Particularly notable in the novel is Fontane's treatment of dialogue. The first two chapters take place in and around a nursery and vegetable farm where Lene, her mother, and Mr. and Mrs. Dörr (the owners of the nursery) live. It is early summer, and "Baron Botho" often visits Lene and spends parts of his evenings in Mrs. Dörr's kitchen, drinking apple cider and conversing with his friends. In these conversations, the characters reveal themselves as not only individuals but also types who share their attitudes and circumstances with many other members of their class. The conversations in Mrs. Dörr's kitchen are juxtaposed with the one among Botho, his uncle, and another young nobleman. They meet in an exclusive Berlin restaurant (whose decor is as carefully described as Mrs. Dörr's kitchen), they drink Chablis, and most of their conversation is concerned with contemporary society and politics. Only at one point does Botho's uncle touch upon the critical issue at hand—when he says that Botho is "practically committed" ("Du bist doch so gut wie gebunden").

This incident is a good example of Fontane's seemingly effortless artistry, because, later on, during a moment of supreme happiness, Lene ties a bunch of flowers with a strand of her own hair. As she gives the flowers to Botho, she uses almost the same words "Now you are tied [committed to me]" ("Nun bist du gebunden"). The irony of the matter is that Botho *is* committed to marry a young noblewoman, and when his mother insists that he honor that commitment, he obeys. When a fellow officer asks Botho for his advice in a similar matter, Botho stoutly defends the existing class distinctions and advises his friend to terminate his relationship with the young bourgeoisie in question. A few years later, however—when he decides to burn a packet of letters that Lene had once written to him, as well as the withered bunch of flowers—he realizes that he still is and always will be "tied" to her.

In *A Suitable Match*, existing social conventions are portrayed as of paramount importance. When they conflict with individual happiness, Botho's happiness must be subordinated to them. The fact that life goes on passably well is adumbrated by Mrs. Dörr in the first chapter. This fact is also demonstrated through the Pietist's account of his first meeting with Lene and through the narrator's account of Botho's marriage.

Stine

The conflict between social conventions and personal happiness is accentuated and rendered more poignant by the tragic conclusion of *Stine*. The main plot of this novel concerns a love affair between a young girl of the working class and a young count. Stine and Waldemar (the two young people) meet during a supper party arranged by Stine's sister Pauline but paid for by Pauline's lover, an aging count who is Waldemar's uncle. Pauline's way of life—specifically, her total financial dependence on the Count—constitutes an important secondary action of this novel. Accounts of Pauline's present and past life are skillfully interwoven in the narration, and the reader learns that she is a widow with a dependent child who simply cannot make ends meet without the Count's financial help—without, in fact, selling herself to him. When Stine first speaks to Waldemar alone, she makes it clear to him that she prefers a life of poverty to the kind of life her sister leads. Later, Waldemar offers to marry her and to immigrate to America with her, but she refuses and explains to him that the difference between their social classes would preclude any kind of permanent happiness for them. Thereupon, Waldemar, who has been unable to obtain his uncle's support for this marriage, commits suicide. Thus, Waldemar dies because all the people who surround him (including his beloved) tell him that a Count cannot marry a working-class girl, that class distinctions are insuperable barriers.

The reader is left with the impression that Waldemar is a victor of sorts, that the old caste system will not survive for long. Contemporary social conventions are attacked, not only by Waldemar but also by the Baron (a friend of Waldemar's uncle to whom Waldemar first turns for help), who says that he is always happy to see someone breaking through the *Krimskrams* (nonsense) of class distinctions. Even Waldemar's uncle admits that "the divine order of the world does not completely correspond to the calendar of the state and to the ranking list of society." He goes even further and states that "at the present time" he and his ilk are still the *beati possidentes* (happy proprietors). He says to Waldemar, "Be a proprietor, and you are in the right. . . . Why deprive ourselves of this possession and . . . conjure up a future which may not benefit anyone, and certainly not us?" Statements such as this one, if read in conjunction with the accounts of Pauline's precarious financial situation, add a considerable dimension of social criticism to the novel. It becomes clear to the reader that the opulence of the nobility is based on the low wages of the working class and on a total absence of a social security system for these people. It is, of course, no accident that *Stine* was written at a time when a comprehensive social security system was being debated in the Prussian parliament. (The social security law was finally passed in 1889.)

Jenny Treibel

In *Stine* as well as in *A Suitable Match*, politics is deftly subsumed in the actions and in the characterizations. That is not quite the case in *Jenny Treibel*, the most lighthearted work in the first category of Fontane's novels. Again, the representatives of two social classes interact and mingle socially, but they cannot intermarry. In *Jenny Treibel*, however, the obstacle is not the insurmountable barrier of class distinction but the determination of one of the protagonists, Mrs. Jenny Treibel, a successful social climber.

In her youth, Jenny had been poor and idealistic and had had an affair with an equally poor and idealistic high school teacher named Schmidt. She had left him and married an industrialist. When the novel opens, Jenny rules over a substantial villa, over her husband, who is only a *Kommerzienrat* but who has higher political ambitions, and over her somewhat spineless son Leopold, who works in his father's firm. Jenny's older son has already married a suitably rich young woman from Hamburg. The other social circle consists mainly of Mr. Schmidt, his vivacious and intelligent daughter, Corinna, and his nephew, Marcell. During a supper party, Corinna flirts with the visiting British businessman, but only in order to attract Leopold's attention. On the way home, she admits to Marcell that she intends to marry Leopold and live a life of luxury, come what may. Marcell is despondent because he loves her and hopes to marry her. Nevertheless, during an outing with both families and some mutual friends, Corinna contrives a sort of engagement to Leopold.

Leaving aside Mr. Treibel's ill-starred political maneuvers, the comedy has two high points, both involving Jenny. In one encounter, she forbids Leopold to marry Corinna, and he refuses to obey her. In the other one, she tries to dissuade Corinna from her endeavor, and the latter refuses to relinquish her "rights" to Leopold. Yet, Jenny wins in the end: Her daughter-in-law conveniently has a sister who will receive a considerable dowry. Jenny invites this young woman to spend a few weeks in her house, and Leopold must at least be polite to her. Meanwhile, he writes letters to Corinna every day, assuring her of his love and steadfastness, but he does not go to see her. Some two weeks later, Marcell receives a tenured appointment as a teacher and is thus able to get married. At this point, Corinna is more than tired of Leopold's letters and more than ready to accept Marcell.

The strength of the novel lies in the indulgent irony with which the various characters are depicted and the loving attention paid to details, lifestyles, food and drink, and nuances of speech. The novel's subject matter is aptly summed up by Corinna when she says that she was not allowed to marry Leopold because she did not have a dowry that would have doubled the Treibels' assets. Such subject matter may be trivial, but Fontane's artistry in presenting it makes the novel a first-rate comedy of manners.

Effi Briest

Fontane's first three novels about marriage and adultery (*The Woman Taken in Adultery*, *Cécile*, and *Beyond Recall*) are uneven in artistic quality. They may be regarded as essentially preparatory to his undisputed masterpiece, *Effi Briest*. The plot of this latter work is based on an anecdote, "a story of adultery like a hundred others," and it is quite simple: Effi von Briest, the seventeen-year-old daughter of a family of the lower nobility, marries Geert von Innstetten, a member of the same social class, thirty-eight years of age. He is a civil servant stationed in the remote seaside town of Kessin. Kessin is a dull place. With one or two exceptions, the townspeople do not measure up to Effi's social and educational levels, and the members of the country gentry in the neighboring estates are narrow-minded and bigoted and receive her coolly. Innstetten tries his best to be attentive to her, but he also has to devote considerable time and effort to his duties and his career.

After a year or so, Effi gives birth to a daughter, but even this happy event does not alter the essentially tranquil and boring quality of her life in Kessin. Then Major von Crampas is stationed there, and he brings some life into the town. He organizes amateur theatrical productions in which Effi and other local notables perform. Effi knows that Crampas is a notorious ladies' man, and she sees through him quite easily. Yet, out of boredom, nonchalance, or frivolity, she allows herself to be seduced by him. Her affair with Crampas, with its attendant problems of secrecy and dissembling, does not bring her much joy. She is therefore relieved when Innstetten informs her that he has been promoted and will be transferred to Berlin.

The Innstettens move into a suitably elegant apartment in the capital and begin leading the kind of social life that befits members of the upper classes. Effi becomes a society lady and is quite happy. Crampas is forgotten. Then, almost seven years after their arrival, Innstetten accidentally discovers a packet of letters that Crampas had written to Effi. Innstetten challenges Crampas to a duel and kills him. He then banishes Effi from his home. She lives in a small apartment in Berlin, financially supported by her parents but forbidden to go to their home and shunned by all members of high society. After three years of this kind of life, she is finally allowed to see her daughter, but the child has been completely turned against her and only parrots words drilled into her by her father or her governess. Effi is so upset by this encounter with her child that she has a complete nervous breakdown. Severely ill, she is finally allowed to return to her parents' home. There she spends a few months in a trancelike kind of happiness, almost beatific, and finally dies.

Effi's fate, as sketched above, certainly produces a certain amount of empathy in the reader, but the real interest of the novel lies in the more general conflict between the concepts of personal happiness and social conventions. Many of the characters in *Effi Briest* are thwarted in their pursuit of happiness by a complex set of rules and regulations, which are presented by the narrator in such a manner as to question their validity. The novel contains a wealth of well-drawn characters, and they are carefully orchestrated to express this crucial problem. The problem arises early in the novel, when Effi meets the various members of the country gentry around Kessin. They are drawn as a stiff, prissy, and bigoted lot, and the reader wonders how much happier they could be and how much happier they could make an intelligent and lively young woman like Effi if they were a little warmer, more natural, and more forthcoming. Juxtaposed to these dull and hidebound characters is the figure of Roswitha, Effi's faithful servant. She is a simple, humane person who does not hesitate to demonstrate such deeply felt emotions as grief, love, and compassion. While Effi's mother is prompted by her concern for the norms of society to forbid her sinful daughter to enter her parental home, Roswitha stays with her in very humble circumstances and remains her servant and companion until the end.

This and similar criticisms of social conventions may be regarded as inferential; they may be discerned from a close consideration of plot and characterization. There is, however, at least one protagonist who undergoes a development to the point where he overtly and consciously attacks contemporary social conventions. After Innstetten has discovered the incriminating letters, he has a long conversation with a colleague, whom he asks to act as a second in the duel. The colleague tries to dissuade Innstetten from the duel, particularly in view of the fact that Effi's adultery occurred almost seven years earlier, but Innstetten retorts,

> I have thought it all over. A man is not just an individual, he belongs to a whole, and we must always pay attention to the whole, we are absolutely dependent on it. If I could manage to live in isolation, I could ignore the matter . . . but that . . . society-something [*Gesellschafts-Etwas*] which tyrannizes us does not ask about charm or love or statutes of limitations. I have no choice. I must.

At this point in the narration, Innstetten follows the dictates of the "society-something" and proceeds to kill Crampas. His and Crampas's seconds notify the authorities, and everything is in perfect legal order. On his way back to Berlin, however, Innstetten begins to have his doubts. He remembers the way Crampas looked at him during his dying moments, and he tells himself that he did not kill him out of hatred, which would at least have been a human emotion, but because of a "concept, a made-up story, a comedy almost." Yet he says to himself, "I must now continue the comedy, and must send Effi away and ruin her, and myself along with her."

It is this "must," this obedience to human-made codes of behavior, no matter how much one doubts their validity, that brings grief and sometimes catastrophe upon many of Fontane's characters. In Innstetten's case, it takes three years of solitary suffering on his part and a moving letter from Roswitha (who begs him to send Effi her favorite old dog) for him to realize that "culture and honor" and "all this nonsense" are the cause of his and Effi's suffering.

It is the supreme irony of this novel that Effi, shortly before her death, expresses her conviction that her husband, in all of his cruelty, has treated her justly. It should be noted that the opposing views reached by the two protagonists are expressed by them, not by the narrator (who intrudes almost nowhere in the novel). In a brief epilogue that is set one month after Effi's death, her mother expresses doubts whether she and her husband gave Effi the right kind of education and whether Effi might not have been too young to marry. Her husband gives his standard response: "That leads us too far afield." In the final analysis, this evasive answer must be given to the question regarding Fontane's own stand on the problem of personal happiness versus social conventions. He raises many questions; he allows some of his major characters to attack contemporary codes of behavior, but those characters who infringe upon them are punished.

Before the Storm

Fontane's Prussian, or historical, novels are vast panoramas of the entire Prussian society. One of these novels takes place in the period of 1812 to 1813 and the other one in the late 1890's. Walter Möller-Seidel has described *Before the Storm* as the best historical novel written in Germany in the nineteenth century. Fontane himself described his intentions as follows: "to introduce a large number of characters from Mark Brandenburg from the winter 1812-1813 [and] to depict the manner in which the great feeling which was born then . . . affected various kinds of people." The "great feeling" was the joy and relief that the Prussian people felt at Napoleon's defeat in Russia in 1812 and the anticipation that Prussia would soon be free of French domination and occupation. (Prussia had previously been defeated by the French and forced into an alliance with them against Russia.)

In the novel, as the demoralized remnants of the defeated French army move westward into Prussia, the Prussian king still respects his pact with Napoleon, but the members of the nobility urge him and his government to attack the French and to rid the fatherland of them. This political aspect constitutes one strand of this long (seven-hundred-page) and diffuse novel: Several members of the rural gentry organize a militia and attempt unsuccessfully to drive the French out of Frankfurt an der Oder.

Several other strands of the action concern the relationships between two noble houses, their plans for intermarriage, and the disparate destinies of the young people in question. In addition, the novel abounds in vivid depictions of contemporary literary life, of members of the middle and peasant classes, and it even contains a breathtaking account of the battle of Borodino, which is at the same time a moving antiwar text. Obviously, this overabundance of material does not make for a tightly constructed plot, but toward the end of the novel, a unifying tenor does emerge—namely, the renewal of society. It is surely no accident that Lewin von Vitzewitz, the young heir to the manor of Hohen-Vietz, marries Marie, the daughter of a traveling circus artist. Lewin's father welcomes her into his family just as Lewin is about to leave for the war of liberation against the French. The timing of these two events seems to symbolize a juncture between the renewal of the Vitzewitz dynasty and that of the entire country. All in all, the various strands of the action, the vivid descriptions, and the loving care expended on each detail add up to a fascinating panorama of Prussian society at a crucial point in its history.

The Stechlin

Turning to *The Stechlin*, Fontane's last work, it may be well to quote from a letter of his in which he described his work to a Berlin publisher: "At the end an old man dies and two young people marry; that is more or less all that happens in five-hundred pages." Fontane's description of his novel is accurate as far as the paucity of the action is concerned, but it is misleading when one considers the abundance of symbolism and political and moral thought that the work contains. For the most part, the novel is set in the village of Stechlin and in the manor house of the same name, which is inhabited by Dubslaw von Stechlin, a retired major in his sixties. The marriage alluded to above is the one between Dubslaw's son Woldemar and Armgard von Barby, the daughter of a retired diplomat living in Berlin. This marriage solves Dubslaw's one major problem: Armgard's dowry will permit Woldemar to repay a mortgage that his father had to take on the manor, and the necessary repairs will be made. As a result, the material base for the continued existence of the Stechlin dynasty in its accustomed style would seem to be assured.

The many questions raised in the novel, however, go far beyond the material base of the Stechlin estate. Throughout the work, there are conversations and discussions about the role of the nobility and about the social contract between various segments of the population, as well as about the individual's relationship to society. The novel encompasses a vast political spectrum, and the reader becomes acquainted with supporters of the three main political parties—namely, the Conservatives, the Progressives, and the Social Democrats. As usual with Fontane, it is difficult to discern his own sympathies, but on the basis of the unequivocally positive characterization accorded to Pastor Lorenzen (the village pastor and Woldemar's mentor), it seems safe to say that the views he expresses are very close to the ones the author reached in his old age. Some of Lorenzen's statements, while a little dated now, bear rereading and rethinking even in the twentieth and twenty-first centuries. Consider, for example, his definition of the modern age:

> The main contrast between the modern and the old [ways of life] consists of the fact that human beings are no longer placed in their positions on the basis of their birth. . . . Previously one was a lord of a manor or a weaver of linen for three-hundred years; now every weaver can one day be the lord of a manor.

This statement is as relevant, and as debatable, in modern times as it was in Fontane's time.

Some of Lorenzen's and Dubslaw's other discussions sound even more relevant today, particularly the discussion about the pollution caused by a chemical plant in their county and Dubslaw's proposal that the workers, instead of working there, should each till half an acre of land, which the state should give them. Lest it appear that *The Stechlin* consists only of dry political or philosophical treatises, it should be pointed out that all of these serious thoughts are presented with light irony, that the interlocutors are depicted with all of their human foibles, and that none of them is presented as a villain. In this way, an air of lightheartedness and serenity pervades the whole work. Upon some reflection, Lorenzen's, Dubslaw's, and Melusine's concerns for their contemporaries emerge as age-old universal concerns—namely, humankind's care for humanity. Thus, in his last work, Fontane's thoughts transcended his previous preoccupation with individual happiness vis-à-vis social conventions to encompass a profound reflection on the question of collective well-being.

Franz P. Haberl

Other major works

NONFICTION: *Ein Sommer in London*, 1854; *Jenseits des Tweed*, 1860 (*Across the Tweed*, 1965); *Wanderungen durch die Mark Brandenburg*, 1865-1882; *Meine liebe Mete: Ein Briefgespräch zwischen Eltern und Tochter*, 2001; *Theodor Fontane und Martha Fontane: Ein Familienbriefnetz*, 2001.

MISCELLANEOUS: *Sämtliche Werke*, 1959-1975 (24 volumes).

Bibliography

Bance, Alan. *Theodor Fontane: The Major Novels*. New York: Cambridge University Press, 1982. Bance discusses all of Fontane's major long fiction. Includes notes and a bibliography.

Chambers, Helen. *The Changing Image of Theodor Fontane*. Columbia, S.C.: Camden House, 1997. Chambers charts the critical reception of Fontane's work from contemporary reviews published when his work first appeared through the 1990's. She focuses on criticism published since 1980, including feminist and psychoanalytic interpretations of his work. Includes a chapter on Fontane and the realistic novel, and features notes and a bibliography.

Craig, Gordon Alexander. *Theodor Fontane: Literature and History in the Bismarck Reich*. New York: Oxford University Press, 1999. Craig places Fontane within the context of historical events and the authors and literature published in nineteenth century Prussia. Contains chapters on the historical novels and the novels of society. Bibliography and index.

Doebeling, Marion, ed. *New Approaches to Theodor Fontane: Cultural Codes in Flux*. New York: Camden House, 1999. A collection of eight essays examines Fontane's realist approach to literature and explores the difficulty and ultimate impossibility of a true mirroring of reality. Includes a bibliography and an index.

Garland, Henry. *The Berlin Novels of Theodor Fontane*. New York: Oxford University Press, 1980. Contains detailed chapters on eleven of Fontane's novels. Includes an index and bibliography.

Krobb, Florian. "Distinctiveness and Change: The Depiction of Jews in Theodor Fontane and Other Bourgeois Realist Authors." In *The Image of the Jew in European Liberal Culture, 1789-1914*, edited by Bryan Cheyette and Nadia Valman. Portland, Oreg.: Valentine Mitchell, 2004. The examination of Fontane's work is included in this collection analyzing anti-Semitism in German, French, British, and Italian literature of the long nineteenth century.

Osborne, John. "Theodor Fontane: Post-War Novelist." In *Germany's Two Unifications: Anticipations, Experiences, Responses*, edited by Ronald Speirs and John Breuilly. New York: Palgrave Macmillan, 2005. Osborne's article about Fontane's postwar long fiction is included in a collection of essays examining the unification of Germany in both the nineteenth and twentieth centuries from literary, historical, and political perspectives.

Velardi, Carol Hawkes. *Techniques of Compression and Prefiguration in the Beginnings of Theodor Fontane's Novels*. New York: Peter Lang, 1992. A somewhat specialized study, but there is a good introduction for the beginning student and a useful bibliography. Velardi analyzes the beginnings of five novels—*The*

Woman Taken in Adultery, *Graf Petöfy*, *Beyond Recall*, *Effi Briest*, and *The Poggenpuhl Family*—to trace Fontane's development as a novelist and social critic.

Wansink, Susan. *Female Victims and Oppressors in Novels by Theodor Fontane and François Mauriac*. New York: Peter Lang, 1998. An interesting combination of literary and cultural criticism situating Fontane in his time while also reading his novels as complex studies of the interaction between characters and societal norms. Includes notes and a bibliography.

Zweibel, William I. *Theodor Fontane*. New York: Twayne, 1992. The starting place not only for beginning students but also for scholars wishing to review research on Fontane. Situates Fontane in his times and explores antiquarianism and romantic destiny, balladry and psychology, Fontane's treatment of the Prussian state, and his later fiction. Provides a chronology, notes, and an annotated bibliography.

SHELBY FOOTE

Born: Greenville, Mississippi; November 17, 1916
Died: Memphis, Tennessee; June 27, 2005
Also known as: Shelby Dade Foote, Jr.

Principal long fiction

Tournament, 1949
Follow Me Down, 1950
Love in a Dry Season, 1951
Shiloh, 1952
Jordan County: A Landscape in Narrative, 1954
Three Novels, 1964 (includes *Follow Me Down*, *Jordan County*, and *Love in a Dry Season*)
September September, 1978

Other literary forms

Shelby Foote began his writing career with poetry, publishing a number of poems in his high school newspaper as well as in *The Oxford Magazine*, an independent periodical published in Oxford, Mississippi. Foote later admitted, however, that he was more attracted to prose than to poetry and that he found prose rhythms more interesting than poetic rhythms; consequently, he abandoned poetry for prose writing.

Foote also wrote a number of short stories; all of his early stories appeared in *The Carolina Magazine*, the University of North Carolina's literary magazine, including such titles as "The Good Pilgrim: A Fury Is Calmed," "The Old Man That Sold Peanuts in New Orleans," "The Village Killers," "The Primrose Hill," and "Bristol's Gargoyle." *Saturday Evening Post* published "Flood Burial," which eventually became an incident in Foote's novel *Tournament*; *Saturday Evening Post* also published "Tell Them Good-By," a shorter version of a story that was eventually titled "Ride Out." Portions of *Shiloh* appeared in *Blue Book Magazine* and in *Esquire*. In 1957, Foote edited a book of short stories titled *The Night Before Chancellorsville, and Other Civil War Stories*, which included a legitimate shorter version of Foote's "Pillar of Fire." Because he favored the novel over the short story, however, he abandoned the latter form.

As writer-in-residence at the University of Virginia, Memphis State University, and Hollins College, Foote lectured extensively, teaching classes on the American Civil War as well as creative writing, the novelist as playwright, Jane Austen's novels, T. S. Eliot's poetry, Ernest Hemingway's short stories, and William Faulkner's works. Foote's Memphis State lectures are all preserved on tape, but his lectures at Hollins College were neither recorded nor published.

While he was writer-in-residence at the Arena Stage theater production company in Washington, D.C., Foote wrote one three-act play titled *Jordan County: A Landscape in the Round*, adapted from his novel *Jordan County*. Directed by Mel Shapiro, it was performed only once, on June 15, 1964, and has not been published. According to one critic, the only surviving texts are mimeographed script copies kept in the Arena Stage's files.

Aside from his major novels, Foote's most imposing and critically acclaimed work is his three-volume *The Civil War: A Narrative* (1958, 1963, 1974). More than 1.5 million words in length, Foote's account of the Civil War took him twenty years to complete; as he humorously remarks in one of the work's bibliographical notes, it took him "five times longer to write the war than the participants to fight it." Intensely interested in history, Foote believed that the historian and the novelist are interested in "the same truth," but they attempt to reach it by different means. Although he did not believe that historians should distort truth, he advised them not only to read the novels of the period they are studying but also to learn the novelists' and poets' techniques.

Acclaimed by reputable and demanding critics, Foote's *The Civil War* combines the research and methods of the historian with the techniques and art of the novelist. His Civil War narrative employs various literary techniques: protagonist (the South) versus antagonist (the Union), with each force embodied in its leaders, Jefferson Davis and Abraham Lincoln; in-depth development of major and minor characters; scenes rendered as a novelist would depict them, with a novelist's feel for the texture of language; and alternation of scene and summary. Because of its scope and power, *The Civil War* has been labeled "one of the finest histories ever fashioned by an American," "one of the most thorough histories of the Civil War yet done," and "a major achievement in the literature of the Civil War."

Achievements

Perhaps Shelby Foote's most notable achievement is that he won great distinction both as a novelist and as a historian. In recognition of Foote's talent and dedication to literature, special issues of the *Mississippi Quarterly* (1971) and *Delta* (1977), a French publication, were devoted entirely to his works.

The Guggenheim Memorial Foundation granted Foote a Guggenheim Fellowship in 1957, 1959, and 1960, and in his "Bibliographical Note" to the second volume of *The Civil War*, Foote thanked the foundation for the extended fellowship, which "made possible the buying of books and bread." In 1963, he was awarded a Ford Foundation Grant, and in 1994, he was elected to the American Academy of Arts and Letters.

Biography

Shelby Dade Foote, Jr., was born in Greenville, Mississippi, on November 17, 1916, to Shelby Dade Foote and Lillian Rosenstock Foote. His father was a prominent Greenville businessman. His grandfather, Huger Lee Foote, an early planter near Greenville, was the model for Hugh Bart, the protagonist of *Tournament*. Foote's great-grandfather had been a cavalry officer at the Battle of Shiloh during the American Civil War, and another ancestor, Isaac Shelby, had been one of Kentucky's early governors and had fought in the Battle of Kings Mountain.

Foote attended grammar and high school in Greenville. When he was about twelve years old, he read Charles Dickens's *David Copperfield* (1849-1850, serial; 1850, book), which made him realize that reading would be "worth a grown man's time," but he freely admitted that neither he nor his family had a literary background. The Foote household did possess, however, the Harvard Classics, Stoddard's Lectures, and current novels by writers such as Rex Beach, Vina del Mar, Percy Marks, and "lots of others mercifully forgotten."

One of Foote's best friends in Greenville was Walker Percy, later to become a distinguished novelist himself. Percy was being reared by his uncle, William Alexander Percy, who had a tremendous influence on Foote's reading and eventual interest in literature. Foote later recalled that there were literally thousands of books in the Percy house and noted that if the Percys had not moved to Greenville he might not have developed an interest in literary things. Very early, William Percy recommended that Foote read what he regarded as the three great modern novels—Marcel Proust's *Remembrance of Things Past* (1913-1927), James Joyce's *Ulysses* (1922), and Thomas Mann's *The Magic Mountain* (1924)—all three of which Foote read in about a six-week period. Foote continued to read extensively.

While in high school, Foote began writing poetry but soon turned from poetry to prose. After he graduated from high school, he enrolled at the University of North Carolina at Chapel Hill. Even though he was impressed with the large university library, he soon realized that he did not want a college degree, and about halfway through his first quarter, he dropped out of his classes in all of the subjects he did not like. He remained on the campus and would sneak into classrooms where undergraduate and even graduate courses that interested him were being taught. He particularly enjoyed medieval history, philosophy, and courses in the novel, but, ironically, he did not take any classes in creative writing. From 1935 to 1937, he worked on *The Carolina Magazine*, the university's literary publication, in which he published book reviews, poetry, and short stories.

When the Germans invaded Poland in September, 1939, Foote joined the Mississippi National Guard. He wrote *Tournament* in 1939 and submitted the manuscript to Alfred A. Knopf, but it was politely rejected by one of the editors, who informed Foote that, even though several other editors had liked it, *Tournament* was so experimental that it would not sell. The editor did suggest, however, that Foote put this first novel away and write another one, which the company would be glad to publish.

In 1940, Foote's National Guard unit was activated, and as an artillery sergeant, he marched off to Camp Blanding in Mississippi and then to World War II. He was eventually promoted to captain and then was discharged because he left his post in Northern Ireland to visit his girlfriend in Belfast (she eventually became his first wife). During the fall and winter of 1944, he worked as an Associated Press reporter in New York. On his days off he again began reading, often rereading those books he had enjoyed as an adolescent.

From January to November, 1945, Foote served in the combat intelligence branch of the U.S. Marine Corps. In the postwar years he was a construction worker, a radio copywriter, and a reporter for Hodding Carter's *Delta Democrat-Times*; Carter later said that Foote missed numerous assignments because he was busy writing fiction. Late in 1945, Foote took out the *Tournament* manuscript, reread it, and began a revision; as he himself admitted, his first version had been influenced too heavily by Joyce, Thomas Wolfe, and various other writers. *Tournament* was published in 1949, and Foote was touted as a "young creative writer of unusual talent." This first novel established Foote's fictional landscape; in *Tournament* and subsequent novels, Washington County and Greenville, Mississippi, became the fictional Jordan County and Bristol, Mississippi. With history as a backdrop, the novel introduced certain motifs that Foote's future narratives would examine: the transition from the Old South to the new South, the crisis of manhood, and the basic loneliness of the individual.

Following the publication of *Tournament*, Foote began a great creative period, publishing *Follow Me Down*, *Love in a Dry Season*, *Shiloh*, and *Jordan County* in quick succession. With the exception of *Shiloh*, all of these novels are about the changing way of life in the South and around Bristol and Jordan County. After the publication of *Jordan County*, Foote moved to Memphis, Tennessee, and in 1954 he began writing his monumental *The Civil War*, which would require three volumes and twenty years to complete.

Shelby Foote. (AP/Wide World Photos)

In 1956, Foote married Gwyn Rainer of Memphis; they had one son, Huger Lee Foote. (His first marriage ended in 1946, and a second marriage, to Marguerite DeSommes, which produced one daughter, Margaret Shelby Foote, lasted from 1948 to 1952. Foote and Rainer remained married until Foote's death in 2005.) In April, 1956, Foote wrote "The Down Slope," a Civil War tale about Mosby's Rangers, which Stanley Kubrick wanted to produce as a film. Although Kubrick had film options for "The Down Slope" and *Love in a Dry Season*, neither was made into a film because, as Foote remarked, his main characters are usually observers who do very little and who do not express what they are thinking in conversation with others. These qualities, according to Foote, do not translate into good films.

In November, 1963, Foote held the position of writer-in-residence at the University of Virginia, where he lectured about his methods of writing historical narrative. During the 1963-1964 season, he was playwright-in-residence at the Arena Stage theater production company in Washington, D.C., where he adapted "Rain Down Home," "A Marriage Portion," and "The Freedom Kick"—three stories from *Jordan County*—into a three-act play titled *Jordan County: A Landscape in the Round*.

Foote moved his family to the Alabama coast in 1964 but ran afoul of the Ku Klux Klan because of his stand on racial equality. After repeated threats, he moved his family back to Memphis. During the 1966-1967 school year, he was writer-in-residence at Memphis State University, and during the spring term of 1968, he held the same position at Hollins College, where he taught a course in the modern novel and gave lectures. In the summer of 1976, he was one of the guest speakers at the University of Mississippi's annual Faulkner Conference. In 1978, Foote published his last novel, *September September*.

Past the age of seventy Foote remained active in historical circles; in 1987, for example, he published a short article in *American Heritage*. In that same year, Random House issued a paperback version of *The Civil War*, to renewed critical acclaim. Foote's monumental work experienced a new surge of sales in 1990, when Foote came to widespread attention in the United States as the result of his appearance as an interview subject throughout Ken Burns's multipart film documentary *The Civil War*, which aired on the stations of the Public Broadcasting Service. Foote died after a heart attack on June 27, 2005, in Memphis.

Analysis

Shelby Foote's *The Civil War* and his six novels are based on three elements: a sense of history, a sense of place, and a sense of change. Foote's sense of history is not that of the antiquarian; rather, he is preoccupied with the historical roots of present conditions. As a novelist, he seeks to "thicken the present" in his narratives by bringing out the historical background. In *Tournament*, for example, Foote concentrates on the historical background of Jordan County and Bristol—the settling of the area in the 1820's, the Civil War, and World War I. *Love in a Dry Season* spans the period from the 1920's to World War II. The historical background for *September September* is the integration crisis at Little Rock Central High School in 1957.

Foote's sense of place is distinctly that of the American South. As William Faulkner created his mythical Yoknapatawpha County and Jefferson, Mississippi, so Foote created his mythical Jordan County and Bristol, Mississippi, which he peopled with blacks and whites, rich and poor, old and young. Like Faulkner's saga, Foote's series of novels includes recurring characters; a major character in one novel may be mentioned only in passing in another. *Tournament*, *Follow Me Down*, *Love in a Dry Season*, and *Jordan County* all take place in Bristol in Jordan County, and even though *September September* takes place in Memphis, four of the main characters are from Bristol. In novel after novel, then, Foote highlights the history of his South as it was first settled in the early 1800's, as it began to flourish and prosper, as it was torn and scarred by the Civil War, as it was decimated by the yellow fever epidemic, and as it changed in the ensuing decades.

In a critical comment, Foote grouped novelists into two categories. The first decides to write about a "situation in which a man does so-and-so"; the second decides to write about a "man who does so-and-so," which is followed by the situation. Foote believed that for a good writer, the man must come before the situation. Foote's interest in history and his rich sense of place are both subservient to his preoccupation with moral action, with men and women making choices, especially under the pressure of change.

Foote's themes arise logically from his analysis of history, place, and change. Beginning with *Tournament*, one of his major themes is the individual's loneliness. Each person is utterly alone, says Foote, in orgasm, in nausea, and in dying. Human beings must accept loneliness as a fact of life, attempting to achieve contact without expecting to lose their essential solitude. Another recurring theme in Foote's works is the crisis of manhood. Rooted in the romantic antebellum South, this concept of masculinity involves a complex code that governs every aspect of a man's life.

Tournament

Foote readily acknowledged that his first novel, *Tournament*, was written when he was "sort of thrashing around in the wilds of the English language." *Tournament* foreshadows Foote's interest in history, place, and change and introduces his themes of loneliness and masculinity. At the center of the story is the rise and fall of Hugh Bart. Structurally, the events are framed by a type of prologue and epilogue, both of which are titled "Asa." Asa is Bart's grandson, who, because he really never knew his grandfather, begins piecing together facts and details. Bart's rise and legend begin when he is elected to a four-year term as sheriff of Issawamba County, Mississippi; the climax of his rise is his restoration of Solitaire Plantation and his acceptance among the wealthy planters. Bart's fall begins with his son's refusal to accept the responsibility of his heritage and culminates when Bart sells Solitaire, leaves the horses and the land, and moves to "the buildings and sidewalks and people."

Foote's sense of history and place are evident in the plot line of *Tournament*. Once Bart purchases Solitaire Plantation, the actions center on Jordan County and Bristol. History figures prominently in the plot, as Foote gives an in-depth account of Isaac Jameson's cotton empire, carved out of the Mississippi wilderness and later destroyed during the Civil War. Symbolically, the fall of the Jamesons and the destruction of Solitaire parallel not only the fall and destruction of the Old South but also the fall and destruction of Bart's dream: Just as the Jamesons' way of life faded with a new era, so too will Bart's.

The changes that doom Bart are not directly related to the Civil War or any other particular historical event; rather, they are indigenous to the times. Bart's first son, Hugh, is expected to assume management of the plantation. Instead, he withdraws from the University of Mississippi after his freshman year, fails at managing Solitaire, and is fired from another job. Even Hugh's accidental death in a 1917 army camp is symbolic of Bart's doomed way of life. Other forces contributing to Bart's fall are his daughter Florence's lesbian sexuality and his daughter-in-law's promiscuity.

Along with the railroads, automobiles, and cinema palaces comes the new world of business and finance, and the ruthless greed that is part of that world is something Bart does not understand. He feels antagonistic toward those who make their livelihoods merely by manipulating money. The ruthlessness of such men is emphasized when Lawrence Tilden refuses to extend the due date on Abraham Wisten's loan, which results in Wisten's suicide. Ironically, too, Bart loses $250,000, the money he got from selling Solitaire, when he deposits it in the Commercial National Bank in Memphis and the bank fails. Foote's emphasis on how such changes mark an end to an era is nowhere more symbolic or poignant than in Bart's funeral procession. "It had to be horse-drawn" was Bart's command, and so the horse-drawn black hearse is followed by people in their automobiles.

Foote's *Tournament* also explores the southern tradition of masculinity; the title suggests the medieval sense of honor, a code of conduct befitting gentlemen. Bart is elected sheriff because of his excellent marksmanship, and his skills in both trap shooting and hunting win him acceptance among the planter aristocracy. Bart's courage is also a mark of his masculinity. This courage is evidenced when he single-handedly crashes through a barricaded cabin door and blows the head off a fugitive, and when he attempts to intervene in a gunfight between Cassendale Tarfeller and Downs Macready. Bart's business ethics are evident in his indignation toward Tilden's mercenary treatment of Wisten.

Finally, *Tournament* analyzes the theme of loneliness. The closing sentences in the Asa sections emphasize the basic loneliness of Bart's life. In the prologue, Asa says that the one conviction he has formed from Bart's life is that "each man, even when pressed closest by other men in their scramble for the things they offer one another with so little grace, is profoundly alone." In his closing section, Asa quotes Bart's dying words: "I'm in the dark, alone." Loneliness thus frames Bart's life and death, even though Bart had achieved some kind of contact with the people in his life.

FOLLOW ME DOWN

Foote stated that his second novel, *Follow Me Down*, was influenced by Robert Browning's *The Ring and the Book* (1868-1869) and by two of Faulkner's novels, *The Sound and the Fury* (1929) and *As I Lay Dying* (1930). *Follow Me Down* was also influenced by Ernest Hemingway, from whom Foote claimed to have learned about the "terrific ambiguity of life"; Foote equated the irony and pity in *Follow Me Down* with the pity and irony in Hemingway's *The Sun Also Rises* (1926).

Considered by some critics to be Foote's most striking novel, *Follow Me Down* is about the adulterous affair between Luther Eustis, a fifty-one-year-old Solitaire tenant farmer, and Beulah Joyner, a twenty-year-old girl. Their affair ends tragically when Luther hears strange voices ordering him to kill Beulah; he drowns her and weighs her body down in the water with two concrete blocks, a crime for which he is sentenced to life in prison at Parchman.

Structurally, this is one of Foote's most interesting novels in that the entire narration is composed of nine monologues. Beulah's monologue is the center of the novel and is framed by two monologues by Luther. Preceding these are monologues by the circuit court clerk, the newspaper reporter, and a deaf-mute; following Beulah's and Luther's monologues are ones by Luther's wife, the lawyer, and the turnkey at the jail. Foote later said that this technique was an experiment that enabled him to "examine a crime of passion by moving into it and then out of it." The beginning monologues become increasingly more personal, climaxing with Beulah's; then the monologues again move to the impersonal, ending with that of the turnkey, Roscoe Jeffcoat. Each character becomes individualized in his or her narration, and various details of the crime are seen from different points of view. Foote later used variations of this technique in *Shiloh* and *September September*.

In *Follow Me Down*, as in *Tournament*, Foote concentrates on the South in transition from traditional southern morality to modern sexuality. This conflict is skillfully and symbolically initiated when Foote describes the disruption of Brother Jimson's prayer meeting four different times by an automobile carrying three soldiers and two women, one of whom is Beulah. The harsh intrusion of the modern world is symbolized by the automobile, which, with horn blaring and engine roaring, scatters dust on the worshipers. The conflict between tradition and modernism is even more apparent when Jimson bodily hurls each of the soldiers into the bushes. The tragic and damning implication of this conflict is typified in the adulterous affair between Luther, who represents traditional religion, and Beulah, who represents modern sexuality. Instead of dealing guardedly with sexuality as he does in *Tournament*, Foote relates the perverse details of both Beulah's and her mother's pasts.

The major theme in *Follow Me Down* is again the basic loneliness of the individual. As Parker Nowell, Luther's lawyer, prepares his defense, he suddenly realizes that the "biographies" of Luther, Mrs. Pitts, and Beulah are actually "histories of inadequacy, the failure of Love." At the same time, he recognizes this condition in his own life; his wife has left him for another man. He concludes: "Love has failed us. We are essentially, irrevocably alone. . . . Love has failed us in this century."

LOVE IN A DRY SEASON

Perhaps Foote's most widely read novel, *Love in a Dry Season* has been ranked with *Follow Me Down*, and one critic has even compared its tone to that of F. Scott Fitzgerald's best work. Indeed, Jeff and Amy Carruthers are reminiscent of Tom and Daisy Buchanan in *The Great Gatsby* (1925), but Foote's novel is unquestionably his own. The plot is an intricate weaving of the stories of the Barcrofts, Jeff and Amy Carruthers, and Harley Drew.

In *Love in a Dry Season*, Foote is once more concerned with history and place as background for his narrative. The center of action is again in Bristol, with side treks to Memphis, Winston-Salem, North Carolina, and Europe. Historically, it is Bristol in a period of transition, from the 1920's to World War II. The Barcroft section, which opens the novel, is a historical measuring stick by which Foote deals with the further erosion of southern values and traditions. Although Major Malcolm

Barcroft is in the mold of Jameson or Bart, he does not equal their stature. He imitates the old order in his conduct and demeanor, but he does not quite succeed because he is between two eras and a part of neither: He was too young for the Civil War and never saw action in the Spanish-American War; he marries into money instead of wrenching his fortune from the Mississippi wilderness; his son dislikes hunting and horses and is killed in a hunting accident; his daughters never marry, so there will be no Barcroft dynasty.

Jeff and Amy Carruthers and Harley Drew highlight the changes that have come to the South and Jordan County in the 1920's. Amy is the only one who has Bristol roots, but she was orphaned as a child and went to live in North Carolina, so her roots are not very deep. She becomes very promiscuous, a sign of the age, and thus becomes another character representing modern sexuality. Jeff is an outlander from Winston-Salem, and his family wealth comes not from growing tobacco but rather from manufacturing tobacco products; the emphasis on manufacturing underscores the rise of business and finance in the South with which Foote earlier dealt in *Tournament*. The wealth from manufacturing contrasts with the wealth the earlier southern planters received from working the land. Moreover, the new wealth turns people such as Josh Carruthers into petty and vindictive figures. Even Amy and Jeff's marriage is symptomatic of the times; it comprises constant rounds of quarreling and physical violence. Amy's promiscuity and Jeff's voyeurism become grotesque and self-defeating. When Jeff is blinded in an automobile accident, he can no longer watch; he complains, "It's no fun in the dark."

Another interesting character is Harley Drew, an outlander whose business ethics and morals are completely self-serving. For him, women are to be used either for his own sexual gratification (his assignations with hotel whores) or for advancing him socially and financially (his methodical courting of Amanda Barcroft). Drew is, moreover, an extension of the unscrupulous businessman such as Josh Carruthers or Lawrence Tilden; Tilden hires Drew for his bank and they work well together. Conducted in other towns and later in the Briartree mansion with Jeff downstairs, Amy and Drew's adulteries mark the nadir of morality in Jordan County. In his characterization of Jeff, Amy, and Drew, Foote depicts the new southern generation whose values and morals are confused. Because they are so corrupt, indeed even comical, they are incapable of significant tragic action.

As the title implies, *Love in a Dry Season* is primarily about the failure of love. Like the characters' values and dreams, love has become distorted and devoid of meaning. Major Barcroft's narrow-eyed views of love make him domineering and ridiculous. Harley Drew's courtship of Amanda is based on personal gain instead of love, and his affair with Amy is couched in lust. Amy and Jeff's marriage contains no love at all. Equally important in the novel is the theme of masculinity or lack of it. Neither Drew nor Jeff conducts himself as his earlier counterparts would have. The duel between Cass Tarfeller and Downs Macready in *Tournament* seems senseless, yet Cass acts properly for a man whose daughter has been violated. Jeff's attempted murder of Drew is a parody of the duel as well as an ineffectual attempt to assert manhood.

Shiloh

Foote included among the influences on his next novel, *Shiloh*, the works of Leo Tolstoy, Stendhal, and Stephen Crane. Acclaimed by critics as a "brilliant book" and the "nearest thing of its kind" to Crane's *The Red Badge of Courage* (1895), *Shiloh* uses multiple viewpoints, as Foote had previously done in *Follow Me Down* and would later do in *September September*. *Shiloh* is composed of seven chapters; with the exception of the first and last chapters, which are narrated by Lieutenant Palmer Metcalfe, the chapters alternate between Union and Confederate narrators. The preparations for the battle in the first two chapters, the actual movement into the battle in chapter 3 followed by details of the battle, and the moving out of the battle in the last chapter echo a progression somewhat similar to that in *Follow Me Down*.

Unlike Foote's other works, *Shiloh* does not take place in Jordan County. Even though some of the combatants are from Mississippi, Foote's aim is not to emphasize his mythical county but rather to deal with a particularly bloody Civil War battle that presaged the defeat of the South and the end of the old order. Lieutenant Metcalfe embodies these concepts, especially when he helps plan a perfect battle strategy on paper and when he recalls the words of his father and of the Union general

William Tecumseh Sherman. His father has foretold the defeat of the South because of its "incurable romanticism and misplaced chivalry," and Sherman has observed that the North has industry while the South has only "spirit and determination."

The crisis of manhood is the major theme of *Shiloh*, because war is a crucible that tests men's mettle. Soldiers of both South and North are quick to praise courageous and ferocious actions on either side. Sergeant Jefferson Polly, for example, feels ashamed for the six thousand Yankee soldiers he sees who have fled from battle and are skulking under the river bluff; he then recalls the bravery of the Yankees who fought in the Hornets Nest and whom he praises as being "as brave as any men." In *Shiloh*, the epitome of southern masculinity is General Forrest, who is inspiring and courageous, the "first cavalryman of his time." Typical of Forrest's courage is the incident in which he leads a charge and finds himself surrounded by enemy troops but cuts and slashes his way to freedom. In comparing Jeff Carruthers, Harley Drew, and Rufus Hutton with Forrest, one can readily see the decline of the South.

Jordan County

Jordan County is a collection of short stories that, much like Joyce's *Dubliners* (1914), Sherwood Anderson's *Winesburg, Ohio* (1919), and Faulkner's *Go Down, Moses* (1942), should be read as a novel. Termed a history in reverse, *Jordan County* begins with "Rain Down Home," set in the post-World War II era, and ends with "The Sacred Mound," set in the 1700's.

"Rain Down Home" is primarily about the effects of change and the lack of love. Pauly Green, a World War II veteran, returns to Bristol and exclaims, "They changed it on me while my back was turned." As he wanders through Bristol he notes the changes, and he also attempts conversations with people. He talks with a waitress in a café, a little girl, and an old man in Wingate Park, but he encounters indifference at every turn. Symbolically, his odyssey through Bristol and his attempts at conversation are based on the initial question he asks the waitress: "Why doesnt [*sic*] everybody love each other?" Later in his conversation with the old derelict, Pauly says that he wants to live in the world but that he does not understand why people cannot be happy, and he adds, "Not cant [*sic*]: wont [*sic*]." Completely frustrated by the lack of love and communication in a changed Bristol, all Pauly can do is shoot up the Greek café; the subsequent headlines label him a "deranged veteran."

"Ride Out" has been widely praised for its artistic excellence and for its tragic rendering of the ambiguities of life. Beginning in Bristol, it moves to New York and then back to Bristol. The story captures the flavor of the Jazz Age; its main character is Duff Conway, a Bristol black man who learns to play the cornet in reform school and rises to become a famous jazz musician in New York, where he contracts tuberculosis. He returns to Bristol, where he falls in love with Julia Kinship, who has a "capacity for cruelty" and who uses Duff until someone better comes along. Chance Jackson, a gambler from Oxford, furnishes the violence Julia demands. Duff shoots Jackson and is subsequently executed for the murder. The decline of traditional southern values is vividly imaged in this final confrontation, in which the notion of manhood has been violently perverted. Foote appears to endorse Duff's simple explanation to Harry Van, his New York friend: "Going off like that I lost touch with everything I was born to be with. . . . I ought to stayed home where I belonged."

"A Marriage Portion" is set in the 1920's and is narrated by a married woman. She talks about dating, marriage, and wedded life. During her narration, certain facts emerge that relate to Foote's recurring themes: She and her husband are confined in a loveless marriage (the failure of love); the husband is unstable and an alcoholic (the fall from greatness and heroic action); she had wanted him to "tame" her, but she is obviously the stronger of the two (the emasculation of the male).

"Child by Fever" is more a novella than a short story. As part of Foote's history in reverse, its time span includes the historical background of the Sturgis and Wingate families and focuses primarily on Hector Sturgis's life from 1878 to 1911. Spoiled and pampered by his grandmother, Esther Wingate, Hector is another example of the emasculated and ineffectual male. Two incidents are crucial in developing this idea. First, as a boy Hector reacts violently to the taunts of his classmates but becomes physically sickened by his actions. Second, he marries Ella Lowry, whose extramarital affairs anger him so that he slaps her, but when she urges him to hit her again, he can only weep. His death is not even tragic because he is incapable of decisive action; he commits suicide after continually blaming himself for Ella's death, even though she and her lover were accidentally asphyxiated while making love.

"The Freedom Kick" examines the change that freedom entails for African Americans in the South. When the narrator's father is roughed up by a black policeman, his mother wants to sue the town of Bristol. From his retrospective viewpoint, the narrator explains that his father's scuffle and his mother's actions were indicative of the confused times. The carpetbaggers were talking about freedom, for example, and the Ku Klux Klan was night-riding and burning crosses.

"Pillar of Fire" is the only story in the collection to deal directly with the Civil War. The plot details the Jameson history—the carving of an empire out of the wilderness and the destruction of the Solitaire mansion by a Union detachment. The destruction of Solitaire symbolizes the defeat and destruction of the South and the dissolution of the planter aristocracy and the old southern way of life. The pity and irony of both defeats climaxes in the description of Isaac Jameson, who, alone, aged, and partially paralyzed, can only sit in a chair in the yard and watch the pillar of fire.

The last story, "The Sacred Mound," takes place in the Province of Mississippi in 1797. It is in the form of a court-recorded deposition made by a Choctaw Indian, Chisahahoma, whose Christian name is John Postoak. He relates the murders of Lancelot Fink and a man identified only as Tyree. Captured by the Indians, these two trappers suffer bloody deaths. Tyree's heart is cut out and shown to him before he dies; Lancelot Fink's sexual organs are cut off and thrown at his feet, and he dies "badly, still crying for mercy when he was far beyond it." Tyree's stoic death contrasts with Fink's, and the deaths relate to Foote's theme of masculinity. In addition, this story deals with civilizations in transition. Just as the coming of the white settlers foretells the end of the Choctaw civilization, so too will changes in later historical eras bring an end to traditional southern lifestyles.

September September

September September is set in Memphis, Tennessee, in 1957. Podjo Harris, Rufus Hutton, and Reeny Perdew—who all live in Bristol—have come to Memphis to kidnap a black boy, Teddy Kinship, son of Eben Kinship and grandson of the wealthy Theo Wiggins. Timing the kidnapping to coincide with the integration crisis at Little Rock Central High School in Arkansas, Podjo and Rufus successfully kidnap the boy and get the sixty thousand dollars in ransom money. Jealous and angry because Reeny prefers Podjo to him, Rufus double-crosses Podjo, takes all of the ransom money except for one thousand dollars, and is killed in an automobile accident.

The backdrop of the integration crisis in Little Rock highlights the changes that have evolved through the centuries in Foote's fictional world. As a successful and wealthy Beale Street businessman, Wiggins typifies the rise of some African Americans. The impending violence in Little Rock indicates that such transitional periods bring extremes of both good and evil. Ironically, the potential violence from the white community is the basis of the threat Podjo and Rufus use to intimidate Eben and Theo.

The transient lives of the characters of *September September* are symbolic of the shift from the small towns of the South to the sprawling cities. As these people desert their southern heritage and as they are caught up in modernism, their dreams and ambitions shrink to a pitiable level. Podjo's dream is to be a big winner in Las Vegas, Reeny's dream is to come "powing out of cakes," and Rufus wants fame and a new automobile. Eben's dreams are of his family's secure future, which contrasts with the ephemeral and hedonistic goals of the other three characters. Part of the novel's irony is that Eben is the only one who succeeds in his endeavors. He has courage enough to confront Theo about a higher salary and a house of his own.

An enduring author both particularizes and universalizes his own fictional world. Like Faulkner, Foote creates an imaginary corner of Mississippi, a fictional place that comes to seem as real as the house next door. Such an achievement is possible only in a cycle of novels, in which generations pass and familiar characters come and go. Like Faulkner, although on a much smaller scale, Foote achieves in his cycle of novels something of the density and complexity of real life, and it is for this achievement that his fiction will be remembered.

Edward C. Reilly

Other major works

play: *Jordan County: A Landscape in the Round*, pr. 1964.

nonfiction: *The Civil War: A Narrative—Fort Sumter to Perryville*, 1958; *The Civil War: A Narrative—Fredericksburg to Meridian*, 1963; *The Civil War: A Narrative—Red River to Appomattox*, 1974; *Conversations with Shelby Foote*, 1989 (William C. Carter, editor); *The Correspondence of Shelby Foote and Walker Percy*, 1997 (Jay Tolson, editor).

edited texts: *The Night Before Chancellorsville, and Other Civil War Stories*, 1957 (also known as *Chickamauga, and Other Civil War Stories*, 1993); *Anton Chekhov: Early Short Stories, 1883-1888*, 1999; *Anton Chekhov: Later Short Stories, 1888-1903*, 1999; *Anton Chekhov: Longer Short Stories from the Last Decade*, 2000.

Bibliography

Chapman, C. Stuart. *Shelby Foote: A Writer's Life*. Jackson: University Press of Mississippi, 2003. Biography describes Foote's ambivalence and contradictory ideas about the South and discusses how these conflicts are expressed in his fiction, including the novels *Jordan County*, *Love in a Dry Season*, and *September September*.

Foote, Shelby. "'Live' with *The American Enterprise*." Interview by Bill Kauffman. *The American Enterprise* 12, no. 1 (January/February, 2001). Foote discusses a wide range of topics in this long interview, including his military service, the origins of his three-volume history of the Civil War, and his views on race relations.

Panabaker, James. *Shelby Foote and the Art of History: Two Gates to the City*. Knoxville: University of Tennessee Press, 2004. Panabaker attempts to burnish what he perceives as tepid critical reception for Foote's work among the academic community. Argues that Foote is uniquely able to combine the sensibilities of a fiction writer with a historian's discipline, producing works that offer a view of the South that was unavailable to William Faulkner and previous writers from that region. Includes index and bibliography.

Phillips, Robert L., Jr. *Shelby Foote: Novelist and Historian*. Jackson: University Press of Mississippi, 1992. Presents literary analyses of Foote's works, including his novels, and describes how Foote used novelistic techniques in the creation of his Civil War history. Includes bibliography and index.

Rubin, Louis D., ed. *The History of Southern Literature*. Baton Rouge: Louisiana State University Press, 1985. Comprehensive literary history of the South contains a brief chapter on Foote by Robert L. Phillips that provides short summaries of his novels.

Tolson, Jay. *Pilgrim in the Ruins: A Life of Walker Percy*. Chapel Hill: University of North Carolina Press, 1992. Well-reviewed biography of Percy chronicles Foote's friendship with the author and provides biographical information on Foote. Includes bibliography and index.

White, Helen, and Redding S. Sugg, Jr. *Shelby Foote*. Boston: Twayne, 1982. Provides analytical and critical insights into Foote's work both as a literary figure and as a historian. Begins with historical information on the Mississippi Delta in the years preceding the Civil War. Includes chronology and helpful bibliography.

FORD MADOX FORD

Ford Madox Hueffer

Born: Merton, England; December 17, 1873
Died: Deauville, France; June 26, 1939
Also known as: Ford Madox Hueffer; Fenil Haig

Principal long fiction

The Shifting of the Fire, 1892
The Inheritors, 1901 (with Joseph Conrad)
Romance, 1903 (with Conrad)
The Benefactor, 1905
The Fifth Queen, 1906
An English Girl, 1907
Privy Seal, 1907
The Fifth Queen Crowned, 1908
Mr. Apollo, 1908
The Half Moon, 1909
The Nature of a Crime, 1909 (serial), 1924 (book; with Conrad)
A Call, 1910
The Portrait, 1910
Ladies Whose Bright Eyes, 1911
The Simple Life Limited, 1911
The New Humpty-Dumpty, 1912
The Panel, 1912
Mr. Fleight, 1913
The Young Lovell, 1913 (also known as *Ring for Nancy*)
The Good Soldier, 1915
The Marsden Case, 1923
Some Do Not . . ., 1924
No More Parades, 1925
A Man Could Stand Up, 1926
The Last Post, 1928
A Little Less than Gods, 1928
No Enemy, 1929
When the Wicked Man, 1931
The Rash Act, 1933
Henry for Hugh, 1934
Vive le Roy, 1936
Parade's End, 1950 (includes *Some Do Not . . .*, *No More Parades*, *A Man Could Stand Up*, and *The Last Post*)

Other literary forms

Ford Madox Ford was an extremely prolific author, working in virtually every literary form. His children's stories and fairy tales include *The Brown Owl* (1891), *The Feather* (1892), *The Queen Who Flew* (1894), *Christina's Fairy Book* (1906), and the pantomime *Mister Bosphorus and the Muses* (1923). His volumes of poetry include *The Questions at the Well* (1893, as Fenil Haig), *Poems for Pictures* (1900), *The Face of the Night* (1904), *From Inland, and Other Poems* (1907), *High Germany* (1911), *On Heaven, and Poems Written on Active Service* (1918), *A House* (1921), *New Poems* (1927), and *Collected Poems* (1936). Acknowledged with Joseph Conrad as coauthor of the novels *The Inheritors* and *Romance*, Ford may also have had some hand in the composition of a number of Conrad's other works during the decade from 1898 to 1908. Ford's biographical, autobiographical, and critical works include *Ford Madox Brown* (1896), *Rossetti* (1902), *Hans Holbein, the Younger* (1905), *The Pre-Raphaelite Brotherhood* (1907), *Ancient Lights* (1911), *The Critical Attitude* (1911), *Henry James* (1913), *Thus to Revisit* (1921), *Joseph Conrad: A Personal Remembrance* (1924), *The English Novel* (1929), *Return to Yesterday* (1931), *It Was the Nightingale* (1933), and *Portraits from Life* (1937; also known as *Mightier than the Sword*, 1938).

During the last years of his life, Ford served as professor of comparative literature at Olivet College in Michigan and prepared his final book, a massive critical history of world literature, *The March of Literature* (1938). His history and travel books include *The Cinque Ports* (1900), *Zeppelin Nights* (1916), *Provence* (1935), and *Great Trade Route* (1937). Collections of Ford's essays include *The Soul of London* (1905), *The Heart of the Country* (1906), *The Spirit of the People* (1907), *Women and Men* (1923), *A Mirror to France* (1926), *New York Is Not America* (1927), and *New York Essays* (1927). Several volumes Ford classified simply as propaganda, including *When Blood Is Their Argument* (1915) and *Between St. Dennis and St. George* (1915). Ford also edited *The English Review* and later

The Transatlantic Review and wrote much ephemeral journalism.

Achievements

It is generally agreed that Ford Madox Ford's *The Good Soldier* is one of the masterpieces of modernism, a major experimental novel of enormous historical and artistic interest. His tetralogy *Parade's End*, composed of *Some Do Not . . .*, *No More Parades*, *A Man Could Stand Up*, and *The Last Post*, is also a key work in the modernist revolution, more massive than *The Good Soldier*, more sweeping in its treatment of historical change, but less daring in its formal innovations. After these five novels, there is a considerable drop in the quality of Ford's remaining fiction. The historical trilogy concerning Henry VIII (*The Fifth Queen*, *Privy Seal*, and *The Fifth Queen Crowned*) is cited by some critics as meriting serious reading. Scattered among his many volumes, works such as *A Call* reward the reader with surprisingly high quality, but most of the lesser books are all too obviously potboilers.

Ford was equally at home in the English, French, and German languages, and he contributed to the cosmopolitan and polyglot texture of European modernism. As an editor of influential literary magazines, he recognized and encouraged many writers who have since become famous. His collaboration with Joseph Conrad in the 1890's corresponded with Conrad's most productive artistic period, but whether Conrad's achievements were stimulated by Ford's collaboration or accomplished in spite of Ford's intrusion is still under debate. Ford also exercised a considerable influence on Ezra Pound during Pound's early London years. Later, after World War I, Ford was associated with all the prominent writers of the Parisian Left Bank: James Joyce, Ernest Hemingway, Jean Rhys, and others.

Ford's achievement then, was as a man of letters whose diverse contributions to modern literature—particularly as an editor and as a champion of modernist writers—far transcended his not inconsiderable legacy as a novelist.

Biography

Ford Madox Hueffer was born in Merton, now a borough of London, on December 17, 1873; he was named for his maternal grandfather, the Pre-Raphaelite painter Ford Madox Brown (1821-1893). Brown had two daughters: The elder married William Michael Rossetti (brother to the poet Dante Gabriel Rossetti); the younger daughter, Catherine, married the German journalist Francis Hueffer, music critic for *The Times* of London, who wrote many books and had a serious scholarly interest in Richard Wagner, Arthur Schopenhauer, and Provençal poetry. Ford was born to this couple and grew up in an intellectual hothouse of painters, musicians, artists, and writers with advanced ideas.

His family expected him to be a genius, which led him to acquire, early in his life, a sense of inadequacy and failure. Ford tended later to falsify information in his biography and to have difficulty separating reality from fantasy in his recollections. He attended the coeducational Praetorius School in Folkestone, apparently an institution with very modern ideas of education. One of his schoolmates there was Elsie Martindale, a young woman whom he married, against her parents' wishes, in 1894. Perhaps this elopement by the impetuous young lovers shows Ford's tendency to play out in reality the conventions of courtly love, a subject of intense study by Ford's father and a preoccupation of the author himself in all his fiction, evident even in his final book, the critical survey *The March of Literature*. Ford and Elsie did not, however, find passionate love a practical way to attain long-term happiness or stability.

In September, 1898, Edward Garnett introduced Ford to Joseph Conrad, now recognized as one of the greatest English-language novelists, even though his native tongue was Polish. Ford, like Conrad, was multilingual, and, at least to some degree, he helped Conrad with the niceties of the English idiom. The two would often write in French and then translate the work into English. By the spring of 1909, however, Ford and Conrad had quarreled and were never again closely associated. They acknowledged that they collaborated on *The Inheritors* and *Romance*, although Ford must have had at least some slight hand in many of Conrad's fictions written between 1898 and 1909. In fairness, it should be noted that Ford, too, must have had his ideas and his style permanently shaped to some degree by his collaboration with the older, more worldly master, Conrad.

Conrad had married Englishwoman Jessie George

in 1896, and he lived in a settled and respectable way with her until his death in 1924. At least in part, Conrad's breach with Ford stemmed from Jessie's dislike for what she regarded as Ford's ever more outrageous sexual behavior. In 1903, Ford had an affair with his wife's sister, Mary Martindale. Throughout his fiction, Ford replays similar real-life issues of passion, adultery, and their tawdry consequences. Thomas C. Moser, in *The Life in the Fiction of Ford Madox Ford* (1980), maintains that Ford's writing follows a cyclical pattern, with each outburst of creativity triggered by the introduction of a new love into his life: Elsie Martindale, Mary Martindale, Arthur Marwood, Violet Hunt, Brigit Patmore, Jean Rhys, Stella Bowen, and Janice Biala. Moser's thesis is a bit too neat to be completely convincing, but its outline suggests the generally messy personal life that Ford must have been living while writing his voluminous works.

Ford Madox Ford. (Archive Photos)

Analysis

From his association with Conrad, his study of Henry James and of the rise of the English novel, and his knowledge of French literature, Ford Madox Ford developed his notion of literary impressionism, which is central to an understanding of his masterpiece, *The Good Soldier*. Ford's clearest statement of his theory of literary impressionism is found in *Joseph Conrad: A Personal Remembrance*, where Ford describes literary impressionism as a revolt against the commonplace nineteenth century novel, or "nuvvle," as he calls it. The impressionist novel should not be a narration or report, but a rendering of impressions. Rather than following a linear plot, giving one event after another as they occur, the impressionist novel enters the mind of a storyteller and follows his or her associated ideas in a tangled stream of consciousness, so that vivid image becomes juxtaposed to vivid image, skipping across space and time in a collage of memory and imagination. The impressionist novel takes as its subject an *affair*, some shocking event that has already happened, and proceeds in concentric rings of growing complication as the storyteller cogitates. The focus of the novel is internal rather than external. The reader must focus on the storyteller's mental processes rather than on the events themselves.

The impressionist novel is limited to the mind of the storyteller, and so is finally solipsistic. The novel refers to itself, so that the reader can never "get out of" the storyteller's limited mentality and judge whether the storyteller is reliable or unreliable, perhaps merely a crazy person telling a tale that has no connection whatever to reality. Limited and unreliable narration, time shifts, fragmentation of details torn from the contexts in which they occur, verbal collages of such fragments in configurations produced by the narrator's association of ideas, defamiliarization of the commonplace—all these are characteristics of Ford's best work.

The traditional nineteenth century English novel depended on the convention of the linear plot. The process of reading from page one to the end of the text was generally assumed to correspond to the passage of time as one event followed another in the story, so that the hero might be born on page one, go to school on page fifty, commit adultery or consider committing adultery on page one hundred, and meet his just reward in the concluding pages of the book. In *The Good Soldier*, Ford rejected this linear structure and substituted for it the "affair": A shocking set of events has already occurred before the book begins, and the narrator weaves back and forth in his memories related to the affair. Gradually, in concentric circles of understanding, the reader learns the complicated situation underlying the superficial first impressions he or she may have formed. The drama of the story shifts from the events of the tale to the process of the telling; such stories necessarily contrast first appearances with deeper "realities" revealed in the narration.

The Good Soldier

The Good Soldier concerns two married couples: Arthur Dowell (the narrator) and his wife, Florence (Hurlbird) Dowell, and Edward Ashburnham and his wife, Leonora (Powys) Ashburnham. The events of the story take place between August, 1904, and August, 1913, a nine-year period throughout most of which the two couples are the best of friends, living the life of the leisured rich at European spas, in elegant, cultivated idleness. There is an elegiac tone to this work, reflecting the autumn sunshine of the Edwardian era and a way of life that would be brutally wiped out with the outbreak of World War I.

The texture of the novel invites the reader to consider the conflict between appearance and reality. For most of the nine-year period of the action, Arthur Dowell believes that his wife is suffering from a heart ailment that confines her travels and requires her to be shut in her room under peculiar circumstances from time to time. He subsequently learns, however, that her heart is sound and that these arrangements are necessary to allow her to commit adultery, first with a young man named Jimmy and later with Edward Ashburnham. Dowell imagines Ashburnham to be a model husband, only gradually learning that he has engaged in a series of affairs and that his wife does not speak to him except when required to do so in public. This novel is like a hall of mirrors, and any statement by the narrator must be doubted.

Because readers are accustomed to novels with linear plots, a summary of the novel is more easily understood if the plot is rearranged into the customary linear sequence of events. Edward Ashburnham is from an ancient Anglican landholding family who owns the estate Branshaw Teleragh. As the novel opens, he has recently returned from serving as a military officer in India and arrives at the health spa, Bad Nauheim, in Germany, where he meets the Dowells for the first time. Although he appears to be brave, sentimental, and heroic, like the knights in ancient romances, the reader learns that he has been involved in a series of unfortunate affairs with women. His parents arranged his marriage to Leonora Powys, a convent-educated Catholic girl, whose impoverished family had an estate in Ireland. Religious and temperamental differences soon cause their marriage to cool. While riding in a third-class carriage, Edward tries in a blundering way to comfort a servant girl and is arrested for sexual misbehavior in what is called the Kilsyte case. This misadventure leads him for the first time in his life to consider himself capable of bad conduct. His next affair involves a short-lived passion for a Spanish dancer, La Dolciquita, who demands cash for spending a week with him at Antibes. Reckless gambling at the casino, combined with the direct expenses of La Dolciquita's passion, substantially depletes Edward's inherited fortune. His wife, Leonora, makes herself the guardian of his estate and sets out to recover their financial losses. She demands that he take a military post in India for eight years and doles out his spending money carefully while squeezing his tenants and lands back in England for as much profit as possible.

In India, Edward finds his next woman, Mrs. Basil, whose husband, a fellow officer, allows the affair to continue in order to blackmail Edward. Eventually, Mrs. Basil's husband is transferred to Africa so that she can no longer stay with Edward. Edward then makes an alliance with Mrs. Maidan, also the wife of a junior officer. Mrs. Maidan has a heart condition and accompanies the Ashburnhams to Bad Nauheim for treatment. On the day that the Dowells and the Ashburnhams first meet, Leonora Ashburnham has found Mrs. Maidan coming out of Edward's bedroom in the hotel. Enraged, Leonora has slapped her and, in doing so, entangled her bracelet in Mrs. Maidan's hair. Florence Dowell sees them struggling in the hallway and comes to help. Leonora lamely explains that she has accidentally caught her bracelet in Mrs. Maidan's hair, and Florence helps them get untangled, after which the sobbing Mrs. Maidan runs to her room. That evening, Leonora insists on sitting at the Dowells' dinner table in the hotel so as to prevent any gossip about that day's events in the hallway. Mrs. Maidan soon commits suicide, leaving Edward free to form a liaison with Florence Dowell herself.

Edward's ward, Nancy Rufford, is being educated in the same convent where Leonora went to school. As Nancy grows to a mature woman, Edward becomes attracted to her, but he is caught in the conflict between love and honor. He desires Nancy, but he is honor-bound not to violate his sacred trust to protect her. After Florence Dowell learns of Edward's affection for Nancy (along with some other distressing developments), she too commits suicide. Edward remains firm, however, and refuses to take advantage of his ward or corrupt her, even when she openly offers herself to him. He arranges for her to be sent to her father in Ceylon. On her voyage there, she cables from Brindisi a cheerful note implying that she feels no sorrow about leaving him. Edward then commits suicide with a penknife, and Nancy goes insane when she hears of his death. His widow, Leonora, marries a rabbitlike neighbor, Rodney Bayham, while Arthur Dowell is left as the proprietor of the Branshaw Teleragh estate, where he nurses the insane Nancy Rufford.

From the exterior, to those who know him only slightly, Edward Ashburnham appears almost superhumanly noble, the ideal of the British country gentleman and good soldier. If the reader believes all that is alleged about him, he is quite the contrary, a raging stallion, recklessly ruining every female he meets. The superficial goodness is merely a veneer masking his corruption. All the other characters, as well, have two sides. Florence Dowell, the respectable wife, has had an affair before her marriage to Arthur with the despicable Jimmy and may have married simply to get back to her lover in Europe. She certainly does not hesitate to become Edward Ashburnham's mistress and commits suicide when she learns in a double-barreled blow that Edward is attracted to Nancy Rufford and that the man in whose house she committed adultery with Jimmy is now talking with her husband in Bad Nauheim. Leonora is purposeful in trying to manage her husband's estate economically, but she is cruel and unloving. The reader can easily imagine that her husband would be driven to seek other company. Arthur Dowell, the narrator himself, is stupid, lazy, and piggish.

Since the story is told entirely from the point of view of Arthur Dowell, and since his is a limited intelligence, the reader can never entirely trust the narration as reliable. Dowell may assert on one page that a character is noble yet show the reader in a hundred ways that the character is despicable. The reader is caught in the web of Dowell's mind. Clearly, Dowell sometimes does not tell the "truth"; but since the total work is fiction, the reader is confronted not simply with a conflict between appearance and reality but with the statuses of competing fictions. Is Edward a noble knight or a despicable roué? The story evaporates into the impressions in Dowell's mind. What Dowell thinks or believes *is* the truth at that moment in the fiction. It could be seriously argued that Edward, Leonora, and Florence have no external "reality" at all, that they are simply the imaginings of the sickly Dowell as he tells or dreams his story. This approach may shock readers of conventional fiction, who are accustomed to reading a novel as if the characters were real people, yet all characters in every fiction are simply projections of the author's creative imagination.

Parade's End

Ford's massive tetralogy *Parade's End* consists of four separate novels: *Some Do Not . . .* , *No More Parades*, *A Man Could Stand Up*, and *The Last Post*. The main theme of these works repeats a major concern of *The Good Soldier*, the destruction of the Tory gentleman. Edward Ashburnham in *The Good Soldier* belongs to the same class as Christopher Tietjens, the protagonist of *Parade's End*. Both are said to have been modeled on Ford's friend Arthur Marwood, who collaborated with Ford in publishing *The English Review*. Ashburnham is the landowner of Branshaw Teleragh, whereas Tietjens's family owns the Groby estate. Both feel an obligation to their dependents and take seriously their stewardship over the land. Both are highly altruistic in certain areas but are tormented by the conflict between their sexual impulses and what is considered proper or honorable behavior. They are Tory gentlemen, landowning, relaxed in manner, Anglican in religion, physically vigorous, classically educated, generous, virile, and possessed of a worldview in which man's place in the universe is clearly defined. Such men are assailed on all sides by women, by modern commercial industry, by Catholics and Jews, by fascists and communists, and finally by the internal contradictions of their own characters. World War I smashed that class of Tory landholding gentlefolk once and for all, in an externalization of that internal battle.

Because the books are a kind of verbal collage, creating a palimpsest of memory and imagination, weaving backward and forward through the minds of characters who are frequently under stress and incapable of reporting events without distorting them, the linear plot of the tetralogy is difficult to summarize. The first novel, *Some Do Not . . .*, opens with Christopher Tietjens traveling in a railway carriage. His destination, unknown to him at the time, is the future world, the wasteland created by World War I and the destruction of the comfortable Tory universe into which he was born. His wife, Sylvia, has a child of whom he is perhaps not the true father, and she has run away with another man to Europe. Christopher meets an attractive young woman named Valentine Wannop. In the course of the tetralogy, Valentine replaces Sylvia as Tietjens's mate. The war, when it breaks out, is a terrifying expression of the conflict already implied in the mind of Christopher.

In *No More Parades*, Christopher sees the men on the battlefield harassed by infidelity at home. The combat scenes in the next volume, *A Man Could Stand Up*, include ones in which Christopher is buried in a collapsed trench under fire, fights desperately to free his companions, and then is demoted for having a dirty uniform. At the end of this book, Valentine and Christopher come together in a nightmare party celebrating the end of the war. The final volume in the tetralogy, *The Last Post*, is composed of a series of dramatic monologues in which the reader learns that the estate has passed to other hands and that the Groby elm, signifying the Tietjenses' ownership of the land, has been cut down.

Ezra Pound suggested that Ford's contribution to modern literature could be measured less by reference to any given works than by "the tradition of his intelligence." While most of Ford's many novels have been consigned to oblivion, *The Good Soldier* and *Parade's End* testify to his manifold gifts as a man of letters and as a godfather to the modernists.

Todd K. Bender

Other major works

POETRY: *The Questions at the Well*, 1893 (as Fenil Haig); *Poems for Pictures*, 1900; *The Face of the Night*, 1904; *From Inland, and Other Poems*, 1907; *Songs from London*, 1910; *High Germany*, 1911; *Collected Poems*, 1913; *Antwerp*, 1915; *On Heaven, and Poems Written on Active Service*, 1918; *A House*, 1921; *New Poems*, 1927; *Collected Poems*, 1936; *Buckshee*, 1966 (wr. 1930).

NONFICTION: *Ford Madox Brown*, 1896; *The Cinque Ports*, 1900; *Rossetti*, 1902; *Hans Holbein, the Younger*, 1905; *The Soul of London*, 1905; *The Heart of the Country*, 1906; *The Pre-Raphaelite Brotherhood*, 1907; *The Spirit of the People*, 1907; *Ancient Lights*, 1911 (also known as *Memories and Impressions*); *The Critical Attitude*, 1911; *Henry James*, 1913; *Between St. Dennis and St. George*, 1915; *When Blood Is Their Argument*, 1915; *Zeppelin Nights*, 1916; *Thus to Revisit*, 1921; *Women and Men*, 1923; *Joseph Conrad: A Personal Remembrance*, 1924; *A Mirror to France*, 1926; *New York Essays*, 1927; *New York Is Not America*, 1927; *The English Novel*, 1929; *No Enemy*, 1929; *Return to Yesterday*, 1931 (autobiography); *It Was the Nightingale*, 1933 (autobiography); *Provence*, 1935; *Great Trade Route*, 1937; *Portraits from Life*, 1937 (also known as *Mightier than the Sword*, 1938); *The March of Literature*, 1938; *The Correspondence of Ford Madox Ford and Stella Bowen*, 1993; *A Literary Friendship: Correspondence Between Caroline Gordon and Ford Madox Ford*, 1999.

CHILDREN'S LITERATURE: *The Brown Owl*, 1891; *The Feather*, 1892; *The Queen Who Flew*, 1894; *Christina's Fairy Book*, 1906; *Mister Bosphorus and the Muses*, 1923.

MISCELLANEOUS: *The Presence of Ford Madox Ford: A Memorial Volume of Essays, Poems, and Memoirs*, 1981.

Bibliography

Brown, Dennis, and Jenny Plastow, eds. *Ford Madox Ford and Englishness*. Atlanta: Rodopi, 2006. Collection of essays focuses on Ford's ideas about England and the concept of "Englishness," describing him as a key participant in Edwardian debates about these subjects. Contributors analyze many of his works in terms of their "Englishness," including the novels *The Good Soldier*, *Parade's End*, and *The Fifth Queen*.

Cassell, Richard A., ed. *Critical Essays on Ford Madox Ford*. Boston: G. K. Hall, 1987. Collection includes essays dealing with Ford's romances, poetry, and social criticism, but the bulk of the contributions focus on *The Good Soldier* and *Parade's End*. In his introduction, Cassell reviews critical responses to Ford's work, which he argues became more laudatory and perceptive after 1939.

_______. *Ford Madox Ford: A Study of His Novels*. Baltimore: Johns Hopkins University Press, 1961. Three chapters covering Ford's biography, aesthetics, and literary theory are followed by close readings not only of the major works (*The Good Soldier*, *Parade's End*) but also of neglected minor fictional works, particularly *Ladies Whose Bright Eyes*, *The Rash Act*, and *Henry for Hugh*.

Green, Robert. *Ford Madox Ford: Prose and Politics*. New York: Cambridge University Press, 1981. Unlike earlier studies that applied New Criticism to Ford's work, Green places Ford within his historical context and identifies his political beliefs. Includes a chronological bibliography of Ford's works as well as an extensive selected bibliography of Ford criticism.

Hampson, Robert, and Max Saunders, eds. *Ford Madox Ford's Modernity*. Atlanta: Rodopi, 2003. Collection of essays examines how Ford's prose reflects the impact of modern experience, including new technologies and new ideas about gender, nation, empire, and subjectivity, with particular focus on *The Good Soldier*.

Haslam, Sara. *Fragmenting Modernism: Ford Madox Ford, the Novel, and the Great War*. New York: Manchester University Press, 2002. Focuses on the modernist characteristics of Ford's works, such as their fragmentation, use of the personal narrative, and literary technique. Includes bibliography and index.

_______, ed. *Ford Madox Ford and the City*. Atlanta: Rodopi, 2005. Fourteen essays explore Ford's depiction of both the real and the ideal city in his novels and other works, including his representations of London, New York, and Paris.

Huntley, H. Robert. *The Alien Protagonist of Ford Madox Ford*. Chapel Hill: University of North Carolina Press, 1970. Focuses on the Ford protagonist, who is typically a man whose alien temperament and ethics produce a conflict with his society. Includes a bibliography.

MacShane, Frank, ed. *Ford Madox Ford: The Critical Heritage*. London: Routledge & Kegan Paul, 1972. An invaluable collection of reviews and responses, gleaned from literary journals, to Ford's fiction and poetry. Contains an 1892 unsigned review of *The Shifting of the Fire* as well as essays by such literary greats as Theodore Dreiser, Arnold Bennett, Ezra Pound, Conrad Aiken, Christina Rossetti, H. L. Mencken, Graham Greene, and Robert Lowell. Includes reviews of individual novels, essays on controversies in which Ford was embroiled, and general studies of Ford's art.

Wiesenfarth, Joseph, ed. *History and Representation in Ford Madox Ford's Writings*. Atlanta: Rodopi, 2004. Collection of essays is devoted to analysis of Ford writings about twentieth century historical events, especially World War I, and how some of his other works represented past history, as best demonstrated by the *Fifth Queen* trilogy.

RICHARD FORD

Born: Jackson, Mississippi; February 16, 1944

PRINCIPAL LONG FICTION

A Piece of My Heart, 1976
The Ultimate Good Luck, 1981
The Sportswriter, 1986
Wildlife, 1990
Independence Day, 1995
The Lay of the Land, 2006

OTHER LITERARY FORMS

In addition to writing novels, Richard Ford has published collections of his own short fiction and has edited several short-story anthologies. *Rock Springs* (1987) brings together some of Ford's short stories that previously appeared in *Esquire*, *Antaeus*, *The New Yorker*, *Granta*, and *TriQuarterly*. Ford has also written screenplays, including an adaptation of his novel *Wildlife*. *Women with Men* (1997) is a collection of three novellas set in Montana, Chicago, and Paris that all revolve around the complications of romantic love. *A Multitude of Sins* (2001) consists of a series of dark short stories that generally concern the issue of infidelity.

ACHIEVEMENTS

Richard Ford has received increasingly high critical praise ever since *The Sportswriter*, which was generally regarded as one of the best novels of 1986. His short-story collection *Rock Springs* received accolades from many of North America's major reviewers. Ford's novels mark a return of the southern writer and a high point for "neorealist" or minimalist fiction. As such, they combine the symbolic and psychological depth of William Faulkner with the blunt, forceful prose of Ernest Hemingway, two writers whom Ford has acknowledged as being primary influences. Ford's evocation of a transient, displaced America is rendered with a deceptive simplicity that itself acts as counterpoint and comment on the complexity of postmodern American society. The hero of his 1995 novel *Independence Day*, Frank Bascombe, is one of the greatest delineations of the suburban, middle-class male in contemporary American fiction, a rival to John Updike's Rabbit Angstrom. *Independence Day* also consolidated Ford's reputation as a major American writer of the post-World War II era.

BIOGRAPHY

Richard Ford was the only son of Parker Carrol Ford, a salesman, and Edna (Akin) Ford, a housewife. Ford spent his youth in Jackson, Mississippi, but after his father suffered a nonfatal heart attack in 1952, Ford lived part of each year at his grandparents' hotel in Little Rock, Arkansas. As a teenager in Mississippi, Ford had several minor scrapes with the law. His father had another heart attack and died in Ford's arms in 1960.

Ford entered college at Michigan State University in 1962 to study hotel management. While there he met his future wife, Kristina Hensley, in 1964. They were married in 1968, and Kristina eventually earned a Ph.D. in urban planning. Ford gave up hotel management to major in English and graduated with a B.A. in 1966. He began and abandoned a law degree, then pursued a master of fine arts degree in fiction writing (awarded 1970) at the University of California at Irvine, where he studied under E. L. Doctorow. In 1970 he applied himself to becoming a full-time writer, attempting, without success, to publish short stories. The following year he began work on his first novel, *A Piece of My Heart*.

Ford has received numerous awards and honors, including a Guggenheim Fellowship, two grants from the National Endowment for the Arts, an American Academy of Arts and Letters Award for Literature, and the 1994 Rea Award, which is given annually to a writer who has made a contribution to the short story as an art form. In 1995, Ford's novel *Independence Day* was the first book to win both the Pulitzer Prize and the PEN/Faulkner Award.

Along with his own writing, Ford has edited issues of the literary journals *Ploughshares* (1996) and *TriQuarterly* (1998) as well as anthologies such as *The Granta Book of the American Short Story* (1992) and *The Granta Book of the American Long Story* (1998). Ford has taught at the University of Michigan, Williams College, and Princeton University.

The lives of Ford and his wife reflect the transience that is one of the major themes of his writings; they have moved frequently and had lived in twelve houses by the late 1990's, when they were living in New Orleans, where Kristina served as executive director of the city planning commission. In the year 2000, Ford and his wife relocated to a year-round home in East Boothbay, Maine, and Ford took a position teaching at Bowdoin College.

Analysis

Richard Ford's novels have been called neorealist and minimalist, and, although Ford disavows a connection to the minimalist school of writing, a deceptive simplicity of style does mark his novels. In response to the clutter of contemporary American life, Ford has retreated into a spare vision in which each image in his stripped-down prose resounds beyond itself. In the same fashion, the simple relationships of family and friendship that form the nexus of his narratives imply larger complexities. Ford often writes in the first person, and his central protagonists tend to be the marginalized: observers, outsiders, people carried away by circumstances. The mood of his novels is often one of impermanence, and this finds its analogue in the bleak, large, often featureless landscapes of the American South and Midwest that Ford favors. Characters move across these landscapes, through relationships, through livelihoods, with a casualness that demonstrates at once the potential and the rootless condition of modern life.

Richard Ford. (James Hamilton)

A Piece of My Heart

In Ford's first novel, *A Piece of My Heart*, two men, Robard Hewes and Sam Newel, arrive on an uncharted island in the Mississippi River peopled only by Mark Lamb, his wife, and their black servant, Landrieu. Hewes arrives to take a short-term job running poachers off the island. He has come to nearby Helena, Arkansas, to take up an old relationship with his cousin, Buena, now married to an industrial-league baseball player named W. W. That relationship is threatened by the possible jealousy of W. W. and the manic sexuality of Buena. Newel, a southerner now living in Chicago, arrives at the prompting of his lover, Beebe Henley, a flight attendant and granddaughter to Mrs. Lamb. One month from completing his requirements for a law degree, Newel becomes emotionally unbalanced, and Henley suggests a rest on the island. Newel is haunted by memories of his youth, memories that revolve around the grotesque and absurd: a midget film star, a pair of lesbians in a motel room, an electrocution.

The novel oscillates between the stories of Hewes and Newel, who are in many ways mirror images or complements of each other; both displaced southerners, they are driven by contradictory passions. On a symbolic level, Hewes is the body and Newel the mind; together, they are the spiritually troubled and physically corrupt South. The island on which they meet their fates is uncharted and lies between the states of Mississippi and Arkansas; like Joseph Conrad's Congo, it is a metaphoric destination, the human condition, the allegorical South. All the characters on the island are bound by their inability to escape the forces that have isolated them, thus they go to their fates with sheeplike acceptance, a fact reflected in the game Ford plays with their names:

Lamb, Hewes, Newel. The island becomes, for the two main characters, not an escape or a place of homecoming but a crucible for the forces that have shaped, and will destroy, both them and the culture they represent.

Having satisfied his lust, Hewes seems bent on escape. He takes Buena to a motel and there recoils from her insistent, and perhaps perverse, sexuality. His rejection prompts her to turn on him and call on her husband for vengeance. Hewes runs back to the island, but, though he escapes Buena's husband, he cannot escape the retarded boy who guards the boat and who himself may be a symbol of the incestuous coupling in which Hewes has been engaging. Newel cannot escape the absurd and the contingent, and he witnesses the comically maladroit death of Lamb while the two are fishing together. Of all the novel's characters, Lamb comes the closest to the cantankerous and colorful southerners of Faulkner, and his death may mark the passing of the southern individualist. Newel lies to Mrs. Lamb about Lamb's last words, apparently too embarrassed to repeat their absurd banality.

The novel begins and ends with the image of the retarded boy on the riverbank with a gun in his hand. If this image summarizes Ford's view of the South, the other image patterns of the novel reflect the contingency of American life as a whole. Beebe Henley's job moves her to different corners of the globe almost every day. Newel's luggage disappears. When Hewes and Newel cross the river to the island, Newel sees a deer, swimming across the river, suddenly pulled under the water by a powerful force, never to rise again. Nothing is permanent or reliable; Ford's characters fight their personal battles on uncharted land surrounded by the constant flow of the river that most signifies the South but that also, in its power and treachery, represents the larger America.

The Ultimate Good Luck

Contingency and displacement become synonymous with violence and deceit in Ford's next novel. In *The Ultimate Good Luck*, Harry Quinn, an alienated Vietnam War veteran, is asked by his former lover Rae to help free her brother, Sonny, from a jail in Oaxaca, Mexico, where he is serving a sentence for drug smuggling. Quinn makes arrangements to free Sonny through bribery with the help of a local lawyer, Bernhardt, but matters become complicated. Sonny's superiors believe that Sonny stole some of the drugs he was carrying and hid them before he was arrested. Oaxaca itself is under terrorist siege and is filled with police. Bernhardt's allegiance and motives are inscrutable. Quinn is terrorized by Deats, an "enforcer" working for Sonny's superiors. Unsuspected layers of power unfold, often in conjunction with arbitrary violence.

Indeed, the novel is dominated by images of violence and chance. The contingency that dominates *A Piece of My Heart* here is marked for higher stakes. With a flat, tough prose reminiscent of Dashiell Hammett's, Ford presents a film noir world of threat and hidden danger. The novel opens with a scene of violence and casual sexuality: Quinn meets an Italian tourist and takes her to a Mexican boxing match that is especially vicious. This casual encounter is indicative of Quinn's life; in flashback the reader discovers that Quinn first met Rae, by chance, at a dog-racing track; he has pursued jobs, such as game warden, that have brought him close to violence. As the novel unfolds, these chance encounters and acts of violence become less controllable. Quinn sees three American girls vanish during their vacation. He and Rae see a family of tourists killed by a terrorist bomb as they stand in front of an ice-cream store; Sonny is attacked and mutilated in jail; Deats binds Quinn and threatens him with a scorpion. Even Quinn's own body, hardened by war and decorated with tattoos, betrays him with a fit of dysentery. Oaxaca becomes a nightmare landscape of violence and confusion, reminiscent of Quinn's Vietnam experience. Like the island of *A Piece of My Heart*, Oaxaca becomes a crucible of the forces that drive the characters, a metaphoric landscape of their souls.

The plot is resolved by death. Sonny is killed in jail, Bernhardt is gunned down, and Quinn ends his search in a shoot-out with strangers. Although Quinn takes some pride in his accomplishment, his survival is simply the ultimate good luck, another chance outcome in a series of gambles.

The Sportswriter

Of Ford's novels, *The Sportswriter* has been the best received, though it may be his least typical. Told in the first person by Frank Bascombe, a thirty-eight-year-old short-story writer turned sportswriter, the novel details Bascombe's adventures over an Easter weekend, beginning with an annual pilgrimage with his former wife (referred to only as X) to the grave of his first son, who died at age eight of Reye's syndrome. It was that death that led to Bascombe's divorce and what he calls his period of "dreaminess," actually a form of detachment or emotional numbness. Over the course of the Easter weekend, Bascombe flies with his lover, Vicki Arcenault, to Detroit, where he interviews a paraplegic former football hero, Herb Wallagher. Cutting the trip short, they return home to Haddam, New Jersey. Bascombe visits the home of Vicki's parents on Easter Sunday, but the visit is interrupted by a call from X: Walter Luckett, a member of the Divorced Men's Club, a casual society to which Bascombe belongs, has committed suicide. Before returning to Haddam, Bascombe fights with Vicki. Bascombe eventually takes a late train into Manhattan to visit his office, something he does not normally do. There a chance encounter with a new female writer sparks what will become an affair. In the novel's epilogue, Bascombe is in Florida, waiting for a young Dartmouth woman to visit. He seems to have stopped grieving for his son, and he may be on the verge of writing fiction once more.

Detached, ironic, and cerebral, Bascombe looks for solace in the mundane and regular: He keeps up the appearances, if not the reality, of a suburban husband and father; he revels in the petty regularities of Haddam; he studies the regularized and "safe" world of professional sports. At these pursuits he is successful, but his adherence to routine and detail itself becomes part of his dreaminess, his detachment. Unable, or unwilling, to extend himself emotionally, he remains aloof from Walter Luckett's grief over a brief homosexual affair, he turns away from the vision of a crippled former athlete he had interviewed, and he ultimately quarrels and breaks with Vicki. His failure to continue writing fiction is an analogue of his inability to connect emotionally, but the novel itself, this fictional memoir, may be his way into a better life.

Wildlife

Wildlife is told as a memoir. Set in 1960, when Joe, the narrator, is sixteen years old (Ford's own age in 1960), the novel details the breakdown of the marriage of Jerry and Jeanette, Joe's parents. The family had recently moved to Grand Falls, Montana, where Jerry works as a golf professional. When he is fired because of a misunderstanding, Jerry signs on to fight the forest fires that rage in the hills outside the town. That sudden decision sends Jeanette into a short affair with a well-to-do local man named Warren Miller. The bulk of the novel is a re-creation of the events of those three days, told with stark simplicity. Joe, like the child protagonists of Ford's short stories, seems caught in the emotional detachment that was precipitated by the marriage breakdown and forced to re-create the situation with the dispassion that has marked his subsequent life. The result is a hesitant accumulation of detail and dialogue, as the retelling of the events becomes a cathartic event for Joe.

The novel is dominated by the image of fire. There are the fires that burn in the foothills and that capture the father's imagination. It seems they cannot be extinguished; they burn through the winter, ignoring the natural seasons, and they come to stand for the unpredictable and confusing in human experience. When Jerry leaves to fight these fires, he sets off a metaphorical fire in his wife, a yearning for passion and completeness that she attempts, unsuccessfully, to fulfill with an affair. When Jerry returns and discovers the adultery, he drives to Warren Miller's house and attempts to burn it down with a bottle of gasoline. That fire, like his wife's adultery, burns itself out and leaves behind recriminations and guilt. Ultimately ineffective, both of these fires succeed only in scarring the psychic landscape of the characters who set them.

The most starkly realistic of Ford's novels, and the closest to minimalist in its style, this novel received mixed reviews when it appeared. Some critics have found in the simplicity of its prose a poetic intensity (particularly in the descriptions of the forest fire and Jerry's attempt to burn down the house); others have argued that the stark dialogue threatens to push the novel into banality. In tone and style, *Wildlife* is certainly more reminiscent of Ford's short stories than of his previous novels.

Independence Day

Independence Day continues the story of Frank Bascombe that Ford began in *The Sportswriter*. Seven years have passed, and Bascombe has turned from sportswriter to real estate agent in Haddam, New Jersey. Set over a few days in the summer of 1988, *Independence Day* revolves around a climactic Fourth of July weekend in which Bascombe attempts to reconnect with his troubled son. The narrative timeline of the novel is not limited to that weekend; it meanders through the time that Bascombe takes preparing for the holiday and includes Bascombe's meditations about the circumstances of his current troubles: his continuing affection for his ex-wife; his relationships with his girlfriends, his troubled children, and his real estate clients; his continued grief over the death of his son Ralph.

The most compelling relationships in the book are between Bascombe and his children. Bascombe wants to be a good father, but because of his divorce from his children's mother, he feels exiled from their daily lives. He is especially worried about Paul, who has been arrested for shoplifting condoms. Paul has grown fat and slovenly, has shaved off most of his hair, and, because he has fixated on his pet dog run over by a car almost a decade before, has taken to barking like a Pomeranian. Bascombe attempts to bring himself closer to his son by taking him to the Baseball Hall of Fame for the Fourth of July weekend. The trip is a disaster. Instead of offering reconciliation, the trip confirms Bascombe's fears that his son is emotionally disturbed, that he will possibly always be that way, and that Bascombe will have to accept this.

Bascombe begins the novel by claiming that he is in an "existence period" of his life, which he describes as a period that can mysteriously go along the way it is for a long time. However, in a time of falling property values and unease in the suburbs, he is overcome by an anxious malaise. Haddam, New Jersey, is an upper-middle-class place where little happens, but its solitude is precisely the danger to Bascombe. Left alone with his thoughts, his worry and concern force him to look with a great deal of introspection at every aspect of his world. Unable to commit to his present girlfriend, he does not commit to anything except his desire to return to the past, even as he sadly realizes that there are things in his life that he cannot fix later.

Bascombe is living in a state where past and present coexist, where memory becomes his experience, recounted with almost dreamlike qualities. He begins to feel that all the determinative things in his life have already taken place, and that now he must deal with the consequences; he cannot change his basic situation, and he wonders if the good times have come and gone. This anxiety is reinforced by his experience with clients who must let go of their dream house and opt to rent, not buy. This subplot parallels Frank's sense that he too must face facts, and that too much water has passed under the bridge for things to be other than they are. Frank and his clients both indicate that underneath the seemingly secure surface of suburbia are distressing emotions connected to a considerable lowering of expectations. While fearing that he is disappearing into the routines of a very ordinary life, however, Bascombe does actually search for a way to interact emotionally with the world and people around him, and he comes to realize that he is more a part of things than he had thought. Finally, in addition to working out his relationships with his family, his clients, and other people around him, Bascombe also believes in the value of his attempt to construct a philosophy that might guide him through his troubling life.

The Lay of the Land

The Lay of the Land brings back Frank Bascombe for Ford's third, final, and longest novel about his American Everyman. It is now the year 2000, and although he still sells real estate, Bascombe has moved to the Jersey Shore. In addition, he feels he has moved from his earlier "existence" period to a "Permanent Period," in which no further major changes will be in the offing. Despite this assumption, however, major changes are taking place: Bascombe has prostate cancer; his second wife, Sally, has left him for a first husband once thought dead; his lesbian daughter is now reconsidering heterosexuality; his ex-wife Ann appears interested in a reconciliation. Other characters from the earlier books also appear, bringing with them a sense not of conclusion but of continuance. By the end of this novel, in fact, Bascombe has traded his Permanent Period for what he refers to as the "Next Level" of his life, one in which all things can be changed.

By novel's end, Bascombe has finally reconciled himself to the death of his young son Ralph, has reconciled with Sally and his increasingly less troubled and rather canny son Paul, and has rescued his daughter from the depredations of an unscrupulous heterosexual, all in time for a big Thanksgiving reunion. It is an offbeat Thanksgiving, however, as it brings with it a life-threatening bullet to Bascombe's heart, the result of his having interfered with the robbery of the greedy, materialistic couple next door. This violent episode takes the reader back to the novel's opening anecdote about a woman who is the victim of a random shooter: Before she is to die, the shooter asks her if she is ready to meet her maker, a question to which she replies in the affirmative. We come to understand that this is also the question Bascombe has been asking himself.

Despite the many episodes, anecdotes, observations, and comic riffs that run through this novel's interior monologue in a loose and seemingly desultory way, the deep subject of this novel is whether Bascombe's life has any integrity. That Bascombe is concerned with these issues has been suggested earlier by his periodic references to the Dalai Lama and by his acquisition of a new business partner, a Tibetan Buddhist named Lobsang Dhargey. While Dhargey has morphed into a perky capitalist now named Mike Mahony, Bascombe has become more spiritual, suggesting that all his comings-and-goings have been in essence a quest for a Dalai Lama-style open heart and for a life he can justify. Bascombe recovers from his shot to the heart, and, as he descends in an airplane with Sally on his way to begin cancer treatments at the Mayo Clinic, the reader understands that although there will be no more Bascombe stories, Bascombe himself will go on to the next thing in pretty good emotional and spiritual shape. In possession of some real thanksgiving, Bascombe is, in this final installment of his saga, indeed ready to meet his maker.

Paul Budra; Jeffrey Greer
Updated by Margaret Boe Birns

Other major works

Short fiction: *Rock Springs*, 1987; *Women with Men: Three Stories*, 1997; *A Multitude of Sins*, 2001; *Vintage Ford*, 2003.

Nonfiction: *Good Raymond*, 1998.

Edited texts: *The Granta Book of the American Short Story*, 1992; *The Essential Tales of Chekhov*, 1998; *The Granta Book of the American Long Story*, 1998; *The New Granta Book of the American Short Story*, 2007.

Bibliography

Dobozy, Tamas, "How Not to Be a 'Dickhead': Partisan Politics in Richard Ford's *Independence Day*." *Critical Survey* 18 (June, 2006): 40-59. Discusses the political conflict between liberalism and conservatism in the novel, asserting that Ford endorses a concept of freedom that requires openness to others and to the uncertainties of life.

Flora, Joseph M., Amber Vogel, and Bryan Albin Giemza, eds. *Southern Writers: A New Biographical Dictionary*. Baton Rouge: Louisiana State University Press, 2006. Ford is included among authors considered to have a significant connection to the American South. Provides information about Ford's birthplace, his upbringing in the South, and his use of the South as a setting.

Ford, Richard. "First Things First." *Harper's Magazine* 276 (August, 1988): 72-77. Ford offers a first-person account of his life and career as a writer, from the early period when his stories were rejected, and how he dealt with such disappointments, to his eventual success and recognition. Also comments on the business of literary production and book publishing in the United States.

Guagliardo, Huey, ed. *Conversations with Richard Ford*. Jackson: University Press of Mississippi, 2001. Collection brings together interviews with Ford and profiles of the author spanning a quarter of a century.

_______. *Perspectives on Richard Ford*. Jackson: University Press of Mississippi, 2000. Comprehensive collection gathers nearly all the published academic criticism on Ford's work up to the end of the twentieth century.

Guinn, Matthew. *After Southern Modernism: Fiction of the Contemporary South*. Jackson: University Press of Mississippi, 2000. Ford is one of several authors whose works are analyzed in this study, which attempts to engage southern fiction on its own terms rather than as a provincial or second-class genre.

_______. "Into the Suburbs: Richard Ford's Sportswriter Novels and the Place of Southern Fiction." In *South to a New Place: Region, Literature, Culture*, edited by Suzanne W. Jones and Sharon Monteith. Baton Rouge: Louisiana State University Press, 2002. Discusses *The Sportswriter* and *Independence Day* with reference to Ford's place in southern literature, the place of the South in Ford's identity as a novelist, and Ford's status as a southern novelist.

Messud, Claire. "A Case of Development." *The New York Review of Books* 54 (January, 2007): 25-27. Presents a thoughtful, thorough discussion of the Bascombe trilogy, with special reference to *The Lay of the Land.*

Schroth, Raymond A. "Run, Frank, Run." *Commonweal* 134 (February, 2007): 30-31. Discusses Ford's protagonist Frank Bascombe as a representative American man; touches on issues of spirituality.

Walker, Elinor Ann. *Richard Ford.* New York: Twayne, 2000. Examines Ford's career, provides readings of individual novels that address Ford's dominant themes, and discusses Ford's relationship to trends in American and southern literature.

E. M. FORSTER

Born: London, England; January 1, 1879

Died: Coventry, Warwickshire, England; June 7, 1970

Also known as: Edward Morgan Forster

Principal long fiction

Where Angels Fear to Tread, 1905
The Longest Journey, 1907
A Room with a View, 1908
Howards End, 1910
A Passage to India, 1924
Maurice, 1971 (wr. 1913)

Other literary forms

In addition to his novels, E. M. Forster wrote short stories, travel books, biographies, essays, and criticism. A number of these works, as well as his novels, appear in the seventeen-volume standard Abinger Edition (1972-1998). *The Celestial Omnibus, and Other Stories* (1911) includes his frequently anthologized story "The Road from Colonus" and five other stories written in a fantastic vein that is found much less frequently in his novels. Forster's *Aspects of the Novel* (1927) remains one of the most widely read discussions of that genre, and the essays of *Abinger Harvest* (1936) and *Two Cheers for Democracy* (1951) have also found many receptive readers. In *Marianne Thornton: A Domestic Biography, 1797-1887* (1956), Forster recalls his great-aunt, a woman whose long life plunged him into the social history of a milieu going back to the closing years of the eighteenth century. A useful description of Forster's uncollected writings by George H. Thomson may be found in *Aspects of E. M. Forster* (1969), a Festschrift honoring the author on his ninetieth birthday. In the same volume, Benjamin Britten recounts one more achievement: the libretto Forster coauthored with Eric Crozier for Britten's opera *Billy Budd* (1951).

Achievements

E. M. Forster will continue to stand a little apart from other major novelists of the twentieth century. Because he made it difficult to decide by which standards his work should be judged, assessing it fairly presents problems. Unlike many of his Bloomsbury friends, he did not rebel against the Victorians or their literary habits; neither did he embrace the literary trends of his own time with any great enthusiasm. He lamented the encroachment of a commercial culture, but he did not declare war on the modern world. Although he composed a set of lectures on the novel, its plural title, *Aspects of the Novel*, anticipates his refusal to develop therein any single theory of the form in which he distinguished himself. On one hand, his work is impossible to pigeonhole; on the other hand, his six novels do not entitle him to a lonely eminence overshadowing his most able contemporaries.

Readers of the novel will not lose sight of Forster, however, because the very ambiguities and inconsistencies that frustrate efforts to find a niche for him continue to intrigue critics. Forster lived long enough to see his reputation fade and then rebound strongly. He had gained critical acclaim while still in his twenties, written a masterpiece in midlife, and published no fiction for nearly two decades before Lionel Trilling's *E. M. Forster* (1943) swung critical attention back to him. Since that time, a formidable body of books and articles dealing with Forster has formed, and many aspects of his work have been studied in great detail. While incapable of putting Forster in a specific place, his critics agree overwhelmingly that he deserves a place of honor among English novelists.

Forster's critics, fortunately, do not hold his unusually protracted silence against him. The author's failure to write a novel in the final forty-six years of his life has been explained in various ways—for example, it has been noted that instead of exercising his talents in succession, husbanding his resources, exhausting one mode before moving to another, Forster put all of himself into the first six novels and then ceased at an age when many novelists are just reaching their prime. Whatever the reason for his early retirement from a literary form successfully practiced by so many older writers, Forster furnished his critics no occasion to regret the decline of his powers.

Those powers yielded fiction marked by a blend of qualities—intelligence, wit, sensitivity, compassion, and ever-alert moral imagination—that few other writers can match. No doubt, many readers begin *A Passage to India* in the line of duty—for it has attained the rank of "classic"—but they are likely to complete it, and then begin the earlier novels, out of a desire to know better a man who could write so movingly and yet so tough-mindedly about the climate created by racial and religious prejudice. Few such readers are disappointed, for while the earlier novels are less fine, the distance between *Where Angels Fear to Tread* and *A Passage to India* is not nearly so great as that between the apprentice efforts and the masterworks of most writers. Even if his final novel is, as one critic has put it, "Forster's sole claim upon posterity," those who delve into his other works will continue to reap rewards in proportion to the attention they bestow on them, for neither wit nor wisdom is ever far away.

The critical consensus is that Forster's most successful mode is comic irony, and his name is often coupled with those of Jane Austen and George Meredith, whose test for comedy—"that it shall awaken thoughtful laughter"—Forster passes with flying colors. Critics invariably hasten to point out that Forster refused to confine himself to this mode; in the midst of deploring these deviations from high comedy, they find in Forster's odd blends of comedy, melodrama, fantasy, lyricism, and tragedy a distinctiveness they would not willingly relinquish.

Biography

Edward Morgan Forster lived a long but rather uneventful life. Born on New Year's Day, 1879, he was reared by his possessive mother and worshipful great-aunt (whose biography he later wrote) after the death of his father from tuberculosis before Forster turned two. Happy, protected, and dominated by women in his early years, he suffered painfully the transition to the masculine, athletically oriented Tonbridge School—later the model for Sawston School in *The Longest Journey*. After a more congenial four years, 1897 to 1901, at King's College, Cambridge, he took a second-class degree. In the next few years, he wrote seriously, traveled in Italy and Greece, tutored the children of a German countess, and indulged in walking tours of his native land.

His first novel, *Where Angels Fear to Tread*, much of which is set in Italy, received favorable reviews in 1905, and Forster produced three more novels in the next five years, of which *A Room with a View* drew also on his Italian experience, while *The Longest Journey* and *Howards End* both reflect his keen delight in the English countryside. Thereafter, having attained a considerable reputation as a novelist, he slowed his pace. He began, but could not finish, a novel called *Arctic Summer*; completed a novel about homosexuality, his own orientation, which he knew to be unpublishable; and brought out a volume of short stories. Among his many friends he numbered Virginia Woolf as well as others of the Bloomsbury group, of which, however, he was never more than a fringe member. World War I found him in Egypt as a Red Cross worker. Although he disliked Egypt, his life there led to the writing of two nonfiction books.

Forster had first visited India in 1912, but his second sojourn there as personal secretary to the maharaja of Dewas gave him the opportunity to observe the political and social life closely enough to inspire him to write another novel. *A Passage to India*, which appeared in 1924, increased his fame and led to an invitation to deliver the Clark Lectures at Trinity College, Cambridge, in 1927; the lectures were published later that year as *Aspects of the Novel*. Although he continued to write for several more decades, he published no more novels. Forster received a number of honors, culminating in the Order of Merit, presented to him on his ninetieth birthday. He died in June of 1970.

E. M. Forster. (Archive Photos)

Analysis

E. M. Forster's most systematic exposition of the novelist's art, *Aspects of the Novel*, is no key to his own practice. Written three years after the publication of *A Passage to India*, the work surveys neither his achievement nor his intentions. While full of the insights, charm, and homely but colorful metaphors that also distinguish Virginia Woolf's *Common Reader* volumes (1925, 1932), the book is an enthusiast's, rather than a working writer's, view of the novel, as if Forster were already distancing himself from the form that earned him his fame as a writer.

A lecture given twenty years later by Lionel Trilling, who had already published his book on Forster, gives a better sense of Forster's achievement. In "Manners, Morals, and the Novel," later published in *The Liberal Imagination* (1950), Trilling explains the novel as the writer's response to the modern world's besetting sin of snobbery, which he defines as "pride in status without pride in function." Europeans, and perhaps especially the English, familiar with snobbery as a manifestation of class structure, require less explanation than do Americans of the novel's relation to snobbery. The central tradition of the English novel from Henry Fielding through Jane Austen, Charles Dickens, William Makepeace Thackeray, and George Meredith—and indeed English comedy as far back as Geoffrey Chaucer's *The Canterbury Tales* (1387-1400)—stands as evidence.

In Forster's time, however, that tradition was being modified. For one thing, the greatest English novelists at work during Forster's formative years were a wealthy American expatriate and a retired Polish mariner. No one as sensitive as Forster could escape the influence of Henry James and Joseph Conrad, but these men made curious heirs to Dickens and Thackeray and George Eliot. James, while intensely interested in the textures of society, focused his attention on the relations between the English (and Continental) leisure class and those American travelers whom Mark Twain had christened "innocents abroad," thus limiting his social scrutiny, in Forster's opinion, to the narrow perceptions of a few wealthy idlers. Conrad diverged even more sharply from the path of previous English novelists, for he neither understood nor cared to understand any level of English society. A man of his temperament and interest might be imagined as a literary force in the midcentury United States of Nathaniel Hawthorne's *The Scarlet Letter* (1850) and Herman Melville's *Moby Dick* (1851), but not in the England of Thackeray's *Vanity Fair* (1847-1848, serial; 1848, book) and Dickens's *Bleak House*

(1852-1853, serial; 1853, book). Nevertheless, Conrad was more in tune with his own literary milieu than was Meredith, who at the end of the century reigned as the grand old man of English letters, and Conrad's work, like that of James, diverted the creative energy of many of the new century's novelists into new channels.

Of native English novelists still regarded as substantial, the most active at the time of Forster's entry into the field were Arnold Bennett, H. G. Wells, and John Galsworthy—all men born in the 1860's and all inheritors of the native tradition of the novel, albeit on a somewhat reduced scale. The next generation of novelists, born slightly after Forster in the 1880's, included Woolf, James Joyce, and D. H. Lawrence, all of whom published their initial works after Forster had already written five of his six novels. This latter group obviously belongs to a new literary dispensation. Society and its network of snobbery, though still significant, have receded into the background, and the conflicts of the protagonists are waged at a more personal, intimate, sometimes semiconscious level. Clearly the work of psychologists such as Sigmund Freud and Henry James's brother William James influenced these later writers and drove them to develop literary techniques adequate to the task of a more truly psychological novel.

Forster, as has been suggested, stands in the middle. A friend of Virginia Woolf and in her mind, certainly, no part of the decaying tradition she trounced so severely in her essay "Mr. Bennett and Mrs. Brown," Forster nevertheless anticipated few of the technical innovations of the novelists who reached their maturity after World War I. His last novel stands with the post-Freudian achievements. *Howards End*, his most ambitious novel, is in most respects a novel of the old school. It is denser, symbolically richer, than the characteristic work of Bennett, Wells, and Galsworthy, but the same might be said of *Bleak House*, written more than half a century earlier.

Only around the time of Forster's birth did novelists begin to insist on the novel as an art form and write theoretical defenses of it. Meredith delivered a lecture on "The Idea of Comedy and the Uses of the Comic Spirit" (1877), which, though mentioning Miguel de Cervantes and Fielding, has more to say of Aristophanes and Molière; Henry James's essay "The Art of Fiction" appeared in 1884. By the century's end, novelists had achieved respectability, and Conrad could soberly echo Longinus: "Art is long and life is short, and success is very far off."

Such new expressions of the novelist's kinship with poet and playwright did not end the nineteenth century habit of producing loose, baggy narratives in a diversity of modes, punctuated by their author's abrupt changes of direction, interpolated moral essays, and episodes introduced for no better reason than a hunch that readers, who cared nothing for artistic integrity, would enjoy them. Stock literary devices that storytellers had accumulated over the centuries—bizarre coincidences, thoroughly improbable recognition scenes thrust into "realistic" contexts, the bundling forth of long-lost (often supposedly deceased) personages in the interests of a happy or surprising denouement, all devices that twentieth century novels would shun—still flourished in Forster's youth, and he used many of them unashamedly.

If Forster's moment in literary history partly explains his wavering between Victorian and modern canons, his skeptical, eclectic temperament must also be cited. His astute analyses of the morals and manners of society involved him in comedy, tragedy, romance, and fantasy—the sort of "God's plenty" that the supposedly neoclassical John Dryden admired in Chaucer and Ben Jonson in William Shakespeare. Such men would write any sort of work and take up with any sort of character. Forster was similarly indiscriminate. His veneration for Leo Tolstoy's *Voyna i mir* (1865-1869; *War and Peace*, 1886), though "such an untidy book," betrays his Englishman's weakness in believing that God's plenty would overcome the artist's scruples.

Of course, Forster's novels are not as long as *War and Peace* or the Victorian ones that readers worked their way through in installments spread over many months. Compared to the seamless garments of Woolf or even the longer works of Joyce and William Faulkner (both of whom exhibit an un-English type of variety but also an astonishing coherence), Forster's juxtapositions of sharply contrasting modes invite criticism by readers who take in his works in two or three successive evenings. Thus, while Forster does not belong with Wells and Galsworthy, neither does he quite keep company with the greatest of his slightly younger contemporaries, for he loved too much the variety and freedom that most earlier English novelists permitted themselves.

Nevertheless, his motto for *Howards End*—"Only connect"—applies to his work generally. If he does not always make the artistic connections, his consistent theme is the necessity of making moral connections with fellow humans, of struggling against the class divisions that so many Englishmen, including a number of his fellow novelists, took for granted. In his novels, prudence is invariably on the side of those who, like Henry Wilcox in *Howards End* and Ronnie Heaslop in *A Passage to India*, resist the breakdown of social barriers; but courage, generosity, friendship, and sympathy are found among Forster's liberal opponents of snobbery. In the world of Forster's novels, the closed class is always sterile and corrupt.

Forster's eclecticism, his versatility, his refusal to ignore the claims either of heart or head make the reading of his novels an ambiguous but rich experience. Never does he seem like a mere exhibitionist, however. Rather, his openness to life's variety amounts to a perpetual invitation to the participation of alert and open-minded readers. He is far less afraid of a gaucherie than of a missed opportunity to "connect."

Where Angels Fear to Tread

Forster's shortest and most tightly focused novel is *Where Angels Fear to Tread.* A young man named Philip Herriton is commissioned by his mother and sister Harriet to bring back from Italy the infant son of Lilia Carella, the widow of another of Mrs. Herriton's sons. Within a year after marrying Gino Carella, the aimless son of a small-town dentist, Lilia died giving birth to a son. Aided by Harriet and by Caroline Abbott, who as Lilia's traveling companion had been able to do nothing to ward off the offensive marriage, Philip finds Gino resistant to Mrs. Herriton's pocketbook and ultimately becomes involved in a shabby kidnapping venture engineered by Harriet—a venture that ends with the accidental death of the child. On the way home, Philip finds himself drawn emotionally to Caroline, who reveals that she too has fallen in love with Gino. In the common effort to minister to the pitifully unregenerate Harriet, however, Philip and Caroline become friends.

Thus summarized, the novel bears some resemblance to one by Henry James. Forster enjoys contrasting Anglo-Saxon and Italian mores, and he shares James's fascinated horror over the machinations and intrigues of sophisticated schemers. He may have owed the idea of centering the story on a somewhat detached emissary to James, whose novel *The Ambassadors* (1903) appeared shortly before Forster began work on his own book.

Forster's handling of his material, however, differs substantially from James's. He cannot resist scathing treatment of the characters whose company he expects his readers to keep and with whom they are to sympathize. Harriet, appalled by Italy's uncleanliness, carries a bottle of ammonia in her trunk, but Forster has it "burst over her prayer-book, so that purple patches appeared on all her clothes." Prayer brings out the worst in many of Forster's characters, an exception being Caroline, who is able to pray in the church in Gino's hometown, "where a prayer to God is thought none the worse of because it comes next to a pleasant word to a neighbor." For Philip to develop neighborliness is a struggle. Not only is he much less experienced and resourceful than Strether or any other Jamesian ambassador, he is also decidedly unattractive: callow, priggish, and cowardly. Caroline's assessment of him in the final chapter, though tardily arrived at, is accurate enough: "You're without passion; you look on life as a spectacle, you don't enter it; you only find it funny or beautiful." By the time he hears this, however, Philip has learned what neither his mother nor his sister ever suspects: that the son of an Italian dentist can love his child more than wealth, that he is capable of trust and friendship, that he can be not merely angered but also hurt by a betrayal. Philip has also felt enough by this time to be hurt by Caroline's words.

Though selfish and shortsighted, Gino is without the treachery of a Jamesian Italian such as Giovanelli in *Daisy Miller* (1878). Indeed, Forster makes him morally superior to the Herriton women. Fixing on a domestic vignette of a sort impossible in any well-appointed English household (or in a James novel, for that matter)—Gino bathing his infant son—Forster draws Caroline into helping him and lets Philip come upon them so engaged, "to all intents and purposes, the Virgin and Child, with Donor." Forster's heroes tend to idealize people who are only behaving a little better than expected, but the capacity to idealize is a symptom of their regeneration.

Harriet tricks Philip into the kidnapping; he discovers

the ruse only after the baby has died and his own arm has been broken in a carriage accident. He returns to confess the transgression, only to have the grief-stricken Gino cruelly twist his broken arm and then nearly choke him to death before Caroline appears to stop him. In a typically Forsterian piece of symbolism, she persuades Gino and Philip together to drink the milk that had been poured for the child. In a pattern that Forster repeats in later novels, Philip, though excessive in his estimate of Caroline's goodness, is nevertheless "saved" by it. Salvation is partly illusion, but such an illusion serves him better than the cynicism that Philip has spent his youth imbibing.

The Longest Journey

Like Philip, Rickie Elliot of *The Longest Journey* is frail and aesthetic. In addition, a deformed foot, a trait inherited from his father, marks him as different from his Cambridge classmates. At the beginning of the novel, both his father, whom he despised, and his beloved mother are dead; his father's sister, Mrs. Failing, is his closest relative. On her Wiltshire estate lives a young man, Stephen Wonham, an illegitimate half brother to Rickie. Rude, truculent, undiscriminating in his choice of companions, and more or less a habitual drunkard, Stephen also proves loyal and almost pathetically trusting. The relationship between the two brothers forms the core of the novel.

The title of the book, from Percy Bysshe Shelley's poem *Epipsychidion* (1821), alludes to the folly of denying the rest of the world for the sake of "a mistress or a friend," with whom, in consequence, one must "the dreariest and longest journey go." In the midst of mulling over the poem, Rickie ironically decides to take his journey with Agnes Pembroke, a girl whose first lover, a strapping athlete, has died suddenly of a football injury. Death, it may be noted, always strikes with unexpected suddenness in Forster's novels. The marriage disgusts Rickie's closest friend, Stewart Ansell, and Rickie himself comes soon enough to regret it. Discouraged by Agnes and her elder brother Herbert from pursuing a career as a writer, Rickie takes a teaching post at Sawston School, where Herbert is a master. By a strange coincidence, a maladjusted boy at the school writes a letter to Stephen Wonham, among other total strangers, asking Stephen to "pray for him." Agnes's practical mind senses trouble if Stephen appears at the school, but mercifully the boy withdraws before Stephen can carry out an offer to come visit him. Rickie, while not fond of Stephen, is willing for him to receive his aunt's property when she dies; not so Agnes. When Mrs. Failing sends the troublesome Stephen packing, he decides to visit Sawston and inform Rickie of their relationship—about which Rickie already knows.

Outside the school, Stephen meets Stewart Ansell, on hand to verify for himself the death of his friend's spirit in his loveless union with the Pembrokes, and, after receiving an insult, knocks him down. Before Stephen can see Rickie, Agnes intercepts him and offers him the money she is sure he wants in return for leaving Sawston and sparing Rickie the embarrassment of acknowledging him. Stunned and stung, the utterly unmercenary Stephen leaves, but Ansell, won over not only by Stephen's fist but also by his principles, breaks into the Sawston dining hall during Sunday dinner and, in front of masters, students, and all, rebukes Rickie for turning away his own brother in the latter's deepest distress. As the assemblage gapes, Ansell reveals what he has correctly intuited: that Stephen is not the son of Rickie's father, as Rickie had supposed, but of his beloved mother. At this news Rickie faints.

Although wildly improbable, the scene has an electric intensity about it. Ansell, with all the clumsy insistence of a true egalitarian and all the insight of a true friend, has, while mistakenly charging Rickie with complicity in Agnes's treachery, stripped away the hypocrisy behind which the couple has hidden. There is about this revelation something of the quality of the recognition scene of a tragedy such as Sophocles' *Oidipous Tyrannos* (c. 429 b.c.e.; *Oedipus Tyrannus*, 1715), with Rickie the lame protagonist faced with the consequences of his disastrous marriage and of his unjust assumption about his father as well as of his denial of his brother.

From the time Rickie listened mutely to his classmates' discussion of whether the cow in the field was "there" if no one was present to perceive her, he has searched unavailingly for reality. He has misinterpreted his love for Agnes as real, watched his son—inevitably deformed like his father and himself—die in infancy, and seen his attempt at a schoolmaster's life tumble. Now he tries, none too successfully, to effect a reconciliation with his brother. He leaves Agnes and the school and tries to rekindle the flame of his short-story writing. When Stephen disappoints him on a visit to Mrs. Failing by breaking a promise not to drink, Rickie concludes that people are not "real." Finding Stephen sprawled drunkenly across the tracks at a railroad crossing, Rickie finds the strength to move him from the path of an oncoming train—but not the strength to save himself.

Rickie's aunt and brother-in-law, incapable of seeing his rescue of Stephen as worthwhile, see him as a failure whose life is mercifully over. Stephen, who is no thinker, is not so sure. In the final chapter, he feels himself to be in some sense the future of England, for he is now the father of a girl who bears the name of his and Rickie's mother. Dimly, he acknowledges that his salvation is from Rickie.

Not only does *The Longest Journey* run to melodrama, but it also incorporates some rather tedious moralizing, both on the part of Mrs. Failing and in an interpolated essay by Forster that forms the whole twenty-eighth chapter (although the chapter is a short one). Probably the greatest burden, however, is the one Stephen Wonham is forced to carry. First of all, he is the disreputable relative who knocks people down and falls down drunk himself. He serves a contrasting and complementary purpose as a kind of spiritual extension of Rickie, particularly after Rickie, recognizing him as his mother's son, begins to invest him with her excellencies, as recollected. In the final chapter, Stephen becomes the consciousness of the novel itself.

Without Stephen, however, Forster's brilliant portrait of Rickie is not only incomplete but also depressing, for Rickie dies, sad to say, murmuring agreement with Mrs. Failing's antihumanist convictions that "we do not live for anything great" and that "people are not important at all." Stephen exists and procreates and retains the idea of greatness to prove Rickie wrong.

A Room with a View

Forster sends his principals off to Italy again in *A Room with a View*. The room in question is one that Lucy Honeychurch and her elder cousin Charlotte Bartlett do not enjoy at the beginning of their stay in a Florentine hotel but that two other travelers, the elderly Mr. Emerson and his son George, are more than willing to exchange for the one that furnishes the ladies with only a disappointing view of the courtyard. Characteristic of Forster's well-bred characters, they lose sight of Emerson's generosity in their horror at the directness and bluntness of his offer, for he has interrupted their conversation at dinner before other guests: "I have a view, I have a view." Having defied the convention that forbids hasty and undue familiarity with a stranger, Mr. Emerson must be certified by an English clergyman, after which the ladies somewhat stiffly accept the view. Mr. Emerson, of course, has throughout the novel a "view" that the cousins, who hate the darkness but blanch at openness, achieve only with difficulty.

Soon an unexpected adventure literally throws Lucy and George Emerson more closely together. While enthusiastically and uncritically buying photographs of Italian masterpieces, Lucy witnesses a stabbing in a public square. She faints; George catches her and, after throwing her blood-spattered photographs into the River Arno, conducts her away gently. Later, Lucy puzzles over the affair and comes to the conclusion that, despite his kind intentions, George Emerson is devoid of "chivalry."

When circumstances throw them together again, George impulsively kisses Lucy. Such behavior drives Lucy and Charlotte to Rome, where they meet Cecil Vyse. He is propriety itself, never once offering to kiss Lucy, and back in England Lucy and Vyse become engaged. By coincidence, Vyse has met the Emersons and introduces them to the neighborhood where Lucy and her mother live. Though well-intentioned, Vyse is one of Forster's snobs. He is also a drab lover, and when Lucy finally tastes one of his unsatisfactory kisses, she is thrown into a panic by the prospect of another meeting with George. They meet again, and George kisses her again, with the result that Lucy deems George impossible and Vyse intolerable and breaks her engagement to the latter with the resolve never to marry anyone.

Clearly Forster is on a different, more wholeheartedly comic, course in this novel, and the denouement fulfills the tradition of romantic comedy, the inevitable marriage of Lucy and George being brought about through the ministrations of a lady who casts off her role as an apparently irredeemable snob—cousin Charlotte. What Forster says of the Honeychurch house, Windy Corner, might almost be said of the novel: "One might laugh at the house, but one never shuddered." Despite the play of Forster's wit throughout the novel and the sympathy he extends to a girl as silly as Lucy, the reader does shudder occasionally. Two murders, the real one Lucy sees and a supposed one, interrupt the proceedings. The latter is a rumor, bruited about by a clergyman named Eager, that Mr. Emerson has murdered his wife. The charge is baseless and seems to have been injected to deepen Emerson's character as a man of sorrows. The real death is even more gratuitous—unless it is meant to validate George Emerson's seriousness and dependability.

Events lead Lucy into a series of lies that she supposes to be little white ones but that threaten general unhappiness until Mr. Emerson, whom she has led to believe that she still intends to marry Vyse, induces heart's truth and persuades her to marry George. The novel ends with the honeymooners back in Florence speculating on Charlotte's motive in bringing about Lucy's climactic meeting with Mr. Emerson. They conclude that "she fought us on the surface, and yet she hoped."

Mr. Emerson, in two respects at least, echoes the writer of the same name. He is convinced of the importance of discovering Nature, and he is an apostle of self-trust. A good man, he grows tedious after the initial chapter, functioning finally as his son's advocate. George himself never quite comes into focus, and the reader is forced to accept on faith Charlotte's change of heart. The lightest of Forster's novels, *A Room with a View*—had it been lighter yet and avoided the rather heavy-handed symbolism of the "view" and the dark—might not have turned out the weakest of the five novels Forster published in his lifetime.

HOWARDS END

Howards End, Forster's most ambitious novel, recounts the adventures of two sisters, Margaret and Helen Schlegel, after two encounters with people not of their quiet, cultivated London set. At the beginning, while a guest at the country home of the Wilcoxes (a family the Schlegels had met while traveling abroad), Helen has become engaged—at least in her own mind—to one of the Wilcox sons, Paul. Her visit and engagement end awkwardly when her aunt whisks her back to London. The second incident grows out of Helen's inadvertently taking home from the theater the umbrella of a bank clerk named Leonard Bast. Standing "at the extreme verge of gentility," Leonard wishes to approach closer. The idealistic Schlegels appreciate the impulse and strike up an acquaintance. Meanwhile, the Wilcox connection is reestablished when the Wilcoxes rent a flat across from the house where the Schlegels, including younger brother Tibby, live, and Margaret, the eldest Schlegel, comes to know Mrs. Wilcox.

A quiet, even dull woman, Ruth Wilcox is an utterly charitable person who conveys to Margaret "the idea of greatness." Her husband Henry, a prosperous businessman, and the three Wilcox children—young adults like Helen and Tibby—radiate energy, good humor, and physical health but lack wit, grace, and any sense of beauty. Suddenly, a quarter of the way through the novel, Ruth Wilcox dies.

In marrying Henry Wilcox, Margaret proves very nearly as improvident as Lilia Herriton or Rickie Elliot. The two have little in common, and before long a series of fortuitous events shakes their precarious union. As a result of offhand bad advice from Henry, duly passed on by the Schlegel sisters, Leonard Bast loses his job. Leonard makes a pilgrimage to Oniton, one of several Wilcox estates on which Henry and Margaret are living. Unfortunately, Leonard chooses to bring along his unbecoming common-law wife, who turns out to be a former mistress of Henry Wilcox. When Henry angrily turns the Basts away, the conscience-stricken Helen insists on trying to compensate Bast. Like Stephen Wonham, he indignantly refuses her money. The impulsive and emotionally overwrought Helen refuses to abandon him. Later Helen disappears into Germany for a time; on her return Margaret discovers that she has conceived a son by Leonard.

When Margaret relays to her husband Helen's request that she be permitted to stay at the unused Howards End for one night, he indignantly refuses, and Margaret realizes that Henry, the betrayer of his own first wife, is unrepentant in his maintenance of a moral double standard. One tragic scene remains. Leonard appears at Howards End to beg forgiveness for sinning with Helen; Charles Wilcox (Henry's other son) totally misunderstands the intruder's motive and strikes him down with the flat of a sword, and Leonard's weak heart gives way. Charles is convicted of manslaughter, and at the end,

Margaret, Helen and her child, and the broken-spirited Henry are living together at Howards End.

Although *Howards End* clearly bears similarities to Forster's first two published novels—the melodrama, the improbable coincidences, the often awkward modulations between comic and tragic tone, and so on—the pattern of events in this work is both more richly and less intrusively symbolic. As many critics have observed, this is a novel about England, written in the uneasy pre-World War I years of growing antagonism between Germany and England. Forster permits himself a series of meditations on, paeans of praise to, his native isle in the manner of John of Gaunt's "This blessed plot, this earth, this realm, this England" speech in Shakespeare's *Richard II* (pr. c. 1595-1596). At the same time, Forster clearly intimates that England is also the Wilcoxes—insular in their outlook, stolid in their prejudices, merciless in their advocacy of the class structure. The Schlegel sisters spring from a German father and revere German Romantic culture. Chapter 5 of the novel celebrates their (and Forster's) extraordinary sensitivity to Ludwig van Beethoven; it is after a performance of the Fifth Symphony that Helen takes Leonard's umbrella.

Margaret also loves England, typified by Howards End, which is no ancient seat of the Wilcoxes but a property that had belonged to Mrs. Wilcox herself, even though she sometimes seems to be amid alien corn there. England, Forster seems to say, needs to unite the best in its Wilcoxes, its providers and healthy consumers of material goods, with the Schlegel principle, expressed in the love of art and civilized discussion. By themselves the Schlegels are ineffectual. They can only watch helplessly as commercial development dooms their London house. After Helen has been carried away by her feeling for Leonard's plight, she flees to her father's ancestral home but cannot live there. Only at Howards End can she live securely and watch her child grow up.

As a symbol for England and for the possibilities of a balanced life, Howards End might seem to have some deficiencies. It is lacking in beauty and tradition. It has become the seat of a philistine family, for even the saintly Ruth demonstrates no artistic interest more highly developed than a fondness for flowers and for a certain adjacent meadow in the early morning. On her first visit to Howards End, Helen Schlegel sees more of nature's beauties than any of the Wilcoxes, who are preoccupied with croquet, tennis, and "calisthenic exercises on a machine that is tacked on to a greengage-tree," ever perceive.

The agent who renders Howards End truly habitable is an uneducated farm woman who refuses to accept her "place." When Margaret first visits Howards End, where, it is thought, they will *not* make their home, she finds Miss Avery there. The old woman, who for a second mistakes Margaret for the first Mrs. Wilcox, has taken it upon herself to guard the empty house. Her presumptuousness, which in the past has taken the form of wedding gifts to both Henry's daughter and daughter-in-law—gaucheries the Wilcoxes are quick to condemn—extends shortly thereafter to unpacking the Schlegel books and other personal belongings, which have been stored there following the expiration of the lease on the London house. After arranging the Schlegel library in bookcases and arranging the Schlegel furniture to suit herself, the woman declines to accept even polite criticism: "You think that you won't come back to live here, Mrs. Wilcox, but you will."

Thus it is an intuitive country person who joins the half-foreign Schlegel culture to the native Wilcox stock. Miss Avery also sends over a country boy, Tom, after Helen and Margaret, in defiance of Henry, spend a night together at Howards End. "Please, I am the milk," says Tom, speaking more truth than he knows. As in *Where Angels Fear to Tread*, the milk is spiritual as well as physical nourishment. Peopled with such life-affirming folk, Howards End becomes a sustaining place, an embodiment of what English life might yet be if the deepening disorder of 1910 is somehow averted. Finally won over to permitting Helen to reside there—and thus at least tacitly acknowledging his own fornication—Henry decrees that at his death the property will pass to Margaret; Ruth Wilcox herself had wanted to give it to her.

The motto of *Howards End* is "Only connect." In the house, "the prose and passion" of life, the Wilcox and Schlegel principles, are joined through the ministrations of another of Forster's characters willing to defy the class system in the interests of a nobler order.

The central symbol of *Howards End* is hay. Ruth Wilcox is first observed "smelling hay," a product that the naturally fertile estate produces in abundance. The rest of the Wilcoxes, Miss Avery at one point observes maliciously, all suffer from hay fever. Forster uses the hay very much as Walt Whitman, whom he occasionally quotes and from whom he appropriated the title of his final novel, uses the grass: to suggest life, sustenance, hope, democracy. At the end of the novel, the chastened Henry's case of hay fever seems to have subsided when Helen, her baby, and Tom burst in from the meadow, with Helen exclaiming, "It'll be such a crop of hay as never!"

MAURICE

Written a few years after *Howards End*, *Maurice* did not see print until the year following Forster's death. In a later "terminal note" to this novel of a gay man, Forster observed a change in the public's reaction to this subject from one of "ignorance and terror" at the time he wrote it to "familiarity and contempt" in his old age, so he continued to withhold the work. Maurice Hall also defies the class system, for his sexual partner is a gamekeeper on a college classmate's estate. Given the rigid penal code of the time, the novel is also about criminality.

Aside from his sexual orientation, Maurice resembles his creator very little, being rather ordinary in intellect, little drawn to the arts, and rather robust physically. Whereas Rickie Elliot had been effeminate, his deformed foot a symbolic impediment to satisfactory heterosexuality, Maurice seems quite "normal" to his friends. His college friend Clive Durham, leaning somewhat to homosexuality in college, ironically changes after an illness and a trip to Greece, and marries. The Durhams are gentlefolk, though somewhat reduced, and Maurice has gotten on well with them, but Clive's marriage drives a wedge between them. After indulging in, and apparently escaping from, a furtive but passionate affair with Alec Scudder, their gamekeeper, Maurice suffers a blackmail threat from his former lover, but in the end Alec proves true, and instead of emigrating with whatever conscience money he might have extracted, Alec returns to the Durham estate, where, in the boathouse, the two come together again. At the end, Maurice's revelation to the conventionally horrified Clive leaves the latter trying "to devise some method of concealing the truth from Anne"—his wife.

Maurice demonstrates Forster's conviction that the desire for loving human relations is proof against the snobbery of all social classes. Although it could not be printed when it was written, the novel now seems more dated than Forster's other works, perhaps because its style is plain and drab. It obviously suffers from its lack of a contemporary audience, although Forster showed it to Lytton Strachey and received some constructive advice. Significantly, when Oliver Stallybrass, the editor of the Abinger Edition of Forster's works, assembled his favorite quotations from Forster, he could find nothing in *Maurice* worth including.

A PASSAGE TO INDIA

Although Forster committed himself wholeheartedly to friendship, it cannot be called the central theme of any of his novels until *A Passage to India*. The friendship of Rickie Elliot and Stewart Ansell, while vital to the former's development and self-discovery, is subordinated to the theme of brotherhood, in its familial sense, and Rickie can find no basis for friendship with Stephen. The incipient friendship of Margaret Schlegel and Ruth Wilcox is aborted by the latter's death. *A Passage to India*, while treating of brotherhood in its largest sense, is at heart a novel of friendship and its possibilities in the context of a racially and religiously fragmented society.

Beginning with the visit to India of the mother and fiancé of Ronnie Heaslop, the young colonial magistrate, and the complications of their encounters with a few educated natives, the narrative comes to focus on the friendship that as a consequence waxes and wanes between the English schoolmaster Cyril Fielding and the young Muslim Dr. Aziz. Forster dedicated the book to another Anglo-Indian friendship: his own with Syed Ross Masood, who first knew Forster as his tutor in Latin prior to Masood's entrance to Oxford in 1906, and who provided the impetus for Forster's own initial passage to India a few years later. Since Anglo-Indian prejudice was one of the loquacious Masood's favorite subjects, Forster understood it well by the time he came to write the novel. Indeed, his friendship with Masood demonstrated the possibility of such a relationship surviving the strains imposed on it by one partner's determination to pull no punches in discussing it.

Aziz, accused by Ronnie's fiancé, Adela Quested, of assaulting or at least offending her (for she remains vague about the matter throughout) in a cave they were exploring, is a less masterful and self-confident figure than Masood, and the reader knows all along that there must be some mistake. Adela has seen how Ronnie's Indian service has exacerbated the weaker aspects of his character, and she has broken off their engagement, but she is not, as Aziz affects to believe, a love-starved female—at least not in the crude sense Aziz intends.

Forster draws an unforgettable picture of the tensions between the colonial rulers and the Indian professional class. The most idealistic Englishmen, it seems, succumb to the prevailing intolerance. It is an effort to consider the natives as human, as when Ronnie, told by his mother, Mrs. Moore, of her meeting with a young doctor, replies: "I know of no young doctor in Chandrapore," though once he learns that his mother has actually been consorting with a Muslim, he identifies him readily enough.

An exception to the rule is Fielding, already over forty when he came to India and a continuing believer in "a globe of men who are trying to reach one another." When Aziz' trial divides the community more openly and dangerously than usual, Fielding supports the young doctor—a move that assures the enmity of the English without guaranteeing the affection of the skeptical Indians. After Adela withdraws her charges against Aziz, the intimacy between the two men reaches its height; almost immediately, however, they quarrel over Aziz' determination to make his tormentor pay damages.

Fielding cannot persuade Aziz to show mercy, but Mrs. Moore can, even though she has left the country before the trial and in fact has died on her return passage. For the sake of the mother of the detested man whom Aziz still believes Adela will marry, he spares the young woman, knowing that the English will interpret this decision as an indication of guilt. With Adela finally gone, Aziz mistakenly assumes that Fielding, now contemplating a visit to England, intends to marry her himself. When the friends meet again two years later, the old frankness and intimacy has been shattered. Although Fielding has married, his bride is the daughter of Mrs. Moore.

The final chapter is a particularly excellent one. As Aziz and Fielding ride horses together, the former vowing that they can be friends but only after the Indians "drive every blasted Englishman into the sea," the horses swerve apart, as if to counter Fielding's objection. Not religion, land, people, even animals want the friendship now. It is difficult to escape the conclusion that under imperial conditions no rapprochement is possible.

Much of the interest in this novel has centered on Mrs. Moore, a rather querulous old woman with a role not much larger than Mrs. Wilcox's in *Howards End*. Although she joins the roster of Forster's admirable characters who defy the taboos that divide people, she refuses to involve herself in the Aziz trial. Nevertheless, the Indians make a legend out of her and invest her with numinous powers. Critics have tended to regard her as a more successful character than Mrs. Wilcox. Part of the explanation may lie in Forster's decision to allow the reader to see her not only at first hand but also through the eyes of the Indians. If their view of Mrs. Moore is partly illusion, the illusion itself—like the more familiar illusions of the English—becomes itself a part of the truth of the situation. It is one of Forster's virtues that he knows and communicates the often conflicting values and attitudes of native Indians.

Nor is the Indian version of Mrs. Moore completely illusory, for in addition to her openness and candor, Mrs. Moore in one respect surpasses all the Europeans, even the gentle Fielding. She loves and respects life, especially unfamiliar life. It is illuminating to contrast her attitude with that of two incidental characters—missionaries who live among the people and never come to the whites' club. They measure up to their calling very well for Forster clergymen, allowing that God has room in his mansions for all people. On the subject of animals they are not so sure; Mr. Sorley, the more liberal of the two, opts for monkeys but stumbles over wasps. Mrs. Moore, more alert to the native birds and animals than she is to many people, is even sympathetic to a wasp ("Pretty dear") that has flown into the house. It is doubtless significant that the wasp is very different from the European type. Long after she is gone, Professor Godbole, Aziz' Hindu friend, remembers her in connection with the wasp. Love of humble forms of life, which the other Westerners in the novel notice only as irritations if at all, is for the Indians of Forster's *A Passage to India* a reliable indication of spirituality.

The sensitivity of Mrs. Moore and the goodwill of Fielding seem like frail counterweights to the prevailing cynicism and prejudice that stifle the necessarily furtive social initiatives of well-intentioned victims such as Aziz. If these flawed but genuine human beings have little impact on the morally bankrupt society in which they move, they have for more than half a century heartened readers of like aspirations.

Robert P. Ellis

Other major works

SHORT FICTION: *The Celestial Omnibus, and Other Stories*, 1911; *The Eternal Moment, and Other Stories*, 1928; *The Collected Tales of E. M. Forster*, 1947; *The Life to Come, and Other Stories*, 1972; *Arctic Summer, and Other Fiction*, 1980.

PLAYS: *Billy Budd*, pb. 1951 (libretto; with Eric Crozier).

NONFICTION: *Alexandria: A History and a Guide*, 1922; *Pharos and Pharillon*, 1923; *Aspects of the Novel*, 1927; *Goldsworthy Lowes Dickinson*, 1934; *Abinger Harvest*, 1936; *Virginia Woolf*, 1942; *Development of English Prose Between 1918 and 1939*, 1945; *Two Cheers for Democracy*, 1951; *The Hill of Devi*, 1953; *Marianne Thornton: A Domestic Biography, 1797-1887*, 1956; *Commonplace Book*, 1978; *Selected Letters of E. M. Forster*, 1983-1985 (2 volumes; Mary Lago and P. N. Furbank, editors); *The Feminine Note in Literature*, 2001.

MISCELLANEOUS: *The Abinger Edition of E. M. Forster*, 1972-1998 (17 volumes; Oliver Stallybrass, editor).

Bibliography

Beauman, Nicola. *E. M. Forster: A Biography*. New York: Alfred A. Knopf, 1994. Biography devoted primarily to the first forty-five years of Forster's life, when he was developing as a fiction writer, discusses the origins of Forster's fictional themes in his family background. Argues that his most successful years as a writer were also his unhappiest as a person owing to his sexual repression and his conflicts over his homosexuality.

Bradshaw, David, ed. *The Cambridge Companion to E. M. Forster*. New York: Cambridge University Press, 2007. Collection of essays examines various aspects of Forster's life and work. Topics discussed include Forster and the novel, Forster and women, and Forsterian sexuality. Among the novels analyzed are *A Room with a View*, *Howards End*, and *A Passage to India*.

Edwards, Mike. *E. M. Forster: The Novels*. New York: Palgrave, 2002. Demonstrates how readers can analyze four of Forster's novels—*A Room with a View*, *Howards End*, *A Passage to India*, and *The Longest Journey*—to understand the author's treatment of characters, locations, relationships, and other aspects of these works. Also provides ideas to help readers engage in further analysis, information about Forster's life, and examples of how four literary critics have approached Forster's writing.

Furbank, Philip N. *E. M. Forster: A Life*. New York: Harcourt Brace Jovanovich, 1978. Authorized biography successfully creates an authentic, intimate, and illuminating portrait of the man behind the writer and controversial public figure. The wealth of previously unavailable material presented makes this an indispensable source on Forster's life, times, and work.

Gardner, Philip, ed. *E. M. Forster: The Critical Heritage*. New York: Routledge, 1997. Collection of critical reviews of Forster's works that were published in British and American newspapers and journals between 1905 and 1971, including articles by D. H. Lawrence and Virginia Woolf. Includes bibliographical references and index.

McDowell, Frederick P. W. *E. M. Forster*. Rev. ed. Boston: Twayne, 1982. Brilliant work provides a well-balanced and compendious overview of Forster's life, times, career, work, and achievements. Includes useful chronology, select bibliography, and index.

Medalie, David. *E. M. Forster's Modernism*. New York: Palgrave, 2002. Examines the relationship of Forster's writings to modernism, analyzing his works to demonstrate their modernist elements. Places Forster within the context of early twentieth century social, political, and aesthetic developments.

Rapport, Nigel. *The Prose and the Passion: Anthropology, Literature, and the Writing of E. M. Forster*. New York: St. Martin's Press, 1994. Looks at Forster's work from both anthropological and literary perspectives, providing excellent interpretation and criticism of the author's writings. Includes bibliography and references.

Stone, Wilfred. *The Cave and the Mountain: A Study of E. M. Forster*. Stanford, Calif.: Stanford University Press, 1966. Well-researched, scholarly work contains a vast amount of useful information about Forster's background, career, aesthetics, and work. Employs psychological and Jungian approaches in offering insightful and masterly critiques of Forster's fiction. Supplemented by notes and a comprehensive index.

Trilling, Lionel. *E. M. Forster: A Study*. Norfolk, Conn.: New Directions, 1943. Pioneer study by a noted American literary critic was instrumental in establishing Forster's reputation. Assesses Forster's artistic achievement in terms of his liberal humanism and moral realism.

FREDERICK FORSYTH

Born: Ashford, Kent, England; August 25, 1938
Also known as: Frederick McCarthy Forsyth

Principal long fiction

The Day of the Jackal, 1971
The Odessa File, 1972
The Dogs of War, 1974
The Devil's Alternative, 1979
The Fourth Protocol, 1984
The Negotiator, 1989
The Deceiver, 1991
The Fist of God, 1994
Icon, 1996
The Phantom of Manhattan, 1999
Avenger, 2003
The Afghan, 2006

Other literary forms

Frederick Forsyth (FOHR-sith) has written and edited short fiction, including *The Shepherd* (1975), one of his most popular short stories. He wrote the screenplay for the 1987 film version of his novel *The Fourth Protocol*. His book sequel to the musical opera *The Phantom of the Opera* (1986), *The Phantom of Manhattan*, is the story of the phantom striking it rich on Wall Street and recruiting his beloved Christine de Chagney to sing at his own opera house. He also has written nonfiction, including *The Biafra Story* (1969), a work based on his experiences in Nigeria. The book was revised as *The Making of an African Legend: The Biafra Story* (1983). He also wrote the biographical *Emeka* (1982; a story of Biafrin president Chukwuemeka Odumegwu Ojukwu) and *I Remember: Reflections on Fishing in Childhood* (1995).

Achievements

Frederick Forsyth created a new kind of fiction, the docudrama, combining journalistic immediacy, precise technical detail, and the fast-paced, suspenseful style of popular thrillers. More than thirty million copies of his books have been sold. *Avenger*, *Icon*, *The Fourth Protocol*, *The Day of the Jackal*, *The Odessa File*, and *The Dogs of War* have been made into films. *The Day of the Jackal* received the Edgar Award from the Mystery Writers of America (1971).

Biography

Frederick McCarthy Forsyth, the son of Frederick William Forsyth and Phyllis Green Forsyth, was born in Ashford, Kent, England, on August 25, 1938. His father taught him to love maps and to find the world's trouble spots on those maps, and he told him exciting stories about Borneo headhunters and tiger shoots. Forsyth attended the Tonbridge School in Kent and loves language (he speaks French, German, Spanish, and some Russian and Italian). He quit school at the age of seventeen.

Having qualified for his pilot's license in a Tiger Moth biplane, Forsyth joined the Royal Air Force (RAF) in 1956 and learned to fly a Vampire jet, becoming at the age of nineteen the youngest fighter pilot in the RAF. Two years later, he left the military to work as a journalist for the *Eastern Daily Press* in Norfolk before joining the international news service Reuters and being posted

Frederick Forsyth. (AP/Wide World Photos)

to Paris. There he covered the campaign against French president Charles de Gaulle, the inspiration for his first novel, *The Day of the Jackal*. Forsyth became chief reporter of the Reuters East Berlin bureau, covering East Germany, Czechoslovakia, and Hungary. In 1965, he joined the British Broadcasting Corporation as a radio reporter and then was assistant diplomatic correspondent for BBC television and assigned to cover the Nigerian civil war. The conflict between the official British stance on the war (motivated by Nigeria's rich oil fields) and his personal sympathy with starving Biafrans in general and their leader, Colonel Ojukwu, in particular led to disillusionment. Having offended Sir David Hunt, British high commissioner in Lagos, Forsyth resigned his position, became a freelance journalist, and recorded his war observations, which became his first book *The Biafra Story*. He also helped illegally fly food to save half a million African children.

Forsyth's *The Day of the Jackal*, recounting French political intrigue, was published two years later, followed quickly by *The Odessa File* and *The Dogs of War*. These three novels made his reputation and allowed him to live well, though high English taxes drove him out of the country, first to Spain for one year, then to Ireland, near Dublin, for five years. Returning to England in 1980, he settled in a fashionable section of London with his wife, Carole Forsyth, and their two sons, Frederick and Shane. He later divorced and was remarried. His memoir, *I Remember*, discusses his favorite pastime, fishing, which provides the author with the calm he needs for thinking through his plots.

Analysis

Frederick Forsyth's financially lucrative suspense thrillers set a technically trained professional on, variously, a collision course with a lone-wolf killer, a secret organization, or deadly representatives of a rogue branch of a government bureaucracy; the novels quicken their pace as characters travel widely across national boundaries, experiencing new geographies, customs, and points of view. The shared competence of protagonist and antagonist means readers learn how to do everything from building a bomb or other specialized weapon to correctly employing distinctive Arab gestures to signal regional origins. Forsyth provides the thrill of insider knowledge about current events and a meaningful pattern that unites seemingly disparate news stories. Journalism taught Forsyth how to insinuate into his fiction a persuasive semblance of reality, provide a broad context and significance for seemingly minor incidents, and make credible and seemingly authentic descriptions of events behind the headlines. Plot and structure create suspense and drive the action forward.

Despite attempts to interject feminine perspectives in his later works, Forsyth's stories depend on an underlying sense of shared male interests and attitudes. He told John Mortimer of the *The Times* of London what he aims for in his fiction—depicting the immoral committing immoral acts no different from those committed by an immoral establishment—so compellingly told that at least four copycat crimes have been associated with his books.

The Day of the Jackal

The Day of the Jackal tracks the movement of the real, infamous international assassin Carlos the Jackal, a mythic figure thought to have tried to assassinate

Charles de Gaulle because de Gaulle supported Algerian independence. (Carlos the Jackal lives on in the works of Robert Ludlum and others.) The novel establishes strategies that became Forsyth's signature: alternating plot lines that promote suspense as the different parties move closer and closer to a deadly encounter, admiration for technically competent professionals, and a contrast between the professional and the amateur.

Forsyth spends a great deal of time on trivial details that prove essential (such as passport forgery), contingency plans that come into play, and logical responses to tight situations. He enables readers to see the action from the perspective of a committed assassin and to appreciate his expertise. Ultimately, however, Commissioner Claude Lebel, a thorough professional, thwarts the Jackal's plan and saves de Gaulle.

The Odessa File

The Odessa File draws on real-life attempts to track Nazi war criminals. The former SS concentration camp commandant tracked in this story is Captain Eduard Roschmann, a historical figure whose actions Forsyth describes with accuracy. In this story, German crime reporter Peter Miller proves his investigative competence as he skillfully deals with the anti-Nazi underground and the Odessa organization (former members of the SS). Readers learn a great deal about the Holocaust and about the Jewish pursuit of Nazis connected with the concentration camps of World War II.

The Dogs of War

The Dogs of War is based on Forsyth's Biafran experiences and his indirect involvement in an attempted coup against then-president of Equatorial Guinea, Francisco Macías Nguema. The story depicts attempts to bring down an Idi Amin-like African dictator. The initial motivation is not sympathy for suffering citizens but a desire to take over newly discovered deposits of platinum. Sir James Manson, a British mining company director, hires mercenary Cat Shannon to depose the tyrant and establish a puppet government. Manson plans to take over mining rights, but Shannon and his crew develop a conscience and support the citizens over the greedy, self-interested Manson and the multinational corporations he represents. During this process, readers learn much about the financing and operation of gunrunning, mortar-shell trajectories, and more.

The Devil's Alternative

Unlike its predecessors, *The Devil's Alternative* describes a fictional terrorist takeover of an oil-filled supertanker that leaves no viable alternative: Yielding to terrorist demands could set off a nuclear war; refusing to yield will create the biggest oil spill in history. Typical of Forsyth, real political figures are present, and are thinly disguised: Joan Carpenter as British prime minister Margaret Thatcher, Bill Matthews as U.S. president Jimmy Carter, Stanislaw Poklewski as U.S. national security adviser Zbigniew Brzezinski, and David Lawrence as U.S. secretary of state Cyrus Vance.

The plot features Jewish Ukrainian nationalists with good cause to strike against the Soviet Union. The nationalists are acting at the same time that plant failures lead to fungicide poisoning of the Soviet wheat crop. Failed harvests drive hardliners to contemplate invading Western Europe and the United States to offer food in exchange for military concessions. British security agent Adam Munro finds himself putting a Russian woman he loves at risk to glean insider information to resolve this dilemma.

The Fourth Protocol

The Fourth Protocol takes its title from a so-called gentleman's agreement not to take portable nuclear weapons into enemy territory. In this case, the violators of protocol are a rogue Soviet group determined to change the direction of British and Western politics by detonating a small atomic device at a U.S. airbase in England. By blaming the Americans, they hope to put the antinuclear Labour Party in power. The novel includes a memorandum on how British Labour Party politics play into Soviet plans.

To accomplish their goals, the rogue Soviets have put into play a lone-wolf assassin tracked by a nondescript but highly competent police officer. The plot alternates between the two characters in typical Forsyth style, closing the distance for the final encounter. The ease with which a small nuclear bomb can be assembled and employed is shocking, and this plot device became a staple of popular fiction and film, raising legitimate concerns.

The Negotiator

Before the novel reached print, the intricate plot of *The Negotiator* was dated by the real-world end of the

Soviet Union, a hazard of topical fiction. In this story, Soviet president Mikhail Gorbachev and U.S. president John Cormack negotiate an unprecedented disarmament treaty, cutting arms and military costs by half and ushering in true peace. Conservative Texans and Soviets dependent on a confrontational status quo to retain national pride and power join forces to kidnap and threaten to execute the president's only son. Low-key hostage negotiator Quinn joins federal agent Samantha Somerville to undermine these villains, but negotiations fail, and these two chase and romance their way through Europe, always a little behind the malefactors and plot organizers. Ironically, Quinn and Somerville end up in a wintry Vermont wilderness in alliance with supportive Russian agents after the same villains, and Russians, Americans, and British join forces to defeat the criminals in their respective secret services.

The Deceiver

The Deceiver reflects nostalgically on the Cold War when heroes and villains were more clearly recognizable, their political positions predictably nationalistic. The novel challenges the assertion that perestroika ushered in peaceful coexistence, ending international crises and the need for the derring-do of traditional spies.

The deceiver of the title, aging British agent Sam McCready, began his career as a field agent, rose rapidly through the ranks, and now heads the Deception, Disinformation, and Psychological Operations desk of the Secret Intelligence Service. However, forced retirement is in the offing. McCready challenges accusations that his type of spying is outmoded by East-West cooperation, requesting that his service record be reexamined. The resultant hearings request that he recount and defend the most notorious of his past exploits: four stories divided by Interludes. These stories describe a clandestine crossing of the Berlin Wall, encounters with Russian defectors and Irish Republic Army arms smugglers, and engagements with a far-reaching terrorist network. McCready retires at about the same time that Iraqi dictator Saddam Hussein invades Kuwait, Forsyth's reminder that spies such as McCready will always be needed to provide intelligence and confront enemies behind the scenes.

The Fist of God

The Fist of God focuses on the West's lack of intelligence information about Hussein's closed Iraq and its troop strength and deployment before the Persian Gulf War. To provide insider information about that country, daring British operative Mike Martin of Britain's elite Special Air Service Regiment draws on his childhood experience in the region to go underground as an Arab militant and try to contact a Mossad plant, codenamed Jericho, who is a deep-cover mole in the Baghdad establishment. Once on the move in Iraq, however, Martin discovers more at stake than up-to-date intelligence.

Hussein has an ultimate secret weapon, probably nuclear, codenamed Fist of God—a doomsday bomb to ignite the Middle East. As the novel shifts rapidly from Washington, D.C., and London to Baghdad and Kuwait (Martin's entryway), Martin skates on the edge of discovery and, in the best spy tradition, achieves much with little. Forsyth takes readers behind bland governmental bulletins to demonstrate how real intelligence is gleaned and how behind-the-scenes battles are waged.

Icon

Icon is the story of right-wing Russian fanatic Igor Komarov, who poses as a moderate to seize power but whose neo-Nazi document, the Black Manifesto, exposes his real plans for the nation if elected. A moment of carelessness places the secret document in the hands of a Jewish janitor, who, horrified, passes it on to an American embassy diplomat. Komarov willingly risks all to retrieve this potentially damaging document, while British and U.S. agents and diplomats debate whether or not it is genuine. Former CIA operative Jason Monk returns to Moscow in disguise, where former master British spy runner Nigel Irvine and a Chechen warlord Irvine had once saved help him track down the janitor and tie together the threads of evidence that damn Komarov.

Avenger

The avenger of this novel's title is Cal Dexter, a Vietnam tunnel rat turned small-town New Jersey attorney and vigilante pursuer who proves unable to save his murdered daughter but is now adept at stalking villains. A billionaire Canadian mining magnate hires Dexter to bring to trial Serbian warlord and mass murderer Zoran Zilic, who brutally butchered the Canadian's idealistic grandson (an aid worker in Bosnia). After searching the United Arab Emirates, Dexter finds Zilic hiding out in a jungle compound in the fictional South American Republic of San Martin, protected by hired security guards and U.S. agents. In the weeks leading up to September 11, 2001, the FBI recruits Zilic to kill Osama Bin Laden, and Dexter pursues Zilic as Zilic pursues Bin Laden. The novel ends on September 10, 2001.

The Afghan

In *The Afghan*, Mike Martin of *The Fist of God* returns from retirement for an even more dangerous mission: to disguise himself as Taliban leader Izmat Khan (imprisoned at Guantanamo Bay) and infiltrate al-Qaeda to learn of a planned strike. Dark-skinned Martin looks like Khan and speaks his language, but he still must convince true believers that he is indeed one of them, anxious to make up for time wasted in prison.

Place, manners, and customs ring true, including a description of the November, 2001, battle to recapture Fort Qala-i-Jangi in northern Afghanistan, highlighting the role of six British Special Boat Service soldiers: Forsyth traveled to Kabul, Islamabad, and Peshawar to collect precise details to bring his story to life. Therein, al-Qaeda plots to bomb world leaders meeting aboard an ocean liner. Their method is to steal and change the shape and name of a small ship, then explode it near the ocean liner outside New York Harbor.

Gina Macdonald and Andrew F. Macdonald

Other major works

SHORT FICTION: *The Shepherd*, 1975; *No Comebacks: Collected Short Stories*, 1982; *Used in Evidence, and Other Stories*, 1998; *The Veteran*, 2001.

SCREENPLAY: *The Fourth Protocol*, 1987 (based on his novel).

NONFICTION: *The Biafra Story*, 1969 (revised as *The Making of an African Legend: The Biafra Story*, 1983); *Emeka*, 1982 (biography of Chukwuemeka Odumegwu Ojukwu); *I Remember: Reflections on Fishing in Childhood*, 1995.

EDITED TEXT: *Great Flying Stories*, 1991.

Bibliography

Butler, Colin. "The Cold War Revisited." *English Review* 10, no. 1 (September, 1999): 2-8. Butler places Forsyth in the context of other popular Cold War authors, arguing that Forsyth's books are well-constructed documents of their time.

Cabell, Craig. *Frederick Forsyth: A Matter of Protocol.* London: Robson, 2001. An authorized biography of Forsyth and a study of his works. Forsyth was "notoriously reticent" about his own past, yet in this book he is candid about the background to each of his novels and even about his political beliefs.

Jones, Dudley. "Professionalism and Popular Fiction: The Novels of Arthur Hailey and Frederick Forsyth." In *Spy Thrillers: From Buchan to Le Carré*, edited by Clive Bloom. New York: St. Martin's Press, 1990. This chapter in a study of spy thrillers examines Forsyth's contributions to the genre and his focus on experts in conflict.

Leeman, Sue. "Forsyth's Foresight." *Hobart Mercury* (Australia), September 16, 2006. Leeman discusses how Forsyth gathered materials for *The Afghan* and how future events have echoed his fictive predictions.

JOHN FOWLES

Born: Leigh-on-Sea, Essex, England; March 31, 1926
Died: Lyme Regis, Dorset, England; November 5, 2005
Also known as: John Robert Fowles

PRINCIPAL LONG FICTION

The Collector, 1963
The Magus, 1965, 1977
The French Lieutenant's Woman, 1969
The Ebony Tower, 1974 (novella, three short stories, and translation of a French medieval romance)
Daniel Martin, 1977
Mantissa, 1982
A Maggot, 1985

OTHER LITERARY FORMS

In addition to his novels, John Fowles wrote works of philosophy, essays for scholarly and popular audiences, criticism, poetry, and short fiction. He also translated the works of several other writers into English. *The Aristos: A Self-Portrait in Ideas*, published in 1964, reflects Fowles's philosophical stance. Patterned on writings of Heraclitus of Ephesus, the fifth century B.C.E. Greek philosopher, it outlines many of the views that Fowles expressed more fully and artistically in his fiction. His collected poetry is published in *Poems* (1973); much of it reflects his period of residence in Greece, the major setting for *The Magus*. His longer nonfiction pieces reflect his love for and interest in nature: *Shipwreck* (1974), a text to accompany the photographs of shipwrecks along the English coast near the town where Fowles made his home until his death in 2005, and *Lyme Regis Camera* (1990), a text to accompany photographs of the town, its inhabitants, and its immediate environs; *Islands* (1978), about the Scilly Islands off the English coast, but more about the nature of islands as a metaphor for literature and the writer; *The Tree* (1979), an extension of the same theme with emphasis on the tree as representative of all nature; and *The Enigma of Stonehenge* (1980), a further extension of nature to encompass the mystery of a sacred place. All these themes are touched on in the varied pieces collected in *Wormholes: Essays and Occasional Writings* (1998). These themes find definition and elaboration in his fiction. Fowles's only collection of short fiction, *The Ebony Tower*, includes a novella from which the title is taken, three short stories, and a translation of a medieval romance. The collection, titled "Variations" in manuscript, also reflects Fowles's central themes in the longer fiction.

ACHIEVEMENTS

John Fowles's place in literary history is difficult to assess. He established an excellent reputation as a writer of serious fiction, one who will continue to be read. His work continues to receive the notice of critics; numerous books have been published about him and about his works. Fowles, however, was no "ivory tower" author; his work enjoys a wide readership, and several of his novels have been made into motion pictures, including *The Collector* (1965), *The Magus* (1968), and *The French Lieutenant's Woman* (1981). Readers can expect to find in Fowles's works a good story with a passionate love interest, complex characters, and a healthy smattering of philosophy, all presented within the context of the plot. Critics can slice away multiple layers to get at the wheels-within-wheels of meaning on existential, historical, philosophical, psychological, and myriad other levels.

Because Fowles rarely told the same story in the same way, genre is a topic of much discussion among his critics. His fiction reflects not only his experimentation with genre but also his questioning of authorial voice, the continuum of time, moments out of time, split viewpoint, stories without endings, stories with choices of endings, and stories with revised endings. Despite such experimentation, most of the novels are in many ways quite old-fashioned, reflecting the ancient boy-meets-girl, boy-loses-girl, boy-seeks-to-find-girl-again-and-in-so-doing-finds-himself quest motif that characterizes so much fiction. They are fairly straightforward "good reads" without the dizzying experimentation of a James Joyce to make them virtually inaccessible to all but the most diligent reader. On any level, Fowles is enjoyable, and what reserves him a place among memorable writers is that he is discoverable again and again.

Biography

John Robert Fowles was born in Leigh-on-Sea, Essex, England, on March 31, 1926, to Robert and Gladys Richards Fowles. During World War II, his family was evacuated to the more remote village of Ippeplen, South Devon, and it was there that Fowles discovered the beauty of the country of Devonshire, his "English Garden of Eden" that figures so prominently in other guises in his fiction. During that same period, he was a student at the exclusive Bedford School, where he studied German and French literature, eventually rising to the stature of head boy, a position of great power over the other boys in the school. It was there that he got his first taste of literature, which he loved, and power, which he despised. The knowledge of both was influential in his own writing.

John Fowles. (Camera Press Ltd./Archive Photos)

From Bedford he went into military service, spending six months at the University of Edinburgh and completing training as a lieutenant in the merchant marine just as the war was ending. Following the war, he continued his education in German and more particularly French literature at New College, Oxford University; he graduated in 1950 with a B.A. with honors. His fiction owes many debts to his study of French literature, particularly his interest in existentialism as espoused by Jean-Paul Sartre and Albert Camus, and his knowledge of the Celtic romance, from which stemmed his expressed belief that all literature has its roots in the theme of the quest.

Upon graduation, Fowles taught English at the University of Poitiers. After a year at Poitiers, he took a job teaching English to Greek boys on the island of Spetsai in the Aegean Sea. The school, the island, the aura of Greece, and the thoughts of the young teacher became the material for *The Magus*, his first novel (although not published first). It was also on Spetsai that he met Elizabeth Whitton, whom he married three years later. For Fowles, Greece was the land of myth, the other world, the place of the quest. Leaving Greece, Fowles suffered the loss of another Eden, but that loss inspired him to write. While writing, he continued to teach in and around London until the publication of *The Collector* in 1963, the success of which enabled him to leave teaching and devote himself to writing. The following year he published *The Aristos*, and in 1965 he finally published *The Magus*, twelve years after its conception.

A year later, he and Elizabeth moved to Lyme Regis in Dorset, a small seaside town away from London, where he lived until his death on November 5, 2005. First living on a rundown farm, the Fowleses later moved to an eighteenth century house overlooking Lyme Bay. The dairy, the house, and the town of Lyme figure prominently in his third novel, *The French Lieutenant's Woman*, a work that established Fowles's international reputation. Following its success he published his *Poems*, *The Ebony Tower*, *Daniel Martin*, the revised version of *The Magus*, *Mantissa*, and *A Maggot*.

Fowles's love of nature was evident in his writing as well as in his life, especially in such nonfiction works as *Islands* and *The Tree*. At his home in Lyme Regis, he oversaw a large, wild garden overlooking Lyme Bay and fostered the natural development of the flora. One passion that he lost, however, was the collection of living things. Once a collector of butterflies, like his character Frederick Clegg in *The Collector*, Fowles later abhorred such activities. Rather, he began collecting Victorian postcards and antique china, read voluminously, went to London infrequently, and shared a very private life with his wife, who was his best critic. It was a life he very much enjoyed until he suffered a mild stroke in early 1988. Although the stroke caused no permanent damage, it left him depressed by the sudden specter of death and by a resulting loss of creative energies. By the mid-1990's, most readers who had followed Fowles's career did not expect him to add to his body of work, despite the statement made at the Fowles seminar in Lyme Regis in 1996 that he was again at work. *Wormholes*, his collection of essays published in 1998, was his last work.

Analysis

John Fowles's fiction has one theme: the quest of his protagonists for self-knowledge. Such a quest is not easy in the modern world because, as many other modern authors have shown, the contemporary quester is cut off from the traditions and rituals of the past that gave people a purpose and sense of direction. Still, desiring the freedom of individual choice that requires an understanding of self, the Fowlesian protagonist moves through the pattern of the quest as best he can.

Following the tradition of the quest theme found in the medieval romance, which Fowles saw as central to his and all of Western fiction, the quester embarks on the journey in response to a call to adventure. Because the quester is in a state of longing for the adventure, often without recognizing the fact, he readily responds to the call. The call takes him across a threshold into another world, the land of myth. For Fowles's questers, this other world is always described as a remote, out-of-the-way place, often lush and primeval. In this place the quester meets the usual dragons, which, in modern terms, are presented as a series of challenges that he must overcome if he is to proceed.

Guided by the figure of the wise old man who has gone before him and can show the way, the quester gradually acquires self-knowledge, which brings freedom of choice. For Fowles's heroes, this choice always centers on the acceptance of a woman. If the quester has attained self-knowledge, he is able to choose the woman—that is, to know and experience love, signifying wholeness. Then he must make the crossing back into the real world and continue to live and choose freely, given the understanding the quest has provided.

What separates the journey of the Fowlesian hero from the journey of the medieval hero is that much of it has become internalized. Where the quester of old did actual battle with dragons, monsters, and mysterious knights, the modern quester is far removed from such obvious obstacles. He cannot see the enemy in front of him because it is often within him, keeping him frozen in a state of inertia that prevents him from questing. The modern journey, then, can be seen in psychological terms; while the events are externalized, the results are measured by the growth of the protagonist toward wholeness or self-knowledge. Thus, as Joseph Campbell describes in *The Hero with a Thousand Faces* (1949), "the problem is . . . nothing if not that of making it possible for men and women to come to full human maturity through the conditions of contemporary life."

Each of Fowles's protagonist/heroes follows the pattern of the mythic quest. Each journeys to a strange land (the unconscious): the Greek island of Phraxos and Conchis' more secret domain for Nicholas Urfe, the isolated countryside house for Frederick Clegg, the primitive Undercliff of Lyme Regis for Charles Smithson, the hidden manor in the forests of Brittany for David Williams, the lost landscape of his youth and the journey up the Nile for Daniel Martin, the interior space of the mind of Miles Green, and the ancient landscape of Stonehenge plus the mystery of the cave for Bartholomew and Rebecca. Each undergoes a series of trials (the warring aspects of his personality) intended to bring him to a state of self-consciousness. With the exception of Clegg, whose story represents the antiquest, each has the aid of a guide (the mythical wise old man): Conchis for Nicholas; Dr. Grogan for Charles; Breasley for David Williams; Professor Kirnberger, György Lukács, a Rembrandt self-portrait, and others for Daniel Martin; the various manifestations of the muse for Miles Green; and Holy Mother Wisdom for Bartholomew and Rebecca. Each has an encounter with a woman (representative of "the other half" needed for wholeness): Alison for Nicholas, Miranda for Frederick, Sarah for Charles, "The Mouse" for David, Jane for Daniel, Erato for Miles, Holy Mother Wisdom for Bartholomew, and Bartholomew for Rebecca. The ability of the quester to calm or assimilate the warring aspects within him, to come to an understanding of himself, and as a result reach out to the experience of love with the woman, represents the degree of growth of each.

Feeling strongly that his fiction must be used as "a method of propagating [his] views of life" to bring a vision of cosmic order out of modern chaos, Fowles saw himself on a journey to accomplish this task. An examination of his fiction reveals the way in which he tackled the task, providing his readers with a description of the journey that they, too, can take.

The Magus

The Magus was Fowles's first novel (although it was published after *The Collector*), and it remains his most popular. Fowles himself was so intrigued by the novel that he spent twelve years writing it; even after its publication, he produced a revised version in 1977 because he was dissatisfied with parts of it. Although some critics see changes between the original and the revision, there is little substantive difference between the two books beyond the addition of more explicit sexual scenes and the elaboration of several sections; thus the discussion of one suffices for the other.

The story derives from Fowles's period of teaching in Greece, and its protagonist, Nicholas Urfe, is much like Fowles in temperament and situation. As is often the case with Fowles, his fiction describes protagonists of the same age and temperament as himself at the time of his writing; thus an examination of the corpus reveals a maturing hero as well as a maturing author. In this first novel, Nicholas is twenty-five, Oxford-educated, attracted to existentialism, and bored with life. He is the typical Fowlesian protagonist, well-bred, aimless, and ripe for the quest.

Discontented with his teaching job in England, he, like Fowles, jumps at the opportunity to teach in Greece. His subconscious desire is for a "new land, a new race, a new language," which the quest will provide. Just before going, he meets Alison, who is to become the important woman in his life, although it takes many pages and much questing through the labyrinth of self-knowledge on Phraxos for Nicholas to realize this. Alison, as the intuitive female, the feeling side Nicholas needs for wholeness, recognizes the importance of their relationship from the beginning, while Nicholas, representing reason, does not. In discussing the elements of the quest that bring Nicholas to an understanding and acceptance of the feeling side of himself, which allows him to experience love, one can chart the pattern of the quest that Fowles presents in variations in all his fiction.

On Phraxos, Nicholas responds to the call to adventure embodied in the voice of a girl, the song of a bird, and some passages of poetry, especially four lines from T. S. Eliot: "We shall not cease from exploration/ And the end of all our exploring/ Will be to arrive where we started/ And know the place for the first time." These lines state the mystery of the journey that awaits him: to quest outside so as to come back to himself with understanding. Put another way, it is the yearning in humankind for the return to the harmony of the Garden of Eden. It is, as well, the thesis of *Four Quartets* (1943), which solves for Eliot the problem of the wasteland. Finally, it is the concept that motivates almost all of Fowles's questers, beginning with Nicholas.

Crossing the threshold beyond the *Salle d'Attente*, or Waiting Room, to the domain of myth at Bournai, Nicholas meets Conchis, his guide through the quest. Under Conchis' tutelage, Nicholas's "discoveries" begin. Nicholas understands that something significant is about to happen, that it is somehow linked to Alison, and that it restores his desire to live. Conchis exposes Nicholas to a series of experiences to teach and test him. Some he describes for Nicholas, others make Nicholas an observer, and still others give him an active, sometimes frightening role. In all, whether he is repulsed, fascinated, or puzzled, Nicholas wants more; he allows himself to be led deeper and deeper into the mysteries. These culminate in a trial scene during which Nicholas is examined, his personality dissected, his person humiliated. Finally, he is put to the test of his ability to choose. Longing to punish Lily/Julie, the personification of woman Nicholas romantically and unrealistically longs for, he is given the opportunity at the end of the trial to flog her. His understanding that his freedom of choice gives him the power to resist the predictable, to go against the dictates of reason alone and follow the voice of the unconscious, signifies that he has become one of the "elect." Nicholas emerges from the underground chamber reborn into a higher state of consciousness. He must then make the return crossing into the real world.

To begin the return journey, he is given a glimpse of Alison, although he has been led to believe that she has committed suicide. Realizing that she is alive and that she offers him "a mirror that did not lie" in her "constant reality," he understands that the remainder of the quest must be toward a reunion with Alison. Apparently, however, he is not yet worthy of her, being dominated still by the ratiocinative side of himself, that part that seeks to unravel logically the mystery that Conchis presents. On his return to London he is put through additional tests until one day, completely unsuspecting of her arrival, he sees Alison again and follows her to Regents Park, where they are reunited.

Signifying the experience of the Garden of Eden, when man and woman existed in wholeness, the park provides an appropriate setting for their reunion. Echoing lines from Eliot, Nicholas has arrived where he started. Now he must prove that he is worthy of Alison, that he can accept the love she once offered freely, but he must win her just as Orpheus attempted to win Eurydice from the dead. Becoming his own magus, he acts out a drama of his own making, challenging Alison to meet him at Paddington Station, where their journey together will begin. Unlike Orpheus, who was unsuccessful in bringing Eurydice from the dead, Nicholas has the confidence gained in his quest to leave Alison and not look back, knowing that she will be at the train station to meet him. While there is some question among critics as to whether Nicholas and Alison do meet and continue their journey together, Fowles has indicated that "Alison is the woman he will first try to love." Certainly, in either case it is the element of mystery that is important, not whether Nicholas wins this particular woman. The significance is in his yearning for her, demonstrating that he has learned to accept and give love, that he has journeyed toward wholeness.

What makes such a journey significant for the reader is that he or she partakes of the experience as an insider, not as an outsider, owing to the narrative technique that Fowles employs. In Fowles's first-person narrative, Nicholas reveals only what he knows at any particular point on his journey; thus the reader sees only what Nicholas sees. Not able to see with any more sophistication than Nicholas the twistings and turnings of Conchis' "godgame," the reader must do exactly what Nicholas does: try to unravel the mystery in its literal sense rather than understand the "mystery" in its sacred sense. Believing every rational explanation Nicholas posits, the reader learns as he learns. As his own magus, Nicholas leads the reader into the mystery he was led into, not spoiling the reader's sense of discovery as his was not spoiled, and providing the reader with the experience of the journey as he experienced it. Of course, behind Nicholas is the master magus Fowles, whose design is to lead each reader to his or her own essential mysteries. The technique provides an immediacy that allows each reader to take the journey toward self-discovery; the novel provides a paradigm by which the mystery of Fowles's other novels can be deciphered.

The Collector

The Collector, in sharp contrast to *The Magus*, presents the other side of the coin, sounding a warning. Here the protagonist is the antihero; his captured lady, the heroine. She goes on the journey he is incapable of taking, which, in his incapacity to understand her or himself, he aborts.

Frederick Clegg, the protagonist, is similar in many ways to Nicholas of *The Magus*. Each is orphaned, in his twenties, and aimless. Each forms an attachment to a blond, gray-eyed woman, and each goes to a remote land in which he explores his relationship with this woman. Each is given the opportunity to become a quester in that land, and each tells a first-person narrative of the experience. In each, the narrative structure is circular, such that the novel arrives where it started.

The major difference, of course, is that Nicholas journeys toward wholeness; Clegg, while given the same opportunities, does not. The reason for Clegg's failure lies in the fact that he cannot understand the mythic signals, and so he cannot move beyond his present confused state. The novel begins and ends in psychic darkness; the hero does not grow or develop. While Clegg remains unchanged, however, the captive Miranda, trapped as Clegg's prisoner, undergoes a transforming experience that puts her on the path of the quest Clegg is unable to take. The tragedy is not so much Clegg's lack of growth as it is the futility of Miranda's growth in view of the fact that she cannot apply in the real world the lessons learned in her quest. She is incapable even of having any beneficial effect on her captor.

Part of the problem between Miranda and Clegg lies in the differences in their cultural backgrounds. Miranda has the background of a typical Fowlesian quester in terms of education and social standing; Clegg's background, however, is atypical in his lower-class roots and lack of education. Part of the thesis of this novel is the clash between these two as representative of the clash between the "Many" and the "Few," which Fowles describes in detail in *The Aristos*. The novel, presented as a divided narrative told first by Clegg and then by Miranda, depicts in its very structure the division between Miranda and Clegg that cannot be bridged.

The first problem for Clegg as a quester is that he captures the object of his quest, keeping her prisoner in a hidden cellar. In psychological terms, Miranda, the feeling side of Clegg, is kept in the cellar "down there," which disallows the possibility of union. Clegg remains a divided man, living above in the house, with Miranda imprisoned below. Miranda, however, discovers that her "tomb" becomes a "womb" in which she grows in self-consciousness and understanding. Thus, the quest centers on her and the antiquest centers on Clegg.

As a butterfly collector, Clegg sees Miranda as his prize acquisition. He hopes that she will come to love him as he thinks he loves her, but what he really prizes is her beauty, which he has hoped to capture and keep as he would a butterfly's. When she begins to turn ugly in her vitality and lack of conformity to his preconceived notions of her, she falls off the pedestal on which he has placed her, and he then feels no compunction about forcing her to pose in the nude for photographs.

Clegg's problems are many. On a social level, he identifies too closely with what he sees as the judgment of the middle class against his lower-class background. On a psychological level, he is possessed by images from his past, the negative influences of his aunt, and his upbringing. His sexual fears and feelings of personal inadequacy combine to lock him into his own psychological prison in the same way he locks Miranda into hers. As he is trapped in his internal prison, the outward presence of Miranda remains just that, outside himself, and he cannot benefit from her proximity. She, however, while externally imprisoned by Clegg, is not prevented from making the inward journey toward self-discovery. At the same time, there is within Clegg, although deeply buried, a desire to break away and move onto the mythic path, and Miranda sees that aspect of him, his essential innocence, which has caused him to be attracted to her in the first place. Nevertheless, it is too deeply buried for Miranda to extract, and his power over her becomes his obsession. When he blurts out, "I love you. It's driven me mad," he indicates the problem he faces. Love is madness when it takes the form of possession, and Clegg is possessed by his feelings in the same way that he possesses Miranda. As Miranda asserts her individuality and Clegg becomes repulsed by her, he is able to shift blame for her death to her as a direct consequence of her actions.

Whereas Clegg learns nothing from his experience and uses his narrative to vindicate himself, Miranda uses her narrative to describe her growing understanding and sense of self-discovery, aborted by her illness and subsequent death. After her death, Clegg cleans out the cellar, restoring it to its original state before Miranda's arrival. This circular structure, returning the reader to the empty cellar, echoes the circular structure of *The Magus*, except that Clegg has learned nothing from his experience, in contrast with Nicholas, who has learned everything. It is not that Nicholas is essentially good and Clegg essentially bad; rather, it is that Clegg cannot respond to the good within him, rendered inert by the warring aspects of his personality. Clegg's failure to respond to the elements of the quest is, in some respects, more tragic than Miranda's death, because he must continue his death-in-life existence, moving in ever-decreasing circles, never profiting or growing from the experience of life. In his next conquest, he will not aim so high; this time it will not be for love but for "the interest of the thing."

Reflecting the bleakness of Clegg's situation, the novel is filled with images of darkness. The pattern of *The Collector* is away from the light toward the darkness. Miranda's dying becomes a struggle against "the black and the black and the black," and her last words to Clegg—"the sun"—are a grim reminder of the struggle between them: the age-old struggle of the forces of light against those of darkness. Miranda's movement in the novel is upward toward light, life, and understanding; Clegg's is one of helpless descent toward darkness, evil, and psychic death.

The French Lieutenant's Woman

With *The French Lieutenant's Woman*, Fowles returns to the theme of the successful quest. Here the quester is Charles Smithson, much like Nicholas in social standing and education. The important differences between the novels are that *The French Lieutenant's Woman* is set in Victorian England and that Charles, in his thirties, a decade older than Nicholas, reflects the older viewpoint of the author. Like Nicholas, his twentieth century counterpart, Charles is representative of his age and class. Also like Nicholas, Charles is somewhat bored with his circumstances, despite the fact that he is finally taking the proper course of marriage to the proper lady, Ernestina. Not nearly so aware of his boredom as is Nicholas, Charles is nevertheless immediately attracted to Sarah upon their first meeting, sensing instantly that she is not like other women. Meeting her again in Ware Commons and its more secret Undercliff, Charles finds in this "other world" the mythic encounter for which he unconsciously yearns. A seeker after fossils, he subconsciously fears his own extinction in the receding waters of the Victorian age, a gentleman left behind in the face of the rising tide of the Industrial Revolution.

Sarah, having recognized her uniqueness in a world of conformity, relishes her position apart from others, particularly in its ability to give her a freedom other women do not possess. As the French lieutenant's woman (a euphemism for whore), she is outside society's bonds. Capitalizing on her position, she has already begun her own quest when she meets Charles; thus, she leads him to his own path for the journey. Ernestina represents the known, the predictable, the respectable. Sarah represents the opposite: the unknown, the mysterious, the forbidden. Torn between the two choices, Charles eventually comes to know himself well enough to be able to make the more hazardous choice, the one more fraught with danger yet far more likely to lead to wholeness.

The feeling and reasoning aspects of Charles's psyche war within him. Seeking advice from Dr. Grogan, he gets the proper scientific viewpoint of Sarah and is prescribed the proper course of action: Return to Ernestina. One side of Charles, the rational, longs to do so; the other side, the feeling, cannot. Thus, after much wrestling with the problem, Charles chooses Sarah, breaks his engagement to Ernestina, and returns to Sarah for what he thinks will be the beginning of their beautiful life in exile together—only to find her gone. At this point, Charles's real journey begins. Sarah has brought him to the point of resisting the predictable and recognizing his feeling side; he must now learn to live alone with such newfound knowledge.

Such a choice is not a simple one, and the reader must choose as well, for there are three "endings" in the novel. The first is not really an ending, as it comes in the middle of the book. In it, Charles rejects Sarah, marries Ernestina and lives, as it were, happily ever after. One knows, if only by the number of pages remaining in the book, that this is not really the ending; it is merely Victorian convention, which the author-god Fowles quickly steps in to tell the reader is not the actual ending. The reader thus passes through another hundred pages before coming to another choice of endings, these more realistic.

The first is happy; the second is not. The endings themselves indicate the evolutionary process that Charles, as well as the novel, takes, for if one includes the hypothetical early ending, one moves from the traditional Victorian view to the emancipated view of Charles and Sarah's union to the final existential view of the cruelty of freedom that denies Charles the happy ending. Fowles wanted his readers to accept the last ending as the right choice but feared that they would opt for the happy ending; he was pleased when they did not.

In the first ending, the gap between Charles and Sarah is bridged through the intercession of Lalage, the child born of their one sexual encounter. The assertion that "the rock of ages can never be anything but love" offers the reader a placebo that does not effect a cure for the novel's dilemma. Fowles then enters, turns the clock back, and sets the wheels in motion for the next ending. In this one, the author-god Fowles drives off, leaving Sarah and Charles to work out their fate alone in much the same way that Conchis absconds from the "godgame" when Nicholas and Alison are reunited in *The Magus*. In both cases, Fowles is trying to demonstrate that the freedom of choice resides with the individual, not with the "author." Since Sarah fears marriage for its potential denial of her hard-won freedom and sense of individuality, she cannot accept Charles's offer to marry, nor can he accept hers of friendship in some lesser relationship. Sarah then gives Charles no choice but to leave, and in his leaving he is released from his bonds to the past, experiencing a new freedom: "It was as if he found himself reborn, though with all his adult faculties and memories." Like Nicholas in *The Magus*, the important point is not whether he wins this particular woman but that he has learned to know himself and to love another. This is what sets him apart as an individual, saves him from extinction, and propels him into the modern age.

The Ebony Tower

Intending to name his collection of short works "Variations" because of its reflection of various themes and genres presented in his longer fiction, Fowles changed the name to *The Ebony Tower* (after the title novella) when first readers thought the original title too obscure. Anyone familiar with Fowles's themes, however, immediately sees their variations in this collection. The volume contains the title novella, followed by a "personal note," followed by Fowles's translation of Marie de France's medieval romance *Eliduc* (c. 1150-1175), followed by three short stories: "Poor Koko," "The Enigma," and "The Cloud." In his "personal note," Fowles explains the inclusion of the medieval romance, relating it first to the novella *The Ebony Tower*, more generally to all of his fiction, and finally to fiction in general.

The novella describes a quester who inadvertently stumbles into the realm of myth only to find that he cannot rise to the challenge of the quest and is therefore ejected from the mythic landscape. The three short stories are all centered on enigmas or mysteries of modern life. These mysteries arise because "mystery" in the sacred sense no longer appears valid in modern humanity's existence. The movement of the stories is generally downward toward darkness, modern humankind being depicted as less and less able to take the journey of self-discovery because it is trapped in the wasteland of contemporary existence. The variations in these stories thus present aspects of the less-than-successful quest.

David Williams of *The Ebony Tower* leaves his comfortable home and lifestyle in England and enters the forests of Brittany, the land of the medieval romance, to face an encounter with Henry Breasley, a famous (and infamous) painter. Because David is a painter himself, he is interested in the journey from an artist's perspective; he does not anticipate the mythic encounter that awaits him in this "other" world. Within this other world, Breasley attacks the "architectonic" nature of David's work in its abstraction, in contrast to Breasley's art, which has been called "mysterious," "archetypal," and "Celtic." In defaming David's art for its rigidity and lack of feeling, Breasley serves as a guide to David. David also finds the essential woman here in the figure of Diana, "The Mouse." The two characters offer him the potential of becoming a quester. The story represents the forsaken opportunity and its aftermath.

David's problem, like that of Nicholas and Charles at the beginning of their quests, is that he is so caught up with the rational that he cannot understand the emotional, in others or in himself. To all that he finds bewildering, he tries to attach a rational explanation. When finally confronted with pure emotion in his meeting with Diana in the edenic garden, he hesitates, fatally pausing to consider rationally what his course of action should be. In that moment, he loses the possibility of responding to his innermost feelings, failing to unite with the woman who represents his feeling side; as a result, he is evicted from the mythic landscape.

Caught between two women, his wife and Diana, David cannot love either. His situation is in sharp contrast to that of Eliduc, who also encounters two women but can love both. For Eliduc, love is a connecting force; for David, it is a dividing force. When David leaves the Brittany manor, he runs over an object in the road, which turns out to be a weasel. Here the weasel is dead with no hope of being restored to life; in *Eliduc*, love restores the weasel to life.

The rest of the story is David's rationalization of his failure. Like Clegg of *The Collector*, David first recognizes his failure but knows that he will soon forget the "wound" he has suffered and the knowledge of his failure. Already the mythic encounter seems far away. By the time he arrives in Paris, he is able to tell his wife that he has "survived." Had David succeeded in his quest, he would have done far more than survive—he would have lived.

The remaining stories in the collection are connected to the title story by the theme of lost opportunities. In "Poor Koko" the narrator, a writer, is robbed by a young thief who burns his only possession of value, his manuscript on Thomas Love Peacock. The story is the writer's attempt to understand the seemingly meaningless actions of the thief, which he finally comes to realize extend from the breakdown in communication between them. On a larger scale, the clash between the boy and the old man is the clash between generations, between a world in which language is meaningful and one in which it is empty.

In the succeeding story, "The Enigma," a mystery of a different kind is presented: the disappearance of John Marcus Fielding, member of Parliament, and the subsequent investigation by Sergeant Jennings. The first mystery focuses on the reason behind the disappearance of Fielding, whose body is never discovered and whose motive is never revealed. What is hinted at by Isobel Dodgson, the former girlfriend of Fielding's son and the last person to have seen Fielding before he disappeared, is that Fielding absconded from life because it offered no mystery; thus he provided his own by disappearing.

The second and more engaging mystery is seen in the developing relationship between Jennings and Isobel. While theirs is not of the dimensions of the relationship between Charles and Sarah, Nicholas and Alison, or even David and Diana, since they are not on the mythic journey, it is nevertheless interesting because it provides a sense of mystery. In a world that motivates a Fielding to walk out, it will have to suffice.

The last story, "The Cloud," is probably the most mysterious in the literal sense, although it describes a world most lacking in mystery in the sacred or mythic sense. The setting is a picnic with two men, Peter and Paul, and two women, sisters, Annabel and Catherine. While the setting describes an idyllic day, one senses from the outset that this is not paradise, because the women are lying in the sun, "stretched as if biered," an image of death that pervades the story. Catherine has apparently suffered the loss of a loved one, presumably her husband, and is in deep depression. She seems unable to make the crossing back into the world. Language does not serve as a bridge, and her feelings elicit no depth of response from the others. Thus, by the end of the story, she enters a myth of her own making, which is described in the story she invents for her niece about the princess abandoned by her prince. Catherine remains behind, unbeknown to the others when they leave the woods, and the reader is left with the assumption that she commits suicide, symbolized by the presence of the dark clouds rolling over the scene. Thus, the dark image of the ebony tower in the first story is replaced by the dark cloud in the last, and the reader has come full circle once again.

DANIEL MARTIN

Having described aspects of the failed quest in *The Ebony Tower*, Fowles once again returns to the theme of the successful quest in *Daniel Martin*. This time the quester is a mature man in his forties, as was the author at the time of the novel's composition, and this time Fowles is able to write the happy ending that had eluded him in his other fiction. The first sentence of the novel contains its thesis and the summation of Fowles's philosophy: "WHOLE SIGHT OR ALL THE REST IS DESOLATION." Like the questers in *The Magus* and *The French Lieutenant's Woman*, Daniel Martin must take the mythic journey to learn the meaning of whole sight and to change his world from a place of desolation to one of fulfillment.

While the first sentence of the novel states the thesis, the epigraph states the problem: "The crisis consists precisely in the fact that the old is dying and the new cannot be born; in this interregnum a great variety of morbid symptoms appears." Trapped in the wasteland of contemporary existence, Daniel experiences "morbid symptoms" in his failure to feel deeply and to be connected to a meaningful past. It is the movement of the novel from the crisis to whole sight that constitutes the quest.

The call to adventure comes with a phone call announcing the impending death of Anthony, an old friend. In going to England to be at his friend's bedside, he returns to the land of his youth and to the time when love was real. That love was with Jane, who later married Anthony, forcing both Daniel and Jane to bury their true feelings for each other. With Anthony's death, Daniel is once again faced with the dilemma of his own happiness and the role that Jane can play in it. At the same time, Daniel is wrestling with the problem of his desire to write a novel; subsequently, as the story unfolds, Daniel's novel unfolds, such that at the completion of the story one also has the completion of Daniel's novel, the demonstrable product of his successful quest.

Moving in and out of time, the novel skips from Daniel's boyhood to his present life in Hollywood with Jenny, a young film actor, to his memories of happy days at Oxford, and to his continuing relationship with Jane in the present. It also has several narrative points of view: Daniel tells certain sections, the omniscient author tells others, and still others are told by Jenny.

Daniel is aided on his journey by several wise old men: among them, Otto Kirnberger, the professor he and Jane meet on their trip up the Nile; and the Hungarian Marxist literary critic György Lukács, whose writings explain Daniel's choices as a writer. Daniel also describes several edenic settings that he calls the experience of the "*bonne vaux*." Remembrance of these experiences at Thorncombe, at Tsankawi, and at Kitchener's Island reinforce his desire to bring them more fully into his life; thus he quests on.

Realizing that the essential element of the quest is his ability to express his love for Jane, he worries that he will be rejected by her. Jane, less certain of her ability to choose her own future, tries to retreat from his declaration of love, telling him that she sees love as a prison. Jane is not yet ready to accept Daniel, but they journey on together, this time to Palmyra, a once beautiful but now desolate and remote outpost. In this wasteland, they experience the renewal of love. The catalyst comes in the form of a sound, "a whimpering, an unhappiness from the very beginning of existence." The sound is that of a litter of forlorn puppies, followed by another sound from their bedraggled mother, who tries to protect her puppies by acting as a decoy to distract the couple. The scene propels Jane out of her own wasteland into an enactment of a private ritual. Burying her wedding ring in the sand, she symbolically severs herself from her restrictive past to connect with the present and Daniel.

On his return to England, Daniel then severs himself from his remaining past by rejecting Jenny, recognizing all the while the importance of compassion in his relations with her and others. Following their last meeting, he enters a nearby church and is confronted with a living picture of all that he has learned: the famous late Rembrandt self-portrait. In this vision of compassion and whole sight, Daniel sees how far he has come and where the path into the future will lead. In Daniel's experience of the happy ending, the reader sees also a beginning. Thus, the last sentence of the novel one reads becomes the first sentence of the novel that Daniel will write. Again the experience is a circle, arriving where it started, with the circle expanding as it does in *The Magus* and in *The French Lieutenant's Woman*.

The movement of Fowles's fiction through *Daniel Martin* suggested the completion of a cycle: from a statement of the thesis in *The Magus*, to a statement of its opposite in *The Collector*, to an examination of the thesis from a different historical perspective in *The French Lieutenant's Woman*, to variations in *The Ebony Tower*, and to arrival at the long-sought happy ending in *Daniel Martin*. One could easily anticipate that the next novel would be very different, and so it was. *Mantissa*, which Fowles defines in a footnote, is a term meaning "an addition of comparatively small importance, especially to a literary effort or discourse." The novel's critical reception was mixed, some critics applauding the obvious departure from Fowles's customary style and others deploring its seeming frivolousness. Fowles contends that it should be taken as "mantissa," a kind of lark on his part. In it, he explores the role of creativity and freedom for the author, expressed through his protagonist Miles Green, as he wakes up to find himself an amnesiac in a hospital. The action of the novel, although it appears to have numerous characters entering and leaving the hospital, is really taking place in the protagonist's head, with the various characters representing manifestations of the muse Erato. The debate between muse and author gives Fowles the opportunity to turn the essential question of "freedom to choose," which he makes the object of the quest for his protagonists in his novels, into the object of the quest for the author/protagonist in this one. It also gives Fowles the opportunity to poke fun at the literary-critical approaches of the day, especially deconstruction. Finally, it gives Fowles the perfect opportunity to write graphically about sexual encounter, which he claims is one of the reasons he revised *The Magus:* to correct a "past failure of nerve."

A Maggot

In his next novel, *A Maggot*, he again chooses a title that requires explanation, his use of the term being in the obsolete sense of "whim or quirk." He goes on to explain in his prologue that he was obsessed with a theme arising out of an image from his unconscious of an unknown party of riders on horseback, and his desire was to capture this "remnant of a lost myth." This same obsession with an image is what led to the writing of *The French Lieutenant's Woman*, the historical novel set in the nineteenth century. In *A Maggot*, the temporal setting is the eighteenth century, and, as in *The French Lieutenant's Woman*, the struggle of a man and a woman to break out of their trapped existence is once again the focus. The man is Bartholomew, the son of a wealthy lord, and the woman is a prostitute named Fanny whose real name is Rebecca Lee. Bartholomew leads Rebecca into the quest, but he disappears, and the remainder of the novel becomes a search for the truth behind the events leading to his disappearance. To conduct this investigation, Bartholomew's father hires the lawyer Henry Ayscough, and the form of the novel shifts from third-person omniscient to first-person depositions, as Ayscough locates and questions everyone connected with the journey leading to the mysterious disappearance of Bartholomew. Everyone has a different view of the event, none of which Ayscough finds convincing. His desire for the truth is based on a belief that there is a rational, logical explanation; yet, despite the thoroughness of his inquiries, he cannot come up with one, finally concluding, without the evidence to prove it, that it must have been a murder.

The crux of the problem lies in his statement to Rebecca: "There are two truths, mistress. One that a person believes is truth; and one that is truth incontestible. We will credit you with the first, but the second is what we seek." Rebecca's belief, that Bartholomew has been transported by a maggot-shaped spaceship to June Eternal and that she has been reborn into a new life, frees her to break out of the trap of her existence by founding what will become the Shaker movement, which the daughter to whom she gives birth at the end of the novel will take to America. The mystery of Bartholomew's disappearance is never solved, and the reader is left to decide where the truth lies. For Rebecca, the central quester, the truth she experienced in the cave gives her the freedom to choose a new life, which is the object of the quest.

Carol M. Barnum
Updated by David W. Cole

Other major works

POETRY: *Poems*, 1973.

NONFICTION: *The Aristos: A Self-Portrait in Ideas*, 1964; *Shipwreck*, 1974; *Islands*, 1978; *The Tree*, 1979; *The Enigma of Stonehenge*, 1980 (with Barry Brukoff); *A Short History of Lyme Regis*, 1982; *Lyme Regis Camera*, 1990; *Wormholes: Essays and Occasional Writings*, 1998; *Conversations with John Fowles*, 1999 (Dianne L. Vipond, editor); *The Journals*, 2003 (Charles Drazin, editor; also known as *The Journals: Volume 1, 1949-1965*, 2005).

Bibliography

Acheson, James. *John Fowles*. New York: St. Martin's Press, 1998. Provides an excellent introduction to the life and works of Fowles. Traces the development of his novels, with a chapter devoted to each major work of long fiction.

Aubrey, James R., ed. *John Fowles and Nature: Fourteen Perspectives on Landscape*. Madison, N.J.: Fairleigh Dickinson University Press, 1999. Collection of essays focuses on Fowles's skill as a nature writer, analyzing the representation of the natural landscape in his fiction and nonfiction. Includes illustrations.

Butler, Lance St. John. "John Fowles and the Fiction of Freedom." In *The British and Irish Novel Since 1960*, edited by James Acheson. New York: St. Martin's Press, 1991. Addresses the centrality of the concept of freedom in Fowles's fiction and discusses the author's coming to terms with freedom in his fiction in an existential sense. Argues that Fowles's development as a writer followed the same course as that of existentialism.

Foster, Thomas C. *Understanding John Fowles*. Columbia: University of South Carolina Press, 1994. Provides an accessible critical introduction to Fowles's principal works, including *The Collector*, *The Magus*, and *The French Lieutenant's Woman*. Includes an annotated bibliography.

Huffaker, Robert. *John Fowles*. Boston: Twayne, 1980. Well-written overview and introduction to Fowles includes a chronology through 1980. Discusses Fowles's fiction through *Daniel Martin*. Includes notes, selected bibliography, and index.

Pifer, Ellen, ed. *Critical Essays on John Fowles*. Boston: G. K. Hall, 1986. Collection of essays previously published in journals. A good introduction by the editor is followed by essays organized under two themes: the unity of Fowles's fiction and discussions of individual works through *Mantissa*. Includes notes and index.

Reynolds, Margaret, and Jonathan Noakes. *John Fowles: The Essential Guide*. London: Vintage Books, 2003. One in a series of guides designed for students, teachers, and general readers, this volume contains an interview with Fowles and reading guides, reading activities, and information about contexts, comparisons, and complementary readings for *The Collector*, *The Magus*, and *The French Lieutenant's Woman*. Also includes glossary and select bibliography.

Tarbox, Katherine. *The Art of John Fowles*. Athens: University of Georgia Press, 1988. Discusses Fowles's novels with an emphasis on the author's dictum to "see whole." Includes an interview with Fowles, bibliography, and index.

Warburton, Eileen. *John Fowles: A Life in Two Worlds*. New York: Viking Press, 2004. Thorough, entertaining, and well-reviewed biography presents many previously untold details of Fowles's life, most notably his thirty-seven-year love affair with his wife. Warburton was given full access to Fowles's journals and personal papers.

Wilson, Thomas M. *The Recurrent Green Universe of John Fowles*. Atlanta: Rodopi, 2006. Described as a work of "ecocriticism," this book focuses on how Fowles's novels and other writings reflect the author's feelings and thoughts about the natural world. Includes bibliography and index.

JANET FRAME

Born: Dunedin, New Zealand; August 28, 1924
Died: Dunedin, New Zealand; January 29, 2004
Also known as: Janet Paterson Frame; Janet Paterson Frame Clutha

Principal long fiction

Owls Do Cry, 1957
Faces in the Water, 1961
The Edge of the Alphabet, 1962
Scented Gardens for the Blind, 1963
The Adaptable Man, 1965
A State of Siege, 1966
The Rainbirds, 1968 (also known as *Yellow Flowers in the Antipodean Room*)
Intensive Care, 1970
Daughter Buffalo, 1972
Living in the Maniototo, 1979
The Carpathians, 1988

Other literary forms

In addition to her novels, Janet Frame produced four collections of stories: *The Lagoon* (1951), *Snowman, Snowman: Fables and Fantasies* (1962), *The Reservoir: Stories and Sketches* (1963), and *You Are Now Entering the Human Heart* (1983). She wrote two volumes of poetry—*The Pocket Mirror* (1967) and *The Goose Bath* (2006). In 1982, Frame penned *To the Is-Land*, the first installment of her three-part autobiography, followed by *An Angel at My Table* (1984) and *The Envoy from Mirror City* (1985). Frame also wrote a volume of children's literature, *Mona Minim and the Smell of the Sun* (1969), and numerous essays and reviews.

Achievements

For her first collection of short stories in 1951, Janet Frame was awarded the Hubert Church Award, New Zealand's highest recognition for prose excellence. She received the award four more times for her novels *Scented Gardens for the Blind*, *A State of Siege*, *Intensive Care*, and *Daughter Buffalo*. For *Owls Do Cry*, her first novel, Frame won the New Zealand Literary Award. She twice received the New Zealand Book Award for Non-Fiction—for *Angel at My Table*, in 1984, and for *The Envoy from Mirror City*, in 1986. She received an honorary doctorate in literature from the University of Otago, Dunedin, in 1978, and another from the University of Waikato, Hamilton, in 1992. She was presented with the Massey University Medal in 1994 from Massey University, Palmerston North. Frame became a member of the Order of New Zealand in 1990 and was recognized by the Arts Foundation of New Zealand as one of its "Icon Artists." In 2003, she received the New Zealand Prime Minister's Award for her achievements in literature.

Biography

Janet Paterson Frame was born August 28, 1924, in Dunedin, New Zealand, the third of five children born to George Samuel, a railway engineer, and Lottie Clarice Frame, a former maid at the house of one of New Zealand's greatest writers, Katherine Mansfield. Lottie Frame had literary inclinations, and in addition to proudly displaying her favorite books, reciting passages from them, and encouraging her children to read them, she sold her own poetry door-to-door.

In 1930, Frame's father was transferred to Oamaru, a small town on the coast of South Island, and the children enrolled in school there. Other students shunned the Frame children, who lived in poverty; the school children wanted little to do with George, an epileptic, and resented the three older Frame girls, who were inseparable and spoke of reading and writing books. In her isolation, and agonizingly shy, Frame, who had red, frizzy hair and bad teeth, began to retreat even farther into an imaginary world of her own making, dreaming of becoming a poet. She finished high school, took a teacher-training course, and began a teaching position in Dunedin. After one stressful year, Frame left teaching to pursue writing full time.

In 1946, a few months after Frame published her first short story, her younger sister drowned. Frame's older sister also had drowned under uncertain circumstances several years earlier, which made her younger sister's death doubly tragic. Unable to cope with the enormity of her loss, Frame suffered an emotional breakdown. Following a failed suicide attempt, she entered Seacliff Mental Hospital, remaining there and in other institutions for a combined period of eight years. Misdiagnosed as schizophrenic and believed to need to be free of her literary ambitions, Frame endured more than two hundred electroshock treatments; when those failed to make her "normal," she was scheduled for a lobotomy—an incision made into the brain to sever nerve fibers in the frontal lobes. A few days before the lobotomy, the institution's director learned from the newspaper that Frame had been awarded the Hubert Church Award for Prose Excellence for a collection of stories she had submitted while in the hospital. He canceled the procedure.

Frame was released from the hospital in 1954, began writing her first novel, and received a literary grant. For more than twenty years, she traveled between New Zealand and England, where she wrote prolifically. In New Zealand, she was heard on a series of radio talks. She then lived and worked at Yaddo, a community of writers and artists in Saratoga Springs, New York, and at the MacDowell Colony in New Hampshire. In the 1980's, she again took up her reclusive residence in Dunedin, New Zealand, where she wrote the three volumes of her autobiography to help clarify the issue of her mental health. The story of her life, *An Angel at My Table*, was filmed by New Zealand director Jane Campion and released in 1990. The film won numerous awards and led to international recognition for Frame. She died of leukemia on January 29, 2004, in Dunedin.

Analysis

Janet Frame's early books are somewhat autobiographical, concerned with poverty, illness, tragedy, and madness. Frame's fictional world is peopled with outcasts and children, whose social alienation permits them to express themselves in a manner at odds with that of "normal" society. Frame's first several books are preoccupied with the inward and outward worlds, and she sets forth dualities—treasures and rubbish heaps, lyrical poetry and mundane prose, enchantment and materialism, normal and abnormal—that form the framework of the books. Frame suggests that the outcasts—whether eccentric, deformed, or mad—are visionaries, whose insights into their own isolation render them superior to other members of society. Her later writings continue her stylistic experimentations but tend toward sharp criticisms of society's repressive values; the later novels focus on the need to keep the mind alive in a sterile and deadening society. Furthermore, to a large degree, all of her books address the role of the artist in society.

Despite her impoverished childhood, Frame enjoyed an intensely literary home life that led her to believe in the "magical" potential of words to reflect imaginative truths that can exist beyond or outside the values of society. In depicting her characters' experiences, Frame experiments with language by using image-filled word play, metaphor, and word combinations to communicate layers of meaning in these truths. Her characters, situated at the boundary of social interaction and annihilation by madness or death, are frequently represented through elements of magical realism and surrealism, as they imagine fantastic events; their imaginings are recounted through lyrical, poetical cadences.

Janet Frame. (Courtesy, George Braziller, Inc.)

Owls Do Cry

Written soon after leaving the mental hospital, Frame's first novel, *Owls Do Cry*, describes the Withers family, whose life circumstances are similar to those of the Frame family. In part 1 of the novel, the four children, Toby, Francie, Daphne, and Teresa, prowl a rubbish heap in search of "treasures" discarded by adults, which, when viewed through the children's eyes, become objects of wonder. During one visit, Francie—who must soon take a job in a woolen mill to help support the family—trips, falls into the heap's fire, and burns to death.

Part 2 of the novel continues beyond Francie's death. Devastated, the family disintegrates: The mother drifts deeper into illness; epileptic Toby supports himself by demolishing old buildings; Teresa marries, moves away, and becomes mired in materialism; and Daphne is sent to a mental hospital. Through her disturbed memory, Daphne poetically recollects the intensity of the three older children as they shared literary ecstasies, or as they clung together, much like small birds, attempting to survive the raw forces of nature. The heart of the novel, the sections narrated by Daphne, signify the status of imagination and vision in a materialistic world.

Daphne, coming from the institution's "dead room," the room in which she fears electrical shock treatments and awaits the frontal lobotomy that is designed to destroy anything true or imaginative within her, is tortured by her thoughts, which reflect her psychic sense of society's efforts to eradicate human individuality. She considers both the mental hospital and the woolen mill to be enforcers of conformity. In her inwardness, also, she envisions the snow-covered, frozen, dead terrain reserved by normal society for the abnormal.

The Edge of the Alphabet

In the third and final novel about the Withers family, *The Edge of the Alphabet*, Frame distances herself from the narrative by creating an author and narrator, Thora Pattern, whose manuscript was found among her papers after her death, and later published. By following the lives of three individuals who are traveling from New Zealand to England, Pattern anticipates a journey of discovery. The three travelers include Toby Withers, sojourning to England, the land of his mother's ancestry, with plans to write a book; Zoe Bryce, returning to England from a holiday in New Zealand; and Pat Keenan,

Toby's Irish roommate, who has been visiting his sister in New Zealand.

Pattern, like Daphne Withers, is a visionary who lives at the "edge of the alphabet"—the edge of society—and is an authentic character. Her insights are inserted into the narrative along with her observations of the three travelers once in England. Pat Keenan, the most rigid of the three, urges the two others forward so they can "get ahead," quoting materialistic slogans and mottos. He takes a job driving a bus—one of Frame's metaphors for going in circles—and eventually works in a stationery store, selling blank sheets of paper. Having succumbed to the dull, ordinary patterns of life, Keenan receives Pattern's harshest assessment.

Zoe Bryce, unmarried and unloved, has dreams that do not include materialistic success. On the journey to England, she is surreptitiously kissed, presumably by an inebriated orderly, who quickly runs away. Troubled by the kiss, Zoe mourns the life of love and children, which, she believes, she will never have. In her despair, she commits suicide. Toby Withers, who is epileptic and ill equipped for steady employment, moves from job to job. He has several relationships with women—and a marriage—but only in his imagination. He talks with his dead mother more and more frequently, and eventually returns to New Zealand, abandoning his dreams of writing a novel.

In the final pages of the novel, Thora Pattern laments the fates of the three individuals she has observed, and calls forth an apocalyptic vision of the destruction of a world, wherein no one can communicate meaningfully with another. Obsessed with death, Pattern suggests that the world is in need of purging, in order to begin again. Through Pattern's insights, Frame's three characters represent social categories that are victimized by the sterility of normal life.

SCENTED GARDENS FOR THE BLIND

Frame's fourth novel, *Scented Gardens for the Blind*, is a strange story of Vera Glace, who appears to be blind; her daughter Erlene, who has become mute; and Vera's husband, Edward, a genealogist who lives in London. Edward has two passions in life: the history of the family he has chosen to explore and his plastic soldiers on miniature battlefields. Edward considers himself a married man, although he has not seen his family in eleven years. When he receives his wife's letter about Erlene's inability to speak, he resolves to return home and encourage his daughter. Both parents believe that Erlene's words will be tremendously significant by ushering in a new language of hope for the world.

In her silence, Erlene imagines conversations with Uncle Blackbeetle. During her visits to an absurd doctor who lacks the skill or insight to help her speak, she is preoccupied with Uncle Blackbeetle's account of the death of his cousin, Albert Dungbeetle, whose dreams of a huge ball of dung literally kill him and his family. In Erlene's mind, she confuses the doctor with Uncle Blackbeetle as she and her mother await the father's return.

In the novel's final chapter, Vera, a former librarian, unmarried and with no family, is suddenly struck dumb at the age of thirty; she remains mute for thirty years. Doctors in a mental hospital persist in their efforts to make her speak. Three months after the destruction of England by an atomic bomb, Vera begins speaking the "language of humanity," which is merely a succession of grunts.

Frame's theme of the tragic view of history and of humankind, a theme begun in *The Edge of the Alphabet*, continues in *Scented Gardens for the Blind*. The novel, almost entirely made up of Vera's extended, imagined monologue—which invents a family Vera never had—also employs magical realism, another common Frame theme.

Mary Hurd

OTHER MAJOR WORKS

SHORT FICTION: *The Lagoon*, 1951; *Snowman, Snowman: Fables and Fantasies*, 1962; *The Reservoir: Stories and Sketches*, 1963; *You Are Now Entering the Human Heart*, 1983.

POETRY: *The Pocket Mirror*, 1967; *Janet Frame, Stories and Poems*, 2004; *The Goose Bath*, 2006 (Pamela Gordon, editor).

NONFICTION: *To the Is-Land*, 1982; *An Angel at My Table*, 1984; *The Envoy from Mirror City*, 1985; *An Autobiography*, 1989 (includes the previous 3 volumes).

CHILDREN'S LITERATURE: *Mona Minim and the Smell of the Sun*, 1969.

MISCELLANEOUS: *The Janet Frame Reader*, 1995 (Carole Ferrier, editor).

Bibliography

Evans, Patrick. *Janet Frame*. Boston: Twayne, 1977. An early, yet still useful, study of Frame and her work that contains biographical and critical material.

King, Michael. *Wrestling with the Angel: A Life of Janet Frame*. Washington, D.C.: Counterpoint, 2000. Written in consultation with Frame, King's meticulously researched biography provides a vast amount of background on the very private author.

Wikse, Maria. *Materialisations of a Woman Writer: Investigating Janet Frame's Biographical Legend*. New York: Peter Lang, 2006. Both a study of Frame's writings and a biography, this book redresses assertions that Frame was a "psychologically disturbed writer." An excellent analysis that focuses on her legend as a writer of autobiography and autobiographical novels.

ANATOLE FRANCE

Born: Paris, France; April 16, 1844
Died: La Béchellerie, near Tours, Saint-Cyr-sur-Loire, France; October 12, 1924
Also known as: Jacques-Anatole-François Thibault

Principal long fiction

Le Crime de Sylvestre Bonnard, 1881 (*The Crime of Sylvestre Bonnard*, 1890)
Les Désirs de Jean Servien, 1882 (*The Aspirations of Jean Servien*, 1912)
Thaïs, 1890 (English translation, 1891)
La Rôtisserie de la Reine Pédauque, 1893 (*At the Sign of the Reine Pédauque*, 1912)
Le Lys rouge, 1894 (*The Red Lily*, 1898)
L'Histoire contemporaine, 1897-1901 (collective title for the first 4 novels that follow; *Contemporary History*)
L'Orme du mail, 1897 (*The Elm Tree on the Mall*, 1910)
Le Mannequin d'osier, 1897 (*The Wicker Work Woman*, 1910)
L'Anneau d'améthyste, 1899 (*The Amethyst Ring*, 1919)
Monsieur Bergeret à Paris, 1901 (*Monsieur Bergeret in Paris*, 1922)
Histoire comique, 1903 (*A Mummer's Tale*, 1921)
L'Île des pingouins, 1908 (*Penguin Island*, 1914)
Les Dieux ont soif, 1912 (*The Gods Are Athirst*, 1913)
La Révolte des anges, 1914 (*The Revolt of the Angels*, 1914)

Other literary forms

Of the twenty-five volumes that make up the standard French edition of the complete works of Anatole France (frahns), more than fifteen are given over to one form or another of prose fiction: ten novels (thirteen if one counts the tetralogy *Contemporary History* as four separate novels), ten collections of short stories, and four volumes of fictionalized autobiography. The remainder of the twenty-five-volume set exhibits a startling variety of literary forms: poetry, theater, biography, history, literary criticism, philosophy, journalism, and polemical writings.

France's first publication was a book-length critical study of the French Romantic poet Alfred de Vigny (1868), after which he published two volumes of his own poetry, one containing lyric poems, the other a play in verse, and several long narrative poems. In the 1880's and 1890's, he wrote a regular weekly column, mostly about books and the literary world, for a prominent Paris newspaper, *Le Temps*. The best of those columns were republished in five volumes under the title *La Vie littéraire* (1888-1892; *On Life and Letters*, 1911-1914). His major venture into the writing of history was *La Vie de Jeanne d'Arc* (1908; *The Life of Joan of Arc*, 1908), published after a quarter of a century of research. That same year, he published his one original prose work for the theater, *La Comédie de celui qui épousa une femme muette* (1903; *The Man Who Married a Dumb Wife*, 1915), a farce based on a well-known medieval fabliau.

France's major speeches and occasional writings, on such issues of the times as the Dreyfus affair, socialism, and pacifism, were collected and published in several volumes under the title *Vers les temps meilleurs* (1906, 1949). Philosophical meditations on human nature and civilization can be found in a volume titled *Le Jardin d'Épicure* (1894; *The Garden of Epicurus*, 1908), consisting of pieces on general subjects originally written for his weekly newspaper column and not included in the volumes of *On Life and Letters*. One may say, in sum, that France was the complete man of letters, who tried his hand at just about every form of writing practiced in the literary world of his time. It is nevertheless accurate to say that the writing of fiction so dominated his output, throughout his career, that it constituted his true vocation.

Achievements

The election of Anatole France to the French Academy in 1896 and his winning of the Nobel Prize in Literature in 1921 were the major public landmarks of the great success and recognition he achieved during his career as a writer, first in his own country and then in the international arena. At the height of his fame, in the early years of the twentieth century, he was widely regarded as France's greatest living author, celebrated for his wit, his wisdom, and his humanitarian vision. The paradoxes of that fame, however, were multiple and heavy with irony: The fame had been an unusually long time in coming (he was nearly fifty years old before he had his first significant success with the public), it was based largely on his association with public events rather than on his genuine but esoteric literary talent, and it lasted only briefly. Indeed, the greatest paradox of his fame was its bewilderingly rapid eclipse after his death. His reputation would not regain the luster of his glory years, around the turn of the twentieth century.

France himself lived long enough to be the saddened witness of a major erosion of his fame in a storm of bitter controversy, which made him an object of both worship and hatred but for purely nonliterary reasons. The truth is that the great fame he enjoyed, during a brief period of his life, was of the public sort, only indirectly occasioned by his writings, which, even at their most popular, appealed to a rather narrowly circumscribed audience. One must separate his fame from his achievements as a writer—which is not to say that his achievements were minor, but only that they were literary and aesthetic, hence accessible to relatively few at any time.

As a novelist and short-story writer, France made his mark in the fiction of ideas, and as a literary critic, he established, by personal example, the validity of subjective impressionism as a method. Those are the two major achievements of his career in letters, the accomplishments that have affected literary history. To those literary achievements, one should add a more personal achievement: the creation of a highly distinctive, instantly identifiable style of classic purity and elegance, with subtle rhythms and limpid clarity, which perfectly translated the skeptical and gently ironic view he held of the human condition.

Biography

Anatole France, born Jacques-Anatole-François Thibault in 1844, was the only child of a well-established Parisian bookdealer and was seemingly predestined to the world of books. His father, Noël-François Thibault, ran the sort of bookshop that was also a gathering place of the literati, who would come as not only customers but also friends. They would sit and talk with the owner, whom they called by the familiar diminutive France, an abbreviation of François. Once the son was old enough to help in the shop and participate in the daily conversations, he was naturally called le jeune France, a custom that suggested to young Anatole the pen name he would choose when he began to write.

Shy and unassertive by nature and unprepossessing physically, France matured into an unworldly and bookish young man, easily intimidated by the "real" world and much given to periods of solitude and quiet reverie. In his twenties, he did occasional research and editing chores for the publishers of dictionaries and encyclopedias, having definitely decided against following in his father's footsteps as a bookseller. Eventually, he became a reader of manuscripts for a publisher, wrote articles for ephemeral journals, and took a civil servant's position, working in the senate library, all the while using his leisure moments to learn the craft of writing. He was thirty-three years old, and a published but thoroughly obscure and unknown author, when he overcame his timidity long enough to marry, in 1877. The marriage produced one child, a daughter born in 1881, but was otherwise an unhappy relationship for both sides that ended in a bitter divorce in 1893, after a prolonged separation.

France's unhappy domestic life was the backdrop for his long personal struggle to find his own "voice" and establish himself as a writer. By the 1880's, he had abandoned poetry and was experimenting with different modes of prose fiction, trying both the novel and the short-story forms but attracting very little attention from the reading public. Only after he became the regular literary critic for *Le Temps* and had published a genuinely popular work, the novel *Thaïs*, did he feel securely established enough as a writer to give up his post at the senate library.

Anatole France. (Library of Congress)

Thereafter, all through the 1890's, France's books sold well, and he rose rapidly in public esteem, aided in part by a newfound interest in and involvement with politics and public affairs. In particular, the Dreyfus affair outraged his sense of justice and galvanized him into public action for the first time in his life. He was then in his fifties, and he discovered, a bit to his own surprise, a radical social thinker beneath the placid and conservative exterior he had always presented to the world. During the first years of the new century, he became outspokenly anticlerical and socialistic in his views but was soon plunged into disillusionment when he saw that even victory, as in the Dreyfus affair, produced little real change in society, and that his own activism served only to make him controversial and the object of vicious attacks, which he found especially painful to endure. This mood of disillusionment drove him to withdraw into himself once more and to give up active involvement in public affairs. His work increasingly concerned the past and took on an unaccustomed satiric edge.

The outbreak of World War I tempted France briefly into the public arena once more, to proclaim his pacifist views, but when he was assailed as unpatriotic, he retreated, this time definitively, into the private world of letters. It is perhaps suggestive of the depth of his wounds from the public fray that his literary preoccupations during the final decade of his life were almost exclusively autobiographical. His career as a novelist had effectively ended with the publication of *The Revolt of the Angels* in 1914.

Analysis

The world of books into which Anatole France was born was surely the strongest influence in determining his vocation as a writer, but that influence went far deeper still, for it also determined the kind of writer he would be. Almost all the subjects he chose to write about, in his long career, were derived from or related to books in some way. He was a voracious reader all of his life, and the many books he wrote not only reflect that wide reading but also reveal that what he read was more immediate and more vital to him—more nourishing to his creative imagination, indeed more *real* to him—than the quotidian reality in which he lived. Even when most actively involved in public events, as he was in the years immediately before the end of the nineteenth century and the beginning of the twentieth, he tended to approach events as abstractions, dealing with them as intellectual issues, somehow detached from specific occurrences involving specific human beings. This conscious need to convert real events into matter for books can be seen most clearly in the tetralogy that he so pointedly titled *Contemporary History* and in which he contrived to write about current events as though they were already in the distant past or even the stuff of legend.

Concomitant with his irreducibly bookish view of the world was his almost instinctive taste for storytelling. Whether as reader or as writer, nothing charmed him more than the unfolding of a narrative. Even factual writing—history and biography, for example—he treated as an exercise in storytelling, going so far as to characterize good literary criticism as a kind of novel in which the critic "recounts the adventures of his soul among masterpieces," as he put it in the famous preface to *On Life and Letters*. The art of storytelling was the art he set out to master in his long and difficult apprenticeship, and the storytelling impulse can be identified as the very heart of his vocation as a writer.

To the mind of the man of letters and the instinct of the teller of tales must be added a third characteristic: the outlook of the determined skeptic. France trained himself, from an early age, to question everything and to discern the contradictions and ironies in all forms of human behavior, including his own. He cultivated a perspective of distance and detachment from both people and events, but he learned to temper the bleakness and isolation of such a perspective with feelings of sympathetic recognition of the folly common to all humankind. A subtle blend of pity and irony came to be the hallmark of his view of the affairs of this world, expressed in the tone of gentle mockery with which his celebrated style was impregnated in the works of his maturity. Indeed, all three central characteristics of France—the literary turn of mind, the narrative impulse, and the ironic perspective—can be found in everything he wrote, including the youthful works of poetry, fiction, and literary criticism through which he gradually learned the writer's trade. Those three traits can be seen fully developed for the first time in the novel that won for him his first public recognition, *The Crime of Sylvestre Bonnard*, in 1881.

The Crime of Sylvestre Bonnard

Published to the accolades of the French Academy, *The Crime of Sylvestre Bonnard* provided France with his first taste of success. The improbable hero of the book is an elderly, unworldly scholar and bibliophile who explains, in his own words, in the form of diary entries, how he came to acquire a coveted medieval manuscript and how he rescued a young girl from poverty and oppression. What holds the reader's interest is not the trivial plot but the character of Sylvestre Bonnard, whose naïve narrative style, in his diary, constantly and unwittingly reveals his own bumbling incompetence in dealing with the practical side of life.

The reader quickly recognizes as comical the dramatic earnestness with which the simpleminded scholar narrates the only two "adventures" that have ever intruded into his serene existence. The ironic discrepancy between the excited tone of the narrator and the mundane character of the events he narrates is echoed suggestively in the title, which promises a thriller but delivers nothing more violent than a book lover's crime: Having promised to sell his personal library in order to create a dowry for the damsel in distress he has rescued, Bonnard confesses, at the end of the diary, that he had "criminally" withheld from the sale several items with which he could not bear to part.

Perhaps the greatest skill the author displays in this book is that of artfully concealing the inherent sentimentality of the material. The key device of concealment is mockery: Bonnard's interest in old books and manuscripts is magnified, in both incidents, into a grand and criminal passion by a transparently mock-heroic tone. This device distracts and amuses the reader, preventing inopportune reflections about the "fairy-tale" unreality of the happy ending of each incident. It is also true that the eccentric character of Bonnard is charming and that the novelty of a gentle fantasy, published at the height of the popularity of the naturalistic novel in France, must have struck many readers of the day as a welcome relief.

It was for such reasons, no doubt, that the novel enjoyed mild critical acclaim and modest sales in 1881, even as its author, sternly self-critical, recognized its limitations of both form and content and set about immediately trying to do better.

What France retained from *The Crime of Sylvestre Bonnard* for future use was the tone of gentle and sympathetic irony about human foibles. In the decade that followed, he experimented with fictionalized autobiography, tales of childhood, and themes borrowed from history or legend, seeking above all a composition that he—and his readers—could recognize as a fully realized work of art. He reached that goal with the publication of *Thaïs* in 1890—his first critical and popular success.

Thaïs

The story of Thaïs, the courtesan of Alexandria, has a bookish source, as does most of France's fiction; he changed the legend of Thaïs, however, by giving the central role in the tale to the monk, Paphnuce, whose ambition for saintliness inspires in him the project of converting the notorious actor and prostitute to Christianity. The well-known plot, in which the saintly monk succumbs to sin even as the notorious sinner seeks salvation in piety, is thus, in France's version, seen almost exclusively from the point of view of the monk. The character of Thaïs is developed hardly at all, while the complex motivations of Paphnuce are analyzed and explored in detail. This imbalance in the point of view, however, does not affect the fundamental irony of the story. Thaïs, though superficially presented, is shown clearly to be a seeker of pagan pleasure and prosperity, who yet was influenced in early youth by piety, having been secretly baptized, and whose growing fear of death and damnation happens to make her receptive to the preaching of Paphnuce at that particular time of her life.

Paphnuce, on the other hand, has had a long struggle against his own sensuality in trying to live as a monk, and is unaware that his sudden project of converting Thaïs is really prompted by his unconscious but still unruly sensual yearnings. When the two meet, therefore, each is ignorant of the other's true disposition, and Paphnuce, moreover, is ignorant of his own desires. Their encounter is thus fated to be sterile, for by that time, Thaïs is already on her way to salvation, and Paphnuce is proceeding precipitously in the opposite direction. France exploits the irony of their opposing trajectories by making the occasion of their meeting the longest and most concentrated episode in the book. The effect is structural: The book is designed as a triptych, with the shorter first and last segments employed to introduce the protagonists and then to record the ultimate fate of each, while the middle segment, equal in length to the other two combined, examines and analyzes their encounter from every angle and demonstrates the impossibility of any fruitful contact between them, because by that time each is in an unanticipatedly different frame of mind.

The structure of the book is perhaps what critics and public admired most about *Thaïs*. It has a satisfying aesthetic quality that announced that France had mastered the sense of form necessary for the achievement of a work of art. The book's success must also, however, be attributed to the subtle complexity of the ideas the author was able to distill from what is, after all, little more than a mildly indecorous comic anecdote. *Thaïs* is a profound and suggestive exploration of the hidden links between religious feeling and sexual desire and, beyond that, of the intricate and unexpected interplay between pagan and Christian ideals and thought and between worldliness and asceticism as patterns of human behavior. In this novel, characterization and realistic description count for comparatively little, and in spite of the daring subject matter, there is not a hint of prurience. The best effects are achieved by a tasteful and harmonious blend of elegant style, well-proportioned structure, and subtle ideas, all presented with gentle irony through the eyes of an amused and skeptical observer. *Thaïs* remains a delight for the thoughtful and attentive reader, one of France's finest achievements.

At about the same time as *Thaïs* was being composed, France was also diligently exploring the short-story form. Employing similar material from history or legend, he was striving to find the ideal fusion of form and content that would yield a work of art in that genre also, and in some of the stories of the volume titled *L'Étui de nacre* (1892; *Tales from a Mother of Pearl Casket*, 1896), notably the famous "Procurator of Judea" and "The Juggler of Our Lady," he succeeded as fully as he had for the novel in *Thaïs*. Thereafter, having earned his artistic spurs in both the novel and the short story, France developed his career in both domains, alternating a novel and a volume of short stories with something approaching regularity over the next twenty years. What is notable in the work of those years is the visible effort he made to avoid the facile repetition of past successes, to explore and experiment with new techniques, and to strive to develop and grow as an artist. During the 1890's, for example, he followed the gemlike stories of *Tales from a Mother of Pearl Casket* with a comic fantasy of a novel called *At the Sign of the Reine Pédauque*, then used a trip to Florence, Italy, as inspiration for a volume of short stories, *Le Puits de Sainte-Claire* (1895; *The Well of Saint Clare*, 1909), and a surprisingly conventional love story, *The Red Lily*, appearing in 1894. Those publications confirmed his newly won stature as a major writer and earned for him election to the French Academy in 1896.

Contemporary History

France's next project, *Contemporary History*, began as a series of weekly newspaper articles commenting on current events by means of anecdotes and illustrative tales. Soon he began interconnecting the articles by using the same set of characters in each. The articles could have formed the basis for a volume of short stories, but instead, France conceived the notion of weaving selected articles from one year's output into a novel that would record the main events of that year in a kind of fictionalized history. It was a bold experiment, which eventually ran to four volumes and occasioned some brilliant writing and the creation of one truly memorable character, Monsieur Bergeret, a scholar and teacher of a wittily ironic turn of mind, who usually articulated the author's own skeptical view of public events.

Some consider *Contemporary History* to be France's finest work, but while it does make unflaggingly entertaining reading, as well as offer a valuable historical record, it may be too randomly structured and too variable in tone to be artistically satisfying for the sophisticated modern reader. It deserves respect, however, both as an interesting experiment in a new kind of fiction and as the inauguration of a new thematic vein in France's work: the overt exploitation of public events, especially politics, in the writing of fiction.

The novels and short stories published between 1900 and 1914 are almost all in this new political vein, sometimes seriously polemical, more often comic and satiric. The most widely read work of that period is the amusing and clever *Penguin Island*, which gives a brief and jaundiced view of French history as though it were a history of a society of penguins. The masterpiece of this period, however, and probably the finest of all France's novels, is his reconstruction of the atmosphere of the French Revolution, called *The Gods Are Athirst*, published in 1912.

The Gods Are Athirst

France's strong interest in the period of the French Revolution was undoubtedly inspired by his youthful browsing in his father's bookshop, which specialized in that subject. During the 1880's, France began work on a novel about the revolutionary period, but he abandoned it, rearranging some of the completed fragments into short stories that turned up, a few years later, in the collection *Tales from a Mother of Pearl Casket*. By 1910, when he began to work on a new novel of the Revolution, he had been through his own personal revolution—involvement in the Dreyfus affair and public espousal of socialism—only to suffer rapid disillusionment with the way human nature seems inevitably to distort and betray ideals. Something of that disillusionment must have shaped *The Gods Are Athirst*, for it concentrates on the process by which the Reign of Terror developed out of revolutionary zeal for liberty, equality, and fraternity and, by means of the inclusion of a large and varied cast of characters, seeks to depict how daily life was affected by this process. The novel is set in Paris and covers a time span of about two years, from 1792 to 1794.

At the very heart of the novel, France places a struggling young painter, a pupil of Jacques Louis David, whose name is Évariste Gamelin and who, in 1792, is active in the revolutionary committees of his quarter. Gamelin is depicted as a mediocre artist but one who is serious in his devotion both to art and to the humanitarian ideals of the new Republic. His seriousness is a function of his youthful innocence, which is unrelieved by any element of gaiety or humor but which endows him with a capacity for tender feelings of affection or sympathy. Those tender feelings are the noble source of his support for the Revolution, but he gets caught up in complex and emotionally charged events that he is incapable of understanding, and, as a member of a revolutionary tribunal, he unwittingly betrays his own humanitarian principles by voting for the execution of innocent people to satisfy the bloodthirsty mob of spectators. Gamelin thus embodies the book's fundamental and deeply pessimistic theme, which is that even decent individuals and noble ideals will fall victim to the winds of fanaticism. At the ironic end of the novel, Gamelin the terrorist is himself condemned and executed by the Reign of Terror.

Gamelin is surrounded by an array of different types who give magnificent density to the novel's re-creation of the past. Most memorable, perhaps, is Maurice Brotteaux, a neighbor of Gamelin and a former member of the nobility, now earning his living by making puppets to sell in toy shops. Brotteaux is a skeptic and a witty ironist—unmistakably the author's alter ego—who, though not unsympathetic to the Revolution, deplores its decline into fanaticism, consoling himself by reading his ever-present copy of Lucretius's *De rerum natura*. The author's intentional irony in this detail is that the Latin poet's work had the original purpose of explaining nature to his contemporaries without reference to the supernatural, in order thus to liberate his compatriots from their superstitious fear of the gods. As the novel's title suggests, Lucretius's noble project is a futile exercise when the gods thirst for blood. Gamelin's fiancé, the voluptuous Élodie, adds a fascinating psychological element to the novel, for as her lover Gamelin grows more and more savage in his condemnation of his fellow citizens, she is surprised to discover that, her horror of him notwithstanding, her sensual attraction to him intensifies: The more blood there is on his hands, the more uncontrollable her passion becomes.

The novel is masterful in its smooth handling of the welter of significant characters and details, the unobtrusive integration of known historical figures and events into an invented narrative, and the creation of both a sense of inevitable tragedy in the action and the feel of epic grandeur in the composition as a whole. It is an impressively vast canvas the author attempts to encompass here—the greatest and most complex of his career. Although there is, of necessity, much weaving back and forth from setting to setting and from one group of characters to another, the clarity and focus of the narrative line are never blurred, and the careful structure accentuates for the reader the inexorability of the mounting dramatic tension enveloping more and more of the novel's characters. In the manner of a classical tragedy, the novel closes with the return of uneasy calm after the catastrophe and the indication that the dead will be quickly forgotten and that life will go on as before. The final paragraph shows Élodie taking a new lover and employing the same endearments to him as she had used at the start of her affair with Gamelin.

The Gods Are Athirst does not quite attain the majestic historical sweep that a subject such as the French Revolution might be expected to command, perhaps because the figure at its center, Évariste Gamelin, is deliberately not cast in the heroic mold. Yet it is a fine and powerful novel, and its unforgettable images carry their intended message to issues beyond the events described, revealing something fundamentally important about human conduct in any revolution and, indeed, in any group situation subject to the volatile incitements of mob psychology. This brilliant novel, written when the author was nearly seventy years old, proved to be the artistic culmination of France's long career. The novel that followed it, *The Revolt of the Angels*, is a merry fantasy of anticlerical bent, amusing to read but making no artistic or intellectual claims to importance. It proved, simply, that this veteran teller of tales still had the skill and magic, at seventy, to hold the attention of the reading public.

The Red Lily

As a writer of fiction, France has always eluded classification. He showed little interest in the precise observation of daily reality that was the hallmark of his naturalist contemporaries, nor did he strive to win fame with sensational plotting, flamboyant characters, or studies in spicily abnormal psychology. Though allied, at certain times, with the Parnassians and the Symbolists, he never submitted himself fully to their aesthetic discipline in his own art. He followed his own bent, and because he was so steeped in books and erudition, so unsociable and so fond of solitude, and so little driven by ambition, he tended to cut a strange and solitary figure in the literary world.

In both manner and matter, he was really quite unlike anyone else then writing. Probably nothing contributed more to his uniqueness as a writer than his absolute addiction to ideas. The originating inspiration for everything he wrote was neither an event nor a character nor a situation nor even a new literary trick to try out, but ever and always an idea, a concept, an abstraction that he wanted to bring to life by means of a story, a play, or a poem. Even his most conventional novel, *The Red Lily*, seems to be only a routine story of frustrated love and jealousy. What truly animates this novel is the daring concept of female independence, which entrenched social attitudes and the habits of male possessiveness in love relationships put out of the reach of even the most lucid and intelligent women, even in that haven of enlightened individualism, Florence.

Though not a great novel, *The Red Lily* penetratingly probes an idea that was very advanced for the time: the idea that a woman who conceives the ambition to be a person in her own right, rather than an accessory to someone else's life, faces tragically insuperable obstacles. One can identify a seminal idea of that kind at the very center of the concerns of every novel and every short story France wrote. Ideas are his trademark—not surprisingly, because his literary imagination was so completely grounded in books, rather than in life, and because his carefully maintained view of the world was a skepticism so systematic, and so bathed in irony, that it kept reality at a distance and made the life of the mind virtually the only life he knew. Such a writer is not for everyone, but in spite of the low ebb of his reputation since his death, his audience will never entirely vanish as long as there are those who relish the pleasures of the intellect.

Murray Sachs

OTHER MAJOR WORKS

SHORT FICTION: *Nos enfants*, 1886; *Balthasar*, 1889 (English translation, 1909); *L'Étui de nacre*, 1892 (*Tales from a Mother of Pearl Casket*, 1896); *Le Puits de Sainte-Claire*, 1895 (*The Well of Saint Clare*, 1909); *Clio*, 1900 (English translation, 1922); *Crainquebille, Putois, Riquet, et plusieurs autres récits profitables*, 1904 (*Crainquebille, Putois, Riquet, and Other Profitable Tales*, 1915); *Les Contes de Jacques Tournebroche*, 1908 (*The Merry Tales of Jacques Tournebroche*, 1910); *Les Sept Femmes de la Barbe-Bleue, et autres contes merveilleux*, 1909 (*The Seven Wives of Bluebeard*, 1920); *The Latin Genius*, 1924; *The Wisdom of the Ages, and Other Stories*, 1925; *Golden Tales*, 1926.

PLAYS: *La Comédie de celui qui épousa une femme muette*, pb. 1903 (*The Man Who Married a Dumb Wife*, 1915); *Crainquebille*, pb. 1903 (English translation, 1915).

NONFICTION: *Alfred de Vigny*, 1868; *La Vie littéraire*, 1888-1892 (5 volumes; *On Life and Letters*, 1911-1914); *Le Jardin d'Épicure*, 1894 (*The Garden of Epicurus*, 1908); *Vers les temps meilleurs*, 1906, 1949; *La Vie de Jeanne d'Arc*, 1908 (*The Life of Joan of Arc*, 1908); *Le Génie latin*, 1913 (*The Latin Genius*, 1924); *Sur la voie glorieuse*, 1915.

MISCELLANEOUS: *The Complete Works*, 1908-1928 (21 volumes); *Œuvres complètes*, 1925-1935 (25 volumes).

BIBLIOGRAPHY

Auchincloss, Louis. "Anatole France." In *Writers and Personality*. Columbia: University of South Carolina Press, 2005. Auchincloss, himself a novelist, has compiled his observations about writers in this collection. The chapter on France discusses how France's personality was reflected in his own fiction.

Axelrad, Jacob. *Anatole France: A Life Without Illusions*. New York: Harper & Brothers, 1944. In this dated but eminently readable biography, Axelrad focuses on France's impact as a social critic and partisan of justice. While the research is carefully undertaken and generally accurate, the point of view is overly sentimental, unabashedly admiring, and insufficiently critical and analytical.

Chevalier, Haakon M. *The Ironic Temper: Anatole France and His Time*. New York: Oxford University Press, 1932. Although dated, this book is insightful and engagingly written. Its purpose is to study a character, not to evaluate the artistic achievement of its subject. It sets an excellent analysis of France's ironic view of the world against a detailed portrait of the political climate in which he lived and wrote. Includes photographs and a bibliography.

Emery, Elizabeth. "Art as Passion in Anatole France's *Le Lys rouge*." *Nineteenth Century French Studies* 35, no. 3/4 (2007): 641-652. An analysis of the novel *The Red Lily*, describing it as a "mordant satire of [France's] contemporaries' aesthetic pronouncements" and focusing on its detailed descriptions of fin-de-siècle aesthetic tastes and attitudes about art.

Hamilton, James F. "Terrorizing the 'Feminine' in Hugo, Dickens, and France." *Symposium* 48, no. 3 (Fall, 1994): 204-215. An analysis of France's novel *The Gods Are Athirst* and novels about the French Revolution by Victor Hugo and Charles Dickens. Hamilton argues that these authors repress the feminine side in their depiction of the Reign of Terror, relying on cold mechanical reasoning that creates a self-defeating force of violence.

Jefferson, Carter. *Anatole France: The Politics of Skepticism*. New Brunswick, N.J.: Rutgers University Press, 1965. This work emphasizes the historical and political, as opposed to the literary, ideas of France and is especially informative with respect to the complex and shifting political positions he assumed in the last two decades of his life. The book's five chapters cover the conservative, anarchist, crusader, socialist, and "bolshevik" stages of France's thought. Contains a bibliography.

Stableford, Brian M. "Anatole France." In *Supernatural Fiction Writers: Fantasy and Horror, 1: Apuleius to May Sinclair*, edited by Everett Franklin Bleiler. New York: Scribner's, 1985. Stableford provides a brief introduction to France's treatment of the Christian myth and to his fantastic fiction, discussing some of the individual works.

Virtanen, Reino. *Anatole France*. New York: Twayne, 1968. Intended as a general introduction to the author's work, this insightful volume is accurate and sound in its evaluation of France's life and career. It is also of use to general readers in its detailed analysis of France's most significant literary works.

JONATHAN FRANZEN

Born: Western Springs, Illinois; August 17, 1959

Principal long fiction

The Twenty-seventh City, 1988
Strong Motion, 1992
The Corrections, 2001

Other literary forms

Jonathan Franzen has published numerous essays in magazines and journals such as *The New Yorker*, *Harper's*, *Details*, and *Graywolf*, essays with a common underlying theme: the conflict between individuality and mass culture. In 2002, these essays were published in the collection *How to Be Alone*. Franzen also has published articles in the form of the memoir. His 2006 book *The Discomfort Zone: A Personal History* explores the difficulties associated with growing up in the American Midwest and assimilating its contradictory values.

Achievements

Jonathan Franzen won a Whiting Writer's Award for *The Twenty-seventh City* and the American Academy's Berlin Prize (2000). *The New Yorker* named him one of the twenty best writers of the twenty-first century, and *Granta* listed him as one of the Best Young American Novelists (2001).

In 2001, Franzen's novel *The Corrections* was selected for Oprah's Book Club, setting off a slew of controversy when Franzen expressed reservations about his work being selected. Eventually, however, Franzen and Winfrey resolved their differences, and she even was one of the people he thanked when *The Corrections* received a National Book Award for Fiction. In 2002, British judges honored this novel with the James Tait Black Memorial Prize for Fiction, awarded by the University of Edinburgh, Scotland. Also in 2002, Franzen's essay, "My Father's Brain," was a finalist for the National Magazine Award from the American Society of Magazine Editors, and *The Discomfort Zone* was named a *New York Times* Notable Book of the Year (2006).

Biography

Born in the Chicago suburb of Western Springs, Illinois, Jonathan Franzen was the third and youngest son of

Irene Franzen, a homemaker, and Earl T. Franzen, a civil engineer. Franzen grew up near St. Louis, Missouri, in the middle-class suburb of Webster Groves. Initially, Franzen carefully guarded his privacy, but he later described his midwestern boyhood in *The Discomfort Zone*, a memoir about growing up in the 1970's; he portrays himself as a sort of Charlie Brown from the *Peanuts* cartoons. Likewise, some of the essays collected in *How to Be Alone* (especially the award-winning "My Father's Brain") address and universalize problems confronted by Franzen and his family.

Jonathan Franzen. (AP/Wide World Photos)

After graduation from Swarthmore College in 1981 and study at the Freie Universität in Berlin, Germany, as a Fulbright scholar, Franzen worked in a seismology lab at Harvard University's Department of Earth and Planetary Sciences. Later, he moved to New York City, where he lived on the upper East Side with his longtime companion, writer Kathryn Chetkovich. In addition to writing novels, he is primarily a freelance writer. His essay, "Perchance to Dream: In the Age of Images, a Reason to Write Novels" (April, 1996), examines the relationship between novelists and mass culture; a revised version, "Why Bother?" appears in *How to Be Alone*.

The impish sense of humor revealed in his nonfiction is also evident in his novels, readings, and appearances on public television. Perhaps the best example of this sense of humor, however, is his starring role in a 2006 episode of the animated television series *The Simpsons*.

Analysis

Jonathan Franzen is one of the best-known proponents of maximalism, also referred to as recherché postmodernism. He writes in a style in which lush, almost overblown prose is combined with a backdrop of realistic, almost journalistic narrative.

The Twenty-seventh City

Set in St. Louis in 1984, *The Twenty-seventh City*, Franzen's first novel, is essentially a political thriller dealing with several major issues of the 1980's, including urban crime and decay, the flight of residents to the suburbs, fears of communist terrorists, and increasing foreign investment in American companies and ownership of American real estate. Franzen describes the effects of these concerns in a city that in one hundred years has declined from the fourth largest city in the United States to the twenty-seventh. Because of this dramatic decline, local business leaders are looking for a way to revitalize the city, opening the doors to ambitious politicians and setting up themselves—and the city—as easy prey.

Within a few months, St. Louis sees an influx of immigrants from India, several of whom have ties to a terrorist cell of communist youth. First, one of the city's wealthiest citizens marries Princess Asha (from Bombay, now Mumbai), who in turn uses her resulting wealth and power to assist her longtime friend S. Jammu in her plot to control the city. After a short but successful career as a police district administrator in Bombay, Jammu has been appointed chief of the St. Louis Police Department. With advice and money from her mother (who is known in Bombay as the laughing jackal of real estate), Jammu begins to build her power base, using a combination of wiretapping, bribery, extortion, intimidation, and even murder. Her goal is to become as important in the United States as her mother's kinswoman Indira Gandhi is in India. Thus, the drive for power is a major theme in this novel.

Ambition is another dominant theme in *The Twenty-seventh City*. Using information derived from wiretaps in their homes, Jammu quickly enlists most of St. Louis's influential men in her scheme to gain power by consolidating the financially struggling city and the more affluent suburbs. They quickly realize that her ambitions extend beyond St. Louis; because her father was American and she was born in Los Angeles, Jammu is actually eligible to run for the U.S. presidency.

Most opponents of Jammu's plans are ordinary citizens who have become suspicious of the changes they have seen in property ownership, but she is not concerned about them because she knows they have no real power. She believes her only important obstacle is Martin Probst, the contractor who built the Gateway Arch and the most influential man in St. Louis. Considering Probst incorruptible by ordinary means, Jammu sets out to destroy his family, cripple him psychologically, and then seduce him sexually. Thus, the novel is a battle between probity and ambition for power, with the outcome in doubt until the final chapter.

Strong Motion

Franzen's second novel takes its title from a seismologist's term for the shaking ground along a fault line near the epicenter of an earthquake. In *Strong Motion*, earthquakes near Boston reveal not only weaknesses along a long-ignored fault line but also the destructive effects of individual and corporate selfishness, irresponsibility, and greed. Franzen focuses on parallels between the disruptions within a family and seismic activity in the Boston area. Just as the unintended effect of Sweeting-Aldren company's illegal, deep-well disposal of toxic waste has been to upset the balance along a local fault line, the self-absorption, indifference, and greed of the Holland family have caused pain to the immediate family and, in a ripple effect, indirectly damaged the lives of their friends and associates.

Alienation is an obvious theme of this novel. The characters are isolated and self-absorbed. Louis Holland feels somewhat superior to his family because he has consciously rejected what he considers their materialism and indifference, but he treats his girlfriend Renee Seitchek with similar indifference. Renee has likewise refused to conform to her mother's image of the ideal young woman, but she insists on the superiority of her ideas and her projects, ridiculing her coworkers and their projects. Thus, both she and Louis are more or less alienated from family, coworkers, temporary roommates, and even each other. Because they are outsiders, with few personal or professional ties, they cannot successfully pursue investigation of Sweeting-Aldren's deep drilling and corporate irresponsibility until they are forced to rely on the family and coworkers they have scorned.

Eventually, the two learn to respect the ethical values of people they have considered corrupted insiders. For instance, when Louis' sister, Eileen, and her fiancé, Peter Stoorhuys, understand the destruction caused by Peter's father and the other company executives, they strongly repudiate this illegal act and eagerly join Louis and Renee in confronting Dave Stoorhuys.

Strong Motion begins Franzen's transition from the plot-driven social novel to novels of character. Though he continues to comment on contemporary social issues, in each case the focus on the interior life of his characters becomes an important parallel to the topical issue being addressed. For example, the Hollands's family environment is being corroded by selfish indifference, just as surely as the Massachusetts landscape is being polluted. Louis is repeatedly told that he must understand Eileen and his mother, Melanie, but until his father, Bob, explains three generations of family snobbery and bitter revenge in Melanie's family, Louis cannot really begin to break this cycle of irresponsibility and emotional detachment. Likewise, Renee's denunciation of the Reverend Philip Stites and the antiabortion protestors reflects her own ambivalence at least as much as her frustration at their telephone harassment of her.

Louis' hostility toward Stites springs from a different source. Louis works briefly at a small AM radio station that plays traditional music and—in keeping with the 1980's demands that the media report more "good news"—broadcasts no reports of crime, politics, or any other depressing subject. Because the station has few listeners and fewer paying advertisers, the owner is forced to sell the station to Stites, who also is head of a fringe religious group known as the Church of Action in Christ, headquartered in a Boston tenement. Stites needs a media outlet for his evangelism, primarily his opposition to abortion.

Interestingly, while Franzen's wit is evident in his discussion of the station's business philosophy, he seems to avoid polemics on the issues of abortion and religion generally. In Stites, he creates a likeable, apparently humble religious leader, who opposes any attempt to combine his moral crusade with partisan politics. Stites seems as astonished as his followers when their building is destroyed by the earthquake and some of them are injured. Franzen is realist enough to add a comment about the litigious nature of the local residents and to observe that plaintiffs range from some of Stites's followers to establishment figures such as Melanie Holland.

Although in *Strong Motion*, Franzen's focus on plot action is substantially balanced by emphasis on character, ultimately, some of the societal and personal conflicts must be resolved. Thus, in addition to strong character development, this novel poses thorny ethical questions, and Franzen's use of multiple narrators and the narrative consciousness of many individual characters are intriguing techniques for presenting both action and character.

THE CORRECTIONS

Franzen's third and arguably best-known novel, *The Corrections*, is a best seller that has been translated into more than thirty languages. The novel continues the theme of ethics versus expediency and profit. In the story, each member of the Lambert family confronts some kind of ethical dilemma. Albert, an engineer with Midland-Pacific, is assigned a major role in corporate downsizing after a merger, but in eliminating railroad lines he tries to maintain service for as many small Iowa towns as possible. Equally ethical is his decision to retire rather than submit to extortion by one of his daughter's former lovers.

Later, Albert is approached by the Axon Corporation, which wants to buy his patent on one of his extracurricular experiments. In his negotiations with the company, he refuses to make exorbitant demands, and he insists on sharing the proceeds with his former employers. In contrast, his wife, Enid, hides the Axon correspondence from her husband. Albert's older son, Gary, is willing to overlook the ethics involved in the consciousness-controlling medications that Axon wants to develop using his father's patented experiment; instead, he tries to buy as much Axon stock as possible and profit from his insider knowledge. Albert's daughter, Denise, also is willing to overlook the ethical questions if her father can be included in Axon's trials of Corecktall, a Parkinson's disease medication.

A more self-centered character is Chip, Albert's younger son. A combination of sexual frustration, drugs, and extreme poverty leads him to a number of unethical actions, including a sexual affair with one of his students, stealing food, and engaging in stock fraud.

Franzen parallels the crises in the life of the Lambert family and the upheavals in national and international financial markets with which each is involved. Enid has used her small inheritance to buy stocks; she has been both conservative and lucky, spending or reinvesting only her profits and gaining a small sense of independence. Although she urges Albert to invest his retirement in the stock market, his memories of the Great Depression and his role in corporate downsizing have led him to remain invested in annuities.

Gary is a financial analyst for a Philadelphia bank; he and his wife, Caroline, are large-scale investors, especially so after Gary learns about Corecktall. Desperate for money, Chip moves to Lithuania, where he becomes involved in an international stock scam involving the national phone company; eventually, though, he loses his illegal gains and barely escapes with his life. Denise is not directly involved with financial markets, but she has become the executive chef and manager of a high-end restaurant in Philadelphia, financed by a local entrepreneur.

The dominant theme of *The Corrections* is disintegration and loss. Franzen uses vivid imagery and incoherent syntax as he allows Albert to reveal his own descent into senility, exacerbated by medications he takes for Parkinson's disease. Almost as chaotic is Chip's drug-induced obsession with a former student, an episode that costs him his tenure-track academic position, his savings, his most prized possessions, and ultimately, his self-respect.

Franzen also explores Enid's consciousness in the commonplace diction and syntax of a conventional midwestern housewife. Her desperation at Albert's physical and mental decline is compounded by her denial that his behavior is anything more than his usual stubbornness. In contrast, Gary, who believes he is the only realist in the family, approaches family relationships with the same cost-analysis language he applies to business dealings. Thus, pragmatism becomes the basis for his interactions not only with his mother and his siblings but also his wife and sons. In the process, however, he must surrender his self-respect. The most enigmatic of the Lamberts, Denise, has always used a facade of propriety to conceal sexual promiscuity, but eventually her ironic attitudes and language are not enough to prevent the loss of her dream job.

At a climactic moment onboard the cruise ship *Gunnar Myrdal*, Enid attends an investment lecture, Surviving the Corrections. She survives the "corrections" in her life primarily by maintaining her lifestyle and her focus on herself. Albert's coping mechanism involves withdrawing ever more deeply into his own psyche. Gary survives by accepting Caroline's versions of reality and allowing her to control their family life. In contrast, Denise finally recognizes Albert's implicit forgiveness of his children and insists on forgiving Chip's twenty-thousand-dollar debt.

The theme of forgiveness is a major element in the novel as well. Those characters unable to forgive bring misery on themselves and others. When Chip forgives his father's indifference, he can also accept his own limitations and forgive himself; thus, he is ready to succeed as a husband and father. Likewise, as Denise accepts her mother's self-absorption, she no longer needs to be geographically close to her brother and the sister-in-law she does not really like. During his Christmas visit in St. Jude, Gary sees his family as they are and is reconciled with them, even with Chip. Finally, Enid learns to accept each of her children, as did Albert.

Charmaine Allmon Mosby

Other major works

NONFICTION: "Perchance to Dream: In the Age of Images, a Reason to Write Novels," 1996; "Scavenging," 1996; "Meet Me in St. Louis," 2001; *How to Be Alone*, 2002; *The Discomfort Zone: A Personal History*, 2006.

TRANSLATION: *Spring Awakening: A Children's Tragedy*, 2007 (of Frank Wedekind's play).

Bibliography

Annesley, James. "Market Corrections: Jonathan Franzen and the 'Novel of Globalization.'" *Journal of Modern Literature* 29, no. 2 (2006): 111-128. A critical examination of what some have called a "novel of globalization," Franzen's *The Corrections*.

Antrim, Donald. "Jonathan Franzen." *Bomb* 77 (Fall, 2001). Franzen discusses, among other topics, how his personal life has affected the writing of his novels. Available at http://www.bombsite.com/issues/77/.

Burn, Stephen J. *Jonathan Franzen at the End of Postmodernism*. New York: Continuum, 2008. Part of the Continuum Literary Authors series, Burn's study surveys the state of postmodern literature in an age when that literature is presumed to be on the wain. The first full-length study of Franzen's work.

Miller, Laura. "Only Correct." *Salon.com*. September 7, 2001. http://archive.salon.com/books/int/2001/09/07/franzen/index.html. Extended interview in which Franzen discusses goals, themes, and writing techniques in *The Corrections*.

HAROLD FREDERIC

Born: Utica, New York; August 19, 1856
Died: Henley-on-Thames, Oxfordshire, England; October 19, 1898
Also known as: George Forth

PRINCIPAL LONG FICTION

Seth's Brother's Wife: A Study of Life in the Greater New York, 1887
In the Valley, 1890
The Lawton Girl, 1890
The Return of the O'Mahony, 1892
The Copperhead, 1893
The Damnation of Theron Ware, 1896
March Hares, 1896 (as George Forth)
Mrs. Albert Grundy: Observations in Philistia, 1896
Gloria Mundi, 1898
The Market Place, 1899

OTHER LITERARY FORMS

Harold Frederic was a journalist by profession, so it is no surprise that he wrote a considerable amount of nonfiction. A large portion of his copy for *The New York Times* was essayistic and well researched and developed. Extended pieces also appeared regularly in English and American magazines. Two sizable groups of dispatches were brought out in book format, *The Young Emperor William II of Germany: A Study in Character Development on a Throne* (1891) and *The New Exodus: A Study of Israel in Russia* (1892). The first of these is not a notable work, despite the fact that its subject became one of the crucial figures of the early twentieth century—and despite the fact that, like almost all of Frederic's fiction, it is a character study. The second work, however—a series of reports on pogroms under Czar Alexander III—was so effective that Frederic became persona non grata in Russia. One is tempted to add to his list of nonfiction the novel *Mrs. Albert Grundy*, a book that hangs by a narrative thread and is precisely what its subtitle proclaims: *Observations in Philistia*, that is, satiric sketches of the London bourgeoisie.

Also not surprising for a journalist, Frederic tried his hand at short fiction. His output ranges from poorly written juvenile beginnings to very readable stories about Ireland to a number of short novels and short stories about the Civil War. These latter pieces are his best; they are collected in variously arranged editions and attracted the attention of writers such as Stephen Crane. In them, Frederic examines the effect of the war on the people at home in central New York through insightful and striking situations and through a skillful handling of description, dialogue, and point of view.

ACHIEVEMENTS

Writing a preface for a uniform edition for Scribner's 1897 edition of his Civil War stories, *In the Sixties*, Harold Frederic remarks about the upstate New York places and people in his fiction that "no exact counterparts exist for them in real life, and no map of the district has as yet been drawn, even in my own mind." This statement was written at a time when Frederic had left his American fiction behind and turned his attention to English matters; the journalist who desired fame as a serious writer did not wish to be taken for someone who merely transcribed the personal experiences of his youth. Although Frederic's fiction is almost evenly divided between American subject matter on one hand and English and Irish on the other, the influence of America is felt even in the non-American works, and Frederic's acknowledged masterpiece, *The Damnation of Theron Ware*, is thoroughly American.

Thomas F. O'Donnell has argued that Frederic is upstate New York's greatest writer since James Fenimore Cooper. In his regional novels, Frederic studies politics (*Seth's Brother's Wife*), history (*In the Valley*), socioeconomics (*The Lawton Girl*), and religion (*The Damnation of Theron Ware*), and thus gives a comprehensive view of his part of the world. Just as Gustave Flaubert anchors his sweeping presentation of human passions in *Madame Bovary* (1857) in the Caux, a rural district of Normandy that easily matches the provinciality of the Mohawk Valley, so, too, does Frederic derive the Jamesian solidity of specification so central to the art of the novel from the authoritatively detailed depiction of his native region.

Although his first model was the successful popular French combination of Erckmann-Chatrian, Frederic grew into a major writer because of his keen observation (sharpened by his reportorial work), his Howellsian sympathy with the common person, and above all, his Hawthornian understanding of the truth of the human heart and the complexity of the American Adam. Hence, Frederic is partly a realist, like Flaubert, and partly a romancer, like Nathaniel Hawthorne, but also, like both of these, a writer with universal themes that are embedded in regional actuality. Were it not for his premature death, he might well have duplicated the achievement of his American fiction with his English fiction. As it is, his reputation will stand on his American works.

Biography

Harold Frederic was born on August 19, 1856, in Utica, a small city of then about twenty thousand people, situated in the picturesque Mohawk Valley of upstate New York. His family tree reached far back into colonial times to Dutch and German farmers and artisans, and he could proudly point out that all four of his great-grandfathers had fought in the Revolutionary War. When Frederic was only a year and a half old, his father died in a train derailment; his mother, however, was energetic and capable and kept the family above water until she remarried. She was a somewhat severe woman, not given to spoiling her children, and Frederic always remembered the early-morning chores he had to do in the family milk and wood businesses before setting out for school. He also remembered the Methodist upbringing he received and the unseemly bickerings among the parishioners of his neighborhood church.

Like many children at the time, Frederic did not receive extensive schooling and graduated from Utica's Advanced School at the age of fourteen. For the next two years, he worked for local photographers, slowly progressing from errand-boy to retoucher. He then tried his luck in Boston, dabbling in art and working for a photographer, but in 1875, he returned to Utica and changed his career by becoming a proofreader for the town's Republican morning paper, shortly afterward switching to its Democratic afternoon counterpart. By this time, Utica had almost doubled its population and had become a political center of the first order, giving the state a governor in Horatio Seymour and the country two senators in Roscoe Conkling and Francis Kernan (it would later add a vice president in James Sherman). Frederic became a firm Democrat and took a lively interest in politics. He soon became a reporter for his paper and also began writing fiction; it was sentimental and imitative beginner's work, but enough of it was published to encourage him.

The centennial celebration of the Battle of Oriskany in 1877 proved to be an intellectual milestone in Frederic's life. He helped prepare the occasion, convinced that the battle had been a turning point of the war and not merely a minor skirmish away from the major battlefields. As he listened to Horatio Seymour's call for a greater awareness on the part of the living of their proud and important history, Frederic resolved to write a historical novel that would give the Mohawk Valley its due and its present inhabitants the historical connectedness Seymour demanded. The regionalist Harold Frederic had come into being, even though *In the Valley* was not published until 1890, respectively and affectionately dedicated to the memory of the late governor.

That fall, Frederic married his neighbor, Grace Williams. At that point, he was able to support a family because of his financial success at the *Observer*, becoming news editor in 1879 and editor in 1880, a seasoned and successful journalist before he turned twenty-four. During that time, Frederic's Methodism was softened through his friendship with Father Terry, an accomplished Irish Catholic priest with a modern and unorthodox outlook who introduced him to Utica's growing Irish community. For the rest of his life, Frederic would be a champion of the Irish, and he paid literary tribute to Father Terry and his circle of friends a few years later in his finest novel.

In 1882, Frederic took another step ahead in his career in becoming editor of the *Evening Journal* in Albany, the state capital. Barely settled in town, the Democratic editor made his Republican paper bolt the party line, thereby helping Grover Cleveland become governor. Cleveland appreciated the support and took a genuine liking to the young newspaperman. Frederic was even bolder—and quite prophetic—the following year when he wrote that Cleveland ought to run for president. In early 1884, the paper changed ownership, and Frederic lost his job. Helped by the recommendation of

Cleveland's chief lieutenant, he secured a position as foreign correspondent with *The New York Times* and sailed for England with his wife and their two daughters.

Frederic's position with the respected American paper and a letter of introduction from Governor Cleveland soon established him in London. A daring tour of cholera-stricken southern France made him a celebrity, and Cleveland's accession to the presidency made Frederic a person of importance. He was admitted to a number of London clubs, where he met many of England's political leaders, the men behind Irish home rule, and the foremost intellectuals, artists, and writers of the day. In this milieu, being only a newspaper correspondent was not satisfactory to Frederic; he set about his literary career with great determination and energy, hoping to become financially independent of journalism and famous as well.

From 1887 on, Frederic's novels appeared in rapid succession, and while they brought him considerable contemporary reputation (*The Damnation of Theron Ware* was a sensation on both sides of the Atlantic Ocean), they did not bring him financial independence. That would have been hard to do even if the sales had been bigger, since Frederic enjoyed a comfortable lifestyle and had a growing family to support. In fact, he had to support two families, for in 1890, he met and fell in love with Kate Lyon, a fellow upstate New Yorker, openly established a second household, and subsequently had three children with her. For some time, Harold and Grace Frederic had been drifting apart. While he split his time between his two families, it was Lyon's place that became the center of his intellectual and artistic life, and it was there, for example, that he entertained his friend, Stephen Crane.

Financial necessities put a great strain on Frederic. Between his continuing journalistic work (which he carried out thoroughly and faithfully and which involved several extended trips to the Continent), his writing (for which he continued to educate himself by reading widely), his club life, and his family life (including return visits to the United States and to his beloved Mohawk Valley as well as vacations in Ireland), he simply wore himself out. Of imposing physique, he drew upon his strength so recklessly that he suffered a stroke in August, 1898, from which he never recovered. Lyon's resistance to doctors and her trust in a Christian Science healer led to a widely publicized manslaughter trial after Frederic's death on October 19; eventually, the defendants were acquitted. Heavily in debt, Frederic had left his family in such financial trouble that friends took up a collection. Five months later, Grace died of cancer. In 1901, the ashes of Harold and Grace Frederic were brought home to their native valley.

Analysis

Harold Frederic was not one of those writers who burst upon the scene with a magnum opus and then fade from view; rather, his writing steadily improved from *Seth's Brother's Wife* to his masterpiece, *The Damnation of Theron Ware*. Ever since the Oriskany Centennial, Frederic's ambition had been the writing of *In the Valley* as the great American historical novel. The prepa-

Harold Frederic. (Library of Congress)

ration for this book was so slow and painstaking that it took years, as well as the experience of writing *Seth's Brother's Wife* first, to complete the Revolutionary War novel. *In the Valley* interprets the Revolutionary War as more of a struggle between the democratic American farmers and the would-be aristocratic American landed gentry than as a conflict between crown and colony. It gives a stirring description of the Battle of Oriskany, but its plot is trite, pitting the sturdy Douw Mauverensen against the slick Philip Cross as political opponents and rivals for the same woman.

In his uniform-edition preface, Frederic states that he firmly controlled everything in *Seth's Brother's Wife* and *In the Valley*, but that in *The Lawton Girl*, "the people took matters into their own hands quite from the start." More than one great novelist has insisted that in truly great fiction, the author does not prescribe to his characters but rather allows them to unfold as they themselves demand, integrating them into the whole. *The Lawton Girl* is a respectable book, despite some plot and character contrivances, for the longer rope Frederic had learned to give to his characters and for his continuing ability to ground his work in regional authenticity.

Before *The Damnation of Theron Ware* appeared, Frederic had published *The Return of the O'Mahony*, a playful work that expresses his strong interest in Ireland and Irish home rule. Even in this pleasant book, there is, as Austin Briggs and others have noted, the abiding sense of a past that conditions the present, a theme familiar from Hawthorne's *The House of the Seven Gables* (1851).

March Hares (published under the pseudonym George Forth), is a comedy of mistaken identities in a make-believe world. These light works were followed by the weightier novels *Gloria Mundi* and *The Market Place*. *Gloria Mundi* is essentially concerned with an investigation of the English aristocracy, which Frederic shows as a hollow, outdated remnant of medieval caste structure. This major theme is accompanied by a variety of probing social observations, at the end of which stands the insight of the new duke of Glastonbury:

> A man is only a man after all. He did not make this world, and he cannot do with it what he likes. . . . There will be many men after me. If one or two of them says of me that I worked hard to do well, and that I left things a trifle better than I found them, then what more can I desire?

This distillation of Frederic's ultimate philosophy of life is evident as early as Seth Fairchild, but it is not a view shared by Theron Ware or the central figure of *The Market Place*, Joel Stormont Thorpe. Ware has visions of greatness and power; Thorpe is the most ruthless and most successful of financiers and prepares by way of sham philanthropy to go into politics and rule England. Frederic's final assessment of people in this world is therefore a very balanced and realistic one: One would like to have the Seth Fairchilds without the Theron Wares and the Stormont Thorpes, but the wish is not going to make those who want to do with the world what they like desist or disappear. The present will always have to find its own way against the past and will always in turn become the next present's past; so passes the glory of the world, and so also does the world go on and on in continuous struggle between good and evil.

Seth's Brother's Wife

Seth's Brother's Wife has all the strengths and weaknesses of a respectable first novel, but only in the late twentieth century did critics begin to take it as something more than a mixture of realistic regionalism and sentimental melodrama. Its very title is confusing, since Seth Fairchild, not Isabel, is the book's main character, since personal integrity rather than amatory complication constitutes the book's principal theme, and since—as the subtitle, *A Study of Life in the Greater New York*, signals—the book's compass reaches well beyond the three people mentioned in the title.

Set in the Mohawk Valley region in the early 1880's, *Seth's Brother's Wife* is the familiar story of a young country lad who goes to town, experiences sometimes severe growing pains, but in the end prevails because of his basic personal decency and his values, which, though tested to the breaking point, hold and are therefore rewarded. Frederic called the novel a romance, and one does well to see it in a line of American stories of initiation that begins, if not with Benjamin Franklin's *The Autobiography* (1791), then with Charles Brockden Brown's *Arthur Mervyn* (1799-1800), and reaches Frederic by way of Hawthorne.

One of three brothers, Seth comes from a farming family whose fortunes have been declining. His brother, John, is editor of the local paper; his other brother, Albert, who is college-educated, is a successful New York City lawyer and comes home to establish residence and a political base for his bid to be a congressman. Albert finds Seth a job with the area's leading daily newspaper; reminiscent of Frederic's own career, Seth eventually becomes editor and is instrumental in the paper's bolting from its traditional political adherence. Seth finds himself opposing his brother, to whom he owes his position in the first place, and supporting his friend, Richard Ansdell, a principled reform candidate who has done much for Seth's intellectual and moral growth.

In a powerful sequence of chapters all set during the same night, the ruthless Albert corners the well-meaning but immature Seth. Seth has fallen under the spell of Albert's young, neglected, city-bred wife, Isabel, and although he never fully succumbs to the temptation, Seth feels the sting of Albert's attack on his political purity: How hypocritical that Seth stand on ethics in politics when he was about to make love to his brother's wife. As Albert leaves to discuss with his henchman, Milton Squires, a scheme of buying the nomination, Seth stumbles out into the darkness conscious of his weakness and foolishness, finds his old love, Annie, and proposes to her on the spot to save himself from himself.

The nominating convention is ruled by the area's political boss, Abe Beekman. Beekman rebuffs Albert's attempt to buy him off (he is in politics for the fun, not the money) and decides to have Ansdell nominated. When news of Albert's death arrives, Beekman turns into the driving force behind the investigation, and after many melodramatic plot complications—including a suspicion that Seth took revenge on his brother—all ends well: Squires is convicted of murdering Albert to get the buy-off money; Seth is united with Annie; Isabel leaves the uncongenial countryside and goes to Washington where, in a pointed undercutting of the validity of happy endings, she will marry Ansdell.

A plot summary of this action-packed book is inadequate to clarify Frederic's major concerns and accomplishments. The conflict between city and country, which is so essential to Arthur Mervyn's initiation, is developed here with forceful realism and admirable balance. Life on the farm is dispiriting, squalid drudgery amid often incredibly vulgar exemplars of humankind, but it is also the smell of blossoms in the orchard and the rustle of autumn leaves underfoot and the taste of fresh cider. Life in the city means not only new cultural and intellectual dimensions but also the distraction of the beer hall and, down the dark alley, the depths of prostitution. In politics, honesty and expediency are played against each other without a facile conclusion; most important, Beekman is no saint and Ansdall no new founding father.

Frederic manages to make none of the major characters a one-dimensional stereotype: The good ones have enough weakness (even Annie does), and the bad ones (even Isabel) have enough strengths to forbid easy and schematic moralizing. Seth is the case in point. The youngest, handsomest, and most promising of the brothers, he is also the most sluggish and the most foolish, almost the proverbial fairy-tale late bloomer. His temporary infatuation with Isabel makes him say things about his sweetheart Annie that are as contemptible as Theron Ware's thoughts and comments about his wife at a similar juncture, but unlike Ware, Seth—with some help from John and Annie and even from Albert—catches himself in time. His ability—which is lacking in Albert, in Ware, and in Arthur Mervyn—to realize that he has been as "weak as water" is his saving grace and the book's chief moral; there is no bedrock in this world other than the hard-won decency of one's own character. That may not be the basis of the American Dream, Frederic seems to say, but it is much more than its sobering simplicity might at first suggest, and after all, the only way to life in this imperfect world.

THE DAMNATION OF THERON WARE

Whatever differences of opinion literary critics have had over the years concerning Frederic's novels, they have been unanimous in designating *The Damnation of Theron Ware* as his masterpiece, and they have generally accorded it a high rank in American literature. The book is so complex, ironic, and ambiguous that no unified critical interpretation has emerged; among the best readings are those of John Henry Raleigh, Stanton Garner, and Austin Briggs, and one cannot afford to overlook Edmund Wilson's caution that no truly great novel was ever built on the humiliation of its hero.

The novel opens on the closing session of the annual conference of Central New York's Methodist Episcopal Church. With leisure and deliberation, Frederic sketches the decline of Methodism in the faces of its ministers. Successively, the deterioration of sterling qualities of devotion, honesty, and simplicity is visible in the faces of the younger generations of ministers, with those of the most recently ordained reverends showing almost no trace of them. This verdict, however, is not confined to the clergy. For most of the parishioners, true worship has long since given way to elbowing for social position within the congregation. It is in this spirit that the standing-room-only crowd listens to the eagerly awaited announcement by the bishop of the ministerial assignments for the upcoming period of service.

The well-to-do and socially ambitious Tecumseh congregation, having housed the conference in style in its fine and new facilities, is bent upon adding to its glory by adorning itself with an "attractive and fashionable preacher." On the basis of the sermons delivered at the conference, the congregation's choice is the Reverend Theron Ware, a young minister who has made a study of pulpit oratory, and whom Frederic describes as a "tall, slender young man with the broad white brow, thoughtful eyes, and features moulded into that regularity of strength which used to characterize the American senatorial type." Ware and his wife, Alice, are quietly informed that they are Tecumseh's choice, but to the bitter disappointment of the couple and the uncharitable outrage of the congregation, the district's plum is awarded to a noncharismatic older pastor. Even here, it is evident that among Theron's and Alice's personal qualities, the spiritual ones are not strongly developed.

Theron is assigned to Octavius, a town twice as large as their previous one, Tyre, and much larger than his first entirely rural post. Like Seth Fairchild, Theron Ware is a country-bred young man who, because of his better than average intellectual abilities, leaves the farm to move on to bigger and presumably better things; like Seth, he—at least initially—neither glorifies nor condemns his country background, and again like Seth, he marries the loveliest and most refined country girl around. Their first year in Tyre is filled with all the radiance of a new life together, until they discover that they are heavily in debt, a discovery that forces them into a joyless attempt at mere survival for the remainder of their time there, and from which they are miraculously released by a gift from Abram Beekman, who had figured so imposingly in *Seth's Brother's Wife*.

The Octavius congregation is old-fashioned in a mean way, believing in "straight-out, flat-footed hell," no milk on Sundays, and no flowery bonnets in church. Theron's first meeting with the trustees is a bitter revelation; the very names of their leaders, Pierce and Winch, suggest the tortures of the Inquisition. Theron rejects their attempt to reduce his already skimpy salary but sacrifices Alice's bonnet without a fight (though not long afterward, he buys himself a new shining hat). To improve his finances, he decides to write a book on Abraham, the Old Testament patriarch. Cogitating about it on a walk, he by chance witnesses the last rites of the Catholic Church upon an Irish workman who has fallen from a tree to his death. The elaborate Latin ceremony with its sonorous, bell-like invocations deeply impresses Theron, as do the priest, Father Forbes, and the organist, the striking Celia Madden. The workman's fall prefigures Theron's own, but it is some time before Frederic's careful structure becomes evident.

The chance acquaintance leads to other meetings between Theron and Celia and Theron and Forbes, entirely destroying Theron's narrowly preconceived notions of the Irish and of Catholicism. His first visit with the urbane and educated priest turns into an eye-opener for Theron: Forbes dismisses Theron's fundamentalist notions of Abraham with a brief survey of modern scholarship on the subject; he discourses learnedly on "this Christ-myth of ours"; he admits to exercising pastoral functions without troubling himself or his congregation overly about fine points of doctrine. Similarly, Forbes's agnostic friend, Dr. Ledsmar, impresses Theron with his scientific learning and the easy authority of his judgments on art, science, and religion. Celia Madden, finally, captivates Theron's emotional side with her sophisticated looks, her self-assured behavior, and her musical proficiency. In their several ways, the lives of these three are firmly grounded in traditions against which Theron's country background and seminary education appear painfully paltry.

The threesome has opened up a new world for Theron, a world that he fervently desires to comprehend and enter. What he calls his "illumination" (Frederic uses light imagery in many key scenes and gave the English edition the title *Illuminations*) is really intoxication: What for others might be light is for him heady wine against which he proves helpless. In his urge to foist himself upon the three, he attempts the sort of manipulation that has made him a slick preacher, substituting public relations techniques for substance. When he condemns everything his life has been, including his wife, Forbes, Ledsmar, and Celia all turn away from him. Forbes—who, despite his latitudinarianism, would never think of maligning his Church—is shocked by Theron's defamation of his congregation and of his Episcopalian roots. Ledsmar, who among other things conducts inhumane scientific experiments, resents Theron's prying into a possible liaison between Forbes and Celia, abruptly terminates their meeting, and gives Theron's name to an evil-looking lizard in his collection.

Celia's case is more complicated; in a memorable scene, she practically seduces Theron with her enchanting personality, her bewitching playing of Frédéric Chopin, and her quasi-Arnoldian Hellenism. At a meeting in the forest, she permits the fawning, craven minister to kiss her lightly, a kiss that she later explains as a goodbye, but one that Theron takes quite the other way. Whatever Theron's considerable shortcomings, Celia does play with fire, and it is fitting that Frederic has her apologize in *The Market Place* for the extravagant ways of her youth.

The more Theron is enamored of Celia, the more he hardens himself against Alice (appropriately, Celia not only is a short form of the name of the patron saint of sacred music but also a classy anagram of "Alice"). Alice in turn has been receiving the innocent, chiefly horticultural attentions of the church's junior trustee. Theron, who rationalizes away his own infidelity, suspects Alice and Gorringe and draws self-justification from the situation. His downward progress is rapid and complete, not only through Celia but also through Sister Soulsby, a professional fund-raiser employed by the trustees to void the church debt. She fixes Theron's strained relations with his congregation but requires of him the casting of an immoral, fraudulent vote with his erstwhile nemesis Pierce.

Theron Ware lacks entirely that which saves Seth Fairchild: the ability to be honest with himself, to admit his weakness, to recognize his complicity with evil, and to be grateful for his wife's love. Celia really dismisses Theron for the wrong reason when she tells him that he is "a bore"; much more to the point is the indictment by her brother, Michael, who, on his deathbed, gives Theron the ringing "damnation" speech that warrants the book's American title. It is to Sister Soulsby's credit that she puts the fallen Theron Ware together again, sending him (and Alice) to Seattle to go into the real estate business. Much has been made of that ending; some critics take it to mean that a chastened Theron will begin a new and—more fitting for him—secular life, whereas others see in his political vision at the very end (he sees himself as a U.S. senator) the continuation of his failure to understand anything about himself. Perhaps one may tolerate immorality more readily in politicians than in clergymen, and perhaps Frederic does not use irony when he describes Theron's features as senatorial in the beginning, but one must also remember that boss Beekman is a rather decent fellow after all, a man whose outstanding characteristic in *Seth's Brother's Wife* is his ability to size up people and whose counsel to Theron to quit the ministry and go into law instead, Theron unfortunately and condescendingly disregards.

Much, too, has been made of Theron Ware as a Faust figure. This is surely a libel on Johann Wolfgang von Goethe's *Faust* (1790) at least. Critics also go too far when they insist that Theron is a fallen Adam. Theron never quests like Faust, and he is never innocent to begin with; his is a myth several numbers smaller than theirs. Conversely, not enough has been made of the money side of Theron Ware. He lives beyond his means and goes into debt in Tyre; he trades his wife's flowery hat off against a sidewalk repair bill; he glories in visions of Celia's wealth; he plays the big spender in New York after "inadvertently" having brought along the church collection. More than any other myth, Frederic's fable is surely about that aberration in the American makeup that accounts for the "In God We Trust" stamped on the quarter dollar.

As in *Seth's Brother's Wife*, so in *The Damnation of Theron Ware*, Frederic makes no one entirely good and no one entirely bad. For the longest time, he manages to make the reader sympathize with Theron. It is only when

Theron turns viciously and deviously against his own wife that he is truly damned.

Frederic produced in *Seth's Brother's Wife* a solid first novel. Its strength lies in its authenticity of place, people, and dialect; its weakness in its insistence on a cloak-and-dagger plot, which at times overshadows the basic theme of growth of character. In *The Damnation of Theron Ware*, Frederic achieves a powerful blending of regional ambience and psychological penetration of character, only slightly marred by an occasional touch of melodrama.

Frank Bergmann

Other major works

SHORT FICTION: *The Copperhead, and Other Stories of the North During the American War*, 1894; *Marsena, and Other Stories of the Wartime*, 1894; *In the Sixties*, 1897; *The Deserter, and Other Stories: A Book of Two Wars*, 1898; *Stories of York State*, 1966 (Thomas F. O'Donnell, editor).

NONFICTION: *The Young Emperor William II of Germany: A Study in Character Development on a Throne*, 1891; *The New Exodus: A Study of Israel in Russia*, 1892.

Bibliography

Bennett, Bridget. *The Damnation of Harold Frederic: His Lives and Works*. Syracuse, N.Y.: Syracuse University Press, 1997. A scholarly biography with a separate chapter on *The Damnation of Theron Ware*. Includes a chronology, detailed notes, and an extensive bibliography.

Briggs, Austin, Jr. *The Novels of Harold Frederic*. Ithaca, N.Y.: Cornell University Press, 1969. A thorough study of Frederic's novels, this book is mostly literary criticism, with a chapter on each of the major novels. Includes a bibliography and an index.

Filetti, Jean S. *An Examination of Political Pessimism in the Works of American Novelist Harold Frederic, 1856-1898*. Lewiston, N.Y.: Edwin Mellen Press, 1998. An examination of Frederic's major novels. Filetti concludes that Frederic's fiction expressed his pessimism and skepticism about the popular conceptions of grassroots democracy, agrarian America, and the West as a democratic frontier in the late nineteenth century.

Foote, Stephanie. "The Region of the Repressed and the Return of the Region: Hamlin Garland and Harold Frederic." In *Regional Fictions: Culture and Identity in Nineteenth-Century American Literature*. Madison: University of Wisconsin Press, 2001. Foote's examination of Frederic's fiction is one of the essays in her investigation of nineteenth and twentieth century regional literature. She argues that Americans' longstanding ideas about the value of local identity originated with the regionalist fiction of Frederic's era.

Myers, Robert M. *Reluctant Expatriate: The Life of Harold Frederic*. Westport, Conn.: Greenwood Press, 1995. Myers's biography examines how Frederic was shaped by his culture and describes how his relationship with his publishers affected his career and fiction. The preface provides a succinct overview of the state of Frederic's reputation. Includes very useful notes and a bibliography.

Oates, Joyce Carol. "Rediscovering Harold Frederic's *The Damnation of Theron Ware*." In *Where I've Been, and Where I'm Going: Essays, Reviews, and Prose*. New York: Plume, 1999. A review of the novel by Oates, herself a highly regarded novelist who provided an introduction to a 2002 reissue of *The Damnation of Theron Ware*. This review contains biographical information about Frederic and praises the novel, which she believes "provided an odd, unexpected link between the crude naturalism of the young Stephen Crane . . . and the elegant dissections of wealthy New York society of Edith Wharton."

O'Donnell, Thomas F., and Hoyt C. Franchere. *Harold Frederic*. New York: Twayne, 1961. The first book-length study of Frederic, this book, although dated, is valuable for its annotated bibliography and its chronology of Frederic's life and writings. Includes an index.

MAX FRISCH

Born: Zurich, Switzerland; May 15, 1911
Died: Zurich, Switzerland; April 4, 1991
Also known as: Max Rudolf Frisch

Principal long fiction

Jürg Reinhart, 1934
J'adore ce qui me brûle: Oder, Die Schwierigen, 1943
Stiller, 1954 (*I'm Not Stiller*, 1958)
Homo Faber, 1957 (*Homo Faber: A Report*, 1959)
Mein Name sei Gantenbein, 1964 (*A Wilderness of Mirrors*, 1965)
Montauk, 1975 (English translation, 1976)
Der Mensch erscheint im Holozän, 1979 (*Man in the Holocene*, 1980)
Blaubart, 1982 (*Bluebeard*, 1983)

Other literary forms

Max Frisch was a versatile writer whose reputation stemmed from both his dramas and his novels. He also wrote diaries, radio plays, short stories, film scenarios, and essays. His essays include discussions of literature, drama, society, architecture, town planning, and travel. A six-volume German edition of his works up to 1976 was published by Suhrkamp in Frankfurt, and an English-language collection titled *Novels, Plays, Essays* was published in 1989.

Frisch's drama and his fiction are closely related thematically. In most of his plays, the quest for identity is the central theme. In his work, Frisch is critical of the roles that people adopt for themselves or have imposed on them by others because role-playing prevents people from growing and realizing their potential as human beings. This concern of Frisch's is particularly evident in the plays *Andorra* (pr., pb. 1961; English translation, 1963) and *Don Juan: Oder, Die Liebe zur Geometrie* (pr., pb. 1953; *Don Juan: Or, The Love of Geometry*, 1967). As in his fiction, Frisch shows in his theater pieces how difficult it is to escape from such roles: However hard his protagonists try, they fail in their attempts to escape because the social restrictions they face are so overwhelming.

Frisch believed that dramatists have a responsibility to address social and political questions; although he was skeptical that the theater can bring about social change, he asserted that it can at least make people more aware. Although most of his plays focus on personal questions, some directly address such social problems as anti-Semitism and prejudice (*Andorra*) and the moral weakness of the middle class (*Biedermann und die Brandstifter*, pr., pb. 1958; *The Firebugs*, 1959; also known as *The Fire Raisers*, 1962). In both his plays and his novels, Frisch sharply criticizes modern society for its hypocrisy, its smugness, and its superficiality—but most of all for the limits it places on the individual.

Achievements

Max Frisch's international reputation was established in 1954 with the publication of *I'm Not Stiller*, which is still considered his most important work. In 1951, Frisch received a Rockefeller grant to study in the United States. He was awarded numerous honors for his works. These include the Georg Büchner Prize and the Zurich Prize in 1958, the Jerusalem Prize and the Schiller Prize in 1965, the Peace Prize of the German Book Trade in 1976, and the Neustadt International Prize for Literature in 1986. In 1989, he was the recipient of the Heinrich Heine Prize, which is an award presented to persons whose works advance social and political progress and promote mutual understanding among peoples.

Frisch's plays have been performed regularly in Europe and the United States. In Germany, Austria, and Switzerland, they have been among the most frequently performed dramas by German-language playwrights. His works have been translated into most European languages, and several have been best sellers.

Biography

Max Rudolf Frisch was born in Zurich, Switzerland, on May 15, 1911, the son of a self-taught architect. After attending secondary school in Zurich between 1924 and 1930, he began studying German literature at the University of Zurich in 1931, at which time he also heard lectures on art history, philosophy, law, and theology.

When his father died in 1933, Frisch had to leave the university to earn a living. He became a freelance journalist and wrote for such newspapers as the *Neue Züricher Zeitung*. In 1933, Frisch traveled to Prague, Budapest, Dalmatia, Istanbul, and Greece, experiences that he used in his first novel, *Jürg Reinhart*, which was published in 1934. In 1936, thanks to the financial support of a friend, Frisch began to study architecture at the Institute of Technology in Zurich; he received his diploma in 1941. In 1942, he opened his own architect's office in Zurich. The highlight of his architectural career was his winning of a competition to build an open-air swimming pool complex in Zurich; this project, Freibad Letzigraben, completed in 1949, remains a tourist attraction in the early twenty-first century. In 1948, Frisch became acquainted with Bertolt Brecht, whose theories were to have an important influence on Frisch's drama.

Max Frisch. (AP/Wide World Photos)

Frisch, an inveterate traveler, wrote in *Tagebuch, 1946-1949* (1950; *Sketchbook, 1946-1949*, 1977) that we travel for two reasons: to meet others who do not assume that they know us intimately and to reexperience what is possible in life. Frisch traveled extensively in Europe and the United States and also visited Arab countries, Mexico, Cuba, the Soviet Union, Japan, and China. His experiences in the United States and Mexico are reflected especially in the novels *I'm Not Stiller* and *Homo Faber* and the short work *Montauk*. In 1954, Frisch gave up his architect's office and began to earn his living solely as a writer. He died of cancer on April 4, 1991.

Analysis

A central theme in Max Frisch's works is the problem of personal identity. The second of the Ten Commandments, "Thou shalt make no graven image," is a key to understanding his works. In an interview with the critic Horst Bienek in 1961, Frisch remarked that people invent plots for their lives, often defending these fictions at great sacrifice. According to Frisch, every "I" that expresses itself is a role. People not only invent roles for themselves but also form images of others; in turn, they suffer from the images others make of them. Frisch asserted that adopting a role or being forced into a role by the expectations of others limits a person's possibilities; instead of being exciting enigmas, people who are forced into roles are reduced to fixed and known entities.

In his fiction, Frisch explores the problem of identity within the framework of human relationships, especially marriage. Real love, according to Frisch, leaves room for both partners to grow and change. Most people, however, are guilty of forming images of their partners that cause their relationships to become static and to deteriorate into repetition, the enemy of growth. The story of Philemon and Baucis, as the narrator of *A Wilderness of Mirrors* relates it, portrays not a loving, loyal marriage, as in the legend, but the deadening boredom and triviality of marriage.

In Frisch's works, individuals are caught in a world of restrictions. Society requires that they conform, adopting definite social roles; society functions to preserve the status quo and is hostile to any notion of change. Frisch portrays society as rigid and banal; instead of growth, it offers only repetition and routine. He depicts those who conform to society as smug and self-righteous. Such people rarely question society's values, which have often deteriorated into clichés. The focus of Frisch's social criticism is his native Switzerland, but his comments can apply to modern society as a whole. An ideal society, according to Frisch, would allow people the freedom to be themselves, to lead authentic lives.

I'M NOT STILLER

The protagonist of *I'm Not Stiller* is a man who tries to escape from the role expected of him and acquire a new identity. (The novel opens with the narrator-protagonist asserting defiantly, "I'm not Stiller.") A man named James Larkin White is arrested at the Swiss border because he has a forged U.S. passport. The Swiss authorities believe that he is the sculptor Anatol Stiller, who disappeared six years previously. They decide to detain him until his identity can be established by court proceedings. In an effort to determine who the man really is, his lawyer, Dr. Bohnenblust, tells him to write down the plain, unvarnished truth about his life. The first and longest part of the novel consists of seven notebooks that Stiller/White writes in prison. The novel is written in diary form (a form favored by Frisch) and includes experiences, memories, and fantasies of the narrator-protagonist as well as descriptions of his life in prison. Also included are protocols of the various witnesses, which make Stiller/White aware of how others view him. The epilogue, written by the prosecutor, Rolf, who is sympathetic to Stiller/White, describes his life once he is released.

At the outset, it is clear that White really is Stiller. Six years earlier, Stiller had suddenly become dissatisfied with his life. Longing for a freer existence, he had fled from himself, his marriage, his profession, and his friends to the United States and Mexico. After failing in an attempt to commit suicide, he returns home, thinking that he is a new person. Even when the authorities confront him with people from his past, he stubbornly denies that he is Stiller. He refuses to be Stiller again—to play the same role, with all its imprisoning repetition. A previous attempt to flee from himself by fighting in the Spanish Civil War failed miserably. When his courage was actually tested, he surrendered in a cowardly fashion to the Fascists. Stiller is also disappointed in his artistic talent; it is not by chance that he is a sculptor, one who makes images of others. When Stiller/White is brought from prison to his old atelier, he destroys all of his sculptures in a futile attempt to break with his past.

Stiller's greatest failure, however, is as a husband and lover. Frisch depicts Stiller's painful marriage to the dancer Julika, a relationship based on a mutual fear of inadequacy. The frigid Julika finds the sexual act distasteful, and Stiller worries about his impotence. Both shy away from close contact with each other; each has formed a rigid image of the other. Julika becomes increasingly narcissistic and withdraws into her dancing—for her, a substitute for life—while Stiller becomes more egocentric. When Stiller is released from prison, they begin their marriage again. Instead of learning from their past, they are fated to make the same mistakes. Because they cannot talk to each other, Julika does not tell Stiller how seriously ill she is (she has tuberculosis), and when she dies, Stiller feels responsible for her death. Because he was discontented with his marriage, Stiller had an affair with Sibylle, Rolf's wife, before he fled to North America, yet his fear of impotence also undermined this relationship.

The defense counsel, Dr. Bohnenblust, typifies the philistine mentality from which Stiller fled. Bohnenblust never questions the values of society, as his long cliché-ridden speech in Stiller's atelier demonstrates. He is hostile to all new ideas. Social conformity and its concomitant safety, security, and comfort are all-important to him. Unlike Stiller, Bohnenblust does not want to confront himself or his values. He fears such a confrontation, for it would cause the disintegration of his social role. In the figure of Bohnenblust, Frisch shows that all that society can offer is the comfortable surface of reality, a life of suffocating normality that is detrimental to all growth.

Afraid of such a life, Stiller seeks freedom to be himself in the United States. The identity he adopts is not his true self, however; rather, it reflects what he would like to become. White is a man of action, an adventurer without scruples, the polar opposite of the tormented, weak, reflective Stiller. In prison, Stiller/White spins tales of his American experiences for the gullible jailer Knobel. He tells of murders he supposedly committed, tales of love, passion, and jealousy. These American stories—

which are partly fact but mostly fiction—indicate how determined Stiller is to cast off his old identity. Indeed, the stories reveal more about Stiller than do the actual facts of his life, reflecting Frisch's belief that an individual's life is more than the sum of facts.

Stiller fails, however, to escape from his old identity. The court finally declares that White is indeed Stiller, thereby sentencing him to be his old self. The epilogue, related by the prosecutor, depicts Stiller's retreat into the mountains with Julika, Julika's death, and Stiller's loneliness. Forced to accept himself, he has become resigned to his role. He has learned that he cannot escape from his past. The excerpt from Søren Kierkegaard's *Enten-Eller* (1843; *Either/Or*, 1944) that precedes the first part of the novel is an ironic commentary on Stiller's search for identity. Kierkegaard writes that when the passion of freedom awakens in a person, that person chooses his own identity and fights for this possession as if for his happiness, and this fight is his happiness. No matter how hard Stiller fights for his chosen identity, however, he cannot break free; he is forced to capitulate in the end. His fight to free himself has not brought him happiness.

Homo Faber

The first-person narrator-protagonist of Frisch's next novel, *Homo Faber*, is Walter Faber, a fifty-year-old Swiss engineer working for the United Nations Educational, Scientific, and Cultural Organization (UNESCO). Unlike Stiller, who wants to adopt a new identity, Faber is satisfied with himself until a series of events makes him confront his past life. The novel's subtitle, *A Report*, indicates that Faber intends to present his story objectively and factually; he eventually realizes, however, that facts alone cannot explain his experiences. The action of the novel, which lasts about four months, is divided into two parts: "First Stop," which Faber writes when he is ill in Caracas, confined to a hotel room, and "Second Stop," written while Faber is waiting for an operation for stomach cancer in an Athenian hospital.

Faber (literally, the novel's title means "man the maker") represents modern man, who defines himself according to technology. He wants to be in control, calmly observing and evaluating life rather than participating in it. The predictability of the technological world is his credo. Faber surrounds himself with technological gadgets; he lives in the United States, the epitome of technological civilization, and speaks the jargon of technology. He even draws his imagery for nature from technology, at one point likening the tributaries of the Mississippi River, which he sees from a plane, to trickles of molten brass or bronze.

The novel begins with Faber on a flight from New York to South America. The plane later develops engine trouble and is forced down in the Tamaulipas Desert. A traveling companion turns out to be Herbert, the brother of an old friend, Joachim, who had married Faber's former girlfriend, Hanna, twenty years ago. To pass the time until they are rescued, they play chess, Faber's favorite game because he can concentrate on the game and not pay attention to the other player. Faber fears becoming involved with others: He dislikes emotions because they are unpredictable. In the desert, without his technological gadgets, Faber feels lost. Because there is no electricity, he cannot use his electric razor; when his beard begins to sprout, he feels as though he is being devoured by nature. Until this point, Faber's world has consisted of routine and predictable events. Faber's rootlessness—the condition of modern humankind—is shown by the airports, hotels, and traveling that make up his world.

Suddenly and inexplicably, Faber decides to accompany Herbert to visit Joachim, who oversees a plantation in Guatemala. On their journey through Mexico and Guatemala, they become increasingly engulfed by the jungle. Nature here is uncontrolled and indifferent to human beings. The travelers experience the stench of fertility, blossoming decay, putrefaction, and vultures hovering overhead. When they reach their goal, they find that Joachim has committed suicide. Faber reacts with typical detachment, filming the corpse. The camera is his way of looking at reality; instead of experiencing life directly, he distances himself by means of the camera lens.

Nevertheless, his time in the jungle begins to change Faber. When he returns to New York and to his mistress, Ivy, with whom he has only a shallow relationship, he is restless. He decides to go to Europe by sea; on the boat he meets Sabeth, travels with her through Europe, and becomes her lover. He is attracted to her youth and beauty; his relationship with her seems to give him new life. Faber suppresses the mounting evidence that Sabeth is his daughter. He does not know that he has a child. When his relationship with Hanna broke up, she was expecting their child, but there was a tacit agreement that she would have an abortion. Because Faber prides himself on evaluating facts clearly, his self-deception and blindness are particularly ironic. After a night on the beach in Greece, Sabeth is bitten by a viper, falls, and later dies—not from the snakebite but from an undiagnosed skull fracture. In Athens, Faber meets Hanna, whom he has not seen for more than twenty years.

"Second Stop" begins with Faber trying, unsuccessfully, to resume his old life in New York. His experiences with Sabeth have shaken him loose from the sterility of his old life, and he increasingly criticizes the superficiality of the American way of life; the world, he says, is becoming an "Americanized vacuum." When he visits Herbert, who has taken over his brother's place on the plantation, he discovers that Herbert, too, has fallen under the spell of the jungle. Faber then makes a detour to Cuba, where for the first time he becomes alive to sensual beauty, experiencing a kind of euphoria, although he is still observing rather than participating in life. When he returns to Europe, he goes to Düsseldorf to show Joachim's firm the pictures of the latter's death. At this point, Faber becomes aware of the limitations of the camera; he realizes that it can record only the surface of life, because the film gives no hint of the stench of Joachim's corpse. Faber moves on to Zurich and finally to Hanna in Athens, where he is hospitalized.

Like Faber, Hanna shies away from personal involvement, as shown by her failed marriages. She wants to be a mother, not a wife and partner. Hanna, however, rejects the technological world. Technology, for her, is the knack of so arranging the world that one does not have to experience it. Life, she says, is not matter and cannot be mastered by technology. Hanna has, however, no positive concept to put in technology's place; instead, she takes refuge in the past, as her profession of piecing together fragments of ancient pottery suggests. Like Faber, she is divorced from life, one-sided, and egocentric.

Throughout the novel, the predictable world of technology is challenged. Faber always relies on statistics to explain events, yet statistics fail him. He quotes statistics to show the improbability of a plane crash, for example, but his plane is forced down; he quotes statistics to show how good his chances are for surviving the operation, but the outcome is not promising. Statistics do not help Faber understand and experience life. In fact, technology as a whole is not as reliable as Faber has assumed. Planes break down, his razor does not work, and, most strikingly, when Faber has to rush Sabeth to the hospital to be treated for the snakebite, technology deserts him altogether and he is forced to use a donkey cart.

Chance plays a large role in *Homo Faber*, further undermining Faber's belief in the predictability of the technological world. Faber's chance meeting with Herbert, for example, initiates his journey into the past. By chance he meets Sabeth, which results in his incestuous affair with his own daughter. The elements of the Oedipus myth of incest and blindness in the novel underscore the role of chance, suggesting the impossibility of controlling life through reason. The novel's story ends in Athens, the cradle of Western civilization—an ironic reminder of how modern technological humankind has divorced itself from its roots.

Although the novel does not end with Faber's death, the imagery used in the novel indicates that his operation is unsuccessful. In the jungle, the waiting vultures and the cycle of birth, decay, and death show the transience of human existence. The Mayan ruins in the jungle suggest not only personal death but the decline of whole civilizations as well. Faber's two meetings with his former professor foreshadow his own demise. The professor's face seems like a death's head, grotesque and emaciated. Later, Faber is shocked by his own emaciated appearance. When Faber is in Rome with Sabeth, they lie on a tomb on the Via Appia; when Faber is taking a bath in Hanna's apartment, the bathtub resembles a sarcophagus. All this imagery of decay, decline, and death mocks the technologist's hope, as Hanna says, of trying to live without death.

Faber's approaching death is, however, especially bitter because he has learned that his overvaluation of technology has prevented him from experiencing life. The man of action has become a man of reflection who is aware of beauty, sensuality, and nature and is ready to make personal commitments. On the threshold of a new way of life, he dies.

A Wilderness of Mirrors

The narrator-protagonist of *A Wilderness of Mirrors* is anonymous. All that the reader knows about him is that he loves a woman who has left him. To try to come to terms with his situation, the narrator creates a variety of fictions; he hopes to find an identity for himself that will help him articulate his experience. For a while, he identifies with the various roles he creates, but then he discards them. Whereas in *I'm Not Stiller*, Stiller/White pretends that his American stories are fact, the narrator of *A Wilderness of Mirrors* presents his creations unequivocally as fiction (he constantly repeats "I imagine"). During the course of the novel, the narrator varies the roles he has created and continually shifts his position among them. The novel, which has no continuous narrative or clear-cut divisions, consists of a number of stories and variations on the themes of love, marriage, jealousy, and identity.

The identities that the narrator invents are those of the art historian Enderlin, who seduces the actress Lila; Gantenbein, Lila's second husband; and Svoboda, Lila's first husband. The narrator imagines Enderlin undergoing an identity crisis: He has reached the pinnacle of success by being appointed to Harvard; at this moment, however, he suddenly loses confidence in his academic role and believes that he has become the prisoner of other people's expectations of him. Instead of accepting the appointment, he retreats into another role, that of a sick man. Like Faber, Enderlin is wary of personal involvement. Through him, the narrator tries on the role of the detached lover. In fact, Enderlin describes his seduction of Lila as if a stranger, and not he, were seducing her.

The narrator imagines Gantenbein playing the role of a blind man. Gantenbein even procures the necessary official documents to prove that he is blind and uses a cane and glasses, the blind man's props. Paradoxically, he pretends to be blind in order to see things clearly. Because people believe he is blind (even when he plays his part badly), they pretend to be what they would like to be, while Gantenbein can see them as they really are. Eventually this role dissatisfies him, however, as it is based on deceit. His supposed blindness allows him to give Lila her freedom—he can pretend not to see her affair with Enderlin. During the course of the novel, however, he is unable to keep his role of the detached, ironic observer; he becomes tormented with jealousy and confesses to Lila that he is not blind. The third role, Svoboda, is never a serious possibility for the narrator. Unlike Enderlin and Gantenbein, the architect Svoboda is a man of action, in the habit, like Faber, of controlling his environment. He is able to accept the breakdown of his marriage.

The importance of role-playing is stressed throughout the novel. In all three roles, the narrator creates models of possible human relationships, trying to find an answer for his own failed relationship. He discards each of the roles because none fits his own experience. The narrator also tells of a *Pechvogel* (an unlucky fellow) who is dogged by bad luck. When he wins a lottery, he begins to doubt himself, and his role threatens to disintegrate. Fortunately for him, he loses his winnings and can thus keep his role intact. Another example of role-playing is seen in the ambassador, who suddenly becomes aware that he is not the man people think he is. He decides to continue playing his role, keeping his knowledge of his real self secret. Unlike Enderlin, the ambassador does not collapse because of his new awareness.

Throughout *A Wilderness of Mirrors*, Frisch shows that human experience and values are too complex to be explained by statistics or mere facts. The world, however, sees the individual only in terms of biographical data, which do not reveal the whole truth about a person. According to Frisch, biography should include not only what a person has done but also what that individual might have done, not only what the person was or is but also what he or she might have been or might still become. The barman with whom the narrator is talking expresses the opinion that biography consists only of facts. The narrator, however, is fascinated not by what individuals have done but by what they might have done. He relates a story about meeting a German in the Alps during the war; he was convinced that the German was a spy. What he might have done (push the man over a cliff) is more vivid to him than what he actually did (accept an apple and watch the man descend).

The narrator tries on various roles like clothes, to see if they will fit. The fictions he invents, he remarks, are sketches for an ego. Unlike the desperate search for identity in *I'm Not Stiller*, however, the tone of *A Wilderness of Mirrors* is more ironic and cheerful. The conclusion, while it remains open, is more optimistic than the endings of the previous novels. Whereas Stiller is condemned to be himself and Faber is dying, the narrator's last words here, as he sits comfortably eating and drinking in Italy on a warm September day, are "I like life."

Frisch asserts in *A Wilderness of Mirrors* that human life is fulfilled or goes wrong in the individual ego, nowhere else. This viewpoint explains his protest against the masks people assume by choice or are forced to assume by society, taking on roles that limit their potential to lead fulfilling lives. Most of Frisch's protagonists who suffer crises of identity fail to live more fully. They allow societal restrictions to imprison them in routine and prevent them from freeing themselves. Frisch's works address the perennial human problems of identity, love, and death. They successfully capture the anxiety of people who are alienated from their partners, from their friends, from their professions, from the society in which they live—but most of all from themselves.

Jennifer Michaels

Other major works

SHORT FICTION: *Bin: Oder, Die Reise nach Peking*, 1945; *Wilhelm Tell für die Schule*, 1971.

PLAYS: *Nun singen sie wieder: Versuch eines Requiems*, pr. 1945 (*Now They Sing Again*, 1972); *Die chinesische Mauer*, pr. 1946 (second version pr., pb. 1955, third version pr. 1965, fourth version pr. 1972; *The Chinese Wall*, 1961); *Santa Cruz*, pr. 1946; *Als der Krieg zu Ende war*, pr., pb. 1949 (*When the War Was Over*, 1967); *Graf Öderland*, pr., pb. 1951 (second version pr. 1956, third version pr. 1961; *Count Oederland*, 1962); *Biedermann und die Brandstifter*, pr., pb. 1958 (*The Firebugs*, 1959; also known as *The Fire Raisers*, 1962); *Don Juan: Oder, Die Liebe zur Geometrie*, pr., pb. 1953 (*Don Juan: Or, The Love of Geometry*, 1967); *Die grosse Wut des Philipp Hotz*, pr., pb. 1958 (*The Great Fury of Philip Hotz*, 1962); *Andorra*, pr., pb. 1961 (English translation, 1963); *Three Plays*, 1962; *Biografie*, pb. 1967 (*Biography*, 1969); *Three Plays*, 1967; *Four Plays*, 1969; *Triptychon: Drei szenische Bilder*, pb. 1978 (pr. 1979 in French, pr. 1981 in German; *Triptych*, 1981); *Three Plays*, 1992.

RADIO PLAY: *Biedermann und die Brandstifter*, 1953.

NONFICTION: *Tagebuch, 1946-1949*, 1950 (*Sketchbook, 1946-1949*, 1977); *Tagebuch, 1966-1971*, 1972 (*Sketchbook, 1966-1971*, 1974); *Dienstbüchlein*, 1974; *Der Briefwechsel: Max Frisch, Uwe Johnson, 1964-1983*, 1999; *Die Briefwechsel mit Carl Jacob Burckhardt und Max Frisch*, 2000.

MISCELLANEOUS: *Gesammelte Werke in zeitlicher Folge*, 1976 (6 volumes); *Novels, Plays, Essays*, 1989.

Bibliography

Brombert, Victor. "Max Frisch: The Courage of Failure." In *In Praise of Antiheroes: Figures and Themes in Modern European Literature, 1830-1980*. Chicago: University of Chicago Press, 1999. Addresses the antiheroes in Frisch's work as part of a larger discussion of the development of the antihero in European literature. Explains how and why the antihero—a "perturber and disturber"—became a common fictional character.

Butler, Michael. "Identity and Authenticity in Swiss and Austrian Novels of the Postwar Era: Max Frisch and Peter Handke." In *The Cambridge Companion to the Modern German Novel*, edited by Graham Bartram. New York: Cambridge University Press, 2004. Frisch's novels are among the works examined in this introductory survey of German-language novels from the late nineteenth and early twentieth centuries. Includes chronology and bibliography.

_______. *The Novels of Max Frisch*. London: O. Wolff, 1976. A scholar who has written extensively about Frisch provides a readable account and analysis of Frisch's novels (through *Montauk*). Includes bibliography and index.

Demetz, Peter. "Max Frisch: The Last Romantic." In *After the Fires: Recent Writing in the Germanies, Austria, and Switzerland*. San Diego, Calif.: Harcourt Brace Jovanovich, 1986. Discusses Frisch within the context of contemporary German-language literature. Broad overview dictates a focus on essentials and high points, providing an excellent introduction and orientation to major aspects of Frisch's career and life.

Köpke, Wulf. *Understanding Max Frisch*. Columbia: University of South Carolina Press, 1991. Explores the structure, themes, character, and style of Frisch's novels and other works as well as their social and political background. Includes bibliography and index.

Paver, Chloe E. M. "Max Frisch: *Mein Name sei Gantenbein*." In *Narrative and Fantasy in the Post-*

war German Novel: A Study of Novels by Johnson, Frisch, Wolf, Becker, and Grass*. New York: Oxford University Press, 1999. Closely analyzes *A Wilderness of Mirrors* as part of an examination of works by Frisch and four other German-language authors. Demonstrates how these writers create stories that ordinary people tell about themselves and their former lives.

Probst, Gerhard F., and Jay F. Bodine, eds. *Perspectives on Max Frisch*. Lexington: University Press of Kentucky, 1982. Collection of essays offers criticism and interpretations of Frisch's life and works, including contributions analyzing the novels *Montauk, A Wilderness of Mirrors*, and *I'm Not Stiller*. Includes bibliography.

Reschke, Claus. *Life as a Man: Contemporary Male-Female Relationships in the Novels of Max Frisch*. New York: Peter Lang, 1990. Examines the psychology of gender roles in Frisch's works, paying special attention to *I'm Not Stiller, Homo Faber, Wilderness of Mirrors*, and *Montauk*. Includes bibliography and index.

Weisstein, Ulrich. *Max Frisch*. New York: Twayne, 1967. Provides a good introductory biographical discussion of Frisch and interpretations of his works.

White, Alfred D. *Max Frisch, the Reluctant Modernist*. Lewiston, N.Y.: Edwin Mellen Press, 1995. Chronological examination of Frisch's life and works argues that Frisch was a conservative regarding aesthetic and political issues. Includes an index of persons, places, concepts, and works by Frisch and a bibliography.

CARLOS FUENTES

Born: Panama City, Panama; November 11, 1928
Also known as: Carlos Fuentes Macías

Principal long fiction

La región más transparente, 1958 (*Where the Air Is Clear*, 1960)
Las buenas conciencias, 1959 (*The Good Conscience*, 1961)
Aura, 1962 (novella; English translation, 1965)
La muerte de Artemio Cruz, 1962 (*The Death of Artemio Cruz*, 1964)
Cambio de piel, 1967 (*A Change of Skin*, 1968)
Zona sagrada, 1967 (novella; *Holy Place*, 1972)
Cumpleaños, 1969 (novella)
Terra nostra, 1975 (English translation, 1976)
La cabeza de la hidra, 1978 (*The Hydra Head*, 1978)
Una familia lejana, 1980 (*Distant Relations*, 1982)
Gringo viejo, 1985 (*The Old Gringo*, 1985)
Cristóbal nonato, 1987 (*Christopher Unborn*, 1989)
La campaña, 1990 (*The Campaign*, 1991)
Diana: O, La Cazadora Solitaria, 1994 (*Diana, the Goddess Who Hunts Alone*, 1995)
Los años con Laura Díaz, 1999 (*The Years with Laura Diaz*, 2000)
Instinto de Inez, 2001 (*Inez*, 2002)
La silla del águila, 2003 (*The Eagle's Throne*, 2006)
La voluntad y la fortuna, 2008

Other literary forms

In addition to his work as a novelist, Carlos Fuentes (FWAYN-tays) has cultivated short fiction throughout his career. His earliest work was a collection of short stories, *Los días enmascarados* (1954; the masked days); this volume and subsequent collections such as *Cantar de ciegos* (1964; songs of the blind) and *Agua quemada* (1980; *Burnt Water*, 1980) have been critically acclaimed. (*Burnt Water*, Fuentes's first short-story collection to be translated into English, contains stories published in earlier collections as well as in *Agua quemada*.) The subjects of these stories are reminiscent of his novels. They are set in contemporary Mexico and are characterized by social and psychological realism. Several stories feature the interpenetration of the real and the fantastic, so much a part of the author's longer fiction. In *La frontera de cristal* (1995; *The Crystal Frontier*, 1997) Fuentes explores in nine fictional stories the relationship gap that has occurred between Mexico and the United States as well as the internal problems that have pushed many Mexicans to emigrate to the United States. In *El naranjo: O, Los círculos del tiempo* (1993; *The Orange Tree*, 1994), a collection of novellas, Fuentes explores the creation of the Mexican culture as a result of language choice.

Fuentes has also written several plays. In 1970, he published *El tuerto es rey* (the blind man is king) and *Todos los gatos son pardos* (all cats are gray). The latter work dramatizes the author's fascination with the subject of the Conquest of Mexico and portrays Hernán Cortés and other historical figures. *Orquídeas a la luz de la luna* (*Orchids in the Moonlight*), which premiered at Harvard University in 1982, was Fuentes's first play produced in the United States.

Achievements

Carlos Fuentes is known the world over as one of Latin America's premier novelists and intellectuals. He has earned this reputation through involvement in international affairs and prodigious creative activity. Fuentes has produced a broad spectrum of literary works in several genres that convey a sense of Mexican life, past and present. He has projected the image of Mexico by means of extremely varied treatments in his works, from the historical and legendary backgrounds of the Spanish Conquest in *Terra Nostra* to the analysis of contemporary social reality and the profound aftershocks of the Mexican Revolution in *The Death of Artemio Cruz*. While Fuentes has manifested his concern for the historical and social realities of Mexico, he has also experimented with fantastic fiction in his short stories and the novella *Aura*, and he has evoked the voluptuousness of decadent settings in *Holy Place*.

In view of Fuentes's achievements in capturing and imagining the myriad faces of Mexican reality, it is hardly any wonder that his literary production must be analyzed from several critical stances. Fuentes has resisted any narrow categorization of his work with the dictum "Don't classify me, read me." Fuentes is one of Latin America's most popular novelists, and his works are eagerly awaited by critics. He is considered to be on the same level with such luminaries of Latin American literature as Mario Vargas Llosa and Gabriel García Márquez in his desire to produce the "total novel" that epitomizes the aspirations and experiences of humankind.

Fuentes has been in the forefront of Mexican letters for decades. As a young writer in the 1950's, he was a cofounder of the prestigious *Revista mexicana de literatura* (Mexican literary review). In 1972, he was elected to the Colegio Nacional of Mexico. He was a fellow at the Woodrow Wilson Center for Scholars in 1974. From 1975 to 1977, Fuentes served as Mexican ambassador to France. Fuentes received an honorary doctoral degree from Harvard University in 1983 and one from Cambridge University in 1987.

The long list of literary prizes that Fuentes has received includes the Biblioteca Breve Award for *A Change of Skin* in 1967; the Villaurrutia Prize, one of Mexico's most important literary awards, for *Terra Nostra* in 1976, and the Venezuelan Rómulo Gallegos Award in 1977 for the same novel; the prestigious Spanish Miguel de Cervantes Prize in 1987; the Rubén Darío Award and the New York City National Arts Club Medal of Honor in 1988; and the Instituto Italo-Latino Americano Award for *The Old Gringo* in 1989. His literary production as a whole was recognized with the Alfonso Reyes Award in 1979 and the National Literature Prize in Mexico in 1984. In 1991, Fuentes was honored with the University of Chile's Presidents Medal, and in 1994 he received the Principe de Asturias Award, the International Grizane Cavor Award, and the Picasso Prize, awarded by the United Nations Educational, Scientific, and Cultural Organization (UNESCO). In 2008, Fuentes became the first recipient of Spain's new International Don Quijote Prize in recognition of his outstanding career.

Biography

Even though Carlos Fuentes has described himself as a product of "petit bourgeois stock," there is nothing common about him. His father was a diplomat, an attaché to the Mexican legation, when he was born. At the age of four, Fuentes learned English in Washington, D.C., where his father served at the Mexican embassy. Oddly enough, the dawning of Fuentes's consciousness of Mexico occurred in the United States. He credits his father with having created a fantasy of his homeland, a "non-existent country invented in order to nourish the imagination of yet another land of fiction, a land of Oz with a green cactus road." As a teenager, Fuentes began to travel on his own. He studied the politics, economics, and society of Spanish America, and he developed a sympathy for socialism that he has fervently maintained ever since. Fuentes's interest in socialism blossomed in Chile, especially after he learned about Pablo Neruda, whose poetry had already become the anthem of the working person.

While living in Santiago, Fuentes attended The Grange, the Chilean capital's bilingual British school, where he cultivated an appreciation of classical and modern writers. While enrolled there, he began to think about becoming a writer, he has recalled, in order to "show himself that his Mexican identity was real." He started to read the Spanish masters of the Golden Age, and he contributed short stories, written in Spanish, to school magazines. After a six-month stay in Buenos Aires, where he read the great works of Argentine literature, he finally returned to Mexico. As a young but mature man, imbued from afar with the myths of his homeland, Fuentes was finally struck by the contrasts between Mexico and more urbane centers of civilization where he had lived. The Mexico that has become the background of his fiction is a land that still bears the scars of the Mexican Revolution, where the promises of progress clash head-on with the problems of an impoverished indigenous population, and where tangible reality is forever overshadowed by the persistence of the past.

After he developed an ample body of writing on modern Mexico, Fuentes, a combative essayist and crusader against Hispanic dependence on foreign interests, trained his sights on the United States. On numerous occasions, he has criticized American military and economic involvement in Latin America, and like many other writers from Latin America, he has suffered accordingly. To prevent him from visiting the United States, the Immigration and Naturalization Service branded Fuentes an "undesirable alien"—a ban eventually lifted in response to aroused public opinion. Fuentes has become a spokesman for the preservation of Mexican—and, by extension, Latin American—cultural diversity, arguing the need for an alternative to the choices offered by the world's two superpowers. He has advocated the coexistence of ancient and modern, indigenous and imported traditions in the Hispanic world as an antidote to powerful foreign influences.

Mexican president Luis Echeverría rewarded Fuentes's interest in improving Mexico's international relations by naming him ambassador to France in 1975, a post he filled until 1977. Since retiring from his diplomatic post, Fuentes has lived in the United States, where he is in great demand on university campuses and at professional meetings as an eminent scholar and stimulating lecturer.

Carlos Fuentes. (Getty Images)

Analysis

Few confrontations in history have been more dramatic or devastating than that between Hernán Cortés and Montezuma II. When the conquistador, Cortés, met the Aztec monarch, Montezuma, two calendars, two worldviews, and two psychologies collided. The Aztec's cyclic concept of catastrophism, which held that the earth and its creatures must die and be reborn every fifty-two years, came into direct conflict with the European vision of linear time and the notion of progress. The Machiavellian Spaniard was perceived by the Aztecs as a god who had returned to his homeland from the East, as prophesied in native mythology. On the other hand, Cortés, with fine irony, depicted Montezuma as a simple and naïve man torn by the workings of superstition, a man whose initiative and aggression against a potential enemy were blocked first by shock and then by curiosity about the mortal who was to become his master. Remote as they seem, these events from sixteenth century Mexico serve as background for the works of Carlos Fuentes. Fuentes claims kinship to both great patriarchs of Mexico's past from biological and cultural standpoints, and the key to their relationship is the notion of diverse worlds in collision, which characterized the Spanish Conquest and which the modern Mexican has assimilated in his works.

To survey the Mexico of Carlos Fuentes is to come in contact with a land of dizzying contrasts and violent conflicts. Fuentes's Mexico is a timeless realm where the steamy and violent past of indigenous Tenochtitlán is evident in a sleazy and materialistic Mexico City built on the ruins of ancient temples. As a theoretician of the modern Latin American novel, Fuentes has advocated such marvelous juxtapositions in fiction. For Fuentes, the novel's continued life depends on a new concept of reality that accommodates a mythic substratum beneath everyday experience. The reader of Fuentes's novels observes a complex Mexican reality in which the barrier between past and present has eroded.

TERRA NOSTRA

Fuentes's reorganization of time is the principal structural element of his masterpiece, *Terra Nostra*. This massive, Byzantine work, an ambitious blend of history and fiction, is indeed nothing less than a compendium of Western civilization, from the Creation to the Apocalypse. In a narrower sense, the focus of the work is Hispanic civilization and the historical background of the epoch of discovery and conquest. In keeping with Fuentes's goals for fiction, the work succeeds in erasing temporal and spatial boundaries and becomes a Mexican *Finnegans Wake* (James Joyce, 1939)—timeless, circular, and meticulously constructed.

In the formal divisions of the work, Fuentes places the reader at the center of a maelstrom of times and places. The novel is divided into three sections, "The Old World," "The New World," and "The Next World." Within "The Old World," time abruptly shifts from twentieth century Paris to sixteenth century Spain. Fuentes intends this descent into the past to resemble an excursion into the wellsprings of Hispanic culture. The reader emerges in the Spain of Philip II, the monarch who built the Escorial. The erection in this novel of the mausoleum by El Señor, the embodiment of the Spanish monarch, is a metaphor of Philip's (and, by extension, Spain's) mad obsession with halting the passage of time. It is here that El Señor holes up and futilely resists change.

The futility of this scheme surfaces in the second part of the novel, which chronicles the discovery and conquest of the New World. The promise of new lands and a new vision of time fire the imagination of the Old World. "The Ancient," an indigenous patriarch reminiscent of Montezuma, captures this vision in his retelling of a tribal legend:

> Between life and death there is no destiny except memory. Memory weaves the destiny of the world. People perish. Suns succeed suns. Cities fall. Power passes from hand to hand. Princes collapse along with the crumbling stone of their palaces abandoned to the fury of fire, tempest and invading jungle. One time ends and another begins. Only memory keeps death alive, and those who must die know it. The end of memory is the end of the world.

This new reckoning of time is an embodiment of perpetual change that threatens the stagnation of the Old World in the novel. El Señor, the defender of temporal paralysis, recoils at the threat in the last part of the novel and ultimately fails to freeze Hispanic tradition within the confines of the sixteenth century. His decree that the New World, with its nonlinear passage of time, does not exist is repudiated in an exuberant celebration of change in the novel's conclusion, when the action returns to Paris in the twentieth century.

In addition to the abrupt shifts in time and space that he employs in a particularly radical form in *Terra Nos-*

tra, Fuentes exploits throughout his fiction other modern literary techniques, such as hallucinatory imagery, stream of consciousness, interior monologue, and numerous devices adapted from the cinema, including flashback, crosscutting, fades, and multiple points of view. When one considers that the twentieth century was the "age of film," it is not surprising that Fuentes's works display a thoroughgoing affinity with cinema. In particular, *Aura*, *Holy Place*, *Distant Relations*, and *The Death of Artemio Cruz* reveal that Fuentes's vision of modern Mexico is perceived through the camera's eye.

AURA

The theme of *Aura*, one of Fuentes's early novels, is the persistence of the past. Fuentes communicates this theme by means of overlaying, as in cinematographic projections, images of light on darkness and old identities on youthful characters. The climax of the story features an astounding and erotic union of personalities as his characters from the twentieth century embody personalities of the nineteenth.

Appropriately enough, the catalyst of this experiment in time is a historian, Felipe Montero, a young man dedicated to preserving the past. Montero's ambition is to sum up the chronicles of the discoverers and conquistadores in the New World, but financial need forces him to undertake a more modest project. He agrees to edit and publish the papers of a Mexican general who has been dead since the beginning of the twentieth century. Consuelo, the general's widow, orders Felipe to live in the ancestral mansion, and he must even learn to write in the style of the general in order to complete the assignment. Surrounded by relics of the past, then, Felipe is gradually seduced by them. What adds ardor to the historian's undertaking is Felipe's discovery of Aura, Consuelo's young niece and companion. During the course of the novel, Felipe learns that Aura is indeed an "aura" of Consuelo's lost youth, a spiritual emanation of the past who is willed into existence to capture Consuelo's early love for the general.

Through a variety of cinematic techniques such as close-ups and montage, Fuentes has the illusion of Aura's presence deceive Montero into believing that she is real. The purpose of this deceit is to render, in a visual way, the author's concept of simultaneity. When Felipe observes how the two women seem to mimic each other at a distance, their separate identities are mirror images of each other. For Fuentes, the two women's divergent personas are surface manifestations of an underlying unity. Fuentes's experiment in cinematic fiction is complete when Felipe stares at Aura's image in photographs from the nineteenth century and discovers his own face superimposed on the image of the general. At the end of the novel, Consuelo has succeeded in uniting past and present in her double identity and in that of Felipe. He now embodies the spirit and flesh of the deceased general.

DISTANT RELATIONS

In *Distant Relations* Fuentes carries the cinematic overlaying of past and present one step further than he does in *Aura*. Fuentes acknowledges his debt to the world of film when he dedicates the novel to the Spanish director Luis Buñuel, with whom he collaborated on a screenplay. In addition to the visual impressions of film in this novel, Fuentes evokes the auditory effect of overdubbing in the recurrent citation of lines from Jules Supervielle's poem "La Chambre Voisine" (the adjoining room). The poem sets the scene for the juxtaposition of several settings, each with its own temporal reality and cast of characters; Fuentes intertwines the various plots that correspond to the different settings so that the barriers of time and space dissolve.

The title of this novel refers to the phenomenon of secret correspondences between people and to their need to bridge the distances that alienate them from one another. The distant relations (or, more literally from the Spanish, "distant family") of the title are a French count, a Mexican archaeologist, and a wealthy Frenchman. Fuentes suggests the relationship of the latter two in his choice of a common family name, Heredia. The choice is most fortuitous because it refers to the Spanish word *herencia* (inheritance) and, more significant, to two poets of the nineteenth century, one French, José Maria de Hérédia, and the other Cuban, José Maréa Heredia, who were cousins. It is curious, then, that Fuentes cites verses from the French Hérédia's *Les Trophées* (1893; English translation, 1897) but makes no reference to the work of the Cuban Heredia (who spent several years of his life in Mexico). An apt reference might have been taken from the Cuban's narrative poem "En el teocalli de Cholula" (upon the temple at Cholula). Heredia's poem, like Fuentes's novel, features a surrealistic clashing of realities that leap across the centuries. The narrator of the poem experiences a vivid hallucination of an Aztec human sacrifice that occurred before the arrival of Cortés. Fuentes engages in this kind of novelistic archaeology in *Distant Relations* when the count's past and the pasts of the two Heredias come together.

HOLY PLACE

A more explicit fascination with film imagery forms the basis for Fuentes's bizarre novel *Holy Place*. The novel claims that filmmaking creates icons that rival those of classical mythology. One case in point is the charismatic Mexican actor Claudia Nervo. She is depicted as a twentieth century siren who lures men to their doom. Her son, Guillermo (affectionately called Mito, a name derived from the diminutive Guillermito and that also means "myth"), is neurotically attracted to her as well. More a decadent Des Esseintes from the pages of Joris-Karl Huysmans's *À Rebours* (1884; *Against the Grain*, 1922) than a Ulysses, he surrounds himself with voluptuous furnishings from the belle époque. This is his personal "sacred zone," his enchanted grotto and refuge, which he needs as an antidote for his mother's rejection.

In the course of the novel, Fuentes analyzes the thralldom exercised by film images on spectators and the actors themselves. For example, Guillermo pathetically tries to possess his mother by immersing himself in her old films. In this regard, *Holy Place* deftly captures the hypnotic attraction of films as they create a personal fantasy world for Guillermo, provide an escape from chronological time for him, and indelibly preserve his hallucinatory fantasies in a mythological space.

THE DEATH OF ARTEMIO CRUZ

Perhaps the most striking example of cinema's influence on Fuentes's work is *The Death of Artemio Cruz*. Written early in his career, it is one of his most successful novels from a technical and thematic standpoint and is widely regarded as a seminal work of modern Spanish American literature. The novel owes some of its fragmented temporal structure and much of its theme of the deterioration of modern life to Orson Welles's landmark film *Citizen Kane* (1941). Through the use of such techniques as close-up, flashback, deep focus (a technique that Welles pioneered in *Citizen Kane*), crosscutting, and recurrent symbolic motifs, Fuentes's novel matches the visual appeal of Welles's cinematographic masterpiece, and it should be read and understood as a motion picture in prose.

Fuentes has discussed his indebtedness to films in general and to Welles in particular in an interview published in the Winter, 1981, issue of *The Paris Review*:

> I'm a great moviegoer. The greatest day in my life as a child was when I was ten and my father took me to New York City to see the World's Fair and *Citizen Kane*. And that struck me in the middle of my imagination and never left me. Since that moment, I've always lived with the ghost of *Citizen Kane*. There are few other great movies which I am conscious of when I write.

Welles's influence on Fuentes can be seen throughout *The Death of Artemio Cruz*, in characterization, themes, and filmic techniques.

Artemio Cruz is a Mexican Citizen Kane in several basic respects. Fuentes chronicles Cruz's rise from an impoverished childhood on the periphery of Mexican society to the heights of power in Mexico City. The mature Artemio becomes the prime mover of a financial empire with holdings in publishing, real estate, banking, and mining. Similarly, Kane, a New York power broker with interests in mining, publishing, real estate, and manufacturing, traces his origins to a simple family in Colorado. During the course of their lives, both men reverse their beliefs from a proletarian admiration for the common person to an authoritarianism that ultimately destroys their relationships with family and friends. Furthermore, their opportunism and cynicism mirror the moral decay of their times. The degeneration of moral values finds its greatest manifestation in the failure of their respective newspapers to print the truth. In this regard, the most salient feature of their resemblance is their manipulation of the press. Both men, thinly veiled replicas of William Randolph Hearst, are publishers who resort to slander for personal gain and to yellow journalism to support their right-wing political causes.

In addition to the characterization of his protagonist, Fuentes borrows various film techniques from *Citizen Kane*. This adaptation of material from the film adds to the novel's complexity and visual richness. For example, one of the most successful reflections of the film is the novel's tightly knit fabric of fragmentary reminiscences. In *Citizen Kane*, Welles breaks up the linear narrative into overlapping vignettes. Here, newsreel footage and interviews with the people who knew Kane best flesh out the portrait of the vulnerable man behind the image of grandeur. Kane's dying word, "rosebud," forces the editors of the newsreel to discover some unifying quality in Kane's life, and it is the quest for the meaning of "rosebud" that serves as the focus of the film. Artemio's conscious and unconscious alternations among past, present, and future tenses and his strange obsession with his son Lorenzo offer a fragmentary record of his life. By deciphering the mysterious relationships among these fragments, deftly scattered throughout the novel, the reader reconstructs the world of Artemio Cruz.

A particularly striking counterpart to Welles's rosebud motif is the recurrent reference to Lorenzo, Artemio's only son. Artemio repeatedly recalls the scene when he and Lorenzo rode on horseback through the hacienda in Vera Cruz near his birthplace. Lorenzo confesses that he must leave Mexico to fight for the Republican cause in Spain. This is their last time together because, as the reader learns in another fragment, Lorenzo dies in the Spanish Civil War. Although the significance of this scene becomes clear only gradually, references to Artemio's last meeting with Lorenzo symbolize a tragic defeat in the same way "rosebud" signifies Kane's disillusionment and his exile from his family. In Lorenzo, Artemio might have been able to combine his own instinct for survival with his son's idealism to produce a morally correct life; with Lorenzo's death, this opportunity is forever lost. Both Kane and Artemio immerse themselves in painful memories that they masochistically cultivate to the end of their lives.

The novel also captures the visual starkness of the film in passages that depict characters and situations through a camera's eye, highlighting grotesque detail and situations through close-ups and other pictorial techniques. For example, Welles's stumbling, bloated Charles Foster Kane is mirrored in Artemio Cruz, described as a walking mummy at his last New Year's Eve party. Cruz's fall from greatness—a counterpart to Kane's collapse during the opening scenes of the film—is captured in a clinical description of his decaying body in close-up: "He must sense this odor of dead scales, of vomit and blood; he must look at this caved-in chest, this matted gray beard, these waxy ears, this fluid oozing from his nose, this dry spit on his lips and chin, these wandering eyes that must attempt another glance."

Fuentes reasserts the cinematographic close-up throughout the novel by means of a tight focus on Cruz in direct descriptions reflected in mirrors. Mirrors and reflections are useful for the narrator to witness his own physical deterioration and for the author to practice his virtuosity in manipulating "camera angles" for special effects. Early in the novel, the prosperous Artemio glances in a storefront window to straighten his tie. What he sees is his reflection, "a man identical to himself but so distant, he also was adjusting his tie, with the same fingers stained with nicotine, the same suit, but colorless." Cruz contemplates his image at a distance, as though he were watching a film of himself. In the reflection—as distant as images on a film screen—he sees himself surrounded by beggars and vendors whom he ignores. Through this cinematographic technique, Fuentes projects the image of a solitary Artemio Cruz, cast in the mold of Charles Kane, divorced from the common folk and insensitive to their suffering.

Other mirror images in the novel emphasize the theme of alienation and disintegration of the protagonist, particularly in the hospital scenes where Cruz stares at his twin image in the fragmented mirrors of his wife's and daughter's purses. The doubling of Artemio in mirror images has its source in one of the most important scenes in *Citizen Kane*, a scene that associates the multiple images of the protagonist with a corresponding fragmentation of his personality. At the end of the film, after his second wife leaves him, Kane breaks up her bedroom, smashing pictures and china and yanking down draperies. From the rubble of her belongings, he picks up a small glass ball that, when shaken, produces within it a miniature snowstorm around a white rose. He utters the word "rosebud" and then strolls leisurely from the room, his face empty of turmoil. Kane then passes between two facing mirrors that reflect his image in infinite series. This scene indicates the extent of Kane's deterioration as he seems to put on a mask of indifference and serenity while he feels his inner self tossed about by failure.

Cruz similarly stands between such facing mirrors in a key scene following the longest fragment of the novel, which deals with Artemio's imprisonment during the Mexican Revolution. Captured by Pancho Villa's forces, Cruz, Gonzalo Bernal (the brother of the woman Cruz will later marry), and his friend Tobias, a Yaqui Indian, face execution by a firing squad. Cruz alone survives by giving false information to his captors. The mirror scene following this episode sums up Artemio's instinct for survival, the aspect of his personality that has won out over whatever charitable impulses he may have had earlier in his life. Artemio now wears the impassible mask of indifference to others, Kane's frozen persona in the mirrors:

> to recognize yourself; to recognize the rest and let them recognize you: and to know that you oppose each individual, because each individual is yet another obstacle to reach your goal: you will choose, in order to survive you will choose, you will choose from among the infinite mirrors one alone, one alone which will reflect you irrevocably, that will cast a black shadow on the other mirrors, you will shatter them rather than surrender.

Fuentes offsets the tight focus in these mirror close-ups with long shots or general establishing shots elsewhere in the novel. His technique of capturing several planes of action occurring simultaneously has its origin in the deep focus of *Citizen Kane*, where this technique is used to juxtapose several characters and situations that impinge on one another. Perhaps the most remarkable example of deep focus in the film shows Charles Kane's parents arranging for their son's enrollment in a boarding school. Framed by the window in the center of the screen, the young Charles plays outside in the snow with his Rosebud sled, oblivious to events indoors before the camera. In a tight shot, with Charles still in focus, his mother signs the power of attorney that establishes a trust fund for him and that symbolizes his entry into high society. Juxtaposed here are the innocent boy and his parents, who prepare his ticket to the good life. The two planes of action make a harsh visual statement about power. Charles, seen from a distance, is surrounded and overwhelmed by his elders and their financial dealings. Later in the film, in another example of deep focus, a gigantic Kane, in the foreground, dwarfs all the other characters in the scene, emblematic of his monumental power.

Fuentes's equivalent of deep focus can be found throughout the novel in fragments that juxtapose characters and situations. One of these fragments depicts Artemio's arrival at the hacienda of Gamaliel Bernal. A masterful juxtaposition of narrative planes focuses on Artemio—the survivor—telling the family of Gonzalo Bernal how their loved one perished in the Villista execution. Crosscutting from Artemio's explanation at the dinner table to his arrival in town and then to his meeting Gamaliel and Catalina Bernal, Fuentes superimposes several moments in time and space in a single scene. The reader thus sees, in the foreground, the conniving Artemio as he ingratiates himself with the Bernal family; in the background, his arrival in Puebla and the rooting out of information about the Bernals; and in the middle ground, the sumptuous furnishings that Artemio will soon possess.

Here, Fuentes achieves effects of simultaneity that compel the reader/spectator to superimpose the planes of action and modify each event in the light of what precedes and what follows it. Such is the effect of other fragments in the novel that depict Artemio's rise to power after he marries Catalina and after he takes over the hacienda after Gamaliel's death. In a scene that depicts Artemio's campaign for political office, he and Catalina ride their buggy through the dusty countryside. They come upon a procession of religious zealots, *penitentes*, who impede their passage. As the narrator describes the grotesque physical deformities of the *penitentes* and their mortification of themselves, he juxtaposes their bloody parade to the religious sanctuary with Artemio's exalted and indifferent ride through their seething masses. The various planes of action appear linked for ironic purposes. In the background, the dust of the arid fields mixes with the clouds of dust raised by the buggy and that of the *penitentes*. The cinematic impact of this scene rivals that of similar settings in Mariano Azuela's photographic *Los de Abajo* (1916; *The Underdogs*, 1929). In the middle ground, the sincerity of the zealots, symbolized by their bloody footprints, is counterbalanced by the cynicism of Artemio's political campaign, which is motivated by hunger for power alone.

Fuentes has said that in all of his works, he offers Mexicans "a mirror in which they can see how they look, how they act, in a country which is a masked country."

Fuentes offers Mexicans more than a mirror, however, for his fiction cinematically projects the spectacle of Mexican life and history on a broad screen in order to preserve and highlight the past.

La voluntad y la fortuna

Fuentes has stated that his 2008 coming-of-age novel *La voluntad y la fortuna* is his best novel so far. Written in a poetical and clean prose, it closes the historical cycle the author began fifty years before with *Where the Air Is Clear*. In *La voluntad y la fortuna*, Fuentes once more turns his eyes toward Mexico and its history, but this time it is contemporary history, the history of a "narco-nation." Drawing from Mexico's bloody reality, Fuentes expresses his preoccupation with the conflict between the Mexican state and the drug mafia, a conflict that has escalated almost into civil war.

To re-create this tragedy, Fuentes uses the biblical story of Cain and Abel in the form of the story of the rivalry between Josue Nadal and his friend Jerico. In their youth, Josue and Jerico agreed that they would not to belong to the masses, that they would make a difference. The competition between them starts as they grow up and they begin to keep secrets from each other. They contend for the love of Asunta Jordan—a dark, predatory woman and principal assistant to Max Monroy, the richest man in Mexico—and for political and economical connections. The novel's tragedy resembles that of Cain and Abel, but it is not an archetypical tragedy, in which the hero dies to cleanse his faults; rather, in this tragedy, both men betray each other.

The novel begins at a beach in Acapulco, on the coast of the state of Guerrero, in the Mexican Pacific. The severed head of Josue lies on the sand afraid of being seen by passersby because of its horrific appearance. The narrator—the head—introduces the reader to the story, tells about the violent events that led to his death, and reflects on his condition as a head without his corpse and about the possibility of having a soul in this condition. Josue describes himself as a twenty-nine-year-old, dark-skinned man who just happens to be the one thousandth person decapitated this year alone in Mexico.

As in *The Years with Laura Diaz* and *Instinto de Inéz*, in this novel Fuentes revisits one of his main philosophical veins through the character of Concepcion, the matriarch. This novel proposes that men contend for power when in reality power belongs to women. Among the other characters are Filopater, the rebellious priest; Antonio Sangines, the lawyer who acts as intermediary between the state and the business; and Miguel Aparecido, who is incarcerated on his own will. The head of Josue knows that the nation of Mexico cannot offer jobs, food, or education to even half of its population. He knows that is why crime reigns and, as if that were not enough, he also knows that evil is celebrated as the greater good, as the natural consequence of will and fortune.

Howard Fraser; Daniel Altamiranda
Updated by Susana Perea-Fox

Other major works

short fiction: *Los días enmascarados*, 1954; *Cantar de ciegos*, 1964; *Poemas de amor: Cuentos del alma*, 1971; *Chac Mool, y otros cuentos*, 1973; *Agua quemada*, 1980 (*Burnt Water*, 1980); *Constancia, y otras novelas para vírgenes*, 1989 (*Constancia, and Other Stories for Virgins*, 1990); *Días enmascarados*, 1990 (includes *Los días enmascarados* and *Cantar de ciegos*); *El naranjo: O, Los círculos del tiempo*, 1993 (*The Orange Tree*, 1994); *La frontera de cristal: Una novela en nueve cuentos*, 1995 (*The Crystal Frontier: A Novel in Nine Stories*, 1997); *Inquieta compañía*, 2004; *Todas las familias felices*, 2006 (*Happy Families: Stories*, 2008).

plays: *Todos los gatos son pardos*, pb. 1970; *El tuerto es rey*, pb. 1970; *Orquídeas a la luz de la luna*, pr., pb. 1982 (*Orchids in the Moonlight*, 1982); *Ceremonias del alba*, 1991 (revised edition).

screenplays: *El acoso*, 1958 (with Luis Buñuel; adaptation of Alejo Carpentier's novel); *Children of Sanchez*, 1961 (with Abbey Mann; adaptation of Oscar Lewis's anthropological work); *Pedro Páramo*, 1966 (adaptation of Juan Rulfo's novel); *Tiempo de morir*, 1966; *Los caifanes*, 1967.

nonfiction: *The Argument of Latin America: Words for North Americans*, 1963; *Paris: La revolución de mayo*, 1968; *El mundo de José Luis Cuevas*, 1969; *La nueva novela hispanoamericana*, 1969; *Casa con dos puertas*, 1970; *Los reinos originarios: Teatro hispanomexicano*, 1971; *Tiempo mexicano*, 1971; *Cervantes: O, La crítica de la lectura*, 1976 (*Cervantes: Or, The Critique of Reading*, 1976); *Myself with Others: Selected Essays*, 1988; *Valiente mundo nuevo: Épica, utopía y mito en la novela*, 1990; *El espejo enterrado*, 1992 (*The Buried Mirror: Reflections on Spain and the New World*, 1992); *Geografía de la novela*, 1993; *Tres discursos para dos aldeas*, 1993; *Nuevo tiempo mexicano*, 1994 (*A New Time for Mexico*, 1996); *Latin America: At War with the Past*, 2001; *En esto creo*, 2002 (*This I Believe: An A to Z of a Life*, 2005); *Viendo visiones*, 2003; *Contra Bush*, 2004; *Los caballeros del siglo XXI*, 2005; *Los 68: París-Praga-México*, 2005.

EDITED TEXT: *The Vintage Book of Latin American Stories*, 2000 (with Julio Ortega).

BIBLIOGRAPHY

Abeyta, Michael. *Fuentes, "Terra Nostra," and the Reconfiguration of Latin American Culture*. Columbia: University of Missouri Press, 2006. Focuses on the theme of the gift in Fuentes's *Terra Nostra*, analyzing how gift giving, excess, expenditure, sacrifice, and exchange shape the novel. Reveals the relevance of this theme to discussions about the relationship between art and the gift.

Bloom, Harold, ed. *Carlos Fuentes' "The Death of Artemio Cruz."* New York: Chelsea House, 2006. Collection of essays analyzes different aspects of *The Death of Artemio Cruz*, including structure and theme, the relationship between fathers and sons, and the expression of memory and time.

Boldy, Steven. *The Narrative of Carlos Fuentes: Family, Texts, Nation*. Durham, England: University of Durham, 2002. Presents analyses of ten works by Fuentes written over almost forty years, from 1958 to 1995. Among the topics discussed are Mexico and memory, the Mexican national identity and history, literature and evil, the carnivalesque, violence and impunity, and intellectual traditions of Mexican national thinking.

Dupont, Denise. "Baroque Ambiguities: The Figure of the Author in *Terra Nostra*." *Latin American Literary Review* 30 (January-June, 2002): 5-19. Examines the interaction between the literal author and the author as envisioned within the text of Fuentes's *Terra Nostra*.

Durán, Victor M. *A Marxist Reading of Fuentes, Vargas Llosa, and Puig*. Lanham, Md.: University Press of America, 1994. Interesting scholarly study of the three authors uses the approach of Marxist literary theory. Chapter 3 analyzes *The Death of Artemio Cruz*.

Gyurko, Lanin A. *Lifting the Obsidian Mask: The Artistic Vision of Carlos Fuentes*. Potomac, Md.: Scripta Humanistica, 2007. Provides analysis of all of Fuentes's writings, including short stories, novels, plays, and essays, from his earliest short stories of the mythic and fantastic to his unique and enigmatic autobiographical dictionary *En esto creo* (2002; *This I Believe: An A to Z of a Life*, 2005) and his narrative *The Eagle's Throne*.

Morton, Adam David. "The Social Function of Carlos Fuentes: A Critical Intellectual or in the 'Shadow of the State'?" *Bulletin of Latin American Research* 22 (January, 2003): 25-51. Uses Fuentes as a case study in a discussion of the role of the public intellectual in Latin American society.

Sheldon, Penn. *Carlos Fuentes's "Terra Nostra" and the Kabbalah: The Recreation of the Hispanic World*. Lewiston, N.Y.: Edwin Mellen Press, 2003. Focuses on the function of Jewish mysticism in *Terra Nostra*. In order to support his case, Penn offers significant insights into Fuentes's other fictional works and, especially, his essays.

Van Delden, Maarten. *Carlos Fuentes, México, and Modernity*. Nashville: Vanderbilt University Press, 1998. Analyzes the ongoing tension in Fuentes's works between nationalism and cosmopolitanism, which stands in a complex relationship to the problem of Latin American modernization.

Williams, Raymond Leslie. *The Writings of Carlos Fuentes*. Austin: University of Texas Press, 1996. Considering *Terra Nostra* a keystone in Fuentes's narrative production, Williams maintains that the early novels contain all the major themes and topics that Fuentes later developed and, by the same token, that the later novels are reworkings and expansions of many of the motifs found in Fuentes's masterpiece.

G

CARLO EMILIO GADDA

Born: Milan, Italy; November 14, 1893
Died: Rome, Italy; May 21, 1973

Principal long fiction

Quer pasticciaccio brutto de via Merulana, 1957 (*That Awful Mess on Via Merulana*, 1965)
La cognizione del dolore, 1963 (revised 1970; *Acquainted with Grief*, 1969)
La meccanica, 1970 (unfinished novella)
Racconto italiano di ignoto del novecento, 1983 (fragment)

Other literary forms

In addition to the novels listed above, Carlo Emilio Gadda (GAHD-dah) published several collections of short stories: *La Madonna dei filosofi* (1931; Our Lady of the philosophers); *Il castello di Udine* (1934; the castle of Udine), awarded the Premio Bagutta; *L'Adalgisa: Disegni milanesi* (1944; tales from Milan); and *Novelle dal ducato in fiamme* (1953; stories from the duchy in flames), awarded the Premio Viareggio. Gadda's most important nonfiction writings are *I viaggi la morte* (1958; travels and death), a collection of literary essays, and the antifascist pamphlet *Eros e Priapo* (1967; Eros and Priapus). His war and prison diary, *Giornale di guerra e di prigionia*, first appeared in 1955 and in its definitive form in 1965.

Gadda also published many topical articles, essays on public works, architectural engineering, a description of a surgical oration, and even a recipe for cooking risotto, all collected in *Le meraviglie d'Italia* (1939, 1964; the marvels of Italy); a book of fables and aphorisms, *Il primo libro delle favole* (1952; the first book of fables); two comic texts for radio broadcast; a small volume of historical caricatures, dedicated to the memories of Louis XIII, XIV, and XV of France (*I Luigi di Francia*, 1964); and a satiric dialogue titled *Il guerriero, l'amazzone, lo spirito della poesia nel verso immortale del Foscolo* (1967; the warrior, the amazon, and the spirit of poetry in the immortal verses of Ugo Foscolo).

Posthumous publications include Gadda's early philosophical notebooks, *Meditazione milanese* (1974; Milanese meditations) and *Le bizze del capitano in congedo, e altri racconti* (1981; the extravagances of a captain on leave, and other stories), and the fragments of an early novel titled *Racconto italiano di ignoto del novecento* (1983; an anonymous twentieth century Italian story). Gadda is also the author of numerous uncollected technical articles that appeared during the 1930's in the dailies *Ambrosiano* and *La gazzetta del popolo*.

Achievements

The recognition of Carlo Emilio Gadda as one of Italy's most important contemporary prose writers came late, when his novel *Acquainted with Grief*, originally published in serial form in *Letteratura*, a small Florentine literary review, was awarded the prestigious Formentor International Literary Prize in 1963. Before then, Gadda was known and admired by a relatively select group of literary critics who praised his work largely for its linguistic eccentricity. The notoriety given to *Acquainted with Grief* called public attention to his earlier writings, especially to *That Awful Mess on Via Merulana*, also previously serialized in *Letteratura*. More important, it caused critics to heed the general significance of his work in relation to the most distinguished manifestations of the European avant-garde.

After decades of serious critical study, Gadda occupies a unique position in the history of Italian literature. At a time when the modern narrative in Italy had found with Italo Svevo, Federigo Tozzi, and Alberto Moravia, authors capable of strengthening a comparatively weak national tradition in the novel, Gadda wrote to contest the very idea of narrative, the traditional notions of author and text, and the very institution of literature itself. His revolution strikes so deeply into the core of conventional literary assumptions and practices that only now, in the light of recent developments in criticism, is it possible to take full measure of its importance.

During the 1950's and 1960's, the epithets "eccentric," "baroque," and "antiliterary" were used to displace Gadda's work outside what was deemed fixed, legitimate, or proper, linking him to the heritage of the macaronic or pasticheur, in part, to such renowned outsiders as Teofilo Folengo, François Rabelais, James Joyce, and Louis-Ferdinand Céline, and, more directly, to the indigenous tradition of the Lombard and Piedmontese *Scapigliatura* (Giovanni Faldella, Achille Giovanni Cagna, and Carlo Dossi). Placing Gadda within this tradition helps one set into perspective the elements of caricature, parody, and derision for which his works are noted. It provides, moreover, a general framework for assessing the linguistic inventiveness that makes Gadda an eminently difficult writer.

BIOGRAPHY

Born in 1893 in Milan, Italy, Carlo Emilio Gadda was the oldest of three children. His father, Francesco Ippolito, was a silk weaver by trade who, through his first marriage, became a partner in a prosperous Milanese textile firm. His mother, Adele Lehr, was half Hungarian. She held a doctorate in letters and philosophy, which enabled her to earn a modest living as a schoolteacher and provide for her children after her husband's death in 1909. What we know of Gadda's life has been filtered in large part through his fiction. His childhood was marked by the financial decline of his family, attributed to his father's imprudent investments and business ventures. In Milan, he attended the Liceo Parini and studied engineering at the Istituto Tecnico Superiore. With the outbreak of World War I, he interrupted his studies to enlist as an officer in the Italian alpine regiment, saw action on several fronts, including Caporetto, and was taken prisoner. In 1920, Gadda began working as an industrial engineer, traveling to Sardinia and abroad to Argentina and, later, to France, Belgium, and Germany, where he supervised the construction of plants for the production of ammonia. In 1933, Gadda was hired by the Vatican to design and oversee the installation of its electrical power system.

In spite of his scientific background and training, Gadda was never wholly satisfied with his career as an engineer. Philosophy and literature interested him more. In fact, he no sooner began working in industry when he left his job to pursue, at Milan's Accademia Scientifico-Letteraria, a second doctorate in philosophy and wrote under the supervision of philosophers Piero Martinetti and Antonio Banfi, a thesis on Gottfried Leibniz's *Nouveaux Essais sur l'entendement humain* (1765; *Essays Concerning Human Understanding*, 1898). For the most part, Gadda succeeded well in combining his literary and scientific talents, but, in 1940, he broke definitively with his profession and moved to Florence, where, in the company of then more distinguished writers such as Elio Vittorini and Tommaso Landolfi, he dedicated himself totally to writing, completing for *Letteratura* the last two installments of *Acquainted with Grief* and writing his best-known novel, *That Awful Mess on Via Merulana* and parts of *Eros e Priapo*.

Ten years later, Gadda moved to Rome to work as a journalist for the Edizioni Radio Italiana. There he lived a modest and secluded life, revising many of his early writings for publication in book form. When Gadda died on May 21, 1973, he left a rich legacy of texts that have influenced generations of writers and have brought him fame as one of contemporary Italy's most original, complex, and compelling authors.

ANALYSIS

Carlo Emilio Gadda's fiction originates in his notion of an objectively chaotic and deformed world. Confronted by a reality that resists organization and rational systemization, the writer, according to Gadda's aesthetics, becomes involved in a never-ending process of unraveling and probing into the interminable succession of links uniting facts, circumstances, and experiences. In this perspective, the subject of authorial self loses its once privileged place as an observer, positioned outside the labyrinth of phenomena and thus capable of exercising judgment, of arranging things to form an organic whole and, therefore, of narrating.

Also, in contrast to the modernist aesthetic, the writer,

in Gadda's view, cannot reflect the fragmentation of the present by refusing to communicate his personality, by remaining aloof and ironic. Instead, he too is a part of the chaos, a single element or moment in an objective chain that can claim no more than its neutral status as a biological and material presence. In other words, the author for Gadda does not disappear completely in his or her attempt to produce a thing-centered universe (as is the case with, say Alain Robbe-Grillet), but rather, becomes part of the "game" called "literature."

What is literature for Gadda? Simply, the alter image of reality that produces fictional entities called characters and plots and disposes them for the purpose of creating particular effects. The subject, as part of this game, can only recognize its degraded position and, in response, try to impose its subjectivity on the reader, knowing full well that the judgments it makes have no special importance, that they are not means of conditioning the reader's comprehension of the fiction but instead merely traces of its own devalued presence. Such expressions of authorial subjectivity at times take the form of violent outbursts or tirades against people or actions that conflict with Gadda's innate sense of order and propriety; at times, they become tragic monologues on existence or the comic deformation of characters and events.

If literature mimics reality and if reality is, as Gadda sees it, a disharmonious continuum, the literary work defies unraveling; it can never be explained for it can never be concluded. Furthermore, because literary works are made up of oppositional and coincidental elements, no one work can contain parts that are truly unique to itself, but rather the parts of one work may be transposed to other, different relational systems that are equally as provisional. This idea explains why Gadda's fictional writings are largely unfinished, deprived of denouement and resolution of conflict. It also accounts for why what became *Acquainted with Grief* was originally intended as chapters in *Le meraviglie d'Italia* and then redesigned to include other parts that subsequently appeared in different collections, while two fragments of the official version of the novel are contained in *L'Adalgisa* and a third in *Novelle dal ducato in fiamme*.

From such a notion of the relation of literature to reality, a fundamental aspect of Gadda's work emerges: the artificial, essentially linguistic, nature of literary production, which elicits the functional utilization of language in the search for contradictions and unexpected connections among things. Gadda's emphasis on language is his way of saying that, in the wake of the crisis of ideology, reality *is* language—that the subject matter of literature is historical realities existing as linguistic codes. The writer, he states in an important literary essay, is faced with a specific number of "languages" that correspond to a variety of codes representing different modes of existence and activity. This collection of "codes" makes up, in his judgment, the "empirical," "chaotic," "baroque," and "grotesque" character of the world. To know this reality means to "coordinate" these various languages and to stamp on the process of "coordination" one's own particular seal. For Gadda, coordinating reality entails finding in things one particular element that distinguishes one system from another. It, therefore, denotes focusing on a specific link in a causal chain, magnifying it out of proportion in order to penetrate its essence; in this sense, knowledge and deformation become one and the same thing.

The principal effect of combining and coordinating different linguistic codes is the pastiche. The pastiche suspends meaning by directing the reader's attention to the process of writing and the particular transgression of literary norms it involves. A situation that is inherently tragic or lyric becomes, with the pastiche, comic representation. Even the use of dialect within the context of standard speech, rather than heightening the realistic effect, is only another means of deforming that discourse to achieve comic incongruity. Gadda's two major novels fully embody the aesthetic principles just summarized.

ACQUAINTED WITH GRIEF

The ideas that make a framework for *Acquainted with Grief* are derived from Gadda's readings of Immanuel Kant and Sigmund Freud. The novel attempts to direct the reader's perception to realities beyond or outside the world of appearance, particularly to that part of the protagonist's mind behind the phenomenal self that can never be directly known but that influences profoundly the sense of self that is experienced and represented. Also, at its base lies the Freudian conviction that the acceptance of society is one and the same with the repression of guilt. History and historiography—Gadda writes in the work's preface—give a distorted picture of humanity's inner life; it shows it in tune with the reality principle and blind to the profound violence that affects the human condition. *Acquainted with Grief* is for Gadda, in its most fundamental meaning, a vindication of human history, "cleansed," in his words, "of the stutter of reticence and the frank syntax of deception."

Acquainted with Grief consists of a series of fragments or "tracts" and, in both its original and book forms, it is incomplete, although on the inside flap of the volume's jacket, the publisher, speaking for the author, writes that in the missing conclusion, the protagonist's mother, left alone in her villa after her son's departure, is murdered by the agents of the night watchmen's organizations (Nistituó Provinciales de Vigilancia para la Noche), that she dies thinking her son, Gonzalo, had plotted the horrendous crime. In 1941, Gadda had composed rough drafts of what were to become the novel's final chapters. These fragments, included in the 1970 edition, appear to substantiate the aforementioned outcome. There is, furthermore, evidence, contained in several unpublished notes, that Gadda had intended to write a third and final episode, centered on the police interrogation of Gonzalo.

The novel's action takes place in Maradagàl, a small, imaginary country in South America, situated near Parapagàl, a country of similar size and resources. Close to the city of Pastrufazio, in a modern villa constructed on the highlands, lived the Pirobutirro family, which, at the time of the novel's action, was reduced to an old widow whom the people call La Señora and her forty-five-year-old son, Gonzalo, who clearly appears as the caricatural reflection of Gadda himself. The whole story, in fact, beginning with its imaginary South American setting in which the people, institutions, geography, and history of early twentieth century Italy (chiefly Lombardy) are easily recognizable, is a kind of autobiographical parody that produces tragicomic deformation. (The family name Pirobutirro, for example, is derived from a type of pear tree, *pere butirro*, that Gadda's father attempted to cultivate at the family's country villa at Longone al Segrino in Brianza.)

Gonzalo is a modern-day misanthrope, extremely jealous of his own privacy and possessions and that of his mother and contemptuous of the outside world, especially of the simple peasant folk whom the Señora charitably supports. He suffers from uneasiness, apprehension, a sense of guilt and unfulfillment, and a general anticipation of danger caused by an undefined image of pain and grief. His manias are for order, silence, and food, and he is obsessed by a wish for death and, allegedly, a desire to kill his mother. He is prone to violent outbursts of rage and long diatribes against anything that appears to intrude on his solitude and sole possession of his mother. In the novel's first part, the Señora appears as a somewhat comic and grotesque figure. She wanders about the house, looking like a bejeweled skeleton in the diamond earrings she cherishes as the last remembrance of past wealth. Gonzalo berates her for her excessive goodness, her need to keep up appearances, and her decision to seek the protection of the night watchmen's organizations, whose members, in Gonzalo's view, are intent on exploiting her fear.

In part 2, however, the author's perspective on the mother changes. No longer the grotesque object of Gonzalo's insensitivity and rejection, she stands out as a tragic character and is portrayed with compassion. With the death of her youngest son, she is left hopeless, confined to isolation and emptiness. Images of darkness, death, desolation, and abandonment abound to express in her character an extreme sense of futility, the very same futility that dominates the characterization of her son, Gonzalo.

The first edition of *Acquainted with Grief* closes with references to several episodes in Gonzalo's life. The most illuminating from a psychoanalytical standpoint is the time when, enraged because his mother had given him a watch that she had bought from a Russian or Armenian refugee, bursts out "in horrible vituperations" and takes from the wall a portrait of his father and tramples it "as if he were pressing grapes in a vat." The first two fragments included in the 1970 edition tell of a robbery in a nearby villa and how Gonzalo had refused the protection of the night watchmen's organizations. In the final fragment, the reader learns that the Señora has been mortally wounded, "debased"—Gadda writes—"by an evil cause operating in the absurdity of the night." The novel ends with the beginning of an inquest.

Criticism has often brought attention to the fact that the world of *Acquainted with Grief*, although disguised in an imaginary South American setting, is in effect the world of Italian fascism, and that Gonzalo's numerous spells of verbal aggression are actually directed toward fascism. It has also been argued that the mother symbolizes Benito Mussolini and fascism in the affection she displays toward others as a means of coercing them into relationships of dependence. It could even be stated that, generally speaking, fascism is the novel's principal referent and that Gonzalo's conflicts derive from fascism's ever-present forms of oppression, as symbolized by the watchmen's organizations and the wall surrounding the villa. Yet, such a political reading of *Acquainted with Grief* falls far short of exhausting the work's total meaning. It tends to ignore the novel's deep psychological structure, the importance of the autobiographical element in seizing the complex patterns of deception and dissemblance that the story embodies.

That Awful Mess on Via Merulana

Gadda began writing his novel *That Awful Mess on Via Merulana* at the peak of Fascist demagoguery, when Italy had made its disastrous entry into World War II. The catastrophic events of those years caused Gadda to shift his narrative focus from the complex problematic of an individual life lived in extremis to the absurdity of human life in general. As in his previous novel, his objectives extend from polemic to benevolent satire, but here the political content is clearly manifested. Yet, the novel is far from being a political work in the strict sense, as are, for example, the stories of Cesare Pavese and Elio Vittorini. Instead, the origins of *That Awful Mess on Via Merulana* are to be located in *Acquainted with Grief*, particularly in Gonzalo's perception of universal guilt. In this respect, the plot of *That Awful Mess on Via Merulana* takes on a special significance because the police investigation at the story's center becomes a vehicle for conveying the guilt of an entire race.

The novel's principal theme is the risk one runs when made the object of inquiry or investigation. The guilty can never be brought to justice because in addition to the perpetrators of the robbery and homicide in Via Merulana, there exist numerous other offenders and criminals, the most evil being the oppressive State, impersonated by the sordid and grotesque figure of its criminal idol Mussolini.

That Awful Mess on Via Merulana follows the action of an elementary detective story. Two crimes are committed in the same apartment house at number 219 Via Merulana in Rome. The first is the theft of some jewels belonging to a certain Countess Menegazzi; the second is the murder of the beautiful Roman gentlewoman Liliana Balducci. Don Ciccio Ingravallo, a friend of the Balduccis, is the detective assigned to the case.

In this novel, more than in his previous work, Gadda shows an exceptional talent for caricature. Don Ciccio, for example, is a typical southern Italian figure: a dilettante philosopher, reflective, sensitive, respectful of ritual, yet somewhat sloppy, and jealous of more charming and handsome men, such as Liliana's cousin Giuliano, whom the detective immediately considers with suspicion. In addition to being a character whose petty jealousies and melancholic disposition set him in polemic contrast to the notion of the ideal Fascist man, Don Ciccio is Gadda's voice in the novel, in that he is continually looking for hidden meanings behind appearances. At a dinner given by Liliana to celebrate her husband's birthday, his inquisitive eye penetrates the signora's mundane graces to observe that at times she appears to sigh and that her face is full of a strange sadness. He attributes her melancholy to her not having children. Her presumed sterility, he concludes, causes her to venerate everything that in the least way is associated with maternity. Her mania, he goes on to note, is even more tragic and grotesque when seen in the context of the fascist myth of fertility and procreation. Don Ciccio's thoughts inspire Gadda to interrupt the flow of the narrative and level a kind of epic satire against fascism's absurd reverence for maternity. The episode is symptomatic of the entire writing procedure in *That Awful Mess on Via Merulana*, whereby a minimal reference to fascism brings on literally pages of fierce, comic invective.

The first crime, which takes place shortly after Liliana's dinner party, is of small importance compared to the pastiche it generates and the opportunities it affords for grotesque caricature. An extraordinary example of Gadda's ability for literary parody and comic deformation is his portrayal of Countess Menegazzi in which he mimics the syntax of Alessandro Manzoni's renowned description of Gertrude in *I promessi sposi* (1840-1842; *The Betrothed*, 1951), creating a picture totally devoid of lyricism or pathos and focusing on the comic absurdity of the human condition as exemplified by this lonely woman who spends her days in a continual state of tormented anxiety.

The presence of physical violence and death also provides a suitable opportunity for Gadda to express his negative vision of life. Here, too, his attitude is one of ironic indifference, which permits his description to become grotesquely comic. The dead body of Liliana at the scene of the crime is open to every sort of disrespect and impiety. Her dress and slip are pulled up and the spectators fix their gaze on her delicately embroidered underwear and the extreme whiteness of her flesh. Only in the next moment do we become aware of the deep wound in her throat. Gadda's description is long and detailed; he examines the body from every possible angle, while the comments of those present are comically abusive.

Liliana's murder turns out to have little meaning when seen from the standpoint of the novel's historical setting, the spring of 1927, when the Fascist regime was promoting an idyllic image of itself based on tender emotions and familial love. Gadda takes great pleasure in mocking Fascist pretensions for law and order and civil austerity. The prime object of Gadda's polemic is Mussolini, the "Death's Head in a Top Hat"; the detective story appears as a pretext for representing the criminality of the state and the uncertainty of human existence in general. In fact, the investigation leads the reader to suspect everyone, while certain of nothing, not even the names of the characters. Only with the arrival of Don Corpi, Liliana's confessor who appears at police headquarters to read her will, does the investigation seem to be headed toward solution. The movement, however, begun in search of the stolen jewels, quickly becomes a kind of voyage to the bottom of the earth, where the multiform horrors of the human condition are graphically revealed. The rediscovered jewels stand out in contrast as primordial essences compared to the grotesque world surrounding them. At a certain point, the detective story breaks down. The murder theme, having been put aside for several chapters, returns in the final pages so that a logical connection may be made between the two crimes.

One's first impulse in commenting on *That Awful Mess on Via Merulana* is to view the novel according to the metaliterary directives it embodies, that is, as a process of excavation into nature, of penetrating into some ever more intimate stratum in search of the secret of existence. In this sense, Gadda is a kind of writer-surgeon who cuts through the crust of appearance to scan and probe the sacrosanct recesses of human matter, demonstrating by means of the scientific precision with which he works his absolute power and control. Gadda's fiction abounds with examples of this sort of descriptive process, an explicit instance of which we find at the conclusion of *That Awful Mess on Via Merulana* when the stolen jewels are recovered.

It would be incomplete, however, to see Gadda's objective as simply one of capturing a universe of meanings or the hidden soul of things, whether either to assign to reality a kind of metaphysical transcendence or to produce, naturalistically, a more complete material image of the phenomenon. A closer look at Gadda's novels will show that what the narrator has in fact done is dilate or deform two modes of writing: one that focuses on the object's meanings, the other centered on the lyric, subjective dimension encased in the consciousness of the reader-spectator. The juxtaposition of these highly stylized perspectives carries out a neutralizing function, reducing them to the level of material causes, that is, to the matter and memory of which the event is constructed, devoid of any specific finality.

Keeping in mind the metacritical structure of Gadda's texts and considering them as a discourse on method, one can note that their syntax calls attention primarily to objects and gestures. What counts is the presence of the material components of discourse, which station themselves before the reader, demanding total, undivided attention. The effect of their extreme presence is what Robbe-Grillet has called, in reference to the new novel, "mocking." It is not by accident, then, that Gadda attained his greatest popularity among the more radical exponents of Italy's neo-avant-garde.

At base, the neo-avant-garde, although showing a wide diversity of theoretical positions, posited its experimental methods on the belief that all ideologic representation falsified reality and that the only strategy possible was one of disengagement that produced an art devoid of meaning and messages and whose sole purpose was to restore reality to its nonideologized and dishistoricized intactness. Whether Gadda can truly be considered a forerunner of the neo-avant-garde is not important. His appropriation by writers such as Alberto Arbasino and Raffaele La Capria marked a decisive turning point in his critical fortunes. It meant his inclusion into the European context of experimentalism as the Italian example and thus it heralded a new way of looking at his work.

No longer a unique Italian specialty, the great, but difficult, pasticheur stood out precisely on account of the very inaccessibility that, according to traditional narrative standards, relegated him to the sphere of minor writers. His greatness now consisted in the deep, seminal value of his language, which, as it expressed an entirely new way of looking at the world, paved the way for the literature of the future.

Robert Dombroski

Other major works

SHORT FICTION: *La Madonna dei filosofi*, 1931; *Il castello di Udine*, 1934; *L'Adalgisa: Disegni milanesi*, 1944; *Il primo libro delle favole*, 1952; *Novelle dal ducato in fiamme*, 1953; *Accoppiamenti giudiziosi*, 1963; *I Luigi di Francia*, 1964; *Le bizze del capitano in congedo e altri racconti*, 1981.

PLAY: *Il guerriero, l'amazzone, lo spirito della poesia nel verso immortale del Foscolo*, pb. 1967.

NONFICTION: *Le meraviglie d'Italia*, 1939 (revised 1964); *Giornale di guerra e di prigionia*, 1955, 1965; *I viaggi la morte*, 1958; *Eros e Priapo*, 1967; *Meditazione milanese*, 1974; *Per favore, mi lasci nell'ombra: Interviste, 1950-1972*, 1993 (interviews; Claudio Vela, editor); *Carissimo Gianfranco: Lettere ritrovate, 1943-1963*, 1998 (letters; Giulio Ungarelli, editor).

Bibliography

Adams, Robert Martin. "Carlo Emilio Gadda." In *After Joyce: Studies in Fiction After "Ulysses."* New York: Oxford University Press, 1977. Gadda's place in modern European literature is discussed.

Bertone, Manuela, and Robert S. Dombroski. *Carlo Gadda: Contemporary Perspectives*. Toronto, Ont.: University of Toronto Press, 1997. A collection of essays in which Gadda's plurilingualism, pastiches, and narrative entanglements are revealed both as a revolt against conventional literary style and as the expression of a chaotic, painful world. Gadda emerges as a transgressive novelist, a humorist, and a mannerist who deforms language through parodic and comic modes.

Bouchard, Norma. *Céline, Gadda, Beckett: Experimental Writings of the 1930's*. Gainsville: University Press of Florida, 2000. Bouchard argues that works by Gadda, Louis-Ferdinand Céline, and Samuel Beckett have stylistic characteristics that can now be considered postmodern, including a changed relationship to language, a burlesque view of the world, and a "decentered" narrative.

Diaconescu-Blumenfeld, Rodica. *Born Illiterate: Gender and Representation in Gadda's "Pasticciaccio."* Market Harborough, England: Troubador, in association with Hull Italian Texts, 1999. Analyzes gender representation in *That Awful Mess on the Via Merulana* and how Gadda's depiction of male and female characters advances the play of unity and difference that is central to the novel.

Di Martino, Loredana. "Modernism/Postmodernism: Rethinking the Canon Through Gadda." *Edinburgh Journal of Gadda Studies*, no. 5 (November, 2007). The author argues in this detailed study of Gadda's place in the modernist canon that "Gadda pushes Modernism to its extremes, accepting the notion of absolute indeterminacy which is a key feature of Postmodernism."

Dombroski, Robert S. *Creative Entanglements: Gadda and the Baroque*. Toronto, Ont.: University of Toronto Press, 1999. Gadda's style has often been described as baroque; this study critically explores that description, demonstrating how Gadda used "baroqueness" as a means of expressing loss, grief, and alienation.

_______. "The Foundations of Italian Modernism: Pirandello, Svevo, Gadda." In *The Cambridge Companion to the Italian Novel*, edited by Peter Bondanella and Andrea Ciccarelli. New York: Cambridge University Press, 2003. This introductory overview of Italian literature includes Dombrowski's essay, which defines Gadda as a modernist writer and compares his work to that of Luigi Pirandello and Italo Svevo.

Ragusa, Olga. *Narrative and Drama: Essays in Modern Italian Literature from Verga to Pasolini*. The Hague, the Netherlands: Mouton, 1976. Gadda's importance to modern Italian literature receives its due coverage in an essay that analyzes his "experimentalism" and compares his work with that of Pier Paolo Pasolini.

Sbragia, Albert. *Carlo Emilio Gadda and the Modern Macaronic*. Gainesville: University of Florida Press, 1996. Sbragia's study examines Gadda's mixture of Milanese vernacular with erudite vocabulary and diction, comparing his writing to the expressionistic fiction of James Joyce and Louis-Ferdinand Céline and placing Gadda's works within the context of plurilingualism in Italian and French literature.

WILLIAM GADDIS

Born: New York, New York; December 29, 1922
Died: East Hampton, New York; December 16, 1998
Also known as: William Thomas Gaddis

Principal long fiction

The Recognitions, 1955
JR, 1975
Carpenter's Gothic, 1985
A Frolic of His Own, 1994
Agapē Agape, 2002

Other literary forms

William Gaddis's literary reputation is based on his novels; he also contributed a number of essays, poems, and short stories to major magazines. Gaddis's papers are housed in the Washington University Library's Modern Language Collection. The archive includes the author's personal library as well as his collected notes, source materials, correspondence, and manuscript drafts and unpublished works.

Achievements

William Gaddis's fiction is convoluted, confusing, and difficult, qualities that have led some readers to criticize it. His work is also sophisticated, multilayered, and technically innovative, qualities that have led most thoughtful readers to see Gaddis one of the most important writers of the post-World War II era, though he is not fully appreciated or understood.

Gaddis's accomplishments began to receive greater attention in the late 1960's and early 1970's, during which time he was at work on his second monumental novel, *JR*. Between 1955 and 1970, only a single article on Gaddis appeared in the United States, but in the 1970's momentum started to build. The first doctoral dissertation on Gaddis was published in 1971, providing valuable information on *The Recognitions* and basic facts about Gaddis's life. The year 1982 saw the publication of new essays on Gaddis in a special issue of the *Review of Contemporary Fiction*, as well as a full-length guide to *The Recognitions*, written by Steven Moore; in that same year, Gaddis was awarded a prestigious MacArthur Fellowship.

Gaddis's success was confirmed when he received the 1976 National Book Award in fiction for *JR*. Indeed, Gaddis responded by publishing his third novel only a decade later, down from the twenty years between his first two efforts. *Carpenter's Gothic* was widely hailed for its bitter yet readable satire of ethical vanity in American business, politics, and popular religion. The novel broadened the readership for a novelist accustomed to a comparatively small audience, and it confirmed him as one of the most gifted and serious writers of contemporary American fiction.

Gaddis's fourth novel, *A Frolic of His Own*, was published in 1994 to a mixed response similar to that given his earlier works. It won for him his second National Book Award and was praised for its savage wit. However, some reviewers raised the old complaints that it was difficult, long-winded, and all too faithful in its representation of the tedium of everyday conversation and legal minutiae.

In addition to the National Book Awards and the

MacArthur Fellowship, Gaddis received a National Institute of Arts and Letters Award (1963), two grants from the National Endowment for the Arts (1963 and 1974), and a Lannan Foundation Lifetime Achievement Award (1993).

BIOGRAPHY

After spending his early childhood in New York City and on Long Island, William Thomas Gaddis attended a private boarding school in Connecticut for nine years. He then returned to Long Island to attend public school from grade eight through high school. He was accepted by Harvard in 1941 and stayed there until 1945, when he took a job as a reader and fact-checker for *The New Yorker*, a position he left after one year in order to travel. In the years that followed, he visited Central America, the Caribbean, North Africa, and parts of Europe, all of which became settings in his first novel. He continued to write after returning to the United States, and in 1955, with ten years of effort behind him, he published *The Recognitions*.

Throughout his life, Gaddis was reluctant to discuss his private life. Although he was sometimes seen at writers' conferences and occasionally did some teaching, he guarded his privacy extremely well. Two scholars of Gaddis's work, David Koenig and Steven Moore, made a number of important inferences about Gaddis's life. For example, the protagonist of *The Recognitions*, Wyatt, has a lonely and isolated childhood. His mother dies on an ocean voyage when he is very young, and his father gradually loses his sanity. When Wyatt is twelve, he suffers from a mysterious ailment that the doctors label *erythema grave*. They mutilate Wyatt's wasted body and send him home to die because they can find neither a cause nor a cure for his illness; unexpectedly, however, Wyatt recovers. Parallels to Gaddis's own childhood emerge from this story line. Apparently he was separated from his parents, at least while he attended a boarding school in Connecticut. He also contracted an illness that the doctors could not identify and therefore called *erythema grave*. Serious effects of the illness recurred in later years to cause further problems and to prevent the young Gaddis from being accepted into the Army during World War II. Forced to remain in college, he began to write pieces for the *Harvard Lampoon* that anticipated the satirical, humorous, and critical tone of his novels. He soon became president of the *Lampoon*.

Gaddis was involved in an incident during his final year at Harvard that required the intervention of local police. Although it was hardly a serious affair, the local newspapers covered it, and this created embarrassing publicity for the university's administration. Gaddis was asked to resign and did so. The end of traditional academic success did not prevent him from acquiring knowledge. Through his travels—and more so through many years of research—Gaddis constructed impressive works of fiction from a vast store of knowledge.

After the publication of *The Recognitions*, Gaddis supported himself by teaching and writing nonfiction. He spent four years working in public relations for the Pfizer Pharmaceutical Company. He was the father of two children. His daughter, Sarah Gaddis, is a novelist whose first book, *Swallow Hard* (1991), takes its title from a phrase in *JR* and features as protagonist an author of difficult, unpopular fiction. Gaddis's son, Matthew Hough Gaddis, is a filmmaker.

Gaddis died of prostate cancer in late 1998 at his home in East Hampton, New York. It was reported at his death that he left behind the completed manuscript of a book called *Agapē Agape*, dealing with the history of the player piano. That was the title, and description, of the book on which Jack Gibbs, in *JR*, was working. Early sources did not agree as to whether the book was fiction or nonfiction. Once *Agapē Agape* was published, it was clear that Gaddis, after decades of drafting and exhaustive research, had turned the nonfictional history of the player piano into a short novel.

ANALYSIS

Critics have placed William Gaddis in the tradition of experimental fiction, linking him closely to James Joyce and comparing him to contemporaries such as Thomas Pynchon. Gaddis himself also indicated the influence of T. S. Eliot on his work, and indeed his books contain both novelistic and poetic structures. The novels employ only vestiges of traditional plots, which go in and out of focus as they are blurred by endless conversations, overpowered by erudite allusions and a multitude of characters, conflicts, and ambiguities. Like Joyce and Eliot, Gaddis uses myth to create a sense of timelessness—

myths of Odysseus, the Grail Knight, the Fisher King, and Christ, along with parallels to the tales of Saint Clement, Faust, and Peer Gynt. Using devices of both modern poetic sequences and modern antirealistic fiction, Gaddis unifies the diversity of parts through recurring images, phrases, and locations; a common tone; historical and literary echoes; and other nonchronological and nonsequential modes of organization.

In *The Recognitions*, point of view is alternated to create tension between the first-person and third-person voices, and there are complicated jokes and symbolism deriving from the unexpected use of "I," "you," "he," and "she." In *JR*, the first-person perspective dominates through incessant talk, with very little relief or explanation in traditional third-person passages. As one reviewer wrote, "[Gaddis] wires his characters for sound and sends his story out on a continuous wave of noise—truncated dialogue, distracted monologue, the racket of TV sets, radios, telephones—from which chaos action, of a sort, eventually emerges."

William Gaddis. (© Marion Ettlinger)

All of Gaddis's work is about cacophony and euphony, fragmentation and integration, art and business, chaos and order. To a casual reader, *Carpenter's Gothic*, *JR*, and *The Recognitions* may appear only cacophonous, fragmented, and chaotic, for their formal experimentation is so dominant. To the reader prepared for the challenge of brilliant fiction, these novels illustrate how very accurate Henry James was in predicting the "elasticity" of the novel and its changing nature in the hands of great writers. From the perspective of the twenty-first century, readers can better appreciate the cultural and global relevance of Gaddis's treatment of mechanical reproduction, the devaluation of individual authorship, and electronic networks of communication.

THE RECOGNITIONS

Considering the complexities of Gaddis's fiction, it is not surprising that the earliest reviews of *The Recognitions* were unenthusiastic. Although they gave Gaddis credit for his extensive knowledge of religion, aesthetics, art, myth, and philosophy, they criticized the absence of clear chronology, the diffuseness of so many intersecting subplots and characters, the large number of references, and the supposed formlessness. In the decade following the publication of *The Recognitions*, very little was written about this allusive novel or its elusive author. Readers had difficulties with the book, and Gaddis offered no explanations. Few copies of the original edition were ever sold, and the novel went out of print. In 1962, Meridian published a paperback edition under its policy to make available neglected but important literary works, and gradually *The Recognitions* became an underground classic, although it again went out of circulation. Not until 1970 did another paperback edition appear. Throughout the precarious life of this novel, Gaddis was probably the person least surprised by its uncertain reception and reader resistance. During a party scene in *The Recognitions*, a poet questions a literary critic about a book he is carrying: "You reading that?" The critic answers, "No, I'm just reviewing it . . . all I need is the jacket blurb."

At its most fundamental level, *The Recognitions* is about every possible kind of recognition. The ultimate recognition is stated in the epigraph by Irenaeus, which translates as "Nothing empty nor without significance with God," but this ultimate recognition is nearly impossible to experience in a secular world where spiritual messages boom forth from the radio and television to become indistinguishable from commercials for soap powder and cereal.

The characters, major and minor, move toward, from, and around various recognitions. Some search for knowledge of how to perform their jobs; others search for knowledge of fraud, of ancestors, of love, self, truth, and sin. Wyatt, settling in New York City, moves sequentially through time and according to place to find his own recognition in Spain. His traditional path is crossed by the paths of many other characters who serve as his foils and reflections. Wyatt paints while Stanley composes music, Otto writes, and Esme loves. Wyatt, however, does more than paint; he forges the masterpieces of Fra Angelico and of Old Flemish painters such as Hugo van der Goes and Dirck Bouts. Thus, his fraudulent activity is reflected in others' fraudulent schemes. Frank Sinisterra, posing as a physician, is forced to operate on Wyatt's mother and inadvertently murders her. Frank is also a counterfeiter; Otto is a plagiarist; Benny is a liar; Big Anna masquerades as a woman, and Agnes Deigh, at a party, is unable to convince people that she is really a woman, not a man in drag; Herschel has no idea who he is (a "negative positivist," a "positive negativist," a "latent homosexual," or a "latent heterosexual"). In similar confusion, Wyatt is addressed as Stephen Asche, Estaban, the Reverend Gilbert Sullivan, and Christ arriving for the Second Coming.

As Wyatt matures from childhood to adulthood, his notions of emptiness and significance, of fraud and authenticity, undergo change. While his mother Camilla and his father are on an ocean voyage across the Atlantic, his mother has an appendicitis attack, is operated on by Sinisterra, and dies. Wyatt is reared by his father but essentially by his Aunt May. She is a fanatical Calvinist who teaches the talented boy that original sketches blaspheme God's original creation, so Wyatt eventually turns to copying from illustrated books. The distinctions between original work and forgery break down. When he is a young man, Wyatt becomes a partner with Recktall Brown, a shrewd art dealer who finds unsuspecting buyers for the forgeries that Wyatt produces. Wyatt is so convinced that "perfect" forgery has nothing to do with sinning, much less with breaking the law, that he has only scorn for the nineteenth century Romantics who prized originality above all else—often, he thinks, at the expense of quality.

It takes many years of disappointments and betrayals for Wyatt to recognize that perfection of line and execution are empty and without significance. The first and crucial step of any great work of art must be the conceptualization behind it, the idea from which the painting derives; there is otherwise no meaningful distinction between the work of the artist and that of the craftsman. Wyatt's abnegation of any original conception implies abnegation of self, which in turn affects his efforts to communicate and to share with his wife Esther and his model Esme. Wyatt's many failures are reflected—in bits and pieces—in the subplots of *The Recognitions*. Characters miss one another as their paths crisscross and they lose track of their appointments. They talk but no one listens, they make love but their partners do not remember, and finally they are trapped within their useless and pretentious self-illusions.

The need for love, forgiveness, purification, and renewal emerges from this frantic activity motivated by greed and selfishness. Thus, Gaddis includes in the novel archetypal questers, priests, mourning women, arid settings, burials, dying and reviving figures, cathedrals, and keepers of the keys. These motifs bring to mind many mythic parallels, though it is hard not to think of specific parallels with Johann Wolfgang von Goethe's *Faust* (1808, 1833) and T. S. Eliot's *The Waste Land* (1922) and *Four Quartets* (1943). Toward the end of his pilgrimage, as well as the end of the novel, Wyatt achieves his recognition of love and authenticity, yet Gaddis does not succumb to the temptation to finish with a conventional denouement but keeps the novel going. In this way, the form of *The Recognitions* reflects its theme, that truth is immutable but exceptionally well hidden. After Wyatt's success follow chapters of others' failures.

Anselm castrates himself and Esme dies; Sinisterra is killed by an assassin and Stanley, while playing his music in a cathedral, is killed as the walls collapse.

Just as *The Recognitions* is rich in meaning, so it is rich in form. The forward movement through chronological time is poised against other combinations of time, primarily the juxtaposition of past and present. The immediate effect of juxtaposition is to interrupt and suspend time while the ultimate effect is to make all time seem simultaneous. For example, in chapter 2, part 2, Wyatt looks out the window at the evening sky as Recktall Brown talks. Brown begins speaking about ancient Greece and Rome but is interrupted by a description of the constellation Orion, by an advertisement for phoney gems, by instructions for passengers riding a bus, by a passage about Alexander the Great, by a quotation from an English travel book of the fourteenth century. The result is that the reader temporarily loses his or her orientation, but the reader need not lose orientation completely. Unity for these disparate time periods is provided by a quality that is part of each passage—glittering beauty marred by a flaw or spurious detail. Thus, organization is based on concept, not on chronology.

Other nonchronological modes of organization in the novel include recurring patterns. Specific words become guides for the reader through difficult sections and also repeat the essential concepts of the novel. For example, "recognitions," "origin," "fished for," "design," "originality," and "fragment" can be found frequently. Larger anecdotes may also be repeated by different speakers, and opinions or metaphysical arguments may be repeated unknowingly or even stolen. The recurring images, words, and stories constitute an internal frame of reference that creates a unity apart from the plot.

In *The Recognitions*, it is possible, though not easy, to discover what activities Gaddis believes to be of enduring value. Deception and fraud are everywhere, but they cannot destroy the truth that is hidden beneath these layers of deception. A first-time reader of this novel will probably have an experience similar to that of first-time readers of Joyce's *Ulysses* (1922) in the years soon after its publication—before full-length guides extolled its merits and explained its obscurities. Like those readers of Joyce's masterpiece, readers of *The Recognitions* will be amply rewarded.

JR

Although *JR* may be even more difficult than Gaddis's first novel, it met with a more positive reception. Critics pointed to its imposing length, diffuse form, and lack of traditional narrative devices, but they believed that it was a novel that could not be ignored by people seriously interested in the future of literature. Reviewers of the novel upon its publication included John Gardner, George Steiner, Earl Miner, and George Stade, further evidence of Gaddis's growing reputation.

Like *The Recognitions*, *JR* is concerned with distinguishing between significant and insignificant activities, all of which take place in a more circumscribed landscape than that of *The Recognitions*. There are no transatlantic crossings and no trips to Central America, only the alternating between a suburb on Long Island and the city of Manhattan. Gaddis shifts his satirical eye to contemporary education through the experience of his protagonist, JR, who attends sixth grade in a school on Long Island. Amy Joubert, JR's social studies teacher, takes the class to visit the stock exchange, and JR is sufficiently impressed by it to interpret the lesson literally. He is fascinated by money and uses the investment of his class in one share of stock to build a corporate empire. Although his immense profits are only on paper, the effects of his transactions on countless others are both concrete and devastating.

Despite the centrality of this obnoxious child, JR remains a shadowy figure. The events he triggers and the people he sucks into his moneymaking whirlwind are more visible. Edward Bast, JR's music teacher and composer, Jack Gibbs, Thomas Eigen, and Shepperman are all artists of some kind, and their realm of activity is quite different from JR's. Bast is forever trying to finish his piece of music, even as he works reluctantly for JR in the Manhattan office that is broken down, cluttered, and chaotic. Eigen has been writing a play, and Gibbs has tried for most of his life to write an ambitious book, but he is always losing pages he has written. While some of Shepperman's paintings have been finished, they remain hidden from sight. The world of art is, however, at odds with the world of business. Bast wants nothing to do with his student's megalomania but proves to be no match for JR. The creative people cannot convince others to leave them alone to their paper, oil paints, and canvases, and as a result they are used and manipulated by those who serve as their liaisons to others who buy, maintain, or publish their efforts.

The primary device for communication is not art but rather the telephone. The world that technology has created is efficient and mechanical since its purpose is to finish jobs so that money can be paid, at least symbolically on paper, and then be reinvested, again on paper. The artist is replaced by the businessman, and it is not even a flesh-and-blood businessman, but only his disembodied voice issuing orders out of a piece of plastic (JR disguises his voice so that he sounds older). The central "authority" is invisible, ubiquitous, and, at least while the conglomerate lasts, omniscient. The triumph of the telephone affords Gaddis endless opportunities for humor and irony, and the failure of art is accompanied by the failure of other means of communication—notably of love. As in *The Recognitions*, lovers miss each other, do not understand each other, and end their affairs or marriages unhappily.

The real tour de force of *JR* is its language. There is almost no third-person description to establish location and speaker and few authorial links or transitions between conversations or monologues. Originally, Gaddis did not even use quotation marks to set off one speaker from the next. *JR* is nearly one thousand pages of talk. The jargon, speech rhythms, and styles of those in the educational establishment and in the stock market are perfectly re-created, but their language is a self-perpetuating system; regardless of their outpouring, the expressive power of words is obliterated by the sheer noise and verbiage. One early reviewer said of *JR* that "everything is insanely jammed together in this novel's closed atmosphere—there's no causality, no progression; and the frantic farcical momentum overlies the entropic unravelling of all 'systems.'" The words pile up as the structures of the culture collapse; the reader is faced with a formidable challenge in making his or her way through it all.

There can be no doubt that *JR*, probably even more than *The Recognitions*, poses serious challenges to the reader. Despite them, and even perhaps because of them, *JR* is an extraordinary novel. Gaddis captures the dizzying pace, the language, and the excesses of modern culture and mercilessly throws them back to his readers in a crazy, nonlinear kind of verisimilitude. The novel operates without causality, chronology, or the logical narrative devices on which many readers depend. The cacophony of the characters and the lack of clarity are certainly meant to be disturbing.

CARPENTER'S GOTHIC

In *Carpenter's Gothic*, this cultural cacophony runs headlong toward a global apocalypse. Again there is the confused eruption of voices into the narrative and the forward-spinning blur of events common to Gaddis's earlier fictions. Gaddis's third novel, however, is not only more focused and brief, at 262 pages, but also the most readable of his works. Its story centers on Elizabeth Vorakers Booth and her husband Paul, renters of a ramshackle "carpenter's gothic" house, in which all of the action unfolds. Daughter of a minerals tycoon who committed suicide when his illegal business practices were exposed, Elizabeth married Paul Booth, a Vietnam War veteran and carrier of Vorakers's bribes, after Paul lied in testifying before Congress.

All the novel's complexities unfold from these tangled business dealings. The Vorakerses' estate is hopelessly snarled in lawsuits, manipulated by swarms of self-serving lawyers. Paul is suing or countersuing everyone in sight (including an airline, for an alleged loss of Liz's "marital services" after she was a passenger during a minor crash). Meanwhile, Paul's earlier testimony before Congress has landed him a job as "media consultant" for a Reverend Ude. Ude's fundamentalist television ministry, based in South Carolina, has mushroomed into an important political interest group, and Paul's meager pay from this group is the only thing keeping him and Liz from bankruptcy. Paul drunkenly schemes and rages at Liz, or at his morning newspaper; as in *JR*, the telephone intrudes with maddeningly insistent threats, deals, wrong numbers, and ads.

Events are intensified with the entry of McCandless, owner of the carpenter's gothic house. A sometime geologist, teacher, and writer, McCandless happens to have surveyed the same southeast African mineral fields on which the Vorakers company had built its fortunes. It also happens to be the same African territory in which Reverend Ude is now building his missions for a great "harvest of souls" expected during "the Rapture," or the anticipated Second Coming of Christ. McCandless is being pursued by U.S. government agents for back taxes and for information about those African territories. He appears at the door one morning, a shambling and wary man, an incessant smoker and an alcoholic, but nevertheless an embodiment of romantic adventure to Liz, who promptly takes him to bed.

Events spin rapidly toward violence. During an unexpected visit, Liz's younger brother, Billy, hears McCandless's tirades against American foreign policy and promptly flies off to Africa, where he is killed when his airplane is gunned down by terrorists. The U.S. Congress has launched an investigation of Ude for bribing a senator to grant his ministry a coveted television license, a bribe that Paul carried. Ude has also managed to drown a young boy during baptismal rites in South Carolina's Pee Dee River. All of Liz and Paul's stored belongings, comprising her last links to family and tradition, have been auctioned off by a storage company in compensation for unpaid bills. Liz's behavior becomes increasingly erratic.

The apocalypse comes when all these events and forces collide. McCandless takes a payoff from the Central Intelligence Agency for his African papers and simply exits the novel, after Liz has refused to accompany him. She dies of a heart attack, the warning signs of which have been planted from the first chapter. Paul immediately files a claim to any of the Vorakerses' inheritance that might have been paid to Billy and Liz, and he too simply exits the novel—notably, after using the same seduction ploy on Liz's best friend as he had originally used on Liz herself. In Africa, however, events truly explode: U.S. forces mobilize to guard various "national interests," and a real apocalypse looms as newspapers proclaim the upcoming use of a "10 K 'DEMO' BOMB OFF AFRICA COAST."

Liz Booth's heart attack symbolizes the absolute loss of empathy and love in such a cynical and careless world. Indeed, her death is further ironized when it is misinterpreted, and also proclaimed in the newspapers, as having taken place during a burglary. As with his earlier works, Gaddis's message involves this seemingly total loss of charitable and compassionate love in a civilization obsessed by success as well as by the technologies for realizing it. Once more his satire targets the counterfeiting of values in American life and the explosive force of mass society on feeling individuals.

The explosion of words that Gaddis re-creates is also a warning. As the efforts of painters, writers, musicians, and other artists are increasingly blocked, unappreciated, and exploited, those urges will be acknowledged by fewer and fewer people. Without an audience of listeners or viewers and without a segment of artists, there will be no possibilities for redemption from the chaos and mechanization. There will be neither sufficient introspection nor a medium through which any introspection can take concrete form. Gaddis's novels are humorous, clever, satiric, and innovative. They are also memorable and frightening reflections of contemporary culture and its values.

A Frolic of His Own

A Frolic of His Own could be seen as the culmination of Gaddis's career, applying to the world of law the same combination of acute detailed observation and merciless satirical invention that he gave the business world in *JR* and that of art in *The Recognitions*. The protagonist, middle-aged college professor Oscar Crease, is suing film producer Constantine Kiester for theft of intellectual property, claiming that Kiester's film *The Blood in the Red, White and Blue* was plagiarized from Crease's unpublished and unproduced play *Once at Antietam*. He is also suing himself (actually his insurance company) because he was run over by his own car while he was attempting to jump-start it.

Meanwhile Oscar's father, ninety-seven-year-old judge Thomas Crease, is deciding two even more bizarre cases, a wrongful-death suit against an evangelist (Reverend Ude from *Carpenter's Gothic*) for the drowning of an infant he was attempting to baptize and a case in which a dog has become trapped in a large nonrepresentational sculpture whose creator, R. Szyrk, is demanding an injunction to forestall any attempt to damage his work in order to free the dog. Gaddis uses these cases to spotlight the increasingly Byzantine nature of the legal process as well as some of the artistic issues dear to his heart. The intellectual property suit focuses attention on issues of plagiarism with the same thoroughness with which *The Recognitions* looks at counterfeiting. The heirs of American dramatist Eugene O'Neill, seeing similarities between *Once at Antietam* and O'Neill's *Mourning Becomes Electra* (pr., pb. 1931), sue Oscar in turn, and elements of both are traced back to Plato, reminding readers of the complexity of determining just what constitutes an original idea. The Szyrk case opposes artistic freedom to animal rights, among other issues, and both Szyrk and Oscar can be seen as somewhat ironic versions of that recurrent Gaddis character, the unappreciated "difficult" artist. In the end, as in most of Gaddis's work, the characters are ground down by the chaos and complexity of the modern world, granted only a few Pyrrhic victories. The award Oscar wins in the plagiarism suit is sharply reduced on appeal, and the father of the baptism victim is awarded less than twenty dollars.

With *A Frolic of His Own*, the creator of Recktall Brown gives us the law firm of Swyne and Dour and the Japanese car brands Isuyu and Sosumi. The reader's already strained suspension of disbelief may stop altogether at a suit by the leaders of the Episcopal Church against the makers of Pepsi-Cola for using a brand name that is an anagram of theirs. Again the dialogue is sparsely annotated and often as vague and garrulous as actual conversation. Trial transcripts and depositions are presented in all their verbosity and redundancy. At least enough of *Once at Antietam* is presented to convince us that it is a tedious play. Those who accuse Gaddis's previous works of difficulty and tedium can make the same charges against this one. Even more than his previous works, *A Frolic of His Own* displays the wit, inventiveness, and complexity of Gaddis at his best, but also the qualities to which readers have objected.

Agapē Agape

If *A Frolic of His Own* is the culmination of Gaddis's career, *Agapē Agape* (in early Christian terms, the community of brotherly love) is its dramatic coda and Gaddis's posthumous work for the twenty-first century. Completed just before the author died in 1998, this is his only fiction published after 2000. It is especially important for providing a final context for understanding his career as a writer of fiction. The work draws post-World War II concepts of modernism and postmodernism, and ideas from his previous works, into a first-person stream-of-consciousness monologue of a man who is doing poorly after major surgery. He witnesses and describes his body's collapse and, despite being heavily medicated, is acutely aware of his imminent death.

With similarities to the Fisher King figure in Eliot's *The Waste Land* and King Lear in Shakespeare's tragedy, the narrator is trying to set his lands (and documents, manuscripts, and estate) in order. He reflects on the past while organizing decades of notes originally meant for a single nonfiction study of the player piano, or pianola. Expressing himself in a prose that is spare and lyrical, focused and allusive, he bears similarities to other characters in Gaddis's fiction concerned with reproduction and fraudulence. However, in this final text, the autobiographical dimensions are unmistakable and certainly intentional. Gaddis himself was very ill, attempting like the narrator to assemble his voluminous notes on the history of the player piano. This subject was initially assigned to him in the mid-1940's when he was a fact-checker at *The New Yorker*. Fascinated and disturbed by a machine that enabled anyone to "play" music, to become the artist, so to speak, and experience the creative process mechanically and without the artist, Gaddis never finished the project. It became an intermittent, lifelong research activity. Like numerous other inventions and activities depicted in his novels, the pianola was an instrument of democratization as well as a cultural metaphor of the devaluing of art and the creator, of the obliteration of the individual genius and the end of humanistic traditions.

It is impossible to read this concentrated monologue without hearing three interweaving texts: Gaddis's social history of the pianola, Gaddis's fictionalizing of his last efforts to make use of his research data, and Gaddis's merging of autobiographical details into a final work of (auto)fictional reflection. Indeed, the monologue is driven by the narrator's (and author's) criticisms of popular culture and the transformation of art into entertainment, largely through mechanical, technological, and electronic reproduction. *Agapē Agape* dramatizes with concentration and erudition the forces of disorder and dislocation. Entropy is everywhere, and every man, woman, and child participates in it with a computer or electronic device in hand. In other words, at the end of his life, Gaddis was still struggling against the chaos he had written about for half a century. He accomplished this by reworking a nonfiction social history into a fiction that reflects on and enacts his own life while warning of the excesses of global commodification and, prophetically, of the expanding universe of virtual realities.

Miriam Fuchs
Updated by Arthur D. Hlavaty

Other major work

NONFICTION: *The Rush for Second Place: Essays and Occasional Writings*, 2002 (Joseph Tabbi, editor).

Bibliography

Beer, John. "William Gaddis." *Review of Contemporary Fiction* 21 (Fall, 2001): 69-110. Very thorough overview article provides a good introduction to Gaddis's body of work. Focuses on Gaddis's satirical style.

Bloom, Harold, ed. *William Gaddis*. Philadelphia: Chelsea House, 2004. Comprehensive collection of critical essays addresses many aspects of Gaddis's fiction. Includes brief biographical information and chronology.

Karl, Frederick R. *American Fictions, 1940-1980: A Comprehensive History and Critical Evaluation*. New York: Harper & Row, 1983. Includes an important essay on Gaddis's place among contemporary writers such as Donald Barthelme and Thomas Pynchon, focusing in particular on Gaddis's satires of counterfeit art, fake sensibility, and empty values in American civilization. Offers an informative discussion of Gaddis's narrative techniques, especially his development of scenes and characters in his first two novels.

Knight, Christopher J. *Hints and Guesses: William Gaddis's Fiction of Longing*. Madison: University of Wisconsin Press, 1997. Analyzes Gaddis's first four novels in depth and addresses the author's significance as a social theorist and satirist. Includes bibliographical references and index.

Moore, Steven. *A Reader's Guide to William Gaddis's "The Recognitions."* Lincoln: University of Nebraska Press, 1982. Indispensable, line-by-line guidebook to Gaddis's difficult first novel provides concise annotations of its extratextual allusions and quotations as well as the novel's intratextual developments of character and events. Also includes an informative introductory essay and reprints three previously published but rare early pieces by Gaddis.

_______. *William Gaddis*. Boston: Twayne, 1989. Readable and critically incisive study examines the writer's career and his principal works from *The Recognitions* through *Carpenter's Gothic*. An opening biographical chapter provides extensive information about Gaddis's childhood, his education, his work, and his affiliations leading up to the first novel.

Review of Contemporary Fiction 2 (Summer, 1982). Special issue is devoted in part to Gaddis's work. Contains a rare though brief interview with the author as well as seven original essays on *The Recognitions* and *JR*. Most of the essays concentrate on the bases of form in novels still regarded, in 1982, as too formless and sprawling.

Tabbi, Joseph, and Rone Shavers, eds. *Paper Empire: William Gaddis and the World System*. Tuscaloosa: University of Alabama Press, 2007. Collection of critical essays locates Gaddis's canon within literary, cultural, and media studies as well as within economic and global contexts.

Wolfe, Peter. *A Vision of His Own*. Cranbury, N.J.: Fairleigh Dickinson University Press, 1997. Thoroughgoing study of Gaddis's first four novels emphasizes such themes as the role of the artist, language and law as efforts to assert meaning and order in the face of entropy, and the soul-destroying aspects of twentieth century American culture.

ERNEST J. GAINES

Born: Oscar, Louisiana; January 15, 1933
Also known as: Ernest James Gaines

Principal long fiction

Catherine Carmier, 1964
Of Love and Dust, 1967
The Autobiography of Miss Jane Pittman, 1971
In My Father's House, 1978
A Gathering of Old Men, 1983
A Lesson Before Dying, 1993

Other literary forms

Ernest J. Gaines published a collection of short stories, *Bloodline*, in 1968. One story from that collection, *A Long Day in November*, was published separately in a children's edition in 1971.

Achievements

Throughout his career, Ernest J. Gaines has been a serious and committed writer of fiction. He has always worked slowly, frustratingly slowly to his admirers, but that is because of his great devotion to and respect for the craft of fiction. His six novels are all set in rural Louisiana, north of Baton Rouge: Gaines, like William Faulkner, has created a single world in which his works are centered. Even though Gaines has written during a time of great racial turmoil and unrest, he has resisted becoming involved in political movements, feeling that he can best serve the cause of art and humanity by devoting himself to perfecting his craft. This does not mean that he has remained detached from political realities. Taken together, his novels cover the period of 1865 to 1980, reflecting the social movements that have affected black Americans during that time. Gaines has said again and again, however, that he is primarily interested in people; certainly it is in his depiction of people that his greatest strength lies. His focus is on the universals of life: love, pride, pity, hatred. He aspires thus not to have an immediate political impact with his writing but to move people emotionally. His supreme achievement in this regard is *The Autobiography of Miss Jane Pittman*. With its publication—and with the highly acclaimed made-for-television film based on the novel—Gaines achieved the recognition he had long deserved.

Biography

From birth until age fifteen, Ernest James Gaines lived in rural Louisiana with his parents. As a boy, he often worked in the plantation fields and spent much of his spare time with his aunt, Miss Augusteen Jefferson. He moved to Vallejo, California, in 1948 to live with his mother and stepfather, and he attended high school and junior college there before serving in the army. After his military service, he earned a B.A. degree at San Francisco State College. On the basis of some stories written while he was a student there, he was awarded the Wallace Stegner Creative Writing Fellowship in 1958 for graduate study at Stanford University.

He was a Guggenheim Fellow in 1971 and won an award from the Black Academy of Arts and Letters in 1972. In 1987 Gaines received a literary award from the American Academy and Institute of Arts and Letters, and in 1993 he was awarded a John D. and Catherine T. MacArthur Foundation fellowship. Also in that year, *A Lesson Before Dying* won the National Book Critics Circle Award.

Since 1958 Gaines has lived, impermanently, by his own testimony, in or near San Francisco, feeling that living elsewhere enables him to gain a perspective on his southern material that would be unavailable were he to live in the South full time. By making yearly trips back to Louisiana, where he holds a visiting professorship in creative writing at the University of Southwestern Louisiana in Lafayette, he retains contact with his native region.

Analysis

Before it became fashionable, Ernest J. Gaines was one southern black writer who wrote about his native area. Although he has lived much of his life in California, he has never been able to write adequately about that region. He has tried to write two novels about the West but has failed to finish either of them. Thus, while he has physically left the South, he has never left emotionally.

His ties remain with the South, and his works remain rooted there. When he first began reading seriously, Gaines gravitated toward those writers who wrote about the soil and the people who lived close to it, among them William Faulkner, John Steinbeck, Willa Cather, and Ivan Turgenev. He was disappointed to discover that few black writers had dealt with the black rural southern experience. (Richard Wright had begun his career by doing so, and his work weakened as he moved further from the South.) Thus, Gaines began his career with the conscious desire to fill a void. He felt that no one had written fiction about his people.

This fact helps explain why his novels always concentrate on rural settings and on the "folk" who inhabit them. One of the great strengths of his work is voice; the sound of the voice telling the story is central to its meaning. Among his works, *Of Love and Dust*, *The Autobiography of Miss Jane Pittman*, and all the stories in *Bloodline* are told in the first person by rural black characters. The voices of the storytellers, especially Miss Jane's, express the perspective not only of the individual speakers but also in some sense of the entire black community, and it is the community on which Gaines most often focuses his attention.

Louisiana society, especially from a racial perspective, is complicated. Not only blacks and whites live there, but also Creoles and Cajuns. Thus there are competing communities, and some of Gaines's more interesting characters find themselves caught between groups, forced to weigh competing demands in order to devise a course of action.

Several themes recur in the Gaines canon, and together they create the total effect of his work. Generally, he deals with the relationship between past and present and the possibility of change, both individual and social. Using a broad historical canvas in his works, especially in *The Autobiography of Miss Jane Pittman*, Gaines treats the changes in race relations over time, but he is most interested in people, in whether and how they change as individuals. The issue of determinism and free will is therefore a central question in his work. Gaines has been very interested in and influenced by Greek tragedy, and in his fiction, a strain of environmental determinism is evident. In his works prior to and including *The Autobiography of Miss Jane Pittman*, a growing freedom on the part of his black characters can be seen, but the tension between fate and free will always underlies his works.

Some of Gaines's most admirable characters—for example, Marcus in *Of Love and Dust*, and Ned, Joe, and Jimmy in *The Autobiography of Miss Jane Pittman*—have the courage, pride, and dignity to fight for change. At the same time, however, Gaines reveres the old, who, while often resistant to change, embody the strength of the black people. In his work, one frequently finds tension between generations, a conflict between old and

Ernest J. Gaines. (© Jerry Bauer)

young that is reconciled only in the character of Miss Jane Pittman, who even in extreme old age retains the courage to fight for change.

Other recurring tensions and dichotomies are evident in Gaines's novels. Conflict often exists between men and women. Because of slavery, which denied them their manhood, black men feel forced to take extreme actions to attain or assert it, a theme most evident in *Of Love and Dust*, *The Autobiography of Miss Jane Pittman*, *A Gathering of Old Men*, and the stories in *Bloodline*. Women, on the other hand, are often presented in Gaines's fiction as preservers and conservers. Each group embodies a strength, but Gaines suggests that wholeness comes about only when the peculiar strengths of the two sexes are united, again most clearly exemplified in Miss Jane and her relationship with the men in her life.

Among the male characters, a tension exists between fathers and sons. Treated explicitly in Gaines's fourth novel, *In My Father's House*, this theme is implicit throughout the canon. Though young men look to the older generation for models, there are few reliable examples for them to follow, and they find it difficult to take responsibility for their lives and for the lives of their loved ones.

Gaines's characters at their best seek freedom and dignity: Some succeed, and some fail in their attempts to overcome both outer and inner obstacles. Viewed in sequence, Gaines's first three novels move from the almost total bleakness and determinism of *Catherine Carmier* to the triumph of *The Autobiography of Miss Jane Pittman*. *In My Father's House*, however, reflects a falling away of hope in both individual and social terms, perhaps corresponding to the diminution of expectations experienced in America during the late 1970's and early 1980's.

Catherine Carmier

Gaines's first novel, *Catherine Carmier*, based on a work he wrote while an adolescent in Vallejo, has many of the characteristic weaknesses of a first novel and is more interesting for what it anticipates in Gaines's later career than for its intrinsic merits. Though it caused barely a ripple of interest when it was first published, the novel introduces many of the themes that Gaines treats more effectively in his mature fiction. The book is set in the country, near Bayonne, Louisiana, an area depicted as virtually a wasteland. Ownership of much of this region has devolved to the Cajuns, who appear throughout Gaines's novels as Snopes-like vermin, interested in owning the land only to exploit it. Like Faulkner, Gaines sees this kind of person as particularly modern, and the growing power of the Cajuns indicates a weakening of values and a loss of determination to live in right relationship to the land.

Onto the scene comes Jackson Bradley, a young black man born and reared in the area but (like Gaines himself) educated in California. Bradley is a hollow, rootless man, a man who does not know where he belongs. He has found the North and the West empty, with people living hurried, pointless lives, but he sees the South as equally empty. Feeling no link to a meaningful past and no hope for a productive future, Bradley is a deracinated modern man. He has returned to Louisiana to bid final farewell to his Aunt Charlotte, a representative of the older generation, and to her way of life.

While there and while trying to find a meaningful path for himself, Bradley meets and falls in love with Catherine Carmier. She, too, is living a blocked life, and he feels that if they can leave the area, they will be able to make a fulfilling life together. Catherine is the daughter of Raoul Carmier, in many ways the most interesting character in the novel. A Creole, he is caught between the races. Because of his black blood, he is not treated as the equal of whites, but because of his white blood, he considers blacks to be beneath him. He has a near incestuous relationship with Catherine, since after her birth his wife was unfaithful to him and he considers none of their subsequent children his. Feeling close only to Catherine, he forbids her to associate with any men, but especially with black men. A man of great pride and love of the land, Raoul is virtually the only man in the region to resist the encroachment of the Cajuns. His attitude isolates him all the more, which in turn makes him fanatically determined to hold to Catherine.

Despite her love for and loyalty to her father, Catherine senses the dead end her life has become and returns Bradley's love. Though she wants to leave with him, she is paralyzed by her love of her father and by her knowledge of what her leaving would do to him. This conflict climaxes with a brutal fight between Raoul and Bradley over Catherine, a fight that Bradley wins. Catherine, however, returns home to nurse her father. The novel ends ambiguously, with at least a hint that Catherine will return to Bradley, although the thrust of the book militates against that eventuality. Gaines implies that history and caste are a prison, a tomb. No change is possible for the characters because they cannot break out of the cages their lives have become. Love is the final victim. Catherine will continue living her narrow, unhealthy life, and Jackson Bradley will continue wandering the earth, searching for something to fill his inner void.

OF LOVE AND DUST

Gaines's second novel, *Of Love and Dust*, was received much more enthusiastically than was *Catherine Carmier*; with it, he began to win the largely positive, respectful reviews that continued with his subsequent work. Like *Catherine Carmier*, *Of Love and Dust* is a story of frustrated love. The setting is the same: rural Louisiana, where the Cajuns are gradually assuming ownership and control of the land. *Of Love and Dust* is a substantial improvement over *Catherine Carmier*, however, in part because it is told in the first person by Jim Kelly, an observer of the central story. In this novel, one can see Gaines working toward the folk voice that became such an integral part of the achievement of *The Autobiography of Miss Jane Pittman*.

The plot of the novel concerns Marcus Payne, a young black man sentenced to prison for murder and then bonded out by a white plantation owner who wants him to work in his fields. Recognizing Marcus's rebelliousness and pride, the owner and his Cajun overseer, Sidney Bonbon, brutally attempt to break his spirit. This only makes Marcus more determined, and in revenge, he decides to seduce Louise, Bonbon's neglected wife. What begins, however, as simply a selfish and egocentric act of revenge on Marcus's part grows into a genuine though grotesque love. When he and Louise decide to run away together, Bonbon discovers them and kills Marcus. Even though he dies, Marcus, by resisting brutalizing circumstances, retains his pride and attempts to prove his manhood and dignity. His attempts begin in a self-centered way, but as his love for Louise grows, he grows in stature in the reader's eyes until he becomes a figure of heroic dimensions.

Through his use of a first-person narrator, Gaines creates a double perspective in the novel, including on the one hand the exploits of Marcus and on the other the black community's reactions to them. The narrator, Jim Kelly, is the straw boss at the plantation, a member of the black community but also accepted and trusted by the whites because of his dependability and his unwillingness to cause any problems. His initial reaction to Marcus—resentment and dislike of him as a troublemaker—represents the reaction of the community at large. The older members of the community never move beyond that attitude because they are committed to the old ways, to submission and accommodation. To his credit, however, Jim's attitude undergoes a transformation. As he observes Marcus, his resentment changes to sympathy and respect, for he comes to see Marcus as an example of black manhood that others would do well to emulate.

Marcus's death gives evidence of the strain of fate and determinism in this novel as well, yet because he dies with his pride and dignity intact, *Of Love and Dust* is more hopeful than *Catherine Carmier*. Gaines indicates that resistance is possible and, through the character of Jim Kelly, that change can occur. Kelly leaves the plantation at the end of the novel, no longer passively accepting what fate brings him but believing that he can act and shape his own life. Though Marcus is an apolitical character, like Jackson Bradley, it is suggested that others will later build on his actions to force social change on the South. *Of Love and Dust* is a major step forward beyond *Catherine Carmier* both artistically and thematically. Through his use of the folk voice, Gaines vivifies his story, and the novel suggests the real possibility of free action by his characters.

THE AUTOBIOGRAPHY OF MISS JANE PITTMAN

Without a doubt, *The Autobiography of Miss Jane Pittman* is Gaines's major contribution to American literature. Except for an introduction written by "the editor," it is told entirely in the first person by Miss Jane and covers approximately one hundred years, from the Civil War to the Civil Rights movement of the 1960's. Basing the novel on stories he heard while he was a child in the company of his aunt, Augusteen Jefferson, and using the format of oral history made popular in recent decades, Gaines created a "folk autobiography" that tells the story of people who are not in the history books. While the work is the story of Miss Jane, she is merely an observer for a substantial portion of its length, and the story becomes that of black Americans from slavery to the present. Gaines's mastery of voice is especially important here, for Miss Jane's voice is the voice of her people.

From the very beginning of the novel, when Miss Jane is determined, even in the face of physical beatings, to keep the name a Union soldier gave her and refuses to be called Ticey, her slave name, to the end of the novel, when she leads her people to Bayonne in a demonstration against segregated facilities, she is courageous and in the best sense of the word "enduring," like Faulkner's Dilsey. In her character and story, many of the dichotomies that run through Gaines's work are unified.

The differing roles of men and women are important elements in the book. Women preserve and sustain—a role symbolized by Miss Jane's longevity. Men, on the other hand, feel the need to assert their manhood in an active way. Three black men are especially important in Miss Jane's life, beginning with Ned, whom she rears from childhood after his mother is killed and who becomes in effect a "son" to her. Like Marcus Payne, Ned is a rebel, but his rebellion is concentrated in the political arena. Returning to Louisiana after the turn of the century, he attempts to lead his people to freedom. Though he is murdered by whites, his legacy and memory are carried on by Miss Jane and the people in the community. Later, in the 1960's, Jimmy Aaron, another young man who tries to encourage his people to effective political action, appears. Again the members of the older generation hang back, fearful of change and danger, but after Jimmy is killed, Jane unites old and young, past and present by her determination to go to Bayonne and carry on Jimmy's work. Thus Marcus's apolitical rebellion in *Of Love and Dust* has been transformed into political action. The third man in Jane's life is Joe Pittman, her husband. A horse-breaker, he is committed to asserting and proving his manhood through his work. Although he too dies, killed by a wild horse he was determined to break, Jane in her understanding and love of him, as well as in her affection for all her men, bridges the gap between man and woman. In her character, the opposites of old and young, past and present, and man and woman are reconciled.

Miss Jane's strength is finally the strength of the past, but it is directed toward the future. When Jimmy returns, he tells the people that he is nothing without their strength, referring not only to their physical numbers but also to the strength of their character as it has been forged by all the hardships they have undergone through history. Even though the people seem weak and fearful, the example of Miss Jane shows that they need not be. They can shake off the chains of bondage and determinism, assert their free spirit through direct action, and effect change. The change has only begun by the conclusion of *The Autobiography of Miss Jane Pittman*, but the pride and dignity of Miss Jane and all those she represents suggest that ultimately they will prevail.

In My Father's House

Gaines's fourth novel, *In My Father's House*, was the first he had written in the third person since *Catherine Carmier*; the effect of its point of view is to distance the reader from the action and characters, creating an ironic perspective. Set during a dreary winter in 1970, in the period of disillusionment following the assassination of Martin Luther King, Jr., the novel suggests that the progress that was implicit in the ending of *The Autobiography of Miss Jane Pittman* was temporary at best, if not downright illusory. The atmosphere of the novel is one of frustration and stagnation.

Both the setting and the protagonist of *In My Father's House* are uncharacteristic for Gaines. Instead of using the rural settings so familiar from his other works, he sets his story in a small town. Rather than focusing on the common people, Gaines chooses as his protagonist Philip Martin, one of the leaders of the black community, a public figure, a minister who is considering running for Congress. A success by practically any measure and pridefully considering himself a *man*, Martin is brought low in the course of the novel. His illegitimate son, Robert X, a ghostlike man, appears and wordlessly accuses him. Robert is evidence that, by abandoning him, his siblings, and their mother many years previously, Martin in effect destroyed their lives. Having been a drinker and gambler, irresponsible, he tries to explain to his son that his earlier weakness was a legacy of slavery. Even though he seems to have surmounted that crippling legacy, his past rises up to haunt him and forces him to face his weakness. Martin wants to effect a reconciliation with his son and thus with his past, but Robert's suicide precludes that. *In My Father's House* makes explicit a concern that was only implicit in Gaines's earlier novels, the relationship between fathers and sons. No communication is possible here, and the failure is illustrative of a more general barrier between the generations. While in the earlier novels the young people led in the struggle for change and the older characters held back, here the situation is reversed. Martin and members of his generation are the leaders, while the young are for the most part sunk in cynicism, apathy, and hopelessness, or devoted to anarchic violence. If the hope of a people is in the young, or in a reconciliation of old and young, hope does not exist in this novel.

A Gathering of Old Men

Hope does exist, however, in Gaines's *A Gathering of Old Men*, for which Gaines returns to his more characteristic rural setting. Here he returns as well to the optimism with which *The Autobiography of Miss Jane Pittman* ends. This time, as at the end of that novel and in *In My Father's House*, it is up to the old among the black community to lead the struggle for change, this time primarily because there are no young men left to lead. All of them have escaped to towns and cities that promise more of a future than does rural Louisiana.

In this small corner of Louisiana, however, as elsewhere in Gaines's fiction, Cajuns are encroaching on the land, replacing men with machines and even threatening to plow up the old graveyard where generations of blacks have been buried. When Beau Boutan, son of the powerful Cajun Fix Boutan, is shot to death in the quarters of Marshall plantation, where Marshall blacks have worked the land since the days of slavery, the old black men who have lived there all of their lives are faced with one last chance to stand up and be men. They stand up for the sake of Matthu, the only one of them who ever stood up before and thus the most logical suspect in the murder. They also stand up because of all the times in their past when they should have stood up but did not. They prove one last time that free action is possible when eighteen or more of them, all in their seventies and eighties, arm themselves with rifles of the same gauge used in the shooting and face down the white sheriff, Mapes, each in his turn claiming to be the killer.

As shut off as the quarters are from the rest of the world, it is easy to forget that the events of the novel take place as recently as the late 1970's. Beau Boutan's brother Gil, however, represents the change that has been taking place in the world outside Marshall. He has achieved gridiron fame at Louisiana State University by working side by side with Cal, a young black man. Youth confronts age when Gil returns home and tries to persuade his father not to ride in revenge against Beau's murderer, as everyone expects him to do. Gil represents the possibility of change from the white perspective. He convinces his father to let the law find and punish Beau's murderer, but he pays a heavy price when his father disowns him. He cannot stop other young Cajuns, led by Luke Will, who are not willing to change but would rather cling to the vigilantism of the old South.

In spite of their dignity and pride, the old men at Marshall risk looking rather silly because after all these years they stand ready for a battle that seems destined never to take place once Fix Boutan decides not to ride on Marshall. Sheriff Mapes taunts them with the knowledge that they have waited too late to take a stand. Ironically, they are ultimately able to maintain their dignity and reveal their growth in freedom by standing up to the one person who has been most valiant in her efforts to help them: Candy Marshall, niece of the landowner. In her effort to protect Matthu, who was largely responsible for rearing her after her parents died, Candy has gone so far as to try to take credit for the murder herself. What she fails to realize is that the days are long past when black men need the protection of a white woman. She is stunned to realize that she too has been living in the past and has been guilty of treating grown black men like children.

The novel does eventually end with a gunfight, because Luke Will and his men refuse to let the murder of a white man by a black one go unavenged. It is fitting that the two men who fall in the battle are Luke Will, the one who was most resistant to change, and Charlie Biggs, the real murderer, who, at fifty, finally proves his manhood by refusing to be beaten by Beau Boutan and then by returning to take the blame for the murder that he has committed. Charlie's body is treated like a sacred relic as each member of the black community, from the oldest to the youngest, touches it, hoping that some of the courage that Charlie found late in life will rub off. Apparently it already has.

With *A Gathering of Old Men*, Gaines returns to first-person narration, but this time the history is told one chapter at a time by various characters involved in or witnessing the action. His original plan was to have the narrator be the white newspaperman Lou Dimes, Candy's boyfriend. He found, however, that there was still much that a black man in Louisiana would not confide to a white man, even a sympathetic one, so he let the people tell their own story, with Dimes narrating an occasional chapter.

A Lesson Before Dying

A Lesson Before Dying, set in Gaines's fictional Bayonne during six months of 1948, reveals the horrors of Jim Crowism in the story of twenty-one-year-old Jefferson, a scarcely literate man-child who works the cane fields of Pichot Plantation. Jefferson hooks up with two criminals who are killed during the robbery of a liquor store, along with the store's white proprietor. Jefferson is left to stand trial before a jury of twelve white men who overlook his naivete despite his lawyer's argument that he is a dumb animal, a "thing" that acts on command, no more deserving of the electric chair than a hog. When this description causes Jefferson to become practically catatonic, his grandmother enlists the local schoolteacher, Grant Wiggins, to help Jefferson gain his manhood before he is put to death. Thus, like *A Gathering of Old Men*, this novel questions the traditional devaluing of black males in the south.

Reluctantly, Wiggins agrees to help Jefferson by encouraging him to speak and to write, visiting him often and giving him a journal in which to record his thoughts. Finally, right before his execution, Jefferson has a breakthrough when he tells Wiggins to thank his students for the pecans they sent him in jail. Wiggins himself becomes the central character as he learns the real lesson of the novel, that all people are connected and responsible for each other. Wiggins comes to terms with his own role in the system that victimizes Jefferson, and the entire community learns from how Jefferson faces his execution. The novel pays a tribute to those who persevere in the face of injustice, and it also puts forward hope for better racial relationships, especially in the character of Paul, the young white jailer who is sympathetic to Jefferson and to Grant Wiggins's attempts to bring forth his humanity.

If *In My Father's House* represents a falling away of hope for human progress and perhaps also a falling away in artistry, one finds once again in *A Gathering of Old Men* and *A Lesson Before Dying* evidence of the same genuine strengths that Gaines exhibited in *The Autobiography of Miss Jane Pittman*: a mastery of the folk voice, a concern for common people, a reverence for the everyday, a love of the land, and a powerful evocation of the strength, pride, and dignity people can develop by working on and living close to the soil.

Frank W. Shelton
Updated by Rebecca G. Smith

Other major works

SHORT FICTION: *Bloodline*, 1968; *A Long Day in November*, 1971.

MISCELLANEOUS: *Porch Talk with Ernest Gaines*, 1990; *Mozart and Leadbelly: Stories and Essays*, 2005.

Bibliography

Auger, Philip. *Native Sons in No Man's Land: Rewriting Afro-American Manhood in the Novels of Baldwin, Walker, Wideman, and Gaines*. New York: Garland, 2000. Examines Gaines's use of religious allegory in commenting on and providing role models for manhood in his novels.

Babb, Valerie Melissa. *Ernest Gaines*. Boston: Twayne, 1991. Provides a solid introduction to the author and his works. Clear, critical analysis devotes one chapter to each of Gaines's major works. Includes bibliography and index.

Beavers, Herman. *Wrestling Angels into Song: The Fictions of Ernest J. Gaines and James Alan McPherson*. Philadelphia: University of Pennsylvania Press, 1995. Thoughtful analysis of the literary kinship of Gaines and McPherson with their precursor Ralph Ellison focuses on all three writers' characters' sense of community, storytelling, and self-recovery. Begins with a look at their southernness and then examines all three as American writers. Discusses Gaines's work through *A Lesson Before Dying*.

Carmean, Karen. *Ernest J. Gaines: A Critical Companion*. Westport, Conn.: Greenwood Press, 1998. Presents an introductory overview of Gaines's work, with analysis of each of his novels and short-story collections. Includes a thorough bibliography of primary and secondary sources.

Clark, Keith. *Black Manhood in James Baldwin, Ernest J. Gaines, and August Wilson*. Urbana: University of Illinois Press, 2002. Chapter on Gaines's work focuses on the "neo-masculinist literary imagination." The opening chapter of the book outlines the aesthetics of black masculinist protest discourse since 1940, contextualizing the later discussion.

Doyle, Mary Ellen. *Voices from the Quarters: The Fiction of Ernest J. Gaines*. Baton Rouge: Louisiana State University Press, 2002. Examines the ways in which Gaines peoples Louisiana's bayous and cane fields with characters that exemplify their real-life counterparts.

Estes, David E., ed. *Critical Reflections on the Fiction of Ernest J. Gaines*. Athens: University of Georgia Press, 1994. Fourteen essays cover all six novels to 1994 and *Bloodline* as well as film adaptations of Gaines's work, offering detailed explications in addition to broad analyses of pastoralism, humor, race, and gender. Excellent introduction highlights important biographical facts, secondary sources, and literary themes in Gaines's work.

Gaines, Ernest J., Marcia G. Gaudet, and Carl Wooton. *Porch Talk with Ernest Gaines: Conversations on the Writer's Craft*. Baton Rouge: Louisiana State University Press, 1990. Transcription of an intimate interview conducted by colleagues of Gaines offers an insightful look at how the author has transmuted his Louisiana heritage, familial experiences, literary influences, and strong folk tradition into fiction with a distinct voice.

Lowe, John, ed. *Conversations with Ernest Gaines*. Jackson: University Press of Mississippi, 1995. Collection of interviews with Gaines provides information about his life, his themes, and his works. Includes index and chronology of his life.

Simpson, Anne K. *A Gathering of Gaines: The Man and the Writer*. Lafayette: Center for Louisiana Studies, University of Southwestern Louisiana, 1991. Well-documented study offers a biographical sketch, an examination of Gaines's stylistic influences and characteristics, and a critical overview of his fiction. Includes a thorough bibliography.

MAVIS GALLANT

Born: Montreal, Quebec, Canada; August 11, 1922
Also known as: Mavis de Trafford Young

Principal long fiction

Green Water, Green Sky, 1959
Its Image on the Mirror, 1964 (novella)
A Fairly Good Time, 1970
The Pegnitz Junction, 1973 (novella)

Other literary forms

The literary reputation of Mavis Gallant (guh-LAHNT) rests more on her short fiction than on her novels. The great majority of Gallant's published short stories have appeared in *The New Yorker*, and many of them have also been collected in books, including *The Other Paris* (1956); *My Heart Is Broken*, which contains the novella *Its Image on the Mirror* (1964); *The End of the World, and Other Stories* (1974); *From the Fifteenth District* (1979); *Home Truths: Selected Canadian Stories* (1981); *In Transit* (1988); *Across the Bridge* (1993); *The Moslem Wife, and Other Stories* (1994); *Paris Stories* (2002); and *Varieties of Exile* (2003). Her one play, *What Is to Be Done?*, was performed in Toronto in 1982. Her nonfiction includes a seventy-two-page essay about a French schoolteacher's affair with a student that appeared as the introduction to *The Affair of Gabrielle Russier* (1971) and a substantial body of periodical essays, book reviews, and newspaper features and articles, some of which are collected in *Paris Notebooks: Essays and Reviews* (1986).

Achievements

Mavis Gallant's chief accomplishment as an author has been to illuminate the physical and psychological effects of the aftermath of World War II and of geographic and cultural dislocation in general. Her recognition of the essential homelessness of the human spirit in the modern world gives her work an appeal on both sides of the Atlantic. She transmutes the banalities of the life of the stranger abroad into metaphors of wandering in a confusing landscape, which is both another country and one's own heart.

After Gallant won the Canadian Fiction Prize in 1978 and the Governor-General's Award in 1981, literary awards continued to come her way. Her publications have garnered the Canada-Australia Literary Prize (1984), the Canada Council Molson Prize for the Arts (1996), the Matt Cohen Award (2001), and the Rea Award for the Short Story (2002). Although Gallant is bilingual, she writes only in English, so it was quite a distinction for her to receive Quebec's Prix-Athanase-David in 2006, which up until that point was given only for literature written in French.

Gallant was made an Officer of the Order of Canada in 1981 and was promoted to the order's highest level of Companion in 1993. In 1989 she became an Honorary Member of the American Academy of Arts and Letters as well as a fellow of the Royal Society of Literature (United Kingdom). In 2004, she was the recipient of a Lannan Literary Fellowship. Since the 1980's, Gallant has been awarded honorary degrees from several universities, including the University of Toronto, the University of Montreal, York University, and Queen's University. Her papers are donated on an ongoing basis to the University of Toronto, where she was a writer-in-residence in 1983-1984. She is considered by critics in Europe and in North America to be one of the greatest Canadian writers of short fiction, along with Alice Munro and Morley Callaghan.

Biography

Mavis Gallant was born Mavis de Trafford Young in Montreal, Quebec, in 1922, to Canadian Scottish Protestant parents. Her early life in a city of diverse languages, religions, and cultures gave her a sense of pluralism that permeates all her fiction. Sent away to a French boarding school at the age of four, she attended a succession of seventeen different schools in both the United States and Canada. The constant change in school venues gave her a keen sensitivity to the sense of displacement and exile that is explored in so much of her fiction.

Gallant chose not to attend college but instead returned to Montreal, intent on a writing career. She took a job with the National Film Board of Canada in 1943, editing documentary films, but soon resumed her search for a writing job. She was hired by the *Montreal Standard* newspaper in 1944 as a feature writer and worked there until 1950. Her story "With a Capital T," collected in *Home Truths*, is a good account of what it was like to be an intelligent, imaginative young woman grudgingly allowed by old newspapermen to fill in while the younger men were away at war. During her time at the *Standard* her five-year marriage to John Gallant, a musician from Winnipeg, ended in divorce in 1948.

Gallant had set herself the goal of being independent by the age of thirty, and, in 1950, despite a chorus of dire warnings from her peers, she resigned her position with the *Standard* and, with a gift of five hundred dollars from her editor, went off to live and write abroad. In 1951, she published her first story with *The New Yorker*, "Madeline's Birthday," and she continued to publish stories in that magazine for the next five decades. By the mid-1970's she abandoned long fiction in favor of short stories. The 1996 publication of *The Collected Stories of Mavis Gallant*, which includes her best pieces from 1953 to 1995, consists of fifty-one short stories and one novella (*The Pegnitz Junction*). She long ago silenced those who doubted her ability to succeed on her own. Beginning with her job on the *Standard*, Gallant has always earned her living solely by her writing.

Although she has always maintained her Canadian citizenship, Gallant has lived in Europe since 1950. She initially traveled around—living in Paris, Salzburg, Rome, Sicily, and Spain—but finally settled in France in 1953, dividing her time between Paris and her house in Menton in southeastern France. Since 1975 Gallant has made her only home in a Paris apartment in the fashionable Faubourg Saint-Germain district of the Left Bank. She maintains a keen interest in European and North American political and literary affairs, daily reading newspapers in French, Italian, German, and En-

Mavis Gallant. (© Allison Harris)

glish. Preferring not to be tied to strict historical accuracy, she writes mostly from memory, but she has kept complete notebooks of her thoughts and observations and is editing them in five volumes. She continues to retain greatest fondness for the works of the authors she read during her youth: Anton Chekhov, Ivan Turgenev, Fyodor Dostoevski, Stendhal, Gustave Flaubert, and Marcel Proust.

Analysis

Because most of Mavis Gallant's works do not have conclusive endings, it is difficult to cite in traditional terms the theme or central idea governing her fiction. It may be more important to understand the point of reference from which Gallant views her characters, most of whom are middle-class men and women, children, and adolescents who are adrift in a confused sea of unmet expectations. Her view of her characters is almost always from without, classically dispassionate. A recurring image in her work is the mirror, which shows her protagonists with pitiless accuracy, faces they often do not recognize as their own, as in the case of "The Late-Homecomer" in *From the Fifteenth District*. Despite the incoherence of the characters' lives, the world they inhabit is carefully and cleanly drawn, technically precise, perfect in detail. Gallant's descriptions of a train station, a café, or a sitting room are exact as to proportion, color, and shape; in contrast, her characters are often indistinct except for their crippling flaws. This indistinctiveness is suggestive, however, never obscuring. Although her characters are emotionally confused and unable to lift themselves out of the morass of indecision and compromise in which they are stranded, they evoke no pity, no sentiment other than a wistful compassion.

Gallant's concern with homelessness or displacement draws her to the strange amid the familiar. Rest stops—a café, a party, a day's outing—become symbols of the only kind of home her characters are ever likely to have. Anticipation is the rule; farther down the coast perhaps, or next season, or even tomorrow at a friend's, things will begin to come clear, problems will begin to resolve themselves. Gallant's figures are often people of little imagination, burdened with insufficient insight and strength of will to take control of their lives. Inevitably, they drift toward disasters, the consequences of which they foresee dimly, if at all. They live more on hope than by the efficacy of their own actions. The warning sounds they should heed in order to save themselves occur to them as echoes, as sounds of a past already too late to change. Gallant's sense of time is geometric rather than linear: Lives collide and rearrange themselves like billiard balls subject to the tyranny of physics. Personal realities may be contemporaneous, but they never interpenetrate.

Often the sole correspondence between characters is a familial one, to which they give no more thought than to the color of their hair or to next Sunday's dinner. For

Gallant, relationship by marriage or blood is almost certain to destroy whatever humanness could exist in the bonds between people. Some of her stories rehearse the chronicle of a thoughtless parent, usually a mother, spending her child's future to pay the debts of her own present, as if another's life were capital to be borrowed and squandered. "Going Ashore" in *The Other Paris* offers the flighty Mrs. Ellenger and her daughter, Emma, as an example of this kind of relationship. The spectacle of shallow interests, selfishness, fraudulent friendships, and the conniving of people trying to live in grand style while on the thin edge of penury does not, as perhaps it might in the work of a more romantic writer, lead young people to throw off the tyranny of their foolish parents; instead, the children become more numbed by the constant movement, the maintenance of surface at the expense of substance. In consequence, the characters take refuge in an interior life contrived out of the rag ends of the only kind of existence they know. Rarely are Gallant's characters guilty of outrageously immoral actions; rather, their small failings accrete to become an attitude, a way of life that denies personal responsibility while insisting that one is doing everything humanly possible to put things right.

In Gallant's fiction, few characters make good on the occasional second chance. In her short story "The Ice Wagon Going Down the Street" in *Home Truths*, Peter and Sheilah Frazier are middle-class vagabonds lately returned from a posting in Hong Kong, out of which, as usual, they have made no profit, either material or spiritual. Their sole talisman of respectability is Sheilah's Balenciaga gown, which at times has been their ticket to some of the better parties. Peter has allowed one opportunity after another to slip through his fingers while he waits for fate or chance or old friends to rescue him. He walks through the world in lordly fashion, unable to see himself as an aging do-nothing, a failure. Even a small inheritance becomes merely the occasion for a brief episode of happiness in Paris, while the couple imitate those of more substantial and lasting means. At one point, Sheilah's beauty and charm bring Peter a job offer with possibilities for making their fortune at last. Without comment, Gallant shows the couple having returned from that episode, sitting in Peter's sister's kitchen, as forlorn as ever, their sole emblem of prosperity a steamer trunk upended in the corner. The two sit holding hands across the table; there are no recriminations, no bitterness, only a sweetly elegiac sense of the loss of something undefined. Even this sense of loss becomes transmuted through naïve optimism into dreams that can only lead to disappointments, further failures. So it goes with most of Gallant's weary protagonists. Hope based on false premises, action inappropriate to the situation, bad decisions, ineffective compromises—these take their toll on the slowly dying, who puzzle over their distantly echoing pain.

Green Water, Green Sky

Although Gallant's first novel, *Green Water, Green Sky*, is only 154 pages long, it spans some eleven years in the life of Florence McCarthy Harris, from her fifteenth to her twenty-sixth year. Like most of Gallant's protagonists, Flor is a halfhearted combatant against her own lingering dissolution. From Venice to Cannes to Paris, Flor drifts, allowing life simply to happen to her. Her mother, Bonnie McCarthy, is a witless pleasure seeker, a woman who strings her days together with no other end in view than making them an adornment, a strand of cheap, gaudy pearls. The novel's image of Flor comes variously from Bonnie; from Flor's cousin George Fairlee; from Wishart, her mother's sexless male companion; and from Bob Harris, Flor's Jewish husband. Flor stands at the center of this square of mirrors, reflecting only what each gives back as its image of her.

Flor's one serious attempt to take control of her fate is her marriage to Harris. Even in this, she is neutralized; her mother disapproves, not so much because Harris is a Jew but because he understands how to make money while Bonnie knows only how to spend it. Flor's attempts to make compromises between the contending forces in her life wear her down until she eventually takes refuge in madness—not the fine, burning madness of a striving consciousness strained beyond its capacity to reconcile the disparate contingencies of existence, but the attenuated surrender of presence in the world of the real.

Its Image on the Mirror

In *Its Image on the Mirror*, her only work of long fiction set in Canada, Gallant turns her imagination to the effect of time on the lives of the Duncan sisters, Jean and Isobel. The action of the novella moves backward and forward, weaving a fabric of time in which the individual threads become muted, indistinct. Jean is now Jean Price, mother of four. Her sister is married to Alfredo, a Venezuelan doctor. Jean's life is ordered and sedate; Isobel's is chaotic and confused. The sisters arrive at their parents' cottage for a family reunion, and the past is revealed from Jean's point of view. Less favored than Isobel with beauty, grace, and wit, Jean has made the best of her gifts and is at peace with herself. Isobel has squandered her blessings and lived to see them become a mockery to her.

In her customary method, Gallant describes the surface of things with great precision; interior life is portrayed in relief, the subtle becoming visible by implication. The present is drawn out of Jean's memories of Montreal during the years of World War II and her humdrum existence of that time. By comparison, those days were Isobel's best. She led the more exciting life, involved in the shady business of procuring apartments for refugees at exorbitant rents. She always knew where to get cigarettes, whiskey, and nylons. She was in; Jean was out. Isobel's marriage to a South American doctor had seemed at the time romantic to the staid Duncans. In reality, they now find Alfredo to be short, unattractive, and boorish. The past again catches up with the present, bringing with it its full freight of disappointment. Gallant takes no sides; she is dispassionate, aloof, holding her characters up to the light so that the reader might better inspect them. In the end, Jean's father sums everything up in his observation that the salt does not taste as salty as it once did.

A FAIRLY GOOD TIME

Shirley Perrigny, the protagonist of *A Fairly Good Time*, is a loser. She loses her first husband on their honeymoon, and, by the end of the novel, she is losing her mind; in between, she loses just about everything else that gives meaning to life. She has married again, this time to Philippe, a hack writer of socially aware articles for a second-rate Paris periodical, *Le Miroir*. (The magazine devotes itself to such burning issues as the analysis of English nursery rhymes as the key to understanding the problems of a developing Africa.) Philippe is everything Shirley is not; he is neat, precise, fastidious, and dim. He is more married to his mother and sister than to his wife. Shirley accepts their combined slights as if she deserves them and finds all her efforts to accommodate Philippe's family turned against her. At one point, after her husband has left her to return home to his mother's house to nurse his tender liver, Shirley cannot even get in to see him; his mother reduces their conversation to a whispered dismissal through a barely open door.

Shirley seems always to be confiding her secrets to the enemy. Chief among these is her own mother, who browbeats and humbugs Shirley through her caustic letters. Shirley befriends young Claudie Maurel, who has ordered a restaurant meal without the money to pay for it, and finds herself in the end an inexplicable object of scorn and ridicule to the entire Maurel family. Having forgotten to get money from Philippe before his departure, she goes to borrow some from her neighbor, a Greek lothario. She proceeds to go to bed with him, not because she actively wants to but because she has nothing better to do. Her attempts to help her friend Renata simply add more mismanagement to a life already as confused as her own. In the end, a distraught and disintegrating Shirley, desperate for understanding, mistakes her own image in a mirror for that of a long-sought true companion. She walks joyfully toward the smiling girl.

THE PEGNITZ JUNCTION

The same spirit of futility informs Gallant's novella *The Pegnitz Junction*. Christine and Herbert have gone to Paris to enjoy an affair. Certain things, however, impinge on their fragile bliss: Christine is engaged to a theological student, and Herbert has brought along his little son, Bert. Christine remains faithful to her fiancé in her own way by reading Dietrich Bonhoeffer. Herbert tries unsuccessfully to nag her into his vision of the liberal pseudoparent. Little Bert enjoys sneaking a nighttime look at the naked, sleeping Christine and in general making a pest of himself.

Gallant employs the return train journey to Strasbourg via Pegnitz as a metaphor for the predictable course of a life along the lines of its own antecedents. The narrative is interleaved with the stories of contingent characters. The complaints of an old woman with whom Christine and Herbert share a compartment are rehearsed in her own italicized thoughts. Christine seems to be aware of these, and at times it is uncertain whether she is imagining them or reading the old woman's mind. At another point, Christine looks out the window at a group of people standing before the gates of an estate, and their story consequently unfolds. When the train is compelled to stop for rerouting, Christine takes notice of an elderly gentleman whose life is told in flashback, again as if occurring in Christine's consciousness. The trip itself is a series of delays, detours, and disappointments; hot drink vendors have coffee but no cups, sandwich hawkers have no sandwiches, the washrooms are locked, and the conductor orders the windows shut despite the heat. Everyone looks forward to Pegnitz; everyone is certain that a comfortable express train will be waiting there, and that there will be food and drink and a chance to freshen up. Their hopes, like their lives, are futile. No train is waiting, only more confusion, delay, and inconvenience. The entire trip has the quality of Christine's life: ill planned and dependent on others to give it direction. She is lost and will remain so.

Long fiction is not Gallant's métier. Her characteristically aloof, precisely rendered sketches of futile lives lose their bite when extended beyond the neat confines of the short story. Nevertheless, her two novels and two novellas repay study, for they work out at length her recurring themes and delve more completely into her recurring categories of dysfunctional characters and families.

Paul LaValley
Updated by Marsha Daigle-Williamson

Other major works

short fiction: *The Other Paris*, 1956; *My Heart Is Broken: Eight Stories and a Short Novel*, 1964 (also known as *An Unmarried Man's Summer*, 1965); *The Pegnitz Junction: A Novella and Five Short Stories*, 1973; *The End of the World, and Other Stories*, 1974; *From the Fifteenth District: A Novella and Eight Short Stories*, 1979; *Home Truths: Selected Canadian Stories*, 1981; *Overhead in a Balloon*, 1985; *In Transit*, 1988; *Across the Bridge*, 1993; *The Moslem Wife, and Other Stories*, 1994; *The Collected Stories of Mavis Gallant*, 1996; *Paris Stories*, 2002; *Varieties of Exile: Stories*, 2003 (also known as *Montreal Stories*, 2004).

play: *What Is to Be Done?*, pr. 1982.

nonfiction: *The Affair of Gabrielle Russier*, 1971; *The War Brides*, 1978; *Paris Notebooks: Essays and Reviews*, 1986.

Bibliography

Clement, Lesley D. *Learning to Look: A Visual Response to Mavis Gallant's Fiction*. Montreal: McGill-Queen's University Press, 2000. Presents chronological discussion of the development of Gallant's style, themes, and characters over a fifty-year period and provides in-depth analysis of *Green Water, Green Sky* and *Its Image on the Mirror*. Includes a bibliography and an excellent index.

Côté, Nicole, and Peter Sabor, eds. *Varieties of Exile: New Essays on Mavis Gallant*. New York: Peter Lang, 2002. Collection offers four essays on Gallant's style and her theme of exile followed by a roundtable discussion (partly in French) with Gallant in which participants include Canadian professors and writers. Includes bibliography and index.

Gunnars, Kristijana, ed. *Transient Questions: New Essays on Mavis Gallant*. Atlanta: Rodopi, 2004. Collection of essays on Gallant's work by Canadian authors, publishers, and scholars covers a range of topics. Six essays address specific stories (one on *The Pegnitz Junction*) and three discuss overall themes in all of the author's work. Includes a brief bibliography.

Jewison, Donald. "Speaking of Mirrors: Imagery and Narration in Two Novellas by Mavis Gallant." *Studies in Canadian Literature* 10, nos. 1/2 (1985): 94-109. Study of *Green Water, Green Sky* and *Its Image on the Mirror* focuses on the significance of mirrors in the works, from the perspective of imagery and narration, and on Gallant's ironic distortion of vision.

Keefer, Janice Kulyk. *Reading Mavis Gallant*. Toronto, Ont.: Oxford University Press, 1989. Presents discussion of Gallant's long fiction, short stories, and nonfiction, arranged thematically and interspersed with comments on her life, her literary theories, and her reception by critics in Canada and in the United States. Includes synopses and analyses of all her works of long fiction, supplemented by excellent footnotes.

Schaub, Danielle. *Mavis Gallant*. New York: Twayne, 1998. Provides commentary on Gallant's fiction and on how the author's irony, stylistic devices, atmosphere, and structure serve to reflect the disconnectedness of her characters. Devotes two chapters to her long fiction. Includes chronology, bibliography, and index.

Smythe, Karen E. "The Silent Cry: Empathy and Elegy in Mavis Gallant's Novels." *Studies in Canadian Literature* 15, no. 2 (1990): 116-135. Discusses the elegiac elements in *Green Water, Green Sky*, *Its Image on the Mirror*, and *A Fairly Good Time* and argues that Gallant uses such elements to elicit reader involvement.

JOHN GALSWORTHY

Born: Kingston Hill, Surrey, England; August 14, 1867
Died: London, England; January 31, 1933
Also known as: John Sinjohn

Principal long fiction

Jocelyn, 1898 (as John Sinjohn)
Villa Rubein, 1900 (as Sinjohn)
The Island Pharisees, 1904
The Man of Property, 1906
The Country House, 1907
Fraternity, 1909
The Patrician, 1911
The Dark Flower, 1913
The Freelands, 1915
The Little Man, 1915
Beyond, 1917
The Burning Spear, 1919, 1923
Saint's Progress, 1919
In Chancery, 1920
To Let, 1921
The Forsyte Saga, 1922 (includes *The Man of Property*, "Indian Summer of a Forsyte," "Awakening," *In Chancery*, and *To Let*)
The White Monkey, 1924
The Silver Spoon, 1926
Swan Song, 1928
A Modern Comedy, 1929 (includes *The White Monkey*, *The Silver Spoon*, *Two Forsyte Interludes*, and *Swan Song*)
Maid in Waiting, 1931
Flowering Wilderness, 1932
Over the River, 1933
End of the Chapter, 1934 (includes *Maid in Waiting*, *Flowering Wilderness*, and *Over the River*)

Other literary forms

John Galsworthy (GAWLZ-wur-thee) attempted and succeeded at writing in all major literary forms. His earlier short fiction is collected in *Caravan: The Assembled Tales of John Galsworthy* (1925); among the individual collections, some of the best known are *A Man of Devon* (1901), published under the pseudonym John Sinjohn, *Five Tales* (1918), *Two Forsyte Interludes* (1927), and *On Forsyte 'Change* (1930). His plays made him, along with George Bernard Shaw, Sir James Barrie, and Harley Granville-Barker, a leading figure in British drama during the early decades of the twentieth century. Galsworthy's most enduring plays include *The Silver Box* (pr. 1906), *Justice* (pr., pb. 1910), *The Skin Game* (pr., pb. 1920), and *Loyalties* (pr., pb. 1922). Collections of Galsworthy's literary sketches and essays include *A Motley* (1910), *The Inn of Tranquility* (1912), and *Tatterdemalion* (1920). Galsworthy wrote poetry throughout his life, and *The Collected Poems of John Galsworthy* was published in 1934.

Achievements

John Galsworthy was a writer who reaped the rewards of literary acclaim in his own time—and suffered the pangs that attend artists who prove truer to the tastes of the public than to an inner vision of personal potential. Galsworthy won the esteem of his countryfolk with a play, *The Silver Box*, and a novel, *The Man of Property*, published in a most notable year, 1906. From that time on, he was a major figure in the British literary establishment, even winning the Nobel Prize in Literature in 1932.

Idealist, optimist, and activist, Galsworthy was a perennial champion of the underprivileged in his works. Women (especially unhappily married ones), children, prisoners, aliens, and animals (especially horses and dogs) engaged Galsworthy's sympathies. His literary indictments of the injustices forced on these victims by an unfeeling society helped to arouse public support for his causes and frequently resulted in elimination of the abuses. After World War I, Galsworthy's crusading spirit was somewhat dampened, but despite the author's disillusionment, his conscience remained sensitive to inequities of all sorts.

Although popular as a writer of fiction and influential as a spokesperson for humane, enlightened personal behavior and public policy, Galsworthy was not the sort of writer who changes the course of literature. His early works contain some powerful satire and some experiments in probing and expressing his internal conflicts. By upbringing and inclination, however, Galsworthy was too "gentlemanly" to be comfortable with self-revelation or even with introspection. Thus, while the English novel was becoming increasingly psychological because of Joseph Conrad, Virginia Woolf, and D. H. Lawrence, Galsworthy continued in the nineteenth century tradition of Ivan Turgenev and Guy de Maupassant, carefully describing social phenomena and assessing their impact on private lives. Most of his characters are individualized representatives of particular social classes, whether the rural gentry, the aristocracy, the intelligentsia, or the London professional elite. He excelled at presenting the fashions, politics, manners, and phrases peculiar to certain milieus at certain times. In creating the Forsytes—and most notably Soames, "the man of property"—Galsworthy's talent transcended that of the memorialist or mere novelist of manners and provided England with a quintessential expression of the shrewd, rich, upright middle class of Victorian London, a group whose qualities subsequent generations found easy to mock, possible to admire, but difficult to love.

Biography

John Galsworthy, son and namesake of a solicitor, company director, and descendant of the Devonshire yeomanry, was born on August 14, 1867, into the rich Victorian middle class he so accurately describes in *The Forsyte Saga*. His early years followed the prescribed pattern of that class. Having spent his childhood at a series of large, grand, ugly country houses outside London, Galsworthy graduated from Harrow School and New College, Oxford. Called to the bar in 1890, he commenced a languid practice of maritime law and traveled widely—to Canada, Australia, and the Far East. On returning to England, he committed an unpardonable breach of middle-class manners and morals: He openly became the lover, or more accurately husband manqué, of Ada, the unhappy wife of his cousin, Major Galsworthy.

Having placed themselves beyond the pale, the lovers traveled abroad and in England and, with Ada's encouragement and assistance, Galsworthy began his literary career by writing books under the pen name John Sinjohn. In 1905, after Ada's divorce, the Galsworthys were able to regularize their relationship, and, in 1906, public acclamation of *The Man of Property* and *The Silver Box* gave Galsworthy a secure place in the British literary establishment. Substantial resources permitted the Galsworthys to maintain London and country residences and to continue what was to be their lifelong habit of extensive traveling.

A kindly, courtly, almost hypersensitive person concerned throughout his life with altruistic ventures large and small, Galsworthy was distressed that his age and physical condition precluded active service in World War I. During these years, Galsworthy donated half or more of his large income to the war effort, wrote patriotic pieces, and for some time served as a masseur for the wounded at a hospital in France.

Friends observed that neither John nor Ada Galsworthy ever truly recovered from the war, and the last decade or so of Galsworthy's life was, beneath a smooth surface, not particularly happy. He had achieved all the trappings of success. Born rich, married to a woman he adored, he owned an elegant town house at Hampstead and an imposing country place at Bury, in Sussex. He was president of the International Association of Poets,

Playwrights, Editors, Essayists and Novelists (PEN). The public honored him as a humanist and philanthropist, acknowledged him as one of the foremost British men of letters, and even—thanks to the nostalgic novels written during the 1920's that, along with *The Man of Property*, constitute *The Forsyte Saga* and its sequel *A Modern Comedy*—made him a best-selling author. Nevertheless, Galsworthy keenly felt that he had never made the most of his talent or fulfilled the promise of his early works.

Furthermore, though he was the sort of gentleman who found complaints and even unarticulated resentment "bad form," Galsworthy must have felt some unconscious hostility toward his wife, who, for all her devotion, was superficial, hypochondriacal, demanding, and possessive in the Forsyte way that Galsworthy found deplorable (at least in people other than Ada) and who, by obliging him to live life on her terms, was perhaps the principal force in the circumspection of his talents. He also felt anxious realizing that the intense, even claustrophobic bond of love that had joined him and Ada would eventually be severed by the death of one or the other. Ironically, in 1932, it became evident that the "stronger" of the two would not survive his "frail" companion. Galsworthy was stricken with an initially vague malaise that, though never satisfactorily diagnosed, was very likely a brain tumor. Galsworthy died at home in London on January 31, 1933, two months after having been awarded in absentia the Nobel Prize in Literature.

Analysis

John Galsworthy is one of those authors whose works are valued most highly by their contemporaries. Once placed in the first rank by such discriminating readers as Joseph Conrad, Edward Garnett, Gilbert Murray, and E. V. Lucas (though Woolf despised him as a mere "materialist"), Galsworthy is now remembered as the workmanlike chronicler of the Forsyte family. Most of his other works are ignored. Changing fashions in literature do not suffice to explain this shift in critical esteem. Rather, the way Galsworthy chose to employ his talents—or the way his upbringing and personal situation obliged him to use them—guaranteed him the esteem of his peers but in large measure lost him the attention of posterity.

Galsworthy's literary strengths are impressive. His works are acutely observant and intensely sympathetic. In his novels, one finds carefully detailed presentations of the manners, codes, pastimes, and material surroundings of England's ruling classes as well as enlightened consideration of the diverse injustices these classes deliberately and inadvertently inflicted on those below them. Temperamentally inclined to support the "underdog"—whether an unhappily married woman, a poor workingman less honest than those in happier circumstances would like him to be, an ostracized German-born Londoner in wartime, or a badly treated horse—Galsworthy does not treat his characters as stereotypes of good or evil. Even when he is a partisan in one of the ethical dilemmas he presents (such as Soames Forsyte's sincerely enamored but brutally proprietary attitude toward Irene, the woman who passively marries him but actively re-

John Galsworthy. (© The Nobel Foundation)

pents of that decision), he strives to show the mixture of good and bad, commendable and culpable, in all parties.

Galsworthy writes best when he deals with characters or situations from his own experience (for example, the various loves in *The Dark Flower*), comments on his own background or family history (as in the satiric group portrait of the Forsytes), or attempts to externalize the intricate course of motivations and ambivalences in his own mind (as does his study of Hilary Dallison, a prosperous writer suffering under the curse of "over-refinement," in *Fraternity*). Nevertheless, Galsworthy's reserve and stoicism, innate qualities further cultivated by his gentlemanly upbringing, made him increasingly unwilling to look within himself and write. His peripatetic existence and desire to grind out work for good causes must have made concentration on truly ambitious projects difficult. His wife's wishes and values, closer than he ever acknowledged to the more blighting aspects of Forsyteism, cut him off from many of the experiences and relationships that writers tend to find enriching. As a result, most of his carefully crafted literary works remain topical productions: He fails to confer suggestions of universality or living particularity on the social types and situations he describes, and thus, as novels of manners tend to do, his works seemed more profound and interesting to the age and society whose likenesses they reflect than they have to succeeding generations.

The first of the Forsyte novels, *The Man of Property*, is generally agreed to be Galsworthy's finest work, and the excellence of this book in great measure guaranteed that its less skillfully realized sequels and the peripheral Forsyte collections such as *Two Forsyte Interludes* and *On Forsyte 'Change* would attract and interest readers. If these social novels typify Galsworthy's achievement, two other works deserve mention, not for their continued popularity or complete artistic success but because they indicate the other avenues Galsworthy might have explored had he not directed his talent as he chose to do. *The Dark Flower*, one of Galsworthy's favorites among his works, displays his ability to handle emotional relationships; *Fraternity*, which he termed "more intimate than anything I've done . . . less *machinery* of story, less history, more life," is his most complex psychological study, a flawed but ambitious attempt at writing a "modern" novel.

Fraternity

In the spring of 1909, ensconced in the Devonshire countryside he loved, Galsworthy worked on the study of London life that would be *Fraternity*. The book's first title, however, was *Shadows*, a word that gives perhaps a clearer indication of the novel's ruling concern. In *Fraternity*, Galsworthy presents two adjacent but contrasting neighborhoods, elegant Campden Hill (where he and Ada then had their town residence) and disreputable Notting Hill Gate, and two sets of characters, the genteel, prosperous, enlightened Dallisons and their "shadows," the impoverished Hughs family.

Aware of the existence of their less fortunate brothers (Mrs. Hughs does household chores for Cecelia, wife of Stephen Dallison, and the Hughses' tenant models for Bianca, the artist wife of Hilary Dallison) and rationally convinced of the unity of humankind and the falseness of the divisions fostered by the class system, the Dallisons would like to take positive actions to help their "shadows" but find themselves unable to succeed at putting their theories into practice. Hilary in particular—like his creator Galsworthy a fortyish writer with a comfortable income and an uncomfortably sensitive conscience—is willing but unable to do some good. Discovering in one of many episodes of self-scrutiny that his benevolent intentions toward his wife's "little model" are far from disinterested and, worse yet, learning that the poor girl loves him, Hilary suffers a fit of repulsion. He is, as Catherine Dupre observes in *John Galsworthy: A Biography* (1976), "horrified by the prospect of any sort of union with someone whose difference of class and outlook would doom from the start their relationship." For Hilary and all the Dallisons, the common bond of shared humanity is ultimately less significant than the web of social life that separates the privileged from their "shadows," that permits observation without true empathy.

Galsworthy's friend, Joseph Conrad, was not alone in appraising *Fraternity* as "the book of a moralist." The great danger and difficulty of such a novel, Conrad argued to Galsworthy, is that its "negative method" of stressing a moral problem without prescribing a remedy leaves the reader dissatisfied: "It is impossible to read a book like that without asking oneself—what then?" In that sentence, Conrad characterizes a recurrent quality of Galsworthy's writing. Except in specific cases (and there were many of these—among them women's suffrage, slaughterhouse reform, docking of horses' tails, vivisection, slum clearance, the condition of prisons, the state of zoos), Galsworthy tended to be a moralist without a gospel. His scrutiny of human behavior and social conditions detracted from the artistic success of his novels without providing anything but a sense of unease. Still, as Galsworthy explained to another critic of *Fraternity*, cultivating this awareness of moral problems is a step, albeit an oblique one, toward "sympathy between man and man."

THE DARK FLOWER

The Dark Flower was one of Galsworthy's particular favorites among his novels. His professed intention in writing the book was to offer "a study [I hoped a true and a deep one] of Passion—that blind force which sweeps upon us out of the dark and turns us pretty well as it will." The book was taken by various readers, the most articulate among them being Sir Arthur Quiller-Couch, who reviewed it in *The Daily Mail*, as a case for free love, an assertion that commitment to a marriage should end when love ends. Interestingly, as Dupre suggests, the gist of *The Dark Flower* is something less general than either the authorial statement of purpose or the critical view would have it be: It is an emotionally faithful representation of Galsworthy's own loves—most immediately, of his 1912 infatuation with a young actor and dancer named Margaret Morris.

The Dark Flower is divided into three parts, "Spring," "Summer," and "Autumn," each depicting a romantic experience in the life of the protagonist, Mark Lennan. Attracted to his tutor's wife in "Spring," the youthful Lennan is rejected and advised to find a woman of his own age. In "Summer," he meets and comes to love a beautiful, charming married woman, Olive Cramier, whose unyielding antipathy for the man to whom she has unwisely yoked herself obviously parallels Ada's revulsion for Major Galsworthy. Olive, the great love of Lennan's life, drowns; in "Autumn" he is happily but not passionately married to a woman, Sylvia, for fifteen years, and is infatuated with a lovely young girl, Nell. The middle-aged lover fondly hopes that he can retain Sylvia without giving up Nell. Like Ada in real life, Sylvia says she can be broad-minded but clearly demonstrates that she cannot. Lennan, like Galsworthy, accordingly sacrifices the more intense love for the long-standing one—in fact, his speeches and Nell's are, as Morris recalls in *My Galsworthy Story* (1967), accurate quotations of real-life dialogue. It is not surprising that having laid out his emotional autobiography, discreetly veiled though it may have been, and having been charged with promoting the sentimental and irresponsible sort of spiritual polygamy advocated by the very young Percy Bysshe Shelley, the reserved and dutiful Galsworthy was afterward reluctant to commit his deepest feelings to print.

THE MAN OF PROPERTY

The trilogy for which Galsworthy is principally known was launched with the publication of *The Man of Property* in 1906. Although Galsworthy thought at the time of continuing his satiric work and mentioned various possibilities in his letters to Conrad, not until 1917, when he returned to England from his stint of hospital service in France and began writing "Indian Summer of a Forsyte," did Galsworthy resume the work that would be his magnum opus.

The Man of Property, the finest and fiercest of the Forsyte novels, combines portraiture of a whole gallery of Galsworthy's Victorian relations with a particular focus on one example of the tenacious Forsyte instinct for possession: Soames Forsyte's refusal to free his beautiful and intensely unhappy wife Irene from a marriage she sees as dead; Irene's affair with a "bohemian" (June Forsyte's fiancé, Bosinney); and the grim but temporary victory of Soames over Irene, of Victorian convention over love. The triangular romance can be seen as symbolic or schematic—the two men, representing the possessive spirit and the creative temperament, both aspire in their different ways for Beauty—but it is also Galsworthy's thinly disguised account of Ada's tragic marriage with his cousin. The personal involvement results in what is least satisfactory about a fine book: Galsworthy's inability, despite an attempt to be philosophical, to moderate his extreme sympathy for Irene and his emotional if not rational assignment of total guilt to Soames, a man both sinned against and sinning.

The Man of Property begins with an "At Home" at the house of Old Jolyon, eldest of the Forsyte brothers and head of the family. At this gathering on June 15, 1886, a party honoring the engagement of old Jolyon's granddaughter, June, to the architect Philip Bosinney, the reader is privileged to observe "the highest efflorescence of the Forsytes." In the senior generation, the sons and daughters of "Superior Dosset" Forsyte, who had come from the country and founded the family's fortunes, are a variety of Victorian types, among them Aunt Ann, an ancient Sibyl tenaciously holding onto the life that remains to her; Jolyon, imperious and philosophical; Soames's father, James, milder than Jolyon but even more single-minded in his devotion to the Forsyte principles of property and family; James's twin, Swithin, an old pouter-pigeon of a bachelor whose hereditary prudence is tinged with antiquated dandyism; and Timothy, the youngest of the ten brothers and sisters and perhaps the Forsyte's Forsyte. He is a man whose caution and whose saving nature are so highly developed that he has retired early and placed all his resources in gilt-edged "Consols," retreating so successfully from the world's demands that even at his own house, the "Exchange," where Forsytes meet and gossip, his presence is felt more often than seen or heard.

The common bond that unites these superficially variegated characters and makes them representative of their whole class is described by young Jolyon, Galsworthy's mouthpiece in the novel: "A Forsyte takes a practical—one might say a common-sense—view of things, and a practical view of things is based fundamentally on a sense of property." The Forsytes, who know good things when they see them, who never give themselves or their possessions away, are the "better half" of England—the "cornerstones of convention."

The novel's principal demonstration of the Forsyte "sense of property" centers on the marriage of Soames, a prospering young solicitor, and the mysterious and lovely Irene. Troubled by his wife's chilly indifference to his strong and genuine love for her and the fine possessions that are his way of showing that feeling, Soames engages June's fiancé Bosinney to design and erect an impressive country house for him and Irene at Robin Hill, in the Surrey countryside outside London. While building this house, a process that posits Bosinney's aesthetic scorn for base monetary matters against Soames's financial precision and passion for a bargain, the architect falls in love with Irene. She, seeing him as an emblem of all that her detested husband is not, reciprocates. The two of them betray their respective Forsytes and enter into a clandestine relationship.

These complicated circumstances pit Soames, determined to retain his property, against Irene, equally determined in her stubbornly passive way to be free of her enslaver. The outcome is tragedy. Bosinney, bankrupt because Soames has justly but vengefully sued him for overspending on the house, and crazed with jealousy and sorrow because Soames has forcibly exercised his conjugal rights, falls under a cab's wheels in a fog and is killed. As the novel ends, the errant Irene has returned to her prison-home, not out of inclination but because like a "bird that is shot and dying" she has nowhere else to fall. Young Jolyon, arriving with a message from his father, has one glimpse into the well-furnished hell that is Soames and Irene's abode before Soames slams the door shut in his face.

Galsworthy's friends and literary advisers Edward and Constance Garnett felt that this ending was unsuitable and wished for the telling defeat of Forsyteism that would be afforded by Irene and Bosinney succeeding in an elopement. Galsworthy, with better instincts, stuck to his "negative method" as a stronger means of arousing public feeling against the possessive passion he attacked. Still, if the crushing forces of property were allowed a victory, albeit a comfortless one, at the novel's end, Soames's triumph was to prove short-lived, though contemporary readers would have to wait eleven years to make the discovery. In "Indian Summer of a Forsyte," Old Jolyon, who has bought Robin Hill from Soames and lives there with his son and grandchildren, encounters Irene, now living on her own, and makes her a bequest that enables her to enjoy a comfortable independence.

IN CHANCERY

In Chancery continues the conflict between the two hostile branches of the Forsyte clan. Soames, who feels the need for a child and heir to his property, is still in love with Irene and hopeful of regaining her. Young Jolyon, made Irene's trustee by his father's will, opposes Soames in his efforts and finds himself attracted by more than sympathy for the lovely, lonely woman. At length, Soames's persistent importunities drive Irene to elope with Jolyon. The infidelity gives Soames grounds for a divorce. Freed at last from any connection with the man she loathes, Irene marries Jolyon. Soames in his turn makes a convenient match with a pretty young Frenchwoman, Annette. The novel ends with the birth of children to both couples.

To Let

To Let, the final volume of the trilogy, brings the family feud to a new generation. Fleur, daughter of Annette and Soames, and Jon, son of Irene and Jolyon, meet first by chance, then, mutually infatuated, by strategy. The cousins intend to marry but are dramatically separated by the dead hand of the past enmity. Jon goes off to America, where after some years he marries a southern girl. Fleur, as passionately proprietary in her feeling for Jon as her father was toward Irene, believes that she has lost her bid for love and settles for a milder sort of happiness. She accepts the proposal of Michael Mont, the amiable, humorous, eminently civilized heir to a baronetcy.

A Modern Comedy

The second Forsyte series, *A Modern Comedy* (consisting of *The White Monkey*, *The Silver Spoon*, *Two Forsyte Interludes*, and *Swan Song*) centers on the adventures of the fashionable young Monts—Michael's stints in publishing and politics, Fleur's career as society host, femme fatale to a promising poet, canteen-keeper during the General Strike, mother, and most of all spoiled daughter to a fond yet wise father. In his love for his child, old Soames proves as selfless and giving as young Soames was possessive in his passion for Irene. Some twenty years after introducing Soames to the world, Galsworthy had come to admire, and at moments even to like, aspects of this gruff, practical, scrupulous incarnation of the possessive instinct, a character who as the years passed had usurped the place of Irene in the artist's imagination. Soames's death at the end of *Swan Song*—he succumbs to a blow on the head inflicted by a falling painting from which he saves Fleur—is at once an ironically appropriate end to the career of a man of property and a noble gesture of self-sacrifice.

When Galsworthy chose to terminate the life of Soames Forsyte, he symbolically presented the close of an age but also implicitly acknowledged the end of what was finest in his own literary career. However wide-ranging his talent might have been if possessed by another person, his personal temperament, training, and circumstances constrained it to a certain limited excellence. Galsworthy the artist was at his best depicting conflicts typical of the Victorian period, that consummate age of property, and relevant to his own life: the contradictory urges of artistic integrity and worldly wisdom, the foolish desire to possess beauty at war with the wise inclination to contemplate and appreciate it, the altruistic motto "do good" contending with the sanely middle-class imperative "be comfortable." Because he knew the overfurnished Victorian and post-Victorian world of the Forsytes and their kind from the inside, Galsworthy's best moral fables are credibly human as well, but when the old order he comprehended if never endorsed gave way to a new and unfathomable one, the novelist of principle dwindled to a kind of literary curator.

Peter W. Graham

Other major works

SHORT FICTION: *From the Four Winds*, 1897 (as John Sinjohn); *A Man of Devon*, 1901 (as Sinjohn); *Five Tales*, 1918; *Captures*, 1923; *Caravan: The Assembled Tales of John Galsworthy*, 1925; *Two Forsyte Interludes*, 1927; *On Forsyte 'Change*, 1930; *Soames and the Flag*, 1930; *Forsytes, Pendyces, and Others*, 1935.

PLAYS: *The Silver Box*, pr. 1906; *Joy*, pr. 1907; *Strife*, pr., pb. 1909; *Justice*, pr., pb. 1910; *The Little Dream*, pr., pb. 1911; *The Eldest Son*, pr., pb. 1912; *The Pigeon*, pr., pb. 1912; *The Fugitive*, pr., pb. 1913; *A Bit o' Love*, pr., pb. 1915; *The Little Man*, pr. 1915; *The Mob*, pr., pb. 1915; *The Foundations*, pr. 1917; *Defeat*, pr. 1920; *The Skin Game*, pr., pb. 1920; *A Family Man*, pr. 1921; *The First and the Last*, pr., pb. 1921; *Hallmarked*, pb. 1921; *Punch and Go*, pb. 1921; *The Sun*, pb. 1921; *Loyalties*, pr., pb. 1922; *Windows*, pr., pb. 1922; *The Forest*, pr., pb. 1924; *Old English*, pr., pb. 1924; *The Show*, pr., pb. 1925; *Escape*, pr., pb. 1926; *Exiled*, pr., pb. 1929; *The Roof*, pr., pb. 1929.

POETRY: *The Collected Poems of John Galsworthy*, 1934 (Ada Galsworthy, editor).

NONFICTION: *A Commentary*, 1908; *A Motley*, 1910; *The Inn of Tranquility*, 1912; *A Sheaf*, 1916; *Another Sheaf*, 1919; *Tatterdemalion*, 1920; *Castles in Spain*, 1927; *Candelabra: Selected Essays and Addresses*, 1932; *Letters from John Galsworthy, 1900-1932*, 1934 (Edward Garnett, editor).

MISCELLANEOUS: *The Works of John Galsworthy*, 1922-1936 (30 volumes).

Bibliography

Barker, Dudley. *The Man of Principle*. New York: Stein & Day, 1969. Barker's book combines elements of autobiography and criticism, giving an impressive picture of the Victorian age and its mores and morals. It also shows how much Galsworthy's work was a reflection of his times, and it explores the relationship between him and his wife, Ada, as well as her influence on his work. Short bibliography and an index.

Batchelor, John. *The Edwardian Novelists*. New York: St. Martin's Press, 1982. Batchelor begins by defining "Edwardian" literature and discusses Galsworthy in terms of his surprising similarities to D. H. Lawrence. Includes an excellent bibliography of Edwardian fiction.

Dupre, Catherine. *John Galsworthy: A Biography*. New York: Coward, McCann and Geoghegan, 1976. A well-researched and thoughtful biography. Less impressive, however, in its critical evaluations of Galsworthy's writings.

Gindin, James. *John Galsworthy's Life and Art*. Ann Arbor: University of Michigan Press, 1987. Having used original sources, Gindin presents a masterful literary biography, particularly appropriate since Galsworthy's fiction is itself so closely tied to his personal life, social criticism, and historic times.

Hapgood, Lynne. "The Unwritten Suburb: Defining Spaces in John Galsworthy's *The Man of Property*." In *Outside Modernism: In Pursuit of the English Novel, 1900-1930*, edited by Lynne Hapgood and Nancy L. Paxton. New York: St. Martin's Press, 2000. A reevaluation of Galsworthy's book and other English novels that were not defined as modernist works when they first appeared. These books are analyzed from the perspectives of postmodern, feminist, Marxist, queer, and cultural theories.

Holloway, David. *John Galsworthy*. London: Morgan-Grampian, 1969. A concise but accurate and perceptive survey of the life and career of Galsworthy. Especially good in identifying ways that Galsworthy's life is directly used in the fiction.

Kaye, Peter. "Dostoevsky and the Gentleman-Writers: E. M. Forster, John Galsworthy, and Henry James." In *Dostoevsky and English Modernism, 1900-1930*. New York: Cambridge University Press, 1999. Focuses on Galsworthy and other English writers who either admired Fyodor Dostoevski or feared him as a destructive literary force. Kaye analyzes these writers' misunderstandings of Dostoevski to better understand the nature of the modern English novel.

Rønning, Anne Holden. *Hidden and Visible Suffrage: Emancipation and the Edwardian Woman in Galsworthy, Wells, and Forster*. New York: Peter Lang, 1995. Three chapters in this examination of the Edwardian literary representation of women discuss Galsworthy: Chapter 1, "The Social Context of Edwardian Literature"; Chapter 4, "Marriage in Galsworthy, Wells, and Forster"; and Chapter 6, "Galsworthy's View on Suffragism." Includes notes and a bibliography.

Ru, Yi-ling. *The Family Novel: Toward a Generic Definition*. New York: Peter Lang, 1992. Ru examines Galsworthy's *The Forsyte Saga* and novels by French writer Roger Martin du Gard and Chinese writer Pa Chin to define the distinct character of the family novel.

Sternlicht, Sanford. *John Galsworthy*. New York: Twayne, 1987. A well-written, complete, yet concise survey of Galsworthy's life and achievement. Still the best single introduction to the subject. Includes a bibliography and an index.

CRISTINA GARCÍA

Born: Havana, Cuba; July 4, 1958

Principal long fiction

Dreaming in Cuban, 1992
The Agüero Sisters, 1997
Monkey Hunting, 2003
A Handbook to Luck, 2007

Other literary forms

Cristina García is known primarily for her novels, but she has also written two children's books—*The Dog Who Loved the Moon* and *I Wanna Be Your Shoebox*—both illustrated works and published in 2008. She also has edited two books: *Cubanisimo! The Vintage Book of Contemporary Cuban Literature* (2003) and *Bordering Fires: The Vintage Book of Contemporary Mexican and Chicana/o Literature* (2006).

Achievements

Cristina García is the first Cuban American to write a novel in English. *Dreaming in Cuban* introduced a fresh voice to the growing field of multicultural literature and became a National Book Award finalist. García received several other prestigious awards, including a Hodder Fellowship (Princeton University, 1992-1993), a Cintas Fellowship (Institute for International Education, 1992-1993), a Guggenheim Fellowship (1994), and a Whiting Writers Award (1996). Though *Dreaming in Cuban* remains García's most popular work, her other novels have received favorable attention as well. *The Agüero Sisters*, chosen as recommended reading by *Library Journal* and *Publisher's Weekly*, won the Janet Heidinger Kafka Prize for Fiction and a *New York Times* Notable Book of the Year award in 1997, and was listed among the American Library Association's Notable Books (1998).

Monkey Hunting marks a widening horizon for García, as she focuses on the often overlooked Chinese presence in Cuba. In 2008, she received the Northern California Book Award in Fiction for her fourth novel, *A Handbook to Luck*.

Biography

Cristina García was born in Havana, Cuba, in 1958 and came to the United States with her parents, who left Cuba after Fidel Castro rose to power there. The family settled in New York City, where García received her schooling at the Dominican Academy. She graduated from Barnard College in 1979 with a bachelor of arts degree in political science. She did graduate work at Johns Hopkins University's School of International Studies, intending to pursue a career in the Foreign Service. However, after receiving her degree in 1981, she switched her attention to journalism.

García held several different jobs at *The New York Times*, the *Boston Globe*, and the *Knoxville Journal* before accepting a job with *Time* magazine in New York in 1983. She worked for *Time* as a researcher, as a reporter, and later as a correspondent in San Francisco, Miami, and Los Angeles. It was in Miami, while living amid the large expatriate Cuban community, that she first became interested in exploring her own family's past.

In 1984, García visited Cuba for the first time since the time of her birth and met many of her relatives. The visit, she said in an interview, was like "finding a missing link." The experience made her aware of the highly charged loyalties of those who believed in the cause of the revolution and the others who left the island nation with the dream of toppling the Castro regime.

In 1990, García left work as a journalist to become a full-time writer of fiction. The same year she married Scott Brown, and in 1992 they had a daughter, Pilarita García-Brown. The publication of *Dreaming in Cuban* brought García widespread acclaim and a nomination for the National Book Award. During 1992-1993, she was a visiting professor at Princeton University. She moved to Los Angeles and taught creative writing at the University of California (both Los Angeles and Santa Barbara) while working on her next novel.

García moved to Napa Valley in Northern California in 2006, and she also taught creative writing at Mills College in Oakland. For her next work, García chose to write about three characters from different ethnic groups

Cristina García. (Time & Life Pictures/Getty Images)

while the other stays behind to serve the revolutionary cause. The novel, though not as popular as her first, was well received. For her next novel, *Monkey Hunting*, García turned her attention to Cuba's colonial past—of the African slaves and the Chinese indentured workers who toiled in the sugarcane fields. *Monkey Hunting* is the story of Chen Pan and his descendants. García covers a period of more than one hundred years, from Chen Pan's rise as a virtual slave to a successful businessperson and the vicissitudes of his children and grandchildren's lives in Cuba, China, and, later, in New York.

García employs multiple shifting narrators in her fiction so that each character's perspective propels the plot. Politics often seeps into the lives of the characters, yet her novels are not political in nature. Her novels are feminist in that they reveal the hardships and oppression endured by women in patriarchal societies. She expanded the range of characters in her last two novels; the use of different narrative voices helps her in revealing their inner lives.

García's familiarity with Latin American literature, particularly the works of Gabriel García Márquez, Jorge Luis Borges, Mario Vargas Llosa, Jorge Amado, and Julio Cortázar, led to her interest in Magical Realism and spirituality. For García, "the fantastic is an extension of reality," and there is no "great divide between what's true and what isn't true." She explores this uncharted territory in all her novels.

A notable aspect of García's novels is her use of language. Her love of poetry, especially the works of Octavio Paz, Pablo Neruda, Federico García Lorca, and Wallace Stevens, is reflected in her lyrical language. She has mentioned in interviews that it was her interest in poetry that turned her into a writer. In a 2003 interview, she said that she begins writing only after reading poetry for an hour or two to help her gain distance from the world of

whose lives run parallel, initially in their homelands and then as their lives cross paths through time.

Analysis

Cuba and Cubans are at the center of all of Cristina García's novels. The search for cultural identity, the complexity of family ties, and the generational divide among the emigrants are the major recurring themes in her works. In a 2003 interview in *Criticas*, García admitted that each of her books "embroiders the themes and obsessions" that prompted her to write in the first place. With characters from differing backgrounds populating her novels, her major concerns remain the question of belonging and "negotiating identities between and among cultures."

García's second novel, *The Agüero Sisters*, draws upon her family's experience and deals with the divided loyalties of a Cuban family. After the overthrow of the dictatorship, one of the Agüero sisters moves to New York to escape the aftermath of the Cuban Revolution logical thinking. Her appreciation of the "music of sentence" and "the jarring juxtaposition of unexpected images" derives from her love of poetry. Vivid descriptions in crisp and poetic language are the hallmark of her writing.

Dreaming in Cuban

Dreaming in Cuban is García's best-known work. Its incorporation in numerous American and multicultural literature courses and the critical attention it has drawn are testaments to its significance in contemporary literature. The novel revolves around the lives of three generations of women—Celia del Pino; her two daughters, Lourdes and Felicia; and Pilar, her granddaughter. The focus of the novel remains on the del Pino family, even though it is set over a period of many years. This focus allows the author to paint a picture of Cuba's evolution from Spanish colonialism to Castro's socialism, and it brings out the two unyielding attitudes of the Cubans toward the revolution: those of the exiles who constantly dream of reinstating the old order and those who steadfastly stay loyal to Castro.

Set in the 1970's, the novel brings out the conflicts between those who renounce the new Cuba and those who stay loyal. The new generation growing up in exile shares neither the nostalgia nor the denunciation of Castro's Cuba by their parents' generation. The young are Americans in spirit, yet remain tethered to their parents and the mother country.

The novel begins with a striking picture of a well-dressed, matronly, Cuban woman sitting on her porch with binoculars in her hand, scanning the blue waters for any traitors likely to invade the island country. The woman is Celia del Pino, the matriarch, a committed follower of Castro, who has stayed on while her family has dispersed. This tale of three generations is not told in chronological order but is revealed in shifting locales and from different perspectives at varying periods in the lives of the characters.

As a young woman, Celia had a passionate affair with Gustavo, a married tourist from Spain. His departure does not dampen her ardor. Even after marrying Jorge del Pino, she continues to write to Gustavo for years. These letters are never mailed but are stored in a satin box under her bed; they record important events in her life and observations about others around her. She knows that the Cuba seen by tourists as a place of natural beauty and abundance is very different from the real lives of the masses mired in oppression and poverty. Her own life has been far from happy. Her husband travels often in connection with his job, and his mother and sister treat her harshly even in his presence. Thus, her nervous breakdown after the birth of her first child, Lourdes, comes as no surprise. Jorge admits her to an asylum for shock therapy, ostensibly to treat her depression, but in reality, he admits later, to punish her for continuing to love Gustavo.

After Celia is released from the asylum, Jorge moves her to a house near the coast. In the years that follow, Celia is a better mother to her other two children, Felicia and Javier. When Castro comes to power, Celia is enthralled by the promises of the revolution: to bring change to the benefit of the people. However, her family offers her no solace. Her eldest daughter, Lourdes, carries the scars of abandonment by her mother and has never felt close to her. Lourdes marries into a wealthy family and lives comfortably until the revolution. After a series of traumatic incidents following the state's takeover of her family's ancestral property, Lourdes leaves Cuba with her husband and daughter.

Celia's second daughter goes through a stormy marriage, abandons her children, and leads an unstable life seeking happiness in drugs and the rituals of Santería, an Afro-Cuban religion. Celia's son leaves Cuba to teach at a university in Czechoslovakia. After many years there, he returns cancer-stricken and embittered by the loss of the custody of his children.

Celia has bestowed a part of her to each child—Lourdes inherits Celia's determination, Felicia gets her mother's sensuousness and love of language, and Javier follows his mother's single-minded devotion to a lost love. Celia's husband dies in New York, where he had gone for cancer treatment. Only Celia remains, keeping the flame of revolution alive.

Unlike most Cuban expatriates, Lourdes does not stay in Miami but moves north to New York to get as far away from Cuba as she can. While her husband turns to tinkering with inventions, Lourdes, with her unflinching faith in capitalism, succeeds in her business. She dreams of expanding her bakery, aptly named Yankie Doodle, to a chain all over the United States. Over the years, as she has prospered, she has nurtured her hatred of Castro, refusing to maintain contact with her mother; because of Lourdes's intractability, her husband and daughter have drifted away from her. Lourdes's daughter, Pilar, who has grown up in the United States, does not share her mother's anti-Castro obsession and derides her materialism. Pilar wants to carve her own path and be a painter of abstract art. Cuba for her is nothing but a fading memory of her grandmother, Celia, whom she has not seen since she was two years old.

As Pilar attains maturity, she realizes that her little acts of rebellion are the manifestation of her rootless existence. After her grandfather's death, she convinces her mother to visit Celia. During their short stay in Cuba, Pilar observes the signs of failure everywhere; despite stalwart supporters such as Celia, the Castro regime seems to be floundering. Cuba changes Pilar; she reconnects with her grandmother but realizes that though she has learned to appreciate her Cuban heritage, she cannot remain there, for her years in the United States have transformed her and given her a new cherished identity.

The Agüero Sisters

The Agüero Sisters is the story of two half-sisters—one who leaves Cuba and the other who stays behind, casting her lot with the Castro regime—and is set in the 1990's. Constancia and Reina are the daughters of two renowned naturalists recognized for their cataloguing of the flora and fauna of Cuba. The prologue depicts the murder of their mother, Blanca, by her husband, Ignacio, on an exploratory trip to Zapata Swamp. Young Reina is told that her mother has drowned, but after seeing her body herself, she notices a wound on her mother's neck. Two years later, after Ignacio commits suicide, the mystery of Blanca's death remains unsolved and overshadows the lives of the estranged sisters.

The narrative turns to Constancia, now about fifty years old and living in Miami, after nearly thirty years in New York; her second husband, Herbert, had owned a thriving tobacco store in Manhattan. Constancia was sent away by her mother after the birth of Reina, the child born of Blanca's extramarital affair. Constancia is now a successful businesswoman with a popular line of cosmetics aimed primarily at aging Cuban matrons, yet she harbors resentment against Reina, who has deprived her of their mother's love.

Reina still lives in Cuba, in a one-room apartment in the family mansion, now shared by seven other families. She is an electrician known for her exceptional skills and seems content with her life in the service of her country—until a freak accident nearly electrocutes her. Reina's burns, all over her body, are patched with skin grafts donated by her daughter and her lover. Unable to resume her previous life, she decides to leave for Miami to start anew. A statuesque, confident woman, Reina exudes sexuality, and despite her burn-scarred body, she still creates a sensation in the circle of Cuban expatriates, particularly among the men.

After Constancia's husband dies in a Cuban expatriate militia's effort to overthrow Castro, she undertakes a secret trip to bring back his remains. It is during this trip that she discovers her father's buried diary containing his confession to shooting Blanca. With the truth now revealed after almost a lifetime, the two sisters reconcile and come to accept each other.

Leela Kapai

Other major works

NONFICTION: *Cars of Cuba*, 1995.

CHILDREN'S/YOUNG ADULT LITERATURE: *The Dog Who Loved the Moon*, 2008; *I Wanna Be Your Shoebox*, 2008.

EDITED TEXTS: *Cubanisimo! The Vintage Book of Contemporary Cuban Literature*, 2003; *Bordering Fires: The Vintage Book of Contemporary Mexican and Chicana/o Literature*, 2006.

Bibliography

Davis, Rocio G. "Back to the Future: Mothers, Languages, and Homes in Cristina García's *Dreaming in Cuban*." *World Literature Today* 74, no. 1 (Winter, 2000): 60-68. Discusses García's *Dreaming in Cuban* as a coming-of-age novel. Examines the complex negotiations of mother-daughter bonds in the novel.

McCracken, Ellen. *New Latina Narrative: The Feminine Space of Postmodern Ethnicity*. Tucson: University of Arizona Press, 1999. García's work is included in this analysis of writings by Latinas. Argues that these authors have helped to redefine concepts of multiculturalism, ethnicity, and diversity in American society.

Payant, Katherine B. "From Alienation to Reconciliation in the Novels of Cristina García." *MELUS* 26, no. 3 (2001): 163-182. A lucid discussion of the major characters in *Dreaming in Cuban* and *The Agüero Sisters*, their reconciliation with estranged members of their family, and the reconciliation of their hopes and desires with reality.

Pérez Firmat, Gustavo. *Life on the Hyphen: The Cuban-American Way*. Austin: University of Texas Press, 1994. Sets García's work in the context of the popular culture created by Cuban Americans who moved to the United States when they were children.

Yagoda, Ben. *The Sound on the Page: Style and Voice in Writing*. New York: HarperResource, 2004. Yagoda, in this study of how writers develop their own unique voice in their works, interviews García and others, who explain how they approach style and how their style has been influenced by other writers.

GABRIEL GARCÍA MÁRQUEZ

Born: Aracataca, Colombia; March 6, 1927
Also known as: Gabriel José García Márquez; Gabo

Principal long fiction

La hojarasca, 1955 (novella; *Leaf Storm*, 1972)
El coronel no tiene quien le escriba, 1961 (novella; *No One Writes to the Colonel*, 1968)
La mala hora, 1962 (revised 1966; *In Evil Hour*, 1979)
Cien años de soledad, 1967 (*One Hundred Years of Solitude*, 1970)
El otoño del patriarca, 1975 (*The Autumn of the Patriarch*, 1975)
Crónica de una muerte anunciada, 1981 (*Chronicle of a Death Foretold*, 1982)
El amor en los tiempos del cólera, 1985 (*Love in the Time of Cholera*, 1988)
El general en su laberinto, 1989 (*The General in His Labyrinth*, 1990)
Collected Novellas, 1990
Del amor y otros demonios, 1994 (*Of Love and Other Demons*, 1995)
Memoria de mis putas tristes, 2004 (*Memories of My Melancholy Whores*, 2005)

Other literary forms

In addition to his novels, Gabriel García Márquez has published short stories, screenplays, and nonfiction works such as essays on cultural and political subjects. Many of his short stories were published originally in newspapers; virtually all of these have been collected in volumes in Spanish. García Márquez's stories have also appeared in *The Atlantic Monthly*, *Esquire*, and *The New Yorker*. Almost all of his stories are available in English.

Achievements

After the publication of *One Hundred Years of Solitude* in 1967, Gabriel García Márquez enjoyed increasing international appeal in the Spanish-speaking world and beyond. The initial reaction to the novel's Spanish edition, which was first issued in Buenos Aires, was overwhelming: New editions were published at the amazing rate of one per week as the public and critics alike applauded the Colombian masterpiece. Reactions around the world were similar as translations were published: In France, the novel was proclaimed the best foreign book of 1969; in Italy, it was awarded the Chianchiano Prize (1969); and in the United States, it was named one of the twelve best books of the year by *The New York Times Book Review* (1970). *One Hundred Years of Solitude* has been translated into more than twenty-seven languages.

The worldwide appeal of García Márquez's masterpiece is widely acknowledged to have been the single most important factor in the extraordinary growth of interest in the Latin American novel. No novelist of the post-World War II era has had an international influence greater than that of García Márquez; his use of Magical Realism gave rise to one of the dominant trends in world fiction in the 1970's and the 1980's. The winner of numerous literary honors, including the Neustadt International Prize for Literature in 1972, García Márquez was awarded the world's highest literary accolade, the Nobel Prize in Literature, in 1982.

Biography

Gabriel José García Márquez was born in Aracataca, near the Caribbean coast of Colombia, on March 6, 1927. His parents were less important to his upbringing than were his grandparents, with whom he lived for the first eight years of his life. García Márquez has emphasized their significance by claiming that nothing interesting happened to him after his grandfather's death, when he was eight years old. In these early years he received a heavy dose of history, myth, legend, and traditional oral storytelling. The Aracataca region, which recently had experienced the economic boom of "banana fever," could no longer rely on American funding, financially or ideologically; therefore myths and nostalgia became essential in forming young García Márquez's reality. His grandparents' home nurtured these interests: His grandmother told the most incredible tales with naturalness and nonchalance. García Márquez has claimed that these were the same qualities that were key to controlling the narrative voice in *One Hundred Years of Solitude*. His grandfather's influence was equally important; it was from him that García Márquez first heard stories of the wars and fables of Colombia, including tales from the War of a Thousand Days, which so profoundly influenced Colombia, including Aracataca, at the beginning of the twentieth century.

García Márquez's parents sent him from the tropical, vibrant coast to the cool and dismal highlands of Bogotá for his secondary education in a private Jesuit school, the National College of Zipaquirá. Neither the frigidness of the Andes nor Bogotá's natives were to his liking, but he graduated in 1946. He began law studies the following year at the National University in Bogotá. Two key events, coupled with his disinterest in law, made 1947 a more important year for literature than for jurisprudence. First, García Márquez met Plinio Apuleyo Mendoza, who became a friend and supporter in the early stages of his writing career and a colleague and collaborator later; in the same year, García Márquez published his first story, "La tercera resignación" ("The Third Resignation"), in one of Bogotá's major newspapers, *El espectador*. Within the next five years, he published fifteen short stories in Colombian newspapers. Years later, traces of the journalistic style would emerge in García Márquez's straightforward retelling of seemingly incredible events.

In April, 1948, an event occurred that would affect García Márquez's life immediately and, in the course of time, mark an important direction of Colombia's history and fiction for the next twenty years. A liberal populist candidate for the Colombian presidency, Jorge Eliécer Gaitán, was assassinated on April 9. This act served as a catalyst for mass violence in Bogotá, civil unrest in much of the country, and civil war in rural areas of Colombia during the next ten years. García Márquez moved back to the coast, taking up residence in Cartagena in May. By then, he had published three stories in *El espectador*. He began writing as a journalist for Cartagena's newspaper *El universal* and pursued both his true interest—reading and writing fiction—and the study of law. He was enrolled in the National University of Cartagena from June, 1948, until he finished his third year studying law in 1949.

The period from 1949 to the mid-1950's was important primarily for the modern novels that García Márquez read for the first time and the literary friends he established in Barranquilla, a nearby coastal city to which he moved in 1950. The influence on García Márquez of such writers as William Faulkner, Virginia Woolf, and Franz Kafka was significant, particularly that of Faulkner. Through his journalism and from statements of his close friends of this period, scholars have documented that García Márquez also read works by James Joyce, John Dos Passos, Ernest Hemingway, John Steinbeck, and William Saroyan, among others. In 1950, he began to write for the newspaper *El heraldo* and to take advantage of the surprisingly cosmopolitan literary life available to him while meeting regularly with the literati of the Happy Bar and La Cueva bar in Barranquilla. The literary father figure of the group was Ramón Vinyes, a Catalonian who stimulated the reading of contemporary world fiction among the young future writers. García

Márquez wrote a regular column, "La jirafa," in Barranquilla's newspaper *El heraldo*. In addition to the short stories he published during this period, he completed the manuscript for a novel titled "La casa," an early version of what would become the novella *Leaf Storm*; the prestigious publishing firm Losada of Buenos Aires rejected the novel. In early 1954, García Márquez's friend Alvaro Mutis convinced him to return to Bogotá to write for *El espectador*.

The year 1955 was a turning point in García Márquez's career for several reasons. He published *Leaf Storm*, his first work of long fiction, and he gained official recognition as a writer when the Association of Artists and Writers of Bogotá awarded him a prize for his story "Un día después del sábado" ("One Day After Saturday"). Also, in July of that year, *El espectador* sent him to Geneva on a journalistic mission, and the subsequent closing of *El espectador* resulted in a change of his original plans for a short stay in Europe and eventually led to his residence in Paris until 1958.

After moving to Caracas, Venezuela, in 1958 and then to New York City in 1961 to work as a correspondent for Cuba's *Prensa latina*, García Márquez lived in Mexico for several years of literary silence. Because of his perceived support of insurrections in Cuba and Nicaragua, he was denied entrance into the United States. In 1965, the pieces of his culminating work—that is, his previous stories—began to fall into place for the creation of *One Hundred Years of Solitude*. García Márquez had found the key to the creation of the magical reality of Macondo, which had been portrayed only partially in his previous fiction. García Márquez has written about the enthusiasm and excitement involved in the culmination of the novel he had been writing for some twenty years. Since its completion and resulting success, he has enjoyed economic and political stability, including being granted permission to enter the United States (by President Bill Clinton, who later declared *One Hundred Years of Solitude* to be his favorite novel). García Márquez continues writing (including an ongoing autobiography). In 1999, he was diagnosed with lymphatic cancer, and he receives treatments in clinics in Colombia, Mexico, and the United States, where his son Rodrigo García is a filmmaker.

Gabriel García Márquez. (© The Nobel Foundation)

Analysis

Gabriel García Márquez denies that the fictional world he describes in his novels is a world of fantasy. In an article about fantasy and artistic creation in Latin America, he concludes: "Reality is a better writer than we are. Our destiny, and perhaps our glory, is to try to imitate it with humility, and the best that is possible for us." Perhaps because García Márquez began writing as a journalist, this attitude permeates much of his writing, and this version of reality is reflected in his fiction. A deep-seated strain of antirationality underlies all of his fiction, which deals with Latin American "reality" in broad terms, rejecting the narrow regionalism of his literary fathers. The result is a type of fiction that transcends its regional base, a Faulknerian fiction that one critic of Spanish American literature, John S. Brushwood, called "transcendent regionalism." A self-proclaimed admirer of Faulkner, García Márquez has worked toward a transcendent regionalism in nearly all his works, with varying degrees of success. His redefinition of realism implies a faithfulness to a higher truth, a mythical level of reality that a more pedestrian realism cannot comprehend. These three factors—antirationality, transcendent regionalism, and myth—are integral to the aesthetics of García Márquez's fiction, aesthetics that balance journalistic depictions of historical events with fantastic stories and cultural myths.

Leaf Storm

García Márquez's first published work of long fiction was the novella *Leaf Storm*. Asked in 1982 to judge how the young García Márquez wrote this tale, the mature writer had the following response:

> With passion, because he wrote it quickly, thinking he wouldn't write anything else in his lifetime, that that one was his only opportunity, and so he tried to put in everything he had learned up to then. Especially literary techniques and tricks taken from American and English writers he was reading.

As anyone who reads *Leaf Storm* recognizes immediately, the apprentice writer used techniques from Faulkner. The parallels between *Leaf Storm* and Faulkner's *As I Lay Dying* (1930) in structure and narrative point of view are blatant.

The setting of *Leaf Storm* is Macondo during approximately the first quarter of the twentieth century, and the action centers on an unnamed doctor, believed to be from France, who had lived in Macondo during this twenty-five-year period and who ultimately committed suicide. All of this is revealed through three narrators who attend the doctor's wake, a nine-year-old boy, his mother, and his grandfather; the multiple points of view involve the reader in a process of discovery. The content of the boy's narration tends to be limited to his immediate situation, revealing primarily what he sees at the wake and how he feels at the moment. The mother's scope is broader; she relates information and anecdotes beyond the immediate circumstance, although limited primarily to her own friends. The grandfather's narration provides a historical account of the doctor's life and Macondo. The effect of this structure is a deeper penetration into the reality of Macondo than either a strictly personal or a strictly historical version would have allowed.

Leaf Storm is a point of departure in establishing elements basic to all of García Márquez's fiction. The underlying antirationality of this structure lies in the fact that effects are often apparent before causes, or, in some cases, causes never surface. The reader can never rationally explain, for example, why the town's priest reads from the Bristol Almanac or why the doctor eats grass for dinner. The novel has the formal elements of transcendent regionalism: García Márquez constructs a story of universal thematic scope—death, solitude—on a clearly defined regional base. One reason the novel does not have the universal appeal of his later fiction is the author's relative ineffectiveness in creating a mythical level of reality. The portrayals of both the doctor and the grandfather make them characters with mythic potential, but neither their characterization nor any other aspect of the novel creates a true sense of myth in *Leaf Storm*. Consequently, *Leaf Storm* is an important, but not totally successful, step in the creation of the Macondo that later will blossom in *One Hundred Years of Solitude*.

The next steps in García Márquez's apprenticeship for the creation of *One Hundred Years of Solitude* were the novella *No One Writes to the Colonel* and the short novel *In Evil Hour*. Both are more firmly based on Colombia's historical reality than most of the writer's later work. This reality is *la violencia*, the period of civil war during the 1950's. *No One Writes to the Colonel* is the story of a stoic retired colonel who waits fifteen years for a pension check that never arrives. In addition to the psychological portrayal of this colonel, the characterization and actions of other characters reveal a town suffering from corruption and repression. This backdrop is García Márquez's subtle means of incorporating the social and political realities of life in Colombia during this period. For example, the colonel's son is killed because of his political activism, but this matter never takes the form of direct political denunciation on the part of the author. A traditional omniscient narrator tells this story in a linear fashion.

In Evil Hour

In Evil Hour also features a controlling omniscient narrator and basically linear development of the story, but here García Márquez employs a juxtaposition of scenes to create a montage effect. Someone puts up placards that undermine the town's stability. These anonymous notes contain personal accusations that lead to conflicts: physical fights, people moving from the town, and even deaths. The mayor, who had been proud of the control he had established in the town before the appearance of the placards, is forced to repress the town's inhabitants in order to maintain order. García Márquez captures the essence of the fear and distrust that pervaded the national consciousness in Colombia at the time.

The antirationality of these stories functions as the catalyst of the anecdotes. In *No One Writes to the Colonel*, it is the inexplicable hope that the colonel has that he will receive the important letter he awaits. The antirational element in *In Evil Hour* is the presence and effect of the placards. Neither of these phenomena is fully explainable in rational terms, although the reader's speculation is invited. Both works transcend their regional base by capturing universal essences: the hope of the colonel and the fear of the town's inhabitants in *In Evil Hour*. The only element that approaches mythic dimensions is the characterization of the colonel in the first of these two books.

One Hundred Years of Solitude

"Many years later, as he faced the firing squad, Colonel Aureliano Buendía was to remember that distant afternoon when his father took him to discover ice." These are the opening words of García Márquez's masterpiece, *One Hundred Years of Solitude*. Most readers have found themselves swept from these lines through the discovery of ice, to the firing squad and beyond, unable to forget the enchantment of Macondo and the attractiveness of the novel. As a matter of fact, few critics have passed the opportunity to comment on the possible sources of this very attractiveness. Many have pointed to the author's masterful synthesis of various literary traditions, from the individual biography to the epic. Other critics seem to contradict one another by attributing the novel's attractiveness, on one hand, to its purely invented reality and, on the other, to its truthful depiction of Colombian history. Many readers are clearly attracted by the humor. In addition, the novel has other interesting characteristics: its people, its fantasy, its plot suspense, its craftsmanship, and its sense of wholeness. It is a novel that is difficult to capture—to describe appropriately or analyze—because of the intangible quality of much of the reader's experience. Some critics have found the term Magical Realism useful in dealing with this novel, in which a narrator describes with perfect naturalness a scene of a character ascending to Heaven and in which no one seems to notice the massacre of thousands of striking workers. Paradoxically, despite the numerous difficulties such a novel presents for the critic, it is not at all difficult to read.

One Hundred Years of Solitude is a family saga that tells the story of five generations of Buendías. It begins with the foundation of Macondo by José Arcadio Buendía and his wife Ursula. Despite their fear that the consummation of their marriage will result in the birth of a child with a pig's tail (there is a family precedent for such an event), José Arcadio Buendía decides to challenge fate to protect his image as a man. A second Macondo is established after José Arcadio Buendía kills a man in the original town. In its early years Macondo is somewhat primitive, albeit a kind of paradise. Macondo's only contact with the outside world is provided by gypsies, who bring items such as the ice and magnets, which the inhabitants find amazing. They suffer an insomnia plague that results in the loss of both sleep and memory.

Modern civilization finally reaches Macondo, along with its numerous institutions, and with the arrival of the national political parties come civil wars caused by their conflicts. The Americans bring economic prosperity and exploitation of the workers on the banana plantations. These intrusions of foreigners and modernity are eliminated by a flood that washes them away and returns Macondo to a state similar to its original paradise. In the end, Macondo is not a paradise, however, but a fiction: A member of the Buendía family deciphers a parchment written in Sanskrit that foretold the entire story of the family and Macondo from beginning to the end—that is, the story of *One Hundred Years of Solitude*. History is the completion of a fiction.

Part of the playfulness in the development of the plot of this novel involves following the intricate Buendía family line. The original José Arcadio Buendía engenders two sons, José Arcadio and Aureliano. The latter becomes identified as Colonel Aureliano. All their offspring also carry similar names—Arcadio, Aureliano

José, Jose Arcadio Segundo, and so on—making following the Buendía family line an exercise in futility or a challenging game of identities. The English translation of the novel, unlike the original Spanish edition, includes a genealogical chart.

One Hundred Years of Solitude is ostensibly a traditional novel that tells a story in a basically linear fashion. It is also a product of technical mastery by a superb craftsman of fiction. The novel's structure is cyclical, from the internal cycles of events that repeat within the novel to the broader cycle completed with the deciphering of the parchments.

García Márquez's handling of narrative point of view is enormously subtle, although it is managed with deceptive simplicity. On one hand, the omniscient narrator tells the story with a perspective similar to a child's view of the world. Consequently, this childlike narrator views and describes the world with freshness and innocence, taking for granted the incredible events of Macondo. Conversely, the narrator is surprised and amazed about things that are normally considered ordinary, such as ice and magnets. García Márquez's style is based on a use of hyperbole, a constant source of humor. One of the most hilarious hyperbolic characterizations is of Colonel Aureliano Buendía, whose machismo is the target of García Márquez's superb satire.

The antirationality of *One Hundred Years of Solitude* is not only a characteristic but also a fundamental principle of the entire narrative system. Entrance into the magical world of Macondo is an acceptance of the negation of rationality. It is soon apparent that everything is possible in Macondo. The work's transcendent regionalism can be visualized as a series of concentric circles emanating from Macondo. The circles near the center inscribe a reality of the Caribbean coast and Colombia—both its historical reality and myths. Larger circles contain patterns associated with all of Latin America, such as the tradition of machismo. Finally, the novel's connotations are universal; on this level one reads the work as a contemporary novelization of the biblical Creation and other universal patterns, such as the fear of incest that pervades the story.

Perhaps the most important achievement of this novel, however, is its expression of a mythic reality. One aspect of this is mythic time that negates linear time. The repetition of numerous cycles, such as the names of the members of the Buendía family, creates this sense of an eternal present. The characterization of Colonel Aureliano Buendía and Ursula makes them characters who function at a mythic level beyond the limits of everyday reality and the capabilities of persons in the everyday world. There is also a biblical level of reading that develops myth from Creation and Original Sin to the apocalyptic ending. García Márquez's creation of a traditional yet fascinating story, his mastery of narrative technique, and his creation of myth make *One Hundred Years of Solitude* not only one of the most important novels from Latin America of the twentieth century but also a work appreciated by an international readership.

The Autumn of the Patriarch

Some critics were disappointed with *The Autumn of the Patriarch* when it appeared, as they found the work to have neither the accessibility nor the magical world of *One Hundred Years of Solitude*. Judged on its own artistic merit, however, *The Autumn of the Patriarch* is an outstanding novel marked by the superb craftsmanship and humor characteristic of almost all García Márquez's fiction.

Several major Latin American writers published novels about dictators in the 1970's. García Márquez's novel deals with a dictator in an unnamed Caribbean nation. The dictator figure is a synthesis of many dictators, historical and fictional; García Márquez had spent many years researching these tyrants. The novel begins with the image of a dictator's corpse rotting in his presidential palace. From the discovery of the corpse by an unidentified narrator within the story, the narrative moves away from the immediate situation to relating events from the dictator's past. His life is bizarre and fantastic, as he is willing to take any measure—including serving one of his generals roasted on a platter—to intimidate others and maintain his power.

The structure and style of *The Autumn of the Patriarch* can present a challenge for readers; its consistently long sentences have caused some to question whether García Márquez bothered with punctuation at all. In reality, the author paid careful attention to even the lengths of the sentences in this prose poem. In each succeeding chapter, García Márquez uses progressively longer sentences, culminating in the last chapter, which is a single sentence. The use of multiple narrative voices within these extensive sentences creates a full portrayal of the pitiful dictator and is a source of much of the novel's humor.

Chronicle of a Death Foretold

Although it is a relatively minor work in García Márquez's oeuvre, the short novel *Chronicle of a Death Foretold* is an interesting tour de force. The story centers on the assassination of its central character, Santiago Nassar. A pair of brothers kill him to save the honor of their sister, Angela Vicario.

Fascinating occurrences abound in *Chronicle of a Death Foretold*, but perhaps the most incredible of all is the series of events surrounding the assassination itself: Everyone in the town, including Nassar himself, knows that he is going to die; nevertheless, nothing is done to obstruct the seemingly inevitable series of events leading to his death. The novel consists of five chapters that relate the story in a generally chronological fashion. The time span is quite limited: The first chapter tells the events of the morning of the assassination; the second chapter relates the courtship of Angela Vicario by Nassar up to the evening of the marriage; the third chapter covers that evening. In the fourth chapter, the narrator moves ahead in time, telling of events after the assassination, such as the autopsy. The last chapter returns to the original chronology, providing the graphic details of the killing on the morning after the wedding. García Márquez's major accomplishment in this work is having written a story that maintains the reader's interest despite the fact that its denouement is announced in the first sentence.

Love in the Time of Cholera

In *Love in the Time of Cholera*, García Márquez accomplishes quite a different objective, exploring the various facets of romantic love, including both those that are readily observable and those that exist solely in the imaginations of those involved. This novel begins with the death of Dr. Juvenal Urbino, husband to Fermina Daza. Daza, in turn, is the long-standing love interest of Florentino Ariza, whose reappearance shortly after the death of Urbino prompts a reexamination of Daza's romantic history. Rather than the guiltily quixotic recollection one might expect under such circumstances, what follows is an examination of the incredible range of passion and tedium experienced during the course of a long marriage. Although criticized for being overly sentimental, this book continues García Márquez's tradition of mixing the real and the imaginary, the extraordinary and the commonplace, this time in the domestic sphere rather than a broader historical or political context, but with similarly effective dramatic results. By focusing such intense attention on what would be insignificant events from an outsider's perspective, García Márquez effectively portrays the self-referential world of love, in which each couple exists as the center of their own universe.

The General in His Labyrinth

In his next novel, García Márquez returns to the overtly rather than the personally political. *The General in His Labyrinth* relates the final days of General Simón Bolívar, who, having wrested his people from Spanish rule, subsequently struggled (and failed) to save them from themselves and each other. Unlike *Love in the Time of Cholera*, in which the intricacies of romantic relationships are the focus of the story, *The General in His Labyrinth* centers on political intrigue and malfeasance, with romantic dalliances playing a subordinate (though discomfiting) role. More disturbing, however, is the notion that because this novel treats Latin American history in greater depth than do any of García Márquez's previous works, it is less susceptible to embellishment because of the inflammatory nature of the events on which the novel is based. In this story, the facts themselves are the stuff of myth, blurring the line between factual, journalistic telling and García Márquez's trademark

Of Love and Other Demons

The contrast reemerges in García Márquez's next novel, *Of Love and Other Demons*. This story has its roots in an event that García Márquez witnessed when he was a reporter, in which the coffin of a young woman was exhumed from a grave in which it had lain for two hundred years. When the casket was opened, it was found to contain not only the body of the woman, long dead, but also yards and yards of her hair, still attached to her skull and as vibrant as that of a living person. From this factual event, with the addition of select details of a story his grandparents had told him of a girl who was killed after having contracted rabies, García Márquez contrives the story of Sierva Maria, a character who, like her real-life counterparts, seems to be defined by the circumstances of her death rather than by those of her life. In this story, as in *The General in His Labyrinth*, the most notable dangers are not from the supernatural or the fantastic but rather from ordinary human passions channeled toward violent (but human) ends.

Memories of My Melancholy Whores

The setting of *Memories of My Melancholy Whores*, García Márquez's return to long fiction after a ten-year absence, is an unknown city in Colombia. The principal character is a ninety-year-old retired man who still writes musical critiques for the local newspaper's Sunday editorial page. He decides to give himself a present for his ninety-first birthday: a night spent with a young virgin (in this case, the fourteen-year-old Delgadina). This novel presents the reader with a sharp juxtaposition of sexual extremes. The protagonist has spent a lifetime insisting on paying for any sexual act, thereby maintaining a posture of physical intimacy without any love. The work is somewhat reminiscent of Vladmir Nabokov's well-known novel *Lolita* (1955), but the expected gender roles—of an older man psychologically dominating a teenage girl—are reversed. That is, the elderly journalist never physically consummates the relationship; instead, he finds himself unable to wake the sleeping Delgadina and comes to realize that love is not a product of sex but rather of emotional connection with another human. While Delgadina continues her innocence through her sleep, the journalist awakens to the simplicity of romance.

Here, García Marquez's Magical Realism is also inverted. Instead of the author presenting irrational and fantasy acts to produce a rational structuring of everyday reality in the mind of the reader, the simple existence and common wishes of a young girl produce an irrational state of fascination and adoration in the protagonist. This duality of realities forces the reader to confront societal and individual preconceptions about sexuality, love, prostitution, age, and obscenity. Through this work, García Márquez brings the reader to question the moral and aesthetic points of love and sex. Could it be that nobody can live a complete life succumbing to some obscene temptation?

By the end of the work, the journalist realizes that it is not money or material wealth that must be constantly renewed in life. Instead, love must be maintained intact from the first moment it is acquired. The protagonist, at an advanced age, discovers that in matters of love, age and time are irrelevant. In the novel's final scene, it is revealed that romance is timeless and that the journalist is condemned to die from a joyous suffering of his only true love—someday after he reaches one hundred years of age.

Each of García Márquez's novels highlights the conflicts that have defined Latin America since the beginning of the twentieth century—the tensions between centuries-old myth and modern rationalism, between authentic and imagined dangers, between the fantastic and the ordinary. These negotiations take place in all arenas, from the domestic sphere to the upper echelons of government. In each case, the relationship between the real and the fantastic must be constantly redefined in relationship to the circumstances of the characters through whom the tale is told. It is this ability to capture the perceptual chaos that arises from such ideological clashes that makes García Márquez one of the greatest authors of all time.

Raymond L. Williams; T. A. Fishman
Updated by Paul Siegrist

Other major works

SHORT FICTION: *Los funerales de la Mamá Grande*, 1962 (*Big Mama's Funeral*, stories included in *No One Writes to the Colonel, and Other Stories*, 1968); *Isabel viendo llover en Macondo*, 1967 (*Monologue of Isabel Watching It Rain in Macondo*, 1972); *No One Writes to the Colonel, and Other Stories*, 1968; *Relato de un náufrago*, 1970 (*The Story of a Shipwrecked Sailor: Who Drifted on a Liferaft for Ten Days Without Food or Water, Was Proclaimed a National Hero, Kissed by Beauty Queens, Made Rich Through Publicity, and Then Spurned by the Government and Forgotten for All Time*, 1986); *La increíble y triste historia de la Cándida Eréndira y de su abuela desalmada*, 1972 (*Innocent Eréndira, and Other Stories*, 1978); *Leaf Storm, and Other Stories*, 1972; *El negro que hizo esperar a los ángeles*, 1972; *Ojos de perro azul*, 1972; *Todos los cuentos de Gabriel García Márquez*, 1975 (*Collected Stories*, 1984); *Doce cuentos peregrinos*, 1992 (*Strange Pilgrims: Twelve Stories*, 1993).

NONFICTION: *La novela en América Latina: Diálogo*, 1968 (with Mario Vargas Llosa); *Cuando era feliz e indocumentado*, 1973; *Chile, el golpe y los gringos*, 1974; *Crónicas y reportajes*, 1976; *Operación Carlota*, 1977; *De viaje por los países socialistas*, 1978; *Periodismo militante*, 1978; *Obra periodística*, 1981-1999 (5 volumes; includes *Textos costeños*, 1981; *Entre cachacos*, 1982; *De Europa y América, 1955-1960*, 1983; *Notas de prensa, 1961-1984*, 1999; *Por la libre, 1974-1995*, 1999); *El olor de la guayaba: Conversaciones con Plinio Apuleyo Mendoza*, 1982 (*The Fragrance of the Guava: Plinio Apuleyo Mendoza in Conversation with Gabriel García Márquez*, 1983; also known as *The Smell of Guava*, 1984); *La aventura de Miguel Littín, clandestino en Chile*, 1986 (*Clandestine in Chile: The Adventures of Miguel Littín*, 1987); *Noticia de un secuestro*, 1996 (*News of a Kidnapping*, 1997); *Por un país al alcance de los niños*, 1996 (*For the Sake of a Country Within Reach of the Children*, 1998); *Vivir para contarla*, 2002 (*Living to Tell the Tale*, 2003).

Bibliography

Bell, Michael. *Gabriel García Márquez: Solitude and Solidarity*. New York: St. Martin's Press, 1993. Explores García Márquez's works from a number of different perspectives, ranging from comparative literary criticism to political and social critiques. Also included are commentaries on García Márquez's styles, including journalism and Magical Realism.

Bell-Villada, Gene H., ed. *Conversations with Gabriel García Márquez*. Jackson: University Press of Mississippi, 2006. Collection reprints interviews with the author that span his career from his earliest successful works to his early twenty-first century novels; topics covered include his life, his attitudes toward his work, and his political views. Some interviews originally conducted in Spanish are translated into English here for the first time.

_______. *Gabriel García Márquez's "One Hundred Years of Solitude": A Casebook*. New York: Oxford University Press, 2002. Collection of a dozen essays provides analysis of García Márquez's masterpiece from a wide range of critical approaches.

Bloom, Harold, ed. *Gabriel García Márquez*. Updated ed. New York: Chelsea House, 2007. Presents essays by twelve critics on the fiction of García Márquez. Novels discussed include *Chronicle of a Death Foretold*, *The Autumn of the Patriarch*, *Love in the Time of Cholera*, and *One Hundred Years of Solitude*. Supplemented with a chronology, an informative editor's introduction, and an interview with García Márquez.

García Márquez, Gabriel. "Gabriel García Márquez (1981)." In *Latin American Writers at Work*, edited by George Plimpton. New York: Modern Library, 2003. Text of a 1981 interview with the author is preceded by a brief biographical sketch. The focus of the interview is on García Márquez's writing style and methods.

McMurray, George R., ed. *Critical Essays on Gabriel García Márquez*. Boston: G. K. Hall, 1987. Collection of book reviews, articles, and essays covers the full range of García Márquez's fictional work. Very useful for an introduction to specific novels and collections of short stories. Also includes an introductory overview by the editor and an index.

McNerney, Kathleen. *Understanding Gabriel García Márquez*. Columbia: University of South Carolina Press, 1989. Overview of the author's work is aimed at students and general readers. After an introduction on Colombia and a brief biography, the five core chapters explain García Márquez's works in depth. Includes a select, annotated bibliography of critical works and an index.

Martin, Gerald. *Gabriel García Márquez: A Life*. London: Bloomsbury, 2008. Comprehensive biography, charting García Márquez's life and his evolution as a writer. Corrects many of the legends and half-truths that García Márquez himself—and others—have disseminated about his background.

Minta, Stephen. *García Márquez: Writer of Colombia*. New York: Harper & Row, 1987. Traces García Márquez's life and work, focusing in particular on the political context of *la violencia* in *No One Writes to the Colonel* and *In Evil Hour*. Devotes two chapters to discussion of Macondo as García Márquez's fictional setting and another chapter to individual analyses of *The Autumn of the Patriarch*, *Chronicle of a Death Foretold*, and *Love in the Time of Cholera*. Includes select bibliography and index.

Solanet, Mariana. *García Márquez for Beginners*. New York: Writers and Readers, 2001. Provides a good, basic introduction to the author's life and works.

Wood, Michael. *Gabriel García Márquez: "One Hundred Years of Solitude."* New York: Cambridge University Press, 1990. Provides much of the background information readers need to understand the history and cultural traditions that inform García Márquez's writings, including insight into the sociopolitical history of Latin America and biographical information about García Márquez himself.

JOHN GARDNER

Born: Batavia, New York; July 21, 1933
Died: Susquehanna, Pennsylvania; September 14, 1982
Also known as: John Champlin Gardner, Jr.

Principal long fiction

The Resurrection, 1966
The Wreckage of Agathon, 1970
Grendel, 1971
The Sunlight Dialogues, 1972
Nickel Mountain: A Pastoral Novel, 1973
October Light, 1976
In the Suicide Mountains, 1977
Freddy's Book, 1980
Mickelsson's Ghosts, 1982
"Stillness" and "Shadows," 1986 (Nicholas Delbanco, editor)

Other literary forms

As a writer, John Gardner was as versatile as he was prolific. In addition to his novels, he published an epic poem (*Jason and Medeia*, 1973), two collections of short stories, poetry, reviews, and four books for children. During the early 1960's, when Gardner was a struggling assistant professor with a growing backlog of unpublished fiction and rejection slips, he turned to more academic pursuits. While some of this work is distinctly scholarly in nature, much of it is directed at a less specialized audience and is designed to make the literature more accessible and more understandable to the general reader or undergraduate student: thus Gardner's translations, or modernized versions, of medieval poetry; a textbook-anthology of fiction; a popular biography of Geoffrey Chaucer; his controversial attack on the contemporary arts and criticism, *On Moral Fiction* (published in 1978 but, like his Chaucer books, begun more than ten years earlier); and a book of advice for young writers, *The Art of Fiction* (1984). Gardner also wrote a number of plays for National Public Radio's *Earplay* series and several opera librettos (one of which, *Rumpelstiltskin*, 1979, was professionally staged by the Opera Company of Philadelphia).

Achievements

At a time when the line between popular and innovative fiction was often considered, in critic Raymond Federman's word, "uncrossable," John Gardner managed to make his mark in both camps. Although his first novel, *The Resurrection*, was indifferently received, his second, *The Wreckage of Agathon*, which deals with law and order in ancient Sparta, gained a small following as a result of its relevance to Vietnam and the Nixon administration. *Grendel*, a parodic retelling of *Beowulf* (c. 1000) from the monster's point of view, was widely praised and in its paperback edition became as popular as *The Catcher in the Rye* (J. D. Salinger, 1951) was in the 1950's. Its success established Gardner's reputation as both an entertaining storyteller and an innovative parodist, a view that was confirmed by the publication of *The King's Indian: Stories and Tales* in 1974.

Gardner's next three novels all became best sellers: *The Sunlight Dialogues*, *Nickel Mountain*, and *October*

Light, which won the 1977 National Book Critics Circle Award for fiction. Among his other awards and honors were a Woodrow Wilson Fellowship (1955), a Danforth Fellowship (1970-1973), an award from the National Endowment for the Arts (1972), a Guggenheim Fellowship (1973-1974), an American Academy of Arts and Letters prize for fiction (1975), the Armstrong Prize for his radio play *The Temptation Game* (1977), and the 1978 Lamport Foundation award for his essay "Moral Fiction."

Upon the publication of the full text of *On Moral Fiction* in 1978, Gardner became a center of literary attention. His plainspoken criticism of fashionable pessimism in the contemporary arts and his generally negative remarks concerning individual writers led to an appearance on *The Dick Cavett Show* in May, 1978, a cover story in *The New York Times Magazine* in August, 1979, a special issue of the journal *Fiction International* devoted to the question of "moral" art, as well as the censure of those who saw Gardner as a reactionary and the praise of others who quickly adopted him as a spokesperson for a more traditional approach to fiction.

Biography

John Gardner was born John Champlin Gardner, Jr., on July 21, 1933, in the western New York community of Batavia, the setting of *The Resurrection*, *The Sunlight Dialogues*, and a number of short stories. Strongly influenced by his father, a farmer and lay preacher, and his mother, an English teacher, Gardner, nicknamed Bud (Welsh for poet), began writing stories when he was eight years old and reading his work aloud to the family in the evening. The death of his younger brother, Gilbert, in a farm accident on April 4, 1945, seems to have been the most formative event in Gardner's life. He felt responsible for his brother's death, which he fictionalized in the story "Redemption" (1977), and as a result became deeply introspective. His mother suggested that Gilbert's death may also account for her son's remarkable energy and productivity, as if he wished to live both his own life and his brother's.

During his high school years, Gardner commuted to the Eastman School of Music in nearby Rochester, where he took French horn lessons. He attended DePauw University for two years, majoring in chemistry, and then, following his marriage to Joan Patterson, a cousin, on June 6, 1953, transferred to Washington University. At Washington, under the tutelage of Jarvis Thurston, he began writing *Nickel Mountain*. From 1955 to 1958 Gardner attended the University of Iowa; at first he studied at the Writers Workshop (his master's thesis and doctoral dissertation were both creative rather than scholarly: one a collection of stories, the other a novel, *The Old Men*) but later switched to the study of Anglo-Saxon and medieval literature under the guidance of John C. McGalliard.

Following his study at Iowa, Gardner held faculty appointments at various colleges and universities: Oberlin (1958-1959); Chico State (1959-1962), where he coedited *MSS* and the student literary review *Selection*; San Francisco State, where he translated the alliterative *Morte d'Arthure* and the works of the Gawain-poet and began writing *The Resurrection*, *The Sunlight Dialogues*, and a study of Chaucer; Southern Illinois (1965-1976), including visiting professorships at the University of Detroit (1970), Northwestern (1973), and Bennington College (1975-1976), a sabbatical in England (1971), and a monthlong tour of Japan for the U.S. Information Service (September-October, 1974); Skidmore and Williams Colleges (1977); George Mason (1977-1978); and, from 1978 until his death, the State University of New York at Binghamton, where he directed the writing program.

Especially significant in Gardner's biography is the period from 1976 through 1978, when *October Light* won popular and critical acclaim. During that time, Gardner lectured on moral fiction at campuses across the United States, and his opera *Rumpelstiltskin* premiered in Lexington, Kentucky. Then Gardner's life took a darker turn: the breakup of his first marriage; a plagiarism charge leveled against him for his Chaucer biography, a charge that for some reason made its way into the pages of *Newsweek* magazine; a successful surgery for intestinal cancer; and the uproar over *On Moral Fiction*, as well as the often hostile reviews of *Freddy's Book* and *Mickelsson's Ghosts*. Until their amicable divorce in 1982, Gardner lived with his second wife, poet L. M. (Liz) Rosenberg, in Susquehanna, Pennsylvania, where he became active in the Laurel Street Theatre both as an actor and as a writer.

John Gardner. (Joel Gardner)

Gardner died in a motorcycle accident on September 14, 1982, a few days before he was to marry Susan Thornton of Rochester, New York. At the time of his death, Gardner had been working (as was his habit) on a variety of projects: operas, radio plays, a revival of his literary journal *MSS*, a television talk show on the arts, a book of advice for young writers (*The Art of Fiction*), a translation of *Gilgamesh* (a poem that figures prominently in *The Sunlight Dialogues*), and the novel *Shadows*.

Analysis

John Gardner is a difficult writer to classify. He was alternately a realist and a fabulist, a novelist of ideas and a writer who maintained that characters and human situations are always more important than philosophy. He was, as well, an academically inclined New Novelist whose work is formally innovative, stylistically extravagant, openly parodic, and highly allusive; yet, at the same time, he was an accessible, popular storyteller, one who some critics, in the wake of *On Moral Fiction*, have labeled a reactionary traditionalist. It is perhaps best to think of Gardner not as a writer who belongs to any one school but instead as a writer who, in terms of style, subject, and moral vision, mediates between the various extremes of innovation and tradition, freedom and order, individual and society. He employed the metafictionist's narrative tricks, for example, not to show that fiction—and, by extension, life—is mere artifice, meaningless play, but to put those tricks to some higher purpose. His fiction raises a familiar but still urgent question: How is humankind to act in a seemingly inhospitable world where chance and uncertainty appear to have rendered all traditional values worthless?

As different as Gardner's characters are in most outward aspects, they are similar in one important way: They are idealists who feel betrayed when their inherited vision of harmony and purpose crumbles beneath the weight of modern incoherence. Once betrayed, they abandon their childlike ideals and embrace the existentialist position that Gardner deplores for its rationalist assumptions and pessimistic moral relativism. His antidote to the modern malaise in general and Jean-Paul Sartre's "nausea" in particular is a twentieth century version of the heroic ideal: common heroes—fathers and husbands, farmers and professors, for example—who intuitively understand that whatever the odds against them, they must act as if they can protect those whom they love. Instead of pure and powerful knights dedicated to a holy quest, Gardner's heroes are confused, sometimes ridiculous figures who learn to overcome their feelings of betrayal and find their strength in love, memory, and forgiveness. Choosing to act responsibly, they achieve a certain measure of human dignity. In effect, the choice these characters face is a simple one: either to affirm "the buzzing blooming confusion" of life, as Gardner, quoting William James, calls it, or to deny it. Whereas the existentialist finds in that confusion meaningless abundance and historical discontinuity, Gardner posits meaningful variety and an interconnectedness that assumes value and makes the individual a part of, not apart from, the human and natural worlds in which he or she lives.

To find, or imagine, these connections is the role Gardner assigns to the artist. This view, propounded at length in *On Moral Fiction*, clearly puts Gardner at odds with other contemporary writers of innovative fiction who, he claims, too readily and uncritically accept the views of Sartre, Freud, Ludwig Wittgenstein, and other twentieth century pessimists. Art, Gardner maintains, ought not merely reflect life as it is but also portray life as it should be. This does not mean that Gardner approves of simpleminded affirmations, for he carefully distinguishes "true" artists from those who simplify complex moral issues, as well as from those who, like William H. Gass, sidestep such issues entirely by creating "linguistic sculpture" in which only the "surface texture" is important.

Believing that art does indeed affect life, and accepting Percy Bysshe Shelley's conception of the artist as legislator for all humankind, Gardner calls for a moral fiction that provides "valid models for imitation, eternal verities worth keeping in mind, and a benevolent vision of the possible" that will cause readers to feel uneasy about their failings and limitations and stimulate them to act virtuously. Moral fiction, however, is not didactic; rather, it involves a search for truth. The author "gropes" for meaning in the act of writing and revising the story; then, by creating suspense, the author devises for the reader a parallel experience. The meaning that author and reader discover in Gardner's work emphasizes the importance of rejecting existential isolation and accepting one's place in the human community, the "common herd" as Gardner calls it in one story. This meaning is not so much rational and intellectual as intuitive and emotional, less a specific message than a feeling—as is entirely appropriate in the case of a writer who defines fiction as "an enormously complex language."

Despite their very different settings—modern Batavia, New York, and ancient Sparta—Gardner's first two published novels, *The Resurrection* and *The Wreckage of Agathon*, share a number of common features—main characters who are professional philosophers, for example—and also share one common fault: Both are overrich in the sense that they include too many undeveloped points that seem to lead nowhere and only tend to clutter the narrative.

The Resurrection

The Resurrection is a fairly straightforward, realistic novel about the ways in which its main character, James Chandler, confronts the fact of death. His disease, leukemia, involves the mindless proliferation of lymph cells and so reflects the universe itself, which may be, as Chandler speculates, similarly chaotic and purposeless. Philosophy does not at first provide Chandler with a Boethian consolation because he, as a distinctly modern person, suspects that philosophy may be nothing more than a meaningless technique, a self-enclosed game. The novel thus raises the question of the purpose of philosophy, art, literature, and even medicine. Chandler's mother knows that the job of philosophers is to help people like her understand what their experiences and their world mean. Meaning, however, is precisely what contemporary philosophy generally denies and what Chandler wisely struggles to find. His breakthrough occurs when he realizes Immanuel Kant's fundamental error, the failure to see that moral and aesthetic affirmations are interconnected and need not—or should not—necessitate that the individual who makes the affirmation be entirely disinterested; that is, the affirmation may have—or should have—some practical application, some usefulness.

Sharing this knowledge becomes rather difficult for Chandler. His sympathetic and loving wife, Marie, is too practical-minded to understand him. Nineteen-year-old Viola Stacey, who, torn between cynicism and her childlike "hunger for absolute goodness," falls in love with Chandler, misinterprets his writing as an escape from reality precipitated by his intense physical suffering. More interesting is John Horne, who, like Chandler, is a terminal patient. According to Horne, a believer in legal technique, love is illusion and humanity is composed of clowns who act with no reason for their behavior. Like Viola, he assumes that art is an escape from life, or an "atonement" for one's failures and mistakes. Although he is interested in philosophy and acquainted with Chandler's published works, his endless prattling precludes Chandler's sharing the discovery with him. Yet Chandler does finally, if indirectly, communicate his vision. By putting it to some practical use (he dies trying to help Viola), Chandler finds what Horne never does: something or someone worth dying for, some vision worth affirming. "It was not the beauty of the world one must affirm," he suddenly understands, "but *the world*, the buzzing blooming confusion itself." Understanding that life is what drives humanity to art and philosophy, to fashion a life for oneself and others that is ennobling and useful (realistically idealistic, Gardner seems to suggest), Chandler fights down his physical and philosophical nausea. His vision worth perpetuating, he lives on—is resurrected—in the memories of those whom he loved, and thus for whom he died.

The Wreckage of Agathon

Early in *The Resurrection*, Gardner quotes the British philosopher R. G. Collingwood: "History is a process . . . in which the things that are destroyed are brought into existence. Only it is easier to see their destruction than to see their construction, because it does not take long." Like Gardner, James Chandler in *The Resurrection* affirms Collingwood's optimistic position, a position that the title character of *The Wreckage of Agathon* unwisely rejects. Insofar as he stands in opposition to the law-and-order society established in Sparta by the tyrant Lykourgus, the seer Agathon is an appealing figure. No system built solely upon reason, least of all one as inflexible as Sparta's, is adequate to the variety and complexity of life, Gardner implies, but this does not mean that the only alternative is the nihilism espoused by Agathon, who had "spent so much time seeing through men's lies he'd forgotten what plain truth looked like." Having once been a lover of truth and beauty, Agathon ("the good") now mocks them; choosing to embody "the absolute idea of *No*," he is the one who sees the wreckage that was, is, and will be, the one who dismisses all art and ideals as mere illusions.

Whereas Chandler learns to put his philosophy to some use, Agathon comes to value his ideas more highly than people. Unlike Chandler, who eventually accepts death, mutability, and human limitations and in this way transcends them, Agathon refuses to see wreckage as being part of life; for him it is the ultimate fact. The cause of Agathon's pessimism is not cosmic but personal; it is the result of his repeated betrayals of his friends, his wife, and his lover. This is the knowledge that haunts Agathon, however much he tries to hide it behind his leering clown's mask, leading him to believe that to be alive is necessarily to be a threat to others. Although he dies of the plague, Agathon's real sickness is of the soul: the inability to believe in love and human dignity as actual possibilities. That they are real is clearly shown in the characters of his friend Dorkis, leader of the Helot revolt, and his young disciple Demodokos, whose prison journal alternates with Agathon's (together they make up Gardner's novel). Demodokos, the "Peeker" to Agathon's "Seer," represents that childlike faith and goodness of heart that the disillusioned Seer has renounced. Patient, understanding (if not completely comprehending), and above all committed to others, the Peeker is the one who, for all his naïveté, or perhaps because of it, serves as Gardner's hero.

Grendel

Agathon reappears in Gardner's next novel as the perversely likable narrator of *Grendel*, a retelling of *Beowulf* from the monster's distinctly modern point of view. In his 1970 essay, "Fulgentius's *Expositio Vergiliana Continentia*," Gardner argues that the *Beowulf* poet used his three monsters as perversions of those virtues affirmed by Vergil in the *Aeneid* (c. 29-19 B.C.E.): valor, wisdom, and goodness (the proper use of things). Specifically, Grendel represents perverted wisdom; in Gardner's novel, he is the one who mistakenly chooses to believe in what he rationally knows and to reject what he intuitively feels. In both the epic and the novel, Grendel is an isolate, a cosmic outlaw, but Gardner's monster is less a hulking beast than a shaggy Holden Caulfield (*The Catcher in the Rye*), a disillusioned and therefore cynical adolescent. Not simply a creature cursed by God, he is a detached Sartrean observer, a relativist for whom "balance" can be both "everything" and "nothing," and a comic ironist trapped within his own mocking point of view. For him the world is a meaningless accident, "wreckage." Although he finds the indignity of the people he observes humorous, he is less tolerant of the factitious patterns they use to make sense of their existence.

Grendel makes his chief mistake when, having become dissatisfied with what is, he goes to the Dragon for advice and guidance. The Dragon is a bored and weary existentialist who espouses the philosophy of Sartre's *Being and Nothingness* (1943). He tells the confused and terrified Grendel that values are merely things, all of which are worthless, and counsels fatalistic passivity in the face of a fragmented, purposeless world. Although Grendel becomes infected by the Dragon's nihilism, he still feels attracted to King Hrothgar's court poet, the Shaper, whose songs he believes are lies. Unlike the Dragon, who is the ultimate realist and materialist, the Shaper is a visionary who sings of the "projected possible" and an alchemist who transforms the base ore of barbarism into the gold of civilization. His songs bespeak hopefulness and, by means of what the Dragon scornfully terms the "gluey whine of connectedness," a dream of order. Moreover, his singing works: The Shaper's words first envision Hrothgar's splendid meadhall and then inspire the men to build it.

Grendel's ambivalence toward the Shaper also marks his attitude toward Wealtheow, the wife bestowed on Hrothgar by her brother in order to save his tribe from the king's army. Whereas Grendel gloats over man's indignity, Wealtheow, whose name means "holy servant of the common good," has the power to absolve it. She brings to Hrothgar's kingdom the illusion of timeless peace, an illusion that, like the Shaper's words, works. Although her "monstrous trick against reason" enrages Grendel, he too is affected by it, temporarily discontinuing his attacks and choosing not to commit "the ultimate act of nihilism," murdering the queen.

The Shaper (art), the queen (peace and love), and the hero Beowulf represent those values "beyond what's possible" that make human existence worthwhile. Interestingly, Gardner's Beowulf is, like Grendel, an isolate, and, in his fight with the monster, appears as a dragon—not Grendel's adviser but the celestial dragon that figures chiefly in Eastern religions. Where Grendel sees accident and waste, the hero finds purpose and regeneration. During their struggle, Beowulf forces Grendel to "sing walls," that is, to forgo his mocking cynicism and to take on the role of Shaper, the one who by his art shapes reality (what is) into an illusion or vision of what can or should be. Thus, Grendel is not simply defeated; he is transformed—his death a ritual dismemberment, a symbolic initiation and rebirth.

Although the novel affirms the heroic ideal, it nevertheless acknowledges the tragic view that informs its Anglo-Saxon source. The meadhall the Shaper sings into existence, to which the queen brings peace, and that Beowulf saves, is a symbol of what a virtuous person can achieve, but it is also tangible evidence that art, love, and heroic action can defeat chaos for a limited time only and that, finally, the Dragon is right: "Things fade." Against this tragic awareness, to which the Dragon and Grendel passively acquiesce, Gardner posits the creative possibilities of human endeavor, especially art. It is, after all, as much the action (plot) of *Beowulf* as Beowulf's heroic act that defeats Gardner's Grendel and the monstrous values he represents.

Gardner's alternative to Grendel's mindless universe and brute mechanics is implied in the novel's very structure. Its twelve chapters suggest not only Grendel's twelve-year war against Hrothgar and the twelve books of literary epics but also the symbol of universal harmony, the zodiac (each chapter of the novel is keyed to an astrological sign). *Grendel*, therefore, is not a postmodern parody of *Beowulf*; rather, it is a work in which parody is used to test the values presented in *Beowulf* (and its other sources: William Shakespeare, William Blake, John Milton, Samuel Beckett, Georges Sorel, Sartre, and others) to discover their usefulness in the modern world.

The Sunlight Dialogues

Like *Grendel*, *The Sunlight Dialogues* (which was written earlier) depends in part on Gardner's skillful interlacing of his literary sources: *Gilgamesh*, Sir Thomas Malory's *Le Morte d'Arthur* (1485), Dante, Herman Melville's *Moby Dick* (1851), William Faulkner, and A. Leo Oppenheim's *Ancient Mesopotamia: Portrait of a Dead Civilization* (1977). It appears to be, at first glance, part family chronicle, part mystery story, but beneath the surface realism, the reader finds elements of fantasy and myth.

By an elaborate system of plots and subplots, each echoing the others, Gardner weaves together his eighty-odd characters into a densely textured whole that contrasts with his characters' sense of social and spiritual fragmentation. The main characters appear as isolates—the marked children of Cain—and as prisoners trapped in cells of their own making. Some blindly strike out for absolute personal freedom (Millie Hodge, for example), while others passively accept the small measure of freedom to be had in the cage of their limitations (Millie's ex-husband, Will Hodge, Sr.). As adults living in a world "decayed to ambiguity," they are like one character's young daughter whose toys frustrate her "to tears of wrath." Their frustration leads not to tantrums but to cynical denial of all hope, all ideals, and all connections between self and other.

The modern condition is illustrated in the fate of the Hodge clan. Just as their farm, Stony Hill, is said to symbolize "virtues no longer found," the late congressman represents the unity and sense of idealistic purpose missing in the Batavia of 1966. His qualities now appear in fragmented and diluted form in his five children: Will, Sr., a lawyer and toggler who can repair but not build; Ben, the weak-willed visionary; Art, Jr., the tinkerer; Ruth, the organizer; and Taggert, who inherits his father's genius, purity of heart, and pride, but not his luck. The failure of the congressman's harmonious vision leads to the moral relativism of the Sunlight Man on one hand and the reductive law-and-order morality of Batavia's chief of police, Fred Clumly, on the other.

The Sunlight Man is the congressman's youngest child, the angelic Tag, transmogrified by misfortune into a forty-year-old devil. Badly disfigured by the fire that kills his two sons, he returns to his hometown in the shape of a Melvillean monomaniac. Having searched for love and truth but having found only betrayal and illusion, he claims that love and truth do not exist; having failed to heal his psychotic wife or protect his sons, he proclaims all actions absurd. His magic tricks are cynical jokes intended to expose all meanings as self-delusions. His four dialogues with the police chief serve the same purpose: to disillusion Clumly, representative of the Judeo-Christian culture. Taking the Babylonian position, the Sunlight Man propounds the complete separation of spirit and matter, the feebleness and inconsequentiality of the individual human life, and the futility of the desire for fame and immortality. Personal responsibility, he says, means nothing more than remaining free to act out one's fated part. Although his dialogues are in fact monologues, it is significant that the Sunlight Man feels it necessary to make any gesture at all toward Clumly and that he finds some relief once he has made it. Similarly, his magic not only evidences his nihilism but also serves to mask the fact that despite his monstrous appearance and philosophy, he is still human enough—vulnerable enough—to feel the need for fellowship and love.

It is this need that Clumly eventually comes to understand. Powerless to stop either the local or the national epidemic of senseless crimes and bewildered by a world that appears to be changing for the worse, the sixty-four-year-old police chief at first seizes upon the Sunlight Man as the embodiment of evil in the modern world. Slowly the molelike, ever-hungry Clumly abandons this Manichaean notion and begins to search for the complicated truth. Clumly strikes through the pasteboard mask and, unlike Melville's Ahab, or the Sunlight Man who is made in his image, finds not the abyss but Taggert Hodge.

Throughout the novel, Clumly feels a strong sense of personal responsibility for his town and all its citizens, but, at the same time, he finds no clear answer to his repeated question, "What's a man to do?" He understands that there is something wrong with the Sunlight Man's philosophy but is not able to articulate what it is; he realizes that in separating the world into actual and ideal, the Sunlight Man has limited the choices too narrowly, but he has no idea what the other choices might be. The conflict between head and heart affects Clumly profoundly and eventually costs him his job. Only at this point can he meet Taggert Hodge as "Fred Clumly, merely mortal." In the novel's final chapter, Clumly, speaking before a local audience, abandons the text of his hackneyed speech on "Law and Order" and delivers instead an impromptu and inspired sermon, or eulogy (Taggert having been killed by a police officer) that transforms the Sunlight Man into "one of our number." Ascending to a healing vision of pure sunlight, Clumly, "shocked to wisdom," spreads the gospel according to Gardner: Man must try to do the best he possibly can; "that's the whole thing."

Nickel Mountain

Although not published until 1973, *Nickel Mountain* was begun nearly twenty years earlier while Gardner was an undergraduate at Washington University. That parts of the novel originally appeared as self-contained short stories is evident in the work's episodic structure and unnecessary repetition of background material. Still, *Nickel Mountain* is one of Gardner's finest achievements, especially in the handling of characters and setting.

The novel's chief figure is the enormously fat, middle-aged bachelor Henry Soames, owner of a diner somewhere in the Catskill Mountains. Alternately sentimental and violent, Henry is a kind of inarticulate poet or priest whose hunger is not for the food he eats but for the love he has never experienced. Similarly, his Stop Off is less a run-down diner than a communal meeting place, a church where the light ("altar lamp") is always on and misfits are always welcome. Willard Freund and Callie Wells, for example, see in Henry the loving father neither has had. Longing to escape their loveless families and fulfill their adolescent dreams, they find shelter at the diner. Willard, however, chooses to follow his father's advice rather than act responsibly toward Callie, whom he has impregnated—a choice that, perversely, confirms Willard in his cynicism and colors his view of human nature. Betrayal comes early to sixteen-year-old Callie (Calliope: the muse of epic poetry) and, as with Willard, leaves its mark. When Henry fumblingly proposes marriage, she interprets her acceptance as an entirely selfish choice. Gardner's description of the wedding, however, shows that, whatever Callie's motivation, the ceremony serves as a communal celebration of those values she and Henry unconsciously affirm and Willard mistakenly denies.

Henry's charity looms as large in the novel as his bulk and seems to extend to everyone but himself. When Simon Bale, a belligerently self-righteous Jehovah's Witness, loses his wife and his home, Henry naturally takes him in, but when Henry accidentally causes Bale to fall to his death, he turns suicidal. Henry's suicide attempt takes a rather comical form—overeating—but his predicament is nevertheless serious. To accept Simon Bale's death as an accident, Henry believes, would be to admit that chance governs the universe and to forfeit all possibility of human dignity. This either/or approach precludes Henry's understanding of one fundamental point: that man is neither hero nor clown, savior nor devil, but a mixture of both; the best he can do is to hope and to act on the strength of that hope.

Henry's friend George Loomis understands Henry's predicament and understands too the flaw in his reasoning, but George is unable to act on this knowledge when he accidentally kills the Goat Lady. As foul-smelling as her goats and even more comically grotesque in appearance than Henry Soames, the Goat Lady passes through the area on her pilgrim's progress in search of her son, Buddy Blatt. Because the drought-stricken farmers turn this mindless creature into a symbol of hopefulness, George's lie—that he knows she is still alive and searching—keeps their illusion and hopes alive; in a sense, he saves his friends from despair, or so Callie believes. From Gardner's perspective, however, George's failure to explain what actually happened and to confess his guilt signals his having lost his place in the human community. That George has always been in danger of losing his humanity, and thus becoming a Grendel, is evident in the way he is described: an ankle smashed during the Korean War, a heart broken by a sixteen-year-old prostitute, an arm torn off by a corn binder, and his lonely existence in a house much too large for one man up on Crow Mountain.

In a key scene, George leaves the Soameses and returns to his house, where, having heard about a recent murder on nearby Nickel Mountain, he becomes terrified, expecting to find murderous thieves looting his "things." Only after he has crawled through the mud, searched the house, and put his rifle down, does he realize his absurdity. More shocking is the knowledge that had Henry Soames acted in precisely the same way, there would have been nothing absurd about it for Henry would have been acting for Callie and their son Jimmie.

It is true that Henry does appear ridiculous throughout much of *Nickel Mountain*; Gardner's purpose here is not to deny his dignity but to qualify it, to make human dignity a realizable ideal in a fictional world where the prevailing mood is one of comic reconciliation rather than existential despair. Against George Loomis's isolation and love of things, the novel counsels responsibility and charitable love. It is, as its subtitle attests, *A Pastoral Novel*, in which the rural setting is used to affirm the value of community in the face of fragmentation and indifference. Gardner's pastoral simplifies the plight of modern humankind without becoming either simplistic or sentimental. Henry's Nickel Mountain represents freedom and clarity, but it also serves as a reminder of humanity's limitations and mortality. If the Christian virtues of faith, hope, and charity constitute one part of Gardner's approach to life, the other is, as one stoic character puts it, having the nerve to ride life down.

October Light

Gardner has called *Nickel Mountain* his "simplest" novel; *October Light*, also a pastoral of sorts, is a much more complex work—more varied in style and characters, at once funnier and yet more serious than *Nickel Mountain*. Most of *October Light* takes place on Prospect Mountain in Vermont, where seventy-two-year-old James L. Page and his eighty-year-old sister, Sally Abbott, are locked in "a battle of the bowels." James, the taciturn New England farmer, suffers from constipation as a result of having to eat his own cooking. A bigot, he simplifies right and wrong and rages against the valuelessness of modern life to the point of shotgunning Sally's television and locking her in her bedroom. James, however, is more than merely a comic buffoon; he is also burdened with guilt and oppressed by mortality—not only his own approaching end but also the accidental death of a young son, the suicides of his son, Richard, and his uncle, Ira, and the passing away of his wife, Ariah, in bitter silence. Self-reliant in the worst sense, James is outwardly unemotional (except for his anger), distant from those around him and from his innermost feelings. Only when he realizes the degree to which he is responsible for Richard's death and the part Richard played in accidentally frightening his Uncle Horace (Sally's husband) to death, does James once again take his place in the natural world and the human community.

Sally, meanwhile, a self-appointed spokeswoman for all oppressed minorities, remains locked in her room where, having nothing to eat but apples, she suffers from loose bowels. A liberal in name if not in fact, she thinks of her stubborn refusal to leave her room as a protest against her tyrannical brother. She is encouraged in her "strike" by the paperback book she reads, *The Smugglers of Lost Souls' Rock*. Comprising nearly 40 percent of the text of *October Light*, this novel-within-a-novel parodies the two kinds of fashionable literature assailed by Gardner in *On Moral Fiction*: the reflexive and the cynically didactic. Although Sally is not an especially discriminating reader, she does understand that *The Smugglers of Lost Souls' Rock* is trash—entertaining perhaps, but certainly not true. As she continues to read, however, the book, which she begins to see as a reflection of her situation, starts to exert its pernicious influence. Slowly Sally adopts its values and point of view as her own: its moral relativism, nihilistic violence, the acceptance of an accidental and therefore purposeless universe, and a casually superficial and irresponsible attitude toward human relationships. The subjects that are so weightlessly and artlessly handled in her paperback novel (suicide, for one) are substantive matters of concern in the "real" lives of James and Sally; but this is a point that Sally, caring less for the Pages to whom she is related than for the pages of her novel, does not understand.

In effect, *October Light* successfully dramatizes the argument of *On Moral Fiction*, that art provides its audience with models and therefore affects human behavior. Reading *The Smugglers of Lost Souls' Rock* leads Sally to devise and implement a plan to kill James; when the plan misfires and nearly results in the death of her niece, Sally, like the characters in her book, feels neither responsibility nor remorse. James is similarly affected by the violence he sees on television and, more particularly, by his Uncle Ira, who appears to have been more a monster than a man and certainly a poor model for James to pattern his own life after. The more James and Sally become like characters in what Gardner calls trivial or immoral fiction, playing out their inflexible parts as victimized woman locked in a tower or rugged New England farmer, the greater the danger that they will lose their humanity and become either caricatures or monsters. One such caricature in *The Smugglers of Lost Souls' Rock* dismisses all fiction, claiming that the trashiest "is all true" and "the noblest is all illusion." In their wiser moments, Sally and James know better; they understand that art is humanity's chief weapon in the battle against chaos and death (what James calls "gravity") and that the true artist is the one who paints "as if his pictures might check the decay—decay that . . . people hadn't yet glimpsed."

As in *Nickel Mountain*, Gardner's affirmation avoids sentimentality. Acknowledging the fact of death, acknowledging how easily the agreements that bind people together can be broken, he exposes the fragility of human existence. What makes his characters' lives even more difficult is the way in which their knowledge is, except for brief flashes of understanding, severely limited. Instead of the easy generalizations of trivial fiction, Gardner offers the complex and interrelated mysteries of Horace's death and Richard's suicide. Memory plays an especially important part in the novel; implying wordless connections between people and times, it is one effective antidote to Sally's "reasonable anger" and James's having stubbornly locked his heart against those he once loved.

Another binding force is forgiveness—the willingness to forgive and to be forgiven—which absolves the individual of the intolerable burden of guilt without freeing him or her of all responsibility. James's son-in-law, Lewis Hicks, for example, can see all sides of an issue and so takes the one course open to humankind (as opposed to monsters): forgiving everyone. Lewis is the dutiful, ever-present handyman who stands ready to shore up everyone else's ruins, understanding them to be his own as well. Significantly, it is Lewis who first sees the October light that, while a sign of winter and therefore a reminder of death, has the power to transform the everyday world into a vision of radiant, magical beauty, a reminder of that life that is yet to be lived.

FREDDY'S BOOK

Many reviewers regarded *Freddy's Book* as one of the least satisfying of Gardner's novels; certainly it is the most perplexing. Like *October Light*, it comprises two distinct stories, but in *Freddy's Book* the two are not interwoven (Gardner thought *October Light* was flawed for just that reason). The first part of *Freddy's Book* is sixty-four pages long and concerns Professor Jack Winesap's visit to Madison, Wisconsin, where he delivers a lecture on "The Psycho-Politics of the Late Welsh Fairy Tale: Fee, Fie, Foe—Revolution." Winesap, a psychohistorian, is a gregarious and sympathetic fellow who appears to accept the relativism and triviality of his age until his meeting with the Agaards makes plain to him the limitations of his easygoing rationalism.

Professor Sven Agaard is a self-righteous dogmatist; his son, Freddy, the victim of a genetic disorder, is another in Gardner's long line of misfits: a sickly looking eight-foot monster dripping baby fat. The manuscript Freddy delivers to Winesap at midnight (*Freddy's Book*) comprises the 180-page second part of Gardner's novel. Freddy's tale of sixteenth century Sweden, titled "King Gustav and the Devil," is a dreadful bore—at least at first. Then the story begins to improve; the style becomes more controlled, the plot more compelling and more complex as Freddy begins to use his fiction writing to explore the possibilities inherent in his story and, analogously, to explore alternatives to his own various confinements.

Many reviewers were puzzled by Gardner's decision to use the ending of Freddy's tale to conclude the larger novel, which, they felt, seemed broken in two. This narrative strategy is both understandable and effective once it is considered in the context of Gardner's "debate on fiction" with his friend, the novelist and critic William Gass. Gass contends that fiction is a self-enclosed and self-referential art object that does not point outside itself toward the world of humans but back into "the world within the word." Gardner, on the other hand, maintains that fiction does extend beyond the page into the reader's real world, affecting the reader in various and usually indirect ways. In *Freddy's Book*, Gardner makes the reader think about what effect Freddy's manuscript has had on its midnight reader, Winesap.

Freddy's Book shares with *Grendel*, *The Sunlight Dialogues*, *Nickel Mountain*, and *October Light* the qualities that have made Gardner a significant as well as a popular contemporary American novelist: the blend of realism and fantasy, narrative game playing and serious purpose, and the interest in character that implies Gardner's interest in humankind. The reader finds characters such as Winesap and Freddy compelling because Gardner draws them honestly, and he draws them honestly because, in part, each represents a side of his own personality. He is as much Grendel as he is the Shaper, as much the anarchic Sunlight Man as the law-and-order police chief Clumly. Gardner sympathizes with those who show the world as it is, but ultimately he rejects their realism in favor of those heroes—poets, farmers, and others—who choose to do what they can to transform the world into their vision of what it should be, those who, like Gardner, affirm the Shaper's "as if."

MICKELSSON'S GHOSTS

In the case of Peter J. Mickelsson, protagonist of Gardner's ninth and last novel, *Mickelsson's Ghosts*, the similarity between author and character is especially close: Both are middle-aged; teach at the State University of New York at Binghamton; own farmhouses in Susquehanna, Pennsylvania; have two college-age children; marriages that end badly; difficulties with the Internal Revenue Service; and both find that their careers, like the rest of their lives, are in a state of decline. The very texture of the novel's 103-word opening sentence makes clear that "something, somewhere had gone wrong with (Mickelsson's) fix on reality."

According to several influential reviewers, it was not only Mickelsson who had lost his fix; in the pages of *Esquire* and *Saturday Review*, for example, Gardner was venomously attacked for his carelessness, boring and pretentious pedantry, implausible language, and failure to resolve or even make sense of his numerous plots: love, ghost, murder, academic life, philosophy, marital stress, sex, environmental issues, and Mormonism. Whether these attacks were directed more against the author of *On Moral Fiction* than the author of *Mickelsson's Ghosts*, as Gardner believed, can only be conjectured. What is certain is that these reviews disturbed Gardner so deeply that for a time he considered giving up novel writing altogether. Moreover, the hostility shown by reviewers James Wolcott, Robert K. Harris, and others is out of proportion to the novel's actual defects (in particular, the unconvincing last scene and Gardner's ill-advised attempts to deal openly with sex). Rather than being a "whopping piece of academic bull slinging" (Wolcott), *Mickelsson's Ghosts* is clearly Gardner's most ambitious work since *The Sunlight Dialogues*, the novel it most resembles both in scope and narrative power.

Mickelsson (who Gardner says is based on his friend, the poet James Dickey) is in most respects a familiar Gardner protagonist. Just as the novel follows no single course but instead branches out in many seemingly unrelated directions, so too is Mickelsson torn apart by his own inner conflicts. He fondly recalls the certainties and ideals of his past, yet at the same time he finds it easier to live in the present by adopting the cynical, existentially free position he abhors. Finding himself in a world that is at best trivial and at worst self-destructive, Mickelsson recoils from all sense of responsibility and from all human relationships (except the most sordid with a teenage prostitute). Having been betrayed by his wife, he himself becomes a betrayer. Mickelsson is, however, too much the good man, desirous of goodness and truth, unwilling to accept any rift between mind and body, thought and deed, to rest easy in his fallen state. Thus, Mickelsson's many ghosts: those of the former owners of his farmhouse, the murderous Spragues; those from his past (wife, children, psychiatrist); the philosophical ghosts of Martin Luther, Friedrich Nietzsche, Wittgenstein, and others; and most important, the ghost of his better self.

By restoring his farmhouse, Mickelsson is in effect attempting his own moral restoration project. Before he can be freed of his ghosts, however, Mickelsson must first feel the need to confess his guilt (he is, among other things, responsible for a man's death)—to confess his guilt rather than to internalize it out of shame (as George Loomis does in *Nickel Mountain*) or to wallow in it as if values did not exist. Only then, through forgiveness, can he enjoy the saving grace of human community. Within the novel's murder-mystery plot, Mickelsson escapes from the murderous design of a fanatical colleague, Professor Lawler, a self-appointed avenging angel, only after making his act of faith in the form of a wholly irrational "psychic cry for help." Acknowledging his dependence on others and, later, accepting his place within the human community, Mickelsson becomes whole again. More than a novel about one man's redemption, *Mickelsson's Ghosts* is an exploration of the way in which a person in the modern world can truly find himself (or herself)—the self that he longs to be—and that discovery can occur only, Gardner believes, in the context of the individual's commitment to others and of their commitment to him.

Stillness *and* Shadows

The posthumously published book *"Stillness" and "Shadows"* was drawn from the University of Rochester's extensive collection of the author's papers. *Stillness* appears as Gardner wrote it in the mid-1970's, in the form of a complete but unrevised draft that Gardner apparently never intended for publication, though he did mine it for two of his finest short stories, "Stillness" and "Redemption." Written as psychotherapy in an effort to save his failing first marriage, it is Gardner's most intimate and autobiographically revealing work. The main characters appear as thinly disguised versions of John and Joan Gardner. Martin Orrick, like Gardner nicknamed Buddy, is professor and novelist; he is stubborn, opinionated, unfaithful, and often drunk. Joan, his wife and cousin, is a musician who has given up her career to allow her husband to pursue his. Although she has reason to complain, she, too, has faults and must share responsibility for their marital difficulties. Both are redeemed, in a sense, in that, as critical as they may be of each other outwardly, each is inwardly critical of him- or herself. The breakup of their marriage is handled with an intensity and sensitivity unusual in Gardner's fiction but not without the typically Gardnerian concern for seeing an isolated fact of domestic life as a sign of the universal decay that the novel's improbable happy ending serves only, ironically, to underscore.

Stillness evidences considerable promise; *Shadows*, on the other hand, suggests a certain pretentiousness on Gardner's part, given his remarks to interviewers on this work in progress. The published novel is nothing more than a patchwork toggled together by fellow novelist Nicholas Delbanco from the author's voluminous notes and drafts. Set in Carbondale, Illinois, the novel concerns Gardner's seriocomic, hard-boiled detective Gerald Craine, as he tries to find a murderer and protect a young Jewish student, Ellen Glass, who has come to him for help. Craine's search for the murderer becomes a search for truth. Delbanco's text makes clear what was to have been the novel's thematic center, Craine's discovery that he cannot protect Ellen, whom he has come to love. The published work, however, does not support Gardner's claim that *Shadows* would be his most experimental work in terms of technique as well as his most conservative in terms of values. That claim is nevertheless important, for much of Gardner's greatness as a novelist derives from the unresolved dialogue between the values he sought to affirm and the often postmodern ways he employed to test and often undermine those values.

Robert A. Morace

Other major works

SHORT FICTION: *The King's Indian: Stories and Tales*, 1974; *The Art of Living, and Other Stories*, 1981.

PLAYS: *Death and the Maiden*, pb. 1979; *Frankenstein*, pb. 1979 (libretto); *Rumpelstiltskin*, pb. 1979 (libretto); *William Wilson*, pb. 1979 (libretto).

POETRY: *Jason and Medeia*, 1973; *Poems*, 1978.

RADIO PLAY: *The Temptation Game*, 1977

NONFICTION: *The Construction of the Wakefield Cycle*, 1974; *The Construction of Christian Poetry in Old English*, 1975; *The Life and Times of Chaucer*, 1977; *The Poetry of Chaucer*, 1977; *On Moral Fiction*, 1978; *On Becoming a Novelist*, 1983; *The Art of Fiction: Notes on Craft for Young Writers*, 1984; *On Writers and Writing*, 1994 (Stewart O'Nan, editor); *Lies! Lies! Lies! A College Journal of John Gardner*, 1999.

TRANSLATIONS: *Tengu Child*, 1983 (of Kikuo Itaya's short stories; with Nobuko Tsukui); *Gilgamesh*, 1984 (with John Maier).

CHILDREN'S LITERATURE: *Dragon, Dragon, and Other Tales*, 1975; *Gudgekin the Thistle Girl, and Other Tales*, 1976; *A Child's Bestiary*, 1977; *The King of the Hummingbirds, and Other Tales*, 1977.

EDITED TEXTS: *The Forms of Fiction*, 1962 (with Lennis Dunlap); *The Complete Works of the Gawain-Poet*, 1965; *Papers on the Art and Age of Geoffrey Chaucer*, 1967 (with Nicholas Joost); *The Alliterative "Morte d'Arthure," "The Owl and the Nightingale," and Five Other Middle English Poems*, 1971.

Bibliography

Chavkin, Allan, ed. *Conversations with John Gardner*. Jackson: University Press of Mississippi, 1990. Although the nineteen interviews collected here represent only a fraction of the number that the loquacious Gardner gave, they are among the most important and are nicely complemented by Chavkin's introductory analysis of the larger Gardner.

Cowart, David. *Arches and Light: The Fiction of John Gardner*. Carbondale: Southern Illinois University Press, 1983. An examination of Gardner's novels and other fictional works. Like so many Gardner critics, Cowart is too willing to take Gardner at his (moral fiction) word. Cowart is, however, an intelligent and astute reader.

Henderson, Jeff, ed. *Thor's Hammer: Essays on John Gardner*. Conway: University of Central Arkansas Press, 1985. A collection of fifteen essays by Gardner scholars that approach his work from a variety of critical perspectives, including biographical, thematic, linguistic, and philosophical. Includes bibliographies.

Howell, John M. *Understanding John Gardner*. Columbia: University of South Carolina Press, 1993. Provides a thorough discussion of the history and criticism of Gardner. Many of the chapters are devoted to analyses of individual novels, including *Grendel*, *The Resurrection*, and *Nickel Mountain*.

McWilliams, Dean. *John Gardner*. Boston: Twayne, 1990. McWilliams includes little biographical material and does not try to be at all comprehensive, yet he has an original thesis: Gardner's fiction may be more fruitfully approached via Mikhail Bakhtin's theory of dialogism than via Gardner's own book *On Moral Fiction*. Unfortunately, the chapters tend to be rather introductory in approach and only rarely dialogical in focus.

Morace, Robert A., and Kathryn Van Spanckeren, eds. *John Gardner: Critical Perspectives*. Carbondale: Southern Illinois University Press, 1982. This first book devoted to criticism of Gardner's work contains twelve essays, including pieces discussing Gardner's early novels, Mesopotamian literature and lore in *The Sunlight Dialogues*, and "*Grendel* and Blake: The Contraries of Existence."

Nutter, Ronald Grant. *A Dream of Peace: Art and Death in the Fiction of John Gardner*. New York: Peter Lang, 1997. Nutter reviews Gardner's life and work, describing his thoughts on religion and peace and other aspects of his personal philosophy. He explains how Gardner was influenced by the thinking of Alfred North Whitehead and Susanne Langer.

Silesky, Barry. *John Gardner: The Life and Death of a Literary Outlaw*. Chapel Hill, N.C.: Algonquin Books of Chapel Hill, 2004. Silesky chronicles Gardner's life and development as a writer, describing how he cultivated the image of the eccentric outsider. While the book provides some description of his major works, it focuses on the events of his life and does not provide a detailed explication of his writings.

Thornton, Susan. *On Broken Glass: Loving and Losing John Gardner*. New York: Carroll & Graf, 2000. A memoir recounting Gardner's tumultuous relationship with Thornton, whom he was to marry until he died in a motorcycle accident a few days before the wedding. Thornton knew Gardner during the last three years of his life, and she traces his decline as an alcoholic during those years.

Winther, Per. *The Art of John Gardner: Instruction and Exploration*. Albany: State University of New York Press, 1992. Winther explores the philosophy and technique of Gardner's major and minor works. Includes a discussion of Gardner's "collage technique," or the relationship of his works to earlier literary classics and other texts, which Winther compares to literary methods commonly used by postmodernist authors.